القرآن
The Koran
(Al-Qur'ān)

طبعة ثنائية اللغة (عربية-انجليزية) مع مقدمة بقلم
محمد عرفه

Arabic-English Bilingual Edition with an Introduction by
Mohamed A. 'Arafa

عربي / إنجليزي
Arabic / English

ترجمة مولانا محمد علي
Maulana Muhammad Ali Translation

القـرآن
THE KORAN
(AL-QUR'ĀN)

طبعة ثنائية اللغة (عربية - انجليزية) مـع مقدمـة بقلم مـحـمـد عرفـه
Arabic-English Bilingual Edition with an Introduction by Mohamed A. 'Arafa

ترجمة مـولانـا مـحمد علـي
Maulana Muhammad Ali Translation

Copyright © 2014-2018 by TellerBooks. All rights reserved. Copyright claimed over text, layout, compilation, and design. No copyright is claimed over Maulana Muhammad Ali's Translation of the Koran, published in 1917, revised in 1920 and belonging to the public domain.

Printing, publishing, or posting this edition on personal or corporate web sites, with the exception of printing for personal use, requires the prior written consent of TellerBooks. For licenses to print, publish, or post, contact: Licenses@TellerBooks.com.

ISBN (13) (Paperback): 978-1-68109-088-7
ISBN (10) (Paperback): 1-68109-088-0
ISBN (13) (ePub): 978-1-68109-089-4
ISBN (10) (ePub): 1-68109-089-9

Published by TIME BOOKS™
an imprint of TELLERBOOKS™

Visit us at TellerBooks.com/Time_Books
TimeBooks@TellerBooks.com

Al-Qur'ān

Introduction to Islam	6
1. The Opening	82
2. The Cow	82
3. The Family of Amran	122
4. The Women	146
5. The Food	170
6. The Cattle	188
7. The Elevated Places	208
8. Voluntary Gifts	231
9. The Immunity	240
10. Jonah	257
11. Hud	269
12. Joseph	281
13. The Thunder	293
14. Abraham	299
15. The Rock	304
16. The Bee	310
17. The Israelites	323
18. The Cave	333
19. Mary	344
20. Ta Ha	351
21. The Prophets	361
22. The Pilgrimage	370
23. The Believers	378
24. The Light	386
25. The Discrimination	394
26. The Poets	401
27. The Naml	412
28. The Narrative	420
29. The Spider	430
30. The Romans	436
31. Luqman	442
32. The Adoration	446
33. The Allies	448
34. The Saba	457
35. The Originator	463
36. Ya Sin	468
37. Those Ranging in Ranks	474
38. Sad	482
39. The Companies	487
40. The Believer	495

القرآن

مدخل إلى الإسلام	٦
١- سورة الفاتحة	٨٢
٢- سورة البقرة	٨٢
٣- سورة آل عمران	١٢٢
٤- سورة النساء	١٤٦
٥- سورة المائدة	١٧٠
٦- سورة الأنعام	١٨٨
٧- سورة الأعراف	٢٠٨
٨- سورة الأنفال	٢٣١
٩- سورة التوبة	٢٤٠
١٠- سورة يونس	٢٥٧
١١- سورة هود	٢٦٩
١٢- سورة يوسف	٢٨١
١٣- سورة الرعد	٢٩٣
١٤- سورة إبراهيم	٢٩٩
١٥- سورة الحجر	٣٠٤
١٦- سورة النحل	٣١٠
١٧- سورة الإسراء	٣٢٣
١٨- سورة الكهف	٣٣٣
١٩- سورة مريم	٣٤٤
٢٠- سورة طه	٣٥١
٢١- سورة الأنبياء	٣٦١
٢٢- سورة الحج	٣٧٠
٢٣- سورة المؤمنون	٣٧٨
٢٤- سورة النور	٣٨٦
٢٥- سورة الفرقان	٣٩٤
٢٦- سورة الشعراء	٤٠١
٢٧- سورة النمل	٤١٢
٢٨- سورة القصص	٤٢٠
٢٩- سورة العنكبوت	٤٣٠
٣٠- سورة الروم	٤٣٦
٣١- سورة لقمان	٤٤٢
٣٢- سورة السجدة	٤٤٦
٣٣- سورة الأحزاب	٤٤٨
٣٤- سورة سبأ	٤٥٧
٣٥- سورة فاطر	٤٦٣
٣٦- سورة يس	٤٦٨
٣٧- سورة الصافات	٤٧٤
٣٨- سورة ص	٤٨٢
٣٩- سورة الزمر	٤٨٧
٤٠- سورة غافر	٤٩٥
٤١- سورة فصلت	٥٠٣
٤٢- سورة الشورى	٥٠٩
٤٣- سورة الزخرف	٥١٤

41. Ha Min	503	٥٢١	٤٤- سورة الدخان
42. The Counsel	509	٥٢٤	٤٥- سورة الجاثية
43. Gold	514	٥٢٧	٤٦- سورة الأحقاف
44. The Drought	521	٥٣١	٤٧- سورة محمد
45. The Kneeling	524	٥٣٥	٤٨- سورة الفتح
46. The Sandhills	527	٥٣٩	٤٩- سورة الحجرات
47. Muhammad	531	٥٤١	٥٠- سورة ق
48. The Victory	535	٥٤٤	٥١- سورة الذاريات
49. The Apartments	539	٥٤٨	٥٢- سورة الطور
50. Qaf	541	٥٥٠	٥٣- سورة النجم
51. The Scatterers	544	٥٥٣	٥٤- سورة القمر
52. The Mountain	548	٥٥٦	٥٥- سورة الرحمن
53. The Star	550	٥٦٠	٥٦- سورة الواقعة
54. The Moon	553	٥٦٤	٥٧- سورة الحديد
55. The Beneficent	556	٥٦٨	٥٨- سورة المجادلة
56. The Event	560	٥٧١	٥٩- سورة الحشر
57. Iron	564	٥٧٤	٦٠- سورة الممتحنة
58. The Pleading Woman	568	٥٧٦	٦١- سورة الصف
59. The Banishment	571	٥٧٨	٦٢- سورة الجمعة
60. The Examined Woman	574	٥٧٩	٦٣- سورة المنافقون
61. The Ranks	576	٥٨٠	٦٤- سورة التغابن
62. The Congregation	578	٥٨٢	٦٥- سورة الطلاق
63. The Hypocrites	579	٥٨٤	٦٦- سورة التحريم
64. Manifestation of Losses	580	٥٨٦	٦٧- سورة الملك
65. Divorce	582	٥٨٨	٦٨- سورة القلم
66. The Prohibition	584	٥٩١	٦٩- سورة الحاقة
67. The Kingdom	586	٥٩٣	٧٠- سورة المعارج
68. The Pen	588	٥٩٥	٧١- سورة نوح
69. The Sure Truth	591	٥٩٧	٧٢- سورة الجن
70. The Ways of Ascent	593	٥٩٩	٧٣- سورة المزمل
71. Noah	595	٦٠١	٧٤- سورة المدثر
72. The Jinn	597	٦٠٣	٧٥- سورة القيامة
73. Folded in Garments	599	٦٠٥	٧٦- سورة الإنسان
74. Wrapped Up	601	٦٠٧	٧٧- سورة المرسلات
75. The Resurrection	603	٦٠٩	٧٨- سورة النبأ
76. Man	605	٦١٠	٧٩- سورة النازعات
77. Those Sent Forth	607	٦١٢	٨٠- سورة عبس
78. The Announcement	609	٦١٤	٨١- سورة التكوير
79. Those Who Yearn	610	٦١٥	٨٢- سورة الإنفطار
80. Frowned	612	٦١٦	٨٣- سورة المطففين
81. The Folding Up	614	٦١٧	٨٤- سورة الإنشقاق
82. The Cleaving	615	٦١٨	٨٥- سورة البروج
83. Default in Duty	616	٦١٩	٨٦- سورة الطارق
84. The Bursting Asunder	617	٦٢٠	٨٧- سورة الأعلى
85. The Stars	618	٦٢١	٨٨- سورة الغاشية
86. The Comer by Night	619	٦٢٢	٨٩- سورة الفجر
		٦٢٣	٩٠- سورة البلد
		٦٢٤	٩١- سورة الشمس
		٦٢٥	٩٢- سورة الليل

87. The Most High	620	
88. The Overwhelming Event	621	
89. The Daybreak	622	
90. The City	623	
91. The Sun	624	
92. The Night	625	
93. The Brightness of the Day	626	
94. The Expansion	626	
95. The Fig	627	
96. The Clot	627	
97. The Majesty	628	
98. The Clear Evidence	628	
99. The Shaking	629	
100. The Assaulters	629	
101. The Calamity	630	
102. Abundance of Wealth	630	
103. The Time	631	
104. The Slanderer	631	
105. The Elephant	631	
106. The Quraish	632	
107. Acts of Kindness	632	
108. The Abundance of Good	632	
109. The Disbelievers	632	
110. The Help	633	
111. The Flame	633	
112. The Unity	633	
113. The Dawn	634	
114. The Men	634	

٩٣- سورة الضحى	٦٢٦
٩٤- سورة الشرح	٦٢٦
٩٥- سورة التين	٦٢٧
٩٦- سورة العلق	٦٢٧
٩٧- سورة القدر	٦٢٨
٩٨- سورة البينة	٦٢٨
٩٩- سورة الزلزلة	٦٢٩
١٠٠- سورة العاديات	٦٢٩
١٠١- سورة القارعة	٦٣٠
١٠٢- سورة التكاثر	٦٣٠
١٠٣- سورة العصر	٦٣١
١٠٤- سورة الهمزة	٦٣١
١٠٥- سورة الفيل	٦٣١
١٠٦- سورة قريش	٦٣٢
١٠٧- سورة الماعون	٦٣٢
١٠٨- سورة الكوثر	٦٣٢
١٠٩- سورة الكافرون	٦٣٢
١١٠- سورة النصر	٦٣٣
١١١- سورة المسد	٦٣٣
١١٢- سورة الإخلاص	٦٣٣
١١٣- سورة الفلق	٦٣٤
١١٤- سورة الناس	٦٣٤

Introduction to Islam

ISLAM AND ISLAMIC LAW: AN INTRODUCTORY OVERVIEW

Mohamed A. 'Arafa[1]

"It's not radical Islam that worries the US—it's independence."
— Noam Chomsky

"Yes I am, I am also a Muslim, a Christian, a Buddhist, and a Jew."
— Mahatma Gandhi"[3]

مدخل إلى الإسلام

الإسلام والقانون الإسلامي: نظرة عامة

محمد عرفه[2]

"ليس الإسلام الراديكالي الذي يقلق الولايات المتحدة ـ إنه الاستقلال"
نعومي تشومسكي

"نعم أنا، أنا أيضا مسلم، مسيحي، بوذي، ويهودي."
-مهاتما غاندي[4]

---

[1] Assistant Professor of Criminal Law and Criminal Justice at Alexandria University Faculty of Law (Egypt); Adjunct Professor of Law at Indiana University Robert H. McKinney School of Law (USA). Ph.D., Indiana University Robert H. McKinney School of Law (2013); LL.M., University of Connecticut School of Law (2008); LL.B., Alexandria University School of Law (2006). Currently, he is a Visiting Professor of Law at the University of Brasília School of Law (UnB). Recently, he has been named to the editorial board of the ARAB LAW QUARTERLY in London as a *"Managing Editor."* Of course, all errors remain the author's. For any comments or questions, please contact the author at marafa@iupui.edu.

[2] أستاذ مساعد في القانون الجنائي والعدالة الجنائية بكلية الحقوق بجامعة الإسكندرية (مصر)؛ أستاذ مساعد للقانون في جامعة إنديانا روبرت ه. مكيني كلية الحقوق (الولايات المتحدة الأمريكية). دكتوراه، جامعة إنديانا روبرت مكيني كلية الحقوق (٢٠١٣)؛ ماجستير، كلية الحقوق بجامعة كونيتيكت (٢٠٠٨)؛ ليسانس حقوق, كلية الحقوق بجامعة الإسكندرية (٢٠٠٦). وهو حاليا أستاذ زائر في القانون بجامعة برازيليا للقانون (أونب). وفي الآونة الأخيرة، تم تعيينه في هيئة تحرير القانون العربي فصليا في لندن ك "مدير التحرير". وبطبيعة الحال، تبقى جميع الأخطاء للمؤلف. للتعليقات أو الأسئلة، يرجى الاتصال بالمؤلف على marafa@iupui.edu.

[3] Noam Chomsky, *It's Not Radical Islam that Worries the US — It's Independence*, THE GUARDIAN, Feb. 4, 2011 https://chomsky.info/20110204/ ("A common refrain among pundits is that fear of radical Islam requires (reluctant) opposition to democracy on pragmatic grounds. While not without some merit, the formulation is misleading. The general threat has always been independence. The US and its allies have regularly supported radical Islamists, sometimes to prevent the threat of secular nationalism."). See also MURTADHA, *Yes I am a Muslim, a Christian, and a Jew*, PHILOSOPHY & RELIGION J., Nov. 27, 2007, https://saudialchemist.org/2007/11/24/yes-i-am-a-muslim-a-christian-and-a-jew/ (last visited Apr. 20, 2017) ("I believe that all of us Muslims (*sunni, shiaat*) Christian, Jews, etc. are seeking a better understanding of humanity so they choose their religion based on assumption that their religion is the best representative of humanity. In fact, their assumption doesn't come arbitrarily . . . it comes from a long experience and several sources . . . Let us all Muslim, Christian, Jews and all others be together and share our happiness and our pains together.").

[4] نعوم تشومسكي، ليس الإسلام التطرفي الذي يزعج الولايات المتحدة – إنه الاستقلال، الجارديان، ٤ فبراير ٢٠١١ https://chomsky.info/20110204/ ("والمانع المشترك بين النقاد هو أن الخوف من

Overview

According to some recent statistical reports, there are around 900 million Muslims nowadays. Several live in the Middle Eastern and the Arab World, as Egypt, Tunisia, Morocco, Jordan, Algeria, among others (assessed at 130 million), but many more live in countries, as Pakistan, Bangladesh, India, Iran, Indonesia, Malaysia, China, the Philippines, the USSR, Cameroon, Chad, Nigeria, and Sudan - along with approximately 3 million Muslims - reside in the United States.[5] The world's three Abrahamic faiths - Judaism, Christianity, and Islam - were born and advanced in the Middle Eastern region, as Abraham was born in the city of Ur, Mesopotamia (Iraq), some 1900 years before Jesus was born in Bethlehem (Palestine).[6] Mohammad was born in Mecca (Saudi Arabia) in 570 A.D., Moses lived in Egypt, as did Jesus for a brief period in his infancy; Mohammad traveled throughout the Arabian Peninsula.[7]

نظرة عامة

يبلغ عدد المسلمين الآن – وفقاً لبعض التقارير الإحصائية الحديثة – حوالى ٩٠٠ مليون مسلم. جزء منهم يعيش فى الشرق الأوسط والعالم العربى فى دول مثل مصر وتونس والمغرب والأردن والجزائر (يقدرون بـ ١٣٠ مليون). ولكن الجزء الأكبر يعيش فى دول آسيا مثل باكستان وبنجلاديش والهند وإيران واندونيسيا وماليزيا والصين والفلبين ودول الإتحاد السوفييتى السابق، وكذلك فى إفريقيا مثل الكاميرون وتشاد ونيجيريا والسودان. بالاضافة إلى مايقدر بـ ٣ مليون مسلم يعيشون فى الولايات المتحدة الأمريكية.[٨] لقد ولدت العقائد الإبراهيمية الثلاثة – اليهودية والمسيحية والإسلام – فى

فى حين أنه ليس من دون بعض الوقائع. الإسلام المتطرف يتطلب المعارضة للديمقراطية على أسس عملية وقد دعمت الولايات المتحدة. وكان التهديد العام دائما الاستقلال. الموضوعية، فإن الصياغة مضللة وحلفاؤ ها بانتظام الإسلاميين الراديكاليين، وأحيانا لمنع تهديد القومية المدنية." انظر أيضا انا مرتضى، نعم أنا مسلم، مسيحي، ويهودي، الفلسفة والدين ج. https://saudialchemist.org/2007/11/24/yes-i-am-a-muslim-a-christian-and-a-jew/) آخر زيارة فى ٢٠ أبريل ٢٠١٧) ("أعتقد أننا جميعا المسلمين (السنة، الشيعة) المسيحيين، اليهود، وما إلى ذلك يسعون إلى فهم أفضل للإنسانية بحيث يختارون دينهم على أساس افتراض أن دينهم هو أفضل ممثل للإنسانية. في دعونا جميعا . . . فإنه يأتي من خبرة طويلة والعديد من المصادر . . . الواقع، افتراضهم لا يأتي بشكل تعسفي. المسلمين والمسيحيين واليهود وجميع الآخرين معا ونتبادل سعادتنا وآلامنا معا").

[5] *See generally* AHMED EL-SHAMSY, THE CANONIZATION OF ISLAMIC LAW: A SOCIAL AND INTELLECTUAL HISTORY (Cambridge Univ. Press, 2013), at 253.

[6] SYED A. ALI, THE SPIRIT OF ISLAM: A HISTORY OF THE EVOLUTION AND IDEALS OF ISLAM, WITH A LIFE OF THE PROPHET (1978).

[7] *Id.* The Middle East region is the foundation of all the ancient civilizations. The oldest of these historic civilizations, the Egyptian, extended over five millennia. The fourth millennium B.C. observed the birth of the great civilizations along the Tigris-Euphrates valley (Turkey, Syria, and Iraq). The most significant of these olden civilizations were the Sumerian, Mesopotamian, Babylonian, Assyrian, Assyro-Babylonian, Aramean, Canaanite, Hebrew, Philistine, among others. Their peoples spoke a number of languages including Akkadian, Aramaic, Sumerian, Hebrew (the *Torah*'s language), and Arabic (the *Qur'an*'s language). *See also generally* GERHARD ENDRESS, ISLAM: AN HISTORICAL INTRODUCTION, (Columbia Univ. Press, 2nd ed., 2002).

تجد كلمة الإسلام جذورها مشتقة من كلمة "سلام" (السلام) أو "سلم" (فرض السلام). ويقصد بالإسلام أن يعهد الشخص بنفسه فى سلم وبالتالى فالمسلم هو ذلك الشخص الذي يعهد بنفسه ويستسلم طواعية لله.[18] فالإسلام بالتالى هو قبول العقيدة أو المعتقد عن حرية وإختيار، قلباً وعقلاً وروحاً.[19] وعلى ذلك فالدخول فى الإسلام

منطقة الشرق الأوسط، إذ ولد نبى الله إبراهيم فى مدينة أور بميزوبوتاميا (العراق) قبل ميلاد المسيح بحوالى ١٩٠٠ فى بيت لحم (فلسطين).[9] وقد ولد محمد – رسول الإسلام – فى مكة (السعودية حالياً) عام ٥٧٠ ميلادياً وكانت اسفاره كثيرة فى شبه الجزيزة العربية، وعاش موسى فى مصر كما فعل المسيح لفترة وجيزة من طفولته.[10]

The word "Islam" is derivative from the same root as the words *salaam* (peace) and *silm* (the condition of peace). Islam means to abandon oneself in peace and thus, a Muslim, is one who in peace gives or surrenders/submits himself or herself to God.[11] Further, Islam means accepting the belief or the faith spontaneously (and freely) –heart, mind, and soul.[12] Accordingly, surrendering to Islam, means giving oneself to belief without reservation, admitting the creeds of faith, and

---

[8] انظر عموما أحمد الشامسي، تقديس القانون الإسلامي: تاريخ اجتماعي وفكري (صحافة جامعة كامبريدج، ٢٠١٣)، فى ٢٥٣.

[9] سيد أ. علي، روح الإسلام: تاريخ تطور ومثل الإسلام، مع حياة النبي (١٩٧٨).

[10] أقدم هذه الحضارات . المرجع السابق، إن منطقة الشرق الأوسط هي أساس كل الحضارات القديمة الألفية الرابعة قبل الميلاد لاحظت ولادة الحضارات التاريخية، المصرية، تمتد على مدى خمسة آلاف سنة أهم هذه الحضارات القديمة هي (الكبرى على طول وادي دجلة والفرات (تركيا وسوريا والعراق السومرية، بلاد الرافدين، البابلية، الآشورية، الآشورية البابلية، الآرامية، الكنعانية، العبرية، الفلسطينية، من وتحدثت شعوبهم عددا من اللغات بما في ذلك الأكادية والآرامية والسومرية والعبرية (لغة. بين أمور أخرى انظر أيضا بشكل عام جيرهارد إندرس، إسلام: مقدمة تاريخية، (صحافة. (التوراة)، والعربية (لغة القرآن جامعة كولومبيا، الطبعة الثانية، ٢٠٠٢.)

[11] *Id.*

[12] JOHN L. ESPOSITO, ISLAM: THE STRAIGHT PATH (Oxford Univ. Press, 3rd ed., 1998). *See also* MALISE RUTHVEN, ISLAM: A VERY SHORT INTRODUCTION, (Oxford Univ. Press, 2nd ed., 2000).

following both the letter and the spirit of the *Qur'anic* values.¹³ Prophet

يعنى أن يؤمن الفرد بعقيدة الإسلام

---

¹³ ANNEMARIE SCHIMMEL, ISLAM: AN INTRODUCTION (1992) & R. M. Savory, ed. *Introduction to Islamic Civilization*, (1976). It should be noted that Abraham, also called "The Patriarch," is the most central of the early prophets to the Jews, Christians, and Muslims. He founded, in what is now Mecca, the first place of worship in the world for the worship of a single God. He was also the father of Isma'il (Ishmael) and Ishaq (Isaac).

¹⁴ *See* M. CHERIF BASSIOUNI, INTRODUCTION TO ISLAM 28 (1985).

¹⁵ THE HOLY QUR'AN: ENGLISH TRANSLATION OF THE MEANINGS AND COMMENTARY (2002), at 96:2 [*al'alaq*: The Clot], http://www.muslim.org/english-quran/quran.htm [hereinafter *Qur'an*]. God says: ("Proclaim! (or Read!) In the name of thy Lord and Cherisher, Who created Created man, out of a (mere) clot of congealed blood Proclaim! And thy Lord is Most Bountiful, He Who taught (the use of) the Pen."). *Id.*, at *Qur'an* 96:1-5.

¹⁶ *See generally* WILLIAM MONTGOMERY WATT, MUHAMMAD AT MECCA (1953); MUHAMMAD AT MEDINA (1956); & MUHAMMAD: PROPHET AND STATESMAN (Oxford Univ. Press, 1961). The Prophet received his revelations from God, sometimes solely sometimes in the presence of others and the words flowed from his mouth in a way that others described as inspired and this was his *wahi* (divine inspiration or revelation).

¹⁷ *Id.* According to classical customs, Prophet Mohammad is a direct descendent of Ishma'el, and his mission was presaged by the deliverance of his dad, 'Abd Allah. The history of the Prophet, his performances and sayings, were at first memorized by his *sahaba* (companions) and passed through oral record. They were first systematically recorded by the historian Ishaq ibn Yasar. Then, the Prophet Sayings (*hadith*) and actions, the circumstances surrounding their incidence, and the evidence of those who first witnessed and reported (narrated, chain of submission) them to others were recorded by several scholars. The most authoritative is *sahih al-Bukhari* and his text is still relied upon today as it is the most authentic one along with *sahih* Muslim.

¹⁸ المرجع السابق.

¹⁹ انظر .)الطبعة الثالثة، ١٩٩٨ يسبوسيتو، الإسلام: الصراط المستقيم (صحافة جامعة أكسفورد، ل. جون

²⁰ أيضا ماليسي روثفن، إسلام: مقدمة قصيرة جدا , (صحافة جامعة أكسفورد، الطبعة الثانية ٢٠٠٠). مقدمة في الحضارة الإسلامية، . مقدمة (١٩٩٢), و ر.م. سافوري، إد: أنيماري ششيميل، إسلام (١٩٧٦). وتجدر الإشارة إلى أن إبراهيم، الذي يدعى أيضا "البطريرك"، هو الرئيسي من الأنبياء في وقت أسس، في ما هو الآن مكة المكرمة، أول مكان للعبادة في العالم لعبادة مبكر لليهود والمسيحيين والمسلمين وكان أيضا والد إسماعيل وإسحاق. إله واحد

²¹ انظر م. شريف بسيوني، تعرف على الإسلام ٢٨ (١٩٨٥).

²² القرآن الكريم: الترجمة الإنجليزية المعاني والتعليق (٢٠٠٢)، في ٩٦: ٢ سورة العلق, http://www.muslim.org/english-quran/quran.htm يقول الله اقْرَأْ بِاسْمِ رَبِّكَ الَّذِي [_فيما يلي القرآن]. ,) خَلَقَ (١) خَلَقَ الْإِنْسَانَ مِنْ عَلَقٍ (٢) اقْرَأْ وَرَبُّكَ الْأَكْرَمُ (٣) الَّذِي عَلَّمَ بِالْقَلَمِ (٤) عَلَّمَ الْإِنْسَانَ مَا لَمْ يَعْلَمْ (٥ المرجع السابق, القرآن السورة ٩٦ الآية ١-٥.

²³ انظر عموما ويليام مونتغومري وات، محمد في مكة (١٩٥٣)؛ محمد في مدينة (١٩٥٦)؛ و محمد: النبي ورجل الدولة (صحافة جامعة أكسفورد، ١٩٦١). وقد تلقى النبي الوحي من الله، أحيانا وحده وأحيانا في وجود الآخرين، ووصف الآخرون الكلمات التي تتدفق من فمه بأنها مستوحاة وكان هذا وحي له (الإلهام الإلهي أو الوحي).

²⁴ المرجع السابق, وفقا للعادات التقليدية، النبي محمد هو نسل مباشر من إسماعيل، وتوقع بنبوته بتحرر تاريخ النبي، أدائه وأقواله، تم حفظها في البداية من قبل الصحابة وتم تمريرها عن طريق .والده، عبد الله ثم تم تسجيل أحاديث النبي .. ثم تم تسجيلها بشكل منهجي من قبل المؤرخ إسحاق بن يسار التسجيل الشفوي وأفعاله، والظروف المحيطة بحدوثها، والأدلة من أولئك الذين شهدوا لأول مرة ونقلها للآخرين من قبل الأكثر موثوقية ونصه لا يزال يعتمد عليه اليوم كما هو الأكثر أصالة العديد من العلماء. صحيح البخاري هو جنبا إلى جنب مع صحيح مسلم.

Mohammad was known to meditate and contemplate solely in the desert and during one of his contemplations, he received the first of his revelations from God.[14] The *Qur'an* recognizes the bearer of the message as the Angel Gabriel, who instructed the Prophet Mohammad to read and when Mohammad replied that he didn't know how, Gabriel replied, *"Read in the name of your Lord Who created man from a clot of blood . . ."* and in this way Mohammad became the conveyer of the divine message.[15] In Islam there can be no misunderstanding or hesitation that Mohammad was a man, and only a man, selected by the Creator to accomplish a divine mission as a prophet.[16] Muslims believe that the *Qur'an* is the Word of *Allah* (God) uttered through the revelations to the Prophet.[17]

Regarding the spread of Islam as a religion, after debating his message secretly with his wife, *Khadijah*, his cousin *'Ali*, and his friend *Abu Bakr*, the Prophet decided to leave *Mecca*, where he had lived in some threat in the year 622.[25] Afterwards, he migrated to *Yathrib* (later *Madina*), whose occupants

---

[25] *See generally* John L. Esposito, THE OXFORD ENCYCLOPEDIA OF THE MODERN ISLAMIC WORLD, 4 Vols. (Oxford Univ. Press, 1995) & ISLAM: THE STRAIGHT PATH (Oxford Univ. Press, 3rd ed., 1998).

بلا تحفظ، أن يؤمن به ويتبع القيم القرآنية نصاً ومضموناً.[20] فنبى الله محمد كان كثيراً ما يتأمل ويتفكر وحيداً فى الصحراء، و كان نزول الوحى عليه من الله لأول مرة أثناء إحدى هذه التأملات.[21] فقد أعلمنا القرآن الكريم أن ملك الوحى جبريل قد جاء رسول الله محمد وقال له "إقرأ" فكان جواب النبى "ما أنا بقارئ (أى: لا أستطيع القراءة)"، فرد عليه جبريل بأولى الرسالات الإلهية قول الله "إقرأ باسم ربك الذى خلق، خلق الإنسان من علق، إقرأ وربك الأكرم، الذى علم بالقلم، علم الإنسان مالم يعلم". وبذلك كان محمد هو حامل الرسالة الإلهية.[22] وليس من شك – فى الإسلام – أن محمد كان رجلاً، وليس سوى رجل إختاره الخالق لكى يضطلع بالمهمة الإلهية وهى الرسالة (أن يكون رسول الله إلى الناس أجمعين).[23] فالقرآن الكريم فى عقيدة المسلمين هو كلام الله المنزل إلينا عن طريق النبى محمد والذى تلقاه بطريق الوحى.[24]

وفيما يتعلق بنشر الدين الإسلامى، فقد قرر النبى – بعد مناقشة الأمر سراً مع زوجته خديجه وابن خاله على وصاحبه ابو بكر – أن يغادر مكة التى عاش فيها مهدداً، وكان ذلك عام ٦٢٢م.[37] وبذلك هاجر

[26] *Id.*
[27] Martin Lings, MUHAMMAD: HIS LIFE BASED ON THE EARLIEST SOURCES (1983).
[28] *Id.* See also Alfred Guillaume, *The Traditions of Islam: An Introduction to the Study of Hadīth Literature* (1924).
[29] Nissim Rejwan, (ed.), *The Many Faces of Islam: Perspectives on a Resurgent Civilization* (Florida Univ. Press 2000); John Renard, *In the Footsteps of Muhammad: Understanding the Islamic Experience* (1992); & John Renard, *Seven Doors to Islam: Spirituality and the Religious Life of Muslims* (California Univ. Press, 1996).
[30] AHMET AKGÜNDÜZ, INTRODUCTION TO ISLAMIC LAW: ISLAMIC LAW IN THEORY AND PRACTICE (2010), at 406.
[31] Shouket Akkuem, *A Legal and Historical Excursus of Muslim Personal Law in the Colonial Cape, South Africa, Eighteenth to Twentieth Century in* MUSLIM FAMILY LAW IN SUB-SAHARAN AFRICA: COLONIAL LEGACIES AND POST-COLONIAL CHALLENGES, Shamil Jeppie, Ebrahim Moosa, & Richard Roberts, (eds.) (Amsterdam Univ. Press 2010), at 63–84.
[32] *Id.* See also AKBAR AHMED, DISCOVERING ISLAM: MAKING SENSE OF MUSLIM HISTORY AND SOCIETY (Routledge 2002) & AKBAR AHMED, ISLAM TODAY: A SHORT INTRODUCTION TO THE MUSLIM WORLD (1999).
[33] Mohamed 'Arafa, *Towards a Culture for Accountability: A New Dawn for Egypt*, 5 PHOENIX L. REV.1 (2011), at 4-5 ("In 40 C.E., the Coptic Christians, followers of St. Marc, originated the first Christian church in Egypt. Then in 742 C.E., the first revolution in Egypt's history occurred when the Coptic Christians called on Arab Muslims to assist them in rebelling against the Byzantine Empire, which resulted in the expulsion of the Byzantines from Egypt.").
[34] *Id.*, at 5-7. For instance, in Egypt, it was the Archbishop of the Coptic Church who invited the Muslims to free Egypt from the Roman occupiers in 641. ("Though a majority is Muslim, Egypt enjoys freedom of religion and is fundamentally non-ideological and secular. About eighty to ninety percent of the population is Muslim, while the remainder is Christian. Historically, the Christians have enjoyed freedom of religion, yet have not always received full equality. In fact, Coptic Christians feel particularly besieged and discriminated against. Still, as a whole the majority of "Egyptians consider themselves Arab, Muslim (for those who are), and Egyptians all at once." Despite each person uniquely ranking these identity categories, most will declare he or she is an Egyptian first. This identification with nationality first supports the belief that ideological religious radicalism is not likely to take over in the near future.").
[35] See Saïd Arjomand, *Perso-Islamicate Political Ethic in Relation to the Sources of Islamic Law in* MIRROR FOR THE MUSLIM PRINCE: ISLAM AND THE THEORY OF STATECRAFT, Mehrzad Boroujerdi, (ed) (Syracuse Univ. Press 2013), at 82–206. In this sense, God says: ("We have honored the sons of Adam; provided them with transport on land and sea; given them for sustenance things good and pure; and conferred on them special favors, above a great part of our Creation") & ("It was We who created man, and We know that dark suggestions his soul makes to him: for We are nearer him than (his) jugular vein"). *Id.*, at *Qur'an* 17:70 & 50:16.
[36] Nandini Chatterjee, *Law, Culture and History: Amir Ali's Interpretation of Islamic Law in* LEGAL HISTORIES OF THE BRITISH EMPIRE: LAWS, ENGAGEMENTS AND LEGACIES, Shaunnagh Dorsett & John McLaren, (eds.) (Routledge, 2014), at 45–59.

[37] انظر بشكل عام جون ل. إسبوسيتو، موسوعة أوكسفورد في القانون الاسلامى المعاصر, المجلد الرابع, الصراط المستقيم (صحافة جامعة أكسفورد، الطبعة الثالثة), :(صحافة جامعة أكسفورد، ١٩٩٥) والإسلام (١٩٩٨).
[38] المرجع السابق.
[39] مارتن لينغز، محمد: حياته مستندة على المصادر المبكرة (١٩٨٣).
[40] المرجع السابق. انظر أيضا ألفريد غيوم، تقاليد الإسلام: مقدمة لدراسة الأدب فيما يتعلق بالحديث الشريف (١٩٢٤).

had invited him to come and expand and spread his message.²⁶ As a result, the history of the Islamic community is considered to have been officially born on the night of the *hejira* (migration's night), when the Prophet left *Mecca* for *Madina*.²⁷ Then, the *Madina's* citizens embraced Islam, and progressively, via a sequence of both military actions and diplomacy acts, Mohammad was able to reenter *Mecca* and to spread the word of Islam in the Arabian Peninsula.²⁸ It should be noted that, since Muslims were by the *Qur'an's* command obliged to respect the *ahl elzhemma*(h)/ *ahl elkitab* (People of the Book) their ancestors in receiving divine revelation, they recognized a

---

⁴¹ نسيم ريجوان، (محرر)، العديد من وجوه الإسلام: وجهات نظر عن الحضارة النامية (صحافة جامعة فلوريدا٢٠٠٠)؛ و جون رينارد، على خطى محمد: فهم التجربة الإسلامية (١٩٩٢)؛ وجون رينار، سبعة أبواب إلى الإسلام: الروحانية والحياة الدينية للمسلمين (صحافة جامعة كاليفورنيا، ١٩٩٦).
⁴² أحمت أكغوندوز، مقدمة للقانون الإسلامي: القانون الإسلامي في النظرية والتطبيق (٢٠١٠)، في ٤٠٦.
⁴³ شوكت أكويم، رحلة قانونية وتاريخية للقانون الشخصي الإسلامي في الرأس الاستعماري، جنوب أفريقيا، القرن الثامن عشر إلى القرن العشرين في قانون الأسرة المسلم في جنوب الصحراء الكبرى في أفريقيا: ميراث الإستعمار والتحديات ما بعد الإستعمار، شامل جبي، إبراهيم موسى، وريتشارد روبرتس، (محرران) (صحافة جامعة أمستردام أمسترداخ٢٠١٠)، في ٦٣-٨٤.
⁴⁴ المرجع السابق, انظر أيضا أكبر أحمد، اكتشاف الإسلام: منطقية من تاريخ المسلمين والمجتمع (روتليدج ٢٠٠٢) و أكبر أحمد، إسلام اليوم: مقدمة قصيرة للعالم المسلم (١٩٩٩).
⁴⁵ محمد عرفة، نحو ثقافة المساءلة: فجر جديد لمصر، ٥ فينيكس ل. ريف. (٢٠١١), في ٤-٥ ("في عام ٤٠ م، أنشأ المسيحيون الأقباط، أتباع سانت مارك، أول كنيسة مسيحية في مصر. ثم في عام ٧٤٢ م، حدثت الثورة الأولى في تاريخ مصر عندما دعا المسيحيون الأقباط المسلمين العرب إلى مساعدتهم في التمرد ضد الإمبراطورية البيزنطية، مما أدى إلى طرد البيزنطيين من مصر.").
⁴⁶ المرجع السابق. في ٥-٧. على سبيل المثال، كان رئيس أساقفة الكنيسة القبطية هو الذي دعا المسلمين إلى تحرير مصر من المحتلين الرومانيين في عام ٦٤١. (على الرغم من أن الأغلبية مسلمة، تتمتع مصر بحرية الدين وهي في الأساس غير أيديولوجية وعلمانية. حوالي من ٨٠ إلى ٩٠ في المئة من السكان مسلمون، والباقي مسيحيون، أما المسيحيون فقد تمتعوا بحرية الدين، لكنهم لم يحصلوا دائما على المساواة الكاملة. في الواقع، يشعر المسيحيون الأقباط بشكل خاص بالحصار والتمييز ضدهم، "معظم المصريين يعتبرون أنفسهم عربا ومسلمون (لمن هم كذلك) ومصريون في آن واحد". وعلى الرغم من أن كل شخص يحمل تصنيفا فريدا لهذه الفئات، فإن معظمهم سيعلن أنه مصري أولا، يدع الإعلان بالجنسية أولا الاعتقاد بأن التطرف العقائدي الديني ليس من المرجح أن يتولى في المستقبل القريب ").
⁴⁷ انظر سعيد أرجومند، الأخلاق السياسية الإسلامية الفارسية فيما يتعلق بمصادر الشريعة الإسلامية في انعكاس لأمير الإسلام: الإسلام ونظرية الكفاءة السياسية، مهرزاد بوروجيردي، (إد) (صحافة جامعة سيراكوس ٢٠١٣)، في ٨٢-٢٠٦. "وَلَقَدْ كَرَّمْنَا بَنِي آدَمَ وَحَمَلْنَاهُمْ فِي الْبَرِّ وَالْبَحْرِ" : في هذا المعنى يقول الله وَرَزَقْنَاهُم مِّنَ الطَّيِّبَاتِ وَفَضَّلْنَاهُمْ عَلَىٰ كَثِيرٍ مِّمَّنْ خَلَقْنَا تَفْضِيلًا " و " وَلَقَدْ خَلَقْنَا الْإِنسَانَ وَنَعْلَمُ مَا تُوَسْوِسُ بِهِ نَفْسُهُ ۖ وَنَحْنُ أَقْرَبُ إِلَيْهِ مِنْ حَبْلِ الْوَرِيدِ". المرجع السابق, سورة الإسراء الآية ٧٠ وسورة ق الآية ١٦.
⁴⁸ نانديني شاترجي، القانون والثقافة والتاريخ: تفسير الأمير علي للشريعة الإسلامية في التاريخ القانوني للإمبراطورية البريطانية: القوانين والإلتزامات المالية والمواريث، شونا دورسيت وجون ماكلارين، ٤٥-٥٩.(محرران) (روتلدج ٢٠١٤)، في

covenant with Christians and Jews.²⁹ 'Omar ibn al-Khattab was the second elected *Caliph* (successor) after the death of the Prophet. In this regard, 'Omar required all Muslims continually to assure and guarantee Christians freedom of religion, practice and use of their houses of worship (churches), and the right of their followers and *hajjis* (pilgrims) to visit their holy places.³⁰ In the same vein, he overturned the Roman decree expelling Jews from Jerusalem and pledged to protect their freedom of religious practice, thus, the 'Omar's Covenant was, in effect, the first international assurance of the protection of religious freedom.³¹ Then, Islam spread to Egypt in 641 and to all of North Africa by 654 and this was due in part to the military proficiency of the Muslim powers.³² But the message the Muslims were spreading and the custom in which they controlled the conquered regions were their strongest asset, as they brought with them not only a fresh faith but a better system of governance which was honest, authentic, and well-organized with a high level of motivation, integrity, transparency, and service.³³ By launching religious freedom and practice for Christians and Jews, they made the followers of these two beliefs their main allies in the countries they pursued to enter.³⁴ The clearness, straightforwardness, and logic of the faith embodied in its creeds and religious performs are its principal attractions along with the emphasis on individual accountability and personal commitment as well as the absence of an organized clergy, makes it readily transmittable.³⁵ In this respect, Islam is a complex historical, political, social, and economic phenomenon; it can be studied and interpreted from various philosophical, historical, and social perceptions. And as a belief, though,

Islam endures to speak to the modern world regardless its other significances, as what institutes the *ummah* (community) is not the existence of a political structure but the cognizant approval of its Muslim participants of God's will and their mission on the earth.36

On the other hand, by the time as a biggest civilization, the culture and evolution of Islam in *al-andalus* (Spain) were in full bloom "Golden Caliphate Era." Science, philosophy, and the liberal arts flourished and the greatest thinkers and minds in every discipline and from all over Europe and the Levant voyaged to *Cordoba* to study and learn.49 It is a twist of history that,

يحمله الدين الإسلامى من عدل ومساواة.46 كان منطق العقيدة الجديدة ووضوحها وإستقامتها أهم عوامل الجذب إليها، بالإضافة إلى التأكيد على مسئولية وواجب الفرد، وغياب طائفة رجال الدين – وهو ما جعلها سريعة الإنتشار.47 وفى هذا الصدد، يعد الإسلام ظاهرة متشعبة تاريخياً واجتماعيا وسياسياً واقتصادياً، فيمكن دراسته وتفسيره من منظور فلسفى أو تاريخى أو إجتماعى. كما أن خطابه الدينى المستمر حتى فى العصر الحديث يرجع إلى تأسيسه الأمة – ليس على نظام سياسى – ولكن على إيمان كافة المسلمين أعضاء المجتمع بمشيئة الله وبمهمتهم على الأرض.48

ومن ناحية أخرى، بلغت الحضارة الإسلامية أوجها فى عهد الخلافة الذهبى، وأصبحت ثقافة الإسلام وتطوره فى الأندلس جاذبة للأنظار، وإزدهرت العلوم والفنون والفلسفة مما دفع أبهى المفكرين من كافة أنحاء أوروبا

---

49 The greatest of these scholars made continuing contributions to science and letters and numerous have become familiar to students in the West under their Latin names, as the philosopher Averroes (Ibn Rushd), the mathematicians Arzachel (al-Zarqali), Alpetragius (al-Bitruji), and the physician Avenzoar (Ibn Zuhr), just to name a few. Perhaps the most distinguished of all contributions of Muslim scholars to science lay in the field of medicine. Muslim physicians made significant additions to the body of knowledge which they inherited from the Greeks. For instance, Ibn al-Nafis, discovered the lesser circulation of the blood hundreds of years before Harvey. Al-Zahrawi wrote a masterwork on anatomy and dissection, the *Tasrif*, which was translated into Latin by Gerard of Cremona and became a typical text in European medical schools throughout the Middle Ages. Ibn Baitar wrote a well-known work on drugs called Collection of Simple Drugs and Food, and this work served for periods of time as a precious reference guide to medicinal plants native to Spain and North Africa.

after periods of exceptional cultural brilliance, periods of deterioration and decay seem to come most rapidly.[50]

Islam As a Religion

The Creator has occasionally selected human beings to reveal His messages to humankind. In this domain, it should be noted that "Islamic" means that if the person (surrenders) himself/herself to God and worships him (purely) with no one else, he/she shall live in (peace and harmony) in this life and in the hereafter, as humans are born pre-formatted to submit to God within original Goodness, free choice, and with no inherited sins or compulsion, as *Qur'an* said "Let be no compulsion in religion" and with no supremacy as Mohammad said "All people are equal like a teeth of a comb"

---

[50] By 1248 the headlock in Seville had fallen, and the area of Spain under Muslim control was condensed to the Kingdom of Granada. There, miraculously, Islamic culture survived for more than two and a half centuries. Ironically, however, it was most likely the Ottoman capture. Soon after, fueled by the Christian fear of Islam, the future supporters of Christopher Columbus brought the screen down on one of the most remarkable and glorious civilizations inspired by Islam on 1492.

(equality principle in positive western doctrine).⁵³

Indeed, the *Qur'an* refers to several Prophets as Abraham, Noah, David, Isaac, Jacob, Moses, and Jesus and these messages and revelations ended in Islam and in Mohammed as the last Prophet.⁵⁵ The historical evolution and integration of prior messages into Islam are obviously identified in the

---

⁵³ *Id.*, at *Qur'an*, 2:256 meaning, Do not force anyone to become Muslim, for Islam is plain and clear, and its proofs and evidence are plain and clear. *Sahih Al-Bukhari & An-Nasa'i*. See also David Eisenberg, *Sources and Principles of Islamic Law in* ISLAMIC FINANCE: LAW AND PRACTICE, Craig R. Nethercott & David M. Eisenberg, (eds.) (2012), at 15–53. It should be noted that the Islamic Beliefs and Rituals are (a) Belief in *Allah* (God), (b) His angels, (c) His scriptures, (d) His messengers, (e) The Day of Resurrection, and (f) The divine destiny. The first means that No deity is worth worshipping except *Allah* (= one true God). Arab Christians and Jews worship *Allah* too. Arabic Christian Bible "IL" in Hebrew = *Allah*. Secondly, Angels are created from light, have no free choice and unlike the human beings, as they have different tasks, as sending messages. Then, Muslims believe in the *Torah*, the *Gospel*, and the *Qur'an* and believe in Messengers, Mohammad (PBUH) is not the founder of Islam, as all messengers are best humans, none of them is divine. Jesus is a messenger like the other messengers and is coming back and Prophet Mohammad is the final messenger. Mohammad said for example, "None of you truly believes until he wishes for his brother what he wishes for himself", "The powerful is not he who knocks the other down, indeed the powerful is he who controls himself in a fit of anger", and "If you are planting a tree and the end of the world came, just go ahead and plant it quickly." Muslims believe that they will be resurrected again and live an eternal life (hereafter) and this is the long term goal of every Muslim and they are supposed to change feelings of sadness and happiness to feelings of acceptance.

⁵⁵ *See generally* ROGER ARNALDEZ, AVERROES: A RATIONALIST IN ISLAM (Notre Dame Press 2000).

Qur'an, consequently, Islam is not a new religion.⁵⁶ *Qur'an* refers to Islam as the religion of Abraham, Jacob, Moses, Jesus, and other prophets and simply the last of the divine messages to reach humanity through Prophet Mohammad, who was chosen by the Creator as the deliverer of his last and all-inclusive revelation.⁵⁷ This elucidates why there exists a strong resemblance/link between Islam, Christianity, and Judaism. Christians and Jews are referred to in the *Qur'an* as the "People of the Book" as they are the inheritors of the messages of the Creator through Moses and the Old Testament prophets and through Jesus (New Testament), who is believed in Islam to be the fruit of a miracle birth by the Blessed Virgin Mary.⁵⁸ It should be noted that Western scholars and philosophers has been citing Mohammad as one of the greatest men on the earth, for instance famous historian Lamartine said: "If greatness of purpose, smallness of means and outstanding results are the three criteria of human genius, who could dare to compare any great man in modern history with Muhammad."⁵⁹ Also, Michael Heart cited that:

---

⁵⁶ Robert Gleave, *Islam and Literalism: Literal Meaning and Interpretation in Islamic Legal Theory*, (Edinburgh Univ. Press 2012), at 210-212.
⁵⁷ Nelly Hanna, *Guild Waqf: Between Religious Law and Common Law in* HELD IN TRUST: WAQF IN THE ISLAMIC WORLD, Pascale Ghazaleh, (ed.), (American Univ. Cairo Press 2011), at 135–153.
⁵⁸ *Id*.
⁵⁹ ALPHONSE DE LAMARTINE, L'HISTOIRE DE LA TURQUIE, Vol. II (1854), at 276.
⁶⁰ انظر عموما روجر أرنالديز، ابن رشد: عقلاني في الإسلام (صحافة نوتردام ٢٠٠٠).
⁶¹ روبرت جليف، الإسلام والحرفية: المعنى الحرفي والتفسير في النظرية القانونية الإسلامية، (صحافة جامعة إدنبرة ٢٠١٢)، في ٢١٠-٢١٢.
⁶² نيللي حنا، نقابة الوقف: بين القانون الديني والقانون العام في مجال الثقة: الوقف في العالم الإسلامي، ١٣٥-١٥٣.باسكال غزالة، (صحافة الجامعة الأمريكية بالقاهرة ٢٠١١)، في
⁶³ المرجع السابق.
⁶⁴ ألفونس دو لامارتين، التاريخ التركي المجلد٢, (١٨٥٤) في ٢٧٦.

الثلاثة لعبقرية الإنسان – فمن يجرؤ أن يقارن أى إنسان فى التاريخ الحديث بمحمد".[64] كذلك نوه مايكل هارت قائلاً:

"إختيارى لمحمد ليكون على رأس قائمة أكثر الأشخاص تأثيراً قد يدهش البعض وقد يثير تساؤلات لدى آخرين، إلا أنه كان الشخص الوحيد فى التاريخ ينجح على المستويين الدينى والدنيوى. إنه ذلك المزيج غير المسبوق من التأثير الدينى والدنيوى والذى يؤهله أن يكون الرجل الأكثر تأثيراً على مر تاريخ البشر".[66]

My Choice of Muhammad to lead the list of the world's most influential persons may surprise some readers and may be questioned by others, but he was the only man in history who was successful on both the religious and secular levels. It is this unparalleled combination of secular and religious influence which I feel entitles Muhammad to be considered the most influential single figure in human history[65]

---

[65] MICHAEL HEART, THE 100: A RANKING OF THE MOST INFLUENTIAL PERSONS IN HISTORY (2000) ("A list of the one hundred most influential people in history features descriptions of the careers, contributions, and accomplishments of the political and religious leaders, inventors, writers, artists, and others who changed the course of history."). In addition, Bernard Shaw said: "I believe that if a man like him were to assume the leadership of the modern world, he would succeed in solving its problems in a way that would bring to this world much needed peace and happiness" and Mahatma Ghandi said:
I became more than convinced that it was not the sword that won a place for Islam in those days in the scheme of life. It was the rigid simplicity, the utter self-effacement of the Prophet, the scrupulous regard for his pledges, his intense devotion to this friends and followers, his intrepidity, his fearlessness, his absolute trust in God and in his own mission. See GEORGE BERNARD SHAW, THE GENUINE ISLAM, Vol. I, No. 8 (1936 & 2002), at 8. He also said: "I have always held the religion of Muhammad in high estimation because of its wonderful vitality. It is the only religion, which appears to me to possess that assimilating capacity to the changing phase of existence, which can make itself appeal to every age" "I have studied him - the wonderful man and in my opinion far from being an anti-Christ, he must be called the Savior of Humanity" and "If any religion had the chance of ruling over England, nay Europe within the next hundred years, it could be Islam." Id.

[66] ال ١٠٠ : ميشيل هيرت، تصنيف الأفراد الأكثر تأثيرا في التاريخ (٢٠٠٠) ("قائمة تضم أكثر مائة شخص تأثيرا في التاريخ وصفا للوظائف، والمساهمات، وإنجازات القادة السياسيين والدينيين، وبالاضافة الى ذلك، قال برنارد والمخترعين، والكتاب، والفنانين، وغيرهم ممن غيروا مسار التاريخ.")

شو "اعتقد انه اذا كان رجل مثله سيتولى قيادة العالم الحديث، فانه سينجح فى حل مشاكله بطريقة تجلب الى هذا العالم السلام والسعادة اللازمين والمهتاما غاندى قال: "أصبحت أكثر من مقتنع أنه ليس السيف الذي حصل على مكانة للإسلام في تلك الأيام في مخطط الحياة. كانت الصرامة البسيطة، والكفاءة الذاتية المطلقة للنبي، والتقدير الدقيق لتعهداته، وتفانيه المكثف للأصدقاء وأتباعه، وبسالته، وجرأته، وثقته المطلقة في الله وفي مهمته الخاصة.

انظر جورج بيرنارد شاو، الإسلام الحقيقي، المجلد الأول، رقم ٨، (١٩٣٦, ٢٠٠٢) ص.٨ وقال أيضا: "لقد هذا هو الدين الوحيد الذي يبدو لي أنه يمتلك. احتفظت دائما بدين محمد في مكانة عالية بسبب حيويته الرائعة استيعاب القدرة على تغيير طور الوجود، والذي يمكن أن تجعل نفسه جذاب لكل العصور" "لقد درسته - و "إذا كان أي دين "رجل رائع وفي رأيي بعيدا عن كونه مناهضا للمسيح، يجب أن يدعى منقذ الإنسانية

In this regard, it should be noted that the three essential unities of Islam are, God, humankind (morality), and religion. Thus, Islam is a universal belief for all times, all places, and all peoples.[67] It is established on the belief that there is but one God, the universe's Creator and of humanity and the *Qur'an* opens with the words, "In the name of *Allah*, the Most Merciful, the Compassionate" and both are the principal qualities and these vital unities are the basis of faith.[68] Islam is the last and most all-inclusive message of God and religion in this sense is a set of rules that govern the relation between the Creator and the created and launch the accountability's basis in the hereafter.[69] Further, it highlights the framework for permitted economic, social, and political structures and articulates the principles and the norms (values) through which folks should deal with one another. In short, it offers a variety of prescriptions and strategies as well as inspiration.[70]

وفى هذا الصدد, ينبغى الإشارة إلى أن الثلاث عناصر الأساسية للإسلام هم الله, الجنس البشرى (الاخلاق), والدين. بناءا عليه فإن الإسلام اعتقاد يناسب جميع الأوقات، وجميع الأماكن، وجميع الشعوب.[71] فقد أس على أنه لا إله إلا الله, خالق الكون والبشرية ويبدأ القرآن أياته ب "بسم الله الرحمن الرحيم" وهما الصفات الرئيسية بل و الوحدات الحيوية التي يقوم علي أساسها الإيمان.[72] إن الإسلام هو الرسالة الأخيرة والأكثر شمولية من الله, والدين في هذا المعنى هو مجموعة من القواعد التي تحكم العلاقة بين الخالق والخلق ويقوم بتحديد أساس المساءلة في الآخرة.[73] وعلاوة على ذلك، فإنه يسلط الضوء على إطار الهياكل الإقتصادية والإجتماعية والسياسية المسموح بها ويبين المبادئ والقواعد (القيم) التي من خلالها يجب تعامل الأفراد مع بعضهم البعض. وباختصار، فإنه وإن كان مصدر

المرجع. "لديه فرصة لحكم انجلترا, بل أوروبا في غضون المائة سنة المقبلة، فيمكن أن يكون الإسلام السابق.

[67] *See generally* Caryle Murphy, *Passion for Islam—Shaping the Modern Middle East: The Egyptian Experience* (2002).

[68] *Id.* The *Qur'an* mentions the creation of the earth and other spiritual bodies out of the darkness of chaos. Scientific theories that store evolved about the creation highlight the unity of the universe.

[69] Sayyid M. Gilani, *Jurists and Legislators in Islam: Origin and Classification of the "Ulama" in* CONTEMPORARY ISSUES IN ISLAMIC LAW, ABDUL HASEEB ANSARI, (ed.) (2011), at 212-234.

[70] Gleave, *supra* note 29.

[71] انظر عموما كاريل ميرفي، الشغف للإسلام تشكيل الشرق الأوسط الحديث: التجربة المصرية (٢٠٠٢).

[72] النظريات . المرجع السابق. ويذكر القرآن خلق الأرض والهيئات الروحية الأخرى من ظلام الفوضى العلمية التي تخزن تطورت حول الخلق تسلط الضوء على وحدة الكون.

[73] م. جيلاني، الفقهاء والمشرعون في الإسلام: أصل وتصنيف "علماء" في القضايا المعاصرة في سيد الشريعة الإسلامية، عبد الحسيب الأنصاري، (محرر) (٢٠١١)، ص٢١٢-٢٣٤.

Islam is very much a law-oriented religion, as delivers the guidelines and philosophies upon which laws and regulations can be recognized.[75] Accordingly, the impact of Islam must not be observed in a scarcely legalistic light but rather as providing a comprehensive memorandum which guarantees basic life values, as fairness and justice to all.[76] It is holistic, needing that its followers have *iman* (faith) to accomplish the necessities of its religious doctrines, as Muslims are required to express their *'ibadat* (God's service) and *mo'malat* (daily transactions), through his deeds, conducts, and words.[77] Reward and punishment shall be meted out in heaven and hell, but God is merciful to those who repent and do good, as regret and mercy are among Islam's great ideals.[78] In this respect, Islam is built on five (pillars) testifying that there is no God but *Allah* and that Mohammad is the Messenger of God, performing the prayers, paying the *zakāh* (commercial obligation), fasting *Ramadan*, and making *hajj* (pilgrimage) to the Worship's House in *Mecca*.[79]

---

[74] غليف، الهامش الأعلى ٢٩.
[75] *See generally* KHALED ABOU EL FADL, SPEAKING IN GOD'S NAME: ISLAMIC LAW, AUTHORITY AND WOMEN (Oxford 2001) (detailing that the ethics at the heart of the Islamic legal system, and proposes that these statutes have been misinterpreted by specific sources to control women and other issues).
[76] Felicitas Opwis, MASLAHA AND THE PURPOSE OF THE LAW: ISLAMIC DISCOURSE ON LEGAL CHANGE FROM THE 4TH/10TH TO 8TH/14TH CENTURY (Brill 2010), at 370.
[77] In other words, *Qur'an* commands that Muslims do good and avoid evil, as life in this world is a channel, and the everlasting soul shall be mediated by the Almighty on the Day of Judgment through intentions as well as deeds.
[78] Gilani, *supra* note 36.
[79] Uriel I. Simonsohn, *A Common Justice: The Legal Allegiances of Christians and Jews Under Early Islam* (2011), at 306.
[80] انظر بوجه عام خالد أبو الفضل، متحدثا باسم الله: الشريعة الإسلامية، السلطة والمرأة (أوكسفورد ٢٠٠١) (تفصيلاً أن الأخلاقيات من صميم النظام القانوني الإسلامي، ويقترح أن هذه القوانين قد أساء تفسيرها من قبل مصادر محددة للسيطرة على النساء وغيرها من القضايا).

Bearing witness to the One and Only God (*shehada*), as *Allah* in Arabic indicates the one and only true God, the start and the end of everything, neither born nor giving birth.[85] The *Qur'an* emphasizes that He is beyond human description, and is referred to in it by ninety-nine attributes, such as the merciful, the compassionate, the forgiving among many others (there is no deity worthy of worship but *Allah*).[86] Together with the command to bear witness and acknowledge the distinctiveness, supremacy, unity, and uniqueness (exclusivity) of God, the believer is enjoined to confess that Mohammad is God's Apostle (messenger) and prophet.[87]

---

[81] فيليسيتاس أوبويس، المصلحة والغرض من القانون: الخطاب الإسلامي على تعديل القانون من القرن الرابع / العاشر إلى الثامن / الرابع عشر (ابريل 2010)، ص 370.

[82] وبعبارة أخرى، فإن القرآن أمر المسلمين بفعل الخير وتجنب الشر، والحياة في هذا العالم هو مسار، ويجب أن تتوسط الروح الأبدية من قبل سبحانه وتعالى في يوم القيامة من خلال النوايا وكذلك الأفعال. جيلاني، الهامش الأعلى 36.

[83]

[84] سيمونسوهن، العدالة المشتركة: الأخلاقيات القانونية للمسيحيين واليهود تحت الإسلام المبكر إ. أوريل (2011)،ص 306.

[85] For further details on the pillars, *see generally* ABDULKADER TAYOB, ISLAM: A SHORT INTRODUCTION (1999); DAVID WAINES, AN INTRODUCTION TO ISLAM (2003); WILLIAM MONTGOMERY WATT, THE FORMATIVE PERIOD OF ISLAMIC THOUGHT (1998); WHAT IS ISLAM? (1970), & JOHN ALDEN WILLIAMS, (ed.) THE WORD OF ISLAM (1994).

[86] *Id.* Whoever says this with sincerity is to be considered as a Muslim and Whoever dies on this belief will enter Paradise if his sins were forgiven by God.

[87] *Id. See also* Abdul Haseeb Ansari & Saad Abu Elgasim, *Command Theory of Legal Positivism and Hukum Shar'i: A Comparison in* CONTEMPORARY ISSUES IN ISLAMIC LAW, ABDUL HASEEB ANSARI, (ed.) (2011), at 63–97 & RAJ BHALA, UNDERSTANDING ISLAMIC LAW: SHARI'A (2011), at 40-55.

[88] مقدمة قصيرة (1999). : لمزيد من التفاصيل حول الركائز، انظر عموما عبد القادر طايوب، إسلام ديفيد وينز، مقدمة إلى الإسلام (2003)؛ ويليام مونتغومري وات، الفترة التكوينية للفكر الإسلامي (1998).(1970)، و جون ألدين ويليامز، (محرر) عالم الإسلام (1994)؛ ما هو الإسلام؟

[89] المرجع السابق، كل من يقول هذا بإخلاص يعتبر مسلم ومن مات على هذا الاعتقاد سوف يدخل الجنة إذا غفر له خطاياه من قبل الله.

On the other hand, while required by the *Qur'an*, *zakāh* (religious tax) is specified in detail only in Mohammad's teachings and the practice and in later Islamic *tafasir* (interpretations).[91] It is the payment of a specific percentage of one's income to sustain the needy and to fulfill other community *masaleh* (purposes).[92] In other words, it means as a mandatory financial obligation on Muslims (purification/alms). It is one of the five fundamental pillars of Islam, and its observance distinct true believers from sole nominal Muslims, as it represents a conduct required by Muslims to validate their faith and dedication to God.[93] In practice, *zakāh* is an amount of money paid by Muslims at the end of the year as an obligatory payment to the needy and susceptible members of society, in particular orphans, widows, and the elderly, who can no longer work and provide for themselves.[94] Muslim society is divided into two halves: one half is obliged to give *zakāh* and the other entitled to take it and the criterion governs whether a Muslim belongs to the half that gives or the half

---

[90] المرجع السابق, انظر أيضا عبد الحسيب أنصاري وسعد أبو القاسم, نظرية القيادة الوضعيه القانونية والحكم الشرعي: مقارنة في القضايا المعاصرة في القانون الإسلامي, عبد الحسيب الأنصاري, (محرر) (٢٠١١), ص٦٣-٩٧ و راج بهالا, فهم الشريعة الإسلامية: الشريعة (٢٠١١), ص٤٠-٥٥.

[91] *Id.* See also Mohamed 'Arafa, *Corporate Social Responsibility and the Fight Against Corruption: Towards the Concept of CSR in Egypt after the January Revolution* in CORPORATE SOCIAL RESPONSIBILITY IN COMPARATIVE PERSPECTIVE, COUNCIL ON INTERNATIONAL LAW AND POLITICS (2014).

[92] Salma Taman, *The Concept of Corporate Social Responsibility in Islamic Law*, 21 IND. INT'L. & COMP. L. REV. 3 (2011) (providing further elaboration concerning the charities in Islamic Law), at 490-492. It should be noted that 2.5% of any cash savings held for one year, 5% to 10% of any agriculture income, and 20% of any extracted resources and minerals as a *zakāh*. In other words, it is the right of the poor on the rich and it is not a not charity.

[93] *Id.*
[94] *Id.*

that receives is whether he or she owns the ("*sahib el-nisab*": "wealthy person").⁹⁵ Further, it is not basically have to be paid in money; it can be paid in the form of agricultural products, especially in the form of food for the hungry.⁹⁶

While this can be rightly equated to a combination of taxation and charity, it should bear in mind that *zakāh* is

---

⁹⁵ 'Arafa, *supra* note 46.

⁹⁶ *Id*. Thus, giving *sadaqah* (charity) to draw consideration to one's fortune does not attract a reward. In other words, it means "purification" or "small daily acts of charity to be blessed and receive the mercy of God." This can be in the form of small sums of money given to the poor but also practical actions, such as carrying a load for an elder person. However, throughout the *Qur'an*, God inspires Muslims to give *sadaqah* to the needy whenever they can, by emphasizing the substantial multiplication of rewards for those who freely give of their assets and time. On the other hand, there is no specific time or amount required by the *Qur'an* for giving *sadaqah*. See TALLAL ALIE TURFE, UNITY IN ISLAM: REFLECTIONS AND INSIGHTS (2004), at 132.

different from *sadaqa* (charity) which is equally mandated by the *Qur'an* but left to the discretion of the individual, depending upon circumstances (case-by-case basis).[103] *Sadaqa* is both tangible and intangible a kind word, but commonly, *zakāh* is physical and often paid at the end of the *Ramadan* fast and non-Muslims (people of the book: Christians and Jews), are not required to pay it but another tax, called *jizyah* (poll tax) through the Islamic history.[104] Modern Muslim scholars indicates that *zakāh* is "an income redistribution mechanism, not necessarily to provide revenue to the state but to

---

[103] *Id.*

[104] Under Islamic law, *Jizya* is a *per capita* tax levied on a division of an Islamic state's non-Muslim citizens, who meet specific criterions and requirements. The tax was to be applied on able bodied adult males of military age and affording power "but with particular exemptions." From the Muslim leaders' perspective, *Jizya* was a substantial (material) proof of the non-Muslims' approval and recognition of subjection and overpowering to the Islamic state and its laws, "just as for the inhabitants it was a concrete continuation of the taxes paid to earlier regimes." In turn, non-Muslim residents were acceptable to practice their faith to enjoy a measure of mutual autonomy, to be entitled to Muslim state's protection and security on their life, kids, property, etc….from outside aggression, to be exempted from military service and the *zakāh* tax is mandatory upon Muslim citizens. In short, *Jizya* is the tax poll in which the tax inflicted on the people of religions ("People of Book "D[Z]himmis") other than Islam for their protection and safety. For further explanation on *Jizyah*, *see* JAVED AHMED GHAMIDI, THE ISLAMIC LAW OF JIHAD (2001).

[105] The philosophy of *zakat*(h) institution brings about protection of property from encroachment and grudge; a means to aid the poor and those in need; cleanses one's heart from frugality and parsimony; gives support and dignity to needy Muslims, and a means of expressing gratitude to *Allah* for all His bounties.

[106] المرجع السابق.

correct imbalances in the social structure... though a ratio of 2.5% is prescribed, income is raised through *zakāh* thus ensuring effective redistribution."[105]

Then, *Salat* (prayers) represents the most significant pillar of Islam, however, the *Qur'an* does not mention the number and its manner; these were established by the Prophet's teachings. Muslims required prayers are said five times a day: at dawn, noon (when the sun is at the center of the sky), afternoon (when the sun is halfway to sunset) sunset, and night (after sunset but before sunrise).[109] The only required communal prayer is the Friday noon prayer and this like the Christians' Sunday or the Jews' Sabbath, Muslims consider Friday the last day of Creation.[110] Prayers can also be collective; that is, in fact, the preferred way, and when so conducted, the prayers are led by an *imam* (leader) like a priest, who is usually either an individual schooled in Islam or basically one among the

والمسيحيين) غير مطالبين بدفع الزكاة ولكن عليهم القيام بإداء نوع أخر من الضرائب المسمي بالجزية من خلال التاريخ الإسلامي.[107] أما علماء الفقه الحديث في الإسلام يشيروا إلي أن الزكاة هي "آلية إعادة توزيع الدخل، وليس بالضرورة أن تكون مصدر دخل للدولة ولكن تقوم بتصحيح اختلال التوازن في البنية الاجتماعية ...من خلال نسبة محددة وهي 2.5%، وبالتالي يرفع الدخل من خلال الزكاة وبناءا عليه يضمن إعادة توزيع للدخل فعال.[108]

ثم الصلاة, التي تمثل أهم أركان الإسلام، ومع ذلك، فإن القرآن الكريم لا يذكر لها عددا ولا طريقة, لكن تم تقريرها من قبل سنة النبي عليه الصلاة والسلام. يتطلب من المسلمين أداء خمس صلوات يوميا: عند الفجر، ظهرا (عندما تكون الشمس في وسط السماء)، عصرا (عندما تكون الشمس في منتصف الطريق إلى غروب الشمس), عند غروب الشمس، وليلا (بعد غروب الشمس ولكن قبل شروق الشمس).[117] و صلاة الظهر يوم الجمعة هي الصلاة الجماعية الوحيدة المطلوبة من المسلمين، وهي مثل يوم الأحد عند المسيحيين أو السبت

---

[109] NISSIM REJWAN (ed.), THE MANY FACES OF ISLAM: PERSPECTIVES ON A RESURGENT CIVILIZATION (2000); John Renard, *In the Footsteps of Muhammad*: *Understanding the Islamic Experience* (1992). The five daily prayers should be on time, at any pure (clean) spot on the earth, and at one direction, all towards *Macca* (Sense of unity). All biblical Prophets like Abraham, Moses, Aron, & Jesus fell on their faces in their prayers, Islam is reviving the prophetic traditions that people forgot.
[110] *Id*. See also Simonsohn, *supra* note 42.

group who is more knowledgeable, older, or recognized by the others as being especially pious.[111] Standing shoulder to shoulder, regardless of status in life, indicates equality before God, as the Prophet of Islam said, "no man is better than another save for his piety, which only *Allah* can judge."[112] All praying Muslims face *Mecca*, where the *kaib'aa* (holds the remnants of Abraham's sanctuary) is placed in which the *qibla* (the direction) which provides unity and homogeneousness (uniformity) for all Muslims.[113] In this domain, the *imam* does not

عند اليهود، وينظر المسلمين إلى يوم الجمعة بأنه اليوم الأخير للخليقة.[118] يمكن كذلك أن أن تكون الصلوات كافة جماعية وهذا هو الأفضل, وعندما تجرى الصلاة في جماعة تكون بواسطة إمام لها مثله مثل الكاهن. والذي يكون عادة إما فرد تدرس في الإسلام أو الشخص الذي يكون الأكثر دراية في المجموعة، أوالأكبر سنا ، أو المعروف عنه من قبل الآخرين بتدينه.[119] ووقوف

---

[111] Muslims stand shoulder to shoulder and kneel several times, depending on whether it is the morning prayer (twice) or the late-night prayer (four times).
[112] SAHAIH AL-BUKRAI & SAHIH MUSLIM. At each kneeling, the Muslim places his forehead on the ground, a sign of the equality of all men, humbleness, devotion of the Creator, and the fact that from earth we come and to earth we return.
[113] At an earlier time, it was the practice to face Jerusalem, the second holiest city in Islam.
[114] It should be noted that One reaches this status after having pursued a wide-ranging education in theology through secondary, college, and graduate study at a theological university.
[115] KENNETH CRAGG, THE EVENT OF THE QUR'AN: ISLAM IN ITS SCRIPTURE (1971).
[116] The call starts with "*Allahu Akbar*" (God is great), words regularly used by Muslims either in prayers or in other frameworks as a restatement of the oneness and omnipotence of the Creator. The expression "*al-hamdu lillah*" (thanks to God) is also among the expressions most commonly used by Muslims used in any circumstances in which a grateful or thankful response is appropriate. They are a prompt that God's will and abundance are everything.

[117] نيسيم ريجوان (محرر), وجوه كثيرة للإسلام: آفاق على المدنية (٢٠٠٠)؛ جون رينارد، على خطى محمد: فهم التجربة الإسلامية (١٩٩٢). يجب أن تكون الصلوات الخمس في الوقت المحدد، في أي بقعة نقية (نظيفة) على الأرض، وفي انجاه واحد، كل نحو مكة (للشعور بالوحدة). سقط كل الأنبياء التورانيين مثل إبراهيم وموسى وهارون ويسوع على وجوههم في صلواتهم، والإسلام ينعش التقاليد النبوية التي نسيها الناس.
[118] المرجع السابق, انظر أيضا سيمونسوهن الهامش الإعلي ٤٢.
[119] يقف المسلمون جنبا إلى جنب ويركعوا عدة مرات، اعتمادا على ما إذا كانت صلاة الصباح (مرتين) أو صلاة في وقت متأخر من الليل (أربع مرات).
[120] في كل الركوع، يضع المسلم جبينه على الأرض، علامة على صحيح البخاري والصحيح مسلم. المساواة بين جميع الرجال، والتواضع، وتفاني الخالق، وحقيقة أن من الأرض نأتي وإلى الأرض نعود.
[121] في وقت سابق، كان من العادة مواجهة القدس، ثاني أقدس مدينة في الإسلام.
[122] وتجدر الإشارة إلى أنه لكي يصل الشخص إلى هذا الوضع بعد أن اتبع تعليم واسع النطاق في علم التوحيد من خلال الدراسة الثانوية والكليات والدراسات العليا في جامعة علم التوحيد.
[123] كينيث كراغ، حدث القرآن: الإسلام في الكتاب (١٩٧١).
[124] الله أكبر", من الكلمات التي يستخدمها المسلمون بانتظام إما في الصلوات أو في أطر " تبدأ الصلاة ب الحمدالله" هو أيضا من بين التعبيرات الأكثر "أخرى لإعادة التصريح بالوحدة والكفاءة للخالق. تعبير استخداما من قبل المسلمين المستخدمة في أي ظرف من الظروف التي تكون فيها استجابة ممتنة أو شكر مناسب. إنها مطالبة بأن إرادة الله وفرة كل شيء.

automatically have any special religious status in *Sunni* tradition just because he is the prayer leader, though, he could be a person whose education or training conversed on him special status, as is the case with the *'ulema'a* (scholars).¹¹⁴ Further, before prayers, Muslims are required to make *wadu'u* (ablutions), which comprise washing the face, arms, and feet in a ritual prescribed by the Prophet and this is not only for the cleaning purposes, but also to provide a break from prior activity and a Muslim must confirm within himself/herself his/her intention before both (praying/ablutions).¹¹⁵ In addition, prayers are usually announced by means of a summons or *adthan* (call to prayer) by the *muadhin* (who chants or intones it). There is no religious status taken by this responsibility; the *muadhin* is usually a pious person of the community who has a particularly good, strong or echoing voice.¹¹⁶

المصليون صفا واحدا كتفا إلي كتف، بغض النظر عن مراكزهم في الحياة، يشير إلي المساواة أمام الله، كما قال النبي صلي الله عليه وسلم: لا يوجد رجل أفضل من آخر حفظ لتقواه، والتي لا يقضى فيها سوي الله.¹²⁰ يوجه المسلمون صلواتهم إلي مكة المكرمة حيث توجد الكعبة (بقايا ملجأ إبراهيم عليه السلام) وتوجه إليها قبلة المسلمين التي تؤدي إلي توافر الوحدة والتجانس (الانتظام) لجميع المسلمين.¹²¹ في هذا المجال، لا يملك الإمام تلقائيا - لكونه قائد الصلاة- أي وضع ديني خاص عند أهل السنة، على الرغم من أنه يمكن أن يكون شخصا تعليمه أو تدريبه يشير إلي وضع خاص له، كما هو الحال بالنسبة لهيئة علماء المسلمين.¹²² وعلاوة على ذلك، يطلب علي المسلمين أن يقوموا بالوضوء قبل الصلاة، ويشمل الوضوء غسل الوجه والذراعين والقدمين بالطريقة التي حددها النبي صلي الله عليه وسلم, وليس النظافة الغرض الوحيد منه ولكن أيضا لتوفير استراحة من النشاط السابق، ويجب على المسلم أن يؤكد نيته قبل (الصلاة / الوضوء).¹²³ وبالاضافة الى ذلك, الإعلان عن الصلاة يكون عادة عن طريق الأذان (الدعوة للصلاة) والذي يقوم به المؤذن (الذي يردد أو يرتل الأذان). ولا يحتاج أداء الأذان إلي أي حالة دينية, فالمؤذن عادة ما يكون شخصا متدينا من المجتمع يحظى بصوت جيد أو

The *masjed* (mosque) is a symbol of the uncompromising nature of Islamic monotheism and has a typical architecture, which contains a minaret for the call to prayer and does not comprise any images that might be associated with religious adoration, which Islam forbids and Muslims remove their shoes before entering so as not to soil the place where they touch their foreheads to the floor to pray.125 Mohammad said "The best of you are those who have the most excellent morals." 126 *Siyam* (fasting) from dawn to sunset during the month of *Ramadan*, the ninth month in the Islamic lunar calendar, is required of those whose health conditions permits.127 It is a comprehensive complete fast, requiring that nothing be taken into the body but needed medication (no eating, drinking [even water], or sexual activities from dawn till sunset) and during this month, there is a stress on piety and religious observances.128 Under Islamic law, based on necessities, those who are sick or traveling, specifically long distances do not have to fast during *Ramadan* but must compensate by fasting and by contributing to the *zakāh* if they have the ability.129

---

125 Cragg, *supra* note 61.
126 AL-BUKRAI & MUSLIM.
127 Oussama Arabi, David S. Powers, & Susan A. Spectorsky, (eds.), *Islamic Legal Thought: A Compendium of Muslim Jurists* (Brill 2013), at 590.
128 In other words, the goal of this fasting is patience and perseverance through discipline.
129 Necessity case in Islamic law is a state that makes a person infringe the law despite himself/herself to avoid an inevitable evil ensuing him/her, however it is in his/her power not to transgress the law and permit the evil to take place over him/her or someone else. Islamic *Shari'a* exempts such an individual from punishment. *See* M. CHERIF BASSIOUNI, THE ISLAMIC CRIMINAL JUSTICE SYSTEM (1982), at 193-194.

Introduction to Islam

الفجر حتى غروب الشمس)، وخلال هذا الشهر يكون هناك إصرار على التقوى وإقامة الشعائر الدينية.[133] بموجب الشريعة الإسلامية، واستنادا إلى الضروريات، فالمريض أو المسافر، وتحديدا لمسافات طويلة ليس عليهم الصيام خلال شهر رمضان ولكن يجب أن يعوضوا عن ذلك عن طريق الصيام والمساهمة في الزكاة إذا كان لديهم القدرة.[134]

The *hajj* (pilgrimage) to *Mecca* once in one's lifetime is required of all those who have the physical (good health) and financial capability to make the trip.[135] The practice derives from the divine mandate given Mohammad to rebuild the first place of God's worship in *Mecca*.[136] The pilgrimage requirement makes this city a gathering place for folks from all parts of the world once a year its rites were established by the Prophet.[137] Folks accentuate repentance, resulting in forgiveness by God and also strengthens the pledge among the faithful from all walks of life and regions of the world.[138]

الحج إلى مكة المكرمة مرة واحدة في العمر وهو مطلوب من جميع أولئك الذين لديهم القدرة الجسدية (صحة جيدة) والقدرة المالية للقيام بالرحلة.[139] هذه الممارسة مستمدة من الولاية الإلهية التي أعطيت لمحمد صلى الله عليه وسلم لإعادة بناء المقام الأول لعبادة الله في مكة المكرمة.[140] وشرط الحج يجعل هذه المدينة مكان تجمع للناس من جميع أنحاء العالم مرة سنويا طبقا لطقوسها وتعليماتها التي أنشأها النبي.[141] يؤكد

---

[132] سبكتورسكي، (محررين)، الفكر القانوني الإسلامي: أ. سوزان بويرس، و .س. أسامة عربي، ديفيد خلاصة وافية من الفقهاء المسلمين (بريل 2013)، ص 590.

[133] وبعبارة أخرى، فإن الهدف من هذا الصيام هو الصبر والمثابرة من خلال الانضباط.

[134] حالة الضرورة في الشريعة الإسلامية هي الحالة التي تجعل الشخص ينتهك القانون على الرغم من نفسه لتفادي شر لا مفر منه يترتب عليه، إلا أنه في سلطته عدم تجاوز القانون والسماح للشر أن يحدث له م. شريف باسيوني، نظام العدالة الجنائية في الإسلام (1982)، ص193-194.

[135] In other words, *hajj* is for those who are able once in lifetime and guarantees the universality of the religion.

[136] SEYYED H. NASR, MUHAMMAD: MAN OF GOD (1995).

[137] M. CHERIF BASSIOUNI, INTRODUCTION TO ISLAM (1988). God says: "Ye who believe! Fasting is prescribed to you as it was prescribed to those before you, That ye may (learn) self-restraint, ..." *Id.*, at *Qur'an* 2:183.

[138] *Id.* It is performed during the Islamic lunar month of *dhu al-hijja* in which the big feast is taking place. And it should be remember that Abraham and Isma'il raised the

Islamic Law

Islam looks to a substantial degree to ethical and decent development within the individual to reinforce resolve and foster self-restraint.[143] Thus, the focus is upon determining the higher-order preferences expounded in the *Qur'an* and the *Sunnah* through the law of the *Shari'a*, reinforced by an influential spiritual enticement system.[144] In this sense, Muslim scholars do not consider Islam to be an developing religion, but rather a religion and legal system which applies to all times, so, the application that is vulnerable to evolution.[145]

---

foundations of the House (With this prayer): "Our Lord! Accept (this service) from us: For Thou art the All-Hearing, the All-knowing." *Id.*, at *Qur'an* 2:127.

[143] AHMAD FARRAG HUSSIEN, AL-MADKL LE DERASSAT AL-SHARI'A AL-ISLAMIA: AL-KITAB AL-AWAL [AN INTRODUCTION TO THE STUDY OF ISLAMIC SHARI'A: BOOK I] (2006) (on file with author), at 33-36.

[144] AHMAD FARRAG HUSSIEN, 'USUL AL-FIQH AL-ISLAMI [PRINCIPLES OF ISLAMIC JURISPRUDENCE] (2006) (on file with author), at 55-67.

[145] RAMADAN 'ALI AL-SHORONBASY, AL-MADKL LE DERASSAT AL-FIQH AL-ISLAMIA: AL-GOZE'E AL-AWAL [AN INTRODUCTION TO THE STUDY OF ISLAMIC JURISPRUDENCE: PART I] (2003) (on file with author), at 16-33 & 38-67.

In fact, the *Qura'nic* provisions are such that by their self-controlled interpretation, with the aid of the *hadith* and other sources of interpretation (Islamic schools), Islam can, as envisioned, provide the solution to modern social difficulties.[149] Fourteen centuries ago Islam was a divine, social, and legal revolution, its potential for achieving progress remains unchanged.[150] This is fundamentally the belief of rational *fundamentalist* Muslims.[151] Thus, Islamic fundamentalism is not, a regressive view of history and contemporary reality. Islam at the height of its civilization, between the seventh and eleventh centuries, was neither oppressive nor regressive, it was a liberal, humanistic, and legalistic force for reform and justice. It should be noted that both legal positive systems—domestic [civil or common] and international—can learn from the Islamic legal system. To get a better understanding of this law, a brief survey of Islamic law and *fiqh* (Islamic Jurisprudence), its sources, and its famous Islamic schools of jurisprudence (*fiqh al-mazaheb/madhhabs*) will be expounded.

---

[148] رمضان الشرنباصي, المدخل لدراسات الفقه الإسلامي الجزء الأول. (٢٠٠٣) (محفوظ لدي المؤلف) ص١٦-٣٣ و٣٨-٦٧.
[149] *Id.*, at 65.
[150] Hussien, *supra* note, 72, at 80-82.
[151] *Id.*
[152] المرجع السابق ص ٦٥.
[153] حسين, الهامش الأعلى ٧٢, ص ٨٠-٨٢.
[154] المرجع السابق.

Islam is the major religion in the Middle East. Muslims are divided into *Sunnis* and *Shi'aas*, though they share the same religion, *Sunnis* and *Shi'aas* vary in their visions of history, politics, and government.[155] Unlike other religions, Islam, commands all behavior undertaken by Muslims, including commercial relations and business transactions.[156] Islam stresses the importance of the spiritual aspect in every realm of human activity, counting the economic one, to guarantee it is in accord with the Islamic ideals.[157] The term "Islamic Law" is normally used in reference to the entire system of law and jurisprudence associated with the religion of Islam, including the key sources of law and the secondary sources of law, as well as the methodology used to infer and apply the law.[158] Islamic law is divided into *'ibadat* (worship) rules regulating the relation between an individual and God and *mo'amalat* (transactions) rules governing the linkage between individuals and societal (private) standards, which are unpredictable and change according to time and

---

[155] Ali ibn AbiTaleb (the fourth rightly guided *Caliph*) and Ma'waia ibn Abi Soufyian. *Shi'aa* constitutes 10% or fewer of the Muslim world and they predominantly live in Iran, Iraq, Syria, Lebanon and are minorities in North Africa, Bahrain, Pakistan, and Saudi Arabia. For a more details about *Shi'aa* and their subgroups, *see* BILAL A. PHILIPS, THE EVOLUTION OF FIQH (1992).

[156] IAN EDGE, ISLAMIC LAW AND LEGAL THEORY (1996).

[157] YOUSSEF KASSEM, MASADER AL-FIQH AL-ISLAMI [SOURCES OF ISLAMIC LAW] 65 (2000). Islamic communities can benefit from the practical stratagems, administrative, and civilian reforms (better governance). They can also benefit from media and press freedom and public debate, which exert pressure for liability and transparency and help to curb and detain the arbitrary misuse of power and privilege options all too often prevalent in the Muslim World.

[158] Norman Calder, *Legal Thought and Jurisprudence in* 2 THE OXFORD ENCYCLOPEDIA OF THE MODERN ISLAMIC WORLD (John L. Esposito ed., 1995).

[159] Al-Shoronbasy, *supra* note 74, at 8 ("The Islamic legal system is unusual in that it its origins are in religious doctrine. Yet like other legal systems, Islamic ("*Shari'a*") law has its own distinctive processes of identifying and developing legal norms. The role of jurists in framing rules of law is also unusual in Islamic law, in large part because it is both a religion and a means toward establishing a legal and social order in civil and criminal

place.¹⁵⁹

In this regard, Islamic law (*Shari'a* or "the right/straight path" in Arabic) is one of the world's main legal systems standing along with common law and civil law systems, even the legal literature have a little coverage on that.¹⁶⁵ *Shari'a* is an accumulation of Islamic law values and comprises principal and supplementary sources. *Qur'an* (holly book of Muslims) is the primary source of Islamic law or jurisprudence.¹⁶⁶ Muslims believe the *Qur'an* is the word of God which

الإسلامية إلى قواعد العبادات التي تنظم العلاقة بين الفرد والله, والمعاملات التي تحكم الارتباط بين الأفراد والمعايير الاجتماعية (الخاصة) والتي لا يمكن التنبؤ بها والتي تتغير حسب الزمان والمكان.¹⁶⁴

في هذا الصدد، فإن الشريعة الإسلامية هي واحدة من النظم القانونية الرئيسية في العالم التي تقف جنبا إلى جنب مع القانون العام ونظم القانون المدني، حتى الأدبيات القانونية لديها تغطية قليلة على ذلك.¹⁷² الشريعة هي تراكم لقيم الشريعة الإسلامية وتتألف من مصادر رئيسية ومكملة. لقرآن (الكتاب المقدس لدي المسلمين) هو

---

matters. As such, it comprises rules concerning devotional obligations as well as rules that create a comprehensive and integrated guide to all aspects of political, economic, national, social, and even international affairs.").

¹⁶⁰ الشيعة يشكلون ١٠٪ أو وعلي بن أبي طالب (رابع الخلفاء الراشدين بحق)، ومعاوية بن أبي سفيان، أقل من العالم الإسلامي ويعيشون في الغالب في إيران والعراق وسوريا ولبنان وهم أقليات في شمال أفريقيا لمزيد من التفاصيل عن الشيعة ومجموعاتهم الفرعية، انظر. والبحرين وباكستان والمملكة العربية السعودية فيليبس، تطور الفقه ١٩٩٢ أ. بلال).

¹⁶¹ إبيان إدج، الشريعة الإسلامية ونظرية القانون (١٩٩٦).

¹⁶² يوسف قاسم، مصادر الفقه الإسلامي ٦٥ (٢٠٠٠). يمكن للمجتمعات الإسلامية أن تستفيد من الحيل العملية والإدارية، والإصلاحات المدنية (الحكم الرشيد). يمكنهم أيضا الاستفادة من وسائل الإعلام وحرية الصحافة والنقاش العام، التي تمارس الضغط على المسؤولية والشفافية وتساعد على كبح واحتجاز إساءة الاستخدام التعسفي للسلطة وخيارات الامتياز، وهي سائدة في العالم الإسلامي.

¹⁶³ نورمان كالدر، الفكر القانوني والفقه في ٢ موسوعة أوكسفورد عن العالم الإسلامي الحديث (جون ل. إسبوسيتو محرر, ١٩٩٥).

¹⁶⁴ الشرنباصي الهامش الأعلى ٧٤ ص٨ ("النظام القانوني الإسلامي غير عادي من حيث أن أصوله في العقيدة الدينية، ولكن مثل الأنظمة القانونية الأخرى، فإن الشريعة لها عملياتها المميزة المتمثلة في تحديد وتطوير القواعد القانونية، ودور الفقهاء في صياغة قواعد القانون هي أيضا غير عادية في الشريعة الإسلامية، ويرجع ذلك في جزء كبير منه إلى كونه دينيا ووسيلة نحو إنشاء نظام قانوني واجتماعي في المسائل المدنية والجنائية، ومن ثم فهو يتضمن قواعد تتعلق بالالتزامات التعبدية وكذلك قواعد تنشئ دليل شامل ومتكامل لجميع جوانب الشؤون السياسية والاقتصادية والوطنية والاجتماعية وحتى الدولية ").

¹⁶⁵ M. Cherif Bassiouni & Gamal Badr, *The Sharia'h: Sources, Interpretation, and Rule-Making*, 1 UCLA J. ISLAMIC & NEAR E.L. (2002).

¹⁶⁶ KHIZR MUAZZAM KHAN, *Juristic Classification of Islamic Law*, 6 HOUS. J. INT'L. L.23 (1983-1984).

Prophet Mohammad (PBUH) relayed primary source of Islamic law.¹⁶⁷ Muslims believe that *Qur'an* is "the word of God which Prophet Mohammad transmitted through revelations via Angel Gabriel from 610 A.D. until 632 A.D. starting with *al-fatiha* (the opening) *surah* (chapter) and ending with *al-naas* (the people).¹⁶⁸ It was exposed in Arabic, so even the *Qur'anic* script is replicated in other languages, only the Arabic manuscript is legally binding as the primary source of law.¹⁶⁹ *Qur'an* is composed of 114

---

¹⁶⁷ Kassem, *supra* note 80. ("In this respect, it should bear in mind that any *Qura'nic* translation is not an actual or original *Qur'an*. Only its original Arabic manuscript [text] is the source of law. Admittedly, it is not easy for non-native Arabs, and even for many Arabs, to understand the its provisions. It takes profound knowledge to understand the actual meanings of its words; knowledge that is available only to jurists or scholars.").
¹⁶⁸ Kristi Kernutt, *Civil Law v. Common Law Systems: Are They So Different?*, 31 OREG. REV. INT'L. L. 1 (1999). *See also* 'ABDULKADER 'AWDAH, AL-TASHRI'AL-JINAI' AL-ISLAMI [ISLAMIC PENAL LAW] (1969) (on file with author).
¹⁶⁹ Bassiouni & Badr, *supra* note 83.
¹⁷⁰ *Id.* Professor Bassiouni said:
The *Qur'an* is a code which governs religious and social life. It has foreseen everything so, that all is implicitly or explicitly regulated. When a new situation arises, or a new need is found, it is met with the help of the principles which are laid down in the *Qur'an*. In its entirety, the *Qur'an* aims at prohibiting all acts detrimental to society ...
¹⁷¹ *Id.*, at 'Awdah, *supra* note 86. The true reading of the *Qur'an* is not possible except by resorting to its *tafsir* (commentaries or interpretations).
١٧٢ ج. شريف بسيوني وجمال بدر، الشريعة: المصادر، التفسير، وصنع القواعد، ١ جامعة كاليفورنيا م. إسلامية و نيار ي.ل. (٢٠٠٢).
١٧٣ خيزر موزام خان، التصنيف الفقهي للشريعة الإسلامية، ٦ مجلة هيوستن في القانون الدولي ل. ٢٣ (١٩٨٣-١٩٨٤).
١٧٤ قاسم الهامش الأعلى ٨٢. ("في هذا الصدد، يجب أن نأخذ في الاعتبار أن أي ترجمة قرآنية ليست قرآن فعليا أو أصيلا، فالمخطوطة العربية الأصلية هي مصدر القانون. على نحو لا يمكن إنكاره، ليس الأمر هل لغير العرب، حتى بالنسبة للعديد من العرب، أن يفهموا أحكامه. فإنه يحتاج إلى معرفة عميقة لفهم المعاني الفعلية من كلماته. المعرفة التي لا تتوفر إلا لدى الفقهاء أو العلماء").
١٧٥ كريستي كيرنوت، القانون المدني ضد أنظمة القانون العام: هل هي مختلفة ؟، ٣١ دورية أوريغون للقانون الدولي ل.١ انظر أيضا "عبد القادر عوده، التشريع الجنائي الإسلامي [١٩٦٩] (محفوظة (1999). لدى المؤلف".
١٧٦ بسيوني وبدر الهامش الأعلى ٨٣.
١٧٧ المرجع السابق الدكتور بسيوني قال:
القرآن هو رمز يحكم الحياة الدينية والاجتماعية. وقد توقع كل شيء على هذا النحو، أن كل شيء ينظم عندما تنشأ حالة جديدة، أو حاجة جديدة وجدت، يتم حلها مع مساعدة من المبادئ ضمنا أو صراحة في المجمل، يهدف القرآن إلى حظر جميع الأفعال التي تضر بالمجتمع. المنصوص عليها في القرآن الكريم.
١٧٨ المرجع السابق. عوده الهامش الأعلى ٨٦. القراءة الحقيقية للقرآن ليست ممكنة إلا باللجوء إلى التفسير (التعليقات أو التفسيرات).

Introduction to Islam

chapters of varying length, each known as *surah* (chapter) and encompasses 6,236 *ayahs* (verses) and numerous sections deal with *khitab* (legal messages) and each of these legal/judicial verses stands as a command, either an *'amr* (order) or a *nahi* (prohibition).[170] *Qur'an* represents the Constitution of all Muslims; a source that prevail over all other sources in case of *real* conflict and is regarded by Muslims as the highest authority in all facets of life, counting legal, social, political, commercial, and economic issues, but within an accurate and flexible interpretation through *ijtihad* (analogical deduction and individual reasoning).[171]

Modern scholars and researches stated that *Qur'an* is the chief source of Islamic law, and covers values and rules by which the Muslim world is administered (or should govern itself) and forms the basis for relationships between God and man, between folks, whether Muslim or non-Muslim, entities, as well as between man and things which are part of creation.[179] *Shari'a* includes rules by which a Muslim *ummah* (community) is organized and governed, and it offers the techniques and the means to resolve disputes among individuals

---

[179] Bassiouni, *supra* note 70.

and between the individual and the state.[180] There is no clash among Muslim jurists that the *Qur'an* is the basis of Islamic legal system and that its explicit provisions are to be conscientiously observed and the *Sunnah* (*hadith*) are harmonizing sources to it and include Mohammad teachings and helps to explain the *Qur'an*, but it may not be interpreted or implemented in any way which is inconsistent with the *Qur'an*.[181]

In the same vein, however there are other sources of law, as consensus, analogy, or progressive reasoning by analogy, *Qur'an* is the first and chief source, followed by the *Sunnah*.[185] Other sources of law and the *Qura'nic* interpretation rules and the *hadith* follow in accordance with a generally acknowledged jurisprudential structure.[186] *Qur'an* encompasses a diversity of law-making provisions and legal prohibitions intermingled through its chapters and a number of rules exist for interpreting these provisions, as the position of a given verse within the context of the chapter, which in turn is understood within its place in the sequence of revelations, its reference to other revelations, and its historical framework regarding

---

[180] *Id. See also* MOHAMED N. 'AWADIN, MASDER AL-FIQH AL-ISLAMI [SOURCES OF ISLAMIC LAW] (2001) (on file with author), at 37.
[181] *Id.*, at 38-40.
[182] بسيوني الهامش الأعلى ٧٠.
[183] المرجع السابق. انظر أيضا محمد ن.عوضين، مصادر الفقه الإسلامي (٢٠٠١) (محفوظة لدي المؤلف)،ص ٣٧.
[184] المرجع الابق, ص٣٨-٤٠.
[185] *Id.*
[186] Hussien, *supra* note 72.

particular conditions which existed at the time of the given revelation.[187] These and other rules are known as *'ilm usul al-fiqh* (the science of interpretation) and according to these rules, one initially is to refer to a precise provision and then to a general provision dealing with a particular situation.[188] No *nas 'aam* (general provision) can be interpreted to contradict a *nas khas* (specific provision), and a specific rule will supersede a general proposition.[189] It should be noted that a general provision, though, is always interpreted in the broadest way, while a specific provision is interpreted in the narrowest manner.[190] *Qiyyas* (reasoning

إلى الوحي الأخر، وإطارها التاريخي فيما يتعلق بالظروف الخاصة التي كانت موجودة في وقت الوحي المعطى.[195] وتعرف هذه القواعد وغيرها باسم "علم أصول الفقه", ووفقا لهذه القواعد بداية يتم الإشارة إلى حكم دقيق ثم إلى حكم عام يتناول حالة معينة.[196] لا يمكن تفسير أي نص عام على أنه يتعارض مع نص خاص, وسيحل حكم الخاص محل مسألة عامة.[197] وتجدر الإشارة إلى أن الحكم العام يفسر دائما على أوسع نطاق، في

---

[187] CH. SARFRAZ AHMAD, ILM-UL-USUL AL-FIQH ISLAMI [ISLAMIC JURISPRUDENCE] (2013), at 408.

[188] In other words, knowledge of the specific incident whose *hukum* (ruling) is to be known.

[189] MUHAMMAD IBN IDRĪS AL-SHĀFI'Ī, *The Epistle on Legal Theory*, Joseph E. Lowry, trans. (2013), at 504.

[190] Baber Johansen, *The Constitution and the Principles of Islamic Normativity Against the Rules of Fiqh: A Judgment of the Supreme Constitutional Court of Egypt*, in DISPENSING JUSTICE IN ISLAM: QADIS AND THEIR JUDGMENTS, Muhammad Khalid Masud, Rudolph Peters & David S. Powers, (eds.), (2012), at 169-193.

[191] Mohd H. Kamal, *Meaning and Method of the Interpretation of Sunnah in the Field of Siyar: A Reappraisal*, in ISLAM AND INTERNATIONAL LAW: ENGAGING SELF-CENTRISM FROM A PLURALITY OF PERSPECTIVES, Marie-Luisa Frick & Andreas Th. Müller, (eds.) (2013), at 64–80.

[192] Nazeem Goolam, *Ijtihad and Its Significance for Islamic Legal Interpretation*, MICH. ST. L. REV. 6 (2006) (discussing *ijtihad*'s concept, its various schools of interpretation, and its sorts in classical and modern *fiqh*).

[193] المرجع السابق.

[194] حسين الهامش الأعلى ٧٢.

[195] ش. سارفراز أحمد، علم الأصول الفقه الإسلامي (2013)ص ٤٠٨,.

[196] وبعبارة أخرى، معرفة الحدث المحدد الذي يكون حكمه معروف .

[197] محمد ابن إدريس الشافعي، رسالة الرسول على النظرية القانونية، جوزيف ي. لوري, ترجمة,٥٠٤ص(2013).

[198] بابر يوهانس, الدستور ومبادئ المعيارية الإسلامية ضد قواعد الفقه: حكم المحكمة الدستورية العليا في مصر, في نشر العدالة في الإسلام: قديس وأحكامهم، محمد خالد مسعود، رودولف بيترز وديفيد س. باورس, (محررين)، (٢٠١٢)، ص ١٦٩-١٩٣.

[199] محمد ه. كمال، معنى وطريقة تفسير السنة في مجال سيار: إعادة تقييم، في الإسلام والقانون الدولي: الانخراط في مركز ذاتي من بلورة وجهات النظر، ماري لويزا فريك وأندرياس ث. مولر (محرران) (٢٠١٣)،ص ٦٤-٨٠.

[200] نظيم غلام، الاجتهاد وأهميته للتفسير القانوني الإسلامي، مجلة ولاية ميشيغان للقانون ٦ (٢٠٠٦) (مناقشة مفهوم الاجتهاد، مختلف مدارس لتفسيره، وأنواعه في الفقه الكلاسيكي والحديث).

by analogy) is allowable, as are applications by analogy, except where explicitly proscribed, and straightforwardness and clear and non-ambiguous language are always preferred along with the clear spirit of certain prescriptions cannot be altered by inconsistent interpretations.[191] A policy-oriented interpretation within the boundaries of the jurisprudential rules is permissible and even recommended, as is the case with the principle of *ijtihad* (progressive reasoning by analogy).[192]

The second primary source of Islamic law is the *Sunnah* (Prophet's traditions). Generally speaking, *sunnah* consists of compilations of Mohammad's actions, sayings, rulings, attitudes, and opinions during his lifetime.[201] It does not rank as high as the Qur'an but is considered an imperative source in the interpretation of the Qur'anic texts.[202] This source is outside revelation, yet is still sacred and divinely inspired and the importance of following Mohammad's instructions and examples is confirmed by the Qur'an, for instance, "Obey Allah and obey the Messenger..."[203] Hadith generally take one of three formulae: (a) a *sunnah* articulated by the Prophet; (b) a *sunnah* of reported facts about the

---

[201] Kassem, *supra* note 80, at 9. In other words, *Sunnah* is the collective word for the mass of texts which tell of the Prophet's spoken words, or are an account of actions or the absence of acts attributed to him (oral or habitual traditions—practice, life style, and conduct of Mohammad—("*sunnat al-nabi*"). These comprise the tradition, or more literally, the Messenger's path which Muslims strives to follow.
[202] 'Awadin, *supra* note 88, at 91.
[203] *Id. Qur'an* has priority over *Sunnah*, because of: its divine origin; as it is recited by the Prophet himself; as *Sunnah* largely plays an explanatory role of the *Qur'an* and the Prophet orders; and as *Qur'an* enjoys the precedence over all sources of Islamic law.

Prophet, as he applied the amputation's penalty of the right hand in case of theft; and (c) a *sunnah* confirmed by the Prophet, who authenticates an act either explicitly or through his silence (tacitly).[204] The *Sunnah* became a means of developing the principles found in the *Qur'anic* manuscripts and thus the most vital source for understanding it, both in the development of religious dogma as well as judicial standards.[205]

Islamic *fiqh* (jurisprudence) has developed over fourteen centuries. Over that time period, various schools of jurisprudence have arose, each with its own interpretation and application of the law.[211] The prosperous profusion of ideas and views confirms to the intellectual depth and breadth of Islamic *fiqh*.[212] However, nothing impedes a given state from codifying the *Shari'a* so as to provide for more inevitability of the law and clarity and consistency in its application.[213]

---

[204] Kassem, *supra* note 80, at 25.
[205] *Id. See also* Gleave, *supra* note 29.
[206] قاسم الهامش الأعلى ٨٠ ص٩. وبعبارة أخرى، السنة هي الكلمة الجماعية لكتلة النصوص التي تخبر بالكلمات المنطوقة، أو هي سرد للأعمال أو غياب الأفعال المنسوبة إلى الرسول (التقاليد الشفهية أو المعتادة - الممارسة، أسلوب الحياة، وسلوك محمد - ("سنة النبي")، وهي تشمل التقليد، أو حرفيا، مسار الرسول الذي يسعى المسلمون إلى اتباعه.
[207] عوضين الهامش الأعلى ٨٨ ص ٩١.
[208] المرجع السابق. القرآن له أولوية على السنة، بسبب: أصله الإلهي. حيث أنه تمت تلاوته من قبل النبي نفسه؛ كما أن السنة تلعب إلى حد كبير دورا تفسيريا للقرآن وأوامر النبي. ولأن القرآن يتمتع بالأسبقية على جميع مصادر الشريعة الإسلامية.
[209] قاسم الهامش الأعلى ٨٠, ص٢٥.
[210] المرجع السابق. انظر أيضا جايف الهامش الأعلى ٢٩.
[211] Ahmed El Shamsy, *The Canonization of Islamic Law: A Social and Intellectual History* (2013), at 253.
[212] Eisenberg, *supra* note 27, at 15–53.
[213] NORMAN CALDER, ISLAMIC JURISPRUDENCE IN THE CLASSICAL ERA (2010), at 233.

Modern Muslim scholars states have done so, the most advanced being Egypt, where the presence of the thousand-year-old *al-azhar* University (originally devoted only to Islamic studies but now to all disciplines) and centuries of legal tradition have congregated to make Islamic law a source of inspiration for the entire Muslim world.[214]

The *Sunni* tradition, which today encompasses approximately 85-90 percent of all Muslims, differs from *Shii'aa* tradition, which includes the remainder of the Muslim world.[219] The distinction between the two societies fundamentally derives from different methods to governance. The *Sunni* believe, based on specific *Quran'ic* and *Sunnah* texts, that Muslim folks are to be governed by *ijma'a* (consensus) through an elected *khalifa* (head of state), according to democratic principles.[220] However, the *Shii'aa*, believe that the leader of Islam, whom they refer to as the *imam* must be a descendant of the Prophet and this concept is the basis for a hereditary hierarchy in the their tradition.[221] The

---

[214] Kassem, *supra* note 80, at 76.

[215] أحمد الشامسي، تقديس الشريعة الإسلامية: تاريخ اجتماعي وفكري (٢٠١٣)، ص ٢٥٣

[216] إيسنبرغ الهامش الأعلى ٢٧ ص ١٥-٣٥.

[217] نورمان كالدر، الفقه الإسلامي في العصر الكلاسيكي (٢٠١٠)، ص ٢٣٣.

[218] قاسم الهامش الأعلى ٨٠، ص٧٦.

[219] *Id.*, at 78.

[220] Bernd Radtke, *Sunni Islam: Law, in* ISLAM IN THE WORLD TODAY: A HANDBOOK OF POLITICS, RELIGION, CULTURE, AND SOCIETY, Werner Ende & Udo Steinbach, (eds.) (2010), at 44–47.

[221] Megan H. Reid, *Law and Piety in Medieval Islam* (2013), at 249. The *Shii'aa* movement dates from the period when a group of Muslims wanted Ali ibn abi Talib, the

most important features distinct between *Sunni* and *Shii'aa* concerning the interpretation of the *Qur'an*, which means that *Sunni* look more to the *al-zaher* (letter of the *Qur'an*); but the *Shii'aa* look more to its *al-baten* (spirit).²²²

Within the *sunni* jurisprudence, they follow any one of four major schools on jurisprudence founded by *imams ibn Hanbal, abu Hanifa, Malek*, and *el-Shaf'ie*, scholars of the ninth to eleventh centuries, and they referred to respectively as the *Hanbali, Hanafi, Maliki*, and *Shaf'ie*, are followed by various Muslim countries partially or entirely.²²⁷ Despite there are differences in Islamic law's interpretation among these schools, they are all recognized as valid.²²⁸

---

cousin and son-in-law of the Prophet, to become the *khalifa* instead of Abu Bakr, who had been elected the first *khalifa* following Mohammad's death in 632. They advanced his candidacy based on heredity.

²²² Radtke, *supra* note 111.

²²³ المرجع السابق, ص٢٨.

²²⁴ بيرند رادتك، الإسلام السني، القانون، في الإسلام اليوم: كتيب للسياسة والدين والثقافة والثقافة، ويرنر إند وأودو شتاينباخ، (محرران) (٢٠١٠)، ص ٤٤-٤٧.

²²⁵ ميغان م. ريد، القانون والتقوى في الإسلام في القرون الوسطى (٢٠١٣)، ص ٢٤٩. حركة الشيعة تعود إلى الفترة التي كانت فيها مجموعة من المسلمين يريدون علي بن أبي طالب، ابن عم وصهر النبي صلى الله عليه وسلم، ليصبح خليفة بدلا من أبو بكر، الذي انتخب أول خليفة بعد وفاة محمد في ٦٣٢. وتقدموا لترشيحه على أساس الوراثة.

²²⁶ رادتك الهامش الأعلى ١١١.

²²⁷ Egypt is traditionally *Hanafi* (the most moderate school), Saudi Arabia is traditionally *Hanbali* (the most rigid and classical *fiqh*) while the country follows more thoroughly the teachings of imam Mohammad Abdal-Wahab, a *Hanbali* activist of the early 1800's, which is more extremist or radical.

²²⁸ Kassem, *supra* note 80.

²²⁹ مصر هي تقليديا حنفي (المدرسة الأكثر اعتدالا)، المملكة العربية السعودية هي تقليديا حنبلي (الفقه الأكثر صلابة والكلاسيكية) في حين أن البلاد تتبع بشكل أكثر تعمقا لتعاليم الإمام محمد عبدالوهاب، الناشط الحنبلي في أوائل ١٨٠٠، وهو أكثر تطرفا أو راديكاليا.

Iijtihad (progressive reasoning by analogy) which produced the most far-reaching developments opened new horizons in the knowledge and understanding of Islam's application to the societal needs.[231] Then, later, Islamic jurisprudence became somewhat rigid until its modern resurgence under the aegis of *al-azhar* moderate scholars, reasonable jurists and other up-to-date reformers of the last two centuries, as *al-Ghazali, al-Afghani,* and *Mohammad 'Abdou*.[232] Contemporary jurisprudential expansions endure the work begun in past ages, meeting individual requirements and collective demands for deciding the problems and conflicts of modern life, while remaining well-matched with Islam and its general norms.[233]

---

[230] قاسم الهامش الأعلى ٨٠. كالدر الهامش الأعلى ١٠٨.

[231] Calder, *supra* note 108.

[232] *Id.*

[233] *Id.* It should be noted that the *Sufi* movement is a spiritual strain in Islam which reflects the need of persons to transcend formal religious practices to reach higher levels of spiritual fulfillment. The *Sufis* are represented in all schools of thought in Islam and found in all Muslim societies. Because of its spiritual atmosphere, *Sufism* appeals more to individuals and small groups and it does not institute either a sect or a school of thought, but is rather a spiritual or mystical practice which persists despite criticism from orthodox theologians. They believe they follow the Prophet's spirituality, predominantly during the Meccan period of the revelations. Therefore, in their practices, there is much meditation and solitary or group recitation of prayers and chants of their own religious formulas. They seek a life of austere pietism, shunning worldly pleasures and seeking the inward purity of a relationship with God through love, patience, forgiveness, and other higher spiritual qualities. In addition, their influence on the development of Islam is more important than is usually recognized. Their ascetic piety and strictly ethical conception of Islamic society have influenced Muslim generations. What symbolizes them the most is their "inwardism" or belief that the *Shari'a* only controls external behavior, whereas inward feelings are matter strictly between each person and the Creator. Based on their emphasis on God's love, they have developed the doctrine of *tawakul* (reliance on God), which is dominant to the relationship between Man and God along with a substantial influence on the practical features of administering a state.

[234] كالدر الهامش الأعلى ١٠٨.

[235] المرجع السابق.

In addition, *Ijm'a* is the third secondary source of Islamic law. It is the common consensus of the *ummah* (community) over its competent representatives (authorized religious councils), thus, it is the agreement of the recognized *fuqah'a'* (jurists) among the companions and the Prophet's followers in a particular age on a specific question of law or fact.[237] It is self-motivated and may be re-formulated at any point in time and has to be supported by either a *Qura'nic* or *Sunnah* verse.[238] Also, it is the source which inspires the laws, regulations, and decrees of the Muslim society, because a congressional body may be considered a competent representative of the community.[239] *Ijm'a* ensures the unity of the Muslim *ummah* and assures the correct

---

[236] المرجع السابق. وتجدر الإشارة إلى أن الحركة الصوفية سلالة روحية في الإسلام تعبر عن حاجة الأشخاص إلى تجاوز الممارسات الدينية الرسمية للوصول إلى مستويات أعلى من الإنجاز الروحي. وتعرض الصوفية في جميع مدارس الفكر في الإسلام ويوجدوا في جميع المجتمعات الإسلامية وبسبب جوها الروحي، تستدعي الصوفية المزيد من الأفراد والمجموعات الصغيرة، ولا تنشئ طائفة ولا مدرسة فكرية، بل هي ممارسة روحية أو غامضة لا تزال قائمة على الرغم من انتقادات اللاهوتيين الأرثوذكسيين لذلك، في ممارساتهم. وهم يعتقدون أنهم يتبعون روحانية النبي، في الغالب خلال الفترة المكية من الوحي. هناك الكثير من التأمل والانفرادية أو مجموعة تلاوة من الصلوات والهتافات من الصيغ الدينية الخاصة بهم انهم يسعون الى حياة بتقوى صارمه، وهجر الملذات الدنيوية والسعي إلى نقاء الداخل للعلاقة مع الله من وبالإضافة إلى ذلك، تأثيرها على خلال الحب والصبر، والمغفرة، وغيرها من الصفات الروحية العليا تطور الإسلام هو أكثر أهمية مما هو معترف به عادة. وقد أثرت تقوى الزهد والمفهوم الأخلاقي الصارم للمجتمع الإسلامي على أجيال المسلمين. ما يرمز لهم أكثر من غيرهم هو "النزعة الداخلية" أو الاعتقاد بأن الشريعة تسيطر فقط على السلوك الخارجي، في حين أن المشاعر الداخلية هي مسألة صارمة بين كل شخص والخالق. واستنادا إلى تركيزهم على حب الله، فقد طوروا عقيدة التوكل (الاعتماد على الله)، التي هي المهيمنة على العلاقة بين الإنسان والله جنبا إلى جنب مع تأثير كبير على السمات العملية لإدارة الدولة.

[237] Irshad Abdal-Haqq, *Islamic Law: An Overview of Its Origin and Elements*, 7 J. ISLAMIC L. & CULTURE 27 (2002).

[238] *Id.* It should be noted that *ijm'a* is formed by two sorts either Express (active) *ijm'a* is one in which the scholars at one time explicitly agree on or admit a particular interpretation, or a Tacit or Implicit (passive) *ijm'a* is one in which the interpretation is admitted by all jurists.

[239] Ahmad, *supra* note, at 410-420.

interpretation of the *Qur'anic* and *hadith* texts.[240] *Qiyyas* (analogical deduction) represents the fourth fundamental source of Islamic law. It factually means measuring or determining the length, weight, or quality of something, but theoretically, it is the extension of a *Shari'a* ruling in one case to a new, similar case due to the similarity (monotony) of both cases's *'ilah* (effective cause), and as the father of international criminal law, Professor M. Cherif Bassiouni elaborated:

هيئة برلمانية ممثلة مختصة للمجتمع.[٢٤٣] ويضمن الإجماع وحدة الأمة الإسلامية ويضمن أيضاً التفسير الصحيح للنصوص القرآنية ونصوص الحديث.[٢٤٤] القياس (الخصم التناظري) يمثل المصدر الأساسي الرابع للشريعة الإسلامية. وهذا يعني في الواقع قياس أو تحديد طول أو وزن أو جودة شيء ما، ولكن من الناحية النظرية، هو تمديد حكم شرعي في حالة واحدة إلى قضية جديدة مماثلة بسبب تشابه (رتابة) كلتا الحالتين وبوصفه ابو القانون الجنائي الدولي، وضع البروفسور شريف بسيوني:

Analogical reasoning in Islamic law is not an autonomous source since it depends on the existence of a model case, or a model body of rules, in either the *Qur'an* or the *Sunnah*. Also, it is a specifically Semitic mode of logic, using only two terms. It operates simply from like to like, from like to

التفكير المنطقي في الشريعة الإسلامية ليس مصدرا مستقلا لأنه يعتمد على وجود حالة نموذجية، أو مجموعة نموذجية من القواعد، سواء في القرآن أو السنة. أيضا، هو وضع سامية على وجه التحديد من المنطق،

---

240 Bassiouni & Badr, *supra* note 83. In other words, *ijm'a* means consensus, and technically refers to the unanimous opinion of the acknowledged religious powers at any given time on a subject matter. When one is faced with a vague or broad *Qur'anic* test or apparently contradictory texts, or is in a position where no available *hadith* expounds or anticipates the case, Islam finds the solution in the form of collective action and this is the legislative process called *ijm'a* (consensus of the Prophet's [*sahaba*]), and their disciples and followers.

241 إرشاد عبد الحق، الشريعة الإسلامية: نظرة عامة على أصله وعناصره، ٧ ج. إالقنون الإسلامي والثقافة ٢٧ (٢٠٠٢).

242 المرجع السابق. وتجدر الإشارة إلى أن الإجماع يتكون من نوعين إما الإجماع الصريح وهو الذي يقوم فيه العلماء في وقت واحد يوافقوا صراحة على أو يعترفوا بتفسير معين، أو الإجماع الضمني هو الذي يتم فيه قبول التفسير من قبل جميع الفقهاء.

243 أحمد الهامش الأعلي ص٤١٠ -٤٢٠.

244 بسيوني وبدر الهامش الأعلي ٨٣. وبعبارة أخرى، يعني الإجماع إتفاق جماعي في الرأي وتقنيا يشير عندما .إلى الرأي بالإجماع من القوى الدينية المعترف بها في أي وقت من الأوقات على حول موضوع ما يواجه المرء اختبارا قرآنيا غامضا أو عريضا أو نصا متناقضا على ما يبدو، أو في موقف لا يتاح فيه الحديث بشرح أو تنبأ للحالة, يجد الإسلام الحل في شكل عمل جماعي وهذه العملية التشريعية تسمى الإجماع (إجماع صحابة النبي صلى الله عليه وسلم)، وتلاميذهم وأتباعهم.

contrary, from more to less, [and] from less to more, without a universal intermediary term as in the typical Aristotelian syllogism, and here always referring to the argument of the Supreme Authority who furnished the text . . .²⁴⁵

In other words, *Qiyyas* is an individual form based on analogical deduction, so, analogical reasoning may be used to expand the implementation of a prevailing rule of law resulting from a *hukum* (decision).²⁴⁷ Systematic reasoning, controlled by the analogy rules, projects the rule beyond its immediate applicability onto a different plane.²⁴⁸ For example, the solution to a case at hand may be found by progressive analogy to a comparable case found in the *Qur'an* or the *hadith* and thus already settled by text.²⁴⁹ Thus, analogy may be active only if no guidance on the point is accessible under discussion in any of the three preceding sources of law.

---

²⁴⁵ Bassiouni, *supra* note 67 at 156.
²⁴⁶ بسيوني، الهامش الأعلى ٦٧ ص١٥٦.
²⁴⁷ *Id.*, at 157.
²⁴⁸ Abdal-Haqq, *supra* note 119.
²⁴⁹ *Id.*
²⁵⁰ المرجع السابق، ص١٥٧.
²⁵¹ عبدالحق الهامش الأعلى ١١٩.
²⁵² المرجع السابق.

In the same vein, same like common law notion, (case law or precedent) is law developed by judges, courts, and analogous tribunals, stated in decisions that ostensibly decide individual cases but that in addition have *precedential* consequence/impact on future cases.[253] In cases (disputes) where the parties disagree on what the law is, a common law court looks to past precedential decisions of relevant courts.[254] If a comparable quarrel has been resolved in the past, the court is usually bound to follow the intellectual reasoning used in the prior decision (a principle known as *stare decisis*).[255] Resolution of the issue in one case becomes precedent that binds future courts, as stare decisis norm means that cases should be decided according to reliable principled rules so that similar facts will yield same results, lies at the heart

---

[253] Charles E. Carpenter, *Court Decisions and the Common Law*, 17 COLUMBIA L. REV. 7 (1917), at 593–607. ("Common law court "decisions are themselves law, or rather the rules which the courts lay down in making the decisions constitute law.""). *See also* Kristi Kernutt, *Civil Law v. Common Law Systems: Are They So Different?* 19 OR. L. REV. 1161 (1990) ("In common law systems, judges take fact patterns, look to applicable statutes, if any, and then have the freedom to apply a measure of judicial authority in deriving the final decision of the court. While in civil law systems they are thought to have very little judicial discretion, and, instead, merely apply the facts to the statutes and briefly state the outcome of the decision. In addition, common law judges are bound by Stare Decisis, while civil law judges are bound by the detailed statutes and written codes that are formulated by their legislative bodies, which are always Parliaments or Congresses.").

[254] *See Marbury v. Madison*, 5 U.S. 137 (1803) ("It is emphatically the province and duty of the judicial department to say what the law is. Those who apply the rule to particular cases, must of necessity expound and interpret that rule. If two laws conflict with each other, the courts must decide on the operation of each.").

[255] Paul M. Perell, *Stare Decisis and Techniques of Legal Reasoning and Legal Argument*, 2 CANADIAN LEGAL RESEARCH (1987), http://legalresearch.org/writing-analysis/stare-decisis-techniques ("Under the doctrine of stare decisis, the decision of a higher court within the same provincial jurisdiction acts as binding authority on a lower court within that same jurisdiction. The decision of a court of another jurisdiction only acts as persuasive authority. The degree of persuasiveness is dependent upon various factors, including, first, the nature of the other jurisdiction. Second, the degree of persuasiveness is dependent upon the level of court which decided the precedent case in the other jurisdiction. Other factors include the date of the precedent case, on the assumption that the more recent the case, the more reliable it will be as authority for a given proposition, although this is not necessarily so. And on some occasions, the judge's reputation may affect the degree of persuasiveness of the authority.").

[256] KARL LLEWELLYN, THE COMMON LAW TRADITION: DECIDING APPEALS (1960), at 7-87.

Introduction to Islam

of all common law systems.²⁵⁶ This is how Islamic law (*Shari'a* legal system) works within its contemporary moderate *fiqh* (jurisprudence).

It should be noted that *Qiyyas* and *Ijm'a* offer criteria to determine positive law, as they both involve rational and balanced interpretation of the

²⁶¹ Bassiouni, *supra* note 67, at 160-164. The prohibition on alcoholic beverages is one such example. The use of analogy explains the methodology of extending an existing rule to an unregulated scenario, and in limiting the application of an existing rule to the situation it was originally meant to regulate. The prohibition on alcoholic drinks is obvious in the *Qur'an*. When narcotic drugs came to be known in the Islamic world, the question arose as to whether they too were banned. By use of the analogical method, Muslim scholars reached the conclusion that they were also proscribed, thus expanding the application of the existing rule to a new case and launching a new rule by progressive analogy. The argument they used was as follows: Alcohol is banned because it is intoxicating *asl* (major premise); narcotic drugs are intoxicating *far'*(minor premise); narcotic drugs are prohibited *hukum* (conclusion). In other words, it is a usage of a particular society, both in speech and in action.

²⁶² *Id.*, at 163. In other words, *Ijtihad* represents a part of Islamic jurisprudence in which the endeavor to derive or formulate a legal rule in an issue whose ruling is not stipulated either in the *Qur'an* or the *Sunnah* but based on the evidence found in those sources by a qualified scholar. Goolam, *supra* note 100. In order to be a "*Mujtahid*" in Islam, the following is required: (1) ultimate awareness of legislating *ayahs*(ts) *al'ahkam*, (2) knowledge of the *Sunnah* and the reliability of the narrators, (3) knowledge of *naskh* (abrogating and abrogated rules, repeal theory), (4) knowledge of *Ijm'a*, (5) knowledge of *'Ilm 'Usul Al-Fiqh* (Science of the Islamic Jurisprudence and principles which determine then methodology of *ijtihad*), (6) complete understanding of reasoning by analogy "i.e., rules and methodology," (7) mastering the Arabic language, (8) through better understanding of the *maqasid al-Shari'a* (objectives) which are five essential things guaranteed in Islam: "religion, life, mind, posterity, and property," (9) piety and Islam. In this regard, it should be noted that there is a distinction between "*Fatwa*" and "*Ijtihad*." Hussien, *supra* note 69. The former means the application of the ruling of the major Islamic schools of doctrine to specific incidents and it is superior than *Ijitahd* and it pertains to a particular situation. In contrast, the latter is more general than the former. Similar conditions as required for *Mujtahid* are required for *Mufti*, in addition to the *Mufti's* knowledge of the particular event. For further elaboration on this issue, *see* Hussien, *supra* note 69, at 100-108.

²⁶³ *Id.* In other words, *Istihsan* is the process of selecting one acceptable alternative solution over another because the former appears more suitable for the situation at hand, even though the selected solution may be technically weaker than the rejected one. This is the process of selecting the best solution for the public interest in the form of *Ijtihad*.

²⁶⁴ Bassiouni & Badr, *supra* note 83, at 11.

²⁶⁵ *Id.* This source assures a Muslim legislator a great deal of freedom in the resolution of new questions in the absence of a primary source of law. For instance, the Prophet's companions issued currencies. On the other hand, it is from *Qiyyas* that the five classifications of acts, *wajib* (obligatory/mandatory), *mobaah* (recommended), *mandoub* (indifferent), *makrouh* (reprehensible), and *haram* (forbidden) emerge.

²⁶⁶ Mohamed 'Arafa, *Corruption and Bribery in Islamic Law: Are Islamic Ideals Being Met in Practice?* 18 GOLDEN GATE ANNUAL SURV. INT'L.& COMP. L. J. (2012), at 181 ("Muslim scholars use this tool to answer new questions. Imam Al-Ghazali, a very well respected Islamic scholar, established this doctrine in his quest for solutions to new economic, social, and political concerns that arose with the development of Islamic community. This source refers to all new ideas that have neither permitted nor prohibited by one or more agreed upon sources of Islamic law. In judging whether an idea or solution is approved according to *masalah mursalah*, scholars look to weather it promotes social welfare. Further, the rule derived from this source must be logical and must not contradict the principles of the *Qur'an*, *Sunnah*, and the overall sprit of *Shari'a*.").

²⁶⁷ Bernard Weiss, *Interpretation in Islamic Law: The Theory of Ijtihad*, 26 A.J. COMP. L. 199 (2010).

²⁶⁸ 'Arafa, *supra* note 136, at 181. ("In many ways, benefits, interests, and social welfare are all soft terms which are relative and not absolute. If there is a conflict between benefits

to some and harm to others, the rule deduced through this technique should achieve a significant public interest or benefit to the majority. Muslim responses to concepts such as foreign investment, communism, and political or economic boycotts have all been developed through this strategy.").

[269] *Id.*

[270] بسيوني الهامش الأعلى ٦٧ ص ١٦٠-١٦٤. ومن الأمثلة على ذلك حظر المشروبات الكحولية ويوضح استخدام القياس طريقة توسيع قاعدة قائمة إلى سيناريو غير منظم، وفي الحد من تطبيق قاعدة قائمة على المشروبات الكحولية واضح في القرآن. على الحالة التي كان القصد منها في الأصل تنظيمها وباستخدام. فعندما ظهرت المخدرات في العالم الإسلامي، نشأت مسألة ما إذا كانت محظورة أيضا .الكريم طريقة القياس، توصل العلماء المسلمون إلى الاستنتاج بأنهم محظورون أيضا، وبالتالي توسيع نطاق تطبيق وكانت الحجة التي. القاعدة الحالية على قضية جديدة وإطلاق قاعدة جديدة من خلال القياس التدريجي استخدموها على النحو التالي: الكحول محظور لأنه هو مسكرة الأصل (الفرضية الرئيسية). المخدرات وبعبارة أخرى، هو استخدام لمجتمع مخدرة الفرع (فرضية طفيفة). الحكم يحظر استخدام العقاقير المخدرة. معين، سواء في الكلام أو في العمل.

[271] المرجع السابق ص١٦٣. وبعبارة أخرى. يمثل الاجتهاد جزءا من الفقه الإسلامي الذي يسعى فيه إلى استنباط أو صياغة قاعدة قانونية في قضية لا ينص على حكمها في القرآن أو السنة، وإنما يستند إلى الأدلة من أجل أن يكون. غولام، الهامش الأعلى ١٠٠ الموجودة في تلك المصادر من قبل باحث مؤهل معرفة السنة ومصداقية (٢)"المجتهد" في الإسلام، ما يلي مطلوب: (١) الوعي النهائي بإحكام الآيات، معرفة الإجماع، (٥) معرفة علم أصول الفقه والمبادئ التي تحدد بعد ذلك (٤)الرواة، (٣) معرفة النسخ ، إتقان اللغة العربية، (٨) من خلال فهم أفضل (٧) " منهجية الاجتهاد، (٦) الفهم الكامل للمنطق بالقياس التي هي خمسة أشياء أساسية مضمونة في الإسلام: "الدين والحياة والعقل) للمقاصد الشريعة (الأهداف وفي هذا الصدد، تجدر الإشارة إلى أن هناك فرقا بين "الفتوى". التقوى والإسلام (٩) والنسل والممتلكات" ، و "الاجتهاد". حسين، الهامش الأعلى ٦٩. الأول يعني تطبيق حكم المدارس الإسلامية الكبرى من المذهب وفي المقابل، فإن هذا الأخير أكثر عمومية .على حوادث محددة، وهو أعلى من الاجتهاد ويتعلق بحالة معينة ذات الشروط كما هي مطلوبة في المجتهد مطلوبة في المفتي، بالإضافة إلى معرفة المفتي. من السابق لمزيد من التفاصيل حول هذه المسألة، انظر حسين، الهامش الأعلى ٦٩ ، في ١٠٠-١٠٨ بالحديث الخاص المرجع السابق.

[272] وبعبارة أخرى، الاستحسان هو عملية اختيار حل بديل مقبول على حل آخر لأن الأول يبدو أكثر ملاءمة للحالة في متناول اليد، على الرغم من أن الحل المحدد قد يكون أضعف من الناحية الفنية .هذه هي عملية اختيار أفضل حل للمصلحة العامة في شكل اجتهاد. من الحل المرفوض

[273] بسيوني وبدر الهامش الأعلى ٨٣, ص ١١.

[274] المرجع السابق. ويضمن هذا المصدر للمشرع الإسلامي قدرا كبيرا من الحرية في حل مسائل جديدة ومن ناحية أخرى، فمن. على سبيل المثال، أصدر صحابة النبي العملات. في غياب مصدر أساسي للقانون القياس أن التصنيفات الخمس للأفعال تنشأ، واجب، مباح، المندوب ، مكروه ، وحرام.

[275] محمد عرفة، الفساد والرشوة في الشريعة الإسلامية: هل المثل الإسلامية تجتمع في الممارسة؟ ١٨ ، ص ١٨١ (٢٠١٢) ("العلماء المسلمين) غولدن غيت السنوي لمجلة القانون الدولي والمقارن يستخدمون هذه الأداة للإجابة على أسئلة جديدة، وقد وضع الإمام الغزالي، وهو عالم إسلامي يحظى باحترام كبير، هذا المبدأ في سعيه لإيجاد حلول لمخاوف اقتصادية واجتماعية وسياسية جديدة نشأت مع تطور المجتمع الإسلامي، ويشير هذا المصدر إلى كل الأفكار الجديدة التي لم يسمح بها ولا يحظرها أحد أو أكثر من مصادر الشريعة الإسلامية المتفق عليها، وفي الحكم على ما إذا كانت فكرة أو حل تتم الموافقة علاوة على ذلك، يجب. عليه وفقا للمصلحة المرسلة،يتطلع العلماء إلى ما إذا كان يعزز الرعاية الاجتماعية أن تكون القاعدة المستمدة من هذا المصدر منطقية ويجب ألا تتناقض مع مبادئ القرآن والسنة والروح العامة للشريعة.").

[276] مجلة القانون المقارن ١٩٩ برنارد فايس، تفسير في الشريعة الإسلامية: نظرية الاجتهاد، ٢٦ (٢٠١٠)

[277] في كثير من النواحي، الفوائد والمصالح والرفاه الاجتماعي ") عرفه الهامش الأعلى ١٣٦ ص١٨١. (" كلها شروط لينة نسبية وليست مطلقة.وإذا كان هناك تعارض بين المنافع للبعض والضرر للآخرين، فإن القاعدة المستنتجة من خلال هذه التقنية يجب أن تحقق مصلحة عامة كبيرة أو استفادتهم من الأغلبية، وقد تم تطوير استجابات المسلمين لمفاهيم مثل الاستثمار الأجنبي والشيوعية والمقاطعات السياسية أو الاقتصادية من خلال هذه الاستراتيجية.")

[278] المرجع السابق.

normative written law from which they themselves derive.²⁶¹ *Qiyyas* is composed of *ijtihad* (individual reasoning), which means technically, putting forth every effort to determine a question of *Shari'a* and it is significant in helping bring to light the universality of Islam through coping, by addressing the world's development and finding solutions to evolving issues, as for example using DNA analysis as a new mode of forensic evidence.²⁶² Moving on to subordinate sources, *Istihsan* (juristic preference) is one of the most imperative. Technically, it is the exercise of individual opinion to avoid any rigid and unfair outcome which could result from literal application of the law and this is most like the doctrine of equity in Western law.²⁶³ *al-Maslahah al-Mursalah/Istialah* (consideration of public interest and common good) represents another source or tool of Islamic law. Etymologically, it means "benefit" or "interest" "free of restrictions," and consists of considerations which secure a benefit or prevent harm.²⁶⁴ Thus, when a new rule is required to legalize a novel situation and cannot be derived from *qiyas*, *ijma'*, or *'urf* (custom), resort to *maslaha* is permitted.²⁶⁵ In some cases, it is comparable to the common law's equity, however it is much comprehensive because it extends beyond the parties to a given conflict.²⁶⁶ Consideration of the common or public good is based on the fact that the law is envisioned to protect and endorse the legitimate interests of the community and its individual members.²⁶⁷ In any extraordinary situation calling for a new rule of law, categorizing that public interest is the first step towards framing a new rule that protects and endorses that public good.²⁶⁸ Hence, *maslaha* is an expression of public policy and the Islamic jurists came up with a list of five basic values that they called *maqasid el-Shari'a* (objectives).[269]

These five values concern the individual's belief, his life, his intellect (linage), his progeny, and his wealth.[279] Any rule of law that defends and promotes any of these five values is a valid rule of Islamic law, if it does not breach or contradict a current peremptory rule (one that derives from the *Qur'an* or *Sunnah*).[280] By implementing this concept of the public good, Muslim scholars were able to objectivize and define an equivocal model otherwise likely to be considered subjectively, which might have opened the door to personal favorites under the cape of an inadequately defined 'common good.'[281] In the infrequent cases where those two interests are in conflict, the public interest is given greater bulk.[282]

---

[279] *See generally* MOHAMMAD HASHIM KAMALI, PRINCIPLES OF ISLAMIC JURISPRUDENCE (3rd ed. 2003).
[280] *Id.*, at 238.
[281] *Id.* The five values recognized by the jurists as the basis for public good relate mostly to the individual and is presumed that in those five areas the interest of the individual and the interest of the community match.
[282] *Id.*

Consequently, when the *biat almal* (public treasury) needed more funds (resources) than what was accessible from taxes provided for in the two major sources of the *Shari'a*, a new rule authorizing the imposition of new taxes was articulated, based on consideration of the public common good, which takes preference over the individual's (private) interest in preserving his/her wealth.[283] It should be noted that the common good is an open-ended source of new rules of law called for by fluctuating social and economic conditions over time.[284] *al-Istihab* (presumption of continuity) is also considered a source of law and this tool is more a rule of evidence than a method of process and is well known by other names in Western law, as "beyond reasonable doubt."[285] In short, it stands for the proposition that a thing or state of affairs known to exist endures to exist until the contrary is proven, as the essential Islamic criminal principle that a person is innocent until proven guilty.[286]

تحت رأس "صالح عام" غير محدد بشكل كاف.[289] وفي الحالات النادرة التي يكون فيها هاتان المصلحتان في حالة نزاع، فإن المصلحة العامة تعطى حجم أكبر.[290] ونتيجة لذلك، عندما احتاج بيت المال (الخزانة العامة) إلى مزيد من الأموال (الموارد) مما كان يمكن الحصول عليه من الضرائب المنصوص عليها في المصدرين الرئيسيين للشريعة، تم وضع قاعدة جديدة تأذن بفرض ضرائب جديدة، مبنية علي اعتبارات الصالح العام، الذي يفضل على مصلحة الفرد (الخاص) في الحفاظ على ثروته.[291] وتجدر الإشارة إلى أن الصالح العام هو مصدر مفتوح لقواعد قانونية جديدة التي تقتضيها الظروف الاجتماعية والاقتصادية المتقلبة مع مرور الوقت.[292] ويعتبر الإصطحاب (افتراض الاستمرارية) أيضا مصدرا للقانون وهذه الأداة هي أكثر قاعدة إثبات عن طريقة عملية والمعروفة جيدا بأسماء أخرى في

---

[283] 'Arafa, *supra* note 136.
[284] *Id.* It should be noted that ("*Ijm'a* is a collective task, whereas *Qiyyas* is largely a process of individual initiative by a jurist. Analogy permits the derivation of a new solution from an already accepted one.").
[285] Khan, *supra* note 84.
[286] *Id.* 'Arafa, *supra* note 136, at 181.
[287] انظر عموما محمد هاشم كمالي، مبادئ الفقه الإسلامي (الطبعة الثالثة ٢٠٠٣).
[288] المرجع السابق, ص٢٣٨.
[289] المرجع السابق. وتتصل القيم الخمسة التي يعترف بها الفقهاء كأساس للمصلحة العامة في الغالب بالفرد، ويفترض أن تتناسب مصالح الفرد ومصلحة المجتمع في تلك المجالات الخمسة.
[290] المرجع السابق.
[291] عرفه الهامش الأعلى ١٣٦.
[292] المرجع السابق. وتجدر الإشارة إلى أن "الإجماع مهمة جماعية، في حين أن القياس هو إلى حد كبير عملية مبادرة فردية من قبل فقيه، ويسمح القياس باستخلاص حل جديد من حل مقبول بالفعل").
[293] خان الهامش الأعلى ٨٤.
[294] المرجع السابق. عرفه الهامش الأعلى ١٣٦ ص١٨١.

Introduction to Islam

Finally, al-'Urf (custom and usage) is a source of Islamic law in which repeated practices are acceptable for people of sound nature.[295] The law that applied in pre-Islamic Arabia entailed customary rules emerged from the practice of the community's members in marketplaces and other areas of social, commercial, interpersonal, and intertribal interaction.[296] Islamic law did not discard out of hand such habitual rules and adopted as its own those of them that were not mismatched with the ethical values of Shari'a spirit.[297] A major example of customary rules revoked as being aggressive to the Islamic values were those approving and resulting in doubling and redoubling of the amount of the inventive obligation from year to year.[298] What differentiates 'urf from ijm'a is that consensus is the field of qualified jurists only, while custom is derived from the traditional practices of common folks in their daily

---

[295] MUHAMMED AZAD, THE MESSAGE OF THE QUR'AN 149-150 (1984).
[296] Bassiouni & Badr, *supra* note 83.
[297] Gamal M. Badr, *Islamic Law and the Challenge of Modern Times*, in *Law, Politics and Personalities in* MIDDLE EAST: ESSAYS IN HONOR OF MAJID KHADDURI 27 (Piscatori & Harris eds., 1987); Gamal M. Badr, *Commercial Law*, in 1 THE OXFORD ENCYCLOPEDIA OF THE MODERN ISLAMIC WORLD 299-300 (John L. Esposito ed., 1995).
[298] Yet other than those moderately few pre-Islamic traditional rules that were not carried over into the evolving Islamic legal system, Islamic law comprises an element of pre-existing customary rules and of other such rules formed by custom in Islamic times through the ages.

communications with each other, thus, a rule arrived at by agreement applies everywhere, while customary rules can be localized.[299] All schools of jurisprudential thought identify custom as a supplementary source of rules of law and a maxim was coined to prompt the place of custom among the sources of legal rules: "What is established by custom is like what" is stipulated (among contractual parties).[300] Like all supplementary sources, custom cannot offer authority for any rule that breaches a binding rule provided by a primary source or by some other supplementary source and it is only to fill in gaps in the body of the law that no other source has dealt with in a mandatory way.[301] Likewise, treaties, pacts and other agreements, contracts, and the judges' jurisprudence are additional sources of Islamic law.

الالتزام الابتكاري من سنة إلى أخرى.[305] إن ما يميز "العرف" عن "الإجماع" هو أن الإجماع هو مجال الفقهاء المؤهلين فقط، في حين أن العرف مستمد من الممارسات التقليدية للناس العاديين في اتصالاتهم اليومية مع بعضهم البعض، وبالتالي، فإن القاعدة التي يتم التوصل إليها بالاتفاق تنطبق في كل مكان، في حين أنه يمكن تحديد موقع القواعد العرفية.[306] فكل مدارس الفقه عرفت العرف كمصدر تكميلي لقواعد القانون، ومبدأ تم صياغته لدفع مكان العرف بين مصادر القواعد القانونية: "ما يثبته العرف" هو مثل ما هو منصوص عليه (بين الأطراف التعاقدية).[307]

---

[299] 'Arafa, *supra* note 133. ("In other words, it is the typical usage of a particular society, both in speech and in action. It is subdivided between general and special rules. Rulings based on Ijtihad are usually influenced by custom. Thus, if custom changes, rulings may also change.").

[300] Badr, *supra* note 147.

[301] So, if there is a rule that is mandatory, then it cannot be changed by customary rules. ("For example, at the outset of Islam, slavery was not prohibited, but after hundreds of years, it was abolished. According to '*urf* (custom), it is prohibited now in all Muslim countries."). 'Arafa, *supra* note 133.

[302] محمد آزاد، رسالة القرآن ١٤٩-١٥٠ (١٩٨٤).

[303] بسيوني وبدر الهامش الأعلى ٨٣.

[304] جمال م. بدر، الشريعة الإسلامية وتحدي العصر الحديث، في القانون والسياسة والشخصيات في هاريس محرران، ١٩٨٧)؛ جمال م. بدر، &الشرق الأوسط: مقالات شرف ماجد خادري ٢٧ (بيسكاتوري إسبوسيتو ل. القانون التجاري، في ١ موعة أوكسفورد عن عالم الإسلام الحديث ٢٩٩-٣٠٠ (جون محرر، ١٩٩٥).

[305] إلا أنه بخلاف تلك القواعد التقليدية المعتدلة نسبيا التي كانت قبل الإسلام، والتي لم يتم نقلها إلى النظام القانوني الإسلامي المتطور، تشكل عنصرا من القواعد العرفية القائمة مسبقا وغيرها من القواعد التي تشكلها العادات في العصر الإسلامي على مر العصور.

[306] عرفه الهامش الأعلى ١٣٣. ("وبعبارة أخرى، هو استخدام نموذجي لمجتمع معين، سواء في الكلام أو في العمل، وينقسم بين القواعد العامة والخاصة. وعادة ما تتأثر الأحكام التي تستند إلى الاجتهاد بالعادات، وبالتالي إذا تغير العرف، فقد تتغير الأحكام أيضا.")

[307] بدر الهامش الأعلى ١٤٧.

[308] لذلك، إذا كانت هناك قاعدة إلزامية، فإنه لا يمكن تغييرها بالقواعد العرفية. ("على سبيل المثال، في بداية الإسلام، لم يكن الاسترقاق محظورا، ولكن بعد مئات السنين، ألغيت، ووفقا للعرف, يحظر الآن في عرفة، الهامش الاعلى ١٣٣. جميع البلدان الإسلامية.")

Therefore, Islamic law is based upon hierarchical sources, and the key sources are unalterable, but *ijtihad* as a main secondary source is very indispensable as events are endless and texts are limited and only a qualified *mujtahid* can find solutions to numerous demanding issues facing Islamic law.309 Based on that, it has been argued that Islamic law may be considered as a jurist's law, while Roman (civil) law is a legislator's law and the Common law is mostly a judge's law.310

It should be noted that Islamic law is different from Islamic *Fiqh* (jurisprudence), as it refers to the understanding of Islamic rules and principles and there are four key schools of *fiqh almadhhabs*

---

309 *Id.*
310 Bassiouni & Badr, *supra* note 80, at 137.
311 المرجع السابق.
312 بسيوني وبدر الهامش الأعلى ٨٠ ص١٣٧.

(jurisprudential thought) and these schools have impacted the *Shari'a* growth.³¹³ Islamic law is jurist-oriented, meaning its rules have been established through history by the writings of Muslim scholars. This law as a comprehensive legal system is not used today in any Muslim country and has a great influence on the political and legal systems of various countries with diverse Islamic and civil law systems, in particular in the Middle East and South Asia.³¹⁴ Several countries in the Middle East—including Egypt, Syria, United Arab Emirates, and Iraq—improved most of their laws from European civil law systems, except for Saudi Arabia, Islamic law is mostly applicable only to family and inheritance issues through most of the Middle East.³¹⁵

---

³¹³ Mohamed Y. Mattar, *Women Entrepreneurs in the Islamic World: Characteristics of Islamic Law and its Main Sources*, 12 JOHN HOPKINS INT'L. J. HUMAN RIGHTS & CIVIL SOCIETY 12 (2010).
³¹⁴ Jean Allain, *Acculturation Through the Middle Ages: The Islamic Law of Nations and Its Place in the History of International Law* in RESEARCH HANDBOOK ON THE THEORY AND HISTORY OF INTERNATIONAL LAW, Alexander Orakhelashvili, (ed.) (2011), at 394–407.
³¹⁵ And even in Saudi Arabia, where the inaccurate Islamic law is overriding, business and corporate laws is based on a mix of Islamic and civil law. Nevertheless, Islamic law is relevant in the current legal applications.

أربع مدارس رئيسية من فقه المذاهب (الفكر الفقهي) وقد أثرت هذه المدارس على نمو الشريعة.³¹⁶ إن الشريعة الإسلامية هي ذات وجهة فقهية، وهذا يعني أن قواعدها قد وضعت من خلال التاريخ من خلال كتابات العلماء المسلمين. هذا القانون باعتباره نظاما قانونيا شاملا لا يستخدم اليوم في أي دولة مسلمة وله تأثير كبير على النظم السياسية والقانونية في مختلف البلدان ذات النظم القانونية الإسلامية والمدنية المتنوعة، ولا سيما في الشرق الأوسط وجنوب آسيا.³¹⁷ وقد حسنت العديد من دول الشرق الأوسط، بما في ذلك مصر وسوريا والإمارات العربية المتحدة والعراق، معظم قوانينها من أنظمة القانون المدني الأوروبي، باستثناء المملكة العربية السعودية، فإن الشريعة الإسلامية غالبا تنطبق فقط في قضايا الأسرة والميراث عبر معظم الشرق الأوسط.³¹⁸

---

³¹⁶ محمد ي. مطر، رائدات الأعمال في العالم الإسلامي: خصائص الشريعة الإسلامية ومصادرها الرئيسية، 12 جون هوبكينز مجلة القانون الدولي لحقوق الإنسان والمجتمع المدني 12 (2010).
³¹⁷ جان آلين، التآزر عبر العصور الوسطى: الشريعة الإسلامية للأمم ومكانها في تاريخ القانون الدولي في كتيب البحث عن نظرية وتاريخ القانون الدولي، ألكسندر أوراكيلاشفيلي، (محرر) (2011)،ص 394-407.
³¹⁸ وحتى في المملكة العربية السعودية، حيث الشريعة الإسلامية غيرال دقيقة هي المهيمنة، قوانين الأعمال والشركات تستند إلى مزيج من القانون الإسلامي والقانون المدني. ومع ذلك، فإن الشريعة الإسلامية ذات صلة في التطبيقات القانونية الحالية.

Furthermore, *Shari'a* outlines the legal culture in the Arab and Muslim [Middle Eastern] World and is often used to set-up the public policy and social order of these countries. *Shari'a* in context, is often inaccurately equated with Islamic law, though both in Western and Muslim discourses it is mutual to use "*Shari'a*" interchangeably with "Islamic law," and it is a much broader concept.[319] For theologians, moralists, and jurists, the extensive meaning of *Shari'a* is the path to well-being or goodness, the life source for well-being and welfare, and the natural and distinctive order created by God.[320] Thus, in Islamic literature the concept is labelling to refer not just to the life's way, or what one may call the attitude and method of Muslims life, but also to any other group of folks attached by a common set of beliefs or principles.[321] So, Islamic literary sources such as the *Qur'an* will often speak of *shra'/shari'at man sabaq/man qablana*" (ways of previous generations), or even *shar' al-falasifa/tariqat al-falasifa* (the methods of the Greek logicians").[322] In Islamic legal system, classically, the expression *shari'at Allah* or *shar' Allah* refers to the wide concept of the extensive and entire path to God, which is likened to the path leading to social *ma'ruf* (goodness) and moral *husn* (goodness).[323] *Shari'a* does not designate a positive set of divine commands with which humans must

---

[319] *See generally* Khaled Abou El-Fadl, *The Islamic Legal Tradition: A Comparative Law Perspective, in* THE CAMBRIDGE COMPANION TO COMPARATIVE LAW (Mauro Bussani & Ugo Mattei eds.) (2012).
[320] Nisrine Abiad, *Sharia, Muslim State, and International Human Rights Treaty Obligations: A Comparative Study*, 51 BRIT. INST. INT'L. & COMP. L. (2008).
[321] Khaled Abou El-Fadel, *Conceptualizing Shari'ah in the Modern State*, 56 VILLANOVA L. REV. (2012).
[322] *Id.*
[323] Ansari & AbuElgasim, *supra* note 45, at 65–96.

comply, but rather the ultimate good God desires for human beings.[324] On the other hand, Islamic law, refers to the growing body of the jurisprudential thought of many communities and schools of thought about the "divine will" and its relation to the common good and thus, is the fallible and defective attempt by human beings over centuries to explore right and wrong and discern what is good.[325] The ethical practicalities and ideologies of al *'adelah tabi'iah* (natural justice) in *Shari'a* are available by human beings, but this does not necessarily lead to an influential system of law.[326]

---

[324] Abou El-Fadel, *supra* note 162.
[325] *Id.*
[326] *Id. Shari'a*, as the pathway to goodness, is perpetual, unchangeable, eternal, and perfect but is not effortlessly cognizable by beings. Additionally, positive legal orders that follow from or are based on these basics are unspecified, changeable, and contextual.

[327] انظر عموما خالد أبو الفضل، العرف القانوني الإسلامي: منظور مقارن للقانون، في دليل كامبريدج (2012) أوغو ماتي محرران للقانون المقارنة (ماورو بوساني و

[328] نسرين أبياد، الشريعة، الدولة المسلمة، والالتزامات المعاهدات الدولية لحقوق الإنسان: دراسة مقارنة، المؤسسة الدولية للقانون والقانون مقارنه (2008). 51. بريت

[329] خالد أبو الفاضل، تصور الشريعة في الدولة الحديثة، 56 فيلانوفا دورية القانون (2012).

[330] المرجع السابق.

[331] أنصاري وأبوالقاسم الهامش الأعلى 45 ص65-96.

[332] أبو الفضل الهامش الأعلى 162.

[333] المرجع السابق.

[334] المرجع السابق، الشريعة، باعتبارها الطريق إلى الخير، هي دائمة، غير قابلة للتغيير، أبدية، وكاملة ولكن لا تدرك دون عناء من قبل الكائنات. بالإضافة إلى ذلك، فإن الأوامر القانونية الإيجابية التي تتبع أو تستند إلى هذه الأساسيات هي غير محددة، قابلة للتغيير، ومتقلب القرينة.

Every Muslim is the beneficiary, guardian, and executor of God's will on earth; his tasks are all encompassing, as the Muslim's duty is to perform in defense of what is right is as much part of his/her belief as is his/her duty to oppose wrong.[335] The conservation of a social order depends on each and every member of the society freely observing the ethical principles and practices. Islam, founded on personal and collective ethics and accountability, introduced a social revolution in the context in which it was first exposed.[336] Communal morality is articulated in the *Qur'an* in such terms as justice, equality, brotherhood, mercy, fairness, compassion, solidarity, and freedom of choice (free will).[337] *alhukaam* (leaders) are in charge of the application of these principles and are responsible to God and man for their management and governance.[338] Under Islamic law, leaders (heads of state or heads of family or private enterprise), have a sophisticated burden/accountability than others.[339] It should be born in mind that in Islam, there is a linkage between individual obligation and the rights and privileges derived from community's membership.[340]

---

[335] *Id.*
[336] Saïd Amir Arjomand, *Perso-Islamicate Political Ethic in Relation to the Sources of Islamic Law in* MEHRZAD MIRROR FOR THE MUSLIM PRINCE: ISLAM AND THE THEORY OF STATECRAFT, (Boroujerdi, ed.) (2013), at 82–206.
[337] *Id.*
[338] Masud, M. Khalid, *Ikhtilaf al-Fuqaha: Diversity in Fiqh as a Social Construction, in* EQUALITY AND JUSTICE IN THE MUSLIM FAMILY, Zainah Anwar, (ed.) (2009), at 65–93.
[339] Abou El-Fadel, *supra* note 162.
[340] *Id.*

Individual responsibilities must be met before one can entitle a portion from the society of which he is part, so each community member must fulfill his/her own duties and rely on others to fulfill theirs before that community can acquire the necessary reservoir of social rights and privileges which can then be shared by all.³⁴¹ The brotherhood and solidarity values not only enforce upon the community the duty to care for its followers, but also require each individual to use his/her creativity to carry out individual and social responsibilities according to his/her capability.³⁴²

المؤسسات الخاصة) عبئا / مساءلة متطورة أكثر عن غيرهم.³⁴⁷ وينبغي أن يوضع في الاعتبار أنه في الإسلام توجد صلة بين الالتزام الفردي والحقوق والامتيازات المستمدة من عضوية المجتمع.³⁴⁸ ويجب الوفاء بالمسؤوليات الفردية قبل أن يتمكن المرء من الحصول على جزء من المجتمع الذي هو جزء منه، لذلك يجب على كل عضو في المجتمع المحلي أن يقوم بواجباته الخاصة وأن يعتمد على الآخرين في الوفاء بواجباتهم قبل أن يتمكن هذا المجتمع من الحصول على المكمن اللازم للحقوق الاجتماعية والإمتيازات التي يمكن بعد ذلك تقاسمها من قبل الجميع.³⁴⁹ إن قيم الأخوة والتضامن لا تفرض على المجتمع واجب رعاية أتباعه فحسب، بل تتطلب أيضا من كل فرد أن يستخدم قدرته الإبداعية في الاضطلاع بمسؤولياته الفردية والاجتماعية وفقا لقدراته.³⁵⁰

---

³⁴¹ *See generally* Anver M. Emon, *Religious Pluralism and Islamic Law*: "Dhimmīs" *and Others in the Empire of Law* (2012).
³⁴² *Id.*
³⁴³ المرجع السابق.
³⁴⁴ سعيد أمير أرجوماند، الأخلاق السياسية الفارسية الإسلامية فيما يتعلق بمصادر الشريعة الإسلامية في ميهرزاد انعكاس لأمير الإسلام: الإسلام ونظرية الكفاءة السياسية، (بوروجيردي، محرر) (٢٠١٣)، في ٨٢-٢٠٦.
³⁴⁵ المرجع السابق.
³⁴⁶ مسعود، م. خالد، إختلاف الفقهاء: التنوع في الفقه كبناء اجتماعي، في المساواة والعدالة في الأسرة المسلمة، زينة أنور،(إصدار) (٢٠٠٩)، في ٦٥-٩٣.
³⁴⁷ أبو الفضل, الهامش الأعلى ١٦٢.
³⁴⁸ المرجع السابق.
³⁴⁹ انظر عموما أنفر م. إمون، التعددية الدينية والشريعة الإسلامية: "ديميس" وآخرون في إمبراطورية القانون (٢٠١٢).
³⁵⁰ المرجع السابق.

The equality of all Muslims is stressed recurrently throughout the *Qur'an* and that's because of that notion that Islam does not have an ordained clergy.[351] It is often argued that Islam is not a faith that offers for full equity among Muslims.[352] Nevertheless, the fact that there is not utter equality in all rights and privileges does not mean that women do not share an inclusive equality with men, as some certain social performs in some Muslim countries are not required by Islam, but have merely evolved in the course of time as a result of indigenous cultural aspects.[353] The exploration for justice is one of the enduring missions of humankind and both social and individual justice are developing concepts which depend largely upon a diversity of external considerations.[354] Islamic law pursues to instruct within every Muslim the need to search for justice and to apply it to himself as well as to others. In the same domain, individual commitment is a cornerstone of Islam, as every Muslim is liable to his Creator for what he himself/herself does or fails to do and for things that he/she has control over.[355] As in Western legal statutes, individual responsibility is established on the intent and motive of the performer in light of his ability to do good and to avoid evil (harm) to others.[356] But it should be taken into

---

[351] *Id.*
[352] Certainly, because Islam makes differences between men and women; not all rights and privileges accessible to men are obtainable to women. For instance, a male Muslim receives (inherits) twice the share of the female, but then a male relative has the financial duty to care for a needy female relative.
[353] *See generally* Michael R. Feener, *Shari'a and Social Engineering*: The Implementation of Islamic Law in Contemporary Aceh (2013).
[354] *Id.*
[355] For further details, *see generally* SEYYED HOSSIEN, ISLAMIC LIFE AND THOUGHT (1981) & THE HEART OF ISLAM: ENDURING VALUES FOR HUMANITY (2002).
[356] Hence, Islam accepts free will, and to the extent that this exists a person is responsible for its exercise in the context of Islamic ethics.

account that the relativity of human justice is not to be disordered with the absoluteness of divine justice whose application every Muslim expects without fail on the day of judgment, as Muslim's belief in responsibility in the hereafter, his/her oath is valid evidence in any judicial or extra-judicial process.[357] So, Muslims are accountable for what they do and what they fails to do in accordance with not only the letter but also the spirit of the law.[358]

الإسلام، حيث أن كل مسلم مسؤول أمام خالقه على ما يقوم به بنفسه أو فشل في القيام به وعن الأشياء التي تكون تحت سيطرته.[363] وكما هو الحال في القوانين القانونية الغربية، تنشأ المسؤولية الفردية عن نية ودوافع المؤدي في ضوء قدرته على فعل الخير وتجنب الشر (الأذى) للآخرين.[364] ولكن يجب أن يؤخذ في الاعتبار أن العدالة البشرية النسبية لا ينبغي أن تكون مختلطة مع العدالة الإلهية المطلقة التي يتوقعها كل مسلم دون فشل يوم القيامة، حيث أن المسلمين يؤمنون بالمسؤولية في الآخرة، وحلف اليمين هو دليل صحيح في أي عملية قضائية أو خارج نطاق القضاء.[365] لذلك،

---

[357] In this regard, God says: "Serve God, and join not any partners with Him; and do good—To parents, orphans, those in need, neighbors who are near, neighbors who are strangers; the companion by your side, the way-farer (ye meet), and what your right hands possess: For God loveth not the arrogant, the vainglorious . . ." *Id.*, at *Qur'an* 4:36. Also, Mohammad said: "None of you (truly) believes until he wishes for his brother what he wishes for himself" and " Actions are but by intention and every man shall have but that which he intended." *Sahih Al-Bukrai & Muslim*.

[358] Hossien, *supra* note 180.

[359] المرجع السابق.

[360] ذلك بالتأكيد لأن الإسلام يخلق إختلافات بين الرجال والنساء؛ لا يمكن للنساء الحصول على جميع الحقوق والإمتيازات المتاحة للرجال. على سبيل المثال، يرث المسلم من الذكور ضعف حصة الإناث، ولكن الذكور عليهم واجب مالي لرعاية النسوة المحتاجة من أقاربهم.

[361] انظر بشكل عام مايكل ر. فينر، الشريعة والهندسة الاجتماعية: تنفيذ الشريعة الإسلامية في إقليم اتشيه الاندونيسى المعاصرة (٢٠١٣).

[362] المرجع السابق.

[363] لمزيد من التفاصيل، انظر عموما سيد حسين، والفكر والحياة الإسلامية (١٩٨١) و قلب الإسلام: القيم الثابتة البشرية (٢٠٠٢).

[364] ومن ثم فإن الإسلام يقبل الإرادة الحرة، وإلى الحد الذي يكون لدي الشخص تلك الإرادة يكون مسؤولا عن ممارسته في سياق الأخلاق الإسلامية.

[365] في هذا الصدد، يقول الله:"وَاعْبُدُوا اللَّهَ وَلَا تُشْرِكُوا بِهِ شَيْئًا ۖ وَبِالْوَالِدَيْنِ إِحْسَانًا وَبِذِي الْقُرْبَىٰ وَالْيَتَامَىٰ وَالْمَسَاكِينِ وَالْجَارِ ذِي الْقُرْبَىٰ وَالْجَارِ الْجُنُبِ وَالصَّاحِبِ بِالْجَنبِ وَابْنِ السَّبِيلِ وَمَا مَلَكَتْ أَيْمَانُكُمْ ۗ إِنَّ اللَّهَ لَا يُحِبُّ مَن كَانَ مُخْتَالًا فَخُورًا " المرجع السابق, القران الأية ٣٦ من سورة النساء. كما قال محمد رسول الله صلى الله عليه وسلم أن النبي صلى الله عليه وسلم قال : (لا يؤمن أحدكم حتى يحب لأخيه ما يحب لنفسه)و(إنَّمَا الأعمالُ بالنِّيَّاتِ، وإنَّمَا لِكُلِّ امرئٍ مَا نَوَى) صحيح البخاري ومسلم.

[366] حسين, الهامش ١٨٠.

In Islam, the values of tolerance and forgiveness must be based on knowledge, awareness, and truth, as these norms depend on the believer's gratitude and acceptance of what he/she has done and his/her honest *twabah* (repentance) with an intent not to repeat the transgression.[367] Nothing in Islamic law averts a woman from achieving herself or attaining her objectives but societies may erect barriers and set obstacles, but nothing in the spirit of the *Qur'an* or the *Sunnah* vanquishes women to men.[368] Over time, social blocks will vanish—as they are disappearing now—because Muslim women will expect and demand it and it can only be anticipated that women will play an progressively larger role in Islamic communities and cultures and surpass the contributions of early Muslim women.[369]

في الإسلام، يجب أن تستند قيم التسامح والمغفرة إلى المعرفة والوعي والحقيقة، لأن هذه المعايير تعتمد على امتنان المؤمن وقبوله لما فعله، وتوباه الصادقة بنية عدم تكرار التجاوز.[370] لا شيء في الشريعة الإسلامية يمنع المرأة من تحقيق نفسها أو تحقيق أهدافها ولكن المجتمعات قد تضع حواجز وعقبات، ولكن لا شيء في روح القرآن أو السنة يقهر النساء في مواجهة الرجال.[371] مع مرور الوقت، سوف تتلاشى الكتل الاجتماعية — كما هي تختفي الآن - لأن النساء المسلمات يتوقعن ويطالبن بذلك، ويمكن توقع أن تلعب

---

[367] That is why Muslims are fortified to pardon the bad actions of others committed against them.
[368] Some provisions show inequitable on the surface but on deep examination reveal a deeper logical understanding and reasonableness. Recently, elevated women's status is apparent in many *Qur'anic* texts which set out women's rights and duties. On protecting her dignity and self-respect, for instance, the *Qur'an* is emphatic and unequivocal: One of the seven *hudud* (fixed) criminal acts is maligning a woman's reputation. God says: "O Mankind: Be careful of your duty to your Lord who created its mate and from them twain hath spread abroad a multitude of men and women. Be careful of your duty toward *Allah* in who ye claim (your rights) of one another" and "O mankind! Lo! We have created you male and female and have made you nations and tribes that ye may know one another. Lo! The noblest of you in the sight of *Allah* is the best in conduct." *Id.*, at *Qur'an*, at 4:1 & 49:13. Furthermore, Mohammad reported: "The most perfect of the believers in faith is the best of them in moral excellence, and the best of you are the kindest of you to their wives." *Sahih Al-Bukari* & *Sahih Muslim*.
[369] Anver M. Emon, *Islamic Law and the Canadian Mosaic: Politics, Jurisprudence, and Multicultural Accommodation*, in Debating Sharia: Islam, Gender Politics, and Family Law Arbitration, Anna C. Korteweg & Jennifer A. Selby, (eds.) (2012).
[370] وهذا هو سبب تحصين المسلمين بالعفو عن الأفعال السيئة التي يرتكبها آخرون ضدهم.
[371] بعض الأحكام تظهر جائرة بنظرة سطحية ولكن الفحص العميق يكشف عن فهم منطقي أعمق وأكثر معقولية. وفي الآونة الأخيرة، يتضح وضع المرأة المرتفع في العديد من النصوص القرآنية التي تحدد حقوق

المرأة دورا أكبر تدريجيا في المجتمعات والثقافات الإسلامية، بل وتتفوق علي مساهمات النساء المسلمات في وقت مبكر.[372]

وفيما يتعلق بظاهرة الأصولية الإسلامية، فإن العديد من غير المسلمين يراقبون التطرف الإسلامي باعتباره شكلا من أشكال الفكر الراديكالي، ويربطونه بالمجموعات والحركات التي تنطوي على أعمال عنف أو تدافع (متعصبة) عن العنف.[382] ويجب تمييز هذا عن التنشيط الإسلامي الذي يمثل حركة سلمية تدعو إلى العودة إلى القيم والممارسات التقليدية الأساسية.[383] ويعتقد المتابعون لهذه الحركة أن

Regarding Islamic fundamentalism phenomenon, many non-Muslims observe Islamic extremism as a form of radical ideology and associate it with groups and movements which involve in violent acts or advocate (fanaticism) violence.[373] This must be distinguished from Islamic revitalization which is a peaceful movement calling for the return to basic traditional values and practices.[374] Followers of such a movement believe that the best way to attain the "true path of Islam" is to develop a unified social and political system based on Islamic ideals and the *Qur'anic* and *Sunnah* teachings and to that extent they are radicals.[375] Reform

---

المرأة وواجباتها. على سبيل المثال، فإن القرآن الكريم، يحمي كرامتها واحترامها لنفسها، على سبيل المثال، القرآن قاطع لا لبس فيه: (إن أحد الحدود الإجرامية السبعة هو تشويه سمعة المرأة. يقول الله : (يَا أَيُّهَا النَّاسُ اتَّقُوا رَبَّكُمُ الَّذِي خَلَقَكُم مِّن نَّفْسٍ وَاحِدَةٍ وَخَلَقَ مِنْهَا زَوْجَهَا وَبَثَّ مِنْهُمَا رِجَالًا كَثِيرًا وَنِسَاءً ۚ وَاتَّقُوا اللَّهَ الَّذِي تَسَاءَلُونَ بِهِ وَالْأَرْحَامَ ۚ إِنَّ اللَّهَ كَانَ عَلَيْكُمْ رَقِيبًا)، (يَا أَيُّهَا النَّاسُ إِنَّا خَلَقْنَاكُم مِّن ذَكَرٍ وَأُنثَىٰ وَجَعَلْنَاكُمْ شُعُوبًا وَقَبَائِلَ لِتَعَارَفُوا ۚ إِنَّ أَكْرَمَكُمْ عِندَ اللَّهِ أَتْقَاكُمْ ۚ إِنَّ اللَّهَ عَلِيمٌ خَبِيرٌ). المرجع السابق, سورة النساء الآية الأولى وسورة الحجرات الآية ١٣. وعلاوة على ذلك، قال محمد أفضل المؤمنين في الإيمان هو أفضلهم في التفوق الأخلاقي، وأفضلهم أطيبهم لزوجاتهم. صحيح البخاري وصحيح مسلم.

[372] أنفر م. إمون، القانون الإسلامي والفسيفساء الكندية: السياسة والفقه والإقامة متعددة الثقافات، في مناقشة الشريعة: الإسلام، وسياسة الجنسنية، وقانون تحكيم الأسرة، آنا ك. كورتيويج وجينيفر أ. سيلبي، (محرران) (٢٠١٢).

[373] See generally David Horowitz, *Islamophobia: Thought Crime of the Totalitarian Future* (2011) (" The ruler of Islamic Iran issued a *fatwa* calling on all Muslims worldwide to murder the novelist Salman Rushdie for insulting the Prophet Muhammad and Islam. Rushdie's crime? Blasphemy or "Islamophobia," as it has come to be known. Since then we have seen worldwide violent Muslim protests over cartoons, blasphemy laws in Europe, prosecutions of notable opponents of Islamic terror like Oriana Fallaci and Geert Wilders, and the demonization of courageous opponents of Islamic imperialism and terror in the West . . . describe the origins of the word "Islamophobia" as a coinage of the Muslim Brotherhood and show how the Brotherhood launched a campaign, by ginning up "Islamophobia" as a hate crime, to stigmatize mention of such issues as radical Islam's violence against women and murder of homosexuals, and the constant incitement of many *imams* to terrorism . . . "Islamophobia" is a dagger aimed at the heart of free speech and also at the heart of our national security.").

[374] *Id.*
[375] *Id.*

أفضل طريقة لتحقيق "المسار الصحيح للإسلام" هي تطوير نظام اجتماعي وسياسي موحد قائم على المثل الإسلامية وتعليمات القرآن والسنة وإلى حد ما هم راديكاليين.[384] إن أفكار الإصلاح التي تنبثق عن حركات النهضة ليست بجديدة على التاريخ الإسلامي، كما أنها لا تشجع اللجوء إلى القسوة لإنجاز مثل هذا الهدف إلا إذا كان هناك تبرير قانوني للاضطراب ضد الحكم الظالم.[385] في القرن الثامن عشر، نشأت حركة الوهاب الراديكاليين في

ideas that emerge from revival movements are not new to the Islamic history, nor do they promote resorting to cruelty to accomplish such an object except where upheaval against unjust rule is lawfully justified.[376] In the 18th century the radical *wahabi* movement developed in Saudi Arabia and its orthodox traditions endure to the present and impacted very badly Islam and Islamic law around the globe, due to the inaccurate and rigid interprerion of the classical Islamic law and they refuses any *tajdid* (reform), as they stick only with literal writings of the divine provisions, especially the repealed or the *nasakh* (abrogated) ones.[377] On the other hand, in the 19th century the

---

[376] *See generally* SEYYED HOSSEIN NASR, THE HEART OF ISLAM: ENDURING VALUES FOR HUMANITY (2002) & SEYYED HOSSEIN NASR, ISLAM: RELIGION, HISTORY, AND CIVILIZATION (2002).

[377] SEYYED HOSSEIN NASR, IDEALS AND REALITIES OF ISLAM (1966).

[378] *Id.*

[379] NISSIM REJWAN (ed.), *The Many Faces of Islam: Perspectives on a Resurgent Civilization* (2000).

[380] *Id.*

[381] Therefore, current political-religious groups focus on social, political, and economic features of Muslim societies and they compete with the secular state and instead call for the launch of a "Muslim State."

[382] (انظر عموما ديفيد هورويتز، الإسلاموفوبيا: جريمة الفكر في المستقبل الاستبدادي ٢٠١١)(" حاكم إيران الإسلامية أصدر فتوى تدعو جميع المسلمين في جميع أنحاء العالم لقتل الروائي سلمان رشدي لإهانة النبي محمد والإسلام. جريمة رشدي؟ التجديف أو "إسلاموفوبيا"، كما أنها قد أصبحت معروفة ومنذ ذلك. الحين، شهدنا احتجاجات عنيفة في جميع أنحاء العالم على الرسوم الكاريكاتورية، وقوانين التجديف في أوروبا، والملاحقات القضائية للمعارضين البارزين للإرهاب الإسلامي مثل أوريانا فالاسي وجيرت فيلدرز. . . وشيطنة المعارضين الشجعان للإمبريالية والإرهاب الإسلامي في الغرب تصف أصول كلمة " الإسلاموفوبيا" كعملة من جماعة الإخوان المسلمين، وتبين كيف أطلقت جماعة الإخوان حملة، من خلال حل "كره الإسلام" كجريمة كراهية، لوصمهم بذكر قضايا مثل العنف الإسلامي المتطرف ضد المرأة وقتل الخوف من الإسلام" هو خنجر يهدف إلى قلب " . . .المثليين، والتحريض المستمر للعديد من أئمة الإرهاب حرية التعبير وأيضا في صميم أمننا القومي").

[383] المرجع السابق.

[384] المرجع السابق.

[385] انظر بشكل عام سيد حسين نصر، قلب الإسلام: استمرار القيم للإنسانية (٢٠٠٢) و سيد حسين نصر، إسلام: دين، تاريخ,والحضارة (٢٠٠٢).

[386] سيد حسين نصر، المثل وحقائق الإسلام (١٩٦٦).

[387] المرجع السابق.

[388] نيسيم ريجوان (محرر). وجوه كثيرة للإسلام: وجهات نظر حول عودة الحضارة ٢٠٠٠ (.)

[389] المرجع السابق.

[390] لذلك، تركز الجماعات السياسية - الدينية الحالية على السمات الاجتماعية والسياسية والاقتصادية للمجتمعات الإسلامية، وتتنافس مع الدولة العلمانية، وبدلا من ذلك تدعو إلى إطلاق "دولة مسلمة".

ideal of the *al-salaf al-salih* (true path to justice) was expressively advocated by the moderate Muslim scholar Mohammad Abduo in Egypt, and his understandings continue to be studied and considered by religious and secular scholars all over the world.[378] Because Islam is an all-inclusive religion integrating all life's aspects, it follows that a revival movement established on religion necessarily confronts the social, economic, and political realisms of the society in which it grows.[379] Muslim and Arab communities, still, have arisen from colonialism and neo-colonialism and are looking for to progress free from certain western inspirations – which according to some inaccurate understandings of them – may corrupt or destabilize basic Islamic values.[380] Moreover in Islam, there is no division/distinction between what in the Western legal system is called "Church and State" and westerners refer to the Islamic form of government as a theocracy which it can be in case of incorrect and rigid interpretations.[381]

المملكة العربية السعودية وتقاليدها الأرثوذكسية الصامدة حتى الوقت الحاضر وأثرت بشدة على الإسلام والشريعة الإسلامية في جميع أنحاء العالم، وذلك بسبب عدم دقة وصرامة التأويل للقانون الإسلامي الكلاسيكي ورفض أي تجديد (وإصلاح)، لأنها لا تلتزم إلا بالكتابات الحرفية للأحكام الإلهية، وخاصة التي ألغيت أو النسخ (إلغاء) منها.[386] من ناحية أخرى، في القرن التاسع عشر، كان المثل الأعلى السلف الصالح (الطريق الحقيقي للعدالة) قد دعا إليه بشكل صريح العالم الإسلامي المعتدل محمد عبده في مصر، ولا تزال مفاهيمه تدرس وينظر فيها من قبل علماء الدين والعلمانيين في جميع أنحاء العالم.[387] ولأن الإسلام دين شامل يدمج جميع جوانب الحياة، فإنه يترتب على ذلك أن حركة النهضة أنشئت على أساس الدين تواجه بالضرورة الواقع الاجتماعي والاقتصادي والسياسي للمجتمع الذي تنمو فيه.[388] ولا تزال المجتمعات الإسلامية والعربية قد نشأت عن الاستعمار والاستعمار الجديد، وهي تبحث عن التقدم بعيدا عن بعض التطلعات الغربية التي قد تفسد أو تزعزع القيم الإسلامية الأساسية وفقا لبعض المفاهيم غير الدقيقة.[389] وعلاوة على ذلك في الإسلام، لا يوجد تقسيم / تمييز بين ما يسمى في النظام القانوني الغربي "الكنيسة والدولة" والغربيين يشيرون إلى الشكل الإسلامي

A distinction must be made between Islamic transformation and Islamic political activism conducted under the outstanding of Islam, as the latter is occasionally categorized by fanaticism, radicalism, and violence, which are conflicting to Islamic teachings and these indicators of a socio-political atmosphere must not be disordered with the Islamic ideals and norms.[391] Progressive reform philosophies continue to develop in the Muslim world, as respectable and prestigious institutions like *al-azhar* University in Cairo, which is the oldest university in the world, is one of the most vital examples of the contemporary, intellectual, educational, and diplomatic forces in the resurgence of Islam, as the contributions they make toward a better understanding of Islam, as well as its peaceful propagation, are free from extremism and violence.[392] The Islamic *alnehada* (renaissance) is prosperous around the globe and devoted Muslims are trying hard to encounter the challenges of modern times while enduring faithful to the classical values.[393] But since all mass activities carry the risk of excess, fanaticism by some is probably to occur at times, however, one should not judge the higher values shared by almost all peaceful Muslim folks based on the extreme deeds committed by the few.[394]

---

[391] Gleave, *supra* note 29, at 212-215.
[392] *Id.*
[393] *Id.* This is enlightened Islamic radicalism as its continuation and growth are continuing.
[394] *Id.*
[395] غليف, الهامش ٢٩ من ٢١٢-٢١٥.
[396] المرجع السابق.

Concerning the Islamic economic aspect, Islamic law comprises prescriptions, prohibitions, commendations, proposals, general principles, and strategies that may be considered the basis for an inclusive modern economic theory. It is significant to recall, though, that such a theory must be part of the full vision of Islam and the combination of all aspects of human effort and collaboration.³⁹⁹ On profit legitimacy, Islam distinguishes between *halal* (legitimate) and *haram* (illegitimate) profit, of which *riba* (usury/interest) is a part, in which the problem of defining it has risen over issues dealing with the financial institutions' activities in the West, specifically the interest's payment which in the classical Islamic view is considered a form of *riba*.⁴⁰⁰ By collecting an encoded, fixed interest, the Muslim neither receives a profit from his/her work nor shares in risk of his/her capital, as speculation is forbidden, and any excessive profiting from the need or misery of others.⁴⁰¹ Indeed, it exists in Islamic law a form of contract called *muqaradah/qard*

---

³⁹⁷ المرجع السابق, هذه هي الراديكالية الإسلامية المستنيرة مع استمرارها ونموها مستمر.
³⁹⁸ المرجع السابق.
³⁹⁹ Bhala, *supra* note 45, at 525-528.
⁴⁰⁰ *Id.*, at 667-701.
⁴⁰¹ *Id.*, at 669-674. Yet, nothing, bans income resulting from what would be equal to joint fund or special trust earnings or other modern forms of financing investments where the investor also bears the burden of potential loss.

hassan (good loan) in which a person entrusts capital to another person for profitable investment and the risk-taking elements justifies the profits, which are neither fixed nor predetermined.402

Moreover, on the obligation's fulfillment, in all businesses and contractual transactions, Muslims required to pay their *dyyoun* (debts) as well as due compensation to those who work for them.407 Rectitude in businesses and personal relationships is as important to the Muslim as is any other principle of faith, thus ethics, morality, and religion are devoted and this is why Muslims regularly do business by oral agreements or a handshake as opposed to a written contract, even writing still highly recommended.408 Also, this elucidates

---

402 *Id.*, at 801-825. The ethical-moral foundation of all business transactions is based on the distinction between *halal* and *haram*. The particular context of a given action, considering the society's common goods and interests and the rights of all folks involved, regulates whether it may be deemed legal or not. Although, this may seem to be imprecise to the non-Muslims, it is however adequately obvious to Muslims as of their belief in God's awareness and wisdom.

403 الهامش ٤٥, من ٥٢٥ – ٥٢٨. بهالا,

404 المرجع السابق, من ٦٦٧-٧٠١.

405 المرجع السابق ٦٦٩-٦٤٧. ومع ذلك, لا شيء, يحظر الدخل الناتج عن ما يساوي الصندوق المشترك أو أرباح الثقة الخاصة أو غيرها من الأشكال الحديثة لتمويل الاستثمارات حيث يتحمل المستثمر أيضا عبء الخسارة المحتملة.

406 المرجع السابق, ٨٠١-٨٢٥. ويستند الأساس الأخلاقي الخلقي لجميع المعاملات التجارية إلى التمييز بين الحلال والحرام. وينظم السياق الخاص لإجراءات معينة, مع مراعاة السلع والمصالح المشتركة للمجتمع وحقوق جميع الأشخاص المعنيين, ما إذا كان يمكن اعتباره قانونيا أم لا. على الرغم من أن هذا قد يبدو غير دقيق لغير المسلمين, إلا أنه واضح بما فيه الكفاية للمسلمين من اعتقادهم في وعي الله والحكمة.

407 *Id.*, at 577-594.

408 *Id.*, at 585-589.

why there is typically a unwillingness to adjudicate claims on an adversarial basis, where artful arguments may be found to justify changing positions.[409] Therefore, in cases of conflict in business dealings, Muslims normally resort to arbitration which means no difference from that which has advanced in non-Muslim societies, as each side chooses an arbitrator who in turn selects a third person.[410] In this context, respect for the person applies to form as well as substance and encompasses all aspects of human dealings.[411]

السبب فإن المسلمين عادة يقومون بأعمالهم التجارية عن طريق اتفاقات شفهية أو المصافحة بدلا من عقد مكتوب، حتى كتابة لا تزال ينصح بها بشدة.[413] ويوضح هذا أيضا سبب عدم الرغبة في الفصل في المطالبات على أساس الخصوم، حيث يمكن إيجاد حجج دقيقة لتبرير المواقف المتغيرة.[414] لذلك، في حالات النزاع في التعاملات التجارية، عادة ما يلجأ المسلمون إلى التحكيم مما يعني عدم وجود اختلاف مما حقق من تقدم في المجتمعات غير الإسلامية، حيث يختار كل طرف محكما الذي بدوره يختار شخص ثالث.[415] وفي هذا السياق، فإن احترام الشخص ينطبق على الشكل وكذلك الجوهر ويشمل

---

[409] Id., at 590.

[410] Id., at 592. Based on the sense of individual dignity, pride, and honor that is very marked to Muslims, it is mutual for both sides to decide on the arbitrator, regularly an individual whose faith, piety, and reputation for fairness is well-established in the community.

[411] In other words, a Muslim's word is still his/her pledge, and his/her dignity is his/her most valued attribute, as human relations are more central than practical considerations. Faithfulness and fidelity are among the most highly appreciated characters and honesty (trust) is not a virtue but an predictable attribute in every Muslim and in today business's world these standards have eroded. In Islam, work, intellectual as well as physical, is considered the foundation of all richness and property. Both work's right, a right to the product of that work, as well as a right to benefit from the rewards of divine wisdom. Work must always have an ethical module, either *per se* or in its outcome (i.e., charity, community service).

[412] المرجع السابق, ٥٧٧-٥٩٤.

[413] المرجع السابق, ٥٨٥-٥٨٩.

[414] المرجع السابق, ٥٩٠.

[415] المرجع السابق, ٥٩٢. واستنادا إلى إحساس الفرد بالكرامة والكبرياء والشرف الذي يتسم به المسلمون، فإنه من المتبادل لكلا الطرفين أن يبت في المحكم، عادة الفرد الذي يكون أيمانه وتقواه وسمعته في الإنصاف راسخة في المجتمع.

[416] وبعبارة أخرى، فإن كلمة المسلم لا تزال تعهده، وكرامته هي صفته الأكثر قيمة، لأن العلاقات الإنسانية الإخلاص والدقة من بين الميزات الأكثر تقديرا والصدق (الثقة) هي أكثر مركزية من الاعتبارات العملية. ليست فضيلة ولكن سمة يمكن التنبؤ بها في كل مسلم وفي عالم الأعمال اليوم هذه المعايير قد تآكلت حقي العمل، الحق في .الإسلام، العمل، الفكري وكذلك الجسدي، يعتبر أساس كل الثراء والممتلكات يجب أن يكون .الحصول على منتج هذا العمل، وكذلك الحق في الاستفادة من ثماره من الحكمة الإلهية للعمل دائما وحدة أخلاقية، سواء في حد ذاته أو في نتائجه (مثال الأعمال الخيرية، خدمة المجتمع).

Under Islamic legal system, there is in the theoretical sense no inherent capital, while the right of *el-mirath* (inheritance) and *al-wassiyyah* (bequests) are maintained, definitely and explicitly prescribed under this law in the *Qur'an*, which permits for the conservation of property, its decentralization and accumulation.[417] The Islamic juristic principle in that context is "the greater one's wealth and power, the greater is the accountability to use them suitably and properly."[418] Thus, economic freedom covers work, property, and the choice of how to use one's proficiencies and resources, as the individual has the choice to select the sort of work he/she does, and he/she has the right to work in an atmosphere that does not impose upon his/her individual dignity.[419]

The *Shari'a* identifies the right to

---

[417] Bhala, *supra* note 45, at 433-456. However, there is the tacit premise that wealth should be lawful through work. Along with the wealth must also be used for good of others, as the needy, and for the community in general.
[418] Hussien, *supra* note 73, at 83.
[419] Bhala, *supra* note 45, at 440. Only in freedom can a person select how to use the fruits of his/her work, that is, to use his/her wealth for personal glorification or for the community's public interest, good, and social welfare. Further, there is a proscription against *jah* (flaunting of one's accomplishment in the face of others, principally the less fortunate) and this reflects the equality and humility norms.

private ownership and its practices save for the public and social welfare to "eminent domain."⁴²³ The use of property in accordance with the best benefits and commands of the proprietor is secured, provided the other's rights are protected based on the Islamic juristic principle of "use is permissible; abuse and destruction are

الخاصة وممارساتها التي توفر للجمهور والرعاية الاجتماعية "مجالا بارزا".⁴³² يتم ضمان استخدام الممتلكات وفقا لأفضل مزايا وأوامر المالك، بشرط حماية حقوق الآخر بناء على المبدأ الفقهي الإسلامي "الاستخدام مسموح به؛

---

⁴²³ *Id.*, at 489-523 & 703-734.

⁴²⁴ *Id.* The utilization of wealth must stabilize the owner's rights against the community's rights, which extends to the conservation of the property itself. Property of whatever kind is not considered only the private privilege of the one who possesses it, but brings a certain responsibility towards the property *per se*, its use and welfares.

⁴²⁵ *Id.* This doesn't mean that every business, industrial, or agricultural initiative must eventually turn into a charitable action, but there must be human and moral, factors that relate to property's use.

⁴²⁶ Bilal Khan & Emir Aly Crowne-Mohammed, *The Value of Islamic Banking in the Current Financial Crisis*, 29 REV. BANKING & FIN. L. 441 (2010).

⁴²⁷ *Id.* The Islamic economic theory values would nullify dealings in which fraud or undue influence is used by one person against another.

⁴²⁸ Barbara L. Seniwski, *Riba Today: Social Equality, The Economy and Doing Business under Islamic Law*, 39 COLUM. J. TRANSNAT'L. L. 701 (2001).

⁴²⁹ Bhala, *supra* note 45, at 577-594. The rational extension of these values is that no one can enrich himself/herself based on harming others, as in such cases, the injured party has a right to compensation for his/her loss, not to surpass the extent of profit of the one causing the unjust loss.

⁴³⁰ Khan & Aly *supra* note 215 & Seniwski, *supra* note 217.

⁴³¹ *Id.* In the same vein, individual agreements, implied pacts, and contracts of *aliz'an* (adhesion) are to be governed in a way as to improve fairness, produce equity, protect the weak and the incautious, and endorse social interests.

⁴³² المرجع السابق, من ٤٨٩-٥٢٣ و ٧٠٣-٧٣٤.

⁴³³ المرجع السابق, يجب استخدام الثروة لتثبيت حقوق المالك على حقوق المجتمع, والذى يمتد الى ولا نعتبر الممتلكات أيا كان نوعها امتيازا خاصا لمن يمتلكها فحسب، بل المحافظة على الممتلكات نفسها تحمل مسؤولية معينة تجاه الممتلكات في حد ذاتها، واستخدامها ورفاهها.

⁴³⁴ المرجع السابق, وهذا لا يعني أن كل مبادرة تجارية أو صناعية أو زراعية يجب أن تتحول في نهاية المطاف إلى عمل خيري، ولكن يجب أن تكون هناك عوامل إنسانية وأخلاقية تتعلق باستخدام الممتلكات

⁴³⁵ بلال خان وإمير علي كرون محمد، قيمة الخدمات المصرفية الإسلامية في الأزمة المالية الحالية، ٢٩ البنوك وفين.ل.٤٤١(٢٠١٠). ريف

⁴³⁶ المرجع السابق, ومن شأن قيم النظرية الاقتصادية الإسلامية أن تلغي التعاملات التي يستخدم فيها شخص ما احتيال أو تأثير غير مبرر ضد شخص آخر.

⁴³⁷ ل. سينويسكي الربا اليوم: المساواة الاجتماعية، الاقتصاد والتجارة بموجب القانون الإسلامي، باربرا ٣٩ كولوم. ج. ترانستنتل. ل. ٧٠١ (٢٠٠١).

⁴³⁸ إن التمديد الرشيد لهذه القيم هو أنه لا يمكن لأحد أن يثري نفسه بهالا، الهامش ٤٥ ، من ٥٧٧-٥٩٤ على أساس الإضرار بالآخرين، في هذه الحالات، يحق للطرف المتضرر الحصول على تعويض عن خسارته، وليس لتجاوز مدى ربح الشخص الذي تسبب في الخسارة الجائرة.

⁴³⁹ سينيوسكي، الهامش ٢١٧ خان وعلي الهامش ٢١٥ و.

⁴⁴⁰ المرجع السابق, وعلى نفس المنوال، فإن الاتفاقات الفردية، والاتفاقات الضمنية، وعقود الإذعان (التصاق) يجب أن تحكم بطريقة تحسن الإنصاف، وتنتج الإنصاف، وتحمي الضعفاء، وتحرض المصالح الاجتماعية وتؤيدها.

prohibited."424 In Islamic law, the relation between man and God and the social responsibilities of a Muslim entail that possessions be used not only for one's individual benefit but also for the community's social good.425 Consequently, based on the Islamic juristic principles, if the choice is between an ethical consideration and profit, the former overcomes over the latter, other things being equivalent. Contractual freedom is mandatory and infers the ability to make free choices without excessive influence.426 Accordingly, the Islamic economic freedom is integrally similar to the idea of free enterprise and socially responsible capitalism.427 Contracts of numerous sorts are governed and fundamentally established on the parties' free will and must manifest the true expression of their intent.428 Economic and business activities based on implied agreements are also composed by a variety of what called in the Western system equitable ideologies to assure against undue influence and lack of fairness, which touch on questions of competence, validity, rescission, and damages.429 It should be noted that the theory of *hisbah* (market observation) suggests that there is a concept of accountability for the market and responsibility for its supervision and this theory initially applied to the classical agricultural markets and their related commercial markets from the 7th to the 12th centuries.430 This can be compared to market and control mechanisms as the Federal Reserve Board's control of currency or the Securities and Exchange Commission's control of stock transactions.431 All of these philosophies of equity, counting protection of the public (consumers, users, etc.), have now developed in the legal systems of the modern world.

الأسواق الزراعية الكلاسيكية والأسواق التجارية ذات الصلة من القرن السابع حتى الثاني عشر.[439] ويمكن مقارنة ذلك بآليات السوق والرقابة، حيث سيطرة مجلس الاحتياط الاتحادي على العملة أو سيطرة لجنة البورصة والأوراق المالية على معاملات الأسهم.[440] كل هذه الفلسفات من العدالة، عد حماية الجمهور (المستهلكين والمستخدمين، وما إلى ذلك)، وضعت الآن في النظم القانونية في العالم الحديث.

الشريعة الإسلامية في مقابل الإرهاب

Shari'a versus Terrorism

Muslims, regardless of whether they are Arabs, Africans, Asians, Chinese, or Westerners (Europeans, Americans, Canadians, Latinos, etc....), still feel powerfully united in their shared beliefs and values. They believe that they have an influence to make in this world, either as persons or as a community, and that their conduct and manner can set an example to others.[441] In the Arab and Muslim world, the difficulties, predicaments, and frustrations are many but Muslims have had to make up for several years during which their social, economic, political, and cultural growth was blunted by both external and internal roots.[442]

المسلمين، بغض النظر عما إذا كانوا من العرب والأفريقة والآسيويين والصينيين أو الغربيين (الأوروبيين والأمريكيين والكنديين واللاتينيين، الخ ...)، لا يزالون يشعرون أنهم مرتبطين بقوة من خلال معتقداتهم وقيمهم المشتركة، لأنهم يعتقدون أن لديهم تأثير يقوموا به في هذا العالم، سواء كأشخاص أو كمجتمع، وأن سلوكهم وطريقتهم يمكن أن تكون مثالا للآخرين.[443] وفي العالم العربي والإسلامي، فإن الصعوبات والمآزق والإحباطات كثيرة، ولكن المسلمين اضطروا إلى تعويض عدة سنوات كان فيها نموهم الاجتماعي والاقتصادي والسياسي والثقافي

---

[441] *See generally* OSMAN BAKAR, THE HISTORY AND PHILOSOPHY OF ISLAMIC SCIENCE (1999).

[442] *Id.* So, they have to fight not only against underdevelopment problems but also forces of quick change.

[443] انظر عموما عثمان بكر، تاريخ وفلسفة العلوم الإسلامية (١٩٩٩).

Introduction to Islam

So, what exactly is the *Shari'a*? In summation, it accurately means "the path," and justice, fairness, and rule of law to most Muslims, as indicated by Harvard Law School and Islamic scholar Professor Noah Feldman.[445] It encompasses both personal, divine aspects and the political and legal realm and only the former is related to most Muslims, particularly in the West.[446] It should be noted that within both, there is a field of various interpretations ranging from the very moderate liberal [secular] to the extreme conservative and there is no uniform understanding of the *Shari'a*, so it can be used and abused by folks with numerous plans and agendas.[447]

Developed over 1,424 years in various societies, it has established itself in a range of understandings. Indeed, the

---

[444] المرجع السابق, لذلك, عليهم أن يقاتلوا ليس فقط ضد مشاكل التخلف ولكن أيضا قوى التغيير السريع.
[445] *See generally* Noah Feldman, THE FALL AND RISE OF THE ISLAMIC STATE (2012) & Noah Feldman, AFTER JIHAD: AMERICA AND THE STRUGGLE FOR ISLAMIC DEMOCRACY (2003).
[446] *Id.*
[447] Labeeb Ahmed Bsoul, *Islamic Diplomacy*: Views of the Classical Jurists in ISLAM AND INTERNATIONAL LAW: ENGAGING SELF-CENTRISM FROM A PLURALITY OF PERSPECTIVES, Marie-Luisa Frick & Andreas Th. Müller, (eds.) (2013), at 127–145.
[448] انظر عموما نوح فلدمان، سقوط الدولة الإسلامية وصعودها (٢٠١٢) ونوح فلدمان، بعد الجهاد: أمريكا والرغبة في الديمقراطية الإسلامية(٢٠٠٣).
[449] المرجع السابق.
[450] لبيب أحمد بسول، الدبلوماسية الإسلامية: آراء الفقهيين الكلاسيكيين في الإسلام والقانون الدولي: مولر، (محرران). الانخراط في مركز ذاتي من وجهات النظر متعددة، ماري لويزا وفريك أندرياس ث (٢٠١٣)، في ١٢٧-١٤٥.

intrinsic multiplicity and pluralism of the *Shari'a* may be the best device we have to counter the vicious and antimodern narratives of fanatics.[451] For those who fear Islamic law creep, it's too late, it's already here. For most, rather like "the golden rule," *Shari'a* requests that their followers obey the laws of the land; live peacefully with their neighbors; don't lie; don't make fraud; pay their taxes; respect each other; care for the needy and the troubled; and focus on making the world better for all.[452] In fact, intellectuals and even western scholars, as Clark Lombardi and Nathan Brown, just to name a few consider the bulk of the *Shari'a* to be evolving human welfare, as for example, at the turn of the 19th, Mohammad 'Abdou, an Egyptian religious scholar, liberal reformer, and prominent *al-azhar* jurist, once said: "I went to the West and saw Islam, but no Muslims; I got back to the East and saw Muslims, but not Islam."[453]

---

[451] Feldaman, *supra* note 223.
[452] *Id.*
[453] See M. A. ZAKI BADAWI, THE REFORMERS OF EGYPT (1976, 1978), [Chapter 2], at 35-95; J. M. S. BALJON, MODERN MUSLIM KORAN INTERPRETATION (1961), & Elie Kedourie, *Afghani and `Abduh: An Essay on Religious Unbelief and Political Activism in Modern Islam* (1966).

In this respect, getting past the *Shari'a* hysteria is not adequate, as opponents still have their "Islamophobia" card to play with. It is a *phobia*, because it is bias and bigotry towards Muslims and the ridiculous and exaggerated fear of an assumed, but nonexistent massive Islam represented by the *Shari'a* bogy.[457] It is an exaggeration, because it takes the deteriorating and extremist understandings of the few who justify terrorism, violence, and classical philosophies and automatically project it onto all Muslims.[458]

---

[457] Sahar Aziz, *Islam on Trial*, BOSTON REV., Feb. 27, 2017, https://bostonreview.net/forum/amna-akbar-jeanne-theoharis-islam-trial ("Islamophobia did not start with Trump nor is it simply the purview of people willing to spout hateful things about Muslims on TV or on the street. It is a historical phenomenon rooted in the history of colonialism. Today, Islamophobia is a widely supported, entrenched social practice invigorated by the rise of the modern national security state and the persistence of global wars against Muslim-majority nations.").

[458] Noah Feldman, *Trump's Travel Ban is an Attack on Religious Liberty*, BLOOMBERG, Jan. 31, 2017, http://www.sltrib.com/opinion/4883881-155/noah-feldman-trumps-travel-ban-is ("President Donald Trump's executive order barring the U.S. entry of refugees from seven [and now six] majority-Muslim countries — while prioritizing refugees who are religious minorities, namely Christians — is a shameful display of discrimination against people who are by legal definition innocent and in danger of their lives. It also violates the constitutional value of equal religious liberty. Whether the constitutional violation could be used by a court to strike down the order is a more difficult question. Classically, the courts haven't interpreted the Constitution to protect the rights of noncitizens living outside the U.S. To get into court to challenge the order, its opponents will need to argue that it violates the rights of people physically in the U.S. As for the Constitution, the 14th Amendment prohibits the government from denying anyone the equal protection of the laws. It was designed to combat racial discrimination. But it also extends to unjust discrimination based on religion. The First Amendment contains two separate guarantees, both of which the order also violates. The free exercise clause has been interpreted to bar the government from preventing a group's religious practice out of religious animus. And the establishment clause prohibits government action that endorses one religion over others. It also bars the government from disfavoring one religion over others.").

This is totally unreasonable because it disregards the peaceful and liberal *Shari'a* interpretations accepted and implemented by the clear majority of Muslims while validating only the radical explanations, as about 1.6 billion Muslims (except "moderates/mainstream") are painted with the same brush.[461] Deferential criticism of Islam and its legal system and even Muslim performs is done regularly by several folks, including Muslims.[462] So far, the Islamophobia

---

[460] نوح فيلدمان، حظر ترامب للسفر هو هجوم على الحرية الدينية، بلومبرغ، 31 يناير 2017، http://www.sltrib.com/opinion/4883881-155/noah-feldman-trumps-travel-ban-is ("إن الأمر الرئاسي للرئيس دونالد ترامب يمنع دخول الولايات المتحدة للاجئين من سبعة [والآن ست دول] أغلبية مسلمة - مع إعطاء الأولوية للاجئين الذين هم أقليات دينية، أي المسيحيين - هو عرض مخجل كما أنه ينتهك القيمة للتمييز ضد الأشخاص الذين هم من خلال التعريف القانوني أبرياء وحياتهم في خطر. أما مسألة ما إذا كان من الممكن أن تستخدم المحكمة انتهاك الدستور. الدستورية للمساواة في الحرية الدينية من الناحية الكلاسيكية، لم تفسر المحاكم الدستور لحماية حقوق غير. من أجل إبطال النظام مسألة أصعب المواطنين الذين يعيشون خارج الولايات المتحدة للدخول في المحكمة للطعن في القرار، فإن خصومهم بحاجة إلى القول بأنه ينتهك حقوق الناس الموجودين بالفعل في الولايات المتحدة. أما بالنسبة للدستور، فإن وهي مصممة. التعديل الرابع عشر يحظر على الحكومة حرمان أي شخص من حماية القانون المتساوية ويتضمن التعديل. ولكنه يمتد أيضا إلى التمييز الظالم القائم على أساس الدين. لمكافحة التمييز العنصري وقد تم تفسير بند حرية الممارسة لمنع الحكومة من. الأول كفالتين منفصلتين، وكلاهما ينتهكهما الأمر أيضا ويحظر بند التأسيس عمل الحكومة علي تأييد دينا. منع ممارسة الشعائر الدينية للمجموعة من العداء الديني على دين آخر. كما يحظر على الحكومة ازدراء دين واحد على الآخرين.

[461] Arsalan Iftikhar, *Sharia Is Nothing to Fear*, TIME, Jul. 16, 2016, http://time.com/4409437/sharia-law-xenophobia/ ("For example, *Sharia* forbids members of a Muslim minority [in Western societies] from engaging in clandestine acts of violence and paramilitary organizing…or from acting as political or military agents for a Muslim-majority country,". . . "Islamic law also forbids the disruption of public safety." (Terrorism would fall into that category.) All this would certainly come as a surprise to the many people who know little about Islam—whether they are extremists who claim to be devout Muslims or those who seek to politically exploit anti-Muslim fear . . ."). *See* Glenn Thrush, *Trump's New Travel Ban Blocks Migrants from Six Nations, Sparing Iraq*, N.Y. TIMES, Mar. 6, 2017, https://www.nytimes.com/2017/03/06/us/politics/travel-ban-muslim-trump.html?_r=0 ("President Trump signed an executive order blocking citizens of six predominantly Muslim countries from entering the United States . . .").

[462] Noah Feldman, *Why Shariah?*, N.Y. TIMES MAG., Mar. 16, 2008, http://www.nytimes.com/2008/03/16/magazine/16Shariah-t.html ("In fact, "*Shariah*" is not the word traditionally used in Arabic to refer to the processes of Islamic legal reasoning or the rulings produced through it: that word is *fiqh*, meaning something like Islamic jurisprudence. The word "*Shariah*" connotes a connection to the divine, a set of unchanging beliefs and principles that order life in accordance with God's will. Westerners

tag is not used, as it is not done with hate and contempt and opinions' diversity are a known forte of Islamic *fiqh* (jurisprudence).463 Liberal scholars for long time have critiqued the typical Islamic opinions on blasphemy, *riddah* (apostasy), women status, etc. and many in the Muslim countries are persecuted and standing on trial for this, but it's *not for Islamophobia*.464	للإسلام ونظامه القانوني وحتى أداء المسلم ينفذ بشكل منتظم من قبل عدة أشخاص, بما فيهم المسلمون.٤٦٦ وحتى الآن, لم يتم استخدام علامة الخوف من الإسلام, حيث أنه لم يتم ذلك بكراهية والاحتقار, وتنوع الآراء موطن معروف في الفقه الإسلامي.٤٦٧ وقد انتقد العلماء الليبراليون منذ فترة طويلة الآراء الإسلامية النموذجية بشأن التجديف, الردة, (وضع المرأة, وما

---

typically imagine that *Shariah* advocates simply want to use the *Koran* as their legal code.").

463 *Id.* ("Under the constitutional theory that the scholars developed to explain the division of labor in the Islamic state, the *caliph* had paramount responsibility to fulfill the divine injunction to "command the right and prohibit the wrong." But this was not a task he could accomplish on his own. It required him to delegate responsibility to scholarly judges, who would apply God's law as they interpreted it. The *caliph* could promote or fire them as he wished, but he could not dictate legal results: judicial authority came from the *caliph*, but the law came from the scholars.").

464 *Id. See also* Iftikhar, *supra* note 231.

٤٦٥ عرسالان افتخار, الشريعة ليست شيئا للخوف, تايم,١٦ يوليو , ٢٠١٦, http://time.com/4409437/sharia-law-xenophobia/ "على سبيل المثال, الشريعة تمنع أعضاء الأقلية المسلمة [في المجتمعات الغربية إن القانون الإسلامي يحظر أيضا تعطيل "..." بدور عملاء سياسيين أو عسكريين لبلد ذي أغلبية مسلمة السلامة العامة". (الإرهاب سوف يندرج ضمن هذه الفئة). كل هذا سيكون بالتأكيد مفاجأة لكثير من الناس الذين يعرفون القليل عن الإسلام ـ سواء كانوا المتطرفين الذين يدعون أنهم مسلمون متدينون أو أولئك الذين انظر جلين ثروش, حظر ترامب الجديد للسفر . . يسعون إلى الاستغلال السياسي للخوف من المسلمين مارس ٢٠١٧, ٦لكتل المهاجرين من ست دول وتجنيب العراق نيويورك تايمز https://www.nytimes.com/2017/03/06/us/politics/travel-ban-muslim-trump.html?_r=0, وقع الرئيس ترامب أمرا تنفيذيا يحظر على مواطني ستة بلدان ذات أغلبية مسلمة دخول الولايات المتحدة") ...(".

٤٦٦ نوح فلدمان, لماذا الشريعة؟ مجلة نيويورك تايمز,١٦ مارس ٢٠٠٨, http://www.nytimes.com/2008/03/16/magazine/16Shariah-t.html , ("في الواقع," الشريعة "ليست كلمة تستخدم عادة في العربية للإشارة إلى عمليات المنطق القانوني الإسلامي أو أحكامه المنتجة من خلال ذلك: هذه الكلمة هي الفقه, وهذا يعني شيء من قبيل الفقه الإسلامي. كلمة "الشريعة" تشير إلى ويتصور اتصال مع الإله, مجموعة من المعتقدات والمبادئ التي لا تتغير التي تأمر الحياة وفقا لإرادة الله الغربيون عادة أن دعاة الشريعة يريدون ببساطة استخدام القرآن كرمزهم القانوني.").

٤٦٧ المرجع السابق, في ظل النظرية الدستورية التي وضعها العلماء لتفسير تقسيم العمل في الدولة الإسلامية, كان على الخليفة مسؤولية قصوى من الوفاء بنصيحة الإله "بالأمر بالمعروف والنهي عن المنكر". ولكن هذه ليست مهمة يمكن أن ينجزها بنفسه. تطلب منه الأمر أن يفوض المسؤولية للقضاة العلميين الذين يطبقون شريعة الله كما يفسرونه. يمكن للخليفة أن يرقيهم أو يطردهم كما يشاء, لكنه لا يستطيع أن يملي النتائج القانونية: فالسلطة القضائية تأتي من الخليفة, ولكن القانون جاء من العلماء.").

٤٦٨ المرجع السابق, انظر أيضا افتخار هامش ٢٣١.

The exploration for an Islamic way is enduring in the Muslim world. It is a complicated and problematic search looking for to link the basics of a glorious past with a future that proposes only optimistic promises reduced by present difficulties. Most Muslims as persons are fearless, for every Muslim trust that he/she should act during his/her lifetime as if he/she will live forever. He/she has a sense of stability and continuity, knowing that the work started by one person will be carried on by another. There is a continuous hope for a better tomorrow; but then, what counts is the hereafter. Ours is not to assure an outcome but to try our best to accomplish it in the right way. Though, the end does not justify the means and the ethical dimension of behavior and method must constantly prevail.

The test of Islam is a challenge to all Muslim cultures: to generate the sorts of economic, social, and political foundations and organizations that will preserve the rudimentary moral and ethical proper Islamic values along with the personal freedom of every Muslim. This includes attaining a faint balance between the community's needs and the right of the individual to the complete accomplishment of freedom, equality, justice and what under the U.S. Constitution is called "the pursuit of happiness." This also is a genuine and valid goal in Islam, as pointed out by the 10th century Muslim philosopher, the mathematician *al-farabi* in which a substantial part of his main text on truth is keen on the achievement of happiness and fulfillment of pleasure.[469] Last but by no means least, Islamic legal theory permanently documented some indeterminacy in man's interpretation of God's law (contingency in sacred law). Indeterminacy is a predictable character of a legal system based on interpretation, as is the common law or U.S. constitutional law; and in general, it is a price we are eager to pay in exchange for elasticity and the law's capability to grow to meet new encounters, so codes and their particularity have perils, too. And, yes, anti-Muslim bigotry or "Muslimophobia" work, but Islamophobia carries the deeper, wealthier, and more accurate nature of the spirits and beliefs that drive the "othering" of Muslims.

---

[469] In this respect, God says: "Every one of you is a shepherd, and every one of you will be questioned about those under his rule: The *amir* (leader/head of state) is a shepherd and he will be questioned about his subjects, the man is a ruler in his family and he will be questioned about those under his care; and the woman is a ruler in the house of her husband and she will be questioned about those under her care." *Id.*, at *Sahih Muslim & Al-Bukari*. By the same token, Prophet Mohammad reported that "O my son! Observe your prayers, order (enjoin or command) with what is just (right and fair) and admonish (forbid) what is wrong; and bear with patience on what befalls upon you; for this is determination of purpose" *Id.*, at *Qur'an* 31:17.

المعنويات والمعتقدات التي تدفع "للتنفير" من المسلمين.

1. The Opening

In the name of Allah, the Beneficent, the Merciful.
1:1. Praise be to God, the Lord of the worlds,
1:2. The Beneficent, the Merciful,
1:3. Master of the day of Requital.
1:4. Thee do we serve and Thee do we beseech for help.
1:5. Guide us on the right path,
1:6. The path of those upon whom Thou hast bestowed favours,
1:7. Not those upon whom wrath is brought down, nor those who go astray.

١- سورة الفاتحة

بِسْمِ اللَّهِ الرَّحْمَنِ الرَّحِيمِ (١)
الْحَمْدُ لِلَّهِ رَبِّ الْعَالَمِينَ (٢)
الرَّحْمَنِ الرَّحِيمِ (٣)
مَالِكِ يَوْمِ الدِّينِ (٤)
إِيَّاكَ نَعْبُدُ وَإِيَّاكَ نَسْتَعِينُ (٥)
اهْدِنَا الصِّرَاطَ الْمُسْتَقِيمَ (٦)
صِرَاطَ الَّذِينَ أَنْعَمْتَ عَلَيْهِمْ غَيْرِ الْمَغْضُوبِ عَلَيْهِمْ وَلَا الضَّالِّينَ (٧)

2. The Cow

Sura 2. The Cow (Al-Baqarah)
In the name of God, the Beneficent, the Merciful.
2:1. I, God, am the best knower.
2:2. This Book, there is no doubt in it, is a guide to those who keep their duty,
2:3. Who believe in the Unseen and keep up prayer and spend out of what We have given them,
2:4. And who believe in that which has been revealed to thee and that which was revealed before thee, and of the Hereafter they are sure.
2:5. These are on a right course from their Lord and these it is that are successful.
2:6. Those who disbelieve -- it being alike to them whether thou warn them or warn them not -- they will not believe.
2:7. God has sealed their hearts and their hearing; and there is a covering on their eyes, and for them is a grievous chastisement.

٢- سورة البقرة

بِسْمِ اللَّهِ الرَّحْمَنِ الرَّحِيمِ
الم (١)
ذَلِكَ الْكِتَابُ لَا رَيْبَ فِيهِ هُدًى لِلْمُتَّقِينَ (٢)
الَّذِينَ يُؤْمِنُونَ بِالْغَيْبِ وَيُقِيمُونَ الصَّلَاةَ وَمِمَّا رَزَقْنَاهُمْ يُنْفِقُونَ (٣)
وَالَّذِينَ يُؤْمِنُونَ بِمَا أُنْزِلَ إِلَيْكَ وَمَا أُنْزِلَ مِنْ قَبْلِكَ وَبِالْآخِرَةِ هُمْ يُوقِنُونَ (٤)
أُولَئِكَ عَلَى هُدًى مِنْ رَبِّهِمْ وَأُولَئِكَ هُمُ الْمُفْلِحُونَ (٥)
إِنَّ الَّذِينَ كَفَرُوا سَوَاءٌ عَلَيْهِمْ أَأَنْذَرْتَهُمْ أَمْ لَمْ تُنْذِرْهُمْ لَا يُؤْمِنُونَ (٦)
خَتَمَ اللَّهُ عَلَى قُلُوبِهِمْ وَعَلَى سَمْعِهِمْ وَعَلَى أَبْصَارِهِمْ غِشَاوَةٌ وَلَهُمْ عَذَابٌ عَظِيمٌ (٧)

2. The Cow

***

2:8. And there are some people who say: We believe in God and the Last Day and they are not believers.

2:9. They seek to deceive God and those who believe, and they deceive only themselves and they perceive not.

2:10. In their hearts is a disease, so God increased their disease, and for them is a painful chastisement because they lie.

2:11. And when it is said to them, Make not mischief in the land, they say: We are but peacemakers.

2:12. Now surely they are the mischief-makers, but they perceive not.

2:13. And when it is said to them, Believe as the people believe, they say: Shall we believe as the fools believe? Now surely they are the fools, but they know not.

2:14. And when they meet those who believe, they say, We believe; and when they are alone with their devils, they say: Surely we are with you, we were only mocking.

2:15. God will pay them back their mockery, and He leaves them alone in their inordinacy, blindly wandering on.

2:16. These are they who buy error for guidance, so their bargain brings no gain, nor are they guided.

2:17. Their parable is as the parable of one who kindles a fire but when it illumines all around him, God takes away their light, and leaves them in darkness -- they cannot see.

2:18. Deaf dumb, (and) blind, so they return not:

2:19. Or like abundant rain from the clouds in which is darkness, and thunder and lightning; they put their fingers into their ears because of the thunder-peal, for fear of death. And God encompasses the disbelievers.

2:20. The lightning almost takes away their sight. Whenever it shines on them

وَمِنَ النَّاسِ مَنْ يَقُولُ آمَنَّا بِاللَّهِ وَبِالْيَوْمِ الْآخِرِ وَمَا هُمْ بِمُؤْمِنِينَ (٨) يُخَادِعُونَ اللَّهَ وَالَّذِينَ آمَنُوا وَمَا يَخْدَعُونَ إِلَّا أَنْفُسَهُمْ وَمَا يَشْعُرُونَ (٩) فِي قُلُوبِهِمْ مَرَضٌ فَزَادَهُمُ اللَّهُ مَرَضًا وَلَهُمْ عَذَابٌ أَلِيمٌ بِمَا كَانُوا يَكْذِبُونَ (١٠) وَإِذَا قِيلَ لَهُمْ لَا تُفْسِدُوا فِي الْأَرْضِ قَالُوا إِنَّمَا نَحْنُ مُصْلِحُونَ (١١) أَلَا إِنَّهُمْ هُمُ الْمُفْسِدُونَ وَلَكِنْ لَا يَشْعُرُونَ (١٢) وَإِذَا قِيلَ لَهُمْ آمِنُوا كَمَا آمَنَ النَّاسُ قَالُوا أَنُؤْمِنُ كَمَا آمَنَ السُّفَهَاءُ أَلَا إِنَّهُمْ هُمُ السُّفَهَاءُ وَلَكِنْ لَا يَعْلَمُونَ (١٣) وَإِذَا لَقُوا الَّذِينَ آمَنُوا قَالُوا آمَنَّا وَإِذَا خَلَوْا إِلَى شَيَاطِينِهِمْ قَالُوا إِنَّا مَعَكُمْ إِنَّمَا نَحْنُ مُسْتَهْزِئُونَ (١٤) اللَّهُ يَسْتَهْزِئُ بِهِمْ وَيَمُدُّهُمْ فِي طُغْيَانِهِمْ يَعْمَهُونَ (١٥) أُولَئِكَ الَّذِينَ اشْتَرَوُا الضَّلَالَةَ بِالْهُدَى فَمَا رَبِحَتْ تِجَارَتُهُمْ وَمَا كَانُوا مُهْتَدِينَ (١٦) مَثَلُهُمْ كَمَثَلِ الَّذِي اسْتَوْقَدَ نَارًا فَلَمَّا أَضَاءَتْ مَا حَوْلَهُ ذَهَبَ اللَّهُ بِنُورِهِمْ وَتَرَكَهُمْ فِي ظُلُمَاتٍ لَا يُبْصِرُونَ (١٧) صُمٌّ بُكْمٌ عُمْيٌ فَهُمْ لَا يَرْجِعُونَ (١٨) أَوْ كَصَيِّبٍ مِنَ السَّمَاءِ فِيهِ ظُلُمَاتٌ وَرَعْدٌ وَبَرْقٌ يَجْعَلُونَ أَصَابِعَهُمْ فِي آذَانِهِمْ مِنَ الصَّوَاعِقِ حَذَرَ الْمَوْتِ وَاللَّهُ مُحِيطٌ بِالْكَافِرِينَ (١٩) يَكَادُ الْبَرْقُ يَخْطَفُ أَبْصَارَهُمْ كُلَّمَا

2. The Cow

they walk in it, and when it becomes dark to them they stand still. And if God had pleased, He would have taken away their hearing and their sight. Surely God is Possessor of power over all things.

* * *

2:21. O men, serve your Lord Who created you and those before you, so that you may guard against evil,

2:22. Who made the earth a resting-place for you and the heaven a structure, and sends down rain from the clouds then brings forth with it fruits for your sustenance; so do not set up rivals to God while you know.

2:23. And if you are in doubt as to that which We have revealed to Our servant, then produce a chapter like it and call on your helpers besides God if you are truthful.

2:24. But if you do (it) not -- and you can never do (it) -- then be on your guard against the fire whose fuel is men and stones; it is prepared for the disbelievers.

2:25. And give good news to those who believe and do good deeds, that for them are Gardens in which rivers flow. Whenever they are given a portion of the fruit thereof, they will say: This is what was given to us before and they are given the like of it. And for them therein are pure companions and therein they will abide.

2:26. Surely God disdains not to set forth any parable -- a gnat or anything above that. Then as for those who believe, they know that it is the truth from their Lord; and as for those who disbelieve, they say: What is it that God means by this parable? Many He leaves in error by it and many He leads aright by it. And He leaves in error by it only the transgressors.

2:27. Who break the covenant of God after its confirmation and cut asunder what God has ordered to be joined,

أَضَاءَ لَهُمْ مَشَوْا فِيهِ وَإِذَا أَظْلَمَ عَلَيْهِمْ قَامُوا وَلَوْ شَاءَ اللَّهُ لَذَهَبَ بِسَمْعِهِمْ وَأَبْصَارِهِمْ إِنَّ اللَّهَ عَلَى كُلِّ شَيْءٍ قَدِيرٌ (٢٠)

يَا أَيُّهَا النَّاسُ اعْبُدُوا رَبَّكُمُ الَّذِي خَلَقَكُمْ وَالَّذِينَ مِنْ قَبْلِكُمْ لَعَلَّكُمْ تَتَّقُونَ (٢١)

الَّذِي جَعَلَ لَكُمُ الْأَرْضَ فِرَاشًا وَالسَّمَاءَ بِنَاءً وَأَنْزَلَ مِنَ السَّمَاءِ مَاءً فَأَخْرَجَ بِهِ مِنَ الثَّمَرَاتِ رِزْقًا لَكُمْ فَلَا تَجْعَلُوا لِلَّهِ أَنْدَادًا وَأَنْتُمْ تَعْلَمُونَ (٢٢)

وَإِنْ كُنْتُمْ فِي رَيْبٍ مِمَّا نَزَّلْنَا عَلَى عَبْدِنَا فَأْتُوا بِسُورَةٍ مِنْ مِثْلِهِ وَادْعُوا شُهَدَاءَكُمْ مِنْ دُونِ اللَّهِ إِنْ كُنْتُمْ صَادِقِينَ (٢٣)

فَإِنْ لَمْ تَفْعَلُوا وَلَنْ تَفْعَلُوا فَاتَّقُوا النَّارَ الَّتِي وَقُودُهَا النَّاسُ وَالْحِجَارَةُ أُعِدَّتْ لِلْكَافِرِينَ (٢٤)

وَبَشِّرِ الَّذِينَ آمَنُوا وَعَمِلُوا الصَّالِحَاتِ أَنَّ لَهُمْ جَنَّاتٍ تَجْرِي مِنْ تَحْتِهَا الْأَنْهَارُ كُلَّمَا رُزِقُوا مِنْهَا مِنْ ثَمَرَةٍ رِزْقًا قَالُوا هَذَا الَّذِي رُزِقْنَا مِنْ قَبْلُ وَأُتُوا بِهِ مُتَشَابِهًا وَلَهُمْ فِيهَا أَزْوَاجٌ مُطَهَّرَةٌ وَهُمْ فِيهَا خَالِدُونَ (٢٥)

إِنَّ اللَّهَ لَا يَسْتَحْيِي أَنْ يَضْرِبَ مَثَلًا مَا بَعُوضَةً فَمَا فَوْقَهَا فَأَمَّا الَّذِينَ آمَنُوا فَيَعْلَمُونَ أَنَّهُ الْحَقُّ مِنْ رَبِّهِمْ وَأَمَّا الَّذِينَ كَفَرُوا فَيَقُولُونَ مَاذَا أَرَادَ اللَّهُ بِهَذَا مَثَلًا يُضِلُّ بِهِ كَثِيرًا وَيَهْدِي بِهِ كَثِيرًا وَمَا يُضِلُّ بِهِ إِلَّا الْفَاسِقِينَ (٢٦)

الَّذِينَ يَنْقُضُونَ عَهْدَ اللَّهِ مِنْ بَعْدِ مِيثَاقِهِ وَيَقْطَعُونَ مَا أَمَرَ اللَّهُ بِهِ أَنْ

and make mischief in the land. These it is that are the losers.

2:28. How can you deny God and you were without life and He gave you life? Again, He will cause you to die and again bring you to life, then you shall be brought back to Him.

2:29. He it is Who created for you all that is in the earth. And He directed Himself to the heaven, so He made them complete seven heavens; and He is Knower of all things.

* * *

2:30. And when thy Lord said to the angels, I am going to place a ruler in the earth, they said: Wilt Thou place in it such as make mischief in it and shed blood? And we celebrate Thy praise and extol Thy holiness. He said: Surely I know what you know not.

2:31. And He taught Adam all the names, then presented them to the angels; He said: Tell Me the names of those if you are right.

2:32. They said: Glory be to Thee We have no knowledge but that which Thou hast taught us. Surely Thou art the Knowing, the Wise.

2:33. He said: O Adam, inform them of their names. So when he informed them of their names, He said: Did I not say to you that I know what is unseen in the heavens and the earth? And I know what you manifest and what you hide.

2:34. And when We said to the angels, Be submissive to Adam, they submitted, but Iblis (did not). He refused and was proud, and he was one of the disbelievers.

2:35. And We said: O Adam, dwell thou and thy wife in the garden, and eat from it a plenteous (food) wherever you wish, and approach not this tree, lest you be of the unjust.

2:36. But the devil made them slip

2. The Cow

from it, and caused them to depart from the state in which they were. And We said: Go forth, some of you are the enemies of others. And there is for you in the earth an abode and a provision for a time.

2:37. Then Adam received (revealed) words from his Lord, and He turned to him (mercifully). Surely He is Oft-returning (to mercy), the Merciful.

2:38. We said: Go forth from this state all. Surely there will come to you guidance from Me, then whoever follows My guidance, no fear shall come upon them, nor shall they grieve.

2:39. And (as to) those who disbelieve in and reject Our messages, they are the companions of the Fire in it they will abide.

* * *

2:40. O Children of Israel, call to mind My favour which I bestowed on you and be faithful to (your) covenant with Me, I shall fulfil (My) covenant with you; and Me, Me alone, should you fear.

2:41. And believe in that which I have revealed, verifying that which is with you, and be not the first to deny it; neither take a mean price for My messages; and keep your duty to Me, Me alone.

2:42. And mix not up truth with falsehood, nor hide the truth while you know.

2:43. And keep up prayer and pay the poor-rate and bow down with those who bow down.

2:44. Do you enjoin men to be good and neglect your own souls while you read the Book? Have you then no sense?

2:45. And seek assistance through patience and prayer, and this is hard except for the humble ones,

2:46. Who know that they will meet their Lord and that to Him they will return.

وَمَتَاعٌ إِلَىٰ حِينٍ (٣٦)
فَتَلَقَّىٰ آدَمُ مِنْ رَبِّهِ كَلِمَاتٍ فَتَابَ عَلَيْهِ إِنَّهُ هُوَ التَّوَّابُ الرَّحِيمُ (٣٧)
قُلْنَا اهْبِطُوا مِنْهَا جَمِيعًا فَإِمَّا يَأْتِيَنَّكُمْ مِنِّي هُدًى فَمَنْ تَبِعَ هُدَايَ فَلَا خَوْفٌ عَلَيْهِمْ وَلَا هُمْ يَحْزَنُونَ (٣٨)
وَالَّذِينَ كَفَرُوا وَكَذَّبُوا بِآيَاتِنَا أُولَٰئِكَ أَصْحَابُ النَّارِ هُمْ فِيهَا خَالِدُونَ (٣٩)
يَا بَنِي إِسْرَائِيلَ اذْكُرُوا نِعْمَتِيَ الَّتِي أَنْعَمْتُ عَلَيْكُمْ وَأَوْفُوا بِعَهْدِي أُوفِ بِعَهْدِكُمْ وَإِيَّايَ فَارْهَبُونِ (٤٠)
وَآمِنُوا بِمَا أَنْزَلْتُ مُصَدِّقًا لِمَا مَعَكُمْ وَلَا تَكُونُوا أَوَّلَ كَافِرٍ بِهِ وَلَا تَشْتَرُوا بِآيَاتِي ثَمَنًا قَلِيلًا وَإِيَّايَ فَاتَّقُونِ (٤١)
وَلَا تَلْبِسُوا الْحَقَّ بِالْبَاطِلِ وَتَكْتُمُوا الْحَقَّ وَأَنْتُمْ تَعْلَمُونَ (٤٢)
وَأَقِيمُوا الصَّلَاةَ وَآتُوا الزَّكَاةَ وَارْكَعُوا مَعَ الرَّاكِعِينَ (٤٣)
أَتَأْمُرُونَ النَّاسَ بِالْبِرِّ وَتَنْسَوْنَ أَنْفُسَكُمْ وَأَنْتُمْ تَتْلُونَ الْكِتَابَ أَفَلَا تَعْقِلُونَ (٤٤)
وَاسْتَعِينُوا بِالصَّبْرِ وَالصَّلَاةِ وَإِنَّهَا لَكَبِيرَةٌ إِلَّا عَلَى الْخَاشِعِينَ (٤٥)
الَّذِينَ يَظُنُّونَ أَنَّهُمْ مُلَاقُو رَبِّهِمْ وَأَنَّهُمْ إِلَيْهِ رَاجِعُونَ (٤٦)
يَا بَنِي إِسْرَائِيلَ اذْكُرُوا نِعْمَتِيَ الَّتِي أَنْعَمْتُ عَلَيْكُمْ وَأَنِّي فَضَّلْتُكُمْ عَلَى الْعَالَمِينَ (٤٧)
وَاتَّقُوا يَوْمًا لَا تَجْزِي نَفْسٌ عَنْ نَفْسٍ شَيْئًا وَلَا يُقْبَلُ مِنْهَا شَفَاعَةٌ وَلَا يُؤْخَذُ مِنْهَا عَدْلٌ وَلَا هُمْ يُنْصَرُونَ (٤٨)
وَإِذْ نَجَّيْنَاكُمْ مِنْ آلِ فِرْعَوْنَ

***

2:47. O Children of Israel, call to mind My favour which I bestowed on you and that I made you excel the nations.

2:48. And guard yourselves against a day when no soul will avail another in the least, neither will intercession be accepted on its behalf, nor will compensation be taken from it, nor will they be helped.

2:49. And when We delivered you from Pharaoh's people, who subjected you to severe torment, killing your sons and sparing your women, and in this there was a great trial from your Lord.

2:50. And when We parted the sea for you, so We saved you and drowned the people of Pharaoh while you saw.

2:51. And when We appointed a time of forty nights with Moses, then you took the calf (for a god) after him, and you were unjust.

2:52. Then We pardoned you after that so that you might give thanks.

2:53. And when We gave Moses the Book and the Discrimination that you might walk aright.

2:54. And when Moses said to his people: O my people, you have surely wronged yourselves by taking the calf (for a god), so turn to your Creator (penitently), and kill your passions. That is best for you with your Creator. So He turned to you (mercifully). Surely He is the Oft-returning (to mercy), the Merciful.

2:55. And when you said: O Moses, we will not believe in thee till we see God manifestly, so the punishment overtook you while you looked on.

2:56. Then We raised you up after your stupor that you might give thanks.

2:57. And We made the clouds to give shade over you and We sent to you manna and quails. Eat of the good things that We have given you. And they did not do Us any harm, but they

يَسُومُونَكُمْ سُوءَ الْعَذَابِ يُذَبِّحُونَ أَبْنَاءَكُمْ وَيَسْتَحْيُونَ نِسَاءَكُمْ وَفِي ذَلِكُمْ بَلَاءٌ مِنْ رَبِّكُمْ عَظِيمٌ (٤٩)

وَإِذْ فَرَقْنَا بِكُمُ الْبَحْرَ فَأَنْجَيْنَاكُمْ وَأَغْرَقْنَا آلَ فِرْعَوْنَ وَأَنْتُمْ تَنْظُرُونَ (٥٠)

وَإِذْ وَاعَدْنَا مُوسَى أَرْبَعِينَ لَيْلَةً ثُمَّ اتَّخَذْتُمُ الْعِجْلَ مِنْ بَعْدِهِ وَأَنْتُمْ ظَالِمُونَ (٥١)

ثُمَّ عَفَوْنَا عَنْكُمْ مِنْ بَعْدِ ذَلِكَ لَعَلَّكُمْ تَشْكُرُونَ (٥٢)

وَإِذْ آتَيْنَا مُوسَى الْكِتَابَ وَالْفُرْقَانَ لَعَلَّكُمْ تَهْتَدُونَ (٥٣)

وَإِذْ قَالَ مُوسَى لِقَوْمِهِ يَا قَوْمِ إِنَّكُمْ ظَلَمْتُمْ أَنْفُسَكُمْ بِاتِّخَاذِكُمُ الْعِجْلَ فَتُوبُوا إِلَى بَارِئِكُمْ فَاقْتُلُوا أَنْفُسَكُمْ ذَلِكُمْ خَيْرٌ لَكُمْ عِنْدَ بَارِئِكُمْ فَتَابَ عَلَيْكُمْ إِنَّهُ هُوَ التَّوَّابُ الرَّحِيمُ (٥٤)

وَإِذْ قُلْتُمْ يَا مُوسَى لَنْ نُؤْمِنَ لَكَ حَتَّى نَرَى اللَّهَ جَهْرَةً فَأَخَذَتْكُمُ الصَّاعِقَةُ وَأَنْتُمْ تَنْظُرُونَ (٥٥)

ثُمَّ بَعَثْنَاكُمْ مِنْ بَعْدِ مَوْتِكُمْ لَعَلَّكُمْ تَشْكُرُونَ (٥٦)

وَظَلَّلْنَا عَلَيْكُمُ الْغَمَامَ وَأَنْزَلْنَا عَلَيْكُمُ الْمَنَّ وَالسَّلْوَى كُلُوا مِنْ طَيِّبَاتِ مَا رَزَقْنَاكُمْ وَمَا ظَلَمُونَا وَلَكِنْ كَانُوا أَنْفُسَهُمْ يَظْلِمُونَ (٥٧)

وَإِذْ قُلْنَا ادْخُلُوا هَذِهِ الْقَرْيَةَ فَكُلُوا مِنْهَا حَيْثُ شِئْتُمْ رَغَدًا وَادْخُلُوا الْبَابَ سُجَّدًا وَقُولُوا حِطَّةٌ نَغْفِرْ لَكُمْ خَطَايَاكُمْ وَسَنَزِيدُ الْمُحْسِنِينَ (٥٨)

فَبَدَّلَ الَّذِينَ ظَلَمُوا قَوْلًا غَيْرَ الَّذِي قِيلَ لَهُمْ فَأَنْزَلْنَا عَلَى الَّذِينَ ظَلَمُوا رِجْزًا مِنَ السَّمَاءِ بِمَا كَانُوا يَفْسُقُونَ

2. The Cow

wronged their own souls.

2:58. And when We said: Enter this city, then eat from it a plenteous (food) whence you wish, and enter the gate submissively, and make petition for forgiveness. We will forgive you your wrongs and increase the reward of those who do good (to others).

2:59. But those who were unjust changed the word which had been spoken to them, for another saying, so We sent upon the wrongdoers a pestilence from heaven, because they transgressed.

* * *

2:60. And when Moses prayed for water for his people, We said: March on to the rock with thy staff. So there flowed from it twelve springs. Each tribe knew their drinking-place. Eat and drink of the provisions of God, and act not corruptly, making mischief in the land.

2:61. And when you said: O Moses, we cannot endure one food, so pray thy Lord on our behalf to bring forth for us out of what the earth grows, of its herbs and its cucumbers and its garlic and its lentils and its onions. He said: Would you exchange that which is better for that which is worse? Enter a city, so you will have what you ask for. And abasement and humiliation were stamped upon them, and they incurred God's wrath. That was so because they disbelieved in the messages of God and would kill the prophets unjustly. That was so because they disobeyed and exceeded the limits.

* * *

2:62. Surely those who believe, and those who are Jews, and the Christians, and the Sabians, whoever believes in God and the Last Day and does good, they have their reward with their Lord, and there is no fear for them, nor shall they grieve.

(٥٩)

وَإِذِ اسْتَسْقَىٰ مُوسَىٰ لِقَوْمِهِ فَقُلْنَا اضْرِبْ بِعَصَاكَ الْحَجَرَ فَانْفَجَرَتْ مِنْهُ اثْنَتَا عَشْرَةَ عَيْنًا قَدْ عَلِمَ كُلُّ أُنَاسٍ مَشْرَبَهُمْ كُلُوا وَاشْرَبُوا مِنْ رِزْقِ اللَّهِ وَلَا تَعْثَوْا فِي الْأَرْضِ مُفْسِدِينَ (٦٠) وَإِذْ قُلْتُمْ يَا مُوسَىٰ لَنْ نَصْبِرَ عَلَىٰ طَعَامٍ وَاحِدٍ فَادْعُ لَنَا رَبَّكَ يُخْرِجْ لَنَا مِمَّا تُنْبِتُ الْأَرْضُ مِنْ بَقْلِهَا وَقِثَّائِهَا وَفُومِهَا وَعَدَسِهَا وَبَصَلِهَا قَالَ أَتَسْتَبْدِلُونَ الَّذِي هُوَ أَدْنَىٰ بِالَّذِي هُوَ خَيْرٌ اهْبِطُوا مِصْرًا فَإِنَّ لَكُمْ مَا سَأَلْتُمْ وَضُرِبَتْ عَلَيْهِمُ الذِّلَّةُ وَالْمَسْكَنَةُ وَبَاءُوا بِغَضَبٍ مِنَ اللَّهِ ذَٰلِكَ بِأَنَّهُمْ كَانُوا يَكْفُرُونَ بِآيَاتِ اللَّهِ وَيَقْتُلُونَ النَّبِيِّينَ بِغَيْرِ الْحَقِّ ذَٰلِكَ بِمَا عَصَوْا وَكَانُوا يَعْتَدُونَ (٦١) إِنَّ الَّذِينَ آمَنُوا وَالَّذِينَ هَادُوا وَالنَّصَارَىٰ وَالصَّابِئِينَ مَنْ آمَنَ بِاللَّهِ وَالْيَوْمِ الْآخِرِ وَعَمِلَ صَالِحًا فَلَهُمْ أَجْرُهُمْ عِنْدَ رَبِّهِمْ وَلَا خَوْفٌ عَلَيْهِمْ وَلَا هُمْ يَحْزَنُونَ (٦٢) وَإِذْ أَخَذْنَا مِيثَاقَكُمْ وَرَفَعْنَا فَوْقَكُمُ الطُّورَ خُذُوا مَا آتَيْنَاكُمْ بِقُوَّةٍ وَاذْكُرُوا

2:63. And when We made a covenant with you and raised the mountain above you: Hold fast that which We have given you, and bear in mind what is in it, so that you may guard against evil.

2:64. Then after that you turned back; and had it not been for the grace of God and His mercy on you, you had certainly been among the losers.

2:65. And indeed you know those among you who violated the Sabbath, so We said to them: Be (as) apes, despised and hated.

2:66. So We made them an example to those who witnessed it and those who came after it and an admonition to those who guard against evil.

2:67. And when Moses said to his people: Surely God commands you to sacrifice a cow. They said: Dost thou ridicule us? He said: I seek refuge with God from being one of the ignorant.

2:68. They said: Call on thy Lord for our sake to make it plain to us what she is. (Moses) said: He says, Surely she is a cow neither advanced in age nor too young, of middle age between these (two); so do what you are commanded.

2:69. They said: Call on thy Lord for our sake to make it clear to us what her colour is. (Moses) said: He says, She is a yellow cow; her colour is intensely yellow delighting the beholders.

2:70. They said: Call on thy Lord for our sake to make it dear to us what she is, for surely to us the cows are all alike, and if God please we shall surely he guided aright.

2:71. (Moses) said: He says: She is a cow not made submissive to plough the land, nor does she water the tilth, sound, without a blemish in her. They said: Now thou hast brought the truth. So they slaughtered her, though they had not the mind to do (it).

***

2:72. And when you (almost) killed a man, then you disagreed about it. And God was to bring forth that which you were going to hide.

2:73. So We said: Smite him with it partially. Thus God brings the dead to life, and He shows you His signs that you may understand.

2:74. Then your hearts hardened after that, so that they were like rocks, rather worse in hardness. And surely there are some rocks from which streams burst forth; and there are some of them which split asunder so water flows from them; and there are some of them which fall down for the fear of God. And God is not heedless of what you do.

2:75. Do you then hope that they would believe in you, and a party from among them indeed used to hear the word of God, then altered it after they had understood it, and they know (this).

2:76. And when they meet those who believe they say, We believe, and when they are apart one with another they say: Do you talk to them of what God has disclosed to you that they may contend with you by this before your Lord? Do you not understand?

2:77. Do they not know that God knows what they keep secret and what they make known?

2:78. And some of them are illiterate; they know not the Book but only (from) hearsay, and they do but conjecture.

2:79. Woe! then to those who write the Book with their hands then say, This is from God; so that they may take for it a small price. So woe! to them for what their hands write and woe! to them for what they earn.

2:80. And they say: Fire will not touch us but for a few days. Say Have you received a promise from God? Then God will not fail to perform His

الْحِجَارَةِ لَمَا يَتَفَجَّرُ مِنْهُ الْأَنْهَارُ وَإِنَّ مِنْهَا لَمَا يَشَّقَّقُ فَيَخْرُجُ مِنْهُ الْمَاءُ وَإِنَّ مِنْهَا لَمَا يَهْبِطُ مِنْ خَشْيَةِ اللّهِ وَمَا اللّهُ بِغَافِلٍ عَمَّا تَعْمَلُونَ (٧٤)

أَفَتَطْمَعُونَ أَنْ يُؤْمِنُوا لَكُمْ وَقَدْ كَانَ فَرِيقٌ مِنْهُمْ يَسْمَعُونَ كَلَامَ اللّهِ ثُمَّ يُحَرِّفُونَهُ مِنْ بَعْدِ مَا عَقَلُوهُ وَهُمْ يَعْلَمُونَ (٧٥)

وَإِذَا لَقُوا الَّذِينَ آمَنُوا قَالُوا آمَنَّا وَإِذَا خَلَا بَعْضُهُمْ إِلَى بَعْضٍ قَالُوا أَتُحَدِّثُونَهُمْ بِمَا فَتَحَ اللّهُ عَلَيْكُمْ لِيُحَاجُّوكُمْ بِهِ عِنْدَ رَبِّكُمْ أَفَلَا تَعْقِلُونَ (٧٦)

أَوَلَا يَعْلَمُونَ أَنَّ اللّهَ يَعْلَمُ مَا يُسِرُّونَ وَمَا يُعْلِنُونَ (٧٧)

وَمِنْهُمْ أُمِّيُّونَ لَا يَعْلَمُونَ الْكِتَابَ إِلَّا أَمَانِيَّ وَإِنْ هُمْ إِلَّا يَظُنُّونَ (٧٨)

فَوَيْلٌ لِلَّذِينَ يَكْتُبُونَ الْكِتَابَ بِأَيْدِيهِمْ ثُمَّ يَقُولُونَ هَذَا مِنْ عِنْدِ اللّهِ لِيَشْتَرُوا بِهِ ثَمَنًا قَلِيلًا فَوَيْلٌ لَهُمْ مِمَّا كَتَبَتْ أَيْدِيهِمْ وَوَيْلٌ لَهُمْ مِمَّا يَكْسِبُونَ (٧٩)

وَقَالُوا لَنْ تَمَسَّنَا النَّارُ إِلَّا أَيَّامًا مَعْدُودَةً قُلْ أَتَّخَذْتُمْ عِنْدَ اللّهِ عَهْدًا فَلَنْ يُخْلِفَ اللّهُ عَهْدَهُ أَمْ تَقُولُونَ عَلَى اللّهِ مَا لَا تَعْلَمُونَ (٨٠)

بَلَى مَنْ كَسَبَ سَيِّئَةً وَأَحَاطَتْ بِهِ خَطِيئَتُهُ فَأُولَئِكَ أَصْحَابُ النَّارِ هُمْ فِيهَا خَالِدُونَ (٨١)

وَالَّذِينَ آمَنُوا وَعَمِلُوا الصَّالِحَاتِ أُولَئِكَ أَصْحَابُ الْجَنَّةِ هُمْ فِيهَا خَالِدُونَ (٨٢)

وَإِذْ أَخَذْنَا مِيثَاقَ بَنِي إِسْرَائِيلَ لَا تَعْبُدُونَ إِلَّا اللّهَ وَبِالْوَالِدَيْنِ إِحْسَانًا وَذِي الْقُرْبَى وَالْيَتَامَى وَالْمَسَاكِينِ

promise. Or do you speak against God. what you know not?

2:81. Yea, whoever earns evil and his sins beset him on every side, those are the companions of the Fire therein they abide."

2:82. And those who believe and do good deeds, these are the owners of the Garden; therein they abide.

* * *

2:83. And when We made a covenant with the Children of Israel. You shall serve none but God. And do good to (your) parents, and to the near of kin and to orphans and the needy, and speak good (words) to (all) men, and keep up prayer and pay the poor-rate. Then you turned back except a few of you, and you are averse.

2:84. And when We made a covenant with you: You shall not shed your blood, nor turn your people out of your cities; then you promised and you bear witness.

2:85. Yet you it is who would slay your people and turn a party from among you out of their homes, backing each other up against them unlawfully and exceeding the limits. And if they should come to you as captives you would ransom them, whereas their turning out itself was unlawful for you. Do you then believe in a part of the Book and disbelieve in the other? What then is the reward of such among you as do this but disgrace in the life of this world, and on the day of Resurrection they shall be sent back to the most grievous chastisement. And God is not heedless of what you do.

2:86. These are they who buy the life of this world for the Hereafter, so their chastisement shall not be lightened, nor shall they be helped.

* * *

2:87. And We indeed gave Moses the Book and We sent messengers after him one after another and We gave

2. The Cow

Jesus, son of Mary, clear arguments and strengthened him with the Holy Spirit. Is it then that whenever there came to you a messenger with what your souls desired not, you were arrogant? And some you gave the lie to and others you would slay.

2:88. And they say: Our hearts are repositories. Nay, God has cursed them on account of their unbelief so little it is that they believe.

2:89. And when there came to them a Book from God verifying that which they have, and aforetime they used to pray for victory against those who disbelieved -- but when there came to them that which they recognized, they disbelieved in it; so God's curse is on the disbelievers.

2:90. Evil is that for which they sell their souls -- that they should deny that which God has revealed, out of envy that God should send down of His grace on whomsoever of His servants He pleases; so they incur wrath upon wrath. And there is an abasing chastisement for the disbelievers.

2:91. And when it is said to them, Believe in that which God has revealed, they say: We believe in that which was revealed to us. And they deny what is besides that, while it is the Truth verifying that which they have. Say: Why then did you kill God's prophets before (this) if you were believers?

2:92. And Moses indeed came to you with clear arguments, then you took the calf (for a god) in his absence and you were wrongdoers.

2:93. And when We made a covenant with you and raised the mountain above you: Take hold of that which We have given you with firmness and obey. They said: We hear and disobey. And they were made to imbibe (the love of) the calf into their hearts on account of their disbelief. Say: Evil is that which your faith bids you if you are believers.

2:94. Say: If the abode of the Here-after with God is specially for you to the exclusion of the people, then invoke death if you are truthful.

2:95. And they will never invoke it on account of what their hands have sent on before, and God knows the wrongdoers.

2:96. And thou wilt certainly find them the greediest of men for life (greedier) even than those who set gods (with God). One of them love to be granted a life of a thousand years, and his being granted a long life will in no way remove him further off from the chastisement. And God is Seer of what they do.

***

2:97. Say: Whoever is an enemy to Gabriel for surely he revealed it to thy heart by God's command, verifying the which is before it and a guidance and glad tidings for the believers.

2:98. Whoever is an enemy to God and His angels and His messengers and Gabriel and Michael, then surely God is an enemy to disbelievers.

2:99. And We indeed have revealed to thee clear messages, and none disbelieve in them except the transgressors.

2:100. Is it that whenever they make a covenant, a party of them cast it aside? Nay, most of them have no faith.

2:101. And when there came to them a messenger from God verifying that which they have, a party of those who were given the Book threw the Book of God behind their backs as if they knew nothing.

2:102. And they follow what the devils fabricated against the kingdom of Solomon. And Solomon disbelieved not, but the devils disbelieved, teaching men enchantment. And it was

يَكْفُرُ بِهَا إِلَّا الْفَاسِقُونَ (٩٩) أَوَكُلَّمَا عَاهَدُوا عَهْدًا نَبَذَهُ فَرِيقٌ مِنْهُمْ بَلْ أَكْثَرُهُمْ لَا يُؤْمِنُونَ (١٠٠) وَلَمَّا جَاءَهُمْ رَسُولٌ مِنْ عِنْدِ اللَّهِ مُصَدِّقٌ لِمَا مَعَهُمْ نَبَذَ فَرِيقٌ مِنَ الَّذِينَ أُوتُوا الْكِتَابَ كِتَابَ اللَّهِ وَرَاءَ ظُهُورِهِمْ كَأَنَّهُمْ لَا يَعْلَمُونَ (١٠١) وَاتَّبَعُوا مَا تَتْلُو الشَّيَاطِينُ عَلَى مُلْكِ سُلَيْمَانَ وَمَا كَفَرَ سُلَيْمَانُ وَلَكِنَّ الشَّيَاطِينَ كَفَرُوا يُعَلِّمُونَ النَّاسَ السِّحْرَ وَمَا أُنْزِلَ عَلَى الْمَلَكَيْنِ بِبَابِلَ هَارُوتَ وَمَارُوتَ وَمَا يُعَلِّمَانِ مِنْ أَحَدٍ حَتَّى يَقُولَا إِنَّمَا نَحْنُ فِتْنَةٌ فَلَا تَكْفُرْ فَيَتَعَلَّمُونَ مِنْهُمَا مَا يُفَرِّقُونَ بِهِ بَيْنَ الْمَرْءِ وَزَوْجِهِ وَمَا هُمْ بِضَارِّينَ بِهِ مِنْ أَحَدٍ إِلَّا بِإِذْنِ اللَّهِ وَيَتَعَلَّمُونَ مَا يَضُرُّهُمْ وَلَا يَنْفَعُهُمْ وَلَقَدْ عَلِمُوا لَمَنِ اشْتَرَاهُ مَا لَهُ فِي الْآخِرَةِ مِنْ خَلَاقٍ وَلَبِئْسَ مَا شَرَوْا بِهِ أَنْفُسَهُمْ لَوْ كَانُوا يَعْلَمُونَ (١٠٢) وَلَوْ أَنَّهُمْ آمَنُوا وَاتَّقَوْا لَمَثُوبَةٌ مِنْ عِنْدِ اللَّهِ خَيْرٌ لَوْ كَانُوا يَعْلَمُونَ (١٠٣)

not revealed to the two angels in Babel, Harut and Marut. Nor did they teach (it to) anyone, so that they should have said, We are only a trial, so disbelieve not. But they learn from these two (sources) that by which they make a distinction between a man and his wife. And they cannot hurt with it anyone except with God's permission. And they learn that which harms them and profits them nor. And certainly they know that he who buys it has no share of good in the Hereafter. And surely evil is the price for which they have sold their souls, did they but know!

2:103. And if they had believed and kept their duty, reward from God would certainly have been better; did they but know!

***

2:104. O you who believe, say not Ra'i-na and say Unzur-na, and listen. And for the disbelievers there is a painful chastisement.

2:105. Neither those who disbelieve from among the people of the Book nor the polytheists, like that any good should be sent down to you from your Lord. And God chooses whom He pleases for His Mercy; and God is the Lord of mighty grace.

2:106. Whatever message We abrogate or cause to be forgotten, We bring one better than it or one like it. Knowest thou not that God is Possessor of power over all things?

2:107. Knowest thou not that God's is the kingdom of the heavens and the earth, and that besides God you have not any friend or helper?

2:108. Rather you wish to put questions to your Messenger, as Moses was questioned before. And whoever adopts disbelief instead of faith he indeed has lost the right direction of the way.

يَا أَيُّهَا الَّذِينَ آمَنُوا لَا تَقُولُوا رَاعِنَا وَقُولُوا انْظُرْنَا وَاسْمَعُوا وَلِلْكَافِرِينَ عَذَابٌ أَلِيمٌ (١٠٤)

مَا يَوَدُّ الَّذِينَ كَفَرُوا مِنْ أَهْلِ الْكِتَابِ وَلَا الْمُشْرِكِينَ أَنْ يُنَزَّلَ عَلَيْكُمْ مِنْ خَيْرٍ مِنْ رَبِّكُمْ وَاللَّهُ يَخْتَصُّ بِرَحْمَتِهِ مَنْ يَشَاءُ وَاللَّهُ ذُو الْفَضْلِ الْعَظِيمِ (١٠٥)

مَا نَنْسَخْ مِنْ آيَةٍ أَوْ نُنْسِهَا نَأْتِ بِخَيْرٍ مِنْهَا أَوْ مِثْلِهَا أَلَمْ تَعْلَمْ أَنَّ اللَّهَ عَلَى كُلِّ شَيْءٍ قَدِيرٌ (١٠٦)

أَلَمْ تَعْلَمْ أَنَّ اللَّهَ لَهُ مُلْكُ السَّمَاوَاتِ وَالْأَرْضِ وَمَا لَكُمْ مِنْ دُونِ اللَّهِ مِنْ وَلِيٍّ وَلَا نَصِيرٍ (١٠٧)

أَمْ تُرِيدُونَ أَنْ تَسْأَلُوا رَسُولَكُمْ كَمَا سُئِلَ مُوسَى مِنْ قَبْلُ وَمَنْ يَتَبَدَّلِ الْكُفْرَ بِالْإِيمَانِ فَقَدْ ضَلَّ سَوَاءَ السَّبِيلِ (١٠٨)

وَدَّ كَثِيرٌ مِنْ أَهْلِ الْكِتَابِ لَوْ يَرُدُّونَكُمْ

2. The Cow

2:109. Many of the people of the Book wish that they could turn you back into disbelievers after you have believed, out of envy from themselves, after truth has become manifest to them. But pardon and forgive till God bring about His command. Surely God is Possessor of power over all things.

2:110. And keep up prayer and pay the poor-rate. And whatever good you send before for yourselves, you will find it with God. Surely God is Seer of what you do.

2:111. And they say: None shall enter the Garden except he who is a Jew, or the Christians. These are their vain desires. Say: Bring your proof if you are truthful.

2:112. Nay, whoever submits himself entirely to God and he is the doer of good (to others); he has his reward from his Lord, and there is no fear for such nor shall they grieve.

* * *

2:113. And the Jews say, The Christians follow nothing (good), and the Christians say, The Jews follow nothing (good), while they recite the (same) Book. Even thus say those who have no knowledge, like what they say. So God will judge between them on the day of Resurrection in that wherein they differ.

2:114. And who is more unjust than he who prevents (men) from the mosques of God, from His name being remembered therein, and strives to ruin them? (As for) these, it was not proper for them to enter them except in fear. For them is disgrace in this world, and theirs is a grievous chastisement in the Hereafter.

2:115. And God's is the East and the West, so whither you turn thither is God's purpose. Surely God is Ample-giving, Knowing.

2:116. And they say: God has taken to Himself a son -- glory be to Him!

مِنْ بَعْدِ إِيمَانِكُمْ كُفَّارًا حَسَدًا مِنْ عِنْدِ أَنْفُسِهِمْ مِنْ بَعْدِ مَا تَبَيَّنَ لَهُمُ الْحَقُّ فَاعْفُوا وَاصْفَحُوا حَتَّى يَأْتِيَ اللَّهُ بِأَمْرِهِ إِنَّ اللَّهَ عَلَى كُلِّ شَيْءٍ قَدِيرٌ (١٠٩)

وَأَقِيمُوا الصَّلَاةَ وَآتُوا الزَّكَاةَ وَمَا تُقَدِّمُوا لِأَنْفُسِكُمْ مِنْ خَيْرٍ تَجِدُوهُ عِنْدَ اللَّهِ إِنَّ اللَّهَ بِمَا تَعْمَلُونَ بَصِيرٌ (١١٠)

وَقَالُوا لَنْ يَدْخُلَ الْجَنَّةَ إِلَّا مَنْ كَانَ هُودًا أَوْ نَصَارَى تِلْكَ أَمَانِيُّهُمْ قُلْ هَاتُوا بُرْهَانَكُمْ إِنْ كُنْتُمْ صَادِقِينَ (١١١)

بَلَى مَنْ أَسْلَمَ وَجْهَهُ لِلَّهِ وَهُوَ مُحْسِنٌ فَلَهُ أَجْرُهُ عِنْدَ رَبِّهِ وَلَا خَوْفٌ عَلَيْهِمْ وَلَا هُمْ يَحْزَنُونَ (١١٢)

وَقَالَتِ الْيَهُودُ لَيْسَتِ النَّصَارَى عَلَى شَيْءٍ وَقَالَتِ النَّصَارَى لَيْسَتِ الْيَهُودُ عَلَى شَيْءٍ وَهُمْ يَتْلُونَ الْكِتَابَ كَذَلِكَ قَالَ الَّذِينَ لَا يَعْلَمُونَ مِثْلَ قَوْلِهِمْ فَاللَّهُ يَحْكُمُ بَيْنَهُمْ يَوْمَ الْقِيَامَةِ فِيمَا كَانُوا فِيهِ يَخْتَلِفُونَ (١١٣)

وَمَنْ أَظْلَمُ مِمَّنْ مَنَعَ مَسَاجِدَ اللَّهِ أَنْ يُذْكَرَ فِيهَا اسْمُهُ وَسَعَى فِي خَرَابِهَا أُولَئِكَ مَا كَانَ لَهُمْ أَنْ يَدْخُلُوهَا إِلَّا خَائِفِينَ لَهُمْ فِي الدُّنْيَا خِزْيٌ وَلَهُمْ فِي الْآخِرَةِ عَذَابٌ عَظِيمٌ (١١٤)

وَلِلَّهِ الْمَشْرِقُ وَالْمَغْرِبُ فَأَيْنَمَا تُوَلُّوا فَثَمَّ وَجْهُ اللَّهِ إِنَّ اللَّهَ وَاسِعٌ عَلِيمٌ (١١٥)

وَقَالُوا اتَّخَذَ اللَّهُ وَلَدًا سُبْحَانَهُ بَلْ لَهُ مَا فِي السَّمَاوَاتِ وَالْأَرْضِ كُلٌّ لَهُ قَانِتُونَ (١١٦)

بَدِيعُ السَّمَاوَاتِ وَالْأَرْضِ وَإِذَا قَضَى أَمْرًا فَإِنَّمَا يَقُولُ لَهُ كُنْ فَيَكُونُ

2. The Cow

Rather, whatever is in the heavens and the earth is His. All are obedient to Him.

2:117. Wonderful Originator of the heavens and the earth! And when He decrees an affair, He says to it only, Be, and it is.

2:118. And those who have no knowledge say: Why does not God speak to us or a sign come to us? Even thus said those before them, the like of what they say. Their hearts are all alike. Indeed We have made the messages clear for a people who are sure.

2:119. Surely We have sent thee with the Truth as a bearer of good news and as a warner, and thou wilt not be called upon to answer for the companions of the flaming Fire.

2:120. And the Jews will not be pleased with thee, nor the Christians, unless thou follow their religion. Say Surely God's guidance, that is the (perfect) guidance. And if thou follow their desires after the knowledge that has come to thee thou shalt have from God no friend, nor helper.

2:121. Those to whom We have given the Book follow it as it ought to be followed. These believe in it. And whoever disbelieves in it, these it is that are the losers.

***

2:122. O Children of Israel, call to mind My favour which I bestowed on you and that I made you excel the nations.

2:123. And be on your guard against a day when no soul will avail another in the least, neither will any compensation be accepted from it, nor will intercession profit it, nor will they be helped.

2:124. And when his Lord tried Abraham with certain commands he fulfilled them. He said: Surely I will make thee a leader of men. (Abraham)

2. The Cow

said: And of my offspring? My covenant does not include the wrongdoers, said He.

2:125. And when We made The House a resort for men and a (place of) security. And: Take ye the place of Abraham for a place of prayer. And We enjoined Abraham and Ishmael, saying: Purify My House for those who visit (it) and those who abide (in it) for devotion and those who bow down (and) those who prostrate themselves.

2:126. And when Abraham said: My Lord, make this a secure town and provide its people with fruits, such of them as believe in God and the Last Day. He said: And whoever disbelieves, I shall grant him enjoyment for a short while, then I shall drive him to the chastisement of the Fire. And it is an evil destination.

2:127. And when Abraham and Ishmael raised the foundations of the House: Our Lord, accept from us surely Thou art the Hearing, the Knowing.

2:128. Our Lord, and make us both submissive to Thee, and (raise) from out offspring, a nation submissive to Thee, and show us our ways of devotion and turn to us (mercifully); surely Thou art the Oft-returning (to mercy), the Merciful.

2:129. Our Lord, and raise up in them a Messenger from among them who shall recite to them Thy messages and teach them the Book and the Wisdom, and purify them Surely Thou art the Mighty, the Wise.

2:130. And who forsakes the religion of Abraham but he who makes a fool of himself. And certainly We made him pure in this world and in the Hereafter he is surely among the righteous.

2:131. When his Lord said to him, Submit, he said: I submit myself to the Lord of the worlds.

وَإِذْ جَعَلْنَا الْبَيْتَ مَثَابَةً لِّلنَّاسِ وَأَمْنًا وَاتَّخِذُوا مِن مَّقَامِ إِبْرَاهِيمَ مُصَلًّى وَعَهِدْنَا إِلَى إِبْرَاهِيمَ وَإِسْمَاعِيلَ أَن طَهِّرَا بَيْتِيَ لِلطَّائِفِينَ وَالْعَاكِفِينَ وَالرُّكَّعِ السُّجُودِ (١٢٥)

وَإِذْ قَالَ إِبْرَاهِيمُ رَبِّ اجْعَلْ هَذَا بَلَدًا آمِنًا وَارْزُقْ أَهْلَهُ مِنَ الثَّمَرَاتِ مَنْ آمَنَ مِنْهُم بِاللَّهِ وَالْيَوْمِ الْآخِرِ قَالَ وَمَن كَفَرَ فَأُمَتِّعُهُ قَلِيلًا ثُمَّ أَضْطَرُّهُ إِلَى عَذَابِ النَّارِ وَبِئْسَ الْمَصِيرُ (١٢٦)

وَإِذْ يَرْفَعُ إِبْرَاهِيمُ الْقَوَاعِدَ مِنَ الْبَيْتِ وَإِسْمَاعِيلُ رَبَّنَا تَقَبَّلْ مِنَّا إِنَّكَ أَنتَ السَّمِيعُ الْعَلِيمُ (١٢٧)

رَبَّنَا وَاجْعَلْنَا مُسْلِمَيْنِ لَكَ وَمِن ذُرِّيَّتِنَا أُمَّةً مُّسْلِمَةً لَّكَ وَأَرِنَا مَنَاسِكَنَا وَتُبْ عَلَيْنَا إِنَّكَ أَنتَ التَّوَّابُ الرَّحِيمُ (١٢٨)

رَبَّنَا وَابْعَثْ فِيهِمْ رَسُولًا مِّنْهُمْ يَتْلُو عَلَيْهِمْ آيَاتِكَ وَيُعَلِّمُهُمُ الْكِتَابَ وَالْحِكْمَةَ وَيُزَكِّيهِمْ إِنَّكَ أَنتَ الْعَزِيزُ الْحَكِيمُ (١٢٩)

وَمَن يَرْغَبُ عَن مِّلَّةِ إِبْرَاهِيمَ إِلَّا مَن سَفِهَ نَفْسَهُ وَلَقَدِ اصْطَفَيْنَاهُ فِي الدُّنْيَا وَإِنَّهُ فِي الْآخِرَةِ لَمِنَ الصَّالِحِينَ (١٣٠)

إِذْ قَالَ لَهُ رَبُّهُ أَسْلِمْ قَالَ أَسْلَمْتُ لِرَبِّ الْعَالَمِينَ (١٣١)

وَوَصَّى بِهَا إِبْرَاهِيمُ بَنِيهِ وَيَعْقُوبُ يَا بَنِيَّ إِنَّ اللَّهَ اصْطَفَى لَكُمُ الدِّينَ فَلَا تَمُوتُنَّ إِلَّا وَأَنتُم مُّسْلِمُونَ (١٣٢)

أَمْ كُنتُمْ شُهَدَاءَ إِذْ حَضَرَ يَعْقُوبَ الْمَوْتُ إِذْ قَالَ لِبَنِيهِ مَا تَعْبُدُونَ مِن بَعْدِي قَالُوا نَعْبُدُ إِلَهَكَ وَإِلَهَ آبَائِكَ

2. The Cow

2:132. And the same did Abraham enjoin on his sons, and (so did) Jacob: O my sons, surely God has chosen for you (this) religion, so die not unless you are submitting ones.

2:133. Or were you witnesses when death visited Jacob, when he said to his sons: What will you serve after me? They said: We shall serve thy God and the God of thy fathers, Abraham and Ishmael and Isaac, one God only, and to Him do we submit.

2:134. Those are a people that have passed away; for them is what they earned and for you what you earn and you will not be asked of what they did.

2:135. And they say: Be Jews or Christians, you will be on the right course. Say: Nay, (we follow) the religion of Abraham, the upright one, and he was not one of the polytheists.

2:136. Say: We believe in God and (in) that which has been revealed to us, and (in) that which was revealed to Abraham, and Ishmael and Isaac and Jacob and the tribes, and (in) that which was given to Moses and Jesus, and (in) that which was given to the prophets from their Lord, we do not make any distinction between any of them and to Him do we submit.

2:137. So if they believe as you believe, they are indeed on the right course; and if they turn back, then they are only in opposition. But God will suffice thee against them and He is the Hearing, the Knowing.

2:138. (We take) God's colour, and who is better than God at colouring, and we are His worshippers.

2:139. Say: Do you dispute with us about God, and He is our Lord and your Lord, and for us are our deeds and for you your deeds; and we are sincere to Him?

2:140. Or do you say that Abraham and Ishmael and Isaac and Jacob and the tribes were Jews or Christians? Say: Do you know better or God? And who is more unjust than he who conceals a testimony that he has from God? And God is not heedless of what you do.

2:141. Those are a people that have passed away; and for them is what they earned and for You what you earn and you will not be asked of what they did.

***

2:142. The fools among the people will say: "What has turned them from their qiblah which they had? " Say: The East and the West belong only to God; He guides whom He pleases to the right path.

2:143. And thus We have made you an exalted nation that you may be the bearers of witness to the people and (that) the Messenger may be a bearer of witness to you. And We did not make that which thou wouldst have to be the qiblah but that We might distinguish him who follows the Messenger from him who turns back upon his heels. And it was indeed a hard test except for those whom God has guided. Nor was God going to make your faith to be fruitless. Surely God is Compassionate, Merciful, to the people.

2:144. Indeed We see the turning of thy face to heaven, so We shall surely make thee master of the qiblah which thou likest; turn then thy face towards the Sacred Mosque. And wherever you are turn your faces towards it. And those who have been given the Book certainly know that it is the truth from their Lord. And God is not heedless of what they do.

2:145. And even if thou shouldst bring to those who have been given the Book every sign they would not follow thy qiblah, nor canst thou be a follower of their qiblah, neither are they the followers of each other's qiblah. And if

سَيَقُولُ السُّفَهَاءُ مِنَ النَّاسِ مَا وَلَّاهُمْ عَنْ قِبْلَتِهِمُ الَّتِي كَانُوا عَلَيْهَا قُلْ لِلَّهِ الْمَشْرِقُ وَالْمَغْرِبُ يَهْدِي مَنْ يَشَاءُ إِلَى صِرَاطٍ مُسْتَقِيمٍ (١٤٢) وَكَذَلِكَ جَعَلْنَاكُمْ أُمَّةً وَسَطًا لِتَكُونُوا شُهَدَاءَ عَلَى النَّاسِ وَيَكُونَ الرَّسُولُ عَلَيْكُمْ شَهِيدًا وَمَا جَعَلْنَا الْقِبْلَةَ الَّتِي كُنْتَ عَلَيْهَا إِلَّا لِنَعْلَمَ مَنْ يَتَّبِعُ الرَّسُولَ مِمَّنْ يَنْقَلِبُ عَلَى عَقِبَيْهِ وَإِنْ كَانَتْ لَكَبِيرَةً إِلَّا عَلَى الَّذِينَ هَدَى اللَّهُ وَمَا كَانَ اللَّهُ لِيُضِيعَ إِيمَانَكُمْ إِنَّ اللَّهَ بِالنَّاسِ لَرَءُوفٌ رَحِيمٌ (١٤٣) قَدْ نَرَى تَقَلُّبَ وَجْهِكَ فِي السَّمَاءِ فَلَنُوَلِّيَنَّكَ قِبْلَةً تَرْضَاهَا فَوَلِّ وَجْهَكَ شَطْرَ الْمَسْجِدِ الْحَرَامِ وَحَيْثُ مَا كُنْتُمْ فَوَلُّوا وُجُوهَكُمْ شَطْرَهُ وَإِنَّ الَّذِينَ أُوتُوا الْكِتَابَ لَيَعْلَمُونَ أَنَّهُ الْحَقُّ مِنْ رَبِّهِمْ وَمَا اللَّهُ بِغَافِلٍ عَمَّا يَعْمَلُونَ (١٤٤) وَلَئِنْ أَتَيْتَ الَّذِينَ أُوتُوا الْكِتَابَ بِكُلِّ آيَةٍ مَا تَبِعُوا قِبْلَتَكَ وَمَا أَنْتَ بِتَابِعٍ قِبْلَتَهُمْ وَمَا بَعْضُهُمْ بِتَابِعٍ قِبْلَةَ بَعْضٍ وَلَئِنِ اتَّبَعْتَ أَهْوَاءَهُمْ مِنْ بَعْدِ مَا جَاءَكَ مِنَ الْعِلْمِ إِنَّكَ إِذًا لَمِنَ الظَّالِمِينَ (١٤٥) الَّذِينَ آتَيْنَاهُمُ الْكِتَابَ يَعْرِفُونَهُ كَمَا يَعْرِفُونَ أَبْنَاءَهُمْ وَإِنَّ فَرِيقًا مِنْهُمْ

thou shouldst follow their desires after the knowledge that has come to thee, then thou wouldst indeed be of the wrongdoers.

2:146. Those whom We have the given the Book recognize him as they recognize their sons. And a party of them surely conceal the truth they while know.

2:147. The truth is from thy Lord, so be thou not of the doubters.

* * *

2:148. And every one has a goal to which he turns (himself), so vie with one another in good works. Wherever you are, God will bring you all together. Surely God is Possessor of power over all things.

2:149. And from whatsoever place thou comest forth, turn thy face towards the Sacred Mosque. And surely it is the truth from thy Lord. And God is not heedless of what you do.

2:150. And from whatsoever place thou comest forth turn thy face towards the Sacred Mosque. And wherever you are turn your faces towards it, so that people may have no plea against you except such of them as are unjust -- so fear them not and fear Me -- and that I may complete My favour to you and that you may go aright.'

2:151. Even as We have sent among you a Messenger from among you, who recites to you Our messages and purifies you and teaches you the Book and the Wisdom and teaches you that which you did not know.

2:152. Therefore glorify Me, I will make you eminent, and give thanks to Me and be not ungrateful to Me.

* * *

2:153. O you who believe, seek assistance through patience and prayer; surely God is with the patient.

2:154. And speak not of those who are slain in God's way as dead. Nay, (they are) alive, but you perceive not.

لَيَكْتُمُونَ الْحَقَّ وَهُمْ يَعْلَمُونَ (١٤٦) الْحَقُّ مِنْ رَبِّكَ فَلَا تَكُونَنَّ مِنَ الْمُمْتَرِينَ (١٤٧) وَلِكُلٍّ وِجْهَةٌ هُوَ مُوَلِّيهَا فَاسْتَبِقُوا الْخَيْرَاتِ أَيْنَ مَا تَكُونُوا يَأْتِ بِكُمُ اللَّهُ جَمِيعًا إِنَّ اللَّهَ عَلَى كُلِّ شَيْءٍ قَدِيرٌ (١٤٨) وَمِنْ حَيْثُ خَرَجْتَ فَوَلِّ وَجْهَكَ شَطْرَ الْمَسْجِدِ الْحَرَامِ وَإِنَّهُ لَلْحَقُّ مِنْ رَبِّكَ وَمَا اللَّهُ بِغَافِلٍ عَمَّا تَعْمَلُونَ (١٤٩) وَمِنْ حَيْثُ خَرَجْتَ فَوَلِّ وَجْهَكَ شَطْرَ الْمَسْجِدِ الْحَرَامِ وَحَيْثُ مَا كُنْتُمْ فَوَلُّوا وُجُوهَكُمْ شَطْرَهُ لِئَلَّا يَكُونَ لِلنَّاسِ عَلَيْكُمْ حُجَّةٌ إِلَّا الَّذِينَ ظَلَمُوا مِنْهُمْ فَلَا تَخْشَوْهُمْ وَاخْشَوْنِي وَلِأُتِمَّ نِعْمَتِي عَلَيْكُمْ وَلَعَلَّكُمْ تَهْتَدُونَ (١٥٠) كَمَا أَرْسَلْنَا فِيكُمْ رَسُولًا مِنْكُمْ يَتْلُو عَلَيْكُمْ آيَاتِنَا وَيُزَكِّيكُمْ وَيُعَلِّمُكُمُ الْكِتَابَ وَالْحِكْمَةَ وَيُعَلِّمُكُمْ مَا لَمْ تَكُونُوا تَعْلَمُونَ (١٥١) فَاذْكُرُونِي أَذْكُرْكُمْ وَاشْكُرُوا لِي وَلَا تَكْفُرُونِ (١٥٢) يَا أَيُّهَا الَّذِينَ آمَنُوا اسْتَعِينُوا بِالصَّبْرِ وَالصَّلَاةِ إِنَّ اللَّهَ مَعَ الصَّابِرِينَ (١٥٣) وَلَا تَقُولُوا لِمَنْ يُقْتَلُ فِي سَبِيلِ اللَّهِ أَمْوَاتٌ بَلْ أَحْيَاءٌ وَلَكِنْ لَا تَشْعُرُونَ (١٥٤) وَلَنَبْلُوَنَّكُمْ بِشَيْءٍ مِنَ الْخَوْفِ وَالْجُوعِ وَنَقْصٍ مِنَ الْأَمْوَالِ وَالْأَنْفُسِ وَالثَّمَرَاتِ وَبَشِّرِ الصَّابِرِينَ (١٥٥) الَّذِينَ إِذَا أَصَابَتْهُمْ مُصِيبَةٌ قَالُوا إِنَّا لِلَّهِ وَإِنَّا إِلَيْهِ رَاجِعُونَ (١٥٦)

2. The Cow

2:155. And We shall certainly try you with something of fear and hunger and loss of property and lives and fruits. And give good news to the patient,

2:156. Who, when a misfortune befalls them say " Surely we are God's, and to Him we shall return."

2:157. Those are they on whom are blessings and mercy from their Lord and those are the followers of the right course.

2:158. The Safa and the Marwah are truly among the signs of God; so whoever makes a pilgrimage to the House or pays a visit (to it), there is no blame on him if he goes round them. And whoever does good spontaneously surely God is Bountiful in rewarding, Knowing.

2:159. Those who conceal the clear proofs and the guidance that We revealed after We have made it clear in the Book for men, these it is whom God curses, and those who curse, curse them (too),

2:160. Except those who repent and amend and make manifest (the truth), these it is to whom I turn (mercifully); and I am the Oft-returning (to mercy), the Merciful.

2:161. Those who disbelieve and die while they are disbelievers, these it is on whom is the curse of God and the angels and men, of all (of them):

2:162. Abiding therein; their chastisement shall not be lightened nor shall they be given respite.

2:163. And your God is one God, there is no God but He! He is the Beneficent, the Merciful.

***

2:164. In the creation of the heavens and the earth, and the alternation of night and day, and the ships that run in the sea with that which profits men, and the water that God sends down from the sky, then gives life therewith to the earth after its death and spreads

أُولَٰئِكَ عَلَيْهِمْ صَلَوَاتٌ مِنْ رَبِّهِمْ وَرَحْمَةٌ وَأُولَٰئِكَ هُمُ الْمُهْتَدُونَ (١٥٧)

إِنَّ الصَّفَا وَالْمَرْوَةَ مِنْ شَعَائِرِ اللَّهِ فَمَنْ حَجَّ الْبَيْتَ أَوِ اعْتَمَرَ فَلَا جُنَاحَ عَلَيْهِ أَنْ يَطَّوَّفَ بِهِمَا وَمَنْ تَطَوَّعَ خَيْرًا فَإِنَّ اللَّهَ شَاكِرٌ عَلِيمٌ (١٥٨)

إِنَّ الَّذِينَ يَكْتُمُونَ مَا أَنْزَلْنَا مِنَ الْبَيِّنَاتِ وَالْهُدَى مِنْ بَعْدِ مَا بَيَّنَّاهُ لِلنَّاسِ فِي الْكِتَابِ أُولَٰئِكَ يَلْعَنُهُمُ اللَّهُ وَيَلْعَنُهُمُ اللَّاعِنُونَ (١٥٩)

إِلَّا الَّذِينَ تَابُوا وَأَصْلَحُوا وَبَيَّنُوا فَأُولَٰئِكَ أَتُوبُ عَلَيْهِمْ وَأَنَا التَّوَّابُ الرَّحِيمُ (١٦٠)

إِنَّ الَّذِينَ كَفَرُوا وَمَاتُوا وَهُمْ كُفَّارٌ أُولَٰئِكَ عَلَيْهِمْ لَعْنَةُ اللَّهِ وَالْمَلَائِكَةِ وَالنَّاسِ أَجْمَعِينَ (١٦١)

خَالِدِينَ فِيهَا لَا يُخَفَّفُ عَنْهُمُ الْعَذَابُ وَلَا هُمْ يُنْظَرُونَ (١٦٢)

وَإِلَٰهُكُمْ إِلَٰهٌ وَاحِدٌ لَا إِلَٰهَ إِلَّا هُوَ الرَّحْمَٰنُ الرَّحِيمُ (١٦٣)

إِنَّ فِي خَلْقِ السَّمَاوَاتِ وَالْأَرْضِ وَاخْتِلَافِ اللَّيْلِ وَالنَّهَارِ وَالْفُلْكِ الَّتِي تَجْرِي فِي الْبَحْرِ بِمَا يَنْفَعُ النَّاسَ وَمَا أَنْزَلَ اللَّهُ مِنَ السَّمَاءِ مِنْ مَاءٍ فَأَحْيَا بِهِ الْأَرْضَ بَعْدَ مَوْتِهَا وَبَثَّ فِيهَا مِنْ كُلِّ دَابَّةٍ وَتَصْرِيفِ الرِّيَاحِ وَالسَّحَابِ الْمُسَخَّرِ بَيْنَ السَّمَاءِ وَالْأَرْضِ لَآيَاتٍ لِقَوْمٍ يَعْقِلُونَ (١٦٤)

وَمِنَ النَّاسِ مَنْ يَتَّخِذُ مِنْ دُونِ اللَّهِ أَنْدَادًا يُحِبُّونَهُمْ كَحُبِّ اللَّهِ وَالَّذِينَ آمَنُوا أَشَدُّ حُبًّا لِلَّهِ وَلَوْ يَرَى الَّذِينَ ظَلَمُوا إِذْ يَرَوْنَ الْعَذَابَ أَنَّ الْقُوَّةَ لِلَّهِ جَمِيعًا وَأَنَّ اللَّهَ شَدِيدُ الْعَذَابِ (١٦٥)

in it all (kinds of) animals, and the changing of the winds and the clouds made subservient between heaven and earth, there are surely signs for a people who understand.

2:165. Yet there are some men who take for themselves objects of worship besides God, whom they love as they should love God. And those who believe are stronger in (their) love for God. And O that the wrongdoers had seen, when they see the chastisement, that power is wholly God's, and that God is severe in chastising!

2:166. When those who were followed renounce those who followed (them), and they see the chastisement and their ties are cut asunder.

2:167. And those who followed will say: If we could but return, we would renounce them as they have renounced us. Thus will God show them their deeds to be intense regret to them, and they will not escape from the Fire.

* * *

2:168. O men, eat the lawful and good things from what is in the earth, and follow not the footsteps of the devil. Surely he is an open enemy to you.

2:169. He enjoins on you only evil and indecency, and that you speak against God what you know not.

2:170. And when it is said to them, 'Follow what God has revealed," they say: "Nay, we follow that wherein we found our fathers. What! Even though their fathers had no sense at all, nor did they follow the right way.

2:171. And the parable of those who disbelieve is as the parable of one who calls out to that which hears no more than a call and a cry. Deaf, dumb, blind, so they have no sense.

2:172. O you who believe, eat of the good things that We have provided you with, and give thanks to God if He it is Whom you serve.

2:173. He has forbidden you only what

إِذْ تَبَرَّأَ الَّذِينَ اتُّبِعُوا مِنَ الَّذِينَ اتَّبَعُوا وَرَأَوُا الْعَذَابَ وَتَقَطَّعَتْ بِهِمُ الْأَسْبَابُ (١٦٦)
وَقَالَ الَّذِينَ اتَّبَعُوا لَوْ أَنَّ لَنَا كَرَّةً فَنَتَبَرَّأَ مِنْهُمْ كَمَا تَبَرَّءُوا مِنَّا كَذَلِكَ يُرِيهِمُ اللَّهُ أَعْمَالَهُمْ حَسَرَاتٍ عَلَيْهِمْ وَمَا هُم بِخَارِجِينَ مِنَ النَّارِ (١٦٧)
يَا أَيُّهَا النَّاسُ كُلُوا مِمَّا فِي الْأَرْضِ حَلَالًا طَيِّبًا وَلَا تَتَّبِعُوا خُطُوَاتِ الشَّيْطَانِ إِنَّهُ لَكُمْ عَدُوٌّ مُبِينٌ (١٦٨)
إِنَّمَا يَأْمُرُكُم بِالسُّوءِ وَالْفَحْشَاءِ وَأَن تَقُولُوا عَلَى اللَّهِ مَا لَا تَعْلَمُونَ (١٦٩)
وَإِذَا قِيلَ لَهُمُ اتَّبِعُوا مَا أَنزَلَ اللَّهُ قَالُوا بَلْ نَتَّبِعُ مَا أَلْفَيْنَا عَلَيْهِ آبَاءَنَا أَوَلَوْ كَانَ آبَاؤُهُمْ لَا يَعْقِلُونَ شَيْئًا وَلَا يَهْتَدُونَ (١٧٠)
وَمَثَلُ الَّذِينَ كَفَرُوا كَمَثَلِ الَّذِي يَنْعِقُ بِمَا لَا يَسْمَعُ إِلَّا دُعَاءً وَنِدَاءً صُمٌّ بُكْمٌ عُمْيٌ فَهُمْ لَا يَعْقِلُونَ (١٧١)
يَا أَيُّهَا الَّذِينَ آمَنُوا كُلُوا مِنْ طَيِّبَاتِ مَا رَزَقْنَاكُمْ وَاشْكُرُوا لِلَّهِ إِن كُنتُمْ إِيَّاهُ تَعْبُدُونَ (١٧٢)
إِنَّمَا حَرَّمَ عَلَيْكُمُ الْمَيْتَةَ وَالدَّمَ وَلَحْمَ الْخِنزِيرِ وَمَا أُهِلَّ بِهِ لِغَيْرِ اللَّهِ فَمَنِ اضْطُرَّ غَيْرَ بَاغٍ وَلَا عَادٍ فَلَا إِثْمَ عَلَيْهِ إِنَّ اللَّهَ غَفُورٌ رَحِيمٌ (١٧٣)
إِنَّ الَّذِينَ يَكْتُمُونَ مَا أَنزَلَ اللَّهُ مِنَ الْكِتَابِ وَيَشْتَرُونَ بِهِ ثَمَنًا قَلِيلًا أُولَٰئِكَ مَا يَأْكُلُونَ فِي بُطُونِهِمْ إِلَّا النَّارَ وَلَا يُكَلِّمُهُمُ اللَّهُ يَوْمَ الْقِيَامَةِ وَلَا يُزَكِّيهِمْ وَلَهُمْ عَذَابٌ أَلِيمٌ (١٧٤)
أُولَٰئِكَ الَّذِينَ اشْتَرَوُا الضَّلَالَةَ بِالْهُدَىٰ وَالْعَذَابَ بِالْمَغْفِرَةِ فَمَا أَصْبَرَهُمْ عَلَى

dies of itself, and blood, and the flesh of swine, and that over which any other (name) than (that of) God has been invoked. Then whoever is driven by necessity, not desiring, nor exceeding the limit, no sin is upon him. Surely God is Forgiving, Merciful.

2:174. Those who conceal aught of the Book that God has revealed and take for it a small price, they eat nothing but fire into their bellies, and God will not speak to them on the day of Resurrection, nor will He purify them; and for them is a painful chastisement.

2:175. Those are they who buy error for guidance and chastisement for forgiveness; how bold they are to challenge the Fire!

2:176. That is because God has revealed the Book with truth. And surely those who disagree about the Book go far in opposition.

* * *

2:177. It is not righteousness that you turn your faces towards the East and the West, but righteous is the one who believes in God, and the Last Day, and the angels and the Book and the prophets, and gives away wealth out of love for Him to the near of kin and the orphans and the needy and the wayfarer and to those who ask and to set slaves free and keeps up prayer and pays the poor-rate and the performers of their promise when they make a promise, and the patient in distress and affliction and in the time of conflict. These are they who are truthful; and these are they who keep their duty.

2:178. O you who believe, retaliation is prescribed for you in the matter of the slain—the free for the free, and the slave for the slave, and the female for the female. But if remission is made to one by his (aggrieved) brother, prosecution (for blood-wit) should be according to usage, and payment to

النَّارِ (١٧٥)
ذَلِكَ بِأَنَّ اللَّهَ نَزَّلَ الْكِتَابَ بِالْحَقِّ وَإِنَّ الَّذِينَ اخْتَلَفُوا فِي الْكِتَابِ لَفِي شِقَاقٍ بَعِيدٍ (١٧٦)
لَيْسَ الْبِرَّ أَنْ تُوَلُّوا وُجُوهَكُمْ قِبَلَ الْمَشْرِقِ وَالْمَغْرِبِ وَلَكِنَّ الْبِرَّ مَنْ آمَنَ بِاللَّهِ وَالْيَوْمِ الْآخِرِ وَالْمَلَائِكَةِ وَالْكِتَابِ وَالنَّبِيِّينَ وَآتَى الْمَالَ عَلَى حُبِّهِ ذَوِي الْقُرْبَى وَالْيَتَامَى وَالْمَسَاكِينَ وَابْنَ السَّبِيلِ وَالسَّائِلِينَ وَفِي الرِّقَابِ وَأَقَامَ الصَّلَاةَ وَآتَى الزَّكَاةَ وَالْمُوفُونَ بِعَهْدِهِمْ إِذَا عَاهَدُوا وَالصَّابِرِينَ فِي الْبَأْسَاءِ وَالضَّرَّاءِ وَحِينَ الْبَأْسِ أُولَئِكَ الَّذِينَ صَدَقُوا وَأُولَئِكَ هُمُ الْمُتَّقُونَ (١٧٧)
يَا أَيُّهَا الَّذِينَ آمَنُوا كُتِبَ عَلَيْكُمُ الْقِصَاصُ فِي الْقَتْلَى الْحُرُّ بِالْحُرِّ وَالْعَبْدُ بِالْعَبْدِ وَالْأُنْثَى بِالْأُنْثَى فَمَنْ عُفِيَ لَهُ مِنْ أَخِيهِ شَيْءٌ فَاتِّبَاعٌ بِالْمَعْرُوفِ وَأَدَاءٌ إِلَيْهِ بِإِحْسَانٍ ذَلِكَ تَخْفِيفٌ مِنْ رَبِّكُمْ وَرَحْمَةٌ فَمَنِ اعْتَدَى بَعْدَ ذَلِكَ فَلَهُ عَذَابٌ أَلِيمٌ (١٧٨)
وَلَكُمْ فِي الْقِصَاصِ حَيَاةٌ يَا أُولِي الْأَلْبَابِ لَعَلَّكُمْ تَتَّقُونَ (١٧٩)
كُتِبَ عَلَيْكُمْ إِذَا حَضَرَ أَحَدَكُمُ الْمَوْتُ إِنْ تَرَكَ خَيْرًا الْوَصِيَّةُ لِلْوَالِدَيْنِ وَالْأَقْرَبِينَ بِالْمَعْرُوفِ حَقًّا عَلَى الْمُتَّقِينَ (١٨٠)
فَمَنْ بَدَّلَهُ بَعْدَمَا سَمِعَهُ فَإِنَّمَا إِثْمُهُ عَلَى الَّذِينَ يُبَدِّلُونَهُ إِنَّ اللَّهَ سَمِيعٌ عَلِيمٌ (١٨١)
فَمَنْ خَافَ مِنْ مُوصٍ جَنَفًا أَوْ إِثْمًا فَأَصْلَحَ بَيْنَهُمْ فَلَا إِثْمَ عَلَيْهِ إِنَّ اللَّهَ

2. The Cow

him in a good manner. This is an alleviation from your Lord and a mercy. Whoever exceeds the limit after this, will have a painful chastisement.

2:179. And there is life for you in retaliation, O men of understanding, that you may guard yourselves.

2:180. It is prescribed for you, when death approaches one of you, if he leaves behind wealth for parents and near relatives, to make a bequest in a kindly manner; it is incumbent upon the dutiful.

2:181. Then whoever changes it after he has heard it, the sin of it is only upon those who change it. Surely God is Hearing, Knowing.

2:182. But if one fears a wrong or a sinful course on the part of the testator, and effects an agreement between the parties, there is no blame on him. Surely God is Forgiving, Merciful.

***

2:183. O you who believe, fasting is prescribed for you, as it was prescribed for those before you, so that you may guard against evil.

2:184. For a certain number of days. But whoever among you is sick or on a journey, (he shall fast) a (like) number of other days And those who find it extremely hard may effect redemption by feeding a poor man. So whoever does good spontaneously, it is better for him; and that you fast is better for you if you know.

2:185. The month of Ramadan is that in which the Qur'an was revealed, a guidance to men and clear proofs of the guidance and the Criterion. So whoever of you is present in the month, he shall fast therein, and whoever is sick or on a journey, (he shall fast) a (like) number of other days. God desires ease for you, and He desires not hardship for you, and (He desires) that you should complete the number and that you should exalt the

غَفُورٌ رَحِيمٌ (١٨٢) يَا أَيُّهَا الَّذِينَ آمَنُوا كُتِبَ عَلَيْكُمُ الصِّيَامُ كَمَا كُتِبَ عَلَى الَّذِينَ مِنْ قَبْلِكُمْ لَعَلَّكُمْ تَتَّقُونَ (١٨٣) أَيَّامًا مَعْدُودَاتٍ فَمَنْ كَانَ مِنْكُمْ مَرِيضًا أَوْ عَلَى سَفَرٍ فَعِدَّةٌ مِنْ أَيَّامٍ أُخَرَ وَعَلَى الَّذِينَ يُطِيقُونَهُ فِدْيَةٌ طَعَامُ مِسْكِينٍ فَمَنْ تَطَوَّعَ خَيْرًا فَهُوَ خَيْرٌ لَهُ وَأَنْ تَصُومُوا خَيْرٌ لَكُمْ إِنْ كُنْتُمْ تَعْلَمُونَ (١٨٤) شَهْرُ رَمَضَانَ الَّذِي أُنْزِلَ فِيهِ الْقُرْآنُ هُدًى لِلنَّاسِ وَبَيِّنَاتٍ مِنَ الْهُدَى وَالْفُرْقَانِ فَمَنْ شَهِدَ مِنْكُمُ الشَّهْرَ فَلْيَصُمْهُ وَمَنْ كَانَ مَرِيضًا أَوْ عَلَى سَفَرٍ فَعِدَّةٌ مِنْ أَيَّامٍ أُخَرَ يُرِيدُ اللَّهُ بِكُمُ الْيُسْرَ وَلَا يُرِيدُ بِكُمُ الْعُسْرَ وَلِتُكْمِلُوا الْعِدَّةَ وَلِتُكَبِّرُوا اللَّهَ عَلَى مَا هَدَاكُمْ وَلَعَلَّكُمْ تَشْكُرُونَ (١٨٥) وَإِذَا سَأَلَكَ عِبَادِي عَنِّي فَإِنِّي قَرِيبٌ أُجِيبُ دَعْوَةَ الدَّاعِ إِذَا دَعَانِ فَلْيَسْتَجِيبُوا لِي وَلْيُؤْمِنُوا بِي لَعَلَّهُمْ يَرْشُدُونَ (١٨٦) أُحِلَّ لَكُمْ لَيْلَةَ الصِّيَامِ الرَّفَثُ إِلَى نِسَائِكُمْ هُنَّ لِبَاسٌ لَكُمْ وَأَنْتُمْ لِبَاسٌ لَهُنَّ عَلِمَ اللَّهُ أَنَّكُمْ كُنْتُمْ تَخْتَانُونَ أَنْفُسَكُمْ فَتَابَ عَلَيْكُمْ وَعَفَا عَنْكُمْ فَالْآنَ بَاشِرُوهُنَّ وَابْتَغُوا مَا كَتَبَ اللَّهُ لَكُمْ وَكُلُوا وَاشْرَبُوا حَتَّى يَتَبَيَّنَ لَكُمُ الْخَيْطُ الْأَبْيَضُ مِنَ الْخَيْطِ الْأَسْوَدِ مِنَ الْفَجْرِ ثُمَّ أَتِمُّوا الصِّيَامَ إِلَى اللَّيْلِ وَلَا تُبَاشِرُوهُنَّ وَأَنْتُمْ عَاكِفُونَ فِي الْمَسَاجِدِ تِلْكَ حُدُودُ اللَّهِ فَلَا تَقْرَبُوهَا كَذَلِكَ يُبَيِّنُ اللَّهُ آيَاتِهِ لِلنَّاسِ لَعَلَّهُمْ يَتَّقُونَ (١٨٧)

greatness of God for having guided you and that you may give thanks.

2:186. And when My servants ask thee concerning Me, surely I am nigh. I answer the prayer of the suppliant when he calls on Me, so they should hear My call and believe in Me that they may walk in the right way.

2:187. It is made lawful for you to go in to your wives on the night of the fast. They are an apparel for you and you are an apparel for them. God knows that you acted unjustly to yourselves, so He turned to you in mercy and removed (the burden) from you. So now be in contact with them and seek what God has ordained for you, and eat and drink until the whiteness of the day becomes distinct from the blackness of the night at dawn, then complete the fast till nightfall, and touch them not while you keep to the mosques. These are the limits of God, so go not near them. Thus does God make clear His messages for men that they may keep their duty.

2:188. And swallow not up your property among yourselves by false means, nor seek to gain access thereby to the judges, so that you may swallow up a part of the property of men wrongfully while you know.

* * *

2:189. They ask thee of the new moons. Say: They are times appointed for men, and (for) the pilgrimage. And it is not righteousness that you enter the houses by their backs, but he is righteous who keeps his duty. And go into the houses by their doors; and keep your duty to God, that you may be successful.

2:190. And fight in the way of God against those who fight against you but be not aggressive. Surely God loves not the aggressors.

2:191. And kill them wherever you find

them, and drive them out from where they drove you out, and persecution is worse than slaughter. And fight not with them at the Sacred Mosque until they fight with you in so if they fight you (in it), slay them. Such is the recompense of the disbelievers.

2:192. But if they desist, then surely God is Forgiving, Merciful.

2:193. And fight them until there is no persecution, and religion is only for Allah. But if they desist, then there should be no hostility except against the oppressors.

2:194. The sacred month for the sacred month, and retaliation (is allowed) in sacred things. Whoever then acts aggressively against you, inflict injury on him according to the injury he has inflicted on you and keep your duty to God, and know that God is with those who keep their duty.

2:195. And spend in the way of God and cast not yourselves to perdition with your own hands and do good (to others). Surely God loves the doers of good.

2:196. And accomplish the pilgrimage and the visit for God. But if you are prevented, (send) whatever offering is easy to obtain; and shave not your heads until the offering reaches its destination. Then whoever among you is sick or has an ailment of the head, he (may effect) a compensation by fasting or alms or sacrificing. And when you are secure, whoever profits by combining the visit with the pilgrimage (should take) whatever offering is easy to obtain. But he who cannot find (an offering) should fast for three days during the pilgrimage and for seven days when you return. These are ten (days) complete. This is for him whose family is not present in the Sacred Mosque. And keep your duty to God, and know that God is severe in requiting (evil).

***

2:197. The months of the pilgrimage are well known; so whoever determines to perform pilgrimage therein there shall be no immodest speech, nor abusing, nor altercation in the pilgrimage. And whatever good you do, God knows it. And make provision for yourselves, the best provision being to keep one's duty. And keep your duty to Me, O men of understanding.

2:198. It is no sin for you that you seek the bounty of your Lord. So when you press on from 'Arafat, remember God near the Holy Monument, and remember Him as He has guided you, though before that you were certainly of the erring ones.

2:199. Then hasten on from where the people hasten on, and ask the forgiveness of God. Surely God is Forgiving, Merciful.

2:200. And when you have performed your devotions, laud God as you lauded your fathers, rather a more hearty lauding. But there are some people who say, Our Lord, give us in the world. And for such there is no portion in the Hereafter.

2:201. And there are some among them who say: Our Lord, grant us good in this world and good in the Hereafter, and save us from the chastisement of the Fire.

2:202. For those there is a portion on account of what they have earned. And God is Swift in reckoning.

2:203. And remember God during the appointed days. Then whoever hastens off in two days, it is no sin for him and whoever stays behind, it is no sin for him, for one who keeps his duty. And keep your duty to God, and know that you will be gathered together to Him.

2:204. And of men is he whose speech about the life of this world pleases thee, and he calls God to witness as to

لَيْسَ عَلَيْكُمْ جُنَاحٌ أَنْ تَبْتَغُوا فَضْلًا مِنْ رَبِّكُمْ فَإِذَا أَفَضْتُمْ مِنْ عَرَفَاتٍ فَاذْكُرُوا اللَّهَ عِنْدَ الْمَشْعَرِ الْحَرَامِ وَاذْكُرُوهُ كَمَا هَدَاكُمْ وَإِنْ كُنْتُمْ مِنْ قَبْلِهِ لَمِنَ الضَّالِّينَ (١٩٨)
ثُمَّ أَفِيضُوا مِنْ حَيْثُ أَفَاضَ النَّاسُ وَاسْتَغْفِرُوا اللَّهَ إِنَّ اللَّهَ غَفُورٌ رَحِيمٌ (١٩٩)
فَإِذَا قَضَيْتُمْ مَنَاسِكَكُمْ فَاذْكُرُوا اللَّهَ كَذِكْرِكُمْ آبَاءَكُمْ أَوْ أَشَدَّ ذِكْرًا فَمِنَ النَّاسِ مَنْ يَقُولُ رَبَّنَا آتِنَا فِي الدُّنْيَا وَمَا لَهُ فِي الْآخِرَةِ مِنْ خَلَاقٍ (٢٠٠)
وَمِنْهُمْ مَنْ يَقُولُ رَبَّنَا آتِنَا فِي الدُّنْيَا حَسَنَةً وَفِي الْآخِرَةِ حَسَنَةً وَقِنَا عَذَابَ النَّارِ (٢٠١)
أُولَئِكَ لَهُمْ نَصِيبٌ مِمَّا كَسَبُوا وَاللَّهُ سَرِيعُ الْحِسَابِ (٢٠٢)
وَاذْكُرُوا اللَّهَ فِي أَيَّامٍ مَعْدُودَاتٍ فَمَنْ تَعَجَّلَ فِي يَوْمَيْنِ فَلَا إِثْمَ عَلَيْهِ وَمَنْ تَأَخَّرَ فَلَا إِثْمَ عَلَيْهِ لِمَنِ اتَّقَى وَاتَّقُوا اللَّهَ وَاعْلَمُوا أَنَّكُمْ إِلَيْهِ تُحْشَرُونَ (٢٠٣)
وَمِنَ النَّاسِ مَنْ يُعْجِبُكَ قَوْلُهُ فِي الْحَيَاةِ الدُّنْيَا وَيُشْهِدُ اللَّهَ عَلَى مَا فِي قَلْبِهِ وَهُوَ أَلَدُّ الْخِصَامِ (٢٠٤)
وَإِذَا تَوَلَّى سَعَى فِي الْأَرْضِ لِيُفْسِدَ فِيهَا وَيُهْلِكَ الْحَرْثَ وَالنَّسْلَ وَاللَّهُ لَا يُحِبُّ الْفَسَادَ (٢٠٥)
وَإِذَا قِيلَ لَهُ اتَّقِ اللَّهَ أَخَذَتْهُ الْعِزَّةُ بِالْإِثْمِ فَحَسْبُهُ جَهَنَّمُ وَلَبِئْسَ الْمِهَادُ (٢٠٦)
وَمِنَ النَّاسِ مَنْ يَشْرِي نَفْسَهُ ابْتِغَاءَ مَرْضَاةِ اللَّهِ وَاللَّهُ رَءُوفٌ بِالْعِبَادِ (٢٠٧)

that which is in his heart, yet he is the most violent of adversaries.

2:205. And when he holds authority, he makes effort in the land to cause mischief in it and destroy tilth and offspring; and God loves not mischief.

2:206. And when it is said to him, Be careful of thy duty to God, pride carries him off to sin -- so hell is sufficient for him. And certainly evil is the resting-place.

2:207. And of men is he who sells himself to seek the pleasure of God. And God is Compassionate to the servants.

2:208. O you who believe, enter into complete peace and follow not the footsteps of the devil. Surely he is your open enemy.

2:209. But if you slip after clear arguments have come to you, then know that God is Mighty, Wise.

2:210. They wait for naught but that God should come to them in the shadows of the clouds with angels, and the matter has (already) been decided. And to God are (all) matters returned.

* * *

2:211. Ask of the Children of Israel how many a clear sign We gave them! And whoever changes the favour of God after it has come to him, then surely God is Severe in requiting (evil).

2:212. The life of this world is made to seem fair to those who disbelieve, and they mock those who believe. And those who keep their duty will be above them on the Day of Resurrection. And God gives to whom He pleases without measure.

2:213. Mankind is a single nation. So God raised prophets as bearers of good news and as warners, and He revealed with them the Book with truth, that it might judge between people concerning that in which they differed. And none but the very people who

يَا أَيُّهَا الَّذِينَ آمَنُوا ادْخُلُوا فِي السِّلْمِ كَافَّةً وَلَا تَتَّبِعُوا خُطُوَاتِ الشَّيْطَانِ إِنَّهُ لَكُمْ عَدُوٌّ مُبِينٌ (٢٠٨) فَإِنْ زَلَلْتُمْ مِنْ بَعْدِ مَا جَاءَتْكُمُ الْبَيِّنَاتُ فَاعْلَمُوا أَنَّ اللَّهَ عَزِيزٌ حَكِيمٌ (٢٠٩) هَلْ يَنْظُرُونَ إِلَّا أَنْ يَأْتِيَهُمُ اللَّهُ فِي ظُلَلٍ مِنَ الْغَمَامِ وَالْمَلَائِكَةُ وَقُضِيَ الْأَمْرُ وَإِلَى اللَّهِ تُرْجَعُ الْأُمُورُ (٢١٠) سَلْ بَنِي إِسْرَائِيلَ كَمْ آتَيْنَاهُمْ مِنْ آيَةٍ بَيِّنَةٍ وَمَنْ يُبَدِّلْ نِعْمَةَ اللَّهِ مِنْ بَعْدِ مَا جَاءَتْهُ فَإِنَّ اللَّهَ شَدِيدُ الْعِقَابِ (٢١١) زُيِّنَ لِلَّذِينَ كَفَرُوا الْحَيَاةُ الدُّنْيَا وَيَسْخَرُونَ مِنَ الَّذِينَ آمَنُوا وَالَّذِينَ اتَّقَوْا فَوْقَهُمْ يَوْمَ الْقِيَامَةِ وَاللَّهُ يَرْزُقُ مَنْ يَشَاءُ بِغَيْرِ حِسَابٍ (٢١٢) كَانَ النَّاسُ أُمَّةً وَاحِدَةً فَبَعَثَ اللَّهُ النَّبِيِّينَ مُبَشِّرِينَ وَمُنْذِرِينَ وَأَنْزَلَ مَعَهُمُ الْكِتَابَ بِالْحَقِّ لِيَحْكُمَ بَيْنَ النَّاسِ فِيمَا اخْتَلَفُوا فِيهِ وَمَا اخْتَلَفَ فِيهِ إِلَّا الَّذِينَ أُوتُوهُ مِنْ بَعْدِ مَا جَاءَتْهُمُ الْبَيِّنَاتُ بَغْيًا بَيْنَهُمْ فَهَدَى اللَّهُ الَّذِينَ آمَنُوا لِمَا اخْتَلَفُوا فِيهِ مِنَ الْحَقِّ بِإِذْنِهِ وَاللَّهُ يَهْدِي مَنْ يَشَاءُ إِلَى صِرَاطٍ مُسْتَقِيمٍ (٢١٣) أَمْ حَسِبْتُمْ أَنْ تَدْخُلُوا الْجَنَّةَ وَلَمَّا يَأْتِكُمْ مَثَلُ الَّذِينَ خَلَوْا مِنْ قَبْلِكُمْ مَسَّتْهُمُ الْبَأْسَاءُ وَالضَّرَّاءُ وَزُلْزِلُوا حَتَّى يَقُولَ الرَّسُولُ وَالَّذِينَ آمَنُوا مَعَهُ مَتَى نَصْرُ اللَّهِ أَلَا إِنَّ نَصْرَ اللَّهِ قَرِيبٌ (٢١٤) يَسْأَلُونَكَ مَاذَا يُنْفِقُونَ قُلْ مَا أَنْفَقْتُمْ مِنْ خَيْرٍ فَلِلْوَالِدَيْنِ وَالْأَقْرَبِينَ وَالْيَتَامَى وَالْمَسَاكِينِ وَابْنِ السَّبِيلِ

were given it differed of about it after clear arguments had come to them, envying one another. So God has guided by His will those who believe to the truth about which they differed. And God guides whom He pleases to the right path.

2:214. Or do you think that you will enter the Garden, while there has not yet befallen you the like of what befell those who have passed away before you. Distress and affliction befell them and they were shaken violently, so that the Messenger and those who believed with him said: When will the help of God come? Now surely the help of God is nigh!

2:215. They ask thee as to what they should spend. Say: Whatever wealth you spend, it is for the parents and the near of kin and the orphans and the needy and the wayfarer. And whatever good you do, God surely is Knower of it.

2:216. Fighting is enjoined on you, though it is disliked by you and it may be that you dislike a thing while it is good for you, and it may be that you love a thing while it is evil for you; and God knows while you know not.

* * *

2:217. They ask thee about fighting in the sacred month. Say: Fighting in it is a grave (offence). And hindering (men) from God's way and denying Him and the Sacred Mosque and turning its people out of it, are still graver with God and persecution is graver than slaughter And they will not cease fighting you until they turn you back from your religion, if they can. And whoever of you turns back from his religion, then he dies while an unbeliever -- these it is whose works go for nothing in this world and the Hereafter. And they are the companions of the Fire: therein they will abide.

وَمَا تَفْعَلُوا مِنْ خَيْرٍ فَإِنَّ اللَّهَ بِهِ عَلِيمٌ (٢١٥) كُتِبَ عَلَيْكُمُ الْقِتَالُ وَهُوَ كُرْهٌ لَكُمْ وَعَسَى أَنْ تَكْرَهُوا شَيْئًا وَهُوَ خَيْرٌ لَكُمْ وَعَسَى أَنْ تُحِبُّوا شَيْئًا وَهُوَ شَرٌّ لَكُمْ وَاللَّهُ يَعْلَمُ وَأَنْتُمْ لَا تَعْلَمُونَ (٢١٦) يَسْأَلُونَكَ عَنِ الشَّهْرِ الْحَرَامِ قِتَالٍ فِيهِ قُلْ قِتَالٌ فِيهِ كَبِيرٌ وَصَدٌّ عَنْ سَبِيلِ اللَّهِ وَكُفْرٌ بِهِ وَالْمَسْجِدِ الْحَرَامِ وَإِخْرَاجُ أَهْلِهِ مِنْهُ أَكْبَرُ عِنْدَ اللَّهِ وَالْفِتْنَةُ أَكْبَرُ مِنَ الْقَتْلِ وَلَا يَزَالُونَ يُقَاتِلُونَكُمْ حَتَّى يَرُدُّوكُمْ عَنْ دِينِكُمْ إِنِ اسْتَطَاعُوا وَمَنْ يَرْتَدِدْ مِنْكُمْ عَنْ دِينِهِ فَيَمُتْ وَهُوَ كَافِرٌ فَأُولَئِكَ حَبِطَتْ أَعْمَالُهُمْ فِي الدُّنْيَا وَالْآخِرَةِ وَأُولَئِكَ أَصْحَابُ النَّارِ هُمْ فِيهَا خَالِدُونَ (٢١٧) إِنَّ الَّذِينَ آمَنُوا وَالَّذِينَ هَاجَرُوا وَجَاهَدُوا فِي سَبِيلِ اللَّهِ أُولَئِكَ يَرْجُونَ رَحْمَةَ اللَّهِ وَاللَّهُ غَفُورٌ رَحِيمٌ (٢١٨) يَسْأَلُونَكَ عَنِ الْخَمْرِ وَالْمَيْسِرِ قُلْ فِيهِمَا إِثْمٌ كَبِيرٌ وَمَنَافِعُ لِلنَّاسِ وَإِثْمُهُمَا أَكْبَرُ مِنْ نَفْعِهِمَا وَيَسْأَلُونَكَ مَاذَا يُنْفِقُونَ قُلِ الْعَفْوَ كَذَلِكَ يُبَيِّنُ اللَّهُ لَكُمُ الْآيَاتِ لَعَلَّكُمْ تَتَفَكَّرُونَ (٢١٩) فِي الدُّنْيَا وَالْآخِرَةِ وَيَسْأَلُونَكَ عَنِ الْيَتَامَى قُلْ إِصْلَاحٌ لَهُمْ خَيْرٌ وَإِنْ تُخَالِطُوهُمْ فَإِخْوَانُكُمْ وَاللَّهُ يَعْلَمُ الْمُفْسِدَ مِنَ الْمُصْلِحِ وَلَوْ شَاءَ اللَّهُ لَأَعْنَتَكُمْ إِنَّ اللَّهَ عَزِيزٌ حَكِيمٌ (٢٢٠) وَلَا تَنْكِحُوا الْمُشْرِكَاتِ حَتَّى يُؤْمِنَّ وَلَأَمَةٌ مُؤْمِنَةٌ خَيْرٌ مِنْ مُشْرِكَةٍ وَلَوْ أَعْجَبَتْكُمْ وَلَا تُنْكِحُوا الْمُشْرِكِينَ حَتَّى

2. The Cow

2:218. Those who believed and those who fled (their homes) and strove hard in God's way -- these surely hope for the mercy of God. And God is Forgiving, Merciful.

2:219. They ask thee about intoxicants and games of chance. Say: In both of them is a great sin and (some) advantage for men, and their sin is greater than their advantage. And they ask thee as to what they should spend. Say: What you can spare. Thus does God make clear to you the messages that you may ponder,

2:220. On this world and the Hereafter. And they ask thee concerning the orphans. Say: To set right their (affairs) is good; and if you mix with them, they are your brethren. And God knows him who makes mischief from him who sets right. And if God pleased, He would have made matters difficult for you. Surely God is Mighty, Wise.

2:221. And marry not the idolatresses until they believe; and certainly a believing maid is better than an idolatress even though she please you. Nor give (believing women) in marriage to idolaters until they believe, and certainly a believing slave is better than an idolater, even though he please you. These invite to the Fire and God invites to the Garden and to forgiveness by His will and He makes clear His messages to men that they may be mindful.

* * *

2:222. And they ask thee about menstruation. Say: It is harmful, so keep aloof from women during menstrual discharge and go not near them until they are clean. But when they have cleansed themselves, go in to them as God has commanded you. Surely God loves those who turn much (to Him), and He loves those who

يُؤْمِنُوا وَلَعَبْدٌ مُؤْمِنٌ خَيْرٌ مِنْ مُشْرِكٍ وَلَوْ أَعْجَبَكُمْ أُولَئِكَ يَدْعُونَ إِلَى النَّارِ وَاللَّهُ يَدْعُو إِلَى الْجَنَّةِ وَالْمَغْفِرَةِ بِإِذْنِهِ وَيُبَيِّنُ آيَاتِهِ لِلنَّاسِ لَعَلَّهُمْ يَتَذَكَّرُونَ (٢٢١)

وَيَسْأَلُونَكَ عَنِ الْمَحِيضِ قُلْ هُوَ أَذًى فَاعْتَزِلُوا النِّسَاءَ فِي الْمَحِيضِ وَلَا تَقْرَبُوهُنَّ حَتَّى يَطْهُرْنَ فَإِذَا تَطَهَّرْنَ فَأْتُوهُنَّ مِنْ حَيْثُ أَمَرَكُمُ اللَّهُ إِنَّ اللَّهَ يُحِبُّ التَّوَّابِينَ وَيُحِبُّ الْمُتَطَهِّرِينَ (٢٢٢)

نِسَاؤُكُمْ حَرْثٌ لَكُمْ فَأْتُوا حَرْثَكُمْ أَنَّى

2. The Cow

purify themselves.

2:223. Your wives are a tilth for you, so go in to your tilth when you like, and send (good) beforehand for yourselves. And keep your duty to God, and know that you will meet Him. And give good news to the believers.

2:224. And make not God by your oaths a hindrance to your doing good and keeping your duty and making peace between men. And God is Hearing, Knowing.

2:225. God will not call you to account for what is vain in your oaths, but He will call you to account for what your hearts have earned. And God is Forgiving, Forbearing.

2:226. Those who swear that they will not go in to their wives should wait four months; then if they go back, God is surely Forgiving, Merciful.

2:227. And if they resolve on a divorce, God is surely Hearing, Knowing.

2:228. And the divorced women should keep themselves in waiting for three courses. And it is not lawful for them to conceal that which God has created in their wombs, if they believe in God and the Last Day. And their husbands have a better right to take them back in the meanwhile if they wish for reconciliation. And women have rights similar to those against them in a just manner, and men are a degree above them. And God is Mighty, Wise.

* * *

2:229. Divorce may be (pronounced) twice; then keep (them) in good fellowship or let (them) go with kindness. And it is not lawful for you to take any part of what you have given them, unless both fear that they cannot keep within the limits of God. Then if you fear that they cannot keep within the limits of God there is no blame on them for what she gives up to become free thereby. These are the

شِئْتُمْ وَقَدِّمُوا لِأَنْفُسِكُمْ وَاتَّقُوا اللَّهَ وَاعْلَمُوا أَنَّكُمْ مُلَاقُوهُ وَبَشِّرِ الْمُؤْمِنِينَ (٢٢٣)

وَلَا تَجْعَلُوا اللَّهَ عُرْضَةً لِأَيْمَانِكُمْ أَنْ تَبَرُّوا وَتَتَّقُوا وَتُصْلِحُوا بَيْنَ النَّاسِ وَاللَّهُ سَمِيعٌ عَلِيمٌ (٢٢٤)

لَا يُؤَاخِذُكُمُ اللَّهُ بِاللَّغْوِ فِي أَيْمَانِكُمْ وَلَكِنْ يُؤَاخِذُكُمْ بِمَا كَسَبَتْ قُلُوبُكُمْ وَاللَّهُ غَفُورٌ حَلِيمٌ (٢٢٥)

لِلَّذِينَ يُؤْلُونَ مِنْ نِسَائِهِمْ تَرَبُّصُ أَرْبَعَةِ أَشْهُرٍ فَإِنْ فَاءُوا فَإِنَّ اللَّهَ غَفُورٌ رَحِيمٌ (٢٢٦)

وَإِنْ عَزَمُوا الطَّلَاقَ فَإِنَّ اللَّهَ سَمِيعٌ عَلِيمٌ (٢٢٧)

وَالْمُطَلَّقَاتُ يَتَرَبَّصْنَ بِأَنْفُسِهِنَّ ثَلَاثَةَ قُرُوءٍ وَلَا يَحِلُّ لَهُنَّ أَنْ يَكْتُمْنَ مَا خَلَقَ اللَّهُ فِي أَرْحَامِهِنَّ إِنْ كُنَّ يُؤْمِنَّ بِاللَّهِ وَالْيَوْمِ الْآخِرِ وَبُعُولَتُهُنَّ أَحَقُّ بِرَدِّهِنَّ فِي ذَلِكَ إِنْ أَرَادُوا إِصْلَاحًا وَلَهُنَّ مِثْلُ الَّذِي عَلَيْهِنَّ بِالْمَعْرُوفِ وَلِلرِّجَالِ عَلَيْهِنَّ دَرَجَةٌ وَاللَّهُ عَزِيزٌ حَكِيمٌ (٢٢٨)

الطَّلَاقُ مَرَّتَانِ فَإِمْسَاكٌ بِمَعْرُوفٍ أَوْ تَسْرِيحٌ بِإِحْسَانٍ وَلَا يَحِلُّ لَكُمْ أَنْ تَأْخُذُوا مِمَّا آتَيْتُمُوهُنَّ شَيْئًا إِلَّا أَنْ يَخَافَا أَلَّا يُقِيمَا حُدُودَ اللَّهِ فَإِنْ خِفْتُمْ أَلَّا يُقِيمَا حُدُودَ اللَّهِ فَلَا جُنَاحَ عَلَيْهِمَا فِيمَا افْتَدَتْ بِهِ تِلْكَ حُدُودُ اللَّهِ فَلَا تَعْتَدُوهَا وَمَنْ يَتَعَدَّ حُدُودَ اللَّهِ فَأُولَئِكَ هُمُ الظَّالِمُونَ (٢٢٩)

فَإِنْ طَلَّقَهَا فَلَا تَحِلُّ لَهُ مِنْ بَعْدُ حَتَّى تَنْكِحَ زَوْجًا غَيْرَهُ فَإِنْ طَلَّقَهَا فَلَا جُنَاحَ عَلَيْهِمَا أَنْ يَتَرَاجَعَا إِنْ ظَنَّا أَنْ يُقِيمَا حُدُودَ اللَّهِ وَتِلْكَ حُدُودُ اللَّهِ يُبَيِّنُهَا

2. The Cow

limits of God, so exceed them not and whoever exceeds the limits of God, these are the wrongdoers.

2:230. So if he divorces her (the third time), she shall not be lawful to him afterwards until she marries anothet husband. If he divorces her, there is no blame on them both if they return to each other (by marriage), if they think that they can keep within the limits of God. And these are the limits of God which He makes clear for a people who know.

2:231. And when you divorce women and they reach their prescribed time, then retain them in kindness or set them free with kindness and retain them not for injury so that you exceed the limits. And whoever does this, he indeed wrongs his own soul. And take not God's messages for a mockery, and remember God's favour to you, and that which He has revealed to you of the Book and the Wisdom, admonishing you thereby. And keep your duty to God, and know that God is the Knower of all things.

***

2:232. And when you divorce women and they end their term, prevent them not from marrying their husbands if they agree among themselves in a lawful manner. With this is admonished he among you who believes in God and the Last Day. This is more profitable for you and purer. And God knows while you know not.

2:233. And mothers shall suckle their children for two whole years, for him who desires to complete the time of suckling. And their maintenance and their clothing must be borne by the father according to usage. No soul shall be burdened beyond its capacity. Neither shall a mother be made to suffer harm on account of her child, nor a father on account of his child and a similar duty (devolves) on the (father's) heir. But if both desire weaning by mutual consent and counsel, there is no blame on them. And if you wish to engage a wet-nurse for your children, there is no blame on you so long as you pay what you promised according to usage. And keep your duty to God and know that God is Seer of what you do.

2:234. And (as for) those of you who die and leave wives behind, such women should keep themselves in waiting for four months and ten days; when they reach their term, there is no blame on you for what they do for themselves in a lawful manner. And God is Aware of what you do.

2:235. And there is no blame on you respecting that which you speak indirectly in the asking of (such) women in marriage or keep (the proposal) concealed within your minds. God knows that you will have them in your minds, but give them not a promise in secret unless you speak in a lawful manner. And confirm not the marriage tie until the prescribed period reaches its end. And know that God knows what is in your minds, so beware of Him; and know that God is Forgiving, Forbearing.

***

2:236. There is no blame on you if you divorce women while yet you have not touched them, nor appointed for them a portion. And provide for them, the wealthy according to his means and the strained according to his means, a provision according to usage. (This is) a duty on the doers of good.

2:237. And if you divorce them before you have touched them and you have appointed for them a portion, (pay) half of what you have appointed unless they forgo or he forgoes in whose hand is the marriage tie. And it is nearer to dutifulness that you forgo. Nor neglect the giving of free gifts

وَلَا جُنَاحَ عَلَيْكُمْ فِيمَا عَرَّضْتُم بِهِ مِنْ خِطْبَةِ النِّسَاءِ أَوْ أَكْنَنتُمْ فِي أَنفُسِكُمْ عَلِمَ اللَّهُ أَنَّكُمْ سَتَذْكُرُونَهُنَّ وَلَٰكِن لَّا تُوَاعِدُوهُنَّ سِرًّا إِلَّا أَن تَقُولُوا قَوْلًا مَّعْرُوفًا وَلَا تَعْزِمُوا عُقْدَةَ النِّكَاحِ حَتَّىٰ يَبْلُغَ الْكِتَابُ أَجَلَهُ وَاعْلَمُوا أَنَّ اللَّهَ يَعْلَمُ مَا فِي أَنفُسِكُمْ فَاحْذَرُوهُ وَاعْلَمُوا أَنَّ اللَّهَ غَفُورٌ حَلِيمٌ (٢٣٥)

لَّا جُنَاحَ عَلَيْكُمْ إِن طَلَّقْتُمُ النِّسَاءَ مَا لَمْ تَمَسُّوهُنَّ أَوْ تَفْرِضُوا لَهُنَّ فَرِيضَةً وَمَتِّعُوهُنَّ عَلَى الْمُوسِعِ قَدَرُهُ وَعَلَى الْمُقْتِرِ قَدَرُهُ مَتَاعًا بِالْمَعْرُوفِ حَقًّا عَلَى الْمُحْسِنِينَ (٢٣٦)

وَإِن طَلَّقْتُمُوهُنَّ مِن قَبْلِ أَن تَمَسُّوهُنَّ وَقَدْ فَرَضْتُمْ لَهُنَّ فَرِيضَةً فَنِصْفُ مَا فَرَضْتُمْ إِلَّا أَن يَعْفُونَ أَوْ يَعْفُوَ الَّذِي بِيَدِهِ عُقْدَةُ النِّكَاحِ وَأَن تَعْفُوا أَقْرَبُ لِلتَّقْوَىٰ وَلَا تَنسَوُا الْفَضْلَ بَيْنَكُمْ إِنَّ اللَّهَ بِمَا تَعْمَلُونَ بَصِيرٌ (٢٣٧)

حَافِظُوا عَلَى الصَّلَوَاتِ وَالصَّلَاةِ الْوُسْطَىٰ وَقُومُوا لِلَّهِ قَانِتِينَ (٢٣٨)

فَإِنْ خِفْتُمْ فَرِجَالًا أَوْ رُكْبَانًا فَإِذَا أَمِنتُمْ فَاذْكُرُوا اللَّهَ كَمَا عَلَّمَكُم مَّا لَمْ تَكُونُوا تَعْلَمُونَ (٢٣٩)

وَالَّذِينَ يُتَوَفَّوْنَ مِنكُمْ وَيَذَرُونَ أَزْوَاجًا وَصِيَّةً لِّأَزْوَاجِهِم مَّتَاعًا إِلَى الْحَوْلِ غَيْرَ إِخْرَاجٍ فَإِنْ خَرَجْنَ فَلَا جُنَاحَ عَلَيْكُمْ فِي مَا فَعَلْنَ فِي أَنفُسِهِنَّ مِن مَّعْرُوفٍ وَاللَّهُ عَزِيزٌ حَكِيمٌ (٢٤٠)

وَلِلْمُطَلَّقَاتِ مَتَاعٌ بِالْمَعْرُوفِ حَقًّا عَلَى الْمُتَّقِينَ (٢٤١)

كَذَٰلِكَ يُبَيِّنُ اللَّهُ لَكُمْ آيَاتِهِ لَعَلَّكُمْ تَعْقِلُونَ (٢٤٢)

2. The Cow

between you. Surely God is Seer of what you do.

2:238. Guard the prayers and the most excellent prayer, and stand up truly obedient to God.

2:239. But if you are in danger (say your prayers) on foot or on horseback. And when you are secure, remember God as He has taught you what you knew not.

2:240. And those of you who die and leave wives behind, should make a bequest in favour of their wives of maintenance for a year without turning (them) out Then if they themselves go away, there is no blame on you for what they do of lawful deeds concerning themselves. And God is Mighty, Wise.

2:241. And for the divorced women, provision (must be made) in kindness, This is incumbent on those who have regard for duty.

2:242. God thus makes clear to you His messages that you may understand.

* * *

2:243. Hast thou not considered those who went forth from their homes, and they were thousands, for fear of death. Then God said to them, Die. Then He gave them life. Surely God is Gracious to people, but most people are not grateful.

2:244. And fight in the way of God, and know that God is Hearing Knowing.

2:245. Who is it that will offer to God a goodly gift, so He multiplies it to him manifold? And God receives and amplifies, and to Him you shall be returned.

2:246. Hast thou not thought of the leaders of the Children of Israel after Moses? When they said to a prophet of theirs: Raise up for us a king, that we may fight in the way of God. He said May it not be that you will not fight if fighting is ordained for you? They

أَلَمْ تَرَ إِلَى الَّذِينَ خَرَجُوا مِنْ دِيَارِهِمْ وَهُمْ أُلُوفٌ حَذَرَ الْمَوْتِ فَقَالَ لَهُمُ اللَّهُ مُوتُوا ثُمَّ أَحْيَاهُمْ إِنَّ اللَّهَ لَذُو فَضْلٍ عَلَى النَّاسِ وَلَكِنَّ أَكْثَرَ النَّاسِ لَا يَشْكُرُونَ (٢٤٣)

وَقَاتِلُوا فِي سَبِيلِ اللَّهِ وَاعْلَمُوا أَنَّ اللَّهَ سَمِيعٌ عَلِيمٌ (٢٤٤)

مَنْ ذَا الَّذِي يُقْرِضُ اللَّهَ قَرْضًا حَسَنًا فَيُضَاعِفَهُ لَهُ أَضْعَافًا كَثِيرَةً وَاللَّهُ يَقْبِضُ وَيَبْسُطُ وَإِلَيْهِ تُرْجَعُونَ (٢٤٥)

أَلَمْ تَرَ إِلَى الْمَلَإِ مِنْ بَنِي إِسْرَائِيلَ مِنْ بَعْدِ مُوسَى إِذْ قَالُوا لِنَبِيٍّ لَهُمُ ابْعَثْ لَنَا مَلِكًا نُقَاتِلْ فِي سَبِيلِ اللَّهِ قَالَ هَلْ عَسَيْتُمْ إِنْ كُتِبَ عَلَيْكُمُ الْقِتَالُ أَلَّا تُقَاتِلُوا قَالُوا وَمَا لَنَا أَلَّا نُقَاتِلَ فِي سَبِيلِ اللَّهِ وَقَدْ أُخْرِجْنَا مِنْ دِيَارِنَا وَأَبْنَائِنَا فَلَمَّا كُتِبَ عَلَيْهِمُ الْقِتَالُ تَوَلَّوْا إِلَّا قَلِيلًا مِنْهُمْ وَاللَّهُ عَلِيمٌ بِالظَّالِمِينَ (٢٤٦)

وَقَالَ لَهُمْ نَبِيُّهُمْ إِنَّ اللَّهَ قَدْ بَعَثَ لَكُمْ طَالُوتَ مَلِكًا قَالُوا أَنَّى يَكُونُ لَهُ الْمُلْكُ عَلَيْنَا وَنَحْنُ أَحَقُّ بِالْمُلْكِ مِنْهُ وَلَمْ يُؤْتَ سَعَةً مِنَ الْمَالِ قَالَ إِنَّ اللَّهَ اصْطَفَاهُ عَلَيْكُمْ وَزَادَهُ بَسْطَةً فِي الْعِلْمِ وَالْجِسْمِ وَاللَّهُ يُؤْتِي مُلْكَهُ مَنْ يَشَاءُ وَاللَّهُ وَاسِعٌ عَلِيمٌ (٢٤٧)

وَقَالَ لَهُمْ نَبِيُّهُمْ إِنَّ آيَةَ مُلْكِهِ أَنْ يَأْتِيَكُمُ التَّابُوتُ فِيهِ سَكِينَةٌ مِنْ رَبِّكُمْ وَبَقِيَّةٌ مِمَّا تَرَكَ آلُ مُوسَى وَآلُ هَارُونَ تَحْمِلُهُ الْمَلَائِكَةُ إِنَّ فِي ذَلِكَ لَآيَةً لَكُمْ إِنْ كُنْتُمْ مُؤْمِنِينَ (٢٤٨)

2. The Cow

said: And what reason have we that we should not fight in God's way and we have indeed been deprived of our homes and our children? But when fighting was ordained for them, they tamed back, except a few of them. And God is Knower of the wrongdoers.

2:247. And their prophet said to them: Surely God has raised Saul to be a king over you. They said: How can he have kingdom over us while we have a greater right to kingdom than he, and he has not been granted abundance of wealth? He said: Surely God has chosen him above you, and has increased him abundantly in knowledge and physique. And God grants His kingdom to whom He pleases. And God is Ample-giving, Knowing.

2:248. And their prophet said to them: Surely the sign of his kingdom is that there shall come to you the hearts in which there is tranquillity from your Lord and the best of what the followers of Moses and the followers of Aaron have left, the angels bearing it. Surely there is a sign in this for you if you are believers.

* * *

2:249. So when Saul set out with the forces, he said: Surely God will try you with a river. Whoever drinks from it, he is not of me, and whoever tastes it not, he is surely of me, except he who takes a handful with his hand, But they drank of it save a few of them. So when he had crossed it, he and those who believed with him, they said: We have to-day no power against Goliath and his forces. Those who were sure that they would meet their Lord said: How often has a small party vanquished a numerous host by God's permission! And God is with the steadfast.

2:250. And when they went out against

2. The Cow

Goliath and his forces, they said: Our Lord, pour out patience on us and make our steps firm and help us against the disbelieving people.

2:251. So they put them to flight by God's permission. And David slew Goliath, and God gave him kingdom and wisdom, and taught him of what He pleased. And were it not for God's repelling some men by others, the earth would certainly be in a state of disorder: but God is Full of grace to the worlds.

2:252. These are the messages of God -- We recite them to thee with truth; and surely thou art of the messengers.

* * *

2:253. We have made some of these messengers to excel others. Among them are they to whom God spoke, and some of them He exalted by (many) degrees of rank. And We gave clear arguments to Jesus son of Mary, and strengthened him with the Holy Spirit. And if God had pleased, those after them would not have fought one with another after clear arguments had come to them, but they disagreed; so some of them believed and some of them denied. And if God had pleased they would nor have fought one with another, but God does what He intends.

* * *

2:254. O you who believe, spend out of what We have given you before the day comes in which there is no bargaining, nor friendship, nor intercession. And the disbelievers -- they are the wrongdoers.

2:255. God -- there is no god but He, the Ever-living, the Self-subsisting by Whom all subsist. Slumber overtakes Him not, nor sleep. To Him belongs whatever is in the heavens and whatever is in the earth. Who is he that can intercede with Him but by His permission? He knows what is before

(٢٥٠) فَهَزَمُوهُم بِإِذْنِ اللَّهِ وَقَتَلَ دَاوُودُ جَالُوتَ وَآتَاهُ اللَّهُ الْمُلْكَ وَالْحِكْمَةَ وَعَلَّمَهُ مِمَّا يَشَاءُ وَلَوْلَا دَفْعُ اللَّهِ النَّاسَ بَعْضَهُم بِبَعْضٍ لَّفَسَدَتِ الْأَرْضُ وَلَٰكِنَّ اللَّهَ ذُو فَضْلٍ عَلَى الْعَالَمِينَ (٢٥١)

تِلْكَ آيَاتُ اللَّهِ نَتْلُوهَا عَلَيْكَ بِالْحَقِّ وَإِنَّكَ لَمِنَ الْمُرْسَلِينَ (٢٥٢)

تِلْكَ الرُّسُلُ فَضَّلْنَا بَعْضَهُمْ عَلَىٰ بَعْضٍ مِّنْهُم مَّن كَلَّمَ اللَّهُ وَرَفَعَ بَعْضَهُمْ دَرَجَاتٍ وَآتَيْنَا عِيسَى ابْنَ مَرْيَمَ الْبَيِّنَاتِ وَأَيَّدْنَاهُ بِرُوحِ الْقُدُسِ وَلَوْ شَاءَ اللَّهُ مَا اقْتَتَلَ الَّذِينَ مِن بَعْدِهِم مِّن بَعْدِ مَا جَاءَتْهُمُ الْبَيِّنَاتُ وَلَٰكِنِ اخْتَلَفُوا فَمِنْهُم مَّنْ آمَنَ وَمِنْهُم مَّن كَفَرَ وَلَوْ شَاءَ اللَّهُ مَا اقْتَتَلُوا وَلَٰكِنَّ اللَّهَ يَفْعَلُ مَا يُرِيدُ (٢٥٣)

يَا أَيُّهَا الَّذِينَ آمَنُوا أَنفِقُوا مِمَّا رَزَقْنَاكُم مِّن قَبْلِ أَن يَأْتِيَ يَوْمٌ لَّا بَيْعٌ فِيهِ وَلَا خُلَّةٌ وَلَا شَفَاعَةٌ وَالْكَافِرُونَ هُمُ الظَّالِمُونَ (٢٥٤)

اللَّهُ لَا إِلَٰهَ إِلَّا هُوَ الْحَيُّ الْقَيُّومُ لَا تَأْخُذُهُ سِنَةٌ وَلَا نَوْمٌ لَّهُ مَا فِي السَّمَاوَاتِ وَمَا فِي الْأَرْضِ مَن ذَا الَّذِي يَشْفَعُ عِندَهُ إِلَّا بِإِذْنِهِ يَعْلَمُ مَا بَيْنَ أَيْدِيهِمْ وَمَا خَلْفَهُمْ وَلَا يُحِيطُونَ بِشَيْءٍ مِّنْ عِلْمِهِ إِلَّا بِمَا شَاءَ وَسِعَ كُرْسِيُّهُ السَّمَاوَاتِ وَالْأَرْضَ وَلَا يَئُودُهُ حِفْظُهُمَا وَهُوَ الْعَلِيُّ الْعَظِيمُ (٢٥٥)

لَا إِكْرَاهَ فِي الدِّينِ قَد تَّبَيَّنَ الرُّشْدُ مِنَ الْغَيِّ فَمَن يَكْفُرْ بِالطَّاغُوتِ وَيُؤْمِن بِاللَّهِ فَقَدِ اسْتَمْسَكَ بِالْعُرْوَةِ الْوُثْقَىٰ لَا

them and what is behind them. And they encompass nothing of His knowledge except what He pleases. His knowledge extends over the heavens and the earth, and the preservation of them both tires Him not. And He is the Most High, the Great.

2:256. There is no compulsion in religion -- the right way is indeed dearly distinct from error. So whoever disbelieves in the devil and believes in God, he indeed lays hold on the firmest handle which shall never break. And God is Hearing, Knowing.

2:257. God is the Friend of those who believe -- He brings them out of darkness into light. And those who disbelieve, their friends are the devils who take them out of light into darkness. They are the companions of the Fire; therein they abide.

* * *

2:258. Hast thou not thought of him who disputed with Abraham about his Lord, because God had given him kingdom? When Abraham said, My Lord is He who gives life and causes to die, he said: I give life and cause death. Abraham said: Surely God causes the sun to rise from the East, so do thou make it rise from the West. Thus he who disbelieved was confounded. And God guides not the unjust people.

2:259. Or like him who passed by a town, and it had fallen in upon its roofs. He said: When will God give it life after its death? So God caused him to die for a hundred years, then raised him. He said: How long hast thou tarried? He said: I have tarried a day, or part of a day. He said: Nay, thou hast tarried a hundred years; but look at thy food and drink -- years have not passed over it! And look at thy ass! And that We may make thee a sign to men. And look at the bones, how We set them together then clothe them

2. The Cow

with flesh. So when it became dear to him, he said: I know that God is Possessor of power over all things.

2:260. And when Abraham said, My Lord, show me how Thou givest life to the dead, He said: Dost thou not believe? He said: Yes, but that my heart may be at ease. He said: Then take four birds, then tame them to incline to thee, then place on every mountain a part of them, then call them, they will come to thee flying and know that God is Mighty, Wise.

* * *

2:261. The parable of those who spend their wealth in the way of God is as the parable of a grain growing seven ears, in every ear a hundred grains. And God multiplies (further) for whom He pleases. And God is Ample-giving, Knowing.

2:262. Those who spend their wealth in the way of God, then follow not up what they have spent with reproach or injury, their reward is with their Lord, and they shall have no fear nor shall they grieve.

2:263. A kind word with forgiveness is better than charity followed by injury. And God is Self-sufficient, Forbearing.

2:264. O you who believe, make not your charity worthless by reproach and injury, like him who spends his wealth to be seen of men and believes not in God and the Last Day. So His parable is as the parable of a smooth rock with earth upon it, then heavy rain falls upon it, so it leaves it bare They are not able to gain anything of that which they earn. And God guides not the disbelieving people.

2:265. And the parable of those who spend their wealth to seek God's pleasure and for the strengthening of their so it is as the parable of a garden on elevated ground, upon which heavy rain falls, so it brings forth its fruit twofold; but if heavy rain falls not on

2. The Cow

it, light rain (suffices). And God is Seer of what you do.

2:266. Does one of you like to have a garden of palms and vines with streams flowing in it -- he has therein all kinds of fruits -- and old age has overtaken him and he has weak offspring; when (lo!) a whirlwind with fire in it smites it so it becomes blasted. Thus God makes the messages clear to you that you may reflect.

* * *

2:267. O you who believe, spend of the good things that you earn and of that which We bring forth for you out of the earth, and aim not at the bad to spend thereof, while you would not take it yourselves unless you connive at it. And know that God is Self-sufficient, Praiseworthy.

2:268. The devil threatens you with poverty and enjoins you to be niggardly, and God promises you forgiveness from Himself and abundance. And. God is Ample-giving, Knowing:

2:269. He grants wisdom to whom He pleases. And whoever is granted wisdom, he indeed is given a great good. And none mind but men of understanding.

2:270. And whatever alms you give or (whatever) vow you vow, God surely knows it. And the wrong-doers shall have no helpers.

2:271. If you manifest charity, how excellent it is! And if you hide it and give it to the poor, it is good for you. And it will do away with some of your evil deeds; and God is Aware of what you do.

2:272. Their guidance is not thy duty, but God guides whom He pleases. And whatever good thing you spend, it is to your good. And you spend nor but to seek God's pleasure. And whatever good thing you spend, it will be paid back to you in full, and you

بِالْفَحْشَاءِ وَاللَّهُ يَعِدُكُمْ مَغْفِرَةً مِنْهُ وَفَضْلًا وَاللَّهُ وَاسِعٌ عَلِيمٌ (٢٦٨) يُؤْتِي الْحِكْمَةَ مَنْ يَشَاءُ وَمَنْ يُؤْتَ الْحِكْمَةَ فَقَدْ أُوتِيَ خَيْرًا كَثِيرًا وَمَا يَذَّكَّرُ إِلَّا أُولُو الْأَلْبَابِ (٢٦٩) وَمَا أَنْفَقْتُمْ مِنْ نَفَقَةٍ أَوْ نَذَرْتُمْ مِنْ نَذْرٍ فَإِنَّ اللَّهَ يَعْلَمُهُ وَمَا لِلظَّالِمِينَ مِنْ أَنْصَارٍ (٢٧٠) إِنْ تُبْدُوا الصَّدَقَاتِ فَنِعِمَّا هِيَ وَإِنْ تُخْفُوهَا وَتُؤْتُوهَا الْفُقَرَاءَ فَهُوَ خَيْرٌ لَكُمْ وَيُكَفِّرُ عَنْكُمْ مِنْ سَيِّئَاتِكُمْ وَاللَّهُ بِمَا تَعْمَلُونَ خَبِيرٌ (٢٧١) لَيْسَ عَلَيْكَ هُدَاهُمْ وَلَكِنَّ اللَّهَ يَهْدِي مَنْ يَشَاءُ وَمَا تُنْفِقُوا مِنْ خَيْرٍ فَلِأَنْفُسِكُمْ وَمَا تُنْفِقُونَ إِلَّا ابْتِغَاءَ وَجْهِ اللَّهِ وَمَا تُنْفِقُوا مِنْ خَيْرٍ يُوَفَّ إِلَيْكُمْ وَأَنْتُمْ لَا تُظْلَمُونَ (٢٧٢) لِلْفُقَرَاءِ الَّذِينَ أُحْصِرُوا فِي سَبِيلِ اللَّهِ لَا يَسْتَطِيعُونَ ضَرْبًا فِي الْأَرْضِ يَحْسَبُهُمُ الْجَاهِلُ أَغْنِيَاءَ مِنَ التَّعَفُّفِ تَعْرِفُهُمْ بِسِيمَاهُمْ لَا يَسْأَلُونَ النَّاسَ إِلْحَافًا وَمَا تُنْفِقُوا مِنْ خَيْرٍ فَإِنَّ اللَّهَ بِهِ عَلِيمٌ (٢٧٣) الَّذِينَ يُنْفِقُونَ أَمْوَالَهُمْ بِاللَّيْلِ وَالنَّهَارِ سِرًّا وَعَلَانِيَةً فَلَهُمْ أَجْرُهُمْ عِنْدَ رَبِّهِمْ وَلَا خَوْفٌ عَلَيْهِمْ وَلَا هُمْ يَحْزَنُونَ (٢٧٤) الَّذِينَ يَأْكُلُونَ الرِّبَا لَا يَقُومُونَ إِلَّا كَمَا يَقُومُ الَّذِي يَتَخَبَّطُهُ الشَّيْطَانُ مِنَ الْمَسِّ ذَلِكَ بِأَنَّهُمْ قَالُوا إِنَّمَا الْبَيْعُ مِثْلُ الرِّبَا وَأَحَلَّ اللَّهُ الْبَيْعَ وَحَرَّمَ الرِّبَا فَمَنْ جَاءَهُ مَوْعِظَةٌ مِنْ رَبِّهِ فَانْتَهَى فَلَهُ مَا سَلَفَ وَأَمْرُهُ إِلَى اللَّهِ وَمَنْ عَادَ فَأُولَئِكَ أَصْحَابُ النَّارِ هُمْ فِيهَا

will not be wronged.

2:273. (Charity) is for the poor who are confined in the way of God, they cannot go about in the land; the ignorant man thinks them to be rich on account of (their) abstaining (from begging) Thou canst recognize them by their mark -- they beg not of men importunately. And whatever good thing you spend, surely God is Knower of it.

* * *

2:274. Those who spend their wealth by night and day, privately and publicly, their reward is with their Lord and they have no fear, nor shall they grieve.

2:275. Those who swallow usury cannot arise except as he arises whom the devil prostrates by (his) touch. That is because they say, Trading is only like usury. And Allah has allowed trading and forbidden usury. To whomsoever then the admonition has come from his Lord, and he desists, he shall have what has already passed. And his affair is in the hands of Allah. And whoever returns (to it) — these are the companions of the Fire: therein they will abide.

2:276. God will blot out usury, and He causes charity to prosper. And God loves not any ungrateful sinner.

2:277. Those who believe and do good deeds and keep up prayer and pay the poor-rate -- their reward is with their Lord; and they have no fear, nor shall they grieve.

2:278. O you who believe, keep your duty to God and relinquish what remains (due) from usury, if you are believers.

2:279. But if you do (it) not, then be apprised of war from God and His Messenger; and if you repent, then you shall have your capital. Wrong not, and you shall not be wronged.

2:280. And if (the debtor) is in

خَالِدُونَ (٢٧٥)
يَمْحَقُ اللَّهُ الرِّبَا وَيُرْبِي الصَّدَقَاتِ وَاللَّهُ لَا يُحِبُّ كُلَّ كَفَّارٍ أَثِيمٍ (٢٧٦)
إِنَّ الَّذِينَ آمَنُوا وَعَمِلُوا الصَّالِحَاتِ وَأَقَامُوا الصَّلَاةَ وَآتَوُا الزَّكَاةَ لَهُمْ أَجْرُهُمْ عِنْدَ رَبِّهِمْ وَلَا خَوْفٌ عَلَيْهِمْ وَلَا هُمْ يَحْزَنُونَ (٢٧٧)
يَا أَيُّهَا الَّذِينَ آمَنُوا اتَّقُوا اللَّهَ وَذَرُوا مَا بَقِيَ مِنَ الرِّبَا إِنْ كُنْتُمْ مُؤْمِنِينَ (٢٧٨)
فَإِنْ لَمْ تَفْعَلُوا فَأْذَنُوا بِحَرْبٍ مِنَ اللَّهِ وَرَسُولِهِ وَإِنْ تُبْتُمْ فَلَكُمْ رُءُوسُ أَمْوَالِكُمْ لَا تَظْلِمُونَ وَلَا تُظْلَمُونَ (٢٧٩)
وَإِنْ كَانَ ذُو عُسْرَةٍ فَنَظِرَةٌ إِلَى مَيْسَرَةٍ وَأَنْ تَصَدَّقُوا خَيْرٌ لَكُمْ إِنْ كُنْتُمْ تَعْلَمُونَ (٢٨٠)
وَاتَّقُوا يَوْمًا تُرْجَعُونَ فِيهِ إِلَى اللَّهِ ثُمَّ تُوَفَّى كُلُّ نَفْسٍ مَا كَسَبَتْ وَهُمْ لَا يُظْلَمُونَ (٢٨١)
يَا أَيُّهَا الَّذِينَ آمَنُوا إِذَا تَدَايَنْتُمْ بِدَيْنٍ إِلَى أَجَلٍ مُسَمًّى فَاكْتُبُوهُ وَلْيَكْتُبْ بَيْنَكُمْ كَاتِبٌ بِالْعَدْلِ وَلَا يَأْبَ كَاتِبٌ أَنْ يَكْتُبَ كَمَا عَلَّمَهُ اللَّهُ فَلْيَكْتُبْ وَلْيُمْلِلِ الَّذِي عَلَيْهِ الْحَقُّ وَلْيَتَّقِ اللَّهَ رَبَّهُ وَلَا يَبْخَسْ مِنْهُ شَيْئًا فَإِنْ كَانَ الَّذِي عَلَيْهِ الْحَقُّ سَفِيهًا أَوْ ضَعِيفًا أَوْ لَا يَسْتَطِيعُ أَنْ يُمِلَّ هُوَ فَلْيُمْلِلْ وَلِيُّهُ بِالْعَدْلِ وَاسْتَشْهِدُوا شَهِيدَيْنِ مِنْ رِجَالِكُمْ فَإِنْ لَمْ يَكُونَا رَجُلَيْنِ فَرَجُلٌ وَامْرَأَتَانِ مِمَّنْ تَرْضَوْنَ مِنَ الشُّهَدَاءِ أَنْ تَضِلَّ إِحْدَاهُمَا فَتُذَكِّرَ إِحْدَاهُمَا الْأُخْرَى وَلَا يَأْبَ الشُّهَدَاءُ إِذَا مَا دُعُوا وَلَا تَسْأَمُوا أَنْ تَكْتُبُوهُ صَغِيرًا أَوْ كَبِيرًا إِلَى أَجَلِهِ

2. The Cow

straitness, let there be postponement till (he is in) ease. And that you remit (it) as alms is better for you, if you only knew.

2:281. And guard yourselves against a day in which you will be returned to God. Then every soul will be paid in full what it has earned, and they will not be wronged.

* * *

2:282. O you who believe, when you contract a debt for a fixed time, write it down. And let a scribe write it down between you with fairness; nor should the scribe refuse to write as God has taught him, so let him write. And let him who owes the debt dictate, and he should observe his duty to God, his Lord, and not diminish any thing from it. But if he who owes the debt is unsound in understanding or weak, or (if) he is not able to dictate himself, let his guardian dictate with fairness. And call to witness from among your men two witnesses; but if there are not two men, then one man and two women from among those whom you choose to be witnesses, so that if one of the two errs, the one may remind the other. And the witnesses must not refuse when they are summoned. And be not averse to writing it whether it is small or large along with the time of its falling due. This is more equitable in the sight of God and makes testimony surer and the best way to keep away from doubts. But when it is ready merchandise which you give and take among yourselves from hand to hand, there is no blame on you in not writing it down. And have witnesses when you sell one to another. And let no harm be done to the scribe or to the witnesses. And if you do (it), then surely it is a transgression on your part. And keep your duty to God. And God teaches you. And God is Knower of all things.

ذَلِكُمْ أَقْسَطُ عِنْدَ اللهِ وَأَقْوَمُ لِلشَّهَادَةِ وَأَدْنَى أَلَّا تَرْتَابُوا إِلَّا أَنْ تَكُونَ تِجَارَةً حَاضِرَةً تُدِيرُونَهَا بَيْنَكُمْ فَلَيْسَ عَلَيْكُمْ جُنَاحٌ أَلَّا تَكْتُبُوهَا وَأَشْهِدُوا إِذَا تَبَايَعْتُمْ وَلَا يُضَارَّ كَاتِبٌ وَلَا شَهِيدٌ وَإِنْ تَفْعَلُوا فَإِنَّهُ فُسُوقٌ بِكُمْ وَاتَّقُوا اللهَ وَيُعَلِّمُكُمُ اللهُ وَاللهُ بِكُلِّ شَيْءٍ عَلِيمٌ (٢٨٢)

وَإِنْ كُنْتُمْ عَلَى سَفَرٍ وَلَمْ تَجِدُوا كَاتِبًا فَرِهَانٌ مَقْبُوضَةٌ فَإِنْ أَمِنَ بَعْضُكُمْ بَعْضًا فَلْيُؤَدِّ الَّذِي اؤْتُمِنَ أَمَانَتَهُ وَلْيَتَّقِ اللهَ رَبَّهُ وَلَا تَكْتُمُوا الشَّهَادَةَ وَمَنْ يَكْتُمْهَا فَإِنَّهُ آثِمٌ قَلْبُهُ وَاللهُ بِمَا تَعْمَلُونَ عَلِيمٌ (٢٨٣)

لِلَّهِ مَا فِي السَّمَاوَاتِ وَمَا فِي الْأَرْضِ وَإِنْ تُبْدُوا مَا فِي أَنْفُسِكُمْ أَوْ تُخْفُوهُ يُحَاسِبْكُمْ بِهِ اللهُ فَيَغْفِرُ لِمَنْ يَشَاءُ وَيُعَذِّبُ مَنْ يَشَاءُ وَاللهُ عَلَى كُلِّ شَيْءٍ قَدِيرٌ (٢٨٤)

آمَنَ الرَّسُولُ بِمَا أُنْزِلَ إِلَيْهِ مِنْ رَبِّهِ وَالْمُؤْمِنُونَ كُلٌّ آمَنَ بِاللهِ وَمَلَائِكَتِهِ وَكُتُبِهِ وَرُسُلِهِ لَا نُفَرِّقُ بَيْنَ أَحَدٍ مِنْ رُسُلِهِ وَقَالُوا سَمِعْنَا وَأَطَعْنَا غُفْرَانَكَ رَبَّنَا وَإِلَيْكَ الْمَصِيرُ (٢٨٥)

لَا يُكَلِّفُ اللهُ نَفْسًا إِلَّا وُسْعَهَا لَهَا مَا كَسَبَتْ وَعَلَيْهَا مَا اكْتَسَبَتْ رَبَّنَا لَا تُؤَاخِذْنَا إِنْ نَسِينَا أَوْ أَخْطَأْنَا رَبَّنَا وَلَا تَحْمِلْ عَلَيْنَا إِصْرًا كَمَا حَمَلْتَهُ عَلَى الَّذِينَ مِنْ قَبْلِنَا رَبَّنَا وَلَا تُحَمِّلْنَا مَا لَا طَاقَةَ لَنَا بِهِ وَاعْفُ عَنَّا وَاغْفِرْ لَنَا وَارْحَمْنَا أَنْتَ مَوْلَانَا فَانْصُرْنَا عَلَى الْقَوْمِ الْكَافِرِينَ (٢٨٦)

2:283. And if you are on a journey and you cannot find a scribe, a security may be taken into possession. But if one of you trusts another, then he who is trusted should deliver his trust, and let him keep his duty to God, his Lord. And conceal not testimony. And whoever conceals it, his heart is surely sinful. And God is Knower of what you do.

* * *

2:284. To God belongs whatever is in the heavens and whatever is in the earth. And whether you manifest what is in your minds or hide it, God will call you to account according to it. So He forgives whom He pleases and chastises whom He pleases. And God is Possessor of power over all things.

2:285. The Messenger believes in what has been revealed to him from his Lord, and (so do) the believers. They all believe in God and His angels and His Books and His messengers. We make no difference between any of His messengers. And they say: We hear and obey; our Lord, Thy forgiveness (do we crave), and to Thee is the eventual course.

2:286. God imposes not on any soul a duty beyond its scope. For it is that which it earns (of good) and against it that which it works (of evil). Our Lord, punish us not if we forget or make a mistake. Our Lord, do not lay on us a burden as Thou didst lay on those before us. Our Lord, impose not on us (afflictions) which we have not the strength to bear. And pardon us! And grant us protection! And have mercy on us! Thou art our Patron, so grant us victory over the disbelieving people.

3. The Family of Amran

In the name of Allah, the Beneficent, the Merciful.

3. The Family of Amran

3:1. I, Allah, am the best Knower,

3:2. Allah, (there is) no god but He, the Ever-living, the Self-subsisting, by Whom all subsist.

3:3. He has revealed to thee the Book with truth, verifying that which is before it, and He revealed the Torah and the Gospel aforetime,

3:4. a guidance for the people, and He sent the Discrimination. Those who disbelieve in the messages of Allah for them is a severe chastisement. And Allah is Mighty, the Lord of retribution.

3:5. Surely nothing in the earth or in the heaven is hidden from Allah.

3:6. He it is Who shapes you in the wombs as He pleases. There is no god but He, the Mighty, the Wise.

3:7. He it is Who has revealed the Book to thee; some of its verses are decisive -- they are the basis of the Book -- and others are allegorical. Then those in whose hearts is perversity follow the part of it which is allegorical, seeking to mislead, and seeking to give it (their own) interpretation. And none knows its interpretation save Allah, and those firmly rooted in knowledge. They say We believe in it, it is all from our Lord. And none mind except men of understanding.

3:8. Our Lord, make not our hearts to deviate after Thou hast guided us and grant us mercy from Thee; surely Thou art the most liberal Giver.

3:9. Our Lord, surely Thou art the Gatherer of men on a day about which there is no doubt. Surely Allah will not fail in (His) promise.

* * *

3:10. Those who disbelieve, neither their wealth nor their children will avail them aught against Allah. And they will be fuel for fire --

3:11. As was the case of the people of Pharaoh, and those before them They rejected Our messages, so Allah

الم (١)

اللَّهُ لَا إِلَهَ إِلَّا هُوَ الْحَيُّ الْقَيُّومُ (٢)

نَزَّلَ عَلَيْكَ الْكِتَابَ بِالْحَقِّ مُصَدِّقًا لِمَا بَيْنَ يَدَيْهِ وَأَنْزَلَ التَّوْرَاةَ وَالْإِنْجِيلَ (٣)

مِنْ قَبْلُ هُدًى لِلنَّاسِ وَأَنْزَلَ الْفُرْقَانَ إِنَّ الَّذِينَ كَفَرُوا بِآيَاتِ اللَّهِ لَهُمْ عَذَابٌ شَدِيدٌ وَاللَّهُ عَزِيزٌ ذُو انْتِقَامٍ (٤)

إِنَّ اللَّهَ لَا يَخْفَى عَلَيْهِ شَيْءٌ فِي الْأَرْضِ وَلَا فِي السَّمَاءِ (٥)

هُوَ الَّذِي يُصَوِّرُكُمْ فِي الْأَرْحَامِ كَيْفَ يَشَاءُ لَا إِلَهَ إِلَّا هُوَ الْعَزِيزُ الْحَكِيمُ (٦)

هُوَ الَّذِي أَنْزَلَ عَلَيْكَ الْكِتَابَ مِنْهُ آيَاتٌ مُحْكَمَاتٌ هُنَّ أُمُّ الْكِتَابِ وَأُخَرُ مُتَشَابِهَاتٌ فَأَمَّا الَّذِينَ فِي قُلُوبِهِمْ زَيْغٌ فَيَتَّبِعُونَ مَا تَشَابَهَ مِنْهُ ابْتِغَاءَ الْفِتْنَةِ وَابْتِغَاءَ تَأْوِيلِهِ وَمَا يَعْلَمُ تَأْوِيلَهُ إِلَّا اللَّهُ وَالرَّاسِخُونَ فِي الْعِلْمِ يَقُولُونَ آمَنَّا بِهِ كُلٌّ مِنْ عِنْدِ رَبِّنَا وَمَا يَذَّكَّرُ إِلَّا أُولُو الْأَلْبَابِ (٧)

رَبَّنَا لَا تُزِغْ قُلُوبَنَا بَعْدَ إِذْ هَدَيْتَنَا وَهَبْ لَنَا مِنْ لَدُنْكَ رَحْمَةً إِنَّكَ أَنْتَ الْوَهَّابُ (٨)

رَبَّنَا إِنَّكَ جَامِعُ النَّاسِ لِيَوْمٍ لَا رَيْبَ فِيهِ إِنَّ اللَّهَ لَا يُخْلِفُ الْمِيعَادَ (٩)

إِنَّ الَّذِينَ كَفَرُوا لَنْ تُغْنِيَ عَنْهُمْ أَمْوَالُهُمْ وَلَا أَوْلَادُهُمْ مِنَ اللَّهِ شَيْئًا وَأُولَئِكَ هُمْ وَقُودُ النَّارِ (١٠)

كَدَأْبِ آلِ فِرْعَوْنَ وَالَّذِينَ مِنْ قَبْلِهِمْ كَذَّبُوا بِآيَاتِنَا فَأَخَذَهُمُ اللَّهُ بِذُنُوبِهِمْ وَاللَّهُ شَدِيدُ الْعِقَابِ (١١)

قُلْ لِلَّذِينَ كَفَرُوا سَتُغْلَبُونَ وَتُحْشَرُونَ إِلَى جَهَنَّمَ وَبِئْسَ الْمِهَادُ (١٢)

3. The Family of Amran

destroyed them on account of their sins. And Allah is Severe in requiting (evil).

3:12. Say to those who disbelieve You shall be vanquished, and driven together to hell; and evil is the resting-place.

3:13. Indeed there was a sign for you in the two hosts (which) met together in encounter -- one party fighting in the way of Allah and the other disbelieving, whom they saw twice as many as themselves with the sight of the eye. And Allah strengthens with His aid whom He pleases. There is a lesson in this for those who have eyes.

3:14. Fair-seeming to men is made the love of desires, of women and sons and hoarded treasures of gold and silver and well-bred horses and cattle and tilth (fields). This is the provision of the life of this world. And Allah -- with Him is the good goal (of life).

3:15. Say: Shall I tell you of what is better than these? For those who guard against evil are Gardens with their Lord, in which rivers flow, to abide in them, and pure companions and Allah's goodly pleasure. And Allah is Seer of the servants.

3:16. Those who say: Our Lord, we believe, so forgive our sins and save us from the chastisement of the fire.

3:17. The patient and the truthful, and the obedient, and those who spend and those who ask Divine protection in the morning times.

3:18. Allah bears witness that there is no god but He, and (so do) the angels and those possessed of knowledge, maintaining justice. There is no god but He, the Mighty, the Wise.

3:19. Surely the (true) religion with Allah is Islam. And those who were given the Book differed only after knowledge had come to them, out of envy among themselves. And whoever disbelieves in the messages of Allah --

قَدْ كَانَ لَكُمْ آيَةٌ فِي فِئَتَيْنِ الْتَقَتَا فِئَةٌ تُقَاتِلُ فِي سَبِيلِ اللَّهِ وَأُخْرَى كَافِرَةٌ يَرَوْنَهُمْ مِثْلَيْهِمْ رَأْيَ الْعَيْنِ وَاللَّهُ يُؤَيِّدُ بِنَصْرِهِ مَنْ يَشَاءُ إِنَّ فِي ذَلِكَ لَعِبْرَةً لِأُولِي الْأَبْصَارِ (١٣)

زُيِّنَ لِلنَّاسِ حُبُّ الشَّهَوَاتِ مِنَ النِّسَاءِ وَالْبَنِينَ وَالْقَنَاطِيرِ الْمُقَنْطَرَةِ مِنَ الذَّهَبِ وَالْفِضَّةِ وَالْخَيْلِ الْمُسَوَّمَةِ وَالْأَنْعَامِ وَالْحَرْثِ ذَلِكَ مَتَاعُ الْحَيَاةِ الدُّنْيَا وَاللَّهُ عِنْدَهُ حُسْنُ الْمَآبِ (١٤)

قُلْ أَؤُنَبِّئُكُمْ بِخَيْرٍ مِنْ ذَلِكُمْ لِلَّذِينَ اتَّقَوْا عِنْدَ رَبِّهِمْ جَنَّاتٌ تَجْرِي مِنْ تَحْتِهَا الْأَنْهَارُ خَالِدِينَ فِيهَا وَأَزْوَاجٌ مُطَهَّرَةٌ وَرِضْوَانٌ مِنَ اللَّهِ وَاللَّهُ بَصِيرٌ بِالْعِبَادِ (١٥)

الَّذِينَ يَقُولُونَ رَبَّنَا إِنَّنَا آمَنَّا فَاغْفِرْ لَنَا ذُنُوبَنَا وَقِنَا عَذَابَ النَّارِ (١٦)

الصَّابِرِينَ وَالصَّادِقِينَ وَالْقَانِتِينَ وَالْمُنْفِقِينَ وَالْمُسْتَغْفِرِينَ بِالْأَسْحَارِ (١٧)

شَهِدَ اللَّهُ أَنَّهُ لَا إِلَهَ إِلَّا هُوَ وَالْمَلَائِكَةُ وَأُولُو الْعِلْمِ قَائِمًا بِالْقِسْطِ لَا إِلَهَ إِلَّا هُوَ الْعَزِيزُ الْحَكِيمُ (١٨)

إِنَّ الدِّينَ عِنْدَ اللَّهِ الْإِسْلَامُ وَمَا اخْتَلَفَ الَّذِينَ أُوتُوا الْكِتَابَ إِلَّا مِنْ بَعْدِ مَا جَاءَهُمُ الْعِلْمُ بَغْيًا بَيْنَهُمْ وَمَنْ يَكْفُرْ بِآيَاتِ اللَّهِ فَإِنَّ اللَّهَ سَرِيعُ الْحِسَابِ (١٩)

فَإِنْ حَاجُّوكَ فَقُلْ أَسْلَمْتُ وَجْهِيَ لِلَّهِ وَمَنِ اتَّبَعَنِ وَقُلْ لِلَّذِينَ أُوتُوا الْكِتَابَ وَالْأُمِّيِّينَ أَأَسْلَمْتُمْ فَإِنْ أَسْلَمُوا فَقَدِ اهْتَدَوْا وَإِنْ تَوَلَّوْا فَإِنَّمَا عَلَيْكَ الْبَلَاغُ وَاللَّهُ بَصِيرٌ بِالْعِبَادِ (٢٠)

إِنَّ الَّذِينَ يَكْفُرُونَ بِآيَاتِ اللَّهِ وَيَقْتُلُونَ

3. The Family of Amran

Allah indeed is Quick at reckoning.

3:20. But if they dispute with thee say: I submit myself entirely to Allah and (so does) he who follows me. And say to those who have been given the Book and the Unlearned (people) Do you submit yourselves? If they submit, then indeed they follow the right way; and if they turn back, thy duty is only to deliver the message. And Allah is Seer of the servants.

* * *

3:21. Those who disbelieve in the messages of Allah and would slay the prophets unjustly and slay those among men who enjoin justice, announce to them a painful chastisement.

3:22. Those are they whose works will be of no avail in this world and the Hereafter, and they will have no helpers.

3:23. Hast thou not seen those who are given a portion of the Book? They are invited to the Book of Allah that it may decide between them, then a party of them turn back and they withdraw.

3:24. This is because they say: The Fire shall not touch us but for a few days; and that which they forge deceives them regarding their religion.

3:25. Then how will it be when We gather them together on a day about which there is no doubt. And every soul shall be fully paid what it has earned, and they shall not be wronged?

3:26. Say O Allah, Owner of the Kingdom, Thou givest the kingdom to whom Thou pleasest, and takest away the kingdom from whom Thou pleasest, and Thou exaltest whom Thou pleasest and abasest whom Thou pleasest. In Thine hand is the good. Surely, Thou art Possessor of power over all things.

3:27. Thou makest the night to pass into the day and Thou makest the day to pass into the night; and Thou

3. The Family of Amran

bringest forth the living from the dead and Thou bringest forth the dead from the living; and Thou givest sustenance to whom Thou pleasest without measure.

3:28. Let not the believers take the disbelievers for friends rather than believers. And whoever does this has no connection with Allah -- except that you guard yourselves against them, guarding carefully. And Allah cautions you against His retribution. And to Allah is the eventual coming.

3:29. Say: Whether you hide what is in your hearts or manifest it, Allah knows it. And He knows whatever is in the heavens and whatever is in the earth. And Allah is Possessor of power over all things.

3:30. On the day when every soul will find present that which it has done of good; and that which it has done of evil -- it will wish that between it and that (evil) there were a long distance. And Allah cautions you against His retribution. And Allah is Compassionate to the servants.

***

3:31. Say: If you love Allah, follow me: Allah will love you, and grant you protection from your sins. And Allah is Forgiving, Merciful.

3:32. Say: Obey Allah and the Messenger; but if they turn back, Allah surely loves not the disbelievers.

3:33. Truly Allah chose Adam and Noah and the descendants of Abraham and the descendants of Amran above the nations,

3:34. Offspring, one of the other. And Allah is Hearing, Knowing.

3:35. When a woman of Amran said: My Lord, I vow to Thee what is in my womb, to be devoted (to Thy service), so accept (it) from me surely Thou, only Thou, art the Hearing, the Knowing.

3:36. So when she brought it forth, she said: My Lord, I have brought it forth a female -- and Allah knew best what she brought forth -- and the male is not like the female, and I have named it Mary, and I commend her and her offspring into Thy protection from the accursed devil.

3:37. So her Lord accepted her with a goodly acceptance and made her grow up a goodly growing, and gave her into the charge of Zacharias. Whenever Zacharias entered the sanctuary to (see) her, he found food with her. He said: O Mary, whence comes this to thee? She said: It is from Allah. Surely Allah gives to whom He pleases without measure.

3:38. There did Zacharias pray to his Lord. He said: My Lord, grant me from Thee goodly offspring; surely Thou art the Hearer of prayer.

3:39. So the angels called to him as he stood praying in the sanctuary Allah gives thee the good news of John, verifying a word from Allah, and honourable and chaste and a prophet from among the good ones.

3:40. He said: My Lord, how can I have a son when old age has already come upon me, and my wife is barren? He said: Even thus does Allah do what He pleases.

3:41. He said: My Lord, appoint a sign for me. Said He: Thy sign is that thou speak not to men for three days except by signs. And remember thy Lord much and glorify (Him) in the evening and early morning.

* * *

3:42. And when the angels said: O Mary, surely Allah has chosen thee and purified thee and chosen thee above the women of the world.

3:43. O Mary, be obedient to thy Lord and humble thyself and bow down with those who bow.

3:44. This is of the tidings of things

وَضَعَتْهَا أُنْثَىٰ وَاللَّهُ أَعْلَمُ بِمَا وَضَعَتْ وَلَيْسَ الذَّكَرُ كَالْأُنْثَىٰ وَإِنِّي سَمَّيْتُهَا مَرْيَمَ وَإِنِّي أُعِيذُهَا بِكَ وَذُرِّيَّتَهَا مِنَ الشَّيْطَانِ الرَّجِيمِ (٣٦)

فَتَقَبَّلَهَا رَبُّهَا بِقَبُولٍ حَسَنٍ وَأَنْبَتَهَا نَبَاتًا حَسَنًا وَكَفَّلَهَا زَكَرِيَّا كُلَّمَا دَخَلَ عَلَيْهَا زَكَرِيَّا الْمِحْرَابَ وَجَدَ عِنْدَهَا رِزْقًا قَالَ يَا مَرْيَمُ أَنَّىٰ لَكِ هَٰذَا قَالَتْ هُوَ مِنْ عِنْدِ اللَّهِ إِنَّ اللَّهَ يَرْزُقُ مَنْ يَشَاءُ بِغَيْرِ حِسَابٍ (٣٧)

هُنَالِكَ دَعَا زَكَرِيَّا رَبَّهُ قَالَ رَبِّ هَبْ لِي مِنْ لَدُنْكَ ذُرِّيَّةً طَيِّبَةً إِنَّكَ سَمِيعُ الدُّعَاءِ (٣٨)

فَنَادَتْهُ الْمَلَائِكَةُ وَهُوَ قَائِمٌ يُصَلِّي فِي الْمِحْرَابِ أَنَّ اللَّهَ يُبَشِّرُكَ بِيَحْيَىٰ مُصَدِّقًا بِكَلِمَةٍ مِنَ اللَّهِ وَسَيِّدًا وَحَصُورًا وَنَبِيًّا مِنَ الصَّالِحِينَ (٣٩)

قَالَ رَبِّ أَنَّىٰ يَكُونُ لِي غُلَامٌ وَقَدْ بَلَغَنِيَ الْكِبَرُ وَامْرَأَتِي عَاقِرٌ قَالَ كَذَٰلِكَ اللَّهُ يَفْعَلُ مَا يَشَاءُ (٤٠)

قَالَ رَبِّ اجْعَلْ لِي آيَةً قَالَ آيَتُكَ أَلَّا تُكَلِّمَ النَّاسَ ثَلَاثَةَ أَيَّامٍ إِلَّا رَمْزًا وَاذْكُرْ رَبَّكَ كَثِيرًا وَسَبِّحْ بِالْعَشِيِّ وَالْإِبْكَارِ (٤١)

وَإِذْ قَالَتِ الْمَلَائِكَةُ يَا مَرْيَمُ إِنَّ اللَّهَ اصْطَفَاكِ وَطَهَّرَكِ وَاصْطَفَاكِ عَلَىٰ نِسَاءِ الْعَالَمِينَ (٤٢)

يَا مَرْيَمُ اقْنُتِي لِرَبِّكِ وَاسْجُدِي وَارْكَعِي مَعَ الرَّاكِعِينَ (٤٣)

ذَٰلِكَ مِنْ أَنْبَاءِ الْغَيْبِ نُوحِيهِ إِلَيْكَ وَمَا كُنْتَ لَدَيْهِمْ إِذْ يُلْقُونَ أَقْلَامَهُمْ أَيُّهُمْ يَكْفُلُ مَرْيَمَ وَمَا كُنْتَ لَدَيْهِمْ إِذْ يَخْتَصِمُونَ (٤٤)

3. The Family of Amran

unseen which We reveal to thee. And thou wast not with them when they cast their pens (to decide) which of them should have Mary in his charge, and thou wast not with them when they contended one with another.

3:45. When the angels said: O Mary, surely Allah gives thee good news with a word from Him (of one) whose name is the Messiah, Jesus, son of Mary, worthy of regard in this world and the Hereafter, and of those who are drawn nigh (to Allah),

3:46. And he will speak to the people when in the cradle and when of old age, and (he will be) one of the good ones.

3:47. She said: My Lord, how can I have a son and man has not yet touched me? He said: Even so; Allah creates what He pleases. When He decrees a matter, He only says to it, Be, and it is.

3:48. And He will teach him the Book and the Wisdom and the Torah and the Gospel:

3:49. And (make him) a messenger to the Children of Israel (saying) I have come to you with a sign from your Lord, that I determine for you out of dust the form of a bird, then I breathe into it and it becomes a bird with Allah's permission, and I heal the blind and the leprous, and bring the dead to life with Allah's permission; and I inform you of what you should eat and what you should store in your houses. Surely there is a sign in this for you, if you are believers.

3:50. And (I am) a verifier of that which is before me of the Torah, and I allow you part of that which was forbidden to you; and I have come to you with a sign from your Lord, so keep your duty to Allah and obey me.

3:51. Surely Allah is my Lord and your Lord, so serve Him. This is the right path.

3:52. But when Jesus perceived

3. The Family of Amran

disbelief on their part, he said Who will be my helpers in Allah's way? The disciples said We are Allah's helpers: we believe in Allah, and bear thou witness that we are submitting ones.

3:53. Our Lord, we believe in that which Thou hast revealed and we follow the messenger, so write us down with those who bear witness.

3:54. And (the Jews) planned and Allah (also) planned. And Allah is the best of planners.

* * *

3:55. When Allah said: O Jesus, I will cause thee to die and exalt thee in My presence and clear thee of those who disbelieve and make those who follow thee above those who disbelieve to the day of Resurrection. Then to Me is your return, so I shall decide between you concerning that wherein you differ.

3:56. Then as to those who disbelieve, I shall chastise them with severe chastisement in this world and the Hereafter, and they will have no helpers.

3:57. And as to those who believe and do good deeds, He will pay them fully their rewards. And Allah loves not the unjust.

3:58. This We recite to thee of the messages and the Reminder full of wisdom.

3:59. The likeness of Jesus with Allah is truly as the likeness of Adam. He created him from dust, then said to him, Be, and he was.

3:60. (This is) the truth from thy Lord, so be not of the disputers.

3:61. Whoever then disputes with thee in this matter after the knowledge that has come to thee, say: Come Let us call our sons and your sons and our women and your women and our people and your people, then let us be earnest in prayer, and invoke the curse of Allah on the liars.

3:62. Surely this is the true account, and

إِذْ قَالَ اللَّهُ يَا عِيسَى إِنِّي مُتَوَفِّيكَ وَرَافِعُكَ إِلَيَّ وَمُطَهِّرُكَ مِنَ الَّذِينَ كَفَرُوا وَجَاعِلُ الَّذِينَ اتَّبَعُوكَ فَوْقَ الَّذِينَ كَفَرُوا إِلَى يَوْمِ الْقِيَامَةِ ثُمَّ إِلَيَّ مَرْجِعُكُمْ فَأَحْكُمُ بَيْنَكُمْ فِيمَا كُنْتُمْ فِيهِ تَخْتَلِفُونَ (٥٥)

فَأَمَّا الَّذِينَ كَفَرُوا فَأُعَذِّبُهُمْ عَذَابًا شَدِيدًا فِي الدُّنْيَا وَالْآخِرَةِ وَمَا لَهُمْ مِنْ نَاصِرِينَ (٥٦)

وَأَمَّا الَّذِينَ آمَنُوا وَعَمِلُوا الصَّالِحَاتِ فَيُوَفِّيهِمْ أُجُورَهُمْ وَاللَّهُ لَا يُحِبُّ الظَّالِمِينَ (٥٧)

ذَلِكَ نَتْلُوهُ عَلَيْكَ مِنَ الْآيَاتِ وَالذِّكْرِ الْحَكِيمِ (٥٨)

إِنَّ مَثَلَ عِيسَى عِنْدَ اللَّهِ كَمَثَلِ آدَمَ خَلَقَهُ مِنْ تُرَابٍ ثُمَّ قَالَ لَهُ كُنْ فَيَكُونُ (٥٩)

الْحَقُّ مِنْ رَبِّكَ فَلَا تَكُنْ مِنَ الْمُمْتَرِينَ (٦٠)

فَمَنْ حَاجَّكَ فِيهِ مِنْ بَعْدِ مَا جَاءَكَ مِنَ الْعِلْمِ فَقُلْ تَعَالَوْا نَدْعُ أَبْنَاءَنَا وَأَبْنَاءَكُمْ وَنِسَاءَنَا وَنِسَاءَكُمْ وَأَنْفُسَنَا وَأَنْفُسَكُمْ ثُمَّ نَبْتَهِلْ فَنَجْعَلْ لَعْنَةَ اللَّهِ عَلَى الْكَاذِبِينَ (٦١)

إِنَّ هَذَا لَهُوَ الْقَصَصُ الْحَقُّ وَمَا مِنْ إِلَهٍ إِلَّا اللَّهُ وَإِنَّ اللَّهَ لَهُوَ الْعَزِيزُ الْحَكِيمُ (٦٢)

فَإِنْ تَوَلَّوْا فَإِنَّ اللَّهَ عَلِيمٌ بِالْمُفْسِدِينَ (٦٣)

قُلْ يَا أَهْلَ الْكِتَابِ تَعَالَوْا إِلَى كَلِمَةٍ سَوَاءٍ بَيْنَنَا وَبَيْنَكُمْ أَلَّا نَعْبُدَ إِلَّا اللَّهَ وَلَا نُشْرِكَ بِهِ شَيْئًا وَلَا يَتَّخِذَ بَعْضُنَا بَعْضًا أَرْبَابًا مِنْ دُونِ اللَّهِ فَإِنْ تَوَلَّوْا فَقُولُوا اشْهَدُوا بِأَنَّا مُسْلِمُونَ (٦٤)

there is no god but Allah. And Allah He surely is the Mighty, the Wise.

3:63. But if they turn away, then surely Allah knows the mischief-makers.

* * *

3:64. Say: O People of the Book, come to an equitable word between us and you, that we shall serve none but Allah and that we shall not associate aught with Him, and that some of us shall not take others for lords besides Allah. But if they turn away, then say: Bear witness, we are Muslims.

3:65. O People of the Book, why do you dispute about Abraham, when the Torah and the Gospel were not revealed till after him? Do you not understand?

3:66. Behold! You are they who disputed about that of which you had knowledge; why then do you dispute about that of which you have no knowledge? And Allah knows while you know not.

3:67. Abraham was not a Jew nor a Christian, but he was (an) upright (man), a Muslim; and he was not one of the polytheists.

3:68. The nearest of people to Abraham are surely those who follow him and this Prophet and those who believe. And Allah is the Friend of the believers.

3:69. A party of the People of the Book desire that they should lead you astray; and they lead not astray but themselves, and they perceive not.

3:70. O People of the Book, why do you disbelieve in the messages of Allah while you witness (their truth)?

3:71. O People of the Book, why do you confound the truth with falsehood, and hide the truth while you know?

* * *

3:72. And a party of the People of the Book say: Avow belief in that which has been revealed to those who believe, in the first part of the day, and

3. The Family of Amran

disbelieve in the latter part of it, perhaps they may turn back.

3:73. And believe not but in him who follows your religion. Say True guidance -- Allah's guidance -- is that one may be given the like of what you were given; or they would prevail on you in argument before your Lord. Say Grace is surely in Allah's hand. He gives it to whom He pleases. And Allah is Ample-giving, Knowing.

3:74. He specially chooses for His mercy whom He pleases. And Allah is the Lord of mighty grace.

3:75. And among the People of the Book there is he who, if thou entrust him with a heap of wealth, would pay it back to thee; and among them is he who, if thou entrust him with a dinar would not pay it back to thee, unless thou kept on demanding it. This is because they say there is no blame on us in the matter of the unlearned people and they forge a lie against Allah while they know.

3:76. Yea, whoever fulfils his promise and keeps his duty -- then Allah surely loves the dutiful.

3:77. Those who take a small price for the covenant of Allah and their own oaths -- they have no portion in the Hereafter, and Allah will not speak to them, nor will He look upon them on the day of Resurrection, nor will He purify them, and for them is a painful chastisement.

3:78. And there is certainly a party of them who lie about the Book that you may consider it to be (a part) of the Book while it is not (a part) of the Book; and they say, It is from Allah, while it is not from Allah; and they forge a lie against Allah whilst they know.

3:79. It is not meet for a mortal that Allah should give him the Book and the judgement and the prophethood, then he should say to men: Be my servants besides Allah's; but (he would

تَأْمَنْهُ بِدِينَارٍ لَا يُؤَدِّهِ إِلَيْكَ إِلَّا مَا دُمْتَ عَلَيْهِ قَائِمًا ذَلِكَ بِأَنَّهُمْ قَالُوا لَيْسَ عَلَيْنَا فِي الْأُمِّيِّينَ سَبِيلٌ وَيَقُولُونَ عَلَى اللَّهِ الْكَذِبَ وَهُمْ يَعْلَمُونَ (٧٥) بَلَى مَنْ أَوْفَى بِعَهْدِهِ وَاتَّقَى فَإِنَّ اللَّهَ يُحِبُّ الْمُتَّقِينَ (٧٦) إِنَّ الَّذِينَ يَشْتَرُونَ بِعَهْدِ اللَّهِ وَأَيْمَانِهِمْ ثَمَنًا قَلِيلًا أُولَئِكَ لَا خَلَاقَ لَهُمْ فِي الْآخِرَةِ وَلَا يُكَلِّمُهُمُ اللَّهُ وَلَا يَنْظُرُ إِلَيْهِمْ يَوْمَ الْقِيَامَةِ وَلَا يُزَكِّيهِمْ وَلَهُمْ عَذَابٌ أَلِيمٌ (٧٧) وَإِنَّ مِنْهُمْ لَفَرِيقًا يَلْوُونَ أَلْسِنَتَهُمْ بِالْكِتَابِ لِتَحْسَبُوهُ مِنَ الْكِتَابِ وَمَا هُوَ مِنَ الْكِتَابِ وَيَقُولُونَ هُوَ مِنْ عِنْدِ اللَّهِ وَمَا هُوَ مِنْ عِنْدِ اللَّهِ وَيَقُولُونَ عَلَى اللَّهِ الْكَذِبَ وَهُمْ يَعْلَمُونَ (٧٨) مَا كَانَ لِبَشَرٍ أَنْ يُؤْتِيَهُ اللَّهُ الْكِتَابَ وَالْحُكْمَ وَالنُّبُوَّةَ ثُمَّ يَقُولَ لِلنَّاسِ كُونُوا عِبَادًا لِي مِنْ دُونِ اللَّهِ وَلَكِنْ كُونُوا رَبَّانِيِّينَ بِمَا كُنْتُمْ تُعَلِّمُونَ الْكِتَابَ وَبِمَا كُنْتُمْ تَدْرُسُونَ (٧٩) وَلَا يَأْمُرَكُمْ أَنْ تَتَّخِذُوا الْمَلَائِكَةَ وَالنَّبِيِّينَ أَرْبَابًا أَيَأْمُرُكُمْ بِالْكُفْرِ بَعْدَ إِذْ أَنْتُمْ مُسْلِمُونَ (٨٠)

3. The Family of Amran

say): Be worshippers of the Lord because you teach the Book and because you study (it);

3:80. Nor would he enjoin you to take the angels and the prophets for lords. Would he enjoin you to disbelieve after you submit?

* * *

3:81. And when Allah made a covenant through the prophets Certainly what I have given you of Book and Wisdom -- then a Messenger comes to you verifying that which is with you, you shall believe in him, and you shall aid him. He said: Do you affirm and accept My compact in this (matter)? They said We do affirm. He said Then bear witness, and I (too) am of the bearers of witness with you.

3:82. Whoever then turns back after this, these are the transgressors.

3:83. Seek they then other than Allah's religion? And to Him submits whoever is in the heavens and the earth, willingly or unwillingly, and to Him they will be returned.

3:84. Say We believe in Allah and that which is revealed to us, and that which was revealed to Abraham and Ishmael and Isaac and Jacob and the tribes, and that which was given to Moses and Jesus and to the prophets from their Lord; we make no distinction between any of them, and to Him we submit.

3:85. And whoever seeks a religion other than Islam, it will not be accepted from him, and in the Hereafter he will be one of the losers.

3:86. How shall Allah guide a people who disbelieved after their believing, and (after) they had borne witness that the Messenger was true, and clear arguments had come to them? And Allah guides not the unjust people.

3:87. As for these their reward is that on them is the curse of Allah and the angels and of men, all together --

وَإِذْ أَخَذَ اللَّهُ مِيثَاقَ النَّبِيِّينَ لَمَا آتَيْتُكُمْ مِنْ كِتَابٍ وَحِكْمَةٍ ثُمَّ جَاءَكُمْ رَسُولٌ مُصَدِّقٌ لِمَا مَعَكُمْ لَتُؤْمِنُنَّ بِهِ وَلَتَنْصُرُنَّهُ قَالَ أَأَقْرَرْتُمْ وَأَخَذْتُمْ عَلَى ذَلِكُمْ إِصْرِي قَالُوا أَقْرَرْنَا قَالَ فَاشْهَدُوا وَأَنَا مَعَكُمْ مِنَ الشَّاهِدِينَ (٨١)

فَمَنْ تَوَلَّى بَعْدَ ذَلِكَ فَأُولَئِكَ هُمُ الْفَاسِقُونَ (٨٢)

أَفَغَيْرَ دِينِ اللَّهِ يَبْغُونَ وَلَهُ أَسْلَمَ مَنْ فِي السَّمَاوَاتِ وَالْأَرْضِ طَوْعًا وَكَرْهًا وَإِلَيْهِ يُرْجَعُونَ (٨٣)

قُلْ آمَنَّا بِاللَّهِ وَمَا أُنْزِلَ عَلَيْنَا وَمَا أُنْزِلَ عَلَى إِبْرَاهِيمَ وَإِسْمَاعِيلَ وَإِسْحَاقَ وَيَعْقُوبَ وَالْأَسْبَاطِ وَمَا أُوتِيَ مُوسَى وَعِيسَى وَالنَّبِيُّونَ مِنْ رَبِّهِمْ لَا نُفَرِّقُ بَيْنَ أَحَدٍ مِنْهُمْ وَنَحْنُ لَهُ مُسْلِمُونَ (٨٤)

وَمَنْ يَبْتَغِ غَيْرَ الْإِسْلَامِ دِينًا فَلَنْ يُقْبَلَ مِنْهُ وَهُوَ فِي الْآخِرَةِ مِنَ الْخَاسِرِينَ (٨٥)

كَيْفَ يَهْدِي اللَّهُ قَوْمًا كَفَرُوا بَعْدَ إِيمَانِهِمْ وَشَهِدُوا أَنَّ الرَّسُولَ حَقٌّ وَجَاءَهُمُ الْبَيِّنَاتُ وَاللَّهُ لَا يَهْدِي الْقَوْمَ الظَّالِمِينَ (٨٦)

أُولَئِكَ جَزَاؤُهُمْ أَنَّ عَلَيْهِمْ لَعْنَةَ اللَّهِ وَالْمَلَائِكَةِ وَالنَّاسِ أَجْمَعِينَ (٨٧)

خَالِدِينَ فِيهَا لَا يُخَفَّفُ عَنْهُمُ الْعَذَابُ

3:88. Abiding therein. Their chastisement shall not be lightened, nor shall they be respited --

3:89. Except those who repent after that and amend, for surely Allah is Forgiving, Merciful.

3:90. Those who disbelieve after their believing, then increase in disbelief, their repentance is not accepted, and these are they that go astray.

3:91. Those who disbelieve and die while they are disbelievers, the earth full of gold will not be accepted from one of them, though he should offer it as ransom. These it is for whom is a painful chastisement, and they shall have no helpers.

* * *

3:92. You cannot attain to righteousness unless you spend out of what you love. And what you spend, Allah surely knows it.

3:93. All food was lawful to the Children of Israel, before the Torah was revealed. -- except that which Israel forbade himself. Say Bring the Torah and read it, if you are truthful.

3:94. So whoever forges a lie against Allah after this, these are the wrong-doers.

3:95. Say Allah speaks the truth; so follow the religion of Abraham, the upright one. And he was not one of the polytheists.

3:96. Certainly the first house appointed for men is the one at Bakkah, blessed and a guidance for the nations.

3:97. In it are clear signs: (It is) the Place of Abraham; and whoever enters it is safe; and pilgrimage to the House is a duty which men owe to Allah -- whoever can find a way to it. And whoever disbelieves, surely Allah is above need of the worlds.

3:98. Say: O People of the Book, why do you disbelieve in the messages of Allah? And Allah is a witness of what

3. The Family of Amran

you do.

3:99. Say: O People of the Book, why do you hinder those who believe from the way of Allah, seeking (to make) it crooked, while you are witnesses? And Allah is not heedless of what you do.

3:100. O you who believe, if you obey a party from among those who have been given the Book, they will turn you back as disbelievers after your belief.

3:101. And how can you disbelieve while to you are recited the messages of Allah, and among you is His Messenger? And whoever holds fast to Allah, he indeed is guided to a right path.

* * *

3:102. O you who believe, keep your duty to Allah, as it ought to be kept, and die not unless you are Muslims.

3:103. And hold fast by the covenant of Allah all together and be not disunited. And remember Allah's favour to you when you were enemies, then He united your hearts so by His favour you became brethren. And you were on the brink of a pit of fire, then He saved you from it. Thus Allah makes clear to you His messages that you may be guided.

3:104. And from among you there should be a party who invite to good and enjoin the right and forbid the wrong. And these are they who are successful.

3:105. And be not like those who became divided and disagreed after clear arguments had come to them. And for them is a grievous chastisement.

3:106. On the day when (some) faces turn white and (some) faces turn black. Then as to those whose faces are black: Did you disbelieve after your belief? So taste the chastisement because you disbelieved.

3:107. And as to those whose faces are white, they shall be in Allah's mercy.

Therein they shall abide.

3:108. These are the messages of Allah which We recite to thee with truth. And Allah desires no injustice to (His) creatures.

3:109. And to Allah belongs whatever is in the heavens and whatever is in the earth. And to Allah are all affairs returned.

***

3:110. You are the best nation raised up for men; you enjoin good and forbid evil and you believe in Allah. And if the People of the Book had believed, it would have been better for them. Some of them are believers but most of them are transgressors.

3:111. They will not harm you save a slight hurt. And if they fight you, they will turn (their) backs to you. Then they will not be helped.

3:112. Abasement will be their lot wherever they are found, except under a covenant with Allah and a covenant with men, and they shall incur the wrath of Allah, and humiliation will be made to cling to them. This is because they disbelieved in the messages of Allah and killed the prophets unjustly. This is because they disobeyed and exceeded the limits.

3:113. They are not all alike. Of the People of the Book there is an upright party who recite Allah's messages in the night time and they adore (Him).

3:114. They believe in Allah and the Last Day, and they enjoin good and forbid evil and vie one with another in good deeds. And those are among the righteous.

3:115. And whatever good they do, they will not be denied it, And Allah knows those who keep their duty.

3:116. Those who disbelieve, neither their wealth nor their children will avail them aught against Allah. And these are the companions of the Fire therein they abide.

3:117. The likeness of that which they spend in the life of this world is as the likeness of wind in which is intense cold it smites the harvest of a people who are unjust to themselves and destroys it. And Allah wronged them not but they wronged themselves.

3:118. O you who believe, take not for intimate friends others than your own people; they spare no pains to cause you loss. They love that which distresses you: Vehement hatred has already appeared from out of their mouths, and that which their hearts conceal is greater still. Indeed We have made the messages clear to you if you understand.

3:119. Lo! you are they who will love them while they love you not, and you believe in the Book, (in) the whole of it. And when they meet you they say, We believe, and when they are alone, they bite (their) finger tips in rage against you. Say Die in your rage. Surely Allah is Knower of what is in the hearts.

3:120. If good befalls you, it grieves them, and if an evil afflicts you, they rejoice at it. And if you are patient and keep your duty, their struggle will not injure you in any way. Surely Allah encompasses what they do.

***

3:121. And when thou didst go forth early in the morning from thy family, to assign to the believers their positions for the battle. And Allah is Hearing, Knowing.

3:122. When two parties from among you thought of showing cowardice, and Allah was the Guardian of them both. And in Allah should the believers trust.

3:123. And Allah certainly helped you at Badr when you were weak. So keep your duty to Allah that you may give thanks.

3:124. When thou didst say to the believers: Does it not suffice you that your Lord should help you with three thousand angels sent down?

3:125. Yea, if you are steadfast and keep your duty, and they come upon you in a headlong manner, your Lord will assist you with five thousand of havoc-making angels.

3:126. And Allah made it only as good news for you, and that your hearts might be at ease thereby. And help comes only from Allah, the Mighty, the Wise,

3:127. That He may cut off a part of those who disbelieve or abase them so that they should return in failure.

3:128. Thou hast no concern in the matter whether He turns to them (mercifully) or chastises them; surely they are wrongdoers.

3:129. And to Allah belongs whatever is in the heavens and whatever is in the earth. He forgives whom He pleases and chastises whom He pleases. And Allah is Forgiving, Merciful.

***

3:130. O you who believe, devour not usury, doubling and redoubling, and keep your duty to Allah, that you may be successful.

3:131. And guard yourselves against the fire which has been prepared for the disbelievers.

3:132. And obey Allah and the Messenger, that you may be shown mercy.

3:133. And hasten to forgiveness from your Lord and a Garden, as wide as the heavens and the earth it is prepared for those who keep their duty:

3:134. Those who spend in ease as well as in adversity and those who restrain (their) anger and pardon men. And Allah loves the doers of good (to others).

3:135. And those who, when they commit an indecency or wrong their souls, remember Allah and ask

3. The Family of Amran

forgiveness for their sins. And who forgives sins but Allah? And they persist not knowingly in what they do.

3:136. Their reward is protection from their Lord, and Gardens wherein flow rivers, to abide in them. And excellent is the reward of the workers!

3:137. Indeed there have been examples before you; so travel in the earth and see what was the end of the deniers.

3:138. This is a clear statement for men, and a guidance and an admonition to those who would keep their duty.

3:139. And be not weak-hearted, nor grieve, and you will have the upper hand if you are believers.

3:140. If a wound has afflicted you, a wound like it has also afflicted the (disbelieving) people. And We bring these days to men by turns, that Allah may know those who believe and take witnesses from among you. And Allah loves not the wrongdoers,

3:141. And that He may purge those who believe and deprive the disbelievers of blessings.

3:142. Do you think that you will enter the Garden while Allah has nor yet known those from among you who strive hard (nor) known the steadfast?

3:143. And certainly you desired death before you met it. So indeed you have seen it now while you look (at it).

* * *

3:144. And Muhammad is but a messenger -- messengers have already passed away before him. If then he dies or is killed, will you turn back upon your heels? And he who turns back upon his heels will do no harm at all to Allah. And Allah will reward the grateful.

3:145. And no soul can die but with Allah's permission -- the term is fixed. And whoever desires the reward of this world, We give him of it, and whoever desires the reward of the Hereafter, We give him of it. And We shall reward the grateful.

3:146. And how many a prophet has fought, with whom were many worshippers of the Lord. So they did not lose heart on account of that which befell them in Allah's way, nor did they weaken, nor did they abase themselves. And Allah loves the steadfast.

3:147. And their cry was only that they said: Our Lord, grant us protection from our sins and our extravagance in our affair, and make firm our feet and grant us victory over the disbelieving people.

3:148. So Allah gave them the reward of the world and a good reward of the Hereafter. And Allah loves the doers of good (to others).

***

3:149. O you who believe, if you obey those who disbelieve, they will make you turn back upon your heels, so you will turn back losers.

3:150. Nay, Allah is your Patron, and He is the Best of the helpers.

3:151. We will cast terror into the hearts of those who disbelieve because they set up with Allah that for which He has sent down no authority, and their abode is the Fire. And evil is the abode of the wrong-doers.

3:152. And Allah certainly made good His promise to you when you slew them by His permission, until you became weak-hearted and disputed about the affair and disobeyed after He had shown you that which you loved. Of you were some who desired this world, and of you were some who desired the Hereafter. Then He turned you away from them that He might try you; and He has indeed pardoned you. And Allah is Gracious to the believers.

3:153. When you went away far, and paid no heed to anyone, and the Messenger was calling you in your rear. So He gave you (another) grief for (your) first grief that you might not grieve at what escaped you, nor (at) what befell you. And Allah is Aware of what you do.

3:154. Then after grief He sent down security on you, slumber overcoming a party of you, while (there was) another party whom their own souls had rendered anxious they entertained about Allah thoughts of ignorance quite unjustly. They said; Have we any hand in the affair? Say: The affair is wholly (in the hands) of Allah. They bide within their souls that which they would not reveal to thee. They say: Had we any hand in the affair. we would not have been slain here. Say Had you remained in your houses, those for whom slaughter was ordained would have gone forth to the places where they would be slain. And (this happened) that Allah might test what was in your breasts and that He might purge what was in your hearts. And Allah is Knower of what is in the breasts.

3:155. Those of you who turned back on the day when the two armies met, only the devil sought to cause them to make a slip on account of some deeds they had done, and certainly Allah has pardoned them. Surely Allah is Forgiving, Forbearing.

***

3:156. O you who believe, be not like those who disbelieve and say of their brethren when they travel in the earth or engage in fighting: Had they been with us, they would not have died, or been slain; that Allah may make it to be a regret in their hearts. And Allah gives life and causes death. And Allah is Seer of what you, do.

3:157. And if you are slain in Allah's way or you die, surely Allah's protection and (His) mercy are better than what they amass.

3:158. And if you die or you are slain, to Allah you are gathered.

3. The Family of Amran

3:159. Thus it is by Allah's mercy that thou art gentle to them. And hadst thou been rough, hard-hearted, they would certainly have dispersed from around thee. So pardon them and ask protection for them, and consult them in (important) matters. But when thou hast determined, put thy trust in Allah. Surely Allah loves those who trust (in Him).

3:160. If Allah helps you, there is none that can overcome you; and if He forsakes you, who is there that can help you after Him? And in Allah should the believers put their trust.

3:161. And it is not for a prophet to act dishonestly. And whoever acts dishonestly will bring his dishonesty on the day of Resurrection. Then shall every soul be paid back fully what it has earned, and they will not be wronged.

3:162. Is then he who follows the pleasure of Allah like him who incurs Allah's displeasure, and his abode is hell? And it is an evil destination.

3:163. There are grades with Allah. And Allah is Seer of what they do.

3:164. Certainly Allah conferred a favour on the believers when He raised among them a Messenger from among themselves, reciting to them His messages and purifying them, and teaching them the Book and the Wisdom, although before that they were surely in manifest error.

3:165. What! When a misfortune befell you, and you had inflicted twice as much, you say: Whence is this? Say It is from yourselves. Surely Allah is Possessor of power over all things.

3:166. And that which befell you on the day when the two armies met was by Allah's permission, that He might know the believers,

3:167. And that He might know the hypocrites. And it was said to them Come, fight in Allah's way, or defend

3. The Family of Amran

yourselves. They said: If we knew fighting, we would have followed you. They were on that day nearer to disbelief than to belief; they say with their mouths what is not in their hearts. And Allah best knows what they conceal.

3:168. Those who said of their brethren whilst they (themselves) held back: Had they obeyed us, they would not have been killed. Say: Avert death from yourselves, if you are truthful.

3:169. And think not of those who are killed in Allah's way as dead. Nay, they are alive being provided sustenance from their Lord,

3:170. Rejoicing in what Allah has given them out of His grace, and they rejoice for the sake of those who, (being left) behind them, have not yet joined them, that they have no fear, nor shall they grieve.

3:171. They rejoice for Allah's favour and (His) grace, and that Allah wastes not the reward of the believers.

* * *

3:172. Those who responded to the call of Allah and the Messenger after the misfortune had befallen them -- for such among them who do good and keep their duty is a great reward.

3:173. Those to whom men said: Surely people have gathered against you, so fear them; but this increased their faith, and they said: Allah is sufficient for us and He is an excellent Guardian.

3:174. So they returned with favour from Allah and (His) grace; no evil touched them, and they followed the pleasure of Allah. And Allah is the Lord of mighty grace.

3:175. It is the devil who only frightens his friends, but fear them not, and fear Me, if you are believers.

3:176. And let not those grieve thee who run into disbelief precipitately surely they can do no harm to Allah. Allah intends not to assign them any

أَمْوَاتًا بَلْ أَحْيَاءٌ عِنْدَ رَبِّهِمْ يُرْزَقُونَ (١٦٩)

فَرِحِينَ بِمَا آتَاهُمُ اللَّهُ مِنْ فَضْلِهِ وَيَسْتَبْشِرُونَ بِالَّذِينَ لَمْ يَلْحَقُوا بِهِمْ مِنْ خَلْفِهِمْ أَلَّا خَوْفٌ عَلَيْهِمْ وَلَا هُمْ يَحْزَنُونَ (١٧٠)

يَسْتَبْشِرُونَ بِنِعْمَةٍ مِنَ اللَّهِ وَفَضْلٍ وَأَنَّ اللَّهَ لَا يُضِيعُ أَجْرَ الْمُؤْمِنِينَ (١٧١)

الَّذِينَ اسْتَجَابُوا لِلَّهِ وَالرَّسُولِ مِنْ بَعْدِ مَا أَصَابَهُمُ الْقَرْحُ لِلَّذِينَ أَحْسَنُوا مِنْهُمْ وَاتَّقَوْا أَجْرٌ عَظِيمٌ (١٧٢)

الَّذِينَ قَالَ لَهُمُ النَّاسُ إِنَّ النَّاسَ قَدْ جَمَعُوا لَكُمْ فَاخْشَوْهُمْ فَزَادَهُمْ إِيمَانًا وَقَالُوا حَسْبُنَا اللَّهُ وَنِعْمَ الْوَكِيلُ (١٧٣)

فَانْقَلَبُوا بِنِعْمَةٍ مِنَ اللَّهِ وَفَضْلٍ لَمْ يَمْسَسْهُمْ سُوءٌ وَاتَّبَعُوا رِضْوَانَ اللَّهِ وَاللَّهُ ذُو فَضْلٍ عَظِيمٍ (١٧٤)

إِنَّمَا ذَلِكُمُ الشَّيْطَانُ يُخَوِّفُ أَوْلِيَاءَهُ فَلَا تَخَافُوهُمْ وَخَافُونِ إِنْ كُنْتُمْ مُؤْمِنِينَ (١٧٥)

وَلَا يَحْزُنْكَ الَّذِينَ يُسَارِعُونَ فِي الْكُفْرِ إِنَّهُمْ لَنْ يَضُرُّوا اللَّهَ شَيْئًا يُرِيدُ اللَّهُ أَلَّا يَجْعَلَ لَهُمْ حَظًّا فِي الْآخِرَةِ وَلَهُمْ عَذَابٌ عَظِيمٌ (١٧٦)

إِنَّ الَّذِينَ اشْتَرَوُا الْكُفْرَ بِالْإِيمَانِ لَنْ يَضُرُّوا اللَّهَ شَيْئًا وَلَهُمْ عَذَابٌ أَلِيمٌ (١٧٧)

وَلَا يَحْسَبَنَّ الَّذِينَ كَفَرُوا أَنَّمَا نُمْلِي لَهُمْ خَيْرٌ لِأَنْفُسِهِمْ إِنَّمَا نُمْلِي لَهُمْ لِيَزْدَادُوا إِثْمًا وَلَهُمْ عَذَابٌ مُهِينٌ (١٧٨)

مَا كَانَ اللَّهُ لِيَذَرَ الْمُؤْمِنِينَ عَلَى مَا

portion in the Hereafter; and for them is a grievous chastisement.

3:177. Those who buy disbelief at the price of faith can do no harm to Allah, and for them is a painful chastisement.

3:178. And let not those who disbelieve think that our granting them respite is good for themselves. We grant them respite only that they may add to their sins; and for them is an humiliating chastisement.

3:179. Allah will not leave the believers in the condition in which you are until He separates the evil from the good. Nor is Allah going to make you acquainted with the unseen, but Allah chooses of His Messengers whom He pleases. So believe in Allah and His Messengers. And if you believe and keep your duty, you will have a great reward.

3:180. And let not those who are niggardly in spending that which Allah has granted them out of His grace, think that it is good for them. Nay, it is evil for them. They shall have a collar of their niggardliness on their necks on the Resurrection day. And Allah's is the heritage of the heavens and the earth. And Allah is Aware of what you do.

***

3:181. Allah has certainly heard the saying of those who said: Allah is poor and we are rich. We shall record what they say, and their killing the prophets unjustly, and We shall say: Taste the chastisement of burning.

3:182. This is for that which your own hands have sent before, and because Allah is not in the least unjust to the servants.

3:183. Those who say: Allah has enjoined us that we should not believe in any messenger until he brings us an offering which is consumed by the fire. Say: Indeed there came to you

3. The Family of Amran

messengers before me with clear arguments and with that which you demand. Why then did you try to kill them, if you are truthful?

3:184. But if they reject thee, so indeed were rejected before thee messengers who came with clear arguments and scriptures and the illuminating Book.

3:185. Every soul will taste of death. And you will be paid your reward fully only on the Resurrection day. Then whoever is removed far from the Fire and is made to enter the Garden, he indeed attains the object. And the life of this world is nothing but a provision of vanities.

3:186. You will certainly be tried in your property and your persons. And you will certainly hear from those who have been given the Book before you and from the idolaters much abuse. And if you are patient and keep your duty, surely this is an affair of great resolution.

187 And when Allah took a covenant from those who were given the Book You shall explain it to men and shall not hide it. But they cast it behind their backs and took a small price for it. So evil is that which they buy.

3:188. Think not that those who exult in what they have done, and love to be praised. for what they have not done -- think not them to be safe from the chastisement; and for them is a painful chastisement.

3:189. And Allah's is the kingdom of the heavens and the earth. And Allah is Possessor of power over all things.

***

3:190. In the creation of the heavens and the earth and the alternation of the night and the day, there are surely signs for men of understanding.

3:191. Those who remember Allah standing and sitting and (lying) on their sides, and reflect on the creation of the heavens and the earth: Our Lord,

بِظَلَّامٍ لِلْعَبِيدِ (١٨٢) الَّذِينَ قَالُوا إِنَّ اللَّهَ عَهِدَ إِلَيْنَا أَلَّا نُؤْمِنَ لِرَسُولٍ حَتَّىٰ يَأْتِيَنَا بِقُرْبَانٍ تَأْكُلُهُ النَّارُ ۗ قُلْ قَدْ جَاءَكُمْ رُسُلٌ مِنْ قَبْلِي بِالْبَيِّنَاتِ وَبِالَّذِي قُلْتُمْ فَلِمَ قَتَلْتُمُوهُمْ إِنْ كُنْتُمْ صَادِقِينَ (١٨٣)

فَإِنْ كَذَّبُوكَ فَقَدْ كُذِّبَ رُسُلٌ مِنْ قَبْلِكَ جَاءُوا بِالْبَيِّنَاتِ وَالزُّبُرِ وَالْكِتَابِ الْمُنِيرِ (١٨٤)

كُلُّ نَفْسٍ ذَائِقَةُ الْمَوْتِ ۗ وَإِنَّمَا تُوَفَّوْنَ أُجُورَكُمْ يَوْمَ الْقِيَامَةِ ۖ فَمَنْ زُحْزِحَ عَنِ النَّارِ وَأُدْخِلَ الْجَنَّةَ فَقَدْ فَازَ ۗ وَمَا الْحَيَاةُ الدُّنْيَا إِلَّا مَتَاعُ الْغُرُورِ (١٨٥)

لَتُبْلَوُنَّ فِي أَمْوَالِكُمْ وَأَنْفُسِكُمْ وَلَتَسْمَعُنَّ مِنَ الَّذِينَ أُوتُوا الْكِتَابَ مِنْ قَبْلِكُمْ وَمِنَ الَّذِينَ أَشْرَكُوا أَذًى كَثِيرًا ۚ وَإِنْ تَصْبِرُوا وَتَتَّقُوا فَإِنَّ ذَٰلِكَ مِنْ عَزْمِ الْأُمُورِ (١٨٦)

وَإِذْ أَخَذَ اللَّهُ مِيثَاقَ الَّذِينَ أُوتُوا الْكِتَابَ لَتُبَيِّنُنَّهُ لِلنَّاسِ وَلَا تَكْتُمُونَهُ فَنَبَذُوهُ وَرَاءَ ظُهُورِهِمْ وَاشْتَرَوْا بِهِ ثَمَنًا قَلِيلًا ۖ فَبِئْسَ مَا يَشْتَرُونَ (١٨٧)

لَا تَحْسَبَنَّ الَّذِينَ يَفْرَحُونَ بِمَا أَتَوْا وَيُحِبُّونَ أَنْ يُحْمَدُوا بِمَا لَمْ يَفْعَلُوا فَلَا تَحْسَبَنَّهُمْ بِمَفَازَةٍ مِنَ الْعَذَابِ ۖ وَلَهُمْ عَذَابٌ أَلِيمٌ (١٨٨)

وَلِلَّهِ مُلْكُ السَّمَاوَاتِ وَالْأَرْضِ ۗ وَاللَّهُ عَلَىٰ كُلِّ شَيْءٍ قَدِيرٌ (١٨٩)

إِنَّ فِي خَلْقِ السَّمَاوَاتِ وَالْأَرْضِ وَاخْتِلَافِ اللَّيْلِ وَالنَّهَارِ لَآيَاتٍ لِأُولِي الْأَلْبَابِ (١٩٠)

الَّذِينَ يَذْكُرُونَ اللَّهَ قِيَامًا وَقُعُودًا وَعَلَىٰ جُنُوبِهِمْ وَيَتَفَكَّرُونَ فِي خَلْقِ

3. The Family of Amran

Thou hast not created this in vain! Glory be to Thee! Save us from the chastisement of the Fire.

3:192. Our Lord, whomsoever Thou makest enter the Fire, him Thou indeed bringest to disgrace. And there will be no helpers for the wrongdoers.

3:193. Our Lord, surely we have heard a Crier calling to the faith, saying Believe in your Lord. So we do believe. Our Lord, grant us protection from our sins and remove our evils and make us die with the righteous.

3:194. Our Lord, grant us what Thou hast promised us by Thy messengers and disgrace us not on the day of Resurrection. Surely Thou never failest in (Thy) promise!

3:195. So their Lord accepted their prayer, (saying) I will not suffer the work of any worker among you to be lost whether male or female, the one of you being from the other. So those who fled and were driven forth from their homes and persecuted in My way and who fought and were slain, I shall truly remove their evil and make them enter Gardens wherein flow rivers -- a reward from Allah. And with Allah is the best reward.

3:196. Let not control in the land, of those who disbelieve, deceive thee.

3:197. A brief enjoyment! Then their abode is hell. And evil is the resting-place.

3:198. But those who keep their duty to their Lord, for them are Gardens wherein flow rivers, to abide therein; an entertainment from their Lord. And that which Allah has in store for the righteous is best.

3:199. And of the People of the Book there are those who believe in Allah and (in) that which has been revealed to you and (in) that which has been revealed to them, humbling themselves before Allah -- they take not a small price for the messages of Allah. These it is that have their reward with their Lord. Surely Allah is Swift to take account

3:200. O you who believe, be steadfast and try to excel in steadfastness and guard (the frontiers). And keep your duty to Allah that you may be successful.

4. The Women

In the name of Allah, the Beneficent, the Merciful.

4:1. O people, keep your duty to your Lord, Who created you from a single being and created its mate of the same (kind), and spread from these two many men and women. And keep your duty to Allah, by Whom you demand one of another (your rights), and (to) the ties of relationship. Surely Allah is ever a Watcher over you.

4:2. And give to the orphans their property, and substitute not worthless (things) for (their) good (ones), and devour not their property (adding) to your own property. This is surely a great sin.

4:3. And if you fear that you cannot do justice to orphans, marry such women as seem good to you, two, or three, or four; but if you fear that you will not do justice, then (marry) only one or that which your right hands possess. This is more proper that you may not do injustice.

4:4. And give women their dowries as a free gift. But if they of themselves be pleased to give you a portion thereof, consume it with enjoyment and pleasure.

4:5. And make not over your property, which Allah has made a (means of) support for you, to the weak of understanding, and maintain them out of it, and clothe them and give them a good education.

4:6. And test the orphans until they reach the age of marriage. Then if you find in them maturity of intellect, make over to them their property, and consume it not extravagantly and hastily against their growing up. And whoever is rich, let him abstain, and whoever is poor let him consume reasonably. And when you make over to them their property, call witnesses in their presence. And Allah is enough as a Reckoner.

4:7. For men is a share of what the parents and the near relatives leave, and for women a share of what the parents and the near relatives leave, whether it be little or much -- an appointed share.

4:8. And when relatives and the orphans and the needy are present at the division, give them out of it and speak to them kind words.

4:9. And let those fear who, should they leave behind them weakly offspring, would fear on their account; so let them observe their duty to Allah and let them speak right words.

4:10. Those who swallow the property of the orphans unjustly, they swallow only fire into their bellies. And they will burn in blazing fire.

***

4:11. Allah enjoins you concerning your children: for the male is the equal of the portion of two females but if there be more than two females, two-thirds of what the deceased leaves is theirs; and if there be one, for her is the half. And as for his parents, for each of them is the sixth of what he leaves, if he has a child; but if he has no child and (only) his two parents inherit him, for his mother is the third; but if he has brothers, for his mother is the sixth, after (payment of) a bequest he may have bequeathed or a debt. Your parents and your children, you know not which of them is the nearer to you

وَمَنْ كَانَ فَقِيرًا فَلْيَأْكُلْ بِالْمَعْرُوفِ فَإِذَا دَفَعْتُمْ إِلَيْهِمْ أَمْوَالَهُمْ فَأَشْهِدُوا عَلَيْهِمْ وَكَفَى بِاللَّهِ حَسِيبًا (٦)

لِلرِّجَالِ نَصِيبٌ مِمَّا تَرَكَ الْوَالِدَانِ وَالْأَقْرَبُونَ وَلِلنِّسَاءِ نَصِيبٌ مِمَّا تَرَكَ الْوَالِدَانِ وَالْأَقْرَبُونَ مِمَّا قَلَّ مِنْهُ أَوْ كَثُرَ نَصِيبًا مَفْرُوضًا (٧)

وَإِذَا حَضَرَ الْقِسْمَةَ أُولُو الْقُرْبَى وَالْيَتَامَى وَالْمَسَاكِينُ فَارْزُقُوهُمْ مِنْهُ وَقُولُوا لَهُمْ قَوْلًا مَعْرُوفًا (٨)

وَلْيَخْشَ الَّذِينَ لَوْ تَرَكُوا مِنْ خَلْفِهِمْ ذُرِّيَّةً ضِعَافًا خَافُوا عَلَيْهِمْ فَلْيَتَّقُوا اللَّهَ وَلْيَقُولُوا قَوْلًا سَدِيدًا (٩)

إِنَّ الَّذِينَ يَأْكُلُونَ أَمْوَالَ الْيَتَامَى ظُلْمًا إِنَّمَا يَأْكُلُونَ فِي بُطُونِهِمْ نَارًا وَسَيَصْلَوْنَ سَعِيرًا (١٠)

يُوصِيكُمُ اللَّهُ فِي أَوْلَادِكُمْ لِلذَّكَرِ مِثْلُ حَظِّ الْأُنْثَيَيْنِ فَإِنْ كُنَّ نِسَاءً فَوْقَ اثْنَتَيْنِ فَلَهُنَّ ثُلُثَا مَا تَرَكَ وَإِنْ كَانَتْ وَاحِدَةً فَلَهَا النِّصْفُ وَلِأَبَوَيْهِ لِكُلِّ وَاحِدٍ مِنْهُمَا السُّدُسُ مِمَّا تَرَكَ إِنْ كَانَ لَهُ وَلَدٌ فَإِنْ لَمْ يَكُنْ لَهُ وَلَدٌ وَوَرِثَهُ أَبَوَاهُ فَلِأُمِّهِ الثُّلُثُ فَإِنْ كَانَ لَهُ إِخْوَةٌ فَلِأُمِّهِ السُّدُسُ مِنْ بَعْدِ وَصِيَّةٍ يُوصِي بِهَا أَوْ دَيْنٍ آبَاؤُكُمْ وَأَبْنَاؤُكُمْ لَا تَدْرُونَ أَيُّهُمْ أَقْرَبُ لَكُمْ نَفْعًا فَرِيضَةً مِنَ اللَّهِ إِنَّ اللَّهَ كَانَ عَلِيمًا حَكِيمًا (١١)

وَلَكُمْ نِصْفُ مَا تَرَكَ أَزْوَاجُكُمْ إِنْ لَمْ يَكُنْ لَهُنَّ وَلَدٌ فَإِنْ كَانَ لَهُنَّ وَلَدٌ فَلَكُمُ الرُّبُعُ مِمَّا تَرَكْنَ مِنْ بَعْدِ وَصِيَّةٍ يُوصِينَ بِهَا أَوْ دَيْنٍ وَلَهُنَّ الرُّبُعُ مِمَّا تَرَكْتُمْ إِنْ لَمْ يَكُنْ لَكُمْ وَلَدٌ فَإِنْ كَانَ لَكُمْ وَلَدٌ فَلَهُنَّ الثُّمُنُ مِمَّا تَرَكْتُمْ مِنْ

4. The Women

in benefit. This is an ordinance from Allah. Allah is surely ever Knowing, Wise.

4:12. And yours is half of what your wives leave if they have no child; but if they have a child, your share is a fourth of what they leave after (payment of) any bequest they may have bequeathed or a debt; and theirs is the fourth of what you leave if you have no child, but if you have a child, their share is the eighth of what you leave after (payment of) a bequest You may have bequeathed or a debt.

4:13. And if a man or a woman, having no children leaves property to be inherited and he (or she) has a brother or a sister, then for each of them is the sixth; but if they are more than that, they shall be sharers in the third after (payment of) a bequest that may have been bequeathed or a debt not injuring (others). This is an ordinance from Allah and Allah is Knowing, Forbearing. These are Allah's limits. And whoever obeys Allah and His Messenger, He will admit him to Gardens wherein flow rivers, to abide in them. And this is the great achievement.

4:14. And whoever disobeys Allah and His Messenger and goes beyond His limits, He will make him enter fire to abide in it, and for him is an abasing chastisement.

***

4:15. And as for those of your women who are guilty of an indecency, call to witness against them four (witnesses) from among you; so if they bear witness, confine them to the houses until death takes them away or Allah opens a way for them.

4:16. And as for the two of you who are guilty of it, give them both a slight punishment; then if they repent and amend, turn aside from them. Surely Allah is ever Oft-returning (to mercy),

بَعْدِ وَصِيَّةٍ تُوصُونَ بِهَا أَوْ دَيْنٍ وَإِنْ كَانَ رَجُلٌ يُورَثُ كَلَالَةً أَوِ امْرَأَةٌ وَلَهُ أَخٌ أَوْ أُخْتٌ فَلِكُلِّ وَاحِدٍ مِنْهُمَا السُّدُسُ فَإِنْ كَانُوا أَكْثَرَ مِنْ ذَلِكَ فَهُمْ شُرَكَاءُ فِي الثُّلُثِ مِنْ بَعْدِ وَصِيَّةٍ يُوصَى بِهَا أَوْ دَيْنٍ غَيْرَ مُضَارٍّ وَصِيَّةً مِنَ اللَّهِ وَاللَّهُ عَلِيمٌ حَلِيمٌ (١٢) تِلْكَ حُدُودُ اللَّهِ وَمَنْ يُطِعِ اللَّهَ وَرَسُولَهُ يُدْخِلْهُ جَنَّاتٍ تَجْرِي مِنْ تَحْتِهَا الْأَنْهَارُ خَالِدِينَ فِيهَا وَذَلِكَ الْفَوْزُ الْعَظِيمُ (١٣) وَمَنْ يَعْصِ اللَّهَ وَرَسُولَهُ وَيَتَعَدَّ حُدُودَهُ يُدْخِلْهُ نَارًا خَالِدًا فِيهَا وَلَهُ عَذَابٌ مُهِينٌ (١٤) وَاللَّاتِي يَأْتِينَ الْفَاحِشَةَ مِنْ نِسَائِكُمْ فَاسْتَشْهِدُوا عَلَيْهِنَّ أَرْبَعَةً مِنْكُمْ فَإِنْ شَهِدُوا فَأَمْسِكُوهُنَّ فِي الْبُيُوتِ حَتَّى يَتَوَفَّاهُنَّ الْمَوْتُ أَوْ يَجْعَلَ اللَّهُ لَهُنَّ سَبِيلًا (١٥) وَاللَّذَانِ يَأْتِيَانِهَا مِنْكُمْ فَآذُوهُمَا فَإِنْ تَابَا وَأَصْلَحَا فَأَعْرِضُوا عَنْهُمَا إِنَّ اللَّهَ كَانَ تَوَّابًا رَحِيمًا (١٦) إِنَّمَا التَّوْبَةُ عَلَى اللَّهِ لِلَّذِينَ يَعْمَلُونَ السُّوءَ بِجَهَالَةٍ ثُمَّ يَتُوبُونَ مِنْ قَرِيبٍ فَأُولَئِكَ يَتُوبُ اللَّهُ عَلَيْهِمْ وَكَانَ اللَّهُ عَلِيمًا حَكِيمًا (١٧) وَلَيْسَتِ التَّوْبَةُ لِلَّذِينَ يَعْمَلُونَ السَّيِّئَاتِ حَتَّى إِذَا حَضَرَ أَحَدَهُمُ الْمَوْتُ قَالَ إِنِّي تُبْتُ الْآنَ وَلَا الَّذِينَ يَمُوتُونَ وَهُمْ كُفَّارٌ أُولَئِكَ أَعْتَدْنَا لَهُمْ عَذَابًا أَلِيمًا (١٨) يَا أَيُّهَا الَّذِينَ آمَنُوا لَا يَحِلُّ لَكُمْ أَنْ تَرِثُوا النِّسَاءَ كَرْهًا وَلَا تَعْضُلُوهُنَّ لِتَذْهَبُوا بِبَعْضِ مَا آتَيْتُمُوهُنَّ إِلَّا أَنْ

4. The Women

the Merciful.

4:17. Repentance with Allah is only for those who do evil in ignorance, then turn (to Allah) soon, so these it is to whom Allah turns (mercifully). And Allah is ever Knowing, Wise.

4:18. And repentance is not for those who go on doing evil deeds, until when death comes to one of them, he says Now I repent; nor (for) those who die while they are disbelievers. For such We have prepared a painful chastisement.

4:19. O you who believe, it is not lawful for you to take women as heritage against (their) will. Nor should you straiten them by taking part of what you have given them, unless they are guilty of manifest indecency. And treat them kindly. Then if you hate them, it may be that you dislike a thing while Allah has placed abundant good in it.

4:20. And if you wish to have (one) wife in the place of another and you have given one of them a heap of gold, take nothing from it. Would you take it by slandering (her) and (doing her) manifest wrong?

4:21. And how can you take it when one of you has already gone in to the other and they have taken from you a strong covenant?

4:22. And marry not women whom your fathers married, except what has already passed. This surely is indecent and hateful; and it is an evil way.

***

4:23. Forbidden to you are your mothers, and your daughters, and your sisters, and your paternal aunts, and your maternal aunts, and brother's daughters and sister's daughters, and your mothers that have suckled you, and your foster-sisters, and mothers of your wives, and your stepdaughters who are in your guardianship (born) of your wives to whom you have gone in -- but if you have not gone in to them,

يَأْتِينَ بِفَاحِشَةٍ مُبَيِّنَةٍ وَعَاشِرُوهُنَّ بِالْمَعْرُوفِ فَإِنْ كَرِهْتُمُوهُنَّ فَعَسَى أَنْ تَكْرَهُوا شَيْئًا وَيَجْعَلَ اللَّهُ فِيهِ خَيْرًا كَثِيرًا (١٩)

وَإِنْ أَرَدْتُمُ اسْتِبْدَالَ زَوْجٍ مَكَانَ زَوْجٍ وَآتَيْتُمْ إِحْدَاهُنَّ قِنْطَارًا فَلَا تَأْخُذُوا مِنْهُ شَيْئًا أَتَأْخُذُونَهُ بُهْتَانًا وَإِثْمًا مُبِينًا (٢٠)

وَكَيْفَ تَأْخُذُونَهُ وَقَدْ أَفْضَى بَعْضُكُمْ إِلَى بَعْضٍ وَأَخَذْنَ مِنْكُمْ مِيثَاقًا غَلِيظًا (٢١)

وَلَا تَنْكِحُوا مَا نَكَحَ آبَاؤُكُمْ مِنَ النِّسَاءِ إِلَّا مَا قَدْ سَلَفَ إِنَّهُ كَانَ فَاحِشَةً وَمَقْتًا وَسَاءَ سَبِيلًا (٢٢)

حُرِّمَتْ عَلَيْكُمْ أُمَّهَاتُكُمْ وَبَنَاتُكُمْ وَأَخَوَاتُكُمْ وَعَمَّاتُكُمْ وَخَالَاتُكُمْ وَبَنَاتُ الْأَخِ وَبَنَاتُ الْأُخْتِ وَأُمَّهَاتُكُمُ اللَّاتِي أَرْضَعْنَكُمْ وَأَخَوَاتُكُمْ مِنَ الرَّضَاعَةِ وَأُمَّهَاتُ نِسَائِكُمْ وَرَبَائِبُكُمُ اللَّاتِي فِي حُجُورِكُمْ مِنْ نِسَائِكُمُ اللَّاتِي دَخَلْتُمْ بِهِنَّ فَإِنْ لَمْ تَكُونُوا دَخَلْتُمْ بِهِنَّ فَلَا جُنَاحَ عَلَيْكُمْ وَحَلَائِلُ أَبْنَائِكُمُ الَّذِينَ مِنْ أَصْلَابِكُمْ وَأَنْ تَجْمَعُوا بَيْنَ الْأُخْتَيْنِ إِلَّا مَا قَدْ سَلَفَ إِنَّ اللَّهَ كَانَ غَفُورًا رَحِيمًا (٢٣)

وَالْمُحْصَنَاتُ مِنَ النِّسَاءِ إِلَّا مَا مَلَكَتْ أَيْمَانُكُمْ كِتَابَ اللَّهِ عَلَيْكُمْ وَأُحِلَّ لَكُمْ مَا وَرَاءَ ذَلِكُمْ أَنْ تَبْتَغُوا بِأَمْوَالِكُمْ مُحْصِنِينَ غَيْرَ مُسَافِحِينَ فَمَا اسْتَمْتَعْتُمْ بِهِ مِنْهُنَّ فَآتُوهُنَّ أُجُورَهُنَّ فَرِيضَةً وَلَا جُنَاحَ عَلَيْكُمْ فِيمَا تَرَاضَيْتُمْ بِهِ مِنْ بَعْدِ الْفَرِيضَةِ إِنَّ اللَّهَ كَانَ عَلِيمًا حَكِيمًا (٢٤)

وَمَنْ لَمْ يَسْتَطِعْ مِنْكُمْ طَوْلًا أَنْ يَنْكِحَ

4. The Women

there is no blame on you -- and the wives of your sons who are of your own loins; and that you should have two sisters together, except what has already passed. Surely Allah is ever Forgiving, Merciful,

4:24. And all married women except those whom your right hands possess (are forbidden); (this is) Allah's ordinance to you. And lawful for you are (all women) besides those, provided that you seek (them) with your property, taking (them) in marriage, not committing fornication. Then as to those whom you profit by (by marrying), give them their dowries as appointed. And there is no blame on you about what you mutually agree after what is appointed (of dowry). Surely Allah is ever Knowing, Wise.

4:25. And whoever among you cannot afford to marry free believing women, (let him marry) such of your believing maidens as your right hands possess. And Allah knows best your faith -- you are (sprung) the one from the other. So marry them with the permission of their masters, and give them their dowries justly, they being chaste, not fornicating, nor receiving paramours; then if they are guilty of adultery when they are taken in marriage, they shall suffer half the punishment for free married women. This is for him among you who fears falling into evil. And that you abstain is better for you. And Allah is Forgiving, Merciful.

* * *

4:26. Allah desires to explain to you, and to guide you into the ways of those before you, and to turn to you (mercifully). And Allah is Knowing, Wise.

4:27. And Allah desires to turn to you (mercifully). And those who follow (their) lusts desire that you should deviate (with) a great deviation.

4:28. Allah desires to make light your

الْمُحْصَنَاتُ الْمُؤْمِنَاتِ فَمِنْ مَا مَلَكَتْ أَيْمَانُكُمْ مِنْ فَتَيَاتِكُمُ الْمُؤْمِنَاتِ وَاللَّهُ أَعْلَمُ بِإِيمَانِكُمْ بَعْضُكُمْ مِنْ بَعْضٍ فَانْكِحُوهُنَّ بِإِذْنِ أَهْلِهِنَّ وَآتُوهُنَّ أُجُورَهُنَّ بِالْمَعْرُوفِ مُحْصَنَاتٍ غَيْرَ مُسَافِحَاتٍ وَلَا مُتَّخِذَاتِ أَخْدَانٍ فَإِذَا أُحْصِنَّ فَإِنْ أَتَيْنَ بِفَاحِشَةٍ فَعَلَيْهِنَّ نِصْفُ مَا عَلَى الْمُحْصَنَاتِ مِنَ الْعَذَابِ ذَلِكَ لِمَنْ خَشِيَ الْعَنَتَ مِنْكُمْ وَأَنْ تَصْبِرُوا خَيْرٌ لَكُمْ وَاللَّهُ غَفُورٌ رَحِيمٌ (٢٥)

يُرِيدُ اللَّهُ لِيُبَيِّنَ لَكُمْ وَيَهْدِيَكُمْ سُنَنَ الَّذِينَ مِنْ قَبْلِكُمْ وَيَتُوبَ عَلَيْكُمْ وَاللَّهُ عَلِيمٌ حَكِيمٌ (٢٦)

وَاللَّهُ يُرِيدُ أَنْ يَتُوبَ عَلَيْكُمْ وَيُرِيدُ الَّذِينَ يَتَّبِعُونَ الشَّهَوَاتِ أَنْ تَمِيلُوا مَيْلًا عَظِيمًا (٢٧)

يُرِيدُ اللَّهُ أَنْ يُخَفِّفَ عَنْكُمْ وَخُلِقَ الْإِنْسَانُ ضَعِيفًا (٢٨)

يَا أَيُّهَا الَّذِينَ آمَنُوا لَا تَأْكُلُوا أَمْوَالَكُمْ بَيْنَكُمْ بِالْبَاطِلِ إِلَّا أَنْ تَكُونَ تِجَارَةً عَنْ تَرَاضٍ مِنْكُمْ وَلَا تَقْتُلُوا أَنْفُسَكُمْ إِنَّ اللَّهَ كَانَ بِكُمْ رَحِيمًا (٢٩)

وَمَنْ يَفْعَلْ ذَلِكَ عُدْوَانًا وَظُلْمًا فَسَوْفَ نُصْلِيهِ نَارًا وَكَانَ ذَلِكَ عَلَى اللَّهِ يَسِيرًا (٣٠)

إِنْ تَجْتَنِبُوا كَبَائِرَ مَا تُنْهَوْنَ عَنْهُ نُكَفِّرْ عَنْكُمْ سَيِّئَاتِكُمْ وَنُدْخِلْكُمْ مُدْخَلًا كَرِيمًا (٣١)

وَلَا تَتَمَنَّوْا مَا فَضَّلَ اللَّهُ بِهِ بَعْضَكُمْ عَلَى بَعْضٍ لِلرِّجَالِ نَصِيبٌ مِمَّا اكْتَسَبُوا وَلِلنِّسَاءِ نَصِيبٌ مِمَّا اكْتَسَبْنَ وَاسْأَلُوا اللَّهَ مِنْ فَضْلِهِ إِنَّ اللَّهَ كَانَ بِكُلِّ شَيْءٍ عَلِيمًا (٣٢)

burdens, and man is created weak.

4:29. O you who believe, devour not your property among yourselves by illegal methods except that it be trading by your mutual consent. And kill not your people. Surely Allah is ever Merciful to you.

4:30. And whoso does this aggressively and unjustly, We shall soon cast him into fire. And this is ever easy for Allah.

4:31. If you shun the great things which you are forbidden, We shall do away with your evil (inclinations) and cause you to enter an honourable place of entering.

4:32. And covet not that by which Allah has made some of you excel others. For men is the benefit of what they earn. And for women is the benefit of what they earn. And ask Allah of His grace. Surely Allah is ever Knower of all things.

4:33. And to every one We have appointed heirs of that which parents and near relatives leave. And as to those with whom your right hands have ratified agreements, give them their due. Surely Allah is ever Witness over all things.

* * *

4:34. Men are the maintainers of women, with what Allah has made some of them to excel others and with what they spend out of their wealth. So the good women are obedient, guarding the unseen as Allah has guarded. And (as to) those on whose part you fear desertion, admonish them, and leave them alone in the beds and chastise them. So if they obey you, seek not a way against them Surely Allah is ever Exalted, Great.

4:35. And if you fear a breach between the two, appoint an arbiter from his people and an arbiter from her people. If they both desire agreement, Allah will effect harmony between them.

4. The Women

Surely Allah is ever Knowing, Aware.

4:36. And serve Allah, and associate naught with Him, and be good to the parents and to the near of kin and the orphans and the needy and the neighbour of (your) kin and the alien neighbour, and the companion in a journey and the wayfarer and those whom your right hands possess. Surely Allah loves not such as are proud, boastful,

4:37. Who are niggardly and bid people to be niggardly and hide that which Allah has given them out of His grace. And We have prepared for the disbelievers an abasing chastisement -- And those who spend their wealth to be seen of men and believe not in Allah nor in the Last Day. And as for him whose companion is the devil, an evil companion is he!

4:39. And what (harm) would it do them if they believe in Allah and the Last Day and spend of that which Allah has given them? And Allah is ever Knower of them.

4:40. Surely Allah wrongs not the weight of an atom; and if it is a good deed, He multiplies it and gives from Himself a great reward.

4:41. But how will it be when We bring from every people a witness and bring thee as a witness against these?

4:42. On that day will those who disbelieved and disobeyed the Messenger desire that the earth were levelled with them. And they can hide no fact from Allah.

* * *

4:43. O you who believe, go not neat prayer when you are intoxicated till you know what you say, nor after sexual intercourse -- except you are merely passing by -- until you have bathed. And if you are sick, or on a journey, or one of you come from the privy, or you have touched the women, and you cannot find water, betake

اللَّهُ بِهِمْ عَلِيمًا (٣٩)

إِنَّ اللَّهَ لَا يَظْلِمُ مِثْقَالَ ذَرَّةٍ وَإِنْ تَكُ حَسَنَةً يُضَاعِفْهَا وَيُؤْتِ مِنْ لَدُنْهُ أَجْرًا عَظِيمًا (٤٠)

فَكَيْفَ إِذَا جِئْنَا مِنْ كُلِّ أُمَّةٍ بِشَهِيدٍ وَجِئْنَا بِكَ عَلَى هَؤُلَاءِ شَهِيدًا (٤١)

يَوْمَئِذٍ يَوَدُّ الَّذِينَ كَفَرُوا وَعَصَوُا الرَّسُولَ لَوْ تُسَوَّى بِهِمُ الْأَرْضُ وَلَا يَكْتُمُونَ اللَّهَ حَدِيثًا (٤٢)

يَا أَيُّهَا الَّذِينَ آمَنُوا لَا تَقْرَبُوا الصَّلَاةَ وَأَنْتُمْ سُكَارَى حَتَّى تَعْلَمُوا مَا تَقُولُونَ وَلَا جُنُبًا إِلَّا عَابِرِي سَبِيلٍ حَتَّى تَغْتَسِلُوا وَإِنْ كُنْتُمْ مَرْضَى أَوْ عَلَى سَفَرٍ أَوْ جَاءَ أَحَدٌ مِنْكُمْ مِنَ الْغَائِطِ أَوْ لَامَسْتُمُ النِّسَاءَ فَلَمْ تَجِدُوا مَاءً فَتَيَمَّمُوا صَعِيدًا طَيِّبًا فَامْسَحُوا بِوُجُوهِكُمْ وَأَيْدِيكُمْ إِنَّ اللَّهَ كَانَ عَفُوًّا غَفُورًا (٤٣)

أَلَمْ تَرَ إِلَى الَّذِينَ أُوتُوا نَصِيبًا مِنَ الْكِتَابِ يَشْتَرُونَ الضَّلَالَةَ وَيُرِيدُونَ أَنْ تَضِلُّوا السَّبِيلَ (٤٤)

وَاللَّهُ أَعْلَمُ بِأَعْدَائِكُمْ وَكَفَى بِاللَّهِ وَلِيًّا وَكَفَى بِاللَّهِ نَصِيرًا (٤٥)

مِنَ الَّذِينَ هَادُوا يُحَرِّفُونَ الْكَلِمَ عَنْ مَوَاضِعِهِ وَيَقُولُونَ سَمِعْنَا وَعَصَيْنَا وَاسْمَعْ غَيْرَ مُسْمَعٍ وَرَاعِنَا لَيًّا بِأَلْسِنَتِهِمْ وَطَعْنًا فِي الدِّينِ وَلَوْ أَنَّهُمْ قَالُوا سَمِعْنَا وَأَطَعْنَا وَاسْمَعْ وَانْظُرْنَا لَكَانَ خَيْرًا لَهُمْ وَأَقْوَمَ وَلَكِنْ لَعَنَهُمُ اللَّهُ بِكُفْرِهِمْ فَلَا يُؤْمِنُونَ إِلَّا قَلِيلًا (٤٦)

يَا أَيُّهَا الَّذِينَ أُوتُوا الْكِتَابَ آمِنُوا بِمَا نَزَّلْنَا مُصَدِّقًا لِمَا مَعَكُمْ مِنْ قَبْلِ أَنْ نَطْمِسَ وُجُوهًا فَنَرُدَّهَا عَلَى أَدْبَارِهَا

4. The Women

yourselves to pure earth, then wipe your faces and your hands. Surely Allah is ever Pardoning, Forgiving.

4:44. Seest thou not those to whom a portion of the Book was given? They buy error and desire to make you err from the (right) way.

4:45. And Allah best knows your enemies. And Allah is sufficient as a Friend and Allah is sufficient as a Helper.

4:46. Some of those who are Jews alter words from their places and say, We have heard and we disobey and (say), Hear without being made to hear, and (say), Ra'ina, distorting with their tongues and slandering religion. And if they had said, We hear and we obey, and hearken, and unzurna; it would have been better for them and more upright; but Allah has cursed them on account of their disbelief, so they believe not but a little.

4:47. O you who have been given the Book, believe in what We have revealed, verifying that which you have, before We destroy the leaders and turn them on their backs, or curse them as We cursed the Sabbath-breakers. And the command of Allah is ever executed.

4:48. Surely Allah forgives not that a partner should be set up with Him, and forgives all besides that to whom He pleases. And whoever sets up a partner with Allah, he devises indeed a great sin.

4:49. Hast thou not seen those who attribute purity to themselves? Nay, Allah purifies whom He pleases, and they will not be wronged a whit.

4:50. See how they forge lies against Allah! And sufficient is this as a manifest sin.

* * *

4:51. Hast thou not seen those to whom a portion of the Book was given? They believe in sorcery and diviners and say

أَوْ نَلْعَنَهُمْ كَمَا لَعَنَّا أَصْحَابَ السَّبْتِ وَكَانَ أَمْرُ اللَّهِ مَفْعُولًا (٤٧)
إِنَّ اللَّهَ لَا يَغْفِرُ أَن يُشْرَكَ بِهِ وَيَغْفِرُ مَا دُونَ ذَلِكَ لِمَن يَشَاءُ وَمَن يُشْرِكْ بِاللَّهِ فَقَدِ افْتَرَى إِثْمًا عَظِيمًا (٤٨)
أَلَمْ تَرَ إِلَى الَّذِينَ يُزَكُّونَ أَنفُسَهُم بَلِ اللَّهُ يُزَكِّي مَن يَشَاءُ وَلَا يُظْلَمُونَ فَتِيلًا (٤٩)
انظُرْ كَيْفَ يَفْتَرُونَ عَلَى اللَّهِ الْكَذِبَ وَكَفَى بِهِ إِثْمًا مُبِينًا (٥٠)
أَلَمْ تَرَ إِلَى الَّذِينَ أُوتُوا نَصِيبًا مِنَ الْكِتَابِ يُؤْمِنُونَ بِالْجِبْتِ وَالطَّاغُوتِ وَيَقُولُونَ لِلَّذِينَ كَفَرُوا هَؤُلَاءِ أَهْدَى مِنَ الَّذِينَ آمَنُوا سَبِيلًا (٥١)
أُولَئِكَ الَّذِينَ لَعَنَهُمُ اللَّهُ وَمَن يَلْعَنِ اللَّهُ فَلَن تَجِدَ لَهُ نَصِيرًا (٥٢)
أَمْ لَهُمْ نَصِيبٌ مِنَ الْمُلْكِ فَإِذًا لَا يُؤْتُونَ النَّاسَ نَقِيرًا (٥٣)
أَمْ يَحْسُدُونَ النَّاسَ عَلَى مَا آتَاهُمُ اللَّهُ مِن فَضْلِهِ فَقَدْ آتَيْنَا آلَ إِبْرَاهِيمَ الْكِتَابَ وَالْحِكْمَةَ وَآتَيْنَاهُم مُلْكًا عَظِيمًا (٥٤)
فَمِنْهُم مَّنْ آمَنَ بِهِ وَمِنْهُم مَّن صَدَّ عَنْهُ وَكَفَى بِجَهَنَّمَ سَعِيرًا (٥٥)
إِنَّ الَّذِينَ كَفَرُوا بِآيَاتِنَا سَوْفَ نُصْلِيهِمْ نَارًا كُلَّمَا نَضِجَتْ جُلُودُهُم بَدَّلْنَاهُمْ جُلُودًا غَيْرَهَا لِيَذُوقُوا الْعَذَابَ إِنَّ اللَّهَ كَانَ عَزِيزًا حَكِيمًا (٥٦)
وَالَّذِينَ آمَنُوا وَعَمِلُوا الصَّالِحَاتِ سَنُدْخِلُهُمْ جَنَّاتٍ تَجْرِي مِن تَحْتِهَا الْأَنْهَارُ خَالِدِينَ فِيهَا أَبَدًا لَهُمْ فِيهَا أَزْوَاجٌ مُطَهَّرَةٌ وَنُدْخِلُهُمْ ظِلًّا ظَلِيلًا (٥٧)
إِنَّ اللَّهَ يَأْمُرُكُمْ أَن تُؤَدُّوا الْأَمَانَاتِ

4. The Women

of those who disbelieve: These are better guided in the path than those who believe.

4:52. Those are they whom Allah has cursed. And whomever Allah curses, thou wilt not find a helper for him.

4:53. Or have they a share in the kingdom? But then they would nor give to people even the speck on a date-stone.

4:54. Or do they envy the people for that which Allah has given them of His grace? But indeed We have given to Abraham's children the Book and the Wisdom, and We have given them a grand kingdom.

4:55. So of them is he who believes in him, and of them is he who turns away from him. And Hell is sufficient to burn.

4:56. Those who disbelieve in Our Messages, we shall make them enter Fire. As often as their skins are burned, We shall change them for other skins, that they may taste the chastisement. Surely Allah is ever Mighty, Wise.

4:57. And those who believe and do good deeds, We shall make them enter Gardens wherein flow rivers, to abide in them for ever. For them therein are pure companions and We shall make them enter a pleasant shade.

4:58. Surely Allah commands you to make over trusts to those worthy of them, and that when you judge between people, you judge with justice. Surely Allah admonishes you with what is excellent. Surely Allah is ever Hearing, Seeing.

4:59. O you who believe, obey Allah and obey the Messenger and those in authority from among you; then if you quarrel about any thing, refer it to Allah and the Messenger, if you believe in Allah and the Last Day. This is best and more suitable to (achieve) the end.

***

4:60. Hast thou not seen those who

assert that they believe in that which has been revealed to thee and that which was revealed before thee? They desire to seek the judgment of the devil, though they have been commanded to deny him. And the devil desires to lead them far astray.

4:61. And when it is said to them, Come to that which Allah has revealed and to the Messenger, thou seest the hypocrites turning away from thee with aversion.

4:62. But how is it that when a misfortune befalls them on account of that which their hands have sent before, they come to thee sweating by Allah: We desired naught but good and concord?

4:63. These are they, the secrets of whose hearts Allah knows; so turn aside from them and admonish them and speak to them effective words concerning themselves.

4:64. And We sent no messenger but that he should be obeyed by Allah's command. And had they, when they wronged themselves, come to thee and asked forgiveness of Allah, and the Messenger had (also) asked forgiveness for them, they would have found Allah Oft-returning (to mercy), Merciful.

4:65. But no, by thy Lord! they believe not until they make thee a judge of what is in dispute between them, then find not any straitness in their hearts as to that which thou decidest and submit with full submission.

4:66. And if We had enjoined them, Lay down your lives or go forth from your homes, they would not have done it except a few of them. And if they had done what they are exhorted to do, it would certainly have been better for them and more strengthening:

4:67. And then We would certainly have given them from Ourselves a great reward,

4:68. And We would certainly have

أَوِ اخْرُجُوا مِنْ دِيَارِكُمْ مَا فَعَلُوهُ إِلَّا قَلِيلٌ مِنْهُمْ وَلَوْ أَنَّهُمْ فَعَلُوا مَا يُوعَظُونَ بِهِ لَكَانَ خَيْرًا لَهُمْ وَأَشَدَّ تَثْبِيتًا (٦٦)

وَإِذًا لَآتَيْنَاهُمْ مِنْ لَدُنَّا أَجْرًا عَظِيمًا (٦٧)

وَلَهَدَيْنَاهُمْ صِرَاطًا مُسْتَقِيمًا (٦٨)

وَمَنْ يُطِعِ اللَّهَ وَالرَّسُولَ فَأُولَئِكَ مَعَ الَّذِينَ أَنْعَمَ اللَّهُ عَلَيْهِمْ مِنَ النَّبِيِّينَ وَالصِّدِّيقِينَ وَالشُّهَدَاءِ وَالصَّالِحِينَ وَحَسُنَ أُولَئِكَ رَفِيقًا (٦٩)

ذَلِكَ الْفَضْلُ مِنَ اللَّهِ وَكَفَى بِاللَّهِ عَلِيمًا (٧٠)

يَا أَيُّهَا الَّذِينَ آمَنُوا خُذُوا حِذْرَكُمْ فَانْفِرُوا ثُبَاتٍ أَوِ انْفِرُوا جَمِيعًا (٧١)

وَإِنَّ مِنْكُمْ لَمَنْ لَيُبَطِّئَنَّ فَإِنْ أَصَابَتْكُمْ مُصِيبَةٌ قَالَ قَدْ أَنْعَمَ اللَّهُ عَلَيَّ إِذْ لَمْ أَكُنْ مَعَهُمْ شَهِيدًا (٧٢)

وَلَئِنْ أَصَابَكُمْ فَضْلٌ مِنَ اللَّهِ لَيَقُولَنَّ كَأَنْ لَمْ تَكُنْ بَيْنَكُمْ وَبَيْنَهُ مَوَدَّةٌ يَا لَيْتَنِي كُنْتُ مَعَهُمْ فَأَفُوزَ فَوْزًا عَظِيمًا (٧٣)

فَلْيُقَاتِلْ فِي سَبِيلِ اللَّهِ الَّذِينَ يَشْرُونَ الْحَيَاةَ الدُّنْيَا بِالْآخِرَةِ وَمَنْ يُقَاتِلْ فِي سَبِيلِ اللَّهِ فَيُقْتَلْ أَوْ يَغْلِبْ فَسَوْفَ نُؤْتِيهِ أَجْرًا عَظِيمًا (٧٤)

وَمَا لَكُمْ لَا تُقَاتِلُونَ فِي سَبِيلِ اللَّهِ وَالْمُسْتَضْعَفِينَ مِنَ الرِّجَالِ وَالنِّسَاءِ وَالْوِلْدَانِ الَّذِينَ يَقُولُونَ رَبَّنَا أَخْرِجْنَا مِنْ هَذِهِ الْقَرْيَةِ الظَّالِمِ أَهْلُهَا وَاجْعَلْ لَنَا مِنْ لَدُنْكَ وَلِيًّا وَاجْعَلْ لَنَا مِنْ لَدُنْكَ نَصِيرًا (٧٥)

الَّذِينَ آمَنُوا يُقَاتِلُونَ فِي سَبِيلِ اللَّهِ وَالَّذِينَ كَفَرُوا يُقَاتِلُونَ فِي سَبِيلِ

4. The Women

guided them in the right path.

4:69. And whoever obeys Allah and the Messenger, they are with those upon whom Allah has bestowed favours from among the prophets and the truthful and the faithful and the righteous, and a goodly company are they!

4:70. Such is the grace from Allah, and Allah is sufficient as Knower.

* * *

4:71. O you who believe, take your precautions, then go forth in detachments or go forth in a body.

4:72. And among you is he who would hang back. Then if a misfortune befalls you he says: Allah indeed bestowed a favour on me as I was not present with them.

4:73. And if bounty from Allah comes to you, he would cry, as if there were no friendship between you and him: Would that I had been with them, then I should have achieved a mighty success

4:74. So let those fight in the way of Allah who sell this world's life for the Hereafter. And whoever fights in the way of Allah, be he slain or be he victorious, We shall grant him a mighty reward.

4:75. And what reason have you not to fight in the way of Allah, and of the weak among the men and the women and the children, who say: Our Lord, take us out of this town, whose people are oppressors, and grant us from Thee a friend, and grant us from Thee a helper!

4:76. Those who believe fight in the way of Allah, and those who disbelieve fight in the way of the devil: So fight against the friends of the devil; surely the struggle of the devil is ever weak.

* * *

4:77. Hast thou not seen those to whom it was said: Withhold your hands, and keep up prayer and pay the poor-rate.

But when fighting is prescribed for them, lo! a party of them fear men as they ought to fear Allah, or with a greater fear, and say: Our Lord, why hast Thou ordained fighting for us? Wouldst Thou not grant us respite to a near term? Say: The enjoyment of this world is short, and the Hereafter is better for him who keeps his duty. And you shall not be wronged a whit.

4:78. Wherever you are, death will overtake you, though you are in towers, raised high. And if good befalls them, they say: This is from Allah; and if a misfortune befalls them, they say: This is from thee. Say: All is from Allah. But what is the matter with these people that they make no effort to understand anything?

4:79. Whatever good befalls thee (O man), it is front Allah, and whatever misfortune befalls thee, it is from thyself. And We have sent thee (O Prophet) to mankind as a Messenger. And Allah is sufficient as a witness.

4:80. Whoever obeys the Messenger, he indeed obeys Allah. And whoever turns away, We have not sent thee as a keeper over them.

4:81. And they say: Obedience. But when they go out from thy presence, a party of them plan by night doing otherwise than what thou sayest." And Allah writes down what they plan by night, so turn aside from them and trust in Allah. And Allah is sufficient as having charge of affairs.

4:82. Will they not then meditate on the Qur'an? And if it were from any other than Allah, they would have found in it many a discrepancy.

4:83. But if any news of security or fear comes to them, they spread it abroad. And if they had referred it to the Messenger and to those in authority among them, those of them who can search out knowledge of it would have known it. And were it not for the grace of Allah upon you and His mercy, you would certainly have followed the devil save a few.

4:84. Fight then in Allah's way -- thou art not responsible except for thyself; and urge on the believers. It may be that Allah will restrain the fighting of those who disbelieve. And Allah is stronger in prowess and stronger to give exemplary punishment.

4:85. Whoever intercedes in a good cause has a share of it, and whoever intercedes in an evil cause has a portion of it. And Allah is ever Keeper over all things.

4:86. And when you are greeted with a greeting, greet with one better than it, or return it. Surely Allah ever takes account of all things.

4:87. Allah, there is no god but He -- He will certainly gather you together on the Resurrection day, there is no doubt in it. And who is more true in word than Allah?

***

4:88. Why should you, then, be two parties in relation to the hypocrites while Allah has made them return (to disbelief) for what they have earned? Do you desire to guide him whom Allah leaves in error? And whomsoever Allah leaves in error thou canst not find a way for him.

4:89. They long that you should disbelieve as they have disbelieved so that you might be on the same level; so take not from among them friends until they flee (their homes) in Allah's way. Then if they turn back (to hostility), seize them and kill them wherever you find them, and take no friend nor helper from among them,

4:90. Except those who join a people between whom and you there is an alliance, or who come to you, their hearts shrinking from fighting you or fighting their own people. And if Allah had pleased, He would have given

سَتَجِدُونَ آخَرِينَ يُرِيدُونَ أَنْ يَأْمَنُوكُمْ وَيَأْمَنُوا قَوْمَهُمْ كُلَّ مَا رُدُّوا إِلَى الْفِتْنَةِ أُرْكِسُوا فِيهَا فَإِنْ لَمْ يَعْتَزِلُوكُمْ وَيُلْقُوا إِلَيْكُمُ السَّلَمَ وَيَكُفُّوا أَيْدِيَهُمْ فَخُذُوهُمْ وَاقْتُلُوهُمْ حَيْثُ ثَقِفْتُمُوهُمْ وَأُولَئِكُمْ جَعَلْنَا لَكُمْ عَلَيْهِمْ سُلْطَانًا مُبِينًا (٩١)

وَمَا كَانَ لِمُؤْمِنٍ أَنْ يَقْتُلَ مُؤْمِنًا إِلَّا خَطَأً وَمَنْ قَتَلَ مُؤْمِنًا خَطَأً فَتَحْرِيرُ رَقَبَةٍ مُؤْمِنَةٍ وَدِيَةٌ مُسَلَّمَةٌ إِلَى أَهْلِهِ إِلَّا أَنْ يَصَّدَّقُوا فَإِنْ كَانَ مِنْ قَوْمٍ عَدُوٍّ لَكُمْ وَهُوَ مُؤْمِنٌ فَتَحْرِيرُ رَقَبَةٍ مُؤْمِنَةٍ وَإِنْ كَانَ مِنْ قَوْمٍ بَيْنَكُمْ وَبَيْنَهُمْ مِيثَاقٌ فَدِيَةٌ مُسَلَّمَةٌ إِلَى أَهْلِهِ وَتَحْرِيرُ رَقَبَةٍ مُؤْمِنَةٍ فَمَنْ لَمْ يَجِدْ فَصِيَامُ شَهْرَيْنِ مُتَتَابِعَيْنِ تَوْبَةً مِنَ اللَّهِ وَكَانَ اللَّهُ عَلِيمًا حَكِيمًا (٩٢)

وَمَنْ يَقْتُلْ مُؤْمِنًا مُتَعَمِّدًا فَجَزَاؤُهُ جَهَنَّمُ خَالِدًا فِيهَا وَغَضِبَ اللَّهُ عَلَيْهِ وَلَعَنَهُ وَأَعَدَّ لَهُ عَذَابًا عَظِيمًا (٩٣)

يَا أَيُّهَا الَّذِينَ آمَنُوا إِذَا ضَرَبْتُمْ فِي سَبِيلِ اللَّهِ فَتَبَيَّنُوا وَلَا تَقُولُوا لِمَنْ أَلْقَى إِلَيْكُمُ السَّلَامَ لَسْتَ مُؤْمِنًا تَبْتَغُونَ عَرَضَ الْحَيَاةِ الدُّنْيَا فَعِنْدَ اللَّهِ مَغَانِمُ كَثِيرَةٌ كَذَلِكَ كُنْتُمْ مِنْ قَبْلُ فَمَنَّ اللَّهُ عَلَيْكُمْ فَتَبَيَّنُوا إِنَّ اللَّهَ كَانَ بِمَا تَعْمَلُونَ خَبِيرًا (٩٤)

لَا يَسْتَوِي الْقَاعِدُونَ مِنَ الْمُؤْمِنِينَ غَيْرُ أُولِي الضَّرَرِ وَالْمُجَاهِدُونَ فِي سَبِيلِ اللَّهِ بِأَمْوَالِهِمْ وَأَنْفُسِهِمْ فَضَّلَ اللَّهُ الْمُجَاهِدِينَ بِأَمْوَالِهِمْ وَأَنْفُسِهِمْ عَلَى الْقَاعِدِينَ دَرَجَةً وَكُلًّا وَعَدَ اللَّهُ الْحُسْنَى وَفَضَّلَ اللَّهُ الْمُجَاهِدِينَ عَلَى الْقَاعِدِينَ أَجْرًا عَظِيمًا (٩٥)

them power over you, so that they would have fought you. So if they withdraw from you and fight you not and offer you peace, then Allah allows you no way against them.

4:91. You will find others who desire to be secure from you and secure from their own people. Whenever they are made to return to hostility, they are plunged into it. So if they withdraw not from you, nor offer you peace and restrain their hands, then seize them and kill them wherever you find them. And against these We have given you a dear authority.

* * *

4:92. And a believer would not kill a believer except by mistake. And he who kills a believer by mistake should free a believing slave, and blood-money should be paid to his people unless they remit it as alms. But if he be from a tribe hostile to you and he is a believer, the freeing of a believing slave (suffices) And if he be from a tribe between whom and you there is a covenant, the blood-money should be paid to his people along with the freeing of a believing slave but he who has nor the means should fast for two months successively: a penance from Allah. And Allah is ever Knowing, Wise.

4:93. And whoever kills a believer intentionally, his punishment is hell, abiding therein: and Allah is wroth with him and He has cursed him and prepared for him a grievous chastisement.

4:94. O you who believe, when you go forth (to fight) in Allah's way, make investigation, and say not to any one who offers you salutation, Thou art not a believer, seeking the good of this world's life. But with Allah there are abundant gains. You too were such before, then Allah conferred a benefit on you; so make investigation. Surely

Allah is ever Aware of what you do.

4:95. The holders back from among the believers, not disabled by injury, and those who strive hard in Allah's way with their property and their persons, are not equal. Allah has made the strivers with their property and their persons to excel the holders-back a (high) degree. And to each Allah has promised good. And Allah has granted to the strivers above the holders-back a mighty reward -- (High) degrees from Him and protection and mercy. And Allah is ever Forgiving, Merciful.

* * *

4:97. (As for) those whom the angels cause to die while they are unjust to themselves, (the angels) will say What were you doing? They will say We were weak in the earth (They will) say: Was not Allah's earth spacious, so that you could have migrated therein? So these it is whose refuge is hell and it is an evil resort.

4:98. Except the weak from among the men and the women and the children who have not the means, nor can they find a way (to escape);

4:99. So these, it may be that Allah will pardon them. And Allah is ever Pardoning, Forgiving.

4:100. And whoever flees in Allah's way, he will find in the earth many a place of escape and abundant resources. And whoever goes forth from his home fleeing to Allah and His Messenger, then death overtakes him, his reward is indeed with Allah. And Allah is ever Forgiving, Merciful.

* * *

4:101. And when you journey in the earth, there is no blame on you if you shorten the prayer, if you fear that those who disbelieve will give you trouble. Surely the disbelievers are an open enemy to you.

4:102. And when thou art among them and leadest the prayer for them, let a party of them stand up with thee, and let them take their arms; Then when they have performed their prostration, let them go to your rear, and let another party who have not prayed come forward and pray with thee, and let them take their precautions and their arms. Those who disbelieve long that you may neglect your arms and your baggage, that they may attack you with a sudden united attack. And there is no blame on you, if you are inconvenienced on account of rain or if you are sick, to put away your arms; and take your precautions. Surely Allah has prepared abasing chastisement for the disbelievers.

4:103. So when you have finished the prayer, remember Allah standing and sitting and reclining. But when you are secure, from danger, keep up (regular) prayer. Prayer indeed has been enjoined on the believers at fixed times.

4:104. And be not weak-hearted in pursuit of the enemy. If you suffer they (too) suffer as you suffer, and you hope from Allah what they hope not. And Allah is ever Knowing, Wise

* * *

4:105. Surely We have revealed the Book to thee with truth that thou mayest judge between people by means of what Allah has taught thee. And be not one pleading the cause of the dishonest,

4:106. And ask the forgiveness of Allah. Surely Allah is ever Forgiving, Merciful.

4:107. And contend not on behalf of those who act unfaithfully to their souls. Surely Allah loves not him who is treacherous, sinful;

4:108. They seek to hide from men and they cannot hide from Allah, and He is with them when they counsel by night matters which please Him not. And Allah ever encompasses what they do.

4:109. Behold! You are they who may

وَلَوْلَا فَضْلُ اللَّهِ عَلَيْكَ وَرَحْمَتُهُ لَهَمَّتْ طَائِفَةٌ مِنْهُمْ أَنْ يُضِلُّوكَ وَمَا يُضِلُّونَ إِلَّا أَنْفُسَهُمْ وَمَا يَضُرُّونَكَ مِنْ شَيْءٍ وَأَنْزَلَ اللَّهُ عَلَيْكَ الْكِتَابَ وَالْحِكْمَةَ وَعَلَّمَكَ مَا لَمْ تَكُنْ تَعْلَمُ وَكَانَ فَضْلُ اللَّهِ عَلَيْكَ عَظِيمًا (١١٣)

لَا خَيْرَ فِي كَثِيرٍ مِنْ نَجْوَاهُمْ إِلَّا مَنْ أَمَرَ بِصَدَقَةٍ أَوْ مَعْرُوفٍ أَوْ إِصْلَاحٍ بَيْنَ النَّاسِ وَمَنْ يَفْعَلْ ذَلِكَ ابْتِغَاءَ مَرْضَاةِ اللَّهِ فَسَوْفَ نُؤْتِيهِ أَجْرًا عَظِيمًا (١١٤)

وَمَنْ يُشَاقِقِ الرَّسُولَ مِنْ بَعْدِ مَا تَبَيَّنَ لَهُ الْهُدَى وَيَتَّبِعْ غَيْرَ سَبِيلِ الْمُؤْمِنِينَ نُوَلِّهِ مَا تَوَلَّى وَنُصْلِهِ جَهَنَّمَ وَسَاءَتْ مَصِيرًا (١١٥)

إِنَّ اللَّهَ لَا يَغْفِرُ أَنْ يُشْرَكَ بِهِ وَيَغْفِرُ مَا دُونَ ذَلِكَ لِمَنْ يَشَاءُ وَمَنْ يُشْرِكْ بِاللَّهِ فَقَدْ ضَلَّ ضَلَالًا بَعِيدًا (١١٦)

إِنْ يَدْعُونَ مِنْ دُونِهِ إِلَّا إِنَاثًا وَإِنْ يَدْعُونَ إِلَّا شَيْطَانًا مَرِيدًا (١١٧)

لَعَنَهُ اللَّهُ وَقَالَ لَأَتَّخِذَنَّ مِنْ عِبَادِكَ نَصِيبًا مَفْرُوضًا (١١٨)

وَلَأُضِلَّنَّهُمْ وَلَأُمَنِّيَنَّهُمْ وَلَآمُرَنَّهُمْ فَلَيُبَتِّكُنَّ آذَانَ الْأَنْعَامِ وَلَآمُرَنَّهُمْ فَلَيُغَيِّرُنَّ خَلْقَ اللَّهِ وَمَنْ يَتَّخِذِ الشَّيْطَانَ وَلِيًّا مِنْ دُونِ اللَّهِ فَقَدْ خَسِرَ خُسْرَانًا مُبِينًا (١١٩)

يَعِدُهُمْ وَيُمَنِّيهِمْ وَمَا يَعِدُهُمُ الشَّيْطَانُ إِلَّا غُرُورًا (١٢٠)

أُولَئِكَ مَأْوَاهُمْ جَهَنَّمُ وَلَا يَجِدُونَ عَنْهَا مَحِيصًا (١٢١)

وَالَّذِينَ آمَنُوا وَعَمِلُوا الصَّالِحَاتِ سَنُدْخِلُهُمْ جَنَّاتٍ تَجْرِي مِنْ تَحْتِهَا

4. The Women

contend on their behalf in this world's life, but who will contend with Allah on their behalf on the Resurrection day, or who will have charge of their affairs?

4:110. And whoever does evil or wrongs his soul, then asks forgiveness of Allah, will find Allah Forgiving, Merciful.

4:111. And whoever commits a sin, commits it only against himself. And Allah is ever Knowing, Wise.

4:112. And whoever commits a fault or a sin, then accuses of it one innocent, he indeed takes upon himself the burden of a calumny and a manifest sin.

* * *

4:113. And were it not for Allah's grace upon thee and His mercy, a party of them had certainly designed to ruin thee. And they ruin only themselves, and they cannot harm thee in any way. And Allah has revealed to thee the Book and the Wisdom, and taught thee what thou knewest not, and Allah's grace on thee is very great.

4:114. There is no good in most of their secret counsels except (in) him who enjoins charity or goodness or reconciliation between people. And whoever does this, seeking Allah's pleasure, We shall give him a mighty reward.

4:115. And whoever acts hostilely to the Messenger after guidance has become manifest to him and follows other than the way of the believers, We turn him to that to which he (himself) turns and make him enter hell and it is an evil resort.

* * *

4:116. Surely Allah forgives not setting up partners with Him, and He forgives all besides this to whom He pleases. And whoever sets up a partner with Allah, he indeed goes far astray

4:117. Besides Him they call on nothing

الْأَنْهَارُ خَالِدِينَ فِيهَا أَبَدًا وَعْدَ اللَّهِ حَقًّا وَمَنْ أَصْدَقُ مِنَ اللَّهِ قِيلًا (١٢٢)

لَيْسَ بِأَمَانِيِّكُمْ وَلَا أَمَانِيِّ أَهْلِ الْكِتَابِ مَنْ يَعْمَلْ سُوءًا يُجْزَ بِهِ وَلَا يَجِدْ لَهُ مِنْ دُونِ اللَّهِ وَلِيًّا وَلَا نَصِيرًا (١٢٣)

وَمَنْ يَعْمَلْ مِنَ الصَّالِحَاتِ مِنْ ذَكَرٍ أَوْ أُنْثَى وَهُوَ مُؤْمِنٌ فَأُولَٰئِكَ يَدْخُلُونَ الْجَنَّةَ وَلَا يُظْلَمُونَ نَقِيرًا (١٢٤)

وَمَنْ أَحْسَنُ دِينًا مِمَّنْ أَسْلَمَ وَجْهَهُ لِلَّهِ وَهُوَ مُحْسِنٌ وَاتَّبَعَ مِلَّةَ إِبْرَاهِيمَ حَنِيفًا وَاتَّخَذَ اللَّهُ إِبْرَاهِيمَ خَلِيلًا (١٢٥)

وَلِلَّهِ مَا فِي السَّمَاوَاتِ وَمَا فِي الْأَرْضِ وَكَانَ اللَّهُ بِكُلِّ شَيْءٍ مُحِيطًا (١٢٦)

وَيَسْتَفْتُونَكَ فِي النِّسَاءِ قُلِ اللَّهُ يُفْتِيكُمْ فِيهِنَّ وَمَا يُتْلَى عَلَيْكُمْ فِي الْكِتَابِ فِي يَتَامَى النِّسَاءِ اللَّاتِي لَا تُؤْتُونَهُنَّ مَا كُتِبَ لَهُنَّ وَتَرْغَبُونَ أَنْ تَنْكِحُوهُنَّ وَالْمُسْتَضْعَفِينَ مِنَ الْوِلْدَانِ وَأَنْ تَقُومُوا لِلْيَتَامَى بِالْقِسْطِ وَمَا تَفْعَلُوا مِنْ خَيْرٍ فَإِنَّ اللَّهَ كَانَ بِهِ عَلِيمًا (١٢٧)

وَإِنِ امْرَأَةٌ خَافَتْ مِنْ بَعْلِهَا نُشُوزًا أَوْ إِعْرَاضًا فَلَا جُنَاحَ عَلَيْهِمَا أَنْ يُصْلِحَا بَيْنَهُمَا صُلْحًا وَالصُّلْحُ خَيْرٌ وَأُحْضِرَتِ الْأَنْفُسُ الشُّحَّ وَإِنْ تُحْسِنُوا وَتَتَّقُوا فَإِنَّ اللَّهَ كَانَ بِمَا تَعْمَلُونَ خَبِيرًا (١٢٨)

وَلَنْ تَسْتَطِيعُوا أَنْ تَعْدِلُوا بَيْنَ النِّسَاءِ وَلَوْ حَرَصْتُمْ فَلَا تَمِيلُوا كُلَّ الْمَيْلِ فَتَذَرُوهَا كَالْمُعَلَّقَةِ وَإِنْ تُصْلِحُوا وَتَتَّقُوا فَإِنَّ اللَّهَ كَانَ غَفُورًا رَحِيمًا

but female divinities and they call on nothing but a rebellious devil,

4:118. Whom Allah has cursed. And he said: Certainly I will take of Thy servants an appointed portion;

4:119. And certainly I will lead them astray and excite in them vain desires and bid them so that they will slit the ears of the cattle, and bid them so that they will alter Allah's creation. And whoever takes the devil for a friend, forsaking Allah, he indeed suffers a manifest loss.

4:120. He promises them and excites vain desires in them. And the devil promises them only to deceive.

4:121. These -- their refuge is hell, and they will find no way of escape from it.

4:122. And those who believe and do good, We shall make them enter Gardens in which rivers flow, to abide therein for ever. It is Allah's promise, in truth. And who is more truthful in word than Allah?

4:123. It will not be in accordance with your vain desires nor the vain desires of the People of the Book. Whoever does evil, will be requited for it and will not find for himself besides Allah a friend or a helper.

4:124. And whoever does good deeds, whether male or female, and he (or she) is a believer these will enter the Garden, and they will not be dealt with a whit unjustly.

4:125. And who is better in religion than he who submits himself entirely to Allah while doing good (to others) and follows the faith of Abraham, the upright one? And Allah took Abraham for a friend

4:126. And to Allah belongs whatever is in the heavens and whatever is in the earth. And Allah ever encompasses all things.

* * *

4:127. And they ask thee a decision about women. Say Allah makes known

(١٢٩)
وَإِنْ يَتَفَرَّقَا يُغْنِ اللَّهُ كُلًّا مِنْ سَعَتِهِ وَكَانَ اللَّهُ وَاسِعًا حَكِيمًا (١٣٠) وَلِلَّهِ مَا فِي السَّمَاوَاتِ وَمَا فِي الْأَرْضِ وَلَقَدْ وَصَّيْنَا الَّذِينَ أُوتُوا الْكِتَابَ مِنْ قَبْلِكُمْ وَإِيَّاكُمْ أَنِ اتَّقُوا اللَّهَ وَإِنْ تَكْفُرُوا فَإِنَّ لِلَّهِ مَا فِي السَّمَاوَاتِ وَمَا فِي الْأَرْضِ وَكَانَ اللَّهُ غَنِيًّا حَمِيدًا (١٣١) وَلِلَّهِ مَا فِي السَّمَاوَاتِ وَمَا فِي الْأَرْضِ وَكَفَى بِاللَّهِ وَكِيلًا (١٣٢) إِنْ يَشَأْ يُذْهِبْكُمْ أَيُّهَا النَّاسُ وَيَأْتِ بِآخَرِينَ وَكَانَ اللَّهُ عَلَى ذَلِكَ قَدِيرًا (١٣٣) مَنْ كَانَ يُرِيدُ ثَوَابَ الدُّنْيَا فَعِنْدَ اللَّهِ ثَوَابُ الدُّنْيَا وَالْآخِرَةِ وَكَانَ اللَّهُ سَمِيعًا بَصِيرًا (١٣٤) يَا أَيُّهَا الَّذِينَ آمَنُوا كُونُوا قَوَّامِينَ بِالْقِسْطِ شُهَدَاءَ لِلَّهِ وَلَوْ عَلَى أَنْفُسِكُمْ أَوِ الْوَالِدَيْنِ وَالْأَقْرَبِينَ إِنْ يَكُنْ غَنِيًّا أَوْ فَقِيرًا فَاللَّهُ أَوْلَى بِهِمَا فَلَا تَتَّبِعُوا الْهَوَى أَنْ تَعْدِلُوا وَإِنْ تَلْوُوا أَوْ تُعْرِضُوا فَإِنَّ اللَّهَ كَانَ بِمَا تَعْمَلُونَ خَبِيرًا (١٣٥) يَا أَيُّهَا الَّذِينَ آمَنُوا آمِنُوا بِاللَّهِ وَرَسُولِهِ وَالْكِتَابِ الَّذِي نَزَّلَ عَلَى رَسُولِهِ وَالْكِتَابِ الَّذِي أَنْزَلَ مِنْ قَبْلُ وَمَنْ يَكْفُرْ بِاللَّهِ وَمَلَائِكَتِهِ وَكُتُبِهِ وَرُسُلِهِ وَالْيَوْمِ الْآخِرِ فَقَدْ ضَلَّ ضَلَالًا بَعِيدًا (١٣٦) إِنَّ الَّذِينَ آمَنُوا ثُمَّ كَفَرُوا ثُمَّ آمَنُوا ثُمَّ كَفَرُوا ثُمَّ ازْدَادُوا كُفْرًا لَمْ يَكُنِ اللَّهُ لِيَغْفِرَ لَهُمْ وَلَا لِيَهْدِيَهُمْ سَبِيلًا (١٣٧) بَشِّرِ الْمُنَافِقِينَ بِأَنَّ لَهُمْ عَذَابًا أَلِيمًا

4. The Women

to you His decision concerning them; and that which is recited to you in the Book is concerning widowed women, whom you give not what is appointed for them, while you are not inclined to marry them, nor to the weak among children, and that you should deal justly with orphans and whatever good you do, Allah is surely ever Knower of it.

4:128. And if a woman fears ill-usage from her husband or desertion no blame is on them if they effect a reconciliation between them. And reconciliation is better. And avarice is met with in (men's) minds. And if you do good (to others) and keep your duty, surely Allah is ever Aware of what you do.

4:129. And you cannot do justice between wives, even though you wish (it), but be not disinclined (from one) with total disinclination, so that you leave her in suspense. And if you are reconciled and keep your duty, surely Allah is ever Forgiving, Merciful.

4:130. And if they separate, Allah will render them both free from want out of His ampleness. And Allah is ever Ample-giving, Wise.

4:131. And to Allah belongs whatever is in the heavens and whatever is in the earth. And certainly We enjoined those who were given the Book before you and (We enjoin) you too to keep your duty to Allah. And if you disbelieve, surely to Allah belongs whatever is in the heavens and whatever is in the earth. And Allah is ever Self-sufficient, Praiseworthy.

4:132. And to Allah belongs whatever is in the heavens and whatever is in the earth. And Allah suffices as having charge of affairs.

4:133. If He please, He will take you away, O people, and bring others. And Allah is ever Powerful to do that.

4:134. Whoever desires the reward of

(١٣٨) الَّذِينَ يَتَّخِذُونَ الْكَافِرِينَ أَوْلِيَاءَ مِنْ دُونِ الْمُؤْمِنِينَ أَيَبْتَغُونَ عِنْدَهُمُ الْعِزَّةَ فَإِنَّ الْعِزَّةَ لِلَّهِ جَمِيعًا (١٣٩) وَقَدْ نَزَّلَ عَلَيْكُمْ فِي الْكِتَابِ أَنْ إِذَا سَمِعْتُمْ آيَاتِ اللَّهِ يُكْفَرُ بِهَا وَيُسْتَهْزَأُ بِهَا فَلَا تَقْعُدُوا مَعَهُمْ حَتَّى يَخُوضُوا فِي حَدِيثٍ غَيْرِهِ إِنَّكُمْ إِذًا مِثْلُهُمْ إِنَّ اللَّهَ جَامِعُ الْمُنَافِقِينَ وَالْكَافِرِينَ فِي جَهَنَّمَ جَمِيعًا (١٤٠) الَّذِينَ يَتَرَبَّصُونَ بِكُمْ فَإِنْ كَانَ لَكُمْ فَتْحٌ مِنَ اللَّهِ قَالُوا أَلَمْ نَكُنْ مَعَكُمْ وَإِنْ كَانَ لِلْكَافِرِينَ نَصِيبٌ قَالُوا أَلَمْ نَسْتَحْوِذْ عَلَيْكُمْ وَنَمْنَعْكُمْ مِنَ الْمُؤْمِنِينَ فَاللَّهُ يَحْكُمُ بَيْنَكُمْ يَوْمَ الْقِيَامَةِ وَلَنْ يَجْعَلَ اللَّهُ لِلْكَافِرِينَ عَلَى الْمُؤْمِنِينَ سَبِيلًا (١٤١)

this world -- then with Allah is the reward of this world and the Hereafter. And Allah is ever Hearing Seeing.

* * *

4:135. O you who believe, be maintainers of justice, bearers of witness for Allah, even though it be against your own selves or (your) parents or near relatives whether he be rich or poor, Allah has a better right over them both. So follow not (your) low desires, lest you deviate. And if you distort or turn away from (truth), surely Allah is ever Aware of what you do.

4:136. O you who believe, believe in Allah and His Messenger and the Book which He has revealed to His Messenger and the Book which He revealed before. And whoever disbelieves in Allah and His angels and His Books and His messengers and the Last Day, he indeed strays far away.

4:137. Those who believe then disbelieve, again believe and again disbelieve, then increase in disbelief, Allah will never forgive them nor guide them in the (right) way.

4:138. Give news to the hypocrites that for them is a painful chastisement --

4:139. Those who take disbelievers for friends rather than believers. Do they seek for might from them? Might surely belongs wholly to Allah.

4:140. And indeed He has revealed to you in the Book that when you hear Allah's messages disbelieved in and mocked at, sit not with them until they enter into some other discourse, for then indeed you would be like them. Surely Allah will gather together the hypocrites and the disbelievers all in hell --

4:141. Those who wait (for misfortunes) for you. Then if you have a victory from Allah they say Were we not with you? And if there is a chance for the disbelievers, they say Did we not

4. The Women

prevail over you and defend you from the believers? So Allah will judge between you on the day of Resurrection. And Allah will by no means give the disbelievers a way against the believers.

***

4:142. The hypocrites seek to deceive Allah, and He will requite their deceit to them. And when they stand up for prayer, they stand up sluggishly -- they do it only to be seen of men and remember Allah but little,

4:143. Wavering between that (and this) (belonging) neither to these nor to those. And whomsoever Allah leaves in error, thou wilt not a way for him.

4:144. O you who believe, take not the disbelievers for friends rather than the believers. Do you desire to give Allah a manifest proof against yourselves?

4:145. The hypocrites are surely in the lowest depths of the Fire, and thou wilt find no helper for them,

4:146. Save those who repent and amend and hold fast to Allah and are sincere in their obedience to Allah -- these are with the believers. And Allah will soon grant the believers a mighty reward.

4:147. Why should Allah chastise you if you are grateful and believe? And Allah is ever Multiplier of rewards, Knowing.

***

4:148. Allah loves not the public utterance of hurtful speech, except by one who has been wronged. And Allah is ever Hearing, Knowing.

4:149. If you do good openly or keep it secret or pardon an evil, Allah surely is ever Pardoning, Powerful.

4:150. Those who disbelieve in Allah and His messengers and desire to make a distinction between Allah and His messengers and say: We believe in

إِنَّ الْمُنَافِقِينَ يُخَادِعُونَ اللَّهَ وَهُوَ خَادِعُهُمْ وَإِذَا قَامُوا إِلَى الصَّلَاةِ قَامُوا كُسَالَى يُرَاءُونَ النَّاسَ وَلَا يَذْكُرُونَ اللَّهَ إِلَّا قَلِيلًا (١٤٢) مُذَبْذَبِينَ بَيْنَ ذَلِكَ لَا إِلَى هَؤُلَاءِ وَلَا إِلَى هَؤُلَاءِ وَمَنْ يُضْلِلِ اللَّهُ فَلَنْ تَجِدَ لَهُ سَبِيلًا (١٤٣) يَا أَيُّهَا الَّذِينَ آمَنُوا لَا تَتَّخِذُوا الْكَافِرِينَ أَوْلِيَاءَ مِنْ دُونِ الْمُؤْمِنِينَ أَتُرِيدُونَ أَنْ تَجْعَلُوا لِلَّهِ عَلَيْكُمْ سُلْطَانًا مُبِينًا (١٤٤) إِنَّ الْمُنَافِقِينَ فِي الدَّرْكِ الْأَسْفَلِ مِنَ النَّارِ وَلَنْ تَجِدَ لَهُمْ نَصِيرًا (١٤٥) إِلَّا الَّذِينَ تَابُوا وَأَصْلَحُوا وَاعْتَصَمُوا بِاللَّهِ وَأَخْلَصُوا دِينَهُمْ لِلَّهِ فَأُولَئِكَ مَعَ الْمُؤْمِنِينَ وَسَوْفَ يُؤْتِ اللَّهُ الْمُؤْمِنِينَ أَجْرًا عَظِيمًا (١٤٦) مَا يَفْعَلُ اللَّهُ بِعَذَابِكُمْ إِنْ شَكَرْتُمْ وَآمَنْتُمْ وَكَانَ اللَّهُ شَاكِرًا عَلِيمًا (١٤٧) لَا يُحِبُّ اللَّهُ الْجَهْرَ بِالسُّوءِ مِنَ الْقَوْلِ إِلَّا مَنْ ظُلِمَ وَكَانَ اللَّهُ سَمِيعًا عَلِيمًا (١٤٨) إِنْ تُبْدُوا خَيْرًا أَوْ تُخْفُوهُ أَوْ تَعْفُوا عَنْ سُوءٍ فَإِنَّ اللَّهَ كَانَ عَفُوًّا قَدِيرًا (١٤٩) إِنَّ الَّذِينَ يَكْفُرُونَ بِاللَّهِ وَرُسُلِهِ وَيُرِيدُونَ أَنْ يُفَرِّقُوا بَيْنَ اللَّهِ وَرُسُلِهِ

some and disbelieve in others; and desire to take a course in between --

4:151. These are truly disbelievers and We have prepared for the disbelievers an abasing chastisement.

4:152. And those who believe in Allah and His messengers and make no distinction between any of them, to them He will grant their rewards. And Allah is ever Forgiving, Merciful.

* * *

4:153. The People of the Book ask thee to bring down to them a Book from heaven; indeed they demanded of Moses a greater thing than that, for they said: Show us Allah manifestly. So destructive punishment overtook them on account of their wrongdoing. Then they took the calf (for a god), after dear signs had come to them, but We pardoned this. And We gave Moses dear authority.

4:154. And We raised the mountain above them at their covenant. And We said to them: Enter the door making obeisance. And We said to them: Violate not the Sabbath; and We took from them a firm covenant.

4:155. Then for their breaking their covenant and their disbelief in the messages of Allah and their killing the prophets wrongfully and their saying, Our hearts are covered; nay, Allah has sealed them owing to their disbelief, so they believe not but a little:

4:156. And for their disbelief and for their uttering against Mary a grievous calumny:

4:157. And for their saying: We have killed the Messiah, Jesus, son of Mary, the messenger of Allah, and they killed him not, nor did they cause his death on the cross, but he was made to appear to them as such. And certainly those who differ therein are in doubt about it. They have no knowledge about it, but only follow a conjecture, and they killed him not for certain:

وَيَقُولُونَ نُؤْمِنُ بِبَعْضٍ وَنَكْفُرُ بِبَعْضٍ وَيُرِيدُونَ أَنْ يَتَّخِذُوا بَيْنَ ذَٰلِكَ سَبِيلًا (١٥٠)

أُولَٰئِكَ هُمُ الْكَافِرُونَ حَقًّا ۚ وَأَعْتَدْنَا لِلْكَافِرِينَ عَذَابًا مُهِينًا (١٥١)

وَالَّذِينَ آمَنُوا بِاللَّهِ وَرُسُلِهِ وَلَمْ يُفَرِّقُوا بَيْنَ أَحَدٍ مِنْهُمْ أُولَٰئِكَ سَوْفَ يُؤْتِيهِمْ أُجُورَهُمْ ۗ وَكَانَ اللَّهُ غَفُورًا رَحِيمًا (١٥٢)

يَسْأَلُكَ أَهْلُ الْكِتَابِ أَنْ تُنَزِّلَ عَلَيْهِمْ كِتَابًا مِنَ السَّمَاءِ ۚ فَقَدْ سَأَلُوا مُوسَىٰ أَكْبَرَ مِنْ ذَٰلِكَ فَقَالُوا أَرِنَا اللَّهَ جَهْرَةً فَأَخَذَتْهُمُ الصَّاعِقَةُ بِظُلْمِهِمْ ۚ ثُمَّ اتَّخَذُوا الْعِجْلَ مِنْ بَعْدِ مَا جَاءَتْهُمُ الْبَيِّنَاتُ فَعَفَوْنَا عَنْ ذَٰلِكَ ۚ وَآتَيْنَا مُوسَىٰ سُلْطَانًا مُبِينًا (١٥٣)

وَرَفَعْنَا فَوْقَهُمُ الطُّورَ بِمِيثَاقِهِمْ وَقُلْنَا لَهُمُ ادْخُلُوا الْبَابَ سُجَّدًا وَقُلْنَا لَهُمْ لَا تَعْدُوا فِي السَّبْتِ وَأَخَذْنَا مِنْهُمْ مِيثَاقًا غَلِيظًا (١٥٤)

فَبِمَا نَقْضِهِمْ مِيثَاقَهُمْ وَكُفْرِهِمْ بِآيَاتِ اللَّهِ وَقَتْلِهِمُ الْأَنْبِيَاءَ بِغَيْرِ حَقٍّ وَقَوْلِهِمْ قُلُوبُنَا غُلْفٌ ۚ بَلْ طَبَعَ اللَّهُ عَلَيْهَا بِكُفْرِهِمْ فَلَا يُؤْمِنُونَ إِلَّا قَلِيلًا (١٥٥)

وَبِكُفْرِهِمْ وَقَوْلِهِمْ عَلَىٰ مَرْيَمَ بُهْتَانًا عَظِيمًا (١٥٦)

وَقَوْلِهِمْ إِنَّا قَتَلْنَا الْمَسِيحَ عِيسَى ابْنَ مَرْيَمَ رَسُولَ اللَّهِ وَمَا قَتَلُوهُ وَمَا صَلَبُوهُ وَلَٰكِنْ شُبِّهَ لَهُمْ ۚ وَإِنَّ الَّذِينَ اخْتَلَفُوا فِيهِ لَفِي شَكٍّ مِنْهُ ۚ مَا لَهُمْ بِهِ مِنْ عِلْمٍ إِلَّا اتِّبَاعَ الظَّنِّ ۚ وَمَا قَتَلُوهُ يَقِينًا (١٥٧)

بَلْ رَفَعَهُ اللَّهُ إِلَيْهِ ۚ وَكَانَ اللَّهُ عَزِيزًا حَكِيمًا (١٥٨)

4. The Women

4:158. Nay, Allah exalted him in His presence. And Allah is ever Mighty, Wise.

4:159. And there is none of the People of the Book but will believe in this before his death; and on the day of Resurrection he will be a witness against them.

4:160. So for the iniquity of the Jews, We forbade them the good things which had been made lawful for them, and for their hindering many (people) from Allah's way.

4:161. And for their taking usury though indeed they were forbidden it and their devouring the property of people falsely. And We have prepared for the disbelievers from among them a painful chastisement.

4:162. But the firm in knowledge among them and the believers believe in that which has been revealed to thee and that which was revealed before thee, and those who keep up prayer and give the poor-rate and the believers in Allah and the Last Day -- these it is to whom We shall give a mighty reward.

***

4:163. Surely We have revealed to thee as We revealed to Noah and the prophets after him, and We revealed to Abraham and Ishmael and Isaac and Jacob and the tribes, and Jesus and Job and Jonah and Aaron and Solomon, and We gave to David a scripture.

4:164. And (We sent) messengers We have mentioned to thee before and messengers We have not mentioned to thee. And to Moses Allah addressed His word, speaking (to him)--

4:165. Messengers, bearers of good news and warners, so that the people may have no plea against Allah after the (coming of) messengers. And Allah is ever Mighty, Wise.

4:166. But Allah bears witness by that which He has revealed to thee that He

وَإِنْ مِنْ أَهْلِ الْكِتَابِ إِلَّا لَيُؤْمِنَنَّ بِهِ قَبْلَ مَوْتِهِ وَيَوْمَ الْقِيَامَةِ يَكُونُ عَلَيْهِمْ شَهِيدًا (١٥٩)

فَبِظُلْمٍ مِنَ الَّذِينَ هَادُوا حَرَّمْنَا عَلَيْهِمْ طَيِّبَاتٍ أُحِلَّتْ لَهُمْ وَبِصَدِّهِمْ عَنْ سَبِيلِ اللَّهِ كَثِيرًا (١٦٠)

وَأَخْذِهِمُ الرِّبَا وَقَدْ نُهُوا عَنْهُ وَأَكْلِهِمْ أَمْوَالَ النَّاسِ بِالْبَاطِلِ وَأَعْتَدْنَا لِلْكَافِرِينَ مِنْهُمْ عَذَابًا أَلِيمًا (١٦١)

لَكِنِ الرَّاسِخُونَ فِي الْعِلْمِ مِنْهُمْ وَالْمُؤْمِنُونَ يُؤْمِنُونَ بِمَا أُنْزِلَ إِلَيْكَ وَمَا أُنْزِلَ مِنْ قَبْلِكَ وَالْمُقِيمِينَ الصَّلَاةَ وَالْمُؤْتُونَ الزَّكَاةَ وَالْمُؤْمِنُونَ بِاللَّهِ وَالْيَوْمِ الْآخِرِ أُولَئِكَ سَنُؤْتِيهِمْ أَجْرًا عَظِيمًا (١٦٢)

إِنَّا أَوْحَيْنَا إِلَيْكَ كَمَا أَوْحَيْنَا إِلَى نُوحٍ وَالنَّبِيِّينَ مِنْ بَعْدِهِ وَأَوْحَيْنَا إِلَى إِبْرَاهِيمَ وَإِسْمَاعِيلَ وَإِسْحَاقَ وَيَعْقُوبَ وَالْأَسْبَاطِ وَعِيسَى وَأَيُّوبَ وَيُونُسَ وَهَارُونَ وَسُلَيْمَانَ وَآتَيْنَا دَاوُودَ زَبُورًا (١٦٣)

وَرُسُلًا قَدْ قَصَصْنَاهُمْ عَلَيْكَ مِنْ قَبْلُ وَرُسُلًا لَمْ نَقْصُصْهُمْ عَلَيْكَ وَكَلَّمَ اللَّهُ مُوسَى تَكْلِيمًا (١٦٤)

رُسُلًا مُبَشِّرِينَ وَمُنْذِرِينَ لِئَلَّا يَكُونَ لِلنَّاسِ عَلَى اللَّهِ حُجَّةٌ بَعْدَ الرُّسُلِ وَكَانَ اللَّهُ عَزِيزًا حَكِيمًا (١٦٥)

لَكِنِ اللَّهُ يَشْهَدُ بِمَا أَنْزَلَ إِلَيْكَ أَنْزَلَهُ بِعِلْمِهِ وَالْمَلَائِكَةُ يَشْهَدُونَ وَكَفَى بِاللَّهِ شَهِيدًا (١٦٦)

إِنَّ الَّذِينَ كَفَرُوا وَصَدُّوا عَنْ سَبِيلِ اللَّهِ قَدْ ضَلُّوا ضَلَالًا بَعِيدًا (١٦٧)

إِنَّ الَّذِينَ كَفَرُوا وَظَلَمُوا لَمْ يَكُنِ اللَّهُ لِيَغْفِرَ لَهُمْ وَلَا لِيَهْدِيَهُمْ طَرِيقًا

4. The Women

has revealed it with His knowledge, and the angels (also) bear witness. And Allah is sufficient as a witness.

4:167. Those who disbelieve and hinder (others) from Allah's way, they indeed have erred, going far astray.

4:168. Those who disbelieve and act unjustly, Allah will never forgive them, nor guide them to a path,

4:169. Except the path of hell, to abide in it for a long time. And that is easy to Allah.

4:170. O mankind, the Messenger has indeed come to you with truth from your Lord, so believe, it is better for you. And if you disbelieve, then surely to Allah belongs whatever is in the heavens and the earth. And Allah is ever Knowing, Wise.

4:171. O People of the Book, exceed not the limits in your religion nor speak anything about Allah, but the truth. The Messiah, Jesus, son of Mary, is only a messenger of Allah and His word which He communicated to Mary and a mercy from Him. So believe in Allah and His messengers. And say not, Three. Desist, it is better for you. Allah is only one God. Far be it from His glory to have a son. To Him belongs whatever is in the heavens and whatever is in the earth. And sufficient is Allah as having charge of affairs.

***

4:172. The Messiah disdains not to be a servant of Allah, not do the angels who are near to Him. And whoever disdains His service and is proud, He will gather them all together to Himself.

4:173. Then as for those who believe and do good, He will pay them fully their rewards and give them more out of His grace. And as for those who disdain and are proud, He will chastise them with a painful chastisement,

4:173.b And they will find for themselves besides Allah no friend nor helper.

(١٦٨) إِلَّا طَرِيقَ جَهَنَّمَ خَالِدِينَ فِيهَا أَبَدًا وَكَانَ ذَلِكَ عَلَى اللَّهِ يَسِيرًا (١٦٩) يَا أَيُّهَا النَّاسُ قَدْ جَاءَكُمُ الرَّسُولُ بِالْحَقِّ مِنْ رَبِّكُمْ فَآمِنُوا خَيْرًا لَكُمْ وَإِنْ تَكْفُرُوا فَإِنَّ لِلَّهِ مَا فِي السَّمَاوَاتِ وَالْأَرْضِ وَكَانَ اللَّهُ عَلِيمًا حَكِيمًا (١٧٠) يَا أَهْلَ الْكِتَابِ لَا تَغْلُوا فِي دِينِكُمْ وَلَا تَقُولُوا عَلَى اللَّهِ إِلَّا الْحَقَّ إِنَّمَا الْمَسِيحُ عِيسَى ابْنُ مَرْيَمَ رَسُولُ اللَّهِ وَكَلِمَتُهُ أَلْقَاهَا إِلَى مَرْيَمَ وَرُوحٌ مِنْهُ فَآمِنُوا بِاللَّهِ وَرُسُلِهِ وَلَا تَقُولُوا ثَلَاثَةٌ انْتَهُوا خَيْرًا لَكُمْ إِنَّمَا اللَّهُ إِلَهٌ وَاحِدٌ سُبْحَانَهُ أَنْ يَكُونَ لَهُ وَلَدٌ لَهُ مَا فِي السَّمَاوَاتِ وَمَا فِي الْأَرْضِ وَكَفَى بِاللَّهِ وَكِيلًا (١٧١) لَنْ يَسْتَنْكِفَ الْمَسِيحُ أَنْ يَكُونَ عَبْدًا لِلَّهِ وَلَا الْمَلَائِكَةُ الْمُقَرَّبُونَ وَمَنْ يَسْتَنْكِفْ عَنْ عِبَادَتِهِ وَيَسْتَكْبِرْ فَسَيَحْشُرُهُمْ إِلَيْهِ جَمِيعًا (١٧٢) فَأَمَّا الَّذِينَ آمَنُوا وَعَمِلُوا الصَّالِحَاتِ فَيُوَفِّيهِمْ أُجُورَهُمْ وَيَزِيدُهُمْ مِنْ فَضْلِهِ وَأَمَّا الَّذِينَ اسْتَنْكَفُوا وَاسْتَكْبَرُوا فَيُعَذِّبُهُمْ عَذَابًا أَلِيمًا وَلَا يَجِدُونَ لَهُمْ مِنْ دُونِ اللَّهِ وَلِيًّا وَلَا نَصِيرًا (١٧٣) يَا أَيُّهَا النَّاسُ قَدْ جَاءَكُمْ بُرْهَانٌ مِنْ رَبِّكُمْ وَأَنْزَلْنَا إِلَيْكُمْ نُورًا مُبِينًا (١٧٤) فَأَمَّا الَّذِينَ آمَنُوا بِاللَّهِ وَاعْتَصَمُوا بِهِ فَسَيُدْخِلُهُمْ فِي رَحْمَةٍ مِنْهُ وَفَضْلٍ وَيَهْدِيهِمْ إِلَيْهِ صِرَاطًا مُسْتَقِيمًا (١٧٥) يَسْتَفْتُونَكَ قُلِ اللَّهُ يُفْتِيكُمْ فِي الْكَلَالَةِ

4:174. O people, manifest proof has indeed come to you from your Lord and We have sent down to you a clear light.

4:175. Then as for those who believe in Allah and hold fast by Him, He will admit them to His mercy and grace, and guide them to Himself on a right path.

4:176. They ask thee for a decision. Say: Allah gives you a decision concerning the person who has neither parents nor children. If a man dies (and) he has no son and he has a sister, hers is half of what he leaves, and he shall be her heir if she has no son. But if there be two (sisters), they shall have two-thirds of what he leaves. And if there are brethren, men and women, then for the male is the like of the portion of two females. Allah makes dear to you, lest you err. And Allah is Knower of all things.

5. The Food

In the name of Allah, the Beneficent, the Merciful.

5:1. O you who believe, fulfil the obligations. The cattle quadrupeds are allowed to you except that which is recited to you, not violating the prohibition against game when you are on the pilgrimage. Surely Allah orders what He pleases.

5:2. O you who believe, violate not the signs of Allah, nor the Sacred Month, nor the offerings, nor the victims with garlands, nor those repairing to the Sacred House seeking the grace and pleasure of their Lord. And when you are free from pilgrimage obligations, then hunt. And let not hatred of a people -- because they hindered you from the Sacred Mosque incite you to transgress. And help one another in righteousness and piety, and help not

5. The Food

one another in sin and aggression, and keep your duty to Allah. Surely Allah is severe in requiting (evil).

5:3. Forbidden to you is that which dies of itself, and blood, and flesh of swine, and that on which any other name than that of Allah has been invoked, and the strangled (animal), and that beaten to death, and that killed by a fall, and that killed by goring with the horn, and that which wild beasts have eaten -- except what you slaughter; and that which is sacrificed on scones set up (for idols), and that you seek to divide by arrows; that is a transgression. This day have those who disbelieve despaired of your religion, so fear them not, and fear Me. This day have I perfected for you your religion and completed My favour to you and chosen for you Islam as a religion. But whoever is compelled by hunger, not inclining wilfully to sin, then surely Allah is Forgiving, Merciful.

5:4. They ask thee as to what is allowed them. Say: The good things are allowed to you, and what you have taught the beasts and birds of prey, training them to hunt -- you teach them of what Allah has taught you; so eat of that which they catch for you and mention the name of Allah over it; and keep your duty to Allah. Surely Allah is Swift in reckoning.

5:5. This day (all) good things are made lawful for you. And the food of those who have been given the Book is lawful for you and your food is lawful for them. And so are the chaste from among the believing women and the chaste from among those who have been given the Book before you, when you give them their dowries, taking (them) in marriage, not fornicating nor taking them for paramours in secret. And whoever denies faith, his work indeed is vain; and in the Hereafter he is of the losers.

حُرِّمَتْ عَلَيْكُمُ الْمَيْتَةُ وَالدَّمُ وَلَحْمُ الْخِنْزِيرِ وَمَا أُهِلَّ لِغَيْرِ اللَّهِ بِهِ وَالْمُنْخَنِقَةُ وَالْمَوْقُوذَةُ وَالْمُتَرَدِّيَةُ وَالنَّطِيحَةُ وَمَا أَكَلَ السَّبُعُ إِلَّا مَا ذَكَّيْتُمْ وَمَا ذُبِحَ عَلَى النُّصُبِ وَأَنْ تَسْتَقْسِمُوا بِالْأَزْلَامِ ذَلِكُمْ فِسْقٌ الْيَوْمَ يَئِسَ الَّذِينَ كَفَرُوا مِنْ دِينِكُمْ فَلَا تَخْشَوْهُمْ وَاخْشَوْنِ الْيَوْمَ أَكْمَلْتُ لَكُمْ دِينَكُمْ وَأَتْمَمْتُ عَلَيْكُمْ نِعْمَتِي وَرَضِيتُ لَكُمُ الْإِسْلَامَ دِينًا فَمَنِ اضْطُرَّ فِي مَخْمَصَةٍ غَيْرَ مُتَجَانِفٍ لِإِثْمٍ فَإِنَّ اللَّهَ غَفُورٌ رَحِيمٌ (٣) يَسْأَلُونَكَ مَاذَا أُحِلَّ لَهُمْ قُلْ أُحِلَّ لَكُمُ الطَّيِّبَاتُ وَمَا عَلَّمْتُمْ مِنَ الْجَوَارِحِ مُكَلِّبِينَ تُعَلِّمُونَهُنَّ مِمَّا عَلَّمَكُمُ اللَّهُ فَكُلُوا مِمَّا أَمْسَكْنَ عَلَيْكُمْ وَاذْكُرُوا اسْمَ اللَّهِ عَلَيْهِ وَاتَّقُوا اللَّهَ إِنَّ اللَّهَ سَرِيعُ الْحِسَابِ (٤) الْيَوْمَ أُحِلَّ لَكُمُ الطَّيِّبَاتُ وَطَعَامُ الَّذِينَ أُوتُوا الْكِتَابَ حِلٌّ لَكُمْ وَطَعَامُكُمْ حِلٌّ لَهُمْ وَالْمُحْصَنَاتُ مِنَ الْمُؤْمِنَاتِ وَالْمُحْصَنَاتُ مِنَ الَّذِينَ أُوتُوا الْكِتَابَ مِنْ قَبْلِكُمْ إِذَا آتَيْتُمُوهُنَّ أُجُورَهُنَّ مُحْصِنِينَ غَيْرَ مُسَافِحِينَ وَلَا مُتَّخِذِي أَخْدَانٍ وَمَنْ يَكْفُرْ بِالْإِيمَانِ فَقَدْ حَبِطَ عَمَلُهُ وَهُوَ فِي الْآخِرَةِ مِنَ الْخَاسِرِينَ (٥) يَا أَيُّهَا الَّذِينَ آمَنُوا إِذَا قُمْتُمْ إِلَى الصَّلَاةِ فَاغْسِلُوا وُجُوهَكُمْ وَأَيْدِيَكُمْ إِلَى الْمَرَافِقِ وَامْسَحُوا بِرُءُوسِكُمْ وَأَرْجُلَكُمْ إِلَى الْكَعْبَيْنِ وَإِنْ كُنْتُمْ جُنُبًا فَاطَّهَّرُوا وَإِنْ كُنْتُمْ مَرْضَى أَوْ عَلَى سَفَرٍ أَوْ جَاءَ أَحَدٌ مِنْكُمْ مِنَ الْغَائِطِ أَوْ لَامَسْتُمُ النِّسَاءَ فَلَمْ تَجِدُوا مَاءً فَتَيَمَّمُوا صَعِيدًا طَيِّبًا فَامْسَحُوا

***

5:6. O you who believe, when you rise up for prayer, wash your faces, and your hands up to the elbows, and wipe your heads, and (wash) your feet up to the ankles. And if you are under an obligation, then wash (yourselves). And if you are sick or on a journey, or one of you comes from the privy, or you have had contact with women and you cannot find water, betake yourselves to pure earth and wipe your faces and your hands therewith. Allah desires not to place a burden on you but He wishes to purify you, and that He may complete His favour on you, so that you may give thanks.

5:7. And remember Allah's favour on you and His covenant with which He bound you when you said: We have heard and we obey. And keep your duty to Allah. Surely Allah knows what is in the breasts.

5:8. O you who believe, be upright for Allah, bearers of witness with justice; and let not hatred of a people incite you not to act equitably. Be just; that is nearer to observance of duty. And keep your duty to Allah. Surely Allah is Aware of what you do.

5:9. Allah has promised to those who believe and do good deeds: For them is forgiveness and a mighty reward.

5:10. And those who disbelieve and reject Our messages, such are the companions of the flaming fire.

5:11. O you who believe, remember Allah's favour on you when a people had determined to stretch out their hands against you, but He withheld their hands from you; and keep your duty to Allah. And on Allah let the believers rely.

***

5:12. And certainly Allah made a covenant with the Children of Israel, and We raised up among them twelve chieftains. And Allah said: Surely I am with you. If you keep up prayer and pay the poor-rate and believe in My messengers and assist them and offer to Allah a goodly gift, I will certainly cover your evil deeds, and cause you to enter Gardens wherein rivers flow. But whoever among you disbelieves after that, he indeed strays from the right way.

5:13. But on account of their breaking their covenant We cursed them and hardened their hearts. They alter the words from their places and neglect a portion of that whereof they were reminded. And thou wilt always discover treachery in them excepting a few of them so pardon them and forgive. Surely Allah loves those who do good (to others).

5:14. And with those who say, We are Christians, We made a covenant, but they neglected a portion of that whereof they were reminded so We stirred up enmity and hatred among them to the day of Resurrection. And Allah will soon inform them of what they did.

5:15. O People of the Book, indeed Our Messenger has come to you, making clear to you much of that which you concealed of the Book and passing over much. Indeed, there has come to you from Allah, a Light and a clear Book,

5:16. Whereby Allah guides such as follow His pleasure into the ways of peace, and brings them out of darkness into light by His will, and guides them to the right path.

5:17. They indeed disbelieve who say: Surely, Allah He is the Messiah, son of Mary. Say: Who then could control anything as against Allah when He wished to destroy the Messiah, son of Mary, and his mother and all those on the earth? And Allah's is the kingdom of the heavens and the earth and what is between them. He creates what He pleases. And Allah is Possessor of

5. The Food

power over all things.

5:18. And the Jews and the Christians say: We are the sons of Allah and His beloved ones. Say: Why does He then chastise you for your sins? Nay, you are mortals from among those whom He has created. He forgives whom He pleases and chastises whom He pleases. And Allah's is the kingdom of the heavens and the earth and what is between them, and to Him is the eventual coming.

5:19. O People of the Book, indeed our Messenger has come to you explaining to you after a cessation of the messengers, lest you say: There came not to us a bearer of good news nor a warner. So indeed a bearer of good news and a warner has come to you. And Allah is Possessor of power over all things.

* * *

5:20. And when Moses said to his people: O my people, remember the favour of Allah to you when He raised prophets among you and made you kings and gave you what He gave not to any other of the nations.

5:21. O my people, enter the Holy Land which Allah has ordained for you and turn not your backs, for then you will turn back losers.

5:22. They said: O Moses, therein are a powerful people, and we shall not enter it until they go out from it; if they go out from it, then surely we will enter.

5:23. Two men of those who feared, on whom Allah had bestowed a favour, said: Enter upon them by the gate, for when you enter it you will surely be victorious; and put your trust in Allah, if you are believers.

5:24. They said: O Moses, we will never enter it so long as they are in it; go therefore thou and thy Lord, and fight; surely here we sit.

5:25. He said: My Lord, I have control

وَإِذْ قَالَ مُوسَىٰ لِقَوْمِهِ يَا قَوْمِ اذْكُرُوا نِعْمَةَ اللَّهِ عَلَيْكُمْ إِذْ جَعَلَ فِيكُمْ أَنْبِيَاءَ وَجَعَلَكُم مُّلُوكًا وَآتَاكُم مَّا لَمْ يُؤْتِ أَحَدًا مِّنَ الْعَالَمِينَ (٢٠)

يَا قَوْمِ ادْخُلُوا الْأَرْضَ الْمُقَدَّسَةَ الَّتِي كَتَبَ اللَّهُ لَكُمْ وَلَا تَرْتَدُّوا عَلَىٰ أَدْبَارِكُمْ فَتَنقَلِبُوا خَاسِرِينَ (٢١)

قَالُوا يَا مُوسَىٰ إِنَّ فِيهَا قَوْمًا جَبَّارِينَ وَإِنَّا لَن نَّدْخُلَهَا حَتَّىٰ يَخْرُجُوا مِنْهَا فَإِن يَخْرُجُوا مِنْهَا فَإِنَّا دَاخِلُونَ (٢٢)

قَالَ رَجُلَانِ مِنَ الَّذِينَ يَخَافُونَ أَنْعَمَ اللَّهُ عَلَيْهِمَا ادْخُلُوا عَلَيْهِمُ الْبَابَ فَإِذَا دَخَلْتُمُوهُ فَإِنَّكُمْ غَالِبُونَ وَعَلَى اللَّهِ فَتَوَكَّلُوا إِن كُنتُم مُّؤْمِنِينَ (٢٣)

قَالُوا يَا مُوسَىٰ إِنَّا لَن نَّدْخُلَهَا أَبَدًا مَّا دَامُوا فِيهَا فَاذْهَبْ أَنتَ وَرَبُّكَ فَقَاتِلَا إِنَّا هَاهُنَا قَاعِدُونَ (٢٤)

قَالَ رَبِّ إِنِّي لَا أَمْلِكُ إِلَّا نَفْسِي وَأَخِي فَافْرُقْ بَيْنَنَا وَبَيْنَ الْقَوْمِ الْفَاسِقِينَ (٢٥)

قَالَ فَإِنَّهَا مُحَرَّمَةٌ عَلَيْهِمْ أَرْبَعِينَ سَنَةً يَتِيهُونَ فِي الْأَرْضِ فَلَا تَأْسَ عَلَى الْقَوْمِ الْفَاسِقِينَ (٢٦)

وَاتْلُ عَلَيْهِمْ نَبَأَ ابْنَيْ آدَمَ بِالْحَقِّ إِذْ قَرَّبَا قُرْبَانًا فَتُقُبِّلَ مِنْ أَحَدِهِمَا وَلَمْ يُتَقَبَّلْ مِنَ الْآخَرِ قَالَ لَأَقْتُلَنَّكَ قَالَ إِنَّمَا يَتَقَبَّلُ اللَّهُ مِنَ الْمُتَّقِينَ (٢٧)

لَئِن بَسَطتَ إِلَيَّ يَدَكَ لِتَقْتُلَنِي مَا أَنَا بِبَاسِطٍ يَدِيَ إِلَيْكَ لِأَقْتُلَكَ إِنِّي أَخَافُ اللَّهَ رَبَّ الْعَالَمِينَ (٢٨)

إِنِّي أُرِيدُ أَن تَبُوءَ بِإِثْمِي وَإِثْمِكَ فَتَكُونَ مِنْ أَصْحَابِ النَّارِ وَذَٰلِكَ جَزَاءُ الظَّالِمِينَ (٢٩)

فَطَوَّعَتْ لَهُ نَفْسُهُ قَتْلَ أَخِيهِ فَقَتَلَهُ

of none but my own self and my brother; so distinguish between us and the transgressing people.

5:26. He said: It will surely be forbidden to them for forty years -- they will wander about in the land. So grieve not for the transgressing people.

* * *

5:27. And relate to them with truth the story of the two sons of Adam, when they offered an offering, but it was accepted from one of them and was not accepted from the other. He said: I will certainly kill thee. (The other) said: Allah accepts only from the dutiful.

5:28. If thou stretch out thy hand against me to kill me I shall not stretch out my hand against thee to kill thee. Surely I fear Allah, the Lord of the worlds:

5:29. I would rather that thou shouldst bear the sin against me and thine own sin, thus thou wouldst be of the companions of the Fire; and that is the recompense of the unjust.

5:30. At length his mind made it easy for him to kill his brother, so he killed him; so he became one of the losers.

5:31. Then Allah sent a crow scratching the ground to show him how to cover the dead body of his brother. He said: Woe is me! Am I not able to be as this crow and cover the dead body of my brother? So he became of those who regret.

5:32. For this reason We prescribed for the Children of Israel that whoever kills a person, unless it be for manslaughter or for mischief in the land, it is as though he had killed all men. And whoever saves a life, it is as though he had saved the lives of all men. And certainly Our messengers came to them with clear arguments, but even after that many of them commit excesses in the land.

5:33. The only punishment of those who wage war against Allah and His

فَأَصْبَحَ مِنَ الْخَاسِرِينَ (٣٠) فَبَعَثَ اللَّهُ غُرَابًا يَبْحَثُ فِي الْأَرْضِ لِيُرِيَهُ كَيْفَ يُوَارِي سَوْأَةَ أَخِيهِ قَالَ يَا وَيْلَتَا أَعَجَزْتُ أَنْ أَكُونَ مِثْلَ هَذَا الْغُرَابِ فَأُوَارِيَ سَوْأَةَ أَخِي فَأَصْبَحَ مِنَ النَّادِمِينَ (٣١)

مِنْ أَجْلِ ذَلِكَ كَتَبْنَا عَلَى بَنِي إِسْرَائِيلَ أَنَّهُ مَنْ قَتَلَ نَفْسًا بِغَيْرِ نَفْسٍ أَوْ فَسَادٍ فِي الْأَرْضِ فَكَأَنَّمَا قَتَلَ النَّاسَ جَمِيعًا وَمَنْ أَحْيَاهَا فَكَأَنَّمَا أَحْيَا النَّاسَ جَمِيعًا وَلَقَدْ جَاءَتْهُمْ رُسُلُنَا بِالْبَيِّنَاتِ ثُمَّ إِنَّ كَثِيرًا مِنْهُمْ بَعْدَ ذَلِكَ فِي الْأَرْضِ لَمُسْرِفُونَ (٣٢)

إِنَّمَا جَزَاءُ الَّذِينَ يُحَارِبُونَ اللَّهَ وَرَسُولَهُ وَيَسْعَوْنَ فِي الْأَرْضِ فَسَادًا أَنْ يُقَتَّلُوا أَوْ يُصَلَّبُوا أَوْ تُقَطَّعَ أَيْدِيهِمْ وَأَرْجُلُهُمْ مِنْ خِلَافٍ أَوْ يُنْفَوْا مِنَ الْأَرْضِ ذَلِكَ لَهُمْ خِزْيٌ فِي الدُّنْيَا وَلَهُمْ فِي الْآخِرَةِ عَذَابٌ عَظِيمٌ (٣٣) إِلَّا الَّذِينَ تَابُوا مِنْ قَبْلِ أَنْ تَقْدِرُوا عَلَيْهِمْ فَاعْلَمُوا أَنَّ اللَّهَ غَفُورٌ رَحِيمٌ (٣٤)

يَا أَيُّهَا الَّذِينَ آمَنُوا اتَّقُوا اللَّهَ وَابْتَغُوا إِلَيْهِ الْوَسِيلَةَ وَجَاهِدُوا فِي سَبِيلِهِ لَعَلَّكُمْ تُفْلِحُونَ (٣٥)

إِنَّ الَّذِينَ كَفَرُوا لَوْ أَنَّ لَهُمْ مَا فِي الْأَرْضِ جَمِيعًا وَمِثْلَهُ مَعَهُ لِيَفْتَدُوا بِهِ مِنْ عَذَابِ يَوْمِ الْقِيَامَةِ مَا تُقُبِّلَ مِنْهُمْ وَلَهُمْ عَذَابٌ أَلِيمٌ (٣٦) يُرِيدُونَ أَنْ يَخْرُجُوا مِنَ النَّارِ وَمَا هُمْ بِخَارِجِينَ مِنْهَا وَلَهُمْ عَذَابٌ مُقِيمٌ (٣٧)

وَالسَّارِقُ وَالسَّارِقَةُ فَاقْطَعُوا أَيْدِيَهُمَا جَزَاءً بِمَا كَسَبَا نَكَالًا مِنَ اللَّهِ وَاللَّهُ

5. The Food

Messenger and strive to make mischief in the land is that they should be murdered, or crucified, or their hands and their feet should be cut off on opposite sides, or they should be imprisoned. This shall he a disgrace for them in this world, and in the Hereafter they shall have a grievous chastisement,

5:34. Except those who repent before you overpower them; so know that Allah is Forgiving, Merciful.

* * *

5:35. O you who believe, keep your duty to Allah, and seek means of nearness to Him, and strive hard in His way that you may be successful.

5:36. Those who disbelieve, even if they had all that is in the earth, and the like of it with it, to ransom themselves therewith from the chastisement of the day of Resurrection, it would not be accepted from them and theirs is a painful chastisement.

5:37. They would desire to come forth from the Fire, and they will not come forth from it, and theirs is a lasting chastisement

5:38. And (as for) the man and the woman addicted to theft, cut off their hands as a punishment for what they have earned, an exemplary punishment from Allah. And Allah is Mighty, Wise.

5:39. But whoever repents after his wrongdoing and reforms, Allah will turn to him (mercifully). Surely Allah is Forgiving, Merciful.

5:40. Knowest thou not that Allah is He to Whom belongs the kingdom of the heavens and the earth? He chastises whom He pleases, and forgives whom He pleases. And Allah is Possessor of power over all things.

5:41. O Messenger, let not those grieve thee who hasten to disbelief, from among those who say with their mouths, We believe, and their hearts

عَزِيزٌ حَكِيمٌ (٣٨)
فَمَنْ تَابَ مِنْ بَعْدِ ظُلْمِهِ وَأَصْلَحَ فَإِنَّ اللَّهَ يَتُوبُ عَلَيْهِ إِنَّ اللَّهَ غَفُورٌ رَحِيمٌ (٣٩)
أَلَمْ تَعْلَمْ أَنَّ اللَّهَ لَهُ مُلْكُ السَّمَاوَاتِ وَالْأَرْضِ يُعَذِّبُ مَنْ يَشَاءُ وَيَغْفِرُ لِمَنْ يَشَاءُ وَاللَّهُ عَلَى كُلِّ شَيْءٍ قَدِيرٌ (٤٠)
يَا أَيُّهَا الرَّسُولُ لَا يَحْزُنْكَ الَّذِينَ يُسَارِعُونَ فِي الْكُفْرِ مِنَ الَّذِينَ قَالُوا آمَنَّا بِأَفْوَاهِهِمْ وَلَمْ تُؤْمِنْ قُلُوبُهُمْ وَمِنَ الَّذِينَ هَادُوا سَمَّاعُونَ لِلْكَذِبِ سَمَّاعُونَ لِقَوْمٍ آخَرِينَ لَمْ يَأْتُوكَ يُحَرِّفُونَ الْكَلِمَ مِنْ بَعْدِ مَوَاضِعِهِ يَقُولُونَ إِنْ أُوتِيتُمْ هَذَا فَخُذُوهُ وَإِنْ لَمْ تُؤْتَوْهُ فَاحْذَرُوا وَمَنْ يُرِدِ اللَّهُ فِتْنَتَهُ فَلَنْ تَمْلِكَ لَهُ مِنَ اللَّهِ شَيْئًا أُولَئِكَ الَّذِينَ لَمْ يُرِدِ اللَّهُ أَنْ يُطَهِّرَ قُلُوبَهُمْ لَهُمْ فِي الدُّنْيَا خِزْيٌ وَلَهُمْ فِي الْآخِرَةِ عَذَابٌ عَظِيمٌ (٤١)
سَمَّاعُونَ لِلْكَذِبِ أَكَّالُونَ لِلسُّحْتِ فَإِنْ جَاءُوكَ فَاحْكُمْ بَيْنَهُمْ أَوْ أَعْرِضْ عَنْهُمْ وَإِنْ تُعْرِضْ عَنْهُمْ فَلَنْ يَضُرُّوكَ شَيْئًا وَإِنْ حَكَمْتَ فَاحْكُمْ بَيْنَهُمْ بِالْقِسْطِ إِنَّ اللَّهَ يُحِبُّ الْمُقْسِطِينَ (٤٢)
وَكَيْفَ يُحَكِّمُونَكَ وَعِنْدَهُمُ التَّوْرَاةُ فِيهَا حُكْمُ اللَّهِ ثُمَّ يَتَوَلَّوْنَ مِنْ بَعْدِ ذَلِكَ وَمَا أُولَئِكَ بِالْمُؤْمِنِينَ (٤٣)
إِنَّا أَنْزَلْنَا التَّوْرَاةَ فِيهَا هُدًى وَنُورٌ يَحْكُمُ بِهَا النَّبِيُّونَ الَّذِينَ أَسْلَمُوا لِلَّذِينَ هَادُوا وَالرَّبَّانِيُّونَ وَالْأَحْبَارُ بِمَا اسْتُحْفِظُوا مِنْ كِتَابِ اللَّهِ وَكَانُوا عَلَيْهِ شُهَدَاءَ فَلَا تَخْشَوُا النَّاسَ وَاخْشَوْنِ

believe not, and from among those who are Jews they are listeners for the Sake of a lie, listeners for another people who have not come to thee. They alter the words after they are put in their (proper) places, saying: If you are given this, take it, and if you are not given this, be cautious. And he for whom Allah intends temptation, thou controllest naught for him against Allah. Those are they whose hearts Allah intends not to purify. For them is disgrace in this world, and for them a grievous chastisement in the Hereafter.

5:42. Listeners for the sake of a lie, devourers of forbidden things, so if they come to thee, judge between them or turn away from them. And if thou turn away from them, they cannot harm thee at all. And if thou judge, judge between them with equity. Surely Allah loves the equitable.

5:43. And how do they make thee a judge and they have the Torah wherein is Allah's judgment? Yet they turn away after that! And these are not believers.

* * *

5:44. Surely We revealed the Torah, having guidance and Light. By it did the prophets who submitted themselves (to Allah) judge for the Jews, and the rabbis and the doctors of law, because they were required to guard the Book of Allah, and they were witnesses thereof. So fear not the people and fear Me, and take not a small price for My messages. And whoever judges not by what Allah has revealed, those are the disbelievers.

5:45. And We prescribed to them in it that life is for life, and eye for eye, and nose for nose, and ear for ear, and tooth for tooth, and for wounds retaliation. But whoso forgoes it, it shall be an expiation for him. And whoever judges not by what Allah has revealed, those are the wrongdoers.

وَلَا تَشْتَرُوا بِآيَاتِي ثَمَنًا قَلِيلًا وَمَنْ لَمْ يَحْكُمْ بِمَا أَنْزَلَ اللَّهُ فَأُولَٰئِكَ هُمُ الْكَافِرُونَ (٤٤)

وَكَتَبْنَا عَلَيْهِمْ فِيهَا أَنَّ النَّفْسَ بِالنَّفْسِ وَالْعَيْنَ بِالْعَيْنِ وَالْأَنْفَ بِالْأَنْفِ وَالْأُذُنَ بِالْأُذُنِ وَالسِّنَّ بِالسِّنِّ وَالْجُرُوحَ قِصَاصٌ فَمَنْ تَصَدَّقَ بِهِ فَهُوَ كَفَّارَةٌ لَهُ وَمَنْ لَمْ يَحْكُمْ بِمَا أَنْزَلَ اللَّهُ فَأُولَٰئِكَ هُمُ الظَّالِمُونَ (٤٥)

وَقَفَّيْنَا عَلَىٰ آثَارِهِمْ بِعِيسَى ابْنِ مَرْيَمَ مُصَدِّقًا لِمَا بَيْنَ يَدَيْهِ مِنَ التَّوْرَاةِ وَآتَيْنَاهُ الْإِنْجِيلَ فِيهِ هُدًى وَنُورٌ وَمُصَدِّقًا لِمَا بَيْنَ يَدَيْهِ مِنَ التَّوْرَاةِ وَهُدًى وَمَوْعِظَةً لِلْمُتَّقِينَ (٤٦)

وَلْيَحْكُمْ أَهْلُ الْإِنْجِيلِ بِمَا أَنْزَلَ اللَّهُ فِيهِ وَمَنْ لَمْ يَحْكُمْ بِمَا أَنْزَلَ اللَّهُ فَأُولَٰئِكَ هُمُ الْفَاسِقُونَ (٤٧)

وَأَنْزَلْنَا إِلَيْكَ الْكِتَابَ بِالْحَقِّ مُصَدِّقًا لِمَا بَيْنَ يَدَيْهِ مِنَ الْكِتَابِ وَمُهَيْمِنًا عَلَيْهِ فَاحْكُمْ بَيْنَهُمْ بِمَا أَنْزَلَ اللَّهُ وَلَا تَتَّبِعْ أَهْوَاءَهُمْ عَمَّا جَاءَكَ مِنَ الْحَقِّ لِكُلٍّ جَعَلْنَا مِنْكُمْ شِرْعَةً وَمِنْهَاجًا وَلَوْ شَاءَ اللَّهُ لَجَعَلَكُمْ أُمَّةً وَاحِدَةً وَلَٰكِنْ لِيَبْلُوَكُمْ فِي مَا آتَاكُمْ فَاسْتَبِقُوا الْخَيْرَاتِ إِلَى اللَّهِ مَرْجِعُكُمْ جَمِيعًا فَيُنَبِّئُكُمْ بِمَا كُنْتُمْ فِيهِ تَخْتَلِفُونَ (٤٨)

وَأَنِ احْكُمْ بَيْنَهُمْ بِمَا أَنْزَلَ اللَّهُ وَلَا تَتَّبِعْ أَهْوَاءَهُمْ وَاحْذَرْهُمْ أَنْ يَفْتِنُوكَ عَنْ بَعْضِ مَا أَنْزَلَ اللَّهُ إِلَيْكَ فَإِنْ تَوَلَّوْا فَاعْلَمْ أَنَّمَا يُرِيدُ اللَّهُ أَنْ يُصِيبَهُمْ بِبَعْضِ ذُنُوبِهِمْ وَإِنَّ كَثِيرًا مِنَ النَّاسِ لَفَاسِقُونَ (٤٩)

أَفَحُكْمَ الْجَاهِلِيَّةِ يَبْغُونَ وَمَنْ أَحْسَنُ مِنَ اللَّهِ حُكْمًا لِقَوْمٍ يُوقِنُونَ (٥٠)

5. The Food

5:46. And We sent after them in their footsteps Jesus, son of Mary, verifying that which was before him of the Torah; and We gave him the Gospel containing guidance and light, and verifying that which was before it of the Torah, and a guidance and an admonition for the dutiful.

5:47. And let the People of the Gospel judge by that which Allah has revealed in it. And whoever judges not by what Allah has revealed, those are the transgressors.

5:48. And We have revealed to thee the Book with the truth, verifying that which is before it of the Book and a guardian over it, so judge between them by what Allah has revealed, and follow not their low desires (turning away) from the truth that has come to thee. For every one of you We appointed a law and a way. And if Allah had pleased He would have made you a single people, but that He might try you in what He gave you. So vie one with another in virtuous deeds. To Allah you will all return, so He will inform you of that wherein you differed;

5:49. And that thou shouldst judge between them by what Allah has revealed, and follow not their low desires, and be cautious of them lest they seduce thee from part of what Allah has revealed to thee. Then if they turn away, know that Allah desires to afflict them for some of their sins. And surely many of the people are transgressors.

5:50. Is it then the judgment of ignorance that they desire? And who is better than Allah to judge for a people who are sure?

* * *

5:51. O you who believe, take not the Jews and the Christians for friends. They are friends of each other. And whoever amongst you takes them for friends he is indeed one of them. Surely Allah guides not the unjust people.

5:52. But thou seest those in whose hearts is a disease, hastening towards them, saying: We fear lest a calamity should befall us. Maybe Allah will bring the victory or a commandment from Himself, so they will regret what they hid in their souls.

5:53. And those who believe will say: Are these they who swore by Allah with their most forcible oaths that they were surely with you? Their deeds will bear no fruit, so they will be losers.

5:54. O you who believe, should any one of you turn back from his religion, then Allah will bring a people, whom He loves and who love Him, humble towards believers, mighty against the disbelievers, striving hard in Allah's way and not fearing the censure of any censurer. This is Allah's grace He gives it to whom He pleases. And Allah is Ample-giving, Knowing.

5:55. Only Allah is your Friend and His Messenger and those who believe, those who keep up prayer and pay the poor-rate, and they bow down.

5:56. And whoever takes Allah and His Messenger and those who believe for friend surely the party of Allah they shall triumph.

* * *

5:57. O you who believe, take not for friends those who take your religion as a mockery and a sport, from among those who were given the Book before you and the disbelievers; and keep your duty to Allah if you are believers.

5:58. And when you call to prayer they take it as a mockery and a sport. That is because they are a people who understand not.

5:59. Say: O People of the Book, do you find fault with us for aught except that we believe in Allah and in that which has been revealed to us and that which

(٥٨)
قُلْ يَا أَهْلَ الْكِتَابِ هَلْ تَنْقِمُونَ مِنَّا إِلَّا أَنْ آمَنَّا بِاللَّهِ وَمَا أُنْزِلَ إِلَيْنَا وَمَا أُنْزِلَ مِنْ قَبْلُ وَأَنَّ أَكْثَرَكُمْ فَاسِقُونَ (٥٩)
قُلْ هَلْ أُنَبِّئُكُمْ بِشَرٍّ مِنْ ذَٰلِكَ مَثُوبَةً عِنْدَ اللَّهِ مَنْ لَعَنَهُ اللَّهُ وَغَضِبَ عَلَيْهِ وَجَعَلَ مِنْهُمُ الْقِرَدَةَ وَالْخَنَازِيرَ وَعَبَدَ الطَّاغُوتَ أُولَٰئِكَ شَرٌّ مَكَانًا وَأَضَلُّ عَنْ سَوَاءِ السَّبِيلِ (٦٠)
وَإِذَا جَاءُوكُمْ قَالُوا آمَنَّا وَقَدْ دَخَلُوا بِالْكُفْرِ وَهُمْ قَدْ خَرَجُوا بِهِ وَاللَّهُ أَعْلَمُ بِمَا كَانُوا يَكْتُمُونَ (٦١)
وَتَرَىٰ كَثِيرًا مِنْهُمْ يُسَارِعُونَ فِي الْإِثْمِ وَالْعُدْوَانِ وَأَكْلِهِمُ السُّحْتَ لَبِئْسَ مَا كَانُوا يَعْمَلُونَ (٦٢)
لَوْلَا يَنْهَاهُمُ الرَّبَّانِيُّونَ وَالْأَحْبَارُ عَنْ قَوْلِهِمُ الْإِثْمَ وَأَكْلِهِمُ السُّحْتَ لَبِئْسَ مَا كَانُوا يَصْنَعُونَ (٦٣)
وَقَالَتِ الْيَهُودُ يَدُ اللَّهِ مَغْلُولَةٌ غُلَّتْ أَيْدِيهِمْ وَلُعِنُوا بِمَا قَالُوا بَلْ يَدَاهُ مَبْسُوطَتَانِ يُنْفِقُ كَيْفَ يَشَاءُ وَلَيَزِيدَنَّ كَثِيرًا مِنْهُمْ مَا أُنْزِلَ إِلَيْكَ مِنْ رَبِّكَ طُغْيَانًا وَكُفْرًا وَأَلْقَيْنَا بَيْنَهُمُ الْعَدَاوَةَ وَالْبَغْضَاءَ إِلَىٰ يَوْمِ الْقِيَامَةِ كُلَّمَا أَوْقَدُوا نَارًا لِلْحَرْبِ أَطْفَأَهَا اللَّهُ وَيَسْعَوْنَ فِي الْأَرْضِ فَسَادًا وَاللَّهُ لَا يُحِبُّ الْمُفْسِدِينَ (٦٤)
وَلَوْ أَنَّ أَهْلَ الْكِتَابِ آمَنُوا وَاتَّقَوْا لَكَفَّرْنَا عَنْهُمْ سَيِّئَاتِهِمْ وَلَأَدْخَلْنَاهُمْ جَنَّاتِ النَّعِيمِ (٦٥)
وَلَوْ أَنَّهُمْ أَقَامُوا التَّوْرَاةَ وَالْإِنْجِيلَ وَمَا أُنْزِلَ إِلَيْهِمْ مِنْ رَبِّهِمْ لَأَكَلُوا مِنْ فَوْقِهِمْ وَمِنْ تَحْتِ أَرْجُلِهِمْ مِنْهُمْ أُمَّةٌ مُقْتَصِدَةٌ وَكَثِيرٌ مِنْهُمْ سَاءَ مَا يَعْمَلُونَ

5. The Food

was revealed before, while most of you are transgressors?

5:60. Say Shall I inform you of those worse than this in retribution from Allah? They are those whom Allah has cursed and upon whom He brought His wrath and of whom He made apes and swine, and who serve the devil. These are in a worse plight and further astray from the straight path.

5:61. And when they come to you, they say, We believe, and surely they come in unbelief and they go forth in it. And Allah knows best what they conceal.

5:62. And thou seest many of them vying one with another in sin and transgression, and their devouring illegal gain. Certainly evil is that which they do.

5:63. Why do not the rabbis and the doctors of law prohibit them from their sinful utterances and their devouring unlawful gain? Certainly evil are the works they do.

5:64. And the Jews say: The hand of Allah is tied up. Their own hands are shackled and they are cursed for what they say. Nay, both His hands are spread out. He disburses as He pleases. And that which has been revealed to thee from thy Lord will certainly make many of them increase in inordinacy and disbelief. And We have cast among them enmity and hatred till the day of Resurrection. Whenever they kindle a fire for war Allah puts it out, and they strive to make mischief in the land. And Allah loves not the mischief-makers.

5:65. And if the People of the Book had believed and kept their duty We would certainly have removed from them their evils, and made them enter gardens of bliss.

5:66. And if they had observed the Torah and the Gospel and that which is revealed to them from their Lord, they would certainly have eaten from above

(٦٦)
يَا أَيُّهَا الرَّسُولُ بَلِّغْ مَا أُنْزِلَ إِلَيْكَ مِنْ رَبِّكَ وَإِنْ لَمْ تَفْعَلْ فَمَا بَلَّغْتَ رِسَالَتَهُ وَاللَّهُ يَعْصِمُكَ مِنَ النَّاسِ إِنَّ اللَّهَ لَا يَهْدِي الْقَوْمَ الْكَافِرِينَ (٦٧)
قُلْ يَا أَهْلَ الْكِتَابِ لَسْتُمْ عَلَى شَيْءٍ حَتَّى تُقِيمُوا التَّوْرَاةَ وَالْإِنْجِيلَ وَمَا أُنْزِلَ إِلَيْكُمْ مِنْ رَبِّكُمْ وَلَيَزِيدَنَّ كَثِيرًا مِنْهُمْ مَا أُنْزِلَ إِلَيْكَ مِنْ رَبِّكَ طُغْيَانًا وَكُفْرًا فَلَا تَأْسَ عَلَى الْقَوْمِ الْكَافِرِينَ (٦٨)
إِنَّ الَّذِينَ آمَنُوا وَالَّذِينَ هَادُوا وَالصَّابِئُونَ وَالنَّصَارَى مَنْ آمَنَ بِاللَّهِ وَالْيَوْمِ الْآخِرِ وَعَمِلَ صَالِحًا فَلَا خَوْفٌ عَلَيْهِمْ وَلَا هُمْ يَحْزَنُونَ (٦٩)
لَقَدْ أَخَذْنَا مِيثَاقَ بَنِي إِسْرَائِيلَ وَأَرْسَلْنَا إِلَيْهِمْ رُسُلًا كُلَّمَا جَاءَهُمْ رَسُولٌ بِمَا لَا تَهْوَى أَنْفُسُهُمْ فَرِيقًا كَذَّبُوا وَفَرِيقًا يَقْتُلُونَ (٧٠)
وَحَسِبُوا أَلَّا تَكُونَ فِتْنَةٌ فَعَمُوا وَصَمُّوا ثُمَّ تَابَ اللَّهُ عَلَيْهِمْ ثُمَّ عَمُوا وَصَمُّوا كَثِيرٌ مِنْهُمْ وَاللَّهُ بَصِيرٌ بِمَا يَعْمَلُونَ (٧١)
لَقَدْ كَفَرَ الَّذِينَ قَالُوا إِنَّ اللَّهَ هُوَ الْمَسِيحُ ابْنُ مَرْيَمَ وَقَالَ الْمَسِيحُ يَا بَنِي إِسْرَائِيلَ اعْبُدُوا اللَّهَ رَبِّي وَرَبَّكُمْ إِنَّهُ مَنْ يُشْرِكْ بِاللَّهِ فَقَدْ حَرَّمَ اللَّهُ عَلَيْهِ الْجَنَّةَ وَمَأْوَاهُ النَّارُ وَمَا لِلظَّالِمِينَ مِنْ أَنْصَارٍ (٧٢)
لَقَدْ كَفَرَ الَّذِينَ قَالُوا إِنَّ اللَّهَ ثَالِثُ ثَلَاثَةٍ وَمَا مِنْ إِلَهٍ إِلَّا إِلَهٌ وَاحِدٌ وَإِنْ لَمْ يَنْتَهُوا عَمَّا يَقُولُونَ لَيَمَسَّنَّ الَّذِينَ كَفَرُوا مِنْهُمْ عَذَابٌ أَلِيمٌ (٧٣)
أَفَلَا يَتُوبُونَ إِلَى اللَّهِ وَيَسْتَغْفِرُونَهُ

them and from beneath their feet. There is a party of them keeping to the moderate course; and most of them -- evil is that which they do.

* * *

5:67. O Messenger, deliver that which has been revealed to thee from thy Lord; and if thou do (it) not, thou hast not delivered His message. And Allah will protect thee from men. Surely Allah guides not the disbelieving people.

5:68. Say: O People of the Book, you follow no good till you observe the Torah and the Gospel and that which is revealed to you from your Lord. And surely that which has been revealed to thee from thy Lord will make many of them increase in inordinacy and disbelief: so grieve not for the disbelieving people.

5:69. Surely those who believe and those who are Jews and the Sabeans and the Christians -- whoever believes in Allah and the Last Day and does good -- they shall have no fear nor shall they grieve.

5:70. Certainly We made a covenant with the Children of Israel and We sent to them messengers. Whenever a messenger came to them with that which their souls desired not, some (of them) they called liars and some they (even) sought to kill.

5:71. And they thought that there would be no affliction, so they became blind and deaf; then Allah turned to them mercifully but many of them (again) became blind and deaf. And Allah is Seer of what they do.

5:72. Certainly they disbelieve who say: Allah, He is the Messiah, son of Mary. And the Messiah said: O Children of Israel, serve Allah, my Lord and your Lord. Surely who ever associates (others) with Allah, Allah has forbidden to him the Garden and his abode is the Fire. And for the wrongdoers there will be no helpers.

5:73. Certainly they disbelieve who say: Allah is the third of the three. And there is no God but One God. And if they desist not from what they say, a painful chastisement will surely befall such of them as disbelieve.

5:74. Will they not then turn to Allah and ask His forgiveness? And Allah is Forgiving, Merciful.

5:75. The Messiah, son of Mary, was only a messenger; messengers before him had indeed passed away. And his mother was a truthful woman. They both used to eat food. See how We make the messages clear to them! Then behold, how they are turned away!

5:76. Say: Do you serve besides Allah that which controls for you neither harm nor good? And Allah -- He is the Hearing, the Knowing.

5:77. Say: O People of the Book, exaggerate not in the matter of your religion unjustly, and follow not the low desires of people who went astray before and led many astray, and went astray from the right path.

***

5:78. Those who disbelieved from among the Children of Israel were cursed by the tongue of David and Jesus, son of Mary. This was because they disobeyed and exceeded the limits.

5:79. They forbade not one another the hateful things they did. Evil indeed was what they did.

5:80. Thou seest many of them befriending those who disbelieve. Certainly evil is that which their souls send before for them, so that Allah is displeased with them, and in chastisement will they abide.

5:81. And if they believed in Allah and the Prophet and that which is revealed to him, they would not take them for friends, but most of them are transgressors.

فَاكْتُبْنَا مَعَ الشَّاهِدِينَ (٨٣) وَمَا لَنَا لَا نُؤْمِنُ بِاللَّهِ وَمَا جَاءَنَا مِنَ الْحَقِّ وَنَطْمَعُ أَنْ يُدْخِلَنَا رَبُّنَا مَعَ الْقَوْمِ الصَّالِحِينَ (٨٤) فَأَثَابَهُمُ اللَّهُ بِمَا قَالُوا جَنَّاتٍ تَجْرِي مِنْ تَحْتِهَا الْأَنْهَارُ خَالِدِينَ فِيهَا وَذَلِكَ جَزَاءُ الْمُحْسِنِينَ (٨٥) وَالَّذِينَ كَفَرُوا وَكَذَّبُوا بِآيَاتِنَا أُولَئِكَ أَصْحَابُ الْجَحِيمِ (٨٦) يَا أَيُّهَا الَّذِينَ آمَنُوا لَا تُحَرِّمُوا طَيِّبَاتِ مَا أَحَلَّ اللَّهُ لَكُمْ وَلَا تَعْتَدُوا إِنَّ اللَّهَ لَا يُحِبُّ الْمُعْتَدِينَ (٨٧) وَكُلُوا مِمَّا رَزَقَكُمُ اللَّهُ حَلَالًا طَيِّبًا وَاتَّقُوا اللَّهَ الَّذِي أَنْتُمْ بِهِ مُؤْمِنُونَ (٨٨) لَا يُؤَاخِذُكُمُ اللَّهُ بِاللَّغْوِ فِي أَيْمَانِكُمْ وَلَكِنْ يُؤَاخِذُكُمْ بِمَا عَقَّدْتُمُ الْأَيْمَانَ فَكَفَّارَتُهُ إِطْعَامُ عَشَرَةِ مَسَاكِينَ مِنْ أَوْسَطِ مَا تُطْعِمُونَ أَهْلِيكُمْ أَوْ كِسْوَتُهُمْ أَوْ تَحْرِيرُ رَقَبَةٍ فَمَنْ لَمْ يَجِدْ فَصِيَامُ ثَلَاثَةِ أَيَّامٍ ذَلِكَ كَفَّارَةُ أَيْمَانِكُمْ إِذَا حَلَفْتُمْ وَاحْفَظُوا أَيْمَانَكُمْ كَذَلِكَ يُبَيِّنُ اللَّهُ لَكُمْ آيَاتِهِ لَعَلَّكُمْ تَشْكُرُونَ (٨٩) يَا أَيُّهَا الَّذِينَ آمَنُوا إِنَّمَا الْخَمْرُ وَالْمَيْسِرُ وَالْأَنْصَابُ وَالْأَزْلَامُ رِجْسٌ مِنْ عَمَلِ الشَّيْطَانِ فَاجْتَنِبُوهُ لَعَلَّكُمْ تُفْلِحُونَ (٩٠) إِنَّمَا يُرِيدُ الشَّيْطَانُ أَنْ يُوقِعَ بَيْنَكُمُ الْعَدَاوَةَ وَالْبَغْضَاءَ فِي الْخَمْرِ وَالْمَيْسِرِ وَيَصُدَّكُمْ عَنْ ذِكْرِ اللَّهِ وَعَنِ الصَّلَاةِ فَهَلْ أَنْتُمْ مُنْتَهُونَ (٩١) وَأَطِيعُوا اللَّهَ وَأَطِيعُوا الرَّسُولَ وَاحْذَرُوا فَإِنْ تَوَلَّيْتُمْ فَاعْلَمُوا أَنَّمَا

5:82. Thou wilt certainly find the most violent of people in enmity against the believers to be the Jews and the idolaters; and thou wilt find the nearest in friendship to the believers to be those who say, We are Christians. That is because there are priests and monks among them and because they are not proud.

***

5:83. And when they hear that which has been revealed to the Messenger thou seest their eyes overflow with tears because of the truth they recognize. They say: Our Lord, we believe, so write us down with the witnesses.

5:84. And what (reason) have we that we should not believe in Allah and in the Truth that has come to us, while we earnestly desire that our Lord should cause us to enter with the righteous people?

5:85. So Allah rewarded them for what they said; with Gardens wherein rivers flow to abide in them. And that is the reward of the doers of good.

5:86. And those who disbelieve and reject Our messages, such are the companions of the flaming fire.

***

5:87. O you who believe, forbid not the good things which Allah has made lawful for you and exceed not the limits. Surely Allah loves not those who exceed the limits.

5:88. And eat of the lawful and good (things) that Allah has given you, and keep your duty to Allah, in Whom you believe.

5:89. Allah will not call you to account for that which is vain in your oaths, but He will call you to account for the making of deliberate oaths so its expiation is the feeding of ten poor men with the average (food) you feed your families with, or their clothing, or the freeing of a neck. But whoso finds

عَلَىٰ رَسُولِنَا الْبَلَاغُ الْمُبِينُ (٩٢) لَيْسَ عَلَى الَّذِينَ آمَنُوا وَعَمِلُوا الصَّالِحَاتِ جُنَاحٌ فِيمَا طَعِمُوا إِذَا مَا اتَّقَوْا وَآمَنُوا وَعَمِلُوا الصَّالِحَاتِ ثُمَّ اتَّقَوْا وَآمَنُوا ثُمَّ اتَّقَوْا وَأَحْسَنُوا وَاللَّهُ يُحِبُّ الْمُحْسِنِينَ (٩٣) يَا أَيُّهَا الَّذِينَ آمَنُوا لَيَبْلُوَنَّكُمُ اللَّهُ بِشَيْءٍ مِنَ الصَّيْدِ تَنَالُهُ أَيْدِيكُمْ وَرِمَاحُكُمْ لِيَعْلَمَ اللَّهُ مَنْ يَخَافُهُ بِالْغَيْبِ فَمَنِ اعْتَدَىٰ بَعْدَ ذَٰلِكَ فَلَهُ عَذَابٌ أَلِيمٌ (٩٤) يَا أَيُّهَا الَّذِينَ آمَنُوا لَا تَقْتُلُوا الصَّيْدَ وَأَنْتُمْ حُرُمٌ وَمَنْ قَتَلَهُ مِنْكُمْ مُتَعَمِّدًا فَجَزَاءٌ مِثْلُ مَا قَتَلَ مِنَ النَّعَمِ يَحْكُمُ بِهِ ذَوَا عَدْلٍ مِنْكُمْ هَدْيًا بَالِغَ الْكَعْبَةِ أَوْ كَفَّارَةٌ طَعَامُ مَسَاكِينَ أَوْ عَدْلُ ذَٰلِكَ صِيَامًا لِيَذُوقَ وَبَالَ أَمْرِهِ عَفَا اللَّهُ عَمَّا سَلَفَ وَمَنْ عَادَ فَيَنْتَقِمُ اللَّهُ مِنْهُ وَاللَّهُ عَزِيزٌ ذُو انْتِقَامٍ (٩٥) أُحِلَّ لَكُمْ صَيْدُ الْبَحْرِ وَطَعَامُهُ مَتَاعًا لَكُمْ وَلِلسَّيَّارَةِ وَحُرِّمَ عَلَيْكُمْ صَيْدُ الْبَرِّ مَا دُمْتُمْ حُرُمًا وَاتَّقُوا اللَّهَ الَّذِي إِلَيْهِ تُحْشَرُونَ (٩٦) جَعَلَ اللَّهُ الْكَعْبَةَ الْبَيْتَ الْحَرَامَ قِيَامًا لِلنَّاسِ وَالشَّهْرَ الْحَرَامَ وَالْهَدْيَ وَالْقَلَائِدَ ذَٰلِكَ لِتَعْلَمُوا أَنَّ اللَّهَ يَعْلَمُ مَا فِي السَّمَاوَاتِ وَمَا فِي الْأَرْضِ وَأَنَّ اللَّهَ بِكُلِّ شَيْءٍ عَلِيمٌ (٩٧) اعْلَمُوا أَنَّ اللَّهَ شَدِيدُ الْعِقَابِ وَأَنَّ اللَّهَ غَفُورٌ رَحِيمٌ (٩٨) مَا عَلَى الرَّسُولِ إِلَّا الْبَلَاغُ وَاللَّهُ يَعْلَمُ مَا تُبْدُونَ وَمَا تَكْتُمُونَ (٩٩) قُلْ لَا يَسْتَوِي الْخَبِيثُ وَالطَّيِّبُ وَلَوْ أَعْجَبَكَ كَثْرَةُ الْخَبِيثِ فَاتَّقُوا اللَّهَ يَا

not (means) should fast for three days. This is the expiation of your oaths when you swear. And keep your oaths. Thus does Allah make clear to you His messages that you may give thanks.

5:90. O you who believe, intoxicants and games of chance and (sacrificing to) stones set up and (dividing by) arrows are only an uncleanness, the devil's work; so shun it that you may succeed.

5:91. The devil desires only to create enmity and hatred among you by means of intoxicants and games of chance, and to keep you back from the remembrance of Allah and from prayer. Will you then keep back?

5:92. And obey Allah and obey the Messenger and be cautious. But if you turn back then know that the duty of Our Messenger is only a clear deliverance of the message.

5:93. On those who believe and do good there is no blame for what they eat, when they keep their duty and believe and do good deeds, then keep their duty and believe, then keep their duty and do good (to others). And Allah loves the doers of good.

* * *

5:94. O you who believe, Allah will certainly try you in respect of some game which your hands and your lances can reach, that Allah may know who fears Him in secret. Whoever exceeds the limit after this, for him is a painful chastisement.

5:95. O you who believe, kill not game while you are on pilgrimage. And whoever among you kills it intentionally, the compensation thereof is the like of what he killed, from the cattle, as two just persons among you judge, as an offering to be brought to the Ka'bah, or the expiation thereof is the feeding of the poor or equivalent of it in fasting, that he may taste the unwholesome result of his deed. Allah

5. The Food

pardons what happened in the past. And whoever returns (to it), Allah will punish him. And Allah is Mighty; Lord of Retribution.

5:96. Lawful to you is the game of the sea and its food, a provision for you and for the travellers, and the game of the land is forbidden to you so long as you are on pilgrimage, and keep your duty to Allah, to Whom you shall be gathered.

5:97. Allah has made the Ka'bah, the Sacred House, a means of support for the people, and the sacred month and the offerings and the victims with garlands. That is that you may know that Allah knows whatever is in the heavens and whatever is in the earth, and that Allah is Knower of all things.

5:98. Know that Allah is severe in requiting (evil) and that Allah is Forgiving, Merciful.

5:99. The duty of the Messenger is only to deliver (the message). And Allah knows what you do openly and what you hide.

5:100. Say: The bad and the good are not equal, though the abundance of the bad may please thee. So keep your duty to Allah, O men of understanding, that you may succeed.

***

5:101. O you who believe, ask not about things which if made known to you would give you trouble; and if you ask about them when the Qur'an is being revealed, they will be made known to you. Allah pardons this; and Allah is Forgiving, Forbearing.

5:102. A people before you indeed asked such questions, then became disbelievers therein.

5:103. Allah has not ordained a bahirah or a sa'ibah or a wasilah or a hami, but those who disbelieve fabricate a lie against Allah. And most of them understand not.

5:104. And when it is said to them,

Come to that which Allah has revealed and to the Messenger, they say Sufficient for us is that wherein we found our fathers. What! even though their fathers knew nothing and had no guidance!

5:105. O you who believe, take care of your souls -- he who errs cannot harm you when you are on the right way. To Allah you will all return, so He will inform you of what you did.

5:106. O you who believe, call to witness between you, when death draws nigh to one of you, at the time of making the will, two just persons from among you, or two others from among others than you, if you are travelling in the land and the calamity of death befalls you. You should detain them after the prayer. Then if you doubt (them), they shall both swear by Allah (saying): We will not take for it a price, though there be a relative nor will we hide the testimony of Allah, for then certainly we shall be sinners.

5:107. If it be discovered that they are guilty of a sin, two others shall stand up in their place from among those against whom the first two have been guilty of a sin; so they shall swear by Allah: Certainly our testimony is truer than the testimony of those two, and we have not exceeded the limit, for then surely we should be unjust.

5:108. Thus it is more probable that they will give true testimony or fear that other oaths will be taken after their oaths. And keep your duty to Allah and hearken. And Allah guides not the transgressing people.

* * *

5:109. On the day when Allah will gather together the messengers and say: What was the response you received? They will say We have no knowledge. Surely Thou art the great Knower of the unseen.

5:110. When Allah will say: O Jesus,

أَحَدًا مِنَ الْعَالَمِينَ (١١٥)
وَإِذْ قَالَ اللَّهُ يَا عِيسَى ابْنَ مَرْيَمَ أَأَنْتَ قُلْتَ لِلنَّاسِ اتَّخِذُونِي وَأُمِّيَ إِلَهَيْنِ مِنْ دُونِ اللَّهِ قَالَ سُبْحَانَكَ مَا يَكُونُ لِي أَنْ أَقُولَ مَا لَيْسَ لِي بِحَقٍّ إِنْ كُنْتُ قُلْتُهُ فَقَدْ عَلِمْتَهُ تَعْلَمُ مَا فِي نَفْسِي وَلَا أَعْلَمُ مَا فِي نَفْسِكَ إِنَّكَ أَنْتَ عَلَّامُ الْغُيُوبِ (١١٦)
مَا قُلْتُ لَهُمْ إِلَّا مَا أَمَرْتَنِي بِهِ أَنِ اعْبُدُوا اللَّهَ رَبِّي وَرَبَّكُمْ وَكُنْتُ عَلَيْهِمْ شَهِيدًا مَا دُمْتُ فِيهِمْ فَلَمَّا تَوَفَّيْتَنِي كُنْتَ أَنْتَ الرَّقِيبَ عَلَيْهِمْ وَأَنْتَ عَلَى كُلِّ شَيْءٍ شَهِيدٌ (١١٧)
إِنْ تُعَذِّبْهُمْ فَإِنَّهُمْ عِبَادُكَ وَإِنْ تَغْفِرْ لَهُمْ فَإِنَّكَ أَنْتَ الْعَزِيزُ الْحَكِيمُ (١١٨)
قَالَ اللَّهُ هَذَا يَوْمُ يَنْفَعُ الصَّادِقِينَ صِدْقُهُمْ لَهُمْ جَنَّاتٌ تَجْرِي مِنْ تَحْتِهَا الْأَنْهَارُ خَالِدِينَ فِيهَا أَبَدًا رَضِيَ اللَّهُ عَنْهُمْ وَرَضُوا عَنْهُ ذَلِكَ الْفَوْزُ الْعَظِيمُ (١١٩)
لِلَّهِ مُلْكُ السَّمَاوَاتِ وَالْأَرْضِ وَمَا فِيهِنَّ وَهُوَ عَلَى كُلِّ شَيْءٍ قَدِيرٌ (١٢٠)

son of Mary, remember My favour to thee and to thy mother, when I strengthened thee with the Holy Spirit; thou spokest to people in the cradle and in old age, and when I taught thee the Book and the Wisdom and the Torah and the Gospel, and when thou didst determine out of clay a thing like the form of a bird by My permission, then thou didst breathe into it and it became a bird by My permission; and thou didst heal the blind and the leprous by My permission; and when thou didst raise the dead by My permission; and when I withheld the Children of Israel from thee when thou camest to them with clear arguments -- but those of them who disbelieved said: This is nothing but clear enchantment.

5:111. And when I revealed to the disciples, saying, Believe in Me and My messenger, they said: We believe and bear witness that we submit.

5:112. When the disciples said: O Jesus, son of Mary, is thy Lord able to send down food to us from heaven? He said: Keep your duty to Allah if you are believers.

5:113. They said: We desire to eat of it, and that our hearts should be at rest, and that we may know that thou hast indeed spoken truth to us, and that we may be witnesses thereof.

5:114. Jesus, son of Mary, said: O Allah, our Lord, send down to us food from heaven which should be to us an ever-recurring happiness to the first of us and the last of us, and a sign from Thee, and give us sustenance and Thou art the Best of the sustainers.

5:115. Allah said: Surely I will send it down to you, but whoever disbelieves afterwards from among you, I will chastise him with a chastisement with which I will not chastise any one among the nations.

* * *

5:116. And when Allah will say: O Jesus, son of Mary, didst thou say to men, Take me and my mother for two gods besides Allah? He will say: Glory be to Thee! it was not for me to say what I had no right to (say). If I had said it, Thou wouldst indeed have known it. Thou knowest what is in my mind, and I know not what is in Thy mind. Surely Thou art the great Knower of the unseen.

5:117. I said to them naught save as Thou didst command me: Serve Allah, my Lord and your Lord; and I was a witness of them so long as I was among them, but when Thou didst cause me to die Thou wast the Watcher over them. And Thou art Witness of all things.

5:118. If Thou chastise them, surely they are Thy servants; and if Thou protect them, surely Thou art the Mighty, the Wise.

5:119. Allah will say: This is a day when their truth will profit the truthful ones. For them are Gardens wherein flow rivers abiding therein forever. Allah is well pleased with them and they are well pleased with Allah. That is the mighty achievement.

5:120. Allah's is the kingdom of the heavens and the earth and whatever is in them; and He is Possessor of power over all things.

6. The Cattle

Sura 6. The Cattle (Al-An'am)
In the name of Allah, the Beneficent, the Merciful.

6:1. Praise be to Allah, Who created the heavens and the earth, and made darkness and light. Yet those who disbelieve set up equals to their Lord.

6:2. He it is Who created you from clay, then He decreed a term. And there is a term named with Him; still you doubt.

6:3. And He is Allah in the heavens and

٦- سورة الأنعام

بِسْمِ اللَّهِ الرَّحْمَنِ الرَّحِيمِ
الْحَمْدُ لِلَّهِ الَّذِي خَلَقَ السَّمَاوَاتِ وَالْأَرْضَ وَجَعَلَ الظُّلُمَاتِ وَالنُّورَ ثُمَّ الَّذِينَ كَفَرُوا بِرَبِّهِمْ يَعْدِلُونَ (١)
هُوَ الَّذِي خَلَقَكُمْ مِنْ طِينٍ ثُمَّ قَضَى أَجَلًا وَأَجَلٌ مُسَمًّى عِنْدَهُ ثُمَّ أَنْتُمْ تَمْتَرُونَ (٢)
وَهُوَ اللَّهُ فِي السَّمَاوَاتِ وَفِي الْأَرْضِ

6. The Cattle

in the earth. He knows your secret (thoughts) and your open (words), and He knows what you earn.

6:4. And there comes not to them any message of the messages of their Lord but they turn away from it.

6:5. So they rejected the truth when it came to them, but soon will come to them the news of that which they mocked.

6:6. See they not how many a generation We destroyed before them, whom We had established in the earth as We have not established you, and We sent the clouds pouring abundant rain on them, and We made the rivers flow beneath them? Then We destroyed them for their sins, and raised up after them another generation.

6:7. And if We had sent down to thee a writing on paper, then they had touched it with their hands, those who disbelieve would have said: This is nothing but clear enchantment.

6:8. And they say: Why has not an angel been sent down to him? And if We send down an angel, the matter would be decided and then they would not be respited.

6:9. And if We had made him an angel, We would certainly have made him a man, and (thus) made confused to them what they confuse.

6:10. And certainly messengers before thee were derided, but that which they derided encompassed those of them who scoffed.

***

6:11. Say: Travel in the land, then see what was the end of the rejectors.

6:12. Say: To whom belongs whatever is in the heavens and the earth? Say: To Allah. He has ordained mercy on Himself. He will certainly gather you on the Resurrection day -- there is no doubt about it. Those who have lost their souls will not believe.

6:13. And to Him belongs whatever dwells in the night and the day. And He is the Hearing, the Knowing.

6:14. Say: Shall I take for a friend other than Allah, the Originator of the heavens and the earth, and He feeds and is not fed? Say: I am commanded to be the first of those who submit. And be thou not of the polytheists.

6:15. Say: Surely I fear, if I disobey my Lord, the chastisement of a grievous day.

6:16. He from whom it is averted on that day, Allah indeed has had mercy on him. And this is a manifest achievement.

6:17. And if Allah touch thee with affliction, there is none to remove it but He. And if He touch thee with good, He is Possessor of power over all things.

6:18. And He is the Supreme, above His servants. And He is the Wise, the Aware.

6:19. Say: What thing is the weightiest in testimony? Say: Allah is witness between you and me. And this Qur'an has been revealed to me that with it I may warn you and whomsoever it reaches. Do you really bear witness that there are other gods with Allah? Say: I bear not witness. Say: He is only One God, and surely I am innocent of that which you set up (with Him).

6:20. Those whom We have given the Book recognize him as they recognize their sons. Those who have lost their souls -- they will not believe.

* * *

6:21. And who is more unjust than he who forges a lie against Allah or gives the lie to His messages? Surely the wrongdoers will not be successful.

6:22. And on the day We gather them all together, then We shall say to those who set up gods (with Allah): Where are your associate-gods whom you asserted?

السَّمَاوَاتِ وَالْأَرْضِ وَهُوَ يُطْعِمُ وَلَا يُطْعَمُ قُلْ إِنِّي أُمِرْتُ أَنْ أَكُونَ أَوَّلَ مَنْ أَسْلَمَ وَلَا تَكُونَنَّ مِنَ الْمُشْرِكِينَ (١٤)

قُلْ إِنِّي أَخَافُ إِنْ عَصَيْتُ رَبِّي عَذَابَ يَوْمٍ عَظِيمٍ (١٥)

مَنْ يُصْرَفْ عَنْهُ يَوْمَئِذٍ فَقَدْ رَحِمَهُ وَذَلِكَ الْفَوْزُ الْمُبِينُ (١٦)

وَإِنْ يَمْسَسْكَ اللَّهُ بِضُرٍّ فَلَا كَاشِفَ لَهُ إِلَّا هُوَ وَإِنْ يَمْسَسْكَ بِخَيْرٍ فَهُوَ عَلَى كُلِّ شَيْءٍ قَدِيرٌ (١٧)

وَهُوَ الْقَاهِرُ فَوْقَ عِبَادِهِ وَهُوَ الْحَكِيمُ الْخَبِيرُ (١٨)

قُلْ أَيُّ شَيْءٍ أَكْبَرُ شَهَادَةً قُلِ اللَّهُ شَهِيدٌ بَيْنِي وَبَيْنَكُمْ وَأُوحِيَ إِلَيَّ هَذَا الْقُرْآنُ لِأُنْذِرَكُمْ بِهِ وَمَنْ بَلَغَ أَئِنَّكُمْ لَتَشْهَدُونَ أَنَّ مَعَ اللَّهِ آلِهَةً أُخْرَى قُلْ لَا أَشْهَدُ قُلْ إِنَّمَا هُوَ إِلَهٌ وَاحِدٌ وَإِنَّنِي بَرِيءٌ مِمَّا تُشْرِكُونَ (١٩)

الَّذِينَ آتَيْنَاهُمُ الْكِتَابَ يَعْرِفُونَهُ كَمَا يَعْرِفُونَ أَبْنَاءَهُمُ الَّذِينَ خَسِرُوا أَنْفُسَهُمْ فَهُمْ لَا يُؤْمِنُونَ (٢٠)

وَمَنْ أَظْلَمُ مِمَّنِ افْتَرَى عَلَى اللَّهِ كَذِبًا أَوْ كَذَّبَ بِآيَاتِهِ إِنَّهُ لَا يُفْلِحُ الظَّالِمُونَ (٢١)

وَيَوْمَ نَحْشُرُهُمْ جَمِيعًا ثُمَّ نَقُولُ لِلَّذِينَ أَشْرَكُوا أَيْنَ شُرَكَاؤُكُمُ الَّذِينَ كُنْتُمْ تَزْعُمُونَ (٢٢)

ثُمَّ لَمْ تَكُنْ فِتْنَتُهُمْ إِلَّا أَنْ قَالُوا وَاللَّهِ رَبِّنَا مَا كُنَّا مُشْرِكِينَ (٢٣)

انْظُرْ كَيْفَ كَذَبُوا عَلَى أَنْفُسِهِمْ وَضَلَّ عَنْهُمْ مَا كَانُوا يَفْتَرُونَ (٢٤)

وَمِنْهُمْ مَنْ يَسْتَمِعُ إِلَيْكَ وَجَعَلْنَا عَلَى قُلُوبِهِمْ أَكِنَّةً أَنْ يَفْقَهُوهُ وَفِي آذَانِهِمْ

6. The Cattle

6:23. Then their excuse would be nothing but that they would say: By Allah, our Lord! we were not polytheists.

6:24. See how they lie against their own souls, and that which they forged shall fail them!

6:25. And of them is he who hearkens to thee and We have cast veils over their hearts so that they understand it not and a deafness into their ears. And (even) if they see every sign they will not believe in it. So much so that when they come to thee they only dispute with thee -- those who disbelieve say: This is naught but stories of the ancients.

6:26. And they forbid (others) from it, and they keep away from it; and they ruin none but their own souls while they perceive not.

6:27. And if thou couldst see when they are made to stand before the Fire, and say: Would that we were sent back! We would not reject the messages of our Lord but would be of the believers.

6:28. Nay, that which they concealed before will become manifest to them. And if they were sent back, they would certainly go back to that which they are forbidden, and surely they are liars.

6:29. And they say: There is nothing but our life of this world and we shall not be raised again.

6:30. And if thou couldst see when they are made to stand before their Lord! He will say: Is not this the truth? They will say: Yea, by our Lord! He will say: Taste then the chastisement because you disbelieved.

***

6:31. They are losers indeed who reject the meeting with Allah, until when the hour comes upon them suddenly, they will say: O our grief for out neglecting it! And they bear their burdens on their backs. Now surely evil is that which they bear!

وَقْرًا وَإِنْ يَرَوْا كُلَّ آيَةٍ لَا يُؤْمِنُوا بِهَا حَتَّى إِذَا جَاءُوكَ يُجَادِلُونَكَ يَقُولُ الَّذِينَ كَفَرُوا إِنْ هَذَا إِلَّا أَسَاطِيرُ الْأَوَّلِينَ (٢٥)

وَهُمْ يَنْهَوْنَ عَنْهُ وَيَنْأَوْنَ عَنْهُ وَإِنْ يُهْلِكُونَ إِلَّا أَنْفُسَهُمْ وَمَا يَشْعُرُونَ (٢٦)

وَلَوْ تَرَى إِذْ وُقِفُوا عَلَى النَّارِ فَقَالُوا يَا لَيْتَنَا نُرَدُّ وَلَا نُكَذِّبَ بِآيَاتِ رَبِّنَا وَنَكُونَ مِنَ الْمُؤْمِنِينَ (٢٧)

بَلْ بَدَا لَهُمْ مَا كَانُوا يُخْفُونَ مِنْ قَبْلُ وَلَوْ رُدُّوا لَعَادُوا لِمَا نُهُوا عَنْهُ وَإِنَّهُمْ لَكَاذِبُونَ (٢٨)

وَقَالُوا إِنْ هِيَ إِلَّا حَيَاتُنَا الدُّنْيَا وَمَا نَحْنُ بِمَبْعُوثِينَ (٢٩)

وَلَوْ تَرَى إِذْ وُقِفُوا عَلَى رَبِّهِمْ قَالَ أَلَيْسَ هَذَا بِالْحَقِّ قَالُوا بَلَى وَرَبِّنَا قَالَ فَذُوقُوا الْعَذَابَ بِمَا كُنْتُمْ تَكْفُرُونَ (٣٠)

قَدْ خَسِرَ الَّذِينَ كَذَّبُوا بِلِقَاءِ اللَّهِ حَتَّى إِذَا جَاءَتْهُمُ السَّاعَةُ بَغْتَةً قَالُوا يَا حَسْرَتَنَا عَلَى مَا فَرَّطْنَا فِيهَا وَهُمْ يَحْمِلُونَ أَوْزَارَهُمْ عَلَى ظُهُورِهِمْ أَلَا سَاءَ مَا يَزِرُونَ (٣١)

وَمَا الْحَيَاةُ الدُّنْيَا إِلَّا لَعِبٌ وَلَهْوٌ وَلَلدَّارُ الْآخِرَةُ خَيْرٌ لِلَّذِينَ يَتَّقُونَ أَفَلَا تَعْقِلُونَ (٣٢)

قَدْ نَعْلَمُ إِنَّهُ لَيَحْزُنُكَ الَّذِي يَقُولُونَ فَإِنَّهُمْ لَا يُكَذِّبُونَكَ وَلَكِنَّ الظَّالِمِينَ بِآيَاتِ اللَّهِ يَجْحَدُونَ (٣٣)

وَلَقَدْ كُذِّبَتْ رُسُلٌ مِنْ قَبْلِكَ فَصَبَرُوا عَلَى مَا كُذِّبُوا وَأُوذُوا حَتَّى أَتَاهُمْ نَصْرُنَا وَلَا مُبَدِّلَ لِكَلِمَاتِ اللَّهِ وَلَقَدْ جَاءَكَ مِنْ نَبَإِ الْمُرْسَلِينَ (٣٤)

6. The Cattle

6:32. And this worlds life is naught but a play and an idle sport. And certainly the abode of the Hereafter is better for those who keep their duty. Do you not then understand?

6:33. We know indeed that what they say grieves thee, for surely they give not thee the lie, but the wrongdoers give the lie to Allah's messages.

6:34. And messengers indeed were rejected before thee, but they were patient when rejected and persecuted, until Our help came to them. And there is none to change the words of Allah. And there has already come to thee some information about the messengers.

6:35. And if their turning away is hard on thee, then, if thou canst, seek an opening into the earth or a ladder to heaven, to bring them a sign! And if Allah pleased, He would certainly have gathered them all to guidance, so be not of the ignorant.

6:36. Only those accept who listen. And as for the dead, Allah will raise them, then to Him they will be returned.

6:37. And they say: Why has not a sign been sent down to him from his Lord? Say: Surely Allah is Able to send down a sign, but most of them know not?'

6:38. And there is no animal in the earth, nor a bird that flies on its two wings, but (they are) communities like yourselves. We have not neglected anything in the Book. Then to their Lord will they be gathered.

6:39. And those who reject Our messages are deaf and dumb, in darkness. Whom Allah pleases He leaves in error. And whom He pleases He places on the right way.

6:40. Say: See, if the chastisement of Allah overtake you or the hour come upon you, will you call on others than Allah, if you are truthful?

6:41. Nay, Him you call upon, so He removes that for which you pray, if He

وَإِنْ كَانَ كَبُرَ عَلَيْكَ إِعْرَاضُهُمْ فَإِنِ اسْتَطَعْتَ أَنْ تَبْتَغِيَ نَفَقًا فِي الْأَرْضِ أَوْ سُلَّمًا فِي السَّمَاءِ فَتَأْتِيَهُمْ بِآيَةٍ وَلَوْ شَاءَ اللَّهُ لَجَمَعَهُمْ عَلَى الْهُدَى فَلَا تَكُونَنَّ مِنَ الْجَاهِلِينَ (٣٥)

إِنَّمَا يَسْتَجِيبُ الَّذِينَ يَسْمَعُونَ وَالْمَوْتَى يَبْعَثُهُمُ اللَّهُ ثُمَّ إِلَيْهِ يُرْجَعُونَ (٣٦)

وَقَالُوا لَوْلَا نُزِّلَ عَلَيْهِ آيَةٌ مِنْ رَبِّهِ قُلْ إِنَّ اللَّهَ قَادِرٌ عَلَى أَنْ يُنَزِّلَ آيَةً وَلَكِنَّ أَكْثَرَهُمْ لَا يَعْلَمُونَ (٣٧)

وَمَا مِنْ دَابَّةٍ فِي الْأَرْضِ وَلَا طَائِرٍ يَطِيرُ بِجَنَاحَيْهِ إِلَّا أُمَمٌ أَمْثَالُكُمْ مَا فَرَّطْنَا فِي الْكِتَابِ مِنْ شَيْءٍ ثُمَّ إِلَى رَبِّهِمْ يُحْشَرُونَ (٣٨)

وَالَّذِينَ كَذَّبُوا بِآيَاتِنَا صُمٌّ وَبُكْمٌ فِي الظُّلُمَاتِ مَنْ يَشَأِ اللَّهُ يُضْلِلْهُ وَمَنْ يَشَأْ يَجْعَلْهُ عَلَى صِرَاطٍ مُسْتَقِيمٍ (٣٩)

قُلْ أَرَأَيْتَكُمْ إِنْ أَتَاكُمْ عَذَابُ اللَّهِ أَوْ أَتَتْكُمُ السَّاعَةُ أَغَيْرَ اللَّهِ تَدْعُونَ إِنْ كُنْتُمْ صَادِقِينَ (٤٠)

بَلْ إِيَّاهُ تَدْعُونَ فَيَكْشِفُ مَا تَدْعُونَ إِلَيْهِ إِنْ شَاءَ وَتَنْسَوْنَ مَا تُشْرِكُونَ (٤١)

وَلَقَدْ أَرْسَلْنَا إِلَى أُمَمٍ مِنْ قَبْلِكَ فَأَخَذْنَاهُمْ بِالْبَأْسَاءِ وَالضَّرَّاءِ لَعَلَّهُمْ يَتَضَرَّعُونَ (٤٢)

فَلَوْلَا إِذْ جَاءَهُمْ بَأْسُنَا تَضَرَّعُوا وَلَكِنْ قَسَتْ قُلُوبُهُمْ وَزَيَّنَ لَهُمُ الشَّيْطَانُ مَا كَانُوا يَعْمَلُونَ (٤٣)

فَلَمَّا نَسُوا مَا ذُكِّرُوا بِهِ فَتَحْنَا عَلَيْهِمْ أَبْوَابَ كُلِّ شَيْءٍ حَتَّى إِذَا فَرِحُوا بِمَا أُوتُوا أَخَذْنَاهُمْ بَغْتَةً فَإِذَا هُمْ مُبْلِسُونَ

6. The Cattle

pleases, and you forget what you set up (with Him).

6:42. And indeed We sent (messengers) to nations before thee then We seized them with distress and affliction that they might humble themselves.

6:43. Yet why did they not, when Our punishment came to them, humble themselves? But their hearts hardened and the devil made all that they did seem fair to them.

6:44. Then, when they neglected that with which they had been admonished, We opened for them the gates of all things. Until, when they rejoiced in that which they were given; We seized them suddenly; then lo! they were in utter despair.

6:45. So the roots of the people who did wrong were cut off. And praise be to Allah, the Lord of the worlds.

6:46. Say: Have you considered that if Allah should take away your hearing and your sight and seal your hearts, who is the god besides Allah that can bring it to you? See how We repeat the messages yet they turn away!

6:47. Say: See, if the chastisement of Allah should overtake you suddenly or openly, will any be destroyed but the wrongdoing people?

6:48. And We send not messengers but as bearers of good news and warners then whoever believes and acts aright, they shall have no fear, nor shall they grieve.

6:49. And as for those who reject Our messages, chastisement will afflict them because they transgressed.

6:50. Say: I say not to you, I have with me the treasures of Allah, nor do I know the unseen, nor do I say to you that I am an angel; I follow only that which is revealed to me. Say: Are the blind and the seeing alike? Do you not then reflect?

6:51. And warn with it those who fear that they will be gathered to their Lord there is no protector for them, nor any intercessor besides Him so that they may keep their duty.

6:52. And drive not away those who call upon their Lord, morning and evening, desiring only His pleasure. Neither art thou accountable for them in aught, nor are they accountable for thee in aught, that thou shouldst drive them away and thus be of the wrongdoers.

6:53. And thus do We try some of them by others so that they say: Are these they upon whom Allah has conferred benefit from among us? Does not Allah best know the grateful?

6:54. And when those who believe in Our messages come to thee say: Peace be to you, your Lord has ordained mercy on Himself, (so) that if any one of you does evil in ignorance, then turns after that and acts aright, then He is Forgiving, Merciful.

6:55. And thus do We make distinct the messages and so that the way of the guilty may become clear.

6:56. Say: I am forbidden to serve those whom you call upon besides Allah. Say: I follow not your low desires, for then indeed I should go astray and should not be of the guided ones.

6:57. Say: Surely I have manifest proof from my Lord and you call it a lie. I have not with me that which you would hasten. The judgment is only Allah's. He relates the truth and He is the Best of deciders.

6:58. Say: If that which you would hasten were with me, the matter would have certainly been decided between you and me. And Allah best knows the wrongdoers.

6:59. And with Him are the treasures of the unseen -- none knows them but He. And He knows what is in the land and the sea. And there falls not a leaf but He knows it, nor is there a grain in the darkness of the earth, nor anything green or dry, but (it is all) in a clear book.

6:60. And He it is Who takes your souls at night, and He knows what you earn by day, then He raises you up therein that an appointed term may be fulfilled. Then to Him is your return, then He will inform you of what you did.

* * *

6:61. And He is the Supreme above His servants, and He sends keepers over you; until when death comes to one of you, Our messengers cause him to die, and they are not remiss.

6:62. Then are they sent back to Allah, their Master, the True one. Now surely His is the judgment and He is Swiftest in taking account

6:63. Say: Who is it that delivers you from the calamities of the land and the sea? (when) you call upon Him, in humility and in secret: If He deliver us from this, we will certainly be of the grateful ones.

6:64. Say: Allah delivers you from this and from every distress, yet you set up others (with Him).

6:65. Say: He has the power to send on you a chastisement from above you or from beneath your feet, or to throw you into confusion, (making you) of different parties, and make some of you taste the violence of others. See how We repeat the messages that they may understand!

6:66. And thy people call it a lie and it is the Truth. Say: I am not put in charge of you.

6:67. For every prophecy is a term, and you will soon come to know (it).

6:68. And when thou seest those who talk nonsense about Our messages, withdraw from them until they enter into some other discourse. And if the devil cause thee to forget, then sit not after recollection with the unjust people.

6:69. And those who keep their duty are not accountable for them in aught but (theirs) is only to remind; haply they may guard against evil.

6:70. And leave those who take their religion for a play and an idle sport, and whom this world's life has deceived, and remind (men) hereby lest a soul be destroyed for what it has earned. It has besides Allah no friend nor intercessor, and though it offer every compensation, it will not be accepted from it. Those are they who are destroyed for what they earn. For them is a drink of boiling water and a painful chastisement, because they disbelieved.

* * *

6:71. Say: Shall we call, besides Allah, on that which profits us not nor harms us, and shall we be turned back on our heels after Allah has guided us? Like one whom the devils cause to follow his low desires, in bewilderment in the earth, he has companions who call him to the right way (saying), Come to us. Say: Surely the guidance of Allah, that is the (true) guidance. And we are commanded to submit to the Lord of the worlds:

6:72. And that you should keep up prayer and keep your duty to Him. And He it is to Whom you shall be gathered.

6:73. And He it is Who created the heavens and the earth with truth. And when He says, Be, it is.

6:73.b His word is the truth and His is the kingdom on the day when the trumpet is blown. The Knower of the unseen and the seen; and He is the Wise, the Aware.

6:74. And when Abraham said to his sire, Azar: Takest thou idols for gods? Surely I see thee and thy people in manifest error.

6:75. And thus did We show Abraham the kingdom of the heavens and the

6. The Cattle

earth and that he might be of those having certainty.

6:76. So when the night overshadowed, him, he saw a star. He said: Is this my Lord? So when it set, he said I love not the setting ones.

6:77. Then when he saw the moon rising, he said: Is this my Lord? So when it set, he said: If my Lord had not guided me, I should certainly be of the erring people.

6:78. Then when he saw the sun rising, he said: Is this my Lord? Is this the greatest? So when it set, he said: O my people, I am clear of what you set up (with Allah).

6:79. Surely I have turned myself, being upright, wholly to Him Who originated the heavens and the earth, and I am not of the polytheists.

6:80. And his people disputed with him. He said: Do you dispute with me respecting Allah and He has guided me indeed? And I fear not in any way those that you set up with Him, unless my Lord please. My Lord comprehends all things in His knowledge. Will you not then mind?

6:81. And how should I fear what you have set up (with Him), while you fear not to set up with Allah that for which He has sent down to you no authority. Which then of the two parties is surer of security, if you know?

6:82. Those who believe and mix not up their faith with iniquity for them is security and they go aright.

***

6:83. And this was Our argument which We gave to Abraham against his people. We exalt in degrees whom We please. Surely thy Lord is Wise, Knowing.

6:84. And We gave him Isaac and Jacob. Each did We guide; and Noah did We guide before, and of his descendants, David and Solomon and Job and Joseph and Moses and Aaron.

And thus do We reward those who do good (to others):

6:85. And Zacharias and John and Jesus and Elias; each one (of them) was of the righteous,

6:86. And Ishmael and Elisha and Jonah and Lot; and each one (of them) We made to excel the people;

6:87. And some of their fathers and their descendants and their brethren. And We chose them and guided them to the right way.

6:88. This is Allah's guidance wherewith He guides whom He pleases of His servants. And if they had associated others (with Him), all that they did would have been vain.

6:89. These are they to, whom We gave the Book and authority and prophecy. Therefore if these disbelieve in it, We have indeed entrusted it to a people who are not disbelievers in it.

6:90. These are they whom Allah guided, so follow their guidance. Say: I ask you not for any reward for it. It is naught but a Reminder to the nations.

***

6:91. And they honour not Allah with the honour due to Him, when they say: Allah has not revealed anything, to a mortal. Say: Who revealed the Book which Moses brought, a light and a guidance to men -- you make it into (scattered) papers, which you show and you conceal much? And you are taught that which neither you nor your fathers knew. Say: Allah. Then leave them sporting in their idle talk.

6:92. And this is a Blessed Book We have revealed, verifying that which is before it, and that thou mayest warn the mother of the towns and those around her. And those who believe in the Hereafter believe in it, and they keep a watch over their prayers.

6:93. And who is more unjust than he who forges a lie against Allah, or says, Revelation has been granted to me

6. The Cattle

while nothing has been revealed to him; and he who says: I can reveal the like of that which Allah has revealed? And if thou couldst see when the wrongdoers are in the agonies of death and the angels stretch forth their hands, (saying): Yield up your souls. This day you are awarded a chastisement of disgrace because you spoke against Allah other than truth, and (because) you scorned His messages.

6:94. And certainly you have come to Us one by one as We created you at first, and you have left behind your backs what We gave you. And We see not with you your intercessors about whom you asserted that they were (Allah's) associates in respect to you. Certainly the ties between you are now cut off and that which you asserted has failed you.

6:95. Surely Allah causes the grain and the date-stone to germinate. He brings forth the living from, the dead and He is the bringer forth of the dead from the living. That is Allah. How are you then turned away!

6:96. He is the Cleaver of the daybreak; and He has made the night for rest, and the sun and the moon reckoning. That is the measuring of the Mighty, the Knowing.

6:97. And He it is Who has made the stars for you that you might follow the right way thereby in the darkness of the land and the sea. Indeed We have made plain the signs for a people who know.

6:98. And He it is Who has brought you into being from a single soul, then there is (for you) a resting-place and a repository. Indeed We have made plain the signs for a people who understand.

6:99. And He it is Who sends down water from the clouds, then We bring forth with it buds of all (plants), then We bring forth from it green (foliage),

فَأَخْرَجْنَا بِهِ نَبَاتَ كُلِّ شَيْءٍ فَأَخْرَجْنَا مِنْهُ خَضِرًا نُخْرِجُ مِنْهُ حَبًّا مُتَرَاكِبًا وَمِنَ النَّخْلِ مِنْ طَلْعِهَا قِنْوَانٌ دَانِيَةٌ وَجَنَّاتٍ مِنْ أَعْنَابٍ وَالزَّيْتُونَ وَالرُّمَّانَ مُشْتَبِهًا وَغَيْرَ مُتَشَابِهٍ انْظُرُوا إِلَى ثَمَرِهِ إِذَا أَثْمَرَ وَيَنْعِهِ إِنَّ فِي ذَلِكُمْ لَآيَاتٍ لِقَوْمٍ يُؤْمِنُونَ (٩٩) وَجَعَلُوا لِلَّهِ شُرَكَاءَ الْجِنَّ وَخَلَقَهُمْ وَخَرَقُوا لَهُ بَنِينَ وَبَنَاتٍ بِغَيْرِ عِلْمٍ سُبْحَانَهُ وَتَعَالَى عَمَّا يَصِفُونَ (١٠٠) بَدِيعُ السَّمَاوَاتِ وَالْأَرْضِ أَنَّى يَكُونُ لَهُ وَلَدٌ وَلَمْ تَكُنْ لَهُ صَاحِبَةٌ وَخَلَقَ كُلَّ شَيْءٍ وَهُوَ بِكُلِّ شَيْءٍ عَلِيمٌ (١٠١) ذَلِكُمُ اللَّهُ رَبُّكُمْ لَا إِلَهَ إِلَّا هُوَ خَالِقُ كُلِّ شَيْءٍ فَاعْبُدُوهُ وَهُوَ عَلَى كُلِّ شَيْءٍ وَكِيلٌ (١٠٢) لَا تُدْرِكُهُ الْأَبْصَارُ وَهُوَ يُدْرِكُ الْأَبْصَارَ وَهُوَ اللَّطِيفُ الْخَبِيرُ (١٠٣) قَدْ جَاءَكُمْ بَصَائِرُ مِنْ رَبِّكُمْ فَمَنْ أَبْصَرَ فَلِنَفْسِهِ وَمَنْ عَمِيَ فَعَلَيْهَا وَمَا أَنَا عَلَيْكُمْ بِحَفِيظٍ (١٠٤) وَكَذَلِكَ نُصَرِّفُ الْآيَاتِ وَلِيَقُولُوا دَرَسْتَ وَلِنُبَيِّنَهُ لِقَوْمٍ يَعْلَمُونَ (١٠٥) اتَّبِعْ مَا أُوحِيَ إِلَيْكَ مِنْ رَبِّكَ لَا إِلَهَ إِلَّا هُوَ وَأَعْرِضْ عَنِ الْمُشْرِكِينَ (١٠٦) وَلَوْ شَاءَ اللَّهُ مَا أَشْرَكُوا وَمَا جَعَلْنَاكَ عَلَيْهِمْ حَفِيظًا وَمَا أَنْتَ عَلَيْهِمْ بِوَكِيلٍ (١٠٧) وَلَا تَسُبُّوا الَّذِينَ يَدْعُونَ مِنْ دُونِ اللَّهِ فَيَسُبُّوا اللَّهَ عَدْوًا بِغَيْرِ عِلْمٍ كَذَلِكَ

6. The Cattle

from which We produce clustered grain; and of the date-palm, of the sheaths of it, come forth clusters (of dates) within reach; and gardens of grapes and the olive and the pomegranate, alike and unlike. Look at the fruit of it when it bears fruit and the ripening of it. Surely there are signs in this for a people who believe!

6:100. And they regard the jinn to he partners with Allah, and He created them, and they falsely attribute to Him sons and daughters without knowledge. Glory be to Him, and highly exalted is He above what they ascribe (to Him)!

* * *

6:101. Wonderful Originator of the heavens and the earth How could He have a son when He has no consort? And He created everything, and He is the Knower of all things.

6:102. That is Allah, your Lord. There is no god but He; the Creator of all things; therefore serve Him, and He has charge of all things.

6:103. Vision comprehends Him not, and He comprehends (all) vision and He is the Subtle, the Aware.

6:104. Clear proofs have indeed come to you from your Lord; so whoever sees, it is for his own good; and whoever is blind, it is to his own harm. And I am not a keeper over you.

6:105. And thus do We repeat the messages; and that they may say, Thou hast studied; and that We may make it clear to a people who know.

6:106. Follow that which is revealed to thee from thy Lord -- there is no god but He; and turn away from the polytheists.

6:107. And if Allah had pleased, they would not have set up others (with Him). And We have not appointed thee a keeper over them, and thou art not placed in charge of them.

6:108. And abuse not those whom they

call upon besides Allah, lest, exceeding the limits, they abuse Allah through ignorance. Thus to every people have We made their deeds fair-seeming; then to their Lord is their return so He will inform them of what they did.

6:109. And they swear their strongest oaths by Allah that if a sign come to them they would certainly believe in it. Say: Signs are with Allah. And what should make you know that when they come they believe not?

6:110. And We turn their hearts and their sights, even as they did not believe in it the first time; and We leave them in their inordinacy, blindly wandering on.

* * *

6:111. And even if We send down to them the angels and the dead speak to them and We bring together all things before them, they would not believe unless Allah please, but most of them are ignorant.

6:112. And thus did We make for every prophet an enemy, the devils from among men and jinn, some of them inspiring others with gilded speech to deceive (them). And if thy Lord pleased, they would not do it, so leave them alone with what they forge --

6:113. And that the hearts of those who believe not in the Hereafter may incline thereto, and that they may be pleased with it, and that they may earn what they are earning.

6:114. Shall I then seek a judge other than Allah, when He it is Who has sent down to you the Book fully explained. And those whom We have given the Book know that it is revealed by thy Lord with truth, so be not thou of the disputers.

6:115. And the word of thy Lord has been accomplished truly and justly. There is none who can change His words; and He is the Hearer, the Knower.

6:116. And if thou obey most of those in the earth, they will lead thee astray from Allah's way. They follow naught but conjecture, and they only lie.

6:117. Surely thy Lord -- He knows best who goes astray from His way, and He knows best the guided ones.

6:118. Eat, then, of that on which Allah's name has been mentioned, if you are believers in His messages.

6:119. And what reason have you that you should not eat of that on which Allah's name is mentioned, when He has already made plain to you what He has forbidden to you -- excepting that which you are compelled to. And surely many lead (people) astray by their low desires through ignorance. Surely thy Lord -- He best knows the transgressors.

6:120. And avoid open sins and secret ones. Surely they who earn sin will be rewarded for what they have earned.

6:121. And eat not of that on which Allah's name has not been mentioned, and that is surely a transgression. And certainly the devils inspire their friends to contend with you; and if you obey them, you will surely be polytheists.

***

6:122. Is he who was dead, then We raised him to life and made for him a light by which he walks among the people, like him whose likeness is that of one in darkness whence he cannot come forth? Thus their doings are made fair-seeming to the disbelievers.

6:123. And thus have We made in every town the leaders of its guilty ones, that they may make plans therein. And they plan not but against themselves, and they perceive not.

6:124. And when a message comes to them they say We will not believe till we are given the like of that which Allah's messengers are given. Allah best knows where to place His Message. Humiliation from Allah and severe chastisement will surely befall the guilty for their planning.

6:125. So whomsoever Allah intends to guide, He expands his breast for Islam, and whomsoever He intends to leave in error, he makes his breast strait (and) narrow as though he were ascending upwards. Thus does Allah lay uncleanness on those who believe not.

6:126. And this is the path of thy Lord, (a) straight (path). Indeed We have made the messages clear for a people who mind.

6:127. Theirs is the abode of peace with their Lord, and He is their Friend because of what they do.

6:128. And on the day when He will gather them all together: O assembly of jinn, you took away a great part of men. And their friends from among men will say: Our Lord, some of us profited by others and we have reached our appointed term which Thou didst appoint for us. He will say: The Fire is your abode -- you shall abide therein, except as Allah please. Surely thy Lord is Wise, Knowing.

6:129. And thus do We make some of the iniquitous to befriend others on account of what they earn.

***

6:130. O community of jinn and men, did there not come to you messengers from among you, relating to you My messages and warning you of the meeting of this day of yours? They will say We bear witness against ourselves. And this world's life deceived them, and they will bear witness against themselves that they were disbelievers.

6:131. This is because thy Lord would not destroy towns unjustly while their people are negligent.

6:132. And for all are degrees according to their doings. And thy Lord is not heedless of what they do.

6:133. And thy Lord is the Self-

بِزَعْمِهِمْ وَهَذَا لِشُرَكَائِنَا فَمَا كَانَ لِشُرَكَائِهِمْ فَلَا يَصِلُ إِلَى اللَّهِ وَمَا كَانَ لِلَّهِ فَهُوَ يَصِلُ إِلَى شُرَكَائِهِمْ سَاءَ مَا يَحْكُمُونَ (١٣٦)

وَكَذَلِكَ زَيَّنَ لِكَثِيرٍ مِنَ الْمُشْرِكِينَ قَتْلَ أَوْلَادِهِمْ شُرَكَاؤُهُمْ لِيُرْدُوهُمْ وَلِيَلْبِسُوا عَلَيْهِمْ دِينَهُمْ وَلَوْ شَاءَ اللَّهُ مَا فَعَلُوهُ فَذَرْهُمْ وَمَا يَفْتَرُونَ (١٣٧)

وَقَالُوا هَذِهِ أَنْعَامٌ وَحَرْثٌ حِجْرٌ لَا يَطْعَمُهَا إِلَّا مَنْ نَشَاءُ بِزَعْمِهِمْ وَأَنْعَامٌ حُرِّمَتْ ظُهُورُهَا وَأَنْعَامٌ لَا يَذْكُرُونَ اسْمَ اللَّهِ عَلَيْهَا افْتِرَاءً عَلَيْهِ سَيَجْزِيهِمْ بِمَا كَانُوا يَفْتَرُونَ (١٣٨)

وَقَالُوا مَا فِي بُطُونِ هَذِهِ الْأَنْعَامِ خَالِصَةٌ لِذُكُورِنَا وَمُحَرَّمٌ عَلَى أَزْوَاجِنَا وَإِنْ يَكُنْ مَيْتَةً فَهُمْ فِيهِ شُرَكَاءُ سَيَجْزِيهِمْ وَصْفَهُمْ إِنَّهُ حَكِيمٌ عَلِيمٌ (١٣٩)

قَدْ خَسِرَ الَّذِينَ قَتَلُوا أَوْلَادَهُمْ سَفَهًا بِغَيْرِ عِلْمٍ وَحَرَّمُوا مَا رَزَقَهُمُ اللَّهُ افْتِرَاءً عَلَى اللَّهِ قَدْ ضَلُّوا وَمَا كَانُوا مُهْتَدِينَ (١٤٠)

وَهُوَ الَّذِي أَنْشَأَ جَنَّاتٍ مَعْرُوشَاتٍ وَغَيْرَ مَعْرُوشَاتٍ وَالنَّخْلَ وَالزَّرْعَ مُخْتَلِفًا أُكُلُهُ وَالزَّيْتُونَ وَالرُّمَّانَ مُتَشَابِهًا وَغَيْرَ مُتَشَابِهٍ كُلُوا مِنْ ثَمَرِهِ إِذَا أَثْمَرَ وَآتُوا حَقَّهُ يَوْمَ حَصَادِهِ وَلَا تُسْرِفُوا إِنَّهُ لَا يُحِبُّ الْمُسْرِفِينَ (١٤١)

وَمِنَ الْأَنْعَامِ حَمُولَةً وَفَرْشًا كُلُوا مِمَّا رَزَقَكُمُ اللَّهُ وَلَا تَتَّبِعُوا خُطُوَاتِ الشَّيْطَانِ إِنَّهُ لَكُمْ عَدُوٌّ مُبِينٌ (١٤٢)

ثَمَانِيَةَ أَزْوَاجٍ مِنَ الضَّأْنِ اثْنَيْنِ وَمِنَ الْمَعْزِ اثْنَيْنِ قُلْ آلذَّكَرَيْنِ حَرَّمَ أَمِ

6. The Cattle

sufficient One, the Lord of mercy. If He please, He may remove you, and make whom He pleases successors after you, even as He raised you up from the seed of other people.

6:134. Surely that which you are promised will come to pass, and you cannot escape (it).

6:135. Say O my people, act according to your ability, I too am acting so you will soon come to know for whom is the (good) end of the abode. Surely the wrongdoers will not succeed.

6:136. And they set apart a portion for Allah out of what He has created of tilth and cattle, and say This is for Allah -- so they assert -- and this for our associate-gods. Then that which is for their associate-gods reaches not Allah, and that which is for Allah reaches their associate-gods. Evil is what they judge.

6:137. And thus their associate-gods have made fair-seeming to many polytheists the killing of their children, that they may cause them to perish and obscure for them their religion. And if Allah had pleased, they would not have done it, so leave them alone with that which they forge.

6:138. And they say: Such and such cattle and crops are prohibited -- none shall eat them except such as we please -- so they assert -- and cattle whose backs are forbidden, and cattle on which they would not mention Allah's name -- forging a lie against Him. He will requite them for what they forge.

6:139. And they say: That which is in the wombs of such and such cattle is reserved for our males, and forbidden to our wives, and if it be stillborn, they are partners in it. He will reward them for their (false) attribution. Surely He is Wise, Knowing.

6:140. They are losers indeed who kill their children foolishly without knowledge, and forbid that which

الْأُنْثَيَيْنِ أَمَّا اشْتَمَلَتْ عَلَيْهِ أَرْحَامُ الْأُنْثَيَيْنِ نَبِّئُونِي بِعِلْمٍ إِنْ كُنْتُمْ صَادِقِينَ (١٤٣)
وَمِنَ الْإِبِلِ اثْنَيْنِ وَمِنَ الْبَقَرِ اثْنَيْنِ قُلْ آلذَّكَرَيْنِ حَرَّمَ أَمِ الْأُنْثَيَيْنِ أَمَّا اشْتَمَلَتْ عَلَيْهِ أَرْحَامُ الْأُنْثَيَيْنِ أَمْ كُنْتُمْ شُهَدَاءَ إِذْ وَصَّاكُمُ اللَّهُ بِهَذَا فَمَنْ أَظْلَمُ مِمَّنِ افْتَرَى عَلَى اللَّهِ كَذِبًا لِيُضِلَّ النَّاسَ بِغَيْرِ عِلْمٍ إِنَّ اللَّهَ لَا يَهْدِي الْقَوْمَ الظَّالِمِينَ (١٤٤)

Allah has provided for them, forging a lie against Allah. They indeed go astray, and are not guided.

* * *

6:141. And He it is Who produces gardens, trellised and untrellised, and palms and seed-produce of which the fruits are of various sorts, and olives and pomegranates, like and unlike. Eat of its fruit when it bears fruit, and pay the due of it on the day of its reaping, and be not prodigal. Surely He loves not the prodigals;

6:142. And of the cattle (He has created) some for burden and some for slaughter. Eat of that which Allah has given you and follow not the foot-steps of the devil. Surely he is your open enemy --

6:143. Eight in pairs -- of the sheep two and of the goats two. Say: Has He forbidden the two males or the two females or that which the wombs of the two females contain? Inform me with knowledge, if you are truthful;

6:144. And of the camels two and of the cows two. Say: Has He forbidden the two males or the two females or that which the wombs of the two females contain? Or were you witnesses when Allah enjoined you this? Who is then more unjust than he who forges a lie against Allah to lead men astray without knowledge? Surely Allah guides not the iniquitous people.

* * *

6:145. Say, I find not in that which is revealed to me aught forbidden for an eater to eat thereof, except that it be what dies of itself, or blood poured forth, or flesh of swine -- for that surely is unclean or what is a transgression, other than (the name of) Allah having been invoked on it. But whoever is driven to necessity, not desiring nor exceeding the limit, then surely thy Lord is Forgiving, Merciful.

قُلْ لَا أَجِدُ فِي مَا أُوحِيَ إِلَيَّ مُحَرَّمًا عَلَى طَاعِمٍ يَطْعَمُهُ إِلَّا أَنْ يَكُونَ مَيْتَةً أَوْ دَمًا مَسْفُوحًا أَوْ لَحْمَ خِنْزِيرٍ فَإِنَّهُ رِجْسٌ أَوْ فِسْقًا أُهِلَّ لِغَيْرِ اللَّهِ بِهِ فَمَنِ اضْطُرَّ غَيْرَ بَاغٍ وَلَا عَادٍ فَإِنَّ رَبَّكَ غَفُورٌ رَحِيمٌ (١٤٥)

وَعَلَى الَّذِينَ هَادُوا حَرَّمْنَا كُلَّ ذِي ظُفُرٍ وَمِنَ الْبَقَرِ وَالْغَنَمِ حَرَّمْنَا عَلَيْهِمْ شُحُومَهُمَا إِلَّا مَا حَمَلَتْ ظُهُورُهُمَا

6:146. And to those who are Jews We forbade every animal having claws, and of oxen and sheep We forbade them the fat thereof, except such as was on their backs or the entrails or what was mixed with bones. This was a punishment We gave them on account of their rebellion, and We are surely Truthful.

6:147. But if they give thee -- the lie, then say: Your Lord is the Lord of all-encompassing mercy; and His punishment cannot be averted from the guilty people.

6:148. Those who are polytheists say: If Allah pleased we would not have set up (aught with Him) nor our fathers, nor would we have made anything unlawful. Thus did those before them reject (the truth) until they tasted Our punishment. Say: Have you any knowledge so you would bring it forth to us? You only follow a conjecture and you only tell lies.

6:149. Say: Then Allah's is the condusive argument; so if He had pleased, He would have guided you all.

6:150. Say: Bring your witnesses who bear witness that Allah forbade this. If they bear witness, then do not thou bear witness with them. And follow not the low desires of those who reject Our messages and those who believe not in the Hereafter, and they make (others) equal with their Lord.

* * *

6:151. Say: Come I will recite what your Lord has forbidden to you: Associate naught with Him and do good to parents and slay not your children for (fear of) poverty -- We provide for you and for them -- and draw not nigh to indecencies, open or secret, and kill not the soul which Allah has made sacred except in the course of justice. This He enjoins upon you that you may understand.

6:152. And approach not the property of the orphan except in the best manner, until he attains his maturity. And give full measure and weight with equity -- We impose not on any soul a duty except to the extent of its ability. And when you speak, be just, though it be (against) a relative. And fulfil Allah's covenant. This He enjoins on you that you may be mindful;

6:153. And (know) that this is My path, the right one, so follow it, and follow not (other) ways, for they will lead you away from His way. This He enjoins on you that you may keep your duty.

6:154. Again, We gave the Book to Moses to complete (Our blessings) on him who would do good, and making plain all things and a guidance and a mercy, so that they might believe in the meeting with their Lord.

***

6:155. And this is a Book We have revealed, full of blessings; so follow it and keep your duty that mercy may be shown to you

6:156. Lest you should say that the Book was revealed only to two parties before us and we were truly unaware of what they read,

6:157. Or, lest you should say: If the Book had been -- revealed to us, we would have been better guided than they. So indeed there has come to you clear proof from your Lord, and guidance and mercy. Who is then more unjust than he -- who rejects Allah's messages and turns away from them? We reward those who turn away from Our messages with an evil chastisement because they turned away.

6:158. They wait not aught but that the angels should come to them, or that thy Lord should come, or that some of the signs of thy Lord should come. On the

وَلَا تَقْرَبُوا مَالَ الْيَتِيمِ إِلَّا بِالَّتِي هِيَ أَحْسَنُ حَتَّى يَبْلُغَ أَشُدَّهُ وَأَوْفُوا الْكَيْلَ وَالْمِيزَانَ بِالْقِسْطِ لَا نُكَلِّفُ نَفْسًا إِلَّا وُسْعَهَا وَإِذَا قُلْتُمْ فَاعْدِلُوا وَلَوْ كَانَ ذَا قُرْبَى وَبِعَهْدِ اللَّهِ أَوْفُوا ذَلِكُمْ وَصَّاكُمْ بِهِ لَعَلَّكُمْ تَذَكَّرُونَ (١٥٢)

وَأَنَّ هَذَا صِرَاطِي مُسْتَقِيمًا فَاتَّبِعُوهُ وَلَا تَتَّبِعُوا السُّبُلَ فَتَفَرَّقَ بِكُمْ عَنْ سَبِيلِهِ ذَلِكُمْ وَصَّاكُمْ بِهِ لَعَلَّكُمْ تَتَّقُونَ (١٥٣)

ثُمَّ آتَيْنَا مُوسَى الْكِتَابَ تَمَامًا عَلَى الَّذِي أَحْسَنَ وَتَفْصِيلًا لِكُلِّ شَيْءٍ وَهُدًى وَرَحْمَةً لَعَلَّهُمْ بِلِقَاءِ رَبِّهِمْ يُؤْمِنُونَ (١٥٤)

وَهَذَا كِتَابٌ أَنْزَلْنَاهُ مُبَارَكٌ فَاتَّبِعُوهُ وَاتَّقُوا لَعَلَّكُمْ تُرْحَمُونَ (١٥٥)

أَنْ تَقُولُوا إِنَّمَا أُنْزِلَ الْكِتَابُ عَلَى طَائِفَتَيْنِ مِنْ قَبْلِنَا وَإِنْ كُنَّا عَنْ دِرَاسَتِهِمْ لَغَافِلِينَ (١٥٦)

أَوْ تَقُولُوا لَوْ أَنَّا أُنْزِلَ عَلَيْنَا الْكِتَابُ لَكُنَّا أَهْدَى مِنْهُمْ فَقَدْ جَاءَكُمْ بَيِّنَةٌ مِنْ رَبِّكُمْ وَهُدًى وَرَحْمَةٌ فَمَنْ أَظْلَمُ مِمَّنْ كَذَّبَ بِآيَاتِ اللَّهِ وَصَدَفَ عَنْهَا سَنَجْزِي الَّذِينَ يَصْدِفُونَ عَنْ آيَاتِنَا سُوءَ الْعَذَابِ بِمَا كَانُوا يَصْدِفُونَ (١٥٧)

هَلْ يَنْظُرُونَ إِلَّا أَنْ تَأْتِيَهُمُ الْمَلَائِكَةُ أَوْ يَأْتِيَ رَبُّكَ أَوْ يَأْتِيَ بَعْضُ آيَاتِ رَبِّكَ يَوْمَ يَأْتِي بَعْضُ آيَاتِ رَبِّكَ لَا يَنْفَعُ نَفْسًا إِيمَانُهَا لَمْ تَكُنْ آمَنَتْ مِنْ قَبْلُ أَوْ كَسَبَتْ فِي إِيمَانِهَا خَيْرًا قُلِ انْتَظِرُوا إِنَّا مُنْتَظِرُونَ (١٥٨)

day when some of the signs of thy Lord come, its faith will not profit a soul which believed not before, nor earned good through its faith. Say: Wait; we too are waiting.

6:159. As for those who split up their religion and became sects, thou hast no concern with them. Their affair is only with Allah, then He will inform them of what they did.

6:160. Whoever brings a good deed will have tenfold like it, and whoever brings an evil deed, will be recompensed only with the like of it, and they shall not be wronged.

6:161. Say: As for me, my Lord has guided me to the right path -- a right religion, the faith of Abraham, the upright one, and he was not of the polytheists.

6:162. Say My prayer and my sacrifice and my life and my death are surely for Allah, the Lord of rhe worlds --

6:163. No associate has He. And this am I commanded, and I am the first of those who submit.

6:164. Say Shall I seek a Lord other than Allah, while He is the Lord of all things? And no soul earns (evil) but against itself. Nor does a bearer of burden bear the burden of another. Then to your Lord is your return, so He will inform you of that in which you differed.

6:165. And He it is Who has made you successors in the land and exalted some of you in rank above others, that He may try you by what He has given you. Surely thy Lord is Quick in requiting (evil), and He is surely the Forgiving, the Merciful.

7. The Elevated Places

7:1. In the name of Allah, the Beneficent, the Merciful. 1 I, Allah, am the best Knower, the Truthful.

إِنَّ الَّذِينَ فَرَّقُوا دِينَهُمْ وَكَانُوا شِيَعًا لَسْتَ مِنْهُمْ فِي شَيْءٍ إِنَّمَا أَمْرُهُمْ إِلَى اللَّهِ ثُمَّ يُنَبِّئُهُمْ بِمَا كَانُوا يَفْعَلُونَ (١٥٩)

مَنْ جَاءَ بِالْحَسَنَةِ فَلَهُ عَشْرُ أَمْثَالِهَا وَمَنْ جَاءَ بِالسَّيِّئَةِ فَلَا يُجْزَى إِلَّا مِثْلَهَا وَهُمْ لَا يُظْلَمُونَ (١٦٠)

قُلْ إِنَّنِي هَدَانِي رَبِّي إِلَى صِرَاطٍ مُسْتَقِيمٍ دِينًا قِيَمًا مِلَّةَ إِبْرَاهِيمَ حَنِيفًا وَمَا كَانَ مِنَ الْمُشْرِكِينَ (١٦١)

قُلْ إِنَّ صَلَاتِي وَنُسُكِي وَمَحْيَايَ وَمَمَاتِي لِلَّهِ رَبِّ الْعَالَمِينَ (١٦٢)

لَا شَرِيكَ لَهُ وَبِذَلِكَ أُمِرْتُ وَأَنَا أَوَّلُ الْمُسْلِمِينَ (١٦٣)

قُلْ أَغَيْرَ اللَّهِ أَبْغِي رَبًّا وَهُوَ رَبُّ كُلِّ شَيْءٍ وَلَا تَكْسِبُ كُلُّ نَفْسٍ إِلَّا عَلَيْهَا وَلَا تَزِرُ وَازِرَةٌ وِزْرَ أُخْرَى ثُمَّ إِلَى رَبِّكُمْ مَرْجِعُكُمْ فَيُنَبِّئُكُمْ بِمَا كُنْتُمْ فِيهِ تَخْتَلِفُونَ (١٦٤)

وَهُوَ الَّذِي جَعَلَكُمْ خَلَائِفَ الْأَرْضِ وَرَفَعَ بَعْضَكُمْ فَوْقَ بَعْضٍ دَرَجَاتٍ لِيَبْلُوَكُمْ فِي مَا آتَاكُمْ إِنَّ رَبَّكَ سَرِيعُ الْعِقَابِ وَإِنَّهُ لَغَفُورٌ رَحِيمٌ (١٦٥)

٧- سورة الأعراف

٧- سُورَةُ الأَعْرَافِ
بِسْمِ اللهِ الرَّحْمَنِ الرَّحِيمِ

7. The Elevated Places

7:2. A Book revealed to thee -- so let there be no straitness in thy breast concerning it -- that thou mayest warn thereby, and a Reminder to the believers.

7:3. Follow what has been revealed to you from your Lord and follow not besides Him any guardians; little do you mind!

7:4. And how many a town have We destroyed! So Our punishment came to it by night or while they slept at midday.

7:5. Yet their cry, when Our punishment came to them, was nothing but that they said: Surely we were wrong doers.

7:6. Then certainly We shall question those to whom messengers were sent, and We shall question the messengers,

7:7. Then surely We shall relate to them with knowledge, and We are never absent.

7:8. And the judging on that day will be just; so as for those whose good deeds are heavy, they are the successful.

7:9. And as for those whose good deeds are light, those are they who ruined their souls because they disbelieved in Our messages.

7:10. And certainly We established you in the earth and made therein means of livelihood for you; little it is that you give thanks!

* * *

7:11. And We indeed created you, then We fashioned you, then We said to the angels: Make submission to Adam. So they submitted, except Iblis; he was not of those who submitted.

7:12. He said: What hindered thee that thou didst not submit when I commanded thee? He said: I am better than he; Thou hast created me of fire, while him Thou didst create of dust.

7:13. He said: Then get forth from this (state), for it is not for thee to behave

المص (١)
كِتَابٌ أُنْزِلَ إِلَيْكَ فَلَا يَكُنْ فِي صَدْرِكَ حَرَجٌ مِنْهُ لِتُنْذِرَ بِهِ وَذِكْرَىٰ لِلْمُؤْمِنِينَ (٢)
اتَّبِعُوا مَا أُنْزِلَ إِلَيْكُمْ مِنْ رَبِّكُمْ وَلَا تَتَّبِعُوا مِنْ دُونِهِ أَوْلِيَاءَ قَلِيلًا مَا تَذَكَّرُونَ (٣)
وَكَمْ مِنْ قَرْيَةٍ أَهْلَكْنَاهَا فَجَاءَهَا بَأْسُنَا بَيَاتًا أَوْ هُمْ قَائِلُونَ (٤)
فَمَا كَانَ دَعْوَاهُمْ إِذْ جَاءَهُمْ بَأْسُنَا إِلَّا أَنْ قَالُوا إِنَّا كُنَّا ظَالِمِينَ (٥)
فَلَنَسْأَلَنَّ الَّذِينَ أُرْسِلَ إِلَيْهِمْ وَلَنَسْأَلَنَّ الْمُرْسَلِينَ (٦)
فَلَنَقُصَّنَّ عَلَيْهِمْ بِعِلْمٍ وَمَا كُنَّا غَائِبِينَ (٧)
وَالْوَزْنُ يَوْمَئِذٍ الْحَقُّ فَمَنْ ثَقُلَتْ مَوَازِينُهُ فَأُولَٰئِكَ هُمُ الْمُفْلِحُونَ (٨)
وَمَنْ خَفَّتْ مَوَازِينُهُ فَأُولَٰئِكَ الَّذِينَ خَسِرُوا أَنْفُسَهُمْ بِمَا كَانُوا بِآيَاتِنَا يَظْلِمُونَ (٩)
وَلَقَدْ مَكَّنَّاكُمْ فِي الْأَرْضِ وَجَعَلْنَا لَكُمْ فِيهَا مَعَايِشَ قَلِيلًا مَا تَشْكُرُونَ (١٠)
وَلَقَدْ خَلَقْنَاكُمْ ثُمَّ صَوَّرْنَاكُمْ ثُمَّ قُلْنَا لِلْمَلَائِكَةِ اسْجُدُوا لِآدَمَ فَسَجَدُوا إِلَّا إِبْلِيسَ لَمْ يَكُنْ مِنَ السَّاجِدِينَ (١١)
قَالَ مَا مَنَعَكَ أَلَّا تَسْجُدَ إِذْ أَمَرْتُكَ قَالَ أَنَا خَيْرٌ مِنْهُ خَلَقْتَنِي مِنْ نَارٍ وَخَلَقْتَهُ مِنْ طِينٍ (١٢)
قَالَ فَاهْبِطْ مِنْهَا فَمَا يَكُونُ لَكَ أَنْ تَتَكَبَّرَ فِيهَا فَاخْرُجْ إِنَّكَ مِنَ الصَّاغِرِينَ (١٣)
قَالَ أَنْظِرْنِي إِلَىٰ يَوْمِ يُبْعَثُونَ (١٤)
قَالَ إِنَّكَ مِنَ الْمُنْظَرِينَ (١٥)

7. The Elevated Places

proudly therein. Go forth, therefore, surely thou art of the abject ones.

7:14. He said: Respite me till the day when they are raised.

7:15. He said: Thou art surely of the respited ones.

7:16. He said: As Thou hast adjudged me to be erring, I will certainly lie in wait for them in Thy straight path,

7:17. Then I shall certainly come upon them from before them and from behind them, and from their right and from their left; and Thou wilt not find most of them thankful.

7:18. He said: Get out of it, despised, driven away. Whoever of them will follow thee, I will certainly fill hell with you all.

7:19. And (We said): O Adam, dwell thou and thy wife in the garden, so eat from whence you desire, but go not near this tree, lest you become of the unjust.

7:20. But the devil made an evil suggestion to them that he might make manifest to them that which had been hidden from them of their shame and he said: Your Lord has forbidden you this tree, lest you become angels or become of the immortals.

7:21. And he swore to them both: Surely I am a sincere adviser to you --

7:22. Thus he caused them to fall by deceit. So when they had tasted of the tree, their shame became manifest to them, and they both began to cover themselves with the leaves of the garden. And their Lord called to them: Did I not forbid you that tree, and say to you that the devil is surely your open enemy?

7:23. They said: Our Lord, we have wronged ourselves; and if Thou forgive us not, and have (not) mercy on us, we shall certainly be of the losers.

7:24. He said: Go forth -- some of you, the enemies of others. And there is for you in the earth an abode and a

قَالَ فَبِمَا أَغْوَيْتَنِي لَأَقْعُدَنَّ لَهُمْ صِرَاطَكَ الْمُسْتَقِيمَ (١٦)
ثُمَّ لَآتِيَنَّهُم مِّن بَيْنِ أَيْدِيهِمْ وَمِنْ خَلْفِهِمْ وَعَنْ أَيْمَانِهِمْ وَعَن شَمَائِلِهِمْ وَلَا تَجِدُ أَكْثَرَهُمْ شَاكِرِينَ (١٧)
قَالَ اخْرُجْ مِنْهَا مَذْءُومًا مَّدْحُورًا لَّمَن تَبِعَكَ مِنْهُمْ لَأَمْلَأَنَّ جَهَنَّمَ مِنكُمْ أَجْمَعِينَ (١٨)
وَيَا آدَمُ اسْكُنْ أَنتَ وَزَوْجُكَ الْجَنَّةَ فَكُلَا مِنْ حَيْثُ شِئْتُمَا وَلَا تَقْرَبَا هَذِهِ الشَّجَرَةَ فَتَكُونَا مِنَ الظَّالِمِينَ (١٩)
فَوَسْوَسَ لَهُمَا الشَّيْطَانُ لِيُبْدِيَ لَهُمَا مَا وُورِيَ عَنْهُمَا مِن سَوْآتِهِمَا وَقَالَ مَا نَهَاكُمَا رَبُّكُمَا عَنْ هَذِهِ الشَّجَرَةِ إِلَّا أَن تَكُونَا مَلَكَيْنِ أَوْ تَكُونَا مِنَ الْخَالِدِينَ (٢٠)
وَقَاسَمَهُمَا إِنِّي لَكُمَا لَمِنَ النَّاصِحِينَ (٢١)
فَدَلَّاهُمَا بِغُرُورٍ فَلَمَّا ذَاقَا الشَّجَرَةَ بَدَتْ لَهُمَا سَوْآتُهُمَا وَطَفِقَا يَخْصِفَانِ عَلَيْهِمَا مِن وَرَقِ الْجَنَّةِ وَنَادَاهُمَا رَبُّهُمَا أَلَمْ أَنْهَكُمَا عَن تِلْكُمَا الشَّجَرَةِ وَأَقُل لَّكُمَا إِنَّ الشَّيْطَانَ لَكُمَا عَدُوٌّ مُّبِينٌ (٢٢)
قَالَا رَبَّنَا ظَلَمْنَا أَنفُسَنَا وَإِن لَّمْ تَغْفِرْ لَنَا وَتَرْحَمْنَا لَنَكُونَنَّ مِنَ الْخَاسِرِينَ (٢٣)
قَالَ اهْبِطُوا بَعْضُكُمْ لِبَعْضٍ عَدُوٌّ وَلَكُمْ فِي الْأَرْضِ مُسْتَقَرٌّ وَمَتَاعٌ إِلَى حِينٍ (٢٤)
قَالَ فِيهَا تَحْيَوْنَ وَفِيهَا تَمُوتُونَ وَمِنْهَا تُخْرَجُونَ (٢٥)

7. The Elevated Places

provision for a time.

7:25. He said: Therein shall you live, and therein shall you die, and there from shall you be raised.

***

7:26. O children of Adam, We have indeed sent down to you clothing to cover your shame, and (clothing) for beauty; and clothing that guards against evil -- that is the best. This is of the messages of Allah that they may be mindful.

7:27. O children of Adam, let not the devil seduce you, as he expelled your parents from the garden, pulling off from them their clothing that he might show them their shame. He surely sees you, he as well as his host, from whence you see them not. Surely We have made the devils to be the friends of those who believe not.

7:28. And when they commit an indecency they say: We found our fathers doing this, and Allah has enjoined it on us. Say: Surely Allah enjoins not indecency. Do you say of Allah what you know not?

7:29. Say: My Lord enjoins justice. And set upright your faces at every time of prayer and call on Him, being sincere to Him in obedience. As He brought you into being, so shall you return.

7:30. A party has He guided, and another party -- perdition is justly their due. Surely they took the devils for friends instead of Allah, and they think that they are rightly guided.

7:31. O children of Adam, attend to your adornment at every time of prayer, and eat and drink and be not prodigal; surely He loves not the prodigals.

***

7:32. Say: Who has forbidden the adornment of Allah, which He has brought forth for His servants, and the good provisions? Say: These are for the

يَا بَنِي آدَمَ قَدْ أَنْزَلْنَا عَلَيْكُمْ لِبَاسًا يُوَارِي سَوْآتِكُمْ وَرِيشًا وَلِبَاسُ التَّقْوَىٰ ذَٰلِكَ خَيْرٌ ذَٰلِكَ مِنْ آيَاتِ اللَّهِ لَعَلَّهُمْ يَذَّكَّرُونَ (٢٦)

يَا بَنِي آدَمَ لَا يَفْتِنَنَّكُمُ الشَّيْطَانُ كَمَا أَخْرَجَ أَبَوَيْكُمْ مِنَ الْجَنَّةِ يَنْزِعُ عَنْهُمَا لِبَاسَهُمَا لِيُرِيَهُمَا سَوْآتِهِمَا إِنَّهُ يَرَاكُمْ هُوَ وَقَبِيلُهُ مِنْ حَيْثُ لَا تَرَوْنَهُمْ إِنَّا جَعَلْنَا الشَّيَاطِينَ أَوْلِيَاءَ لِلَّذِينَ لَا يُؤْمِنُونَ (٢٧)

وَإِذَا فَعَلُوا فَاحِشَةً قَالُوا وَجَدْنَا عَلَيْهَا آبَاءَنَا وَاللَّهُ أَمَرَنَا بِهَا قُلْ إِنَّ اللَّهَ لَا يَأْمُرُ بِالْفَحْشَاءِ أَتَقُولُونَ عَلَى اللَّهِ مَا لَا تَعْلَمُونَ (٢٨)

قُلْ أَمَرَ رَبِّي بِالْقِسْطِ وَأَقِيمُوا وُجُوهَكُمْ عِنْدَ كُلِّ مَسْجِدٍ وَادْعُوهُ مُخْلِصِينَ لَهُ الدِّينَ كَمَا بَدَأَكُمْ تَعُودُونَ (٢٩)

فَرِيقًا هَدَىٰ وَفَرِيقًا حَقَّ عَلَيْهِمُ الضَّلَالَةُ إِنَّهُمُ اتَّخَذُوا الشَّيَاطِينَ أَوْلِيَاءَ مِنْ دُونِ اللَّهِ وَيَحْسَبُونَ أَنَّهُمْ مُهْتَدُونَ (٣٠)

يَا بَنِي آدَمَ خُذُوا زِينَتَكُمْ عِنْدَ كُلِّ مَسْجِدٍ وَكُلُوا وَاشْرَبُوا وَلَا تُسْرِفُوا إِنَّهُ لَا يُحِبُّ الْمُسْرِفِينَ (٣١)

قُلْ مَنْ حَرَّمَ زِينَةَ اللَّهِ الَّتِي أَخْرَجَ لِعِبَادِهِ وَالطَّيِّبَاتِ مِنَ الرِّزْقِ قُلْ هِيَ لِلَّذِينَ آمَنُوا فِي الْحَيَاةِ الدُّنْيَا خَالِصَةً يَوْمَ الْقِيَامَةِ كَذَٰلِكَ نُفَصِّلُ الْآيَاتِ لِقَوْمٍ يَعْلَمُونَ (٣٢)

7. The Elevated Places

believers in the life of this world, purely (theirs) on the Resurrection day. Thus do We make the messages clear for a people who know.

7:33. Say: My Lord forbids only indecencies, such of them as are apparent and such as are concealed, and sin and unjust rebellion, and that you associate with Allah that for which He has sent down no authority, and that you say of Allah what you know not.

7:34. And every nation has a term so when its term comes, they cannot remain behind the least while, nor can they precede (it).

7:35. O children of Adam, if messengers come to you from among you relating to you My messages, then whosoever guards against evil and acts aright they shall have no fear, nor shall they grieve.

7:36. And those who reject Our messages and turn away from them haughtily these are the companions of the Fire; they shall abide in it.

7:37. Who is then more unjust than he who forges a lie against Allah or rejects His messages? These -- their portion of the Book shall reach them; until when Our messengers come to them causing them to die; they say: Where is that which you used to call upon besides Allah? They would say: They are gone away from us. And they shall bear witness against themselves that they were disbelievers.

7:38. He will say: Enter into the Fire among the nations that have passed away before you from among the jinn and men. Every time a nation enters, it curses its sister until when they all follow one another into it, the last of them will say with regard to the first of them: Our Lord, these led us astray, so give them a double chastisement of the Fire. He will say: Each one has double but you know not.

قُلْ إِنَّمَا حَرَّمَ رَبِّيَ الْفَوَاحِشَ مَا ظَهَرَ مِنْهَا وَمَا بَطَنَ وَالْإِثْمَ وَالْبَغْيَ بِغَيْرِ الْحَقِّ وَأَن تُشْرِكُوا بِاللَّهِ مَا لَمْ يُنَزِّلْ بِهِ سُلْطَانًا وَأَن تَقُولُوا عَلَى اللَّهِ مَا لَا تَعْلَمُونَ (٣٣)

وَلِكُلِّ أُمَّةٍ أَجَلٌ فَإِذَا جَاءَ أَجَلُهُمْ لَا يَسْتَأْخِرُونَ سَاعَةً وَلَا يَسْتَقْدِمُونَ (٣٤)

يَا بَنِي آدَمَ إِمَّا يَأْتِيَنَّكُمْ رُسُلٌ مِنْكُمْ يَقُصُّونَ عَلَيْكُمْ آيَاتِي فَمَنِ اتَّقَى وَأَصْلَحَ فَلَا خَوْفٌ عَلَيْهِمْ وَلَا هُمْ يَحْزَنُونَ (٣٥)

وَالَّذِينَ كَذَّبُوا بِآيَاتِنَا وَاسْتَكْبَرُوا عَنْهَا أُولَٰئِكَ أَصْحَابُ النَّارِ هُمْ فِيهَا خَالِدُونَ (٣٦)

فَمَنْ أَظْلَمُ مِمَّنِ افْتَرَى عَلَى اللَّهِ كَذِبًا أَوْ كَذَّبَ بِآيَاتِهِ أُولَٰئِكَ يَنَالُهُمْ نَصِيبُهُمْ مِنَ الْكِتَابِ حَتَّى إِذَا جَاءَتْهُمْ رُسُلُنَا يَتَوَفَّوْنَهُمْ قَالُوا أَيْنَ مَا كُنْتُمْ تَدْعُونَ مِنْ دُونِ اللَّهِ قَالُوا ضَلُّوا عَنَّا وَشَهِدُوا عَلَى أَنْفُسِهِمْ أَنَّهُمْ كَانُوا كَافِرِينَ (٣٧)

قَالَ ادْخُلُوا فِي أُمَمٍ قَدْ خَلَتْ مِنْ قَبْلِكُمْ مِنَ الْجِنِّ وَالْإِنْسِ فِي النَّارِ كُلَّمَا دَخَلَتْ أُمَّةٌ لَعَنَتْ أُخْتَهَا حَتَّى إِذَا ادَّارَكُوا فِيهَا جَمِيعًا قَالَتْ أُخْرَاهُمْ لِأُولَاهُمْ رَبَّنَا هَٰؤُلَاءِ أَضَلُّونَا فَآتِهِمْ عَذَابًا ضِعْفًا مِنَ النَّارِ قَالَ لِكُلٍّ ضِعْفٌ وَلَٰكِنْ لَا تَعْلَمُونَ (٣٨)

وَقَالَتْ أُولَاهُمْ لِأُخْرَاهُمْ فَمَا كَانَ لَكُمْ عَلَيْنَا مِنْ فَضْلٍ فَذُوقُوا الْعَذَابَ بِمَا كُنْتُمْ تَكْسِبُونَ (٣٩)

إِنَّ الَّذِينَ كَذَّبُوا بِآيَاتِنَا وَاسْتَكْبَرُوا عَنْهَا لَا تُفَتَّحُ لَهُمْ أَبْوَابُ السَّمَاءِ وَلَا

7. The Elevated Places

7:39. And the first of them will say to the last of them: You have no preference over us, so taste the chastisement for what you earned.

* * *

7:40. Those who reject Our messages and turn away from them haughtily, the doors of heaven will not be opened for them, nor will they enter the Garden until the camel pass through the eye of the needle. And thus do We reward the guilty.

7:41. They shall have a bed of hell and over them coverings (of it). And thus do We requite the wrongdoers.

7:42. And as for those who believe and do good -- We impose not on any soul a duty beyond its scope -- they are the owners of the Garden; therein they abide.

7:43. And We shall remove whatever of ill-feeling is in their hearts -- rivers flow beneath them. And they say: All praise is due to Allah, Who guided us to this! And we would not have found the way if Allah had not guided us. Certainly the messengers of our Lord brought the truth. And it will be cried out to them: This is the Garden which you are made to inherit for what you did.

7:44. And the owners of the Garden call out to the companions of the Fire: We have found that which our Lord promised us to be true; have you, too, found that which your Lord promised to be true? They will say: Yes. Then a crier will cry out among them: The curse of Allah is on the wrongdoers,

7:45. Who hinder (men) from Allah's way and seek to make it crooked, and they are disbelievers in the Hereafter.

7:46. And between them is a veil. And on the Elevated Places are men who know all by their marks. And they call out to the owners of the Garden: Peace be to you! They have not yet entered it, though they hope.

7:47. And when their eyes are turned towards the companions of the Fire, they say: Our Lord, place us not with the unjust people.

***

7:48. And the owners of the Elevated Places call out to men whom they recognize by their marks, saying: Of no avail were to you your amassings and your arrogance.

7:49. Are these they about whom you swore that Allah would not bestow mercy on them? Enter the Garden; you have no fear, nor shall you grieve.

7:50. And the companions of the Fire call out to the owners of the Garden: Pour on us some water or some of that which Allah has provided for you. They say: Surely Allah has forbidden them both to the disbelievers,

7:51. Who take their religion for an idle sport and a play, and this world's life deceives them. So this day We shall forsake them, as they neglected the meeting of this day of theirs, and as they denied Our messages.

7:52. And certainly We have brought them a Book which We make clear with knowledge, a guidance and a mercy for a people who believe.

7:53. Do they wait for aught but its final sequel? On the day when its final sequel comes, those who neglected it before will say: Indeed the messengers of our Lord brought the truth. Are there any intercessors on our behalf so that they should intercede for us? Or could we be sent back so that we should do (deeds) other than those which we did? Indeed they have lost their souls, and that which they forged has failed them.

***

7:54. Surely your Lord is Allah, Who created the heavens and the earth in six periods, and He is established on the Throne of Power. He makes the night

7. The **Elevated Places**

cover the day, which it pursues incessantly. And (He created) the sun and the moon and the stars, made subservient by His command. Surely His is the creation and the command. Blessed is Allah, the Lord of the worlds!

7:55. Call on your Lord humbly and in secret. Surely He loves not the transgressors.

7:56. And make not mischief in the earth after its reformation and call on Him, fearing and hoping. Surely the mercy of Allah is nigh to the doers of good.

7:57. And He it is Who sends forth the winds hearing good news before His mercy; till, when they bear a laden cloud, We drive it to a dead land, then We send down water on it, then bring forth thereby fruits of all kinds. Thus do We bring forth the dead that you may be mindful.

7:58. And the good land -- its vegetation comes forth (abundantly) by the permission of its Lord. And that which is inferior -- (its herbage) comes forth but scantily. Thus do We repeat the messages for a people who give thanks.

***

7:59. Certainly We sent Noah to his people, so he said: O my people, serve Allah, you have no god other than Him. Indeed I fear for you the chastisement of a grievous day.

7:60. The chiefs of his people said Surely we see thee in clear error.

7:61. He said: O my people, there is no error in me, but I am a messenger from the Lord of the worlds.

7:62. I deliver to you the messages of my Lord, and I offer you good advice, and I know from Allah what you know not.

7:63. Do you wonder that a reminder has come to you from your Lord through a man from among you, that

7. The Elevated Places

he may warn you and that you may guard against evil, and that mercy may be shown to you?

7:64. But they called him a liar, so We delivered him and those with him in the ark, and We drowned those who rejected Our messages. Surely they were a blind people!

* * *

7:65. And to 'Ad (We sent) their brother Hud. He said: O my people, serve Allah, you have no god other than Him. Will you not then guard against evil?

7:66. The chiefs of those who disbelieved from among his people said: Certainly we see thee in folly, and we certainly think thee to be of the liars.

7:67. He said: O my people, there is no folly in me, but I am a messenger of the Lord of the worlds.

7:68. I deliver to you the messages of my Lord and I am a faithful adviser to you.

7:69. Do you wonder that a reminder has come to you from your Lord through a man from among you that he may warn you? And remember when He made you successors after Noah's people and increased you in excellence of make. So remember the bounties of Allah, that you may be successful.

7:70. They said: Hast thou come to us that we may serve Allah alone, and give up that which out fathers used to serve? Then bring to us what thou threatenest us with, if thou art of the truthful.

7:71. He said: Indeed uncleanness and wrath from your Lord have lighted upon you. Do you dispute with me about names which you and your fathers have named? Allah has not sent any authority for them. Wait, then; I too with you am of those who wait.

7:72. So We delivered him and those with him by mercy from Us, and We

وَإِلَىٰ عَادٍ أَخَاهُمْ هُودًا ۗ قَالَ يَا قَوْمِ اعْبُدُوا اللَّهَ مَا لَكُمْ مِنْ إِلَٰهٍ غَيْرُهُ ۚ أَفَلَا تَتَّقُونَ (٦٥)

قَالَ الْمَلَأُ الَّذِينَ كَفَرُوا مِنْ قَوْمِهِ إِنَّا لَنَرَاكَ فِي سَفَاهَةٍ وَإِنَّا لَنَظُنُّكَ مِنَ الْكَاذِبِينَ (٦٦)

قَالَ يَا قَوْمِ لَيْسَ بِي سَفَاهَةٌ وَلَٰكِنِّي رَسُولٌ مِنْ رَبِّ الْعَالَمِينَ (٦٧)

أُبَلِّغُكُمْ رِسَالَاتِ رَبِّي وَأَنَا لَكُمْ نَاصِحٌ أَمِينٌ (٦٨)

أَوَعَجِبْتُمْ أَنْ جَاءَكُمْ ذِكْرٌ مِنْ رَبِّكُمْ عَلَىٰ رَجُلٍ مِنْكُمْ لِيُنْذِرَكُمْ ۚ وَاذْكُرُوا إِذْ جَعَلَكُمْ خُلَفَاءَ مِنْ بَعْدِ قَوْمِ نُوحٍ وَزَادَكُمْ فِي الْخَلْقِ بَسْطَةً ۖ فَاذْكُرُوا آلَاءَ اللَّهِ لَعَلَّكُمْ تُفْلِحُونَ (٦٩)

قَالُوا أَجِئْتَنَا لِنَعْبُدَ اللَّهَ وَحْدَهُ وَنَذَرَ مَا كَانَ يَعْبُدُ آبَاؤُنَا ۖ فَأْتِنَا بِمَا تَعِدُنَا إِنْ كُنْتَ مِنَ الصَّادِقِينَ (٧٠)

قَالَ قَدْ وَقَعَ عَلَيْكُمْ مِنْ رَبِّكُمْ رِجْسٌ وَغَضَبٌ ۖ أَتُجَادِلُونَنِي فِي أَسْمَاءٍ سَمَّيْتُمُوهَا أَنْتُمْ وَآبَاؤُكُمْ مَا نَزَّلَ اللَّهُ بِهَا مِنْ سُلْطَانٍ ۚ فَانْتَظِرُوا إِنِّي مَعَكُمْ مِنَ الْمُنْتَظِرِينَ (٧١)

فَأَنْجَيْنَاهُ وَالَّذِينَ مَعَهُ بِرَحْمَةٍ مِنَّا وَقَطَعْنَا دَابِرَ الَّذِينَ كَذَّبُوا بِآيَاتِنَا ۖ وَمَا كَانُوا مُؤْمِنِينَ (٧٢)

وَإِلَىٰ ثَمُودَ أَخَاهُمْ صَالِحًا ۗ قَالَ يَا قَوْمِ اعْبُدُوا اللَّهَ مَا لَكُمْ مِنْ إِلَٰهٍ غَيْرُهُ ۖ قَدْ جَاءَتْكُمْ بَيِّنَةٌ مِنْ رَبِّكُمْ ۖ هَٰذِهِ نَاقَةُ اللَّهِ لَكُمْ آيَةً ۖ فَذَرُوهَا تَأْكُلْ فِي أَرْضِ اللَّهِ ۖ وَلَا تَمَسُّوهَا بِسُوءٍ فَيَأْخُذَكُمْ عَذَابٌ أَلِيمٌ (٧٣)

وَاذْكُرُوا إِذْ جَعَلَكُمْ خُلَفَاءَ مِنْ بَعْدِ عَادٍ وَبَوَّأَكُمْ فِي الْأَرْضِ تَتَّخِذُونَ مِنْ

7. The Elevated Places

cut off the roots of those who rejected Our messages and were not believers.

* * *

7:73. And to Thamud (We sent) their brother Salih. He said: O my people, serve Allah, you have no god other than Him. Clear proof has indeed come to you from your Lord. This is Allah's she-camel -- a sign for you -- so leave her alone to pasture in Allah's earth, and do her no harm, lest painful chastisement over-take you.

7:74. And remember when He made you successors after 'Ad and settled you in the land -- you make mansions on its plains and hew out houses in the mountains. So remember Allah's bounties and act not corruptly in the land, making mischief.

7:75. The arrogant chiefs of his people said to those who were weak, to those who believed from among them: Do you know that Salih is one sent by his Lord? They said: Surely we are believers in that wherewith he has been sent.

7:76. Those who were haughty said: Surely we are disbelievers in that which you believe.

7:77. Then they hamstrung the she-camel and revolted against their Lord's commandment, and said: O Salih, bring us that with which thou threatenest us, if thou art of the messengers.

7:78. So the earthquake seized them, and they were motionless bodies in their abodes.

7:79. So he turned away from them and said: O my people, I delivered to you the message of my Lord and gave you good advice, but you love not good advisers.

7:80. And (We sent) Lot, when he said to his people: Do you commit an abomination which no one in the world did before you?

7:81. Surely you come to males with

سُهُولِهَا قُصُورًا وَتَنْحِتُونَ الْجِبَالَ بُيُوتًا فَاذْكُرُوا آلَاءَ اللَّهِ وَلَا تَعْثَوْا فِي الْأَرْضِ مُفْسِدِينَ (٧٤) قَالَ الْمَلَأُ الَّذِينَ اسْتَكْبَرُوا مِنْ قَوْمِهِ لِلَّذِينَ اسْتُضْعِفُوا لِمَنْ آمَنَ مِنْهُمْ أَتَعْلَمُونَ أَنَّ صَالِحًا مُرْسَلٌ مِنْ رَبِّهِ قَالُوا إِنَّا بِمَا أُرْسِلَ بِهِ مُؤْمِنُونَ (٧٥) قَالَ الَّذِينَ اسْتَكْبَرُوا إِنَّا بِالَّذِي آمَنْتُمْ بِهِ كَافِرُونَ (٧٦) فَعَقَرُوا النَّاقَةَ وَعَتَوْا عَنْ أَمْرِ رَبِّهِمْ وَقَالُوا يَا صَالِحُ ائْتِنَا بِمَا تَعِدُنَا إِنْ كُنْتَ مِنَ الْمُرْسَلِينَ (٧٧) فَأَخَذَتْهُمُ الرَّجْفَةُ فَأَصْبَحُوا فِي دَارِهِمْ جَاثِمِينَ (٧٨) فَتَوَلَّى عَنْهُمْ وَقَالَ يَا قَوْمِ لَقَدْ أَبْلَغْتُكُمْ رِسَالَةَ رَبِّي وَنَصَحْتُ لَكُمْ وَلَكِنْ لَا تُحِبُّونَ النَّاصِحِينَ (٧٩) وَلُوطًا إِذْ قَالَ لِقَوْمِهِ أَتَأْتُونَ الْفَاحِشَةَ مَا سَبَقَكُمْ بِهَا مِنْ أَحَدٍ مِنَ الْعَالَمِينَ (٨٠) إِنَّكُمْ لَتَأْتُونَ الرِّجَالَ شَهْوَةً مِنْ دُونِ النِّسَاءِ بَلْ أَنْتُمْ قَوْمٌ مُسْرِفُونَ (٨١) وَمَا كَانَ جَوَابَ قَوْمِهِ إِلَّا أَنْ قَالُوا أَخْرِجُوهُمْ مِنْ قَرْيَتِكُمْ إِنَّهُمْ أُنَاسٌ يَتَطَهَّرُونَ (٨٢) فَأَنْجَيْنَاهُ وَأَهْلَهُ إِلَّا امْرَأَتَهُ كَانَتْ مِنَ الْغَابِرِينَ (٨٣) وَأَمْطَرْنَا عَلَيْهِمْ مَطَرًا فَانْظُرْ كَيْفَ كَانَ عَاقِبَةُ الْمُجْرِمِينَ (٨٤) وَإِلَى مَدْيَنَ أَخَاهُمْ شُعَيْبًا قَالَ يَا قَوْمِ اعْبُدُوا اللَّهَ مَا لَكُمْ مِنْ إِلَهٍ غَيْرُهُ قَدْ جَاءَتْكُمْ بَيِّنَةٌ مِنْ رَبِّكُمْ فَأَوْفُوا الْكَيْلَ وَالْمِيزَانَ وَلَا تَبْخَسُوا النَّاسَ أَشْيَاءَهُمْ وَلَا تُفْسِدُوا فِي الْأَرْضِ بَعْدَ

7. The Elevated Places

lust instead of females. Nay, you are a people exceeding bounds.

7:82. And the answer of his people was no other than that they said: Turn them out of your town; surely they are a people who aspire to purity!

7:83. So We delivered him and his followers, except his wife -- she was of those who remained behind.

7:84. And We rained upon them a rain. See, then, what was the end of the guilty!

* * *

7:85. And to Midian (We sent) their brother Shu'aib. He said: O my people, serve Allah, you have no god other than Him. Clear proof indeed has come to you from your Lord, so give full measure and weight and diminish not to men their things, and make not mischief in the land after its reform. This is better for you, if you are believers.

7:86. And lie not in wait on every road, threatening and turning away from Allah's way him who believes in Him and seeking to make it crooked. And remember when you were few, then He multiplied you, and see what was the end of the mischief-makers!

7:87. And if there is a party of you who believe in that wherewith I am sent and another party who believe not, then wait patiently till Allah judges between us; and He is the Best of Judges.

* * *

7:88. The arrogant chiefs of his people said: We will certainly turn thee out O Shu'aib, and those who believe with thee from our town, or you shall come back to our religion. He said: Even though we dislike (it)?

7:89. Indeed we should have forged a lie against Allah, if we go back to your religion after Allah has delivered us from it. And it is not for us to go back to it, unless Allah our Lord please. Our

Lord comprehends all things in His knowledge. In Allah do we trust. Our Lord, decide between us and our people with truth, and Thou art the Best of Deciders.

7:90. And the chiefs of his people, who disbelieved, said: If you follow Shu'aib, you are surely losers.

7:91. So the earthquake overtook them, and they were motionless bodies in their abode --

7:92. Those who called Shu'aib a liar were as though they had never dwelt therein those who called Shu'aib a liar, they were the losers.

7:93. So he turned away from them and said: O my people, indeed I delivered to you the messages of my Lord and I gave you good advice; how, then, should I be sorry for a disbelieving people?

* * *

7:94. And We did not send a prophet to a town but We seized its people with distress and affliction that they might humble themselves.

7:95. Then We changed the evil for good, till they became affluent and said: Distress and happiness did indeed touch our fathers. So We took them by surprise while they perceived not.

7:96. And if the people of the towns had believed and kept their duty, We would certainly have opened for them blessings from the heavens and the earth. But they rejected, so We seized them for what they earned.

7:97. Are the people of the towns, then, secure from Our punishment coming to them by night while they sleep?

7:98. Or, are the people of the towns secure from Our punishment coming to them in the morning while they play?

7:99. Are they secure from Allah's plan? But none feels secure from Allah's plan except the people who perish.

7. The Elevated Places

***

7:100. Is it not dear to those who inherit the earth after its (former) residents that, if We please, We would afflict them for their sins, and seal their hearts so they would not hear?

7:101. Such were the towns some of whose news We have related to thee. And certainly their messengers came to them with clear arguments, but they would not believe what they had rejected before. Thus does Allah seal the hearts of the disbelievers.

7:102. And We found not in most of them (faithfulness to) covenant; and We found most of them to be transgressors.

7:103. Then, after them, We sent Moses with Our messages to Pharaoh and his chiefs, but they disbelieved them. See, then, what was the end of the mischief-makers!

7:104. And Moses said: O Pharaoh, surely I am a messenger from the Lord of the worlds,

7:105. Worthy of not saying anything about Allah except the truth. I have come to you indeed with clear proof from your Lord, so let the Children of Israel go with me.

7:106. He said: If thou hast come with a sign, produce it, if thou art truthful.

7:107. So he threw his rod, then lo! it was a serpent manifest,

7:108. And he drew forth his hand, and lo! it was white to the beholders.

***

7:109. The chiefs of Pharaoh's people said: Surely this is a skilful enchanter!

7:110. He intends to turn you out of your land. What do you advise?

7:111. They said: Put him off and his brother, and send summoners into the cities,

7:112. To bring to thee every skilful enchanter.

7:113. And the enchanters came to Pharaoh, saying: We must surely have a reward if we prevail.

7:114. He said: Yes, and you shall certainly be of those who are near (to me).

7:115. They said: O Moses, wilt thou cast, or shall we (be the first to) cast?

7:116. He said: Cast. So when they cast, they deceived the people's eyes and overawed them, and they produced a mighty enchantment.

7:117. And We revealed to Moses: Cast thy rod. Then lo! it swallowed up their lies.

7:118. So the truth was established, and that which they did became null.

7:119. There they were vanquished, and they went back abased.

7:120. And the enchanters fell down prostrate --

7:121. They said: We believe in the Lord of the worlds,

7:122. The Lord of Moses and Aaron.

7:123. Pharaoh said: You believe in Him before I give you permission! Surely this is a plot which you have plotted in the city, to turn out of it its people, but you shall know!

7:124. I shall certainly cut off your hands and your feet on opposite sides, then I shall crucify you all together

7:125. They said: Surely to our Lord do we return.

7:126. And thou takest revenge on us only because we believed in the messages of our Lord when they came to us. Our Lord, pour out on us patience and cause us to die in submission. (to Thee)!

***

7:127. And the chiefs of Pharaoh's people said: Wilt thou leave Moses and his people to make mischief in the land and forsake thee and thy gods? He said: We will slay their sons and spare their women, and surely we are dominant over them.

7:128. Moses said to his people: Ask help from Allah and be patient. Surely

قَالَ أَلْقُوا فَلَمَّا أَلْقَوْا سَحَرُوا أَعْيُنَ النَّاسِ وَاسْتَرْهَبُوهُمْ وَجَاءُوا بِسِحْرٍ عَظِيمٍ (١١٦)

وَأَوْحَيْنَا إِلَى مُوسَى أَنْ أَلْقِ عَصَاكَ فَإِذَا هِيَ تَلْقَفُ مَا يَأْفِكُونَ (١١٧)

فَوَقَعَ الْحَقُّ وَبَطَلَ مَا كَانُوا يَعْمَلُونَ (١١٨)

فَغُلِبُوا هُنَالِكَ وَانْقَلَبُوا صَاغِرِينَ (١١٩)

وَأُلْقِيَ السَّحَرَةُ سَاجِدِينَ (١٢٠)

قَالُوا آمَنَّا بِرَبِّ الْعَالَمِينَ (١٢١)

رَبِّ مُوسَى وَهَارُونَ (١٢٢)

قَالَ فِرْعَوْنُ آمَنْتُمْ بِهِ قَبْلَ أَنْ آذَنَ لَكُمْ إِنَّ هَذَا لَمَكْرٌ مَكَرْتُمُوهُ فِي الْمَدِينَةِ لِتُخْرِجُوا مِنْهَا أَهْلَهَا فَسَوْفَ تَعْلَمُونَ (١٢٣)

لَأُقَطِّعَنَّ أَيْدِيَكُمْ وَأَرْجُلَكُمْ مِنْ خِلَافٍ ثُمَّ لَأُصَلِّبَنَّكُمْ أَجْمَعِينَ (١٢٤)

قَالُوا إِنَّا إِلَى رَبِّنَا مُنْقَلِبُونَ (١٢٥)

وَمَا تَنْقِمُ مِنَّا إِلَّا أَنْ آمَنَّا بِآيَاتِ رَبِّنَا لَمَّا جَاءَتْنَا رَبَّنَا أَفْرِغْ عَلَيْنَا صَبْرًا وَتَوَفَّنَا مُسْلِمِينَ (١٢٦)

وَقَالَ الْمَلَأُ مِنْ قَوْمِ فِرْعَوْنَ أَتَذَرُ مُوسَى وَقَوْمَهُ لِيُفْسِدُوا فِي الْأَرْضِ وَيَذَرَكَ وَآلِهَتَكَ قَالَ سَنُقَتِّلُ أَبْنَاءَهُمْ وَنَسْتَحْيِي نِسَاءَهُمْ وَإِنَّا فَوْقَهُمْ قَاهِرُونَ (١٢٧)

قَالَ مُوسَى لِقَوْمِهِ اسْتَعِينُوا بِاللَّهِ وَاصْبِرُوا إِنَّ الْأَرْضَ لِلَّهِ يُورِثُهَا مَنْ يَشَاءُ مِنْ عِبَادِهِ وَالْعَاقِبَةُ لِلْمُتَّقِينَ (١٢٨)

قَالُوا أُوذِينَا مِنْ قَبْلِ أَنْ تَأْتِيَنَا وَمِنْ بَعْدِ مَا جِئْتَنَا قَالَ عَسَى رَبُّكُمْ أَنْ

7. The Elevated Places

the land is Allah's — He gives it for an inheritance to such of His servants as He pleases. And the end is for those who keep their duty.

7:129. They said: We were persecuted before thou camest to us and since thou hast come to us. He said: It may be that your Lord will destroy your enemy and make you rulers in the land, then He will see how you act.

* * *

7:130. And certainly We overtook Pharaoh's people with droughts and diminution of fruits that they might be mindful.

7:131. But when good befell them they said: This is due to us. And when evil afflicted them, they attributed it to the ill-luck of Moses and those with him. Surely their evil fortune is only from Allah, but most of them know not.

7:132. And they said: Whatever sign thou mayest bring to us to charm us therewith we shall not believe in thee.

7:133. So We sent upon them widespread death, and the locusts and the lice and the frogs and the blood — clear signs. But they behaved haughtily and they were a guilty people.

7:134. And when the plague fell upon them, they said: O Moses, pray for us to thy Lord as He has made promise with thee. If thou remove the plague from us, we will certainly believe in thee and will let the Children of Israel go with thee.

7:135. But when We removed the plague from them till a term which they should attain, lo they broke (their promise).

7:136. So We exacted retribution from them and drowned them in the sea, because they rejected Our signs and were heedless of them.

7:137. And We made the people who were deemed weak to inherit the eastern lands and the western ones which We had blessed. And the good word of thy Lord was fulfilled in the Children of Israel because of their patience. And We destroyed what Pharaoh and his people had wrought and what they had built.

7:138. And We took the Children of Israel across the sea. Then they came to a people who were devoted to their idols. They said: O Moses, make for us a god as they have gods. He said: Surely you are an ignorant people!

7:139. (As to) these, that wherein they are engaged shall be destroyed and that which they do is vain.

7:140. He said: Shall I seek for you a god other than Allah, while He has made you excel (all) created things?

7:141. And when We delivered you from Pharaoh's people, who subjected you to severe torment, killing your sons and sparing your women. And therein was a great trial from your Lord.

* * *

7:142. And We appointed for Moses thirty nights, and completed them with ten, so the appointed time of his Lord was complete forty nights. And Moses said to his brother Aaron: Take my place among my people, and act well and follow not the way of the mischief-makers.

7:143. And when Moses came at Our appointed time and his Lord spoke to him, he said: My Lord, show me (Thyself) so that I may look at Thee. He said: Thou canst not see Me; but look at the mountain; if it remains firm in its place, then wilt thou see Me. So when his Lord manifested His glory to the mountain, He made it crumble and Moses fell down in a swoon. Then when he recovered, he said.: Glory be to Thee! I turn to Thee, and I am the first of the believers.

7:144. He said: O Moses, surely I have chosen thee above the people by My

7. The Elevated Places

messages and My words. So take hold of what I give thee and he of the grateful.

7:145. And We ordained for him in the tablets admonition of every kind and clear explanation of all things. So take hold of them with firmness and enjoin thy people to rake hold of what is best thereof. I shall show you the abode of the transgressors.

7:146. I shall turn away from My messages those who are unjustly proud in the earth. And if they see every sign, they will not believe in it; and if they see the way of rectitude, they take it not for a way and if they see the way of error, they take it for a way. This is because they reject Our messages and are heedless of them.

7:147. And those who reject Our messages and the meeting of the Hereafter their deeds are fruitless. Can they be rewarded except for what they do?

* * *

7:148. And Moses' people made of their ornaments a calf after him -- a (lifeless) body, having a lowing sound. Could they not see that it spoke not to them, nor guided them in the way? They took it (for worship) and they were unjust.

7:149. And when they repented and saw that they had gone astray, they said: If our Lord have not mercy on us and forgive us, we shall certainly be of the losers.

7:150. And when Moses returned to his people, wrathful, grieved, he said Evil is that which you have done after me! Did you hasten on the judgment of your Lord? And he threw down the tablets and seized his brother by the head, dragging him towards him. He said: Son of my mother, the people reckoned me weak and had well-nigh slain me. So make not the enemies to rejoice over me and count me not among the unjust people.

سَأَصْرِفُ عَنْ آيَاتِيَ الَّذِينَ يَتَكَبَّرُونَ فِي الْأَرْضِ بِغَيْرِ الْحَقِّ وَإِنْ يَرَوْا كُلَّ آيَةٍ لَا يُؤْمِنُوا بِهَا وَإِنْ يَرَوْا سَبِيلَ الرُّشْدِ لَا يَتَّخِذُوهُ سَبِيلًا وَإِنْ يَرَوْا سَبِيلَ الْغَيِّ يَتَّخِذُوهُ سَبِيلًا ذَلِكَ بِأَنَّهُمْ كَذَّبُوا بِآيَاتِنَا وَكَانُوا عَنْهَا غَافِلِينَ (١٤٦)

وَالَّذِينَ كَذَّبُوا بِآيَاتِنَا وَلِقَاءِ الْآخِرَةِ حَبِطَتْ أَعْمَالُهُمْ هَلْ يُجْزَوْنَ إِلَّا مَا كَانُوا يَعْمَلُونَ (١٤٧)

وَاتَّخَذَ قَوْمُ مُوسَى مِنْ بَعْدِهِ مِنْ حُلِيِّهِمْ عِجْلًا جَسَدًا لَهُ خُوَارٌ أَلَمْ يَرَوْا أَنَّهُ لَا يُكَلِّمُهُمْ وَلَا يَهْدِيهِمْ سَبِيلًا اتَّخَذُوهُ وَكَانُوا ظَالِمِينَ (١٤٨)

وَلَمَّا سُقِطَ فِي أَيْدِيهِمْ وَرَأَوْا أَنَّهُمْ قَدْ ضَلُّوا قَالُوا لَئِنْ لَمْ يَرْحَمْنَا رَبُّنَا وَيَغْفِرْ لَنَا لَنَكُونَنَّ مِنَ الْخَاسِرِينَ (١٤٩)

وَلَمَّا رَجَعَ مُوسَى إِلَى قَوْمِهِ غَضْبَانَ أَسِفًا قَالَ بِئْسَمَا خَلَفْتُمُونِي مِنْ بَعْدِي أَعَجِلْتُمْ أَمْرَ رَبِّكُمْ وَأَلْقَى الْأَلْوَاحَ وَأَخَذَ بِرَأْسِ أَخِيهِ يَجُرُّهُ إِلَيْهِ قَالَ ابْنَ أُمَّ إِنَّ الْقَوْمَ اسْتَضْعَفُونِي وَكَادُوا يَقْتُلُونَنِي فَلَا تُشْمِتْ بِيَ الْأَعْدَاءَ وَلَا تَجْعَلْنِي مَعَ الْقَوْمِ الظَّالِمِينَ (١٥٠)

قَالَ رَبِّ اغْفِرْ لِي وَلِأَخِي وَأَدْخِلْنَا فِي رَحْمَتِكَ وَأَنْتَ أَرْحَمُ الرَّاحِمِينَ (١٥١)

إِنَّ الَّذِينَ اتَّخَذُوا الْعِجْلَ سَيَنَالُهُمْ غَضَبٌ مِنْ رَبِّهِمْ وَذِلَّةٌ فِي الْحَيَاةِ الدُّنْيَا وَكَذَلِكَ نَجْزِي الْمُفْتَرِينَ (١٥٢)

وَالَّذِينَ عَمِلُوا السَّيِّئَاتِ ثُمَّ تَابُوا مِنْ بَعْدِهَا وَآمَنُوا إِنَّ رَبَّكَ مِنْ بَعْدِهَا

7. The Elevated Places

7:151. He said: My Lord, forgive me and my brother, and admit us to Thy mercy, and Thou art the Most Merciful of those who show mercy.

***

7:152. Those who took the calf (for a god) -- wrath from their Lord, and disgrace in this world's life, will surely overtake them. And thus do We recompense those who invent lies.

7:153. And those who do evil deeds, then repent after that and believe -- thy Lord after that is surely Forgiving, Merciful.

7:154. And when Moses' anger calmed down, he took up the tablets; and in the writing thereof was guidance and mercy for those who fear their Lord.

7:155. And Moses chose of his people seventy men for Our appointment. So when the earthquake overtook them, he said: My Lord, if Thou hadst pleased, Thou hadst destroyed them before and myself (too). Wilt Thou destroy us for that which the foolish among us have done? It is naught but Thy trial. Thou causest to perish thereby whom Thou pleasest and guidest whom Thou pleasest. Thou art our Protector, so forgive us and have mercy on us, and Thou art the Best of those who forgive.

7:156. And ordain for us good in this world's life and in the Hereafter, for surely we turn to Thee. He said: I afflict with My chastisement whom I please, and My mercy encompasses all things. So I ordain it for those who keep their duty and pay the poor-rate, and those who believe in Our messages --

7:157. Those who follow the Messenger-Prophet, the [Ummi] whom they find mentioned in the Torah and the Gospel. He enjoins them good and forbids them evil, and makes lawful to them the good things and prohibits for them impure things, and removes from them their burden and the shackles

لَغَفُورٌ رَحِيمٌ (١٥٣)

وَلَمَّا سَكَتَ عَنْ مُوسَى الْغَضَبُ أَخَذَ الْأَلْوَاحَ وَفِي نُسْخَتِهَا هُدًى وَرَحْمَةٌ لِلَّذِينَ هُمْ لِرَبِّهِمْ يَرْهَبُونَ (١٥٤)

وَاخْتَارَ مُوسَى قَوْمَهُ سَبْعِينَ رَجُلًا لِمِيقَاتِنَا فَلَمَّا أَخَذَتْهُمُ الرَّجْفَةُ قَالَ رَبِّ لَوْ شِئْتَ أَهْلَكْتَهُمْ مِنْ قَبْلُ وَإِيَّايَ أَتُهْلِكُنَا بِمَا فَعَلَ السُّفَهَاءُ مِنَّا إِنْ هِيَ إِلَّا فِتْنَتُكَ تُضِلُّ بِهَا مَنْ تَشَاءُ وَتَهْدِي مَنْ تَشَاءُ أَنْتَ وَلِيُّنَا فَاغْفِرْ لَنَا وَارْحَمْنَا وَأَنْتَ خَيْرُ الْغَافِرِينَ (١٥٥)

وَاكْتُبْ لَنَا فِي هَذِهِ الدُّنْيَا حَسَنَةً وَفِي الْآخِرَةِ إِنَّا هُدْنَا إِلَيْكَ قَالَ عَذَابِي أُصِيبُ بِهِ مَنْ أَشَاءُ وَرَحْمَتِي وَسِعَتْ كُلَّ شَيْءٍ فَسَأَكْتُبُهَا لِلَّذِينَ يَتَّقُونَ وَيُؤْتُونَ الزَّكَاةَ وَالَّذِينَ هُمْ بِآيَاتِنَا يُؤْمِنُونَ (١٥٦)

الَّذِينَ يَتَّبِعُونَ الرَّسُولَ النَّبِيَّ الْأُمِّيَّ الَّذِي يَجِدُونَهُ مَكْتُوبًا عِنْدَهُمْ فِي التَّوْرَاةِ وَالْإِنْجِيلِ يَأْمُرُهُمْ بِالْمَعْرُوفِ وَيَنْهَاهُمْ عَنِ الْمُنْكَرِ وَيُحِلُّ لَهُمُ الطَّيِّبَاتِ وَيُحَرِّمُ عَلَيْهِمُ الْخَبَائِثَ وَيَضَعُ عَنْهُمْ إِصْرَهُمْ وَالْأَغْلَالَ الَّتِي كَانَتْ عَلَيْهِمْ فَالَّذِينَ آمَنُوا بِهِ وَعَزَّرُوهُ وَنَصَرُوهُ وَاتَّبَعُوا النُّورَ الَّذِي أُنْزِلَ مَعَهُ أُولَئِكَ هُمُ الْمُفْلِحُونَ (١٥٧)

قُلْ يَا أَيُّهَا النَّاسُ إِنِّي رَسُولُ اللَّهِ إِلَيْكُمْ جَمِيعًا الَّذِي لَهُ مُلْكُ السَّمَاوَاتِ وَالْأَرْضِ لَا إِلَهَ إِلَّا هُوَ يُحْيِي وَيُمِيتُ فَآمِنُوا بِاللَّهِ وَرَسُولِهِ النَّبِيِّ الْأُمِّيِّ الَّذِي يُؤْمِنُ بِاللَّهِ وَكَلِمَاتِهِ وَاتَّبِعُوهُ لَعَلَّكُمْ تَهْتَدُونَ (١٥٨)

7. The Elevated Places

which were on them. So those who believe in him and honour him and help him, and follow the light which has been sent down with him -- these are the successful.

***

7:158. Say: O mankind, surely I am the Messenger of Allah to you all, of Him, Whose is the kingdom of the heavens and the earth. There is no god but He. He gives life and causes death. So believe in Allah and His Messenger, the [Ummi] Prophet who believes in Allah and His words, and follow him so that you may be guided aright.

7:159. And of Moses' people is a party who guide with truth, and therewith they do justice.

7:160. And We divided them into twelve tribes, as nations. And We revealed to Moses when his people asked him for water: Strike the rock with thy staff; so out flowed from it twelve springs. Each tribe knew its drinking-place. And We made the clouds to give shade over them and We sent to them manna and quails. Eat of the good things We have given you. And they did not do Us any harm, but they wronged themselves.

7:161. And when it was said to them: Dwell in this town and eat from it whence you wish, and make petition for forgiveness, and enter the gate submissively, We shall forgive you your wrongs. We shall give more to the doers of good.

7:162. But those who were unjust among them changed it for a word other than that which they were told, so We sent upon them a pestilence from heaven for their wrongdoing.

***

7:163. And ask them about the town which stood by the sea. When they violated the Sabbath, when their fish came to them on their Sabbath day on

وَمِنْ قَوْمِ مُوسَى أُمَّةٌ يَهْدُونَ بِالْحَقِّ وَبِهِ يَعْدِلُونَ (١٥٩)

وَقَطَّعْنَاهُمُ اثْنَتَيْ عَشْرَةَ أَسْبَاطًا أُمَمًا وَأَوْحَيْنَا إِلَى مُوسَى إِذِ اسْتَسْقَاهُ قَوْمُهُ أَنِ اضْرِبْ بِعَصَاكَ الْحَجَرَ فَانْبَجَسَتْ مِنْهُ اثْنَتَا عَشْرَةَ عَيْنًا قَدْ عَلِمَ كُلُّ أُنَاسٍ مَشْرَبَهُمْ وَظَلَّلْنَا عَلَيْهِمُ الْغَمَامَ وَأَنْزَلْنَا عَلَيْهِمُ الْمَنَّ وَالسَّلْوَى كُلُوا مِنْ طَيِّبَاتِ مَا رَزَقْنَاكُمْ وَمَا ظَلَمُونَا وَلَكِنْ كَانُوا أَنْفُسَهُمْ يَظْلِمُونَ (١٦٠)

وَإِذْ قِيلَ لَهُمُ اسْكُنُوا هَذِهِ الْقَرْيَةَ وَكُلُوا مِنْهَا حَيْثُ شِئْتُمْ وَقُولُوا حِطَّةٌ وَادْخُلُوا الْبَابَ سُجَّدًا نَغْفِرْ لَكُمْ خَطِيئَاتِكُمْ سَنَزِيدُ الْمُحْسِنِينَ (١٦١) فَبَدَّلَ الَّذِينَ ظَلَمُوا مِنْهُمْ قَوْلًا غَيْرَ الَّذِي قِيلَ لَهُمْ فَأَرْسَلْنَا عَلَيْهِمْ رِجْزًا مِنَ السَّمَاءِ بِمَا كَانُوا يَظْلِمُونَ (١٦٢)

وَاسْأَلْهُمْ عَنِ الْقَرْيَةِ الَّتِي كَانَتْ حَاضِرَةَ الْبَحْرِ إِذْ يَعْدُونَ فِي السَّبْتِ إِذْ تَأْتِيهِمْ حِيتَانُهُمْ يَوْمَ سَبْتِهِمْ شُرَّعًا

the surface, and when it was not their Sabbath they came not to them. Thus did We try them because they transgressed.

7:164. And when a party of them said: Why preach you to a people whom Allah would destroy or whom He would chastise with a severe chastisement? They said: To be free from blame before your Lord, and that haply they may guard against evil.

7:165. So when they neglected that whereof they had been reminded, We delivered those who forbade evil and We overtook those who were iniquitous with an evil chastisement because they transgressed.

7:166. So when they revoltingly persisted in that which they had been forbidden, We said to them: Be (as) apes, despised and hated.

7:167. And when thy Lord declared that He would send against them to the day of Resurrection those who would subject them to severe torment. Surely thy Lord is Quick in requiting; and surely He is Forgiving, Merciful.

7:168. And We divided them in the earth into parties -- some of them are righteous and some of them are otherwise. And We tried them with blessings and misfortunes that they might turn.

7:169. Then after them came an evil posterity who inherited the Book, taking the frail goods of this low life and saying: It will be forgiven us. And if the like good came to them, they would take it (too). Was not a promise taken from them in the Book that they would not speak anything about Allah but the truth? And they study what is in it. And the abode of the Hereafter is better for those who keep their duty. Do you not then understand?

7:170. And as for those who hold fast by the Book and keep up prayer -- surely We waste not the reward of the

وَيَوْمَ لَا يَسْبِتُونَ لَا تَأْتِيهِمْ كَذَلِكَ نَبْلُوهُمْ بِمَا كَانُوا يَفْسُقُونَ (١٦٣)

وَإِذْ قَالَتْ أُمَّةٌ مِنْهُمْ لِمَ تَعِظُونَ قَوْمًا اللَّهُ مُهْلِكُهُمْ أَوْ مُعَذِّبُهُمْ عَذَابًا شَدِيدًا قَالُوا مَعْذِرَةً إِلَى رَبِّكُمْ وَلَعَلَّهُمْ يَتَّقُونَ (١٦٤)

فَلَمَّا نَسُوا مَا ذُكِّرُوا بِهِ أَنْجَيْنَا الَّذِينَ يَنْهَوْنَ عَنِ السُّوءِ وَأَخَذْنَا الَّذِينَ ظَلَمُوا بِعَذَابٍ بَئِيسٍ بِمَا كَانُوا يَفْسُقُونَ (١٦٥)

فَلَمَّا عَتَوْا عَنْ مَا نُهُوا عَنْهُ قُلْنَا لَهُمْ كُونُوا قِرَدَةً خَاسِئِينَ (١٦٦)

وَإِذْ تَأَذَّنَ رَبُّكَ لَيَبْعَثَنَّ عَلَيْهِمْ إِلَى يَوْمِ الْقِيَامَةِ مَنْ يَسُومُهُمْ سُوءَ الْعَذَابِ إِنَّ رَبَّكَ لَسَرِيعُ الْعِقَابِ وَإِنَّهُ لَغَفُورٌ رَحِيمٌ (١٦٧)

وَقَطَّعْنَاهُمْ فِي الْأَرْضِ أُمَمًا مِنْهُمُ الصَّالِحُونَ وَمِنْهُمْ دُونَ ذَلِكَ وَبَلَوْنَاهُمْ بِالْحَسَنَاتِ وَالسَّيِّئَاتِ لَعَلَّهُمْ يَرْجِعُونَ (١٦٨)

فَخَلَفَ مِنْ بَعْدِهِمْ خَلْفٌ وَرِثُوا الْكِتَابَ يَأْخُذُونَ عَرَضَ هَذَا الْأَدْنَى وَيَقُولُونَ سَيُغْفَرُ لَنَا وَإِنْ يَأْتِهِمْ عَرَضٌ مِثْلُهُ يَأْخُذُوهُ أَلَمْ يُؤْخَذْ عَلَيْهِمْ مِيثَاقُ الْكِتَابِ أَنْ لَا يَقُولُوا عَلَى اللَّهِ إِلَّا الْحَقَّ وَدَرَسُوا مَا فِيهِ وَالدَّارُ الْآخِرَةُ خَيْرٌ لِلَّذِينَ يَتَّقُونَ أَفَلَا تَعْقِلُونَ (١٦٩)

وَالَّذِينَ يُمَسِّكُونَ بِالْكِتَابِ وَأَقَامُوا الصَّلَاةَ إِنَّا لَا نُضِيعُ أَجْرَ الْمُصْلِحِينَ (١٧٠)

وَإِذْ نَتَقْنَا الْجَبَلَ فَوْقَهُمْ كَأَنَّهُ ظُلَّةٌ وَظَنُّوا أَنَّهُ وَاقِعٌ بِهِمْ خُذُوا مَا آتَيْنَاكُمْ بِقُوَّةٍ وَاذْكُرُوا مَا فِيهِ لَعَلَّكُمْ تَتَّقُونَ

7. The Elevated Places

reformers.

7:171. And when We shook the mountain over them as if it were a covering, and they thought that it was going to fall down upon them: Hold on firmly to that which We have given you, and be mindful of that which is in it, so that you may guard against evil.

* * *

7:172. And when thy Lord brought forth from the children of Adam, from their loins, their descendants, and made them bear witness about themselves: Am I not your Lord? They said: Yes; we bear witness. Lest you should say on the day of Resurrection: We were unaware of this,

7:173. Or (lest) you should say: Only our fathers ascribed partners (to Allah) before (us), and we were (their) descendants after them. Wilt Thou destroy us for what liars did?

7:174. And thus do We make the messages clear, and that haply they may return.

7:175. And recite to them the news of him to whom We give Our messages, but he withdraws himself from them, so the devil follows him up, and he is of those who perish.

7:176. And if We had pleased, We would have exalted him thereby; but he clings to the earth and follows his low desire. His parable is as the parable of the dog if thou drive him away, he lolls out his tongue, and if thou leave him alone, he lolls out his tongue. Such is the parable of the people who reject Our messages. So relate the narrative that they may reflect.

7:177. Evil is the likeness of the people who reject Our messages and wrong their own souls.

7:178. He whom Allah guides is on the right way; and he whom He leaves in error -- they are the losers.

7:179. And certainly We have created

for hell many of the jinn and the men -- they have hearts wherewith they understand not, and they have eyes wherewith they see not, and they have ears wherewith they hear not. They are as cattle; nay, they are more astray. These are the heedless ones.

7:180. And Allah's are the best names, so call on Him thereby and leave alone those who violate the sanctity of His names. They will be recompensed for what they do.

7:181. And of those whom We have created is a community who guide with the truth and therewith do justice.

* * *

7:182. And those who reject Our messages -- We lead them (to destruction) step by step from whence they know not.

7:183. And I grant them respite. Surely My scheme is effective.

7:184. Do they not reflect (that) there is no madness in their companion? He is only a plain warner.

7:185. Do they not consider the kingdom of the heavens and the earth and what things Allah has created, and that it may be that their doom has drawn nigh? In what announcement after this will they then believe?

7:186. Whomsoever Allah leaves in error, there is no guide for him. And He leaves them alone in their inordinacy, blindly wandering on.

7:187. They ask thee about the Hour, when will it come to pass? Say: The knowledge thereof is with my Lord only. None but He will manifest it at its time. It is momentous in the heavens and the earth. It will not come to you but of a sudden. They ask thee as if thou wert solicitous about it. Say: Its knowledge is with Allah only, but most people know not.

7:188. Say: I control not benefit or harm for myself except as Allah please. And had I known the unseen, I should have

7. The Elevated Places

much of good, and no evil would touch me. I am but a warner and the giver of good news to a people who believe.

* * *

7:189. He it is Who created you from a single soul, and of the same did He make his mate, that he might find comfort in her. So when he covers her she bears a light burden, then moves about with it. Then when it grows heavy, they both call upon Allah, their Lord: If Thou givest us a good one, we shall certainly be of the grateful.

7:190. But when He gives them a good one, they set up with Him associates in that which He has given them. High is Allah above what they associate (with Him).

7:191. Do they associate (with Him) that which has created naught, while they are themselves created?

7:192. And they cannot give them help, nor can they help themselves.

7:193. And if you invite them to guidance, they will not follow you. It is the same to you whether you invite them or you are silent.

7:194. Those whom you call on besides Allah are slaves like yourselves -- call on them, then let them answer you, if you are truthful.

7:195. Have they feet with which they walk, or have they hands with which they hold, or have they eyes with which they see, or have they ears with which they hear? Say: Call upon your associate-gods then plot against me and give me no respite.

7:196. Surely my Friend is Allah, Who revealed the Book, and He befriends the righteous.

7:197. And those whom you call upon besides Him are not able to help you, nor can they help themselves.

7:198. And if you invite them to guidance, they hear not and thou seest them looking towards thee, yet they see not.

7:199. Take to forgiveness and enjoin good and turn away from the ignorant.

7:200. And if a false imputation from the devil afflict thee, seek refuge in Allah. Surely He is Hearing, Knowing.

7:201. Those who guard against evil, when a visitation from the devil afflicts them, they become mindful, then lo they see.

7:202. And their brethren increase them in error, then they cease not.

7:203. And when thou bringest them not a sign, they say Why dost thou not demand it? Say I follow only that which is revealed to me from my Lord. These are clear proofs from your Lord and a guidance and a mercy for a people who believe.

7:204. And when the Qur'an is recited, listen to it and remain silent, that mercy may be shown to you.

7:205. And remember thy Lord within thyself humbly and fearing, and in a voice not loud, in the morning and the evening, and be not of the heedless.

7:206. Surely those who are with thy Lord are not too proud to serve Him, and they glorify Him and prostrate themselves before Him.

8. Voluntary Gifts

In the name of Allah, the Beneficent, the Merciful.

8:1. They ask thee about voluntary gifts. Say Voluntary gifts are for Allah and the Messenger. So keep your duty to Allah and set aright your differences, and obey Allah and His Messenger, if you are believers.

8:2. They only are believers whose hearts are full of fear when Allah is mentioned, and when His messages are recited to them they increase them in faith, and in their Lord do they trust,

8:3. Those who keep up prayer and spend out of what We have given

8. Voluntary Gifts

them.

8:4. These are the believers in truth. For them are with their Lord exalted grades and protection and an honourable sustenance.

8:5. Even as thy Lord caused thee to go forth from thy house with truth, though a party of the believers were surely averse,

8:6. Disputing with thee about the truth after it had become clear -- as if they were being driven to death while they saw (it).

8:7. And when Allah promised you one of the two parties that it should be yours, and you loved that the one not armed should be yours, and Allah desired to establish the Truth by His words, and to cut off the root of the disbelievers --

8:8. That He might cause the Truth to triumph and bring the falsehood to naught though the guilty disliked.

8:9. When you sought the aid of your Lord, so He answered you I will assist you with a thousand of the angels following one another.

8:10. And Allah gave it only as good news, and that your hearts might be at ease thereby. And victory is only from Allah surely Allah is Mighty, Wise.

* * *

8:11. When He made slumber fall on you as a security from Him, and sent down upon you water from the clouds that He might thereby purify you, and take away from you the uncleanness of the devil, and that He might fortify your hearts and make firm (your) feet thereby.

8:12. When thy Lord revealed to the angels; I am with you, so make firm those who believe I will cast terror into the hearts of those who disbelieve. So smite above the necks and smite every finger-tip of them.

8:13. This is because they opposed Allah and His Messenger. And

أُولَٰئِكَ هُمُ الْمُؤْمِنُونَ حَقًّا لَهُمْ دَرَجَاتٌ عِنْدَ رَبِّهِمْ وَمَغْفِرَةٌ وَرِزْقٌ كَرِيمٌ (٤)
كَمَا أَخْرَجَكَ رَبُّكَ مِنْ بَيْتِكَ بِالْحَقِّ وَإِنَّ فَرِيقًا مِنَ الْمُؤْمِنِينَ لَكَارِهُونَ (٥)
يُجَادِلُونَكَ فِي الْحَقِّ بَعْدَمَا تَبَيَّنَ كَأَنَّمَا يُسَاقُونَ إِلَى الْمَوْتِ وَهُمْ يَنْظُرُونَ (٦)
وَإِذْ يَعِدُكُمُ اللَّهُ إِحْدَى الطَّائِفَتَيْنِ أَنَّهَا لَكُمْ وَتَوَدُّونَ أَنَّ غَيْرَ ذَاتِ الشَّوْكَةِ تَكُونُ لَكُمْ وَيُرِيدُ اللَّهُ أَنْ يُحِقَّ الْحَقَّ بِكَلِمَاتِهِ وَيَقْطَعَ دَابِرَ الْكَافِرِينَ (٧)
لِيُحِقَّ الْحَقَّ وَيُبْطِلَ الْبَاطِلَ وَلَوْ كَرِهَ الْمُجْرِمُونَ (٨)
إِذْ تَسْتَغِيثُونَ رَبَّكُمْ فَاسْتَجَابَ لَكُمْ أَنِّي مُمِدُّكُمْ بِأَلْفٍ مِنَ الْمَلَائِكَةِ مُرْدِفِينَ (٩)
وَمَا جَعَلَهُ اللَّهُ إِلَّا بُشْرَى وَلِتَطْمَئِنَّ بِهِ قُلُوبُكُمْ وَمَا النَّصْرُ إِلَّا مِنْ عِنْدِ اللَّهِ إِنَّ اللَّهَ عَزِيزٌ حَكِيمٌ (١٠)
إِذْ يُغَشِّيكُمُ النُّعَاسَ أَمَنَةً مِنْهُ وَيُنَزِّلُ عَلَيْكُمْ مِنَ السَّمَاءِ مَاءً لِيُطَهِّرَكُمْ بِهِ وَيُذْهِبَ عَنْكُمْ رِجْزَ الشَّيْطَانِ وَلِيَرْبِطَ عَلَى قُلُوبِكُمْ وَيُثَبِّتَ بِهِ الْأَقْدَامَ (١١)
إِذْ يُوحِي رَبُّكَ إِلَى الْمَلَائِكَةِ أَنِّي مَعَكُمْ فَثَبِّتُوا الَّذِينَ آمَنُوا سَأُلْقِي فِي قُلُوبِ الَّذِينَ كَفَرُوا الرُّعْبَ فَاضْرِبُوا فَوْقَ الْأَعْنَاقِ وَاضْرِبُوا مِنْهُمْ كُلَّ بَنَانٍ (١٢)
ذَٰلِكَ بِأَنَّهُمْ شَاقُّوا اللَّهَ وَرَسُولَهُ وَمَنْ يُشَاقِقِ اللَّهَ وَرَسُولَهُ فَإِنَّ اللَّهَ شَدِيدُ الْعِقَابِ (١٣)
ذَٰلِكُمْ فَذُوقُوهُ وَأَنَّ لِلْكَافِرِينَ عَذَابَ

8. Voluntary Gifts

whoever opposes Allah and His Messenger -- then surely Allah is Severe in requiting.

8:14. This -- taste it, and (know) that for the disbelievers is the chastisement of the Fire.

8:15. O you who believe, when you meet those who disbelieve marching for war, turn not your backs to them.

8:16. And whoso turns his back to them on that day unless manoeuvring for battle or turning to join a company -- he, indeed, incurs Allah's wrath and his refuge is hell. And an evil destination it is.

8:17. So you slew them not but Allah slew them, and thou smotest not when thou didst smite (the enemy), but Allah smote (him), and that He might confer upon the believers a benefit from Himself. Surely Allah is Hearing, Knowing.

8:18. This -- and (know) that Allah will weaken the struggle of the disbelievers.

8:19. If you sought a judgment, the judgment has indeed come to you and if you desist, it is better for you. And if you return (to fight), We (too) shall return and your forces will avail you nothing, though they may be many; and (know) that Allah is with the believers.

* * *

8:20. O you who believe, obey Allah and His Messenger and turn not away from Him while you hear.

8:21. And be not like those who say, We hear; and they hear not.

8:22. Surely the vilest of beasts, in Allah's sight, are the deaf, the dumb, who understand not.

8:23. And if Allah had known any good in them, He would have made them hear. And if He makes them hear, they would turn away while they are averse.

8:24. O you who believe, respond to Allah and His Messenger, when he calls you to that which gives you life. And know that Allah comes in between a man and his heart, and that to Him you will be gathered.

8:25. And guard yourselves against an affliction which may not smite those of you exclusively who are unjust; and know that Allah is Severe in requiting.

8:26. And remember when you were few, deemed weak in the land, fearing lest people should carry you off by force, He sheltered you and strengthened you with His help, and gave you of the good things that you might give thanks.

8:27. O you who believe, be not unfaithful to Allah and the Messenger, nor be unfaithful to your trusts, while you know.

8:28. And know that your wealth and your children are a temptation, and that Allah is He with Whom there is a mighty reward

***

8:29. O you who believe, if you keep your duty to Allah, He will grant you a distinction and do away with your evils and protect you. And Allah is the Lord of mighty grace.

8:30. And when those who disbelieved devised plans against thee that they might confine thee or slay thee or drive thee away and they devised plans and Allah, too, had arranged a plan; and Allah is the best of planners --

8:31. And when Our messages are recited to them, they say: We have heard. If we wished, we could say the like of it; this is nothing but the stories of the ancients.

8:32. And when they said: O Allah, if this is indeed the truth from Thee, then rain down on us stones from heaven or inflict on us a painful chastisement.

8:33. And Allah would not chastise them while thou wast among them; nor would Allah chastise them while they seek forgiveness.

الْعِقَابِ (٢٥)
وَاذْكُرُوا إِذْ أَنْتُمْ قَلِيلٌ مُسْتَضْعَفُونَ فِي الْأَرْضِ تَخَافُونَ أَنْ يَتَخَطَّفَكُمُ النَّاسُ فَآوَاكُمْ وَأَيَّدَكُمْ بِنَصْرِهِ وَرَزَقَكُمْ مِنَ الطَّيِّبَاتِ لَعَلَّكُمْ تَشْكُرُونَ (٢٦)
يَا أَيُّهَا الَّذِينَ آمَنُوا لَا تَخُونُوا اللَّهَ وَالرَّسُولَ وَتَخُونُوا أَمَانَاتِكُمْ وَأَنْتُمْ تَعْلَمُونَ (٢٧)
وَاعْلَمُوا أَنَّمَا أَمْوَالُكُمْ وَأَوْلَادُكُمْ فِتْنَةٌ وَأَنَّ اللَّهَ عِنْدَهُ أَجْرٌ عَظِيمٌ (٢٨)
يَا أَيُّهَا الَّذِينَ آمَنُوا إِنْ تَتَّقُوا اللَّهَ يَجْعَلْ لَكُمْ فُرْقَانًا وَيُكَفِّرْ عَنْكُمْ سَيِّئَاتِكُمْ وَيَغْفِرْ لَكُمْ وَاللَّهُ ذُو الْفَضْلِ الْعَظِيمِ (٢٩)
وَإِذْ يَمْكُرُ بِكَ الَّذِينَ كَفَرُوا لِيُثْبِتُوكَ أَوْ يَقْتُلُوكَ أَوْ يُخْرِجُوكَ وَيَمْكُرُونَ وَيَمْكُرُ اللَّهُ وَاللَّهُ خَيْرُ الْمَاكِرِينَ (٣٠)
وَإِذَا تُتْلَى عَلَيْهِمْ آيَاتُنَا قَالُوا قَدْ سَمِعْنَا لَوْ نَشَاءُ لَقُلْنَا مِثْلَ هَذَا إِنْ هَذَا إِلَّا أَسَاطِيرُ الْأَوَّلِينَ (٣١)
وَإِذْ قَالُوا اللَّهُمَّ إِنْ كَانَ هَذَا هُوَ الْحَقَّ مِنْ عِنْدِكَ فَأَمْطِرْ عَلَيْنَا حِجَارَةً مِنَ السَّمَاءِ أَوِ ائْتِنَا بِعَذَابٍ أَلِيمٍ (٣٢)
وَمَا كَانَ اللَّهُ لِيُعَذِّبَهُمْ وَأَنْتَ فِيهِمْ وَمَا كَانَ اللَّهُ مُعَذِّبَهُمْ وَهُمْ يَسْتَغْفِرُونَ (٣٣)
وَمَا لَهُمْ أَلَّا يُعَذِّبَهُمُ اللَّهُ وَهُمْ يَصُدُّونَ عَنِ الْمَسْجِدِ الْحَرَامِ وَمَا كَانُوا أَوْلِيَاءَهُ إِنْ أَوْلِيَاؤُهُ إِلَّا الْمُتَّقُونَ وَلَكِنَّ أَكْثَرَهُمْ لَا يَعْلَمُونَ (٣٤)
وَمَا كَانَ صَلَاتُهُمْ عِنْدَ الْبَيْتِ إِلَّا مُكَاءً وَتَصْدِيَةً فَذُوقُوا الْعَذَابَ بِمَا كُنْتُمْ تَكْفُرُونَ (٣٥)

8. Voluntary Gifts

8:34. And what excuse have they that Allah should not chastise them while they hinder (men) from the Sacred Mosque and they are not its (true) guardians? Its guardians are only those who keep their duty, but most of them know not.

8:35. And their prayer at the House is nothing but whistling and clapping of hands. Taste, then, the chastisement, because you disbelieved.

8:36. Surely those who disbelieve spend their wealth to hinder (people) from the way of Allah. So they will go on spending it, then it will be to them a regret, then they will be overcome. And those who disbelieve will be gathered together to hell,

8:37. That Allah may separate the wicked from the good, and put the wicked one upon another, then heap them together, then cast them into hell. These indeed are the losers.

***

8:38. Say to those who disbelieve, if they desist, that which is past will be forgiven them; and if they return, then the example of those of old has already gone.

8:39. And fight with them until there is no more persecution [temptation, chaos], and all religions are for Allah. But if they desist, then surely Allah is Seer of what they do.

8:40. And if they turn back, then know that Allah is your Patron. Most excellent the Patron and most excellent the Helper!

***

8:41. And know that whatever you acquire in war, a fifth of it is for Allah and for the Messenger and for the near of kin and the orphans and the needy and the wayfarer, if you believe in Allah and in that which We revealed to Our servant, on the day of Discrimination, the day on which the

إِنَّ الَّذِينَ كَفَرُوا يُنْفِقُونَ أَمْوَالَهُمْ لِيَصُدُّوا عَنْ سَبِيلِ اللَّهِ فَسَيُنْفِقُونَهَا ثُمَّ تَكُونُ عَلَيْهِمْ حَسْرَةً ثُمَّ يُغْلَبُونَ وَالَّذِينَ كَفَرُوا إِلَى جَهَنَّمَ يُحْشَرُونَ (٣٦)

لِيَمِيزَ اللَّهُ الْخَبِيثَ مِنَ الطَّيِّبِ وَيَجْعَلَ الْخَبِيثَ بَعْضَهُ عَلَى بَعْضٍ فَيَرْكُمَهُ جَمِيعًا فَيَجْعَلَهُ فِي جَهَنَّمَ أُولَٰئِكَ هُمُ الْخَاسِرُونَ (٣٧)

قُلْ لِلَّذِينَ كَفَرُوا إِنْ يَنْتَهُوا يُغْفَرْ لَهُمْ مَا قَدْ سَلَفَ وَإِنْ يَعُودُوا فَقَدْ مَضَتْ سُنَّةُ الْأَوَّلِينَ (٣٨)

وَقَاتِلُوهُمْ حَتَّى لَا تَكُونَ فِتْنَةٌ وَيَكُونَ الدِّينُ كُلُّهُ لِلَّهِ فَإِنِ انْتَهَوْا فَإِنَّ اللَّهَ بِمَا يَعْمَلُونَ بَصِيرٌ (٣٩)

وَإِنْ تَوَلَّوْا فَاعْلَمُوا أَنَّ اللَّهَ مَوْلَاكُمْ نِعْمَ الْمَوْلَى وَنِعْمَ النَّصِيرُ (٤٠)

وَاعْلَمُوا أَنَّمَا غَنِمْتُمْ مِنْ شَيْءٍ فَأَنَّ لِلَّهِ خُمُسَهُ وَلِلرَّسُولِ وَلِذِي الْقُرْبَى وَالْيَتَامَى وَالْمَسَاكِينِ وَابْنِ السَّبِيلِ إِنْ كُنْتُمْ آمَنْتُمْ بِاللَّهِ وَمَا أَنْزَلْنَا عَلَى عَبْدِنَا يَوْمَ الْفُرْقَانِ يَوْمَ الْتَقَى الْجَمْعَانِ وَاللَّهُ عَلَى كُلِّ شَيْءٍ قَدِيرٌ (٤١)

8. Voluntary Gifts

two patties met. And Allah is Possessor of power over all things.

8:42. When you were on the nearer side (of the valley) and they were on the farther side, while the caravan was in a lower place than you. And if you had tried to make a mutual appointment, you would certainly have broken away from the appointment, -- but in order that Allah might bring about a matter which had to be done; that he who perished by clear argument might perish, and he who lived by clear argument might live. And surely Allah is Hearing, Knowing

8:43. When Allah showed them to thee in thy dream as few and if He had shown them to thee as many, you would certainly have become weak hearted and you would have disputed about the matter, but Allah saved (you). Surely He is Knower of what is in the breasts.

8:44. And when He showed them to you, when you met, as few in your eyes, and He made you to appear few in their eyes, in order that Allah might bring about a matter which had to be done. And to Allah are all affairs returned.

* * *

8:45. O you who believe, when you meet an army, be firm, and remember Allah much, that you may be successful.

8:46. And obey Allah and His Messenger and dispute not one with another, lest you get weak-hearted and your power depart; and be steadfast. Surely Allah is with the steadfast.

8:47. And be not like those who came forth from their homes exultingly and to be seen of men, and they hinder (people) from the way of Allah. And Allah encompasses what they do.

8:48. And when the devil made their works fair-seeming to them, and said: None among men can overcome you

إِذْ أَنْتُمْ بِالْعُدْوَةِ الدُّنْيَا وَهُمْ بِالْعُدْوَةِ الْقُصْوَىٰ وَالرَّكْبُ أَسْفَلَ مِنْكُمْ ۚ وَلَوْ تَوَاعَدْتُمْ لَاخْتَلَفْتُمْ فِي الْمِيعَادِ ۙ وَلَٰكِنْ لِيَقْضِيَ اللَّهُ أَمْرًا كَانَ مَفْعُولًا لِيَهْلِكَ مَنْ هَلَكَ عَنْ بَيِّنَةٍ وَيَحْيَىٰ مَنْ حَيَّ عَنْ بَيِّنَةٍ ۗ وَإِنَّ اللَّهَ لَسَمِيعٌ عَلِيمٌ (٤٢)

إِذْ يُرِيكَهُمُ اللَّهُ فِي مَنَامِكَ قَلِيلًا ۖ وَلَوْ أَرَاكَهُمْ كَثِيرًا لَفَشِلْتُمْ وَلَتَنَازَعْتُمْ فِي الْأَمْرِ وَلَٰكِنَّ اللَّهَ سَلَّمَ ۗ إِنَّهُ عَلِيمٌ بِذَاتِ الصُّدُورِ (٤٣)

وَإِذْ يُرِيكُمُوهُمْ إِذِ الْتَقَيْتُمْ فِي أَعْيُنِكُمْ قَلِيلًا وَيُقَلِّلُكُمْ فِي أَعْيُنِهِمْ لِيَقْضِيَ اللَّهُ أَمْرًا كَانَ مَفْعُولًا ۗ وَإِلَى اللَّهِ تُرْجَعُ الْأُمُورُ (٤٤)

يَا أَيُّهَا الَّذِينَ آمَنُوا إِذَا لَقِيتُمْ فِئَةً فَاثْبُتُوا وَاذْكُرُوا اللَّهَ كَثِيرًا لَعَلَّكُمْ تُفْلِحُونَ (٤٥)

وَأَطِيعُوا اللَّهَ وَرَسُولَهُ وَلَا تَنَازَعُوا فَتَفْشَلُوا وَتَذْهَبَ رِيحُكُمْ ۖ وَاصْبِرُوا ۚ إِنَّ اللَّهَ مَعَ الصَّابِرِينَ (٤٦)

وَلَا تَكُونُوا كَالَّذِينَ خَرَجُوا مِنْ دِيَارِهِمْ بَطَرًا وَرِئَاءَ النَّاسِ وَيَصُدُّونَ عَنْ سَبِيلِ اللَّهِ ۚ وَاللَّهُ بِمَا يَعْمَلُونَ مُحِيطٌ (٤٧)

وَإِذْ زَيَّنَ لَهُمُ الشَّيْطَانُ أَعْمَالَهُمْ وَقَالَ لَا غَالِبَ لَكُمُ الْيَوْمَ مِنَ النَّاسِ وَإِنِّي جَارٌ لَكُمْ ۖ فَلَمَّا تَرَاءَتِ الْفِئَتَانِ نَكَصَ عَلَىٰ عَقِبَيْهِ وَقَالَ إِنِّي بَرِيءٌ مِنْكُمْ إِنِّي أَرَىٰ مَا لَا تَرَوْنَ إِنِّي أَخَافُ اللَّهَ ۚ وَاللَّهُ شَدِيدُ الْعِقَابِ (٤٨)

8. Voluntary Gifts

this day, and I am your protector. But when the two armies came in sight of one another, he turned upon his heels, and said: Surely I am clear of you, I see what you see not; surely I fear Allah. And Allah is Severe in requiting.

***

8:49. And when the hypocrites and those in whose hearts is a disease said Their religion has deluded them. And whoever trusts in Allah, then surely Allah is Mighty, Wise.

8:50. And if thou couldst see when the angels cause to die those who disbelieve, smiting their faces and their backs, and (saying): Taste the punishment of burning.

8:51. This is for that which your own hands have sent on before, and because Allah is not in the least unjust to the servants --

8:52. In the manner of the people of Pharaoh and those before them, they disbelieved in Allah's messages, so Allah punished them for their sins. Surely Allah is Strong, Severe in requiting.

8:53. This is because Allah never changes a favour which He has conferred upon a people until they change their own condition and because Allah is Hearing, Knowing --

8:54. In the manner of the people of pharaoh, and those before them. They rejected the messages of their Lord, so We destroyed them for their sins. And We drowned Pharaoh's people and they were all wrongdoers.

8:55. Surely the vilest of beasts in Allah's sight are those who disbelieve, then they would not believe.

8:56. Those with whom thou makest an agreement, then they break their agreement every time, and they keep not their duty.

8:57. So if thou overtake them in war, scatter by them those who are behind

إِذْ يَقُولُ الْمُنَافِقُونَ وَالَّذِينَ فِي قُلُوبِهِمْ مَرَضٌ غَرَّ هَؤُلَاءِ دِينُهُمْ وَمَنْ يَتَوَكَّلْ عَلَى اللَّهِ فَإِنَّ اللَّهَ عَزِيزٌ حَكِيمٌ (٤٩) وَلَوْ تَرَى إِذْ يَتَوَفَّى الَّذِينَ كَفَرُوا الْمَلَائِكَةُ يَضْرِبُونَ وُجُوهَهُمْ وَأَدْبَارَهُمْ وَذُوقُوا عَذَابَ الْحَرِيقِ (٥٠)

ذَلِكَ بِمَا قَدَّمَتْ أَيْدِيكُمْ وَأَنَّ اللَّهَ لَيْسَ بِظَلَّامٍ لِلْعَبِيدِ (٥١) كَدَأْبِ آلِ فِرْعَوْنَ وَالَّذِينَ مِنْ قَبْلِهِمْ كَفَرُوا بِآيَاتِ اللَّهِ فَأَخَذَهُمُ اللَّهُ بِذُنُوبِهِمْ إِنَّ اللَّهَ قَوِيٌّ شَدِيدُ الْعِقَابِ (٥٢) ذَلِكَ بِأَنَّ اللَّهَ لَمْ يَكُ مُغَيِّرًا نِعْمَةً أَنْعَمَهَا عَلَى قَوْمٍ حَتَّى يُغَيِّرُوا مَا بِأَنْفُسِهِمْ وَأَنَّ اللَّهَ سَمِيعٌ عَلِيمٌ (٥٣) كَدَأْبِ آلِ فِرْعَوْنَ وَالَّذِينَ مِنْ قَبْلِهِمْ كَذَّبُوا بِآيَاتِ رَبِّهِمْ فَأَهْلَكْنَاهُمْ بِذُنُوبِهِمْ وَأَغْرَقْنَا آلَ فِرْعَوْنَ وَكُلٌّ كَانُوا ظَالِمِينَ (٥٤)

إِنَّ شَرَّ الدَّوَابِّ عِنْدَ اللَّهِ الَّذِينَ كَفَرُوا فَهُمْ لَا يُؤْمِنُونَ (٥٥) الَّذِينَ عَاهَدْتَ مِنْهُمْ ثُمَّ يَنْقُضُونَ عَهْدَهُمْ فِي كُلِّ مَرَّةٍ وَهُمْ لَا يَتَّقُونَ (٥٦)

فَإِمَّا تَثْقَفَنَّهُمْ فِي الْحَرْبِ فَشَرِّدْ بِهِمْ مَنْ خَلْفَهُمْ لَعَلَّهُمْ يَذَّكَّرُونَ (٥٧) وَإِمَّا تَخَافَنَّ مِنْ قَوْمٍ خِيَانَةً فَانْبِذْ إِلَيْهِمْ عَلَى سَوَاءٍ إِنَّ اللَّهَ لَا يُحِبُّ الْخَائِنِينَ (٥٨)

8. Voluntary Gifts

them, that they may be mindful.

8:58. And if thou fear treachery on the part of a people, throw back to them (their treaty) on terms of equality. Surely Allah loves not the treacherous.

* * *

8:59. And let not those who disbelieve think that they can outstrip (Us). Surely they cannot escape.

8:60. And make ready for them whatever force you can and horses tied at the frontier, to frighten thereby the enemy of Allah and your enemy and others besides them, whom you know not Allah knows them. And whatever you spend in Allah's way, it will be paid back to you fully and you will not be wronged.

8:61. And if they incline to peace, incline thou also to it, and trust in Allah. Surely He is the Hearer, the Knower.

8:62. And if they intend to deceive thee, then surely Allah is sufficient for thee. He it is Who strengthened thee with His help and with the believers,

8:63. And He has united their hearts. If thou hadst spent all that is in the earth, thou couldst not have united their hearts, but Allah united them. Surely He is Mighty, Wise.

8:64. O Prophet, Allah is sufficient for thee and those who follow thee of the believers.

* * *

8:65. O Prophet, urge the believers to fight. If there be of you twenty steadfast, they shall overcome two hundred; and if there be of you a hundred, they shall overcome a thousand of those who disbelieve, because they are a people who do not understand.

8:66. Now Allah has lightened your burden and He knows that there is weakness in you. So if there be of you a hundred steadfast, they shall overcome two hundred; and if there be of you a

وَلَا يَحْسَبَنَّ الَّذِينَ كَفَرُوا سَبَقُوا إِنَّهُمْ لَا يُعْجِزُونَ (٥٩)
وَأَعِدُّوا لَهُمْ مَا اسْتَطَعْتُمْ مِنْ قُوَّةٍ وَمِنْ رِبَاطِ الْخَيْلِ تُرْهِبُونَ بِهِ عَدُوَّ اللَّهِ وَعَدُوَّكُمْ وَآخَرِينَ مِنْ دُونِهِمْ لَا تَعْلَمُونَهُمُ اللَّهُ يَعْلَمُهُمْ وَمَا تُنْفِقُوا مِنْ شَيْءٍ فِي سَبِيلِ اللَّهِ يُوَفَّ إِلَيْكُمْ وَأَنْتُمْ لَا تُظْلَمُونَ (٦٠)
وَإِنْ جَنَحُوا لِلسَّلْمِ فَاجْنَحْ لَهَا وَتَوَكَّلْ عَلَى اللَّهِ إِنَّهُ هُوَ السَّمِيعُ الْعَلِيمُ (٦١)
وَإِنْ يُرِيدُوا أَنْ يَخْدَعُوكَ فَإِنَّ حَسْبَكَ اللَّهُ هُوَ الَّذِي أَيَّدَكَ بِنَصْرِهِ وَبِالْمُؤْمِنِينَ (٦٢)
وَأَلَّفَ بَيْنَ قُلُوبِهِمْ لَوْ أَنْفَقْتَ مَا فِي الْأَرْضِ جَمِيعًا مَا أَلَّفْتَ بَيْنَ قُلُوبِهِمْ وَلَكِنَّ اللَّهَ أَلَّفَ بَيْنَهُمْ إِنَّهُ عَزِيزٌ حَكِيمٌ (٦٣)
يَا أَيُّهَا النَّبِيُّ حَسْبُكَ اللَّهُ وَمَنِ اتَّبَعَكَ مِنَ الْمُؤْمِنِينَ (٦٤)
يَا أَيُّهَا النَّبِيُّ حَرِّضِ الْمُؤْمِنِينَ عَلَى الْقِتَالِ إِنْ يَكُنْ مِنْكُمْ عِشْرُونَ صَابِرُونَ يَغْلِبُوا مِائَتَيْنِ وَإِنْ يَكُنْ مِنْكُمْ مِئَةٌ يَغْلِبُوا أَلْفًا مِنَ الَّذِينَ كَفَرُوا بِأَنَّهُمْ قَوْمٌ لَا يَفْقَهُونَ (٦٥)
الْآنَ خَفَّفَ اللَّهُ عَنْكُمْ وَعَلِمَ أَنَّ فِيكُمْ ضَعْفًا فَإِنْ يَكُنْ مِنْكُمْ مِئَةٌ صَابِرَةٌ يَغْلِبُوا مِائَتَيْنِ وَإِنْ يَكُنْ مِنْكُمْ أَلْفٌ يَغْلِبُوا أَلْفَيْنِ بِإِذْنِ اللَّهِ وَاللَّهُ مَعَ الصَّابِرِينَ (٦٦)
مَا كَانَ لِنَبِيٍّ أَنْ يَكُونَ لَهُ أَسْرَى حَتَّى يُثْخِنَ فِي الْأَرْضِ تُرِيدُونَ عَرَضَ الدُّنْيَا وَاللَّهُ يُرِيدُ الْآخِرَةَ وَاللَّهُ عَزِيزٌ حَكِيمٌ (٦٧)
لَوْلَا كِتَابٌ مِنَ اللَّهِ سَبَقَ لَمَسَّكُمْ فِيمَا

thousand, they shall overcome two thousand by Allah's permission. And Allah is with the steadfast.

8:67. It is not fit for a prophet to take captives unless he has fought and triumphed in the land. You desire the frail goods of this world, while Allah desires (for you) the Hereafter. And Allah is Mighty, Wise.

8:68. Were it not for an ordinance from Allah that had gone before, surely there would have befallen you a great chastisement for what you were going to do.

8:69. Eat then of the lawful and good (things) which you have acquired in war, and keep your duty to Allah. Surely Allah is Forgiving, Merciful.

***

8:70. O Prophet, say to those of the captives who are in your hands: If Allah knows anything good in your hearts, He will give you better than that which has been taken from you, and will forgive you. And Allah is Forgiving, Merciful.

8:71. And if they intend to be treacherous to thee, so indeed they have been treacherous to Allah before, but He gave (you) mastery over them. And Allah is Knowing, Wise.

8:72. Surely those who believed and fled (their homes) and struggled hard in Allah's way with their wealth and their lives, and those who gave shelter and helped -- these are friends one of another. And those who believed and did not flee, you are not responsible for their protection until they flee. And if they seek help from you in the matter of religion, it is your duty to help (them) except against a people between whom and you there is a treaty. And Allah is Seer of what you do.

8:73. And those who disbelieve are friends one of another. If you do it not, there will be persecution in the land

and great mischief.

8:74. And those who believed and fled and struggled hard in Allah's way, and those who gave shelter and helped -- these are the believers truly. For them is forgiveness and an honourable provision.

8:75. And those who believed afterwards and fled and struggled hard along with you, they are of you. And the relatives are nearer one to another in the ordinance of Allah. Surely Allah is Knower of all things.

9. The Immunity

9:1. A declaration of immunity from Allah and His Messenger to those of the idolaters with whom you made an agreement.

9:2. So go about in the land for four months and know that you cannot escape Allah and that Allah will disgrace the disbelievers.

9:3. And an announcement from Allah and His Messenger to the people on the day of the greater pilgrimage that Allah is free from liability to the idolaters, and so is His Messenger. So if you repent, it will be better for you and if you turn away, then know that you will not escape Allah. And announce painful chastisement to those who disbelieve --

9:4. Except those of the idolaters with whom you made an agreement, then they have not failed you in anything and have not backed up any one against you so fulfil their agreement to the end of their term. Surely Allah loves those who keep their duty.

9:5. So when the sacred months have passed, slay the idolaters, wherever you find them, and take them captive and besiege them and lie in wait for them in every ambush. But if they repent and keep up prayer and pay the

9. The Immunity

poor-rare, leave their way free. Surely Allah is Forgiving, Merciful.

9:6. And if anyone of the idolaters seek thy protection, protect him till he hears the word of Allah, then convey him to his place of safety. This is because they are a people who know not.

* * *

9:7. How can there be an agreement for the idolaters with Allah and with His Messenger, except those with whom you made an agreement at the Sacred Mosque? So as long as they are true to you, be true to them. Surely Allah loves those who keep their duty.

9:8. How (can it be)? And if they prevail against you, they respect neither ties of relationship nor covenant in your case. They would please you with their mouths while their hearts refuse and most of them are transgressors.

9:9. They have taken a small price for the messages of Allah, so they hinder (men) from His way. Surely evil is that which they do.

9:10. They respect neither ties of relationship nor covenant, in the case of a believer. And these are they who go beyond the limits.

9:11. But if they repent and keep up prayer and pay the poor-rare, they are your brethren in faith. And We make the messages clear for a people who know.

9:12. And if they break their oaths after their agreement and revile your religion, then fight the leaders of disbelief -- surely their oaths are nothing -- so that they may desist.

9:13. Will you not fight a people who broke their oaths and aimed at the expulsion of the Messenger, and they attacked you first? Do you fear them? But Allah has more right that you should fear Him, if you are believers.

9:14. Fight them; Allah will chastise them at your hands and bring them to disgrace, and assist you against them and relieve the hearts of a believing people,

9:15. And remove the rage of their hearts. And Allah turns (mercifully) to whom He pleases. And Allah is Knowing, Wise.

9:16. Do you think that you would be left alone while Allah has not yet known those of you who struggle hard and take not anyone as an intimate friend besides Allah and His Messenger and the believers? And Allah is Aware of what you do.

* * *

9:17. The idolaters have no right to maintain the mosques of Allah, while bearing witness to disbelief against themselves. These it is whose works are vain; and in the Fire will they abide.

9:18. Only he can maintain the mosques of Allah who believes in Allah and the Last Day, and keeps up prayer and pays the poor-rate and fears none but Allah. So these it is who may be of the guided ones.

9:19. Do you hold the giving of drink to the pilgrims and the maintenance of the Sacred Mosque equal to (the service of) one who believes in Allah and the Last Day and strives hard in Allah's way? They are not equal in the sight of Allah. And Allah guides not the iniquitous people.

9:20. Those who believed and fled (their homes), and strove hard in Allah's way with their wealth and their lives, are much higher in rank with Allah. And it is these that shall triumph.

9:21. Their Lord gives them good news of mercy and pleasure, from Himself, and Gardens wherein lasting blessings will be theirs,

9:22. Abiding therein for ever. Surely Allah has a mighty reward with Him.

9. The Immunity

9:23. O you who believe, take not your fathers and your brothers for friends if they love disbelief above faith. And whoever of you takes them for friends, such are the wrongdoers.

9:24. Say If your fathers and your sons and your brethren and your wives and your kinsfolk and the wealth you have acquired, and trade whose dullness you fear, and dwellings you love, are dearer to you than Allah and His Messenger and striving in His way, then wait till Allah brings His command to pass. And Allah guides nor the transgressing people.

* * *

9:25. Certainly Allah helped you in many battlefields, and on the day of Hunain, when your great numbers made you proud, but they availed you nothing, and the earth with all its spaciousness was straitened for you, then you turned back retreating.

9:26. Then Allah sent down His calm upon His Messenger and upon the believers, and sent hosts which you saw not, and chastised those who disbelieved. And such is the reward of the disbelievers.

9:27. Then will Allah after this turn mercifully to whom He pleases. And Allah is Forgiving, Merciful.

9:28. O you who believe, the idolaters are surely unclean, so they shall not approach the Sacred Mosque after this year of theirs. And if you fear poverty, then Allah will enrich you out of His grace, if He please. Surely Allah is Knowing, Wise.

9:29. Fight those who believe not in Allah, nor in the Last Day, nor forbid that which Allah and His Messenger have forbidden, nor follow the Religion of Truth, out of those who have been given the Book, until they pay the tax in acknowledgment of superiority and they are in a state of subjection.

* * *

9:30. And the Jews say: Ezra is the son of Allah; and the Christians say The Messiah is the son of Allah. These are the words of their mouths. They imitate the saying of those who disbelieved before. Allah's curse be on them! How they are turned away!

9:31. They take their doctors of law and their monks for Lords besides Allah, and (also) the Messiah, son of Mary, And they were enjoined that they should serve one God only -- there is no god but He. Be He glorified from what they set up (with Him)!

9:32. They desire to put out the light of Allah with their mouths, and Allah will allow nothing save the perfection of His light, though the disbelievers are averse.

9:33. He it is Who sent His Messenger with guidance and the Religion of Truth, that He may cause it to prevail over all religions, though the polytheists are averse.

9:34. O you who believe, surely many of the doctors of law and the monks eat away the property of men falsely, and hinder (them) from Allah's way. And those who hoard up gold and silver and spend it not in Allah's way -- announce to them a painful chastisement,

9:35. On the day when it will be heated in the Fire of hell, then their foreheads and their sides and their backs will be branded with it: This is what you hoarded up for yourselves, so taste what you used to hoard.

9:36. Surely the number of months with Allah is twelve months by Allah's ordinance, since the day when He created the heavens and the earth -- of these four are sacred. That is the right religion; so wrong not yourselves therein. And fight the polytheists all together as they fight you all together. And know that Allah is with those who keep their duty.

9. The Immunity

9:37. Postponing (of the sacred month) is only an addition in disbelief, whereby those who disbelieve are led astray. They allow it one year and forbid it (another) year, that they may agree in the number (of months) which Allah has made sacred, and thus make lawful what Allah has forbidden. The evil of their doings is made fair-seeming to them. And Allah guides not the disbelieving people.

* * *

9:38. O you who believe, what (excuse) have you that when it is said to you, Go forth in Allah's way, you should incline heavily to earth? Are you contented with this world's life instead of the Hereafter? The provision of this world's life is but little as compared with the Hereafter.

9:39. If you go not forth, He will chastise you with a painful chastisement, and bring in your place a people other than you, and you can do Him no harm. And Allah is Possessor of power over all things.

9:40. If you help him not, Allah certainly helped him when those who disbelieved expelled him -- he being the second of the two; when they were both in the cave, when he said to his companion Grieve not, surely Allah is with us. So Allah sent down His tranquillity on him and strengthened him with hosts which you saw not, and made lowest the word of those who disbelieved. And the word of Allah, that is the uppermost. And Allah is Mighty, Wise.

9:41. Go forth, light and heavy, and strive hard in Allah's way with your wealth and your lives. This is better for you, if you know.

9:42. Had it been a near gain and a short journey, they would certainly have followed thee, but the hard journey was too long for them. And

الْكَافِرِينَ (٣٧)

يَا أَيُّهَا الَّذِينَ آمَنُوا مَا لَكُمْ إِذَا قِيلَ لَكُمُ انْفِرُوا فِي سَبِيلِ اللَّهِ اثَّاقَلْتُمْ إِلَى الْأَرْضِ أَرَضِيتُمْ بِالْحَيَاةِ الدُّنْيَا مِنَ الْآخِرَةِ فَمَا مَتَاعُ الْحَيَاةِ الدُّنْيَا فِي الْآخِرَةِ إِلَّا قَلِيلٌ (٣٨)

إِلَّا تَنْفِرُوا يُعَذِّبْكُمْ عَذَابًا أَلِيمًا وَيَسْتَبْدِلْ قَوْمًا غَيْرَكُمْ وَلَا تَضُرُّوهُ شَيْئًا وَاللَّهُ عَلَى كُلِّ شَيْءٍ قَدِيرٌ (٣٩)

إِلَّا تَنْصُرُوهُ فَقَدْ نَصَرَهُ اللَّهُ إِذْ أَخْرَجَهُ الَّذِينَ كَفَرُوا ثَانِيَ اثْنَيْنِ إِذْ هُمَا فِي الْغَارِ إِذْ يَقُولُ لِصَاحِبِهِ لَا تَحْزَنْ إِنَّ اللَّهَ مَعَنَا فَأَنْزَلَ اللَّهُ سَكِينَتَهُ عَلَيْهِ وَأَيَّدَهُ بِجُنُودٍ لَمْ تَرَوْهَا وَجَعَلَ كَلِمَةَ الَّذِينَ كَفَرُوا السُّفْلَى وَكَلِمَةُ اللَّهِ هِيَ الْعُلْيَا وَاللَّهُ عَزِيزٌ حَكِيمٌ (٤٠)

انْفِرُوا خِفَافًا وَثِقَالًا وَجَاهِدُوا بِأَمْوَالِكُمْ وَأَنْفُسِكُمْ فِي سَبِيلِ اللَّهِ ذَلِكُمْ خَيْرٌ لَكُمْ إِنْ كُنْتُمْ تَعْلَمُونَ (٤١)

لَوْ كَانَ عَرَضًا قَرِيبًا وَسَفَرًا قَاصِدًا لَاتَّبَعُوكَ وَلَكِنْ بَعُدَتْ عَلَيْهِمُ الشُّقَّةُ وَسَيَحْلِفُونَ بِاللَّهِ لَوِ اسْتَطَعْنَا لَخَرَجْنَا مَعَكُمْ يُهْلِكُونَ أَنْفُسَهُمْ وَاللَّهُ يَعْلَمُ إِنَّهُمْ لَكَاذِبُونَ (٤٢)

عَفَا اللَّهُ عَنْكَ لِمَ أَذِنْتَ لَهُمْ حَتَّى يَتَبَيَّنَ لَكَ الَّذِينَ صَدَقُوا وَتَعْلَمَ الْكَاذِبِينَ

9. The Immunity

they wilt swear by Allah: If we had been able, we would have gone forth with you. They cause their own souls to perish; and Allah knows that they are liars.

* * *

9:43. Allah pardon thee! Why didst thou permit them until those who spoke the truth had become manifest to thee and thou hadst known the liars?

9:44. Those who believe in Allah and the Last Day ask not leave of thee (to stay away) from striving hard with their wealth and their persons. And Allah is Knower of those who keep their duty.

9:45. They alone ask leave of thee who believe not in Allah and the Last Day, and their hearts are in doubt, so in their doubt they waver.

9:46. And if they had intended to go forth, they would certainly have provided equipment for it; but Allah did not like their going forth. So He withheld them, and it was said: Hold back with those who hold back.

9:47. Had they gone forth with you, they would have added to you naught but trouble, and would have hurried to and fro among you seeking (to sow) dissension among you. And among you there are those who would listen to them. And Allah well knows the wrongdoers.

9:48. Certainly they sought (to sow) dissension before, and they devised plots against thee till the Truth came, and Allah's command prevailed, though they did not like (it).

9:49. And among them is he who says: Excuse me and try me not. Surely into trial have they already fallen, and truly hell encompasses the disbelievers.

9:50. If good befalls thee, it grieves them; and if hardship afflicts thee, they say: Indeed we had taken care of our affair before. And they turn away rejoicing.

(٤٣)
لَا يَسْتَأْذِنُكَ الَّذِينَ يُؤْمِنُونَ بِاللَّهِ وَالْيَوْمِ الْآخِرِ أَنْ يُجَاهِدُوا بِأَمْوَالِهِمْ وَأَنْفُسِهِمْ وَاللَّهُ عَلِيمٌ بِالْمُتَّقِينَ (٤٤)
إِنَّمَا يَسْتَأْذِنُكَ الَّذِينَ لَا يُؤْمِنُونَ بِاللَّهِ وَالْيَوْمِ الْآخِرِ وَارْتَابَتْ قُلُوبُهُمْ فَهُمْ فِي رَيْبِهِمْ يَتَرَدَّدُونَ (٤٥)
وَلَوْ أَرَادُوا الْخُرُوجَ لَأَعَدُّوا لَهُ عُدَّةً وَلَٰكِنْ كَرِهَ اللَّهُ انْبِعَاثَهُمْ فَثَبَّطَهُمْ وَقِيلَ اقْعُدُوا مَعَ الْقَاعِدِينَ (٤٦)
لَوْ خَرَجُوا فِيكُمْ مَا زَادُوكُمْ إِلَّا خَبَالًا وَلَأَوْضَعُوا خِلَالَكُمْ يَبْغُونَكُمُ الْفِتْنَةَ وَفِيكُمْ سَمَّاعُونَ لَهُمْ وَاللَّهُ عَلِيمٌ بِالظَّالِمِينَ (٤٧)
لَقَدِ ابْتَغَوُا الْفِتْنَةَ مِنْ قَبْلُ وَقَلَّبُوا لَكَ الْأُمُورَ حَتَّى جَاءَ الْحَقُّ وَظَهَرَ أَمْرُ اللَّهِ وَهُمْ كَارِهُونَ (٤٨)
وَمِنْهُمْ مَنْ يَقُولُ ائْذَنْ لِي وَلَا تَفْتِنِّي أَلَا فِي الْفِتْنَةِ سَقَطُوا وَإِنَّ جَهَنَّمَ لَمُحِيطَةٌ بِالْكَافِرِينَ (٤٩)
إِنْ تُصِبْكَ حَسَنَةٌ تَسُؤْهُمْ وَإِنْ تُصِبْكَ مُصِيبَةٌ يَقُولُوا قَدْ أَخَذْنَا أَمْرَنَا مِنْ قَبْلُ وَيَتَوَلَّوْا وَهُمْ فَرِحُونَ (٥٠)
قُلْ لَنْ يُصِيبَنَا إِلَّا مَا كَتَبَ اللَّهُ لَنَا هُوَ مَوْلَانَا وَعَلَى اللَّهِ فَلْيَتَوَكَّلِ الْمُؤْمِنُونَ (٥١)
قُلْ هَلْ تَرَبَّصُونَ بِنَا إِلَّا إِحْدَى الْحُسْنَيَيْنِ وَنَحْنُ نَتَرَبَّصُ بِكُمْ أَنْ يُصِيبَكُمُ اللَّهُ بِعَذَابٍ مِنْ عِنْدِهِ أَوْ بِأَيْدِينَا فَتَرَبَّصُوا إِنَّا مَعَكُمْ مُتَرَبِّصُونَ (٥٢)
قُلْ أَنْفِقُوا طَوْعًا أَوْ كَرْهًا لَنْ يُتَقَبَّلَ مِنْكُمْ إِنَّكُمْ كُنْتُمْ قَوْمًا فَاسِقِينَ (٥٣)
وَمَا مَنَعَهُمْ أَنْ تُقْبَلَ مِنْهُمْ نَفَقَاتُهُمْ إِلَّا

9. The Immunity

9:51. Say: Nothing will afflict us save that which Allah has ordained for us. He is our Patron; and on Allah let the believers rely.

9:52. Say: Do you await for us but one of two most excellent things? And we await for you that Allah will afflict you with chastisement from Himself or by our hands. So wait; we too are waiting with you.

9:53. Say: Spend willingly or unwillingly, it will not be accepted from you. Surely you are a transgressing people.

9:54. And nothing hinders their contributions being accepted from them, except that they disbelieve in Allah and in His Messenger and they come not to prayer except as lazy people, and they spend not but while they are reluctant.

9:55. Let not then their wealth nor their children excite thine admiration. Allah only wishes to chastise them therewith in this world's life and (that) their souls may depart while they are disbelievers.

9:56. And they swear by Allah that they are truly of you. And they are not of you, but they are a people who are afraid.

9:57. If they could find a refuge or caves or a place to enter, they would certainly have turned thereto, running away in all haste.

9:58. And of them are those who blame thee in the matter of the alms. So if they are given thereof, they are pleased, and if they are not given thereof, lo! they are enraged.

9:59. And if they were content with that which Allah and His Messenger gave them, and had said: Allah is sufficient for us; Allah will soon give us (more) out of His grace and His Messenger too: surely to Allah we make petition.

* * *

9:60. (Zakat) charity is only for the poor

9. The Immunity

and the needy, and those employed to administer it, and those whose hearts are made to incline (to truth), and (to free) the captives, and those in debt, and in the way of Allah and for the wayfarer -- an ordinance from Allah. And Allah is Knowing, Wise.'

9:61. And of them are those who molest the Prophet and say, He is (all) ear. Say: A hearer of good for you -- he believes in Allah and believes the faithful, and is a mercy for those of you who believe. And those who molest the Messenger of Allah, for them is a painful chastisement.

9:62. They swear by Allah to you to please you; and Allah as well as His Messenger has a greater right that they should please Him, if they are believers.

9:63. Know they not that whoever opposes Allah and His Messenger, for him is the Fire of hell to abide in it? That is the grievous abasement.

9:64. The hypocrites fear lest a chapter should be sent down concerning them, telling them plainly of what is in their hearts. Say: Go on mocking, surely Allah will bring to light what you fear.

9:65. And if thou ask them, would certainly say: We were only talking idly and sporting. Say: Was it Allah and His messages and His Messenger that you mocked?

9:66. Make no excuse, you disbelieved after your believing. If We pardon a party of you, We shall chastise a party, because they are guilty.

* * *

9:67. The hypocrites, men and women, are all alike. They enjoin evil and forbid good and withhold their hands. They have forsaken Allah, so He has forsaken them. Surely the hypocrites are the transgressors.

9:68. Allah promises the hypocrites, men and women, and the disbelievers, the Fire of hell to abide therein. It is enough for them. And Allah curses them, and for them is a lasting chastisement.

9:69. Like those before you they were stronger than you in power and had more wealth and children. So they enjoyed their portion thus have you enjoyed your portion as those before you enjoyed their portion, and you indulge in idle talk as they did. These are they whose works are null in this world and the Hereafter, and these are they who are the losers.

9:70. Has not the story reached them of those before them -- of the people of Noah and 'Ad and Thamud, and the people of Abraham and the dwellers of Midian and the overthrown cities? Their messengers came to them with clear arguments. So Allah wronged them not but they wronged themselves.

9:71. And the believers, men and women, are friends one of another. They enjoin good and forbid evil and keep up prayer and pay the poor-rate, and obey Allah and His Messenger. As for these, Allah will have mercy on them. Surely Allah is Mighty, Wise.

9:72. Allah has promised to the believers, men and women, Gardens, wherein flow rivers, to abide therein, and goodly dwellings in Gardens of perpetual abode. And greatest of all is Allah's goodly pleasure. That is the grand achievement.

* * *

9:73. O Prophet, strive hard against the disbelievers and the hypocrites and be firm against them. And their abode is hell, and evil is the destination.

9:74. They swear by Allah that they said nothing. And certainly they did speak the word of disbelief, and disbelieved after their Islam, and they purposed that which they could not attain. And they sought revenge only because Allah -- as well as His

9. The **Immunity**

Messenger -- had enriched them out of His grace. So if they repent, it will be good for them and if they turn away, Allah will chastise them with a painful chastisement in this world and the Hereafter and they shall have in the earth neither a friend not a helper.

9:75. And of them are those who made a covenant with Allah: If He give us out of His grace, we will certainly give alms and be of the righteous.

9:76. But when He gave them out of His grace, they became niggardly of it and they turned away and they are averse.

9:77. So He requited them with hypocrisy in their hearts till the day when they meet Him, because they broke their promise with Allah and because they lied.

9:78. Know they not that Allah knows their hidden thoughts and their secret counsels, and that Allah is the great Knower of the unseen things?

9:79. Those who taunt the free givers of alms among the believers as well as those who cannot find anything (to give) but with their hard labour they scoff at them. Allah will pay them back their mockery and for them is a painful chastisement.

9:80. Ask forgiveness for them or ask not forgiveness for them. Even if thou ask forgiveness for them seventy times Allah will not forgive them. This is because they disbelieve in Allah and His Messenger. And Allah guides not the transgressing people.

* * *

9:81. Those who were left behind were glad on account of their sitting behind Allah's Messenger, and they were averse to striving in Allah's way with their property and their persons, and said: Go not forth in the heat. Say: The Fire of hell is fiercer in heat. If only they could understand!

9:82. Then let them laugh a little and

وَمِنْهُمْ مَنْ عَاهَدَ اللَّهَ لَئِنْ آتَانَا مِنْ فَضْلِهِ لَنَصَّدَّقَنَّ وَلَنَكُونَنَّ مِنَ الصَّالِحِينَ (٧٥)

فَلَمَّا آتَاهُمْ مِنْ فَضْلِهِ بَخِلُوا بِهِ وَتَوَلَّوْا وَهُمْ مُعْرِضُونَ (٧٦)

فَأَعْقَبَهُمْ نِفَاقًا فِي قُلُوبِهِمْ إِلَىٰ يَوْمِ يَلْقَوْنَهُ بِمَا أَخْلَفُوا اللَّهَ مَا وَعَدُوهُ وَبِمَا كَانُوا يَكْذِبُونَ (٧٧)

أَلَمْ يَعْلَمُوا أَنَّ اللَّهَ يَعْلَمُ سِرَّهُمْ وَنَجْوَاهُمْ وَأَنَّ اللَّهَ عَلَّامُ الْغُيُوبِ (٧٨)

الَّذِينَ يَلْمِزُونَ الْمُطَّوِّعِينَ مِنَ الْمُؤْمِنِينَ فِي الصَّدَقَاتِ وَالَّذِينَ لَا يَجِدُونَ إِلَّا جُهْدَهُمْ فَيَسْخَرُونَ مِنْهُمْ سَخِرَ اللَّهُ مِنْهُمْ وَلَهُمْ عَذَابٌ أَلِيمٌ (٧٩)

اسْتَغْفِرْ لَهُمْ أَوْ لَا تَسْتَغْفِرْ لَهُمْ إِنْ تَسْتَغْفِرْ لَهُمْ سَبْعِينَ مَرَّةً فَلَنْ يَغْفِرَ اللَّهُ لَهُمْ ذَٰلِكَ بِأَنَّهُمْ كَفَرُوا بِاللَّهِ وَرَسُولِهِ وَاللَّهُ لَا يَهْدِي الْقَوْمَ الْفَاسِقِينَ (٨٠)

فَرِحَ الْمُخَلَّفُونَ بِمَقْعَدِهِمْ خِلَافَ رَسُولِ اللَّهِ وَكَرِهُوا أَنْ يُجَاهِدُوا بِأَمْوَالِهِمْ وَأَنْفُسِهِمْ فِي سَبِيلِ اللَّهِ وَقَالُوا لَا تَنْفِرُوا فِي الْحَرِّ قُلْ نَارُ جَهَنَّمَ أَشَدُّ حَرًّا لَوْ كَانُوا يَفْقَهُونَ (٨١)

فَلْيَضْحَكُوا قَلِيلًا وَلْيَبْكُوا كَثِيرًا جَزَاءً بِمَا كَانُوا يَكْسِبُونَ (٨٢)

فَإِنْ رَجَعَكَ اللَّهُ إِلَىٰ طَائِفَةٍ مِنْهُمْ فَاسْتَأْذَنُوكَ لِلْخُرُوجِ فَقُلْ لَنْ تَخْرُجُوا مَعِيَ أَبَدًا وَلَنْ تُقَاتِلُوا مَعِيَ عَدُوًّا إِنَّكُمْ رَضِيتُمْ بِالْقُعُودِ أَوَّلَ مَرَّةٍ فَاقْعُدُوا مَعَ الْخَالِفِينَ (٨٣)

9. The **Immunity**

weep much a recompense for what they earned.

9:83. So if Allah bring thee back to a party of them, then they ask thy permission to go forth, say: Never shall you go forth with me and never shall you fight an enemy with me. You chose to sit (at home) the first time so sit (now) with those who remain behind.

9:84. And never offer prayer for any one of them who dies, nor stand by his grave. Surely they disbelieved in Allah and His Messenger and they died in transgression.

9:85. And let not their wealth and their children excite thy admiration. Allah only intends to chastise them thereby in this world, and (that) their souls may depart while they are disbelievers.

9:86. And when a chapter is revealed, saying, Believe in Allah and strive hard along with His Messenger, the wealthy among them ask permission of thee and say: Leave us (behind), that we may be with those who sit (at home).

9:87. They prefer to be with those who remain behind, and their hearts are sealed so they understand not.

9:88. But the Messenger and those who believe with him strive hard with their property and their persons. And these it is for whom are the good things and these it is who are successful.

9:89. Allah has prepared for them Gardens wherein flow rivers, to abide therein. That is the great achievement.

***

9:90. And the defaulters from among the dwellers of the desert came that permission might be given to them, and they sat (at home) who lied to Allah and His Messenger. A painful chastisement will afflict those of them who disbelieve.

9:91. No blame lies on the weak, nor on the sick, nor on those who can find nothing to spend, if they are sincere to

وَلَا تُصَلِّ عَلَىٰ أَحَدٍ مِنْهُمْ مَاتَ أَبَدًا وَلَا تَقُمْ عَلَىٰ قَبْرِهِ إِنَّهُمْ كَفَرُوا بِاللَّهِ وَرَسُولِهِ وَمَاتُوا وَهُمْ فَاسِقُونَ (٨٤) وَلَا تُعْجِبْكَ أَمْوَالُهُمْ وَأَوْلَادُهُمْ إِنَّمَا يُرِيدُ اللَّهُ أَنْ يُعَذِّبَهُمْ بِهَا فِي الدُّنْيَا وَتَزْهَقَ أَنْفُسُهُمْ وَهُمْ كَافِرُونَ (٨٥) وَإِذَا أُنْزِلَتْ سُورَةٌ أَنْ آمِنُوا بِاللَّهِ وَجَاهِدُوا مَعَ رَسُولِهِ اسْتَأْذَنَكَ أُولُو الطَّوْلِ مِنْهُمْ وَقَالُوا ذَرْنَا نَكُنْ مَعَ الْقَاعِدِينَ (٨٦) رَضُوا بِأَنْ يَكُونُوا مَعَ الْخَوَالِفِ وَطُبِعَ عَلَىٰ قُلُوبِهِمْ فَهُمْ لَا يَفْقَهُونَ (٨٧) لَكِنِ الرَّسُولُ وَالَّذِينَ آمَنُوا مَعَهُ جَاهَدُوا بِأَمْوَالِهِمْ وَأَنْفُسِهِمْ وَأُولَٰئِكَ لَهُمُ الْخَيْرَاتُ وَأُولَٰئِكَ هُمُ الْمُفْلِحُونَ (٨٨) أَعَدَّ اللَّهُ لَهُمْ جَنَّاتٍ تَجْرِي مِنْ تَحْتِهَا الْأَنْهَارُ خَالِدِينَ فِيهَا ذَٰلِكَ الْفَوْزُ الْعَظِيمُ (٨٩)

وَجَاءَ الْمُعَذِّرُونَ مِنَ الْأَعْرَابِ لِيُؤْذَنَ لَهُمْ وَقَعَدَ الَّذِينَ كَذَبُوا اللَّهَ وَرَسُولَهُ سَيُصِيبُ الَّذِينَ كَفَرُوا مِنْهُمْ عَذَابٌ أَلِيمٌ (٩٠) لَيْسَ عَلَى الضُّعَفَاءِ وَلَا عَلَى الْمَرْضَىٰ وَلَا عَلَى الَّذِينَ لَا يَجِدُونَ مَا يُنْفِقُونَ حَرَجٌ إِذَا نَصَحُوا لِلَّهِ وَرَسُولِهِ مَا عَلَى الْمُحْسِنِينَ مِنْ

9. The Immunity

Allah and His Messenger. There is no way (to blame) against the doers of good. And Allah is Forgiving, Merciful

--

9:92. Nor on those to whom, when they came to thee that thou shouldst mount them, thou didst say: I cannot find that on which to mount you. They went back while their eyes overflowed with tears of grief that they could not find aught to spend.

9:93. The way (to blame) is only against those who ask permission of thee, though they are rich. They have chosen to be with those who remained behind; and Allah has sealed their hearts, so they know not.

* * *

9:94. They will make excuses to you when you return to them. Say: Make no excuse, we shall not believe you; Allah has informed us of matters relating to you. And Allah and His Messenger will now see your actions, then you will be brought back to the Knower of the unseen and the seen, then He will inform you of what you did.

9:95. They will swear by Allah to you, when you return to them, so that you may leave them alone. So leave them alone. Surely they are unclean and their refuge is hell a recompense for what they earned.

9:96. They will swear to you that you may be pleased with them. But if you are pleased with them, yet surely Allah is nor pleased with the transgressing people.

9:97. The dwellers of the desert are hardest in disbelief and hypocrisy, and most disposed not to know the limits of what Allah has revealed to His Messenger. And Allah is Knowing, Wise.

9:98. And of the dwellers of the desert are those who take what they spend to be a fine, and they wait for an evil turn of fortune for you. On them is the evil

9. The Immunity

turn. And Allah is Hearing, Knowing.

9:99. And of the desert Arabs are those who believe in Allah and the Last Day, and consider what they spend and the prayers of the Messenger, as bringing them nearer to Allah. Surely they bring them nearer (to Allah). Allah will bring them into His mercy. Surely Allah is Forgiving, Merciful.

* * *

9:100. And the foremost, the first of the Emigrants and the Helpers, and those who followed them in goodness -- Allah is well pleased with them and they are well pleased with Him, and He has prepared for them Gardens wherein flow rivers, abiding therein for ever. That is the mighty achievement.

9:101. And of those around you of the desert Arabs, there are hypocrites and of the people of Madinah (also) -- they persist in hypocrisy. Thou knowest them not; We know them. We will chastise them twice, then they will be turned back to a grievous chastisement.

9:102. And others have acknowledged their faults, -- they mixed a good deed with another that was evil. It may be that Allah will turn to them (mercifully). Surely Allah is Forgiving, Merciful.

9:103. Take alms out of their property -- thou wouldst cleanse them and purify them thereby -- and pray for them. Surely thy prayer is a relief to them. And Allah is Hearing, Knowing.

9:104. Know they not that Allah is He Who accepts repentance from His servants and takes the alms, and that Allah -- He is the Oft-returning (to mercy), the Merciful?

9:105. And say, Work so Allah will see your work and (so will) His Messenger and the believers. And you will be brought back to the Knower of the unseen and the seen, then He will inform you of what you did.

9:106. And others are made to await

9. The Immunity

Allah's command, whether He chastise them or turn to them (mercifully). And Allah is Knowing, Wise.

9:107. And those who built a mosque to cause harm (to Islam) and (to help) disbelief, and to cause disunion among the believers, and a refuge for him who made war against Allah and His Messenger before. And they will certainly swear: We desired naught but good. And Allah bears witness that they are certainly liars.

9:108. Never stand in it. Certainly a mosque founded on observance of duty from the first day is more deserving that thou shouldst stand in it. In it are men who love to purify themselves. And Allah loves those who purify themselves.

9:109. Is he, then, who lays his foundation on duty to Allah and (His) good pleasure better, or he who lays his foundation on the edge of a cracking hollowed bank, so it broke down with him into the Fire of hell? And Allah guides not the unjust people.

9:110. The building which they have built will ever continue to be a source of disquiet in their hearts, unless their hearts be torn to pieces. And Allah is Knowing, Wise.

* * *

9:111. Surely Allah has bought from the believers their persons and their property -- theirs (in return) is the Garden. They fight in Allah's way, so they slay and are slain. It is a promise which is binding on Him in the Torah and the Gospel and the Qur'an. And who is more faithful to his promise than Allah? Rejoice therefore in your bargain which you have made. And that is the mighty achievement.

9:112. They who turn (to Allah), who serve (Him), who praise (Him), who fast, who bow down, who prostrate themselves, who enjoin what is good and forbid what is evil, and who keep the limits of Allah and give good news to the believers.

9:113. It is not for the Prophet and those who believe to ask forgiveness for the polytheists, even though they should be near relatives, after it has become clear to them that they are companions of the flaming fire.'

9:114. And Abraham's asking forgiveness for his sire was only owing to a promise which he had made to him but when it became clear to him that he was an enemy of Allah, he dissociated himself from him. Surely Abraham was tender-hearted, forbearing.

9:115. And it is not (attributable to) Allah that He should lead a people astray after He has guided them, so far so that He makes clear to them what they should guard against. Surely Allah is Knower of all things.

9:116. Surely Allah's is the kingdom of the heavens and the earth. He gives life and causes death. And besides Allah you have no friend nor helper.

9:117. Certainly Allah has turned in mercy to the Prophet and the Emigrants and the Helpers who followed him in the hour of hardship, after the hearts of a part of them were about to deviate then He turned to them in mercy. Surely to them He is Compassionate, Merciful;

9:118. And (He turned in mercy) to the three who were left behind; until the earth, vast as it is, became strait to them and their souls were also straitened to them; and they knew that there was no refuge from Allah but in Him. Then He turned to them in mercy that they might turn (to Him). Surely Allah -- He is the Oft-returning to mercy, the Merciful.

***

9:119. O you who believe, keep your

9. The Immunity

duty to Allah and be with the truthful.

9:120. It was not proper for the people of Madinah and those round about them of the desert Arabs to remain behind the Messenger of Allah, not to prefer their own lives to his life. That is because there afflicts them neither thirst nor fatigue nor hunger in Allah's way nor tread they a path which enrages the disbelievers nor cause they any harm to an enemy, but a good work is written down for them on account of it. Surely Allah wastes not the reward of the doers of good;

9:121. Nor spend they any thing, small or great, nor do they traverse a valley but it is written down for them, that Allah may reward them for the best of what they did.

9:122. And the believers should not go forth all together. Why, then, does not a company from every party from among them go forth that they may apply themselves to obtain understanding in religion, and that they may warn their people, when they come back to them, that they may be cautious?

* * *

9:123. O you who believe, fight those of the disbelievers who are near to you and let them find firmness in you. And know that Allah is with those who keep their duty.

9:124. And whenever a chapter is revealed, there are some of them who say: Which of you has it strengthened in faith? So as for those who believe, it strengthens them in faith and they rejoice.

9:125. And as for those in whose hearts is a disease, it adds uncleanness to their uncleanness, and they die while they are disbelievers.

9:126. See they not that they are tried once or twice in every year, yet they repent not, nor do they mind.

9:127. And whenever a chapter is

revealed, they look one at another: Does any one see you? Then they turn away. Allah has turned away their hearts because they are a people who understand not.

9:128. Certainly a Messenger has come to you from among yourselves grievous to him is your falling into distress, most solicitous for you, to the believers (he is) compassionate, merciful.

9:129. But if they turn away, say: Allah is sufficient for me -- there is no god but He. On Him do I rely, and He is the Lord of the mighty Throne.

10. Jonah

In the name of Allah, the Beneficent, the Merciful.

10:1. I, Allah, am the Seer. These are the verses of the Book, full of wisdom.

10:2. Is it a wonder to the people what We have revealed to a man from among themselves: Warn the people and give good news to those who believe that for them is advancement in excellence with their Lord? The disbelievers say: This is surely a manifest enchanter.

10:3. Surely your Lord is Allah, Who created the heavens and the earth in six periods, and He is established on the Throne of Power regulating the Affair. There is no intercessor except after His permission. This is Allah, your Lord, therefore serve Him. Will you not mind?

10:4. To Him is your return, of all (of you). It is the promise of Allah (made) in truth. Surely He produces the first creation, then He reproduces it, that He may reward with equity those who believe and do good. And as for those who disbelieve, for them is a drink of hot water and a painful chastisement because they disbelieved.

10:5. He it is Who made the sun a

shining brightness, and the moon a light, and ordained for it stages that you might know the computation of years and the reckoning. Allah created not this but with truth. He makes the signs manifest for a people who know.

10:6. Surely in the variation of the night and the day, and that which Allah has created in the heavens and the earth, there are signs for a people who keep their duty.

10:7. Those who expect not the meeting with Us, and are pleased with this world's life and are satisfied with it, and those who are heedless of Our communications --

10:8. These, their abode is the Fire because of what they earned.

10:9. Those who believe and do good, their Lord guides them by their faith; rivers will flow beneath them in Gardens of bliss.

10:10. Their cry therein will be, Glory to Thee, O Allah and their greeting, Peace! And the last of their cry will be Praise be to Allah, the Lord of the worlds!

* * *

10:11. And if Allah were to hasten for men the (consequences of) evil, as they would hasten on the good, their doom would certainly have been decreed for them. But We leave those alone, who have no hope of meeting with Us, in their inordinacy, blindly wandering on.

10:12. And when affliction touches a man, he calls on Us, whether lying on his side or sitting or standing; but, when We remove his affliction from him, he passes on as though he had never called on Us on account of an affliction that touched him. Thus is what they do, made fair-seeming to the extravagant.

10:13. And certainly We destroyed generations before you when they did wrong, and their messengers came to them with clear arguments, yet they

10. Jonah

would nor believe, Thus do We recompense the guilty people.

10:14. Then We made you rulers in the land after them, so that We might see how you act.

10:15. And when Our clear messages are recited to them, those who have no hope of meeting with Us say: Bring a Qur'an other than this or change it. Say: It is not for me to change it of my own accord. I follow naught but what is revealed to me. Indeed I fear, if I disobey my Lord, the chastisement of a grievous day.

10:16. Say: If Allah had desired, I would not have recited it to you, nor would He have made it known to you. I have lived among you a lifetime before it. Do you not then understand?

10:17. Who is then more unjust than he who forges a lie against Allah or gives the lie to His messages? Surely the guilty never succeed.

10:18. And they serve besides Allah that which can neither harm them nor profit them, and they say: These are our intercessors with Allah. Say Would you inform Allah of what He knows not in the heavens and the earth? Glory be to Him, and supremely exalted is He above what they set up (with Him)!

10:19. And (all) people are but a single nation, then they disagree. And had not a word already gone forth from thy Lord, the matter would have certainly been decided between them in respect of that wherein they disagree.

10:20. And they say: Why is not a sign sent to him from his Lord? Say: The unseen is only for Allah, so wait; surely I too with you am of those who wait.

* * *

10:21. And when We make people taste of mercy after an affliction touches them, lo! they devise plans against Our messages. Say: Allah is quicker to plan. Surely Our messengers write down what you plan.

يُوحَى إِلَيَّ إِنِّي أَخَافُ إِنْ عَصَيْتُ رَبِّي عَذَابَ يَوْمٍ عَظِيمٍ (١٥) قُلْ لَوْ شَاءَ اللَّهُ مَا تَلَوْتُهُ عَلَيْكُمْ وَلَا أَدْرَاكُمْ بِهِ فَقَدْ لَبِثْتُ فِيكُمْ عُمُرًا مِنْ قَبْلِهِ أَفَلَا تَعْقِلُونَ (١٦) فَمَنْ أَظْلَمُ مِمَّنِ افْتَرَى عَلَى اللَّهِ كَذِبًا أَوْ كَذَّبَ بِآيَاتِهِ إِنَّهُ لَا يُفْلِحُ الْمُجْرِمُونَ (١٧) وَيَعْبُدُونَ مِنْ دُونِ اللَّهِ مَا لَا يَضُرُّهُمْ وَلَا يَنْفَعُهُمْ وَيَقُولُونَ هَؤُلَاءِ شُفَعَاؤُنَا عِنْدَ اللَّهِ قُلْ أَتُنَبِّئُونَ اللَّهَ بِمَا لَا يَعْلَمُ فِي السَّمَاوَاتِ وَلَا فِي الْأَرْضِ سُبْحَانَهُ وَتَعَالَى عَمَّا يُشْرِكُونَ (١٨) وَمَا كَانَ النَّاسُ إِلَّا أُمَّةً وَاحِدَةً فَاخْتَلَفُوا وَلَوْلَا كَلِمَةٌ سَبَقَتْ مِنْ رَبِّكَ لَقُضِيَ بَيْنَهُمْ فِيمَا فِيهِ يَخْتَلِفُونَ (١٩) وَيَقُولُونَ لَوْلَا أُنْزِلَ عَلَيْهِ آيَةٌ مِنْ رَبِّهِ فَقُلْ إِنَّمَا الْغَيْبُ لِلَّهِ فَانْتَظِرُوا إِنِّي مَعَكُمْ مِنَ الْمُنْتَظِرِينَ (٢٠) وَإِذَا أَذَقْنَا النَّاسَ رَحْمَةً مِنْ بَعْدِ ضَرَّاءَ مَسَّتْهُمْ إِذَا لَهُمْ مَكْرٌ فِي آيَاتِنَا قُلِ اللَّهُ أَسْرَعُ مَكْرًا إِنَّ رُسُلَنَا يَكْتُبُونَ مَا تَمْكُرُونَ (٢١) هُوَ الَّذِي يُسَيِّرُكُمْ فِي الْبَرِّ وَالْبَحْرِ حَتَّى إِذَا كُنْتُمْ فِي الْفُلْكِ وَجَرَيْنَ بِهِمْ بِرِيحٍ طَيِّبَةٍ وَفَرِحُوا بِهَا جَاءَتْهَا رِيحٌ عَاصِفٌ وَجَاءَهُمُ الْمَوْجُ مِنْ كُلِّ مَكَانٍ وَظَنُّوا أَنَّهُمْ أُحِيطَ بِهِمْ دَعَوُا اللَّهَ مُخْلِصِينَ لَهُ الدِّينَ لَئِنْ أَنْجَيْتَنَا مِنْ هَذِهِ لَنَكُونَنَّ مِنَ الشَّاكِرِينَ (٢٢) فَلَمَّا أَنْجَاهُمْ إِذَا هُمْ يَبْغُونَ فِي الْأَرْضِ بِغَيْرِ الْحَقِّ يَا أَيُّهَا النَّاسُ إِنَّمَا بَغْيُكُمْ عَلَى أَنْفُسِكُمْ مَتَاعَ الْحَيَاةِ الدُّنْيَا ثُمَّ إِلَيْنَا مَرْجِعُكُمْ فَنُنَبِّئُكُمْ بِمَا

10:22. He it is Who makes you travel by land and sea; until, when you are in the ships, and they sail on with them in a pleasant breeze, and they rejoice at it, a violent wind overtakes them and the billows surge in on them from all sides, and they deem that they are encompassed about. Then they pray to Allah, being sincere to Him in obedience: If Thou deliver us from this, we will certainly be of the grateful ones.

10:23. But when He delivers them, lo! they are unjustly rebellious in the earth. O men, your rebellion is against yourselves a provision (only) of this world's life. Then to Us is your return, so We shall inform you of what you did.

10:24. The likeness of this world's life is only as water which We send down from the clouds, then the herbage of the earth, of which men and cattle eat, grows luxuriantly thereby; until when the earth puts on its golden raiment and it becomes adorned, and its people think that they are masters of it, Our command comes to it, by night or by day, so We render it as reaped seed-produce, as though it had not flourished yesterday. Thus do We make clear the messages for a people who reflect.

10:25. And Allah invites to the abode of peace, and guides whom He pleases to the right path.

10:26. For those who do good is good (reward) and more (than this). Neither blackness nor ignominy will cover their faces. These are the owners of the Garden; therein they will abide.

10:27. And those who earn evil, the punishment of an evil is the like thereof, and abasement will cover them they will have none to protect them from Allah -- as if their faces had been covered with slices of the dense darkness of night. These are the companions of the Fire; therein they will abide.

10:28. And on the day when We gather them all together, then We shall say to those who associated others (with Allah): Keep where you are, you and your associate-gods. Then We shall separate them one from another, and their associates will say: It was not us that you served.

10:29. So Allah suffices as a witness between us and you that we were quite unaware of your serving (us).

10:30. There will every soul become acquainted with what it sent before, and they will be brought back to Allah, their true Patron, and that which they devised will escape from them.

***

10:31. Say: Who gives you sustenance from the heaven and the earth, or who controls the hearing and the sight, and who brings forth the living from the dead, and brings forth the dead from the living? And who regulates the affair? They will say: Allah. Say then: Will you not then guard against evil?

10:32. Such then is Allah, your true Lord. And what is there after the truth but error? How then are you turned away!

10:33. Thus does the word of thy Lord prove true against those who transgress that they believe not.

10:34. Say: Is there anyone among your associate-gods who produces the first creation, then reproduces it? Say Allah produces the first creation, then He reproduces it. How are you then turned away!

10:35. Say: Is there any of your associate-gods who guides to the Truth? Say: Allah guides to the Truth. Is He then Who guides to the Truth more worthy to be followed, or he who finds not the way unless he is guided? What is the matter with you? How do you judge?

فَسَيَقُولُونَ اللَّهُ فَقُلْ أَفَلَا تَتَّقُونَ (٣١)
فَذَلِكُمُ اللَّهُ رَبُّكُمُ الْحَقُّ فَمَاذَا بَعْدَ الْحَقِّ إِلَّا الضَّلَالُ فَأَنَّى تُصْرَفُونَ (٣٢)
كَذَلِكَ حَقَّتْ كَلِمَةُ رَبِّكَ عَلَى الَّذِينَ فَسَقُوا أَنَّهُمْ لَا يُؤْمِنُونَ (٣٣)
قُلْ هَلْ مِنْ شُرَكَائِكُمْ مَنْ يَبْدَأُ الْخَلْقَ ثُمَّ يُعِيدُهُ قُلِ اللَّهُ يَبْدَأُ الْخَلْقَ ثُمَّ يُعِيدُهُ فَأَنَّى تُؤْفَكُونَ (٣٤)
قُلْ هَلْ مِنْ شُرَكَائِكُمْ مَنْ يَهْدِي إِلَى الْحَقِّ قُلِ اللَّهُ يَهْدِي لِلْحَقِّ أَفَمَنْ يَهْدِي إِلَى الْحَقِّ أَحَقُّ أَنْ يُتَّبَعَ أَمَّنْ لَا يَهِدِّي إِلَّا أَنْ يُهْدَى فَمَا لَكُمْ كَيْفَ تَحْكُمُونَ (٣٥)
وَمَا يَتَّبِعُ أَكْثَرُهُمْ إِلَّا ظَنًّا إِنَّ الظَّنَّ لَا يُغْنِي مِنَ الْحَقِّ شَيْئًا إِنَّ اللَّهَ عَلِيمٌ بِمَا يَفْعَلُونَ (٣٦)
وَمَا كَانَ هَذَا الْقُرْآنُ أَنْ يُفْتَرَى مِنْ دُونِ اللَّهِ وَلَكِنْ تَصْدِيقَ الَّذِي بَيْنَ يَدَيْهِ وَتَفْصِيلَ الْكِتَابِ لَا رَيْبَ فِيهِ مِنْ رَبِّ الْعَالَمِينَ (٣٧)
أَمْ يَقُولُونَ افْتَرَاهُ قُلْ فَأْتُوا بِسُورَةٍ مِثْلِهِ وَادْعُوا مَنِ اسْتَطَعْتُمْ مِنْ دُونِ اللَّهِ إِنْ كُنْتُمْ صَادِقِينَ (٣٨)
بَلْ كَذَّبُوا بِمَا لَمْ يُحِيطُوا بِعِلْمِهِ وَلَمَّا يَأْتِهِمْ تَأْوِيلُهُ كَذَلِكَ كَذَّبَ الَّذِينَ مِنْ قَبْلِهِمْ فَانْظُرْ كَيْفَ كَانَ عَاقِبَةُ الظَّالِمِينَ (٣٩)
وَمِنْهُمْ مَنْ يُؤْمِنُ بِهِ وَمِنْهُمْ مَنْ لَا يُؤْمِنُ بِهِ وَرَبُّكَ أَعْلَمُ بِالْمُفْسِدِينَ (٤٠)
وَإِنْ كَذَّبُوكَ فَقُلْ لِي عَمَلِي وَلَكُمْ عَمَلُكُمْ أَنْتُمْ بَرِيئُونَ مِمَّا أَعْمَلُ وَأَنَا بَرِيءٌ مِمَّا تَعْمَلُونَ (٤١)
وَمِنْهُمْ مَنْ يَسْتَمِعُونَ إِلَيْكَ أَفَأَنْتَ

10:36. And most of them follow naught but conjecture. Surely conjecture will not avail aught against the Truth. Truly Allah is Knower of what they do.

10:37. And this Qur'an is not such as could be forged by those besides Allah, but it is a verification of that which is before it and a dear explanation of the Book, there is no doubt in it, from the Lord of the worlds.

10:38. Or say they: He has forged it? Say: Then bring a chapter like it, and invite whom you can besides Allah, if you are truthful.

10:39. Nay, they reject that, whose knowledge they cannot compass and whose final sequel has not yet come to them. Even thus did those before them reject; then see what was the end of the wrongdoers.

10:40. And of them is he who believes in it, and of them is he who believes not in it. And thy Lord best knows the mischief-makers.

* * *

10:41. And if they reject thee, say My work is for me and your work for you. You are clear of what I do and I am clear of what you do.

10:42. And of them are some who listen to thee. But canst thou make the deaf to hear, though they will not understand?

10:43. And of them are some who look at thee. But canst thou show the way to the blind, though they will not see?

10:44. Surely Allah wrongs not men in aught, but men wrong themselves.

10:45. And on the day when He will gather them, as though they had not stayed but an hour of the day, they will recognize one another. They perish indeed who reject the meeting with Allah, and they follow not the right way.

10:46. And if We show thee something of that which We promise them, or Cause thee to die, yet to Us is their return, and Allah is Witness to what

تُسْمِعُ الصُّمَّ وَلَوْ كَانُوا لَا يَعْقِلُونَ (٤٢)
وَمِنْهُمْ مَنْ يَنْظُرُ إِلَيْكَ أَفَأَنْتَ تَهْدِي الْعُمْيَ وَلَوْ كَانُوا لَا يُبْصِرُونَ (٤٣)
إِنَّ اللَّهَ لَا يَظْلِمُ النَّاسَ شَيْئًا وَلَكِنَّ النَّاسَ أَنْفُسَهُمْ يَظْلِمُونَ (٤٤)
وَيَوْمَ يَحْشُرُهُمْ كَأَنْ لَمْ يَلْبَثُوا إِلَّا سَاعَةً مِنَ النَّهَارِ يَتَعَارَفُونَ بَيْنَهُمْ قَدْ خَسِرَ الَّذِينَ كَذَّبُوا بِلِقَاءِ اللَّهِ وَمَا كَانُوا مُهْتَدِينَ (٤٥)
وَإِمَّا نُرِيَنَّكَ بَعْضَ الَّذِي نَعِدُهُمْ أَوْ نَتَوَفَّيَنَّكَ فَإِلَيْنَا مَرْجِعُهُمْ ثُمَّ اللَّهُ شَهِيدٌ عَلَى مَا يَفْعَلُونَ (٤٦)
وَلِكُلِّ أُمَّةٍ رَسُولٌ فَإِذَا جَاءَ رَسُولُهُمْ قُضِيَ بَيْنَهُمْ بِالْقِسْطِ وَهُمْ لَا يُظْلَمُونَ (٤٧)
وَيَقُولُونَ مَتَى هَذَا الْوَعْدُ إِنْ كُنْتُمْ صَادِقِينَ (٤٨)
قُلْ لَا أَمْلِكُ لِنَفْسِي ضَرًّا وَلَا نَفْعًا إِلَّا مَا شَاءَ اللَّهُ لِكُلِّ أُمَّةٍ أَجَلٌ إِذَا جَاءَ أَجَلُهُمْ فَلَا يَسْتَأْخِرُونَ سَاعَةً وَلَا يَسْتَقْدِمُونَ (٤٩)
قُلْ أَرَأَيْتُمْ إِنْ أَتَاكُمْ عَذَابُهُ بَيَاتًا أَوْ نَهَارًا مَاذَا يَسْتَعْجِلُ مِنْهُ الْمُجْرِمُونَ (٥٠)
أَثُمَّ إِذَا مَا وَقَعَ آمَنْتُمْ بِهِ آلْآنَ وَقَدْ كُنْتُمْ بِهِ تَسْتَعْجِلُونَ (٥١)
ثُمَّ قِيلَ لِلَّذِينَ ظَلَمُوا ذُوقُوا عَذَابَ الْخُلْدِ هَلْ تُجْزَوْنَ إِلَّا بِمَا كُنْتُمْ تَكْسِبُونَ (٥٢)
وَيَسْتَنْبِئُونَكَ أَحَقٌّ هُوَ قُلْ إِي وَرَبِّي إِنَّهُ لَحَقٌّ وَمَا أَنْتُمْ بِمُعْجِزِينَ (٥٣)
وَلَوْ أَنَّ لِكُلِّ نَفْسٍ ظَلَمَتْ مَا فِي الْأَرْضِ لَافْتَدَتْ بِهِ وَأَسَرُّوا النَّدَامَةَ

they do.

10:47. And for every nation there is a messenger. So when their messenger comes, the matter is decided between them with justice, and they are not wronged.

10:48. And they say: When will this promise be fulfilled, if you are truthful?

10:49. Say: I control not for myself any harm, or any benefit, except what Allah pleases. Every nation has a term. When their term comes, they cannot put it off an hour, nor can they bring it before (its time).

10:50. Say: Do you see if His chastisement overtakes you by night or by day? What then is there of it that the guilty would hasten?

10:51. And when it comes to pass, will you believe in it? What! now! and you hastened it on.

10:52. Then will it be said to those who were unjust: Taste abiding chastisement; you are not requited except for what you earned.

10:53. And they ask thee: Is that true? Say: Aye, by my Lord it is surely the Truth, and you will not escape.

* * *

10:54. And if every soul that has done injustice had all that is in the earth, it would offer it for ransom. And they will manifest regret when they see the chastisement. And it will be decided between them with justice, and they will not be wronged.

10:55. Now surely whatever is in the heavens and the earth is Allah's. Now surely Allah's promise is true, but most of them know not.

10:56. He gives life and causes death, and to Him you will be returned.

10:57. O men, there has come to you indeed an admonition from your Lord and a healing for what is in the breasts; and a guidance and a mercy for the believers.

10:58. Say: In the grace of Allah and In

His mercy, in that they should rejoice. It is better than that which they hoard.

10:59. Say: See you what Allah has sent down for you of sustenance, then you make (a part) of it unlawful and (a part) lawful. Say: Has Allah commanded you or do you forge a lie against Allah?

10:60. And what think those who forge lies against Allah of the day of Resurrection? Surely Allah is Bountiful to men, but most of them give not thanks.

* * *

10:61. And thou art not (engaged) in any affair and thou recitest not concerning it any portion of the Qur'an, and you do no work, but We are Witness of you when you are engaged therein. And not the weight of an atom in the earth or in the heaven is hidden from thy Lord, nor anything less than that nor greater, but it is (all) in a dear book.

10:62. Now surely the friends of Allah, they have no fear nor do they grieve --

10:63. Those who believe and keep their duty.

10:64. For them is good news in this world's life and in the Hereafter. There is no changing the words of Allah. That is the mighty achievement.

10:65. And let not their speech grieve thee. Surely might belongs wholly to Allah. He is the Hearer, the Knower.

10:66. Now, surely, whatever is in the heavens and whatever is in the earth is Allah's. And what do follow those who call on associates besides Allah? They follow naught but conjecture, and they only lie.

10:67. He it is Who made for you the night that you might rest therein and the day giving light. Surely in this are signs for a people who hear.

10:68. They say Allah has taken a son (to Himself). Glory be to Him! He is the Self-sufficient. His is what is in the heavens and what is in the earth. You have no authority for this. Say you against Allah what you know not?

10:69. Say Those who forge a lie against Allah will not succeed.

10:70. A little enjoyment in this world, then to Us is their return, then We shall make them taste severe chastisement because they disbelieved.

* * *

10:71. And recite to them the story of Noah, when he said to his people: O my people, if my staying (here) and my reminding (you) by the messages of Allah is hard on you, on Allah do I rely; so decide upon your course of action and (gather) your associates. Then let not your course of action be dubious to you, so have it executed against me and give me no respite.

10:72. But if you turn back, I ask for no reward from you. My reward is only with Allah, and I am commanded to be of those who submit.

10:73. But they rejected him, so We delivered him and those with him in the ark, and We made them rulers and drowned those who rejected Our messages. See, then, what was the end of those who were warned.

10:74. Then, after him We sent messengers to their people. They came to them with clear arguments, but they would not believe what they had rejected before. Thus do We seal the hearts of those who exceed the limits.

10:75. Then after them We sent Moses and Aaron to Pharaoh and his chiefs with Our signs, but they were arrogant, and they were a guilty people.

10:76. So when the truth came to them from Us, they said: This is surely clear enchantment!

10:77. Moses said: Say you (this) of the truth when it has come to you? Is it enchantment? And the enchanters never succeed.

10:78. They said: Hast thou come to us

ثُمَّ بَعَثْنَا مِنْ بَعْدِهِمْ مُوسَى وَهَارُونَ إِلَى فِرْعَوْنَ وَمَلَئِهِ بِآيَاتِنَا فَاسْتَكْبَرُوا وَكَانُوا قَوْمًا مُجْرِمِينَ (٧٥) فَلَمَّا جَاءَهُمُ الْحَقُّ مِنْ عِنْدِنَا قَالُوا إِنَّ هَذَا لَسِحْرٌ مُبِينٌ (٧٦) قَالَ مُوسَى أَتَقُولُونَ لِلْحَقِّ لَمَّا جَاءَكُمْ أَسِحْرٌ هَذَا وَلَا يُفْلِحُ السَّاحِرُونَ (٧٧) قَالُوا أَجِئْتَنَا لِتَلْفِتَنَا عَمَّا وَجَدْنَا عَلَيْهِ آبَاءَنَا وَتَكُونَ لَكُمَا الْكِبْرِيَاءُ فِي الْأَرْضِ وَمَا نَحْنُ لَكُمَا بِمُؤْمِنِينَ (٧٨) وَقَالَ فِرْعَوْنُ ائْتُونِي بِكُلِّ سَاحِرٍ عَلِيمٍ (٧٩) فَلَمَّا جَاءَ السَّحَرَةُ قَالَ لَهُمْ مُوسَى أَلْقُوا مَا أَنْتُمْ مُلْقُونَ (٨٠) فَلَمَّا أَلْقَوْا قَالَ مُوسَى مَا جِئْتُمْ بِهِ السِّحْرُ إِنَّ اللَّهَ سَيُبْطِلُهُ إِنَّ اللَّهَ لَا يُصْلِحُ عَمَلَ الْمُفْسِدِينَ (٨١) وَيُحِقُّ اللَّهُ الْحَقَّ بِكَلِمَاتِهِ وَلَوْ كَرِهَ الْمُجْرِمُونَ (٨٢) فَمَا آمَنَ لِمُوسَى إِلَّا ذُرِّيَّةٌ مِنْ قَوْمِهِ عَلَى خَوْفٍ مِنْ فِرْعَوْنَ وَمَلَئِهِمْ أَنْ يَفْتِنَهُمْ وَإِنَّ فِرْعَوْنَ لَعَالٍ فِي الْأَرْضِ وَإِنَّهُ لَمِنَ الْمُسْرِفِينَ (٨٣) وَقَالَ مُوسَى يَا قَوْمِ إِنْ كُنْتُمْ آمَنْتُمْ بِاللَّهِ فَعَلَيْهِ تَوَكَّلُوا إِنْ كُنْتُمْ مُسْلِمِينَ (٨٤) فَقَالُوا عَلَى اللَّهِ تَوَكَّلْنَا رَبَّنَا لَا تَجْعَلْنَا فِتْنَةً لِلْقَوْمِ الظَّالِمِينَ (٨٥) وَنَجِّنَا بِرَحْمَتِكَ مِنَ الْقَوْمِ الْكَافِرِينَ (٨٦) وَأَوْحَيْنَا إِلَى مُوسَى وَأَخِيهِ أَنْ تَبَوَّآ لِقَوْمِكُمَا بِمِصْرَ بُيُوتًا وَاجْعَلُوا

to turn us away from that which we found our fathers following, and (that) greatness in the land may be for you two? And we are not going to believe in you.

10:79. And Pharaoh said: Bring to me every skilful enchanter.

10:80. So when the enchanters came, Moses said to them: Cast what you are going to cast.

10:81. So when they had cast down, Moses said: What you have brought is deception. Surely Allah will make it naught. Surely Allah allows not the work of mischief-makers to thrive.

10:82. And Allan will establish the truth by His words, though the guilty be averse.

* * *

10:83. But, on account of the fear of Pharaoh and their chiefs persecuting them, none believed in Moses except a few of his people. And Pharaoh was truly high-handed in the land; and surely he was extravagant.

10:84. And Moses said: O my people, if you believe in Allah, then rely on Him if you submit (to Him).

10:85. They said: On Allah we rely; our Lord, make us not a trial for the unjust people.

10:86. And deliver us by Thy mercy from the disbelieving people.

10:87. And We revealed to Moses and his brother: Take for your people houses to abide in Egypt and make your houses places of worship and keep up prayer. And give good news to the believers.

10:88. And Moses said: Our Lord, surely Thou hast given Pharaoh and his chiefs finery and riches in this world's life, our Lord, that they may lead (people) astray from Thy way. Our Lord, destroy their riches and harden their hearts, so that they believe not till they see the painful chastisement.

10:89. He said: Your prayer is accepted; so continue in the right way and follow not the path of those who know not.

10:90. And We brought the Children of Israel across the sea. Then Pharaoh and his hosts followed them for oppression and tyranny, till, when drowning overtook him, he said: I believe that there is no god but He in Whom the Children of Israel believe, and I am of those who submit.

10:91. What! Now! And indeed before (this) thou didst disobey and thou wast of the mischief-makers!

10:92. But this day We shall save thee in thy body that thou mayest be a sign to those after thee. And surely most of the people are heedless of Our signs.

* * *

10:93. And certainly We lodged the Children of Israel in a goodly abode and provided them with good things. Then they differed not till the knowledge came to them. Surely thy Lord will judge between them on the day of Resurrection concerning that in which they differed.

10:94. But if thou art in doubt as to that which We have revealed to thee, ask those who read the Book before thee. Certainly the Truth has come to thee from thy Lord, so be not thou of the doubters.

10:95. And be not of those who reject the messages of Allah, (for) then thou wilt be of the losers.

10:96. Surely those against whom the word of thy Lord has proved true will not believe,

10:97. Though every sign should come to them, till they see the painful chastisement.

10:98. And why was there not a town which believed, so that their belief should have profited them, but the people of Jonah? When they believed, We removed from them the chastisement of disgrace in this world's

10. Jonah

life, and We gave them provision for a while.

10:99. And if thy Lord had pleased, all those who are in the earth would have believed, all of them. Wilt thou then force men till they are believers?

10:100. And it is not for any soul to believe except by Allah's permission. And He casts uncleanness on those who will not understand.

10:101. Say: Behold what is in the heavens and the earth! And signs and warners avail not a people who believe not.

10:102. What do they wait for, then, but the like of the days of those who passed away before them? Say: Wait then: I, too, am with you of those who wait.

10:103. Then We deliver Our messengers and those who believe -- even so (now); it is binding on Us to deliver the believers.

* * *

10:104. Say: O people, if you are in doubt as to my religion, (know that) I serve not those whom you serve besides Allah, but I serve Allah, Who causes you to die; and I am commanded to be of the believers,

10:105. And that thou set thy purpose towards the Religion uprightly; and be not of the polytheists.

10:106. And call not besides Allah on that which can neither benefit thee nor harm thee; for if thou dost, thou shalt then be of the unjust.

10:107. And if Allah afflicts thee with harm, there is none to remove it but He; and if He intends good to thee, there is none to repel His grace. He brings it to whom He pleases of His servants. And He is the Forgiving, the Merciful.

10:108. Say: O people, the Truth has indeed come to you from your Lord; so whoever goes aright, goes aright only for the good of his own soul; and

رَبِّكُمْ فَمَنِ اهْتَدَى فَإِنَّمَا يَهْتَدِي لِنَفْسِهِ وَمَنْ ضَلَّ فَإِنَّمَا يَضِلُّ عَلَيْهَا وَمَا أَنَا عَلَيْكُمْ بِوَكِيلٍ (١٠٨)

وَاتَّبِعْ مَا يُوحَى إِلَيْكَ وَاصْبِرْ حَتَّى يَحْكُمَ اللَّهُ وَهُوَ خَيْرُ الْحَاكِمِينَ (١٠٩)

whoever errs, errs only against it. And I am not a custodian over you.

10:109. And follow what is revealed to thee and be patient till Allah give judgment, and He is the Best of the judges.

11. Hud

In the name of Allah, the Beneficent, the Merciful.

11:1. I, Allah, am the Seer. A Book, whose verses are characterized by wisdom, then they are made plain, from One Wise, Aware:

11:2. That you should serve none but Allah. Surely I am to you from Him a warner and a giver of good news.

11:3. And ask forgiveness of your Lord, then turn to Him. He will provide you with a goodly provision to an appointed term, and will bestow His grace on every one endowed with grace. And if you turn away, I fear for you the chastisement of a great day.

11:4. To Allah is your return, and He is Possessor of power over all things.

11:5. Now surely they cover up their breasts to conceal (their enmity) from Him. Now surely, when they put their garments as a covering, He knows what they hide and what they make public. Surely He is Knower of what is in the breasts.

11:6. And there is no animal in the earth but on Allah is the sustenance of it, and He knows its resting-place and its depository. All is in a clear record.

11:7. And He it is Who created the heavens and the earth in six periods and His Throne of Power is ever on water that He might manifest (the good qualities in) you whoever of you is best in deeds. And if thou sayest, You shall surely be raised up after death, those who disbelieve say This is nothing but clear deceit.

11:8. And if We delay for them the

chastisement for a stated period, they will certainly say: What prevents it? Now surely on the day when it will come to them, it will not be averted from them, and that which they scoffed at will beset them.

***

11:9. And if We make man taste mercy from Us, then withdraw it from him, he is surely despairing, ungrateful.

11:10. And if We make him taste a favour after distress has afflicted him, he says: The evils are gone away from me. Certainly he is exultant, boastful,

11:11. Except those who are patient and do good. For them is forgiveness and a great reward.

11:12. Then, may it be that thou wilt give up part of what is revealed to thee and thy breast will he straitened by it, because they say: Why has not a tteasure been sent down for him or an angel come with him? Thou art only a warner And Allah is in charge of all things.

11:13. Or, say they He has forged it. Say: Then bring ten forged chapters like it, and call upon whom you can besides Allah, if you are truthful.

11:14. But if they answer you not, then know that it is revealed by Allah's knowledge, and that there is no God but He. Will you then submit?

11:15. Whoever desires this world's life and its finery We repay them their deeds therein, and they are not made to suffer loss in it.

11:16. These are they for whom there is nothing but Fire in the Hereafter. And what they work therein is fruitless and their deeds are vain.

11:17. Is he then (like these) who has with him clear proof from his Lord, and a witness from Him recites it, and before it (is) the Book of Moses, a guide and a mercy? These believe in it. And whoever of the parties disbelieves in it, the Fire is his promised place. So be not in doubt about It. Surely it is the truth from thy Lord, but most men believe not.

11:18. And who is more unjust than he who forges a lie against Allah? These will be brought before their Lord, and the witnesses will say: These are they who lied against their Lord. Now surely the curse of Allah is on the wrongdoers,

11:19. Who hinder (men) from the path of Allah and desire to make it crooked. And they are disbelievers in the Hereafter.

11:20. These will not escape in the earth, nor have they guardians besides Allah. The chastisement will be doubled for them. They could not beat to hear, and they did not see.

11:21. These are they who have lost their souls, and that which they forged is gone from them.

11:22. Truly in the Hereafter they are the greatest losers.

11:23. Surely those who believe and do good and humble themselves before their Lord, these are the owners of the Garden; therein they will abide.

11:24. The likeness of the two parties is as the blind and the deaf, and the seer and the hearer. Are they equal in condition? Will you not then mind?

***

11:25. And certainly We sent Noah to his people: Surely I am a plain warner to you,

11:26. To serve none but Allah. Verily I fear for you the chastisement of a painful day.

11:27. But the chiefs of his people who disbelieved said: We see thee not but a mortal like us, and we see not that any follow thee but those who are the meanest of us at first thought. Nor do we see in you any superiority over us; nay, we deem you liars.

11:28. He said: O my people, see you if I have with me clear proof from my

وَمَنْ أَظْلَمُ مِمَّنِ افْتَرَى عَلَى اللَّهِ كَذِبًا أُولَٰئِكَ يُعْرَضُونَ عَلَىٰ رَبِّهِمْ وَيَقُولُ الْأَشْهَادُ هَٰؤُلَاءِ الَّذِينَ كَذَبُوا عَلَىٰ رَبِّهِمْ أَلَا لَعْنَةُ اللَّهِ عَلَى الظَّالِمِينَ (١٨)

الَّذِينَ يَصُدُّونَ عَنْ سَبِيلِ اللَّهِ وَيَبْغُونَهَا عِوَجًا وَهُمْ بِالْآخِرَةِ هُمْ كَافِرُونَ (١٩)

أُولَٰئِكَ لَمْ يَكُونُوا مُعْجِزِينَ فِي الْأَرْضِ وَمَا كَانَ لَهُمْ مِنْ دُونِ اللَّهِ مِنْ أَوْلِيَاءَ يُضَاعَفُ لَهُمُ الْعَذَابُ مَا كَانُوا يَسْتَطِيعُونَ السَّمْعَ وَمَا كَانُوا يُبْصِرُونَ (٢٠)

أُولَٰئِكَ الَّذِينَ خَسِرُوا أَنْفُسَهُمْ وَضَلَّ عَنْهُمْ مَا كَانُوا يَفْتَرُونَ (٢١)

لَا جَرَمَ أَنَّهُمْ فِي الْآخِرَةِ هُمُ الْأَخْسَرُونَ (٢٢)

إِنَّ الَّذِينَ آمَنُوا وَعَمِلُوا الصَّالِحَاتِ وَأَخْبَتُوا إِلَىٰ رَبِّهِمْ أُولَٰئِكَ أَصْحَابُ الْجَنَّةِ هُمْ فِيهَا خَالِدُونَ (٢٣)

مَثَلُ الْفَرِيقَيْنِ كَالْأَعْمَىٰ وَالْأَصَمِّ وَالْبَصِيرِ وَالسَّمِيعِ هَلْ يَسْتَوِيَانِ مَثَلًا أَفَلَا تَذَكَّرُونَ (٢٤)

وَلَقَدْ أَرْسَلْنَا نُوحًا إِلَىٰ قَوْمِهِ إِنِّي لَكُمْ نَذِيرٌ مُبِينٌ (٢٥)

أَنْ لَا تَعْبُدُوا إِلَّا اللَّهَ إِنِّي أَخَافُ عَلَيْكُمْ عَذَابَ يَوْمٍ أَلِيمٍ (٢٦)

فَقَالَ الْمَلَأُ الَّذِينَ كَفَرُوا مِنْ قَوْمِهِ مَا نَرَاكَ إِلَّا بَشَرًا مِثْلَنَا وَمَا نَرَاكَ اتَّبَعَكَ إِلَّا الَّذِينَ هُمْ أَرَاذِلُنَا بَادِيَ الرَّأْيِ وَمَا نَرَىٰ لَكُمْ عَلَيْنَا مِنْ فَضْلٍ بَلْ نَظُنُّكُمْ كَاذِبِينَ (٢٧)

قَالَ يَا قَوْمِ أَرَأَيْتُمْ إِنْ كُنْتُ عَلَىٰ بَيِّنَةٍ مِنْ رَبِّي وَآتَانِي رَحْمَةً مِنْ عِنْدِهِ

Lord, and He has granted me mercy from Himself and it has been made obscure to you. Can we compel you to (accept) it while you are averse to it?

11:29. And, O my people, I ask you not for wealth (in return) for it. My reward is only with Allah, and I am not going to drive away those who believe. Surely they will meet their Lord, but I see you a people who are ignorant.

11:30. And, O my people, who will help me against Allah, if I drive them away? Will you not then mind?

11:31. And I say not to you that I have the treasures of Allah; and I know not the unseen; nor do I say that I am an angel. Nor do I say about those whom your eyes scorn that Allah will not grant them (any) good. Allah knows best what is in their souls -- for then indeed I should be of the wrongdoers.

11:32. They said: O Noah, indeed thou hast disputed with us and prolonged dispute with us, so bring upon us that which thou threatenest us with, if thou art truthful.

11:33. He said: Only Allah will bring it on you, if He please, and you will not escape:

11:34. And my advice will not profit you, if I intend to give you good advice, if Allah intends to destroy you. He is your Lord; and to Him you will be brought back.

11:35. Or say they: He has forged it? Say: If I have forged it, on me is my guilt; and I am free of that of which you are guilty.

* * *

11:36. And it was revealed to Noah: None of thy people will believe except those who have already believed, so grieve not at what they do:

11:37. And make the ark under Our eyes and Our revelation, and speak not to Me on behalf of those who are unjust. Surely they will be drowned.

11:38. And he began to make the ark.

فَعُمِّيَتْ عَلَيْكُمْ أَنُلْزِمُكُمُوهَا وَأَنْتُمْ لَهَا كَارِهُونَ (٢٨)

وَيَا قَوْمِ لَا أَسْأَلُكُمْ عَلَيْهِ مَالًا إِنْ أَجْرِيَ إِلَّا عَلَى اللَّهِ وَمَا أَنَا بِطَارِدِ الَّذِينَ آمَنُوا إِنَّهُمْ مُلَاقُو رَبِّهِمْ وَلَكِنِّي أَرَاكُمْ قَوْمًا تَجْهَلُونَ (٢٩)

وَيَا قَوْمِ مَنْ يَنْصُرُنِي مِنَ اللَّهِ إِنْ طَرَدْتُهُمْ أَفَلَا تَذَكَّرُونَ (٣٠)

وَلَا أَقُولُ لَكُمْ عِنْدِي خَزَائِنُ اللَّهِ وَلَا أَعْلَمُ الْغَيْبَ وَلَا أَقُولُ إِنِّي مَلَكٌ وَلَا أَقُولُ لِلَّذِينَ تَزْدَرِي أَعْيُنُكُمْ لَنْ يُؤْتِيَهُمُ اللَّهُ خَيْرًا اللَّهُ أَعْلَمُ بِمَا فِي أَنْفُسِهِمْ إِنِّي إِذًا لَمِنَ الظَّالِمِينَ (٣١)

قَالُوا يَا نُوحُ قَدْ جَادَلْتَنَا فَأَكْثَرْتَ جِدَالَنَا فَأْتِنَا بِمَا تَعِدُنَا إِنْ كُنْتَ مِنَ الصَّادِقِينَ (٣٢)

قَالَ إِنَّمَا يَأْتِيكُمْ بِهِ اللَّهُ إِنْ شَاءَ وَمَا أَنْتُمْ بِمُعْجِزِينَ (٣٣)

وَلَا يَنْفَعُكُمْ نُصْحِي إِنْ أَرَدْتُ أَنْ أَنْصَحَ لَكُمْ إِنْ كَانَ اللَّهُ يُرِيدُ أَنْ يُغْوِيَكُمْ هُوَ رَبُّكُمْ وَإِلَيْهِ تُرْجَعُونَ (٣٤)

أَمْ يَقُولُونَ افْتَرَاهُ قُلْ إِنِ افْتَرَيْتُهُ فَعَلَيَّ إِجْرَامِي وَأَنَا بَرِيءٌ مِمَّا تُجْرِمُونَ (٣٥)

وَأُوحِيَ إِلَى نُوحٍ أَنَّهُ لَنْ يُؤْمِنَ مِنْ قَوْمِكَ إِلَّا مَنْ قَدْ آمَنَ فَلَا تَبْتَئِسْ بِمَا كَانُوا يَفْعَلُونَ (٣٦)

وَاصْنَعِ الْفُلْكَ بِأَعْيُنِنَا وَوَحْيِنَا وَلَا تُخَاطِبْنِي فِي الَّذِينَ ظَلَمُوا إِنَّهُمْ مُغْرَقُونَ (٣٧)

وَيَصْنَعُ الْفُلْكَ وَكُلَّمَا مَرَّ عَلَيْهِ مَلَأٌ مِنْ قَوْمِهِ سَخِرُوا مِنْهُ قَالَ إِنْ تَسْخَرُوا مِنَّا فَإِنَّا نَسْخَرُ مِنْكُمْ كَمَا

And whenever the chiefs of his people passed by him, they laughed at him. He said: If you laugh at us, surely we, too, laugh at you as you laugh (at us).

11:39. So you shall know who it is on whom will come a chastisement which will disgrace him, and on whom a lasting chastisement will fall.

11:40. At length when Our command came and water gushed forth from the valley, We said: Carry in it two of all things, a pair, and thine own family except those against whom the word has already gone forth -- and those who believe. And there believed not with him but a few.

11:41. And he said: Embark in it, in the name of Allah be its sailing and its anchoring. Surely my Lord is Forgiving, Merciful.

11:42. And it moved on with them amid waves like mountains. And Noah called out to his son, and he was aloof: O my son, embark with us and be not with the disbelievers.

11:43. He said: I will betake myself for refuge to a mountain that will save me from the water. He said: There is none safe to-day from Allah's command, but he on whom He has mercy. And a wave intervened between them, so he was among the drowned.

11:44. And it was said: O earth, swallow thy water, and O cloud, clear away. And the water was made to abate, and the affair was decided, and it rested on the Judi, and it was said: Away with the iniquitous people!

11:45. And Noah cried to his Lord and said: My Lord, surely my son is of my family, and Thy promise is true, and Thou art the Justest of the judges.

11:46. He said: O Noah, he is not of thy family; he is (an embodiment of) unrighteous conduct. So ask not of Me that of which thou hast no knowledge. I admonish thee lest thou be of the ignorant.

تَسْخَرُونَ (٣٨) فَسَوْفَ تَعْلَمُونَ مَنْ يَأْتِيهِ عَذَابٌ يُخْزِيهِ وَيَحِلُّ عَلَيْهِ عَذَابٌ مُقِيمٌ (٣٩) حَتَّى إِذَا جَاءَ أَمْرُنَا وَفَارَ التَّنُّورُ قُلْنَا احْمِلْ فِيهَا مِنْ كُلٍّ زَوْجَيْنِ اثْنَيْنِ وَأَهْلَكَ إِلَّا مَنْ سَبَقَ عَلَيْهِ الْقَوْلُ وَمَنْ آمَنَ وَمَا آمَنَ مَعَهُ إِلَّا قَلِيلٌ (٤٠) وَقَالَ ارْكَبُوا فِيهَا بِسْمِ اللَّهِ مَجْرَاهَا وَمُرْسَاهَا إِنَّ رَبِّي لَغَفُورٌ رَحِيمٌ (٤١) وَهِيَ تَجْرِي بِهِمْ فِي مَوْجٍ كَالْجِبَالِ وَنَادَى نُوحٌ ابْنَهُ وَكَانَ فِي مَعْزِلٍ يَا بُنَيَّ ارْكَبْ مَعَنَا وَلَا تَكُنْ مَعَ الْكَافِرِينَ (٤٢) قَالَ سَآوِي إِلَى جَبَلٍ يَعْصِمُنِي مِنَ الْمَاءِ قَالَ لَا عَاصِمَ الْيَوْمَ مِنْ أَمْرِ اللَّهِ إِلَّا مَنْ رَحِمَ وَحَالَ بَيْنَهُمَا الْمَوْجُ فَكَانَ مِنَ الْمُغْرَقِينَ (٤٣) وَقِيلَ يَا أَرْضُ ابْلَعِي مَاءَكِ وَيَا سَمَاءُ أَقْلِعِي وَغِيضَ الْمَاءُ وَقُضِيَ الْأَمْرُ وَاسْتَوَتْ عَلَى الْجُودِيِّ وَقِيلَ بُعْدًا لِلْقَوْمِ الظَّالِمِينَ (٤٤) وَنَادَى نُوحٌ رَبَّهُ فَقَالَ رَبِّ إِنَّ ابْنِي مِنْ أَهْلِي وَإِنَّ وَعْدَكَ الْحَقُّ وَأَنْتَ أَحْكَمُ الْحَاكِمِينَ (٤٥) قَالَ يَا نُوحُ إِنَّهُ لَيْسَ مِنْ أَهْلِكَ إِنَّهُ عَمَلٌ غَيْرُ صَالِحٍ فَلَا تَسْأَلْنِ مَا لَيْسَ لَكَ بِهِ عِلْمٌ إِنِّي أَعِظُكَ أَنْ تَكُونَ مِنَ الْجَاهِلِينَ (٤٦) قَالَ رَبِّ إِنِّي أَعُوذُ بِكَ أَنْ أَسْأَلَكَ مَا لَيْسَ لِي بِهِ عِلْمٌ وَإِلَّا تَغْفِرْ لِي وَتَرْحَمْنِي أَكُنْ مِنَ الْخَاسِرِينَ (٤٧) قِيلَ يَا نُوحُ اهْبِطْ بِسَلَامٍ مِنَّا وَبَرَكَاتٍ

11:47. He said: My Lord, I seek refuge in Thee from asking of Thee that of which I have no knowledge. And unless Thou forgive me and have mercy on me, I shall be of the losers.

11:48. It was said: O Noah, descend with peace from Us and blessings on thee and on nations (springing) from those with thee. And there are nations whom We afford provisions, then a painful punishment from Us afflicts them.

11:49. These are announcements relating to the unseen which We reveal to thee; thou didst not know them (neither) thou nor thy people before this. So be patient. Surely, the (good) end is for the dutiful.

* * *

11:50. And to 'Ad (We sent) their brother Hud. He said: O my people, serve Allah, you have no god save Him. You are only fabricators.

11:51. O my people, I ask of you no reward for it. My reward is only with Him Who created me. Do you not then understand?

11:52. And, O my people, ask forgiveness of your Lord, then turn to Him, He will send on you clouds pouring down abundance of rain and add strength to your strength, and turn not back, guilty.

11:53. They said: O Hud, thou hast brought us no clear argument, and we are not going to desert our gods for thy word, and we are not believers in thee.

11:54. We say naught but that some of our gods have smitten thee with evil. He said: Surely I call Allah to witness, and do you, too, bear witness that I am innocent of what you associate (with Allah)

11:55. Besides Him. So scheme against me all together, then give me no respite.

11:56. Surely I put my trust in Allah, my Lord and your Lord. There is no

عَلَيْكَ وَعَلَى أُمَمٍ مِمَّنْ مَعَكَ وَأُمَمٌ سَنُمَتِّعُهُمْ ثُمَّ يَمَسُّهُمْ مِنَّا عَذَابٌ أَلِيمٌ (٤٨)

تِلْكَ مِنْ أَنْبَاءِ الْغَيْبِ نُوحِيهَا إِلَيْكَ مَا كُنْتَ تَعْلَمُهَا أَنْتَ وَلَا قَوْمُكَ مِنْ قَبْلِ هَذَا فَاصْبِرْ إِنَّ الْعَاقِبَةَ لِلْمُتَّقِينَ (٤٩)

وَإِلَى عَادٍ أَخَاهُمْ هُودًا قَالَ يَا قَوْمِ اعْبُدُوا اللَّهَ مَا لَكُمْ مِنْ إِلَهٍ غَيْرُهُ إِنْ أَنْتُمْ إِلَّا مُفْتَرُونَ (٥٠)

يَا قَوْمِ لَا أَسْأَلُكُمْ عَلَيْهِ أَجْرًا إِنْ أَجْرِيَ إِلَّا عَلَى الَّذِي فَطَرَنِي أَفَلَا تَعْقِلُونَ (٥١)

وَيَا قَوْمِ اسْتَغْفِرُوا رَبَّكُمْ ثُمَّ تُوبُوا إِلَيْهِ يُرْسِلِ السَّمَاءَ عَلَيْكُمْ مِدْرَارًا وَيَزِدْكُمْ قُوَّةً إِلَى قُوَّتِكُمْ وَلَا تَتَوَلَّوْا مُجْرِمِينَ (٥٢)

قَالُوا يَا هُودُ مَا جِئْتَنَا بِبَيِّنَةٍ وَمَا نَحْنُ بِتَارِكِي آلِهَتِنَا عَنْ قَوْلِكَ وَمَا نَحْنُ لَكَ بِمُؤْمِنِينَ (٥٣)

إِنْ نَقُولُ إِلَّا اعْتَرَاكَ بَعْضُ آلِهَتِنَا بِسُوءٍ قَالَ إِنِّي أُشْهِدُ اللَّهَ وَاشْهَدُوا أَنِّي بَرِيءٌ مِمَّا تُشْرِكُونَ (٥٤)

مِنْ دُونِهِ فَكِيدُونِي جَمِيعًا ثُمَّ لَا تُنْظِرُونِ (٥٥)

إِنِّي تَوَكَّلْتُ عَلَى اللَّهِ رَبِّي وَرَبِّكُمْ مَا مِنْ دَابَّةٍ إِلَّا هُوَ آخِذٌ بِنَاصِيَتِهَا إِنَّ رَبِّي عَلَى صِرَاطٍ مُسْتَقِيمٍ (٥٦)

فَإِنْ تَوَلَّوْا فَقَدْ أَبْلَغْتُكُمْ مَا أُرْسِلْتُ بِهِ إِلَيْكُمْ وَيَسْتَخْلِفُ رَبِّي قَوْمًا غَيْرَكُمْ وَلَا تَضُرُّونَهُ شَيْئًا إِنَّ رَبِّي عَلَى كُلِّ شَيْءٍ حَفِيظٌ (٥٧)

وَلَمَّا جَاءَ أَمْرُنَا نَجَّيْنَا هُودًا وَالَّذِينَ آمَنُوا مَعَهُ بِرَحْمَةٍ مِنَّا وَنَجَّيْنَاهُمْ مِنْ عَذَابٍ غَلِيظٍ (٥٨)

living creature but He grasps it by its forelock. Surely my Lord is on the right path.

11:57. But if you turn away, then indeed I have delivered to you that with which I am sent to you. And my Lord will bring another people in your place, and you cannot do Him any harm. Surely my Lord is the Preserver of all things.

11:58. And when Our commandment came to pass, We delivered Hud and those who believed with him with mercy from Us; and We delivered them from a hard chastisement.

11:59. And such were 'Ad. They denied the messages of their Lord, and disobeyed His messengers and followed the bidding of every insolent opposer (of truth).

11:60. And they were overtaken by a curse in this world and on the day of Resurrection. Now surely 'Ad disbelieved in their Lord. Now surely, away with 'Ad, the people of Hud!

***

11:61. And to Thamud (We sent) their brother Salih. He said: O my people, serve Allah, you have no god other than Him. He brought you forth from the earth and made you dwell in it, so ask forgiveness of Him, then turn to Him. Surely my Lord is Nigh, Answering.

11:62. They said: O Salih, thou wast among us a centre of (our) hopes before this. Dost thou forbid us to worship what our fathers worshipped? And surely we are in grave doubt about that to which thou callest us.

11:63. He said: O my people, see you if I have clear proof from my Lord and He has granted me mercy from Himself who will then help me against Allah, if I disobey Him? So you would add to me naught but perdition.

11:64. And, O my people, this is Allah's she-camel, a sign for you, so leave her

وَتِلْكَ عَادٌ جَحَدُوا بِآيَاتِ رَبِّهِمْ وَعَصَوْا رُسُلَهُ وَاتَّبَعُوا أَمْرَ كُلِّ جَبَّارٍ عَنِيدٍ (٥٩)

وَأُتْبِعُوا فِي هَذِهِ الدُّنْيَا لَعْنَةً وَيَوْمَ الْقِيَامَةِ أَلَا إِنَّ عَادًا كَفَرُوا رَبَّهُمْ أَلَا بُعْدًا لِعَادٍ قَوْمِ هُودٍ (٦٠)

وَإِلَى ثَمُودَ أَخَاهُمْ صَالِحًا قَالَ يَا قَوْمِ اعْبُدُوا اللَّهَ مَا لَكُمْ مِنْ إِلَهٍ غَيْرُهُ هُوَ أَنْشَأَكُمْ مِنَ الْأَرْضِ وَاسْتَعْمَرَكُمْ فِيهَا فَاسْتَغْفِرُوهُ ثُمَّ تُوبُوا إِلَيْهِ إِنَّ رَبِّي قَرِيبٌ مُجِيبٌ (٦١)

قَالُوا يَا صَالِحُ قَدْ كُنْتَ فِينَا مَرْجُوًّا قَبْلَ هَذَا أَتَنْهَانَا أَنْ نَعْبُدَ مَا يَعْبُدُ آبَاؤُنَا وَإِنَّنَا لَفِي شَكٍّ مِمَّا تَدْعُونَا إِلَيْهِ مُرِيبٍ (٦٢)

قَالَ يَا قَوْمِ أَرَأَيْتُمْ إِنْ كُنْتُ عَلَى بَيِّنَةٍ مِنْ رَبِّي وَآتَانِي مِنْهُ رَحْمَةً فَمَنْ يَنْصُرُنِي مِنَ اللَّهِ إِنْ عَصَيْتُهُ فَمَا تَزِيدُونَنِي غَيْرَ تَخْسِيرٍ (٦٣)

وَيَا قَوْمِ هَذِهِ نَاقَةُ اللَّهِ لَكُمْ آيَةً فَذَرُوهَا تَأْكُلْ فِي أَرْضِ اللَّهِ وَلَا تَمَسُّوهَا بِسُوءٍ فَيَأْخُذَكُمْ عَذَابٌ قَرِيبٌ (٦٤)

فَعَقَرُوهَا فَقَالَ تَمَتَّعُوا فِي دَارِكُمْ ثَلَاثَةَ أَيَّامٍ ذَلِكَ وَعْدٌ غَيْرُ مَكْذُوبٍ (٦٥)

فَلَمَّا جَاءَ أَمْرُنَا نَجَّيْنَا صَالِحًا وَالَّذِينَ آمَنُوا مَعَهُ بِرَحْمَةٍ مِنَّا وَمِنْ خِزْيِ يَوْمِئِذٍ إِنَّ رَبَّكَ هُوَ الْقَوِيُّ الْعَزِيزُ (٦٦)

وَأَخَذَ الَّذِينَ ظَلَمُوا الصَّيْحَةُ فَأَصْبَحُوا فِي دِيَارِهِمْ جَاثِمِينَ (٦٧)

كَأَنْ لَمْ يَغْنَوْا فِيهَا أَلَا إِنَّ ثَمُودَ كَفَرُوا رَبَّهُمْ أَلَا بُعْدًا لِثَمُودَ (٦٨)

وَلَقَدْ جَاءَتْ رُسُلُنَا إِبْرَاهِيمَ بِالْبُشْرَى

to pasture on Allah's earth and touch her not with evil, lest a near chastisement overtake you.

11:65. But they hamstrung her, so he said: Enjoy yourselves in your houses for three days. That is a promise not to be belied.

11:66. So when Our commandment came to pass, We saved Salih and those who believed with him by mercy from Us from the disgrace of that day. Surely thy Lord -- He is the Strong, the Mighty.

11:67. And the cry overtook those who did wrong, so they were motionless bodies in their abodes,

11:68. As though they had never dwelt therein. Now surely Thamud disbelieved in their Lord. So away with Thamud!

* * *

11:69. And certainly Our messengers came to Abraham with good news. They said: Peace! Peace! said he, And he made no delay in bringing a roasted calf.

11:70. But when he saw that their hands reached not to it, he mistrusted them and conceived fear of them. They said: Fear not we have been sent to Lot's people.

11:71. And his wife was standing (by), so she wondered. Then We gave her the good news of Isaac, and beyond Isaac, of Jacob.

11:72. She said; O wonder! Shall I bear a son when I am an extremely old woman, and this my husband an extremely old man? This is a wonderful thing indeed!

11:73. They said: Wonderest thou at Allah's commandment? The mercy of Allah and His blessings on you, O people of the house. Surely He is Praised, Glorious.

11:74. So when feat departed from Abraham and good news came to him, he began to plead with Us for Lot's

قَالُوا سَلَامًا قَالَ سَلَامٌ فَمَا لَبِثَ أَنْ جَاءَ بِعِجْلٍ حَنِيذٍ (٦٩)

فَلَمَّا رَأَى أَيْدِيَهُمْ لَا تَصِلُ إِلَيْهِ نَكِرَهُمْ وَأَوْجَسَ مِنْهُمْ خِيفَةً قَالُوا لَا تَخَفْ إِنَّا أُرْسِلْنَا إِلَى قَوْمِ لُوطٍ (٧٠)

وَامْرَأَتُهُ قَائِمَةٌ فَضَحِكَتْ فَبَشَّرْنَاهَا بِإِسْحَاقَ وَمِنْ وَرَاءِ إِسْحَاقَ يَعْقُوبَ (٧١)

قَالَتْ يَا وَيْلَتَى أَأَلِدُ وَأَنَا عَجُوزٌ وَهَذَا بَعْلِي شَيْخًا إِنَّ هَذَا لَشَيْءٌ عَجِيبٌ (٧٢)

قَالُوا أَتَعْجَبِينَ مِنْ أَمْرِ اللَّهِ رَحْمَةُ اللَّهِ وَبَرَكَاتُهُ عَلَيْكُمْ أَهْلَ الْبَيْتِ إِنَّهُ حَمِيدٌ مَجِيدٌ (٧٣)

فَلَمَّا ذَهَبَ عَنْ إِبْرَاهِيمَ الرَّوْعُ وَجَاءَتْهُ الْبُشْرَى يُجَادِلُنَا فِي قَوْمِ لُوطٍ (٧٤)

إِنَّ إِبْرَاهِيمَ لَحَلِيمٌ أَوَّاهٌ مُنِيبٌ (٧٥)

يَا إِبْرَاهِيمُ أَعْرِضْ عَنْ هَذَا إِنَّهُ قَدْ جَاءَ أَمْرُ رَبِّكَ وَإِنَّهُمْ آتِيهِمْ عَذَابٌ غَيْرُ مَرْدُودٍ (٧٦)

وَلَمَّا جَاءَتْ رُسُلُنَا لُوطًا سِيءَ بِهِمْ وَضَاقَ بِهِمْ ذَرْعًا وَقَالَ هَذَا يَوْمٌ عَصِيبٌ (٧٧)

وَجَاءَهُ قَوْمُهُ يُهْرَعُونَ إِلَيْهِ وَمِنْ قَبْلُ كَانُوا يَعْمَلُونَ السَّيِّئَاتِ قَالَ يَا قَوْمِ هَؤُلَاءِ بَنَاتِي هُنَّ أَطْهَرُ لَكُمْ فَاتَّقُوا اللَّهَ وَلَا تُخْزُونِ فِي ضَيْفِي أَلَيْسَ مِنْكُمْ رَجُلٌ رَشِيدٌ (٧٨)

قَالُوا لَقَدْ عَلِمْتَ مَا لَنَا فِي بَنَاتِكَ مِنْ حَقٍّ وَإِنَّكَ لَتَعْلَمُ مَا نُرِيدُ (٧٩)

قَالَ لَوْ أَنَّ لِي بِكُمْ قُوَّةً أَوْ آوِي إِلَى رُكْنٍ شَدِيدٍ (٨٠)

قَالُوا يَا لُوطُ إِنَّا رُسُلُ رَبِّكَ لَنْ

people.

11:75. Surely Abraham was forbearing, tender-hearted, oft-returning (to Allah).

11:76. O Abraham, cease from this. Surely the decree of thy Lord has gone forth and there must come to them a chastisement that cannot be averted.

11:77. And when Our messengers came to Lot, he was grieved for them, and he was unable to protect them, and said: This is a distressful day!

11:78. And his people came to him, (as if) driven on towards him, and they were used to the doing of evil deeds before. He said: O my people, these are my daughters -- they are purer for you; so guard against (the punishment of) Allah and disgrace me not about my guests. Is there not among you any right-minded man?

11:79. They said: Certainly thou knowest that we have no claim on thy daughters, and thou knowest what we desire.

11:80. He said: Would that I had the power to repel you! -- rather I shall have recourse to a strong support.

11:81. They said: O Lot, we are the messengers of thy Lord. They shall not reach thee. So travel with thy people for a part of the night and let none of you turn back except thy wife. Surely whatsoever befalls them shall befall her. Surely their appointed time is the morning. Is not the morning nigh?

11:82. So when Our decree came to pass, We turned them upside down, and rained on them stones, as decreed, one after another,

11:83. Marked (for punishment) with thy Lord. And it is not far off from the wrongdoers.

* * *

11:84. And to Midian (We sent) their brother Shu'aib. He said: O my people, serve Allah, you have no other god save Him. And give not short measure

يَصِلُوا إِلَيْكَ فَأَسْرِ بِأَهْلِكَ بِقِطْعٍ مِنَ اللَّيْلِ وَلَا يَلْتَفِتْ مِنْكُمْ أَحَدٌ إِلَّا امْرَأَتَكَ إِنَّهُ مُصِيبُهَا مَا أَصَابَهُمْ إِنَّ مَوْعِدَهُمُ الصُّبْحُ أَلَيْسَ الصُّبْحُ بِقَرِيبٍ (٨١) فَلَمَّا جَاءَ أَمْرُنَا جَعَلْنَا عَالِيَهَا سَافِلَهَا وَأَمْطَرْنَا عَلَيْهَا حِجَارَةً مِنْ سِجِّيلٍ مَنْضُودٍ (٨٢) مُسَوَّمَةً عِنْدَ رَبِّكَ وَمَا هِيَ مِنَ الظَّالِمِينَ بِبَعِيدٍ (٨٣) وَإِلَى مَدْيَنَ أَخَاهُمْ شُعَيْبًا قَالَ يَا قَوْمِ اعْبُدُوا اللَّهَ مَا لَكُمْ مِنْ إِلَهٍ غَيْرُهُ وَلَا تَنْقُصُوا الْمِكْيَالَ وَالْمِيزَانَ إِنِّي أَرَاكُمْ بِخَيْرٍ وَإِنِّي أَخَافُ عَلَيْكُمْ عَذَابَ يَوْمٍ مُحِيطٍ (٨٤) وَيَا قَوْمِ أَوْفُوا الْمِكْيَالَ وَالْمِيزَانَ بِالْقِسْطِ وَلَا تَبْخَسُوا النَّاسَ أَشْيَاءَهُمْ وَلَا تَعْثَوْا فِي الْأَرْضِ مُفْسِدِينَ (٨٥) بَقِيَّتُ اللَّهِ خَيْرٌ لَكُمْ إِنْ كُنْتُمْ مُؤْمِنِينَ وَمَا أَنَا عَلَيْكُمْ بِحَفِيظٍ (٨٦) قَالُوا يَا شُعَيْبُ أَصَلَاتُكَ تَأْمُرُكَ أَنْ نَتْرُكَ مَا يَعْبُدُ آبَاؤُنَا أَوْ أَنْ نَفْعَلَ فِي أَمْوَالِنَا مَا نَشَاءُ إِنَّكَ لَأَنْتَ الْحَلِيمُ الرَّشِيدُ (٨٧) قَالَ يَا قَوْمِ أَرَأَيْتُمْ إِنْ كُنْتُ عَلَى بَيِّنَةٍ مِنْ رَبِّي وَرَزَقَنِي مِنْهُ رِزْقًا حَسَنًا وَمَا أُرِيدُ أَنْ أُخَالِفَكُمْ إِلَى مَا أَنْهَاكُمْ عَنْهُ إِنْ أُرِيدُ إِلَّا الْإِصْلَاحَ مَا اسْتَطَعْتُ وَمَا تَوْفِيقِي إِلَّا بِاللَّهِ عَلَيْهِ تَوَكَّلْتُ وَإِلَيْهِ أُنِيبُ (٨٨) وَيَا قَوْمِ لَا يَجْرِمَنَّكُمْ شِقَاقِي أَنْ يُصِيبَكُمْ مِثْلُ مَا أَصَابَ قَوْمَ نُوحٍ أَوْ قَوْمَ هُودٍ أَوْ قَوْمَ صَالِحٍ وَمَا قَوْمُ لُوطٍ مِنْكُمْ بِبَعِيدٍ (٨٩)

and weight. I see you in prosperity, and I fear for you the chastisement of an all-encompassing day:

11:85. And, O my people, give full measure and weight justly, and defraud not men of their things, and act not corruptly in the land, making mischief:

11:86. What remains with Allah is better for you, if you are believers. And I am not a keeper over you.

11:87. They said: O Shu'aib, does thy prayer enjoin thee that we should forsake what our fathers worshipped or that we should not do what we please with regard to our property? Forsooth thou art the forbearing, the right-directing one!

11:88. He said: O my people, see you if I have a dear proof from my Lord and He has given me a goodly sustenance from Himself. And I desire not to act in opposition to you, in that which I forbid you. I desire nothing but reform, so far as I am able. And with none but Allah is the direction of my affair to a right issue. In Him I trust and to Him I turn.

11:89. And, O my people, let not opposition to me make you guilty so that there may befall you the like of that which befell the people of Noah, or the people of Hud, or the people of Salih. Nor are the people of Lot far off from you.

11:90. And ask forgiveness of your Lord, then turn to Him. Surely my Lord is Merciful, Loving-kind.

11:91. They said; O Shu'aib we understand not much of what thou sayest and surely we see thee to be weak among us. And were it not for thy family, we would surely stone thee, and thou art not mighty against us.

11:92. He said; O my people, is my family more esteemed by you than Allah? And you neglect Him as a thing cast behind your backs! Surely my

وَاسْتَغْفِرُوا رَبَّكُمْ ثُمَّ تُوبُوا إِلَيْهِ إِنَّ رَبِّي رَحِيمٌ وَدُودٌ (٩٠)

قَالُوا يَا شُعَيْبُ مَا نَفْقَهُ كَثِيرًا مِمَّا تَقُولُ وَإِنَّا لَنَرَاكَ فِينَا ضَعِيفًا وَلَوْلَا رَهْطُكَ لَرَجَمْنَاكَ وَمَا أَنْتَ عَلَيْنَا بِعَزِيزٍ (٩١)

قَالَ يَا قَوْمِ أَرَهْطِي أَعَزُّ عَلَيْكُمْ مِنَ اللَّهِ وَاتَّخَذْتُمُوهُ وَرَاءَكُمْ ظِهْرِيًّا إِنَّ رَبِّي بِمَا تَعْمَلُونَ مُحِيطٌ (٩٢)

وَيَا قَوْمِ اعْمَلُوا عَلَى مَكَانَتِكُمْ إِنِّي عَامِلٌ سَوْفَ تَعْلَمُونَ مَنْ يَأْتِيهِ عَذَابٌ يُخْزِيهِ وَمَنْ هُوَ كَاذِبٌ وَارْتَقِبُوا إِنِّي مَعَكُمْ رَقِيبٌ (٩٣)

وَلَمَّا جَاءَ أَمْرُنَا نَجَّيْنَا شُعَيْبًا وَالَّذِينَ آمَنُوا مَعَهُ بِرَحْمَةٍ مِنَّا وَأَخَذَتِ الَّذِينَ ظَلَمُوا الصَّيْحَةُ فَأَصْبَحُوا فِي دِيَارِهِمْ جَاثِمِينَ (٩٤)

كَأَنْ لَمْ يَغْنَوْا فِيهَا أَلَا بُعْدًا لِمَدْيَنَ كَمَا بَعِدَتْ ثَمُودُ (٩٥)

وَلَقَدْ أَرْسَلْنَا مُوسَى بِآيَاتِنَا وَسُلْطَانٍ مُبِينٍ (٩٦)

إِلَى فِرْعَوْنَ وَمَلَئِهِ فَاتَّبَعُوا أَمْرَ فِرْعَوْنَ وَمَا أَمْرُ فِرْعَوْنَ بِرَشِيدٍ (٩٧)

يَقْدُمُ قَوْمَهُ يَوْمَ الْقِيَامَةِ فَأَوْرَدَهُمُ النَّارَ وَبِئْسَ الْوِرْدُ الْمَوْرُودُ (٩٨)

وَأُتْبِعُوا فِي هَذِهِ لَعْنَةً وَيَوْمَ الْقِيَامَةِ بِئْسَ الرِّفْدُ الْمَرْفُودُ (٩٩)

ذَلِكَ مِنْ أَنْبَاءِ الْقُرَى نَقُصُّهُ عَلَيْكَ مِنْهَا قَائِمٌ وَحَصِيدٌ (١٠٠)

وَمَا ظَلَمْنَاهُمْ وَلَكِنْ ظَلَمُوا أَنْفُسَهُمْ فَمَا أَغْنَتْ عَنْهُمْ آلِهَتُهُمُ الَّتِي يَدْعُونَ مِنْ دُونِ اللَّهِ مِنْ شَيْءٍ لَمَّا جَاءَ أَمْرُ رَبِّكَ وَمَا زَادُوهُمْ غَيْرَ تَتْبِيبٍ

Lord encompasses what you do.

11:93. And, O my people, act according to your ability, I too am acting. You will come to know soon who it is on whom will light the punishment that will disgrace him, and who it is that is a liar. And watch, surely I too am watching with you.

11:94. And when Our decree came to pass, We delivered Shu'aib and those who believed with him by mercy from Us. And the cry overtook those who were iniquitous, so they were motionless bodies in their abodes,

11:95. As though they had never dwelt in them. So away with Midian, just as Thamud perished!

***

11:96. And certainly We sent Moses with Our signs and a clear authority,

11:97. To Pharaoh and his chiefs, but they followed the bidding of Pharaoh; and Pharaoh's bidding was not right-directing.

11:98. He will lead his people on the day of Resurrection, and bring them down to the Fire. And evil the place to which they are brought!

11:99. And they are overtaken by a curse in this (world), and on the day of Resurrection. Evil the gift which shall be given!

11:100. This is an account of the towns which we relate to thee. Of them are some that stand and (others) mown down.

11:101. And We wronged them not but they wronged themselves. And their gods whom they called upon besides Allah availed them naught when the decree of thy Lord came to pass. And they added to them naught but ruin.

11:102. And such is the punishment of thy Lord, when He punishes the towns while they are iniquitous. Surely His punishment is painful, severe.

11:103. Surely there is a sign in this for him who fears the chastisement of the

(١٠١) وَكَذَلِكَ أَخْذُ رَبِّكَ إِذَا أَخَذَ الْقُرَى وَهِيَ ظَالِمَةٌ إِنَّ أَخْذَهُ أَلِيمٌ شَدِيدٌ

(١٠٢) إِنَّ فِي ذَلِكَ لَآيَةً لِّمَنْ خَافَ عَذَابَ الْآخِرَةِ ذَلِكَ يَوْمٌ مَّجْمُوعٌ لَّهُ النَّاسُ وَذَلِكَ يَوْمٌ مَّشْهُودٌ (١٠٣) وَمَا نُؤَخِّرُهُ إِلَّا لِأَجَلٍ مَّعْدُودٍ (١٠٤) يَوْمَ يَأْتِ لَا تَكَلَّمُ نَفْسٌ إِلَّا بِإِذْنِهِ فَمِنْهُمْ شَقِيٌّ وَسَعِيدٌ (١٠٥) فَأَمَّا الَّذِينَ شَقُوا فَفِي النَّارِ لَهُمْ فِيهَا زَفِيرٌ وَشَهِيقٌ (١٠٦) خَالِدِينَ فِيهَا مَا دَامَتِ السَّمَوَاتُ وَالْأَرْضُ إِلَّا مَا شَاءَ رَبُّكَ إِنَّ رَبَّكَ فَعَّالٌ لِّمَا يُرِيدُ (١٠٧) وَأَمَّا الَّذِينَ سُعِدُوا فَفِي الْجَنَّةِ خَالِدِينَ فِيهَا مَا دَامَتِ السَّمَوَاتُ وَالْأَرْضُ إِلَّا مَا شَاءَ رَبُّكَ عَطَاءً غَيْرَ مَجْذُوذٍ (١٠٨) فَلَا تَكُ فِي مِرْيَةٍ مِّمَّا يَعْبُدُ هَؤُلَاءِ مَا يَعْبُدُونَ إِلَّا كَمَا يَعْبُدُ آبَاؤُهُم مِّن قَبْلُ وَإِنَّا لَمُوَفُّوهُمْ نَصِيبَهُمْ غَيْرَ مَنقُوصٍ (١٠٩) وَلَقَدْ آتَيْنَا مُوسَى الْكِتَابَ فَاخْتُلِفَ فِيهِ وَلَوْلَا كَلِمَةٌ سَبَقَتْ مِن رَّبِّكَ لَقُضِيَ بَيْنَهُمْ وَإِنَّهُمْ لَفِي شَكٍّ مِّنْهُ مُرِيبٍ (١١٠) وَإِنَّ كُلًّا لَّمَّا لَيُوَفِّيَنَّهُمْ رَبُّكَ أَعْمَالَهُمْ إِنَّهُ بِمَا يَعْمَلُونَ خَبِيرٌ (١١١) فَاسْتَقِمْ كَمَا أُمِرْتَ وَمَن تَابَ مَعَكَ وَلَا تَطْغَوْا إِنَّهُ بِمَا تَعْمَلُونَ بَصِيرٌ (١١٢) وَلَا تَرْكَنُوا إِلَى الَّذِينَ ظَلَمُوا فَتَمَسَّكُمُ النَّارُ وَمَا لَكُم مِّن دُونِ اللَّهِ مِنْ أَوْلِيَاءَ

Hereafter. That is a day on which people will be gathered together, and that is a day to be witnessed.

11:104. And We delay it not but for an appointed term.

11:105. On the day when it comes, no soul will speak except by His permission; so (some) of them will be unhappy and (others) happy.

11:106. Then as for those who are unhappy, they will be in the Fire; for them therein will be sighing and groaning --

11:107. Abiding therein so long as the heavens and the earth endure, except as thy Lord please. Surely thy Lord is Doer of what He intends.

11:108. And as for those who are made happy, they will be in the Garden abiding therein so long as the heavens and the earth endure, except as thy Lord please -- a gift never to be cut off.

11:109. So be not thou in doubt as to that which these worship. They worship only as their fathers worshipped before. And surely We shall pay them in full their due undiminished.

***

11:110. And We certainly gave the Book to Moses, but differences arose therein. And had not a word gone forth from thy Lord, the matter would have been decided between them. And they are surely in a disquieting doubt about it.

11:111. And thy Lord will surely pay back to all their deeds in full. He indeed is Aware of what they do.

11:112. Continue then in the right way as thou art commanded, as also (should) those who turn (to Allah) with thee. And be not inordinate, (O men). Surely He is Seer of what you do.

11:113. And incline not to those who do wrong, lest the fire touch you; and you have no protectors besides Allah, then you would not be helped.

ثُمَّ لَا تُنْصَرُونَ (١١٣)
وَأَقِمِ الصَّلَاةَ طَرَفَيِ النَّهَارِ وَزُلَفًا مِنَ اللَّيْلِ إِنَّ الْحَسَنَاتِ يُذْهِبْنَ السَّيِّئَاتِ ذَلِكَ ذِكْرَى لِلذَّاكِرِينَ (١١٤)
وَاصْبِرْ فَإِنَّ اللَّهَ لَا يُضِيعُ أَجْرَ الْمُحْسِنِينَ (١١٥)
فَلَوْلَا كَانَ مِنَ الْقُرُونِ مِنْ قَبْلِكُمْ أُولُو بَقِيَّةٍ يَنْهَوْنَ عَنِ الْفَسَادِ فِي الْأَرْضِ إِلَّا قَلِيلًا مِمَّنْ أَنْجَيْنَا مِنْهُمْ وَاتَّبَعَ الَّذِينَ ظَلَمُوا مَا أُتْرِفُوا فِيهِ وَكَانُوا مُجْرِمِينَ (١١٦)
وَمَا كَانَ رَبُّكَ لِيُهْلِكَ الْقُرَى بِظُلْمٍ وَأَهْلُهَا مُصْلِحُونَ (١١٧)
وَلَوْ شَاءَ رَبُّكَ لَجَعَلَ النَّاسَ أُمَّةً وَاحِدَةً وَلَا يَزَالُونَ مُخْتَلِفِينَ (١١٨)
إِلَّا مَنْ رَحِمَ رَبُّكَ وَلِذَلِكَ خَلَقَهُمْ وَتَمَّتْ كَلِمَةُ رَبِّكَ لَأَمْلَأَنَّ جَهَنَّمَ مِنَ الْجِنَّةِ وَالنَّاسِ أَجْمَعِينَ (١١٩)
وَكُلًّا نَقُصُّ عَلَيْكَ مِنْ أَنْبَاءِ الرُّسُلِ مَا نُثَبِّتُ بِهِ فُؤَادَكَ وَجَاءَكَ فِي هَذِهِ الْحَقُّ وَمَوْعِظَةٌ وَذِكْرَى لِلْمُؤْمِنِينَ (١٢٠)
وَقُلْ لِلَّذِينَ لَا يُؤْمِنُونَ اعْمَلُوا عَلَى مَكَانَتِكُمْ إِنَّا عَامِلُونَ (١٢١)
وَانْتَظِرُوا إِنَّا مُنْتَظِرُونَ (١٢٢)
وَلِلَّهِ غَيْبُ السَّمَاوَاتِ وَالْأَرْضِ وَإِلَيْهِ يُرْجَعُ الْأَمْرُ كُلُّهُ فَاعْبُدْهُ وَتَوَكَّلْ عَلَيْهِ وَمَا رَبُّكَ بِغَافِلٍ عَمَّا تَعْمَلُونَ (١٢٣)

11:114. And keep up prayer at the two ends of the day and in the first hours of the night. Surely good deeds take away evil deeds. This is a reminder for the mindful.

11:115. And be patient, for surely Allah wastes not the reward of the doers of good.

11:116. Why were there not then among the generations before you those possessing understanding, forbidding mischief in the earth, except a few among them whom We delivered? And the unjust pursued the enjoyment of plenty, and they were guilty.

11:117. And thy Lord would not destroy the towns unjustly, while their people acted well.

11:118. And if thy Lord had pleased, He would have made people a single nation. And they cease not to differ,

11:119. Except those on whom thy Lord has mercy; and for this did He create them. And the word of thy Lord is fulfilled: I shall fill hell with jinn and men, all together.

11:120. And all We relate to thee of the account of the messengers is to strengthen thy heart therewith. And in this has come to thee the truth and an admonition and a reminder for the believers.

11:121. And say to those who believe not: Act according to your power, surely we too are acting

11:122. And wait, surely we are waiting (also).

11:123. And Allah's is the unseen in the heavens and the earth, and to Him the whole affair will be returned. So serve Him and put thy trust in Him. And thy Lord is not heedless of what you do.

12. Joseph

In the name of Allah, the Beneficent, the Merciful.

12. Joseph

12:1. I, Allah, am the Seer. These are the verses of the Book that makes manifest.

12:2. Surely We have revealed it -- an Arabic Qur'an -- that you may understand.

12:3. We narrate to thee the best of narratives, in that We have revealed to thee this Qur'an, though before this thou wast of those unaware.

12:4. When Joseph said to his father: O my father, I saw eleven stars and the sun and the moon -- I saw them making obeisance to me.

12:5. He said: O my son, relate not thy dream to thy brethren, lest they devise a plan against thee. The devil indeed is an open enemy to man.

12:6. And thus will thy Lord choose thee and teach thee the interpretation of sayings, and make His favour complete to thee and to the Children of Jacob, as He made it complete before to thy fathers, Abraham and Isaac. Surely thy Lord is Knowing, Wise.

* * *

12:7. Verily in Joseph and his brethren there are signs for the inquirers.

12:8. When they said: Certainly Joseph and his brother are dearer to our father than we, though we are a (strong) company. Surely our father is in manifest error --

12:9. Slay Joseph or banish him to some (other) land, so that your father's regard may be exclusively for you, and after that you may be a righteous people.

12:10. A speaker among them said: Slay not Joseph, but, if you are going to do anything, cast him down to the bottom of the well. Some of the travellers may pick him up.

12:11. They said: O our father, why dost thou not trust us with Joseph, and surely we are his sincere well-wishers?

12:12. Send him with us to-morrow that he may enjoy himself and play and we shall surely guard him well.

12. Joseph

12:13. He said: Indeed it grieves me that you should take him away and I fear lest the wolf devour him, while you are heedless of him.

12:14. They said: If the wolf should devour him, while we are a (strong) company, we should then certainly be losers.

12:15. So when they took him away and agreed to put him down at the bottom of the pit, We revealed to him: Thou wilt certainly inform them of this affair of theirs while they perceive not.

12:16. And they came to their father at nightfall, weeping.

12:17. They said: O our father, we went off racing one with another and left Joseph by our goods, so the wolf devoured him. And thou wilt not believe us, though we are truthful.

12:18. And they came with false blood on his shirt. He said: Nay, your souls have made a matter light for you. So patience is goodly. And Allah is He Whose help is sought against what you describe.

12:19. And there came travellers, and they sent their water-drawer and he let down his bucket. He said: O good news! This is a youth. And they concealed him as an article of merchandise, and Allah was Cognizant of what they did.

12:20. And they sold him for a small price, a few pieces of silver, and they showed no desire for him.

* * *

12:21. And the Egyptian who bought him said to his wife: Make his stay honourable. Maybe he will be useful to us, or we may adopt him as a son. And thus We established Joseph in the land, and that We might teach him the interpretation of sayings. And Allah has full control over His affair, but most people know not.

12:22. And when he attained his maturity, We gave him wisdom and

غَافِلُونَ (١٣)
قَالُوا لَئِنْ أَكَلَهُ الذِّئْبُ وَنَحْنُ عُصْبَةٌ إِنَّا إِذًا لَخَاسِرُونَ (١٤)
فَلَمَّا ذَهَبُوا بِهِ وَأَجْمَعُوا أَنْ يَجْعَلُوهُ فِي غَيَابَةِ الْجُبِّ وَأَوْحَيْنَا إِلَيْهِ لَتُنَبِّئَنَّهُمْ بِأَمْرِهِمْ هَذَا وَهُمْ لَا يَشْعُرُونَ (١٥)
وَجَاءُوا أَبَاهُمْ عِشَاءً يَبْكُونَ (١٦)
قَالُوا يَا أَبَانَا إِنَّا ذَهَبْنَا نَسْتَبِقُ وَتَرَكْنَا يُوسُفَ عِنْدَ مَتَاعِنَا فَأَكَلَهُ الذِّئْبُ وَمَا أَنْتَ بِمُؤْمِنٍ لَنَا وَلَوْ كُنَّا صَادِقِينَ (١٧)
وَجَاءُوا عَلَى قَمِيصِهِ بِدَمٍ كَذِبٍ قَالَ بَلْ سَوَّلَتْ لَكُمْ أَنْفُسُكُمْ أَمْرًا فَصَبْرٌ جَمِيلٌ وَاللَّهُ الْمُسْتَعَانُ عَلَى مَا تَصِفُونَ (١٨)
وَجَاءَتْ سَيَّارَةٌ فَأَرْسَلُوا وَارِدَهُمْ فَأَدْلَى دَلْوَهُ قَالَ يَا بُشْرَى هَذَا غُلَامٌ وَأَسَرُّوهُ بِضَاعَةً وَاللَّهُ عَلِيمٌ بِمَا يَعْمَلُونَ (١٩)
وَشَرَوْهُ بِثَمَنٍ بَخْسٍ دَرَاهِمَ مَعْدُودَةٍ وَكَانُوا فِيهِ مِنَ الزَّاهِدِينَ (٢٠)
وَقَالَ الَّذِي اشْتَرَاهُ مِنْ مِصْرَ لِامْرَأَتِهِ أَكْرِمِي مَثْوَاهُ عَسَى أَنْ يَنْفَعَنَا أَوْ نَتَّخِذَهُ وَلَدًا وَكَذَلِكَ مَكَّنَّا لِيُوسُفَ فِي الْأَرْضِ وَلِنُعَلِّمَهُ مِنْ تَأْوِيلِ الْأَحَادِيثِ وَاللَّهُ غَالِبٌ عَلَى أَمْرِهِ وَلَكِنَّ أَكْثَرَ النَّاسِ لَا يَعْلَمُونَ (٢١)
وَلَمَّا بَلَغَ أَشُدَّهُ آتَيْنَاهُ حُكْمًا وَعِلْمًا وَكَذَلِكَ نَجْزِي الْمُحْسِنِينَ (٢٢)
وَرَاوَدَتْهُ الَّتِي هُوَ فِي بَيْتِهَا عَنْ نَفْسِهِ وَغَلَّقَتِ الْأَبْوَابَ وَقَالَتْ هَيْتَ لَكَ قَالَ مَعَاذَ اللَّهِ إِنَّهُ رَبِّي أَحْسَنَ مَثْوَايَ إِنَّهُ لَا يُفْلِحُ الظَّالِمُونَ (٢٣)

12. Joseph

knowledge. And thus do We reward the doers of good.

12:23. And she in whose house he was, sought to seduce him, and made fast the doors and said: Come. He said: Allah forbid! Surely my Lord made good my abode. The wrongdoers never prosper.

12:24. And certainly she desired him, and he would have desired her, were it nor that he had seen the manifest evidence of his Lord. Thus (it was) that We might turn away from him evil and indecency. Surely he was one of Our chosen servants.

12:25. And they raced with one another to the door, and she rent his shirt from behind, and they met her husband at the door. She said: What is the punishment for one who intends evil to thy wife, except imprisonment or a painful chastisement?

12:26. He said: She sought to seduce me. And a witness of her own family bore witness: If his shirt is rent in front, she speaks the truth and he is of the liars.

12:27. And if his shirt is rent behind, she tells a lie and he is of the truthful.

12:28. So when he saw his shirt rent behind, he said: Surely it is a device of you women. Your device is indeed great!

12:29. O Joseph, turn aside from this. And (O my wife), ask forgiveness for thy sin. Surely thou art one of the sinful.

***

12:30. And women in the city said: The chief's wife seeks to seduce her slave. He has indeed affected her deeply with (his) love. Truly we see her in manifest error.

12:31. So when she heard of their device, she sent for them and prepared for them a repast, and gave each of them a knife; and said (to Joseph): Come out to them. So when they saw

وَلَقَدْ هَمَّتْ بِهِ وَهَمَّ بِهَا لَوْلَا أَنْ رَأَى بُرْهَانَ رَبِّهِ كَذَلِكَ لِنَصْرِفَ عَنْهُ السُّوءَ وَالْفَحْشَاءَ إِنَّهُ مِنْ عِبَادِنَا الْمُخْلَصِينَ (٢٤)
وَاسْتَبَقَا الْبَابَ وَقَدَّتْ قَمِيصَهُ مِنْ دُبُرٍ وَأَلْفَيَا سَيِّدَهَا لَدَى الْبَابِ قَالَتْ مَا جَزَاءُ مَنْ أَرَادَ بِأَهْلِكَ سُوءًا إِلَّا أَنْ يُسْجَنَ أَوْ عَذَابٌ أَلِيمٌ (٢٥)
قَالَ هِيَ رَاوَدَتْنِي عَنْ نَفْسِي وَشَهِدَ شَاهِدٌ مِنْ أَهْلِهَا إِنْ كَانَ قَمِيصُهُ قُدَّ مِنْ قُبُلٍ فَصَدَقَتْ وَهُوَ مِنَ الْكَاذِبِينَ (٢٦)
وَإِنْ كَانَ قَمِيصُهُ قُدَّ مِنْ دُبُرٍ فَكَذَبَتْ وَهُوَ مِنَ الصَّادِقِينَ (٢٧)
فَلَمَّا رَأَى قَمِيصَهُ قُدَّ مِنْ دُبُرٍ قَالَ إِنَّهُ مِنْ كَيْدِكُنَّ إِنَّ كَيْدَكُنَّ عَظِيمٌ (٢٨)
يُوسُفُ أَعْرِضْ عَنْ هَذَا وَاسْتَغْفِرِي لِذَنْبِكِ إِنَّكِ كُنْتِ مِنَ الْخَاطِئِينَ (٢٩)
وَقَالَ نِسْوَةٌ فِي الْمَدِينَةِ امْرَأَةُ الْعَزِيزِ تُرَاوِدُ فَتَاهَا عَنْ نَفْسِهِ قَدْ شَغَفَهَا حُبًّا إِنَّا لَنَرَاهَا فِي ضَلَالٍ مُبِينٍ (٣٠)
فَلَمَّا سَمِعَتْ بِمَكْرِهِنَّ أَرْسَلَتْ إِلَيْهِنَّ وَأَعْتَدَتْ لَهُنَّ مُتَّكَأً وَآتَتْ كُلَّ وَاحِدَةٍ مِنْهُنَّ سِكِّينًا وَقَالَتِ اخْرُجْ عَلَيْهِنَّ فَلَمَّا رَأَيْنَهُ أَكْبَرْنَهُ وَقَطَّعْنَ أَيْدِيَهُنَّ وَقُلْنَ حَاشَ لِلَّهِ مَا هَذَا بَشَرًا إِنْ هَذَا إِلَّا مَلَكٌ كَرِيمٌ (٣١)
قَالَتْ فَذَلِكُنَّ الَّذِي لُمْتُنَّنِي فِيهِ وَلَقَدْ رَاوَدْتُهُ عَنْ نَفْسِهِ فَاسْتَعْصَمَ وَلَئِنْ لَمْ يَفْعَلْ مَا آمُرُهُ لَيُسْجَنَنَّ وَلَيَكُونًا مِنَ الصَّاغِرِينَ (٣٢)
قَالَ رَبِّ السِّجْنُ أَحَبُّ إِلَيَّ مِمَّا يَدْعُونَنِي إِلَيْهِ وَإِلَّا تَصْرِفْ عَنِّي كَيْدَهُنَّ أَصْبُ إِلَيْهِنَّ وَأَكُنْ مِنَ

him, they deemed him great, and cut their hands (in amazement), and said: Holy Allah! This is not a mortal! This is but a noble angel.

12:32. She said: This is he about whom you blamed me. And certainly I sought to seduce him, but he was firm in continence. And if he do not what I bid him, he shall certainly be imprisoned, and he shall certainly be of the abject.

12:33. He said: My Lord, the prison is dearer to me than that to which they invite me. And if Thou turn not away their device from me, I shall yearn towards them and be of the ignorant.

12:34. So his Lord accepted his prayer and turned away their device from him. Surely He is the Hearer, the Knower.

12:35. Then it occurred to them after they had seen the signs that they should imprison him till a time.

* * *

12:36. And two youths entered the prison with him. One of them said: I saw myself pressing wine. And the other said: I saw myself carrying bread on my head, of which birds were eating. Inform us of its interpretation surely we see thee to be of the doers of good.

12:37. He said: The food with which you are fed shall not come to you, but I shall inform you of its' interpretation before it comes to you. This is of what my Lord has taught me. Surely I have forsaken the religion of a people who believe not in Allah, and are deniers of the Hereafter.

12:38. And I follow the religion of my fathers, Abraham and Isaac and Jacob. It beseems us not to associate aught with Allah. This is by Allah's grace upon us and on mankind, but most people give not thanks.

12:39. O my two fellow-prisoners, are sundry lords better or Allah the One, the Supreme?

12:40. You serve not besides Him but names which you have named, you and your fathers Allah has sent down no authority for them. Judgment is only Allah's. He has commanded that you serve none but Him. This is the right religion, but most people know not.

12:41. O my two fellow-prisoners, as for one of you, he will serve wine for his lord to drink; and as for the other, he will be crucified, so that the birds will eat from his head. The matter is decreed concerning which you inquired.

12:42. And he said to him whom he knew would be delivered of the two Remember me with thy lord. But the devil caused him to forget mentioning (it) to his lord, so he remained in the prison a few years.

***

12:43. And the King said: I have seen seven fat kine which seven lean ones devoured; -- and seven green ears and (seven) others dry. O chiefs, explain to me my dream, if you can interpret the dream.

12:44. They said: Confused dreams, and we know not the interpretation of dreams.

12:45. And of the two, he who had found deliverance and remembered after a long time said: I will inform you of its interpretation, so send me.

12:46. Joseph, O truthful one, explain to us seven fat kine which seven lean ones devoured, and seven green ears and (seven) others dry, that I may go back to the people so that they may know.

12:47. He said: You shall sow for seven years as usual, then that which you reap, leave it in its ear, except a little which you eat.

12:48. Then after that will come seven years of hardship, which will eat away all you have beforehand stored for them, except a little which you have

ذِكْرَ رَبِّهِ فَلَبِثَ فِي السِّجْنِ بِضْعَ سِنِينَ (٤٢)
وَقَالَ الْمَلِكُ إِنِّي أَرَى سَبْعَ بَقَرَاتٍ سِمَانٍ يَأْكُلُهُنَّ سَبْعٌ عِجَافٌ وَسَبْعَ سُنْبُلَاتٍ خُضْرٍ وَأُخَرَ يَابِسَاتٍ يَا أَيُّهَا الْمَلَأُ أَفْتُونِي فِي رُؤْيَايَ إِنْ كُنْتُمْ لِلرُّؤْيَا تَعْبُرُونَ (٤٣)
قَالُوا أَضْغَاثُ أَحْلَامٍ وَمَا نَحْنُ بِتَأْوِيلِ الْأَحْلَامِ بِعَالِمِينَ (٤٤)
وَقَالَ الَّذِي نَجَا مِنْهُمَا وَادَّكَرَ بَعْدَ أُمَّةٍ أَنَا أُنَبِّئُكُمْ بِتَأْوِيلِهِ فَأَرْسِلُونِ (٤٥)
يُوسُفُ أَيُّهَا الصِّدِّيقُ أَفْتِنَا فِي سَبْعِ بَقَرَاتٍ سِمَانٍ يَأْكُلُهُنَّ سَبْعٌ عِجَافٌ وَسَبْعِ سُنْبُلَاتٍ خُضْرٍ وَأُخَرَ يَابِسَاتٍ لَعَلِّي أَرْجِعُ إِلَى النَّاسِ لَعَلَّهُمْ يَعْلَمُونَ (٤٦)
قَالَ تَزْرَعُونَ سَبْعَ سِنِينَ دَأَبًا فَمَا حَصَدْتُمْ فَذَرُوهُ فِي سُنْبُلِهِ إِلَّا قَلِيلًا مِمَّا تَأْكُلُونَ (٤٧)
ثُمَّ يَأْتِي مِنْ بَعْدِ ذَلِكَ سَبْعٌ شِدَادٌ يَأْكُلْنَ مَا قَدَّمْتُمْ لَهُنَّ إِلَّا قَلِيلًا مِمَّا تُحْصِنُونَ (٤٨)
ثُمَّ يَأْتِي مِنْ بَعْدِ ذَلِكَ عَامٌ فِيهِ يُغَاثُ النَّاسُ وَفِيهِ يَعْصِرُونَ (٤٩)
وَقَالَ الْمَلِكُ ائْتُونِي بِهِ فَلَمَّا جَاءَهُ الرَّسُولُ قَالَ ارْجِعْ إِلَى رَبِّكَ فَاسْأَلْهُ مَا بَالُ النِّسْوَةِ اللَّاتِي قَطَّعْنَ أَيْدِيَهُنَّ إِنَّ رَبِّي بِكَيْدِهِنَّ عَلِيمٌ (٥٠)
قَالَ مَا خَطْبُكُنَّ إِذْ رَاوَدْتُنَّ يُوسُفَ عَنْ نَفْسِهِ قُلْنَ حَاشَ لِلَّهِ مَا عَلِمْنَا عَلَيْهِ مِنْ سُوءٍ قَالَتِ امْرَأَةُ الْعَزِيزِ الْآنَ حَصْحَصَ الْحَقُّ أَنَا رَاوَدْتُهُ عَنْ نَفْسِهِ وَإِنَّهُ لَمِنَ الصَّادِقِينَ (٥١)
ذَلِكَ لِيَعْلَمَ أَنِّي لَمْ أَخُنْهُ بِالْغَيْبِ وَأَنَّ

12. Joseph

preserved.

12:49. Then after that will come a year in which people will have rain and in which they will press (grapes).

***

12:50. And the king said: Bring him to me. So when the messenger came to him, he said: Go back to thy lord and ask him, what is the case of the women who cut their hands. Surely my Lord knows their device.

12:51. (The king) said: What was your affair when you sought to seduce Joseph? They said: Holy Allah! We knew of no evil on his part. The chief's wife said: Now has the truth become manifest. I sought to seduce him and he is surely of the truthful.

12:52. This is that he might know that I have not been unfaithful to him in secret, and that Allah guides not the device of the unfaithful.

***

12:53. And I call not myself sinless surely (man's) self is wont to command evil, except those on whom my Lord has mercy. Surely my Lord is Forgiving, Merciful.

12:54. And the king said: Bring him to me, I will choose him for myself. So when he talked with him, he said: Surely thou art in our presence to-day dignified, trusted.

12:55. He said: Place me (in authority) over the treasures of the land; surely I am a good keeper, knowing well.

12:56. And thus did We give to Joseph power in the land -- he had mastery in it wherever he liked. We bestow Our mercy on whom We please, and We waste not the reward of the doers of good.

12:57. And certainly the reward of the Hereafter is better for those who believe and guard against evil.

***

12:58. And Joseph's brethren came and went in to him, and he knew them,

اللَّهَ لَا يَهْدِي كَيْدَ الْخَائِنِينَ (٥٢)
وَمَا أُبَرِّئُ نَفْسِي إِنَّ النَّفْسَ لَأَمَّارَةٌ بِالسُّوءِ إِلَّا مَا رَحِمَ رَبِّي إِنَّ رَبِّي غَفُورٌ رَحِيمٌ (٥٣)
وَقَالَ الْمَلِكُ ائْتُونِي بِهِ أَسْتَخْلِصْهُ لِنَفْسِي فَلَمَّا كَلَّمَهُ قَالَ إِنَّكَ الْيَوْمَ لَدَيْنَا مَكِينٌ أَمِينٌ (٥٤)
قَالَ اجْعَلْنِي عَلَى خَزَائِنِ الْأَرْضِ إِنِّي حَفِيظٌ عَلِيمٌ (٥٥)
وَكَذَلِكَ مَكَّنَّا لِيُوسُفَ فِي الْأَرْضِ يَتَبَوَّأُ مِنْهَا حَيْثُ يَشَاءُ نُصِيبُ بِرَحْمَتِنَا مَنْ نَشَاءُ وَلَا نُضِيعُ أَجْرَ الْمُحْسِنِينَ (٥٦)
وَلَأَجْرُ الْآخِرَةِ خَيْرٌ لِلَّذِينَ آمَنُوا وَكَانُوا يَتَّقُونَ (٥٧)
وَجَاءَ إِخْوَةُ يُوسُفَ فَدَخَلُوا عَلَيْهِ فَعَرَفَهُمْ وَهُمْ لَهُ مُنْكِرُونَ (٥٨)
وَلَمَّا جَهَّزَهُمْ بِجَهَازِهِمْ قَالَ ائْتُونِي بِأَخٍ لَكُمْ مِنْ أَبِيكُمْ أَلَا تَرَوْنَ أَنِّي أُوفِي الْكَيْلَ وَأَنَا خَيْرُ الْمُنْزِلِينَ (٥٩)
فَإِنْ لَمْ تَأْتُونِي بِهِ فَلَا كَيْلَ لَكُمْ عِنْدِي وَلَا تَقْرَبُونِ (٦٠)
قَالُوا سَنُرَاوِدُ عَنْهُ أَبَاهُ وَإِنَّا لَفَاعِلُونَ (٦١)
وَقَالَ لِفِتْيَانِهِ اجْعَلُوا بِضَاعَتَهُمْ فِي رِحَالِهِمْ لَعَلَّهُمْ يَعْرِفُونَهَا إِذَا انْقَلَبُوا إِلَى أَهْلِهِمْ لَعَلَّهُمْ يَرْجِعُونَ (٦٢)
فَلَمَّا رَجَعُوا إِلَى أَبِيهِمْ قَالُوا يَا أَبَانَا مُنِعَ مِنَّا الْكَيْلُ فَأَرْسِلْ مَعَنَا أَخَانَا نَكْتَلْ وَإِنَّا لَهُ لَحَافِظُونَ (٦٣)
قَالَ هَلْ آمَنُكُمْ عَلَيْهِ إِلَّا كَمَا أَمِنْتُكُمْ عَلَى أَخِيهِ مِنْ قَبْلُ فَاللَّهُ خَيْرٌ حَافِظًا وَهُوَ أَرْحَمُ الرَّاحِمِينَ (٦٤)

while they recognized him not.

12:59. And when he furnished them with their provision, he said: Bring to me a brother of yours from your father. See you not that I give full measure and that I am the best of hosts?

12:60. But if you bring him not to me, you shall have no measure (of corn) from me, nor shall you come near me.

12:61. They said: We shall strive to make his father yield about him, and we are sure to do (it).

12:62. And he said to his servants: Put their money into their bags that they may recognize it when they go back to their family, so that they may come back.

12:63. So when they returned to their father, they said: O our father, the measure is withheld from us, so send with us our brother that we may get the measure, and we will surely guard him.

12:64. He said: Can I trust you with him, except as I trusted you with his brother before. So Allah is the Best Keeper, and He is the most Merciful of those who show mercy.

12:65. And when they opened their goods, they found their money returned to them. They said: O our father, what (more) can we desire? This is our property returned to us, and we shall bring corn for our family and guard our brother, and have in addition the measure of a camel-load. This is an easy measure.

12:66. He said: I will by no means send him with you, until you give me a firm covenant in Allah's name that you will bring him back to me, unless you are completely surrounded. And when they gave him their covenant, he said: Allah is Guardian over what we say.

12:67. And he said: O my sons, enter not by one gate but enter by different gates. And I can avail you naught against Allah. Judgment is only Allah's.

وَلَمَّا فَتَحُوا مَتَاعَهُمْ وَجَدُوا بِضَاعَتَهُمْ رُدَّتْ إِلَيْهِمْ قَالُوا يَا أَبَانَا مَا نَبْغِي هَذِهِ بِضَاعَتُنَا رُدَّتْ إِلَيْنَا وَنَمِيرُ أَهْلَنَا وَنَحْفَظُ أَخَانَا وَنَزْدَادُ كَيْلَ بَعِيرٍ ذَلِكَ كَيْلٌ يَسِيرٌ (٦٥)

قَالَ لَنْ أُرْسِلَهُ مَعَكُمْ حَتَّى تُؤْتُونِ مَوْثِقًا مِنَ اللَّهِ لَتَأْتُنَّنِي بِهِ إِلَّا أَنْ يُحَاطَ بِكُمْ فَلَمَّا آتَوْهُ مَوْثِقَهُمْ قَالَ اللَّهُ عَلَى مَا نَقُولُ وَكِيلٌ (٦٦)

وَقَالَ يَا بَنِيَّ لَا تَدْخُلُوا مِنْ بَابٍ وَاحِدٍ وَادْخُلُوا مِنْ أَبْوَابٍ مُتَفَرِّقَةٍ وَمَا أُغْنِي عَنْكُمْ مِنَ اللَّهِ مِنْ شَيْءٍ إِنِ الْحُكْمُ إِلَّا لِلَّهِ عَلَيْهِ تَوَكَّلْتُ وَعَلَيْهِ فَلْيَتَوَكَّلِ الْمُتَوَكِّلُونَ (٦٧)

وَلَمَّا دَخَلُوا مِنْ حَيْثُ أَمَرَهُمْ أَبُوهُمْ مَا كَانَ يُغْنِي عَنْهُمْ مِنَ اللَّهِ مِنْ شَيْءٍ إِلَّا حَاجَةً فِي نَفْسِ يَعْقُوبَ قَضَاهَا وَإِنَّهُ لَذُو عِلْمٍ لِمَا عَلَّمْنَاهُ وَلَكِنَّ أَكْثَرَ النَّاسِ لَا يَعْلَمُونَ (٦٨)

وَلَمَّا دَخَلُوا عَلَى يُوسُفَ آوَى إِلَيْهِ أَخَاهُ قَالَ إِنِّي أَنَا أَخُوكَ فَلَا تَبْتَئِسْ بِمَا كَانُوا يَعْمَلُونَ (٦٩)

فَلَمَّا جَهَّزَهُمْ بِجَهَازِهِمْ جَعَلَ السِّقَايَةَ فِي رَحْلِ أَخِيهِ ثُمَّ أَذَّنَ مُؤَذِّنٌ أَيَّتُهَا الْعِيرُ إِنَّكُمْ لَسَارِقُونَ (٧٠)

قَالُوا وَأَقْبَلُوا عَلَيْهِمْ مَاذَا تَفْقِدُونَ (٧١)

قَالُوا نَفْقِدُ صُوَاعَ الْمَلِكِ وَلِمَنْ جَاءَ بِهِ حِمْلُ بَعِيرٍ وَأَنَا بِهِ زَعِيمٌ (٧٢)

قَالُوا تَاللَّهِ لَقَدْ عَلِمْتُمْ مَا جِئْنَا لِنُفْسِدَ فِي الْأَرْضِ وَمَا كُنَّا سَارِقِينَ (٧٣)

قَالُوا فَمَا جَزَاؤُهُ إِنْ كُنْتُمْ كَاذِبِينَ (٧٤)

قَالُوا جَزَاؤُهُ مَنْ وُجِدَ فِي رَحْلِهِ فَهُوَ

On Him I rely, and on Him let the reliant rely.

12:68. And when they entered as their father had bidden them, it availed them naught against Allah, but (it was only) a desire in the soul of Jacob, which he satisfied. And surely he was possessed of knowledge, because We had given him knowledge, but most people know not.

* * *

12:69. And when they went in to Joseph, he lodged his brother with himself saying: I am thy brother, so grieve not at what they do.

12:70. Then when he furnished them with their provision, (some one) placed the drinking-cup in his brother's bag. Then a crier cried out: O caravan, you are surely thieves!

12:71. They said, while they turned towards them: What is it that you miss?

12:72. They said: We miss the king's drinking-cup, and he who brings it shall have a camel-load, and I am responsible for it.

12:73. They said: By Allah! You know for certain that we have not come to make mischief in the land, and we are not thieves.

12:74. They said: But what is the penalty for this, if you are liars?

12:75. They said: The penalty for this -- the person in whose bag it is found, he himself is the penalty for it. Thus do we punish the wrongdoers.

12:76. So he began with their sacks before the sack of his brother, then be brought it out from his brother's sack. Thus did We plan for the sake of Joseph. He could not take his brother under the king's law, unless Allah pleased. We raise in degree whom We please. And above every one possessed of knowledge is the All-Knowing One.

12:77. They said: If he steal, a brother of his did indeed steal before. But Joseph

جَزَاؤُهُ كَذَٰلِكَ نَجْزِي الظَّالِمِينَ (٧٥) فَبَدَأَ بِأَوْعِيَتِهِمْ قَبْلَ وِعَاءِ أَخِيهِ ثُمَّ اسْتَخْرَجَهَا مِنْ وِعَاءِ أَخِيهِ كَذَٰلِكَ كِدْنَا لِيُوسُفَ مَا كَانَ لِيَأْخُذَ أَخَاهُ فِي دِينِ الْمَلِكِ إِلَّا أَنْ يَشَاءَ اللَّهُ نَرْفَعُ دَرَجَاتٍ مَنْ نَشَاءُ وَفَوْقَ كُلِّ ذِي عِلْمٍ عَلِيمٌ (٧٦)

قَالُوا إِنْ يَسْرِقْ فَقَدْ سَرَقَ أَخٌ لَهُ مِنْ قَبْلُ فَأَسَرَّهَا يُوسُفُ فِي نَفْسِهِ وَلَمْ يُبْدِهَا لَهُمْ قَالَ أَنْتُمْ شَرٌّ مَكَانًا وَاللَّهُ أَعْلَمُ بِمَا تَصِفُونَ (٧٧) قَالُوا يَا أَيُّهَا الْعَزِيزُ إِنَّ لَهُ أَبًا شَيْخًا كَبِيرًا فَخُذْ أَحَدَنَا مَكَانَهُ إِنَّا نَرَاكَ مِنَ الْمُحْسِنِينَ (٧٨) قَالَ مَعَاذَ اللَّهِ أَنْ نَأْخُذَ إِلَّا مَنْ وَجَدْنَا مَتَاعَنَا عِنْدَهُ إِنَّا إِذًا لَظَالِمُونَ (٧٩) فَلَمَّا اسْتَيْأَسُوا مِنْهُ خَلَصُوا نَجِيًّا قَالَ كَبِيرُهُمْ أَلَمْ تَعْلَمُوا أَنَّ أَبَاكُمْ قَدْ أَخَذَ عَلَيْكُمْ مَوْثِقًا مِنَ اللَّهِ وَمِنْ قَبْلُ مَا فَرَّطْتُمْ فِي يُوسُفَ فَلَنْ أَبْرَحَ الْأَرْضَ حَتَّىٰ يَأْذَنَ لِي أَبِي أَوْ يَحْكُمَ اللَّهُ لِي وَهُوَ خَيْرُ الْحَاكِمِينَ (٨٠) ارْجِعُوا إِلَىٰ أَبِيكُمْ فَقُولُوا يَا أَبَانَا إِنَّ ابْنَكَ سَرَقَ وَمَا شَهِدْنَا إِلَّا بِمَا عَلِمْنَا وَمَا كُنَّا لِلْغَيْبِ حَافِظِينَ (٨١) وَاسْأَلِ الْقَرْيَةَ الَّتِي كُنَّا فِيهَا وَالْعِيرَ الَّتِي أَقْبَلْنَا فِيهَا وَإِنَّا لَصَادِقُونَ (٨٢) قَالَ بَلْ سَوَّلَتْ لَكُمْ أَنْفُسُكُمْ أَمْرًا فَصَبْرٌ جَمِيلٌ عَسَى اللَّهُ أَنْ يَأْتِيَنِي بِهِمْ جَمِيعًا إِنَّهُ هُوَ الْعَلِيمُ الْحَكِيمُ (٨٣) وَتَوَلَّىٰ عَنْهُمْ وَقَالَ يَا أَسَفَىٰ عَلَىٰ يُوسُفَ وَابْيَضَّتْ عَيْنَاهُ مِنَ الْحُزْنِ فَهُوَ كَظِيمٌ (٨٤)

kept it secret in his soul, and disclosed it not to them. He said: You are in an evil condition, and Allah knows best what you state.

12:78. They said: O chief, he has a father, a very old man, so take one of us in his place. Surely we see thee to he of the doers of good.

12:79. He said: Allah forbid that we should seize other than him with whom we found our property, for then surely we should be unjust

* * *

12:80. So when they despaired of him, they conferred together privately. The eldest of them said: Know you not that your father took from you a covenant in Allah's name, and how you fell short of your duty about Joseph before? So I shall not leave this land, until my father permits me or Allah decides for me; and He is the Best of the judges.

12:81. Go back to your father and say: O our father, thy son committed theft. And we bear witness only to what we know, and we could not keep watch over the unseen.

12:82. And ask the town where we were, and the caravan with which we proceeded. And surely we are truthful.

12:83. He said: Nay, your souls have contrived an affair for you, so patience is good. Maybe Allah will bring them together to me. Surely He is the Knowing, the Wise.

12:84. And he ruined away from them, and said: O my sorrow for Joseph! And his eyes were filled (with tears) on account of the grief, then he repressed (grief).

12:85, They said: By Allah! Thou wilt not cease remembering Joseph till thou art a prey to disease or thou art of those who perish.

12:86 He said: I complain of my grief and sorrow only to Allah, and I know from Allah what you know not.

12:87. O my sons, go and inquire about

12. Joseph

Joseph and his brother; and despair not of Allah's mercy. Surely none despairs of Allah's mercy except the disbelieving people.

12:88. So when they came to him, they said: O chief, distress has afflicted us and our family, and we have brought scanty money, so give us full measure and be charitable to us. Surely Allah rewards the charitable.

12:89. He said: Do you know how you treated Joseph and his brother, when you were ignorant?

12:90. They said: Art thou indeed Joseph? He said: I am Joseph and this is my brother; Allah has indeed been gracious to us. Surely he who keeps his duty and is patient -- Allah never wastes the reward of the doers of good.

12:91. They said: By Allah! Allah has indeed chosen thee over us, and we were certainly sinners.

12:92. He said: No reproof be against you this day. Allah may forgive you, and He is the most Merciful of those who show mercy.

12:93. Take this my shirt and cast it before my father's face -- he will come to know. And come to me with all your family.

***

12:94. And when the caravan left (Egypt); their father said Surely I scent (the power of) Joseph, if you call me not a dotard.

12:95. They said: By Allah thou art surely in thy old error.

12:96. Then when the bearer of good news came, he cast it before his face so he became certain. He said: Did I not say to you that I know from Allah what you know not?

12:97. They said: O Our father, ask forgiveness of our sins for us, surely we are sinners.

12:98. He said I shall ask forgiveness for you of my Lord. Surely He is the Forgiving, the Merciful.

أَعْلَمُ مِنَ اللَّهِ مَا لَا تَعْلَمُونَ (٩٦) قَالُوا يَا أَبَانَا اسْتَغْفِرْ لَنَا ذُنُوبَنَا إِنَّا كُنَّا خَاطِئِينَ (٩٧) قَالَ سَوْفَ أَسْتَغْفِرُ لَكُمْ رَبِّي إِنَّهُ هُوَ الْغَفُورُ الرَّحِيمُ (٩٨) فَلَمَّا دَخَلُوا عَلَى يُوسُفَ آوَى إِلَيْهِ أَبَوَيْهِ وَقَالَ ادْخُلُوا مِصْرَ إِنْ شَاءَ اللَّهُ آمِنِينَ (٩٩) وَرَفَعَ أَبَوَيْهِ عَلَى الْعَرْشِ وَخَرُّوا لَهُ سُجَّدًا وَقَالَ يَا أَبَتِ هَذَا تَأْوِيلُ رُؤْيَايَ مِنْ قَبْلُ قَدْ جَعَلَهَا رَبِّي حَقًّا وَقَدْ أَحْسَنَ بِي إِذْ أَخْرَجَنِي مِنَ السِّجْنِ وَجَاءَ بِكُمْ مِنَ الْبَدْوِ مِنْ بَعْدِ أَنْ نَزَغَ الشَّيْطَانُ بَيْنِي وَبَيْنَ إِخْوَتِي إِنَّ رَبِّي لَطِيفٌ لِمَا يَشَاءُ إِنَّهُ هُوَ الْعَلِيمُ الْحَكِيمُ (١٠٠) رَبِّ قَدْ آتَيْتَنِي مِنَ الْمُلْكِ وَعَلَّمْتَنِي مِنْ تَأْوِيلِ الْأَحَادِيثِ فَاطِرَ السَّمَاوَاتِ وَالْأَرْضِ أَنْتَ وَلِيِّي فِي الدُّنْيَا وَالْآخِرَةِ تَوَفَّنِي مُسْلِمًا وَأَلْحِقْنِي بِالصَّالِحِينَ (١٠١) ذَلِكَ مِنْ أَنْبَاءِ الْغَيْبِ نُوحِيهِ إِلَيْكَ وَمَا كُنْتَ لَدَيْهِمْ إِذْ أَجْمَعُوا أَمْرَهُمْ وَهُمْ يَمْكُرُونَ (١٠٢) وَمَا أَكْثَرُ النَّاسِ وَلَوْ حَرَصْتَ بِمُؤْمِنِينَ (١٠٣) وَمَا تَسْأَلُهُمْ عَلَيْهِ مِنْ أَجْرٍ إِنْ هُوَ إِلَّا ذِكْرٌ لِلْعَالَمِينَ (١٠٤) وَكَأَيِّنْ مِنْ آيَةٍ فِي السَّمَاوَاتِ وَالْأَرْضِ يَمُرُّونَ عَلَيْهَا وَهُمْ عَنْهَا مُعْرِضُونَ (١٠٥) وَمَا يُؤْمِنُ أَكْثَرُهُمْ بِاللَّهِ إِلَّا وَهُمْ مُشْرِكُونَ (١٠٦) أَفَأَمِنُوا أَنْ تَأْتِيَهُمْ غَاشِيَةٌ مِنْ عَذَابِ

12:99. Then when they went in to Joseph, he lodged his parents with himself and said: Enter Egypt in safety, if Allah please.

12:100. And he raised his parents on the throne, and they fell prostrate for his sake. And he said: O my father, this is the significance of my vision of old -- my Lord has made it true. And He was indeed kind to me, when He brought me forth from the prison, and brought you from the desert after the devil had sown dissensions between me and my brethren. Surely my Lord is Benignant to whom He pleases. Truly He is the Knowing, the Wise.

12:101. My Lord, Thou hast given me of the kingdom and taught me of the interpretation of sayings. Originator of the heavens and the earth, Thou art my Friend in this world and the Hereafter. Make me die in submission and join me with the righteous.

12:102. This is of the announcements relating to the unseen (which) We reveal to thee, and thou wast not with them when they resolved upon their affair, and they were devising plans.

12:103. And most men believe not, though thou desirest it eagerly.

12:104. And thou askest them no reward for it. It is nothing but a reminder for all mankind.

* * *

12:105. And how many a sign in the heavens and the earth do they pass by! yet they turn away from it.

12:106. And most of them believe not in Allah without associating others (with Him).

12:107. Do they then feel secure from the coming to them of an all-encompassing chastisement from Allah or from the coming to them of the hour suddenly, while they perceive not?

12:108. Say: This is my way: I call to Allah, with certain knowledge -- I and those who follow me. And glory be to

Allah! and I am not of the polytheists.

12:109. And We sent not before thee any but men, from the people of the towns, to whom We sent revelation. Have they not then travelled in the land and seen what was the end of those before them? And certainly the abode of the Hereafter is best for those who keep their duty. Do you not then understand?

12:110. Until, when the messengers despaired and (the people) thought that they were told a lie, Our help came to them, and whom. We pleased was delivered. And Our punishment is not averted from the guilty people.

12:111. In their histories there is certainly a lesson for men of understanding. It is not a narrative which could be forged, but a verification of what is before it, and a distinct explanation of all things, and a guide and a mercy to a people who believe.

13. The Thunder

In the name of Allah, the Beneficent, the Merciful.

13:1. 1, Allah, am the Best Knower, the Seer. These are verses of the Book. And that which is revealed to thee from thy Lord is the Truth, but most people believe nor.

13:2. Allah is He who raised the heavens without any pillars that you can see, and He is established on the Throne of Power, and He made the sun and the moon subservient (to you). Each one runs to an appointed term. He regulates the affair, making clear the messages that you may be certain of the meeting with your Lord.

13:3. And He it is who spread the earth, and made in it firm mountains and rivers. And of all fruits He has made in it pairs, two (of every kind). He makes

١٣ـ سورة الرعد

بِسْمِ اللَّهِ الرَّحْمَنِ الرَّحِيمِ
المر تِلْكَ آيَاتُ الْكِتَابِ وَالَّذِي أُنْزِلَ إِلَيْكَ مِنْ رَبِّكَ الْحَقُّ وَلَكِنَّ أَكْثَرَ النَّاسِ لَا يُؤْمِنُونَ (١)
اللَّهُ الَّذِي رَفَعَ السَّمَاوَاتِ بِغَيْرِ عَمَدٍ تَرَوْنَهَا ثُمَّ اسْتَوَى عَلَى الْعَرْشِ وَسَخَّرَ الشَّمْسَ وَالْقَمَرَ كُلٌّ يَجْرِي لِأَجَلٍ مُسَمًّى يُدَبِّرُ الْأَمْرَ يُفَصِّلُ الْآيَاتِ لَعَلَّكُمْ بِلِقَاءِ رَبِّكُمْ تُوقِنُونَ (٢)
وَهُوَ الَّذِي مَدَّ الْأَرْضَ وَجَعَلَ فِيهَا رَوَاسِيَ وَأَنْهَارًا وَمِنْ كُلِّ الثَّمَرَاتِ جَعَلَ فِيهَا زَوْجَيْنِ اثْنَيْنِ يُغْشِي اللَّيْلَ النَّهَارَ إِنَّ فِي ذَلِكَ لَآيَاتٍ لِقَوْمٍ يَتَفَكَّرُونَ (٣)

13. The Thunder

the night cover the day. Surely there are signs in this for a people who reflect.

13:4. And in the earth are tracts side by side, and gardens of vines, and corn, and palm-trees growing from one root and distinct roots they are watered with one water; and We make some of them to excel others in fruit. Surely there are signs in this for a people who understand.

13:5. And if thou wonderest, then wondrous is their saying: When we are dust, shall we then be raised in a new creation? These are they who disbelieve in their Lord, and these have chains on their necks, and they are the companions of the Fire; in it they will abide.

13:6. And they ask thee to hasten on the evil before the good, and indeed there have been exemplary punishments before them. And surely thy Lord is full of forgiveness for mankind notwithstanding their iniquity. And surely thy Lord is Severe in requiting.

13:7. And those who disbelieve say: Why has not a sign been sent down to him from his Lord? Thou art only a warner and for every people a guide.

***

13:8. Allah knows what every female beats, and that of which the wombs fall short of completion and that which they grow. And everything with Him has a measure.

13:9. The Knower of the Unseen and the seen, the Great, the Most High.

13:10. Alike (to Him) among you is he who conceals (the) word and he who speaks openly, and he who hides himself by night and (who) goes forth by day.

13:11. For him are (angels) guarding the consequences (of his deeds), before him and behind him, who guard him by Allah's command. Surely Allah changes not the condition of a people,

وَفِي الْأَرْضِ قِطَعٌ مُتَجَاوِرَاتٌ وَجَنَّاتٌ مِنْ أَعْنَابٍ وَزَرْعٌ وَنَخِيلٌ صِنْوَانٌ وَغَيْرُ صِنْوَانٍ يُسْقَى بِمَاءٍ وَاحِدٍ وَنُفَضِّلُ بَعْضَهَا عَلَى بَعْضٍ فِي الْأُكُلِ إِنَّ فِي ذَلِكَ لَآيَاتٍ لِقَوْمٍ يَعْقِلُونَ (٤)

وَإِنْ تَعْجَبْ فَعَجَبٌ قَوْلُهُمْ أَئِذَا كُنَّا تُرَابًا أَئِنَّا لَفِي خَلْقٍ جَدِيدٍ أُولَئِكَ الَّذِينَ كَفَرُوا بِرَبِّهِمْ وَأُولَئِكَ الْأَغْلَالُ فِي أَعْنَاقِهِمْ وَأُولَئِكَ أَصْحَابُ النَّارِ هُمْ فِيهَا خَالِدُونَ (٥)

وَيَسْتَعْجِلُونَكَ بِالسَّيِّئَةِ قَبْلَ الْحَسَنَةِ وَقَدْ خَلَتْ مِنْ قَبْلِهِمُ الْمَثُلَاتُ وَإِنَّ رَبَّكَ لَذُو مَغْفِرَةٍ لِلنَّاسِ عَلَى ظُلْمِهِمْ وَإِنَّ رَبَّكَ لَشَدِيدُ الْعِقَابِ (٦)

وَيَقُولُ الَّذِينَ كَفَرُوا لَوْلَا أُنْزِلَ عَلَيْهِ آيَةٌ مِنْ رَبِّهِ إِنَّمَا أَنْتَ مُنْذِرٌ وَلِكُلِّ قَوْمٍ هَادٍ (٧)

اللَّهُ يَعْلَمُ مَا تَحْمِلُ كُلُّ أُنْثَى وَمَا تَغِيضُ الْأَرْحَامُ وَمَا تَزْدَادُ وَكُلُّ شَيْءٍ عِنْدَهُ بِمِقْدَارٍ (٨)

عَالِمُ الْغَيْبِ وَالشَّهَادَةِ الْكَبِيرُ الْمُتَعَالِ (٩)

سَوَاءٌ مِنْكُمْ مَنْ أَسَرَّ الْقَوْلَ وَمَنْ جَهَرَ بِهِ وَمَنْ هُوَ مُسْتَخْفٍ بِاللَّيْلِ وَسَارِبٌ بِالنَّهَارِ (١٠)

لَهُ مُعَقِّبَاتٌ مِنْ بَيْنِ يَدَيْهِ وَمِنْ خَلْفِهِ يَحْفَظُونَهُ مِنْ أَمْرِ اللَّهِ إِنَّ اللَّهَ لَا يُغَيِّرُ مَا بِقَوْمٍ حَتَّى يُغَيِّرُوا مَا بِأَنْفُسِهِمْ وَإِذَا أَرَادَ اللَّهُ بِقَوْمٍ سُوءًا فَلَا مَرَدَّ لَهُ وَمَا لَهُمْ مِنْ دُونِهِ مِنْ وَالٍ (١١)

هُوَ الَّذِي يُرِيكُمُ الْبَرْقَ خَوْفًا وَطَمَعًا وَيُنْشِئُ السَّحَابَ الثِّقَالَ (١٢)

وَيُسَبِّحُ الرَّعْدُ بِحَمْدِهِ وَالْمَلَائِكَةُ مِنْ

until they change their own condition. And when Allah intends evil to a people, there is no averting it, and besides Him they have no protector.

13:12. He it is Who shows you the lightning causing feat and hope and (Who) brings up the heavy cloud.

13:13. And the thunder celebrates His praise, and the angels too for awe of Him. And He sends the thunderbolts and smites with them whom He pleases, yet they dispute concerning Allah, and He is Mighty in prowess.

13:14. To Him is due the true prayer. And those to whom they pray besides Him give them no answer, but (they are) like one who stretches forth his two hands towards water that it may reach his mouth, but it will not reach it. And the prayer of the disbelievers is only wasted.

13:15. And whoever is in the heavens and the earth makes obeisance to Allah only, willingly and unwillingly, and their shadows, too, at morn and eve.

13:16. Say: Who is the Lord of the heavens and the earth? Say: Allah. Say: Do you then take besides Him guardians who control no benefit or harm even for themselves? Say: Are the blind and the seeing alike? Or, are darkness and light equal? Or, have they set up with Allah associates who have created creation like His, so that what is created became confused to them? Say: Allah is the Creator of all things, and He is the One, the Supreme.

13:17. He sends down water from the clouds, then watercourses flow according to their measure, and the torrent bears along the swelling foam. And from that which they melt in the fire for the sake of making ornaments or apparatus arises a scum like it. Thus does Allah compare truth and falsehood. Then as for the scum, it passes away as a worthless thing; and

13. The Thunder

as for that which does good to men, it tarries in the earth. Thus does Allah set forth parables.

13:18. For those who respond to their Lord is good. And as for those who respond not to Him, even if they had all that is in the earth and the like thereof with it, they would certainly offer it for a ransom. As for those, theirs is an evil reckoning and their abode is hell; and evil is the resting-place.

* * *

13:19. Is he who knows that what is revealed to thee from thy Lord is the truth like him who is blind? Only men of understanding mind --

13:20. Those who fulfil the pact of Allah, and break not the covenant,

13:21. And those who join that which Allah has bidden to be joined and have awe of their Lord, and fear the evil reckoning.

13:22. And those who are steadfast seeking the pleasure of their Lord, and keep up prayer and spend of that which We have given them, secretly and openly, and repel evil with good; for such is the (happy) issue of the abode --

13:23. Gardens of perpetuity, which they will enter along with those who do good from among their fathers and their spouses and their offspring and the angels will enter in upon them from every gate.

13:24. Peace be to you, because you were constant -- how excellent is then the final Abode!

13:25. And those who break the covenant of Allah after its confirmation, and cut asunder that which Allah has ordered to be joined, and make mischief in the land, for them is the curse, and theirs is the evil end of the Abode.

13:26. Allah amplifies and straitens provision for whom He pleases. And

أُولُو الْأَلْبَابِ (١٩)
الَّذِينَ يُوفُونَ بِعَهْدِ اللَّهِ وَلَا يَنْقُضُونَ الْمِيثَاقَ (٢٠)
وَالَّذِينَ يَصِلُونَ مَا أَمَرَ اللَّهُ بِهِ أَنْ يُوصَلَ وَيَخْشَوْنَ رَبَّهُمْ وَيَخَافُونَ سُوءَ الْحِسَابِ (٢١)
وَالَّذِينَ صَبَرُوا ابْتِغَاءَ وَجْهِ رَبِّهِمْ وَأَقَامُوا الصَّلَاةَ وَأَنْفَقُوا مِمَّا رَزَقْنَاهُمْ سِرًّا وَعَلَانِيَةً وَيَدْرَءُونَ بِالْحَسَنَةِ السَّيِّئَةَ أُولَٰئِكَ لَهُمْ عُقْبَى الدَّارِ (٢٢)
جَنَّاتُ عَدْنٍ يَدْخُلُونَهَا وَمَنْ صَلَحَ مِنْ آبَائِهِمْ وَأَزْوَاجِهِمْ وَذُرِّيَّاتِهِمْ وَالْمَلَائِكَةُ يَدْخُلُونَ عَلَيْهِمْ مِنْ كُلِّ بَابٍ (٢٣)
سَلَامٌ عَلَيْكُمْ بِمَا صَبَرْتُمْ فَنِعْمَ عُقْبَى الدَّارِ (٢٤)
وَالَّذِينَ يَنْقُضُونَ عَهْدَ اللَّهِ مِنْ بَعْدِ مِيثَاقِهِ وَيَقْطَعُونَ مَا أَمَرَ اللَّهُ بِهِ أَنْ يُوصَلَ وَيُفْسِدُونَ فِي الْأَرْضِ أُولَٰئِكَ لَهُمُ اللَّعْنَةُ وَلَهُمْ سُوءُ الدَّارِ (٢٥)
اللَّهُ يَبْسُطُ الرِّزْقَ لِمَنْ يَشَاءُ وَيَقْدِرُ وَفَرِحُوا بِالْحَيَاةِ الدُّنْيَا وَمَا الْحَيَاةُ الدُّنْيَا فِي الْآخِرَةِ إِلَّا مَتَاعٌ (٢٦)
وَيَقُولُ الَّذِينَ كَفَرُوا لَوْلَا أُنْزِلَ عَلَيْهِ آيَةٌ مِنْ رَبِّهِ قُلْ إِنَّ اللَّهَ يُضِلُّ مَنْ يَشَاءُ وَيَهْدِي إِلَيْهِ مَنْ أَنَابَ (٢٧)
الَّذِينَ آمَنُوا وَتَطْمَئِنُّ قُلُوبُهُمْ بِذِكْرِ اللَّهِ أَلَا بِذِكْرِ اللَّهِ تَطْمَئِنُّ الْقُلُوبُ (٢٨)
الَّذِينَ آمَنُوا وَعَمِلُوا الصَّالِحَاتِ طُوبَى لَهُمْ وَحُسْنُ مَآبٍ (٢٩)
كَذَٰلِكَ أَرْسَلْنَاكَ فِي أُمَّةٍ قَدْ خَلَتْ مِنْ قَبْلِهَا أُمَمٌ لِتَتْلُوَ عَلَيْهِمُ الَّذِي أَوْحَيْنَا إِلَيْكَ وَهُمْ يَكْفُرُونَ بِالرَّحْمَٰنِ قُلْ هُوَ رَبِّي لَا إِلَٰهَ إِلَّا هُوَ عَلَيْهِ تَوَكَّلْتُ وَإِلَيْهِ

they rejoice in this world's life. And this world's life, compared with the Hereafter, is only a temporary enjoyment.

***

13:27. And those who disbelieve say: Why is not a sign sent down to him by his Lord? Say: Allah leaves in error whom He pleases, and guides to Himself those who turn (to Him) --

13:28. Those who believe and whose hearts find rest in the remembrance of Allah. Now surely in Allah's remembrance do hearts find rest.

13:29. Those who believe and do good, a good final state is theirs and a goodly return.

13:30. Thus We have sent thee among a nation before which other nations have passed away, that thou mightest recite to them what We have revealed to thee, and (still) they deny the Beneficent. Say: He is my Lord, there is no god but He; in Him do I trust and to Him is my return.

13:31. And if there could be a Qur'an with which the mountains were made to pass away, or the earth were cloven asunder, or the dead were made to speak -- nay, the commandment is wholly Allah's. Do not those who believe know that, if Allah please, He would certainly guide all the people? And as for those who disbelieve, disaster will not cease to afflict them because of what they do, or it will alight close by their abodes, until the promise of Allah come to pass. Surely Allah will not fail in (His) promise.

***

13:32. And messengers before thee were certainly mocked, but I gave respite to those who disbelieved, then I seized them How (awful) was then My requital!

13:33. Is, then, He Who watches every soul as to what it earns? And yet they ascribe partners to Allah! Say: Name

مَتَابٍ (٣٠) وَلَوْ أَنَّ قُرْآنًا سُيِّرَتْ بِهِ الْجِبَالُ أَوْ قُطِّعَتْ بِهِ الْأَرْضُ أَوْ كُلِّمَ بِهِ الْمَوْتَى بَلْ لِلَّهِ الْأَمْرُ جَمِيعًا أَفَلَمْ يَيْأَسِ الَّذِينَ آمَنُوا أَنْ لَوْ يَشَاءُ اللَّهُ لَهَدَى النَّاسَ جَمِيعًا وَلَا يَزَالُ الَّذِينَ كَفَرُوا تُصِيبُهُمْ بِمَا صَنَعُوا قَارِعَةٌ أَوْ تَحُلُّ قَرِيبًا مِنْ دَارِهِمْ حَتَّى يَأْتِيَ وَعْدُ اللَّهِ إِنَّ اللَّهَ لَا يُخْلِفُ الْمِيعَادَ (٣١) وَلَقَدِ اسْتُهْزِئَ بِرُسُلٍ مِنْ قَبْلِكَ فَأَمْلَيْتُ لِلَّذِينَ كَفَرُوا ثُمَّ أَخَذْتُهُمْ فَكَيْفَ كَانَ عِقَابِ (٣٢) أَفَمَنْ هُوَ قَائِمٌ عَلَى كُلِّ نَفْسٍ بِمَا كَسَبَتْ وَجَعَلُوا لِلَّهِ شُرَكَاءَ قُلْ سَمُّوهُمْ أَمْ تُنَبِّئُونَهُ بِمَا لَا يَعْلَمُ فِي الْأَرْضِ أَمْ بِظَاهِرٍ مِنَ الْقَوْلِ بَلْ زُيِّنَ لِلَّذِينَ كَفَرُوا مَكْرُهُمْ وَصُدُّوا عَنِ السَّبِيلِ وَمَنْ يُضْلِلِ اللَّهُ فَمَا لَهُ مِنْ هَادٍ (٣٣) لَهُمْ عَذَابٌ فِي الْحَيَاةِ الدُّنْيَا وَلَعَذَابُ الْآخِرَةِ أَشَقُّ وَمَا لَهُمْ مِنَ اللَّهِ مِنْ وَاقٍ (٣٤) مَثَلُ الْجَنَّةِ الَّتِي وُعِدَ الْمُتَّقُونَ تَجْرِي مِنْ تَحْتِهَا الْأَنْهَارُ أُكُلُهَا دَائِمٌ وَظِلُّهَا تِلْكَ عُقْبَى الَّذِينَ اتَّقَوْا وَعُقْبَى الْكَافِرِينَ النَّارُ (٣٥) وَالَّذِينَ آتَيْنَاهُمُ الْكِتَابَ يَفْرَحُونَ بِمَا أُنْزِلَ إِلَيْكَ وَمِنَ الْأَحْزَابِ مَنْ يُنْكِرُ بَعْضَهُ قُلْ إِنَّمَا أُمِرْتُ أَنْ أَعْبُدَ اللَّهَ وَلَا أُشْرِكَ بِهِ إِلَيْهِ أَدْعُو وَإِلَيْهِ مَآبِ (٣٦) وَكَذَلِكَ أَنْزَلْنَاهُ حُكْمًا عَرَبِيًّا وَلَئِنِ اتَّبَعْتَ أَهْوَاءَهُمْ بَعْدَمَا جَاءَكَ مِنَ الْعِلْمِ مَا لَكَ مِنَ اللَّهِ مِنْ وَلِيٍّ وَلَا وَاقٍ

13. The Thunder

them. Would you inform Him of that which He knows not in the earth, or of an outward saying? Rather, their plan is made fair-seeming to those who disbelieve, and they are kept back from the path. And whom Allah leaves in error, he has no guide.

13:34. For them is chastisement in this world's life, and the chastisement of the Hereafter is certainly more grievous. And they have no protector against Allah.

13:35. A parable of the Garden which is promised to those who keep their duty: Therein flow rivers. Its fruits are perpetual and its plenty. Such is the end for those who keep their duty; and the end for the disbelievers is the Fire.

13:36. And those to whom We have given the Book rejoice in that which has been revealed to thee, and of the confederates are some who deny a part of it. Say: I am commanded only to serve Allah and not associate anything with Him. To Him do I invite (you), and to Him is my return.

13:37. And thus have We revealed it, a true judgment, in Arabic. And if thou follow their low desires after that which has come to thee of knowledge, thou wouldst have against Allah no guardian nor protector.

* * *

13:38. And certainly We sent messengers before thee and appointed for them wives and children. And it is not in (the power of) a messenger to bring a sign except by Allah's permission. For every term there is an appointment.

13:39. Allah effaces what He pleases and establishes (what He pleases), and with Him is the basis of the Book.

13:40. Whether We let thee see part of that which We promise them, or cause thee to die, thine is but the delivery of the message, and Ours to call (them) to account.

(٣٧) وَلَقَدْ أَرْسَلْنَا رُسُلًا مِنْ قَبْلِكَ وَجَعَلْنَا لَهُمْ أَزْوَاجًا وَذُرِّيَّةً وَمَا كَانَ لِرَسُولٍ أَنْ يَأْتِيَ بِآيَةٍ إِلَّا بِإِذْنِ اللَّهِ لِكُلِّ أَجَلٍ كِتَابٌ (٣٨) يَمْحُوا اللَّهُ مَا يَشَاءُ وَيُثْبِتُ وَعِنْدَهُ أُمُّ الْكِتَابِ (٣٩) وَإِنْ مَا نُرِيَنَّكَ بَعْضَ الَّذِي نَعِدُهُمْ أَوْ نَتَوَفَّيَنَّكَ فَإِنَّمَا عَلَيْكَ الْبَلَاغُ وَعَلَيْنَا الْحِسَابُ (٤٠) أَوَلَمْ يَرَوْا أَنَّا نَأْتِي الْأَرْضَ نَنْقُصُهَا مِنْ أَطْرَافِهَا وَاللَّهُ يَحْكُمُ لَا مُعَقِّبَ لِحُكْمِهِ وَهُوَ سَرِيعُ الْحِسَابِ (٤١) وَقَدْ مَكَرَ الَّذِينَ مِنْ قَبْلِهِمْ فَلِلَّهِ الْمَكْرُ جَمِيعًا يَعْلَمُ مَا تَكْسِبُ كُلُّ نَفْسٍ وَسَيَعْلَمُ الْكُفَّارُ لِمَنْ عُقْبَى الدَّارِ (٤٢) وَيَقُولُ الَّذِينَ كَفَرُوا لَسْتَ مُرْسَلًا قُلْ كَفَى بِاللَّهِ شَهِيدًا بَيْنِي وَبَيْنَكُمْ وَمَنْ عِنْدَهُ عِلْمُ الْكِتَابِ (٤٣)

13:41. See they not that We are visiting the land, curtailing it of its sides? And Allah pronounces a doom -- there is no repeller of His decree. And He is Swift in calling to account.

13:42. And those before them planned indeed, but all planning is Allah's. He knows what every soul earns. And the disbelievers will come to know for whom is the (good) end of the Abode.

13:43. And those who disbelieve say: Thou art not a messenger. Say: Allah is sufficient for a witness between me and you and whoever has knowledge of the Book.'

14. Abraham

In the name of Allah, the Beneficent, the Merciful.

14:1. I, Allah, am the Seer. A Book which We have revealed to thee that thou mayest bring forth men, by their Lord's permission, from darkness into light, to the way of the Mighty, the Praised One,

14:2. Of Allah, Whose is whatever is in the heavens and whatever is in the earth. And woe to the disbelievers for the severe chastisement!

14:3. Those who love this world's life more than the Hereafter, and turn away from Allah's path, and would have it crooked. Those are far astray.

14:4. And We sent no messenger but with the language of his people, so that he might explain to them clearly. Then Allah leaves in error whom He pleases and He guides whom He pleases. And He is the Mighty, the Wise.

14:5. And certainly We sent Moses with Our messages, saying Bring forth thy people from darkness into light and remind them of the days of Allah. In this are surely signs for every steadfast, grateful one.

14:6. And when Moses said to his people: Call to mind Allah's favour to

١٤- سورة إبراهيم

بِسْمِ اللَّهِ الرَّحْمَنِ الرَّحِيمِ

الر كِتَابٌ أَنْزَلْنَاهُ إِلَيْكَ لِتُخْرِجَ النَّاسَ مِنَ الظُّلُمَاتِ إِلَى النُّورِ بِإِذْنِ رَبِّهِمْ إِلَى صِرَاطِ الْعَزِيزِ الْحَمِيدِ (١)

اللَّهِ الَّذِي لَهُ مَا فِي السَّمَاوَاتِ وَمَا فِي الْأَرْضِ وَوَيْلٌ لِلْكَافِرِينَ مِنْ عَذَابٍ شَدِيدٍ (٢)

الَّذِينَ يَسْتَحِبُّونَ الْحَيَاةَ الدُّنْيَا عَلَى الْآخِرَةِ وَيَصُدُّونَ عَنْ سَبِيلِ اللَّهِ وَيَبْغُونَهَا عِوَجًا أُولَئِكَ فِي ضَلَالٍ بَعِيدٍ (٣)

وَمَا أَرْسَلْنَا مِنْ رَسُولٍ إِلَّا بِلِسَانِ قَوْمِهِ لِيُبَيِّنَ لَهُمْ فَيُضِلُّ اللَّهُ مَنْ يَشَاءُ وَيَهْدِي مَنْ يَشَاءُ وَهُوَ الْعَزِيزُ الْحَكِيمُ (٤)

وَلَقَدْ أَرْسَلْنَا مُوسَى بِآيَاتِنَا أَنْ أَخْرِجْ قَوْمَكَ مِنَ الظُّلُمَاتِ إِلَى النُّورِ وَذَكِّرْهُمْ بِأَيَّامِ اللَّهِ إِنَّ فِي ذَلِكَ لَآيَاتٍ لِكُلِّ صَبَّارٍ شَكُورٍ (٥)

وَإِذْ قَالَ مُوسَى لِقَوْمِهِ اذْكُرُوا نِعْمَةَ اللَّهِ عَلَيْكُمْ إِذْ أَنْجَاكُمْ مِنْ آلِ فِرْعَوْنَ

14. Abraham

you, when He delivered you from Pharaoh's people, who subjected you to severe torment, and slew your sons and spared your women. And therein was a great trial from your Lord.

* * *

14:7. And when your Lord made it known: If you are grateful, I will give you more, and if you are ungrateful, My chastisement is truly severe.

14:8. And Moses said: If you are Ungrateful, you and all those on earth, then Allah is surely Self-sufficient, Praised.

14:9. Has not the account reached you of those before you, of the people of Noah and 'Ad and Thamud -- and those after them? None knows them but Allah. Their messengers came to them with clear arguments, but they thrust their hands into their mouths and said: We deny that with which you are sent, and surely we are in serious doubt as to that to which you invite us.

14:10. Their messengers said: Is there doubt about Allah, the Maker of the heavens and the earth? He invites you to forgive you your faults and to respite you till an appointed term. They said: You are nothing but mortals like us; you wish to turn us away from that which our fathers used to worship; so bring us clear authority.

14:11. Their messengers said to them We are nothing but mortals like yourselves, but Allah bestows (His) favours on whom He pleases of His servants. And it is not for us to bring you an authority, except by Allah's permission. And on Allah let the believers rely.

14:12. And why should we not rely on Allah? and He has indeed guided us in our ways. And we would certainly bear with patience your persecution of us. And on Allah should the reliant rely.

* * *

يَسُومُونَكُمْ سُوءَ الْعَذَابِ وَيُذَبِّحُونَ أَبْنَاءَكُمْ وَيَسْتَحْيُونَ نِسَاءَكُمْ وَفِي ذَٰلِكُمْ بَلَاءٌ مِنْ رَبِّكُمْ عَظِيمٌ (٦) وَإِذْ تَأَذَّنَ رَبُّكُمْ لَئِنْ شَكَرْتُمْ لَأَزِيدَنَّكُمْ وَلَئِنْ كَفَرْتُمْ إِنَّ عَذَابِي لَشَدِيدٌ (٧) وَقَالَ مُوسَىٰ إِنْ تَكْفُرُوا أَنْتُمْ وَمَنْ فِي الْأَرْضِ جَمِيعًا فَإِنَّ اللَّهَ لَغَنِيٌّ حَمِيدٌ (٨) أَلَمْ يَأْتِكُمْ نَبَأُ الَّذِينَ مِنْ قَبْلِكُمْ قَوْمِ نُوحٍ وَعَادٍ وَثَمُودَ وَالَّذِينَ مِنْ بَعْدِهِمْ لَا يَعْلَمُهُمْ إِلَّا اللَّهُ جَاءَتْهُمْ رُسُلُهُمْ بِالْبَيِّنَاتِ فَرَدُّوا أَيْدِيَهُمْ فِي أَفْوَاهِهِمْ وَقَالُوا إِنَّا كَفَرْنَا بِمَا أُرْسِلْتُمْ بِهِ وَإِنَّا لَفِي شَكٍّ مِمَّا تَدْعُونَنَا إِلَيْهِ مُرِيبٍ (٩) قَالَتْ رُسُلُهُمْ أَفِي اللَّهِ شَكٌّ فَاطِرِ السَّمَاوَاتِ وَالْأَرْضِ يَدْعُوكُمْ لِيَغْفِرَ لَكُمْ مِنْ ذُنُوبِكُمْ وَيُؤَخِّرَكُمْ إِلَىٰ أَجَلٍ مُسَمًّى قَالُوا إِنْ أَنْتُمْ إِلَّا بَشَرٌ مِثْلُنَا تُرِيدُونَ أَنْ تَصُدُّونَا عَمَّا كَانَ يَعْبُدُ آبَاؤُنَا فَأْتُونَا بِسُلْطَانٍ مُبِينٍ (١٠) قَالَتْ لَهُمْ رُسُلُهُمْ إِنْ نَحْنُ إِلَّا بَشَرٌ مِثْلُكُمْ وَلَٰكِنَّ اللَّهَ يَمُنُّ عَلَىٰ مَنْ يَشَاءُ مِنْ عِبَادِهِ وَمَا كَانَ لَنَا أَنْ نَأْتِيَكُمْ بِسُلْطَانٍ إِلَّا بِإِذْنِ اللَّهِ وَعَلَى اللَّهِ فَلْيَتَوَكَّلِ الْمُؤْمِنُونَ (١١) وَمَا لَنَا أَلَّا نَتَوَكَّلَ عَلَى اللَّهِ وَقَدْ هَدَانَا سُبُلَنَا وَلَنَصْبِرَنَّ عَلَىٰ مَا آذَيْتُمُونَا وَعَلَى اللَّهِ فَلْيَتَوَكَّلِ الْمُتَوَكِّلُونَ (١٢) وَقَالَ الَّذِينَ كَفَرُوا لِرُسُلِهِمْ لَنُخْرِجَنَّكُمْ مِنْ أَرْضِنَا أَوْ لَتَعُودُنَّ فِي مِلَّتِنَا فَأَوْحَىٰ إِلَيْهِمْ رَبُّهُمْ لَنُهْلِكَنَّ الظَّالِمِينَ (١٣) وَلَنُسْكِنَنَّكُمُ الْأَرْضَ مِنْ بَعْدِهِمْ ذَٰلِكَ

14. Abraham

14:13. And those who disbelieved said to their messengers: We will certainly drive you out of our land, unless you come back into our religion. So their Lord revealed to them: We shall certainly destroy the wrongdoers,

14:14. And We shall certainly settle you in the land after them. This is for him who fears standing in My presence and fears My threat.

14:15. And they sought judgment, and every insolent opposer was disappointed:

14:16. Hell is before him and he is given to drink of boiling water;

14:17. He drinks it little by little and is not able to swallow it; and death comes to him from every quarter, yet he dies not. And before him is vehement chastisement.

14:18. The parable of those who disbelieve in their Lord: Their works are as ashes on which the wind blows hard on a stormy day. They have no power over aught they have earned. That is straying far away.

14:19. Seest thou not that Allah created the heavens and the earth with truth? If He please, He will take you away arid bring a new creation,

14:20. And that is not difficult for Allah.

14:21. And they will all come forth to Allah, then the weak will say to those who were proud: We were your followers, can you then avert from us aught of the chastisement of Allah? They will say: If Allah had guided us, we would have guided you. It is the same to us whether we cry or bear patiently; there is no escape for us.

***

14:22. And the devil will say, when the matter is decided: Surely Allah promised you a promise of truth, and I promised you, then failed you. And I had no authority over you, except that I called you and you obeyed me; so

لِمَنْ خَافَ مَقَامِي وَخَافَ وَعِيدِ (١٤)

وَاسْتَفْتَحُوا وَخَابَ كُلُّ جَبَّارٍ عَنِيدٍ (١٥)

مِنْ وَرَائِهِ جَهَنَّمُ وَيُسْقَىٰ مِنْ مَاءٍ صَدِيدٍ (١٦)

يَتَجَرَّعُهُ وَلَا يَكَادُ يُسِيغُهُ وَيَأْتِيهِ الْمَوْتُ مِنْ كُلِّ مَكَانٍ وَمَا هُوَ بِمَيِّتٍ وَمِنْ وَرَائِهِ عَذَابٌ غَلِيظٌ (١٧)

مَثَلُ الَّذِينَ كَفَرُوا بِرَبِّهِمْ أَعْمَالُهُمْ كَرَمَادٍ اشْتَدَّتْ بِهِ الرِّيحُ فِي يَوْمٍ عَاصِفٍ لَا يَقْدِرُونَ مِمَّا كَسَبُوا عَلَىٰ شَيْءٍ ذَٰلِكَ هُوَ الضَّلَالُ الْبَعِيدُ (١٨)

أَلَمْ تَرَ أَنَّ اللَّهَ خَلَقَ السَّمَاوَاتِ وَالْأَرْضَ بِالْحَقِّ إِنْ يَشَأْ يُذْهِبْكُمْ وَيَأْتِ بِخَلْقٍ جَدِيدٍ (١٩)

وَمَا ذَٰلِكَ عَلَى اللَّهِ بِعَزِيزٍ (٢٠)

وَبَرَزُوا لِلَّهِ جَمِيعًا فَقَالَ الضُّعَفَاءُ لِلَّذِينَ اسْتَكْبَرُوا إِنَّا كُنَّا لَكُمْ تَبَعًا فَهَلْ أَنْتُمْ مُغْنُونَ عَنَّا مِنْ عَذَابِ اللَّهِ مِنْ شَيْءٍ قَالُوا لَوْ هَدَانَا اللَّهُ لَهَدَيْنَاكُمْ سَوَاءٌ عَلَيْنَا أَجَزِعْنَا أَمْ صَبَرْنَا مَا لَنَا مِنْ مَحِيصٍ (٢١)

وَقَالَ الشَّيْطَانُ لَمَّا قُضِيَ الْأَمْرُ إِنَّ اللَّهَ وَعَدَكُمْ وَعْدَ الْحَقِّ وَوَعَدْتُكُمْ فَأَخْلَفْتُكُمْ وَمَا كَانَ لِي عَلَيْكُمْ مِنْ سُلْطَانٍ إِلَّا أَنْ دَعَوْتُكُمْ فَاسْتَجَبْتُمْ لِي فَلَا تَلُومُونِي وَلُومُوا أَنْفُسَكُمْ مَا أَنَا بِمُصْرِخِكُمْ وَمَا أَنْتُمْ بِمُصْرِخِيَّ إِنِّي كَفَرْتُ بِمَا أَشْرَكْتُمُونِ مِنْ قَبْلُ إِنَّ الظَّالِمِينَ لَهُمْ عَذَابٌ أَلِيمٌ (٢٢)

وَأُدْخِلَ الَّذِينَ آمَنُوا وَعَمِلُوا الصَّالِحَاتِ جَنَّاتٍ تَجْرِي مِنْ تَحْتِهَا الْأَنْهَارُ خَالِدِينَ فِيهَا بِإِذْنِ رَبِّهِمْ

blame me not but blame yourselves. I cannot come to your help, nor can you come to my help. I deny your associating me with Allah before. Surely for the unjust is a painful chastisement.

14:23. And those who believe and do good are made to enter Gardens, wherein flow rivers, abiding therein by their lord's permission. Their greeting therein is, Peace!

14:24. Seest thou not how Allah sets forth a parable of a good word as a good tree, whose root is firm and whose branches are high,

14:25. Yielding its fruit in every season by the permission of its Lord? And Allah sets forth parables for men that they may be mindful.

14:26. And the parable of an evil word is as an evil tree pulled up from the earth's surface; it has no stability.

14:27. Allah confirms those who believe with the sure word in this world's life and in the Hereafter; and Allah leaves the wrongdoers in error and Allah does what He pleases.

* * *

14:28. Seest thou not those who change Allah's favour for disbelief and make their people to alight in the abode of perdition

14:29. Hell. They will burn in it And an evil place it is to settle in!

14:30. And they set up equals with Allah to lead astray from His path. Say: Enjoy yourselves, for surely your return is to the Fire.

14:31. Tell My servants who believe to keep up prayer and spend out of what We have given them, secretly and openly, before the coming of the day in which there is no bartering, nor befriending.

14:32. Allah is He Who created the heavens and the earth and sent down water from the clouds, then brought forth with it fruits as a sustenance for

تَحِيَّتُهُمْ فِيهَا سَلَامٌ (٢٣)
أَلَمْ تَرَ كَيْفَ ضَرَبَ اللَّهُ مَثَلًا كَلِمَةً طَيِّبَةً كَشَجَرَةٍ طَيِّبَةٍ أَصْلُهَا ثَابِتٌ وَفَرْعُهَا فِي السَّمَاءِ (٢٤)
تُؤْتِي أُكُلَهَا كُلَّ حِينٍ بِإِذْنِ رَبِّهَا وَيَضْرِبُ اللَّهُ الْأَمْثَالَ لِلنَّاسِ لَعَلَّهُمْ يَتَذَكَّرُونَ (٢٥)
وَمَثَلُ كَلِمَةٍ خَبِيثَةٍ كَشَجَرَةٍ خَبِيثَةٍ اجْتُثَّتْ مِنْ فَوْقِ الْأَرْضِ مَا لَهَا مِنْ قَرَارٍ (٢٦)
يُثَبِّتُ اللَّهُ الَّذِينَ آمَنُوا بِالْقَوْلِ الثَّابِتِ فِي الْحَيَاةِ الدُّنْيَا وَفِي الْآخِرَةِ وَيُضِلُّ اللَّهُ الظَّالِمِينَ وَيَفْعَلُ اللَّهُ مَا يَشَاءُ (٢٧)
أَلَمْ تَرَ إِلَى الَّذِينَ بَدَّلُوا نِعْمَةَ اللَّهِ كُفْرًا وَأَحَلُّوا قَوْمَهُمْ دَارَ الْبَوَارِ (٢٨)
جَهَنَّمَ يَصْلَوْنَهَا وَبِئْسَ الْقَرَارُ (٢٩)
وَجَعَلُوا لِلَّهِ أَنْدَادًا لِيُضِلُّوا عَنْ سَبِيلِهِ قُلْ تَمَتَّعُوا فَإِنَّ مَصِيرَكُمْ إِلَى النَّارِ (٣٠)
قُلْ لِعِبَادِيَ الَّذِينَ آمَنُوا يُقِيمُوا الصَّلَاةَ وَيُنْفِقُوا مِمَّا رَزَقْنَاهُمْ سِرًّا وَعَلَانِيَةً مِنْ قَبْلِ أَنْ يَأْتِيَ يَوْمٌ لَا بَيْعٌ فِيهِ وَلَا خِلَالٌ (٣١)
اللَّهُ الَّذِي خَلَقَ السَّمَاوَاتِ وَالْأَرْضَ وَأَنْزَلَ مِنَ السَّمَاءِ مَاءً فَأَخْرَجَ بِهِ مِنَ الثَّمَرَاتِ رِزْقًا لَكُمْ وَسَخَّرَ لَكُمُ الْفُلْكَ لِتَجْرِيَ فِي الْبَحْرِ بِأَمْرِهِ وَسَخَّرَ لَكُمُ الْأَنْهَارَ (٣٢)
وَسَخَّرَ لَكُمُ الشَّمْسَ وَالْقَمَرَ دَائِبَيْنِ وَسَخَّرَ لَكُمُ اللَّيْلَ وَالنَّهَارَ (٣٣)
وَآتَاكُمْ مِنْ كُلِّ مَا سَأَلْتُمُوهُ وَإِنْ تَعُدُّوا نِعْمَةَ اللَّهِ لَا تُحْصُوهَا إِنَّ الْإِنْسَانَ لَظَلُومٌ كَفَّارٌ (٣٤)

14. Abraham

you, and He has made the ships subservient to you to run their course in the sea by His command, and He has made the rivers subservient to you.

14:33. And He has made subservient to you the sun and the moon, pursuing their courses; and He has made subservient to you the night and the day.

14:34. And He gives you of all you ask of Him. And if you count Allah's favours, you will not be able to number them. Surely man is very unjust, very ungrateful.

* * *

14:35. And when Abraham said: My Lord, make this city secure, and save me and my sons from worshipping idols.

14:36. My Lord, surely they have led many men astray. So whoever follows me, he is surely of me; and whoever disobeys me, Thou surely art Forgiving, Merciful.

14:37. Our Lord, I have settled a part of my offspring in a valley unproductive of fruit near Thy Sacred House, our Lord, that they may keep up prayer; so make the hearts of some people yearn towards them, and provide them with fruits; haply they may be grateful,

14:38. Our Lord, surely Thou knowest what we hide and what we proclaim. And nothing is hidden from Allah, either in the earth, or in the heaven.

14:39. Praise be to Allah, Who has given me, in old age, Ishmael and Isaac! Surely my Lord is the Hearer of prayer.

14:40. My Lord, make me keep up prayer and from my offspring (too), our Lord, and accept my prayer.

14:41. Our Lord, grant me protection and my parents and the believers on the day when the reckoning comes to pass.

* * *

14:42. And think not Allah to be

وَإِذْ قَالَ إِبْرَاهِيمُ رَبِّ اجْعَلْ هَذَا الْبَلَدَ آمِنًا وَاجْنُبْنِي وَبَنِيَّ أَنْ نَعْبُدَ الْأَصْنَامَ (٣٥)

رَبِّ إِنَّهُنَّ أَضْلَلْنَ كَثِيرًا مِنَ النَّاسِ فَمَنْ تَبِعَنِي فَإِنَّهُ مِنِّي وَمَنْ عَصَانِي فَإِنَّكَ غَفُورٌ رَحِيمٌ (٣٦)

رَبَّنَا إِنِّي أَسْكَنْتُ مِنْ ذُرِّيَّتِي بِوَادٍ غَيْرِ ذِي زَرْعٍ عِنْدَ بَيْتِكَ الْمُحَرَّمِ رَبَّنَا لِيُقِيمُوا الصَّلَاةَ فَاجْعَلْ أَفْئِدَةً مِنَ النَّاسِ تَهْوِي إِلَيْهِمْ وَارْزُقْهُمْ مِنَ الثَّمَرَاتِ لَعَلَّهُمْ يَشْكُرُونَ (٣٧)

رَبَّنَا إِنَّكَ تَعْلَمُ مَا نُخْفِي وَمَا نُعْلِنُ وَمَا يَخْفَى عَلَى اللَّهِ مِنْ شَيْءٍ فِي الْأَرْضِ وَلَا فِي السَّمَاءِ (٣٨)

الْحَمْدُ لِلَّهِ الَّذِي وَهَبَ لِي عَلَى الْكِبَرِ إِسْمَاعِيلَ وَإِسْحَاقَ إِنَّ رَبِّي لَسَمِيعُ الدُّعَاءِ (٣٩)

رَبِّ اجْعَلْنِي مُقِيمَ الصَّلَاةِ وَمِنْ ذُرِّيَّتِي رَبَّنَا وَتَقَبَّلْ دُعَاءِ (٤٠)

رَبَّنَا اغْفِرْ لِي وَلِوَالِدَيَّ وَلِلْمُؤْمِنِينَ يَوْمَ يَقُومُ الْحِسَابُ (٤١)

وَلَا تَحْسَبَنَّ اللَّهَ غَافِلًا عَمَّا يَعْمَلُ الظَّالِمُونَ إِنَّمَا يُؤَخِّرُهُمْ لِيَوْمٍ تَشْخَصُ فِيهِ الْأَبْصَارُ (٤٢)

مُهْطِعِينَ مُقْنِعِي رُءُوسِهِمْ لَا يَرْتَدُّ إِلَيْهِمْ طَرْفُهُمْ وَأَفْئِدَتُهُمْ هَوَاءٌ (٤٣)

وَأَنْذِرِ النَّاسَ يَوْمَ يَأْتِيهِمُ الْعَذَابُ فَيَقُولُ الَّذِينَ ظَلَمُوا رَبَّنَا أَخِّرْنَا إِلَى أَجَلٍ قَرِيبٍ نُجِبْ دَعْوَتَكَ وَنَتَّبِعِ الرُّسُلَ أَوَلَمْ تَكُونُوا أَقْسَمْتُمْ مِنْ قَبْلُ مَا لَكُمْ مِنْ زَوَالٍ (٤٤)

وَسَكَنْتُمْ فِي مَسَاكِنِ الَّذِينَ ظَلَمُوا أَنْفُسَهُمْ وَتَبَيَّنَ لَكُمْ كَيْفَ فَعَلْنَا بِهِمْ وَضَرَبْنَا لَكُمُ الْأَمْثَالَ (٤٥)

heedless of what the unjust do. He only respites them to a day when the eyes will stare (in terror),

14:43. Hastening forward, their heads upraised, their gaze not returning to them, and their hearts vacant.

14:44. And warn people of a day when the chastisement will come to them, then the wrongdoers will say: Our Lord, respite us to a near term, we will respond to Thy call and follow the messengers. Did you not swear before that there will be no passing away for you?

14:45. And you dwell in the abodes of those who wronged themselves, and it is clear to you how We dealt with them and We made (them) examples for you.

14:46. And they have indeed planned their plan, and their plan is with Allah, though their plan is such that the mountains should be moved thereby.

14:47. So think not that Allah will fail in His promise to His messengers. Surely Allah is Mighty, the Lord of retribution.

14:48. On the day when the earth will be changed into a different earth, and the heavens (as well), and they will come forth to Allah, the One, the Supreme.

14:49. And thou wilt see the guilty on that day linked together in chains --

14:50. Their shirts made of pitch, and fire covering their faces,

14:51. That Allah may repay each soul what it has earned. Surely Allah is Swift in reckoning.

14:52. This is a message for the people and that they may be warned thereby, and that they may know that He is One God, and that men of understanding may mind.

15. The Rock

In the name of Allah, the Beneficent,

15. The Rock

the Merciful.

15:1. I, Allah, am the Seer. These are the verses of the Book and (of) a Qur'an that makes manifest.

15:2. Often will those who disbelieve wish that they were Muslims.

15:3. Leave them to eat and enjoy themselves, and let (false) hope beguile them, for they will soon know.

15:4. And never did We destroy a town but it had a decree made known.

15:5. No people can hasten on their doom, nor can they postpone (it).

15:6. And they say: O thou to whom the Reminder is revealed, thou art indeed mad.

15:7. Why bringest thou not the angels to us, if thou art of the truthful?

15:8. We send not angels but with truth, and then they would not be respited.

15:9. Surely We have revealed the Reminder, and surely We are its Guardian.

15:10. And certainly We sent (messengers) before thee among the sects of yore.

ii And there never came a messenger to them but they mocked him. 12 Thus do We make it enter the hearts of the guilty --

15:13. They believe not in it; and the example of the ancients has gone before.

15:14. And even if We open to them a gate of heaven, and they keep on ascending into it,

15:15. They would say: Only our eyes have been covered over, rather we are an enchanted people.

* * *

15:16. And certainly We have made strongholds in the heaven, and We have made it fair-seeming to the beholders,

15:17. And We guard it against every accursed devil,

15:18. But he who steals a hearing; so

الر تِلْكَ آيَاتُ الْكِتَابِ وَقُرْآنٍ مُبِينٍ (١)

رُبَمَا يَوَدُّ الَّذِينَ كَفَرُوا لَوْ كَانُوا مُسْلِمِينَ (٢)

ذَرْهُمْ يَأْكُلُوا وَيَتَمَتَّعُوا وَيُلْهِهِمُ الْأَمَلُ فَسَوْفَ يَعْلَمُونَ (٣)

وَمَا أَهْلَكْنَا مِنْ قَرْيَةٍ إِلَّا وَلَهَا كِتَابٌ مَعْلُومٌ (٤)

مَا تَسْبِقُ مِنْ أُمَّةٍ أَجَلَهَا وَمَا يَسْتَأْخِرُونَ (٥)

وَقَالُوا يَا أَيُّهَا الَّذِي نُزِّلَ عَلَيْهِ الذِّكْرُ إِنَّكَ لَمَجْنُونٌ (٦)

لَوْ مَا تَأْتِينَا بِالْمَلَائِكَةِ إِنْ كُنْتَ مِنَ الصَّادِقِينَ (٧)

مَا نُنَزِّلُ الْمَلَائِكَةَ إِلَّا بِالْحَقِّ وَمَا كَانُوا إِذًا مُنْظَرِينَ (٨)

إِنَّا نَحْنُ نَزَّلْنَا الذِّكْرَ وَإِنَّا لَهُ لَحَافِظُونَ (٩)

وَلَقَدْ أَرْسَلْنَا مِنْ قَبْلِكَ فِي شِيَعِ الْأَوَّلِينَ (١٠)

وَمَا يَأْتِيهِمْ مِنْ رَسُولٍ إِلَّا كَانُوا بِهِ يَسْتَهْزِئُونَ (١١)

كَذَلِكَ نَسْلُكُهُ فِي قُلُوبِ الْمُجْرِمِينَ (١٢)

لَا يُؤْمِنُونَ بِهِ وَقَدْ خَلَتْ سُنَّةُ الْأَوَّلِينَ (١٣)

وَلَوْ فَتَحْنَا عَلَيْهِمْ بَابًا مِنَ السَّمَاءِ فَظَلُّوا فِيهِ يَعْرُجُونَ (١٤)

لَقَالُوا إِنَّمَا سُكِّرَتْ أَبْصَارُنَا بَلْ نَحْنُ قَوْمٌ مَسْحُورُونَ (١٥)

وَلَقَدْ جَعَلْنَا فِي السَّمَاءِ بُرُوجًا وَزَيَّنَّاهَا لِلنَّاظِرِينَ (١٦)

وَحَفِظْنَاهَا مِنْ كُلِّ شَيْطَانٍ رَجِيمٍ

15. The Rock

there follows him a visible flame.

15:19. And the earth -- We have spread it out and made in it firm mountains and caused to grow in it of every suitable thing

15:20. And We have made in it means of subsistence for you and for him for whom you provide not.

15:21. And there is not a thing but with Us are the treasures of it, and We send it not down but in a known measure.

15:22. And We send the winds fertilizing, then send down water from the clouds, so We give it to you to drink; nor is it you who store it up.

15:23. And surely it is We, Who give life and cause death, and We are the Inheritors.

15:24. And certainly We know those among you who go forward and We certainly know those who lag behind.

15:25. And surely thy Lord will gather them together. He indeed is Wise,

* * *

15:26. And surely We created man of sounding clay, of black mud fashioned into shape.

15:27. And the jinn, We created before of intensely hot fire.

15:28. And when thy Lord said to the angels I am going to create a mortal of sound clay, of black mud fashioned into shape.

15:29. So when I have made him complete and breathed into him of My spirit, fall down making obeisance to him.

15:30. So the angels made obeisance, all of them together --

15:31. But Iblis (did it not). He refused to be with those who made obeisance.

15:32. He said: O Iblis, what is the reason that thou art not with those who make obeisance?

15:33. He said: I am not going to make obeisance to a mortal, whom Thou hast created of sounding clay, of black mud fashioned into shape.

(١٧)
إِلَّا مَنِ اسْتَرَقَ السَّمْعَ فَأَتْبَعَهُ شِهَابٌ مُبِينٌ (١٨)
وَالْأَرْضَ مَدَدْنَاهَا وَأَلْقَيْنَا فِيهَا رَوَاسِيَ وَأَنْبَتْنَا فِيهَا مِنْ كُلِّ شَيْءٍ مَوْزُونٍ (١٩)
وَجَعَلْنَا لَكُمْ فِيهَا مَعَايِشَ وَمَنْ لَسْتُمْ لَهُ بِرَازِقِينَ (٢٠)
وَإِنْ مِنْ شَيْءٍ إِلَّا عِنْدَنَا خَزَائِنُهُ وَمَا نُنَزِّلُهُ إِلَّا بِقَدَرٍ مَعْلُومٍ (٢١)
وَأَرْسَلْنَا الرِّيَاحَ لَوَاقِحَ فَأَنْزَلْنَا مِنَ السَّمَاءِ مَاءً فَأَسْقَيْنَاكُمُوهُ وَمَا أَنْتُمْ لَهُ بِخَازِنِينَ (٢٢)
وَإِنَّا لَنَحْنُ نُحْيِي وَنُمِيتُ وَنَحْنُ الْوَارِثُونَ (٢٣)
وَلَقَدْ عَلِمْنَا الْمُسْتَقْدِمِينَ مِنْكُمْ وَلَقَدْ عَلِمْنَا الْمُسْتَأْخِرِينَ (٢٤)
وَإِنَّ رَبَّكَ هُوَ يَحْشُرُهُمْ إِنَّهُ حَكِيمٌ عَلِيمٌ (٢٥)
وَلَقَدْ خَلَقْنَا الْإِنْسَانَ مِنْ صَلْصَالٍ مِنْ حَمَإٍ مَسْنُونٍ (٢٦)
وَالْجَانَّ خَلَقْنَاهُ مِنْ قَبْلُ مِنْ نَارِ السَّمُومِ (٢٧)
وَإِذْ قَالَ رَبُّكَ لِلْمَلَائِكَةِ إِنِّي خَالِقٌ بَشَرًا مِنْ صَلْصَالٍ مِنْ حَمَإٍ مَسْنُونٍ (٢٨)
فَإِذَا سَوَّيْتُهُ وَنَفَخْتُ فِيهِ مِنْ رُوحِي فَقَعُوا لَهُ سَاجِدِينَ (٢٩)
فَسَجَدَ الْمَلَائِكَةُ كُلُّهُمْ أَجْمَعُونَ (٣٠)
إِلَّا إِبْلِيسَ أَبَى أَنْ يَكُونَ مَعَ السَّاجِدِينَ (٣١)
قَالَ يَا إِبْلِيسُ مَا لَكَ أَلَّا تَكُونَ مَعَ السَّاجِدِينَ (٣٢)

15. The Rock

15:34. He said: Then go forth, for surely thou art driven away,

15:35. And surely on thee is a curse till the day of Judgment.

15:36. He said: My Lord, respite me till the time when they are raised.

15:37. He said: Surely thou art of the respited ones,

15:38. Till the period of the time made known.

15:39. He said: My Lord, as Thou hast judged me erring, I shall certainly make (evil) fair-seeming to them on earth, and I shall cause them all to deviate,

15:40. Except Thy servants from among them, the purified ones.

15:41. He said: This is a right way with Me.

15:42. As regards My servants, thou hast no authority over them except such of the deviators as follow thee.

15:43. And surely hell is the promised place for them all --

15:44. It has seven gates. For each gate is an appointed portion of them.

* * *

15:45. Surely those who keep their duty are in Gardens and fountains.

15:46. Enter them in peace, secure.

15:47. And We shall root out whatever of rancour is in their breasts -- as brethren, on raised couches, face to face.

15:48. Toil afflicts them not therein, nor will they be ejected therefrom.

15:49. Inform My servants that I am the Forgiving, the Merciful,

15:50. And that My chastisement -- that is the painful chastisement.

15:51. And inform them of the guests of Abraham.

15:52. When they entered upon him, they said, Peace He said: We are afraid of you.

15:53. They said: Be not afraid, we give thee good news of a boy, possessing knowledge.

15. The Rock

15:54. He said: Do you give me good news when old age has come upon me? Of what then do you give me good news?

15:55. They said: We give thee good news with truth, so be not thou of the despairing ones.

15:56. He said: And who despairs of the mercy of his Lord but the erring ones?

15:57. He said: What is your business, then, O messengers?

15:58. They said: We have been sent to a guilty people,

15:59. Except Lot's followers. We shall deliver them all,

15:60. Except his wife: We ordained that she shall surely be of those who remain behind.

* * *

15:61. So when the messengers came to Lot's followers,

15:62. He said: Surely you are an unknown people.

15:63. They said: Nay, we have come to thee with that about which they disputed.

15:64. And we have come to thee with the truth, and we are surely truthful.

15:65. So travel with thy followers for a part of the night and thyself follow their rear; and let not any one of you turn round, and go whither you are commanded.

15:66. And We made known to him this decree, that the roots of these should be cut off in the morning.

15:67. And the people of the town came rejoicing.

15:68. He said: These are my guests, so disgrace me not,

15:69. And keep your duty to Allah and shame me not.

15:70. They said: Did we not forbid thee from (entertaining) people?

15:71. He said: These are my daughters, if you will do (aught).

15:72. By thy life they blindly

قَالَ أَبَشَّرْتُمُونِي عَلَى أَنْ مَسَّنِيَ الْكِبَرُ فَبِمَ تُبَشِّرُونَ (٥٤)

قَالُوا بَشَّرْنَاكَ بِالْحَقِّ فَلَا تَكُنْ مِنَ الْقَانِطِينَ (٥٥)

قَالَ وَمَنْ يَقْنَطُ مِنْ رَحْمَةِ رَبِّهِ إِلَّا الضَّالُّونَ (٥٦)

قَالَ فَمَا خَطْبُكُمْ أَيُّهَا الْمُرْسَلُونَ (٥٧)

قَالُوا إِنَّا أُرْسِلْنَا إِلَى قَوْمٍ مُجْرِمِينَ (٥٨)

إِلَّا آلَ لُوطٍ إِنَّا لَمُنَجُّوهُمْ أَجْمَعِينَ (٥٩)

إِلَّا امْرَأَتَهُ قَدَّرْنَا إِنَّهَا لَمِنَ الْغَابِرِينَ (٦٠)

فَلَمَّا جَاءَ آلَ لُوطٍ الْمُرْسَلُونَ (٦١)

قَالَ إِنَّكُمْ قَوْمٌ مُنْكَرُونَ (٦٢)

قَالُوا بَلْ جِئْنَاكَ بِمَا كَانُوا فِيهِ يَمْتَرُونَ (٦٣)

وَأَتَيْنَاكَ بِالْحَقِّ وَإِنَّا لَصَادِقُونَ (٦٤)

فَأَسْرِ بِأَهْلِكَ بِقِطْعٍ مِنَ اللَّيْلِ وَاتَّبِعْ أَدْبَارَهُمْ وَلَا يَلْتَفِتْ مِنْكُمْ أَحَدٌ وَامْضُوا حَيْثُ تُؤْمَرُونَ (٦٥)

وَقَضَيْنَا إِلَيْهِ ذَلِكَ الْأَمْرَ أَنَّ دَابِرَ هَؤُلَاءِ مَقْطُوعٌ مُصْبِحِينَ (٦٦)

وَجَاءَ أَهْلُ الْمَدِينَةِ يَسْتَبْشِرُونَ (٦٧)

قَالَ إِنَّ هَؤُلَاءِ ضَيْفِي فَلَا تَفْضَحُونِ (٦٨)

وَاتَّقُوا اللَّهَ وَلَا تُخْزُونِ (٦٩)

قَالُوا أَوَلَمْ نَنْهَكَ عَنِ الْعَالَمِينَ (٧٠)

قَالَ هَؤُلَاءِ بَنَاتِي إِنْ كُنْتُمْ فَاعِلِينَ (٧١)

لَعَمْرُكَ إِنَّهُمْ لَفِي سَكْرَتِهِمْ يَعْمَهُونَ (٧٢)

15. The Rock

wandered on in their frenzy.
15:73. So the cry overtook them at sunrise
15:74. Thus We turned it upside down, and rained upon them hard stones.
15:75. Surely in this are signs for those who take a lesson.
15:76. And it is on a road that still abides.
15:77. Verily therein is a sign for the believers.
15:78. And the dwellers of the thicker were indeed iniquitous;
15:79. So We inflicted retribution on them. And they are both on an open high road.

* * *

15:80. And the dwellers of the Rock indeed rejected the messengers;
15:81. And We gave them Our messages, but they turned away from them;
15:82. And they hewed houses in the mountains, in security.
15:83. So the cry overtook them in the morning;
15:84. And what they earned availed them not.
15:85. And We created not the heavens and the earth and what is between them but with truth. And the Hour is surely coming, so turn away with kindly forgiveness.
15:86. Surely thy Lord -- He is the Creator, the Knower.
15:87. And certainly We have given thee seven oft-repeated (verses) and the grand Qur'an.
15:88. Strain not thine eyes at what We have given certain classes of them to enjoy, and grieve not for them, and make thyself gentle to the believers.
15:89. And say: I am indeed the plain warner.
15:90. Like as We sent down on them who took oaths,
15:91. Those who divided the Qur'an into parts.

فَأَخَذَتْهُمُ الصَّيْحَةُ مُشْرِقِينَ (٧٣)
فَجَعَلْنَا عَالِيَهَا سَافِلَهَا وَأَمْطَرْنَا عَلَيْهِمْ حِجَارَةً مِنْ سِجِّيلٍ (٧٤)
إِنَّ فِي ذَلِكَ لَآيَاتٍ لِلْمُتَوَسِّمِينَ (٧٥)
وَإِنَّهَا لَبِسَبِيلٍ مُقِيمٍ (٧٦)
إِنَّ فِي ذَلِكَ لَآيَةً لِلْمُؤْمِنِينَ (٧٧)
وَإِنْ كَانَ أَصْحَابُ الْأَيْكَةِ لَظَالِمِينَ (٧٨)
فَانْتَقَمْنَا مِنْهُمْ وَإِنَّهُمَا لَبِإِمَامٍ مُبِينٍ (٧٩)
وَلَقَدْ كَذَّبَ أَصْحَابُ الْحِجْرِ الْمُرْسَلِينَ (٨٠)
وَآتَيْنَاهُمْ آيَاتِنَا فَكَانُوا عَنْهَا مُعْرِضِينَ (٨١)
وَكَانُوا يَنْحِتُونَ مِنَ الْجِبَالِ بُيُوتًا آمِنِينَ (٨٢)
فَأَخَذَتْهُمُ الصَّيْحَةُ مُصْبِحِينَ (٨٣)
فَمَا أَغْنَى عَنْهُمْ مَا كَانُوا يَكْسِبُونَ (٨٤)
وَمَا خَلَقْنَا السَّمَاوَاتِ وَالْأَرْضَ وَمَا بَيْنَهُمَا إِلَّا بِالْحَقِّ وَإِنَّ السَّاعَةَ لَآتِيَةٌ فَاصْفَحِ الصَّفْحَ الْجَمِيلَ (٨٥)
إِنَّ رَبَّكَ هُوَ الْخَلَّاقُ الْعَلِيمُ (٨٦)
وَلَقَدْ آتَيْنَاكَ سَبْعًا مِنَ الْمَثَانِي وَالْقُرْآنَ الْعَظِيمَ (٨٧)
لَا تَمُدَّنَّ عَيْنَيْكَ إِلَى مَا مَتَّعْنَا بِهِ أَزْوَاجًا مِنْهُمْ وَلَا تَحْزَنْ عَلَيْهِمْ وَاخْفِضْ جَنَاحَكَ لِلْمُؤْمِنِينَ (٨٨)
وَقُلْ إِنِّي أَنَا النَّذِيرُ الْمُبِينُ (٨٩)
كَمَا أَنْزَلْنَا عَلَى الْمُقْتَسِمِينَ (٩٠)
الَّذِينَ جَعَلُوا الْقُرْآنَ عِضِينَ (٩١)
فَوَرَبِّكَ لَنَسْأَلَنَّهُمْ أَجْمَعِينَ (٩٢)

15:92. So, by thy Lord! We shall question them all.
15:93. As to what they did.
15:94. Therefore declare openly what thou art commanded, and turn away from the polytheists.
15:95. Surely We are sufficient for thee against the scoffers --
15:96. Those who set up another god with Allah; so they will come to know.
15:97. And We know indeed that thy breast straitens at what they say;
15:98. So celebrate the praise of thy Lord, and be of those who make obeisance.
15:99. And serve thy Lord, until there comes to thee that which is certain.

16. The Bee

In the name of Allah, the Beneficent, the Merciful.
16:1. Allah's commandment will come to pass, so seek not to hasten it. Glory be to Him, and highly exalted be He above what they associate (with Him)!
16:2. He sends down angels with revelation by His command on whom He pleases of His servants, saying Give the warning that there is no God but Me, so keep your duty to Me.
16:3. He created the heavens and the earth with truth. Highly exalted be He above what they associate (with Him)!
16:4. He created man from a small life-germ, and lo! he is an open contender.
16:5. And the cattle, He has created them for you. You have in them warm clothing and (other) advantages, and of them you eat.
16:6. And therein is beauty for you, when you drive them back (home) and when you send them out (to pasture).
16:7. And they carry your heavy loads to regions which you could not reach but with distress to yourselves. Surely your Lord is Compassionate, Merciful.

عَمَّا كَانُوا يَعْمَلُونَ (٩٣)
فَاصْدَعْ بِمَا تُؤْمَرُ وَأَعْرِضْ عَنِ الْمُشْرِكِينَ (٩٤)
إِنَّا كَفَيْنَاكَ الْمُسْتَهْزِئِينَ (٩٥)
الَّذِينَ يَجْعَلُونَ مَعَ اللَّهِ إِلَهًا آخَرَ فَسَوْفَ يَعْلَمُونَ (٩٦)
وَلَقَدْ نَعْلَمُ أَنَّكَ يَضِيقُ صَدْرُكَ بِمَا يَقُولُونَ (٩٧)
فَسَبِّحْ بِحَمْدِ رَبِّكَ وَكُنْ مِنَ السَّاجِدِينَ (٩٨)
وَاعْبُدْ رَبَّكَ حَتَّى يَأْتِيَكَ الْيَقِينُ (٩٩)

١٦ـ سورة النحل

بِسْمِ اللهِ الرَّحْمَنِ الرَّحِيمِ
أَتَى أَمْرُ اللهِ فَلَا تَسْتَعْجِلُوهُ سُبْحَانَهُ وَتَعَالَى عَمَّا يُشْرِكُونَ (١)
يُنَزِّلُ الْمَلَائِكَةَ بِالرُّوحِ مِنْ أَمْرِهِ عَلَى مَنْ يَشَاءُ مِنْ عِبَادِهِ أَنْ أَنْذِرُوا أَنَّهُ لَا إِلَهَ إِلَّا أَنَا فَاتَّقُونِ (٢)
خَلَقَ السَّمَاوَاتِ وَالْأَرْضَ بِالْحَقِّ تَعَالَى عَمَّا يُشْرِكُونَ (٣)
خَلَقَ الْإِنْسَانَ مِنْ نُطْفَةٍ فَإِذَا هُوَ خَصِيمٌ مُبِينٌ (٤)
وَالْأَنْعَامَ خَلَقَهَا لَكُمْ فِيهَا دِفْءٌ وَمَنَافِعُ وَمِنْهَا تَأْكُلُونَ (٥)
وَلَكُمْ فِيهَا جَمَالٌ حِينَ تُرِيحُونَ وَحِينَ تَسْرَحُونَ (٦)
وَتَحْمِلُ أَثْقَالَكُمْ إِلَى بَلَدٍ لَمْ تَكُونُوا بَالِغِيهِ إِلَّا بِشِقِّ الْأَنْفُسِ إِنَّ رَبَّكُمْ لَرَؤُوفٌ رَحِيمٌ (٧)
وَالْخَيْلَ وَالْبِغَالَ وَالْحَمِيرَ لِتَرْكَبُوهَا وَزِينَةً وَيَخْلُقُ مَا لَا تَعْلَمُونَ (٨)

16. The Bee

16:8. And (He made) horses and mules and asses that you might ride upon them and as an ornament. And He creates what you know not.

16:9. And upon Allah it tests to show the right way, and there are some deviating (ways). And if He please, He would guide you all aright.

* * *

16:10. He it is who sends down water from the clouds for you; it gives drink, and by it (grow) the trees on which you feed.

16:11. He causes to grow for you thereby herbage, and the olives, and the date-palms, and the grapes, and all the fruits. Surely there is a sign in this for a people who reflect.

16:12. And He has made subservient for you the night and the day and the sun and the moon. And the stars are made subservient by His command. Surely there are signs in this for a people who understand.

16:13. And what He has created for you in the earth is of varied hues. Surely there is a sign in this for a people who are mindful.

16:14. And He it is Who has made the sea subservient that you may eat fresh flesh from it and bring forth from it ornaments which you wear. And thou seest the ships cleaving through it, so that you seek of His bounty and that you may give thanks.

16:15. And He has cast firm mountains in the earth lest it quake with you, and rivers and roads that you may go aright,

16:16. And landmarks. And by the stars they find the right way.

16:17. Is He then Who creates like him who creates not? Do you not then mind? --

16:18. And if you would count Allah's favours, you would not be able to number them. Surely Allah is Forgiving, Merciful.

وَعَلَى اللَّهِ قَصْدُ السَّبِيلِ وَمِنْهَا جَائِرٌ وَلَوْ شَاءَ لَهَدَاكُمْ أَجْمَعِينَ (٩)

هُوَ الَّذِي أَنْزَلَ مِنَ السَّمَاءِ مَاءً لَكُمْ مِنْهُ شَرَابٌ وَمِنْهُ شَجَرٌ فِيهِ تُسِيمُونَ (١٠)

يُنْبِتُ لَكُمْ بِهِ الزَّرْعَ وَالزَّيْتُونَ وَالنَّخِيلَ وَالْأَعْنَابَ وَمِنْ كُلِّ الثَّمَرَاتِ إِنَّ فِي ذَلِكَ لَآيَةً لِقَوْمٍ يَتَفَكَّرُونَ (١١)

وَسَخَّرَ لَكُمُ اللَّيْلَ وَالنَّهَارَ وَالشَّمْسَ وَالْقَمَرَ وَالنُّجُومُ مُسَخَّرَاتٌ بِأَمْرِهِ إِنَّ فِي ذَلِكَ لَآيَاتٍ لِقَوْمٍ يَعْقِلُونَ (١٢)

وَمَا ذَرَأَ لَكُمْ فِي الْأَرْضِ مُخْتَلِفًا أَلْوَانُهُ إِنَّ فِي ذَلِكَ لَآيَةً لِقَوْمٍ يَذَّكَّرُونَ (١٣)

وَهُوَ الَّذِي سَخَّرَ الْبَحْرَ لِتَأْكُلُوا مِنْهُ لَحْمًا طَرِيًّا وَتَسْتَخْرِجُوا مِنْهُ حِلْيَةً تَلْبَسُونَهَا وَتَرَى الْفُلْكَ مَوَاخِرَ فِيهِ وَلِتَبْتَغُوا مِنْ فَضْلِهِ وَلَعَلَّكُمْ تَشْكُرُونَ (١٤)

وَأَلْقَى فِي الْأَرْضِ رَوَاسِيَ أَنْ تَمِيدَ بِكُمْ وَأَنْهَارًا وَسُبُلًا لَعَلَّكُمْ تَهْتَدُونَ (١٥)

وَعَلَامَاتٍ وَبِالنَّجْمِ هُمْ يَهْتَدُونَ (١٦)

أَفَمَنْ يَخْلُقُ كَمَنْ لَا يَخْلُقُ أَفَلَا تَذَكَّرُونَ (١٧)

وَإِنْ تَعُدُّوا نِعْمَةَ اللَّهِ لَا تُحْصُوهَا إِنَّ اللَّهَ لَغَفُورٌ رَحِيمٌ (١٨)

وَاللَّهُ يَعْلَمُ مَا تُسِرُّونَ وَمَا تُعْلِنُونَ (١٩)

وَالَّذِينَ يَدْعُونَ مِنْ دُونِ اللَّهِ لَا يَخْلُقُونَ شَيْئًا وَهُمْ يُخْلَقُونَ (٢٠) أَمْوَاتٌ غَيْرُ أَحْيَاءٍ وَمَا يَشْعُرُونَ

16. The Bee

16:19. And Allah knows what you conceal and what you do openly.

16:20. And those whom they call on besides Allah created naught, while they are themselves created.

16:21. Dead (are they), not living. And they know not when they will be raised.

***

16:22. Your God is one God: so those who believe not in the Hereafter, their hearts refuse to know and they are proud.

16:23. Undoubtedly Allah knows what they hide and what they manifest. Surely He loves not the proud.

16:24. And when it is said to them, What is it that your Lord has revealed? they say, Stories of the ancients!

16:25. That they may bear their burdens in full on the day of Resurrection, and also of the burdens of those whom they lead astray without knowledge. Ah! evil is what they bear.

***

16:26. Those before them plotted, so Allah demolished their building from the foundations, so the roof fell down on them from above them, and the chastisement came to them from whence they perceived not.

16:27. Then on the Resurrection day He will bring them to disgrace and say: Where are My partners, for whose sake you became hostile? Those who are given the knowledge will say: Surely disgrace this day and evil are upon the disbelievers,

16:28. Whom the angels cause to die, while they are unjust to themselves. Then would they offer submission: We did not do any evil. Nay! Surely Allah knows what you did.

16:29. So enter the gates of hell, to abide therein. Evil indeed is the dwelling-place of the proud.

16:30. And it is said to those who guard

أَيَّانَ يُبْعَثُونَ (٢١)

إِلَهُكُمْ إِلَهٌ وَاحِدٌ فَالَّذِينَ لَا يُؤْمِنُونَ بِالْآخِرَةِ قُلُوبُهُمْ مُنْكِرَةٌ وَهُمْ مُسْتَكْبِرُونَ (٢٢)

لَا جَرَمَ أَنَّ اللَّهَ يَعْلَمُ مَا يُسِرُّونَ وَمَا يُعْلِنُونَ إِنَّهُ لَا يُحِبُّ الْمُسْتَكْبِرِينَ (٢٣)

وَإِذَا قِيلَ لَهُمْ مَاذَا أَنْزَلَ رَبُّكُمْ قَالُوا أَسَاطِيرُ الْأَوَّلِينَ (٢٤)

لِيَحْمِلُوا أَوْزَارَهُمْ كَامِلَةً يَوْمَ الْقِيَامَةِ وَمِنْ أَوْزَارِ الَّذِينَ يُضِلُّونَهُمْ بِغَيْرِ عِلْمٍ أَلَا سَاءَ مَا يَزِرُونَ (٢٥)

قَدْ مَكَرَ الَّذِينَ مِنْ قَبْلِهِمْ فَأَتَى اللَّهُ بُنْيَانَهُمْ مِنَ الْقَوَاعِدِ فَخَرَّ عَلَيْهِمُ السَّقْفُ مِنْ فَوْقِهِمْ وَأَتَاهُمُ الْعَذَابُ مِنْ حَيْثُ لَا يَشْعُرُونَ (٢٦)

ثُمَّ يَوْمَ الْقِيَامَةِ يُخْزِيهِمْ وَيَقُولُ أَيْنَ شُرَكَائِيَ الَّذِينَ كُنْتُمْ تُشَاقُّونَ فِيهِمْ قَالَ الَّذِينَ أُوتُوا الْعِلْمَ إِنَّ الْخِزْيَ الْيَوْمَ وَالسُّوءَ عَلَى الْكَافِرِينَ (٢٧)

الَّذِينَ تَتَوَفَّاهُمُ الْمَلَائِكَةُ ظَالِمِي أَنْفُسِهِمْ فَأَلْقَوُا السَّلَمَ مَا كُنَّا نَعْمَلُ مِنْ سُوءٍ بَلَى إِنَّ اللَّهَ عَلِيمٌ بِمَا كُنْتُمْ تَعْمَلُونَ (٢٨)

فَادْخُلُوا أَبْوَابَ جَهَنَّمَ خَالِدِينَ فِيهَا فَلَبِئْسَ مَثْوَى الْمُتَكَبِّرِينَ (٢٩)

وَقِيلَ لِلَّذِينَ اتَّقَوْا مَاذَا أَنْزَلَ رَبُّكُمْ قَالُوا خَيْرًا لِلَّذِينَ أَحْسَنُوا فِي هَذِهِ الدُّنْيَا حَسَنَةٌ وَلَدَارُ الْآخِرَةِ خَيْرٌ وَلَنِعْمَ دَارُ الْمُتَّقِينَ (٣٠)

جَنَّاتُ عَدْنٍ يَدْخُلُونَهَا تَجْرِي مِنْ تَحْتِهَا الْأَنْهَارُ لَهُمْ فِيهَا مَا يَشَاءُونَ كَذَلِكَ يَجْزِي اللَّهُ الْمُتَّقِينَ (٣١)

الَّذِينَ تَتَوَفَّاهُمُ الْمَلَائِكَةُ طَيِّبِينَ

16. The Bee

against evil What has your Lord revealed? They say, Good. For those who do good in this world is good. And certainly the abode of the Hereafter is better. And excellent indeed is the abode of those who keep their duty --

16:31. Gardens of perpetuity which they enter, wherein flow rivers: they have therein what they please. Thus does Allah reward those who keep their duty,

16:32. Whom the angels cause to die in purity, saying: Peace be to you enter the Garden for what you did.

16:33. Await they aught but that the angels should come to them or that thy Lord's command should come to pass. Thus did those before them. And Allah wronged them not, but they wronged themselves.

16:34. So the evil of what they did afflicted them, and that which they mocked encompassed them.

* * *

16:35. And the idolaters say: Had Allah pleased, we had nor served aught but Him, (neither) we nor our fathers, nor had we prohibited aught without (order from) Him. Thus did those before them. But have the messengers any duty except a plain delivery (of the message)?

16:36. And certainly We raised in every nation a messenger, saying: Serve Allah and shun the devil. Then of them was he whom Allah guided, and of them was he whose remaining in error was justly due. So travel in the land, then see what was the end of the rejectors.

16:37. If thou desirest their guidance, yet Allah will not guide him who leads astray, nor have they any helpers.

16:38. And they swear by Allah their most energetic oaths: Allah will not raise up him who dies Yea! it is a promise binding on Him, quite true,

16. The Bee

but most people know not:

16:39. So that He might make manifest to them that about which they differ, and that those who disbelieve might know that they were liars.

16:40. Our word for a thing, when We intend it, is only that We say to it, Be; and it is.

* * *

16:41. And those who flee for Allah's sake after they are oppressed, We shall certainly give them a good abode in the world; and the reward of the Hereafter is much greater. Did they but know!

16:42. Those who are steadfast and on their Lord they rely.

16:43. And We sent not before thee any but men to whom We sent revelation -- so ask the followers of the Reminder if you know not --

16:44. With clear arguments and Scriptures. And We have revealed to thee the Reminder that thou mayest make clear to men that which has been revealed to them, and that haply they may reflect.

16:45. Are they, then, who plan evil (plans), secure that Allah will not abase them in the earth, or that chastisement will not overtake them from whence they perceive not?

16:46. Or that He will not seize them in their going to and fro, then they will not be able to escape?

16:47. Or that He will not seize them with a gradual diminution? Your Lord is surely Compassionate, Merciful.

16:48. See they not everything that Allah has created? Its (very) shadows return from right and left, making obeisance to Allah, while they are in utter abasement.

16:49. And to Allah makes obeisance every living creature that is in the heavens and that is in the earth, and the angels (too) and they are not proud.

16:50. They fear their Lord above them and do what they are commanded.

الَّذِينَ صَبَرُوا وَعَلَىٰ رَبِّهِمْ يَتَوَكَّلُونَ (٤٢)

وَمَا أَرْسَلْنَا مِن قَبْلِكَ إِلَّا رِجَالًا نُوحِي إِلَيْهِمْ فَاسْأَلُوا أَهْلَ الذِّكْرِ إِن كُنتُمْ لَا تَعْلَمُونَ (٤٣)

بِالْبَيِّنَاتِ وَالزُّبُرِ وَأَنزَلْنَا إِلَيْكَ الذِّكْرَ لِتُبَيِّنَ لِلنَّاسِ مَا نُزِّلَ إِلَيْهِمْ وَلَعَلَّهُمْ يَتَفَكَّرُونَ (٤٤)

أَفَأَمِنَ الَّذِينَ مَكَرُوا السَّيِّئَاتِ أَن يَخْسِفَ اللَّهُ بِهِمُ الْأَرْضَ أَوْ يَأْتِيَهُمُ الْعَذَابُ مِنْ حَيْثُ لَا يَشْعُرُونَ (٤٥)

أَوْ يَأْخُذَهُمْ فِي تَقَلُّبِهِمْ فَمَا هُم بِمُعْجِزِينَ (٤٦)

أَوْ يَأْخُذَهُمْ عَلَىٰ تَخَوُّفٍ فَإِنَّ رَبَّكُمْ لَرَءُوفٌ رَحِيمٌ (٤٧)

أَوَلَمْ يَرَوْا إِلَىٰ مَا خَلَقَ اللَّهُ مِن شَيْءٍ يَتَفَيَّأُ ظِلَالُهُ عَنِ الْيَمِينِ وَالشَّمَائِلِ سُجَّدًا لِلَّهِ وَهُمْ دَاخِرُونَ (٤٨)

وَلِلَّهِ يَسْجُدُ مَا فِي السَّمَاوَاتِ وَمَا فِي الْأَرْضِ مِن دَابَّةٍ وَالْمَلَائِكَةُ وَهُمْ لَا يَسْتَكْبِرُونَ (٤٩)

يَخَافُونَ رَبَّهُم مِّن فَوْقِهِمْ وَيَفْعَلُونَ مَا يُؤْمَرُونَ (٥٠)

وَقَالَ اللَّهُ لَا تَتَّخِذُوا إِلَٰهَيْنِ اثْنَيْنِ إِنَّمَا هُوَ إِلَٰهٌ وَاحِدٌ فَإِيَّايَ فَارْهَبُونِ (٥١)

وَلَهُ مَا فِي السَّمَاوَاتِ وَالْأَرْضِ وَلَهُ الدِّينُ وَاصِبًا أَفَغَيْرَ اللَّهِ تَتَّقُونَ (٥٢)

وَمَا بِكُم مِّن نِّعْمَةٍ فَمِنَ اللَّهِ ثُمَّ إِذَا مَسَّكُمُ الضُّرُّ فَإِلَيْهِ تَجْأَرُونَ (٥٣)

ثُمَّ إِذَا كَشَفَ الضُّرَّ عَنكُمْ إِذَا فَرِيقٌ مِّنكُم بِرَبِّهِمْ يُشْرِكُونَ (٥٤)

لِيَكْفُرُوا بِمَا آتَيْنَاهُمْ فَتَمَتَّعُوا فَسَوْفَ تَعْلَمُونَ (٥٥)

16. The Bee

***

16:51. And Allah has said: Take not two gods. He is only one God: So Me alone should you fear.

16:52. And whatever is in the heavens and the earth is His, and to Him is obedience due always. Will you then fear other than Allah?

16:53. And whatever good you have, it is from Allah; then, when evil afflicts you, to Him do you cry for aid.

16:54. Then when He removes the evil from you, lo! some of you associate others with their Lord,

16:55. So as to deny what We have given them. Then enjoy yourselves, for soon will you know.

16:56. And they set apart for what they know not, a portion of what we have given them. By Allah! you shall certainly be questioned about that which you forged.

16:57. And they ascribe daughters to Allah. Glory be to Him! And for themselves is what they desire!

16:58. And when the birth of a daughter is announced to one of them, his face becomes black and he is full of wrath.

16:59. He hides himself from the people because of the evil of what is announced to him. Shall he keep it with disgrace or bury it (alive) in the dust? Now surely evil is what they judge!

16:60. For those who believe not in the Hereafter are evil attributes and Allah's are the sublime attributes. And He is the Mighty, the Wise.

***

16:61. And if Allah were to destroy men for their iniquity, He would not leave therein a single creature, but He respites them till an appointed time. So when their doom comes, they are not able to delay (it) an hour, nor can they advance (it).

16:62. And they ascribe to Allah what

وَيَجْعَلُونَ لِمَا لَا يَعْلَمُونَ نَصِيبًا مِمَّا رَزَقْنَاهُمْ تَاللَّهِ لَتُسْأَلُنَّ عَمَّا كُنْتُمْ تَفْتَرُونَ (٥٦)

وَيَجْعَلُونَ لِلَّهِ الْبَنَاتِ سُبْحَانَهُ وَلَهُمْ مَا يَشْتَهُونَ (٥٧)

وَإِذَا بُشِّرَ أَحَدُهُمْ بِالْأُنْثَى ظَلَّ وَجْهُهُ مُسْوَدًّا وَهُوَ كَظِيمٌ (٥٨)

يَتَوَارَى مِنَ الْقَوْمِ مِنْ سُوءِ مَا بُشِّرَ بِهِ أَيُمْسِكُهُ عَلَى هُونٍ أَمْ يَدُسُّهُ فِي التُّرَابِ أَلَا سَاءَ مَا يَحْكُمُونَ (٥٩)

لِلَّذِينَ لَا يُؤْمِنُونَ بِالْآخِرَةِ مَثَلُ السَّوْءِ وَلِلَّهِ الْمَثَلُ الْأَعْلَى وَهُوَ الْعَزِيزُ الْحَكِيمُ (٦٠)

وَلَوْ يُؤَاخِذُ اللَّهُ النَّاسَ بِظُلْمِهِمْ مَا تَرَكَ عَلَيْهَا مِنْ دَابَّةٍ وَلَكِنْ يُؤَخِّرُهُمْ إِلَى أَجَلٍ مُسَمًّى فَإِذَا جَاءَ أَجَلُهُمْ لَا يَسْتَأْخِرُونَ سَاعَةً وَلَا يَسْتَقْدِمُونَ (٦١)

وَيَجْعَلُونَ لِلَّهِ مَا يَكْرَهُونَ وَتَصِفُ أَلْسِنَتُهُمُ الْكَذِبَ أَنَّ لَهُمُ الْحُسْنَى لَا جَرَمَ أَنَّ لَهُمُ النَّارَ وَأَنَّهُمْ مُفْرَطُونَ (٦٢)

تَاللَّهِ لَقَدْ أَرْسَلْنَا إِلَى أُمَمٍ مِنْ قَبْلِكَ فَزَيَّنَ لَهُمُ الشَّيْطَانُ أَعْمَالَهُمْ فَهُوَ وَلِيُّهُمُ الْيَوْمَ وَلَهُمْ عَذَابٌ أَلِيمٌ (٦٣)

وَمَا أَنْزَلْنَا عَلَيْكَ الْكِتَابَ إِلَّا لِتُبَيِّنَ لَهُمُ الَّذِي اخْتَلَفُوا فِيهِ وَهُدًى وَرَحْمَةً لِقَوْمٍ يُؤْمِنُونَ (٦٤)

وَاللَّهُ أَنْزَلَ مِنَ السَّمَاءِ مَاءً فَأَحْيَا بِهِ الْأَرْضَ بَعْدَ مَوْتِهَا إِنَّ فِي ذَلِكَ لَآيَةً لِقَوْمٍ يَسْمَعُونَ (٦٥)

وَإِنَّ لَكُمْ فِي الْأَنْعَامِ لَعِبْرَةً نُسْقِيكُمْ مِمَّا فِي بُطُونِهِ مِنْ بَيْنِ فَرْثٍ وَدَمٍ لَبَنًا خَالِصًا سَائِغًا لِلشَّارِبِينَ (٦٦)

16. The Bee

they (themselves) hate, and their tongues relate the lie that for them is good. Assuredly for them is the Fire, and they will be (therein) abandoned.
16:63. By Allah! We certainly sent (messengers) to nations before thee, but the devil made their deeds fair-seeming to them. So he is their patron to-day, and for them is a painful chastisement.
16:64. And We have not revealed to thee the Book except that thou mayest make clear to them that wherein they differ, and (as) a guidance and a mercy for a people who believe.
16:65. And Allah sends down water from above, and therewith gives life to the earth after its death. Surely there is a sign in this for a people who listen.

* * *

16:66. And surely there is a lesson for you in the cattle: We give you to drink of what is in their bellies -- from betwixt the faeces and the blood -- pure milk, agreeable to the drinkers.
16:67. And of the fruits of the palms and the grapes, you obtain from them intoxicants and goodly provision. There is surely a sign in this for a people who ponder.
16:68. And thy Lord revealed to the bee: Make hives in the mountains and in the trees and in what they build,
16:69. Then eat of all the fruits and walk in the ways of thy Lord submissively. There comes forth from their bellies a beverage of many hues, in which there is healing for men. Therein is surely a sign for a people who reflect.
16:70. And Allah creates you, then He causes you to die and of you is he who is brought back to the worst part of life, so that he knows nothing after having knowledge. Surely Allah is Knowing, Powerful.

* * *

16:71. And Allah has made some of

وَمِنْ ثَمَرَاتِ النَّخِيلِ وَالْأَعْنَابِ تَتَّخِذُونَ مِنْهُ سَكَرًا وَرِزْقًا حَسَنًا إِنَّ فِي ذَلِكَ لَآيَةً لِقَوْمٍ يَعْقِلُونَ (٦٧) وَأَوْحَى رَبُّكَ إِلَى النَّحْلِ أَنِ اتَّخِذِي مِنَ الْجِبَالِ بُيُوتًا وَمِنَ الشَّجَرِ وَمِمَّا يَعْرِشُونَ (٦٨) ثُمَّ كُلِي مِنْ كُلِّ الثَّمَرَاتِ فَاسْلُكِي سُبُلَ رَبِّكِ ذُلُلًا يَخْرُجُ مِنْ بُطُونِهَا شَرَابٌ مُخْتَلِفٌ أَلْوَانُهُ فِيهِ شِفَاءٌ لِلنَّاسِ إِنَّ فِي ذَلِكَ لَآيَةً لِقَوْمٍ يَتَفَكَّرُونَ (٦٩) وَاللَّهُ خَلَقَكُمْ ثُمَّ يَتَوَفَّاكُمْ وَمِنْكُمْ مَنْ يُرَدُّ إِلَى أَرْذَلِ الْعُمُرِ لِكَيْ لَا يَعْلَمَ بَعْدَ عِلْمٍ شَيْئًا إِنَّ اللَّهَ عَلِيمٌ قَدِيرٌ (٧٠) وَاللَّهُ فَضَّلَ بَعْضَكُمْ عَلَى بَعْضٍ فِي الرِّزْقِ فَمَا الَّذِينَ فُضِّلُوا بِرَادِّي رِزْقِهِمْ عَلَى مَا مَلَكَتْ أَيْمَانُهُمْ فَهُمْ فِيهِ سَوَاءٌ أَفَبِنِعْمَةِ اللَّهِ يَجْحَدُونَ (٧١) وَاللَّهُ جَعَلَ لَكُمْ مِنْ أَنْفُسِكُمْ أَزْوَاجًا وَجَعَلَ لَكُمْ مِنْ أَزْوَاجِكُمْ بَنِينَ وَحَفَدَةً وَرَزَقَكُمْ مِنَ الطَّيِّبَاتِ أَفَبِالْبَاطِلِ يُؤْمِنُونَ وَبِنِعْمَةِ اللَّهِ هُمْ يَكْفُرُونَ (٧٢) وَيَعْبُدُونَ مِنْ دُونِ اللَّهِ مَا لَا يَمْلِكُ لَهُمْ رِزْقًا مِنَ السَّمَاوَاتِ وَالْأَرْضِ شَيْئًا وَلَا يَسْتَطِيعُونَ (٧٣) فَلَا تَضْرِبُوا لِلَّهِ الْأَمْثَالَ إِنَّ اللَّهَ يَعْلَمُ وَأَنْتُمْ لَا تَعْلَمُونَ (٧٤) ضَرَبَ اللَّهُ مَثَلًا عَبْدًا مَمْلُوكًا لَا يَقْدِرُ عَلَى شَيْءٍ وَمَنْ رَزَقْنَاهُ مِنَّا رِزْقًا حَسَنًا فَهُوَ يُنْفِقُ مِنْهُ سِرًّا وَجَهْرًا هَلْ يَسْتَوُونَ الْحَمْدُ لِلَّهِ بَلْ أَكْثَرُهُمْ لَا

16. The Bee

you excel others in the means of subsistence; so those who are made to excel give not away their sustenance to those whom their right hands possess, so that they may be equal therein. Will they then deny the favour of Allah?

16:72. And Allah has made wives for you from among yourselves, and has given you sons and daughters from your wives, and has provided you with good things. Will they then believe in falsehood and deny the favour of Allah?

16:73. And they serve besides Allah that which controls for them no sustenance at all from the heavens and the earth; nor have they any power.

16:74. So coin not similitudes for Allah. Surely Allah knows and you know not.

16:75. Allah sets forth a parable: There is a slave, the property of another, controlling naught, and there is one to whom We have granted from Ourselves goodly provisions, so he spends from it secretly and openly. Are the two alike? Praise be to Allah! Nay, most of them know not.

16:76. And Allah sets forth a parable of two men: One of them dumb, controlling naught, and he is a burden to his master; wherever he sends him, he brings no good. Is he equal with him who enjoins justice, and he is on the right path?

***

16:77. And Allah's is the unseen of the heavens and the earth. And the matter of the Hour is but as a twinkling of the eye or it is nigher still. Surely Allah is Possessor of power over all things.

16:78. And Allah brought you forth from the wombs of your mothers you knew nothing -- and He gave you hearing and sight and hearts that you might give thanks.

16:79. See they not the birds, constrained in the middle of the sky? None witholds them but Allah. Surely

16. The Bee

in this are signs for a people who believe.

16:80. And Allah has given you an abode in your houses, and He has given you houses of the skins of cattle, which you find light to carry on the day of your march and on the day of your halting, and of their wool and their fur and their hair, household stuff and a provision for a time.

16:81. And Allah has made for you, of what He has created, shelters, and He has given you in the mountains, places of retreat, and He has given you garments to save you from the heat, and coats of mail to save you in your fighting. Thus does He complete His favour to you that you may submit.

16:82. Then if they turn away, thy duty is only clear deliverance (of the message).

16:83. Trey recognize the favour of Allah, yet they deny it, and most of them are ungrateful.

***

16:84. And on the day when We raise up a witness out of every nation, then permission (to offer excuse) will not be given to the disbelievers, nor will they be allowed to make amends.

16:85. And when the wrong-doers see the chastisement, it will not be lightened for them, not will they be respited.

16:86. And when those who ascribed partners (to Allah) see their associate-gods, they will say: Our Lord, these are our associate-gods on whom we called besides Thee. But they will throw back at them the word: Surely you are liars.

16:87. And they will tender submission to Allah on that day, and what they used to forge will fail them.

16:88. Those who disbelieve and hinder (men) from Allah's way, We will add chastisement to their chastisement because they made mischief.

16:89. And on the day when We raise

(٨٤)
وَإِذَا رَأَى الَّذِينَ ظَلَمُوا الْعَذَابَ فَلَا يُخَفَّفُ عَنْهُمْ وَلَا هُمْ يُنظَرُونَ (٨٥)
وَإِذَا رَأَى الَّذِينَ أَشْرَكُوا شُرَكَاءَهُمْ قَالُوا رَبَّنَا هَؤُلَاءِ شُرَكَاؤُنَا الَّذِينَ كُنَّا نَدْعُوا مِن دُونِكَ فَأَلْقَوْا إِلَيْهِمُ الْقَوْلَ إِنَّكُمْ لَكَاذِبُونَ (٨٦)
وَأَلْقَوْا إِلَى اللَّهِ يَوْمَئِذٍ السَّلَمَ وَضَلَّ عَنْهُم مَّا كَانُوا يَفْتَرُونَ (٨٧)
الَّذِينَ كَفَرُوا وَصَدُّوا عَن سَبِيلِ اللَّهِ زِدْنَاهُمْ عَذَابًا فَوْقَ الْعَذَابِ بِمَا كَانُوا يُفْسِدُونَ (٨٨)
وَيَوْمَ نَبْعَثُ فِي كُلِّ أُمَّةٍ شَهِيدًا عَلَيْهِم مِّنْ أَنفُسِهِمْ وَجِئْنَا بِكَ شَهِيدًا عَلَى هَؤُلَاءِ وَنَزَّلْنَا عَلَيْكَ الْكِتَابَ تِبْيَانًا لِّكُلِّ شَيْءٍ وَهُدًى وَرَحْمَةً وَبُشْرَى لِلْمُسْلِمِينَ (٨٩)
إِنَّ اللَّهَ يَأْمُرُ بِالْعَدْلِ وَالْإِحْسَانِ وَإِيتَاءِ ذِي الْقُرْبَى وَيَنْهَى عَنِ الْفَحْشَاءِ وَالْمُنكَرِ وَالْبَغْيِ يَعِظُكُمْ لَعَلَّكُمْ تَذَكَّرُونَ (٩٠)
وَأَوْفُوا بِعَهْدِ اللَّهِ إِذَا عَاهَدتُّمْ وَلَا تَنقُضُوا الْأَيْمَانَ بَعْدَ تَوْكِيدِهَا وَقَدْ جَعَلْتُمُ اللَّهَ عَلَيْكُمْ كَفِيلًا إِنَّ اللَّهَ يَعْلَمُ مَا تَفْعَلُونَ (٩١)
وَلَا تَكُونُوا كَالَّتِي نَقَضَتْ غَزْلَهَا مِن بَعْدِ قُوَّةٍ أَنكَاثًا تَتَّخِذُونَ أَيْمَانَكُمْ دَخَلًا بَيْنَكُمْ أَن تَكُونَ أُمَّةٌ هِيَ أَرْبَى مِنْ أُمَّةٍ إِنَّمَا يَبْلُوكُمُ اللَّهُ بِهِ وَلَيُبَيِّنَنَّ لَكُمْ يَوْمَ الْقِيَامَةِ مَا كُنتُمْ فِيهِ تَخْتَلِفُونَ (٩٢)
وَلَوْ شَاءَ اللَّهُ لَجَعَلَكُمْ أُمَّةً وَاحِدَةً وَلَٰكِن يُضِلُّ مَن يَشَاءُ وَيَهْدِي مَن يَشَاءُ وَلَتُسْأَلُنَّ عَمَّا كُنتُمْ تَعْمَلُونَ

16. The Bee

up in every people a witness against them from among themselves, and bring thee as a witness against these. And We have revealed the Book to thee explaining all things, and a guidance and mercy and good news for those who submit.

* * *

16:90. Surely Allah enjoins justice and the doing of good (to others) and the giving to the kindred, and He forbids indecency and evil and rebellion. He admonishes you that you may be mindful.

16:91. And fulfil the covenant of Allah, when you have made a covenant, and break not the oaths after making them fast, and you have indeed made Allah your surety. Surely Allah knows what you do.

16:92. And be not like her who unravels her yarn, disintegrating it into pieces, after she has spun It strongly. You make your oaths to be means of deceit between you because (one) nation is more numerous than (another) nation. Allah only tries you by this. And He will certainly make clear to you on the day of Resurrection that wherein you differed.

16:93. And if Allah please, He would make you a single nation, but He leaves in error whom He pleases and guides whom He pleases. And certainly you will be questioned as to what you did.

16:94. And make not your oaths a means of deceit between you, lest a foot should slip after its stability, and you should taste evil because you hinder (men) from Allah's way and grievous chastisement be your (lot).

16:95. And take not a small price for Allah's covenant. Surely what is with Allah is better for you, did you but know!

16:96. What is with you passes away and what is with Allah is enduring.

(٩٣)

وَلَا تَتَّخِذُوا أَيْمَانَكُمْ دَخَلًا بَيْنَكُمْ فَتَزِلَّ قَدَمٌ بَعْدَ ثُبُوتِهَا وَتَذُوقُوا السُّوءَ بِمَا صَدَدتُّمْ عَن سَبِيلِ اللَّهِ وَلَكُمْ عَذَابٌ عَظِيمٌ (٩٤)

وَلَا تَشْتَرُوا بِعَهْدِ اللَّهِ ثَمَنًا قَلِيلًا إِنَّمَا عِندَ اللَّهِ هُوَ خَيْرٌ لَّكُمْ إِن كُنتُمْ تَعْلَمُونَ (٩٥)

مَا عِندَكُمْ يَنفَدُ وَمَا عِندَ اللَّهِ بَاقٍ وَلَنَجْزِيَنَّ الَّذِينَ صَبَرُوا أَجْرَهُم بِأَحْسَنِ مَا كَانُوا يَعْمَلُونَ (٩٦)

مَنْ عَمِلَ صَالِحًا مِّن ذَكَرٍ أَوْ أُنثَىٰ وَهُوَ مُؤْمِنٌ فَلَنُحْيِيَنَّهُ حَيَاةً طَيِّبَةً وَلَنَجْزِيَنَّهُمْ أَجْرَهُم بِأَحْسَنِ مَا كَانُوا يَعْمَلُونَ (٩٧)

فَإِذَا قَرَأْتَ الْقُرْآنَ فَاسْتَعِذْ بِاللَّهِ مِنَ الشَّيْطَانِ الرَّجِيمِ (٩٨)

إِنَّهُ لَيْسَ لَهُ سُلْطَانٌ عَلَى الَّذِينَ آمَنُوا وَعَلَىٰ رَبِّهِمْ يَتَوَكَّلُونَ (٩٩)

إِنَّمَا سُلْطَانُهُ عَلَى الَّذِينَ يَتَوَلَّوْنَهُ وَالَّذِينَ هُم بِهِ مُشْرِكُونَ (١٠٠)

وَإِذَا بَدَّلْنَا آيَةً مَّكَانَ آيَةٍ وَاللَّهُ أَعْلَمُ بِمَا يُنَزِّلُ قَالُوا إِنَّمَا أَنتَ مُفْتَرٍ بَلْ أَكْثَرُهُمْ لَا يَعْلَمُونَ (١٠١)

قُلْ نَزَّلَهُ رُوحُ الْقُدُسِ مِن رَّبِّكَ بِالْحَقِّ لِيُثَبِّتَ الَّذِينَ آمَنُوا وَهُدًى وَبُشْرَىٰ لِلْمُسْلِمِينَ (١٠٢)

وَلَقَدْ نَعْلَمُ أَنَّهُمْ يَقُولُونَ إِنَّمَا يُعَلِّمُهُ بَشَرٌ لِّسَانُ الَّذِي يُلْحِدُونَ إِلَيْهِ أَعْجَمِيٌّ وَهَـٰذَا لِسَانٌ عَرَبِيٌّ مُّبِينٌ (١٠٣)

إِنَّ الَّذِينَ لَا يُؤْمِنُونَ بِآيَاتِ اللَّهِ لَا يَهْدِيهِمُ اللَّهُ وَلَهُمْ عَذَابٌ أَلِيمٌ (١٠٤)

إِنَّمَا يَفْتَرِي الْكَذِبَ الَّذِينَ لَا يُؤْمِنُونَ

16. The Bee

And We shall certainly give to those who are patient their reward for the best of what they did.

16:97. Whoever does good, whether male or female, and is a believer, We shall certainly make him live a good life, and We shall certainly give them their reward for the best of what they did.

16:98. So when thou recitest the Qur'an, seek refuge in Allah from the accursed devil.

16:99. Surely he has no authority over those who believe and rely on their Lord.

16:100. His authority is only over those who befriend him and those who associate others with Him.

* * *

16:101. And when We change a message for a message and Allah knows best what He reveals -- they say Thou art only a forger. Nay, most of them know not.

16:102. Say: The Holy Spirit has revealed it from thy Lord with truth, that it may establish those who believe, and as a guidance and good news for those who submit.

16:103. And indeed We know that they say: Only a mortal teaches him. The tongue of him whom they hint at is foreign, and this is clear Arabic language.

16:104. Those who believe not in Allah's messages, Allah guides them not, and for them is a painful chastisement.

16:105. Only they forge lies who believe not in Allah's messages, and they are the liars.

16:106. Whoso disbelieves in Allah after his belief -- not he who is compelled while his heart is content with faith, but he who opens (his) breast for disbelief -- on them is the wrath of Allah, and for them is a grievous chastisement.

بِآيَاتِ اللَّهِ وَأُولَٰئِكَ هُمُ الْكَاذِبُونَ (١٠٥)

مَن كَفَرَ بِاللَّهِ مِن بَعْدِ إِيمَانِهِ إِلَّا مَنْ أُكْرِهَ وَقَلْبُهُ مُطْمَئِنٌّ بِالْإِيمَانِ وَلَٰكِن مَّن شَرَحَ بِالْكُفْرِ صَدْرًا فَعَلَيْهِمْ غَضَبٌ مِّنَ اللَّهِ وَلَهُمْ عَذَابٌ عَظِيمٌ (١٠٦)

ذَٰلِكَ بِأَنَّهُمُ اسْتَحَبُّوا الْحَيَاةَ الدُّنْيَا عَلَى الْآخِرَةِ وَأَنَّ اللَّهَ لَا يَهْدِي الْقَوْمَ الْكَافِرِينَ (١٠٧)

أُولَٰئِكَ الَّذِينَ طَبَعَ اللَّهُ عَلَىٰ قُلُوبِهِمْ وَسَمْعِهِمْ وَأَبْصَارِهِمْ وَأُولَٰئِكَ هُمُ الْغَافِلُونَ (١٠٨)

لَا جَرَمَ أَنَّهُمْ فِي الْآخِرَةِ هُمُ الْخَاسِرُونَ (١٠٩)

ثُمَّ إِنَّ رَبَّكَ لِلَّذِينَ هَاجَرُوا مِن بَعْدِ مَا فُتِنُوا ثُمَّ جَاهَدُوا وَصَبَرُوا إِنَّ رَبَّكَ مِن بَعْدِهَا لَغَفُورٌ رَحِيمٌ (١١٠)

يَوْمَ تَأْتِي كُلُّ نَفْسٍ تُجَادِلُ عَن نَّفْسِهَا وَتُوَفَّىٰ كُلُّ نَفْسٍ مَّا عَمِلَتْ وَهُمْ لَا يُظْلَمُونَ (١١١)

وَضَرَبَ اللَّهُ مَثَلًا قَرْيَةً كَانَتْ آمِنَةً مُّطْمَئِنَّةً يَأْتِيهَا رِزْقُهَا رَغَدًا مِّن كُلِّ مَكَانٍ فَكَفَرَتْ بِأَنْعُمِ اللَّهِ فَأَذَاقَهَا اللَّهُ لِبَاسَ الْجُوعِ وَالْخَوْفِ بِمَا كَانُوا يَصْنَعُونَ (١١٢)

وَلَقَدْ جَاءَهُمْ رَسُولٌ مِّنْهُمْ فَكَذَّبُوهُ فَأَخَذَهُمُ الْعَذَابُ وَهُمْ ظَالِمُونَ (١١٣)

فَكُلُوا مِمَّا رَزَقَكُمُ اللَّهُ حَلَالًا طَيِّبًا وَاشْكُرُوا نِعْمَتَ اللَّهِ إِن كُنتُمْ إِيَّاهُ تَعْبُدُونَ (١١٤)

إِنَّمَا حَرَّمَ عَلَيْكُمُ الْمَيْتَةَ وَالدَّمَ وَلَحْمَ الْخِنزِيرِ وَمَا أُهِلَّ لِغَيْرِ اللَّهِ بِهِ فَمَنِ

16:107. That is because they love this world's life more than the Hereafter, and because Allah guides not the disbelieving people.

16:108. These are they whose hearts and ears and eyes Allah has sealed and these are the heedless ones.

16:109. No doubt that in the Hereafter they are the losers.

16:110. Then surely thy Lord, to those who flee after they are persecuted, then struggle hard and are patient, surely thy Lord after that is Protecting, Merciful.

***

16:111. On the day when every soul will come pleading for itself, and every soul will be paid in full what it has done, and they will not be dealt with unjustly.

16:112. And Allah sets forth a parable: A town safe and secure, to which its means of subsistence came in abundance from every quarter; but it disbelieved in Allah's favours, so Allah made it taste a pall of hunger and fear because of what they wrought.

16:113. And certainly there came to them a Messenger from among them, but they rejected him, so the chastisement overtook them, while they were wrongdoers.

16:114. So eat of what Allah has given you, lawful and good (things), and give thanks for Allah's favour, if He it is you serve.

16:115. He has forbidden you only what dies of itself and blood and the flesh of swine and that over which any other name than that of Allah has been invoked; but whoever is driven to (it), not desiring nor exceeding the limit, then surely Allah is Forgiving, Merciful.

16:116. And utter not, for what your tongues describe, the lie: This is lawful and this unlawful; so that you forge a lie against Allah. Surely those who forge a lie against Allah will not prosper.

16:117. A little enjoyment -- and for them is a painful chastisement.

16:118. And to those who are Jews We prohibited what We have related to thee already, and We did them no wrong, but they wronged themselves.

16:119. And surely thy Lord, for those who do evil in ignorance, then turn after that and make amends, surely thy Lord after that is Forgiving, Merciful.

* * *

16:120. Surely Abraham was a model (of virtue), obedient to Allah, upright, and he was not of the polytheist,

16:121. Grateful for His favours. He chose him and guided him on the right path.

16:122. And We gave him good in this world; and in the Hereafter he is surely among the righteous.

16:123. Then We revealed to thee: Follow the faith of Abraham, the upright one; and he was not of the polytheists.

16:124. The Sabbath was ordained only against those who differed about it. And surely thy Lord will judge between them on the day of Resurrection concerning that wherein they differed.

16:125. Call to the way of thy Lord with wisdom and goodly exhortation, and argue with them in the best manner. Surely thy Lord knows best him who strays from His path, and He knows best those who go atight.

16:126. And if you take your turn, then punish with the like of that with which you were afflicted. But if you show patience, it is certainly best for the patient.

16:127. And be patient and thy patience is not but by (the help of) Allah, and grieve not for them, nor be in distress for what they plan.

16:128. Surely Allah is with those who

(١٢٦)
وَاصْبِرْ وَمَا صَبْرُكَ إِلَّا بِاللَّهِ وَلَا تَحْزَنْ عَلَيْهِمْ وَلَا تَكُ فِي ضَيْقٍ مِمَّا يَمْكُرُونَ (١٢٧)
إِنَّ اللَّهَ مَعَ الَّذِينَ اتَّقَوْا وَالَّذِينَ هُم مُّحْسِنُونَ (١٢٨)

keep their duty and those who do good (to others).

17. The Israelites

In the name of Allah, the Beneficent, the Merciful.

17:1. Glory to Him Who carried His servant by night from the Sacred Mosque to the Remote Mosque, whose precincts We blessed, that We might show him of Our signs! 1410 Surely He is the Heating, the Seeing.

17:2. And We gave Moses the Book and made it a guidance to the Children of Israel (saying): Take no guardian beside Me --

17:3. The offspring of those whom We bore with Noah. Surely he was a grateful servant.

17:4. And We made known to the Children of Israel in the Book: Certainly you will make mischief in the land twice, and behave insolently with mighty arrogance.

17:5. So when of the two, the first warning came to pass, We raised against you Our servants, of mighty prowess, so they made havoc in (your) houses. And it was an accomplished threat.

17:6. Then We gave you back the turn against them, and aided you with wealth and children and made you a numerous band.

17:7. If you do good, you do good for your own souls. And if you do evil, it is for them. So when the second warning came, (We raised another people) that they might bring you to grief and that they might enter the Mosque as they entered it the first time, and that they might destroy, whatever they conquered, with utter destruction.

17:8. It may be that your Lord will have mercy on you. And if you return (to mischief), We will return (to

١٧- سورة الإسراء

بِسْمِ اللَّهِ الرَّحْمَنِ الرَّحِيمِ

سُبْحَانَ الَّذِي أَسْرَى بِعَبْدِهِ لَيْلًا مِنَ الْمَسْجِدِ الْحَرَامِ إِلَى الْمَسْجِدِ الْأَقْصَى الَّذِي بَارَكْنَا حَوْلَهُ لِنُرِيَهُ مِنْ آيَاتِنَا إِنَّهُ هُوَ السَّمِيعُ الْبَصِيرُ (١)

وَآتَيْنَا مُوسَى الْكِتَابَ وَجَعَلْنَاهُ هُدًى لِبَنِي إِسْرَائِيلَ أَلَّا تَتَّخِذُوا مِنْ دُونِي وَكِيلًا (٢)

ذُرِّيَّةَ مَنْ حَمَلْنَا مَعَ نُوحٍ إِنَّهُ كَانَ عَبْدًا شَكُورًا (٣)

وَقَضَيْنَا إِلَى بَنِي إِسْرَائِيلَ فِي الْكِتَابِ لَتُفْسِدُنَّ فِي الْأَرْضِ مَرَّتَيْنِ وَلَتَعْلُنَّ عُلُوًّا كَبِيرًا (٤)

فَإِذَا جَاءَ وَعْدُ أُولَاهُمَا بَعَثْنَا عَلَيْكُمْ عِبَادًا لَنَا أُولِي بَأْسٍ شَدِيدٍ فَجَاسُوا خِلَالَ الدِّيَارِ وَكَانَ وَعْدًا مَفْعُولًا (٥)

ثُمَّ رَدَدْنَا لَكُمُ الْكَرَّةَ عَلَيْهِمْ وَأَمْدَدْنَاكُمْ بِأَمْوَالٍ وَبَنِينَ وَجَعَلْنَاكُمْ أَكْثَرَ نَفِيرًا (٦)

إِنْ أَحْسَنْتُمْ أَحْسَنْتُمْ لِأَنْفُسِكُمْ وَإِنْ أَسَأْتُمْ فَلَهَا فَإِذَا جَاءَ وَعْدُ الْآخِرَةِ لِيَسُوءُوا وُجُوهَكُمْ وَلِيَدْخُلُوا الْمَسْجِدَ كَمَا دَخَلُوهُ أَوَّلَ مَرَّةٍ وَلِيُتَبِّرُوا مَا عَلَوْا تَتْبِيرًا (٧)

عَسَى رَبُّكُمْ أَنْ يَرْحَمَكُمْ وَإِنْ عُدْتُمْ عُدْنَا وَجَعَلْنَا جَهَنَّمَ لِلْكَافِرِينَ حَصِيرًا (٨)

إِنَّ هَذَا الْقُرْآنَ يَهْدِي لِلَّتِي هِيَ أَقْوَمُ وَيُبَشِّرُ الْمُؤْمِنِينَ الَّذِينَ يَعْمَلُونَ

17. The Israelites

punishment). And We have made hell a prison for the disbelievers.

17:9. Surely this Qur'an guides to that which is most upright, and gives good news to the believers who do good that theirs is a great reward,

17:10. And that those who believe not in the Hereafter, We have prepared for them a painful chastisement.

* * *

17:11. And man prays for evil as he ought to pray for good; and man is ever hasty.

17:12. And We made the night and the day two signs, then We have made the sign of the night to pass away and We have made the sign of the day manifest, so that you may seek grace from your Lord, and that you may know the numbering of years and the reckoning. And We have explained everything with distinctness.

17:13. And We have made every man's actions to cling to his neck, and We shall bring forth to him on the day of Resurrection a book which he will find wide open. Read thy book. Thine own soul is sufficient as a reckoner against thee this day.

17:15. Whoever goes aright, for his own soul does he go aright; and whoever goes astray, to its detriment only does he go astray. And no bearer of a burden can bear the burden of another. Nor do We chastise until We raise a messenger.

17:16. And when We wish to destroy a town, We send commandments to its people who lead easy lives, but they transgress therein; thus the word proves true against it, so We destroy it with utter destruction.

17:17. And how many generations did We destroy after Noah And thy Lord suffices as being Aware and Seer of His servants' sins.

17:18. Whoso desires this transitory life, We hasten to him therein what We

الصَّالِحَاتِ أَنَّ لَهُمْ أَجْرًا كَبِيرًا (9) وَأَنَّ الَّذِينَ لَا يُؤْمِنُونَ بِالْآخِرَةِ أَعْتَدْنَا لَهُمْ عَذَابًا أَلِيمًا (10) وَيَدْعُ الْإِنْسَانُ بِالشَّرِّ دُعَاءَهُ بِالْخَيْرِ وَكَانَ الْإِنْسَانُ عَجُولًا (11) وَجَعَلْنَا اللَّيْلَ وَالنَّهَارَ آيَتَيْنِ فَمَحَوْنَا آيَةَ اللَّيْلِ وَجَعَلْنَا آيَةَ النَّهَارِ مُبْصِرَةً لِتَبْتَغُوا فَضْلًا مِنْ رَبِّكُمْ وَلِتَعْلَمُوا عَدَدَ السِّنِينَ وَالْحِسَابَ وَكُلَّ شَيْءٍ فَصَّلْنَاهُ تَفْصِيلًا (12) وَكُلَّ إِنْسَانٍ أَلْزَمْنَاهُ طَائِرَهُ فِي عُنُقِهِ وَنُخْرِجُ لَهُ يَوْمَ الْقِيَامَةِ كِتَابًا يَلْقَاهُ مَنْشُورًا (13) اقْرَأْ كِتَابَكَ كَفَى بِنَفْسِكَ الْيَوْمَ عَلَيْكَ حَسِيبًا (14) مَنِ اهْتَدَى فَإِنَّمَا يَهْتَدِي لِنَفْسِهِ وَمَنْ ضَلَّ فَإِنَّمَا يَضِلُّ عَلَيْهَا وَلَا تَزِرُ وَازِرَةٌ وِزْرَ أُخْرَى وَمَا كُنَّا مُعَذِّبِينَ حَتَّى نَبْعَثَ رَسُولًا (15) وَإِذَا أَرَدْنَا أَنْ نُهْلِكَ قَرْيَةً أَمَرْنَا مُتْرَفِيهَا فَفَسَقُوا فِيهَا فَحَقَّ عَلَيْهَا الْقَوْلُ فَدَمَّرْنَاهَا تَدْمِيرًا (16) وَكَمْ أَهْلَكْنَا مِنَ الْقُرُونِ مِنْ بَعْدِ نُوحٍ وَكَفَى بِرَبِّكَ بِذُنُوبِ عِبَادِهِ خَبِيرًا بَصِيرًا (17) مَنْ كَانَ يُرِيدُ الْعَاجِلَةَ عَجَّلْنَا لَهُ فِيهَا مَا نَشَاءُ لِمَنْ نُرِيدُ ثُمَّ جَعَلْنَا لَهُ جَهَنَّمَ يَصْلَاهَا مَذْمُومًا مَدْحُورًا (18) وَمَنْ أَرَادَ الْآخِرَةَ وَسَعَى لَهَا سَعْيَهَا وَهُوَ مُؤْمِنٌ فَأُولَئِكَ كَانَ سَعْيُهُمْ مَشْكُورًا (19) كُلًّا نُمِدُّ هَؤُلَاءِ وَهَؤُلَاءِ مِنْ عَطَاءِ رَبِّكَ وَمَا كَانَ عَطَاءُ رَبِّكَ مَحْظُورًا (20)

17. The Israelites

please for whomsoever We desire, then We assign to him the hell; he will enter it despised, driven away.

17:19. And whoso desires the Hereafter and strives for it as he ought to strive and he is a believer those are they whose striving is amply rewarded.

17:20. All do We aid -- these as well as those -- out of the bounty of thy Lord, and the bounty of thy Lord is not limited.

17:21. See how We have made some of them to excel others. And certainly the Hereafter is greater in degrees and greater in excellence.

17:22. Associate not any other god with Allah, lest thou sit down despised, forsaken.

* * *

17:23. And thy Lord has decreed that you serve none but Him, and do good to patents. If either or both of them reach old age with thee, say not "Fie" to them, nor chide them, and speak to them a generous word.

17:24. And lower to them the wing of humility out of mercy, and say: My Lord, have mercy on them, as they brought me up (when I was) little.

17:25. Your Lord knows best what is in your minds. If you are righteous, He is surely Forgiving to those who turn (to Him).

17:26. And give to the near of kin his due and (to) the needy and the wayfarer, and squander not wastefully.

17:27. Surely the squanderers are the devil's brethren. And the devil is ever ungrateful to his Lord.

17:28. And if thou turn away from them to seek mercy from thy Lord, which thou hopest for, speak to them a gentle word.

17:29. And make not thy hand to be shackled to thy neck, nor stretch it forth to the utmost (limit) of its stretching forth, lest thou sit down blamed, stripped off.

انْظُرْ كَيْفَ فَضَّلْنَا بَعْضَهُمْ عَلَى بَعْضٍ وَلَلْآخِرَةُ أَكْبَرُ دَرَجَاتٍ وَأَكْبَرُ تَفْضِيلًا (٢١)

لَا تَجْعَلْ مَعَ اللَّهِ إِلَهًا آخَرَ فَتَقْعُدَ مَذْمُومًا مَخْذُولًا (٢٢)

وَقَضَى رَبُّكَ أَلَّا تَعْبُدُوا إِلَّا إِيَّاهُ وَبِالْوَالِدَيْنِ إِحْسَانًا إِمَّا يَبْلُغَنَّ عِنْدَكَ الْكِبَرَ أَحَدُهُمَا أَوْ كِلَاهُمَا فَلَا تَقُلْ لَهُمَا أُفٍّ وَلَا تَنْهَرْهُمَا وَقُلْ لَهُمَا قَوْلًا كَرِيمًا (٢٣)

وَاخْفِضْ لَهُمَا جَنَاحَ الذُّلِّ مِنَ الرَّحْمَةِ وَقُلْ رَبِّ ارْحَمْهُمَا كَمَا رَبَّيَانِي صَغِيرًا (٢٤)

رَبُّكُمْ أَعْلَمُ بِمَا فِي نُفُوسِكُمْ إِنْ تَكُونُوا صَالِحِينَ فَإِنَّهُ كَانَ لِلْأَوَّابِينَ غَفُورًا (٢٥)

وَآتِ ذَا الْقُرْبَى حَقَّهُ وَالْمِسْكِينَ وَابْنَ السَّبِيلِ وَلَا تُبَذِّرْ تَبْذِيرًا (٢٦)

إِنَّ الْمُبَذِّرِينَ كَانُوا إِخْوَانَ الشَّيَاطِينِ وَكَانَ الشَّيْطَانُ لِرَبِّهِ كَفُورًا (٢٧)

وَإِمَّا تُعْرِضَنَّ عَنْهُمُ ابْتِغَاءَ رَحْمَةٍ مِنْ رَبِّكَ تَرْجُوهَا فَقُلْ لَهُمْ قَوْلًا مَيْسُورًا (٢٨)

وَلَا تَجْعَلْ يَدَكَ مَغْلُولَةً إِلَى عُنُقِكَ وَلَا تَبْسُطْهَا كُلَّ الْبَسْطِ فَتَقْعُدَ مَلُومًا مَحْسُورًا (٢٩)

إِنَّ رَبَّكَ يَبْسُطُ الرِّزْقَ لِمَنْ يَشَاءُ وَيَقْدِرُ إِنَّهُ كَانَ بِعِبَادِهِ خَبِيرًا بَصِيرًا (٣٠)

وَلَا تَقْتُلُوا أَوْلَادَكُمْ خَشْيَةَ إِمْلَاقٍ نَحْنُ نَرْزُقُهُمْ وَإِيَّاكُمْ إِنَّ قَتْلَهُمْ كَانَ خِطْئًا كَبِيرًا (٣١)

وَلَا تَقْرَبُوا الزِّنَا إِنَّهُ كَانَ فَاحِشَةً وَسَاءَ سَبِيلًا (٣٢)

17. The Israelites

17:30. Surely thy Lord makes plentiful the means of subsistence for whom He pleases, and He straitens. Surely He is ever Aware, Seer, of His servants.

* * *

17:31. And kill not your children for fear of poverty -- We provide for them and for you. Surely the killing of them is a great wrong.

17:32. And go not nigh to fornication; surely it is an obscenity. And evil is the way.

17:33. And kill not the soul which Allah has forbidden except for a just cause. And whoever is slain unjustly, We have indeed given to his heir authority -- but let him not exceed the limit in slaying. Surely he will be helped.

17:34. And draw not nigh to the orphan's property, except in a goodly way, till he attains his maturity. And fulfil the promise; surely, the promise will be enquired into.

17:35. And give full measure when you measure out, and weigh with a true balance. This is fair and better in the end.

17:36. And follow not that of which thou hast no knowledge. Surely the hearing and the sight and the heart, of all of these it will be asked.

17:37. And go not about in the land exultingly, for thou canst not tend the earth, nor reach the mountains in height.

17:38. All this, the evil thereof, is hateful in the sight of thy Lord.

17:39. This is of the wisdom which thy Lord has revealed to thee. And associate not any other god with AlIlib lest thou be thrown into hell, blamed, cast away.

17:40. Has then your Lord preferred to give you sons, and (for Himself) taken daughters from among the angels? Surely you utter a grievous saying.

* * *

17:41. And certainly We have repeated

وَلَا تَقْتُلُوا النَّفْسَ الَّتِي حَرَّمَ اللَّهُ إِلَّا بِالْحَقِّ وَمَنْ قُتِلَ مَظْلُومًا فَقَدْ جَعَلْنَا لِوَلِيِّهِ سُلْطَانًا فَلَا يُسْرِفْ فِي الْقَتْلِ إِنَّهُ كَانَ مَنْصُورًا (٣٣)

وَلَا تَقْرَبُوا مَالَ الْيَتِيمِ إِلَّا بِالَّتِي هِيَ أَحْسَنُ حَتَّى يَبْلُغَ أَشُدَّهُ وَأَوْفُوا بِالْعَهْدِ إِنَّ الْعَهْدَ كَانَ مَسْئُولًا (٣٤)

وَأَوْفُوا الْكَيْلَ إِذَا كِلْتُمْ وَزِنُوا بِالْقِسْطَاسِ الْمُسْتَقِيمِ ذَلِكَ خَيْرٌ وَأَحْسَنُ تَأْوِيلًا (٣٥)

وَلَا تَقْفُ مَا لَيْسَ لَكَ بِهِ عِلْمٌ إِنَّ السَّمْعَ وَالْبَصَرَ وَالْفُؤَادَ كُلُّ أُولَئِكَ كَانَ عَنْهُ مَسْئُولًا (٣٦)

وَلَا تَمْشِ فِي الْأَرْضِ مَرَحًا إِنَّكَ لَنْ تَخْرِقَ الْأَرْضَ وَلَنْ تَبْلُغَ الْجِبَالَ طُولًا (٣٧)

كُلُّ ذَلِكَ كَانَ سَيِّئُهُ عِنْدَ رَبِّكَ مَكْرُوهًا (٣٨)

ذَلِكَ مِمَّا أَوْحَى إِلَيْكَ رَبُّكَ مِنَ الْحِكْمَةِ وَلَا تَجْعَلْ مَعَ اللَّهِ إِلَهًا آخَرَ فَتُلْقَى فِي جَهَنَّمَ مَلُومًا مَدْحُورًا (٣٩)

أَفَأَصْفَاكُمْ رَبُّكُمْ بِالْبَنِينَ وَاتَّخَذَ مِنَ الْمَلَائِكَةِ إِنَاثًا إِنَّكُمْ لَتَقُولُونَ قَوْلًا عَظِيمًا (٤٠)

وَلَقَدْ صَرَّفْنَا فِي هَذَا الْقُرْآنِ لِيَذَّكَّرُوا وَمَا يَزِيدُهُمْ إِلَّا نُفُورًا (٤١)

قُلْ لَوْ كَانَ مَعَهُ آلِهَةٌ كَمَا يَقُولُونَ إِذًا لَابْتَغَوْا إِلَى ذِي الْعَرْشِ سَبِيلًا (٤٢)

سُبْحَانَهُ وَتَعَالَى عَمَّا يَقُولُونَ عُلُوًّا كَبِيرًا (٤٣)

تُسَبِّحُ لَهُ السَّمَوَاتُ السَّبْعُ وَالْأَرْضُ وَمَنْ فِيهِنَّ وَإِنْ مِنْ شَيْءٍ إِلَّا يُسَبِّحُ بِحَمْدِهِ وَلَكِنْ لَا تَفْقَهُونَ تَسْبِيحَهُمْ إِنَّهُ

(warnings) in this Qur'an that they may be mindful. And it adds not save to their aversion.

17:42. Say If there were with Him gods, as they say, then certainly they would have been able to seek a way to the Lord of the Throne.

17:43. Glory to Him! and He is highly exalted above what they say!

17:44. The seven heavens and the earth and those in them declare His glory. And there is not a single thing but glorifies Him with His praise, but you do not understand their glorification. Surely He is Forbearing, Forgiving.

17:45. And when thou recitest the Qur'an, We place between thee and those who believe not in the Hereafter a hidden barrier

17:46. And We put coverings on their hearts and a deafness in their ears lest they understand it; and when thou makest mention of thy Lord alone in the Qur'an, they turn their backs in aversion.

17:47. We know best what they listen to when they listen to thee, and when they take counsel secretly, when the wrongdoers say: You follow only a man deprived of reason.

17:48. See, what they liken thee to So they have gone astray, and cannot find the way.

17:49. And they say: When we are bones and decayed particles, shall we then be raised up as a new creation?

17:50. Say: Be stones or iron,

17:51. Or some other creature of those which are too hard (to receive life) in your minds! But they will say: Who will return us? Say: He Who created you at first. Still they will shake their heads at thee and say When will it be? Say: Maybe it has drawn nigh.

17:52. On the day when He will call you forth, then will you obey Him, giving Him praise, and you will think that you tarried but a little (while).

كَانَ حَلِيمًا غَفُورًا (٤٤)
وَإِذَا قَرَأْتَ الْقُرْآنَ جَعَلْنَا بَيْنَكَ وَبَيْنَ الَّذِينَ لَا يُؤْمِنُونَ بِالْآخِرَةِ حِجَابًا مَسْتُورًا (٤٥)
وَجَعَلْنَا عَلَى قُلُوبِهِمْ أَكِنَّةً أَنْ يَفْقَهُوهُ وَفِي آذَانِهِمْ وَقْرًا وَإِذَا ذَكَرْتَ رَبَّكَ فِي الْقُرْآنِ وَحْدَهُ وَلَّوْا عَلَى أَدْبَارِهِمْ نُفُورًا (٤٦)
نَحْنُ أَعْلَمُ بِمَا يَسْتَمِعُونَ بِهِ إِذْ يَسْتَمِعُونَ إِلَيْكَ وَإِذْ هُمْ نَجْوَى إِذْ يَقُولُ الظَّالِمُونَ إِنْ تَتَّبِعُونَ إِلَّا رَجُلًا مَسْحُورًا (٤٧)
انْظُرْ كَيْفَ ضَرَبُوا لَكَ الْأَمْثَالَ فَضَلُّوا فَلَا يَسْتَطِيعُونَ سَبِيلًا (٤٨)
وَقَالُوا أَئِذَا كُنَّا عِظَامًا وَرُفَاتًا أَئِنَّا لَمَبْعُوثُونَ خَلْقًا جَدِيدًا (٤٩)
قُلْ كُونُوا حِجَارَةً أَوْ حَدِيدًا (٥٠)
أَوْ خَلْقًا مِمَّا يَكْبُرُ فِي صُدُورِكُمْ فَسَيَقُولُونَ مَنْ يُعِيدُنَا قُلِ الَّذِي فَطَرَكُمْ أَوَّلَ مَرَّةٍ فَسَيُنْغِضُونَ إِلَيْكَ رُءُوسَهُمْ وَيَقُولُونَ مَتَى هُوَ قُلْ عَسَى أَنْ يَكُونَ قَرِيبًا (٥١)
يَوْمَ يَدْعُوكُمْ فَتَسْتَجِيبُونَ بِحَمْدِهِ وَتَظُنُّونَ إِنْ لَبِثْتُمْ إِلَّا قَلِيلًا (٥٢)
وَقُلْ لِعِبَادِي يَقُولُوا الَّتِي هِيَ أَحْسَنُ إِنَّ الشَّيْطَانَ يَنْزَغُ بَيْنَهُمْ إِنَّ الشَّيْطَانَ كَانَ لِلْإِنْسَانِ عَدُوًّا مُبِينًا (٥٣)
رَبُّكُمْ أَعْلَمُ بِكُمْ إِنْ يَشَأْ يَرْحَمْكُمْ أَوْ إِنْ يَشَأْ يُعَذِّبْكُمْ وَمَا أَرْسَلْنَاكَ عَلَيْهِمْ وَكِيلًا (٥٤)
وَرَبُّكَ أَعْلَمُ بِمَنْ فِي السَّمَاوَاتِ وَالْأَرْضِ وَلَقَدْ فَضَّلْنَا بَعْضَ النَّبِيِّينَ عَلَى بَعْضٍ وَآتَيْنَا دَاوُودَ زَبُورًا (٥٥)

17. The Israelites

***

17:53. And say to My servants that they speak what is best. Surely the devil sows dissensions among them. The devil is surely an open enemy to man.

17:54. Your Lord knows you best. He will have mercy on you, if He please, or He will chastise you, if He please. And We have not sent thee as being in charge of them.

17:55. And thy Lord best knows those who are in the heavens and the earth. And certainly We made some of the prophets to excel others, and to David We gave the Zabur.

17:56. Say: Call on those whom you assert besides Him they have no power to remove distress from you nor to change.

17:57. Those whom they call upon, themselves seek the means of access to their Lord whoever of them is nearest -- and they hope for His mercy and fear His chastisement. Surely the chastisement of thy Lord is a thing to be cautious of.

17:58. And there is not a town but We will destroy it before the day of Resurrection or chastise it with a severe chastisement. That is written in the Book.

17:59. And nothing hindered Us from sending signs, but the ancients rejected them. And We gave to Thamud the she-camel, a manifest sign, but they did her wrong, and We send not signs but to warn.

17:60. And when We said to thee: Surely thy Lord encompasses men. And We made not the vision which We showed thee but a trial for men, as also the tree cursed in the Qur'an. And We warn them, but it only adds to their great inordinacy.

***

17:61. And when We said to the angels: Be submissive to Adam; they submitted, except Iblis. He said: Shall I

17. The Israelites

submit to him whom Thou hast created of dust?
17:62. He said; Seest Thou? This is he whom Thou hast honoured above me! If Thou respite me to the day of Resurrection, I will certainly cause his progeny to perish except a few.
17:63. He said; Begone! whoever of them follows thee surely hell is your recompense, a full recompense.
17:64. And incite whom thou canst of them with thy voice, and collect against them thy horse and thy foot and share with them in wealth and children, and promise them. And the devil promises them only to deceive. My servants -- thou hast surely no authority over them. And thy Lord suffices as having charge of affairs.
17:66. Your Lord is He who speeds the ships for you in the sea that you may seek of His grace. Surely He is ever Merciful to you.
17:67. And when distress afflicts you in the sea, away go those whom you call on except He; but when He brings you safe to the land, you turn away. And man is ever ungrateful.
17:68. Do you then feel secure that He will not bring you low on a tract of land, or send on you a violent wind? Then you will not find a protector for yourselves;
17:69. Or, do you feel secure that He will not take you back into it another time, then send on you a fierce gale and thus overwhelm you for your ungratefulness? Then you will not find any aider against Us in the matter.
17:70. And surely We have honoured the children of Adam, and We carry them in the land and the sea, and We provide them with good things, and We have made them to excel highly most of those whom We have created.

* * *

17:71. On the day when We shall call every people with their leader: then

رَبُّكُمُ الَّذِي يُزْجِي لَكُمُ الْفُلْكَ فِي الْبَحْرِ لِتَبْتَغُوا مِنْ فَضْلِهِ إِنَّهُ كَانَ بِكُمْ رَحِيمًا (٦٦)
وَإِذَا مَسَّكُمُ الضُّرُّ فِي الْبَحْرِ ضَلَّ مَنْ تَدْعُونَ إِلَّا إِيَّاهُ فَلَمَّا نَجَّاكُمْ إِلَى الْبَرِّ أَعْرَضْتُمْ وَكَانَ الْإِنْسَانُ كَفُورًا (٦٧)
أَفَأَمِنْتُمْ أَنْ يَخْسِفَ بِكُمْ جَانِبَ الْبَرِّ أَوْ يُرْسِلَ عَلَيْكُمْ حَاصِبًا ثُمَّ لَا تَجِدُوا لَكُمْ وَكِيلًا (٦٨)
أَمْ أَمِنْتُمْ أَنْ يُعِيدَكُمْ فِيهِ تَارَةً أُخْرَى فَيُرْسِلَ عَلَيْكُمْ قَاصِفًا مِنَ الرِّيحِ فَيُغْرِقَكُمْ بِمَا كَفَرْتُمْ ثُمَّ لَا تَجِدُوا لَكُمْ عَلَيْنَا بِهِ تَبِيعًا (٦٩)
وَلَقَدْ كَرَّمْنَا بَنِي آدَمَ وَحَمَلْنَاهُمْ فِي الْبَرِّ وَالْبَحْرِ وَرَزَقْنَاهُمْ مِنَ الطَّيِّبَاتِ وَفَضَّلْنَاهُمْ عَلَى كَثِيرٍ مِمَّنْ خَلَقْنَا تَفْضِيلًا (٧٠)
يَوْمَ نَدْعُوا كُلَّ أُنَاسٍ بِإِمَامِهِمْ فَمَنْ أُوتِيَ كِتَابَهُ بِيَمِينِهِ فَأُولَئِكَ يَقْرَءُونَ كِتَابَهُمْ وَلَا يُظْلَمُونَ فَتِيلًا (٧١)
وَمَنْ كَانَ فِي هَذِهِ أَعْمَى فَهُوَ فِي الْآخِرَةِ أَعْمَى وَأَضَلُّ سَبِيلًا (٧٢)
وَإِنْ كَادُوا لَيَفْتِنُونَكَ عَنِ الَّذِي أَوْحَيْنَا إِلَيْكَ لِتَفْتَرِيَ عَلَيْنَا غَيْرَهُ وَإِذًا لَاتَّخَذُوكَ خَلِيلًا (٧٣)
وَلَوْلَا أَنْ ثَبَّتْنَاكَ لَقَدْ كِدْتَ تَرْكَنُ إِلَيْهِمْ شَيْئًا قَلِيلًا (٧٤)
إِذًا لَأَذَقْنَاكَ ضِعْفَ الْحَيَاةِ وَضِعْفَ الْمَمَاتِ ثُمَّ لَا تَجِدُ لَكَ عَلَيْنَا نَصِيرًا (٧٥)
وَإِنْ كَادُوا لَيَسْتَفِزُّونَكَ مِنَ الْأَرْضِ لِيُخْرِجُوكَ مِنْهَا وَإِذًا لَا يَلْبَثُونَ خِلَافَكَ إِلَّا قَلِيلًا (٧٦)

whoever is given his book in his right hand, these will read their book and they will not be dealt with a whit unjustly.

17:72. And whoever is blind in this (world) he will be blind in the Hereafter, and further away from the path.

17:73. And surely they had purposed to turn thee away from that which We have revealed to thee, that thou shouldst forge against Us other than that, and then they would have taken thee for a friend.

17:74. And if We had not made thee firm, thou mightest have indeed inclined to them a little

17:75. Then We would have made thee taste a double (punishment) in life and a double (punishment) after death, and then thou wouldst not have found any helper against Us.

17:76. And surely they purposed to unsettle thee from the land that they might expel thee from it, and then they will not tarry after thee but a little.

17:77. (This is Our) way with Our messengers whom We sent before thee, and thou wilt not find a change in Our course.

***

17:78. Keep up prayer from the declining of the sun till the darkness of the night, and the recital of the Qur'an at dawn. Surely the recital of the Qur'an at dawn is witnessed.

17:79. And during a part of the, night, keep awake by it, beyond what is incumbent on thee; maybe thy Lord will raise thee to a position of great glory.

17:80. And say: My Lord, make me enter a truthful entering, and make me go forth a truthful going forth, and grant me from Thy presence an authority to help (me).

17:81. And say: The Truth has come and falsehood vanished. Surely

سُنَّةَ مَنْ قَدْ أَرْسَلْنَا قَبْلَكَ مِنْ رُسُلِنَا وَلَا تَجِدُ لِسُنَّتِنَا تَحْوِيلًا (٧٧)
أَقِمِ الصَّلَاةَ لِدُلُوكِ الشَّمْسِ إِلَىٰ غَسَقِ اللَّيْلِ وَقُرْآنَ الْفَجْرِ إِنَّ قُرْآنَ الْفَجْرِ كَانَ مَشْهُودًا (٧٨)
وَمِنَ اللَّيْلِ فَتَهَجَّدْ بِهِ نَافِلَةً لَكَ عَسَىٰ أَنْ يَبْعَثَكَ رَبُّكَ مَقَامًا مَحْمُودًا (٧٩)
وَقُلْ رَبِّ أَدْخِلْنِي مُدْخَلَ صِدْقٍ وَأَخْرِجْنِي مُخْرَجَ صِدْقٍ وَاجْعَلْ لِي مِنْ لَدُنْكَ سُلْطَانًا نَصِيرًا (٨٠)
وَقُلْ جَاءَ الْحَقُّ وَزَهَقَ الْبَاطِلُ إِنَّ الْبَاطِلَ كَانَ زَهُوقًا (٨١)
وَنُنَزِّلُ مِنَ الْقُرْآنِ مَا هُوَ شِفَاءٌ وَرَحْمَةٌ لِلْمُؤْمِنِينَ وَلَا يَزِيدُ الظَّالِمِينَ إِلَّا خَسَارًا (٨٢)
وَإِذَا أَنْعَمْنَا عَلَى الْإِنْسَانِ أَعْرَضَ وَنَأَىٰ بِجَانِبِهِ وَإِذَا مَسَّهُ الشَّرُّ كَانَ يَئُوسًا (٨٣)
قُلْ كُلٌّ يَعْمَلُ عَلَىٰ شَاكِلَتِهِ فَرَبُّكُمْ أَعْلَمُ بِمَنْ هُوَ أَهْدَىٰ سَبِيلًا (٨٤)
وَيَسْأَلُونَكَ عَنِ الرُّوحِ قُلِ الرُّوحُ مِنْ أَمْرِ رَبِّي وَمَا أُوتِيتُمْ مِنَ الْعِلْمِ إِلَّا قَلِيلًا (٨٥)
وَلَئِنْ شِئْنَا لَنَذْهَبَنَّ بِالَّذِي أَوْحَيْنَا إِلَيْكَ ثُمَّ لَا تَجِدُ لَكَ بِهِ عَلَيْنَا وَكِيلًا (٨٦)
إِلَّا رَحْمَةً مِنْ رَبِّكَ إِنَّ فَضْلَهُ كَانَ عَلَيْكَ كَبِيرًا (٨٧)
قُلْ لَئِنِ اجْتَمَعَتِ الْإِنْسُ وَالْجِنُّ عَلَىٰ أَنْ يَأْتُوا بِمِثْلِ هَٰذَا الْقُرْآنِ لَا يَأْتُونَ بِمِثْلِهِ وَلَوْ كَانَ بَعْضُهُمْ لِبَعْضٍ ظَهِيرًا (٨٨)
وَلَقَدْ صَرَّفْنَا لِلنَّاسِ فِي هَٰذَا الْقُرْآنِ مِنْ كُلِّ مَثَلٍ فَأَبَىٰ أَكْثَرُ النَّاسِ إِلَّا

falsehood is ever bound to vanish.

17:82. And We reveal of the Qur'an that which is a healing and a mercy to the believers, and it adds only to the perdition of the wrongdoers.

17:83. And when We bestow favours on man, he turns away and behaves proudly; and when evil afflicts him, he is in despair.

17:84. Say: Everyone acts according to his manner. But your Lord best knows who is best guided on the path.

* * *

17:85. And they ask thee about the revelation. Say: The revelation is by the commandment of my Lord, and of knowledge you are given but a little.

17:86. And if We please, We could certainly take away that which We have revealed to thee, then thou wouldst find none to plead (thy cause) against Us --

17:87. But it is a mercy from thy Lord. Surely His bounty to thee is abundant.

17:88. Say: If men and jinn should combine together to bring the like of this Qur'an, they could not bring the like of it, though some of them were aiders of others.!

17:89. And certainly We have made clear for men in this Qur'an every kind of description, but most men consent to naught save denying.

17:90. And they say: We will by no means believe in thee, till thou cause a spring to gush forth from the earth for us,

17:91. Or thou have a garden of palms and grapes in the midst of which thou cause rivers to flow forth abundantly,

17:92. Or thou cause the heaven to come down upon us in pieces, as thou thinkest, or bring Allah and the angels face to face (with us),

17:93. Or thou have a house of gold, or thou ascend into heaven. And we will not believe in thy ascending till thou bring down to us a book we can read.

كَفُورًا (٨٩)
وَقَالُوا لَنْ نُؤْمِنَ لَكَ حَتَّى تَفْجُرَ لَنَا مِنَ الْأَرْضِ يَنْبُوعًا (٩٠)
أَوْ تَكُونَ لَكَ جَنَّةٌ مِنْ نَخِيلٍ وَعِنَبٍ فَتُفَجِّرَ الْأَنْهَارَ خِلَالَهَا تَفْجِيرًا (٩١)
أَوْ تُسْقِطَ السَّمَاءَ كَمَا زَعَمْتَ عَلَيْنَا كِسَفًا أَوْ تَأْتِيَ بِاللَّهِ وَالْمَلَائِكَةِ قَبِيلًا (٩٢)
أَوْ يَكُونَ لَكَ بَيْتٌ مِنْ زُخْرُفٍ أَوْ تَرْقَى فِي السَّمَاءِ وَلَنْ نُؤْمِنَ لِرُقِيِّكَ حَتَّى تُنَزِّلَ عَلَيْنَا كِتَابًا نَقْرَؤُهُ قُلْ سُبْحَانَ رَبِّي هَلْ كُنْتُ إِلَّا بَشَرًا رَسُولًا (٩٣)
وَمَا مَنَعَ النَّاسَ أَنْ يُؤْمِنُوا إِذْ جَاءَهُمُ الْهُدَى إِلَّا أَنْ قَالُوا أَبَعَثَ اللَّهُ بَشَرًا رَسُولًا (٩٤)
قُلْ لَوْ كَانَ فِي الْأَرْضِ مَلَائِكَةٌ يَمْشُونَ مُطْمَئِنِّينَ لَنَزَّلْنَا عَلَيْهِمْ مِنَ السَّمَاءِ مَلَكًا رَسُولًا (٩٥)
قُلْ كَفَى بِاللَّهِ شَهِيدًا بَيْنِي وَبَيْنَكُمْ إِنَّهُ كَانَ بِعِبَادِهِ خَبِيرًا بَصِيرًا (٩٦)
وَمَنْ يَهْدِ اللَّهُ فَهُوَ الْمُهْتَدِ وَمَنْ يُضْلِلْ فَلَنْ تَجِدَ لَهُمْ أَوْلِيَاءَ مِنْ دُونِهِ وَنَحْشُرُهُمْ يَوْمَ الْقِيَامَةِ عَلَى وُجُوهِهِمْ عُمْيًا وَبُكْمًا وَصُمًّا مَأْوَاهُمْ جَهَنَّمُ كُلَّمَا خَبَتْ زِدْنَاهُمْ سَعِيرًا (٩٧)
ذَلِكَ جَزَاؤُهُمْ بِأَنَّهُمْ كَفَرُوا بِآيَاتِنَا وَقَالُوا أَئِذَا كُنَّا عِظَامًا وَرُفَاتًا أَئِنَّا لَمَبْعُوثُونَ خَلْقًا جَدِيدًا (٩٨)
أَوَلَمْ يَرَوْا أَنَّ اللَّهَ الَّذِي خَلَقَ السَّمَاوَاتِ وَالْأَرْضَ قَادِرٌ عَلَى أَنْ يَخْلُقَ مِثْلَهُمْ وَجَعَلَ لَهُمْ أَجَلًا لَا رَيْبَ فِيهِ فَأَبَى الظَّالِمُونَ إِلَّا كُفُورًا (٩٩)
قُلْ لَوْ أَنْتُمْ تَمْلِكُونَ خَزَائِنَ رَحْمَةِ

17. The Israelites

Say: Glory to my Lord am I aught but a mortal messenger?

***

17:94. And nothing prevents people from believing, when the guidance comes to them, except that they say: Has Allah raised up a mortal to be a messenger?

17:95. Say: Had there been in the earth angels walking about secure, We would have sent down to them from the heaven an angel as messenger.

17:96. Say: Allah suffices for a witness between me and you. Surely He is ever Aware of His servants, Seeing.

17:97. And he whom Allah guides, he is on the right way; and he whom He leaves in error, for them thou wilt find no guardians besides Him. And We shall gather them together on the day of Resurrection on their faces, blind and dumb and deaf. Their abode is hell. Whenever it abates, We make them burn the more.

17:98. This is their retribution because they disbelieve in Our messages and say: When we are bones and decayed particles, shall we then be raised up into a new creation?

17:99. See they not that Allah, Who created the heavens and the earth, is able to create the like of them? And He has appointed for them a term, whereof there is no doubt. But the wrongdoers consent to naught but denying.

17:100. Say: If you control the treasures of the mercy of my Lord, then you would withhold (them) for fear of spending. And man is eve? niggardly.

***

17:101. And certainly We gave Moses nine clear signs; so ask the Children of Israel. When he came to them, Pharaoh said to him: Surely I deem thee, O Moses, to be one bewitched.

17:102. He said: Truly thou knowest that none but the Lord of the heavens and the earth has sent these as clear proofs; and surely I believe thee, O Pharaoh, to be lost.

17:103. So he desired to scare them from the land, but We drowned him and those with him, all together;

17:104. And We said to the Children of Israel after him: Abide in the land. But when the latter promise came, We brought you all rolled up.

17:105. And with truth have We revealed it, and with truth did it come. And We have nor sent thee but as a giver of good news and as a warner.

17:106. And it is a Qur'an We have made distinct, so that thou mayest read it to the people by slow degrees, and We have revealed it in portions.

17:107. Say: Believe in it or believe not. Surely those who are given the knowledge before it, fall down prostrate on their faces, when it is recited to them,

17:108. And say: Glory to our Lord! Surely the promise of our Lord was to be fulfilled.

17:109. And they fall down on their faces, weeping, and it adds to their humility.

17:110. Say: Call on Allah or call on the Beneficent. 1476 By whatever (name) you call on Him, He has the best names. And utter not thy prayer loudly nor be silent in it, and seek a way between these.

17:111. And say: Praise be to Allah Who has not taken to Himself a son, and Who has not a partner in the kingdom, and Who has not a helper because of weakness; and proclaim His greatness, magnifying (Him).

18. The Cave

١٨ـ سورة الكهف

In the name of Allah, the Beneficent, the Merciful.

بِسْمِ اللَّهِ الرَّحْمَنِ الرَّحِيمِ

18:1. Praise be to Allah! Who revealed

الْحَمْدُ لِلَّهِ الَّذِي أَنْزَلَ عَلَى عَبْدِهِ

18. The Cave

the Book to His servant, and allowed not therein any crookedness,

18:2. Rightly directing, to give warning of severe punishment from Him and to give good news to the believers who do good that theirs is a goodly reward,

18:3. Staying in it for ever

18:4. And to warn those who say: Allah has taken to Himself a son.

18:5. They have no knowledge of it, nor had their fathers. Grievous is the word that comes out of their mouths. They speak nothing but a lie.

18:6. Then maybe thou wilt kill thyself with grief, sorrowing after them, if they believe not in this announcement.

18:7. Surely We have made whatever is on the earth an embellishment for it, so that We may try which of them is best in works.

18:8. And We shall surely make what is on it dust, without herbage.

18:9. Or, thinkest thou that the companions of the Cave and the Inscription were of Our wonderful signs?

18:10. When the youths sought refuge in the Cave, they said: Our Lord, grant us mercy from Thyself, and provide for us a right course in our affair.

18:11. So We prevented them from hearing in the Cave for a number of years,

18:12. Then We raised them up that We might know which of the two parties was best able to calculate the time for which they remained.

* * *

18:13. We relate to thee their story with truth. Surely they were youths who believed in their Lord and We increased them in guidance.

18:14. And We strengthened their hearts when they stood up and said: Our Lord is the Lord of the heavens and the earth we call upon no god beside Him, for then indeed we should utter an enormity.

18. The Cave

18:15. These our people have taken gods beside Him. Why do they not bring clear authority for them? Who is then mote unjust than he who forges a lie against Allah?

18:16. And when you withdraw from them and what they worship save Allah, take refuge in the Cave; your Lord will spread forth for you of His mercy, and provide for you a profitable course in your affair.

18:17. And thou mightest see the sun, when it rose, decline from their Cave to the right, and when it set leave them behind on the left, while they were in a wide space thereof. This is of the signs of Allah. He whom Allah guides, he is on the right way; and whom He leaves in error, thou wilt not find for him a friend to guide aright.

* * *

18:18. And thou mightest think them awake while they were asleep, and We turned them about to the right and to the left, with their dog outstretching its paws at the entrance. If thou didst look at them, thou wouldst turn back from them in flight, and thou wouldst be filled with awe because of them.

18:19. And thus did We rouse them that they might question each other. A speaker from among them said: How long have you tarried? They said: We have tarried for a day or a part of a day. (Others) said: Your Lord knows best how long you have tarried. Now send one of you with this silver (coin) of yours to the city, then let him see what food is purest, and bring, you provision from it, and let him behave with gentleness, and not make your case known to anyone.

18:20. For if they prevail against you, they would stone you to death or force you back to their religion, and then you would never succeed.

18:21. And thus did We make (men) to get knowledge of them, that they might

أَظْلَمُ مِمَّنِ افْتَرَى عَلَى اللَّهِ كَذِبًا (١٥) وَإِذِ اعْتَزَلْتُمُوهُمْ وَمَا يَعْبُدُونَ إِلَّا اللَّهَ فَأْوُوا إِلَى الْكَهْفِ يَنْشُرْ لَكُمْ رَبُّكُمْ مِنْ رَحْمَتِهِ وَيُهَيِّئْ لَكُمْ مِنْ أَمْرِكُمْ مِرْفَقًا (١٦) وَتَرَى الشَّمْسَ إِذَا طَلَعَتْ تَزَاوَرُ عَنْ كَهْفِهِمْ ذَاتَ الْيَمِينِ وَإِذَا غَرَبَتْ تَقْرِضُهُمْ ذَاتَ الشِّمَالِ وَهُمْ فِي فَجْوَةٍ مِنْهُ ذَلِكَ مِنْ آيَاتِ اللَّهِ مَنْ يَهْدِ اللَّهُ فَهُوَ الْمُهْتَدِ وَمَنْ يُضْلِلْ فَلَنْ تَجِدَ لَهُ وَلِيًّا مُرْشِدًا (١٧) وَتَحْسَبُهُمْ أَيْقَاظًا وَهُمْ رُقُودٌ وَنُقَلِّبُهُمْ ذَاتَ الْيَمِينِ وَذَاتَ الشِّمَالِ وَكَلْبُهُمْ بَاسِطٌ ذِرَاعَيْهِ بِالْوَصِيدِ لَوِ اطَّلَعْتَ عَلَيْهِمْ لَوَلَّيْتَ مِنْهُمْ فِرَارًا وَلَمُلِئْتَ مِنْهُمْ رُعْبًا (١٨) وَكَذَلِكَ بَعَثْنَاهُمْ لِيَتَسَاءَلُوا بَيْنَهُمْ قَالَ قَائِلٌ مِنْهُمْ كَمْ لَبِثْتُمْ قَالُوا لَبِثْنَا يَوْمًا أَوْ بَعْضَ يَوْمٍ قَالُوا رَبُّكُمْ أَعْلَمُ بِمَا لَبِثْتُمْ فَابْعَثُوا أَحَدَكُمْ بِوَرِقِكُمْ هَذِهِ إِلَى الْمَدِينَةِ فَلْيَنْظُرْ أَيُّهَا أَزْكَى طَعَامًا فَلْيَأْتِكُمْ بِرِزْقٍ مِنْهُ وَلْيَتَلَطَّفْ وَلَا يُشْعِرَنَّ بِكُمْ أَحَدًا (١٩) إِنَّهُمْ إِنْ يَظْهَرُوا عَلَيْكُمْ يَرْجُمُوكُمْ أَوْ يُعِيدُوكُمْ فِي مِلَّتِهِمْ وَلَنْ تُفْلِحُوا إِذًا أَبَدًا (٢٠) وَكَذَلِكَ أَعْثَرْنَا عَلَيْهِمْ لِيَعْلَمُوا أَنَّ وَعْدَ اللَّهِ حَقٌّ وَأَنَّ السَّاعَةَ لَا رَيْبَ فِيهَا إِذْ يَتَنَازَعُونَ بَيْنَهُمْ أَمْرَهُمْ فَقَالُوا ابْنُوا عَلَيْهِمْ بُنْيَانًا رَبُّهُمْ أَعْلَمُ بِهِمْ قَالَ الَّذِينَ غَلَبُوا عَلَى أَمْرِهِمْ لَنَتَّخِذَنَّ عَلَيْهِمْ مَسْجِدًا (٢١) سَيَقُولُونَ ثَلَاثَةٌ رَابِعُهُمْ كَلْبُهُمْ

18. The Cave

know that Allah's promise is true and that the Hour -- there is no doubt about it. When they disputed among themselves about their affair and said: Erect an edifice over them. Their Lord knows best about them. Those who prevailed in their affair said: We shall certainly build a place of worship over them.

18:22. (Some) say: (They were) three, the fourth of them their dog; and (others) say: Five, the sixth of them their dog, making conjectures about the unseen. And (others) say: Seven, and the eighth of them their dog. Say: My Lord best knows their number none knows them but a few. So contend not in their matter but with an outward contention, and question not any of them concerning them.

18:25. And they remained in their cave three hundred years, and they add nine.

18:26. Say: Allah knows best how long they remained. His is the unseen of the heavens and the earth. How clear His sight and His hearing! There is no guardian for them beside Him, and He associates none in His judgment.

18:27. And recite that which has been revealed to thee of the Book of thy Lord. There is none who can alter His words. And thou wilt find no refuge beside Him.

18:28. And keep thyself with those who call on their Lord morning and evening desiring His goodwill, and let not thine eyes pass from them, desiring the beauties of this world's life. And follow not him whose heart We have made unmindful of Our remembrance, and he follows his low desires and his case exceeds due bounds.

18:29. And say: The Truth is from your Lord; so let him who please believe, and let him who please disbelieve. Surely We have prepared for the iniquitous a Fire, an enclosure of which will encompass them. And if they cry for water, they are given water like molten brass, scalding their faces. Evil the drink! And ill the resting-place!

18:30. As for those who believe and do good, We waste not the reward of him who does a good work.

18:31. These it is for whom are Gardens of perpetuity wherein flow rivers; they are adorned therein with bracelets of gold, and they wear green robes of fine silk and thick brocade, reclining therein on raised couches. Excellent the recompense! And goodly the resting-place!

* * *

18:32. And set forth to them the parable of two men for one of them We made two gardens of grape-vines, and We surrounded them with date-palms, and between them We made cornfields.

18:33. Both these gardens yielded their fruits, and failed not in aught thereof, and We caused a river to gush forth in their midst,

18:34. And he had fruit. So he said to his companion, while he argued with him: I have greater wealth than thou; and am mightier in followers.

18:35. And he went into his garden, while he was unjust to himself. He said: I think not that this will ever perish,

18:36. And I think not the Hour will come; and even if I am returned to my Lord, I will certainly find a returning-place better than this.

18:37. His companion said to him, while arguing with him: Disbelieve thou in Him Who created thee of dust, then of a small life-germ, then He made thee a perfect man?

18:38. But as for me, He, Allah, is my Lord, and I associate none with my Lord.

18:39. And wherefore didst thou not say, when thou entered thy garden? It is as Allah has pleased -- there is no

18. The Cave

power save in Allah? If thou consider me as less than thee in wealth and children --

18:40. Then maybe my Lord will give me better than thy garden, and will send on (thine) a reckoning from heaven so that it is dust without plant:

18:41. Or its water will sink down into the ground, so that thou art unable to find it.

18:42. And his fruit was destroyed; so he began to wring his hands for what he had spent on it, while it lay waste, its roofs fallen down, and he said: Ah me! would that I had ascribed no partners to my Lord!

18:43. And he had no host to help him against Allah, nor could he defend himself.

18:44. Thus protection is only Allah's, the True One. He is Best to reward and Best in requiting.

* * *

18:45. And set forth to them the parable of the life of this world as water which We send down from the cloud, so the herbage of the earth becomes luxuriant thereby, then it becomes dry, broken into pieces which the winds scatter. And Allah is the Holder of power over all things.

18:46. Wealth and children are an adornment of the life of this world but the ever-abiding, the good works, are better with thy Lord in reward and better in hope.

18:47. And the day when We cause the mountains to pass away, and thou seest the earth a levelled plain and We gather them together and leave none of them behind.

18:48. And they are brought before thy Lord in ranks. Now certainly you have come to Us as We created you at first. Nay, you thought that We had not made an appointment for you.

18:49. And the book is placed, and thou seest the guilty fearing for what is in it,

وَأُحِيطَ بِثَمَرِهِ فَأَصْبَحَ يُقَلِّبُ كَفَّيْهِ عَلَىٰ مَا أَنفَقَ فِيهَا وَهِيَ خَاوِيَةٌ عَلَىٰ عُرُوشِهَا وَيَقُولُ يَا لَيْتَنِي لَمْ أُشْرِكْ بِرَبِّي أَحَدًا (٤٢)

وَلَمْ تَكُن لَّهُ فِئَةٌ يَنصُرُونَهُ مِن دُونِ اللَّهِ وَمَا كَانَ مُنتَصِرًا (٤٣)

هُنَالِكَ الْوَلَايَةُ لِلَّهِ الْحَقِّ هُوَ خَيْرٌ ثَوَابًا وَخَيْرٌ عُقْبًا (٤٤)

وَاضْرِبْ لَهُم مَّثَلَ الْحَيَاةِ الدُّنْيَا كَمَاءٍ أَنزَلْنَاهُ مِنَ السَّمَاءِ فَاخْتَلَطَ بِهِ نَبَاتُ الْأَرْضِ فَأَصْبَحَ هَشِيمًا تَذْرُوهُ الرِّيَاحُ وَكَانَ اللَّهُ عَلَىٰ كُلِّ شَيْءٍ مُّقْتَدِرًا (٤٥)

الْمَالُ وَالْبَنُونَ زِينَةُ الْحَيَاةِ الدُّنْيَا وَالْبَاقِيَاتُ الصَّالِحَاتُ خَيْرٌ عِندَ رَبِّكَ ثَوَابًا وَخَيْرٌ أَمَلًا (٤٦)

وَيَوْمَ نُسَيِّرُ الْجِبَالَ وَتَرَى الْأَرْضَ بَارِزَةً وَحَشَرْنَاهُمْ فَلَمْ نُغَادِرْ مِنْهُمْ أَحَدًا (٤٧)

وَعُرِضُوا عَلَىٰ رَبِّكَ صَفًّا لَّقَدْ جِئْتُمُونَا كَمَا خَلَقْنَاكُمْ أَوَّلَ مَرَّةٍ بَلْ زَعَمْتُمْ أَلَّن نَّجْعَلَ لَكُم مَّوْعِدًا (٤٨)

وَوُضِعَ الْكِتَابُ فَتَرَى الْمُجْرِمِينَ مُشْفِقِينَ مِمَّا فِيهِ وَيَقُولُونَ يَا وَيْلَتَنَا مَالِ هَـٰذَا الْكِتَابِ لَا يُغَادِرُ صَغِيرَةً وَلَا كَبِيرَةً إِلَّا أَحْصَاهَا وَوَجَدُوا مَا عَمِلُوا حَاضِرًا وَلَا يَظْلِمُ رَبُّكَ أَحَدًا (٤٩)

وَإِذْ قُلْنَا لِلْمَلَائِكَةِ اسْجُدُوا لِآدَمَ فَسَجَدُوا إِلَّا إِبْلِيسَ كَانَ مِنَ الْجِنِّ فَفَسَقَ عَنْ أَمْرِ رَبِّهِ أَفَتَتَّخِذُونَهُ وَذُرِّيَّتَهُ أَوْلِيَاءَ مِن دُونِي وَهُمْ لَكُمْ عَدُوٌّ بِئْسَ لِلظَّالِمِينَ بَدَلًا (٥٠)

مَا أَشْهَدتُّهُمْ خَلْقَ السَّمَاوَاتِ

and they say: O woe to us what a book is this It leaves out neither a small thing nor a great one, but numbers them (all), and they find what they did confronting them. And thy Lord wrongs not any one.

* * *

18:50. And when We said to the angels: Make submission to Adam, they submitted except Iblis. He was of the jinn, so he transgressed the commandment of his Lord. Will you then take him and his offspring for friends rather than Me, and they are your enemies? Evil is the exchange for the unjust.

18:51. I made them not to witness the creation of the heavens and the earth, nor their own creation. Nor could I take those who mislead for aiders.

18:52. And one day He will say: Call on those whom you considered to be My partners. So they will call on them, but they will not answer them, and We shall cause a separation between them.

18:53. And the guilty will see the Fire, and know that they are about to fall into it, and they will find no escape from it.

* * *

18:54. And certainly We have made distinct in this Qur'an for mankind every kind of description; and man is in most things contentious.

18:55. And nothing prevents men from believing when the guidance comes to them, and from asking forgiveness of their Lord, but that (they wait) for the way of the ancients to overtake them, or that the chastisement should confront them.

18:56. And We send not messengers but as givers of good news and warning, and those who disbelieve contend with falsehood to weaken thereby the Truth, and they take My messages and the warning for a mockery.

18. The Cave

18:57. And who is more unjust than he who is reminded of the messages of his Lord, then he turns away from them and forgets what his hands have sent before? Surely We have placed veils over their hearts, lest they understand it, and a deafness in their ears. And if thou call them to the guidance, they will even then never follow the right course.

18:58. And thy Lord is Forgiving, Full of Mercy. Were He to punish them for what they earn, He would certainly hasten the chastisement for them. But for them there is an appointed time from which they will find no refuge.

18:59. And these towns We destroyed them when they did wrong. And We have appointed a time for their destruction.

***

18:60. And when Moses said to his servant: I will not cease until I reach the junction of the two rivers, otherwise I will go on for years.

18:61. So when they reached the junction of the two (rivers), they forgot their fish, and it took its way into the river, being free.

18:62. But when they had gone further, he said to his servant Bring to us our morning meal, certainly we have found fatigue in this our journey.

18:63. He said; Sawest thou when we took refuge on the rock, I forgot the fish, and none but the devil made me forget to speak of it, and it took its way into the river; what a wonder!

18:64. He said This is what we sought for. So they returned retracing their footsteps.

18:65. Then they found one of Our servants whom We had granted mercy from Us and whom We had taught knowledge from Ourselves.

18:66. Moses said to him: May I follow thee that thou mayest teach me of the good thou hast been taught?

فَاتَّخَذَ سَبِيلَهُ فِي الْبَحْرِ سَرَبًا (٦١) فَلَمَّا جَاوَزَا قَالَ لِفَتَاهُ آتِنَا غَدَاءَنَا لَقَدْ لَقِينَا مِنْ سَفَرِنَا هَذَا نَصَبًا (٦٢) قَالَ أَرَأَيْتَ إِذْ أَوَيْنَا إِلَى الصَّخْرَةِ فَإِنِّي نَسِيتُ الْحُوتَ وَمَا أَنْسَانِيهُ إِلَّا الشَّيْطَانُ أَنْ أَذْكُرَهُ وَاتَّخَذَ سَبِيلَهُ فِي الْبَحْرِ عَجَبًا (٦٣) قَالَ ذَلِكَ مَا كُنَّا نَبْغِ فَارْتَدَّا عَلَى آثَارِهِمَا قَصَصًا (٦٤) فَوَجَدَا عَبْدًا مِنْ عِبَادِنَا آتَيْنَاهُ رَحْمَةً مِنْ عِنْدِنَا وَعَلَّمْنَاهُ مِنْ لَدُنَّا عِلْمًا (٦٥) قَالَ لَهُ مُوسَى هَلْ أَتَّبِعُكَ عَلَى أَنْ تُعَلِّمَنِ مِمَّا عُلِّمْتَ رُشْدًا (٦٦) قَالَ إِنَّكَ لَنْ تَسْتَطِيعَ مَعِيَ صَبْرًا (٦٧) وَكَيْفَ تَصْبِرُ عَلَى مَا لَمْ تُحِطْ بِهِ خُبْرًا (٦٨) قَالَ سَتَجِدُنِي إِنْ شَاءَ اللَّهُ صَابِرًا وَلَا أَعْصِي لَكَ أَمْرًا (٦٩) قَالَ فَإِنِ اتَّبَعْتَنِي فَلَا تَسْأَلْنِي عَنْ شَيْءٍ حَتَّى أُحْدِثَ لَكَ مِنْهُ ذِكْرًا (٧٠) فَانْطَلَقَا حَتَّى إِذَا رَكِبَا فِي السَّفِينَةِ خَرَقَهَا قَالَ أَخَرَقْتَهَا لِتُغْرِقَ أَهْلَهَا لَقَدْ جِئْتَ شَيْئًا إِمْرًا (٧١) قَالَ أَلَمْ أَقُلْ إِنَّكَ لَنْ تَسْتَطِيعَ مَعِيَ صَبْرًا (٧٢) قَالَ لَا تُؤَاخِذْنِي بِمَا نَسِيتُ وَلَا تُرْهِقْنِي مِنْ أَمْرِي عُسْرًا (٧٣) فَانْطَلَقَا حَتَّى إِذَا لَقِيَا غُلَامًا فَقَتَلَهُ قَالَ أَقَتَلْتَ نَفْسًا زَكِيَّةً بِغَيْرِ نَفْسٍ لَقَدْ جِئْتَ شَيْئًا نُكْرًا (٧٤)

18. The Cave

18:67. He said: Thou canst not have patience with me.
18:68. And how canst thou have patience in that whereof, thou hast not a comprehensive knowledge?
18:69. He said: If Allah please, thou wilt find me patient, nor shall I disobey thee in aught.
18:70. He said: If thou wouldst follow me, question me not about aught until I myself speak to thee about it

* * *

18:71. So they set out until, when they embarked in a boat, he made a hole in it. (Moses) said: Hast thou made a hole in it to drown its occupants? Thou hast surely done a grievous thing.
18:72. He said: Did I not say that thou couldst not have patience with me?
18:73. He said: Blame me not for what I forgot, and be not hard upon me for what I did.
18:74. So they went on, until, when they met a boy, he slew him. (Moses) said: Hast thou slain an innocent person, not guilty of slaying another? Thou hast indeed done a horrible thing.

* * *

18:75. He said: Did I not say to thee that thou couldst not have patience with me?
18:76. He said If I ask thee about anything after this, keep not company with me. Thou wilt then indeed have found an excuse in my case.
18:77. So they went on, until, when they came to the people of a town, they asked its people for food, but they refused to entertain them as guests. Then they found in it a wall which was on the point of falling, so he put it into a right state. (Moses) said: If thou hadst wished, thou couldst have taken a recompense for it.
18:78. He said: This is the parting between me and thee. Now I will inform thee of the significance of that

قَالَ أَلَمْ أَقُلْ لَكَ إِنَّكَ لَنْ تَسْتَطِيعَ مَعِيَ صَبْرًا (٧٥)
قَالَ إِنْ سَأَلْتُكَ عَنْ شَيْءٍ بَعْدَهَا فَلَا تُصَاحِبْنِي قَدْ بَلَغْتَ مِنْ لَدُنِّي عُذْرًا (٧٦)
فَانْطَلَقَا حَتَّى إِذَا أَتَيَا أَهْلَ قَرْيَةٍ اسْتَطْعَمَا أَهْلَهَا فَأَبَوْا أَنْ يُضَيِّفُوهُمَا فَوَجَدَا فِيهَا جِدَارًا يُرِيدُ أَنْ يَنْقَضَّ فَأَقَامَهُ قَالَ لَوْ شِئْتَ لَاتَّخَذْتَ عَلَيْهِ أَجْرًا (٧٧)
قَالَ هَذَا فِرَاقُ بَيْنِي وَبَيْنِكَ سَأُنَبِّئُكَ بِتَأْوِيلِ مَا لَمْ تَسْتَطِعْ عَلَيْهِ صَبْرًا (٧٨)
أَمَّا السَّفِينَةُ فَكَانَتْ لِمَسَاكِينَ يَعْمَلُونَ فِي الْبَحْرِ فَأَرَدْتُ أَنْ أَعِيبَهَا وَكَانَ وَرَاءَهُمْ مَلِكٌ يَأْخُذُ كُلَّ سَفِينَةٍ غَصْبًا (٧٩)
وَأَمَّا الْغُلَامُ فَكَانَ أَبَوَاهُ مُؤْمِنَيْنِ فَخَشِينَا أَنْ يُرْهِقَهُمَا طُغْيَانًا وَكُفْرًا (٨٠)
فَأَرَدْنَا أَنْ يُبْدِلَهُمَا رَبُّهُمَا خَيْرًا مِنْهُ زَكَاةً وَأَقْرَبَ رُحْمًا (٨١)
وَأَمَّا الْجِدَارُ فَكَانَ لِغُلَامَيْنِ يَتِيمَيْنِ فِي الْمَدِينَةِ وَكَانَ تَحْتَهُ كَنْزٌ لَهُمَا وَكَانَ أَبُوهُمَا صَالِحًا فَأَرَادَ رَبُّكَ أَنْ يَبْلُغَا أَشُدَّهُمَا وَيَسْتَخْرِجَا كَنْزَهُمَا رَحْمَةً مِنْ رَبِّكَ وَمَا فَعَلْتُهُ عَنْ أَمْرِي ذَلِكَ تَأْوِيلُ مَا لَمْ تَسْطِعْ عَلَيْهِ صَبْرًا (٨٢)
وَيَسْأَلُونَكَ عَنْ ذِي الْقَرْنَيْنِ قُلْ سَأَتْلُو عَلَيْكُمْ مِنْهُ ذِكْرًا (٨٣)
إِنَّا مَكَّنَّا لَهُ فِي الْأَرْضِ وَآتَيْنَاهُ مِنْ كُلِّ شَيْءٍ سَبَبًا (٨٤)
فَأَتْبَعَ سَبَبًا (٨٥)

18. The Cave

with which thou couldst not have patience.

18:79. As for the boat, it belonged to poor people working on the river, and I intended to damage it, for there was behind them a king who seized every boat by force.

18:80. And as for the boy, his parents were believers and We feared lest he should involve them in wrongdoing and disbelief.

18:81. So We intended that their Lord might give them in his place one better in purity and nearer to mercy.

18:82. And as for the wall; it belonged to two orphan boys in the city, and there was beneath it a treasure belonging to them, and their father had been a righteous man. So thy Lord intended that they should attain their maturity and take out their treasure a mercy from thy Lord and I did not do it of my own accord. This is the significance of that with which thou couldst not have patience.

***

18:83. And they ask thee about Dhu-l-qarnain Say: I will recite to you an account of him.

18:84. Truly We established him in the land and granted him means of access to everything

18:85. So he followed a course.

18:86. Until, when he reached the setting-place of the sun, he found it going down into a black sea, and found by it a people. We said: O Dhu-l-qarnain, either punish them or do them a benefit.

18:87. He said: As for him who is unjust, we shall chastise him, then he will be returned to his Lord, and He will chastise him with an exemplary chastisement.

18:88. And as for him who believes and does good, for him is a good reward, and We shall speak to him an easy word of Our command.

18. The Cave

18:89. Then he followed a course.
18:90. Until, when he reached the (land of) the rising sun, he found it rising on a people to whom We had given no shelter from it --
18:91. So it was. And We had full knowledge of what he had.
18:92. Then he followed a course.
18:93. Until, when he reached (a place) between the two mountains, he found on that side of them a people who could hardly understand a word.
18:94. They said: O Dhu-l-qarnain, Gog and Magog do mischief in the land. May we then pay thee tribute on condition that thou raise a barrier between us and them?' --
18:95. He said: That wherein my Lord has established me is better, so if only you help me with strength (of men), I will make a fortified barrier between you and them:
18:96. Bring me blocks of iron. At length, when he had filled up the space between the two mountain sides, he said, Blow. Till, when he had made it (as) fire, he said: Bring me molten brass to pour over it.
18:97. So they were not able to scale it, nor could they make a hole in it.
18:98. He said: This is a mercy from my Lord, but when the promise of my Lord comes to pass He will crumble it, and the promise of my Lord is ever true.
18:99. And on that day We shall let some of them surge against others and the trumpet will be blown, then We shall gather them all together,
18:100. And We shall bring forth hell, exposed to view, on that day before the disbelievers,
18:101. Whose eyes were under a cover from My Reminder, and they could not bear to heat.

* * *

18:102. Do those who disbelieve think that they can take My servants to be friends besides Me? Surely We have prepared hell as an entertainment for the disbelievers.

18:103. Say: Shall We inform you who are the greatest losers in respect of deeds?

18:104. Those whose effort goes astray in this world's life, and they think that they are making good manufactures.

18:105. Those are they who disbelieve in the messages of their Lord and meeting with Him, so their works are vain. Nor shall We set up a balance for them on the day of Resurrection.

18:106. That is their reward -- hell, because they disbelieved and held My messages and My messengers in mockery.

18:107. As for those who believe and do good deeds, for them are Garden of Paradise, an entertainment,

18:108. To abide therein; they will not desire removal therefrom.

18:109. Say: If the sea were ink for the words of my Lord, the sea would surely be exhausted before the words of my Lord were exhausted, though We brought the like of it to add (thereto).

18:110. Say I am only a mortal like you -- it is revealed to me that your God is one God. So whoever hopes to meet his Lord, he should do good deeds, and join no one in the service of his Lord.

19. Mary

In the name of Allah, the Beneficent, the Merciful.

19:1. Sufficient, Guide, Blessed, Knowing, Truthful God.

19:2. A mention of the mercy of thy Lord to His servant Zacharias --

19:3. When he called upon his Lord, crying in secret.

19:4. He said: My Lord, my bones are weakened, and my head flares with hoariness, and I have never been

19. Mary

unsuccessful in my prayer to Thee, my Lord.

19:5. And I fear my kinsfolk after me, and my wife is barren, so grant me from Thyself an heir

19:6. Who should inherit me and inherit of the Children of Jacob, and make him, my Lord, acceptable (to Thee).

19:7. O Zacharias, We give thee good news of a boy, whose name is John: We have not made before anyone his equal.

19:8. He said: My Lord, how shall I have a son, and my wife is barren, and I have reached extreme old age?

19:9. He said: So (it will be). Thy Lord says: It is easy to Me, and indeed I created thee before, when thou wast nothing.

19:10. He said: My Lord, give me a sign. He said: Thy sign is that thou speak not to people three nights, being in sound health.

19:11. So he went forth to his people from the sanctuary and proclaimed to them: Glorify (Allah) morning and evening.

19:12. O John, take hold of the Book with strength. And We granted him wisdom when a child,

19:13. And kind-heartedness from Us and purity. And he was dutiful,

19:14. And kindly to his parents, and he was not insolent, disobedient.

19:15. And peace on him the day he was born and the day he died, and the day he is raised to life

***

19:16. And mention Mary in the Book. When she drew aside from her family to an eastern place;

19:17. So she screened herself from them. Then We sent to her Our spirit and it appeared to her as a well made man.

19:18. She said: I flee for refuge from thee to the Beneficent, if thou art one

19. Mary

guarding against evil.
19:19. He said: I am only bearer of a message of thy Lord: That I will give thee a pure boy.
19:20. She said: How can I have a son and no mortal has yet touched me, nor have I been unchaste?
19:21. He said: So (it will be). Thy Lord says: It is easy to Me; and that We may make him a sign to men and a mercy from Us. And it is a matter decreed.
19:22. Then she conceived him; and withdrew with him to a remote place.
19:23. And the throes of childbirth drove her to the trunk of a palm tree. She said: Oh, would that I had died before this, and had been a thing quite forgotten!
19:24. So a voice came to her from beneath her: Grieve not, surely thy Lord has provided a stream beneath thee.
19:25. And shake towards thee the trunk of the palm-tree, it will drop on thee fresh ripe dates.
19:26. So eat and drink and cool the eye. Then if thou seest any mortal, say: Surely I have vowed a fast to the Beneficent, so I will not speak to any man to-day.
19:27. Then she came to her people with him, carrying him. They said: O Mary, thou hast indeed brought a strange thing!
19:28. O sister of Aaron, thy father was not a wicked man, nor was thy mother an unchaste woman!
19:29. But she pointed to him. They said: How should we speak to one who is a child in the cradle?
19:30. He said: I am indeed a servant of Allah. He has given me the Book and made me a prophet:
19:31. And He has made me blessed wherever I may be, and He has enjoined on me prayer and poor-rate so long as I live.
19:32. And to be kind to my mother;

غُلَامًا زَكِيًّا (١٩) قَالَتْ أَنَّىٰ يَكُونُ لِي غُلَامٌ وَلَمْ يَمْسَسْنِي بَشَرٌ وَلَمْ أَكُ بَغِيًّا (٢٠) قَالَ كَذَٰلِكِ قَالَ رَبُّكِ هُوَ عَلَيَّ هَيِّنٌ وَلِنَجْعَلَهُ آيَةً لِلنَّاسِ وَرَحْمَةً مِنَّا وَكَانَ أَمْرًا مَقْضِيًّا (٢١) فَحَمَلَتْهُ فَانْتَبَذَتْ بِهِ مَكَانًا قَصِيًّا (٢٢) فَأَجَاءَهَا الْمَخَاضُ إِلَىٰ جِذْعِ النَّخْلَةِ قَالَتْ يَا لَيْتَنِي مِتُّ قَبْلَ هَٰذَا وَكُنْتُ نَسْيًا مَنْسِيًّا (٢٣) فَنَادَاهَا مِنْ تَحْتِهَا أَلَّا تَحْزَنِي قَدْ جَعَلَ رَبُّكِ تَحْتَكِ سَرِيًّا (٢٤) وَهُزِّي إِلَيْكِ بِجِذْعِ النَّخْلَةِ تُسَاقِطْ عَلَيْكِ رُطَبًا جَنِيًّا (٢٥) فَكُلِي وَاشْرَبِي وَقَرِّي عَيْنًا فَإِمَّا تَرَيِنَّ مِنَ الْبَشَرِ أَحَدًا فَقُولِي إِنِّي نَذَرْتُ لِلرَّحْمَٰنِ صَوْمًا فَلَنْ أُكَلِّمَ الْيَوْمَ إِنْسِيًّا (٢٦) فَأَتَتْ بِهِ قَوْمَهَا تَحْمِلُهُ قَالُوا يَا مَرْيَمُ لَقَدْ جِئْتِ شَيْئًا فَرِيًّا (٢٧) يَا أُخْتَ هَارُونَ مَا كَانَ أَبُوكِ امْرَأَ سَوْءٍ وَمَا كَانَتْ أُمُّكِ بَغِيًّا (٢٨) فَأَشَارَتْ إِلَيْهِ قَالُوا كَيْفَ نُكَلِّمُ مَنْ كَانَ فِي الْمَهْدِ صَبِيًّا (٢٩) قَالَ إِنِّي عَبْدُ اللَّهِ آتَانِيَ الْكِتَابَ وَجَعَلَنِي نَبِيًّا (٣٠) وَجَعَلَنِي مُبَارَكًا أَيْنَ مَا كُنْتُ وَأَوْصَانِي بِالصَّلَاةِ وَالزَّكَاةِ مَا دُمْتُ حَيًّا (٣١) وَبَرًّا بِوَالِدَتِي وَلَمْ يَجْعَلْنِي جَبَّارًا شَقِيًّا (٣٢) وَالسَّلَامُ عَلَيَّ يَوْمَ وُلِدْتُ وَيَوْمَ أَمُوتُ

and He has not made me insolent, unblessed.

19:33. And peace on me the day I was born, and the day I die, and the day I am raised to life.

19:34. Such is Jesus son of Mary a statement of truth about which they dispute.

19:35. It beseems not Allah that He should take to Himself a son. Glory be to Him! when He decrees a matter He only says to it, Be, and it is.

19:36. And surely Allah is my Lord and your Lord, so serve Him. This is the right path.

19:37. But parties from among them differed; so woe to those who disbelieve, because of their presence on a grievous day!

19:38. How clearly will they hear and see on the day when they come to Us but the wrongdoers are to-day in manifest error.

19:39. And warn them of the day of Regret, when the matter is decided. And they are (now) in negligence and they believe not.

19:40. Surely We inherit the earth and those thereon, and to Us they are returned.

* * *

19:41. And mention Abraham in the Book. Surely he was a truthful man, a prophet.

19:42. When he said to his sire O my sire, why worshippest thou that which hears not, nor sees, nor can it avail thee aught?

19:43. O my sire, to me indeed has come the knowledge which has not come to thee; so follow me, I will guide thee on a right path.

19:44. O my sire, serve not the devil. Surely the devil is disobedient to the Beneficent.

19:45. O my sire, surely I fear lest a punishment from the Beneficent should afflict thee, so that thou become

وَيَوْمَ أُبْعَثُ حَيًّا (٣٣)
ذَٰلِكَ عِيسَى ابْنُ مَرْيَمَ قَوْلَ الْحَقِّ الَّذِي فِيهِ يَمْتَرُونَ (٣٤)
مَا كَانَ لِلَّهِ أَنْ يَتَّخِذَ مِنْ وَلَدٍ سُبْحَانَهُ إِذَا قَضَىٰ أَمْرًا فَإِنَّمَا يَقُولُ لَهُ كُنْ فَيَكُونُ (٣٥)
وَإِنَّ اللَّهَ رَبِّي وَرَبُّكُمْ فَاعْبُدُوهُ هَٰذَا صِرَاطٌ مُسْتَقِيمٌ (٣٦)
فَاخْتَلَفَ الْأَحْزَابُ مِنْ بَيْنِهِمْ ۖ فَوَيْلٌ لِلَّذِينَ كَفَرُوا مِنْ مَشْهَدِ يَوْمٍ عَظِيمٍ (٣٧)
أَسْمِعْ بِهِمْ وَأَبْصِرْ يَوْمَ يَأْتُونَنَا لَٰكِنِ الظَّالِمُونَ الْيَوْمَ فِي ضَلَالٍ مُبِينٍ (٣٨)
وَأَنْذِرْهُمْ يَوْمَ الْحَسْرَةِ إِذْ قُضِيَ الْأَمْرُ وَهُمْ فِي غَفْلَةٍ وَهُمْ لَا يُؤْمِنُونَ (٣٩)
إِنَّا نَحْنُ نَرِثُ الْأَرْضَ وَمَنْ عَلَيْهَا وَإِلَيْنَا يُرْجَعُونَ (٤٠)
وَاذْكُرْ فِي الْكِتَابِ إِبْرَاهِيمَ ۚ إِنَّهُ كَانَ صِدِّيقًا نَبِيًّا (٤١)
إِذْ قَالَ لِأَبِيهِ يَا أَبَتِ لِمَ تَعْبُدُ مَا لَا يَسْمَعُ وَلَا يُبْصِرُ وَلَا يُغْنِي عَنْكَ شَيْئًا (٤٢)
يَا أَبَتِ إِنِّي قَدْ جَاءَنِي مِنَ الْعِلْمِ مَا لَمْ يَأْتِكَ فَاتَّبِعْنِي أَهْدِكَ صِرَاطًا سَوِيًّا (٤٣)
يَا أَبَتِ لَا تَعْبُدِ الشَّيْطَانَ ۖ إِنَّ الشَّيْطَانَ كَانَ لِلرَّحْمَٰنِ عَصِيًّا (٤٤)
يَا أَبَتِ إِنِّي أَخَافُ أَنْ يَمَسَّكَ عَذَابٌ مِنَ الرَّحْمَٰنِ فَتَكُونَ لِلشَّيْطَانِ وَلِيًّا (٤٥)
قَالَ أَرَاغِبٌ أَنْتَ عَنْ آلِهَتِي يَا إِبْرَاهِيمُ ۖ لَئِنْ لَمْ تَنْتَهِ لَأَرْجُمَنَّكَ

a friend of the devil.

19:46. He said: Dislikest thou my gods, O Abraham? If thou desist not, I will certainly drive thee away. And leave me for a time.

19:47. He said: Peace be to thee! I shall pray my Lord to forgive thee. Surely He is ever Kind to me.

19:48. And I withdraw from you and that which you call on beside Allah and I call upon my Lord. Maybe I shall not remain unblessed in calling upon my Lord.

19:49. So, when he withdrew from them and that which they worshipped besides Allah, We gave him Isaac and Jacob. And each (of them) We made a prophet.

19:50. And We gave them of Our mercy, and We granted them a truthful mention of eminence.

* * *

19:51. And mention Moses in the Book. Surely he was one purified, and was a messenger, a prophet.

19:52. And We called to him from the blessed side of the mountain, and We made him draw nigh in communion.

19:53. And We gave him out of Our mercy his brother Aaron, a prophet.

19:54. And mention Ishmael in the Book. Surely he was truthful in promise, and he was a messenger, a prophet.

19:55. And he enjoined on his people prayer and almsgiving, and was one in whom his Lord was well pleased.

19:56. And mention Idris in the Book. Surely he was a truthful man, a prophet,

19:57. And We raised him to an elevated state.

19:58. These are they on whom Allah bestowed favours, from among the prophets, of the seed of Adam, and of those whom We carried with Noah, and of the seed of Abraham and Israel, and of those whom We guided and

وَاهْجُرْنِي مَلِيًّا (٤٦)
قَالَ سَلَامٌ عَلَيْكَ سَأَسْتَغْفِرُ لَكَ رَبِّي إِنَّهُ كَانَ بِي حَفِيًّا (٤٧)
وَأَعْتَزِلُكُمْ وَمَا تَدْعُونَ مِنْ دُونِ اللَّهِ وَأَدْعُو رَبِّي عَسَى أَلَّا أَكُونَ بِدُعَاءِ رَبِّي شَقِيًّا (٤٨)
فَلَمَّا اعْتَزَلَهُمْ وَمَا يَعْبُدُونَ مِنْ دُونِ اللَّهِ وَهَبْنَا لَهُ إِسْحَاقَ وَيَعْقُوبَ وَكُلًّا جَعَلْنَا نَبِيًّا (٤٩)
وَوَهَبْنَا لَهُمْ مِنْ رَحْمَتِنَا وَجَعَلْنَا لَهُمْ لِسَانَ صِدْقٍ عَلِيًّا (٥٠)
وَاذْكُرْ فِي الْكِتَابِ مُوسَى إِنَّهُ كَانَ مُخْلَصًا وَكَانَ رَسُولًا نَبِيًّا (٥١)
وَنَادَيْنَاهُ مِنْ جَانِبِ الطُّورِ الْأَيْمَنِ وَقَرَّبْنَاهُ نَجِيًّا (٥٢)
وَوَهَبْنَا لَهُ مِنْ رَحْمَتِنَا أَخَاهُ هَارُونَ نَبِيًّا (٥٣)
وَاذْكُرْ فِي الْكِتَابِ إِسْمَاعِيلَ إِنَّهُ كَانَ صَادِقَ الْوَعْدِ وَكَانَ رَسُولًا نَبِيًّا (٥٤)
وَكَانَ يَأْمُرُ أَهْلَهُ بِالصَّلَاةِ وَالزَّكَاةِ وَكَانَ عِنْدَ رَبِّهِ مَرْضِيًّا (٥٥)
وَاذْكُرْ فِي الْكِتَابِ إِدْرِيسَ إِنَّهُ كَانَ صِدِّيقًا نَبِيًّا (٥٦)
وَرَفَعْنَاهُ مَكَانًا عَلِيًّا (٥٧)
أُولَئِكَ الَّذِينَ أَنْعَمَ اللَّهُ عَلَيْهِمْ مِنَ النَّبِيِّينَ مِنْ ذُرِّيَّةِ آدَمَ وَمِمَّنْ حَمَلْنَا مَعَ نُوحٍ وَمِنْ ذُرِّيَّةِ إِبْرَاهِيمَ وَإِسْرَائِيلَ وَمِمَّنْ هَدَيْنَا وَاجْتَبَيْنَا إِذَا تُتْلَى عَلَيْهِمْ آيَاتُ الرَّحْمَنِ خَرُّوا سُجَّدًا وَبُكِيًّا (٥٨)
فَخَلَفَ مِنْ بَعْدِهِمْ خَلْفٌ أَضَاعُوا الصَّلَاةَ وَاتَّبَعُوا الشَّهَوَاتِ فَسَوْفَ

chose. When the messages of the Beneficent were recited to them, they fell down in submission, weeping.

19:59. But there came after them an evil generation, who wasted prayers and followed lusts, so they will meet perdition,

19:60. Except those who repent and believe and do good such will enter the Garden, and they will not be wronged in aught:

19:61. Gardens of perpetuity which the Beneficent has promised to His servants in the Unseen. Surely His promise ever comes to pass.

19:62. They will hear therein no vain discourse, but only, Peace! And they have their sustenance therein, morning and evening.

19:63. This is the Garden which We cause those of Our servants to inherit who keep their duty.

19:64. And we descend not but by the command of thy Lord. To Him belongs what is before us and what is behind us and what is between these, and thy Lord is never forgetful.

19:65. Lord of the heavens and the earth and what is between them, so serve Him and be patient in His service. Knowest thou any one equal to Him?

***

19:66. And says man: When I am dead, shall I truly be brought forth alive?

19:67. Does not man remember that We created him before, when he was nothing?

19:68. So by thy Lord! We shall certainly gather them together and the devils, then shall We bring them around hell on their knees.

19:69. Then We shall draw forth from every sect those most rebellious against the Beneficent.

19:70. Again, We certainly know best those who deserve most to be burned therein.

يَلْقَوْنَ غَيًّا (٥٩)
إِلَّا مَنْ تَابَ وَآمَنَ وَعَمِلَ صَالِحًا فَأُولَٰئِكَ يَدْخُلُونَ الْجَنَّةَ وَلَا يُظْلَمُونَ شَيْئًا (٦٠)
جَنَّاتِ عَدْنٍ الَّتِي وَعَدَ الرَّحْمَٰنُ عِبَادَهُ بِالْغَيْبِ إِنَّهُ كَانَ وَعْدُهُ مَأْتِيًّا (٦١)
لَا يَسْمَعُونَ فِيهَا لَغْوًا إِلَّا سَلَامًا وَلَهُمْ رِزْقُهُمْ فِيهَا بُكْرَةً وَعَشِيًّا (٦٢)
تِلْكَ الْجَنَّةُ الَّتِي نُورِثُ مِنْ عِبَادِنَا مَنْ كَانَ تَقِيًّا (٦٣)
وَمَا نَتَنَزَّلُ إِلَّا بِأَمْرِ رَبِّكَ لَهُ مَا بَيْنَ أَيْدِينَا وَمَا خَلْفَنَا وَمَا بَيْنَ ذَٰلِكَ وَمَا كَانَ رَبُّكَ نَسِيًّا (٦٤)
رَبُّ السَّمَاوَاتِ وَالْأَرْضِ وَمَا بَيْنَهُمَا فَاعْبُدْهُ وَاصْطَبِرْ لِعِبَادَتِهِ هَلْ تَعْلَمُ لَهُ سَمِيًّا (٦٥)
وَيَقُولُ الْإِنْسَانُ أَئِذَا مَا مِتُّ لَسَوْفَ أُخْرَجُ حَيًّا (٦٦)
أَوَلَا يَذْكُرُ الْإِنْسَانُ أَنَّا خَلَقْنَاهُ مِنْ قَبْلُ وَلَمْ يَكُ شَيْئًا (٦٧)
فَوَرَبِّكَ لَنَحْشُرَنَّهُمْ وَالشَّيَاطِينَ ثُمَّ لَنُحْضِرَنَّهُمْ حَوْلَ جَهَنَّمَ جِثِيًّا (٦٨)
ثُمَّ لَنَنْزِعَنَّ مِنْ كُلِّ شِيعَةٍ أَيُّهُمْ أَشَدُّ عَلَى الرَّحْمَٰنِ عِتِيًّا (٦٩)
ثُمَّ لَنَحْنُ أَعْلَمُ بِالَّذِينَ هُمْ أَوْلَىٰ بِهَا صِلِيًّا (٧٠)
وَإِنْ مِنْكُمْ إِلَّا وَارِدُهَا كَانَ عَلَىٰ رَبِّكَ حَتْمًا مَقْضِيًّا (٧١)
ثُمَّ نُنَجِّي الَّذِينَ اتَّقَوْا وَنَذَرُ الظَّالِمِينَ فِيهَا جِثِيًّا (٧٢)
وَإِذَا تُتْلَىٰ عَلَيْهِمْ آيَاتُنَا بَيِّنَاتٍ قَالَ الَّذِينَ كَفَرُوا لِلَّذِينَ آمَنُوا أَيُّ الْفَرِيقَيْنِ خَيْرٌ مَقَامًا وَأَحْسَنُ نَدِيًّا (٧٣)

19:71. And there is not one of you but shall come to it. This is an unavoidable decree of thy Lord.

19:72. And We shall deliver those who guard against evil, and leave the wrongdoers therein on their knees.

19:73. And when Our clear messages are recited to them, those who disbelieve say to those who believe: Which of the two parties is better in position and better in assembly?

19:74. And how many a generation have We destroyed before them, who had better possessions and appearance!

19:75. Say: As for him who is in error, the Beneficent will prolong his length of days; until they see what they were threatened with, either the punishment or the Hour. Then they will know who is worse in position and weaker in forces.

19:76. And Allah increases in guidance those who go aright. And deeds that endure, the good deeds, are, with thy Lord, better in recompense and yield better return.

19:77. Hast thou seen him who disbelieves in Our messages and says: I shall certainly be given wealth and children?

19:78. Has he gained knowledge of the unseen, or made a covenant with the Beneficent?

19:79. By no means! We write down what he says, and We shall lengthen to him the length of the chastisement

19:80. And We shall inherit from him what he says, and he will come to Us alone.

19:81. And they have taken gods besides Allah, that they should be to them a source of strength --

19:82. By no means! They will soon deny their worshipping them, and be their adversaries.

***

19:83. Seest thou not that We send the devils against the disbelievers, inciting

وَكَمْ أَهْلَكْنَا قَبْلَهُمْ مِنْ قَرْنٍ هُمْ أَحْسَنُ أَثَاثًا وَرِئْيًا (٧٤)

قُلْ مَنْ كَانَ فِي الضَّلَالَةِ فَلْيَمْدُدْ لَهُ الرَّحْمَنُ مَدًّا حَتَّى إِذَا رَأَوْا مَا يُوعَدُونَ إِمَّا الْعَذَابَ وَإِمَّا السَّاعَةَ فَسَيَعْلَمُونَ مَنْ هُوَ شَرٌّ مَكَانًا وَأَضْعَفُ جُنْدًا (٧٥)

وَيَزِيدُ اللَّهُ الَّذِينَ اهْتَدَوْا هُدًى وَالْبَاقِيَاتُ الصَّالِحَاتُ خَيْرٌ عِنْدَ رَبِّكَ ثَوَابًا وَخَيْرٌ مَرَدًّا (٧٦)

أَفَرَأَيْتَ الَّذِي كَفَرَ بِآيَاتِنَا وَقَالَ لَأُوتَيَنَّ مَالًا وَوَلَدًا (٧٧)

أَطَّلَعَ الْغَيْبَ أَمِ اتَّخَذَ عِنْدَ الرَّحْمَنِ عَهْدًا (٧٨)

كَلَّا سَنَكْتُبُ مَا يَقُولُ وَنَمُدُّ لَهُ مِنَ الْعَذَابِ مَدًّا (٧٩)

وَنَرِثُهُ مَا يَقُولُ وَيَأْتِينَا فَرْدًا (٨٠)

وَاتَّخَذُوا مِنْ دُونِ اللَّهِ آلِهَةً لِيَكُونُوا لَهُمْ عِزًّا (٨١)

كَلَّا سَيَكْفُرُونَ بِعِبَادَتِهِمْ وَيَكُونُونَ عَلَيْهِمْ ضِدًّا (٨٢)

أَلَمْ تَرَ أَنَّا أَرْسَلْنَا الشَّيَاطِينَ عَلَى الْكَافِرِينَ تَؤُزُّهُمْ أَزًّا (٨٣)

فَلَا تَعْجَلْ عَلَيْهِمْ إِنَّمَا نَعُدُّ لَهُمْ عَدًّا (٨٤)

يَوْمَ نَحْشُرُ الْمُتَّقِينَ إِلَى الرَّحْمَنِ وَفْدًا (٨٥)

وَنَسُوقُ الْمُجْرِمِينَ إِلَى جَهَنَّمَ وِرْدًا (٨٦)

لَا يَمْلِكُونَ الشَّفَاعَةَ إِلَّا مَنِ اتَّخَذَ عِنْدَ الرَّحْمَنِ عَهْدًا (٨٧)

وَقَالُوا اتَّخَذَ الرَّحْمَنُ وَلَدًا (٨٨)

لَقَدْ جِئْتُمْ شَيْئًا إِدًّا (٨٩)

them incitingly?

19:84. So make no haste against them. We only number out to them a number (of days).

19:85. The day when We gather the dutiful to the Beneficent to receive honours,

19:86. And drive the guilty to hell, as thirsty beasts.

19:87. They have no power of intercession, save him who has made a covenant with the Beneficent.

19:88. And they say: The Beneficent has taken to Himself a son.

19:89. Certainly you make an abominable assertion!

19:90. The heavens may almost be rent thereat, and the earth cleave asunder, and the mountains fall down in pieces,

19:91. That they ascribe a son to the Beneficent!

19:92. And it is not worthy of the Beneficent that He should take to Himself a son.

19:93. There is none in the heavens and the earth but comes to the Beneficent as a servant.

19:94. Certainly He comprehends them, and has numbered them all.

19:95. And every one of them will come to Him on the day of Resurrection, alone.

19:96. Those who believe and do good deeds, for them the Beneficent will surely bring about love.

19:97. So We have made it easy in thy tongue only that thou shouldst give good news thereby to those who guard against evil, and shouldst warn thereby a contentious people.

19:98. And how many a generation before them have We destroyed! Canst thou see any one of them or hear a sound of them?

تَكَادُ السَّمَوَاتُ يَتَفَطَّرْنَ مِنْهُ وَتَنْشَقُّ الْأَرْضُ وَتَخِرُّ الْجِبَالُ هَدًّا (٩٠) أَنْ دَعَوْا لِلرَّحْمَنِ وَلَدًا (٩١) وَمَا يَنْبَغِي لِلرَّحْمَنِ أَنْ يَتَّخِذَ وَلَدًا (٩٢) إِنْ كُلُّ مَنْ فِي السَّمَاوَاتِ وَالْأَرْضِ إِلَّا آتِي الرَّحْمَنِ عَبْدًا (٩٣) لَقَدْ أَحْصَاهُمْ وَعَدَّهُمْ عَدًّا (٩٤) وَكُلُّهُمْ آتِيهِ يَوْمَ الْقِيَامَةِ فَرْدًا (٩٥) إِنَّ الَّذِينَ آمَنُوا وَعَمِلُوا الصَّالِحَاتِ سَيَجْعَلُ لَهُمُ الرَّحْمَنُ وُدًّا (٩٦) فَإِنَّمَا يَسَّرْنَاهُ بِلِسَانِكَ لِتُبَشِّرَ بِهِ الْمُتَّقِينَ وَتُنْذِرَ بِهِ قَوْمًا لُدًّا (٩٧) وَكَمْ أَهْلَكْنَا قَبْلَهُمْ مِنْ قَرْنٍ هَلْ تُحِسُّ مِنْهُمْ مِنْ أَحَدٍ أَوْ تَسْمَعُ لَهُمْ رِكْزًا (٩٨)

20. Ta Ha

In the name of Allah, the Beneficent, the Merciful.

20:1. O man,

20:2. We have not revealed the Qur'an to thee that thou mayest be unsuccessful;

20:3. But it is a reminder to him who fears:

20:4. A revelation from Him Who created the earth and the high heavens.

20:5. The Beneficent is established on the Throne of Power.

20:6. To Him belongs whatever is in the heavens and whatever is in the earth and whatever is between them and whatever is beneath the soil.

20:7. And if thou utter the saying aloud, surely He knows the secret, and what is yet more hidden.

20:8. Allah there is no God but He. His are the most beautiful names.

20:9. And has the story of Moses come to thee?

20:10. When he saw a fire, he said to his people: Stay, I see a fire; haply I may bring to you therefrom a live coal or find guidance at the fire.

20:11. So when he came to it, a voice came: O Moses,

20:12. Surely I am thy Lord, so take off thy shoes; surely thou art in the sacred valley Tuwa.

20:13. And I have chosen thee so listen to what is revealed:

20:14. Surely I am Allah, there is no God but I, so serve Me, and keep up prayer for My remembrance,

20:15. Surely the Hour is coming -- I am about to make it manifest -- so that every soul may be rewarded as it strives.

20:16. So let not him, who believes not in it and follows his low desire, turn thee away from it, lest thou perish.

20:17. And what is this in thy right hand, O Moses?

٢٠- سورة طه

بِسْمِ اللَّهِ الرَّحْمَنِ الرَّحِيمِ

طه (١)

مَا أَنزَلْنَا عَلَيْكَ الْقُرْآنَ لِتَشْقَى (٢)

إِلَّا تَذْكِرَةً لِمَن يَخْشَى (٣)

تَنزِيلًا مِّمَّنْ خَلَقَ الْأَرْضَ وَالسَّمَاوَاتِ الْعُلَى (٤)

الرَّحْمَنُ عَلَى الْعَرْشِ اسْتَوَى (٥)

لَهُ مَا فِي السَّمَاوَاتِ وَمَا فِي الْأَرْضِ وَمَا بَيْنَهُمَا وَمَا تَحْتَ الثَّرَى (٦)

وَإِن تَجْهَرْ بِالْقَوْلِ فَإِنَّهُ يَعْلَمُ السِّرَّ وَأَخْفَى (٧)

اللَّهُ لَا إِلَهَ إِلَّا هُوَ لَهُ الْأَسْمَاءُ الْحُسْنَى (٨)

وَهَلْ أَتَاكَ حَدِيثُ مُوسَى (٩)

إِذْ رَأَى نَارًا فَقَالَ لِأَهْلِهِ امْكُثُوا إِنِّي آنَسْتُ نَارًا لَعَلِّي آتِيكُم مِّنْهَا بِقَبَسٍ أَوْ أَجِدُ عَلَى النَّارِ هُدًى (١٠)

فَلَمَّا أَتَاهَا نُودِيَ يَا مُوسَى (١١)

إِنِّي أَنَا رَبُّكَ فَاخْلَعْ نَعْلَيْكَ إِنَّكَ بِالْوَادِ الْمُقَدَّسِ طُوًى (١٢)

وَأَنَا اخْتَرْتُكَ فَاسْتَمِعْ لِمَا يُوحَى (١٣)

إِنَّنِي أَنَا اللَّهُ لَا إِلَهَ إِلَّا أَنَا فَاعْبُدْنِي وَأَقِمِ الصَّلَاةَ لِذِكْرِي (١٤)

إِنَّ السَّاعَةَ آتِيَةٌ أَكَادُ أُخْفِيهَا لِتُجْزَى كُلُّ نَفْسٍ بِمَا تَسْعَى (١٥)

فَلَا يَصُدَّنَّكَ عَنْهَا مَن لَّا يُؤْمِنُ بِهَا وَاتَّبَعَ هَوَاهُ فَتَرْدَى (١٦)

وَمَا تِلْكَ بِيَمِينِكَ يَا مُوسَى (١٧)

قَالَ هِيَ عَصَايَ أَتَوَكَّأُ عَلَيْهَا وَأَهُشُّ بِهَا عَلَى غَنَمِي وَلِيَ فِيهَا مَآرِبُ

20. Ta Ha

20:18. He said: This is my staff I lean on it, and I beat the leaves with it for my sheep, and I have other uses for it.
20:19. He said: Cast it down, O Moses.
20:20. So he cast it down, and lo! it was a serpent, gliding.
20:21. He said: Seize it and fear not. We shall return it to its former state.
20:22. And press thy hand to thy side, it will come out white without evil -- another sign:
20:23. That We may show thee of Our greater signs.
20:24. Go to Pharaoh, surely he has exceeded the limits.

***

20:25. He said: My Lord, expand my breast for me:
20:26. And ease my affair for me:
20:27. And loose the knot from my tongue,
20:28. (That) they may understand my word.
20:29. And give to me an aider from my family:
20:30. Aaron, my brother;
20:31. Add to my strength by him,
20:32. And make him share my task --
20:33. So that we may glorify Thee much,
20:34. And much remember Thee.
20:35. Surely, Thou art ever Seeing us.
20:36. He said: Thou art indeed granted thy petition, O Moses.
20:37. And indeed We bestowed on thee a favour at another time,
20:38. When We revealed to thy mother that which was revealed:
20:39. Put him into a chest, then cast it into the river, the river will cast it upon the shore -- there an enemy to Me and an enemy to him shall take him up. And I shed on thee love from Me; and that thou mayest be brought up before My eyes.
20:40. When thy sister went and said: Shall I direct you to one who will take charge of him? So We brought thee

أُخْرَى (١٨)
قَالَ أَلْقِهَا يَا مُوسَى (١٩)
فَأَلْقَاهَا فَإِذَا هِيَ حَيَّةٌ تَسْعَى (٢٠)
قَالَ خُذْهَا وَلَا تَخَفْ سَنُعِيدُهَا سِيرَتَهَا الْأُولَى (٢١)
وَاضْمُمْ يَدَكَ إِلَى جَنَاحِكَ تَخْرُجْ بَيْضَاءَ مِنْ غَيْرِ سُوءٍ آيَةً أُخْرَى (٢٢)
لِنُرِيَكَ مِنْ آيَاتِنَا الْكُبْرَى (٢٣)
اذْهَبْ إِلَى فِرْعَوْنَ إِنَّهُ طَغَى (٢٤)
قَالَ رَبِّ اشْرَحْ لِي صَدْرِي (٢٥)
وَيَسِّرْ لِي أَمْرِي (٢٦)
وَاحْلُلْ عُقْدَةً مِنْ لِسَانِي (٢٧)
يَفْقَهُوا قَوْلِي (٢٨)
وَاجْعَلْ لِي وَزِيرًا مِنْ أَهْلِي (٢٩)
هَارُونَ أَخِي (٣٠)
اشْدُدْ بِهِ أَزْرِي (٣١)
وَأَشْرِكْهُ فِي أَمْرِي (٣٢)
كَيْ نُسَبِّحَكَ كَثِيرًا (٣٣)
وَنَذْكُرَكَ كَثِيرًا (٣٤)
إِنَّكَ كُنْتَ بِنَا بَصِيرًا (٣٥)
قَالَ قَدْ أُوتِيتَ سُؤْلَكَ يَا مُوسَى (٣٦)
وَلَقَدْ مَنَنَّا عَلَيْكَ مَرَّةً أُخْرَى (٣٧)
إِذْ أَوْحَيْنَا إِلَى أُمِّكَ مَا يُوحَى (٣٨)
أَنِ اقْذِفِيهِ فِي التَّابُوتِ فَاقْذِفِيهِ فِي الْيَمِّ فَلْيُلْقِهِ الْيَمُّ بِالسَّاحِلِ يَأْخُذْهُ عَدُوٌّ لِي وَعَدُوٌّ لَهُ وَأَلْقَيْتُ عَلَيْكَ مَحَبَّةً مِنِّي وَلِتُصْنَعَ عَلَى عَيْنِي (٣٩)
إِذْ تَمْشِي أُخْتُكَ فَتَقُولُ هَلْ أَدُلُّكُمْ عَلَى مَنْ يَكْفُلُهُ فَرَجَعْنَاكَ إِلَى أُمِّكَ كَيْ تَقَرَّ عَيْنُهَا وَلَا تَحْزَنَ وَقَتَلْتَ نَفْسًا فَنَجَّيْنَاكَ مِنَ الْغَمِّ وَفَتَنَّاكَ فُتُونًا فَلَبِثْتَ

20. Ta Ha

back to thy mother that her eye might be cooled and she should not grieve. And thou didst kill a man, then We delivered thee from grief, and tried thee with (many) trials. Then thou didst stay for years among the people of Midian. Then thou camest hither as ordained, O Moses.

20:41. And I have chosen thee for Myself.

20:42. Go thou and thy brother with My messages and be not remiss in remembering Me.

20:43. Go both of you to Pharaoh, surely he is inordinate;

20:44. Then speak to him a gentle word, haply he may mind or fear.

20:45. They said: Our Lord, we fear lest he hasten to do evil to us or be inordinate.

20:46. He said: Fear not, surely I am with you -- I do hear and see.

20:47. So go you to him and say: Surely we are two messengers of thy Lord; so send forth the Children of Israel with us; and torment them not. Indeed we have brought to thee a message from thy Lord, and peace to him who follows the guidance.

20:48. It has indeed been revealed to us that punishment will overtake him who rejects and turns away.

20:49. (Pharaoh) said: Who is your Lord, O Moses?

20:50. He said: Our Lord is He Who gives to everything its creation, then guides (it).

20:51. He said: What then is the state of the former generations?

20:52. He said: The knowledge thereof is with my Lord in a book; my Lord neither errs nor forgets --

20:53. Who made the earth for you an expanse and made for you therein paths and sent down water from the clouds. Then thereby We bring forth pairs of various herbs.

20:54. Eat and pasture your cattle.

سِنِينَ فِي أَهْلِ مَدْيَنَ ثُمَّ جِئْتَ عَلَى قَدَرٍ يَا مُوسَى (٤٠) وَاصْطَنَعْتُكَ لِنَفْسِي (٤١) اذْهَبْ أَنْتَ وَأَخُوكَ بِآيَاتِي وَلَا تَنِيَا فِي ذِكْرِي (٤٢) اذْهَبَا إِلَى فِرْعَوْنَ إِنَّهُ طَغَى (٤٣) فَقُولَا لَهُ قَوْلًا لَيِّنًا لَعَلَّهُ يَتَذَكَّرُ أَوْ يَخْشَى (٤٤) قَالَا رَبَّنَا إِنَّنَا نَخَافُ أَنْ يَفْرُطَ عَلَيْنَا أَوْ أَنْ يَطْغَى (٤٥) قَالَ لَا تَخَافَا إِنَّنِي مَعَكُمَا أَسْمَعُ وَأَرَى (٤٦) فَأْتِيَاهُ فَقُولَا إِنَّا رَسُولَا رَبِّكَ فَأَرْسِلْ مَعَنَا بَنِي إِسْرَائِيلَ وَلَا تُعَذِّبْهُمْ قَدْ جِئْنَاكَ بِآيَةٍ مِنْ رَبِّكَ وَالسَّلَامُ عَلَى مَنِ اتَّبَعَ الْهُدَى (٤٧) إِنَّا قَدْ أُوحِيَ إِلَيْنَا أَنَّ الْعَذَابَ عَلَى مَنْ كَذَّبَ وَتَوَلَّى (٤٨) قَالَ فَمَنْ رَبُّكُمَا يَا مُوسَى (٤٩) قَالَ رَبُّنَا الَّذِي أَعْطَى كُلَّ شَيْءٍ خَلْقَهُ ثُمَّ هَدَى (٥٠) قَالَ فَمَا بَالُ الْقُرُونِ الْأُولَى (٥١) قَالَ عِلْمُهَا عِنْدَ رَبِّي فِي كِتَابٍ لَا يَضِلُّ رَبِّي وَلَا يَنْسَى (٥٢) الَّذِي جَعَلَ لَكُمُ الْأَرْضَ مَهْدًا وَسَلَكَ لَكُمْ فِيهَا سُبُلًا وَأَنْزَلَ مِنَ السَّمَاءِ مَاءً فَأَخْرَجْنَا بِهِ أَزْوَاجًا مِنْ نَبَاتٍ شَتَّى (٥٣) كُلُوا وَارْعَوْا أَنْعَامَكُمْ إِنَّ فِي ذَلِكَ لَآيَاتٍ لِأُولِي النُّهَى (٥٤) مِنْهَا خَلَقْنَاكُمْ وَفِيهَا نُعِيدُكُمْ وَمِنْهَا نُخْرِجُكُمْ تَارَةً أُخْرَى (٥٥) وَلَقَدْ أَرَيْنَاهُ آيَاتِنَا كُلَّهَا فَكَذَّبَ وَأَبَى

Surely there are signs in this for men of understanding.

***

20:55. From it We created you, and into it We shall return you, and from it raise you a second time.

20:56. And truly We showed him all Our signs but he rejected and refused.

20:57. Said he: Hast thou come to us to turn us out of our land by thy enchantment, O Moses?

20:58. We too can bring to thee enchantment like it, so make an appointment between us and thee, which we break not, (neither) we nor thou, (in) a central place.

20:59. (Moses) said: Your appointment is the day of the Festival, and let the people be gathered in the early forenoon.

20:60. So Pharaoh went back and settled his plan, then came.

20:61. Moses said to them: Woe to you! Forge not a lie against Allah, lest He destroy you by punishment, and he fails indeed who forges (a lie).

20:62. So they disputed one with another about their affair and kept the discourse secret.

20:63. They said: These are surely two enchanters who would drive you out from your land by their enchantment, and destroy your excellent institutions.

20:64. So settle your plan, then come in ranks, and he will succeed indeed this day who is uppermost.

20:65. They said: O Moses, wilt thou cast, or shall we be the first to cast down?

20:66. He said: Nay! Cast you down. Then lo! their cords and their rods it appeared to him by their enchantment as if they ran.

20:67. So Moses conceived fear in his mind.

20:68. We said: Fear not, surely thou art the uppermost.

20:69. And cast down what is in thy

(٥٦)
قَالَ أَجِئْتَنَا لِتُخْرِجَنَا مِنْ أَرْضِنَا بِسِحْرِكَ يَا مُوسَىٰ (٥٧)
فَلَنَأْتِيَنَّكَ بِسِحْرٍ مِثْلِهِ فَاجْعَلْ بَيْنَنَا وَبَيْنَكَ مَوْعِدًا لَا نُخْلِفُهُ نَحْنُ وَلَا أَنْتَ مَكَانًا سُوًى (٥٨)
قَالَ مَوْعِدُكُمْ يَوْمُ الزِّينَةِ وَأَنْ يُحْشَرَ النَّاسُ ضُحًى (٥٩)
فَتَوَلَّىٰ فِرْعَوْنُ فَجَمَعَ كَيْدَهُ ثُمَّ أَتَىٰ (٦٠)
قَالَ لَهُمْ مُوسَىٰ وَيْلَكُمْ لَا تَفْتَرُوا عَلَى اللَّهِ كَذِبًا فَيُسْحِتَكُمْ بِعَذَابٍ وَقَدْ خَابَ مَنِ افْتَرَىٰ (٦١)
فَتَنَازَعُوا أَمْرَهُمْ بَيْنَهُمْ وَأَسَرُّوا النَّجْوَىٰ (٦٢)
قَالُوا إِنْ هَذَانِ لَسَاحِرَانِ يُرِيدَانِ أَنْ يُخْرِجَاكُمْ مِنْ أَرْضِكُمْ بِسِحْرِهِمَا وَيَذْهَبَا بِطَرِيقَتِكُمُ الْمُثْلَىٰ (٦٣)
فَأَجْمِعُوا كَيْدَكُمْ ثُمَّ ائْتُوا صَفًّا وَقَدْ أَفْلَحَ الْيَوْمَ مَنِ اسْتَعْلَىٰ (٦٤)
قَالُوا يَا مُوسَىٰ إِمَّا أَنْ تُلْقِيَ وَإِمَّا أَنْ نَكُونَ أَوَّلَ مَنْ أَلْقَىٰ (٦٥)
قَالَ بَلْ أَلْقُوا فَإِذَا حِبَالُهُمْ وَعِصِيُّهُمْ يُخَيَّلُ إِلَيْهِ مِنْ سِحْرِهِمْ أَنَّهَا تَسْعَىٰ (٦٦)
فَأَوْجَسَ فِي نَفْسِهِ خِيفَةً مُوسَىٰ (٦٧)
قُلْنَا لَا تَخَفْ إِنَّكَ أَنْتَ الْأَعْلَىٰ (٦٨)
وَأَلْقِ مَا فِي يَمِينِكَ تَلْقَفْ مَا صَنَعُوا إِنَّمَا صَنَعُوا كَيْدُ سَاحِرٍ وَلَا يُفْلِحُ السَّاحِرُ حَيْثُ أَتَىٰ (٦٩)
فَأُلْقِيَ السَّحَرَةُ سُجَّدًا قَالُوا آمَنَّا بِرَبِّ هَارُونَ وَمُوسَىٰ (٧٠)
قَالَ آمَنْتُمْ لَهُ قَبْلَ أَنْ آذَنَ لَكُمْ إِنَّهُ

20. Ta Ha

right hand -- it will eat up what they have wrought. What they have wrought is only the trick of an enchanter, and the enchanter succeeds not wheresoever he comes from.

20:70. So the enchanters fell down prostrate, saying: We believe in the Lord of Aaron and Moses.

20:71. (Pharaoh) said: You believe in him before I give you leave! Surely he is your chief who taught you enchantment. So I shall cut off your hands and your feet on opposite sides and I shall crucify you on the trunks of palm-trees, and you shall certainly know which of us can give the severer and the more abiding chastisement.

20:72. They said: We cannot prefer thee to what has come to us of clear arguments and to Him Who made us, so decide as thou wilt decide. Thou canst only decide about this world's life.

20:73. Surely we believe in our Lord that He may forgive us our faults and the magic to which thou didst compel us. And Allah is Best and ever Abiding.

20:74. Whoso comes guilty to his Lord, for him is surely hell. He will neither die therein, nor live.

20:75. And whoso comes to Him a believer, having done good deeds, for them are high ranks --

20:76. Gardens of perpetuity, wherein flow rivers, to abide therein. And such is the reward of him who purifies himself.

20:77. And certainly We revealed to Moses: Travel by night with My servants, then strike for them a dry path in the sea, not fearing to overtaken, nor being afraid.

20:78. So Pharaoh followed them with his armies, then there covered them of the sea that which covered them.

20:79. And Pharaoh led his people astray and he guided not aright.

20:80. O Children of Israel, We truly

لَكَبِيرُكُمُ الَّذِي عَلَّمَكُمُ السِّحْرَ فَلَأُقَطِّعَنَّ أَيْدِيَكُمْ وَأَرْجُلَكُمْ مِنْ خِلَافٍ وَلَأُصَلِّبَنَّكُمْ فِي جُذُوعِ النَّخْلِ وَلَتَعْلَمُنَّ أَيُّنَا أَشَدُّ عَذَابًا وَأَبْقَى (٧١) قَالُوا لَنْ نُؤْثِرَكَ عَلَى مَا جَاءَنَا مِنَ الْبَيِّنَاتِ وَالَّذِي فَطَرَنَا فَاقْضِ مَا أَنْتَ قَاضٍ إِنَّمَا تَقْضِي هَذِهِ الْحَيَاةَ الدُّنْيَا (٧٢) إِنَّا آمَنَّا بِرَبِّنَا لِيَغْفِرَ لَنَا خَطَايَانَا وَمَا أَكْرَهْتَنَا عَلَيْهِ مِنَ السِّحْرِ وَاللَّهُ خَيْرٌ وَأَبْقَى (٧٣) إِنَّهُ مَنْ يَأْتِ رَبَّهُ مُجْرِمًا فَإِنَّ لَهُ جَهَنَّمَ لَا يَمُوتُ فِيهَا وَلَا يَحْيَا (٧٤) وَمَنْ يَأْتِهِ مُؤْمِنًا قَدْ عَمِلَ الصَّالِحَاتِ فَأُولَئِكَ لَهُمُ الدَّرَجَاتُ الْعُلَا (٧٥) جَنَّاتُ عَدْنٍ تَجْرِي مِنْ تَحْتِهَا الْأَنْهَارُ خَالِدِينَ فِيهَا وَذَلِكَ جَزَاءُ مَنْ تَزَكَّى (٧٦) وَلَقَدْ أَوْحَيْنَا إِلَى مُوسَى أَنْ أَسْرِ بِعِبَادِي فَاضْرِبْ لَهُمْ طَرِيقًا فِي الْبَحْرِ يَبَسًا لَا تَخَافُ دَرَكًا وَلَا تَخْشَى (٧٧) فَأَتْبَعَهُمْ فِرْعَوْنُ بِجُنُودِهِ فَغَشِيَهُمْ مِنَ الْيَمِّ مَا غَشِيَهُمْ (٧٨) وَأَضَلَّ فِرْعَوْنُ قَوْمَهُ وَمَا هَدَى (٧٩) يَا بَنِي إِسْرَائِيلَ قَدْ أَنْجَيْنَاكُمْ مِنْ عَدُوِّكُمْ وَوَاعَدْنَاكُمْ جَانِبَ الطُّورِ الْأَيْمَنَ وَنَزَّلْنَا عَلَيْكُمُ الْمَنَّ وَالسَّلْوَى (٨٠) كُلُوا مِنْ طَيِّبَاتِ مَا رَزَقْنَاكُمْ وَلَا تَطْغَوْا فِيهِ فَيَحِلَّ عَلَيْكُمْ غَضَبِي وَمَنْ يَحْلِلْ عَلَيْهِ غَضَبِي فَقَدْ هَوَى (٨١) وَإِنِّي لَغَفَّارٌ لِمَنْ تَابَ وَآمَنَ وَعَمِلَ

delivered you from your enemy, and made a covenant with you on the blessed side of the mountain, and sent to you the manna and the quails.

20:81. Eat of the good things We have provided for you, and be not inordinate in respect thereof, lest My wrath come upon you; and he on whom My wrath comes, he perishes indeed.

20:82. And surely I am Forgiving toward him who repents and believes and does good, then walks aright.

20:83. And what made thee hasten from thy people, O Moses?

20:84. He said: They are here on my track, and I hastened on to Thee, my Lord, that Thou mightest be pleased.

20:85. He said: Surely We have tried thy people in thy absence, and the Samiri has led them astray.

20:86. So Moses returned to his people angry, sorrowing. He said: O my people, did not your Lord promise you a goodly promise? Did the promised time, then, seem long to you, or did you wish that displeasure from your Lord should come upon you, so that you broke (your) promise to me?

20:87. They said: We broke not the promise to thee of our own accord, but we were made to bear the burdens of the ornaments uf the people, then we cast them away, and thus did the Samiri suggest

20:88. Then he brought forth for them a calf, a body, which had a hollow sound, so they said: This is your god and the god of Moses but he forgot.

20:89. Could they not see that it returned no reply to them, nor controlled any harm or benefit for them?

***

20:90. And Aaron indeed had said to them before: O my people, you are only tried by it, and surely your Lord is the Beneficent God, so follow me and

صَالِحًا ثُمَّ اهْتَدَى (٨٢)
وَمَا أَعْجَلَكَ عَنْ قَوْمِكَ يَا مُوسَى (٨٣)
قَالَ هُمْ أُولَاءِ عَلَى أَثَرِي وَعَجِلْتُ إِلَيْكَ رَبِّ لِتَرْضَى (٨٤)
قَالَ فَإِنَّا قَدْ فَتَنَّا قَوْمَكَ مِنْ بَعْدِكَ وَأَضَلَّهُمُ السَّامِرِيُّ (٨٥)
فَرَجَعَ مُوسَى إِلَى قَوْمِهِ غَضْبَانَ أَسِفًا قَالَ يَا قَوْمِ أَلَمْ يَعِدْكُمْ رَبُّكُمْ وَعْدًا حَسَنًا أَفَطَالَ عَلَيْكُمُ الْعَهْدُ أَمْ أَرَدْتُمْ أَنْ يَحِلَّ عَلَيْكُمْ غَضَبٌ مِنْ رَبِّكُمْ فَأَخْلَفْتُمْ مَوْعِدِي (٨٦)
قَالُوا مَا أَخْلَفْنَا مَوْعِدَكَ بِمَلْكِنَا وَلَكِنَّا حُمِّلْنَا أَوْزَارًا مِنْ زِينَةِ الْقَوْمِ فَقَذَفْنَاهَا فَكَذَلِكَ أَلْقَى السَّامِرِيُّ (٨٧)
فَأَخْرَجَ لَهُمْ عِجْلًا جَسَدًا لَهُ خُوَارٌ فَقَالُوا هَذَا إِلَهُكُمْ وَإِلَهُ مُوسَى فَنَسِيَ (٨٨)
أَفَلَا يَرَوْنَ أَلَّا يَرْجِعُ إِلَيْهِمْ قَوْلًا وَلَا يَمْلِكُ لَهُمْ ضَرًّا وَلَا نَفْعًا (٨٩)
وَلَقَدْ قَالَ لَهُمْ هَارُونُ مِنْ قَبْلُ يَا قَوْمِ إِنَّمَا فُتِنْتُمْ بِهِ وَإِنَّ رَبَّكُمُ الرَّحْمَنُ فَاتَّبِعُونِي وَأَطِيعُوا أَمْرِي (٩٠)
قَالُوا لَنْ نَبْرَحَ عَلَيْهِ عَاكِفِينَ حَتَّى يَرْجِعَ إِلَيْنَا مُوسَى (٩١)
قَالَ يَا هَارُونُ مَا مَنَعَكَ إِذْ رَأَيْتَهُمْ ضَلُّوا (٩٢)
أَلَّا تَتَّبِعَنِ أَفَعَصَيْتَ أَمْرِي (٩٣)
قَالَ يَا ابْنَ أُمَّ لَا تَأْخُذْ بِلِحْيَتِي وَلَا بِرَأْسِي إِنِّي خَشِيتُ أَنْ تَقُولَ فَرَّقْتَ بَيْنَ بَنِي إِسْرَائِيلَ وَلَمْ تَرْقُبْ قَوْلِي (٩٤)
قَالَ فَمَا خَطْبُكَ يَا سَامِرِيُّ (٩٥)

20. Ta Ha

obey my order.

20:91. They said We shall not cease to keep to its worship until Moses returns to us.

20:92. (Moses) said: O Aaron, what prevented thee, when thou sawest them going astray,

20:93. That thou didst not follow me? Hast thou, then, disobeyed my order?

20:94. He said: O son of my mother, seize me not by my beard, nor by my head. Surely I was afraid lest thou shouldst say Thou hast caused division among the Children of Israel and not waited for my word.

20:95. (Moses) said: What was thy object, O Samiri?

20:96. He said: I perceived what they perceived not, so I took a handful from the footprints of the messenger then I cast it away. Thus did my soul embellish (it) to me.

20:97. He said: Begone then! It is for thee in this life to say, Touch (me) not. And for thee is a promise which shall not fail. And look at thy god to whose worship thou hast kept. We will certainly burn it, then we will scatter it in the sea.

20:98. Your Lord is only Allah, there is no God but He. He comprehends all things in (His) knowledge.

20:99. Thus relate We to thee of the news of what has gone before. And indeed We have given thee a Reminder from Ourselves.

20:100. Whoever turns away from it, he will surely bear a burden on the day of Resurrection,

20:101. Abiding therein. And evil will be their burden on the day of Resurrection -

20:102. The day when the trumpet is blown; and We shall gather the guilty, blue-eyed, on that day,

20:103. Consulting together secretly: You tarried but ten (days).

20:104. We know best what they say

قَالَ بَصُرْتُ بِمَا لَمْ يَبْصُرُوا بِهِ فَقَبَضْتُ قَبْضَةً مِنْ أَثَرِ الرَّسُولِ فَنَبَذْتُهَا وَكَذَلِكَ سَوَّلَتْ لِي نَفْسِي (٩٦)

قَالَ فَاذْهَبْ فَإِنَّ لَكَ فِي الْحَيَاةِ أَنْ تَقُولَ لَا مِسَاسَ وَإِنَّ لَكَ مَوْعِدًا لَنْ تُخْلَفَهُ وَانْظُرْ إِلَى إِلَهِكَ الَّذِي ظَلْتَ عَلَيْهِ عَاكِفًا لَنُحَرِّقَنَّهُ ثُمَّ لَنَنْسِفَنَّهُ فِي الْيَمِّ نَسْفًا (٩٧)

إِنَّمَا إِلَهُكُمُ اللَّهُ الَّذِي لَا إِلَهَ إِلَّا هُوَ وَسِعَ كُلَّ شَيْءٍ عِلْمًا (٩٨)

كَذَلِكَ نَقُصُّ عَلَيْكَ مِنْ أَنْبَاءِ مَا قَدْ سَبَقَ وَقَدْ آتَيْنَاكَ مِنْ لَدُنَّا ذِكْرًا (٩٩)

مَنْ أَعْرَضَ عَنْهُ فَإِنَّهُ يَحْمِلُ يَوْمَ الْقِيَامَةِ وِزْرًا (١٠٠)

خَالِدِينَ فِيهِ وَسَاءَ لَهُمْ يَوْمَ الْقِيَامَةِ حِمْلًا (١٠١)

يَوْمَ يُنْفَخُ فِي الصُّورِ وَنَحْشُرُ الْمُجْرِمِينَ يَوْمَئِذٍ زُرْقًا (١٠٢)

يَتَخَافَتُونَ بَيْنَهُمْ إِنْ لَبِثْتُمْ إِلَّا عَشْرًا (١٠٣)

نَحْنُ أَعْلَمُ بِمَا يَقُولُونَ إِذْ يَقُولُ أَمْثَلُهُمْ طَرِيقَةً إِنْ لَبِثْتُمْ إِلَّا يَوْمًا (١٠٤)

وَيَسْأَلُونَكَ عَنِ الْجِبَالِ فَقُلْ يَنْسِفُهَا رَبِّي نَسْفًا (١٠٥)

فَيَذَرُهَا قَاعًا صَفْصَفًا (١٠٦)

لَا تَرَى فِيهَا عِوَجًا وَلَا أَمْتًا (١٠٧)

يَوْمَئِذٍ يَتَّبِعُونَ الدَّاعِيَ لَا عِوَجَ لَهُ وَخَشَعَتِ الْأَصْوَاتُ لِلرَّحْمَنِ فَلَا تَسْمَعُ إِلَّا هَمْسًا (١٠٨)

يَوْمَئِذٍ لَا تَنْفَعُ الشَّفَاعَةُ إِلَّا مَنْ أَذِنَ لَهُ الرَّحْمَنُ وَرَضِيَ لَهُ قَوْلًا (١٠٩)

يَعْلَمُ مَا بَيْنَ أَيْدِيهِمْ وَمَا خَلْفَهُمْ وَلَا

20. Ta Ha

when the fairest of them in course would say: You tarried but a day.

***

20:105. And they ask thee about the mountains. Say: My Lord will scatter them, as scattered dust,

20:106. Then leave it a plain, smooth, level,

20:107. Wherein thou seest no crookedness nor unevenness.

20:108. On that day they will follow the Inviter, in whom is no crookedness; and the voices are low before the Beneficent God, so that thou hearest naught but a soft sound.

20:109. On that day no intercession avails except of him whom the Beneficent allows, and whose word He is pleased with.

20:110. He knows what is before them and what is behind them, while they cannot comprehend it in knowledge.

20:111. And faces shall be humbled before the Living, the Self-subsistent. And he who bears iniquity is indeed undone.

20:112. And whoever does good works and he is a believer, he has no fear of injustice, nor of the withholding of his due.

20:113. And thus have We sent it down an Arabic Qur'an, and have distinctly set forth therein of threats that they may guard against evil, or that it may be a reminder for them.

20:114. Supremely exalted then is Allah, the King, the Truth. And make not haste with the Qur'an before its revelation is made complete to thee, and say: My Lord, increase me in knowledge.

20:115. And certainly We gave a commandment to Adam before, but he forgot; and We found in him no resolve (to disobey).

***

20:116. And when We said to the angels: Be submissive to Adam, they

يُحِيطُونَ بِهِ عِلْمًا (١١٠)
وَعَنَتِ الْوُجُوهُ لِلْحَيِّ الْقَيُّومِ وَقَدْ خَابَ مَنْ حَمَلَ ظُلْمًا (١١١)
وَمَنْ يَعْمَلْ مِنَ الصَّالِحَاتِ وَهُوَ مُؤْمِنٌ فَلَا يَخَافُ ظُلْمًا وَلَا هَضْمًا (١١٢)
وَكَذَلِكَ أَنْزَلْنَاهُ قُرْآنًا عَرَبِيًّا وَصَرَّفْنَا فِيهِ مِنَ الْوَعِيدِ لَعَلَّهُمْ يَتَّقُونَ أَوْ يُحْدِثُ لَهُمْ ذِكْرًا (١١٣)
فَتَعَالَى اللَّهُ الْمَلِكُ الْحَقُّ وَلَا تَعْجَلْ بِالْقُرْآنِ مِنْ قَبْلِ أَنْ يُقْضَى إِلَيْكَ وَحْيُهُ وَقُلْ رَبِّ زِدْنِي عِلْمًا (١١٤)
وَلَقَدْ عَهِدْنَا إِلَى آدَمَ مِنْ قَبْلُ فَنَسِيَ وَلَمْ نَجِدْ لَهُ عَزْمًا (١١٥)
وَإِذْ قُلْنَا لِلْمَلَائِكَةِ اسْجُدُوا لِآدَمَ فَسَجَدُوا إِلَّا إِبْلِيسَ أَبَى (١١٦)
فَقُلْنَا يَا آدَمُ إِنَّ هَذَا عَدُوٌّ لَكَ وَلِزَوْجِكَ فَلَا يُخْرِجَنَّكُمَا مِنَ الْجَنَّةِ فَتَشْقَى (١١٧)
إِنَّ لَكَ أَلَّا تَجُوعَ فِيهَا وَلَا تَعْرَى (١١٨)
وَأَنَّكَ لَا تَظْمَأُ فِيهَا وَلَا تَضْحَى (١١٩)
فَوَسْوَسَ إِلَيْهِ الشَّيْطَانُ قَالَ يَا آدَمُ هَلْ أَدُلُّكَ عَلَى شَجَرَةِ الْخُلْدِ وَمُلْكٍ لَا يَبْلَى (١٢٠)
فَأَكَلَا مِنْهَا فَبَدَتْ لَهُمَا سَوْآتُهُمَا وَطَفِقَا يَخْصِفَانِ عَلَيْهِمَا مِنْ وَرَقِ الْجَنَّةِ وَعَصَى آدَمُ رَبَّهُ فَغَوَى (١٢١)
ثُمَّ اجْتَبَاهُ رَبُّهُ فَتَابَ عَلَيْهِ وَهَدَى (١٢٢)
قَالَ اهْبِطَا مِنْهَا جَمِيعًا بَعْضُكُمْ

20. Ta Ha

submitted except Iblis; he refused.

20:117. We said: O Adam, this is an enemy to thee and to thy wife; so let him not drive you both out of the garden so that thou art unhappy.

20:118. Surely it is granted to thee therein that thou art not hungry, nor naked,

20:119. And that thou art not thirsty therein, nor exposed to the sun's heat.

20:120. But the devil made an evil suggestion to him; he said: O Adam, shall I lead thee to the tree of immortality and a kingdom which decays not?

20:121. So they both ate of it, then their evil inclinations became manifest to them, and they began to cover themselves with the leaves of the garden. And Adam disobeyed his Lord, and was disappointed.

20:122. Then his Lord chose him, so He turned to him and guided (him).

20:123. He said: Go forth herefrom both -- all (of you) one of you (is) enemy to another. So there will surely come to you guidance from Me; then whoever follows My guidance, he will not go astray nor be unhappy.

20:124. And whoever turns away from My Reminder, for him is surely a straitened life, and We shall raise him up blind on the day of Resurrection.

20:125. He will say: My Lord, why hast Thou raised me up blind, while I used to see?

20:126. He will say: Thus did Our messages come to thee, but thou didst neglect them. And thus art thou forsaken this day.

20:127. And thus do We recompense him who is extravagant and believes not in the messages of his Lord. And certainly the chastisement of the Hereafter is severer and mote lasting.

20:128. Does it not manifest to them how many of the generations, in whose dwellings they go about, We destroyed

لِبَعْضٍ عَدُوٌّ فَإِمَّا يَأْتِيَنَّكُم مِّنِّي هُدًى فَمَنِ اتَّبَعَ هُدَايَ فَلَا يَضِلُّ وَلَا يَشْقَى (١٢٣)

وَمَنْ أَعْرَضَ عَن ذِكْرِي فَإِنَّ لَهُ مَعِيشَةً ضَنكًا وَنَحْشُرُهُ يَوْمَ الْقِيَامَةِ أَعْمَى (١٢٤)

قَالَ رَبِّ لِمَ حَشَرْتَنِي أَعْمَى وَقَدْ كُنتُ بَصِيرًا (١٢٥)

قَالَ كَذَلِكَ أَتَتْكَ آيَاتُنَا فَنَسِيتَهَا وَكَذَلِكَ الْيَوْمَ تُنسَى (١٢٦)

وَكَذَلِكَ نَجْزِي مَنْ أَسْرَفَ وَلَمْ يُؤْمِن بِآيَاتِ رَبِّهِ وَلَعَذَابُ الْآخِرَةِ أَشَدُّ وَأَبْقَى (١٢٧)

أَفَلَمْ يَهْدِ لَهُمْ كَمْ أَهْلَكْنَا قَبْلَهُم مِّنَ الْقُرُونِ يَمْشُونَ فِي مَسَاكِنِهِمْ إِنَّ فِي ذَلِكَ لَآيَاتٍ لِّأُولِي النُّهَى (١٢٨)

وَلَوْلَا كَلِمَةٌ سَبَقَتْ مِن رَّبِّكَ لَكَانَ لِزَامًا وَأَجَلٌ مُّسَمًّى (١٢٩)

فَاصْبِرْ عَلَى مَا يَقُولُونَ وَسَبِّحْ بِحَمْدِ رَبِّكَ قَبْلَ طُلُوعِ الشَّمْسِ وَقَبْلَ غُرُوبِهَا وَمِنْ آنَاءِ اللَّيْلِ فَسَبِّحْ وَأَطْرَافَ النَّهَارِ لَعَلَّكَ تَرْضَى (١٣٠)

وَلَا تَمُدَّنَّ عَيْنَيْكَ إِلَى مَا مَتَّعْنَا بِهِ أَزْوَاجًا مِّنْهُمْ زَهْرَةَ الْحَيَاةِ الدُّنْيَا لِنَفْتِنَهُمْ فِيهِ وَرِزْقُ رَبِّكَ خَيْرٌ وَأَبْقَى (١٣١)

وَأْمُرْ أَهْلَكَ بِالصَّلَاةِ وَاصْطَبِرْ عَلَيْهَا لَا نَسْأَلُكَ رِزْقًا نَّحْنُ نَرْزُقُكَ وَالْعَاقِبَةُ لِلتَّقْوَى (١٣٢)

وَقَالُوا لَوْلَا يَأْتِينَا بِآيَةٍ مِّن رَّبِّهِ أَوَلَمْ تَأْتِهِم بَيِّنَةُ مَا فِي الصُّحُفِ الْأُولَى (١٣٣)

وَلَوْ أَنَّا أَهْلَكْنَاهُم بِعَذَابٍ مِّن قَبْلِهِ

before them? Surely there are signs in this for men of understanding.

* * *

20:129. And had not a word gone forth from thy Lord, and a term been fixed, it would surely have overtaken them.

20:130. So bear patiently what they say, and celebrate the praise of thy Lord before the rising of the sun and before its setting, and glorify (Him) during the hours of the night and parts of the day, that thou mayest be well pleased.

20:131. And strain not thine eyes toward that with which We have provided different classes of them, (of) the splendour of this world's life, that We may thereby try them. And the sustenance of thy Lord is better and more abiding.

20:132. And enjoin prayer on thy people, and steadily adhere to it. We ask not of thee a sustenance. We provide for thee. And the (good) end is for guarding against evil.

20:133. And they say: Why does he not bring us a sign from his Lord? Has not there come to them a clear evidence of what is in the previous Books?

20:134. And if We had destroyed them with chastisement before it, they would have said: Our Lord, why didst Thou not send to us a messenger, so that we might have followed Thy messages before we met disgrace and shame?

20:135. Say: Every one (of us) is waiting, so wait. Soon you will come to know who is the follower of the even path and who goes aright.

21. The Prophets

In the name of Allah the Beneficent, the Merciful.

21:1. Their reckoning draws nigh to men, and they turn away in heedlessness.

21:2. There comes not to them a new

21. The Prophets

Reminder from their Lord but they hear it while they sport,

21:3. Their hearts trifling. And they -- the wrongdoers -- counsel in secret: He is nothing but a mortal like yourselves; will you then yield to enchantment while you see?

21:4. He said: My Lord knows (every) utterance in the heaven and the earth, and He is the Hearer, the Knower.

21:5. Nay, say they: Medleys of dreams! nay, he has forged it! nay, he is a poet! so let him bring to us a sign such as the former (prophets) were sent (with).

21:6. Not a town believed before them which We destroyed: will they then believe?

21:7. And We sent not before thee any but men to whom We sent revelation; so ask the followers of the Reminder if you know not.

21:8. Not did We give them bodies not eating food, nor did they abide.

21:9. Then We made Our promise good to them; so We delivered them and whom We pleased, and We destroyed the extravagant.

21:10. Certainly We have revealed to you a Book which will give you eminence. Do you not then understand?

* * *

21:11. And how many a town which was iniquitous did We demolish, and We raised up after it another people!

21:12. So when they felt Our might, lo! they began to flee from it.

21:13. Flee not and return to the easy lives which you led, and to your dwellings, that you may be questioned.

21:14. They said: O woe to us! Surely we were unjust.

21:15. And this cry of theirs ceased not till We made them cut off, extinct.

21:16. And We created not the heaven and the earth and what is between them for sport.

إِلَّا اسْتَمَعُوهُ وَهُمْ يَلْعَبُونَ (٢) لَاهِيَةً قُلُوبُهُمْ وَأَسَرُّوا النَّجْوَى الَّذِينَ ظَلَمُوا هَلْ هَذَا إِلَّا بَشَرٌ مِثْلُكُمْ أَفَتَأْتُونَ السِّحْرَ وَأَنْتُمْ تُبْصِرُونَ (٣) قَالَ رَبِّي يَعْلَمُ الْقَوْلَ فِي السَّمَاءِ وَالْأَرْضِ وَهُوَ السَّمِيعُ الْعَلِيمُ (٤) بَلْ قَالُوا أَضْغَاثُ أَحْلَامٍ بَلِ افْتَرَاهُ بَلْ هُوَ شَاعِرٌ فَلْيَأْتِنَا بِآيَةٍ كَمَا أُرْسِلَ الْأَوَّلُونَ (٥) مَا آمَنَتْ قَبْلَهُمْ مِنْ قَرْيَةٍ أَهْلَكْنَاهَا أَفَهُمْ يُؤْمِنُونَ (٦) وَمَا أَرْسَلْنَا قَبْلَكَ إِلَّا رِجَالًا نُوحِي إِلَيْهِمْ فَاسْأَلُوا أَهْلَ الذِّكْرِ إِنْ كُنْتُمْ لَا تَعْلَمُونَ (٧) وَمَا جَعَلْنَاهُمْ جَسَدًا لَا يَأْكُلُونَ الطَّعَامَ وَمَا كَانُوا خَالِدِينَ (٨) ثُمَّ صَدَقْنَاهُمُ الْوَعْدَ فَأَنْجَيْنَاهُمْ وَمَنْ نَشَاءُ وَأَهْلَكْنَا الْمُسْرِفِينَ (٩) لَقَدْ أَنْزَلْنَا إِلَيْكُمْ كِتَابًا فِيهِ ذِكْرُكُمْ أَفَلَا تَعْقِلُونَ (١٠) وَكَمْ قَصَمْنَا مِنْ قَرْيَةٍ كَانَتْ ظَالِمَةً وَأَنْشَأْنَا بَعْدَهَا قَوْمًا آخَرِينَ (١١) فَلَمَّا أَحَسُّوا بَأْسَنَا إِذَا هُمْ مِنْهَا يَرْكُضُونَ (١٢) لَا تَرْكُضُوا وَارْجِعُوا إِلَى مَا أُتْرِفْتُمْ فِيهِ وَمَسَاكِنِكُمْ لَعَلَّكُمْ تُسْأَلُونَ (١٣) قَالُوا يَاوَيْلَنَا إِنَّا كُنَّا ظَالِمِينَ (١٤) فَمَا زَالَتْ تِلْكَ دَعْوَاهُمْ حَتَّى جَعَلْنَاهُمْ حَصِيدًا خَامِدِينَ (١٥) وَمَا خَلَقْنَا السَّمَاءَ وَالْأَرْضَ وَمَا بَيْنَهُمَا لَاعِبِينَ (١٦) لَوْ أَرَدْنَا أَنْ نَتَّخِذَ لَهْوًا لَاتَّخَذْنَاهُ مِنْ لَدُنَّا إِنْ كُنَّا فَاعِلِينَ (١٧)

21. The Prophets

21:17. Had We wished to take a pastime, We would have taken it from before Ourselves; by no means would We do (so).

21:18. Nay, We hurl the Truth against falsehood, so it knocks out its brains, and lo! it vanishes. And woe to you for what you describe!

21:19. And to Him belongs whoever is in the heavens and the earth. And those who are with Him are not too proud to serve Him, nor are they weary.

21:20. They glorify (Him) night and day: they flag not.

21:21. Or have they taken gods from the earth who give life?

21:22. If there were in them gods besides Allah, they would both have been in disorder. So glory be to Allah, the Lord of the Throne, being above what they describe!

21:23. He cannot be questioned as to what He does, and they will be questioned.

21:24. Or, have they taken gods besides Him? Say Bring your proof. This is the reminder of those with me and the reminder of those before me. Nay, most of them know not the Truth, so they turn away.

21:25. And We sent no messenger before thee but We revealed to him that there is no God but Me, so serve Me.

21:26. And they say: The Beneficent has taken to Himself a son. Glory be to Him! Nay, they are honoured servants --

21:27. They speak not before He speaks, and according to His command they act.

21:28. He knows what is before them and what is behind them, and they intercede not except for him whom He approves, and for fear of Him they tremble.

21:29. And whoever of them should say I am a god besides Him, such a one We

بَلْ نَقْذِفُ بِالْحَقِّ عَلَى الْبَاطِلِ فَيَدْمَغُهُ فَإِذَا هُوَ زَاهِقٌ وَلَكُمُ الْوَيْلُ مِمَّا تَصِفُونَ (١٨)

وَلَهُ مَنْ فِي السَّمَاوَاتِ وَالْأَرْضِ وَمَنْ عِنْدَهُ لَا يَسْتَكْبِرُونَ عَنْ عِبَادَتِهِ وَلَا يَسْتَحْسِرُونَ (١٩)

يُسَبِّحُونَ اللَّيْلَ وَالنَّهَارَ لَا يَفْتُرُونَ (٢٠)

أَمِ اتَّخَذُوا آلِهَةً مِنَ الْأَرْضِ هُمْ يُنْشِرُونَ (٢١)

لَوْ كَانَ فِيهِمَا آلِهَةٌ إِلَّا اللَّهُ لَفَسَدَتَا فَسُبْحَانَ اللَّهِ رَبِّ الْعَرْشِ عَمَّا يَصِفُونَ (٢٢)

لَا يُسْأَلُ عَمَّا يَفْعَلُ وَهُمْ يُسْأَلُونَ (٢٣)

أَمِ اتَّخَذُوا مِنْ دُونِهِ آلِهَةً قُلْ هَاتُوا بُرْهَانَكُمْ هَذَا ذِكْرُ مَنْ مَعِيَ وَذِكْرُ مَنْ قَبْلِي بَلْ أَكْثَرُهُمْ لَا يَعْلَمُونَ الْحَقَّ فَهُمْ مُعْرِضُونَ (٢٤)

وَمَا أَرْسَلْنَا مِنْ قَبْلِكَ مِنْ رَسُولٍ إِلَّا نُوحِي إِلَيْهِ أَنَّهُ لَا إِلَهَ إِلَّا أَنَا فَاعْبُدُونِ (٢٥)

وَقَالُوا اتَّخَذَ الرَّحْمَنُ وَلَدًا سُبْحَانَهُ بَلْ عِبَادٌ مُكْرَمُونَ (٢٦)

لَا يَسْبِقُونَهُ بِالْقَوْلِ وَهُمْ بِأَمْرِهِ يَعْمَلُونَ (٢٧)

يَعْلَمُ مَا بَيْنَ أَيْدِيهِمْ وَمَا خَلْفَهُمْ وَلَا يَشْفَعُونَ إِلَّا لِمَنِ ارْتَضَى وَهُمْ مِنْ خَشْيَتِهِ مُشْفِقُونَ (٢٨)

وَمَنْ يَقُلْ مِنْهُمْ إِنِّي إِلَهٌ مِنْ دُونِهِ فَذَلِكَ نَجْزِيهِ جَهَنَّمَ كَذَلِكَ نَجْزِي الظَّالِمِينَ (٢٩)

أَوَلَمْ يَرَ الَّذِينَ كَفَرُوا أَنَّ السَّمَاوَاتِ وَالْأَرْضَ كَانَتَا رَتْقًا فَفَتَقْنَاهُمَا

recompense with hell. Thus We reward the unjust.

***

21:30. Do not those who disbelieve see that the heavens and the earth were closed up, so We rent them. And We made from water everything living. Will they not then believe?

21:31. And We made firm mountains in the earth lest it be convulsed with them, and We made in it wide ways that they might follow a right direction.

21:32. And We have made the heaven a guarded canopy; yet they turn away from its signs.

21:33. And He it is Who created the night and the day and the sun and the moon. All float in orbits.

21:34. And We granted abiding for ever to no mortal before thee. If thou diest, will they abide?

21:35. Every soul must taste of death. And We test you by evil and good by way of trial. And to Us you are returned.

21:36. And when those who disbelieve see thee, they treat thee not but with mockery: Is this he who speaks of your gods? And they deny when the Beneficent God is mentioned.

21:37. Man is created of haste. Soon will I show you My signs, so ask Me not to hasten them.

21:38. And they say When will this threat come to pass, if you are truthful?

21:39. If those who disbelieve but knew the time when they will not be able to ward off the fire from their faces, nor from their backs, and they will not he helped!

21:40. Nay, it will come to them all of a sudden and confound them, so they will not have the power to avert it, nor will they be respited.

21:41. And messengers before thee were indeed mocked, so there befell those of them who scoffed, that whereat they scoffed.

وَجَعَلْنَا مِنَ الْمَاءِ كُلَّ شَيْءٍ حَيٍّ أَفَلَا يُؤْمِنُونَ (٣٠) وَجَعَلْنَا فِي الْأَرْضِ رَوَاسِيَ أَنْ تَمِيدَ بِهِمْ وَجَعَلْنَا فِيهَا فِجَاجًا سُبُلًا لَعَلَّهُمْ يَهْتَدُونَ (٣١) وَجَعَلْنَا السَّمَاءَ سَقْفًا مَحْفُوظًا وَهُمْ عَنْ آيَاتِهَا مُعْرِضُونَ (٣٢) وَهُوَ الَّذِي خَلَقَ اللَّيْلَ وَالنَّهَارَ وَالشَّمْسَ وَالْقَمَرَ كُلٌّ فِي فَلَكٍ يَسْبَحُونَ (٣٣) وَمَا جَعَلْنَا لِبَشَرٍ مِنْ قَبْلِكَ الْخُلْدَ أَفَإِنْ مِتَّ فَهُمُ الْخَالِدُونَ (٣٤) كُلُّ نَفْسٍ ذَائِقَةُ الْمَوْتِ وَنَبْلُوكُمْ بِالشَّرِّ وَالْخَيْرِ فِتْنَةً وَإِلَيْنَا تُرْجَعُونَ (٣٥) وَإِذَا رَآكَ الَّذِينَ كَفَرُوا إِنْ يَتَّخِذُونَكَ إِلَّا هُزُوًا أَهَذَا الَّذِي يَذْكُرُ آلِهَتَكُمْ وَهُمْ بِذِكْرِ الرَّحْمَنِ هُمْ كَافِرُونَ (٣٦) خُلِقَ الْإِنْسَانُ مِنْ عَجَلٍ سَأُرِيكُمْ آيَاتِي فَلَا تَسْتَعْجِلُونِ (٣٧) وَيَقُولُونَ مَتَى هَذَا الْوَعْدُ إِنْ كُنْتُمْ صَادِقِينَ (٣٨) لَوْ يَعْلَمُ الَّذِينَ كَفَرُوا حِينَ لَا يَكُفُّونَ عَنْ وُجُوهِهِمُ النَّارَ وَلَا عَنْ ظُهُورِهِمْ وَلَا هُمْ يُنْصَرُونَ (٣٩) بَلْ تَأْتِيهِمْ بَغْتَةً فَتَبْهَتُهُمْ فَلَا يَسْتَطِيعُونَ رَدَّهَا وَلَا هُمْ يُنْظَرُونَ (٤٠) وَلَقَدِ اسْتُهْزِئَ بِرُسُلٍ مِنْ قَبْلِكَ فَحَاقَ بِالَّذِينَ سَخِرُوا مِنْهُمْ مَا كَانُوا بِهِ يَسْتَهْزِئُونَ (٤١) قُلْ مَنْ يَكْلَؤُكُمْ بِاللَّيْلِ وَالنَّهَارِ مِنَ الرَّحْمَنِ بَلْ هُمْ عَنْ ذِكْرِ رَبِّهِمْ مُعْرِضُونَ (٤٢)

21. The Prophets

***

21:42. Say: Who guards you by night and by day from the Beneficent? Nay, they turn away at the mention of their Lord.

21:43. Or, have they gods who can defend them against Us? They cannot help themselves, nor can they be defended from Us.

21:44. Nay, We gave provision to these and their fathers, until life was prolonged to them. See they not then that We are visiting the land, curtailing it of its sides? Can they then prevail?

21:45. Say: I warn you only by revelation; and the deaf hear not the call when they are warned.

21:46. And if a blast of the chastisement of thy Lord were to touch them, they would say: O woe to us! Surely we were unjust.

21:47. And We will set up a just balance on the day of Resurrection, so no soul will be wronged in the least. And if there be the weight of a grain of mustard seed, We will bring it. And Sufficient are We to take account.

21:48. And certainly We gave Moses and Aaron the criterion and a light and a reminder for those who keep from evil,

21:49. Who fear their Lord in secret and they are fearful of the Hour.

21:50. And this is a blessed Reminder which We have revealed. Will you then deny it?

***

21:51. And certainly We gave Abraham his rectitude before, and We knew him well.

21:52. When he said to his sire and his people What are these images to whose worship you cleave?

21:53. They said We found our fathers worshipping them.

21:54. He said Certainly you have been, you and your fathers, in manifest error.

21:55. They said: Hast thou brought us

أَمْ لَهُمْ آلِهَةٌ تَمْنَعُهُمْ مِنْ دُونِنَا لَا يَسْتَطِيعُونَ نَصْرَ أَنْفُسِهِمْ وَلَا هُمْ مِنَّا يُصْحَبُونَ (٤٣)

بَلْ مَتَّعْنَا هَؤُلَاءِ وَآبَاءَهُمْ حَتَّى طَالَ عَلَيْهِمُ الْعُمُرُ أَفَلَا يَرَوْنَ أَنَّا نَأْتِي الْأَرْضَ نَنْقُصُهَا مِنْ أَطْرَافِهَا أَفَهُمُ الْغَالِبُونَ (٤٤)

قُلْ إِنَّمَا أُنْذِرُكُمْ بِالْوَحْيِ وَلَا يَسْمَعُ الصُّمُّ الدُّعَاءَ إِذَا مَا يُنْذَرُونَ (٤٥)

وَلَئِنْ مَسَّتْهُمْ نَفْحَةٌ مِنْ عَذَابِ رَبِّكَ لَيَقُولُنَّ يَاوَيْلَنَا إِنَّا كُنَّا ظَالِمِينَ (٤٦)

وَنَضَعُ الْمَوَازِينَ الْقِسْطَ لِيَوْمِ الْقِيَامَةِ فَلَا تُظْلَمُ نَفْسٌ شَيْئًا وَإِنْ كَانَ مِثْقَالَ حَبَّةٍ مِنْ خَرْدَلٍ أَتَيْنَا بِهَا وَكَفَى بِنَا حَاسِبِينَ (٤٧)

وَلَقَدْ آتَيْنَا مُوسَى وَهَارُونَ الْفُرْقَانَ وَضِيَاءً وَذِكْرًا لِلْمُتَّقِينَ (٤٨)

الَّذِينَ يَخْشَوْنَ رَبَّهُمْ بِالْغَيْبِ وَهُمْ مِنَ السَّاعَةِ مُشْفِقُونَ (٤٩)

وَهَذَا ذِكْرٌ مُبَارَكٌ أَنْزَلْنَاهُ أَفَأَنْتُمْ لَهُ مُنْكِرُونَ (٥٠)

وَلَقَدْ آتَيْنَا إِبْرَاهِيمَ رُشْدَهُ مِنْ قَبْلُ وَكُنَّا بِهِ عَالِمِينَ (٥١)

إِذْ قَالَ لِأَبِيهِ وَقَوْمِهِ مَا هَذِهِ التَّمَاثِيلُ الَّتِي أَنْتُمْ لَهَا عَاكِفُونَ (٥٢)

قَالُوا وَجَدْنَا آبَاءَنَا لَهَا عَابِدِينَ (٥٣)

قَالَ لَقَدْ كُنْتُمْ أَنْتُمْ وَآبَاؤُكُمْ فِي ضَلَالٍ مُبِينٍ (٥٤)

قَالُوا أَجِئْتَنَا بِالْحَقِّ أَمْ أَنْتَ مِنَ اللَّاعِبِينَ (٥٥)

قَالَ بَلْ رَبُّكُمْ رَبُّ السَّمَاوَاتِ وَالْأَرْضِ الَّذِي فَطَرَهُنَّ وَأَنَا عَلَى ذَلِكُمْ مِنَ الشَّاهِدِينَ (٥٦)

21. The Prophets

the truth, or art thou of the jesters?

21:56. He said Nay, your Lord is the Lord of the heavens and the earth, Who created them and I am of those who bear witness to this.

21:57. And, by Allah! I will certainly plan against your idols after you go away, turning your backs.

21:58. So he broke them into pieces, except the chief of them, that haply they might return to it

21:59. They said: Who has done this to our gods? Surely he is one of the unjust.

21:60. They said: We heard a youth, who is called Abraham, speak of them.

21:61. They said: Then bring him before the people's eyes, perhaps they may bear witness.

21:62. They said: Hast thou done this to our gods, O Abraham?

21:63. He said: Surely (someone) has done it. The chief of them is this; so ask them, if they can speak.

21:64. Then they turned to themselves and said: Surely you yourselves are wrongdoers;

21:65. Then they were made to hang down their heads: Thou knowest indeed that they speak not.

21:66. He said: Serve you then besides Allah what does you no good, nor harm you?

21:67. Fie on you and on what you serve besides Allah! Have you no sense?

21:68. They said: Burn him, and help your gods, if you are going to do (anything).

21:69. We said: O fire, be coolness and peace for Abraham:

21:70. And they intended a plan against him, but We made them the greater losers.

21:71. And We delivered him and Lot (directing them) to the land which We had blessed for the nations.

21:72. And We gave him Isaac; and

وَتَاللَّهِ لَأَكِيدَنَّ أَصْنَامَكُمْ بَعْدَ أَنْ تُوَلُّوا مُدْبِرِينَ (٥٧)

فَجَعَلَهُمْ جُذَاذًا إِلَّا كَبِيرًا لَهُمْ لَعَلَّهُمْ إِلَيْهِ يَرْجِعُونَ (٥٨)

قَالُوا مَنْ فَعَلَ هَذَا بِآلِهَتِنَا إِنَّهُ لَمِنَ الظَّالِمِينَ (٥٩)

قَالُوا سَمِعْنَا فَتًى يَذْكُرُهُمْ يُقَالُ لَهُ إِبْرَاهِيمُ (٦٠)

قَالُوا فَأْتُوا بِهِ عَلَى أَعْيُنِ النَّاسِ لَعَلَّهُمْ يَشْهَدُونَ (٦١)

قَالُوا أَأَنْتَ فَعَلْتَ هَذَا بِآلِهَتِنَا يَا إِبْرَاهِيمُ (٦٢)

قَالَ بَلْ فَعَلَهُ كَبِيرُهُمْ هَذَا فَاسْأَلُوهُمْ إِنْ كَانُوا يَنْطِقُونَ (٦٣)

فَرَجَعُوا إِلَى أَنْفُسِهِمْ فَقَالُوا إِنَّكُمْ أَنْتُمُ الظَّالِمُونَ (٦٤)

ثُمَّ نُكِسُوا عَلَى رُءُوسِهِمْ لَقَدْ عَلِمْتَ مَا هَؤُلَاءِ يَنْطِقُونَ (٦٥)

قَالَ أَفَتَعْبُدُونَ مِنْ دُونِ اللَّهِ مَا لَا يَنْفَعُكُمْ شَيْئًا وَلَا يَضُرُّكُمْ (٦٦)

أُفٍّ لَكُمْ وَلِمَا تَعْبُدُونَ مِنْ دُونِ اللَّهِ أَفَلَا تَعْقِلُونَ (٦٧)

قَالُوا حَرِّقُوهُ وَانْصُرُوا آلِهَتَكُمْ إِنْ كُنْتُمْ فَاعِلِينَ (٦٨)

قُلْنَا يَا نَارُ كُونِي بَرْدًا وَسَلَامًا عَلَى إِبْرَاهِيمَ (٦٩)

وَأَرَادُوا بِهِ كَيْدًا فَجَعَلْنَاهُمُ الْأَخْسَرِينَ (٧٠)

وَنَجَّيْنَاهُ وَلُوطًا إِلَى الْأَرْضِ الَّتِي بَارَكْنَا فِيهَا لِلْعَالَمِينَ (٧١)

وَوَهَبْنَا لَهُ إِسْحَاقَ وَيَعْقُوبَ نَافِلَةً وَكُلًّا جَعَلْنَا صَالِحِينَ (٧٢)

وَجَعَلْنَاهُمْ أَئِمَّةً يَهْدُونَ بِأَمْرِنَا

21. The Prophets

Jacob, a son's son. And We made (them) all good.

21:73. And We made them leaders who guided (people) by Our command, and We revealed to them the doing of good and the keeping up of prayer and the giving of alms, and Us (alone) they served;

21:74. And to Lot We gave wisdom and knowledge, and We delivered him from the town which wrought abomination. Surely they were an evil people, transgressors

21:75. And We admitted him to Our mercy; surely he was of the righteous.

* * *

21:76. And Noah, when he cried aforetime, so We answered him, and delivered him and his people from the great calamity.

21:77. And We helped him against the people who rejected Our messages. Surely they were an evil people, so We drowned them all.

21:78. And David and Solomon, when they gave judgment concerning the field, when the people's sheep strayed therein by night, and We were bearers of witness to their judgment.

21:79. So We made Solomon to understand it. And to each (of them) We gave wisdom and knowledge. And We made the mountains, declaring (Our) glory, and the birds, subservient to David. And We were the Doers.

21:80. And We taught him the making of coats of mail for you, to protect you in your wars will you then be grateful?

21:81. And to Solomon (We subdued) the wind blowing violent, pursuing its course by His command to the land which We had blessed, and We are ever Knower of all things.

21:82. And of the devils there were those who dived for him and did other work besides that; and We kept guard over them:

21:83. And Job, when he cried to his

وَأَوْحَيْنَا إِلَيْهِمْ فِعْلَ الْخَيْرَاتِ وَإِقَامَ الصَّلَاةِ وَإِيتَاءَ الزَّكَاةِ وَكَانُوا لَنَا عَابِدِينَ (٧٣)

وَلُوطًا آتَيْنَاهُ حُكْمًا وَعِلْمًا وَنَجَّيْنَاهُ مِنَ الْقَرْيَةِ الَّتِي كَانَتْ تَعْمَلُ الْخَبَائِثَ إِنَّهُمْ كَانُوا قَوْمَ سَوْءٍ فَاسِقِينَ (٧٤) وَأَدْخَلْنَاهُ فِي رَحْمَتِنَا إِنَّهُ مِنَ الصَّالِحِينَ (٧٥)

وَنُوحًا إِذْ نَادَى مِنْ قَبْلُ فَاسْتَجَبْنَا لَهُ فَنَجَّيْنَاهُ وَأَهْلَهُ مِنَ الْكَرْبِ الْعَظِيمِ (٧٦)

وَنَصَرْنَاهُ مِنَ الْقَوْمِ الَّذِينَ كَذَّبُوا بِآيَاتِنَا إِنَّهُمْ كَانُوا قَوْمَ سَوْءٍ فَأَغْرَقْنَاهُمْ أَجْمَعِينَ (٧٧)

وَدَاوُودَ وَسُلَيْمَانَ إِذْ يَحْكُمَانِ فِي الْحَرْثِ إِذْ نَفَشَتْ فِيهِ غَنَمُ الْقَوْمِ وَكُنَّا لِحُكْمِهِمْ شَاهِدِينَ (٧٨)

فَفَهَّمْنَاهَا سُلَيْمَانَ وَكُلًّا آتَيْنَا حُكْمًا وَعِلْمًا وَسَخَّرْنَا مَعَ دَاوُودَ الْجِبَالَ يُسَبِّحْنَ وَالطَّيْرَ وَكُنَّا فَاعِلِينَ (٧٩) وَعَلَّمْنَاهُ صَنْعَةَ لَبُوسٍ لَكُمْ لِتُحْصِنَكُمْ مِنْ بَأْسِكُمْ فَهَلْ أَنْتُمْ شَاكِرُونَ (٨٠) وَلِسُلَيْمَانَ الرِّيحَ عَاصِفَةً تَجْرِي بِأَمْرِهِ إِلَى الْأَرْضِ الَّتِي بَارَكْنَا فِيهَا وَكُنَّا بِكُلِّ شَيْءٍ عَالِمِينَ (٨١)

وَمِنَ الشَّيَاطِينِ مَنْ يَغُوصُونَ لَهُ وَيَعْمَلُونَ عَمَلًا دُونَ ذَلِكَ وَكُنَّا لَهُمْ حَافِظِينَ (٨٢)

وَأَيُّوبَ إِذْ نَادَى رَبَّهُ أَنِّي مَسَّنِيَ الضُّرُّ وَأَنْتَ أَرْحَمُ الرَّاحِمِينَ (٨٣) فَاسْتَجَبْنَا لَهُ فَكَشَفْنَا مَا بِهِ مِنْ ضُرٍّ وَآتَيْنَاهُ أَهْلَهُ وَمِثْلَهُمْ مَعَهُمْ رَحْمَةً مِنْ عِنْدِنَا وَذِكْرَى لِلْعَابِدِينَ (٨٤)

وَإِسْمَاعِيلَ وَإِدْرِيسَ وَذَا الْكِفْلِ كُلٌّ

21. The Prophets

Lord; Distress has afflicted me and Thou art the most Merciful of those who show mercy.

21:84. So We responded to him and removed the distress he had, and We gave him his people and the like of them with them; a mercy from Us and a reminder to the worshippers.

21:85. And Ishmael and Idris and Dhu-l-Kifl; all were of the patient ones;

21:86. And We admitted them to Our mercy; surely they were of the good ones.

21:87. And Dhu-l-Nun, when he went away in wrath, and he thought that We would not straiten him, so he called out among afflictions. There is no God but Thou, glory be to Thee! Surely I am of the sufferers of loss.

21:88. So We responded to him and delivered him from grief. And thus do We deliver the believers

21:89. And Zacharias, when he cried to his Lord: My Lord, leave me not alone and Thou art the Best of inheritors.

21:90. So We responded to him and gave him John and made his wife fit for him. Surely they used to vie, one with another, in good deeds and called upon Us, hoping and fearing and they were humble before Us.

21:91. And she who guarded her chastity, so We breathed into her of Our inspiration, and made her and her son a sign for the nations.

21:92. Surely this your community is a single community, and I am your Lord, so serve Me.

21:93. And they cut off their affair among them: to Us will all return.

***

21:94. So whoever does good deeds and is a believer, there is no rejection of his effort, and We surely write (it) down for him.

21:95. And it is forbidden to a town which We destroy: they shall not return.

21:96. Even when Gog and Magog are let loose and they sally forth from every elevated place.
21:97. And the True Promise draws nigh, then lo the eyes of those who disbelieve will be fixedly open: O woe to us Surely we were heedless of this; nay, we were unjust.
21:98. Surely you and what you worship besides Allah are fuel of hell: to it you will come.
21:99. Had these been gods, they would not have come to it. And all will abide therein,
21:100. For them therein is groaning and therein they hear not.
21:101. Those for whom the good has already gone forth from Us, they will he kept far off from it
21:102. They will nor hear the faintest sound of it and they will abide in that which their souls desire.
21:103. The great Terror will not grieve them, and the angels will meet them: This is your day which you were promised.
21:104. The day when We roll up heaven like the rolling up of the scroll of writings. As We began the first creation, We shall reproduce it. A promise (binding) on Us. We shall bring it about.
21:105. And certainly We wrote in the Book after the reminder that My righteous servants will inherit the land.
21:106. Surely in this is a message for a people who serve (Us).
21:107. And We have not sent thee but as a mercy to the nations.
21:108. Say It is only revealed to me that your God is one God will you then submit?
21:109. But if they turn back, say: I have warned you in fairness, and I know not whether that which you are promised is near or far.
21:110. Surely He knows what is spoken openly and He knows what

ظَالِمِينَ (٩٧)
إِنَّكُمْ وَمَا تَعْبُدُونَ مِنْ دُونِ اللَّهِ حَصَبُ جَهَنَّمَ أَنْتُمْ لَهَا وَارِدُونَ (٩٨)
لَوْ كَانَ هَٰؤُلَاءِ آلِهَةً مَا وَرَدُوهَا وَكُلٌّ فِيهَا خَالِدُونَ (٩٩)
لَهُمْ فِيهَا زَفِيرٌ وَهُمْ فِيهَا لَا يَسْمَعُونَ (١٠٠)
إِنَّ الَّذِينَ سَبَقَتْ لَهُمْ مِنَّا الْحُسْنَىٰ أُولَٰئِكَ عَنْهَا مُبْعَدُونَ (١٠١)
لَا يَسْمَعُونَ حَسِيسَهَا وَهُمْ فِي مَا اشْتَهَتْ أَنْفُسُهُمْ خَالِدُونَ (١٠٢)
لَا يَحْزُنُهُمُ الْفَزَعُ الْأَكْبَرُ وَتَتَلَقَّاهُمُ الْمَلَائِكَةُ هَٰذَا يَوْمُكُمُ الَّذِي كُنْتُمْ تُوعَدُونَ (١٠٣)
يَوْمَ نَطْوِي السَّمَاءَ كَطَيِّ السِّجِلِّ لِلْكُتُبِ كَمَا بَدَأْنَا أَوَّلَ خَلْقٍ نُعِيدُهُ وَعْدًا عَلَيْنَا إِنَّا كُنَّا فَاعِلِينَ (١٠٤)
وَلَقَدْ كَتَبْنَا فِي الزَّبُورِ مِنْ بَعْدِ الذِّكْرِ أَنَّ الْأَرْضَ يَرِثُهَا عِبَادِيَ الصَّالِحُونَ (١٠٥)
إِنَّ فِي هَٰذَا لَبَلَاغًا لِقَوْمٍ عَابِدِينَ (١٠٦)
وَمَا أَرْسَلْنَاكَ إِلَّا رَحْمَةً لِلْعَالَمِينَ (١٠٧)
قُلْ إِنَّمَا يُوحَىٰ إِلَيَّ أَنَّمَا إِلَٰهُكُمْ إِلَٰهٌ وَاحِدٌ فَهَلْ أَنْتُمْ مُسْلِمُونَ (١٠٨)
فَإِنْ تَوَلَّوْا فَقُلْ آذَنْتُكُمْ عَلَىٰ سَوَاءٍ وَإِنْ أَدْرِي أَقَرِيبٌ أَمْ بَعِيدٌ مَا تُوعَدُونَ (١٠٩)
إِنَّهُ يَعْلَمُ الْجَهْرَ مِنَ الْقَوْلِ وَيَعْلَمُ مَا تَكْتُمُونَ (١١٠)
وَإِنْ أَدْرِي لَعَلَّهُ فِتْنَةٌ لَكُمْ وَمَتَاعٌ إِلَىٰ حِينٍ (١١١)

you hide.

21:111. And I know not if this may be a trial for you and a provision till a time.

21:112. He said: My Lord, judge Thou with truth. And our Lord is the Beneficent, Whose help is sought against what you ascribe (to Him).

22. The Pilgrimage

In the name of Allah, the Beneficent, the Merciful.

22:1. O people, keep your duty to your Lord; surely the shock of the Hour is a grievous thing.

22:2. The day you see it, every woman giving suck will forget her suckling and every pregnant one will lay down her burden, and thou wilt see men as drunken, yet they will not be drunken, but the chastisement of Allah will be severe.

22:3. And among men is he who disputes about Allah without knowledge, and follows every rebellious devil --

22:4. For him it is written that whoever takes him for a friend, he will lead him astray and conduct him to the chastisement of the burning Fire.

22:5. O people, if you are in doubt about the Resurrection, then surely We created you from dust, then from a small life-germ, then from a clot, then from a lump of flesh, complete in make and incomplete, that We may make clear to you. And We cause what We please to remain in the wombs till an appointed time, then We bring you forth as babies, then that you may attain your maturity. And of you is he who is caused to die, and of you is he who is brought back to the worst part of life, so that after knowledge he knows nothing. And thou seest the earth barren, but when We send down thereon water, it stirs and swells and

22. The Pilgrimage

brings forth a beautiful (growth) of every kind.

22:6. That is because Allah, He is the Truth, and He gives life to the dead, and He is Possessor of power over all things,

22:7. And the Hour is coming, there is no doubt about it; and Allah will raise up those who are in the graves.

22:8. And among men is he who disputes about Allah without knowledge, and without guidance, and without an illuminating Book.

22:9. Turning away haughtily to lead men astray from the way of Allah. For him is disgrace in this world, and on the day of Resurrection We shall make him taste the punishment of burning.

22:10. This is for that which thy two hands have sent before, and Allah is not in the least unjust to the servants.

* * *

22:11. And among men is he who serves Allah, (standing) on the verge, so that if good befalls him he is satisfied therewith, but if a trial afflicts him he turns back headlong. He loses this world and the Hereafter. That is a manifest loss.

22:12. He calls besides Allah on that which harms him not, nor benefits him; that is straying far.

22:13. He calls on him whose harm is nearer than his benefit. Certainly an evil guardian and an evil associate

22:14. Surely Allah causes those who believe and do good deeds to enter Gardens wherein flow rivers. Allah indeed does what He pleases.

22:15. Whoever thinks that Allah will not assist him in this life and the Hereafter, let him raise (himself) by some means to the heaven, then let him cut (it) off, then let him see if his plan will take away that at which he is enraged.

22:16. And thus have We revealed it, clear arguments, and Allah guides

اللَّهَ يَبْعَثُ مَنْ فِي الْقُبُورِ (٧)
وَمِنَ النَّاسِ مَنْ يُجَادِلُ فِي اللَّهِ بِغَيْرِ عِلْمٍ وَلَا هُدًى وَلَا كِتَابٍ مُنِيرٍ (٨)
ثَانِيَ عِطْفِهِ لِيُضِلَّ عَنْ سَبِيلِ اللَّهِ لَهُ فِي الدُّنْيَا خِزْيٌ وَنُذِيقُهُ يَوْمَ الْقِيَامَةِ عَذَابَ الْحَرِيقِ (٩)
ذَلِكَ بِمَا قَدَّمَتْ يَدَاكَ وَأَنَّ اللَّهَ لَيْسَ بِظَلَّامٍ لِلْعَبِيدِ (١٠)
وَمِنَ النَّاسِ مَنْ يَعْبُدُ اللَّهَ عَلَى حَرْفٍ فَإِنْ أَصَابَهُ خَيْرٌ اطْمَأَنَّ بِهِ وَإِنْ أَصَابَتْهُ فِتْنَةٌ انْقَلَبَ عَلَى وَجْهِهِ خَسِرَ الدُّنْيَا وَالْآخِرَةَ ذَلِكَ هُوَ الْخُسْرَانُ الْمُبِينُ (١١)
يَدْعُو مِنْ دُونِ اللَّهِ مَا لَا يَضُرُّهُ وَمَا لَا يَنْفَعُهُ ذَلِكَ هُوَ الضَّلَالُ الْبَعِيدُ (١٢)
يَدْعُو لَمَنْ ضَرُّهُ أَقْرَبُ مِنْ نَفْعِهِ لَبِئْسَ الْمَوْلَى وَلَبِئْسَ الْعَشِيرُ (١٣)
إِنَّ اللَّهَ يُدْخِلُ الَّذِينَ آمَنُوا وَعَمِلُوا الصَّالِحَاتِ جَنَّاتٍ تَجْرِي مِنْ تَحْتِهَا الْأَنْهَارُ إِنَّ اللَّهَ يَفْعَلُ مَا يُرِيدُ (١٤)
مَنْ كَانَ يَظُنُّ أَنْ لَنْ يَنْصُرَهُ اللَّهُ فِي الدُّنْيَا وَالْآخِرَةِ فَلْيَمْدُدْ بِسَبَبٍ إِلَى السَّمَاءِ ثُمَّ لِيَقْطَعْ فَلْيَنْظُرْ هَلْ يُذْهِبَنَّ كَيْدُهُ مَا يَغِيظُ (١٥)
وَكَذَلِكَ أَنْزَلْنَاهُ آيَاتٍ بَيِّنَاتٍ وَأَنَّ اللَّهَ يَهْدِي مَنْ يُرِيدُ (١٦)
إِنَّ الَّذِينَ آمَنُوا وَالَّذِينَ هَادُوا وَالصَّابِئِينَ وَالنَّصَارَى وَالْمَجُوسَ وَالَّذِينَ أَشْرَكُوا إِنَّ اللَّهَ يَفْصِلُ بَيْنَهُمْ يَوْمَ الْقِيَامَةِ إِنَّ اللَّهَ عَلَى كُلِّ شَيْءٍ شَهِيدٌ (١٧)
أَلَمْ تَرَ أَنَّ اللَّهَ يَسْجُدُ لَهُ مَنْ فِي السَّمَاوَاتِ وَمَنْ فِي الْأَرْضِ

22. The Pilgrimage

whom He will.

22:17. Those who believe and those who are Jews and the Sabeans and the Christians and the Magians and the polytheists -- surely Allah will decide between them on the day of Resurrection. Surely Allah is Witness over all things.

22:18. Seest thou not that to Allah makes submission whoever is in the heavens and whoever is in the earth, and the sun and the moon and the stars, and the mountains and the trees, and the animals and many of the people? And many there are to whom chastisement is due. And he whom Allah abases, none can give him honour. Sorely Allah does what He pleases.

22:19. These are two adversaries who dispute about their Lord. So those who disbelieve, for them are cut out garments of lire. Boiling water will be poured out over their heads.

22:20. With it will be melted what is in their bellies and (their) skins as well.

22:21. And for them are whips of iron.

22:22. Whenever they desire to go forth from it, from grief, they are turned back into it, and (it is said) Taste the chastisement of burning.

***

22:23. Surely Allah will make those who believe and do good deeds enter Gardens wherein flow rivers they are adorned therein with bracelets of gold and (with) pearls. And their garments therein are of silk.

22:24. And they are guided to pure words, and they are guided to the path of the Praised One.

22:25. Those who disbelieve and hinder (men) from Allah's way and from the Sacred Mosque, which We have made equally for all men, (for) the dweller therein and the visitor. And whoever inclines therein. to wrong, unjustly, We shall make him taste of painful

22. The Pilgrimage

chastisement.

***

22:26. And when We pointed to Abraham the place of the House, saying: Associate naught with Me; and purify My House for those who make circuits and stand to pray and bow and prostrate themselves.

22:27. And proclaim to men the Pilgrimage: they will come to thee on foot and on every lean camel, coming from every remote path:

22:28. That they may witness benefits (provided) for them, and mention the name of Allah on appointed days over what He has given them of the cattle quadrupeds; then eat of them and feed the distressed one, the needy.

22:29. Then let them accomplish their needful acts of cleansing, and let them fulfil their vows and go round the Ancient House.

22:30. That (shall be so). And whoever respects the sacred ordinances of Allah, it is good for him with his Lord. And the cattle are made lawful for you, except that which is recited to you, so shun the filth of the idols and shun false words,

22:31. Being upright for Allah, not associating aught with Him. And whoever associates (aught) with Allah, it is as if he had fallen from on high, then the birds had snatched him away, or the wind had carried him off to a distant place.

22:32. That (shall be so). And whoever respects the ordinances of Allah, this is surely from the piety of hearts.

22:33. Therein are benefits for you for a term appointed, then their place of sacrifice is the Ancient House.

***

22:34. And for every nation We appointed acts of devotion that they might mention the name of Allah on what He has given them of the cattle quadrupeds. So your God is One God,

22. The Pilgrimage

therefore to Him should you submit. And give good news to the humble,

22:35. Whose hearts tremble when Allah is mentioned, and who are patient in their afflictions, and who keep up prayer, and spend of what We have given them.

22:36. And the camels, We have made them of the signs appointed by Allah for you -- for you therein is much good. So mention the name of Allah on them standing in a row. Then when they fall down on their sides, eat of them and feed the contented one and the beggar. Thus have We made them subservient to you that you may be grateful.

22:37. Not their flesh, nor their blood, reaches Allah, but to Him is acceptable observance of duty on your part. Thus has He made them subservient to you, that you may magnify Allah for guiding you aright. And give good news to those who do good (to others).

22:38. Surely Allah defends those who believe. Surely Allah loves not anyone who is unfaithful, ungrateful.

* * *

22:39. Permission (to fight) is given to those on whom war is made, because they are oppressed. And surely Allah is Able to assist them --

22:40. Those who are driven from their homes without a just cause except that they say Our Lord is Allah. And if Allah did not repel some people by others, cloisters, and churches, and synagogues, and mosques in which Allah's name is much remembered, would have been pulled down. And surely Allah will help him who helps Him. Surely Allah is Strong, Mighty.

22:41. Those who, if We establish them in the land, will keep up prayer and pay the poor-rate and enjoin good and forbid evil. And Allah's is the end of affairs.

22:42. And if they reject thee, already before them did the people of Noah

سَخَّرَهَا لَكُمْ لِتُكَبِّرُوا اللَّهَ عَلَىٰ مَا هَدَاكُمْ وَبَشِّرِ الْمُحْسِنِينَ (٣٧) إِنَّ اللَّهَ يُدَافِعُ عَنِ الَّذِينَ آمَنُوا إِنَّ اللَّهَ لَا يُحِبُّ كُلَّ خَوَّانٍ كَفُورٍ (٣٨) أُذِنَ لِلَّذِينَ يُقَاتَلُونَ بِأَنَّهُمْ ظُلِمُوا وَإِنَّ اللَّهَ عَلَىٰ نَصْرِهِمْ لَقَدِيرٌ (٣٩) الَّذِينَ أُخْرِجُوا مِنْ دِيَارِهِمْ بِغَيْرِ حَقٍّ إِلَّا أَنْ يَقُولُوا رَبُّنَا اللَّهُ وَلَوْلَا دَفْعُ اللَّهِ النَّاسَ بَعْضَهُمْ بِبَعْضٍ لَهُدِّمَتْ صَوَامِعُ وَبِيَعٌ وَصَلَوَاتٌ وَمَسَاجِدُ يُذْكَرُ فِيهَا اسْمُ اللَّهِ كَثِيرًا وَلَيَنْصُرَنَّ اللَّهُ مَنْ يَنْصُرُهُ إِنَّ اللَّهَ لَقَوِيٌّ عَزِيزٌ (٤٠) الَّذِينَ إِنْ مَكَّنَّاهُمْ فِي الْأَرْضِ أَقَامُوا الصَّلَاةَ وَآتَوُا الزَّكَاةَ وَأَمَرُوا بِالْمَعْرُوفِ وَنَهَوْا عَنِ الْمُنْكَرِ وَلِلَّهِ عَاقِبَةُ الْأُمُورِ (٤١) وَإِنْ يُكَذِّبُوكَ فَقَدْ كَذَّبَتْ قَبْلَهُمْ قَوْمُ نُوحٍ وَعَادٌ وَثَمُودُ (٤٢) وَقَوْمُ إِبْرَاهِيمَ وَقَوْمُ لُوطٍ (٤٣) وَأَصْحَابُ مَدْيَنَ وَكُذِّبَ مُوسَى فَأَمْلَيْتُ لِلْكَافِرِينَ ثُمَّ أَخَذْتُهُمْ فَكَيْفَ كَانَ نَكِيرِ (٤٤) فَكَأَيِّنْ مِنْ قَرْيَةٍ أَهْلَكْنَاهَا وَهِيَ ظَالِمَةٌ فَهِيَ خَاوِيَةٌ عَلَىٰ عُرُوشِهَا وَبِئْرٍ مُعَطَّلَةٍ وَقَصْرٍ مَشِيدٍ (٤٥) أَفَلَمْ يَسِيرُوا فِي الْأَرْضِ فَتَكُونَ لَهُمْ قُلُوبٌ يَعْقِلُونَ بِهَا أَوْ آذَانٌ يَسْمَعُونَ بِهَا فَإِنَّهَا لَا تَعْمَى الْأَبْصَارُ وَلَكِنْ تَعْمَى الْقُلُوبُ الَّتِي فِي الصُّدُورِ (٤٦) وَيَسْتَعْجِلُونَكَ بِالْعَذَابِ وَلَنْ يُخْلِفَ اللَّهُ وَعْدَهُ وَإِنَّ يَوْمًا عِنْدَ رَبِّكَ كَأَلْفِ سَنَةٍ مِمَّا تَعُدُّونَ (٤٧)

22. The Pilgrimage

and 'Ad and Thamud reject (prophets),
22:43. And the people of Abraham and the people of Lot,
22:44. And the dwellers of Midian. And Moses (too) was rejected. But I gave respite to the disbelievers, then I seized them; so how (severe) was My disapproval!
22:45. How many a town We destroyed while it was iniquitous, so it is fallen down upon its roofs; and (how many) a deserted well and palace raised high!
22:46. Have they not travelled in the land so that they should have hearts with which to understand, or ears with which to hear? For surely it is not the eyes that are blind, but blind are the hearts which are in the breasts.
22:47. And they ask thee to hasten on the chastisement, and Allah by no means fails in His promise. And surely a day with thy Lord is as a thousand years of what you reckon.
22:48. And how many a town to which I gave respite while it was unjust, then I seized it! And to Me is the return.

***

22:49. Say: O people, I am only a plain warner to you.
22:50. So those who believe and do good, for them is forgiveness and an honourable sustenance.
22:51. And those who strive to oppose Our messages, they are the inmates of the flaming Fire.
22:52. And We never sent a messenger or a prophet before thee but when he desired, the devil made a suggestion respecting his desire; but Allah annuls that which the devil casts, then does Allah establish His messages. And Allah is Knowing, Wise --
22:53. That He may make what the devil casts a trial for those in whose hearts is a disease and the hardhearted. And surely the wrongdoers are in severe opposition,
22:54. And that those who have been

وَكَأَيِّنْ مِنْ قَرْيَةٍ أَمْلَيْتُ لَهَا وَهِيَ ظَالِمَةٌ ثُمَّ أَخَذْتُهَا وَإِلَيَّ الْمَصِيرُ (٤٨)
قُلْ يَا أَيُّهَا النَّاسُ إِنَّمَا أَنَا لَكُمْ نَذِيرٌ مُبِينٌ (٤٩)
فَالَّذِينَ آمَنُوا وَعَمِلُوا الصَّالِحَاتِ لَهُمْ مَغْفِرَةٌ وَرِزْقٌ كَرِيمٌ (٥٠)
وَالَّذِينَ سَعَوْا فِي آيَاتِنَا مُعَاجِزِينَ أُولَئِكَ أَصْحَابُ الْجَحِيمِ (٥١)
وَمَا أَرْسَلْنَا مِنْ قَبْلِكَ مِنْ رَسُولٍ وَلَا نَبِيٍّ إِلَّا إِذَا تَمَنَّى أَلْقَى الشَّيْطَانُ فِي أُمْنِيَّتِهِ فَيَنْسَخُ اللَّهُ مَا يُلْقِي الشَّيْطَانُ ثُمَّ يُحْكِمُ اللَّهُ آيَاتِهِ وَاللَّهُ عَلِيمٌ حَكِيمٌ (٥٢)
لِيَجْعَلَ مَا يُلْقِي الشَّيْطَانُ فِتْنَةً لِلَّذِينَ فِي قُلُوبِهِمْ مَرَضٌ وَالْقَاسِيَةِ قُلُوبُهُمْ وَإِنَّ الظَّالِمِينَ لَفِي شِقَاقٍ بَعِيدٍ (٥٣)
وَلِيَعْلَمَ الَّذِينَ أُوتُوا الْعِلْمَ أَنَّهُ الْحَقُّ مِنْ رَبِّكَ فَيُؤْمِنُوا بِهِ فَتُخْبِتَ لَهُ قُلُوبُهُمْ وَإِنَّ اللَّهَ لَهَادِ الَّذِينَ آمَنُوا إِلَى صِرَاطٍ مُسْتَقِيمٍ (٥٤)
وَلَا يَزَالُ الَّذِينَ كَفَرُوا فِي مِرْيَةٍ مِنْهُ حَتَّى تَأْتِيَهُمُ السَّاعَةُ بَغْتَةً أَوْ يَأْتِيَهُمْ عَذَابُ يَوْمٍ عَقِيمٍ (٥٥)
الْمُلْكُ يَوْمَئِذٍ لِلَّهِ يَحْكُمُ بَيْنَهُمْ فَالَّذِينَ آمَنُوا وَعَمِلُوا الصَّالِحَاتِ فِي جَنَّاتِ النَّعِيمِ (٥٦)
وَالَّذِينَ كَفَرُوا وَكَذَّبُوا بِآيَاتِنَا فَأُولَئِكَ لَهُمْ عَذَابٌ مُهِينٌ (٥٧)
وَالَّذِينَ هَاجَرُوا فِي سَبِيلِ اللَّهِ ثُمَّ قُتِلُوا أَوْ مَاتُوا لَيَرْزُقَنَّهُمُ اللَّهُ رِزْقًا حَسَنًا وَإِنَّ اللَّهَ لَهُوَ خَيْرُ الرَّازِقِينَ (٥٨)
لَيُدْخِلَنَّهُمْ مُدْخَلًا يَرْضَوْنَهُ وَإِنَّ اللَّهَ لَعَلِيمٌ حَلِيمٌ (٥٩)

given knowledge may know that it is the Truth from thy Lord, so they should believe in it that their hearts may be lowly before Him. And surely Allah is the Guide of those who believe, into a right path.

22:55. And those who disbelieve will not cease to be in doubt concerning it, until the Hour overtakes them suddenly, or there comes to them the chastisement of a destructive day.

22:56. The kingdom on that day is Allah's. He will judge between them. So those who believe and do good will be in Gardens of bliss.

22:57. And those who disbelieve and reject Our messages, for them is an abasing chastisement.

* * *

22:58. And those who flee in Allah's way and are then slain or die, Allah will certainly grant them a goodly sustenance. And surely Allah is the Best of providers.

22:59. He will certainly cause them to enter a place which they are pleased with. And surely Allah is Knowing, Forbearing.

22:60. That (is so). And whoever retaliates with the like of that with which he is afflicted and he is oppressed, Allah will certainly help him. Surely Allah is Pardoning, Forgiving.

22:61. That is because Allah causes the night to enter into the day and causes the day to enter into the night, and because Allah is Hearing, Seeing.

22:62. That is because Allah is the Truth, and that which they call upon besides Him that is the falsehood, and because Allah -- He is the High, the Great.

22:63. Seest thou not that Allah sends down water from the cloud, then the earth becomes green? Surely Allah is Knower of subtleties, Aware.

22:64. To Him belongs whatever is in

ذَلِكَ وَمَنْ عَاقَبَ بِمِثْلِ مَا عُوقِبَ بِهِ ثُمَّ بُغِيَ عَلَيْهِ لَيَنصُرَنَّهُ اللَّهُ إِنَّ اللَّهَ لَعَفُوٌّ غَفُورٌ (٦٠)

ذَلِكَ بِأَنَّ اللَّهَ يُولِجُ اللَّيْلَ فِي النَّهَارِ وَيُولِجُ النَّهَارَ فِي اللَّيْلِ وَأَنَّ اللَّهَ سَمِيعٌ بَصِيرٌ (٦١)

ذَلِكَ بِأَنَّ اللَّهَ هُوَ الْحَقُّ وَأَنَّ مَا يَدْعُونَ مِنْ دُونِهِ هُوَ الْبَاطِلُ وَأَنَّ اللَّهَ هُوَ الْعَلِيُّ الْكَبِيرُ (٦٢)

أَلَمْ تَرَ أَنَّ اللَّهَ أَنْزَلَ مِنَ السَّمَاءِ مَاءً فَتُصْبِحُ الْأَرْضُ مُخْضَرَّةً إِنَّ اللَّهَ لَطِيفٌ خَبِيرٌ (٦٣)

لَهُ مَا فِي السَّمَاوَاتِ وَمَا فِي الْأَرْضِ وَإِنَّ اللَّهَ لَهُوَ الْغَنِيُّ الْحَمِيدُ (٦٤)

أَلَمْ تَرَ أَنَّ اللَّهَ سَخَّرَ لَكُمْ مَا فِي الْأَرْضِ وَالْفُلْكَ تَجْرِي فِي الْبَحْرِ بِأَمْرِهِ وَيُمْسِكُ السَّمَاءَ أَنْ تَقَعَ عَلَى الْأَرْضِ إِلَّا بِإِذْنِهِ إِنَّ اللَّهَ بِالنَّاسِ لَرَءُوفٌ رَحِيمٌ (٦٥)

وَهُوَ الَّذِي أَحْيَاكُمْ ثُمَّ يُمِيتُكُمْ ثُمَّ يُحْيِيكُمْ إِنَّ الْإِنْسَانَ لَكَفُورٌ (٦٦)

لِكُلِّ أُمَّةٍ جَعَلْنَا مَنْسَكًا هُمْ نَاسِكُوهُ فَلَا يُنَازِعُنَّكَ فِي الْأَمْرِ وَادْعُ إِلَى رَبِّكَ إِنَّكَ لَعَلَى هُدًى مُسْتَقِيمٍ (٦٧)

وَإِنْ جَادَلُوكَ فَقُلِ اللَّهُ أَعْلَمُ بِمَا تَعْمَلُونَ (٦٨)

اللَّهُ يَحْكُمُ بَيْنَكُمْ يَوْمَ الْقِيَامَةِ فِيمَا كُنْتُمْ فِيهِ تَخْتَلِفُونَ (٦٩)

أَلَمْ تَعْلَمْ أَنَّ اللَّهَ يَعْلَمُ مَا فِي السَّمَاءِ وَالْأَرْضِ إِنَّ ذَلِكَ فِي كِتَابٍ إِنَّ ذَلِكَ عَلَى اللَّهِ يَسِيرٌ (٧٠)

وَيَعْبُدُونَ مِنْ دُونِ اللَّهِ مَا لَمْ يُنَزِّلْ بِهِ سُلْطَانًا وَمَا لَيْسَ لَهُمْ بِهِ عِلْمٌ وَمَا لِلظَّالِمِينَ مِنْ نَصِيرٍ (٧١)

the heavens and whatever is in the earth. And surely Allah -- He is the Self-Sufficient, the Praised.

***

22:65. Seest thou not that Allah has made subservient to you all that is in the earth, and the ships gliding in the sea by His command? And He withholds the heaven from falling on the earth except with His permission. Surely Allah is Compassionate, Merciful to men.

22:66. And He it is Who brings you to life, then He causes you to die, then He will bring you to life. Surely man is ungrateful.

22:67. To every nation We appointed acts of devotion, which they observe, so let them not dispute with thee in the matter, and call to thy Lord. Surely thou art on a right guidance.

22:68. And if they contend with thee, say: Allah best knows what you do.

22:69. Allah will judge between you on the day of Resurrection respecting that in which you differ.

22:70. Knowest thou not that Allah knows what is in the heaven and the earth? Surely this is in a book. That is surely easy to Allah.

22:71. And they serve besides Allah that for which He has not sent any authority, and of which they have no knowledge. And for the unjust there is no helper.

22:72. And when Our clear messages are recited to them, thou wilt notice a denial on the faces of those who disbelieve -- they almost attack those who recite to them Our messages. Say: Shall I inform you of what is worse than this? The Fire. Allah has promised it to those who disbelieve. And evil is the resort.

***

22:73. O people, a parable is set forth,

so listen to it. Surely those whom you call upon besides Allah cannot create a fly, though they should all gather for it. And if the fly carry off aught from them, they cannot take it back from it. Weak are (both) the invoker and the invoked.

22:74. They estimate not Allah with His due estimation. Surely Allah is Strong, Mighty.

22:75. Allah chooses messengers from angels and from men. Surely Allah is Hearing, Seeing.

22:76. He knows what is before them and what is behind them. And to Allah are all affairs returned.

22:77. O you who believe, bow down and prostrate yourselves and serve your Lord, and do good that you may succeed.

22:78. And strive hard for Allah with due striving. He has chosen you and has not laid upon you any hardship in religion -- the faith of your father Abraham. He named you Muslims before and in this, that the Messenger may be a bearer of witness to you, and you may be bearers of witness to the people; so keep up prayer and pay the poor-rate and hold fast to Allah. He is your Protector excellent the Protector and excellent the Helper!

23. The Believers

In the name of Allah the Beneficent, the Merciful.

23:1. Successful indeed are the believers,
23:2. Who are humble in their prayers,
23:3. And who shun what is vain,
23:4. And who act for the sake of purity,
23:5. And who restrain their sexual passions --
23:6. Except in the presence of their mates or those whom their right hands

23. The Believers

possess, for such surely are not blameable,

23:7. But whoever seeks to go beyond that, such are transgressors --

23:8. And those who are keepers of their trusts and their covenant,

23:9. And those who keep a guard on their prayers.

23:10. These are the heirs,

23:11. Who inherit Paradise. Therein they will abide.

23:12. And certainly We create man of an extract of clay,

23:13. Then We make him a small life-germ in a firm resting-place,

23:14. Then We make the life-germ a clot, then We make the clot a lump of flesh, then We make (in) the lump of flesh bones, then We clothe the bones with flesh, then We cause it to grow into another creation. So blessed be Allah, the Best of creators.

23:15. Then after that you certainly die.

23:16. Then on the day of Resurrection you will surely be raised up.

23:17. And indeed We have made above you seven ways -- and never are We heedless of creation.

23:18. And We send down water from the cloud according to a measure, then We cause it to settle in the earth, and We are indeed able to carry it away.

23:19. Then We cause to grow thereby gardens of palm-trees and grapes for you. You have therein many fruits and of them you eat;

23:20. And a tree that grows out of Mount Sinai, which produces oil and relish for the eaters.

23:21. And surely there is a lesson for you in the cattle. We make you to drink of what is in their bellies, and you have in them many advantages and of them you eat,

23:22. And on them and on the ships you are borne.

* * *

23:23. And certainly We sent Noah to

فَمَنِ ابْتَغَىٰ وَرَاءَ ذَٰلِكَ فَأُولَٰئِكَ هُمُ الْعَادُونَ (٧)

وَالَّذِينَ هُمْ لِأَمَانَاتِهِمْ وَعَهْدِهِمْ رَاعُونَ (٨)

وَالَّذِينَ هُمْ عَلَىٰ صَلَوَاتِهِمْ يُحَافِظُونَ (٩)

أُولَٰئِكَ هُمُ الْوَارِثُونَ (١٠)

الَّذِينَ يَرِثُونَ الْفِرْدَوْسَ هُمْ فِيهَا خَالِدُونَ (١١)

وَلَقَدْ خَلَقْنَا الْإِنْسَانَ مِنْ سُلَالَةٍ مِنْ طِينٍ (١٢)

ثُمَّ جَعَلْنَاهُ نُطْفَةً فِي قَرَارٍ مَكِينٍ (١٣)

ثُمَّ خَلَقْنَا النُّطْفَةَ عَلَقَةً فَخَلَقْنَا الْعَلَقَةَ مُضْغَةً فَخَلَقْنَا الْمُضْغَةَ عِظَامًا فَكَسَوْنَا الْعِظَامَ لَحْمًا ثُمَّ أَنْشَأْنَاهُ خَلْقًا آخَرَ ۚ فَتَبَارَكَ اللَّهُ أَحْسَنُ الْخَالِقِينَ (١٤)

ثُمَّ إِنَّكُمْ بَعْدَ ذَٰلِكَ لَمَيِّتُونَ (١٥)

ثُمَّ إِنَّكُمْ يَوْمَ الْقِيَامَةِ تُبْعَثُونَ (١٦)

وَلَقَدْ خَلَقْنَا فَوْقَكُمْ سَبْعَ طَرَائِقَ وَمَا كُنَّا عَنِ الْخَلْقِ غَافِلِينَ (١٧)

وَأَنْزَلْنَا مِنَ السَّمَاءِ مَاءً بِقَدَرٍ فَأَسْكَنَّاهُ فِي الْأَرْضِ ۖ وَإِنَّا عَلَىٰ ذَهَابٍ بِهِ لَقَادِرُونَ (١٨)

فَأَنْشَأْنَا لَكُمْ بِهِ جَنَّاتٍ مِنْ نَخِيلٍ وَأَعْنَابٍ لَكُمْ فِيهَا فَوَاكِهُ كَثِيرَةٌ وَمِنْهَا تَأْكُلُونَ (١٩)

وَشَجَرَةً تَخْرُجُ مِنْ طُورِ سَيْنَاءَ تَنْبُتُ بِالدُّهْنِ وَصِبْغٍ لِلْآكِلِينَ (٢٠)

وَإِنَّ لَكُمْ فِي الْأَنْعَامِ لَعِبْرَةً ۖ نُسْقِيكُمْ مِمَّا فِي بُطُونِهَا وَلَكُمْ فِيهَا مَنَافِعُ كَثِيرَةٌ وَمِنْهَا تَأْكُلُونَ (٢١)

his people, so he said: O my people, serve Allah, you have no God other than Him. Will you not guard against evil?

23:24. But the chiefs of those who disbelieved from among his people said: He is nothing but a mortal like yourselves, who desires to have superiority over you. And if Allah had pleased, He could have sent down angels. We have not heard of this among our fathers of yore.

23:25. He is only a madman, so bear with him for a time.

23:26. He said: My Lord, help me against their calling me a liar.

23:27. So We revealed to him: Make the ark under Our eyes and according to Our revelation; then when Our command comes, and water gushes forth from the valley, take into it of every kind a pair, two, and thy people, except those among them against whom the word has gone forth, and speak not to Me in respect of those who are unjust; surely they will be drowned.

23:28. Then when thou art firmly seated, thou and those with thee, in the ark, say: Praise be to Allah, Who delivered us from the unjust people!

23:29. And say: My Lord, cause me to land a blessed landing and Thou art the Best of those who bring to land.

23:30. Surely there are signs in this, and surely We are ever trying (men).

23:31. Then We raised after them another generation.

23:32. So We sent among them a messenger from among them, saying: Serve Allah -- you have no God other than Him. Will you not guard against evil?

***

23:33. And the chiefs of His people who disbelieved and called the meeting of the Hereafter a lie, and whom We had given plenty to enjoy in this world's

وَعَلَيْهَا وَعَلَى الْفُلْكِ تُحْمَلُونَ (٢٢)
وَلَقَدْ أَرْسَلْنَا نُوحًا إِلَى قَوْمِهِ فَقَالَ يَا قَوْمِ اعْبُدُوا اللَّهَ مَا لَكُمْ مِنْ إِلَهٍ غَيْرُهُ أَفَلَا تَتَّقُونَ (٢٣)
فَقَالَ الْمَلَأُ الَّذِينَ كَفَرُوا مِنْ قَوْمِهِ مَا هَذَا إِلَّا بَشَرٌ مِثْلُكُمْ يُرِيدُ أَنْ يَتَفَضَّلَ عَلَيْكُمْ وَلَوْ شَاءَ اللَّهُ لَأَنْزَلَ مَلَائِكَةً مَا سَمِعْنَا بِهَذَا فِي آبَائِنَا الْأَوَّلِينَ (٢٤)
إِنْ هُوَ إِلَّا رَجُلٌ بِهِ جِنَّةٌ فَتَرَبَّصُوا بِهِ حَتَّى حِينٍ (٢٥)
قَالَ رَبِّ انْصُرْنِي بِمَا كَذَّبُونِ (٢٦)
فَأَوْحَيْنَا إِلَيْهِ أَنِ اصْنَعِ الْفُلْكَ بِأَعْيُنِنَا وَوَحْيِنَا فَإِذَا جَاءَ أَمْرُنَا وَفَارَ التَّنُّورُ فَاسْلُكْ فِيهَا مِنْ كُلٍّ زَوْجَيْنِ اثْنَيْنِ وَأَهْلَكَ إِلَّا مَنْ سَبَقَ عَلَيْهِ الْقَوْلُ مِنْهُمْ وَلَا تُخَاطِبْنِي فِي الَّذِينَ ظَلَمُوا إِنَّهُمْ مُغْرَقُونَ (٢٧)
فَإِذَا اسْتَوَيْتَ أَنْتَ وَمَنْ مَعَكَ عَلَى الْفُلْكِ فَقُلِ الْحَمْدُ لِلَّهِ الَّذِي نَجَّانَا مِنَ الْقَوْمِ الظَّالِمِينَ (٢٨)
وَقُلْ رَبِّ أَنْزِلْنِي مُنْزَلًا مُبَارَكًا وَأَنْتَ خَيْرُ الْمُنْزِلِينَ (٢٩)
إِنَّ فِي ذَلِكَ لَآيَاتٍ وَإِنْ كُنَّا لَمُبْتَلِينَ (٣٠)
ثُمَّ أَنْشَأْنَا مِنْ بَعْدِهِمْ قَرْنًا آخَرِينَ (٣١)
فَأَرْسَلْنَا فِيهِمْ رَسُولًا مِنْهُمْ أَنِ اعْبُدُوا اللَّهَ مَا لَكُمْ مِنْ إِلَهٍ غَيْرُهُ أَفَلَا تَتَّقُونَ (٣٢)
وَقَالَ الْمَلَأُ مِنْ قَوْمِهِ الَّذِينَ كَفَرُوا وَكَذَّبُوا بِلِقَاءِ الْآخِرَةِ وَأَتْرَفْنَاهُمْ فِي الْحَيَاةِ الدُّنْيَا مَا هَذَا إِلَّا بَشَرٌ مِثْلُكُمْ يَأْكُلُ مِمَّا تَأْكُلُونَ مِنْهُ وَيَشْرَبُ مِمَّا تَشْرَبُونَ (٣٣)

23. The Believers

life, said: This is only a mortal like you, eating of that whereof you eat and drinking of what you drink.

23:34. And if you obey a mortal like yourselves, then surely you are losers.

23:35. Does he promise you that, when you are dead and become dust and bones, you will then be brought forth?

23:36. Far, very far, is that which you are promised:

23:37. There is naught but our life in this world: we die and we live and we shall not be raised again:

23:38. He is naught but a man who has forged a lie against Allah, and we are not going to believe in him.

23:39. He said: My Lord, help me against their calling me a liar.

23:40. He said: In a little while they will certainly be repenting.

23:41. So the punishment overtook them in justice, and We made them as rubbish; so away with the unjust people!

23:42. Then We raised after them other generations.

23:43. No people can hasten on their doom, nor can they postpone (it).

23:44. Then We sent Our messengers one after another. Whenever its messenger came to a people, they called him a liar, so We made them follow one another and We made them stories. So away with a people who believe not!

23:45. Then We sent Moses and his brother Aaron with Our messages and a clear authority

23:46. To Pharaoh and his chiefs, but they behaved haughtily and they were an insolent people.

23:47. So they said: Shall We believe in two mortals like ourselves while their people serve us?

23:48. So they rejected them and became of those who were destroyed.

23:49. And certainly We gave Moses the Book that they might go aright.

23. The Believers

23:50. And We made the son of Mary and his mother a sign, and We gave them refuge on a lofty ground having meadows and springs.

***

23:51. O ye messengers, eat of the good things and do good. Surely I am Knower of what you do.

23:52. And surely this your community -- one community, and I am your Lord, so keep your duty to Me.

23:53. But they became divided into sects, each party rejoicing in that which was with them.

23:54. So leave them in their ignorance till a time.

23:55. Think they that by the wealth and children wherewith We aid them,

23:56. We are hastening to them of good things? Nay, they perceive not.

23:57. Surely they who live in awe for fear of their Lord,

23:58. And those who believe in the messages of their Lord,

23:59. And those who associate naught with their Lord,

23:60. And those who give what they give while their hearts are full of fear that to their Lord they must return --

23:61. These hasten to good things and they are foremost in attaining them.

23:62. And We lay not on any soul a burden except to the extent of its ability, and with Us is a book which speaks the truth, and they are not wronged.

23:63. Nay, their hearts are in ignorance about it, and they have besides this other deeds which they do.

23:64. Until, when We seize those who lead easy lives among them with chastisement, lo! they cry for succour.

23:65. Cry not for succour this day. Surely you will not be helped by Us.

23:66. My messages were indeed recited to you, but you used to turn back on your heels

23:67. Haughtily, passing nights in

يَا أَيُّهَا الرُّسُلُ كُلُوا مِنَ الطَّيِّبَاتِ وَاعْمَلُوا صَالِحًا إِنِّي بِمَا تَعْمَلُونَ عَلِيمٌ (٥١)

وَإِنَّ هَذِهِ أُمَّتُكُمْ أُمَّةً وَاحِدَةً وَأَنَا رَبُّكُمْ فَاتَّقُونِ (٥٢)

فَتَقَطَّعُوا أَمْرَهُمْ بَيْنَهُمْ زُبُرًا كُلُّ حِزْبٍ بِمَا لَدَيْهِمْ فَرِحُونَ (٥٣)

فَذَرْهُمْ فِي غَمْرَتِهِمْ حَتَّى حِينٍ (٥٤)

أَيَحْسَبُونَ أَنَّمَا نُمِدُّهُمْ بِهِ مِنْ مَالٍ وَبَنِينَ (٥٥)

نُسَارِعُ لَهُمْ فِي الْخَيْرَاتِ بَلْ لَا يَشْعُرُونَ (٥٦)

إِنَّ الَّذِينَ هُمْ مِنْ خَشْيَةِ رَبِّهِمْ مُشْفِقُونَ (٥٧)

وَالَّذِينَ هُمْ بِآيَاتِ رَبِّهِمْ يُؤْمِنُونَ (٥٨)

وَالَّذِينَ هُمْ بِرَبِّهِمْ لَا يُشْرِكُونَ (٥٩)

وَالَّذِينَ يُؤْتُونَ مَا آتَوْا وَقُلُوبُهُمْ وَجِلَةٌ أَنَّهُمْ إِلَى رَبِّهِمْ رَاجِعُونَ (٦٠)

أُولَئِكَ يُسَارِعُونَ فِي الْخَيْرَاتِ وَهُمْ لَهَا سَابِقُونَ (٦١)

وَلَا نُكَلِّفُ نَفْسًا إِلَّا وُسْعَهَا وَلَدَيْنَا كِتَابٌ يَنْطِقُ بِالْحَقِّ وَهُمْ لَا يُظْلَمُونَ (٦٢)

بَلْ قُلُوبُهُمْ فِي غَمْرَةٍ مِنْ هَذَا وَلَهُمْ أَعْمَالٌ مِنْ دُونِ ذَلِكَ هُمْ لَهَا عَامِلُونَ (٦٣)

حَتَّى إِذَا أَخَذْنَا مُتْرَفِيهِمْ بِالْعَذَابِ إِذَا هُمْ يَجْأَرُونَ (٦٤)

لَا تَجْأَرُوا الْيَوْمَ إِنَّكُمْ مِنَّا لَا تُنْصَرُونَ (٦٥)

قَدْ كَانَتْ آيَاتِي تُتْلَى عَلَيْكُمْ فَكُنْتُمْ عَلَى أَعْقَابِكُمْ تَنْكِصُونَ (٦٦)

23. The Believers

talking nonsense about it.

23:68. Do they not then ponder the Word? Or has there come to them that which did nor come to their fathers of old?

23:69. Or do they not recognize their Messenger, that they deny him?

23:70. Or say they: There is madness in him? Nay, he has brought them the Truth, and most of them hate the Truth.

23:71. And if the Truth follow their desires, the heavens and the earth and all those who are therein would perish. Nay, We have brought them their reminder, but they turn away from their reminder.

23:72. Or dost thou ask them a recompense? But the recompense of thy Lord is best, and He is the Best of providers.

23:73. And surely thou callest them to a right way.

23:74. And surely those who believe not in the Hereafter are deviating from the way.

23:75. And if We show mercy to them and remove the distress they have, they would persist in their inordinacy, blindly wandering on.

23:76. And already We seized them with chastisement, but they were not submissive to their Lord, nor did they humble themselves.

23:77. Until, when We open for them a door of severe chastisement, lo! they are in despair at it.

* * *

23:78. And He it is Who made for you the ears and the eyes and the hearts. Little it is that you give thanks!

23:79. And He it is Who multiplied you in the earth, and to Him you will be gathered.

23:80. And He it is Who gives life and causes death, and His is the alternation of the night and the day. Do you not then understand?

مُسْتَكْبِرِينَ بِهِ سَامِرًا تَهْجُرُونَ (٦٧)
أَفَلَمْ يَدَّبَّرُوا الْقَوْلَ أَمْ جَاءَهُمْ مَا لَمْ يَأْتِ آبَاءَهُمُ الْأَوَّلِينَ (٦٨)
أَمْ لَمْ يَعْرِفُوا رَسُولَهُمْ فَهُمْ لَهُ مُنْكِرُونَ (٦٩)
أَمْ يَقُولُونَ بِهِ جِنَّةٌ بَلْ جَاءَهُمْ بِالْحَقِّ وَأَكْثَرُهُمْ لِلْحَقِّ كَارِهُونَ (٧٠)
وَلَوِ اتَّبَعَ الْحَقُّ أَهْوَاءَهُمْ لَفَسَدَتِ السَّمَوَاتُ وَالْأَرْضُ وَمَنْ فِيهِنَّ بَلْ أَتَيْنَاهُمْ بِذِكْرِهِمْ فَهُمْ عَنْ ذِكْرِهِمْ مُعْرِضُونَ (٧١)
أَمْ تَسْأَلُهُمْ خَرْجًا فَخَرَاجُ رَبِّكَ خَيْرٌ وَهُوَ خَيْرُ الرَّازِقِينَ (٧٢)
وَإِنَّكَ لَتَدْعُوهُمْ إِلَى صِرَاطٍ مُسْتَقِيمٍ (٧٣)
وَإِنَّ الَّذِينَ لَا يُؤْمِنُونَ بِالْآخِرَةِ عَنِ الصِّرَاطِ لَنَاكِبُونَ (٧٤)
وَلَوْ رَحِمْنَاهُمْ وَكَشَفْنَا مَا بِهِمْ مِنْ ضُرٍّ لَلَجُّوا فِي طُغْيَانِهِمْ يَعْمَهُونَ (٧٥)
وَلَقَدْ أَخَذْنَاهُمْ بِالْعَذَابِ فَمَا اسْتَكَانُوا لِرَبِّهِمْ وَمَا يَتَضَرَّعُونَ (٧٦)
حَتَّى إِذَا فَتَحْنَا عَلَيْهِمْ بَابًا ذَا عَذَابٍ شَدِيدٍ إِذَا هُمْ فِيهِ مُبْلِسُونَ (٧٧)
وَهُوَ الَّذِي أَنْشَأَ لَكُمُ السَّمْعَ وَالْأَبْصَارَ وَالْأَفْئِدَةَ قَلِيلًا مَا تَشْكُرُونَ (٧٨)
وَهُوَ الَّذِي ذَرَأَكُمْ فِي الْأَرْضِ وَإِلَيْهِ تُحْشَرُونَ (٧٩)
وَهُوَ الَّذِي يُحْيِي وَيُمِيتُ وَلَهُ اخْتِلَافُ اللَّيْلِ وَالنَّهَارِ أَفَلَا تَعْقِلُونَ (٨٠)
بَلْ قَالُوا مِثْلَ مَا قَالَ الْأَوَّلُونَ (٨١)
قَالُوا أَئِذَا مِتْنَا وَكُنَّا تُرَابًا وَعِظَامًا

23. The Believers

23:81. Nay, they say the like of what the ancients said.

23:82. They say: When we die and become dust and bones, shall we then be raised up?

23:83. We are indeed promised this, and (so were) our fathers before. This is naught but stories of those of old!

23:84. Say: Whose is the earth, and whoever is therein, if you know?

23:85. They will say Allah's. Say: Will you not then mind?

23:86. Say: Who is the Lord of the seven heavens and the Lord of the mighty Throne of power?

23:87. They will say: (This is) Allah's. Say: Will you not then guard against evil?

23:88. Say: Who is it in Whose hand is the kingdom of all things and He protects, and none is prorected against Him, if you know?

23:89. They will say: (This is) Allah's. Say: Whence are you then deceived?

23:90. Nay, We have brought them the Truth and surely they are liars.

23:91. Allah has not taken to Himself a son, nor is there with Him any (other) god -- in that case would each god have taken away what he created, and some of them would have overpowered others. Glory be to Allah above what they describe

23:92. The Knower of the unseen and the seen; so may He be exalted above what they associate (with Him)!

* * *

23:93. Say: My Lord, if Thou show me that which they are promised --

23:94. My Lord, then place me not with the unjust people.

23:95. And surely We are well Able to show thee what We promise them.

23:96. Repel evil with that which is best. We know best what they describe.

23:97. And say: My Lord, I seek refuge in Thee from the evil suggestions of the devils,

23:98. And I seek refuge in Thee, my Lord, lest they come to me.
23:99. Until when death overtakes one of them, he says: My Lord, send toe back,
23:100. That I may do good in that which I have left. By no means! It is but a word that he speaks. And before them is a barrier, until the day they are raised.
23:101. So when the trumpet is blown, there will be no ties of relationship among them that day, nor will they ask of one another.
23:102. Then those whose good deeds are heavy, those are the successful.
23:103. And those whose good deeds are light, those are they who have lost their souls, abiding in hell.
23:104. The Fire will scorch their faces, and they therein will be in severe affliction.
23:105. Were not My messages recited to you, but you used to reject them?
23:106. They will say: Our Lord, our adversity overcame us, and we were an erring people.
23:107. Our Lord, take us out of it; then if we return (to evil), we shall be unjust.
23:108. He will say: Begone therein, and speak not to Me.
23:109. Surely there was a party of My servants who said: Our Lord, we believe, so forgive us and have mercy on us, and Thou are the Best of those who show mercy.
23:110. But you ridiculed them, until they made you forget remembrance of Me, and you used to laugh at them.
23:111. Surely I have rewarded them this day because they were patient, that they are the achievers.
23:112. He will say: How many years did you tarry in the earth?
23:113. They will say: We tarried a day or part of a day, but ask those who keep account.

حَتَّىٰ إِذَا جَاءَ أَحَدَهُمُ الْمَوْتُ قَالَ رَبِّ ارْجِعُونِ (٩٩)
لَعَلِّي أَعْمَلُ صَالِحًا فِيمَا تَرَكْتُ ۚ كَلَّا ۚ إِنَّهَا كَلِمَةٌ هُوَ قَائِلُهَا ۖ وَمِن وَرَائِهِم بَرْزَخٌ إِلَىٰ يَوْمِ يُبْعَثُونَ (١٠٠)
فَإِذَا نُفِخَ فِي الصُّورِ فَلَا أَنسَابَ بَيْنَهُمْ يَوْمَئِذٍ وَلَا يَتَسَاءَلُونَ (١٠١)
فَمَن ثَقُلَتْ مَوَازِينُهُ فَأُولَٰئِكَ هُمُ الْمُفْلِحُونَ (١٠٢)
وَمَنْ خَفَّتْ مَوَازِينُهُ فَأُولَٰئِكَ الَّذِينَ خَسِرُوا أَنفُسَهُمْ فِي جَهَنَّمَ خَالِدُونَ (١٠٣)
تَلْفَحُ وُجُوهَهُمُ النَّارُ وَهُمْ فِيهَا كَالِحُونَ (١٠٤)
أَلَمْ تَكُنْ آيَاتِي تُتْلَىٰ عَلَيْكُمْ فَكُنتُم بِهَا تُكَذِّبُونَ (١٠٥)
قَالُوا رَبَّنَا غَلَبَتْ عَلَيْنَا شِقْوَتُنَا وَكُنَّا قَوْمًا ضَالِّينَ (١٠٦)
رَبَّنَا أَخْرِجْنَا مِنْهَا فَإِنْ عُدْنَا فَإِنَّا ظَالِمُونَ (١٠٧)
قَالَ اخْسَئُوا فِيهَا وَلَا تُكَلِّمُونِ (١٠٨)
إِنَّهُ كَانَ فَرِيقٌ مِنْ عِبَادِي يَقُولُونَ رَبَّنَا آمَنَّا فَاغْفِرْ لَنَا وَارْحَمْنَا وَأَنتَ خَيْرُ الرَّاحِمِينَ (١٠٩)
فَاتَّخَذْتُمُوهُمْ سِخْرِيًّا حَتَّىٰ أَنسَوْكُمْ ذِكْرِي وَكُنتُم مِنْهُمْ تَضْحَكُونَ (١١٠)
إِنِّي جَزَيْتُهُمُ الْيَوْمَ بِمَا صَبَرُوا أَنَّهُمْ هُمُ الْفَائِزُونَ (١١١)
قَالَ كَمْ لَبِثْتُمْ فِي الْأَرْضِ عَدَدَ سِنِينَ (١١٢)
قَالُوا لَبِثْنَا يَوْمًا أَوْ بَعْضَ يَوْمٍ فَاسْأَلِ

23:114. He will say: You tarried but a little if you only knew!
23:115. Do you then think that We have created you in vain, and that you will not be returned to Us?
23:116. So exalted be Allah, the True King! No God is there but He, the Lord of the Throne of Grace.
23:117. And whoever invokes, besides Allah, another god -- he has no proof of this -- his reckoning is only with his Lord. Surely the disbelievers will not be successful.
23:118. And say: My Lord, forgive and have mercy, and Thou art the Best of those who show mercy.

24. The Light

In the name of Allah, the Beneficent, the Merciful.(This is) a chapter which We have revealed and made obligatory and wherein We have revealed clear messages that you may be mindful.
24:2. The adulteress and the adulterer, flog each of them (with) a hundred stripes, and let not pity for them detain you from obedience to Allah, if you believe in Allah and the Last Day, and let a party of believers wit ness their chastisement.
24:3. The adulterer cannot have sexual relations with any but an adulteress or an idolatress, and the adulteress, none can have sexual relations with her but an adulterer or an idolater; and it is forbidden to believers.
24:4. And those who accuse free women and bring not four witnesses, flog them (with) eighty stripes and never accept their evidence, and these are the transgressors --
24:5. Except those who afterwards repent and act aright; surely Allah is Forgiving, Merciful.
24:6. And those who accuse their wives

الْعَادِّينَ (١١٣)
قَالَ إِنْ لَبِثْتُمْ إِلَّا قَلِيلًا لَوْ أَنَّكُمْ كُنْتُمْ تَعْلَمُونَ (١١٤)
أَفَحَسِبْتُمْ أَنَّمَا خَلَقْنَاكُمْ عَبَثًا وَأَنَّكُمْ إِلَيْنَا لَا تُرْجَعُونَ (١١٥)
فَتَعَالَى اللَّهُ الْمَلِكُ الْحَقُّ لَا إِلَهَ إِلَّا هُوَ رَبُّ الْعَرْشِ الْكَرِيمِ (١١٦)
وَمَنْ يَدْعُ مَعَ اللَّهِ إِلَهًا آخَرَ لَا بُرْهَانَ لَهُ بِهِ فَإِنَّمَا حِسَابُهُ عِنْدَ رَبِّهِ إِنَّهُ لَا يُفْلِحُ الْكَافِرُونَ (١١٧)
وَقُلْ رَبِّ اغْفِرْ وَارْحَمْ وَأَنْتَ خَيْرُ الرَّاحِمِينَ (١١٨)

٢٤- سورة النور

بِسْمِ اللَّهِ الرَّحْمَنِ الرَّحِيمِ
سُورَةٌ أَنْزَلْنَاهَا وَفَرَضْنَاهَا وَأَنْزَلْنَا فِيهَا آيَاتٍ بَيِّنَاتٍ لَعَلَّكُمْ تَذَكَّرُونَ (١)
الزَّانِيَةُ وَالزَّانِي فَاجْلِدُوا كُلَّ وَاحِدٍ مِنْهُمَا مِئَةَ جَلْدَةٍ وَلَا تَأْخُذْكُمْ بِهِمَا رَأْفَةٌ فِي دِينِ اللَّهِ إِنْ كُنْتُمْ تُؤْمِنُونَ بِاللَّهِ وَالْيَوْمِ الْآخِرِ وَلْيَشْهَدْ عَذَابَهُمَا طَائِفَةٌ مِنَ الْمُؤْمِنِينَ (٢)
الزَّانِي لَا يَنْكِحُ إِلَّا زَانِيَةً أَوْ مُشْرِكَةً وَالزَّانِيَةُ لَا يَنْكِحُهَا إِلَّا زَانٍ أَوْ مُشْرِكٌ وَحُرِّمَ ذَلِكَ عَلَى الْمُؤْمِنِينَ (٣)
وَالَّذِينَ يَرْمُونَ الْمُحْصَنَاتِ ثُمَّ لَمْ يَأْتُوا بِأَرْبَعَةِ شُهَدَاءَ فَاجْلِدُوهُمْ ثَمَانِينَ جَلْدَةً وَلَا تَقْبَلُوا لَهُمْ شَهَادَةً أَبَدًا وَأُولَئِكَ هُمُ الْفَاسِقُونَ (٤)
إِلَّا الَّذِينَ تَابُوا مِنْ بَعْدِ ذَلِكَ وَأَصْلَحُوا فَإِنَّ اللَّهَ غَفُورٌ رَحِيمٌ (٥)
وَالَّذِينَ يَرْمُونَ أَزْوَاجَهُمْ وَلَمْ يَكُنْ

and have no witnesses except themselves, let one of them testify four times, bearing Allah to witness, that he is of those who speak the truth.

24:7. And the fifth (time) that the curse of Allah be on him, if he is of those who lie.

24:8. And it shall avert the chastisement from her, if she testify four times, bearing Allah to witness that he is of those who lie.

24:9. And the fifth (time) that the wrath of Allah to be on her, if he is of those who speak the truth.

24:10. And were it not for Allah's grace upon you and His mercy -- and that Allah is Oft-returning (to mercy) Wise

***

24:11. Surely they who concocted the lie are a party from among you. Deem it not an evil to you. Nay, it is good for you. For every man of them is what he has earned of sin and as for him among them who took upon himself the main part thereof, he shall have a grievous punishment.

24:12. Why did not the believing men and the believing women, when you heard it, think well of their own people, and say: This is an evident falsehood?

24:13. Why did they not bring four witnesses of it? So, as they have not brought witnesses, they are liars in the sight of Allah.

24:14. And were it not for Allah's grace upon you and His mercy in this world and the Hereafter, a grievous chastisement would certainly have touched you on account of the talk you indulged in.

24:15. When you received it on your tongues and spoke with your mouths that of which you had no knowledge, and you deemed it a trifle, while with Allah it was serious. --

24:16. And why did you not, when you heard it, say: It beseems us not to talk

لَهُمْ شُهَدَاءُ إِلَّا أَنْفُسُهُمْ فَشَهَادَةُ أَحَدِهِمْ أَرْبَعُ شَهَادَاتٍ بِاللَّهِ إِنَّهُ لَمِنَ الصَّادِقِينَ (٦)

وَالْخَامِسَةُ أَنَّ لَعْنَةَ اللَّهِ عَلَيْهِ إِنْ كَانَ مِنَ الْكَاذِبِينَ (٧)

وَيَدْرَأُ عَنْهَا الْعَذَابَ أَنْ تَشْهَدَ أَرْبَعَ شَهَادَاتٍ بِاللَّهِ إِنَّهُ لَمِنَ الْكَاذِبِينَ (٨)

وَالْخَامِسَةَ أَنَّ غَضَبَ اللَّهِ عَلَيْهَا إِنْ كَانَ مِنَ الصَّادِقِينَ (٩)

وَلَوْلَا فَضْلُ اللَّهِ عَلَيْكُمْ وَرَحْمَتُهُ وَأَنَّ اللَّهَ تَوَّابٌ حَكِيمٌ (١٠)

إِنَّ الَّذِينَ جَاءُوا بِالْإِفْكِ عُصْبَةٌ مِنْكُمْ لَا تَحْسَبُوهُ شَرًّا لَكُمْ بَلْ هُوَ خَيْرٌ لَكُمْ لِكُلِّ امْرِئٍ مِنْهُمْ مَا اكْتَسَبَ مِنَ الْإِثْمِ وَالَّذِي تَوَلَّى كِبْرَهُ مِنْهُمْ لَهُ عَذَابٌ عَظِيمٌ (١١)

لَوْلَا إِذْ سَمِعْتُمُوهُ ظَنَّ الْمُؤْمِنُونَ وَالْمُؤْمِنَاتُ بِأَنْفُسِهِمْ خَيْرًا وَقَالُوا هَذَا إِفْكٌ مُبِينٌ (١٢)

لَوْلَا جَاءُوا عَلَيْهِ بِأَرْبَعَةِ شُهَدَاءَ فَإِذْ لَمْ يَأْتُوا بِالشُّهَدَاءِ فَأُولَئِكَ عِنْدَ اللَّهِ هُمُ الْكَاذِبُونَ (١٣)

وَلَوْلَا فَضْلُ اللَّهِ عَلَيْكُمْ وَرَحْمَتُهُ فِي الدُّنْيَا وَالْآخِرَةِ لَمَسَّكُمْ فِي مَا أَفَضْتُمْ فِيهِ عَذَابٌ عَظِيمٌ (١٤)

إِذْ تَلَقَّوْنَهُ بِأَلْسِنَتِكُمْ وَتَقُولُونَ بِأَفْوَاهِكُمْ مَا لَيْسَ لَكُمْ بِهِ عِلْمٌ وَتَحْسَبُونَهُ هَيِّنًا وَهُوَ عِنْدَ اللَّهِ عَظِيمٌ (١٥)

وَلَوْلَا إِذْ سَمِعْتُمُوهُ قُلْتُمْ مَا يَكُونُ لَنَا أَنْ نَتَكَلَّمَ بِهَذَا سُبْحَانَكَ هَذَا بُهْتَانٌ عَظِيمٌ (١٦)

يَعِظُكُمُ اللَّهُ أَنْ تَعُودُوا لِمِثْلِهِ أَبَدًا إِنْ كُنْتُمْ مُؤْمِنِينَ (١٧)

وَيُبَيِّنُ اللَّهُ لَكُمُ الْآيَاتِ وَاللَّهُ عَلِيمٌ

24. The Light

of it. Glory be to Thee 'This is a great calumny.

24:17. Allah admonishes you that you return not to the like of it ever again, if you are believers.

24:18. And Allah makes clear to you the messages; and Allah is Knowing, Wise.

24:19. Those who love that scandal should circulate respecting those who believe, for them is a grievous chastisement in this world and the Hereafter. And Allah knows, while you know not.

24:20. And were it not for Allah's grace on you and His mercy -- and that Allah is Compassionate, Merciful.

* * *

24:21. O you who believe, follow not the footsteps of the devil. And whoever follows the footsteps of the devil, surely he commands indecency and evil. And were it not for Allah's grace on you and His mercy, not one of you would ever have been pure, but Allah purifies whom He pleases. And Allah is Hearing, Knowing.

24:22. And let not possessors of grace and abundance among you swear against giving to the near of kin and the poor and those who have fled in Allah's way; and pardon and overlook. Do you not love that Allah should forgive you? And Allah is Forgiving, Merciful.

24:23. Surely those who accuse chaste believing women, unaware (of the evil), are cursed in this world and the Hereafter, arid for them is a grievous chastisement,

24:24. On the day when their tongues and their hands and their feet bear witness against them as to what they did,

24:25. On that day Allah will pay back to them in full their just reward, and they will know that Allah, He is the Evident Truth.

حَكِيمٌ (١٨)

إِنَّ الَّذِينَ يُحِبُّونَ أَنْ تَشِيعَ الْفَاحِشَةُ فِي الَّذِينَ آمَنُوا لَهُمْ عَذَابٌ أَلِيمٌ فِي الدُّنْيَا وَالْآخِرَةِ وَاللَّهُ يَعْلَمُ وَأَنْتُمْ لَا تَعْلَمُونَ (١٩)

وَلَوْلَا فَضْلُ اللَّهِ عَلَيْكُمْ وَرَحْمَتُهُ وَأَنَّ اللَّهَ رَءُوفٌ رَحِيمٌ (٢٠)

يَا أَيُّهَا الَّذِينَ آمَنُوا لَا تَتَّبِعُوا خُطُوَاتِ الشَّيْطَانِ وَمَنْ يَتَّبِعْ خُطُوَاتِ الشَّيْطَانِ فَإِنَّهُ يَأْمُرُ بِالْفَحْشَاءِ وَالْمُنْكَرِ وَلَوْلَا فَضْلُ اللَّهِ عَلَيْكُمْ وَرَحْمَتُهُ مَا زَكَا مِنْكُمْ مِنْ أَحَدٍ أَبَدًا وَلَكِنَّ اللَّهَ يُزَكِّي مَنْ يَشَاءُ وَاللَّهُ سَمِيعٌ عَلِيمٌ (٢١)

وَلَا يَأْتَلِ أُولُو الْفَضْلِ مِنْكُمْ وَالسَّعَةِ أَنْ يُؤْتُوا أُولِي الْقُرْبَى وَالْمَسَاكِينَ وَالْمُهَاجِرِينَ فِي سَبِيلِ اللَّهِ وَلْيَعْفُوا وَلْيَصْفَحُوا أَلَا تُحِبُّونَ أَنْ يَغْفِرَ اللَّهُ لَكُمْ وَاللَّهُ غَفُورٌ رَحِيمٌ (٢٢)

إِنَّ الَّذِينَ يَرْمُونَ الْمُحْصَنَاتِ الْغَافِلَاتِ الْمُؤْمِنَاتِ لُعِنُوا فِي الدُّنْيَا وَالْآخِرَةِ وَلَهُمْ عَذَابٌ عَظِيمٌ (٢٣)

يَوْمَ تَشْهَدُ عَلَيْهِمْ أَلْسِنَتُهُمْ وَأَيْدِيهِمْ وَأَرْجُلُهُمْ بِمَا كَانُوا يَعْمَلُونَ (٢٤)

يَوْمَئِذٍ يُوَفِّيهِمُ اللَّهُ دِينَهُمُ الْحَقَّ وَيَعْلَمُونَ أَنَّ اللَّهَ هُوَ الْحَقُّ الْمُبِينُ (٢٥)

الْخَبِيثَاتُ لِلْخَبِيثِينَ وَالْخَبِيثُونَ لِلْخَبِيثَاتِ وَالطَّيِّبَاتُ لِلطَّيِّبِينَ وَالطَّيِّبُونَ لِلطَّيِّبَاتِ أُولَئِكَ مُبَرَّءُونَ مِمَّا يَقُولُونَ لَهُمْ مَغْفِرَةٌ وَرِزْقٌ كَرِيمٌ (٢٦)

يَا أَيُّهَا الَّذِينَ آمَنُوا لَا تَدْخُلُوا بُيُوتًا غَيْرَ بُيُوتِكُمْ حَتَّى تَسْتَأْنِسُوا وَتُسَلِّمُوا

24. The Light

24:26. Unclean things are for unclean ones and unclean ones are for unclean things, and good things are for good ones and good ones are for good things; these are free from what they say. For them is forgiveness and an honourable sustenance.

***

24:27. O you who believe, enter not houses other than your own houses, until you have asked permission and saluted their inmates. This is better for you that you may be mindful.

24:28. But if you find no one therein, enter them not, until permission is given to you; -- and if it is said to you, Go back, then go back; this is purer for you. And Allah is Knower of what you do.

24:29. It is no sin for you to enter uninhabited houses wherein you have your necessaries. And Allah knows what you do openly and what you hide.

24:30. Say to the believing men that they lower their gaze and restrain their sexual passions. That is purer for them. Surely Allah is Aware of what they do.

24:31. And say to the believing women that they lower their gaze and restrain their sexual passions and do not display their adornment except what appears thereof. -- And let them wear their head-coverings over their bosoms. And they should not display their adornment except to their husbands or their fathers, or the fathers of their husbands, or their sons, or the sons of their husbands, or their brothers, or their brothers' sons, or their sisters' sons, or their women, or those whom their -- right hands possess, or guileless male servants, or the children who know not women's nakedness. And let them not strike their feet so that the adornment that they hide may be known. And turn to Allah all, O believers, so that you may be

عَلَىٰ أَهْلِهَا ذَٰلِكُمْ خَيْرٌ لَكُمْ لَعَلَّكُمْ تَذَكَّرُونَ (٢٧)

فَإِنْ لَمْ تَجِدُوا فِيهَا أَحَدًا فَلَا تَدْخُلُوهَا حَتَّىٰ يُؤْذَنَ لَكُمْ وَإِنْ قِيلَ لَكُمُ ارْجِعُوا فَارْجِعُوا هُوَ أَزْكَىٰ لَكُمْ وَاللَّهُ بِمَا تَعْمَلُونَ عَلِيمٌ (٢٨)

لَيْسَ عَلَيْكُمْ جُنَاحٌ أَنْ تَدْخُلُوا بُيُوتًا غَيْرَ مَسْكُونَةٍ فِيهَا مَتَاعٌ لَكُمْ وَاللَّهُ يَعْلَمُ مَا تُبْدُونَ وَمَا تَكْتُمُونَ (٢٩)

قُلْ لِلْمُؤْمِنِينَ يَغُضُّوا مِنْ أَبْصَارِهِمْ وَيَحْفَظُوا فُرُوجَهُمْ ذَٰلِكَ أَزْكَىٰ لَهُمْ إِنَّ اللَّهَ خَبِيرٌ بِمَا يَصْنَعُونَ (٣٠)

وَقُلْ لِلْمُؤْمِنَاتِ يَغْضُضْنَ مِنْ أَبْصَارِهِنَّ وَيَحْفَظْنَ فُرُوجَهُنَّ وَلَا يُبْدِينَ زِينَتَهُنَّ إِلَّا مَا ظَهَرَ مِنْهَا وَلْيَضْرِبْنَ بِخُمُرِهِنَّ عَلَىٰ جُيُوبِهِنَّ وَلَا يُبْدِينَ زِينَتَهُنَّ إِلَّا لِبُعُولَتِهِنَّ أَوْ آبَائِهِنَّ أَوْ آبَاءِ بُعُولَتِهِنَّ أَوْ أَبْنَائِهِنَّ أَوْ أَبْنَاءِ بُعُولَتِهِنَّ أَوْ إِخْوَانِهِنَّ أَوْ بَنِي إِخْوَانِهِنَّ أَوْ بَنِي أَخَوَاتِهِنَّ أَوْ نِسَائِهِنَّ أَوْ مَا مَلَكَتْ أَيْمَانُهُنَّ أَوِ التَّابِعِينَ غَيْرِ أُولِي الْإِرْبَةِ مِنَ الرِّجَالِ أَوِ الطِّفْلِ الَّذِينَ لَمْ يَظْهَرُوا عَلَىٰ عَوْرَاتِ النِّسَاءِ وَلَا يَضْرِبْنَ بِأَرْجُلِهِنَّ لِيُعْلَمَ مَا يُخْفِينَ مِنْ زِينَتِهِنَّ وَتُوبُوا إِلَى اللَّهِ جَمِيعًا أَيُّهَ الْمُؤْمِنُونَ لَعَلَّكُمْ تُفْلِحُونَ (٣١)

وَأَنْكِحُوا الْأَيَامَىٰ مِنْكُمْ وَالصَّالِحِينَ مِنْ عِبَادِكُمْ وَإِمَائِكُمْ إِنْ يَكُونُوا فُقَرَاءَ يُغْنِهِمُ اللَّهُ مِنْ فَضْلِهِ وَاللَّهُ وَاسِعٌ عَلِيمٌ (٣٢)

وَلْيَسْتَعْفِفِ الَّذِينَ لَا يَجِدُونَ نِكَاحًا حَتَّىٰ يُغْنِيَهُمُ اللَّهُ مِنْ فَضْلِهِ وَالَّذِينَ يَبْتَغُونَ الْكِتَابَ مِمَّا مَلَكَتْ أَيْمَانُكُمْ

successful.

24:32. And marry those among you who are single, and those who are fit among your male slaves and your female slaves. If they are needy, Allah will make them free from want out of His grace. And Allah is Ample-giving, Knowing.

24:33. And let those who cannot find a match keep chaste, until Allah makes them free from want out of His grace. And those of your slaves who ask for a writing (of freedom), give them the writing, if you know any good in them, and give them of the wealth of Allah which He has given you. And compel not your slave-girls to prostitution when they desire to keep chaste, in order to seek the frail goods of this world's life. And whoever compels them, then surely after their compulsion Allah is Forgiving, Merciful.

24:34. And certainly We have sent to you clear messages and a description of those who passed away before you, and an admonition to those who guard against evil.

* * *

24:35. Allah is the light of the heavens and the earth. A likeness of His light is as a pillar on which is a lamp -- the lamp is in a glass, the glass is as it were a brightly shining star -- lit from a blessed olive-tree, neither eastern nor western, the oil whereof gives light, though fire touch it not -- light upon light. Allah guides to His light whom He pleases. And Allah sets forth parables for men, and Allah is Knower of all things --

24:36. (It is) in houses which Allah has permitted to be exalted and His name to be remembered therein. Therein do glorify Him, in the mornings and the evenings,

24:37. Men whom neither merchandise nor selling diverts -- from the

24. The Light

remembrance of Allah and the keeping up -- of prayer and the paying of the poor-rate -- they fear a day in which the hearts and the eyes will turn about,
24:38. That Allah may give them the best reward for what they did, and give them more out of His grace. And Allah provides without measure for whom He pleases.
24:39. And those who disbelieve, their deeds are as a mirage in a desert, which the thirsty man deems to be water, until, when he comes to it, he finds it naught, and he finds Allah with him, so He pays him his due. And Allah is Swift at reckoning --
24:40. Or like darkness in the deep sea there covers him a wave, above which is a wave, above which is a cloud -- (layers of) darkness one above another -- when he holds out his hand, he is almost unable to see it. And to whom Allah gives not light, he has no light.

***

24:41. Seest thou not that Allah is He, Whom do glorify all those who are in the heavens and the earth, and the birds with wings outspread? Each one knows its prayer and its glorification. And Allah is Knower of what they do.
24:42. And Allah's is the kingdom of the heavens and the earth, and to Allah is the eventual coming.
24:43. Seest thou not that Allah drives along the clouds, then gathers them together, then piles them up, so that thou seest the rain coming forth from their midst? And He sends down from the heaven (clouds like) mountains, wherein is hail, afflicting therewith whom He pleases and turning it away from whom He pleases. The flash of His lightning almost takes away the sight.
24:44. Allah causes the night and the day to succeed one another. Surely there is a lesson in this for those who have sight.

ظُلُمَاتٌ بَعْضُهَا فَوْقَ بَعْضٍ إِذَا أَخْرَجَ يَدَهُ لَمْ يَكَدْ يَرَاهَا وَمَنْ لَمْ يَجْعَلِ اللَّهُ لَهُ نُورًا فَمَا لَهُ مِنْ نُورٍ (٤٠)

أَلَمْ تَرَ أَنَّ اللَّهَ يُسَبِّحُ لَهُ مَنْ فِي السَّمَاوَاتِ وَالْأَرْضِ وَالطَّيْرُ صَافَّاتٍ كُلٌّ قَدْ عَلِمَ صَلَاتَهُ وَتَسْبِيحَهُ وَاللَّهُ عَلِيمٌ بِمَا يَفْعَلُونَ (٤١)

وَلِلَّهِ مُلْكُ السَّمَاوَاتِ وَالْأَرْضِ وَإِلَى اللَّهِ الْمَصِيرُ (٤٢)

أَلَمْ تَرَ أَنَّ اللَّهَ يُزْجِي سَحَابًا ثُمَّ يُؤَلِّفُ بَيْنَهُ ثُمَّ يَجْعَلُهُ رُكَامًا فَتَرَى الْوَدْقَ يَخْرُجُ مِنْ خِلَالِهِ وَيُنَزِّلُ مِنَ السَّمَاءِ مِنْ جِبَالٍ فِيهَا مِنْ بَرَدٍ فَيُصِيبُ بِهِ مَنْ يَشَاءُ وَيَصْرِفُهُ عَنْ مَنْ يَشَاءُ يَكَادُ سَنَا بَرْقِهِ يَذْهَبُ بِالْأَبْصَارِ (٤٣)

يُقَلِّبُ اللَّهُ اللَّيْلَ وَالنَّهَارَ إِنَّ فِي ذَلِكَ لَعِبْرَةً لِأُولِي الْأَبْصَارِ (٤٤)

وَاللَّهُ خَلَقَ كُلَّ دَابَّةٍ مِنْ مَاءٍ فَمِنْهُمْ مَنْ يَمْشِي عَلَى بَطْنِهِ وَمِنْهُمْ مَنْ يَمْشِي عَلَى رِجْلَيْنِ وَمِنْهُمْ مَنْ يَمْشِي عَلَى أَرْبَعٍ يَخْلُقُ اللَّهُ مَا يَشَاءُ إِنَّ اللَّهَ عَلَى كُلِّ شَيْءٍ قَدِيرٌ (٤٥)

لَقَدْ أَنْزَلْنَا آيَاتٍ مُبَيِّنَاتٍ وَاللَّهُ يَهْدِي مَنْ يَشَاءُ إِلَى صِرَاطٍ مُسْتَقِيمٍ (٤٦)

وَيَقُولُونَ آمَنَّا بِاللَّهِ وَبِالرَّسُولِ وَأَطَعْنَا ثُمَّ يَتَوَلَّى فَرِيقٌ مِنْهُمْ مِنْ بَعْدِ ذَلِكَ وَمَا أُولَئِكَ بِالْمُؤْمِنِينَ (٤٧)

وَإِذَا دُعُوا إِلَى اللَّهِ وَرَسُولِهِ لِيَحْكُمَ بَيْنَهُمْ إِذَا فَرِيقٌ مِنْهُمْ مُعْرِضُونَ (٤٨)

وَإِنْ يَكُنْ لَهُمُ الْحَقُّ يَأْتُوا إِلَيْهِ مُذْعِنِينَ (٤٩)

24. The Light

24:45. And Allah has created every animal of water. So of them is that which crawls upon its belly, and of them is that which walks upon two feet, and of them is that which walks upon four. Allah creates what He pleases. Surely Allah is Possessor of power over all things.

24:46. We have indeed revealed clear messages. And Allah guides whom He pleases to the right way.

24:47. And they say: We believe in Allah and in the Messenger and we obey then a party of them turn away after this, and they are not believers.

24:48. And when they are invited to Allah and His Messenger that he may judge between them, lo a party of them turn aside.

24:49. And if the right is on their side, they hasten to him in submission.

24:50. Is there in their hearts a disease, or are they in doubt, or fear they that Allah and His Messenger will deal with them unjustly? Nay! they themselves are; the wrongdoers.

* * *

24:51. The response of the believers, when they are invited to Allah and His Messenger that he may judge between them, is only that they say: We hear and we obey. And these it is that are successful.

* * *

24:52. And he who obeys Allah and His Messenger, and fears Allah and keeps duty to Him, these it is that are the achievers.

24:53. And they swear by Allah with their strongest oaths that, if thou command them, they would certainly go forth. Say: Swear not; reasonable obedience (is desired). Surely Allah is Aware of what you do.

24:54. Say: Obey Allah and obey the Messenger. But if you turn away, he is responsible for the duty imposed on him, and you are responsible for the

24. The Light

duty imposed on you. And if you obey him, you go aright. And the Messenger's duty is only to deliver (the message) plainly.

24:55. Allah has promised to those of you who believe and do good that He will surely make them rulers in the earth as He made those before them rulers and that He will surely establish for them their religion, which He has chosen for them, and that He will surely give them security in exchange after their fear. They will serve Me, not associating aught with Me. And whoever is ungrateful after this, they are the transgressors.

24:56. And keep up prayer and pay the poor-rate and obey the Messenger, so that mercy may be shown to you.

24:57. Think not that those who disbelieve will weaken (the Truth) in the earth; and their abode is the Fire. And it is indeed an evil resort

* * *

24:58. O you who believe, let those whom your right hands possess and those of you who have not attained to puberty ask permission of you three times: Before the morning prayer, and when you put off your clothes for the heat of noon, and after the prayer of night. These are three times of privacy for you; besides these it is no sin for you nor for them -- some of you go round about (waiting) upon others. Thus does Allah make clear to you the messages. And Allah is Knowing, Wise.

24:59. And when the children among you attain to puberty, let them seek permission as those before them sought permission. Thus does Allah make clear to you His messages. And Allah is Knowing, Wise.

24:60. And (as for) women past childbearing, who hope not for marriage, it is no sin for them if they put off their clothes without displaying their adornment. And if they are modest, it is better for them. And Allah is Hearing, Knowing.

24:61. There is no blame on the blind man, nor any blame on the lame, nor blame on the sick, nor on yourselves that you eat in your own houses, or your fathers' houses, or your mothers' houses, or your brothers' houses, or your sisters' houses; or your paternal uncles' houses, or your paternal aunts' houses, or your maternal uncles' houses, or your maternal aunts' houses, or (houses) whereof you possess the keys, or your friends' (houses). It is no sin in you that you eat together or separately. So when you enter houses, greet your people with a salutation from Allah, blessed (and) goodly. Thus does Allah make clear to you the messages that you may understand.

* * *

24:62. Only those are believers who believe in Allah and His Messenger, and when they are with him on a momentous affair, they go not away until they have asked leave of him. Surely they who ask leave of thee, are they who believe in Allah and His Messenger; so when they ask leave of thee for some affair of theirs, give leave to whom thou wilt of them, and ask forgiveness for them from Allah. Surely Allah is Forgiving, Merciful.

24:63. Make not the calling among you of the Messenger as your calling one of another. Allah indeed knows those who steal away from among you, concealing themselves. So let those who go against his order beware, lest a trial afflict them or there befall them a painful chastisement.

24:64. Now surely Allah's is whatever is in the heavens and the earth. He knows indeed your condition. And on the day when they are returned to Him, He will inform them of what they did. And Allah is Knower of all things.

وَاسْتَغْفِرْ لَهُمُ اللَّهَ إِنَّ اللَّهَ غَفُورٌ رَحِيمٌ (٦٢)

لَا تَجْعَلُوا دُعَاءَ الرَّسُولِ بَيْنَكُمْ كَدُعَاءِ بَعْضِكُمْ بَعْضًا قَدْ يَعْلَمُ اللَّهُ الَّذِينَ يَتَسَلَّلُونَ مِنْكُمْ لِوَاذًا فَلْيَحْذَرِ الَّذِينَ يُخَالِفُونَ عَنْ أَمْرِهِ أَنْ تُصِيبَهُمْ فِتْنَةٌ أَوْ يُصِيبَهُمْ عَذَابٌ أَلِيمٌ (٦٣)

أَلَا إِنَّ لِلَّهِ مَا فِي السَّمَاوَاتِ وَالْأَرْضِ قَدْ يَعْلَمُ مَا أَنْتُمْ عَلَيْهِ وَيَوْمَ يُرْجَعُونَ إِلَيْهِ فَيُنَبِّئُهُمْ بِمَا عَمِلُوا وَاللَّهُ بِكُلِّ شَيْءٍ عَلِيمٌ (٦٤)

25. The Discrimination

In the name of Allah, the Beneficent, the Merciful.

25:1. Blessed is He Who sent down the Discrimination upon His servant that he might be a warner to the nations --

25:2. He, Whose is the kingdom of the heavens and the earth, and Who did not take to Himself a son, and Who has no associate in the kingdom, and Who created everything, then ordained for it a measure.

25:3. And they take besides Him gods who create naught, while they are themselves created, and they control for themselves no harm nor profit, and they control not death, nor life, nor raising to life.

25:4. And those who disbelieve say this is nothing but a lie, which he has forged, and other people have helped him at it. So indeed they have brought an iniquity and a falsehood.

25:5. And they say Stories of the ancients, which he has got written, so they are read out to him morning and evening!

25:6. Say: He has revealed it, Who knows the secret of the heavens and the earth. Surely He is ever Forgiving, Merciful.

25:7. And they say: What a Messenger is this? He eats food and goes about in the markets. Why has not an angel been sent down to him to be a warner with him?

25:8. Or a treasure given to him, or a garden from which to eat? And the evildoers say: You follow but a man bewitched!

25:9. See what parables they set forth for thee -- they have gone astray, so they cannot find a way.

* * *

25:10. Blessed is He Who if He please, will give thee what is better than this: Gardens wherein flow rivers. And He

25. The Discrimination

will give thee palaces.

25:11. But they deny the Hour, and We have prepared a burning Fire for him who denies the Hour.

25:12. When it sees them from a faroff place, they will hear its raging and roaring.

25:13. And when they are cast into a narrow place thereof in chains, they will there pray for destruction.

25:14. Pray nor this day for destruction once but pray for destruction again and again.

25:15. Say: Is this better or the Garden of Perpetuity, which the dutiful are promised? That is a reward and a resort for them.

25:16. For them therein is what they desire, to abide. It is a promise to be prayed for from thy Lord.

25:17. And on the day when He will gather them, and that which they serve besides Allah, He will say: Was it you who led astray these My servants, or did they themselves stray from the path?

25:18. They will say: Glory be to Thee! it was not beseeming for us that we should take for protectors others besides Thee, but Thou didst make them and their fathers to enjoy until they forgot the Reminder, and they became a lost people.

25:19. So they will give you the lie in what you say, then you can neither ward off (evil), nor (obtain) help. And whoever among you does wrong, We shall make him taste a great chastisement.

25:20. And We did not send before thee any messengers but they surely ate food and went about in the markets. And We make some of you a trial for others. Will you bear patiently? And thy Lord is ever Seeing.

* * *

25:21. And those who look not for meeting with Us, say: Why have not

إِذَا رَأَتْهُمْ مِنْ مَكَانٍ بَعِيدٍ سَمِعُوا لَهَا تَغَيُّظًا وَزَفِيرًا (١٢)

وَإِذَا أُلْقُوا مِنْهَا مَكَانًا ضَيِّقًا مُقَرَّنِينَ دَعَوْا هُنَالِكَ ثُبُورًا (١٣)

لَا تَدْعُوا الْيَوْمَ ثُبُورًا وَاحِدًا وَادْعُوا ثُبُورًا كَثِيرًا (١٤)

قُلْ أَذَلِكَ خَيْرٌ أَمْ جَنَّةُ الْخُلْدِ الَّتِي وُعِدَ الْمُتَّقُونَ كَانَتْ لَهُمْ جَزَاءً وَمَصِيرًا (١٥)

لَهُمْ فِيهَا مَا يَشَاءُونَ خَالِدِينَ كَانَ عَلَى رَبِّكَ وَعْدًا مَسْئُولًا (١٦)

وَيَوْمَ يَحْشُرُهُمْ وَمَا يَعْبُدُونَ مِنْ دُونِ اللَّهِ فَيَقُولُ أَأَنْتُمْ أَضْلَلْتُمْ عِبَادِي هَؤُلَاءِ أَمْ هُمْ ضَلُّوا السَّبِيلَ (١٧)

قَالُوا سُبْحَانَكَ مَا كَانَ يَنْبَغِي لَنَا أَنْ نَتَّخِذَ مِنْ دُونِكَ مِنْ أَوْلِيَاءَ وَلَكِنْ مَتَّعْتَهُمْ وَآبَاءَهُمْ حَتَّى نَسُوا الذِّكْرَ وَكَانُوا قَوْمًا بُورًا (١٨)

فَقَدْ كَذَّبُوكُمْ بِمَا تَقُولُونَ فَمَا تَسْتَطِيعُونَ صَرْفًا وَلَا نَصْرًا وَمَنْ يَظْلِمْ مِنْكُمْ نُذِقْهُ عَذَابًا كَبِيرًا (١٩)

وَمَا أَرْسَلْنَا قَبْلَكَ مِنَ الْمُرْسَلِينَ إِلَّا إِنَّهُمْ لَيَأْكُلُونَ الطَّعَامَ وَيَمْشُونَ فِي الْأَسْوَاقِ وَجَعَلْنَا بَعْضَكُمْ لِبَعْضٍ فِتْنَةً أَتَصْبِرُونَ وَكَانَ رَبُّكَ بَصِيرًا (٢٠)

وَقَالَ الَّذِينَ لَا يَرْجُونَ لِقَاءَنَا لَوْلَا أُنْزِلَ عَلَيْنَا الْمَلَائِكَةُ أَوْ نَرَى رَبَّنَا لَقَدِ اسْتَكْبَرُوا فِي أَنْفُسِهِمْ وَعَتَوْا عُتُوًّا كَبِيرًا (٢١)

يَوْمَ يَرَوْنَ الْمَلَائِكَةَ لَا بُشْرَى يَوْمَئِذٍ لِلْمُجْرِمِينَ وَيَقُولُونَ حِجْرًا مَحْجُورًا (٢٢)

وَقَدِمْنَا إِلَى مَا عَمِلُوا مِنْ عَمَلٍ فَجَعَلْنَاهُ هَبَاءً مَنْثُورًا (٢٣)

25. The Discrimination

angels been sent down to us, or (why) do we not see our Lord? Indeed they are too proud of themselves and revolt in great revolt.

25:22. On the day when they will see the angels, there will be no good news for the guilty, and they will say: Let there be a strong barrier!

25:23. And We shall turn to the work they have done, so We shall render it as scattered motes.

25:24. The owners of the Garden will on that day be in a better abiding-place and a fairer resting-place.

25:25. And on the day when the heaven bursts asunder with clouds, and the angels are sent down, as they are sent.

25:26. The kingdom on that day rightly belongs to the Beneficent, and it will be a hard day for the disbelievers.

25:27. And on the day when the wrongdoer will bite his hands, saying: Would that I had taken a way with the Messenger!

25:28. O woe is me! would that I had not taken such a one for a friend!

25:29. Certainly he led me astray from the Reminder after it had come to me. And the devil ever deserts man.

25:30. And the Messenger will say My Lord, surely my people treat this Qur'an as a forsaken thing.

25:31. And thus have We made for every prophet an enemy from among the guilty, and sufficient is thy Lord as a Guide and a Helper.

25:32. And those who disbelieve say: Why has not the Qur'an been revealed to him all at once? Thus, that We may strengthen thy heart thereby and We have arranged it well in arranging.

25:33. And they cannot bring thee a question, but We have brought thee the truth and the best explanation.

25:34. Those who will be gathered to hell on their faces they are in an evil plight and straying farther away from the path.

أَصْحَابُ الْجَنَّةِ يَوْمَئِذٍ خَيْرٌ مُسْتَقَرًّا وَأَحْسَنُ مَقِيلًا (٢٤)

وَيَوْمَ تَشَقَّقُ السَّمَاءُ بِالْغَمَامِ وَنُزِّلَ الْمَلَائِكَةُ تَنْزِيلًا (٢٥)

الْمُلْكُ يَوْمَئِذٍ الْحَقُّ لِلرَّحْمَنِ وَكَانَ يَوْمًا عَلَى الْكَافِرِينَ عَسِيرًا (٢٦)

وَيَوْمَ يَعَضُّ الظَّالِمُ عَلَى يَدَيْهِ يَقُولُ يَا لَيْتَنِي اتَّخَذْتُ مَعَ الرَّسُولِ سَبِيلًا (٢٧)

يَا وَيْلَتَى لَيْتَنِي لَمْ أَتَّخِذْ فُلَانًا خَلِيلًا (٢٨)

لَقَدْ أَضَلَّنِي عَنِ الذِّكْرِ بَعْدَ إِذْ جَاءَنِي وَكَانَ الشَّيْطَانُ لِلْإِنْسَانِ خَذُولًا (٢٩)

وَقَالَ الرَّسُولُ يَا رَبِّ إِنَّ قَوْمِي اتَّخَذُوا هَذَا الْقُرْآنَ مَهْجُورًا (٣٠)

وَكَذَلِكَ جَعَلْنَا لِكُلِّ نَبِيٍّ عَدُوًّا مِنَ الْمُجْرِمِينَ وَكَفَى بِرَبِّكَ هَادِيًا وَنَصِيرًا (٣١)

وَقَالَ الَّذِينَ كَفَرُوا لَوْلَا نُزِّلَ عَلَيْهِ الْقُرْآنُ جُمْلَةً وَاحِدَةً كَذَلِكَ لِنُثَبِّتَ بِهِ فُؤَادَكَ وَرَتَّلْنَاهُ تَرْتِيلًا (٣٢)

وَلَا يَأْتُونَكَ بِمَثَلٍ إِلَّا جِئْنَاكَ بِالْحَقِّ وَأَحْسَنَ تَفْسِيرًا (٣٣)

الَّذِينَ يُحْشَرُونَ عَلَى وُجُوهِهِمْ إِلَى جَهَنَّمَ أُولَئِكَ شَرٌّ مَكَانًا وَأَضَلُّ سَبِيلًا (٣٤)

وَلَقَدْ آتَيْنَا مُوسَى الْكِتَابَ وَجَعَلْنَا مَعَهُ أَخَاهُ هَارُونَ وَزِيرًا (٣٥)

فَقُلْنَا اذْهَبَا إِلَى الْقَوْمِ الَّذِينَ كَذَّبُوا بِآيَاتِنَا فَدَمَّرْنَاهُمْ تَدْمِيرًا (٣٦)

وَقَوْمَ نُوحٍ لَمَّا كَذَّبُوا الرُّسُلَ أَغْرَقْنَاهُمْ وَجَعَلْنَاهُمْ لِلنَّاسِ آيَةً

25. The Discrimination

***

25:35. And certainly We gave Moses the Book and We appointed with him his brother Aaron, an aider.

25:36. Then We said: Go you both to the people who reject Our messages. So We destroyed them with utter destruction.

25:37. And the people of Noah, when they rejected the messengers, We drowned them, and made them a sign for men. And We have prepared a painful chastisement for the wrongdoers --

25:38. And 'Ad and Thamud and the dwellers of Rass and many generations in between.

25:39. And to each We gave examples and each did We destroy with utter destruction.

25:40. And indeed they pass by the town wherein was rained an evil rain. Do they not see it? Nay, they hope not to be raised again.

25:41. And when they see thee, they take thee for naught but a jest Is this he whom Allah has raised to be a messenger?

25:42. He had well-nigh led us astray from our gods had we not adhered to them patiently! And they will know, when they see the chastisement, who is mote astray from the path.

25:43. Hast thou seen him who takes his low desires for his god? Wilt thou be a guardian over him?

25:44. Or thinkest thou that most of them hear or understand? They are but as the cattle; nay, they are farther astray from the path.

***

25:45. Seest thou not how thy Lord extends the shade? And if He pleased, He would have made it stationary. Then We have made the sun an indication of it,

25:46. Then We take it to Ourselves, taking little by little.

25:47. And He it is Who made the night a covering for you, and sleep a rest, and He made the day to rise up again.

25:48. And He it is Who sends the winds as good news before His mercy and We send down pure water from the clouds,

25:49. That We may give life thereby to a dead land, and give it for drink to cattle and many people that We have created.

25:50. And certainly We repeat this to them that they may be mindful, but most men consent to naught but denying.

25:51. And if We pleased, We could raise a warner in every town.

25:52. So obey not the disbelievers, and strive against them a mighty striving with it.

25:53. And He it is Who has made the two seas to flow freely, the one sweet, very sweet, and the other saltish, bitter. And between the two He has made a barrier and inviolable obstruction.

25:54. And He it is Who has created man from water, then He has made for him blood-relationship and marriage-relationship. And thy Lord is ever Powerful.

25:55. And they serve besides Allah that which can neither profit them, nor harm them. And the disbeliever is ever an aider against his Lord.

25:56. And We have not sent thee but as a giver of good news and as a warner.

25:57. Say: I ask of you naught in return for it except that he who will may take a way to his Lord.

25:58. And rely on the Ever-Living Who dies not, and celebrate His praise. And sufficient is He as being Aware of His servants' sins,

25:59. Who created the heavens and the earth and what is between them in six periods, and He is established on the Throne of Power, the Beneficent. So ask

(٥١)
فَلَا تُطِعِ الْكَافِرِينَ وَجَاهِدْهُم بِهِ جِهَادًا كَبِيرًا (٥٢)
وَهُوَ الَّذِي مَرَجَ الْبَحْرَيْنِ هَذَا عَذْبٌ فُرَاتٌ وَهَذَا مِلْحٌ أُجَاجٌ وَجَعَلَ بَيْنَهُمَا بَرْزَخًا وَحِجْرًا مَحْجُورًا (٥٣)
وَهُوَ الَّذِي خَلَقَ مِنَ الْمَاءِ بَشَرًا فَجَعَلَهُ نَسَبًا وَصِهْرًا وَكَانَ رَبُّكَ قَدِيرًا (٥٤)
وَيَعْبُدُونَ مِن دُونِ اللَّهِ مَا لَا يَنفَعُهُمْ وَلَا يَضُرُّهُمْ وَكَانَ الْكَافِرُ عَلَى رَبِّهِ ظَهِيرًا (٥٥)
وَمَا أَرْسَلْنَاكَ إِلَّا مُبَشِّرًا وَنَذِيرًا (٥٦)
قُلْ مَا أَسْأَلُكُمْ عَلَيْهِ مِنْ أَجْرٍ إِلَّا مَن شَاءَ أَن يَتَّخِذَ إِلَى رَبِّهِ سَبِيلًا (٥٧)
وَتَوَكَّلْ عَلَى الْحَيِّ الَّذِي لَا يَمُوتُ وَسَبِّحْ بِحَمْدِهِ وَكَفَى بِهِ بِذُنُوبِ عِبَادِهِ خَبِيرًا (٥٨)
الَّذِي خَلَقَ السَّمَاوَاتِ وَالْأَرْضَ وَمَا بَيْنَهُمَا فِي سِتَّةِ أَيَّامٍ ثُمَّ اسْتَوَى عَلَى الْعَرْشِ الرَّحْمَنُ فَاسْأَلْ بِهِ خَبِيرًا (٥٩)
وَإِذَا قِيلَ لَهُمُ اسْجُدُوا لِلرَّحْمَنِ قَالُوا وَمَا الرَّحْمَنُ أَنَسْجُدُ لِمَا تَأْمُرُنَا وَزَادَهُمْ نُفُورًا (٦٠)
تَبَارَكَ الَّذِي جَعَلَ فِي السَّمَاءِ بُرُوجًا وَجَعَلَ فِيهَا سِرَاجًا وَقَمَرًا مُنِيرًا (٦١)
وَهُوَ الَّذِي جَعَلَ اللَّيْلَ وَالنَّهَارَ خِلْفَةً لِمَنْ أَرَادَ أَن يَذَّكَّرَ أَوْ أَرَادَ شُكُورًا (٦٢)
وَعِبَادُ الرَّحْمَنِ الَّذِينَ يَمْشُونَ عَلَى الْأَرْضِ هَوْنًا وَإِذَا خَاطَبَهُمُ

25. The Discrimination

respecting Him one aware.

25:60. And when it is said to them: Make obeisance to the Beneficent, they say: And what is the Beneficent? Shall we make obeisance to what thou biddest us? And it adds to their aversion.

* * *

25:61. Blessed is He Who made the stars in the heavens and made therein a sun and a moon giving light!

25:62. And He it is, Who made the night and the day to follow each other, for him who desires to be mindful or desires to be thankful.

25:63. And the servants of the Beneficent are they who walk on the earth in humility, and when the ignorant address them, they say, Peace!

25:64. And they who pass the night prostrating themselves before their Lord and standing.

25:65. And they who say Our Lord, avert from us the chastisement of hell; surely the chastisement thereof is a lasting evil:

25:66. It is surely an evil abode and resting-place!

25:67. And they who, when they spend are neither extravagant nor parsimonious, and the just mean is ever between these.

25:68. And they who call not upon another god with Allah and slay not the soul which Allah has forbidden, except in the cause of justice, nor commit fornication; and he who does this shall meet a requital of sin --

25:69. The chastisement will be doubled to him on the day of Resurrection, and he will abide therein in abasement --

25:70. Except him who repents and believes and does good deeds; for such Allah changes their evil deeds to good ones. And Allah is ever Forgiving, Merciful.

25:71. And whoever repents and does

الْجَاهِلُونَ قَالُوا سَلَامًا (٦٣) وَالَّذِينَ يَبِيتُونَ لِرَبِّهِمْ سُجَّدًا وَقِيَامًا (٦٤) وَالَّذِينَ يَقُولُونَ رَبَّنَا اصْرِفْ عَنَّا عَذَابَ جَهَنَّمَ إِنَّ عَذَابَهَا كَانَ غَرَامًا (٦٥) إِنَّهَا سَاءَتْ مُسْتَقَرًّا وَمُقَامًا (٦٦) وَالَّذِينَ إِذَا أَنْفَقُوا لَمْ يُسْرِفُوا وَلَمْ يَقْتُرُوا وَكَانَ بَيْنَ ذَلِكَ قَوَامًا (٦٧) وَالَّذِينَ لَا يَدْعُونَ مَعَ اللَّهِ إِلَهًا آخَرَ وَلَا يَقْتُلُونَ النَّفْسَ الَّتِي حَرَّمَ اللَّهُ إِلَّا بِالْحَقِّ وَلَا يَزْنُونَ وَمَنْ يَفْعَلْ ذَلِكَ يَلْقَ أَثَامًا (٦٨) يُضَاعَفْ لَهُ الْعَذَابُ يَوْمَ الْقِيَامَةِ وَيَخْلُدْ فِيهِ مُهَانًا (٦٩) إِلَّا مَنْ تَابَ وَآمَنَ وَعَمِلَ عَمَلًا صَالِحًا فَأُولَئِكَ يُبَدِّلُ اللَّهُ سَيِّئَاتِهِمْ حَسَنَاتٍ وَكَانَ اللَّهُ غَفُورًا رَحِيمًا (٧٠) وَمَنْ تَابَ وَعَمِلَ صَالِحًا فَإِنَّهُ يَتُوبُ إِلَى اللَّهِ مَتَابًا (٧١) وَالَّذِينَ لَا يَشْهَدُونَ الزُّورَ وَإِذَا مَرُّوا بِاللَّغْوِ مَرُّوا كِرَامًا (٧٢) وَالَّذِينَ إِذَا ذُكِّرُوا بِآيَاتِ رَبِّهِمْ لَمْ يَخِرُّوا عَلَيْهَا صُمًّا وَعُمْيَانًا (٧٣) وَالَّذِينَ يَقُولُونَ رَبَّنَا هَبْ لَنَا مِنْ أَزْوَاجِنَا وَذُرِّيَّاتِنَا قُرَّةَ أَعْيُنٍ وَاجْعَلْنَا لِلْمُتَّقِينَ إِمَامًا (٧٤) أُولَئِكَ يُجْزَوْنَ الْغُرْفَةَ بِمَا صَبَرُوا وَيُلَقَّوْنَ فِيهَا تَحِيَّةً وَسَلَامًا (٧٥) خَالِدِينَ فِيهَا حَسُنَتْ مُسْتَقَرًّا وَمُقَامًا (٧٦) قُلْ مَا يَعْبَأُ بِكُمْ رَبِّي لَوْلَا دُعَاؤُكُمْ فَقَدْ

good, he surely turns to Allah a (goodly) turning.

25:72. And they who witness no falsehood, and when they pass by what is vain, they pass by nobly.

25:73. And they who, when reminded of the messages of their Lord, fall not down thereat deaf and blind.

25:74. And they who say, Our Lord, grant us in our wives and our offspring the joy of our eyes, and make us leaders for those who guard against evil.

25:75. These are rewarded with high places because they are patient, and are met therein with greetings and salutation,

25:76. Abiding therein. Goodly the abode and the resting-place!

25:77. Say: My Lord would not care for you, were it not for your prayer. Now indeed you have rejected, so the punishment will come.

26. The Poets

In the name of Allah, the Beneficent, the Merciful.

26:1. Benignant, Hearing, Knowing God.

26:2. These are the verses of the Book that makes manifest.

26:3. Perhaps thou wilt kill thyself with grief because they believe not.

26:4. If We please, We could send down on them a sign from heaven, so that their necks would bend before it.

26:5. And there comes not to them a new Reminder from the Beneficent but they turn away from it.

26:6. They indeed reject, so the news will soon come to them of that at which they mock.

26:7. See they not the earth, how many of every noble kind We cause to grow in it?

26:8. surely in this is a sign; yet most of

26. The Poets

them believe not.
26:9. And surely thy Lord is the Mighty, the Merciful.

***

26:10. And when thy Lord called Moses, saying: Go to the iniquitous people
26:11. The people of Pharaoh. Will they nor guard against evil?
26:12. He said: My Lord, I fear that they will reject me.
26:13. And my breast straitens, and my tongue is not eloquent, so send for Aaron (too).
26:14. And they have a crime against me, so I fear that they will kill me.
26:15. He said: By no means; so go you both with Our signs surely We are with you, Hearing.
26:16. Then come to Pharaoh, and say: We are bearers of a message of the Lord of the worlds:
26:17. Send with us the Children of Israel.
26:18. (Pharaoh) said: Did we not bring thee up as a child among us, and thou didst tarry (many) years of thy life among us?
26:19. And thou didst (that) deed of thine which thou didst and thou art of the ungrateful ones.
26:20. He said: I did it then when I was of those who err.
26:21. So I fled from you when I feared you, then my Lord granted me judgment and made me of the messengers.
26:22. And is it a favour of which thou remindest me that thou hast enslaved the Children of Israel?
26:23. Pharaoh said: And what is the Lord of the worlds?
26:24. He said: The Lord of the heavens and the earth and what is between them, if you would be sure.
26:25. (Pharaoh) said to those around him: Do you not hear?
26:26. He said: Your Lord and the Lord

مُؤْمِنِينَ (٨)
وَإِنَّ رَبَّكَ لَهُوَ الْعَزِيزُ الرَّحِيمُ (٩)
وَإِذْ نَادَىٰ رَبُّكَ مُوسَىٰ أَنِ ائْتِ الْقَوْمَ الظَّالِمِينَ (١٠)
قَوْمَ فِرْعَوْنَ ۚ أَلَا يَتَّقُونَ (١١)
قَالَ رَبِّ إِنِّي أَخَافُ أَنْ يُكَذِّبُونِ (١٢)
وَيَضِيقُ صَدْرِي وَلَا يَنْطَلِقُ لِسَانِي فَأَرْسِلْ إِلَىٰ هَارُونَ (١٣)
وَلَهُمْ عَلَيَّ ذَنْبٌ فَأَخَافُ أَنْ يَقْتُلُونِ (١٤)
قَالَ كَلَّا ۖ فَاذْهَبَا بِآيَاتِنَا ۖ إِنَّا مَعَكُمْ مُسْتَمِعُونَ (١٥)
فَأْتِيَا فِرْعَوْنَ فَقُولَا إِنَّا رَسُولُ رَبِّ الْعَالَمِينَ (١٦)
أَنْ أَرْسِلْ مَعَنَا بَنِي إِسْرَائِيلَ (١٧)
قَالَ أَلَمْ نُرَبِّكَ فِينَا وَلِيدًا وَلَبِثْتَ فِينَا مِنْ عُمُرِكَ سِنِينَ (١٨)
وَفَعَلْتَ فَعْلَتَكَ الَّتِي فَعَلْتَ وَأَنْتَ مِنَ الْكَافِرِينَ (١٩)
قَالَ فَعَلْتُهَا إِذًا وَأَنَا مِنَ الضَّالِّينَ (٢٠)
فَفَرَرْتُ مِنْكُمْ لَمَّا خِفْتُكُمْ فَوَهَبَ لِي رَبِّي حُكْمًا وَجَعَلَنِي مِنَ الْمُرْسَلِينَ (٢١)
وَتِلْكَ نِعْمَةٌ تَمُنُّهَا عَلَيَّ أَنْ عَبَّدْتَ بَنِي إِسْرَائِيلَ (٢٢)
قَالَ فِرْعَوْنُ وَمَا رَبُّ الْعَالَمِينَ (٢٣)
قَالَ رَبُّ السَّمَاوَاتِ وَالْأَرْضِ وَمَا بَيْنَهُمَا ۖ إِنْ كُنْتُمْ مُوقِنِينَ (٢٤)
قَالَ لِمَنْ حَوْلَهُ أَلَا تَسْتَمِعُونَ (٢٥)
قَالَ رَبُّكُمْ وَرَبُّ آبَائِكُمُ الْأَوَّلِينَ (٢٦)
قَالَ إِنَّ رَسُولَكُمُ الَّذِي أُرْسِلَ إِلَيْكُمْ

26. The Poets

of your fathers of old.
26:27. (Pharaoh) said: Surely your messenger, who is sent to you, is mad.
26:28. He said: The Lord of the East and the West and what is between them, if you have any sense.
26:29. (Pharaoh) said: If thou takest a god besides me, I will certainly put thee in prison.
26:30. He said: Even if I show thee something plain?
26:31. (Pharaoh) said: Show it, then, if thou art of the truthful.
26:32. So he cast down his rod, and lo! it was an obvious serpent;
26:33. And he drew forth his hand, and lo! it appeared white to the beholders.

* * *

26:34. (Pharaoh) said to the chiefs around him: Surely this is a skilful enchanter,
26:35. Who desires to turn you out of your land with his enchantment. What is it then that you counsel?
26:36. They said: Give him and his brother respite and send heralds into the cities,
26:37. That they bring to thee every skilful enchanter.
26:38. So the enchanters were gathered together for the appointment of a well-known day,
26:39. And it was said to the people Will you gather together?
26:40. Haply we may follow the enchanters, if they are the vanquishers.
26:41. So when the enchanters came, they said to Pharaoh: Will there be a reward for us, if we are the vanquishers?
26:42. He said: Yes, and surely you will then be of those who are nearest (to me).
26:43. Moses said to them: Cast what you are going to cast.
26:44. So they cast down their cords and their rods and said: By Pharaoh's power we shall most surely be

26. The Poets

victorious.

26:45. Then Moses cast down his rod, and lo! it swallowed up their fabrication.

26:46. And the enchanters were thrown down prostrate --

26:47. They said: We believe in the Lord of the worlds,

26:48. The Lord of Moses and Aaron.

26:49. (Pharaoh) said: You believe in him before I give you leave; surely he is the chief of you who taught you enchantment, so you shall know. Certainly I will cut off your hands and your feet on opposite sides, and I will crucify you all.

26:50. They said: No harm; surely to our Lord we return.

26:51. We hope that out Lord will forgive us our wrongs because we are the first of the believers.

* * *

26:52. And We revealed to Moses, saying: Travel by night with My servants -- you will be pursued.

26:53. And Pharaoh sent heralds into the cities (proclaiming):

26:54. These are indeed a small band,

26:55. And they have surely enraged us:

26:56. And we are truly a vigilant multitude.

26:57. So We turned them out of gardens and springs,

26:58. And treasures and goodly dwellings --

26:59. Even so. And We gave them as a heritage to the Children of Israel.

26:60. Then they pursued them at sunrise.

26:61. So when the two hosts saw each other, the companions of Moses cried out: Surely we are overtaken.

26:62. He said: By no means; surely my Lord is with me -- He will guide me.

26:63. Then We revealed to Moses March on to the sea with thy staff. So it parted, and each party was like a huge

26. The Poets

mound.

26:64. And there We brought near the others.

26:65. And We saved Moses and those with him, all.

26:66. Then We drowned the others.

26:67. Surely there is a sign in this yet most of them believe not.

26:68. And surely thy Lord is the Mighty, the Merciful.

* * *

26:69. And recite to them the story of Abraham.

26:70. When he said to his sire and his people: What do you worship?

26:71. They said: We worship idols, so we shall remain devoted to them.

26:72. He said: Do they hear you when you call (on them),

26:73. Or do they benefit or harm you?

26:74. They said: Nay, we found our fathers doing so.

26:75. He said: Do you then see what you worship --

26:76. You and your ancient sires?

26:77. Surely they are an enemy to me, but not (so) the Lord of the worlds,

26:78. Who created me, then He shows me the way,

26:79. And Who gives me to eat and to drink,

26:80. And when I am sick, He heals me,

26:81. And Who will cause me to die, then give me life,

26:82. And Who, I hope, will forgive me my mistakes on the day of Judgment.

26:83. My Lord, grant me wisdom, and join me with the righteous,

26:84. And ordain for me a goodly mention in later generations,

26:85. And make me of the heirs of the Garden of bliss,

26:86. And forgive my sire, surely he is of the erring ones,

26:87. And disgrace me not on the day when they are raised --

(٦٥)
ثُمَّ أَغْرَقْنَا الْآخَرِينَ (٦٦)
إِنَّ فِي ذَٰلِكَ لَآيَةً وَمَا كَانَ أَكْثَرُهُمْ مُؤْمِنِينَ (٦٧)
وَإِنَّ رَبَّكَ لَهُوَ الْعَزِيزُ الرَّحِيمُ (٦٨)
وَاتْلُ عَلَيْهِمْ نَبَأَ إِبْرَاهِيمَ (٦٩)
إِذْ قَالَ لِأَبِيهِ وَقَوْمِهِ مَا تَعْبُدُونَ (٧٠)
قَالُوا نَعْبُدُ أَصْنَامًا فَنَظَلُّ لَهَا عَاكِفِينَ (٧١)
قَالَ هَلْ يَسْمَعُونَكُمْ إِذْ تَدْعُونَ (٧٢)
أَوْ يَنْفَعُونَكُمْ أَوْ يَضُرُّونَ (٧٣)
قَالُوا بَلْ وَجَدْنَا آبَاءَنَا كَذَٰلِكَ يَفْعَلُونَ (٧٤)
قَالَ أَفَرَأَيْتُمْ مَا كُنْتُمْ تَعْبُدُونَ (٧٥)
أَنْتُمْ وَآبَاؤُكُمُ الْأَقْدَمُونَ (٧٦)
فَإِنَّهُمْ عَدُوٌّ لِي إِلَّا رَبَّ الْعَالَمِينَ (٧٧)
الَّذِي خَلَقَنِي فَهُوَ يَهْدِينِ (٧٨)
وَالَّذِي هُوَ يُطْعِمُنِي وَيَسْقِينِ (٧٩)
وَإِذَا مَرِضْتُ فَهُوَ يَشْفِينِ (٨٠)
وَالَّذِي يُمِيتُنِي ثُمَّ يُحْيِينِ (٨١)
وَالَّذِي أَطْمَعُ أَنْ يَغْفِرَ لِي خَطِيئَتِي يَوْمَ الدِّينِ (٨٢)
رَبِّ هَبْ لِي حُكْمًا وَأَلْحِقْنِي بِالصَّالِحِينَ (٨٣)
وَاجْعَلْ لِي لِسَانَ صِدْقٍ فِي الْآخِرِينَ (٨٤)
وَاجْعَلْنِي مِنْ وَرَثَةِ جَنَّةِ النَّعِيمِ (٨٥)
وَاغْفِرْ لِأَبِي إِنَّهُ كَانَ مِنَ الضَّالِّينَ (٨٦)
وَلَا تُخْزِنِي يَوْمَ يُبْعَثُونَ (٨٧)
يَوْمَ لَا يَنْفَعُ مَالٌ وَلَا بَنُونَ (٨٨)

26:88. The day when wealth will not avail, nor sons,
26:89. Save him who comes to Allah with a sound heart.
26:90. And the Garden is brought near for the dutiful,
26:91. And hell is made manifest to the deviators,
26:92. And it is said to them: Where are those that you worshipped
26:93. Besides Allah? Can they help you or help themselves?
26:94. So they are hurled into it, they and the deviators,
26:95. And the hosts of the devil, all.
26:96. They will say, while they quarrel therein
26:97. By Allah We were certainly in manifest error,
26:98. When we made you equal with the Lord of the worlds.
26:99. And none but the guilty led us astray.
26:100. So we have no intercessors,
26:101. Nor a true friend.
26:102. Now, if we could but once return, we would be believers.
26:103. Surely there is a sign in this yet most of them believe not.
26:104. And surely thy Lord is the Mighty, the Merciful.

***

26:105. The people of Noah rejected the messengers.
26:106. When their brother Noah said to them: Will you not guard against evil?
26:107. Surely I am a faithful messenger to you:
26:108. So keep your duty to Allah and obey me.
26:109. And I ask of you no reward for it my reward is only with the Lord of the worlds.
26:110. So keep your duty to Allah and obey me.
26:111. They said: Shall we believe in thee and the meanest follow thee?

إِلَّا مَنْ أَتَى اللَّهَ بِقَلْبٍ سَلِيمٍ (٨٩)
وَأُزْلِفَتِ الْجَنَّةُ لِلْمُتَّقِينَ (٩٠)
وَبُرِّزَتِ الْجَحِيمُ لِلْغَاوِينَ (٩١)
وَقِيلَ لَهُمْ أَيْنَ مَا كُنْتُمْ تَعْبُدُونَ (٩٢)
مِنْ دُونِ اللَّهِ هَلْ يَنْصُرُونَكُمْ أَوْ يَنْتَصِرُونَ (٩٣)
فَكُبْكِبُوا فِيهَا هُمْ وَالْغَاوُونَ (٩٤)
وَجُنُودُ إِبْلِيسَ أَجْمَعُونَ (٩٥)
قَالُوا وَهُمْ فِيهَا يَخْتَصِمُونَ (٩٦)
تَاللَّهِ إِنْ كُنَّا لَفِي ضَلَالٍ مُبِينٍ (٩٧)
إِذْ نُسَوِّيكُمْ بِرَبِّ الْعَالَمِينَ (٩٨)
وَمَا أَضَلَّنَا إِلَّا الْمُجْرِمُونَ (٩٩)
فَمَا لَنَا مِنْ شَافِعِينَ (١٠٠)
وَلَا صَدِيقٍ حَمِيمٍ (١٠١)
فَلَوْ أَنَّ لَنَا كَرَّةً فَنَكُونَ مِنَ الْمُؤْمِنِينَ (١٠٢)
إِنَّ فِي ذَلِكَ لَآيَةً وَمَا كَانَ أَكْثَرُهُمْ مُؤْمِنِينَ (١٠٣)
وَإِنَّ رَبَّكَ لَهُوَ الْعَزِيزُ الرَّحِيمُ (١٠٤)
كَذَّبَتْ قَوْمُ نُوحٍ الْمُرْسَلِينَ (١٠٥)
إِذْ قَالَ لَهُمْ أَخُوهُمْ نُوحٌ أَلَا تَتَّقُونَ (١٠٦)
إِنِّي لَكُمْ رَسُولٌ أَمِينٌ (١٠٧)
فَاتَّقُوا اللَّهَ وَأَطِيعُونِ (١٠٨)
وَمَا أَسْأَلُكُمْ عَلَيْهِ مِنْ أَجْرٍ إِنْ أَجْرِيَ إِلَّا عَلَى رَبِّ الْعَالَمِينَ (١٠٩)
فَاتَّقُوا اللَّهَ وَأَطِيعُونِ (١١٠)
قَالُوا أَنُؤْمِنُ لَكَ وَاتَّبَعَكَ الْأَرْذَلُونَ (١١١)
قَالَ وَمَا عِلْمِي بِمَا كَانُوا يَعْمَلُونَ (١١٢)

26. The Poets

26:112. He said: And what knowledge have I of what they did?

26:113. Their reckoning is only with my Lord, if you but perceive.

26:114. And I am not going to drive away the believers

26:115. I am only a plain warner.

26:116. They said: If thou desist not, O Noah, thou wilt certainly be stoned to death.

26:117. He said: My Lord, my people give me the lie.

26:118. So judge Thou between me and them openly, and deliver me and the believers who are with me.

26:119. So We delivered him and those with him in the laden ark.

26:120. Then We drowned the rest afterwards.

26:121. Surely there is sign in this, yet most of them believe not.

26:122. And surely thy Lord is the Mighty, the Merciful.

* * *

26:123. 'Ad gave the lie to the messengers.

26:124. When their brother Hud said to them: Will you not guard against evil?

26:125. Surely I am a faithful messenger to you:

26:126. So keep your duty to Allah and obey me.

26:127. And I ask of you no reward for it; surely my reward is only with the Lord of the worlds.

26:128. Do you build on every height a monument? You (only) sport.

26:129. And you make fortresses that you may abide.

26:130. And when you seize, you seize as tyrants.

26:131. So keep your duty to Allah and obey me.

26:132. And keep your duty to Him Who aids you with that which you know --

26:133. He aids you with cattle and children

26:134. And gardens and fountains.
26:135. Surely I fear for you the chastisement of a grievous day.
26:136. They said: It is the same to us whether thou admonish, or art not one of the admonishers:
26:137. This is naught but a fabrication of the ancients:
26:138. And we will not be chastised.
26:139. So they rejected him, then We destroyed them. Surely there is a sign in this; yet most of them believe not.
26:140. And surely thy Lord is the Mighty, the Merciful;

* * *

26:141. Thamud gave the lie to the messengers.
26:142. When their brother Salih said to them: Will you not guard against evil?
26:143. Surely I am a faithful messenger to you:
26:144. So keep your duty to Allah and obey me.
26:145. And I ask of you no reward for it; my reward is only with the Lord of the worlds.
26:146. Will you be left secure in what is here,
26:147. In gardens and fountains,
26:148. And corn-fields and palm-trees having fine flower-spikes?
26:149. And you hew houses out of the mountains exultingly.
26:150. So keep your duty to Allah and obey me.
26:151. And obey not the bidding of the extravagant,
26:152. Who make mischief in the land and act nor aright.
26:153. They said: Thou art only a deluded person.
26:154. Thou art naught but a mortal like ourselves -- so bring a sign if thou art truthful.
26:155. He said: This is a she-camel she has her portion of water, and you have your portion of water at an appointed time.

إِنِّي أَخَافُ عَلَيْكُمْ عَذَابَ يَوْمٍ عَظِيمٍ (١٣٥)
قَالُوا سَوَاءٌ عَلَيْنَا أَوَعَظْتَ أَمْ لَمْ تَكُنْ مِنَ الْوَاعِظِينَ (١٣٦)
إِنْ هَذَا إِلَّا خُلُقُ الْأَوَّلِينَ (١٣٧)
وَمَا نَحْنُ بِمُعَذَّبِينَ (١٣٨)
فَكَذَّبُوهُ فَأَهْلَكْنَاهُمْ إِنَّ فِي ذَلِكَ لَآيَةً وَمَا كَانَ أَكْثَرُهُمْ مُؤْمِنِينَ (١٣٩)
وَإِنَّ رَبَّكَ لَهُوَ الْعَزِيزُ الرَّحِيمُ (١٤٠)
كَذَّبَتْ ثَمُودُ الْمُرْسَلِينَ (١٤١)
إِذْ قَالَ لَهُمْ أَخُوهُمْ صَالِحٌ أَلَا تَتَّقُونَ (١٤٢)
إِنِّي لَكُمْ رَسُولٌ أَمِينٌ (١٤٣)
فَاتَّقُوا اللَّهَ وَأَطِيعُونِ (١٤٤)
وَمَا أَسْأَلُكُمْ عَلَيْهِ مِنْ أَجْرٍ إِنْ أَجْرِيَ إِلَّا عَلَى رَبِّ الْعَالَمِينَ (١٤٥)
أَتُتْرَكُونَ فِي مَا هَاهُنَا آمِنِينَ (١٤٦)
فِي جَنَّاتٍ وَعُيُونٍ (١٤٧)
وَزُرُوعٍ وَنَخْلٍ طَلْعُهَا هَضِيمٌ (١٤٨)
وَتَنْحِتُونَ مِنَ الْجِبَالِ بُيُوتًا فَارِهِينَ (١٤٩)
فَاتَّقُوا اللَّهَ وَأَطِيعُونِ (١٥٠)
وَلَا تُطِيعُوا أَمْرَ الْمُسْرِفِينَ (١٥١)
الَّذِينَ يُفْسِدُونَ فِي الْأَرْضِ وَلَا يُصْلِحُونَ (١٥٢)
قَالُوا إِنَّمَا أَنْتَ مِنَ الْمُسَحَّرِينَ (١٥٣)
مَا أَنْتَ إِلَّا بَشَرٌ مِثْلُنَا فَأْتِ بِآيَةٍ إِنْ كُنْتَ مِنَ الصَّادِقِينَ (١٥٤)
قَالَ هَذِهِ نَاقَةٌ لَهَا شِرْبٌ وَلَكُمْ شِرْبُ

26. The Poets

26:156. And touch her not with evil, lest the chastisement of a grievous day overtake you.
26:157. But they hamstrung her, then regretted,
26:158. So the chastisement overtook them. Surely there is a sign in this yet most of them believe not.
26:159. And surely thy Lord is the Mighty, the Merciful.

* * *

26:160. The people of Lot gave the lie to the messengers.
26:161. When their brother Lot said to them: Will you not guard against evil?
26:162. Surely I am a faithful messenger to you:
26:163. So keep your duty to Allah and obey me.
26:164. And I ask of you no reward for it my reward is only with the Lord of the worlds.
26:165. Do you come to the males from among the creatures,
26:166. And leave your wives whom your Lord has created for you? Nay, you are a people exceeding limits.
26:167. They said: If thou desist not, O Lot, thou wilt surely be banished.
26:168. He said: Surely I abhor what you do.
26:169. My Lord, deliver me and my followers from what they do.
26:170. So We delivered him and his followers all,
26:171. Except an old woman, among those who remained behind.
26:172. Then We destroyed the others.
26:173. And We rained on them a rain, and evil was the rain on those warned.
26:174. Surely there is a sign in this yet most of them believe not.
26:175. And surely thy Lord is the Mighty, the Merciful.

* * *

26:176. The dwellers of the thicket gave the lie to the messengers.
26:177. When Shu'aib said to them: Will

يَوْمٍ مَعْلُومٍ (١٥٥)
وَلَا تَمَسُّوهَا بِسُوءٍ فَيَأْخُذَكُمْ عَذَابُ يَوْمٍ عَظِيمٍ (١٥٦)
فَعَقَرُوهَا فَأَصْبَحُوا نَادِمِينَ (١٥٧)
فَأَخَذَهُمُ الْعَذَابُ إِنَّ فِي ذَٰلِكَ لَآيَةً وَمَا كَانَ أَكْثَرُهُم مُّؤْمِنِينَ (١٥٨)
وَإِنَّ رَبَّكَ لَهُوَ الْعَزِيزُ الرَّحِيمُ (١٥٩)
كَذَّبَتْ قَوْمُ لُوطٍ الْمُرْسَلِينَ (١٦٠)
إِذْ قَالَ لَهُمْ أَخُوهُمْ لُوطٌ أَلَا تَتَّقُونَ (١٦١)
إِنِّي لَكُمْ رَسُولٌ أَمِينٌ (١٦٢)
فَاتَّقُوا اللَّهَ وَأَطِيعُونِ (١٦٣)
وَمَا أَسْأَلُكُمْ عَلَيْهِ مِنْ أَجْرٍ إِنْ أَجْرِيَ إِلَّا عَلَىٰ رَبِّ الْعَالَمِينَ (١٦٤)
أَتَأْتُونَ الذُّكْرَانَ مِنَ الْعَالَمِينَ (١٦٥)
وَتَذَرُونَ مَا خَلَقَ لَكُمْ رَبُّكُم مِّنْ أَزْوَاجِكُم بَلْ أَنتُمْ قَوْمٌ عَادُونَ (١٦٦)
قَالُوا لَئِن لَّمْ تَنتَهِ يَا لُوطُ لَتَكُونَنَّ مِنَ الْمُخْرَجِينَ (١٦٧)
قَالَ إِنِّي لِعَمَلِكُم مِّنَ الْقَالِينَ (١٦٨)
رَبِّ نَجِّنِي وَأَهْلِي مِمَّا يَعْمَلُونَ (١٦٩)
فَنَجَّيْنَاهُ وَأَهْلَهُ أَجْمَعِينَ (١٧٠)
إِلَّا عَجُوزًا فِي الْغَابِرِينَ (١٧١)
ثُمَّ دَمَّرْنَا الْآخَرِينَ (١٧٢)
وَأَمْطَرْنَا عَلَيْهِم مَّطَرًا فَسَاءَ مَطَرُ الْمُنذَرِينَ (١٧٣)
إِنَّ فِي ذَٰلِكَ لَآيَةً وَمَا كَانَ أَكْثَرُهُم مُّؤْمِنِينَ (١٧٤)
وَإِنَّ رَبَّكَ لَهُوَ الْعَزِيزُ الرَّحِيمُ

26. The Poets

you not guard against evil?
26:178. Surely I am a faithful messenger to you;
26:179. So keep your duty to Allah and obey me.
26:180. And I ask of you no reward for it; my reward is only with the Lord of the worlds.
26:181. Give full measure and be not of those who diminish.
26:182. And weigh with a true balance.
26:183. And wrong not men of their dues, and act not corruptly in the earth, making mischief.
26:184. And keep your duty to Him Who created you and the former generations.
26:185. They said: Thou art only a deluded person,
26:186. And thou art naught but a mortal like ourselves, and we deem thee to be a liar.
26:187. So cause a portion of heaven to fall on us, if thou art truthful.
26:188. He said: My Lord knows best what you do.
26:189. But they rejected him, so the chastisement of the day of Covering overtook them. Surely it was the chastisement of a grievous day!
26:190. Surely there is a sign in this yet must of them believe not.
26:191. And surely thy Lord is the Mighty, the Merciful.

* * *

26:192. And surely this is a revelation from the Lord of the worlds.
26:193. The Faithful Spirit has brought it
26:194. On thy heart that thou mayest be a warner,
26:195. In plain Arabic language.
26:196. And surely the same is in the Scriptures of the ancients.
26:197. Is it not a sign to them that the learned men of the Children of Israel know it?
26:198. And if We had revealed it to

(١٧٥) كَذَّبَ أَصْحَابُ الْأَيْكَةِ الْمُرْسَلِينَ (١٧٦) إِذْ قَالَ لَهُمْ شُعَيْبٌ أَلَا تَتَّقُونَ (١٧٧) إِنِّي لَكُمْ رَسُولٌ أَمِينٌ (١٧٨) فَاتَّقُوا اللَّهَ وَأَطِيعُونِ (١٧٩) وَمَا أَسْأَلُكُمْ عَلَيْهِ مِنْ أَجْرٍ إِنْ أَجْرِيَ إِلَّا عَلَى رَبِّ الْعَالَمِينَ (١٨٠) أَوْفُوا الْكَيْلَ وَلَا تَكُونُوا مِنَ الْمُخْسِرِينَ (١٨١) وَزِنُوا بِالْقِسْطَاسِ الْمُسْتَقِيمِ (١٨٢) وَلَا تَبْخَسُوا النَّاسَ أَشْيَاءَهُمْ وَلَا تَعْثَوْا فِي الْأَرْضِ مُفْسِدِينَ (١٨٣) وَاتَّقُوا الَّذِي خَلَقَكُمْ وَالْجِبِلَّةَ الْأَوَّلِينَ (١٨٤) قَالُوا إِنَّمَا أَنْتَ مِنَ الْمُسَحَّرِينَ (١٨٥) وَمَا أَنْتَ إِلَّا بَشَرٌ مِثْلُنَا وَإِنْ نَظُنُّكَ لَمِنَ الْكَاذِبِينَ (١٨٦) فَأَسْقِطْ عَلَيْنَا كِسَفًا مِنَ السَّمَاءِ إِنْ كُنْتَ مِنَ الصَّادِقِينَ (١٨٧) قَالَ رَبِّي أَعْلَمُ بِمَا تَعْمَلُونَ (١٨٨) فَكَذَّبُوهُ فَأَخَذَهُمْ عَذَابُ يَوْمِ الظُّلَّةِ إِنَّهُ كَانَ عَذَابَ يَوْمٍ عَظِيمٍ (١٨٩) إِنَّ فِي ذَلِكَ لَآيَةً وَمَا كَانَ أَكْثَرُهُمْ مُؤْمِنِينَ (١٩٠) وَإِنَّ رَبَّكَ لَهُوَ الْعَزِيزُ الرَّحِيمُ (١٩١) وَإِنَّهُ لَتَنْزِيلُ رَبِّ الْعَالَمِينَ (١٩٢) نَزَلَ بِهِ الرُّوحُ الْأَمِينُ (١٩٣) عَلَى قَلْبِكَ لِتَكُونَ مِنَ الْمُنْذِرِينَ (١٩٤)

26. The Poets

any of the foreigners,
26:199. And he had read it to them, they would not have believed in it.
26:200. Thus do We cause it to enter into the hearts of the guilty.
26:201. They will not believe in it till they see the painful chastisement:
26:202. So it will come to them suddenly, while they perceive not;
26:203. Then they will say: Shall we be respited?
26:204. Do they still seek to hasten on Our chastisement?
26:205. Seest thou, if We let them enjoy themselves for years,
26:206. Then that which they are promised comes to them
26:207. That which they were made to enjoy will not avail them?
26:208. And We destroyed no town but it had (its) warners
26:209. To remind. And We are never unjust.
26:210. And the devils have not brought it.
26:211. And it behoves them not, nor have they the power to do (it).
26:212. Surely they are far removed from hearing it.
26:213. So call not upon another god with Allah, lest thou be of those who are chastised.
26:214. And warn thy nearest relations,
26:215. And lower thy wing to the believers who follow thee.
26:216. But if they disobey thee, say I am clear of what you do.
26:217. And rely on the Mighty, the Merciful,
26:218. Who sees thee when thou standest up,
26:219. And thy movements among those who prostrate themselves.
26:220. Surely He is the Hearing, the Knowing.
26:221. Shall I inform you upon whom the devils descend?
26:222. They descend upon every lying,

بِلِسَانٍ عَرَبِيٍّ مُبِينٍ (١٩٥)
وَإِنَّهُ لَفِي زُبُرِ الْأَوَّلِينَ (١٩٦)
أَوَلَمْ يَكُنْ لَهُمْ آيَةً أَنْ يَعْلَمَهُ عُلَمَاءُ بَنِي إِسْرَائِيلَ (١٩٧)
وَلَوْ نَزَّلْنَاهُ عَلَى بَعْضِ الْأَعْجَمِينَ (١٩٨)
فَقَرَأَهُ عَلَيْهِمْ مَا كَانُوا بِهِ مُؤْمِنِينَ (١٩٩)
كَذَلِكَ سَلَكْنَاهُ فِي قُلُوبِ الْمُجْرِمِينَ (٢٠٠)
لَا يُؤْمِنُونَ بِهِ حَتَّى يَرَوُا الْعَذَابَ الْأَلِيمَ (٢٠١)
فَيَأْتِيَهُمْ بَغْتَةً وَهُمْ لَا يَشْعُرُونَ (٢٠٢)
فَيَقُولُوا هَلْ نَحْنُ مُنْظَرُونَ (٢٠٣)
أَفَبِعَذَابِنَا يَسْتَعْجِلُونَ (٢٠٤)
أَفَرَأَيْتَ إِنْ مَتَّعْنَاهُمْ سِنِينَ (٢٠٥)
ثُمَّ جَاءَهُمْ مَا كَانُوا يُوعَدُونَ (٢٠٦)
مَا أَغْنَى عَنْهُمْ مَا كَانُوا يُمَتَّعُونَ (٢٠٧)
وَمَا أَهْلَكْنَا مِنْ قَرْيَةٍ إِلَّا لَهَا مُنْذِرُونَ (٢٠٨)
ذِكْرَى وَمَا كُنَّا ظَالِمِينَ (٢٠٩)
وَمَا تَنَزَّلَتْ بِهِ الشَّيَاطِينُ (٢١٠)
وَمَا يَنْبَغِي لَهُمْ وَمَا يَسْتَطِيعُونَ (٢١١)
إِنَّهُمْ عَنِ السَّمْعِ لَمَعْزُولُونَ (٢١٢)
فَلَا تَدْعُ مَعَ اللَّهِ إِلَهًا آخَرَ فَتَكُونَ مِنَ الْمُعَذَّبِينَ (٢١٣)
وَأَنْذِرْ عَشِيرَتَكَ الْأَقْرَبِينَ (٢١٤)
وَاخْفِضْ جَنَاحَكَ لِمَنِ اتَّبَعَكَ مِنَ الْمُؤْمِنِينَ (٢١٥)

sinful one --
26:223. They give ear, and most of them are liars.
26:224. And the poets -- the deviators follow them.
26:225. Seest thou not that they wander in every valley,
26:226. And that they say that which they do not?
26:227. Except those who believe and do good and remember Allah much, and defend themselves after they are oppressed. And they who do wrong, will know to what final place of turning they will turn back.

27. The Naml

In the name of Allah, the Beneficent, the Merciful.
27:1. Benignant, Hearing God! These are the verses of the Qur'an and the Book that makes manifest:
27:2. A guidance and good news for the believers,
27:3. Who keep up prayer and pay the poor-rate, and they are sure of the Hereafter.
27:4. Those who believe not in the Hereafter, We make their deeds fair-seeming to them, but they blindly wander on.
27:5. These are they for whom is an evil chastisement, and in the Hereafter they

فَإِنْ عَصَوْكَ فَقُلْ إِنِّي بَرِيءٌ مِمَّا تَعْمَلُونَ (٢١٦)
وَتَوَكَّلْ عَلَى الْعَزِيزِ الرَّحِيمِ (٢١٧)
الَّذِي يَرَاكَ حِينَ تَقُومُ (٢١٨)
وَتَقَلُّبَكَ فِي السَّاجِدِينَ (٢١٩)
إِنَّهُ هُوَ السَّمِيعُ الْعَلِيمُ (٢٢٠)
هَلْ أُنَبِّئُكُمْ عَلَى مَنْ تَنَزَّلُ الشَّيَاطِينُ (٢٢١)
تَنَزَّلُ عَلَى كُلِّ أَفَّاكٍ أَثِيمٍ (٢٢٢)
يُلْقُونَ السَّمْعَ وَأَكْثَرُهُمْ كَاذِبُونَ (٢٢٣)
وَالشُّعَرَاءُ يَتَّبِعُهُمُ الْغَاوُونَ (٢٢٤)
أَلَمْ تَرَ أَنَّهُمْ فِي كُلِّ وَادٍ يَهِيمُونَ (٢٢٥)
وَأَنَّهُمْ يَقُولُونَ مَا لَا يَفْعَلُونَ (٢٢٦)
إِلَّا الَّذِينَ آمَنُوا وَعَمِلُوا الصَّالِحَاتِ وَذَكَرُوا اللَّهَ كَثِيرًا وَانْتَصَرُوا مِنْ بَعْدِ مَا ظُلِمُوا وَسَيَعْلَمُ الَّذِينَ ظَلَمُوا أَيَّ مُنْقَلَبٍ يَنْقَلِبُونَ (٢٢٧)

٢٧- سورة النمل

بِسْمِ اللَّهِ الرَّحْمَنِ الرَّحِيمِ
طس تِلْكَ آيَاتُ الْقُرْآنِ وَكِتَابٍ مُبِينٍ (١)
هُدًى وَبُشْرَى لِلْمُؤْمِنِينَ (٢)
الَّذِينَ يُقِيمُونَ الصَّلَاةَ وَيُؤْتُونَ الزَّكَاةَ وَهُمْ بِالْآخِرَةِ هُمْ يُوقِنُونَ (٣)
إِنَّ الَّذِينَ لَا يُؤْمِنُونَ بِالْآخِرَةِ زَيَّنَّا لَهُمْ أَعْمَالَهُمْ فَهُمْ يَعْمَهُونَ (٤)
أُولَئِكَ الَّذِينَ لَهُمْ سُوءُ الْعَذَابِ وَهُمْ فِي الْآخِرَةِ هُمُ الْأَخْسَرُونَ (٥)
وَإِنَّكَ لَتُلَقَّى الْقُرْآنَ مِنْ لَدُنْ حَكِيمٍ

are the greatest losers.

27:6. And thou art surely made to receive the Qur'an from the Wise, the Knowing.

27:7. When Moses said to his family Surely I see a fire; I will bring you news thence, or bring you therefrom a burning brand, so that you may warm yourselves.

27:8. So when he came to it, a voice issued, saying Blessed is he who is in search of fire and those around it. And glory be to Allah, the Lord of the worlds!

27:9. O Moses, surely I am Allah, the Mighty, the Wise:

27:10. And cast down thy rod. So when he saw it in motion as if it were a serpent, he turned back retreating and did not return. O Moses, fear not. Surely the messengers fear not in My presence --

27:11. Not he who does wrong, then does good instead after evil; surely I am Forgiving, Merciful,

27:12. And put thy hand into thy bosom, it will come forth white without evil, among nine signs to Pharaoh and his people. Surely they are a transgressing people.

27:13. So when Our clear signs came to them, they said This is clear enchantment.

27:14. And they denied them unjustly and proudly, while their souls were convinced of them. See then, what was the end of the mischief-makers

* * *

27:15. And certainly We gave knowledge to David and Solomon. And they said Praise be to Allah, Who has made us excel many of His believing servants!

27:16. And Solomon was David's heir, and he said: O men, we have been taught the speech of birds, and we have been granted of all things. Surely this is manifest grace.

27:17. And his hosts of the jinn and the men and the birds were gathered to Solomon, and they were formed into groups.
27:18. Until when they came to the valley of the Naml, a Namlite said: O Naml, enter your houses, (lest) Solomon and his hosts crush you, while they know not.
27:19. So he smiled, wondering at her word, and said My Lord, grant me that I may be grateful for Thy favour which Thou hast bestowed on me and on my parents, and that I may do good such as Thou art pleased with, and admit me, by Thy mercy, among Thy righteous servants.
27:20. And he reviewed the birds, then said How is it I see not Hudhud, or is it that he is one of the absentees?
27:21. I will certainly punish him with a severe punishment, or kill him, or he shall bring me a clear excuse.
27:22. And he tarried not long, then said: I have compassed that which thou hast not compassed and I have come to thee from Saba' with sure information --
27:23. I found a woman ruling over them, and she has been given of everything and she has a mighty throne.
27:24. I found her and her people adoring the sun instead of Allah, and the devil has made their deeds fair-seeming to them and turned them from the way, so they go not aright
27:25. So that they worship not Allah, Who brings forth what is hidden in the heavens and the earth and knows what you hide and what you proclaim.
27:26. Allah, there is no God but He, the Lord of the mighty Throne.
27:27. He said: We shall see whether thou speakest the truth or whether thou art a liar.
27:28. Take this my letter and hand it over to them, then turn from them and

نَمْلَةٌ يَا أَيُّهَا النَّمْلُ ادْخُلُوا مَسَاكِنَكُمْ لَا يَحْطِمَنَّكُمْ سُلَيْمَانُ وَجُنُودُهُ وَهُمْ لَا يَشْعُرُونَ (١٨)
فَتَبَسَّمَ ضَاحِكًا مِنْ قَوْلِهَا وَقَالَ رَبِّ أَوْزِعْنِي أَنْ أَشْكُرَ نِعْمَتَكَ الَّتِي أَنْعَمْتَ عَلَيَّ وَعَلَى وَالِدَيَّ وَأَنْ أَعْمَلَ صَالِحًا تَرْضَاهُ وَأَدْخِلْنِي بِرَحْمَتِكَ فِي عِبَادِكَ الصَّالِحِينَ (١٩)
وَتَفَقَّدَ الطَّيْرَ فَقَالَ مَا لِيَ لَا أَرَى الْهُدْهُدَ أَمْ كَانَ مِنَ الْغَائِبِينَ (٢٠)
لَأُعَذِّبَنَّهُ عَذَابًا شَدِيدًا أَوْ لَأَذْبَحَنَّهُ أَوْ لَيَأْتِيَنِّي بِسُلْطَانٍ مُبِينٍ (٢١)
فَمَكَثَ غَيْرَ بَعِيدٍ فَقَالَ أَحَطْتُ بِمَا لَمْ تُحِطْ بِهِ وَجِئْتُكَ مِنْ سَبَإٍ بِنَبَإٍ يَقِينٍ (٢٢)
إِنِّي وَجَدْتُ امْرَأَةً تَمْلِكُهُمْ وَأُوتِيَتْ مِنْ كُلِّ شَيْءٍ وَلَهَا عَرْشٌ عَظِيمٌ (٢٣)
وَجَدْتُهَا وَقَوْمَهَا يَسْجُدُونَ لِلشَّمْسِ مِنْ دُونِ اللَّهِ وَزَيَّنَ لَهُمُ الشَّيْطَانُ أَعْمَالَهُمْ فَصَدَّهُمْ عَنِ السَّبِيلِ فَهُمْ لَا يَهْتَدُونَ (٢٤)
أَلَّا يَسْجُدُوا لِلَّهِ الَّذِي يُخْرِجُ الْخَبْءَ فِي السَّمَاوَاتِ وَالْأَرْضِ وَيَعْلَمُ مَا تُخْفُونَ وَمَا تُعْلِنُونَ (٢٥)
اللَّهُ لَا إِلَهَ إِلَّا هُوَ رَبُّ الْعَرْشِ الْعَظِيمِ (٢٦)
قَالَ سَنَنْظُرُ أَصَدَقْتَ أَمْ كُنْتَ مِنَ الْكَاذِبِينَ (٢٧)
اذْهَبْ بِكِتَابِي هَذَا فَأَلْقِهْ إِلَيْهِمْ ثُمَّ تَوَلَّ عَنْهُمْ فَانْظُرْ مَاذَا يَرْجِعُونَ (٢٨)
قَالَتْ يَا أَيُّهَا الْمَلَأُ إِنِّي أُلْقِيَ إِلَيَّ كِتَابٌ كَرِيمٌ (٢٩)
إِنَّهُ مِنْ سُلَيْمَانَ وَإِنَّهُ بِسْمِ اللَّهِ الرَّحْمَنِ

27. The Naml

see what (answer) they return.

27:29. She said: O chiefs, an honourable letter has been delivered to me.

27:30. It is from Solomon, and it is in the name of Allah, the Beneficent, the Merciful

27:31. Proclaiming, Exalt not yourselves against me and come to me in submission.

* * *

27:32. She said: O chiefs, advise me respecting my affair; I never decide an affair uhtil you are in my presence.

27:33. They said: We are possessors of strength and possessors of mighty prowess. And the command is thine, so consider what thou wilt command.

27:34. She said: Surely the kings, when they enter a town, ruin it and make the noblest of its people to be low; and thus they do.

27:35. And surely I am going to send them a present, and to see what (answer) the messengers bring back.

27:36. So when (the envoy) came to Solomon, he said: Will you help me with wealth? But what Allah has given me is better than that which He has given you. Nay, you are exultant because of your present.

27:37. Go back to them, so we shall certainly come to them with hosts which they have no power to oppose, and we shall certainly expel them therefrom in disgrace, while they are abased.

27:38. He said: O chiefs, which of you can bring me her throne before they come to me in submission?

27:39. One audacious among the jinn said: I will bring it to thee before thou rise up from thy place; and surely I am strong, trusty for it --

27:40. One having knowledge of the Book said: I will bring it to thee in the twinkling of an eye. Then when he saw it settled beside him, he said: This is of the grace of my Lord, that He may try

27. The Naml

me whither I am grateful or ungrateful. And whoever is grateful, he is grateful only for his own soul, and whoever is ungrateful, then surely my Lord is Self-sufficient, Bountiful.

27:41. He said: Alter her throne for her; we may see 'whether she follows the right way or is of those who go not aright.

27:42. So when she came, it was said Was thy throne like this? She said: It is as it were the same; and we were given the knowledge before about it, and we submitted.

27:43. And that which she worshipped besides Allah prevented her; for she was of a disbelieving people.

27:44. It was said to her: Enter the palace. But when she saw it she deemed it to be a great expanse of water, and prepared herself to meet the difficulty. He said: Surely it is a palace made smooth with glass. She said: My Lord, surely I have wronged myself, and I submit with Solomon to Allah, the Lord of thu worlds.

***

27:45. And certainly We sent to Thamud their brother Salih, saying; Serve Allah. Then lo they became two parties, contending.

27:46. He said: O my people, why do you hasten on the evil before the good? Why do you not ask forgiveness of Allah so that you may have mercy?

27:47. They said: We augur evil of thee and those with thee. He said: Your evil augury is with Allah; nay, you are a people who are tried.

27:48. And there were in the city nine persons who made mischief in the land and did not act aright.

27:49. They said: Swear one to another by Allah that we shall attack him and his family by night, then we shall say to his heir: We witnessed not the destruction of his family, and we are surely truthful.

27:50. And they planned a plan, and We planned a plan, while they perceived not.

27:51. See, then, what was the end of their plan, that We destroyed them and their people, all (of them).

27:52. So those are their houses fallen down because they were iniquitous. Surely there is a sign in this for a people who know.

27:53. And We delivered those who believed and kept their duty.

27:54. And Lot, when he said to his people: Do you commit foul deeds, while you see?

27:55. Will you come to men lustfully rather than women? Nay, you are a people who act ignorantly.

27:56. But the answer of his people was naught except that they said: Drive out Lot's followers from your town; surely they are a people who would keep pure!

27:57. But We delivered him and his followers except his wife; We ordained her to be of those who remained behind.

27:58. And We rained on them a rain; so evil was the rain on those who had been warned.

* * *

27:59. Say: Praise be to Allah and peace on His servants whom He has chosen! Is Allah better, or what they associate (with Him,)?

* * *

27:60. Or, Who created the heavens and the earth, and sends down for you water from the cloud? Then We cause to grow thereby beautiful gardens -- it is not possible for you to make the trees thereof to grow. Is there a god with Allah? Nay, they are a people who deviate!

27:61. Or, Who made the earth a resting-place, and made in it rivers, and raised on it mountains, and placed between the two seas a barrier? Is there

وَأَنْتُمْ تُبْصِرُونَ (٥٤) أَئِنَّكُمْ لَتَأْتُونَ الرِّجَالَ شَهْوَةً مِنْ دُونِ النِّسَاءِ بَلْ أَنْتُمْ قَوْمٌ تَجْهَلُونَ (٥٥) فَمَا كَانَ جَوَابَ قَوْمِهِ إِلَّا أَنْ قَالُوا أَخْرِجُوا آلَ لُوطٍ مِنْ قَرْيَتِكُمْ إِنَّهُمْ أُنَاسٌ يَتَطَهَّرُونَ (٥٦) فَأَنْجَيْنَاهُ وَأَهْلَهُ إِلَّا امْرَأَتَهُ قَدَّرْنَاهَا مِنَ الْغَابِرِينَ (٥٧) وَأَمْطَرْنَا عَلَيْهِمْ مَطَرًا فَسَاءَ مَطَرُ الْمُنْذَرِينَ (٥٨) قُلِ الْحَمْدُ لِلَّهِ وَسَلَامٌ عَلَى عِبَادِهِ الَّذِينَ اصْطَفَى آللَّهُ خَيْرٌ أَمَّا يُشْرِكُونَ (٥٩) أَمَّنْ خَلَقَ السَّمَاوَاتِ وَالْأَرْضَ وَأَنْزَلَ لَكُمْ مِنَ السَّمَاءِ مَاءً فَأَنْبَتْنَا بِهِ حَدَائِقَ ذَاتَ بَهْجَةٍ مَا كَانَ لَكُمْ أَنْ تُنْبِتُوا شَجَرَهَا أَإِلَهٌ مَعَ اللَّهِ بَلْ هُمْ قَوْمٌ يَعْدِلُونَ (٦٠) أَمَّنْ جَعَلَ الْأَرْضَ قَرَارًا وَجَعَلَ خِلَالَهَا أَنْهَارًا وَجَعَلَ لَهَا رَوَاسِيَ وَجَعَلَ بَيْنَ الْبَحْرَيْنِ حَاجِزًا أَإِلَهٌ مَعَ اللَّهِ بَلْ أَكْثَرُهُمْ لَا يَعْلَمُونَ (٦١) أَمَّنْ يُجِيبُ الْمُضْطَرَّ إِذَا دَعَاهُ وَيَكْشِفُ السُّوءَ وَيَجْعَلُكُمْ خُلَفَاءَ الْأَرْضِ أَإِلَهٌ مَعَ اللَّهِ قَلِيلًا مَا تَذَكَّرُونَ (٦٢) أَمَّنْ يَهْدِيكُمْ فِي ظُلُمَاتِ الْبَرِّ وَالْبَحْرِ وَمَنْ يُرْسِلُ الرِّيَاحَ بُشْرًا بَيْنَ يَدَيْ رَحْمَتِهِ أَإِلَهٌ مَعَ اللَّهِ تَعَالَى اللَّهُ عَمَّا يُشْرِكُونَ (٦٣) أَمَّنْ يَبْدَأُ الْخَلْقَ ثُمَّ يُعِيدُهُ وَمَنْ يَرْزُقُكُمْ مِنَ السَّمَاءِ وَالْأَرْضِ أَإِلَهٌ مَعَ اللَّهِ قُلْ هَاتُوا بُرْهَانَكُمْ إِنْ كُنْتُمْ صَادِقِينَ (٦٤)

a god with Allah? Nay, most of them know not!

27:62. Or, Who answers the distressed one when he calls upon Him and removes the evil, and will make you successors in the earth? Is there a god with Allah? Little is it that you mind!

27:63. Or, Who guides you in the darkness of the land and the sea, and Who sends the winds as good news before His mercy? Is there a god with Allah? Exalted be Allah above what they associate (with Him)

27:64. Or, Who originates the creation, then reproduces it, and Who gives you sustenance from the heaven and the earth? Is there a god with Allah? Say Bring your proof, if you are truthful.

27:65. Say: No one in the heavens and the earth knows the unseen but Allah; and they know not when they will be raised.

27:66. Nay, their knowledge reaches not the Hereafter. Nay, they are in doubt about it. Nay, they are blind to it.

* * *

27:67. And those who disbelieve say: When we have become dust and our fathers (too), shall we indeed be brought forth?

27:68. We have certainly been promised this -- we and our fathers before; these are naught but stories of the ancients!

27:69. Say: Travel in the earth, then see what was the end of the guilty!

27:70. And grieve not for them, nor be distressed because of what they plan.

27:71. And they say: When will this promise come to pass, if you are truthful?

27:72. Say: Maybe somewhat of that which you seek to hasten has drawn nigh to you.

27:73. And surely thy Lord is full of grace to men, but most of them do not give thanks.

27:74. And surely thy Lord knows what

قُلْ لَا يَعْلَمُ مَنْ فِي السَّمَاوَاتِ وَالْأَرْضِ الْغَيْبَ إِلَّا اللَّهُ وَمَا يَشْعُرُونَ أَيَّانَ يُبْعَثُونَ (٦٥)

بَلِ ادَّارَكَ عِلْمُهُمْ فِي الْآخِرَةِ بَلْ هُمْ فِي شَكٍّ مِنْهَا بَلْ هُمْ مِنْهَا عَمُونَ (٦٦)

وَقَالَ الَّذِينَ كَفَرُوا أَئِذَا كُنَّا تُرَابًا وَآبَاؤُنَا أَئِنَّا لَمُخْرَجُونَ (٦٧)

لَقَدْ وُعِدْنَا هَذَا نَحْنُ وَآبَاؤُنَا مِنْ قَبْلُ إِنْ هَذَا إِلَّا أَسَاطِيرُ الْأَوَّلِينَ (٦٨)

قُلْ سِيرُوا فِي الْأَرْضِ فَانْظُرُوا كَيْفَ كَانَ عَاقِبَةُ الْمُجْرِمِينَ (٦٩)

وَلَا تَحْزَنْ عَلَيْهِمْ وَلَا تَكُنْ فِي ضَيْقٍ مِمَّا يَمْكُرُونَ (٧٠)

وَيَقُولُونَ مَتَى هَذَا الْوَعْدُ إِنْ كُنْتُمْ صَادِقِينَ (٧١)

قُلْ عَسَى أَنْ يَكُونَ رَدِفَ لَكُمْ بَعْضُ الَّذِي تَسْتَعْجِلُونَ (٧٢)

وَإِنَّ رَبَّكَ لَذُو فَضْلٍ عَلَى النَّاسِ وَلَكِنَّ أَكْثَرَهُمْ لَا يَشْكُرُونَ (٧٣)

وَإِنَّ رَبَّكَ لَيَعْلَمُ مَا تُكِنُّ صُدُورُهُمْ وَمَا يُعْلِنُونَ (٧٤)

وَمَا مِنْ غَائِبَةٍ فِي السَّمَاءِ وَالْأَرْضِ إِلَّا فِي كِتَابٍ مُبِينٍ (٧٥)

إِنَّ هَذَا الْقُرْآنَ يَقُصُّ عَلَى بَنِي إِسْرَائِيلَ أَكْثَرَ الَّذِي هُمْ فِيهِ يَخْتَلِفُونَ (٧٦)

وَإِنَّهُ لَهُدًى وَرَحْمَةٌ لِلْمُؤْمِنِينَ (٧٧)

إِنَّ رَبَّكَ يَقْضِي بَيْنَهُمْ بِحُكْمِهِ وَهُوَ الْعَزِيزُ الْعَلِيمُ (٧٨)

فَتَوَكَّلْ عَلَى اللَّهِ إِنَّكَ عَلَى الْحَقِّ الْمُبِينِ (٧٩)

إِنَّكَ لَا تُسْمِعُ الْمَوْتَى وَلَا تُسْمِعُ

their breasts conceal and what they manifest.

27:75. And there is nothing concealed in the heaven and the earth but it is in a clear book.

27:76. Surely this Qur'an declares to the Children of Israel most of that wherein they differ.

27:77. And surely it is a guidance and a mercy for the believers.

27:78. Truly thy Lord will judge between them by His judgment, and He is the Mighty, the Knowing.

27:79. So rely on Allah. Surely thou art on the plain truth.

27:80. Certainly thou canst not make the dead to hear the call, nor canst thou make the deaf to hear, when they go back retreating.

27:81. Nor canst thou lead the blind out of their error. Thou canst make none to hear except those who believe in Our messages, so they submit.

27:82. And when the word comes to pass against them, We shall bring forth for them a creature from the earth that will speak to them, because people did not believe in Our messages.

***

27:83. And the day when We gather from every nation a party from among those who rejected Our messages, then they will be formed into groups.

27:84. Until, when they come, He will say did you reject My messages, while you did not comprehend them in knowledge? Or what was it that you did?

27:85. And the word will come to pass against them because they were unjust, so they will not speak.

27:86. See they not that We have made the night that they may rest therein, and the day to give light? Surely there are signs in this for a people who believe.

27:87. And the day when the trumpet is blown, then those in the heavens and those in the earth will be struck with terror, except such as Allah please. And all shall come to Him abased.

27:88. And thou seest the mountains -- thou thinkest them firmly fixed -- passing away as the passing away of the cloud; the handiwork of Allah, Who has made everything thoroughly. Surely He is Aware of what you do.

27:89. Whoever brings good, he will have better than it; and they will be secure from terror that day.

27:90. And whoever brings evil, these will be thrown down on their faces into the Fire. Are you rewarded aught except for what you did?

27:91. I am commanded only to serve the Lord of this city, Who has made it sacred, and His are all things, and I am commanded to be of those who submit,

27:92. And to recite the Qur'an. So whoever goes aright, he goes aright for his own soul, and whoever goes astray -- say: I am only one of the warners.

27:93. And say: Praise be to Allah! He will show you His signs so that you shall recognize them. And thy Lord is not heedless of what you do.

28. The Narrative

In the name of Allah, the Beneficent, the Merciful.

28:1. Benignant, Hearing, Knowing God!

28:2. These are the verses of the Book that makes manifest.

28:3. We recite to thee the story of Moses and Pharaoh with truth, for a people who believe.

28:4. Surely Pharaoh exalted himself in the land and made its people into parties, weakening one party from among them; he slaughtered their sons and let their women live. Surely he was one of the mischief-makers.

28:5. And We desired to bestow a

28. The Narrative

favour upon those who were deemed weak in the land, and to make them the leaders, and to make them the heirs,

28:6. And to grant them power in the land, and to make Pharaoh and Haman and their hosts see from them what they feared.

28:7. And We revealed to Moses' mother, saying: Give him suck; then when thou fearest for him, cast him into the river and fear not, nor grieve surely We shall bring him back to thee and make him one of the messengers.

28:8. So Pharaoh's people took him up that he might be an enemy and a grief for them. Surely Pharaoh and Haman and their hosts were wrongdoers.

28:9. And Pharaoh's wife said: A refreshment of the eye to me and to thee -- slay him not maybe he will be useful to us, or we may take him for a son. And they perceived not.

28:10. And the heart of Moses' mother was free (from anxiety). She would almost have disclosed it, had We not strengthened her heart, so that she might be of the believers.

28:11. And she said to his sister: Follow him up. So she watched him from a distance, while they perceived not.

28:12. And We did not allow him to suck before, so she said: Shall I point out to you the people of a house who will bring him up for you, and they will wish him well?

28:13. So We gave him back to his mother that her eye might be refreshed, and that she might not grieve, and that she might know that the promise of Allah is true. But most of them know not.

* * *

28:14. And when he attained his maturity and became full-grown, We granted him wisdom and knowledge. And thus do We reward those who do good (to others).

28:15. And he went into the city at a

28. The Narrative

time of carelessness on the part of its people, so he found therein two men fighting -- one being of his party and the other of his foes; and he who was of his party cried out to him for help against him who was of his enemies, so Moses struck him with his fist and killed him. He said: This is on account of the devil's doing; surely he is an enemy, openly leading astray.

28:16. He said: My Lord, surely I have done harm to myself, so do Thou protect me; so He protected him. Surely He is the Forgiving, the Merciful.

28:17. He said: My Lord, because Thou hast bestowed a favour on me, I shall never be a backer of the guilty.

28:18. And he was in the city, fearing, awaiting, when lo, he who had asked his assistance the day before was crying out to him for help. Moses said to him: Thou art surely one erring manifestly.

28:19. So when he desired to seize him who was an enemy to them both, he said: O Moses, dost thou intend to kill me as thou didst kill a person yesterday? Thou only desirest to be a tyrant in the land, and thou desirest not to be of those who act aright.

28:20. And a man came running from the remotest part of the city. He said: O Moses, the chiefs are consulting together to slay thee, so depart (at once); surely I am of those who wish thee well.

28:21. So he went forth therefrom, fearing, awaiting. He said: My Lord, deliver me from the iniquitous people.

* * *

28:22. And when he turned his face towards Midian, he said: Maybe my Lord will guide me in the right path.

28:23. And when he came to the water of Midian, he found there a group of men watering, and he found besides them two women keeping back (their

28. The Narrative

flocks). He said: What is the matter with you? They said: We cannot water until the shepherds take away (their sheep) from the water; and our father is a very old man.

28:24. So he watered (their sheep) for them, then went back to the shade, and said: My Lord, I stand in need of whatever good Thou mayest send to me.

28:25. Then one of the two women came to him walking bashfully. She said: My father invites thee that he may reward thee for having watered for us. So when he came to him and related to him the story, he said: Fear not, thou art secure from the iniquitous people.

28:26. One of them said: O my father, employ him; surely the best of those that thou canst employ is the strong, the faithful one.

28:27. He said: I desire to marry one of these two daughters of mine to thee on condition that thou serve me for eight years; but, if thou complete ten, it will be of thy own free will; and I wish not to be hard on thee. If Allah please, thou wilt find me one of the righteous.

28:28. He said: That is (agreed) between me and thee; whichever of the two terms I fulfil, there will be no injustice to me; and Allah is surety over what we say.

***

28:29. Then when Moses had completed the term, and was travelling with his family, he perceived a fire on the side of the mountain. He said to his family: Wait, I see a fire; maybe I will bring to you from it some news or a brand of fire, so that you may warm yourselves.

28:30. And when he came to it, he was called from the right side of the valley in the blessed spot of the bush. O Moses, surely I am Allah, the Lord of the worlds

28:31. And cast down thy rod. So when

الْقَصَصَ قَالَ لَا تَخَفْ نَجَوْتَ مِنَ الْقَوْمِ الظَّالِمِينَ (٢٥)

قَالَتْ إِحْدَاهُمَا يَا أَبَتِ اسْتَأْجِرْهُ إِنَّ خَيْرَ مَنِ اسْتَأْجَرْتَ الْقَوِيُّ الْأَمِينُ (٢٦)

قَالَ إِنِّي أُرِيدُ أَنْ أُنكِحَكَ إِحْدَى ابْنَتَيَّ هَاتَيْنِ عَلَى أَنْ تَأْجُرَنِي ثَمَانِيَ حِجَجٍ فَإِنْ أَتْمَمْتَ عَشْرًا فَمِنْ عِندِكَ وَمَا أُرِيدُ أَنْ أَشُقَّ عَلَيْكَ سَتَجِدُنِي إِنْ شَاءَ اللَّهُ مِنَ الصَّالِحِينَ (٢٧)

قَالَ ذَلِكَ بَيْنِي وَبَيْنَكَ أَيَّمَا الْأَجَلَيْنِ قَضَيْتُ فَلَا عُدْوَانَ عَلَيَّ وَاللَّهُ عَلَى مَا نَقُولُ وَكِيلٌ (٢٨)

فَلَمَّا قَضَى مُوسَى الْأَجَلَ وَسَارَ بِأَهْلِهِ آنَسَ مِنْ جَانِبِ الطُّورِ نَارًا قَالَ لِأَهْلِهِ امْكُثُوا إِنِّي آنَسْتُ نَارًا لَعَلِّي آتِيكُمْ مِنْهَا بِخَبَرٍ أَوْ جَذْوَةٍ مِنَ النَّارِ لَعَلَّكُمْ تَصْطَلُونَ (٢٩)

فَلَمَّا أَتَاهَا نُودِيَ مِنْ شَاطِئِ الْوَادِ الْأَيْمَنِ فِي الْبُقْعَةِ الْمُبَارَكَةِ مِنَ الشَّجَرَةِ أَنْ يَا مُوسَى إِنِّي أَنَا اللَّهُ رَبُّ الْعَالَمِينَ (٣٠)

وَأَنْ أَلْقِ عَصَاكَ فَلَمَّا رَآهَا تَهْتَزُّ كَأَنَّهَا جَانٌّ وَلَّى مُدْبِرًا وَلَمْ يُعَقِّبْ يَا مُوسَى أَقْبِلْ وَلَا تَخَفْ إِنَّكَ مِنَ الْآمِنِينَ (٣١)

اسْلُكْ يَدَكَ فِي جَيْبِكَ تَخْرُجْ بَيْضَاءَ مِنْ غَيْرِ سُوءٍ وَاضْمُمْ إِلَيْكَ جَنَاحَكَ مِنَ الرَّهْبِ فَذَانِكَ بُرْهَانَانِ مِنْ رَبِّكَ إِلَى فِرْعَوْنَ وَمَلَئِهِ إِنَّهُمْ كَانُوا قَوْمًا فَاسِقِينَ (٣٢)

قَالَ رَبِّ إِنِّي قَتَلْتُ مِنْهُمْ نَفْسًا فَأَخَافُ أَنْ يَقْتُلُونِ (٣٣)

وَأَخِي هَارُونُ هُوَ أَفْصَحُ مِنِّي لِسَانًا

28. The Narrative

he saw it in motion as if it were a serpent, he turned away retreating, and looked not back. O Moses, come forward and fear not; surely thou art of those who are secure.

28:32. Insert thy hand into thy bosom, it will come forth white without evil, and remain calm in fear. These two are two arguments from thy Lord to Pharaoh and his chiefs. Surely they are a transgressing people.

28:33. He said: My Lord, I killed one of them, so I fear lest they slay me.

28:34. And my brother, Aaron, he is more eloquent in speech than I, so send him with me as a helper to confirm me. Surely I fear that they would reject me.

28:35. He said: We will strengthen thine arm with thy brother, and We will give you both an authority, so that they shall not reach you. With Our signs, you two and those who follow you, will triumph.

28:36. So when Moses came to them with Our clear signs, they said This is nothing but forged enchantment, and we never heard of it among out fathers of old!

28:37. And Moses said: My Lord knows best who comes with guidance from Him, and whose shall be the good end of the abode. Surely the wrongdoers will not be successful.

28:38. And Pharaoh said: O chiefs, I know no god for you besides myself; so kindle a fire for me, O Haman, on (bricks of) clay, then prepare for me a lofty building, so that I may obtain knowledge of Moses' God, and surely I think him a liar.

28:39. And he was unjustly proud in the land, he and his hosts, and they deemed that they would not be brought back to Us.

28:40. So We caught hold of him and his hosts, then We cast them into the sea, and see what was the end of the iniquitous.

فَأَرْسِلْهُ مَعِيَ رِدْءًا يُصَدِّقُنِي إِنِّي أَخَافُ أَنْ يُكَذِّبُونِ (٣٤)

قَالَ سَنَشُدُّ عَضُدَكَ بِأَخِيكَ وَنَجْعَلُ لَكُمَا سُلْطَانًا فَلَا يَصِلُونَ إِلَيْكُمَا بِآيَاتِنَا أَنْتُمَا وَمَنِ اتَّبَعَكُمَا الْغَالِبُونَ (٣٥)

فَلَمَّا جَاءَهُمْ مُوسَى بِآيَاتِنَا بَيِّنَاتٍ قَالُوا مَا هَذَا إِلَّا سِحْرٌ مُفْتَرًى وَمَا سَمِعْنَا بِهَذَا فِي آبَائِنَا الْأَوَّلِينَ (٣٦)

وَقَالَ مُوسَى رَبِّي أَعْلَمُ بِمَنْ جَاءَ بِالْهُدَى مِنْ عِنْدِهِ وَمَنْ تَكُونُ لَهُ عَاقِبَةُ الدَّارِ إِنَّهُ لَا يُفْلِحُ الظَّالِمُونَ (٣٧)

وَقَالَ فِرْعَوْنُ يَا أَيُّهَا الْمَلَأُ مَا عَلِمْتُ لَكُمْ مِنْ إِلَهٍ غَيْرِي فَأَوْقِدْ لِي يَا هَامَانُ عَلَى الطِّينِ فَاجْعَلْ لِي صَرْحًا لَعَلِّي أَطَّلِعُ إِلَى إِلَهِ مُوسَى وَإِنِّي لَأَظُنُّهُ مِنَ الْكَاذِبِينَ (٣٨)

وَاسْتَكْبَرَ هُوَ وَجُنُودُهُ فِي الْأَرْضِ بِغَيْرِ الْحَقِّ وَظَنُّوا أَنَّهُمْ إِلَيْنَا لَا يُرْجَعُونَ (٣٩)

فَأَخَذْنَاهُ وَجُنُودَهُ فَنَبَذْنَاهُمْ فِي الْيَمِّ فَانْظُرْ كَيْفَ كَانَ عَاقِبَةُ الظَّالِمِينَ (٤٠)

وَجَعَلْنَاهُمْ أَئِمَّةً يَدْعُونَ إِلَى النَّارِ وَيَوْمَ الْقِيَامَةِ لَا يُنْصَرُونَ (٤١)

وَأَتْبَعْنَاهُمْ فِي هَذِهِ الدُّنْيَا لَعْنَةً وَيَوْمَ الْقِيَامَةِ هُمْ مِنَ الْمَقْبُوحِينَ (٤٢)

وَلَقَدْ آتَيْنَا مُوسَى الْكِتَابَ مِنْ بَعْدِ مَا أَهْلَكْنَا الْقُرُونَ الْأُولَى بَصَائِرَ لِلنَّاسِ وَهُدًى وَرَحْمَةً لَعَلَّهُمْ يَتَذَكَّرُونَ (٤٣)

وَمَا كُنْتَ بِجَانِبِ الْغَرْبِيِّ إِذْ قَضَيْنَا إِلَى مُوسَى الْأَمْرَ وَمَا كُنْتَ مِنَ

28. The Narrative

28:41. And We made them leaders who call to the Fire, and on the day of Resurrection they will not be helped.

28:42. And We made a curse to follow them in this world, and on the day of Resurrection they will be hideous.

* * *

28:43. And certainly We gave Moses the Book after We had destroyed the former generations clear arguments for men and a guidance and a mercy, that they may be mindful.

28:44. And thou wast not on the western side when We revealed to Moses the commandment, nor wast thou among those present

28:45. But We raised up generations, then life became prolonged to them. And thou wast not dwelling among the people of Midian, reciting to them Our messages, but We are the Sender (of messengers).

28:46. And thou wast not at the side of the mountain when We called, but a mercy from thy Lord that thou mayest warn a people to whom no warner came before thee, that they may be mindful.

28:47. And lest, if a disaster should befall them for what their hands have sent before, they should say: Our Lord, why didst Thou not send to us a messenger so that we might have followed Thy messages and been of the believers?

28:48. But (now) when the Truth has come to them from Us, they say: Why is he not given the like of what was given to Moses? Did they not disbelieve in that which was given to Moses before? They say: Two enchantments backing up each other! And they say: Surely we are disbelievers in both.

28:49. Say: Then bring some (other) Book from Allah which is a better guide than these two, I will follow it if you are truthful.

28. The Narrative

28:50. But if they answer thee not, know that they only follow their low desires. And who is more erring than he who follows his low desires without any guidance from Allah? Surely Allah guides not the iniquitous people.

* * *

28:51. And certainly We have made the Word to have many connections for their sake, so that they may be mindful.
28:52. Those to whom We gave the Book before it, they are believers in it.
28:53. And when it is recited to them they say We believe in it; surely it is the Truth from our Lord; we were indeed before this submitting ones.
28:54. These will be granted their reward twice, because they are steadfast, and they repel evil with good and spend out of what We have given them.
28:55. And when they hear idle talk, they turn aside from it and say: For us are our deeds and for you your deeds. Peace be to you! We desire not the ignorant.
28:56. Surely thou canst not guide whom thou lovest, but Allah guides whom He pleases; and He knows best those who walk aright.
28:57. And they say: If we follow the guidance with thee, we should be carried off from our country. Have We not settled them in a safe, sacred territory to which fruits of every kind are drawn? A sustenance from Us but most of them know not.
28:58. And how many a town have We destroyed which exulted in its means of subsistence! So those are their abodes: they have not been dwelt in after them except a little. And We are ever the inheritors.
28:59. And thy Lord never destroyed the towns, until He had raised in their metropolis a messenger, reciting to them Our messages, and We never destroyed the towns except when their

وَمِمَّا رَزَقْنَاهُمْ يُنْفِقُونَ (٥٤)
وَإِذَا سَمِعُوا اللَّغْوَ أَعْرَضُوا عَنْهُ وَقَالُوا لَنَا أَعْمَالُنَا وَلَكُمْ أَعْمَالُكُمْ سَلَامٌ عَلَيْكُمْ لَا نَبْتَغِي الْجَاهِلِينَ (٥٥)
إِنَّكَ لَا تَهْدِي مَنْ أَحْبَبْتَ وَلَكِنَّ اللَّهَ يَهْدِي مَنْ يَشَاءُ وَهُوَ أَعْلَمُ بِالْمُهْتَدِينَ (٥٦)
وَقَالُوا إِنْ نَتَّبِعِ الْهُدَى مَعَكَ نُتَخَطَّفْ مِنْ أَرْضِنَا أَوَلَمْ نُمَكِّنْ لَهُمْ حَرَمًا آمِنًا يُجْبَى إِلَيْهِ ثَمَرَاتُ كُلِّ شَيْءٍ رِزْقًا مِنْ لَدُنَّا وَلَكِنَّ أَكْثَرَهُمْ لَا يَعْلَمُونَ (٥٧)
وَكَمْ أَهْلَكْنَا مِنْ قَرْيَةٍ بَطِرَتْ مَعِيشَتَهَا فَتِلْكَ مَسَاكِنُهُمْ لَمْ تُسْكَنْ مِنْ بَعْدِهِمْ إِلَّا قَلِيلًا وَكُنَّا نَحْنُ الْوَارِثِينَ (٥٨)
وَمَا كَانَ رَبُّكَ مُهْلِكَ الْقُرَى حَتَّى يَبْعَثَ فِي أُمِّهَا رَسُولًا يَتْلُو عَلَيْهِمْ آيَاتِنَا وَمَا كُنَّا مُهْلِكِي الْقُرَى إِلَّا وَأَهْلُهَا ظَالِمُونَ (٥٩)
وَمَا أُوتِيتُمْ مِنْ شَيْءٍ فَمَتَاعُ الْحَيَاةِ الدُّنْيَا وَزِينَتُهَا وَمَا عِنْدَ اللَّهِ خَيْرٌ وَأَبْقَى أَفَلَا تَعْقِلُونَ (٦٠)
أَفَمَنْ وَعَدْنَاهُ وَعْدًا حَسَنًا فَهُوَ لَاقِيهِ كَمَنْ مَتَّعْنَاهُ مَتَاعَ الْحَيَاةِ الدُّنْيَا ثُمَّ هُوَ يَوْمَ الْقِيَامَةِ مِنَ الْمُحْضَرِينَ (٦١)
وَيَوْمَ يُنَادِيهِمْ فَيَقُولُ أَيْنَ شُرَكَائِيَ الَّذِينَ كُنْتُمْ تَزْعُمُونَ (٦٢)
قَالَ الَّذِينَ حَقَّ عَلَيْهِمُ الْقَوْلُ رَبَّنَا هَؤُلَاءِ الَّذِينَ أَغْوَيْنَا أَغْوَيْنَاهُمْ كَمَا غَوَيْنَا تَبَرَّأْنَا إِلَيْكَ مَا كَانُوا إِيَّانَا يَعْبُدُونَ (٦٣)
وَقِيلَ ادْعُوا شُرَكَاءَكُمْ فَدَعَوْهُمْ فَلَمْ يَسْتَجِيبُوا لَهُمْ وَرَأَوُا الْعَذَابَ لَوْ أَنَّهُمْ كَانُوا يَهْتَدُونَ (٦٤)

28. The Narrative

people were iniquitous.

28:60. And whatever things you have been given are only a provision of this world's life and its adornment, and whatever is with Allah is better and more lasting. Do you not then understand?

* * *

28:61. Is he to whom We have promised a goodly promise, which he will meet with, like him whom We have provided with the provisions of this world's life, then on the day of Resurrection he will be of those brought up (for punishment)?

28:62. And the day when He will call them and say: Where are those whom you deemed to be My associates?

28:63. Those against whom the word has proved true will say: Our Lord, these are they whom we caused to deviate -- we caused them to deviate as we ourselves deviated. We declare our innocence before Thee. Us they never worshipped.

28:64. And it will be said: Call your associate-gods. So they will call upon them, but they will not answer them, and they will see the chastisement. Would that they had followed the right way.

28:65. And the day He will call them, then say: What was the answer you gave to the messengers?

28:66. On that day excuses will become obscure to them, so they will not ask each other.

28:67. But as to him who repents and believes and does good, maybe he will be among the successful.

28:68. And thy Lord creates and chooses whom He pleases. To choose is not theirs. Glory be to Allah and exalted be He above what they associate (with Him)!

28:69. And thy Lord knows what their breasts conceal and what they proclaim.

وَيَوْمَ يُنَادِيهِمْ فَيَقُولُ مَاذَا أَجَبْتُمُ الْمُرْسَلِينَ (٦٥)

فَعَمِيَتْ عَلَيْهِمُ الْأَنْبَاءُ يَوْمَئِذٍ فَهُمْ لَا يَتَسَاءَلُونَ (٦٦)

فَأَمَّا مَنْ تَابَ وَآمَنَ وَعَمِلَ صَالِحًا فَعَسَى أَنْ يَكُونَ مِنَ الْمُفْلِحِينَ (٦٧)

وَرَبُّكَ يَخْلُقُ مَا يَشَاءُ وَيَخْتَارُ مَا كَانَ لَهُمُ الْخِيَرَةُ سُبْحَانَ اللَّهِ وَتَعَالَى عَمَّا يُشْرِكُونَ (٦٨)

وَرَبُّكَ يَعْلَمُ مَا تُكِنُّ صُدُورُهُمْ وَمَا يُعْلِنُونَ (٦٩)

وَهُوَ اللَّهُ لَا إِلَهَ إِلَّا هُوَ لَهُ الْحَمْدُ فِي الْأُولَى وَالْآخِرَةِ وَلَهُ الْحُكْمُ وَإِلَيْهِ تُرْجَعُونَ (٧٠)

قُلْ أَرَأَيْتُمْ إِنْ جَعَلَ اللَّهُ عَلَيْكُمُ اللَّيْلَ سَرْمَدًا إِلَى يَوْمِ الْقِيَامَةِ مَنْ إِلَهٌ غَيْرُ اللَّهِ يَأْتِيكُمْ بِضِيَاءٍ أَفَلَا تَسْمَعُونَ (٧١)

قُلْ أَرَأَيْتُمْ إِنْ جَعَلَ اللَّهُ عَلَيْكُمُ النَّهَارَ سَرْمَدًا إِلَى يَوْمِ الْقِيَامَةِ مَنْ إِلَهٌ غَيْرُ اللَّهِ يَأْتِيكُمْ بِلَيْلٍ تَسْكُنُونَ فِيهِ أَفَلَا تُبْصِرُونَ (٧٢)

وَمِنْ رَحْمَتِهِ جَعَلَ لَكُمُ اللَّيْلَ وَالنَّهَارَ لِتَسْكُنُوا فِيهِ وَلِتَبْتَغُوا مِنْ فَضْلِهِ وَلَعَلَّكُمْ تَشْكُرُونَ (٧٣)

وَيَوْمَ يُنَادِيهِمْ فَيَقُولُ أَيْنَ شُرَكَائِيَ الَّذِينَ كُنْتُمْ تَزْعُمُونَ (٧٤)

وَنَزَعْنَا مِنْ كُلِّ أُمَّةٍ شَهِيدًا فَقُلْنَا هَاتُوا بُرْهَانَكُمْ فَعَلِمُوا أَنَّ الْحَقَّ لِلَّهِ وَضَلَّ عَنْهُمْ مَا كَانُوا يَفْتَرُونَ (٧٥)

إِنَّ قَارُونَ كَانَ مِنْ قَوْمِ مُوسَى فَبَغَى عَلَيْهِمْ وَآتَيْنَاهُ مِنَ الْكُنُوزِ مَا إِنَّ مَفَاتِحَهُ لَتَنُوءُ بِالْعُصْبَةِ أُولِي الْقُوَّةِ إِذْ قَالَ لَهُ قَوْمُهُ لَا تَفْرَحْ إِنَّ اللَّهَ لَا يُحِبُّ

28. The Narrative

28:70. And He is Allah, there is no god but He! His is the praise in this (life) and the Hereafter; and His is the judgment, and to Him you will be brought back.

28:71. Say: Do you see if Allah were to make the day to continue incessantly on you till the day of Resurrection, who is the god besides Allah that could bring you the night in which you take rest? Do you not then see?

28:72. Say: Do you see if Allah were to make the night to continue incessantly on you till the day of Resurrection, who is the god besides Allah who could bring you light? Will you not then hear?

28:73. And out of His mercy He has made for you the night and the day, that you may rest therein, and that you may seek of His grace, and that you may give thanks.

28:74. And the day when He will call them and say: Where are My associates whom you pretended?

28:75. And We shall draw forth from among every nation a witness and say: Bring your proof. Then shall they know that the Truth is Allah's and that which they forged will fail them.

***

28:76. Korah was surely of the people of Moses, but he oppressed them, and We gave him treasures, so much so that his hoards of wealth would weigh down a body of strong men. When his people said to him: Exult not; surely Allah loves not the exultant.

28:77. And seek the abode of the Hereafter by means of what Allah has given thee, and neglect not thy portion of the world, and do good (to others) as Allah has done good to thee, and seek not to make mischief in the land. Surely Allah loves nor the mischief-makers.

28:78. He said: I have been given this only on account of the knowledge I have. Did he not know that Allah had destroyed before him generations who were mightier in strength than he and greater in assemblage? And the guilty are not questioned about their sins.

28:79. So he went forth to his people in his finery. Those who desired this world's life said: O would that we had the like of what Korah is given! Surely he is possessed of mighty good fortune!

28:80. But those who were given the knowledge said: Woe to you! Allah's reward is better for him who believes and does good, and none is made to receive this except the patient.

28:81. So We made the earth to swallow him up and his abode. He had no host to help him against Allah, nor was he of those who can defend themselves.

28:82. And those who had yearned for his place the day before began to say: Ah! (know) that Allah amplifies and straitens the means of subsistence for whom He pleases of His servants had not Allah been gracious to us, He would have abased us. Ah! (know) that the ungrateful are never successful.

* * *

28:83. That abode of the Hereafter, We assign it to those who have no desire to exalt themselves in the earth nor to make mischief. And the good end is for those who keep their duty.

28:84. Whoever brings good, he will have better than it; and whoever brings evil, those who do evil will be required only for what they did.

28:85. He who has made the Qur'an binding in thee will surely bring thee back to the Place of Return. Say: My Lord knows best him who has brought the guidance and him who is in manifest error.

28:86. And thou didst not expect that the Book would be inspired to thee, but it is a mercy from thy Lord, so be not a backer up of the disbelievers.

بِالْهُدَى وَمَنْ هُوَ فِي ضَلَالٍ مُبِينٍ (٨٥)

وَمَا كُنْتَ تَرْجُو أَنْ يُلْقَى إِلَيْكَ الْكِتَابُ إِلَّا رَحْمَةً مِنْ رَبِّكَ فَلَا تَكُونَنَّ ظَهِيرًا لِلْكَافِرِينَ (٨٦)

وَلَا يَصُدُّنَّكَ عَنْ آيَاتِ اللَّهِ بَعْدَ إِذْ أُنْزِلَتْ إِلَيْكَ وَادْعُ إِلَى رَبِّكَ وَلَا تَكُونَنَّ مِنَ الْمُشْرِكِينَ (٨٧)

وَلَا تَدْعُ مَعَ اللَّهِ إِلَهًا آخَرَ لَا إِلَهَ إِلَّا هُوَ كُلُّ شَيْءٍ هَالِكٌ إِلَّا وَجْهَهُ لَهُ الْحُكْمُ وَإِلَيْهِ تُرْجَعُونَ (٨٨)

28:87. And let them not turn thee aside from the messages of Allah after they have been revealed to thee, and call (men) to thy Lord and be not of the polytheists.

28:88. And call not with Allah any other god. There is no God but He. Everything will perish but He. His is the judgment, and to Him you will be brought back.

29. The Spider

In the name of Allah, the Beneficent, the Merciful.

29:1. I, Allah, am the best Knower.

29:2. Do men think that they will be left alone on saying, We believe, and will not be tried?

29:3. And indeed We tried those before them, so Allah will certainly know those who are true and He will know the liars.

29:4. Or do they who work evil think that they will escape Us? Evil is it that they judge!

29:5. Whoever hopes to meet with Allah, the term of Allah is then surely coming. And He is the Hearing, the Knowing.

29:6. And whoever strives hard, strives for himself. Surely Allah is Self-sufficient, above (need of) (His) creatures.

29:7. And those who believe and do good, We shall certainly do away. with their afflictions and reward them for the best of what they did.

29:8. And We have enjoined on man goodness to his parents. But if they contend with thee to associate (others) with Me, of which thou hast no knowledge, obey them not. To Me is your return, so I will inform you of what you did.

29:9. And those who believe and do good, We shall surely make them enter

٢٩ - سورة العنكبوت

بِسْمِ اللَّهِ الرَّحْمَنِ الرَّحِيمِ

الم (١)

أَحَسِبَ النَّاسُ أَنْ يُتْرَكُوا أَنْ يَقُولُوا آمَنَّا وَهُمْ لَا يُفْتَنُونَ (٢)

وَلَقَدْ فَتَنَّا الَّذِينَ مِنْ قَبْلِهِمْ فَلَيَعْلَمَنَّ اللَّهُ الَّذِينَ صَدَقُوا وَلَيَعْلَمَنَّ الْكَاذِبِينَ (٣)

أَمْ حَسِبَ الَّذِينَ يَعْمَلُونَ السَّيِّئَاتِ أَنْ يَسْبِقُونَا سَاءَ مَا يَحْكُمُونَ (٤)

مَنْ كَانَ يَرْجُو لِقَاءَ اللَّهِ فَإِنَّ أَجَلَ اللَّهِ لَآتٍ وَهُوَ السَّمِيعُ الْعَلِيمُ (٥)

وَمَنْ جَاهَدَ فَإِنَّمَا يُجَاهِدُ لِنَفْسِهِ إِنَّ اللَّهَ لَغَنِيٌّ عَنِ الْعَالَمِينَ (٦)

وَالَّذِينَ آمَنُوا وَعَمِلُوا الصَّالِحَاتِ لَنُكَفِّرَنَّ عَنْهُمْ سَيِّئَاتِهِمْ وَلَنَجْزِيَنَّهُمْ أَحْسَنَ الَّذِي كَانُوا يَعْمَلُونَ (٧)

وَوَصَّيْنَا الْإِنْسَانَ بِوَالِدَيْهِ حُسْنًا وَإِنْ جَاهَدَاكَ لِتُشْرِكَ بِي مَا لَيْسَ لَكَ بِهِ عِلْمٌ فَلَا تُطِعْهُمَا إِلَيَّ مَرْجِعُكُمْ فَأُنَبِّئُكُمْ بِمَا كُنْتُمْ تَعْمَلُونَ (٨)

وَالَّذِينَ آمَنُوا وَعَمِلُوا الصَّالِحَاتِ لَنُدْخِلَنَّهُمْ فِي الصَّالِحِينَ (٩)

وَمِنَ النَّاسِ مَنْ يَقُولُ آمَنَّا بِاللَّهِ فَإِذَا أُوذِيَ فِي اللَّهِ جَعَلَ فِتْنَةَ النَّاسِ كَعَذَابِ اللَّهِ وَلَئِنْ جَاءَ نَصْرٌ مِنْ رَبِّكَ

29. The Spider

among the righteous.

29:10. And among men is he who says: We believe in Allah; but when he is persecuted for the sake of Allah, he thinks the persecution of men to be as the chastisement of Allah. And if there comes help from thy Lord, they will say: Surely we were with you. Is not Allah the Best Knower of what is in the hearts of mankind?

29:11. And certainly Allah will know those who believe, and He will know the hypocrites.

29:12. And those who disbelieve say to those who believe: Follow our path and we will bear your wrongs. And they can never bear aught of their wrongs. Surely they are liars.

29:13. And they will certainly bear their own burdens, and other burdens besides their own burdens; and they will certainly be questioned on the day of Resurrection as to what they forged.

* * *

29:14. And We indeed sent Noah to his people, so he remained among them a thousand years save fifty years. And the deluge overtook them, and they were wrongdoers.

29:15. So We delivered him and the inmates of the ark, and made it a sign to the nations.

29:16. And (We sent) Abraham, when he said to his people: Serve Allah and keep your duty to Him. That is better for you, if you did but know.

29:17. You only worship idols besides Allah and you invent a lie. Surely they whom you serve besides Allah control no sustenance for you; so seek sustenance from Allah and serve Him and be grateful to Him. To Him you will be brought back.

29:18. And if you reject, nations before you did indeed reject (the Truth). And the duty of the Messenger is only to deliver (the message) plainly.

29:19. See they not how Allah

29. The Spider

originates the creation, then reproduces it? Surely that is easy to Allah.

29:20. Say: Travel in the earth then see how He makes the first creation, then Allah creates the latter creation. Surely Allah is Possessor of power over all things.

29:21. He chastises whom He pleases and has mercy on whom He pleases, to Him you will be turned back.

29:22. And you cannot escape in the earth nor in the heaven, and you have no protector or helper besides Allah.

* * *

29:23. And those who disbelieve in the messages of Allah and the meeting with Him, they despair of My mercy, and for them is a painful chastisement.

29:24. So naught was the answer of his people except that they said: Slay him or burn him! But Allah delivered him from the fire. Surely therein are signs for a people who believe.

29:25. And he said: You have only taken idols besides Allah by way of friendship between you in this world's life, then on the day of Resurrection some of you will deny others, and some of you will curse others and your abode is the Fire, and you will have no helpers.

29:26. So Lot believed in him. And he said: I am fleeing to my Lord. Surely He is the Mighty, the Wise.

29:27. And We granted him Isaac and Jacob, and ordained prophethood and the Book among his seed. And We gave him his reward in this world, and in the Hereafter he will surely be among the righteous.

29:28. And (We sent) Lot when he said to his people: Surely you are guilty of an abomination which none of the nations has done before you.

29:29. Do you come to males and commit robbery on the highway, and commit evil deeds in your assemblies? But the answer of his people was only

يُعَذِّبُ مَنْ يَشَاءُ وَيَرْحَمُ مَنْ يَشَاءُ وَإِلَيْهِ تُقْلَبُونَ (٢١) وَمَا أَنْتُمْ بِمُعْجِزِينَ فِي الْأَرْضِ وَلَا فِي السَّمَاءِ وَمَا لَكُمْ مِنْ دُونِ اللَّهِ مِنْ وَلِيٍّ وَلَا نَصِيرٍ (٢٢) وَالَّذِينَ كَفَرُوا بِآيَاتِ اللَّهِ وَلِقَائِهِ أُولَئِكَ يَئِسُوا مِنْ رَحْمَتِي وَأُولَئِكَ لَهُمْ عَذَابٌ أَلِيمٌ (٢٣) فَمَا كَانَ جَوَابَ قَوْمِهِ إِلَّا أَنْ قَالُوا اقْتُلُوهُ أَوْ حَرِّقُوهُ فَأَنْجَاهُ اللَّهُ مِنَ النَّارِ إِنَّ فِي ذَلِكَ لَآيَاتٍ لِقَوْمٍ يُؤْمِنُونَ (٢٤) وَقَالَ إِنَّمَا اتَّخَذْتُمْ مِنْ دُونِ اللَّهِ أَوْثَانًا مَوَدَّةَ بَيْنِكُمْ فِي الْحَيَاةِ الدُّنْيَا ثُمَّ يَوْمَ الْقِيَامَةِ يَكْفُرُ بَعْضُكُمْ بِبَعْضٍ وَيَلْعَنُ بَعْضُكُمْ بَعْضًا وَمَأْوَاكُمُ النَّارُ وَمَا لَكُمْ مِنْ نَاصِرِينَ (٢٥) فَآمَنَ لَهُ لُوطٌ وَقَالَ إِنِّي مُهَاجِرٌ إِلَى رَبِّي إِنَّهُ هُوَ الْعَزِيزُ الْحَكِيمُ (٢٦) وَوَهَبْنَا لَهُ إِسْحَاقَ وَيَعْقُوبَ وَجَعَلْنَا فِي ذُرِّيَّتِهِ النُّبُوَّةَ وَالْكِتَابَ وَآتَيْنَاهُ أَجْرَهُ فِي الدُّنْيَا وَإِنَّهُ فِي الْآخِرَةِ لَمِنَ الصَّالِحِينَ (٢٧) وَلُوطًا إِذْ قَالَ لِقَوْمِهِ إِنَّكُمْ لَتَأْتُونَ الْفَاحِشَةَ مَا سَبَقَكُمْ بِهَا مِنْ أَحَدٍ مِنَ الْعَالَمِينَ (٢٨) أَئِنَّكُمْ لَتَأْتُونَ الرِّجَالَ وَتَقْطَعُونَ السَّبِيلَ وَتَأْتُونَ فِي نَادِيكُمُ الْمُنْكَرَ فَمَا كَانَ جَوَابَ قَوْمِهِ إِلَّا أَنْ قَالُوا ائْتِنَا بِعَذَابِ اللَّهِ إِنْ كُنْتَ مِنَ الصَّادِقِينَ (٢٩) قَالَ رَبِّ انْصُرْنِي عَلَى الْقَوْمِ الْمُفْسِدِينَ (٣٠) وَلَمَّا جَاءَتْ رُسُلُنَا إِبْرَاهِيمَ بِالْبُشْرَى

29. The Spider

that they said: Bring on us Allah's chastisement, if thou art truthful.

29:30. He said: My Lord, help me against the mischievous people.

* * *

29:31. And when Our messengers came to Abraham with good news, they said: We are going to destroy the people of this town, for its people are iniquitous.

29:32. He said: Surely in it is Lot. They said: We know well who is in it; we shall certainly deliver him and his followers, except his wife; she is of those who remain behind.

29:33. And when Our messengers came to Lot, he was grieved on account of them, and he lacked strength to protect them. And they said: Fear not, nor grieve; surely we will deliver thee and thy followers, except thy wife -- she is of those who remain behind.

29:34. Surely We are going to bring down upon the people of this town a punishment from heaven, because they transgressed.

29:35. And certainly We have left a clear sign of it for a people who understand.

29:36. And to Midian (We sent) their brother Shu'aib, so he said: O my people, serve Allah and fear the Latter day, and act not corruptly, making mischief, in the land.

29:37. But they rejected him, so a severe earthquake overtook them and they lay prostrate in their abodes.

29:38. And 'Ad and Thamud! And some of their dwellings are indeed apparent to you. And the devil made their deeds fair-seeming to them, so he kept them back from the path, and they could see clearly.

29:39. And Korah and Pharaoh and Haman! And certainly Moses came to them with clear arguments, but they behaved haughtily in the land; and they could not outstrip (Us).

29:40. So each one We punished for his

قَالُوا إِنَّا مُهْلِكُو أَهْلِ هَذِهِ الْقَرْيَةِ إِنَّ أَهْلَهَا كَانُوا ظَالِمِينَ (٣١) قَالَ إِنَّ فِيهَا لُوطًا قَالُوا نَحْنُ أَعْلَمُ بِمَن فِيهَا لَنُنَجِّيَنَّهُ وَأَهْلَهُ إِلَّا امْرَأَتَهُ كَانَتْ مِنَ الْغَابِرِينَ (٣٢) وَلَمَّا أَن جَاءَتْ رُسُلُنَا لُوطًا سِيءَ بِهِمْ وَضَاقَ بِهِمْ ذَرْعًا وَقَالُوا لَا تَخَفْ وَلَا تَحْزَنْ إِنَّا مُنَجُّوكَ وَأَهْلَكَ إِلَّا امْرَأَتَكَ كَانَتْ مِنَ الْغَابِرِينَ (٣٣) إِنَّا مُنزِلُونَ عَلَى أَهْلِ هَذِهِ الْقَرْيَةِ رِجْزًا مِنَ السَّمَاءِ بِمَا كَانُوا يَفْسُقُونَ (٣٤) وَلَقَد تَّرَكْنَا مِنْهَا آيَةً بَيِّنَةً لِّقَوْمٍ يَعْقِلُونَ (٣٥) وَإِلَى مَدْيَنَ أَخَاهُمْ شُعَيْبًا فَقَالَ يَا قَوْمِ اعْبُدُوا اللَّهَ وَارْجُوا الْيَوْمَ الْآخِرَ وَلَا تَعْثَوْا فِي الْأَرْضِ مُفْسِدِينَ (٣٦) فَكَذَّبُوهُ فَأَخَذَتْهُمُ الرَّجْفَةُ فَأَصْبَحُوا فِي دَارِهِمْ جَاثِمِينَ (٣٧) وَعَادًا وَثَمُودَ وَقَد تَّبَيَّنَ لَكُم مِّن مَّسَاكِنِهِمْ وَزَيَّنَ لَهُمُ الشَّيْطَانُ أَعْمَالَهُمْ فَصَدَّهُمْ عَنِ السَّبِيلِ وَكَانُوا مُسْتَبْصِرِينَ (٣٨) وَقَارُونَ وَفِرْعَوْنَ وَهَامَانَ وَلَقَدْ جَاءَهُم مُّوسَى بِالْبَيِّنَاتِ فَاسْتَكْبَرُوا فِي الْأَرْضِ وَمَا كَانُوا سَابِقِينَ (٣٩) فَكُلًّا أَخَذْنَا بِذَنبِهِ فَمِنْهُم مَّنْ أَرْسَلْنَا عَلَيْهِ حَاصِبًا وَمِنْهُم مَّنْ أَخَذَتْهُ الصَّيْحَةُ وَمِنْهُم مَّنْ خَسَفْنَا بِهِ الْأَرْضَ وَمِنْهُم مَّنْ أَغْرَقْنَا وَمَا كَانَ اللَّهُ لِيَظْلِمَهُمْ وَلَكِن كَانُوا أَنفُسَهُمْ يَظْلِمُونَ (٤٠) مَثَلُ الَّذِينَ اتَّخَذُوا مِن دُونِ اللَّهِ أَوْلِيَاءَ كَمَثَلِ الْعَنكَبُوتِ اتَّخَذَتْ بَيْتًا وَإِنَّ

29. The Spider

sin. Of them was he on whom We sent a violent storm, and of them was he whom the rumbling overtook, and of them was he whom We caused the earth to swallow, and of them was he whom We drowned. And it was not Allah, Who wronged them, but they wronged themselves.

29:41. The parable of those who take guardians besides Allah is as the parable of the spider that makes for itself a house; and surely the frailest of the houses is the spider's house -- if they but knew!

29:42. Surely Allah knows whatever they call upon besides Him. And He is the Mighty, the Wise.

29:43. And these parables, We set them forth for men, and none understand them but the learned.

29:44. Allah created the heavens and the earth with truth. Surely there is a sign in this for the believers.

* * *

29:45. Recite that which has been revealed to thee of the Book and keep up prayer. Surely prayer keeps (one) away from indecency and evil; and certainly the remembrance of Allah is the greatest (force). And Allah knows what you do.

29:46. And argue not with the People of the Book except by what is best, save such of them as act unjustly. But say: We believe in that which has been revealed to us and revealed to you, and our God and your God is One, and to Him we submit.

29:47. And thus have We revealed the Book to thee. So those whom We have given the Book believe in it, and of these there are those who believe in it; and none deny Our messages except the disbelievers.

29:48. And thou didst not recite before it any book, nor didst thou transcribe one with thy right hand, for then could the liars have doubted.

أَوْهَنَ الْبُيُوتِ لَبَيْتُ الْعَنْكَبُوتِ لَوْ كَانُوا يَعْلَمُونَ (٤١)

إِنَّ اللَّهَ يَعْلَمُ مَا يَدْعُونَ مِنْ دُونِهِ مِنْ شَيْءٍ وَهُوَ الْعَزِيزُ الْحَكِيمُ (٤٢)

وَتِلْكَ الْأَمْثَالُ نَضْرِبُهَا لِلنَّاسِ وَمَا يَعْقِلُهَا إِلَّا الْعَالِمُونَ (٤٣)

خَلَقَ اللَّهُ السَّمَاوَاتِ وَالْأَرْضَ بِالْحَقِّ إِنَّ فِي ذَلِكَ لَآيَةً لِلْمُؤْمِنِينَ (٤٤)

اتْلُ مَا أُوحِيَ إِلَيْكَ مِنَ الْكِتَابِ وَأَقِمِ الصَّلَاةَ إِنَّ الصَّلَاةَ تَنْهَى عَنِ الْفَحْشَاءِ وَالْمُنْكَرِ وَلَذِكْرُ اللَّهِ أَكْبَرُ وَاللَّهُ يَعْلَمُ مَا تَصْنَعُونَ (٤٥)

وَلَا تُجَادِلُوا أَهْلَ الْكِتَابِ إِلَّا بِالَّتِي هِيَ أَحْسَنُ إِلَّا الَّذِينَ ظَلَمُوا مِنْهُمْ وَقُولُوا آمَنَّا بِالَّذِي أُنْزِلَ إِلَيْنَا وَأُنْزِلَ إِلَيْكُمْ وَإِلَهُنَا وَإِلَهُكُمْ وَاحِدٌ وَنَحْنُ لَهُ مُسْلِمُونَ (٤٦)

وَكَذَلِكَ أَنْزَلْنَا إِلَيْكَ الْكِتَابَ فَالَّذِينَ آتَيْنَاهُمُ الْكِتَابَ يُؤْمِنُونَ بِهِ وَمِنْ هَؤُلَاءِ مَنْ يُؤْمِنُ بِهِ وَمَا يَجْحَدُ بِآيَاتِنَا إِلَّا الْكَافِرُونَ (٤٧)

وَمَا كُنْتَ تَتْلُو مِنْ قَبْلِهِ مِنْ كِتَابٍ وَلَا تَخُطُّهُ بِيَمِينِكَ إِذًا لَارْتَابَ الْمُبْطِلُونَ (٤٨)

بَلْ هُوَ آيَاتٌ بَيِّنَاتٌ فِي صُدُورِ الَّذِينَ أُوتُوا الْعِلْمَ وَمَا يَجْحَدُ بِآيَاتِنَا إِلَّا الظَّالِمُونَ (٤٩)

وَقَالُوا لَوْلَا أُنْزِلَ عَلَيْهِ آيَاتٌ مِنْ رَبِّهِ قُلْ إِنَّمَا الْآيَاتُ عِنْدَ اللَّهِ وَإِنَّمَا أَنَا نَذِيرٌ مُبِينٌ (٥٠)

أَوَلَمْ يَكْفِهِمْ أَنَّا أَنْزَلْنَا عَلَيْكَ الْكِتَابَ يُتْلَى عَلَيْهِمْ إِنَّ فِي ذَلِكَ لَرَحْمَةً وَذِكْرَى لِقَوْمٍ يُؤْمِنُونَ (٥١)

قُلْ كَفَى بِاللَّهِ بَيْنِي وَبَيْنَكُمْ شَهِيدًا يَعْلَمُ

29:49. Nay, it is clear messages in the hearts of those who are granted knowledge. And none deny Our messages except the iniquitous.

29:50. And they say: Why are not signs sent down upon him from his Lord? Say: Signs are with Allah only, and I am only a plain warner.

29:51. Is it not enough for them that We have revealed to thee the Book which is recited to them? Surely there is mercy in this and a reminder for a people who believe.

***

29:52. Say: Allah is sufficient as a witness between me and you. He knows what is in the heavens and the earth. And those who believe in falsehood and disbelieve in Allah, these it is that are the losers.

29:53. And they ask thee to hasten on the chastisement. And had not a term been appointed, the chastisement would certainly have come to them. And certainly it will come to them all of a sudden, while they perceive not.

29:54. They ask thee to hasten on the chastisement, and surely hell encompasses the disbelievers --

29:55. The day when the chastisement will cover them from above them, and from beneath their feet And He will say: Taste what you did.

29:56. O My servants who believe, surely My earth is vast, so serve Me only.

29:57. Every soul must taste of death then to Us you will be returned.

29:58. And those who believe and do good, We shall certainly give them an abode in high places in the Garden wherein flow rivers, abiding therein. Excellent the reward of the workers.

29:59. Who are patient, and on their Lord they rely!

29:60. And how many a living creature carries not its sustenance! Allah sustains it and yourselves. And He is

مَا فِي السَّمَاوَاتِ وَالْأَرْضِ وَالَّذِينَ آمَنُوا بِالْبَاطِلِ وَكَفَرُوا بِاللَّهِ أُولَٰئِكَ هُمُ الْخَاسِرُونَ (٥٢)

وَيَسْتَعْجِلُونَكَ بِالْعَذَابِ وَلَوْلَا أَجَلٌ مُسَمًّى لَجَاءَهُمُ الْعَذَابُ وَلَيَأْتِيَنَّهُمْ بَغْتَةً وَهُمْ لَا يَشْعُرُونَ (٥٣)

يَسْتَعْجِلُونَكَ بِالْعَذَابِ وَإِنَّ جَهَنَّمَ لَمُحِيطَةٌ بِالْكَافِرِينَ (٥٤)

يَوْمَ يَغْشَاهُمُ الْعَذَابُ مِنْ فَوْقِهِمْ وَمِنْ تَحْتِ أَرْجُلِهِمْ وَيَقُولُ ذُوقُوا مَا كُنْتُمْ تَعْمَلُونَ (٥٥)

يَا عِبَادِيَ الَّذِينَ آمَنُوا إِنَّ أَرْضِي وَاسِعَةٌ فَإِيَّايَ فَاعْبُدُونِ (٥٦)

كُلُّ نَفْسٍ ذَائِقَةُ الْمَوْتِ ثُمَّ إِلَيْنَا تُرْجَعُونَ (٥٧)

وَالَّذِينَ آمَنُوا وَعَمِلُوا الصَّالِحَاتِ لَنُبَوِّئَنَّهُمْ مِنَ الْجَنَّةِ غُرَفًا تَجْرِي مِنْ تَحْتِهَا الْأَنْهَارُ خَالِدِينَ فِيهَا نِعْمَ أَجْرُ الْعَامِلِينَ (٥٨)

الَّذِينَ صَبَرُوا وَعَلَىٰ رَبِّهِمْ يَتَوَكَّلُونَ (٥٩)

وَكَأَيِّنْ مِنْ دَابَّةٍ لَا تَحْمِلُ رِزْقَهَا اللَّهُ يَرْزُقُهَا وَإِيَّاكُمْ وَهُوَ السَّمِيعُ الْعَلِيمُ (٦٠)

وَلَئِنْ سَأَلْتَهُمْ مَنْ خَلَقَ السَّمَاوَاتِ وَالْأَرْضَ وَسَخَّرَ الشَّمْسَ وَالْقَمَرَ لَيَقُولُنَّ اللَّهُ فَأَنَّىٰ يُؤْفَكُونَ (٦١)

اللَّهُ يَبْسُطُ الرِّزْقَ لِمَنْ يَشَاءُ مِنْ عِبَادِهِ وَيَقْدِرُ لَهُ إِنَّ اللَّهَ بِكُلِّ شَيْءٍ عَلِيمٌ (٦٢)

وَلَئِنْ سَأَلْتَهُمْ مَنْ نَزَّلَ مِنَ السَّمَاءِ مَاءً فَأَحْيَا بِهِ الْأَرْضَ مِنْ بَعْدِ مَوْتِهَا لَيَقُولُنَّ اللَّهُ قُلِ الْحَمْدُ لِلَّهِ بَلْ أَكْثَرُهُمْ لَا يَعْقِلُونَ (٦٣)

29. The Spider

the Hearing, the Knowing.

29:61. And if thou ask them, Who created the heavens and the earth and made the sun and the moon subservient? they would say, Allah. Whence are they then turned away?

29:62. Allah makes abundant the means of subsistence for whom He pleases of His servants, or straitens (them) for him; Surely Allah is Knower of all things.

29:63. And if thou ask them, Who is it that sends down water from the clouds, then gives life to the earth with it after its death? they will say, Allah. Say: Praise be to Allah! Nay, most of them understand not.

* * *

29:64. And the life of this world is but a sport and a play. And the home of the Hereafter, that surely is the Life, did they but know!

29:65. So when they ride in the ships, they call upon Allah, being sincerely obedient to Him but when He brings them safe to the land, lo they associate others (with Him),

29:66. That they may be ungrateful for what We have given them, and that they may enjoy. But they shalt soon know.

29:67. See they not that We have made a sacred territory secure while men are carried off by force from around them? Will they still believe in the falsehood and disbelieve in the favour of Allah?

29:68. And who is more iniquitous than one who forges a lie against Allah, or gives the lie to the Truth, when it has come to him? Is there not an abode in hell for the disbelievers?

29:69. And those who strive hard for Us, We shall certainly guide them in Our ways. And Allah is surely with the doers of good.

وَمَا هَذِهِ الْحَيَاةُ الدُّنْيَا إِلَّا لَهْوٌ وَلَعِبٌ وَإِنَّ الدَّارَ الْآخِرَةَ لَهِيَ الْحَيَوَانُ لَوْ كَانُوا يَعْلَمُونَ (٦٤)

فَإِذَا رَكِبُوا فِي الْفُلْكِ دَعَوُا اللَّهَ مُخْلِصِينَ لَهُ الدِّينَ فَلَمَّا نَجَّاهُمْ إِلَى الْبَرِّ إِذَا هُمْ يُشْرِكُونَ (٦٥)

لِيَكْفُرُوا بِمَا آتَيْنَاهُمْ وَلِيَتَمَتَّعُوا فَسَوْفَ يَعْلَمُونَ (٦٦)

أَوَلَمْ يَرَوْا أَنَّا جَعَلْنَا حَرَمًا آمِنًا وَيُتَخَطَّفُ النَّاسُ مِنْ حَوْلِهِمْ أَفَبِالْبَاطِلِ يُؤْمِنُونَ وَبِنِعْمَةِ اللَّهِ يَكْفُرُونَ (٦٧)

وَمَنْ أَظْلَمُ مِمَّنِ افْتَرَى عَلَى اللَّهِ كَذِبًا أَوْ كَذَّبَ بِالْحَقِّ لَمَّا جَاءَهُ أَلَيْسَ فِي جَهَنَّمَ مَثْوًى لِلْكَافِرِينَ (٦٨)

وَالَّذِينَ جَاهَدُوا فِينَا لَنَهْدِيَنَّهُمْ سُبُلَنَا وَإِنَّ اللَّهَ لَمَعَ الْمُحْسِنِينَ (٦٩)

30. The Romans

In the name of Allah, the Beneficent, the Merciful.

30:1. I, Allah, am the Best Knower.

30:2. The Romans are vanquished

30:3. In a near land, and they, after their defeat, will gain victory

30:4. Within nine years. Allah's is the command before and after. And on that day the believers will rejoice

30:5. In Allah's help. He helps whom He pleases, and He is the Mighty, the Merciful

30:6. (It is) Allah's promise. Allah will not fail in His promise, but most people know not.

30:7. They know the outward of this world's life, but of the Hereafter they are heedless.

30:8. Do they not reflect within themselves? Allah did not create the heavens and the earth and what is between them but with truth, and (for) an appointed term. And surely most of the people are deniers of the meeting with their Lord.

30:9. Have they not travelled in the earth and seen what was the end of those before them? They were stronger than these in prowess, and dug up the earth, and built on it more than these have built. And their messengers came to them with clear arguments. So it was not Allah, Who wronged them, but they wronged themselves.

30:10. Then evil was the end of those who did evil, because they rejected the messages of Allah and mocked at them.

* * *

30:11. Allah originates the creation, then reproduces it, then to Him you will be returned.

30:12. And the day when the Hour comes, the guilty will despair.

30:13. And they will have no intercessors from among their associate-gods, and they will deny

۳۰- سورة الروم

بِسْمِ اللَّهِ الرَّحْمَنِ الرَّحِيمِ

الم (١)

غُلِبَتِ الرُّومُ (٢)

فِي أَدْنَى الْأَرْضِ وَهُمْ مِنْ بَعْدِ غَلَبِهِمْ سَيَغْلِبُونَ (٣)

فِي بِضْعِ سِنِينَ لِلَّهِ الْأَمْرُ مِنْ قَبْلُ وَمِنْ بَعْدُ وَيَوْمَئِذٍ يَفْرَحُ الْمُؤْمِنُونَ (٤)

بِنَصْرِ اللَّهِ يَنْصُرُ مَنْ يَشَاءُ وَهُوَ الْعَزِيزُ الرَّحِيمُ (٥)

وَعْدَ اللَّهِ لَا يُخْلِفُ اللَّهُ وَعْدَهُ وَلَكِنَّ أَكْثَرَ النَّاسِ لَا يَعْلَمُونَ (٦)

يَعْلَمُونَ ظَاهِرًا مِنَ الْحَيَاةِ الدُّنْيَا وَهُمْ عَنِ الْآخِرَةِ هُمْ غَافِلُونَ (٧)

أَوَلَمْ يَتَفَكَّرُوا فِي أَنْفُسِهِمْ مَا خَلَقَ اللَّهُ السَّمَاوَاتِ وَالْأَرْضَ وَمَا بَيْنَهُمَا إِلَّا بِالْحَقِّ وَأَجَلٍ مُسَمًّى وَإِنَّ كَثِيرًا مِنَ النَّاسِ بِلِقَاءِ رَبِّهِمْ لَكَافِرُونَ (٨)

أَوَلَمْ يَسِيرُوا فِي الْأَرْضِ فَيَنْظُرُوا كَيْفَ كَانَ عَاقِبَةُ الَّذِينَ مِنْ قَبْلِهِمْ كَانُوا أَشَدَّ مِنْهُمْ قُوَّةً وَأَثَارُوا الْأَرْضَ وَعَمَرُوهَا أَكْثَرَ مِمَّا عَمَرُوهَا وَجَاءَتْهُمْ رُسُلُهُمْ بِالْبَيِّنَاتِ فَمَا كَانَ اللَّهُ لِيَظْلِمَهُمْ وَلَكِنْ كَانُوا أَنْفُسَهُمْ يَظْلِمُونَ (٩)

ثُمَّ كَانَ عَاقِبَةَ الَّذِينَ أَسَاءُوا السُّوأَى أَنْ كَذَّبُوا بِآيَاتِ اللَّهِ وَكَانُوا بِهَا يَسْتَهْزِئُونَ (١٠)

اللَّهُ يَبْدَأُ الْخَلْقَ ثُمَّ يُعِيدُهُ ثُمَّ إِلَيْهِ تُرْجَعُونَ (١١)

وَيَوْمَ تَقُومُ السَّاعَةُ يُبْلِسُ الْمُجْرِمُونَ (١٢)

their associate-gods.

30:14. And the day when the Hour comes, that day they will be separated one from the other.

30:15. Then as to those who believed and did good, they will be made happy in a garden.

30:16. And as for those who disbelieved and rejected Our messages and the meeting of the Hereafter, they will he brought to chastisement.

30:17. So glory be to Allah when you enter the evening and when you enter the morning.

30:18. And to Him be praise in the heavens and the earth, and in the afternoon, and when the sun declines.

30:19. He brings forth the living from the dead and brings forth the dead from the living, and gives life to the earth after its death. And thus will you be brought forth.

* * *

30:20. And of His signs is this, that He created you from dust, then lo! you are mortals (who) scatter.

30:21. And of His signs is this, that He created mates for you from yourselves that you might find quiet of mind in them, and He put between you love and compassion. Surely there are signs in this for a people who reflect.

30:22. And of His signs is the creation of the heavens and the earth and the diversity of your tongues and colours. Surely there are signs in this for the learned.

30:23. And of His signs is your sleep by night and by day and your seeking of His bounty. Surely there are signs in this for a people who would hear.

30:24. And of His signs is this, that He shows you the lightning for fear and for hope, and sends down water from the cloud, then gives life there-with to the earth after its death. Surely there are signs in this for a people who understand.

30. The Romans

30:25. And of His signs is this, that the heaven and the earth subsist by His command. Then when He calls you from the earth -- lo! you come forth.

30:26. And His is whosoever is in the heavens and the earth. All are obedient to Him.

30:27. And He it is, Who originates the creation, then reproduces it, and it is very easy to Him. And His is the most exalted state in the heavens and the earth; and He is the Mighty, the Wise.

* * *

30:28. He sets forth to you a parable relating to yourselves. Have you among those whom your right hands possess partners in that which We have provided you with, so that with respect to it you are alike -- you fear them as you fear each other? Thus do We make the messages clear for a people who understand.

30:29. Nay, those who are unjust follow their low desires without any knowledge; so who can guide him whom Allah leaves in error? And they shall have no helpers.

30:30. So set thy face for religion, being upright, the nature made by Allah in which He has created men. There is no altering Allah's creation. That is the right religion but most people know not --

30:31. Turning to Him; and keep your duty to Him, and keep up prayer and be not of the polytheists,

30:32. Of those who split up their religion and become parties; every sect rejoicing in that which is with it.

30:33. And when harm afflicts men, they call upon their Lord, turning to Him, then when He makes them taste of mercy from Him, lo! some of them begin to associate (others) with their Lord,

30:34. So as to be ungrateful for that which We have given them. So enjoy yourselves a while -- you will soon

30. The Romans

come to know.

30:35. Or, have We sent to them an authority so that it speaks of that which they associate with Him?

30:36. And when We make people taste of mercy they rejoice in it, and if an evil befall them for what their hands have already wrought, lo! they despair.

30:37. See they not that Allah enlarges provision and straitens (it) for whom He pleases? Certainly there are signs in this for a people who believe.

30:38. So give to the near of kin his due, and to the needy and the wayfarer. This is best for those who desire Allah's pleasure, and these it is who are successful.

30:39. And whatever you lay out at usury, so that it may increase in the property of men, it increases not with Allah; and whatever you give in charity, desiring Allah's pleasure these will get manifold.

30:40. Allah is He Who created you, then He sustains you, then He causes you to die, then brings you to life. Is there any of your associate-gods who does aught of it? Glory be to Him, and exalted be He above what they associate (with Him)!

***

Corruption has appeared in the land and the sea on account of that which men's hands have wrought, that He may make them taste a part of that which they have done, so that they may return. 42 Say Travel in the land, then see what was the end of those before. Most of them were polytheists.

30:43. Then set thyself, being upright, to the right religion before there come from Allah the day which cannot be averted on that day they will be separated.

30:44. Whoever disbelieves will be responsible for his disbelief; and whoever does good, such prepare (good) for their own souls,

أَوَلَمْ يَرَوْا أَنَّ اللَّهَ يَبْسُطُ الرِّزْقَ لِمَنْ يَشَاءُ وَيَقْدِرُ إِنَّ فِي ذَلِكَ لَآيَاتٍ لِقَوْمٍ يُؤْمِنُونَ (٣٧)

فَآتِ ذَا الْقُرْبَى حَقَّهُ وَالْمِسْكِينَ وَابْنَ السَّبِيلِ ذَلِكَ خَيْرٌ لِلَّذِينَ يُرِيدُونَ وَجْهَ اللَّهِ وَأُولَئِكَ هُمُ الْمُفْلِحُونَ (٣٨)

وَمَا آتَيْتُمْ مِنْ رِبًا لِيَرْبُوَ فِي أَمْوَالِ النَّاسِ فَلَا يَرْبُو عِنْدَ اللَّهِ وَمَا آتَيْتُمْ مِنْ زَكَاةٍ تُرِيدُونَ وَجْهَ اللَّهِ فَأُولَئِكَ هُمُ الْمُضْعِفُونَ (٣٩)

اللَّهُ الَّذِي خَلَقَكُمْ ثُمَّ رَزَقَكُمْ ثُمَّ يُمِيتُكُمْ ثُمَّ يُحْيِيكُمْ هَلْ مِنْ شُرَكَائِكُمْ مَنْ يَفْعَلُ مِنْ ذَلِكُمْ مِنْ شَيْءٍ سُبْحَانَهُ وَتَعَالَى عَمَّا يُشْرِكُونَ (٤٠)

ظَهَرَ الْفَسَادُ فِي الْبَرِّ وَالْبَحْرِ بِمَا كَسَبَتْ أَيْدِي النَّاسِ لِيُذِيقَهُمْ بَعْضَ الَّذِي عَمِلُوا لَعَلَّهُمْ يَرْجِعُونَ (٤١)

قُلْ سِيرُوا فِي الْأَرْضِ فَانْظُرُوا كَيْفَ كَانَ عَاقِبَةُ الَّذِينَ مِنْ قَبْلُ كَانَ أَكْثَرُهُمْ مُشْرِكِينَ (٤٢)

فَأَقِمْ وَجْهَكَ لِلدِّينِ الْقَيِّمِ مِنْ قَبْلِ أَنْ يَأْتِيَ يَوْمٌ لَا مَرَدَّ لَهُ مِنَ اللَّهِ يَوْمَئِذٍ يَصَّدَّعُونَ (٤٣)

مَنْ كَفَرَ فَعَلَيْهِ كُفْرُهُ وَمَنْ عَمِلَ صَالِحًا فَلِأَنْفُسِهِمْ يَمْهَدُونَ (٤٤)

لِيَجْزِيَ الَّذِينَ آمَنُوا وَعَمِلُوا الصَّالِحَاتِ مِنْ فَضْلِهِ إِنَّهُ لَا يُحِبُّ الْكَافِرِينَ (٤٥)

وَمِنْ آيَاتِهِ أَنْ يُرْسِلَ الرِّيَاحَ مُبَشِّرَاتٍ وَلِيُذِيقَكُمْ مِنْ رَحْمَتِهِ وَلِتَجْرِيَ الْفُلْكُ بِأَمْرِهِ وَلِتَبْتَغُوا مِنْ فَضْلِهِ وَلَعَلَّكُمْ تَشْكُرُونَ (٤٦)

وَلَقَدْ أَرْسَلْنَا مِنْ قَبْلِكَ رُسُلًا إِلَى قَوْمِهِمْ فَجَاءُوهُمْ بِالْبَيِّنَاتِ فَانْتَقَمْنَا مِنَ

30:45. That He may reward out of His grace those who believe and do good. Surely He loves not the disbelievers.

30:46. And of His signs is this, that He sends forth the winds bearing good news, and that He may make you taste of His mercy, and that the ships may glide by His command, and that you may seek His grace, and that you may be grateful.

30:47. And certainly We sent before thee messengers to their people, so they came to them with clear arguments, then We punished those who were guilty. And to help believers is ever incumbent on Us.

30:48. Allah is He Who sends forth the winds, so they raise a cloud, then He spreads it forth in the sky as He pleases, and He breaks it, so that you see the rain coming forth from inside it; then when He causes it to fall upon whom He pleases of His servants, lo! they rejoice --

30:49. Though they were before this, before it was sent down upon them, in sure despair.

30:50. Look then at the signs of Allah's mercy, how He gives life to the earth after its death. Surely He is the Quickener of the dead; and He is Possessor of power over all things.

30:51. And if We send a wind and they see it yellow, they would after that certainly continue to disbelieve.

30:52. So surely thou canst not make the dead to hear, nor canst thou make the deaf to hear the call, when they turn back retreating.

30:53. Nor canst thou guide the blind out of their error. Thou canst make none to hear but those who believe in Our messages, so they submit.

***

30:54. Allah is He Who created you from a state of weakness, then He gave strength after weakness, then ordained weakness and hoary hair after strength.

He creates what He pleases, and He is the Knowing, the Powerful.

30:55. And the day when the Hour comes, the guilty will swear: They did not tarry but an hour. Thus are they ever turned away.

30:56. And those who are given knowledge and faith will say: Certainly you tarried according to the ordinance of Allah till the day of Resurrection -- so this is the day of Resurrection -- but you did not know.

30:57. So that day their excuse will not profit those who were unjust, nor will they be granted goodwill.

30:58. And certainly We have set forth for men in this Qur'an every kind of parable. And if thou bring them a sign, those who disbelieve would certainly say: You are naught but deceivers.

30:59. Thus does Allah seal the hearts of those who know not.

30:60. So be patient; surely the promise of Allah is true; and let not those disquiet thee who have no certainty.

31. Luqman

In the name of Allah, the Beneficent, the Merciful.

31:1. I, Allah, am the Best Knower.

31:2. 'These are verses of the Book of Wisdom --

31:3. A guidance and a mercy for the doers of good,

31:4. Who keep up prayer and pay the poor-rate and who are certain of the Hereafter.

31:5. These are on a guidance from their Lord, and these are they who are successful.

31:6. And of men is he who takes instead frivolous discourse to lead astray from Allah's path without knowledge, and to make it a mockery. For such is an abasing chastisement.

31:7. And when Our messages are recited to him, he turns back proudly, as if he had not heard them, as if there were deafness in his ears; so announce to him a painful chastisement.

31:8. Those who believe and do good, for them are Gardens of bliss,

31:9. To abide therein. A promise of Allah in truth! And He is the Mighty, the Wise.

31:10. He created the heavens without pillars that you see, and cast mountains on the earth lest it should be convulsed with you, and He spread on it animals of every kind. And We send down water from the clouds, then cause to grow therein of every noble kind.

31:11. This is Allah's creation; now show Me that which those besides Him have created. Nay, the unjust are in manifest error.

* * *

31:12. And certainly We gave Luqman wisdom, saying: Give thanks to Allah. And whoever is thankful, is thankful for his own soul; and whoever denies, then surely Allah is Self-Sufficient, Praised.

31:13. And when Luqman said to his son, while he admonished him: O my son, ascribe no partner to Allah. Surely ascribing partners (to Him) is a grievous iniquity.

31:14. And We have enjoined on man concerning his parents -- his mother bears him with faintings upon faintings and his weaning takes two years -- Saying: Give thanks to Me and to thy parents. To Me is the eventual coming.

31:15. And if they strive with thee to make thee associate with Me that of which thou hast no knowledge, obey them not, and keep kindly company with them in this world, and follow the way of him who turns to Me; then to Me is your return, then I shall inform you of what you did.

31:16. O my son, even if it be the weight of a grain of mustard-seed, even though it be in a rock, or in the

كَأَنْ لَمْ يَسْمَعْهَا كَأَنَّ فِي أُذُنَيْهِ وَقْرًا فَبَشِّرْهُ بِعَذَابٍ أَلِيمٍ (٧)
إِنَّ الَّذِينَ آمَنُوا وَعَمِلُوا الصَّالِحَاتِ لَهُمْ جَنَّاتُ النَّعِيمِ (٨)
خَالِدِينَ فِيهَا وَعْدَ اللَّهِ حَقًّا وَهُوَ الْعَزِيزُ الْحَكِيمُ (٩)
خَلَقَ السَّمَاوَاتِ بِغَيْرِ عَمَدٍ تَرَوْنَهَا وَأَلْقَى فِي الْأَرْضِ رَوَاسِيَ أَنْ تَمِيدَ بِكُمْ وَبَثَّ فِيهَا مِنْ كُلِّ دَابَّةٍ وَأَنْزَلْنَا مِنَ السَّمَاءِ مَاءً فَأَنْبَتْنَا فِيهَا مِنْ كُلِّ زَوْجٍ كَرِيمٍ (١٠)
هَذَا خَلْقُ اللَّهِ فَأَرُونِي مَاذَا خَلَقَ الَّذِينَ مِنْ دُونِهِ بَلِ الظَّالِمُونَ فِي ضَلَالٍ مُبِينٍ (١١)
وَلَقَدْ آتَيْنَا لُقْمَانَ الْحِكْمَةَ أَنِ اشْكُرْ لِلَّهِ وَمَنْ يَشْكُرْ فَإِنَّمَا يَشْكُرُ لِنَفْسِهِ وَمَنْ كَفَرَ فَإِنَّ اللَّهَ غَنِيٌّ حَمِيدٌ (١٢)
وَإِذْ قَالَ لُقْمَانُ لِابْنِهِ وَهُوَ يَعِظُهُ يَا بُنَيَّ لَا تُشْرِكْ بِاللَّهِ إِنَّ الشِّرْكَ لَظُلْمٌ عَظِيمٌ (١٣)
وَوَصَّيْنَا الْإِنْسَانَ بِوَالِدَيْهِ حَمَلَتْهُ أُمُّهُ وَهْنًا عَلَى وَهْنٍ وَفِصَالُهُ فِي عَامَيْنِ أَنِ اشْكُرْ لِي وَلِوَالِدَيْكَ إِلَيَّ الْمَصِيرُ (١٤)
وَإِنْ جَاهَدَاكَ عَلَى أَنْ تُشْرِكَ بِي مَا لَيْسَ لَكَ بِهِ عِلْمٌ فَلَا تُطِعْهُمَا وَصَاحِبْهُمَا فِي الدُّنْيَا مَعْرُوفًا وَاتَّبِعْ سَبِيلَ مَنْ أَنَابَ إِلَيَّ ثُمَّ إِلَيَّ مَرْجِعُكُمْ فَأُنَبِّئُكُمْ بِمَا كُنْتُمْ تَعْمَلُونَ (١٥)
يَا بُنَيَّ إِنَّهَا إِنْ تَكُ مِثْقَالَ حَبَّةٍ مِنْ خَرْدَلٍ فَتَكُنْ فِي صَخْرَةٍ أَوْ فِي السَّمَاوَاتِ أَوْ فِي الْأَرْضِ يَأْتِ بِهَا اللَّهُ إِنَّ اللَّهَ لَطِيفٌ خَبِيرٌ (١٦)
يَا بُنَيَّ أَقِمِ الصَّلَاةَ وَأْمُرْ بِالْمَعْرُوفِ

heaven or in the earth, Allah will bring it forth. Surely Allah is Knower of subtilities, Aware.

31:17. O my son, keep up prayer and enjoin good and forbid evil, and bear patiently that which befalls thee. Surely this is an affair of great resolution.

31:18. And turn not thy face away from people in contempt, nor go about in the land exultingly. Surely Allah loves not any self-conceited boaster.

31:19. And pursue the right course in thy going about and lower thy voice. Surely the most hateful of voices is braying of asses.

* * *

31:20. See you not that Allah has made subservient to you whatever is in the heavens and whatever is in the earth, and granted to you His favours complete outwardly and inwardly? And among men is he who disputes concerning Allah without knowledge or guidance or a Book giving light.

31:21. And when it is said to them, Follow that which Allah has revealed, they say: Nay, we follow that where-in we found our fathers. What Though the devil calls them to the chastisement of the burning Fire

31:22. And whoever submits himself to Allah and does good (to others), he indeed takes hold of the firmest handle. And Allah's is the end of affairs.

31:23. And whoever disbelieves, let not his disbelief grieve thee. To Us is their return, then We shall inform them of what they did. Surely Allah is Knower of what is in the breasts.

31:24. We give them to enjoy a little, then We shall drive them to a severe chastisement.

31:25. And if thou ask them who created the heavens and the earth? they will say: Allah. Say: Praise be to Allah! Nay, most of them know not.

31:26. To Allah belongs whatever is in

the heavens and the earth Surely Allah is the Self-Sufficient, the Praised.

31:27. And if all the trees in the earth were pens, and the sea with seven more seas added to it (were ink), the words of Allah would not be exhausted. Surely Allah is Mighty, Wise.

31:28. Your creation or your raising is only like a single soul. Surely Allah is Hearing, Seeing.

31:29. Seest thou not that Allah makes the night to enter into the day, and He makes the day to enter into the night, and He has made the sun and the moon subservient (to you) -- each pursues its course till an appointed time -- and that Allah is Aware of what you do?

31:30. This is because Allah is the Truth, and that which they call upon besides Him is falsehood, and that Allah is the High, the Great.

* * *

31:31. Seest thou not that the ships glide on the sea by Allah's grace, that He may show you of His signs? Surely there are signs in this for every patient, endurer, grateful one.

31:32. And when a wave like awnings covers them, they call upon Allah, being sincere to Him in obedience. But when He brings them safe to land, some of them follow the middle course. And none denies Our signs but every perfidious, ungrateful one.

31:33. O people, keep your duty to your Lord and dread the day when no father can avail his son in aught, nor the child will avail his father. Surely the promise of Allah is true, so let not this world's life deceive you, nor let the arch-deceiver deceive you about Allah.

31:34. Surely Allah is He with Whom is the knowledge of the Hour, and He sends down the rain, and He knows what is in the wombs. And no one knows what he will earn on the

عَزِيزٌ حَكِيمٌ (٢٧)
مَا خَلْقُكُمْ وَلَا بَعْثُكُمْ إِلَّا كَنَفْسٍ وَاحِدَةٍ إِنَّ اللَّهَ سَمِيعٌ بَصِيرٌ (٢٨)
أَلَمْ تَرَ أَنَّ اللَّهَ يُولِجُ اللَّيْلَ فِي النَّهَارِ وَيُولِجُ النَّهَارَ فِي اللَّيْلِ وَسَخَّرَ الشَّمْسَ وَالْقَمَرَ كُلٌّ يَجْرِي إِلَى أَجَلٍ مُسَمًّى وَأَنَّ اللَّهَ بِمَا تَعْمَلُونَ خَبِيرٌ (٢٩)
ذَلِكَ بِأَنَّ اللَّهَ هُوَ الْحَقُّ وَأَنَّ مَا يَدْعُونَ مِنْ دُونِهِ الْبَاطِلُ وَأَنَّ اللَّهَ هُوَ الْعَلِيُّ الْكَبِيرُ (٣٠)
أَلَمْ تَرَ أَنَّ الْفُلْكَ تَجْرِي فِي الْبَحْرِ بِنِعْمَةِ اللَّهِ لِيُرِيَكُمْ مِنْ آيَاتِهِ إِنَّ فِي ذَلِكَ لَآيَاتٍ لِكُلِّ صَبَّارٍ شَكُورٍ (٣١)
وَإِذَا غَشِيَهُمْ مَوْجٌ كَالظُّلَلِ دَعَوُا اللَّهَ مُخْلِصِينَ لَهُ الدِّينَ فَلَمَّا نَجَّاهُمْ إِلَى الْبَرِّ فَمِنْهُمْ مُقْتَصِدٌ وَمَا يَجْحَدُ بِآيَاتِنَا إِلَّا كُلُّ خَتَّارٍ كَفُورٍ (٣٢)
يَا أَيُّهَا النَّاسُ اتَّقُوا رَبَّكُمْ وَاخْشَوْا يَوْمًا لَا يَجْزِي وَالِدٌ عَنْ وَلَدِهِ وَلَا مَوْلُودٌ هُوَ جَازٍ عَنْ وَالِدِهِ شَيْئًا إِنَّ وَعْدَ اللَّهِ حَقٌّ فَلَا تَغُرَّنَّكُمُ الْحَيَاةُ الدُّنْيَا وَلَا يَغُرَّنَّكُمْ بِاللَّهِ الْغَرُورُ (٣٣)
إِنَّ اللَّهَ عِنْدَهُ عِلْمُ السَّاعَةِ وَيُنَزِّلُ الْغَيْثَ وَيَعْلَمُ مَا فِي الْأَرْحَامِ وَمَا تَدْرِي نَفْسٌ مَاذَا تَكْسِبُ غَدًا وَمَا تَدْرِي نَفْسٌ بِأَيِّ أَرْضٍ تَمُوتُ إِنَّ اللَّهَ عَلِيمٌ خَبِيرٌ (٣٤)

morrow. And no one knows in what land he will die. Surely Allah is Knowing, Aware.

32. The Adoration

In the name of Allah, the Beneficent, the Merciful.

32:1. I, Allah, am the Best Knower.

32:2. The revelation of the Book, there is no doubt in it, is from the Lord of the worlds.

32:3. Or do they say: He has forged it? Nay, it is the Truth from thy Lord that thou mayest warn a people to whom no warner has come before thee that they may walk aright.

32:4. Allah is He Who created the heavens and the earth and what is between them in six periods, and He is established on the Throne of Power. You have not besides Him a guardian or an intercessor. Will you not then mind?

32:5. He orders the Affair from the heaven to the earth; then it will ascend to Him in a day the measure of which is a thousand years as you count.

32:6. Such is the Knower of the unseen and the seen, the Mighty, the Merciful,

32:7. Who made beautiful everything that He created, and He began the creation of man from dust.

32:8. Then He made his progeny of an extract, of worthless water.

32:9. Then He made him complete and breathed into him of His spirit, and gave you ears and eyes and hearts; little it is that you give thanks!

32:10. And they say: When we are lost in the earth, shall we then be in a new creation? Nay, they are disbelievers in the meeting with their Lord.

32:11. Say: The angel of death, who is given charge of you, will cause you to die, then to your Lord you will be returned.

32- سورة السجدة

بِسْمِ اللَّهِ الرَّحْمَنِ الرَّحِيمِ
الم (١)
تَنزِيلُ الْكِتَابِ لَا رَيْبَ فِيهِ مِن رَبِّ الْعَالَمِينَ (٢)
أَمْ يَقُولُونَ افْتَرَاهُ بَلْ هُوَ الْحَقُّ مِن رَّبِّكَ لِتُنذِرَ قَوْمًا مَّا أَتَاهُم مِّن نَّذِيرٍ مِّن قَبْلِكَ لَعَلَّهُمْ يَهْتَدُونَ (٣)
اللَّهُ الَّذِي خَلَقَ السَّمَاوَاتِ وَالْأَرْضَ وَمَا بَيْنَهُمَا فِي سِتَّةِ أَيَّامٍ ثُمَّ اسْتَوَى عَلَى الْعَرْشِ مَا لَكُم مِّن دُونِهِ مِن وَلِيٍّ وَلَا شَفِيعٍ أَفَلَا تَتَذَكَّرُونَ (٤)
يُدَبِّرُ الْأَمْرَ مِنَ السَّمَاءِ إِلَى الْأَرْضِ ثُمَّ يَعْرُجُ إِلَيْهِ فِي يَوْمٍ كَانَ مِقْدَارُهُ أَلْفَ سَنَةٍ مِّمَّا تَعُدُّونَ (٥)
ذَلِكَ عَالِمُ الْغَيْبِ وَالشَّهَادَةِ الْعَزِيزُ الرَّحِيمُ (٦)
الَّذِي أَحْسَنَ كُلَّ شَيْءٍ خَلَقَهُ وَبَدَأَ خَلْقَ الْإِنسَانِ مِن طِينٍ (٧)
ثُمَّ جَعَلَ نَسْلَهُ مِن سُلَالَةٍ مِّن مَّاءٍ مَّهِينٍ (٨)
ثُمَّ سَوَّاهُ وَنَفَخَ فِيهِ مِن رُّوحِهِ وَجَعَلَ لَكُمُ السَّمْعَ وَالْأَبْصَارَ وَالْأَفْئِدَةَ قَلِيلًا مَّا تَشْكُرُونَ (٩)
وَقَالُوا أَئِذَا ضَلَلْنَا فِي الْأَرْضِ أَئِنَّا لَفِي خَلْقٍ جَدِيدٍ بَلْ هُم بِلِقَاءِ رَبِّهِمْ كَافِرُونَ (١٠)
قُلْ يَتَوَفَّاكُم مَّلَكُ الْمَوْتِ الَّذِي وُكِّلَ بِكُمْ ثُمَّ إِلَى رَبِّكُمْ تُرْجَعُونَ (١١)
وَلَوْ تَرَى إِذِ الْمُجْرِمُونَ نَاكِسُو

32. The Adoration

32:12. And couldst thou but see when the guilty hang their heads before their Lord: Our Lord, we have seen and heard, so send us back, we will do good we are (now) certain.

32:13. And if We had pleased, We could have given every soul its guidance, but the word from Me was just; I will certainly fill hell with the jinn and men together.

32:14. So taste, because you forgot the meeting of this Day of yours surely We forsake you; and taste the abiding chastisement for what you did.

32:15. Only they believe in Our messages who, when they are reminded of them, fall down prostrate and celebrate the praise of their Lord, and they are not proud.

32:16. They forsake (their) beds, calling upon their Lord in fear and in hope, and spend out of what We have given them.

32:17. So no soul knows what refreshment of the eyes is hidden for them a reward for what they did.

32:18. Is he then, who is a believer, like him who is a transgressor? They are not equal.

32:19. As for those who believe and do good deeds, for them are Gardens, a refuge -- an entertainment for what they did.

32:20. And as for those who transgress, their refuge is the Fire. Whenever they desire to go forth from it, they are brought back into it, and it is said to them: Taste the chastisement of the Fire, which you called a lie.

32:21. And certainly We will make them taste the nearer punishment before the greater chastisement, that haply they may turn.

32:22. And who is more iniquitous than he who is reminded of the messages of his Lord, then he turns away from them? Surely We exact retribution from

رُءُوسِهِمْ عِنْدَ رَبِّهِمْ رَبَّنَا أَبْصَرْنَا وَسَمِعْنَا فَارْجِعْنَا نَعْمَلْ صَالِحًا إِنَّا مُوقِنُونَ (١٢)

وَلَوْ شِئْنَا لَآتَيْنَا كُلَّ نَفْسٍ هُدَاهَا وَلَٰكِنْ حَقَّ الْقَوْلُ مِنِّي لَأَمْلَأَنَّ جَهَنَّمَ مِنَ الْجِنَّةِ وَالنَّاسِ أَجْمَعِينَ (١٣)

فَذُوقُوا بِمَا نَسِيتُمْ لِقَاءَ يَوْمِكُمْ هَٰذَا إِنَّا نَسِينَاكُمْ وَذُوقُوا عَذَابَ الْخُلْدِ بِمَا كُنْتُمْ تَعْمَلُونَ (١٤)

إِنَّمَا يُؤْمِنُ بِآيَاتِنَا الَّذِينَ إِذَا ذُكِّرُوا بِهَا خَرُّوا سُجَّدًا وَسَبَّحُوا بِحَمْدِ رَبِّهِمْ وَهُمْ لَا يَسْتَكْبِرُونَ (١٥)

تَتَجَافَىٰ جُنُوبُهُمْ عَنِ الْمَضَاجِعِ يَدْعُونَ رَبَّهُمْ خَوْفًا وَطَمَعًا وَمِمَّا رَزَقْنَاهُمْ يُنْفِقُونَ (١٦)

فَلَا تَعْلَمُ نَفْسٌ مَا أُخْفِيَ لَهُمْ مِنْ قُرَّةِ أَعْيُنٍ جَزَاءً بِمَا كَانُوا يَعْمَلُونَ (١٧)

أَفَمَنْ كَانَ مُؤْمِنًا كَمَنْ كَانَ فَاسِقًا لَا يَسْتَوُونَ (١٨)

أَمَّا الَّذِينَ آمَنُوا وَعَمِلُوا الصَّالِحَاتِ فَلَهُمْ جَنَّاتُ الْمَأْوَىٰ نُزُلًا بِمَا كَانُوا يَعْمَلُونَ (١٩)

وَأَمَّا الَّذِينَ فَسَقُوا فَمَأْوَاهُمُ النَّارُ كُلَّمَا أَرَادُوا أَنْ يَخْرُجُوا مِنْهَا أُعِيدُوا فِيهَا وَقِيلَ لَهُمْ ذُوقُوا عَذَابَ النَّارِ الَّذِي كُنْتُمْ بِهِ تُكَذِّبُونَ (٢٠)

وَلَنُذِيقَنَّهُمْ مِنَ الْعَذَابِ الْأَدْنَىٰ دُونَ الْعَذَابِ الْأَكْبَرِ لَعَلَّهُمْ يَرْجِعُونَ (٢١)

وَمَنْ أَظْلَمُ مِمَّنْ ذُكِّرَ بِآيَاتِ رَبِّهِ ثُمَّ أَعْرَضَ عَنْهَا إِنَّا مِنَ الْمُجْرِمِينَ مُنْتَقِمُونَ (٢٢)

وَلَقَدْ آتَيْنَا مُوسَى الْكِتَابَ فَلَا تَكُنْ فِي مِرْيَةٍ مِنْ لِقَائِهِ وَجَعَلْنَاهُ هُدًى لِبَنِي إِسْرَائِيلَ (٢٣)

the guilty.

***

32:23. And We indeed gave Moses the Book -- so doubt not the meeting with Him -- and We made it a guide for the Children of Israel.

32:24. And We made from among them leaders to guide by Our command when they were patient. And they were certain of Our messages.

32:25. Surely thy Lord will judge between them on the day of Resurrection concerning that wherein they differed.

32:26. Is it not clear to them, how many of the generations, in whose abodes they go about, We destroyed before them? Surely there are signs in this. Will they not then hear?

32:27. See they not that We drive the water to a land having no herbage, then We bring forth thereby seed-produce, of which their cattle and they themselves eat. Will they not then see?

32:28. And they say: When will this victory come, if you are truthful?

32:29. Say: On the day of victory the faith of those who (now) disbelieve will not profit them, nor will they be respired.

32:30. So turn away from them and wait, surely they too are waiting.

33. The Allies

In the name of Allah, the Beneficent, the Merciful.

33:1. O Prophet, keep thy duty to Allah and obey not the disbelievers and the hypocrites. Surely Allah is ever Knowing, Wise;

33:2. And follow that which is revealed to thee from thy Lord. Surely Allah is ever Aware of what you do;

33:3. And trust in Allah. And Allah is enough as having charge (of affairs).

33:4. Allah has not made for any man

33. The Allies

two hearts within him nor has He made your wives whom you desert by Zihar, your mothers, nor has He made those whom you assert (to be your sons) your sons. These are the words of your mouths. And Allah speaks the truth and He shows the way.

33:5. Call them by (the names of) their fathers; this is more equitable with Allah; but if you know not their fathers, then they are your brethren in faith and your friends. And there is no blame on you in that wherein you make a mistake, but (you are answerable for) that which your hearts purpose. And Allah is ever Forgiving, Merciful.

33:6. The Prophet is closer to the faithful than their own selves, and his wives are (as) their mothers. And the possessors of relationship are doser one to another in the ordinance of Allah than (other) believers, and those who fled (their homes), except that you do some good to your friends. This is written in the Book.

33:7. And when We took a covenant from the prophets and from thee, and from Noah and Abraham and Moses and Jesus, son of Mary, and We took from them a solemn covenant,

33:8. That He may question the truthful of their truth, and He has prepared for the disbelievers a painful chastisement.

* * *

33:9. O you who believe, call to mind the favour of Allah to you when there came against you hosts, so We sent against them a strong wind and hosts that you saw not. And Allah is ever Seer of what you do.

33:10. When they came upon you from above you and from below you, and when the eyes turned dull and the hearts rose up to the throats, and you began to think diverse thoughts about Allah.

33:11. There were the believers tried

مَا جَعَلَ اللَّهُ لِرَجُلٍ مِنْ قَلْبَيْنِ فِي جَوْفِهِ وَمَا جَعَلَ أَزْوَاجَكُمُ اللَّائِي تُظَاهِرُونَ مِنْهُنَّ أُمَّهَاتِكُمْ وَمَا جَعَلَ أَدْعِيَاءَكُمْ أَبْنَاءَكُمْ ذَلِكُمْ قَوْلُكُمْ بِأَفْوَاهِكُمْ وَاللَّهُ يَقُولُ الْحَقَّ وَهُوَ يَهْدِي السَّبِيلَ (٤)

ادْعُوهُمْ لِآبَائِهِمْ هُوَ أَقْسَطُ عِنْدَ اللَّهِ فَإِنْ لَمْ تَعْلَمُوا آبَاءَهُمْ فَإِخْوَانُكُمْ فِي الدِّينِ وَمَوَالِيكُمْ وَلَيْسَ عَلَيْكُمْ جُنَاحٌ فِيمَا أَخْطَأْتُمْ بِهِ وَلَكِنْ مَا تَعَمَّدَتْ قُلُوبُكُمْ وَكَانَ اللَّهُ غَفُورًا رَحِيمًا (٥) النَّبِيُّ أَوْلَى بِالْمُؤْمِنِينَ مِنْ أَنْفُسِهِمْ وَأَزْوَاجُهُ أُمَّهَاتُهُمْ وَأُولُو الْأَرْحَامِ بَعْضُهُمْ أَوْلَى بِبَعْضٍ فِي كِتَابِ اللَّهِ مِنَ الْمُؤْمِنِينَ وَالْمُهَاجِرِينَ إِلَّا أَنْ تَفْعَلُوا إِلَى أَوْلِيَائِكُمْ مَعْرُوفًا كَانَ ذَلِكَ فِي الْكِتَابِ مَسْطُورًا (٦)

وَإِذْ أَخَذْنَا مِنَ النَّبِيِّينَ مِيثَاقَهُمْ وَمِنْكَ وَمِنْ نُوحٍ وَإِبْرَاهِيمَ وَمُوسَى وَعِيسَى ابْنِ مَرْيَمَ وَأَخَذْنَا مِنْهُمْ مِيثَاقًا غَلِيظًا (٧)

لِيَسْأَلَ الصَّادِقِينَ عَنْ صِدْقِهِمْ وَأَعَدَّ لِلْكَافِرِينَ عَذَابًا أَلِيمًا (٨)

يَا أَيُّهَا الَّذِينَ آمَنُوا اذْكُرُوا نِعْمَةَ اللَّهِ عَلَيْكُمْ إِذْ جَاءَتْكُمْ جُنُودٌ فَأَرْسَلْنَا عَلَيْهِمْ رِيحًا وَجُنُودًا لَمْ تَرَوْهَا وَكَانَ اللَّهُ بِمَا تَعْمَلُونَ بَصِيرًا (٩)

إِذْ جَاءُوكُمْ مِنْ فَوْقِكُمْ وَمِنْ أَسْفَلَ مِنْكُمْ وَإِذْ زَاغَتِ الْأَبْصَارُ وَبَلَغَتِ الْقُلُوبُ الْحَنَاجِرَ وَتَظُنُّونَ بِاللَّهِ الظُّنُونَا (١٠)

هُنَالِكَ ابْتُلِيَ الْمُؤْمِنُونَ وَزُلْزِلُوا زِلْزَالًا شَدِيدًا (١١)

وَإِذْ يَقُولُ الْمُنَافِقُونَ وَالَّذِينَ فِي

33. The Allies

and they were shaken with a severe shaking.

33:12. And when the hypocrites and those in whose hearts was a disease began to say: Allah and His Messenger did not promise us (victory) but only to deceive.

33:13. And when a party of them said: O people of Yathrib, you cannot make a stand, so go back. And a party of them asked permission of the Prophet, saying, Our houses are exposed. And they were not exposed. They only desired to run away.

33:14. And if an entry were made upon them from the outlying parts of it, then they were asked to wage war (against the Muslims), they would certainly have done it, and they would not have stayed in it but a little while.

33:15. And they had indeed made a covenant with Allah before, (that) they would not turn (their) backs. And a covenant with Allah must be answered for.

33:16. Say: Flight will not profit you, if you flee from death or slaughter, and then you will not be allowed to enjoy yourselves but a little.

33:17. Say: Who is it that can protect you from Allah, if He intends harm for you or He intends to show you mercy? And they will not find for themselves a guardian or a helper besides Allah.

33:18. Allah indeed knows those among you who hinder others and those who say to their brethren, Come to us. And they come not to the fight but a little,

33:19. Being niggardly with respect to you. But when fear comes, thou wilt see them looking to thee, their eyes rolling like one swooning because of death. But when fear is gone they smite you with sharp tongues, being covetous of wealth. These have not believed, so Allah makes their deeds naught. And that is easy for Allah.

33. The Allies

33:20. They think the allies are not gone, and if the allies should come (again), they would fain be in the deserts with the desert Arabs, asking for news about you. And if they were among you, they would not fight save a little.

* * *

33:21. Certainly you have in the Messenger of Allah an excellent exemplar for him who hopes in Allah and the Latter day, and remembers Allah much.

33:22. And when the believers saw the allies, they said: This is what Allah and His Messenger promised us, and Allah and His Messenger spoke the truth. And it only added to their faith and submission.

33:23. Of the believers are men who are true to the covenant they made with Allah so of them is he who has accomplished his vow, and of them is he who yet waits, and they have not changed in the least --

33:24. That Allah may reward the truthful for their truth, and chastise the hypocrites if He please, or turn to them (mercifully). Surely Allah is ever Forgiving, Merciful.

33:25. And Allah turned back the disbelievers in their rage -- they gained no advantage. And Allah sufficed the believers in fighting. And Allah is ever Strong, Mighty.

33:26. And He drove down those of the People of the Book who backed them from their fortresses and He cast awe into their hearts; some you killed and you took captive some.

33:27. And He made you heirs to their land and their dwellings and their property, and (to) a land which you have not yet trodden. And Allah is ever Possessor of power over all things.

* * *

33:28. O Prophet, say to thy wives If you desire this world's life and its

(٢٠)
لَقَدْ كَانَ لَكُمْ فِي رَسُولِ اللَّهِ أُسْوَةٌ حَسَنَةٌ لِمَنْ كَانَ يَرْجُو اللَّهَ وَالْيَوْمَ الْآخِرَ وَذَكَرَ اللَّهَ كَثِيرًا (٢١) وَلَمَّا رَأَى الْمُؤْمِنُونَ الْأَحْزَابَ قَالُوا هَذَا مَا وَعَدَنَا اللَّهُ وَرَسُولُهُ وَصَدَقَ اللَّهُ وَرَسُولُهُ وَمَا زَادَهُمْ إِلَّا إِيمَانًا وَتَسْلِيمًا (٢٢) مِنَ الْمُؤْمِنِينَ رِجَالٌ صَدَقُوا مَا عَاهَدُوا اللَّهَ عَلَيْهِ فَمِنْهُمْ مَنْ قَضَى نَحْبَهُ وَمِنْهُمْ مَنْ يَنْتَظِرُ وَمَا بَدَّلُوا تَبْدِيلًا (٢٣) لِيَجْزِيَ اللَّهُ الصَّادِقِينَ بِصِدْقِهِمْ وَيُعَذِّبَ الْمُنَافِقِينَ إِنْ شَاءَ أَوْ يَتُوبَ عَلَيْهِمْ إِنَّ اللَّهَ كَانَ غَفُورًا رَحِيمًا (٢٤) وَرَدَّ اللَّهُ الَّذِينَ كَفَرُوا بِغَيْظِهِمْ لَمْ يَنَالُوا خَيْرًا وَكَفَى اللَّهُ الْمُؤْمِنِينَ الْقِتَالَ وَكَانَ اللَّهُ قَوِيًّا عَزِيزًا (٢٥) وَأَنْزَلَ الَّذِينَ ظَاهَرُوهُمْ مِنْ أَهْلِ الْكِتَابِ مِنْ صَيَاصِيهِمْ وَقَذَفَ فِي قُلُوبِهِمُ الرُّعْبَ فَرِيقًا تَقْتُلُونَ وَتَأْسِرُونَ فَرِيقًا (٢٦) وَأَوْرَثَكُمْ أَرْضَهُمْ وَدِيَارَهُمْ وَأَمْوَالَهُمْ وَأَرْضًا لَمْ تَطَئُوهَا وَكَانَ اللَّهُ عَلَى كُلِّ شَيْءٍ قَدِيرًا (٢٧) يَا أَيُّهَا النَّبِيُّ قُلْ لِأَزْوَاجِكَ إِنْ كُنْتُنَّ تُرِدْنَ الْحَيَاةَ الدُّنْيَا وَزِينَتَهَا فَتَعَالَيْنَ أُمَتِّعْكُنَّ وَأُسَرِّحْكُنَّ سَرَاحًا جَمِيلًا (٢٨) وَإِنْ كُنْتُنَّ تُرِدْنَ اللَّهَ وَرَسُولَهُ وَالدَّارَ الْآخِرَةَ فَإِنَّ اللَّهَ أَعَدَّ لِلْمُحْسِنَاتِ مِنْكُنَّ أَجْرًا عَظِيمًا (٢٩) يَا نِسَاءَ النَّبِيِّ مَنْ يَأْتِ مِنْكُنَّ بِفَاحِشَةٍ

33. The Allies

adornment, come, I will give you a provision and allow you to depart a goodly departing.

33:29. And if you desire Allah and His Messenger and the abode of the Hereafter, then surely Allah has prepared for the doers of good among you a mighty reward.

33:30. O wives of the Prophet, whoever of you is guilty of manifestly improper conduct, the chastisement will be doubled for her. And this is easy for Allah.

* * *

33:31. And whoever of you is obedient to Allah and His Messenger and does good, We shall give her a double reward, and We have prepared for her an honourable sustenance.

33:32. O wives of the Prophet, you are not like any other women. If you would keep your duty, be nor soft in speech, lest he in whose heart is a disease yearn; and speak a word of goodness.

33:33. And stay in your houses and display not your beauty like the displaying of the ignorance of yore; and keep up prayer, and pay the poor-rate, and obey Allah and His Messenger Allah only desires to take away uncleanness from you, O people of the household, and to purify you a (thorough) purifying.

33:34. And remember that which is recited in your houses of the messages of Allah and the Wisdom. Surely Allah is ever Knower of subtilities, Aware.

* * *

33:35. Surely the men who submit and the women who submit, and the believing men and the believing women, and the obeying men and the obeying women, and the truthful men and the truthful women, and the patient men and the patient women, and the humble men and the humble women, and the charitable men and the

33. The Allies

charitable women, and the fasting men and the fasting women, and the men who guard their chastity and the women who guard, and the men who remember Allah much and the women who remember -- Allah has prepared for them forgiveness and a mighty reward.

33:36. And it behoves not a believing man or a believing woman, when Allah and His Messenger have decided an affair to exercise a choice in their matter. And whoever disobeys Allah and His Messenger, he surely strays off to manifest error.

33:37. And when thou saidst to him to whom Allah had shown favour and to whom thou hadst shown a favour: Keep thy wife to thyself and keep thy duty to Allah and thou concealedst in thy heart what Allah would bring to light, and thou fearedst men, and Allah has a greater right that thou shouldst fear Him. So when Zaid dissolved her marriage-tie, We gave her to thee as a wife, so that there should be no difficulty for the believers about the wives of their adopted sons, when they have dissolved their marriage-tie. And Allah's command is ever performed.

33:38. There is no harm for the prophet in that which Allah has ordained for him. Such has been the way of Allah with those who have gone before. And the command of Allah is a decree that is made absolute --

33:39. Those who deliver the messages of Allah and fear Him, and fear none but Allah. And Allah is Sufficient to take account.

33:40. Muhammad is not the father of any of your men, but he is the Messenger of Allah and the Seal of the prophets And Allah is ever Knower of all things.

* * *

33:41. O you who believe, remember Allah with much remembrance,

33. The Allies

33:42. And glorify Him morning and evening.
33:43. He it is Who sends blessings on you, and (so do) His angels, that He may bring you forth out of darkness into light. And He is ever Merciful to the believers.
33:44. Their salutation on the day they meet Him will be, Peace! and He has prepared for them an honourable reward.
33:45. O Prophet, surely We have sent thee as a witness, and a bearer of good news and a warner,
33:46. And as an inviter to Allah by His permission, and as a light-giving sun.
33:47. And give the believers the good news that they will have great grace from Allah.
33:48. And obey not the disbelievers and the hypocrites, and disregard their annoying talk, and rely on Allah. And Allah is enough as having charge (of affairs).
33:49. O you who believe, when you marry believing women, then divorce them before you touch them, you have in their case no term which you should reckon. But make provision for them and set them free in a goodly manner.
33:50. O Prophet, We have made lawful to thee thy wives whom thou hast given their dowries, and those whom thy right hand possesses, out of those whom Allah has given thee as prisoners of war, and the daughters of thy paternal uncle and the daughters of thy paternal aunts, and the daughters of thy maternal uncle and the daughters of thy maternal aunts who fled with thee; and a believing woman, if she gives herself to the Prophet, if the Prophet desires to marry her. (It is) especially for thee, not for the believers -- We know what We have ordained for them concerning their wives and those whom their right hands possess in order that no blame may attach to

الْمُؤْمِنَاتِ ثُمَّ طَلَّقْتُمُوهُنَّ مِنْ قَبْلِ أَنْ تَمَسُّوهُنَّ فَمَا لَكُمْ عَلَيْهِنَّ مِنْ عِدَّةٍ تَعْتَدُّونَهَا فَمَتِّعُوهُنَّ وَسَرِّحُوهُنَّ سَرَاحًا جَمِيلًا (٤٩)
يَا أَيُّهَا النَّبِيُّ إِنَّا أَحْلَلْنَا لَكَ أَزْوَاجَكَ اللَّاتِي آتَيْتَ أُجُورَهُنَّ وَمَا مَلَكَتْ يَمِينُكَ مِمَّا أَفَاءَ اللَّهُ عَلَيْكَ وَبَنَاتِ عَمِّكَ وَبَنَاتِ عَمَّاتِكَ وَبَنَاتِ خَالِكَ وَبَنَاتِ خَالَاتِكَ اللَّاتِي هَاجَرْنَ مَعَكَ وَامْرَأَةً مُؤْمِنَةً إِنْ وَهَبَتْ نَفْسَهَا لِلنَّبِيِّ إِنْ أَرَادَ النَّبِيُّ أَنْ يَسْتَنْكِحَهَا خَالِصَةً لَكَ مِنْ دُونِ الْمُؤْمِنِينَ قَدْ عَلِمْنَا مَا فَرَضْنَا عَلَيْهِمْ فِي أَزْوَاجِهِمْ وَمَا مَلَكَتْ أَيْمَانُهُمْ لِكَيْلَا يَكُونَ عَلَيْكَ حَرَجٌ وَكَانَ اللَّهُ غَفُورًا رَحِيمًا (٥٠)
تُرْجِي مَنْ تَشَاءُ مِنْهُنَّ وَتُؤْوِي إِلَيْكَ مَنْ تَشَاءُ وَمَنِ ابْتَغَيْتَ مِمَّنْ عَزَلْتَ فَلَا جُنَاحَ عَلَيْكَ ذَلِكَ أَدْنَى أَنْ تَقَرَّ أَعْيُنُهُنَّ وَلَا يَحْزَنَّ وَيَرْضَيْنَ بِمَا آتَيْتَهُنَّ كُلُّهُنَّ وَاللَّهُ يَعْلَمُ مَا فِي قُلُوبِكُمْ وَكَانَ اللَّهُ عَلِيمًا حَلِيمًا (٥١)
لَا يَحِلُّ لَكَ النِّسَاءُ مِنْ بَعْدُ وَلَا أَنْ تَبَدَّلَ بِهِنَّ مِنْ أَزْوَاجٍ وَلَوْ أَعْجَبَكَ حُسْنُهُنَّ إِلَّا مَا مَلَكَتْ يَمِينُكَ وَكَانَ اللَّهُ عَلَى كُلِّ شَيْءٍ رَقِيبًا (٥٢)
يَا أَيُّهَا الَّذِينَ آمَنُوا لَا تَدْخُلُوا بُيُوتَ النَّبِيِّ إِلَّا أَنْ يُؤْذَنَ لَكُمْ إِلَى طَعَامٍ غَيْرَ نَاظِرِينَ إِنَاهُ وَلَكِنْ إِذَا دُعِيتُمْ فَادْخُلُوا فَإِذَا طَعِمْتُمْ فَانْتَشِرُوا وَلَا مُسْتَأْنِسِينَ لِحَدِيثٍ إِنَّ ذَلِكُمْ كَانَ يُؤْذِي النَّبِيَّ فَيَسْتَحْيِي مِنْكُمْ وَاللَّهُ لَا يَسْتَحْيِي مِنَ الْحَقِّ وَإِذَا سَأَلْتُمُوهُنَّ مَتَاعًا فَاسْأَلُوهُنَّ مِنْ وَرَاءِ حِجَابٍ ذَلِكُمْ أَطْهَرُ لِقُلُوبِكُمْ وَقُلُوبِهِنَّ وَمَا كَانَ لَكُمْ أَنْ تُؤْذُوا رَسُولَ اللَّهِ وَلَا أَنْ

33. The Allies

thee. And Allah is ever Forgiving, Merciful.

33:51. Thou mayest put off whom thou pleasest of them, and take to thee whom thou pleasest. And whom thou desirest of those whom thou hadst separated provisionally, no blame attaches to thee. This is most proper so that their eyes may be cool and they may not grieve, and that they should be pleased, all of them, with what thou givest them. And Allah knows what is in your hearts. And Allah is ever Knowing, Forbearing.

33:52. It is not allowed to thee to take wives after this, nor to change them for other wives, though their beauty be pleasing to thee, except those whom thy right hand possesses. And Allah is ever Watchful over all things.

* * *

33:53. O you who believe, enter not the houses of the Prophet unless permission is given to you for a meal, not waiting for its cooking being finished but when you are invited, enter, and when you have taken food, disperse not seeking to listen to talk. Surely this gives the Prophet trouble, but he forbears from you, and Allah forbears not from the truth. And when you ask of them any goods, ask of them from behind a curtain. This is purer for your hearts and their hearts. And it behoves you not to give trouble to the Messenger of Allah, nor to marry his wives after him ever. Surely this is grievous in the sight of Allah.

33:54. If you do a thing openly or do it in secret, then surely Allah is ever Knower of all things.

33:55. There is no blame on them in respect of their fathers, nor their sons, nor their brothers, nor their brothers' sons, nor their sisters' sons, nor their own women, nor of what their right hands possess — and (ye women) keep your duty to Allah. Surely Allah is ever

تَنكِحُوا أَزْوَاجَهُ مِنْ بَعْدِهِ أَبَدًا إِنَّ ذَٰلِكُمْ كَانَ عِنْدَ اللَّهِ عَظِيمًا (٥٣)

إِنْ تُبْدُوا شَيْئًا أَوْ تُخْفُوهُ فَإِنَّ اللَّهَ كَانَ بِكُلِّ شَيْءٍ عَلِيمًا (٥٤)

لَا جُنَاحَ عَلَيْهِنَّ فِي آبَائِهِنَّ وَلَا أَبْنَائِهِنَّ وَلَا إِخْوَانِهِنَّ وَلَا أَبْنَاءِ إِخْوَانِهِنَّ وَلَا أَبْنَاءِ أَخَوَاتِهِنَّ وَلَا نِسَائِهِنَّ وَلَا مَا مَلَكَتْ أَيْمَانُهُنَّ وَاتَّقِينَ اللَّهَ إِنَّ اللَّهَ كَانَ عَلَىٰ كُلِّ شَيْءٍ شَهِيدًا (٥٥)

إِنَّ اللَّهَ وَمَلَائِكَتَهُ يُصَلُّونَ عَلَى النَّبِيِّ يَا أَيُّهَا الَّذِينَ آمَنُوا صَلُّوا عَلَيْهِ وَسَلِّمُوا تَسْلِيمًا (٥٦)

إِنَّ الَّذِينَ يُؤْذُونَ اللَّهَ وَرَسُولَهُ لَعَنَهُمُ اللَّهُ فِي الدُّنْيَا وَالْآخِرَةِ وَأَعَدَّ لَهُمْ عَذَابًا مُهِينًا (٥٧)

وَالَّذِينَ يُؤْذُونَ الْمُؤْمِنِينَ وَالْمُؤْمِنَاتِ بِغَيْرِ مَا اكْتَسَبُوا فَقَدِ احْتَمَلُوا بُهْتَانًا وَإِثْمًا مُبِينًا (٥٨)

يَا أَيُّهَا النَّبِيُّ قُلْ لِأَزْوَاجِكَ وَبَنَاتِكَ وَنِسَاءِ الْمُؤْمِنِينَ يُدْنِينَ عَلَيْهِنَّ مِنْ جَلَابِيبِهِنَّ ذَٰلِكَ أَدْنَىٰ أَنْ يُعْرَفْنَ فَلَا يُؤْذَيْنَ وَكَانَ اللَّهُ غَفُورًا رَحِيمًا (٥٩)

لَئِنْ لَمْ يَنْتَهِ الْمُنَافِقُونَ وَالَّذِينَ فِي قُلُوبِهِمْ مَرَضٌ وَالْمُرْجِفُونَ فِي الْمَدِينَةِ لَنُغْرِيَنَّكَ بِهِمْ ثُمَّ لَا يُجَاوِرُونَكَ فِيهَا إِلَّا قَلِيلًا (٦٠)

مَلْعُونِينَ أَيْنَمَا ثُقِفُوا أُخِذُوا وَقُتِّلُوا تَقْتِيلًا (٦١)

سُنَّةَ اللَّهِ فِي الَّذِينَ خَلَوْا مِنْ قَبْلُ وَلَنْ تَجِدَ لِسُنَّةِ اللَّهِ تَبْدِيلًا (٦٢)

يَسْأَلُكَ النَّاسُ عَنِ السَّاعَةِ قُلْ إِنَّمَا عِلْمُهَا عِنْدَ اللَّهِ وَمَا يُدْرِيكَ لَعَلَّ

33. The Allies

Witness over all things.

33:56. Surely Allah and His angels bless the Prophet. O you who believe, call for blessings on him and salute him with a (becoming) salutation.

33:57. Surely those who annoy Allah and His Messenger, Allah has cursed them in this world and the Hereafter, and He has prepared for them an abasing chastisement.

33:58. And those who annoy believing men and believing women undeservedly, they bear the guilt of slander and manifest sin.

33:59. O Prophet, tell thy wives and thy daughters and the women of believers to let down upon them their over-garments. This is more proper, so that they may be known, and not be given trouble. And Allah is ever Forgiving, Merciful.

33:60. If the hypocrites and those in whose hearts is a disease and the agitators in Madinah desist not, We shall certainly urge thee on against them, then they shall not be thy neighbours in it but for a little while —

33:61. Accursed, wherever they are found they will be seized and slain.

33:62. That was the way of Allah concerning those who have gone before; and thou wilt find no change in the way of Allah.

33:63. Men ask thee about the Hour. Say: The knowledge of it is only with Allah. And what will make thee comprehend that the Hour may be nigh?

33:64. Surely Allah has cursed the disbelievers and prepared for them a burning Fire,

33:65. To abide therein for a long time; they will find no protector nor helper.

33:66. On the day when their leaders are turned back into the Fire, they say: O would that we had obeyed Allah and obeyed the Messenger!

33:67. And they say: Our Lord, we only

obeyed our leaders and our great men, so they led us astray from the path.

33:68. Our Lord, give them a double chastisement and curse them with a great curse.

* * *

33:69. O you who believe, be not like those who maligned Moses, but Allah cleared him of what they said. And he was worthy of regard with Allah.

33:70. O you who believe, keep your duty to Allah and speak straight words:

33:71. He will put your deeds into a right state for you, and forgive you your sins. And whoever obeys Allah and His Messenger, he indeed achieves a mighty success.

33:72. Surely We offered the trust to the heavens and the earth and the mountains, but they refused to be unfaithful to it and feared from it, and man has turned unfaithful to it. Surely he is ever unjust, ignorant --

33:73. That Allah may chastise the hypocritical men and the hypocritical women and the polytheistic men and the polytheistic women, and Allah will turn (mercifully) to the believing men and the believing women. And Allah is ever Forgiving, Merciful.

34. The Saba

In the name of Allah, the Beneficent, the Merciful.

34:1. Praise be to Allah! Whose is whatsoever is in the heavens and whatsoever is in the earth, and to Him be praise in the Hereafter! And He is the Wise, the Aware.

34:2. He knows that which goes down into the earth and that which comes out of it, and that which comes down from heaven and that which goes up to it. And He is the Merciful, the Forgiving.

٣٤- سورة سبأ

بِسْمِ اللَّهِ الرَّحْمَٰنِ الرَّحِيمِ
الْحَمْدُ لِلَّهِ الَّذِي لَهُ مَا فِي السَّمَاوَاتِ وَمَا فِي الْأَرْضِ وَلَهُ الْحَمْدُ فِي الْآخِرَةِ وَهُوَ الْحَكِيمُ الْخَبِيرُ (١)
يَعْلَمُ مَا يَلِجُ فِي الْأَرْضِ وَمَا يَخْرُجُ مِنْهَا وَمَا يَنْزِلُ مِنَ السَّمَاءِ وَمَا يَعْرُجُ فِيهَا وَهُوَ الرَّحِيمُ الْغَفُورُ (٢)
وَقَالَ الَّذِينَ كَفَرُوا لَا تَأْتِينَا السَّاعَةُ قُلْ بَلَىٰ وَرَبِّي لَتَأْتِيَنَّكُمْ عَالِمِ الْغَيْبِ لَا

34. The Saba

34:3. And those who disbelieve say: The Hour will never come to us. Say: Yea, by my Lord, the Knower of the unseen! it will certainly come to you. Not an atom's weight escapes Him in the heavens or in the earth, nor is there less than that nor greater, but (all) is in a clear book,

34:4. That He may reward those who believe and do good. For them is forgiveness and an honourable sustenance.

34:5. And those who strive hard in opposing Our Messages, for them is a painful chastisement of an evil kind.

34:6. And those who have been given knowledge see that what is revealed to thee from thy Lord, is the Truth, and it guides into the path of the Mighty, the Praised.

34:7. And those who disbelieve say: Shall we show to you a man who informs you that, when you are scattered the utmost scattering, you will then be in a new creation?

34:8. Has he forged a lie against Allah or is there madness in him? Nay, those who believe not in the Hereafter are in torment and in far error.

34:9. See they not what is before them and what is behind them of the heaven and the earth? If We please, We can make them low in the land or bring down upon them a portion of heaven. Surely there is a sign in this for every servant turning (to Allah).

* * *

34:10. And certainly We gave David abundance from Us: O mountains, repeat praises with him, and the birds, and We made the iron pliant to him,

34:11. Saying: Make ample (coats of mail), and assign a time to the making of coats of mail and do ye good. Surely I am Seer of what you do.

34:12. And (We made) the wind (subservient) to Solomon; it made a month's journey in the morning and a

يَعْزُبُ عَنْهُ مِثْقَالُ ذَرَّةٍ فِي السَّمَاوَاتِ وَلَا فِي الْأَرْضِ وَلَا أَصْغَرُ مِنْ ذَلِكَ وَلَا أَكْبَرُ إِلَّا فِي كِتَابٍ مُبِينٍ (٣) لِيَجْزِيَ الَّذِينَ آمَنُوا وَعَمِلُوا الصَّالِحَاتِ أُولَئِكَ لَهُمْ مَغْفِرَةٌ وَرِزْقٌ كَرِيمٌ (٤) وَالَّذِينَ سَعَوْا فِي آيَاتِنَا مُعَاجِزِينَ أُولَئِكَ لَهُمْ عَذَابٌ مِنْ رِجْزٍ أَلِيمٌ (٥) وَيَرَى الَّذِينَ أُوتُوا الْعِلْمَ الَّذِي أُنْزِلَ إِلَيْكَ مِنْ رَبِّكَ هُوَ الْحَقَّ وَيَهْدِي إِلَى صِرَاطِ الْعَزِيزِ الْحَمِيدِ (٦) وَقَالَ الَّذِينَ كَفَرُوا هَلْ نَدُلُّكُمْ عَلَى رَجُلٍ يُنَبِّئُكُمْ إِذَا مُزِّقْتُمْ كُلَّ مُمَزَّقٍ إِنَّكُمْ لَفِي خَلْقٍ جَدِيدٍ (٧) أَفْتَرَى عَلَى اللَّهِ كَذِبًا أَمْ بِهِ جِنَّةٌ بَلِ الَّذِينَ لَا يُؤْمِنُونَ بِالْآخِرَةِ فِي الْعَذَابِ وَالضَّلَالِ الْبَعِيدِ (٨) أَفَلَمْ يَرَوْا إِلَى مَا بَيْنَ أَيْدِيهِمْ وَمَا خَلْفَهُمْ مِنَ السَّمَاءِ وَالْأَرْضِ إِنْ نَشَأْ نَخْسِفْ بِهِمُ الْأَرْضَ أَوْ نُسْقِطْ عَلَيْهِمْ كِسَفًا مِنَ السَّمَاءِ إِنَّ فِي ذَلِكَ لَآيَةً لِكُلِّ عَبْدٍ مُنِيبٍ (٩) وَلَقَدْ آتَيْنَا دَاوُودَ مِنَّا فَضْلًا يَا جِبَالُ أَوِّبِي مَعَهُ وَالطَّيْرَ وَأَلَنَّا لَهُ الْحَدِيدَ (١٠) أَنِ اعْمَلْ سَابِغَاتٍ وَقَدِّرْ فِي السَّرْدِ وَاعْمَلُوا صَالِحًا إِنِّي بِمَا تَعْمَلُونَ بَصِيرٌ (١١) وَلِسُلَيْمَانَ الرِّيحَ غُدُوُّهَا شَهْرٌ وَرَوَاحُهَا شَهْرٌ وَأَسَلْنَا لَهُ عَيْنَ الْقِطْرِ وَمِنَ الْجِنِّ مَنْ يَعْمَلُ بَيْنَ يَدَيْهِ بِإِذْنِ رَبِّهِ وَمَنْ يَزِغْ مِنْهُمْ عَنْ أَمْرِنَا نُذِقْهُ مِنْ عَذَابِ السَّعِيرِ (١٢) يَعْمَلُونَ لَهُ مَا يَشَاءُ مِنْ مَحَارِيبَ

month's journey in the evening and We made a fountain of molten brass to flow for him. And of the jinn there were those who worked before him by the command of his Lord. And whoever turned aside from Our command from among them, We made him taste of the chastisement of burning.

34:13. They made for him what he pleased, of synagogues and images, and bowls (large) as watering-troughs and fixed cooking-pots. Give thanks, O people of David! And very few of My servants are grateful.

34:14. But when We decreed death for him, naught showed them his death but a creature of the earth that ate away his staff. So when it fell down, the jinn saw clearly that, if they had known the unseen, they would not have tarried in humiliating torment.

34:15. Certainly there was a sign for Saba' in their abode -- two gardens on the right and the left. Eat of the sustenance of your Lord and give thanks to Him. A good land and a Forgiving Lord!

34:16. But they turned aside, so We sent upon them a violent torrent, and in place of their two gardens We gave them two gardens yielding bitter fruit and (growing) tamarisk and a few lote-trees.

34:17. With this We requited them because they were ungrateful; and We punish none but the ingrate.

34:18. And We made between them and the towns which We had blessed, (other) towns easy to be seen, and We apportioned the journey therein: Travel through them nights and days, secure.

34:19. But they said: Our Lord, make longer stages between our journeys. And they wronged themselves; so We made them stories and scattered them a total scattering. Surely there are signs in this for every patient, grateful one.

34:20. And the devil indeed found true

34. The Saba

his conjecture concerning them, so they follow him, except a party of the believers.

34:21. And he has no authority over them, but that We may know him who believes in the Hereafter from him who is in doubt concerning it. And thy Lord is the Preserver of all things.

* * *

34:22. Say: Call upon those whom you assert besides Allah; they control not the weight of an atom in the heavens or in the earth, nor have they any partnership in either, nor has He a helper among them.

34:23. And intercession avails naught with Him, save of him whom He permits. Until when fear is removed from their hearts, they say: What is it that your Lord said? They say: The Truth. And He is the Most High, the Great.

34:24. Say: Who gives you sustenance from the heavens and the earth? Say: Allah. And surely we or you are on a right way or in manifest error.

34:25. Say: You will not be asked of what we are guilty, nor shall we be asked of what you do.

34:26. Say: Our Lord will gather us together, then He will judge between us with truth. And He is the Best Judge, the Knower.

34:27. Say: Show me those whom you join with Him as associates. By no means (can you)! Nay, He is Allah, the Mighty, the Wise.

34:28. And We have not sent thee but as a bearer of good news and as a warner to all mankind, but most men know not.

34:29. And they say: When will this promise be (fulfilled), if you are truthful?

34:30. Say: You have the appointment of a day which you cannot postpone by an hour, nor hasten on.

* * *

وَلَا فِي الْأَرْضِ وَمَا لَهُمْ فِيهِمَا مِنْ شِرْكٍ وَمَا لَهُ مِنْهُمْ مِنْ ظَهِيرٍ (٢٢) وَلَا تَنْفَعُ الشَّفَاعَةُ عِنْدَهُ إِلَّا لِمَنْ أَذِنَ لَهُ حَتَّى إِذَا فُزِّعَ عَنْ قُلُوبِهِمْ قَالُوا مَاذَا قَالَ رَبُّكُمْ قَالُوا الْحَقَّ وَهُوَ الْعَلِيُّ الْكَبِيرُ (٢٣) قُلْ مَنْ يَرْزُقُكُمْ مِنَ السَّمَاوَاتِ وَالْأَرْضِ قُلِ اللَّهُ وَإِنَّا أَوْ إِيَّاكُمْ لَعَلَى هُدًى أَوْ فِي ضَلَالٍ مُبِينٍ (٢٤) قُلْ لَا تُسْأَلُونَ عَمَّا أَجْرَمْنَا وَلَا نُسْأَلُ عَمَّا تَعْمَلُونَ (٢٥) قُلْ يَجْمَعُ بَيْنَنَا رَبُّنَا ثُمَّ يَفْتَحُ بَيْنَنَا بِالْحَقِّ وَهُوَ الْفَتَّاحُ الْعَلِيمُ (٢٦) قُلْ أَرُونِيَ الَّذِينَ أَلْحَقْتُمْ بِهِ شُرَكَاءَ كَلَّا بَلْ هُوَ اللَّهُ الْعَزِيزُ الْحَكِيمُ (٢٧) وَمَا أَرْسَلْنَاكَ إِلَّا كَافَّةً لِلنَّاسِ بَشِيرًا وَنَذِيرًا وَلَكِنَّ أَكْثَرَ النَّاسِ لَا يَعْلَمُونَ (٢٨) وَيَقُولُونَ مَتَى هَذَا الْوَعْدُ إِنْ كُنْتُمْ صَادِقِينَ (٢٩) قُلْ لَكُمْ مِيعَادُ يَوْمٍ لَا تَسْتَأْخِرُونَ عَنْهُ سَاعَةً وَلَا تَسْتَقْدِمُونَ (٣٠) وَقَالَ الَّذِينَ كَفَرُوا لَنْ نُؤْمِنَ بِهَذَا الْقُرْآنِ وَلَا بِالَّذِي بَيْنَ يَدَيْهِ وَلَوْ تَرَى إِذِ الظَّالِمُونَ مَوْقُوفُونَ عِنْدَ رَبِّهِمْ يَرْجِعُ بَعْضُهُمْ إِلَى بَعْضٍ الْقَوْلَ يَقُولُ الَّذِينَ اسْتُضْعِفُوا لِلَّذِينَ اسْتَكْبَرُوا لَوْلَا أَنْتُمْ لَكُنَّا مُؤْمِنِينَ (٣١) قَالَ الَّذِينَ اسْتَكْبَرُوا لِلَّذِينَ اسْتُضْعِفُوا أَنَحْنُ صَدَدْنَاكُمْ عَنِ الْهُدَى بَعْدَ إِذْ جَاءَكُمْ بَلْ كُنْتُمْ مُجْرِمِينَ (٣٢) وَقَالَ الَّذِينَ اسْتُضْعِفُوا لِلَّذِينَ

34:31. And those who disbelieve say: We believe not in this Qur'an, nor in that which is before it. And if thou couldst see when the wrongdoers are made to stand before their Lord, throwing back the blame one to another! Those who were reckoned weak say to those who were proud: Had it not been for you, we would have been believers.

34:32. Those who were proud say to those who were deemed weak: Did we turn you away from the guidance after it had come to you? Nay, you (yourselves) were guilty.

34:33. And those who were deemed weak say to those who were proud: Nay, (it was your) planning by night and day when you told us to disbelieve in Allah and to set up likes with Him. And they will manifest regret when they see the chastisement. And We put shackles on the necks of those who disbelieve. They will not be requited but for what they did.

34:34. And We never sent a warner to a town but those who led easy lives in it said: We are disbelievers in that with which you are sent.

34:35. And they say: We have more wealth and children, and we cannot be punished.

34:36. Say: Surely my Lord amplifies and straitens provision for whom He pleases, but most men know not.

***

34:37. And it is not your wealth, nor your children, that bring you near to Us in rank; but whoever believes and does good, for such is a double reward for what they do, and they are secure in the highest places.

34:38. And those who strive in opposing Our messages, they will be brought to the chastisement.

34:39. Say: Surely my Lord amplifies provision for whom He pleases of His servants and straitens (it) for him. And

اسْتَكْبَرُوا بَلْ مَكْرُ اللَّيْلِ وَالنَّهَارِ إِذْ تَأْمُرُونَنَا أَنْ نَكْفُرَ بِاللَّهِ وَنَجْعَلَ لَهُ أَنْدَادًا وَأَسَرُّوا النَّدَامَةَ لَمَّا رَأَوُا الْعَذَابَ وَجَعَلْنَا الْأَغْلَالَ فِي أَعْنَاقِ الَّذِينَ كَفَرُوا هَلْ يُجْزَوْنَ إِلَّا مَا كَانُوا يَعْمَلُونَ (٣٣)

وَمَا أَرْسَلْنَا فِي قَرْيَةٍ مِنْ نَذِيرٍ إِلَّا قَالَ مُتْرَفُوهَا إِنَّا بِمَا أُرْسِلْتُمْ بِهِ كَافِرُونَ (٣٤)

وَقَالُوا نَحْنُ أَكْثَرُ أَمْوَالًا وَأَوْلَادًا وَمَا نَحْنُ بِمُعَذَّبِينَ (٣٥)

قُلْ إِنَّ رَبِّي يَبْسُطُ الرِّزْقَ لِمَنْ يَشَاءُ وَيَقْدِرُ وَلَكِنَّ أَكْثَرَ النَّاسِ لَا يَعْلَمُونَ (٣٦)

وَمَا أَمْوَالُكُمْ وَلَا أَوْلَادُكُمْ بِالَّتِي تُقَرِّبُكُمْ عِنْدَنَا زُلْفَى إِلَّا مَنْ آمَنَ وَعَمِلَ صَالِحًا فَأُولَئِكَ لَهُمْ جَزَاءُ الضِّعْفِ بِمَا عَمِلُوا وَهُمْ فِي الْغُرُفَاتِ آمِنُونَ (٣٧)

وَالَّذِينَ يَسْعَوْنَ فِي آيَاتِنَا مُعَاجِزِينَ أُولَئِكَ فِي الْعَذَابِ مُحْضَرُونَ (٣٨)

قُلْ إِنَّ رَبِّي يَبْسُطُ الرِّزْقَ لِمَنْ يَشَاءُ مِنْ عِبَادِهِ وَيَقْدِرُ لَهُ وَمَا أَنْفَقْتُمْ مِنْ شَيْءٍ فَهُوَ يُخْلِفُهُ وَهُوَ خَيْرُ الرَّازِقِينَ (٣٩)

وَيَوْمَ يَحْشُرُهُمْ جَمِيعًا ثُمَّ يَقُولُ لِلْمَلَائِكَةِ أَهَؤُلَاءِ إِيَّاكُمْ كَانُوا يَعْبُدُونَ (٤٠)

قَالُوا سُبْحَانَكَ أَنْتَ وَلِيُّنَا مِنْ دُونِهِمْ بَلْ كَانُوا يَعْبُدُونَ الْجِنَّ أَكْثَرُهُمْ بِهِمْ مُؤْمِنُونَ (٤١)

فَالْيَوْمَ لَا يَمْلِكُ بَعْضُكُمْ لِبَعْضٍ نَفْعًا وَلَا ضَرًّا وَنَقُولُ لِلَّذِينَ ظَلَمُوا ذُوقُوا عَذَابَ النَّارِ الَّتِي كُنْتُمْ بِهَا تُكَذِّبُونَ

34. The Saba

whatsoever you spend, He increases it in reward, and He is the Best of Providers.

34:40. And on the day when He will gather them all together, then will He say to the angels: Did these worship you?

34:41. They will say: Glory be to Thee! Thou art our Protecting Friend, not they; nay, they worshipped the jinn; most of them were believers in them.

34:42. So on that day you will not control profit nor harm for one another. And We will say to those who were iniquitous: Taste the chastisement of the Fire, which you called a lie.

34:43. And when Our clear messages are recited to them, they say: This is naught but a man who desires to turn you away from that which your fathers worshipped. And they say: This is naught but a forged lie! And those who disbelieve say of the Truth when it comes to them: This is only clear enchantment

34:44. And We have not given them any Books which they read, nor did We send to them before thee a warner.

34:45. And those before them rejected (the truth), and these have not yet attained a tenth of that which We gave them, but they gave the lie to My messengers. How (terrible) was then My disapproval!

***

34:46. Say: I exhort you only to one thing, that you rise up for Allah's sake by twos and singly, then ponder! There is no madness in your companion. He is only a warner to you before a severe chastisement.

34:47. Say: Whatever reward I ask of you, that is only for yourselves. My reward is only with Allah, and He is a Witness over all things.

34:48. Say: Surely my Lord casts the Truth, the great Knower of the unseen.

34:49. Say: The Truth has come, and

falsehood neither originates, nor reproduces.

34:50. Say: If I err, I err only to my own loss and if I go aright, it is because of what my Lord reveals to me. Surely He is Hearing, Nigh.

34:51. And couldst thou see when they become terrified, but (then) there will be no escape and they will be seized from a near place;

34:52. And they will say: We believe in it. And how can they attain (to faith) from a distant place?

34:53. And they indeed disbelieved in it before, and they utter conjectures with regard to the unseen from a distant place.

34:54. And a barrier is placed between them and that which they desire, as was done with their partisans before. Surely they are in a disquieting doubt.

35. The Originator

In the name of Allah, the Beneficent, the Merciful.

35:1. Praise be to Allah, the Originator of the heavens and the earth, the Maker of the angels, messengers flying on wings, two, and three, and four. He increases in creation what He pleases. Surely Allah is Possessor of power over all things.

35:2. Whatever Allah grants to men of (His) mercy, there is none to withhold it, and what He withholds, none can grant thereafter. And He is the Mighty, the Wise.

35:3. O Men, call to mind the favour of Allah to you. Is there any Creator besides Allah who provides for you from the heaven and the earth? There is no God but He. How are you then turned away?

35:4. And if they reject thee -- truly messengers before thee were rejected. And to Allah are all affairs returned.

35. The Originator

35:5. O men, surely the promise of Allah is true, so let not the life of this world deceive you. And let not the arch-deceiver deceive you about Allah.

35:6. Surely the devil is your enemy, so take him for an enemy. He only invites his party to be companions of the burning Fire.

35:7. Those who disbelieve, for them is a severe chastisement. And those who believe and do good, for them is forgiveness and a great reward.

* * *

35:8. Is he whose evil deed is made fair-seeming to him so that he considers it good? Now surely Allah leaves in error whom He pleases and guides aright whom He pleases, so let not thy soul waste away in grief for them. Surely Allah is Knower of what they do.

35:9. And Allah is He Who sends the winds, so they raise a cloud, then We drive it on to a dead land, and therewith give life to the earth after its death. Even so is the quickening.

35:10. Whoever desires might, then to Allah belongs the might wholly. To Him do ascend the goodly words, and the goodly deed -- He exalts it. And those who plan evil -- for them is a severe chastisement. And their plan will perish.

35:11. And Allah created you from dust, then from the life-germ, then He made you pairs. And no female bears, nor brings forth, except with His knowledge. And no one living long is granted a long life, nor is aught diminished of one's life, but it is all in a book. Surely this is easy to Allah.

35:12. And the two seas are not alike the one sweet, very sweet, pleasant to drink; and the other salt, bitter. Yet from both you eat fresh flesh and bring forth ornaments which you wear. And thou seest the ships cleave through it, that you may seek of His bounty and that you may give thanks.

تَغُرَّنَّكُمُ الْحَيَاةُ الدُّنْيَا وَلَا يَغُرَّنَّكُم بِاللَّهِ الْغَرُورُ (٥)

إِنَّ الشَّيْطَانَ لَكُمْ عَدُوٌّ فَاتَّخِذُوهُ عَدُوًّا إِنَّمَا يَدْعُو حِزْبَهُ لِيَكُونُوا مِنْ أَصْحَابِ السَّعِيرِ (٦)

الَّذِينَ كَفَرُوا لَهُمْ عَذَابٌ شَدِيدٌ وَالَّذِينَ آمَنُوا وَعَمِلُوا الصَّالِحَاتِ لَهُم مَّغْفِرَةٌ وَأَجْرٌ كَبِيرٌ (٧)

أَفَمَن زُيِّنَ لَهُ سُوءُ عَمَلِهِ فَرَآهُ حَسَنًا فَإِنَّ اللَّهَ يُضِلُّ مَن يَشَاءُ وَيَهْدِي مَن يَشَاءُ فَلَا تَذْهَبْ نَفْسُكَ عَلَيْهِمْ حَسَرَاتٍ إِنَّ اللَّهَ عَلِيمٌ بِمَا يَصْنَعُونَ (٨)

وَاللَّهُ الَّذِي أَرْسَلَ الرِّيَاحَ فَتُثِيرُ سَحَابًا فَسُقْنَاهُ إِلَى بَلَدٍ مَّيِّتٍ فَأَحْيَيْنَا بِهِ الْأَرْضَ بَعْدَ مَوْتِهَا كَذَلِكَ النُّشُورُ (٩)

مَن كَانَ يُرِيدُ الْعِزَّةَ فَلِلَّهِ الْعِزَّةُ جَمِيعًا إِلَيْهِ يَصْعَدُ الْكَلِمُ الطَّيِّبُ وَالْعَمَلُ الصَّالِحُ يَرْفَعُهُ وَالَّذِينَ يَمْكُرُونَ السَّيِّئَاتِ لَهُمْ عَذَابٌ شَدِيدٌ وَمَكْرُ أُولَئِكَ هُوَ يَبُورُ (١٠)

وَاللَّهُ خَلَقَكُم مِّن تُرَابٍ ثُمَّ مِن نُّطْفَةٍ ثُمَّ جَعَلَكُمْ أَزْوَاجًا وَمَا تَحْمِلُ مِنْ أُنْثَى وَلَا تَضَعُ إِلَّا بِعِلْمِهِ وَمَا يُعَمَّرُ مِن مُّعَمَّرٍ وَلَا يُنقَصُ مِنْ عُمُرِهِ إِلَّا فِي كِتَابٍ إِنَّ ذَلِكَ عَلَى اللَّهِ يَسِيرٌ (١١)

وَمَا يَسْتَوِي الْبَحْرَانِ هَذَا عَذْبٌ فُرَاتٌ سَائِغٌ شَرَابُهُ وَهَذَا مِلْحٌ أُجَاجٌ وَمِن كُلٍّ تَأْكُلُونَ لَحْمًا طَرِيًّا وَتَسْتَخْرِجُونَ حِلْيَةً تَلْبَسُونَهَا وَتَرَى الْفُلْكَ فِيهِ مَوَاخِرَ لِتَبْتَغُوا مِن فَضْلِهِ وَلَعَلَّكُمْ تَشْكُرُونَ (١٢)

35. The Originator

35:13. He causes the night to enter in upon the day, and causes the day to enter in upon the night, and He has made subservient the sun and the moon, each one moves to an appointed time. This is Allah, your Lord; His is the kingdom. And those whom you call upon besides Him own not a straw.
35:14. If you call on them, they hear not your call; and if they heard, they could not answer you. And on the day of Resurrection they will deny your associating them (with Allah). And none can inform thee like the All-Aware One.

* * *

35:15. O men, it is you that have need of Allah, and Allah is the Self-Sufficient, the Praised One.
35:16. If He please, He will remove you and bring a new creation.
35:17. And this is not hard to Allah.
35:18. And no burdened soul can bear another's burden. And if one weighed down by a burden calls another to carry his load, naught of it will be carried, even though he be near of kin. Thou warnest only those who fear their Lord in secret and keep up prayer. And whoever purifies himself, purifies himself only for his own good. And to Allah is the eventual coming.
35:19. And the blind and the seeing are not alike,
35:20. Nor the darkness and the light,
35:21. Nor the shade and the heat.
35:22. Neither are the living and the dead alike. Surely Allah makes whom He pleases hear; and thou canst not make those hear who are in the graves.
35:23. Thou art naught but a warner.
35:24. Surely We have sent thee with the Truth as a bearer of good news and a warner. And there is not a people but a warner has gone among them.
35:25. And if they reject thee, those before them also rejected -- their messengers came to them with clear

يُولِجُ اللَّيْلَ فِي النَّهَارِ وَيُولِجُ النَّهَارَ فِي اللَّيْلِ وَسَخَّرَ الشَّمْسَ وَالْقَمَرَ كُلٌّ يَجْرِي لِأَجَلٍ مُسَمًّى ذَلِكُمُ اللَّهُ رَبُّكُمْ لَهُ الْمُلْكُ وَالَّذِينَ تَدْعُونَ مِنْ دُونِهِ مَا يَمْلِكُونَ مِنْ قِطْمِيرٍ (١٣)

إِنْ تَدْعُوهُمْ لَا يَسْمَعُوا دُعَاءَكُمْ وَلَوْ سَمِعُوا مَا اسْتَجَابُوا لَكُمْ وَيَوْمَ الْقِيَامَةِ يَكْفُرُونَ بِشِرْكِكُمْ وَلَا يُنَبِّئُكَ مِثْلُ خَبِيرٍ (١٤)

يَا أَيُّهَا النَّاسُ أَنْتُمُ الْفُقَرَاءُ إِلَى اللَّهِ وَاللَّهُ هُوَ الْغَنِيُّ الْحَمِيدُ (١٥)

إِنْ يَشَأْ يُذْهِبْكُمْ وَيَأْتِ بِخَلْقٍ جَدِيدٍ (١٦)

وَمَا ذَلِكَ عَلَى اللَّهِ بِعَزِيزٍ (١٧)

وَلَا تَزِرُ وَازِرَةٌ وِزْرَ أُخْرَى وَإِنْ تَدْعُ مُثْقَلَةٌ إِلَى حِمْلِهَا لَا يُحْمَلْ مِنْهُ شَيْءٌ وَلَوْ كَانَ ذَا قُرْبَى إِنَّمَا تُنْذِرُ الَّذِينَ يَخْشَوْنَ رَبَّهُمْ بِالْغَيْبِ وَأَقَامُوا الصَّلَاةَ وَمَنْ تَزَكَّى فَإِنَّمَا يَتَزَكَّى لِنَفْسِهِ وَإِلَى اللَّهِ الْمَصِيرُ (١٨)

وَمَا يَسْتَوِي الْأَعْمَى وَالْبَصِيرُ (١٩)

وَلَا الظُّلُمَاتُ وَلَا النُّورُ (٢٠)

وَلَا الظِّلُّ وَلَا الْحَرُورُ (٢١)

وَمَا يَسْتَوِي الْأَحْيَاءُ وَلَا الْأَمْوَاتُ إِنَّ اللَّهَ يُسْمِعُ مَنْ يَشَاءُ وَمَا أَنْتَ بِمُسْمِعٍ مَنْ فِي الْقُبُورِ (٢٢)

إِنْ أَنْتَ إِلَّا نَذِيرٌ (٢٣)

إِنَّا أَرْسَلْنَاكَ بِالْحَقِّ بَشِيرًا وَنَذِيرًا وَإِنْ مِنْ أُمَّةٍ إِلَّا خَلَا فِيهَا نَذِيرٌ (٢٤)

وَإِنْ يُكَذِّبُوكَ فَقَدْ كَذَّبَ الَّذِينَ مِنْ قَبْلِهِمْ جَاءَتْهُمْ رُسُلُهُمْ بِالْبَيِّنَاتِ وَبِالزُّبُرِ وَبِالْكِتَابِ الْمُنِيرِ (٢٥)

ثُمَّ أَخَذْتُ الَّذِينَ كَفَرُوا فَكَيْفَ كَانَ

arguments, and with scriptures, and with the illuminating Book.

35:26. Then I seized those who disbelieved, so how (terrible) was My disapproval!

***

35:27. Seest thou not that Allah sends down water from the clouds, then We bring forth therewith fruits of various hues? And in the mountains are streaks, white and red, of various hues and (others) intensely black.

35:28. And of men and beasts and cattle there are various colours likewise. Those of His servants only who are possessed of knowledge fear Allah. Surely Allah is Mighty, Forgiving.

35:29. Surely those who recite the Book of Allah and keep up prayer and spend out of what We have given them, secretly and openly, hope for a gain which perishes not --

35:30. That He may pay them back fully their rewards and give them more out of His grace. Surely He is Forgiving, Multiplier of reward.

35:31. And that which We have revealed to thee of the Book, that is the truth, verifying that which is before it. Surely Allah is Aware, Seer of His servants.

35:32. Then We have given the Book as inheritance to those whom We have chosen from among Our servants: so of them is he who wrongs himself, and of them is he who takes a middle course, and of them is he who is foremost in deeds of goodness by Allah's permission. That is the great grace.

35:33. Gardens of perpetuity, which they enter -- they are made to wear therein bracelets of gold and pearls, and their dress therein is silk.

35:34. And they say: Praise be to Allah, Who has removed grief from us! Surely our Lord is Forgiving, Multiplier of reward,

35:35. Who out of His grace has made

us alight in a house abiding for ever; therein toil touches us not nor does fatigue afflict us therein.

35:36. And those who disbelieve, for them is Fire of hell; it is not finished with them so that they should die, nor is chastisement thereof lightened to them. Thus We deal retribution on every ungrateful one.

35:37. And therein they cry for succour: Our Lord, take us out! we will do good deeds other than those which we used to do! Did We not give you a life long enough, for him to be mindful who would mind? And there came to you the warner. So taste; because for the iniquitous there is no helper.

***

35:38. Surely Allah is the Knower of the unseen in the heavens and the earth. Surely He is Knower of what is in the hearts.

35:39. He it is Who made you successors in the earth. So whoever disbelieves, his disbelief is against himself. And their disbelief increases the disbelievers with their Lord in naught but hatred; and their disbelief increases the disbelievers in naught but loss.

35:40. Say: Have you seen your associates which you call upon besides Allah? Show me what they have created of the earth! Or have they any share in the heavens? Or, have We given them a Book so that they follow a clear argument thereof? Nay, the wrongdoers hold out promises one to another only to deceive.

35:41. Surely Allah upholds the heavens and the earth lest they come to naught. And if they come to naught, none can uphold them after Him. Surely He is ever Forbearing, Forgiving.

35:42. And they swore by Allah, their strongest oaths, that, if a warner came to them, they would be better guided than any of the nations. But when a warner came to them, it increased them in naught but aversion,

35:43. Behaving proudly in the land and planning evil. And the evil plan besets none save the authors of it. So they wait for naught but the way of the ancients. But thou wilt find no alteration in the course of Allah and thou wilt find no change in the course of Allah.

35:44. Have they not travelled in the land and seen what was the end of those before them and they were stronger than those in power? And Allah is not such that anything in the heavens or the earth can escape Him. Surely He is ever Knowing, Powerful.

35:45. And were Allah to punish men for what they earn, He would not leave on the back of it any creature, but He respires them till an appointed term so when their doom comes, then surely Allah is ever Seer of His servants.

36. Ya Sin

In the name of Allah, the Beneficent, the Merciful.

36:1. O man,

36:2. By the Qur'an, full of wisdom!

36:3. Surely thou art one of the messengers,

36:4. On a right way.

36:5. A revelation of the Mighty, the Merciful,

36:6. That thou mayest warn a people whose fathers were not warned, so they are heedless.

36:7. The word has indeed proved true of most of them, so they believe not,

36:8. Surely We have placed on their necks chains reaching up to the chins, so they have their heads raised aloft.

36:9. And We have set a barrier before them and a barrier behind them, thus We have covered them, so that they see

36. Ya Sin

not.

36:10. And it is alike to them whether thou warn them or warn them nor -- they believe not.

36:11. Thou canst warn him only who follows the Reminder and fears the Beneficent in secret; so give him good news of forgiveness and a generous reward.

36:12. Surely We give life to the dead, and We write down that which they send before and their footprints, and We record everything in a clear writing.

* * *

36:13. And set out to them a parable of the people of the town when apostles came to it.

36:14. When We sent to them two, they rejected them both; then We strengthened (them) with a third, so they said: Surely we are sent to you.

36:15. They said: You are only mortals like ourselves, nor has the Beneficent revealed anything -- you only lie.

36:16. They said: Our Lord knows that we are surely sent to you.

36:17. And our duty is only a clear deliverance (of the message).

36:18. They said: Surely we augur evil from you. If you desist not, we will surely stone you, and a painful chastisement from us will certainly afflict you.

36:19. They said: Your evil fortune is with you. What! If you are reminded! Nay, you are an extravagant people.

36:20. And from the remote part of the city there came a man running. He said: O my people, follow the apostles.

36:21. Follow him who asks of you no reward, and they are on the right course.

* * *

36:22. And what reason have I that I should not serve Him Who created me and to Whom you will be brought back.

36. Ya Sin

36:23. Shall I take besides Him gods whose intercession, if the Beneficent should desire to afflict me with harm, will avail me naught, not can they deliver me?

36:24. Then I shall surely be in clear error.

36:25. Surely I believe in your Lord, so hear me.

36:26. It was said: Enter the Garden. He said: Would that my people knew,

36:27. How my Lord has forgiven me and made me of the honoured ones!

36:28. And We sent not down upon his people after him any host from heaven, nor do We ever send.

36:29. It was naught but a single cry, and lo! they were still.

36:30. Alas for the servants! Never does a messenger come to them but they mock him.

36:31. See they not how many generations We destroyed before them, that they return not to them?

36:32. And all -- surely all -- will be brought before Us.

* * *

36:33. And a sign to them is the dead earth: We give life to it and bring forth from it grain so they eat of it.

36:34. And We make therein gardens of date-palms and grapes and We make springs to flow forth therein,

36:35. That they may eat of the fruit thereof, and their hands made it not. Will they not then give thanks?

36:36. Glory be to Him Who created pairs of all things, of what the earth grows, and of their kind and of what they know not!

36:37. And a sign to them is the night: We draw forth from it the day, then lo! they are in darkness;

36:38. And the sun moves on to its destination. That is the ordinance of the Mighty, the Knower.

36:39. And the moon, We have ordained for it stages till it becomes again as an old dry palm-branch.

36:40. Neither is it for the sun to overtake the moon, nor can the night outstrip the day. And all float on in an orbit.

36:41. And a sign to them is that We bear their offspring in the laden ship,

36:42. And We have created for them the like thereof, whereon they ride.

36:43. And if We please, We may drown them, then there is no succour for them, nor can they be rescued --

36:44. But by mercy from Us and for enjoyment till a time.

36:45. And when it is said to them Guard against that which is before you and that which is behind you, that mercy may be shown to you.

36:46. And there comes to them no message of the messages of their Lord but they turn away from it.

36:47. And when it is said to them: Spend out of that which Allah has given you, those who disbelieve say to those who believe: Shall we feed him whom, if Allah please, He could feed? You are in naught but clear error.

36:48. And they say: When will this promise come to pass, if you are truthful?

36:49. They await but a single cry, which will overtake them while they contend.

36:50. So they will not be able to make a bequest, nor will they return to their families.

***

36:51. And the trumpet is blown, when lo! from their graves they will hasten on to their Lord.

36:52. They will say: O woe to us Who has raised us up from our sleeping-place? This is what the Beneficent promised and the messengers told the truth.

36:53. It is but a single cry, when lo! they are all brought before Us.

36:54. So this day no soul is wronged in

aught and you are not rewarded aught but for what you did.

36:55. Surely the owners of the Garden are on that day in a happy occupation.

36:56. They and their wives are in shades, reclining on raised couches.

36:57. They have fruits therein, and they have whatever they desire.

36:58. Peace! A word from a Merciful Lord.

36:59. And withdraw to-day, O guilty ones!

36:60. Did I not charge you, O children of Adam, that you serve not the devil? Surely he is your open enemy.

36:61. And that you serve Me. This is the right way.

36:62. And certainly he led astray numerous people from among you. Could you not then understand?

36:63. This is the hell which you were promised.

36:64. Enter it this day because you disbelieved.

36:65. That day We shall seal their mouths, and their hands will speak to Us, and their feet will bear witness as to what they earned.

36:66. And if We pleased, We would put out their eyes, then they would strive to get first to the way, but how should they see?

36:67. And if We pleased, We would transform them in their place, then they would not be able to go on, or turn back.

* * *

36:68. And whomsoever We cause to live long, We reduce to an abject state in creation. Do they not understand?

36:69. And We have not taught him poetry, nor is it meet for him. This is naught but a Reminder and a plain Qur'an,

36:70. To warn him who would have life, and (that) the word may prove true against the disbelievers.

36:71. See they not that We have

36. Ya Sin

created cattle for them, out of what Our hands have wrought, so they are their masters?
36:72. And We have subjected them to them, so some of them they ride, and some they eat.
36:73. And therein they have advantages and drinks. Will they not then give thanks?
36:74. And they take gods besides Allah that they may be helped.
36:75. They are not able to help them, and they are a host brought up before them.
36:76. So let not their speech grieve thee. Surely We know what they do in secret and what they do openly.
36:77. Does not man see that We have created him from the small life germ? Then lo! he is an open disputant.
36:78. And he strikes our a likeness for Us and forgets his own creation. Says he: Who will give life to the bones, when they are rotten?
36:79. Say He will give life to them, Who brought them into existence at first, and He is Knower of all creation,
36:80. Who produced fire for you out of the green tree, so that with it you kindle.
36:81. Is not He Who created the heavens and the earth able to create the like of them? Yea! And He is the Creator (of all), the Knower.
36:82. His command, when He intends anything, is only to say to it, Be, and it is.
36:83. So glory be to Him in Whose hand is the kingdom of all things and to Him you will be returned.

وَمَنْ نُعَمِّرْهُ نُنَكِّسْهُ فِي الْخَلْقِ أَفَلَا يَعْقِلُونَ (٦٨)
وَمَا عَلَّمْنَاهُ الشِّعْرَ وَمَا يَنْبَغِي لَهُ إِنْ هُوَ إِلَّا ذِكْرٌ وَقُرْآنٌ مُبِينٌ (٦٩)
لِيُنْذِرَ مَنْ كَانَ حَيًّا وَيَحِقَّ الْقَوْلُ عَلَى الْكَافِرِينَ (٧٠)
أَوَلَمْ يَرَوْا أَنَّا خَلَقْنَا لَهُمْ مِمَّا عَمِلَتْ أَيْدِينَا أَنْعَامًا فَهُمْ لَهَا مَالِكُونَ (٧١)
وَذَلَّلْنَاهَا لَهُمْ فَمِنْهَا رَكُوبُهُمْ وَمِنْهَا يَأْكُلُونَ (٧٢)
وَلَهُمْ فِيهَا مَنَافِعُ وَمَشَارِبُ أَفَلَا يَشْكُرُونَ (٧٣)
وَاتَّخَذُوا مِنْ دُونِ اللَّهِ آلِهَةً لَعَلَّهُمْ يُنْصَرُونَ (٧٤)
لَا يَسْتَطِيعُونَ نَصْرَهُمْ وَهُمْ لَهُمْ جُنْدٌ مُحْضَرُونَ (٧٥)
فَلَا يَحْزُنْكَ قَوْلُهُمْ إِنَّا نَعْلَمُ مَا يُسِرُّونَ وَمَا يُعْلِنُونَ (٧٦)
أَوَلَمْ يَرَ الْإِنْسَانُ أَنَّا خَلَقْنَاهُ مِنْ نُطْفَةٍ فَإِذَا هُوَ خَصِيمٌ مُبِينٌ (٧٧)
وَضَرَبَ لَنَا مَثَلًا وَنَسِيَ خَلْقَهُ قَالَ مَنْ يُحْيِي الْعِظَامَ وَهِيَ رَمِيمٌ (٧٨)
قُلْ يُحْيِيهَا الَّذِي أَنْشَأَهَا أَوَّلَ مَرَّةٍ وَهُوَ بِكُلِّ خَلْقٍ عَلِيمٌ (٧٩)
الَّذِي جَعَلَ لَكُمْ مِنَ الشَّجَرِ الْأَخْضَرِ نَارًا فَإِذَا أَنْتُمْ مِنْهُ تُوقِدُونَ (٨٠)
أَوَلَيْسَ الَّذِي خَلَقَ السَّمَاوَاتِ وَالْأَرْضَ بِقَادِرٍ عَلَى أَنْ يَخْلُقَ مِثْلَهُمْ بَلَى وَهُوَ الْخَلَّاقُ الْعَلِيمُ (٨١)
إِنَّمَا أَمْرُهُ إِذَا أَرَادَ شَيْئًا أَنْ يَقُولَ لَهُ كُنْ فَيَكُونُ (٨٢)
فَسُبْحَانَ الَّذِي بِيَدِهِ مَلَكُوتُ كُلِّ شَيْءٍ وَإِلَيْهِ تُرْجَعُونَ (٨٣)

37. Those Ranging in Ranks

In the name of Allah, the Beneficent, the Merciful. 1 By those ranging in ranks,

37:2. And those who restrain holding in restraint,

37:3. And those who recite the Reminder,

37:4. Surely your God is One.

37:5. The Lord of the heavens and the earth and what is between them, and the Lord of the eastern lands.

37:6. Surely We have adorned the lower heaven with an adornment, the stars,

37:7. And (there is) a safeguard against every rebellious devil.

37:8. They cannot listen to the exalted assembly and they are reproached from every side,

37:9. Driven off; and for them is a perpetual chastisement,

37:10. Except him who snatches away but once, then there follows him a brightly shining flame.

37:11. So ask them whether they are stronger in creation or those (others) whom We have created. Surely We created them of firm clay.

37:12. Nay, thou wonderest, while they mock,

37:13. And when they are reminded, they mind not,

37:14. And when they see a sign, they seek to scoff,

37:15. And say: This is nothing but clear enchantment.

37:16. When we are dead and have become dust and bones; shall we then be raised,

37:17. Or our fathers of yore?

37:18. Say: Yea, and you will be humiliated.

37:19. So it will be but one cry, when lo! they will see.

37:20. And they will say: O woe to us! This is the day of Requital.

٣٧- سورة الصافات

بِسْمِ اللهِ الرَّحْمَنِ الرَّحِيمِ
وَالصَّافَّاتِ صَفًّا (١)
فَالزَّاجِرَاتِ زَجْرًا (٢)
فَالتَّالِيَاتِ ذِكْرًا (٣)
إِنَّ إِلَهَكُمْ لَوَاحِدٌ (٤)
رَبُّ السَّمَاوَاتِ وَالْأَرْضِ وَمَا بَيْنَهُمَا وَرَبُّ الْمَشَارِقِ (٥)
إِنَّا زَيَّنَّا السَّمَاءَ الدُّنْيَا بِزِينَةٍ الْكَوَاكِبِ (٦)
وَحِفْظًا مِنْ كُلِّ شَيْطَانٍ مَارِدٍ (٧)
لَا يَسَّمَّعُونَ إِلَى الْمَلَإِ الْأَعْلَى وَيُقْذَفُونَ مِنْ كُلِّ جَانِبٍ (٨)
دُحُورًا وَلَهُمْ عَذَابٌ وَاصِبٌ (٩)
إِلَّا مَنْ خَطِفَ الْخَطْفَةَ فَأَتْبَعَهُ شِهَابٌ ثَاقِبٌ (١٠)
فَاسْتَفْتِهِمْ أَهُمْ أَشَدُّ خَلْقًا أَمْ مَنْ خَلَقْنَا إِنَّا خَلَقْنَاهُمْ مِنْ طِينٍ لَازِبٍ (١١)
بَلْ عَجِبْتَ وَيَسْخَرُونَ (١٢)
وَإِذَا ذُكِّرُوا لَا يَذْكُرُونَ (١٣)
وَإِذَا رَأَوْا آيَةً يَسْتَسْخِرُونَ (١٤)
وَقَالُوا إِنْ هَذَا إِلَّا سِحْرٌ مُبِينٌ (١٥)
أَإِذَا مِتْنَا وَكُنَّا تُرَابًا وَعِظَامًا أَإِنَّا لَمَبْعُوثُونَ (١٦)
أَوَآبَاؤُنَا الْأَوَّلُونَ (١٧)
قُلْ نَعَمْ وَأَنْتُمْ دَاخِرُونَ (١٨)
فَإِنَّمَا هِيَ زَجْرَةٌ وَاحِدَةٌ فَإِذَا هُمْ يَنْظُرُونَ (١٩)
وَقَالُوا يَا وَيْلَنَا هَذَا يَوْمُ الدِّينِ (٢٠)
هَذَا يَوْمُ الْفَصْلِ الَّذِي كُنْتُمْ بِهِ تُكَذِّبُونَ (٢١)
احْشُرُوا الَّذِينَ ظَلَمُوا وَأَزْوَاجَهُمْ وَمَا

37:21. This is the day of Judgment, which you called a lie.

***

37:22. Gather together those who did wrong and their associates, and what they worshipped

37:23. Besides Allah, then lead them to the way to hell.

37:24. And stop them, for they shall be questioned:

37:25. What is the matter with you that you help not one another?

37:26. Nay, on that day they will be submissive.

37:27. And some of them will turn to others mutually questioning --

37:28. Saying: Surely you used to come to us from the right side.

37:29. They will say: Nay, you (yourselves) were not believers.

37:30. And we had no authority over you, but you were an inordinate people.

37:31. So the word of our Lord has proved true against us: we shall surely taste.

37:32. We led you astray, for we ourselves were erring.

37:33. So, that day they will be sharers in the chastisement.

37:34. Thus do We deal with the guilty.

37:35. They indeed were arrogant, when it was said to them: There is no god but Allah;

37:36. And said: Shall we give up our gods for a mad poet?

37:37. Nay, he has brought the Truth ind verifies the messengers.

37:38. Surely you will taste the painful chastisement.

37:39. And you are requited naught but for what you did --

37:40. Save the servants of Allah, the purified ones.

37:41. For them is a known sustenance:

37:42. Fruits. And they are honoured,

37:43. In Gardens of delight,

37:44. On thrones, facing each other.

37:45. A bowl of running water will be made to go round them,
37:46. White, delicious to those who drink.
37:47. It deprives not of reason, nor are they exhausted therewith.
37:48. And with them are those modest in gaze, having beautiful eyes,
37:49. As if they were eggs, carefully protected.
37:50. Then some of them will turn to others, questioning mutually.
37:51. A speaker of them will say: Surely I had a comrade,
37:52. Who said: Art thou indeed of those who accept?
37:53. When we are dead and have become dust and bones, shall we then be requited?
37:54. He will say: Will you look?
37:55. Then he looked down and saw him in the midst of hell.
37:56. He will say: By Allah! thou hadst almost caused me to perish
37:57. And had it not been for favour of my Lord, I should have been among those brought up.
37:58. Are we not to die,
37:59. Except our previous death? And are we not to be chastised?
37:60. Surely this is the mighty achievement.
37:61. For the like of this, then, let the workers work.
37:62. Is this the better entertainment or the tree of Zaqqum?
37:63. Surely We have made it a trial for the wrongdoers.
37:64. It is a tree that grows in the bottom of hell --
37:65. Its produce is as it were the heads of serpents.
37:66. Then truly they will eat of it and fill (their) bellies with it.
37:67. Then surely they shall have after it a drink of boiling water.
37:68. Then their return is surety to the flaming Fire.

عَلَىٰ سُرُرٍ مُتَقَابِلِينَ (٤٤)
يُطَافُ عَلَيْهِمْ بِكَأْسٍ مِنْ مَعِينٍ (٤٥)
بَيْضَاءَ لَذَّةٍ لِلشَّارِبِينَ (٤٦)
لَا فِيهَا غَوْلٌ وَلَا هُمْ عَنْهَا يُنْزَفُونَ (٤٧)
وَعِنْدَهُمْ قَاصِرَاتُ الطَّرْفِ عِينٌ (٤٨)
كَأَنَّهُنَّ بَيْضٌ مَكْنُونٌ (٤٩)
فَأَقْبَلَ بَعْضُهُمْ عَلَىٰ بَعْضٍ يَتَسَاءَلُونَ (٥٠)
قَالَ قَائِلٌ مِنْهُمْ إِنِّي كَانَ لِي قَرِينٌ (٥١)
يَقُولُ أَئِنَّكَ لَمِنَ الْمُصَدِّقِينَ (٥٢)
أَئِذَا مِتْنَا وَكُنَّا تُرَابًا وَعِظَامًا أَئِنَّا لَمَدِينُونَ (٥٣)
قَالَ هَلْ أَنْتُمْ مُطَّلِعُونَ (٥٤)
فَاطَّلَعَ فَرَآهُ فِي سَوَاءِ الْجَحِيمِ (٥٥)
قَالَ تَاللَّهِ إِنْ كِدْتَ لَتُرْدِينِ (٥٦)
وَلَوْلَا نِعْمَةُ رَبِّي لَكُنْتُ مِنَ الْمُحْضَرِينَ (٥٧)
أَفَمَا نَحْنُ بِمَيِّتِينَ (٥٨)
إِلَّا مَوْتَتَنَا الْأُولَىٰ وَمَا نَحْنُ بِمُعَذَّبِينَ (٥٩)
إِنَّ هَٰذَا لَهُوَ الْفَوْزُ الْعَظِيمُ (٦٠)
لِمِثْلِ هَٰذَا فَلْيَعْمَلِ الْعَامِلُونَ (٦١)
أَذَٰلِكَ خَيْرٌ نُزُلًا أَمْ شَجَرَةُ الزَّقُّومِ (٦٢)
إِنَّا جَعَلْنَاهَا فِتْنَةً لِلظَّالِمِينَ (٦٣)
إِنَّهَا شَجَرَةٌ تَخْرُجُ فِي أَصْلِ الْجَحِيمِ (٦٤)
طَلْعُهَا كَأَنَّهُ رُءُوسُ الشَّيَاطِينِ (٦٥)
فَإِنَّهُمْ لَآكِلُونَ مِنْهَا فَمَالِئُونَ مِنْهَا

37:69. They indeed found their fathers astray,
37:70. So in their footsteps they are hastening on.
37:71. And most of the ancients surely went astray before them,
37:72. And indeed We sent among them warners.
37:73. Then see what was the end of those warned --
37:74. Except the servants of Allah, the purified ones.

* * *

37:75. And Noah certainly called upon Us, and excellent Answerer of prayers are We!
37:76. And We delivered him and his people from the great distress;
37:77. And made his offspring the survivors,
37:78. And left for him (praise) among the later generations,
37:79. Peace be to Noah among the nations!
37:80. Thus indeed do We reward the doers of good.
37:81. Surely he was of Our believing servants.
37:82. Then We drowned the others.
37:83. And surely of his party was Abraham.
37:84. When he came to his Lord with a secure heart.
37:85. When he said to his sire and his people: What is it that you worship?
37:86. A lie -- gods besides Allah do you desire?
37:87. What is then your idea about the Lord of the worlds?
37:88. Then he glanced a glance at the stars,
37:89. And said: Surely I am sick (of your deities).
37:90. So they turned their backs on him, going away.
37:91. Then he turned to their gods and said: Do you not eat?
37:92. What is the matter with you that

الْبُطُونَ (٦٦)
ثُمَّ إِنَّ لَهُمْ عَلَيْهَا لَشَوْبًا مِنْ حَمِيمٍ (٦٧)
ثُمَّ إِنَّ مَرْجِعَهُمْ لَإِلَى الْجَحِيمِ (٦٨)
إِنَّهُمْ أَلْفَوْا آبَاءَهُمْ ضَالِّينَ (٦٩)
فَهُمْ عَلَى آثَارِهِمْ يُهْرَعُونَ (٧٠)
وَلَقَدْ ضَلَّ قَبْلَهُمْ أَكْثَرُ الْأَوَّلِينَ (٧١)
وَلَقَدْ أَرْسَلْنَا فِيهِمْ مُنْذِرِينَ (٧٢)
فَانْظُرْ كَيْفَ كَانَ عَاقِبَةُ الْمُنْذَرِينَ (٧٣)
إِلَّا عِبَادَ اللَّهِ الْمُخْلَصِينَ (٧٤)
وَلَقَدْ نَادَانَا نُوحٌ فَلَنِعْمَ الْمُجِيبُونَ (٧٥)
وَنَجَّيْنَاهُ وَأَهْلَهُ مِنَ الْكَرْبِ الْعَظِيمِ (٧٦)
وَجَعَلْنَا ذُرِّيَّتَهُ هُمُ الْبَاقِينَ (٧٧)
وَتَرَكْنَا عَلَيْهِ فِي الْآخِرِينَ (٧٨)
سَلَامٌ عَلَى نُوحٍ فِي الْعَالَمِينَ (٧٩)
إِنَّا كَذَلِكَ نَجْزِي الْمُحْسِنِينَ (٨٠)
إِنَّهُ مِنْ عِبَادِنَا الْمُؤْمِنِينَ (٨١)
ثُمَّ أَغْرَقْنَا الْآخَرِينَ (٨٢)
وَإِنَّ مِنْ شِيعَتِهِ لَإِبْرَاهِيمَ (٨٣)
إِذْ جَاءَ رَبَّهُ بِقَلْبٍ سَلِيمٍ (٨٤)
إِذْ قَالَ لِأَبِيهِ وَقَوْمِهِ مَاذَا تَعْبُدُونَ (٨٥)
أَئِفْكًا آلِهَةً دُونَ اللَّهِ تُرِيدُونَ (٨٦)
فَمَا ظَنُّكُمْ بِرَبِّ الْعَالَمِينَ (٨٧)
فَنَظَرَ نَظْرَةً فِي النُّجُومِ (٨٨)
فَقَالَ إِنِّي سَقِيمٌ (٨٩)
فَتَوَلَّوْا عَنْهُ مُدْبِرِينَ (٩٠)
فَرَاغَ إِلَى آلِهَتِهِمْ فَقَالَ أَلَا تَأْكُلُونَ (٩١)

you speak not?

37:93. So he turned upon them, smiting with the right hand.

37:94. Then they came to him, hastening.

37:95. He said: Do you worship that which you hew out?

37:96. And Allah has created you and what you make.

37:97. They said: Build for him a building, then cast him into the flaming fire.

37:98. And they designed a plan against him, but We brought them low.

37:99. And he said: Surely I flee to my Lord -- He will guide me.

37:100. My Lord, grant me a doer of good deeds.

37:101. So We gave him the good news of a forbearing son.

37:102. But when he became of (age to) work with him, he said: O my son, I have seen in a dream that I should sacrifice thee: so consider what thou seest. He said: O my father, do as thou art commanded; if Allah please, thou wilt find me patient.

37:103. So when they both submitted and he had thrown him down upon his forehead,

37:104. And We called out to him saying, O Abraham,

37:105. Thou hast indeed fulfilled the vision. Thus do We reward the doers of good.

37:106. Surely this is a manifest trial.

37:107. And We ransomed him with a great sacrifice.

37:108. And We granted him among the later generations (the salutation),

37:109. Peace be to Abraham!

37:110. Thus do We reward the doers of good.

37:111. Surely he was one of Our believing servants.

37:112. And We gave him the good news of Isaac, a prophet, a righteous one.

37. Those Ranging in Ranks

37:113. And We blessed him and Isaac. And of their offspring some are doers of good, but some are clearly unjust to themselves.

***

37:114. And certainly We conferred a favour on Moses and Aaron.

37:115. And We delivered them, and their people from the mighty distress.

37:116. And We helped them, so they were the vanquishers.

37:117. And We gave them both the clear Book.

37:118. And We guided them on the right way.

37:119. And We granted them among the later generations (the salutation),

37:120. Peace be to Moses and Aaron!

37:121. Thus do We reward the doers of good.

37:122. Surely they were both of Our believing servants.

37:123. And Elias was surely of those sent.

37:124. When he said to his people: Will you not guard against evil?

37:125. Do you call upon Ba'l and forsake the Best of the creators,

37:126. Allah, your Lord and the Lord of your fathers of yore?

37:127. But they rejected him, so they shall be brought up,

37:128. But not the servants of Allah, the purified ones.

37:129. And We granted him among the later generations (the salutation),

37:130. Peace be to Elias!

37:131. Even thus We reward the doers of good.

37:132. Surely he was one of Our believing servants.

37:133. And Lot was surely of those sent.

37:134. When We delivered him and his people, all --

37:135. Except an old woman among those who remained behind.

37:136. Then We destroyed the others.

37. Those Ranging in Ranks

37:137. And surely you pass by them in the morning,
37:138. And at night. Do you not then understand?

***

37:139. And Jonah was surely of those sent.
37:140. When he fled to the laden ship,
37:141. So he shared with others but was of those cast away.
37:142. So the fish took him into its mouth while he was blamable.
37:143. But had he not been of those who glorify (Us),
37:144. He would have tarried in its belly till the day when they are raised.
37:145. Then We cast him on the naked shore, while he was sick.
37:146. And We caused a gourd to grow up for him.
37:147. And We sent him to a hundred thousand or more.
37:148. And they believed, so We gave them provision till a time.
37:149. Now ask them whether thy Lord has daughters and they have sons?
37:150. Or did We create the angels females, while they witnessed?
37:151. Now surely it is of their own lie that they say:
37:152. Allah has begotten. And truly they are liars.
37:153. Has He preferred daughters to sons?
37:154. What is the matter with you? How you judge!
37:155. Will you not then mind?
37:156. Or have you a clear authority?
37:157. Then bring your Book, if you are truthful.
37:158. And they assert a relationship between Him and the jinn. And certainly the jinn know that they will be brought up (for judgment) --
37:159. Glory be to Allah from what they describe! --
37:160. But not so the servants of Allah,

وَبِاللَّيْلِ أَفَلَا تَعْقِلُونَ (١٣٨)
وَإِنَّ يُونُسَ لَمِنَ الْمُرْسَلِينَ (١٣٩)
إِذْ أَبَقَ إِلَى الْفُلْكِ الْمَشْحُونِ (١٤٠)
فَسَاهَمَ فَكَانَ مِنَ الْمُدْحَضِينَ (١٤١)
فَالْتَقَمَهُ الْحُوتُ وَهُوَ مُلِيمٌ (١٤٢)
فَلَوْلَا أَنَّهُ كَانَ مِنَ الْمُسَبِّحِينَ (١٤٣)
لَلَبِثَ فِي بَطْنِهِ إِلَى يَوْمِ يُبْعَثُونَ (١٤٤)
فَنَبَذْنَاهُ بِالْعَرَاءِ وَهُوَ سَقِيمٌ (١٤٥)
وَأَنْبَتْنَا عَلَيْهِ شَجَرَةً مِنْ يَقْطِينٍ (١٤٦)
وَأَرْسَلْنَاهُ إِلَى مِئَةِ أَلْفٍ أَوْ يَزِيدُونَ (١٤٧)
فَآمَنُوا فَمَتَّعْنَاهُمْ إِلَى حِينٍ (١٤٨)
فَاسْتَفْتِهِمْ أَلِرَبِّكَ الْبَنَاتُ وَلَهُمُ الْبَنُونَ (١٤٩)
أَمْ خَلَقْنَا الْمَلَائِكَةَ إِنَاثًا وَهُمْ شَاهِدُونَ (١٥٠)
أَلَا إِنَّهُمْ مِنْ إِفْكِهِمْ لَيَقُولُونَ (١٥١)
وَلَدَ اللَّهُ وَإِنَّهُمْ لَكَاذِبُونَ (١٥٢)
أَصْطَفَى الْبَنَاتِ عَلَى الْبَنِينَ (١٥٣)
مَا لَكُمْ كَيْفَ تَحْكُمُونَ (١٥٤)
أَفَلَا تَذَكَّرُونَ (١٥٥)
أَمْ لَكُمْ سُلْطَانٌ مُبِينٌ (١٥٦)
فَأْتُوا بِكِتَابِكُمْ إِنْ كُنْتُمْ صَادِقِينَ (١٥٧)
وَجَعَلُوا بَيْنَهُ وَبَيْنَ الْجِنَّةِ نَسَبًا وَلَقَدْ عَلِمَتِ الْجِنَّةُ إِنَّهُمْ لَمُحْضَرُونَ (١٥٨)
سُبْحَانَ اللَّهِ عَمَّا يَصِفُونَ (١٥٩)
إِلَّا عِبَادَ اللَّهِ الْمُخْلَصِينَ (١٦٠)
فَإِنَّكُمْ وَمَا تَعْبُدُونَ (١٦١)

the purified ones.
37:161. So surely you and that which you serve,
37:162. Not against Him can you cause (any) to fall into trial,
37:163. Save him who will burn in the flaming Fire.
37:164. And there is none of us but has an assigned place,
37:165. And verily we are ranged in ranks,
37:166. And we truly glorify (Him).
37:167. And surely they used to say:
37:168. Had we a reminder from those of yore,
37:169. We would have been sincere servants of Allah.
37:170. But (now) they disbelieve in it, so they will come to know.
37:171. And certainly Our word has already gone forth to Our servants, to those sent,
37:172. That they, surely they, will be helped,
37:173. And Our hosts, surely they, will be triumphant.
37:174. So turn away from them till a time,
37:175. And watch them, they too will see.
37:176. Would they hasten on Our chastisement?
37:177. So when it descends in their court, evil will be the morning of the warned ones.
37:178. And turn away from them till a time,
37:179. And watch, for they too will see.
37:180. Glory be to thy Lord, the Lord of Might, above what they describe
37:181. And peace be to those sent
37:182. And praise be to Allah, the Lord of the worlds!

مَا أَنتُمْ عَلَيْهِ بِفَاتِنِينَ (١٦٢)
إِلَّا مَنْ هُوَ صَالِ الْجَحِيمِ (١٦٣)
وَمَا مِنَّا إِلَّا لَهُ مَقَامٌ مَعْلُومٌ (١٦٤)
وَإِنَّا لَنَحْنُ الصَّافُّونَ (١٦٥)
وَإِنَّا لَنَحْنُ الْمُسَبِّحُونَ (١٦٦)
وَإِنْ كَانُوا لَيَقُولُونَ (١٦٧)
لَوْ أَنَّ عِندَنَا ذِكْرًا مِنَ الْأَوَّلِينَ (١٦٨)
لَكُنَّا عِبَادَ اللَّهِ الْمُخْلَصِينَ (١٦٩)
فَكَفَرُوا بِهِ فَسَوْفَ يَعْلَمُونَ (١٧٠)
وَلَقَدْ سَبَقَتْ كَلِمَتُنَا لِعِبَادِنَا الْمُرْسَلِينَ (١٧١)
إِنَّهُمْ لَهُمُ الْمَنصُورُونَ (١٧٢)
وَإِنَّ جُندَنَا لَهُمُ الْغَالِبُونَ (١٧٣)
فَتَوَلَّ عَنْهُمْ حَتَّى حِينٍ (١٧٤)
وَأَبْصِرْهُمْ فَسَوْفَ يُبْصِرُونَ (١٧٥)
أَفَبِعَذَابِنَا يَسْتَعْجِلُونَ (١٧٦)
فَإِذَا نَزَلَ بِسَاحَتِهِمْ فَسَاءَ صَبَاحُ الْمُنذَرِينَ (١٧٧)
وَتَوَلَّ عَنْهُمْ حَتَّى حِينٍ (١٧٨)
وَأَبْصِرْ فَسَوْفَ يُبْصِرُونَ (١٧٩)
سُبْحَانَ رَبِّكَ رَبِّ الْعِزَّةِ عَمَّا يَصِفُونَ (١٨٠)
وَسَلَامٌ عَلَى الْمُرْسَلِينَ (١٨١)
وَالْحَمْدُ لِلَّهِ رَبِّ الْعَالَمِينَ (١٨٢)

38. Sad

In the name of Allah, the Beneficent, the Merciful.

38:1. Truthful God! By the Qur'an, possessing eminence!

38:2. Nay, those who disbelieve are in self-exaltation and opposition.

38:3. How many a generation We destroyed before them, then they cried when there was no longer time for escape!

38:4. And they wonder that a warner from among themselves has come to them, and the disbelievers say: This is an enchanter, a liar.

38:5. Makes he the gods a single God? Surely this is a strange thing.

38:6. And the chiefs among them say: Go and steadily adhere to your gods: surely this is a thing intended.

38:7. We never heard of this in the former faith: this is nothing but a forgery.

38:8. Has the Reminder been revealed to him from among us? Nay, they are in doubt as to My Reminder. Nay, they have not yet tasted My chastisement.

38:9. Or, have they the treasures of the mercy of thy Lord, the Mighty, the Great Giver?

38:10. Or is the kingdom of the heavens and the earth and what is between them theirs? Then let them rise higher in means.

38:11. What an army of the allies is here put to flight!

38:12. The people of Noah, and 'Ad, and Pharaoh, the lord of hosts, rejected (prophets) before them,

38:13. And Thamud and the people of Lot and the dwellers of the thicket. These were the parties (opposing Truth).

38:14. Not one of them but rejected the messengers, so just was My retribution.

***

38:15. And these wait but for one cry,

بِسْمِ اللهِ الرَّحْمَنِ الرَّحِيمِ
ص وَالْقُرْآنِ ذِي الذِّكْرِ (١)
بَلِ الَّذِينَ كَفَرُوا فِي عِزَّةٍ وَشِقَاقٍ (٢)
كَمْ أَهْلَكْنَا مِنْ قَبْلِهِمْ مِنْ قَرْنٍ فَنَادَوْا وَلَاتَ حِينَ مَنَاصٍ (٣)
وَعَجِبُوا أَنْ جَاءَهُمْ مُنْذِرٌ مِنْهُمْ وَقَالَ الْكَافِرُونَ هَذَا سَاحِرٌ كَذَّابٌ (٤)
أَجَعَلَ الْآلِهَةَ إِلَهًا وَاحِدًا إِنَّ هَذَا لَشَيْءٌ عُجَابٌ (٥)
وَانْطَلَقَ الْمَلَأُ مِنْهُمْ أَنِ امْشُوا وَاصْبِرُوا عَلَى آلِهَتِكُمْ إِنَّ هَذَا لَشَيْءٌ يُرَادُ (٦)
مَا سَمِعْنَا بِهَذَا فِي الْمِلَّةِ الْآخِرَةِ إِنْ هَذَا إِلَّا اخْتِلَاقٌ (٧)
أَأُنْزِلَ عَلَيْهِ الذِّكْرُ مِنْ بَيْنِنَا بَلْ هُمْ فِي شَكٍّ مِنْ ذِكْرِي بَلْ لَمَّا يَذُوقُوا عَذَابِ (٨)
أَمْ عِنْدَهُمْ خَزَائِنُ رَحْمَةِ رَبِّكَ الْعَزِيزِ الْوَهَّابِ (٩)
أَمْ لَهُمْ مُلْكُ السَّمَاوَاتِ وَالْأَرْضِ وَمَا بَيْنَهُمَا فَلْيَرْتَقُوا فِي الْأَسْبَابِ (١٠)
جُنْدٌ مَا هُنَالِكَ مَهْزُومٌ مِنَ الْأَحْزَابِ (١١)
كَذَّبَتْ قَبْلَهُمْ قَوْمُ نُوحٍ وَعَادٌ وَفِرْعَوْنُ ذُو الْأَوْتَادِ (١٢)
وَثَمُودُ وَقَوْمُ لُوطٍ وَأَصْحَابُ الْأَيْكَةِ أُولَئِكَ الْأَحْزَابُ (١٣)
إِنْ كُلٌّ إِلَّا كَذَّبَ الرُّسُلَ فَحَقَّ عِقَابِ (١٤)
وَمَا يَنْظُرُ هَؤُلَاءِ إِلَّا صَيْحَةً وَاحِدَةً مَا لَهَا مِنْ فَوَاقٍ (١٥)

38. Sad

wherein there is no delay.
38:16. And they say: Our Lord, hasten on for us our portion before the day of Reckoning.
38:17. Bear patiently what they say, and remember Our servant David, the possessor of power. He ever turned (to Allah).
38:18. Truly We made the mountains subject to him, glorifying (Allah) at nightfall and sunrise,
38:19. And the birds gathered together. All were obedient to him.
38:20. And We strengthened his kingdom and We gave him wisdom and a clear judgment.
38:21. And has the story of the adversaries come to thee? When they made an entry into the private chamber by climbing the wall --
38:22. When they came upon David so he was afraid of them. They said Fear not; two litigants, of whom one has wronged the other, so decide between us with justice, and act not unjustly, and guide us to the right way.
38:23. This is my brother. He has ninety-nine ewes and I have a single ewe. Then he said, Make it over to me, and he has prevailed against me in dispute.
38:24. He said: Surely he has wronged thee in demanding thy ewe (to add) to his own ewes. And surely many partners wrong one another save those who believe and do good, and very few are they! And David knew that We had tried him, so he asked his Lord for protection, and he fell down bowing and turned (to God).
38:25. So We gave him this protection, and he had a nearness to Us and an excellent resort.
38:26. O David, surely We have made thee a ruler in the land; so judge between men justly and follow not desire, lest it lead thee astray from the path of Allah. Those who go astray

وَقَالُوا رَبَّنَا عَجِّلْ لَنَا قِطَّنَا قَبْلَ يَوْمِ الْحِسَابِ (١٦)
اصْبِرْ عَلَى مَا يَقُولُونَ وَاذْكُرْ عَبْدَنَا دَاوُودَ ذَا الْأَيْدِ إِنَّهُ أَوَّابٌ (١٧)
إِنَّا سَخَّرْنَا الْجِبَالَ مَعَهُ يُسَبِّحْنَ بِالْعَشِيِّ وَالْإِشْرَاقِ (١٨)
وَالطَّيْرَ مَحْشُورَةً كُلٌّ لَهُ أَوَّابٌ (١٩)
وَشَدَدْنَا مُلْكَهُ وَآتَيْنَاهُ الْحِكْمَةَ وَفَصْلَ الْخِطَابِ (٢٠)
وَهَلْ أَتَاكَ نَبَأُ الْخَصْمِ إِذْ تَسَوَّرُوا الْمِحْرَابَ (٢١)
إِذْ دَخَلُوا عَلَى دَاوُودَ فَفَزِعَ مِنْهُمْ قَالُوا لَا تَخَفْ خَصْمَانِ بَغَى بَعْضُنَا عَلَى بَعْضٍ فَاحْكُمْ بَيْنَنَا بِالْحَقِّ وَلَا تُشْطِطْ وَاهْدِنَا إِلَى سَوَاءِ الصِّرَاطِ (٢٢)
إِنَّ هَذَا أَخِي لَهُ تِسْعٌ وَتِسْعُونَ نَعْجَةً وَلِيَ نَعْجَةٌ وَاحِدَةٌ فَقَالَ أَكْفِلْنِيهَا وَعَزَّنِي فِي الْخِطَابِ (٢٣)
قَالَ لَقَدْ ظَلَمَكَ بِسُؤَالِ نَعْجَتِكَ إِلَى نِعَاجِهِ وَإِنَّ كَثِيرًا مِنَ الْخُلَطَاءِ لَيَبْغِي بَعْضُهُمْ عَلَى بَعْضٍ إِلَّا الَّذِينَ آمَنُوا وَعَمِلُوا الصَّالِحَاتِ وَقَلِيلٌ مَا هُمْ وَظَنَّ دَاوُودُ أَنَّمَا فَتَنَّاهُ فَاسْتَغْفَرَ رَبَّهُ وَخَرَّ رَاكِعًا وَأَنَابَ (٢٤)
فَغَفَرْنَا لَهُ ذَلِكَ وَإِنَّ لَهُ عِنْدَنَا لَزُلْفَى وَحُسْنَ مَآبٍ (٢٥)
يَا دَاوُودُ إِنَّا جَعَلْنَاكَ خَلِيفَةً فِي الْأَرْضِ فَاحْكُمْ بَيْنَ النَّاسِ بِالْحَقِّ وَلَا تَتَّبِعِ الْهَوَى فَيُضِلَّكَ عَنْ سَبِيلِ اللَّهِ إِنَّ الَّذِينَ يَضِلُّونَ عَنْ سَبِيلِ اللَّهِ لَهُمْ عَذَابٌ شَدِيدٌ بِمَا نَسُوا يَوْمَ الْحِسَابِ (٢٦)
وَمَا خَلَقْنَا السَّمَاءَ وَالْأَرْضَ وَمَا

from the path of Allah, for them is surely a severe chastisement because they forgot the day of Reckoning.

***

38:27. And We created not the heaven and the earth and what is between them in vain. That is the opinion of those who disbelieve. So woe to those who disbelieve on account of the Fire!

38:28. Shall We treat those who believe and do good like the mischief-makers in the earth? Or shall We make the dutiful like the wicked?

38:29. (This is) a Book that We have revealed to thee abounding in good, that they may ponder over its verses, and that the men of understanding may mind.

38:30. And We gave to David Solomon. Most excellent the servant! Surely he ever turned (to Allah).

38:31. When well-bred, swift (horses) were brought to him at evening --

38:32. So he said, I love the good things on account of the remembrance of my Lord -- until they were hidden behind the veil.

38:33. (He said): Bring them back to me. So he began to stroke (their) legs and necks.

38:34. And certainly we tried Solomon, and We put on his throne a (mere) body, so he turned (to Allah).

38:35. He said My Lord, forgive me and grant me a kingdom which is not fit for any one after me; surely Thou art the Great Giver.

38:36. So We made the wind subservient to him it made his command to run gently wherever he desired,

38:37. And the devils, every builder and diver,

38:38. And others fettered in chains.

38:39. This is Our free gift, so give freely or withhold, without reckoning.

38:40. And surely he had a nearness to Us and an excellent resort.

***

38:41. And remember Our servant Job. When he cried to his Lord: The devil has afflicted me with toil and torment.
38:42. Urge with thy foot; here is a cool washing-place and a drink.
38:43. And We gave him his people and the like of them with them, a mercy from Us, and a reminder for men of understanding.
38:44. And take in thy hand few worldly goods and earn goodness therewith and incline not to falsehood. Surely We found him patient; most excellent the servant Surely he (ever) turned (to Us).
4) And remember Our servants Abraham and Isaac and Jacob, men of power and insight. 46 We indeed purified them by a pure quality, the keeping in mind of the (final) abode.
38:47. And surely they were with Us, of the elect, the best.
38:48. And remember Ishmael and Elisha and Dhu-l-Kifl; and they were all of the best.
38:49. This is a reminder. And surely there is an excellent resort for the dutiful:
38:50. Gardens of perpetuity -- the doors are opened for them.
38:51. Reclining therein, calling therein for many fruits and drink.
38:52. And with them are those modest in gaze, equals in age.
38:53. This is what you are promised for the day of Reckoning.
38:54. Surely this is Our sustenance it will never come to an end --
38:55. This (is for the good)! And surely there is an evil resort for the inordinate --
38:56. Hell. They will enter it. So evil is the resting-place.
38:57. This -- so let them taste it, boiling and intensely cold (drink),
38:58. And other similar (punishment), of various sorts.

وَشَرَابٌ (٤٢)
وَوَهَبْنَا لَهُ أَهْلَهُ وَمِثْلَهُم مَّعَهُمْ رَحْمَةً مِّنَّا وَذِكْرَى لِأُولِي الْأَلْبَابِ (٤٣)
وَخُذْ بِيَدِكَ ضِغْثًا فَاضْرِب بِّهِ وَلَا تَحْنَثْ إِنَّا وَجَدْنَاهُ صَابِرًا نِّعْمَ الْعَبْدُ إِنَّهُ أَوَّابٌ (٤٤)
وَاذْكُرْ عِبَادَنَا إِبْرَاهِيمَ وَإِسْحَاقَ وَيَعْقُوبَ أُولِي الْأَيْدِي وَالْأَبْصَارِ (٤٥)
إِنَّا أَخْلَصْنَاهُم بِخَالِصَةٍ ذِكْرَى الدَّارِ (٤٦)
وَإِنَّهُمْ عِندَنَا لَمِنَ الْمُصْطَفَيْنَ الْأَخْيَارِ (٤٧)
وَاذْكُرْ إِسْمَاعِيلَ وَالْيَسَعَ وَذَا الْكِفْلِ وَكُلٌّ مِّنَ الْأَخْيَارِ (٤٨)
هَذَا ذِكْرٌ وَإِنَّ لِلْمُتَّقِينَ لَحُسْنَ مَآبٍ (٤٩)
جَنَّاتِ عَدْنٍ مُّفَتَّحَةً لَّهُمُ الْأَبْوَابُ (٥٠)
مُتَّكِئِينَ فِيهَا يَدْعُونَ فِيهَا بِفَاكِهَةٍ كَثِيرَةٍ وَشَرَابٍ (٥١)
وَعِندَهُمْ قَاصِرَاتُ الطَّرْفِ أَتْرَابٌ (٥٢)
هَذَا مَا تُوعَدُونَ لِيَوْمِ الْحِسَابِ (٥٣)
إِنَّ هَذَا لَرِزْقُنَا مَا لَهُ مِن نَّفَادٍ (٥٤)
هَذَا وَإِنَّ لِلطَّاغِينَ لَشَرَّ مَآبٍ (٥٥)
جَهَنَّمَ يَصْلَوْنَهَا فَبِئْسَ الْمِهَادُ (٥٦)
هَذَا فَلْيَذُوقُوهُ حَمِيمٌ وَغَسَّاقٌ (٥٧)
وَآخَرُ مِن شَكْلِهِ أَزْوَاجٌ (٥٨)
هَذَا فَوْجٌ مُّقْتَحِمٌ مَّعَكُمْ لَا مَرْحَبًا بِهِمْ إِنَّهُمْ صَالُوا النَّارِ (٥٩)
قَالُوا بَلْ أَنتُمْ لَا مَرْحَبًا بِكُمْ أَنتُمْ قَدَّمْتُمُوهُ لَنَا فَبِئْسَ الْقَرَارُ (٦٠)

38:59. This is an army rushing headlong with you -- no welcome for them! Surely they will burn in fire.
38:60. They say: Nay! you -- no welcome to you! You prepared it for us, so evil is the resting-place.
38:61. They say: Our Lord, whoever prepared it for us, give him more, a double, punishment in the Fire.
38:62. And they say: What is the matter with us? -- we see not men whom we used to count among the vicious.
38:63. Did we (only) take them in scorn, or do our eyes miss them?
38:64. That surely is the truth the contending one with another of the inmates of the Fire.

* * *

38:65. Say: I am only a warner; and there is no God but Allah, the One, the Subduer (of all) --
38:66. The Lord of the heavens and the earth and what is between them, the Mighty, the Forgiving.
38:67. Say: It is a message of importance,--
38:68. From which you turn away.
38:69. I have no knowledge of the exalted chiefs when they contend.
38:70. Only this is revealed to me that I am a plain warner.
38:71. When thy Lord said to the angels: Surely I am going to create a mortal from dust.
38:72. So when I have made him complete and breathed into him of My spirit, fall down submitting to him.
38:73. And the angels submitted, all of them,
38:74. But not Iblis. He was proud and he was one of the disbelievers.
38:75. He said: O Iblis, what prevented thee from submitting to him whom I created with both My hands? Art thou proud or art thou of the exalted Ones?
38:76. He said: I am better than he; Thou hast created me of fire, and him Thou didst create of dust.

قَالُوا رَبَّنَا مَنْ قَدَّمَ لَنَا هَذَا فَزِدْهُ عَذَابًا ضِعْفًا فِي النَّارِ (٦١)
وَقَالُوا مَا لَنَا لَا نَرَى رِجَالًا كُنَّا نَعُدُّهُمْ مِنَ الْأَشْرَارِ (٦٢)
أَتَّخَذْنَاهُمْ سِخْرِيًّا أَمْ زَاغَتْ عَنْهُمُ الْأَبْصَارُ (٦٣)
إِنَّ ذَلِكَ لَحَقٌّ تَخَاصُمُ أَهْلِ النَّارِ (٦٤)
قُلْ إِنَّمَا أَنَا مُنْذِرٌ وَمَا مِنْ إِلَهٍ إِلَّا اللَّهُ الْوَاحِدُ الْقَهَّارُ (٦٥)
رَبُّ السَّمَاوَاتِ وَالْأَرْضِ وَمَا بَيْنَهُمَا الْعَزِيزُ الْغَفَّارُ (٦٦)
قُلْ هُوَ نَبَأٌ عَظِيمٌ (٦٧)
أَنْتُمْ عَنْهُ مُعْرِضُونَ (٦٨)
مَا كَانَ لِيَ مِنْ عِلْمٍ بِالْمَلَإِ الْأَعْلَى إِذْ يَخْتَصِمُونَ (٦٩)
إِنْ يُوحَى إِلَيَّ إِلَّا أَنَّمَا أَنَا نَذِيرٌ مُبِينٌ (٧٠)
إِذْ قَالَ رَبُّكَ لِلْمَلَائِكَةِ إِنِّي خَالِقٌ بَشَرًا مِنْ طِينٍ (٧١)
فَإِذَا سَوَّيْتُهُ وَنَفَخْتُ فِيهِ مِنْ رُوحِي فَقَعُوا لَهُ سَاجِدِينَ (٧٢)
فَسَجَدَ الْمَلَائِكَةُ كُلُّهُمْ أَجْمَعُونَ (٧٣)
إِلَّا إِبْلِيسَ اسْتَكْبَرَ وَكَانَ مِنَ الْكَافِرِينَ (٧٤)
قَالَ يَا إِبْلِيسُ مَا مَنَعَكَ أَنْ تَسْجُدَ لِمَا خَلَقْتُ بِيَدَيَّ أَسْتَكْبَرْتَ أَمْ كُنْتَ مِنَ الْعَالِينَ (٧٥)
قَالَ أَنَا خَيْرٌ مِنْهُ خَلَقْتَنِي مِنْ نَارٍ وَخَلَقْتَهُ مِنْ طِينٍ (٧٦)
قَالَ فَاخْرُجْ مِنْهَا فَإِنَّكَ رَجِيمٌ (٧٧)
وَإِنَّ عَلَيْكَ لَعْنَتِي إِلَى يَوْمِ الدِّينِ (٧٨)

39. The Companies

38:77. He said: Go forth from hence surely thou art driven away:
38:78. And surely My curse is on thee to the day of Judgment.
38:79. He said: My Lord, respite me to the day that they are raised.
38:80. He said: Surely thou art of the respited ones.
38:81. Till the day of the time made known.
38:82. He said: Then, by Thy Might! I will surely lead them all astray,
38:83. Except Thy servants from among them, the purified ones.
38:84. He said: The Truth is, and the truth I speak --
38:85. That I shall fill hell with thee and with all those among them who follow thee.
38:86. Say: I ask you no reward for it nor am I of the impostors.
38:87. It is naught but a Reminder to the nations.
38:88. And certainly you will come to know about it after a time.

39. The Companies

In the name of Allah, the Beneficent, the Merciful.

39:1. The revelation of the Book is from Allah, the Mighty, the Wise.
39:2. Surely We have revealed to thee the Book with truth, so serve Allah, being sincere to Him in obedience.
39:3. Now surely sincere obedience is due to Allah (alone). And those who choose protectors besides Him (say): We serve them only that they may bring us nearer to Allah. Surely Allah will judge between them in that in which they differ. Surely Allah guides not him who is a liar, ungrateful.
39:4. If Allah desired to take a son to Himself, He could have chosen those He pleased out of those whom He has created -- Glory be to Him He is Allah,

39. The Companies

the One, the Subduer (of all).

39:5. He has created the heavens and the earth with truth; He makes the night cover the day and makes the day overtake the night, and He has made the sun and the moon subservient; each one moves on to an assigned term. Now surely He is the Mighty, the Forgiver.

39:6. He created you from a single being, then made its mate of the same (kind). And He sent down for you eight of the cattle in pairs. He creates you in the wombs of your mothers -- creation after creation -in triple darkness. That is Allah, your Lord; His is the kingdom. There is no God but He. How are you then turned away?

39:7. If you are ungrateful, then surely Allah is above need of you. And He likes not ungratefulness in His servants. And if you are grateful, He likes it for you. And no bearer of a burden will bear another's burden. Then to your Lord is your return, then will He inform you of what you did. Surely He is Knower of what is in the breasts.

39:8. And when distress afflicts a man he calls upon his Lord, turning to Him; then when He grants him a favour from Him, he forgets that for which he called upon Him before, and sets up rivals to Allah that he may cause (men) to stray from His path. Say: Enjoy thine ungratefulness for a little, surely thou art of the companions of the Fire.

39:9. Is he who is obedient during hours of the night, prostrating himself and standing, taking care of the Hereafter and hoping for the mercy of his Lord --? Say: Are those who know and those who know not alike? Only men of understanding mind.

* * *

39:10. Say: O My servants who believe; keep your duty to your Lord. For those who do good in this world is good, and

39. The Companies

Allah's earth is spacious. Truly the steadfast will be paid their reward without measure.

39:11. Say: I am commanded to serve Allah, being sincere to Him in obedience,

39:12. And I am commanded to be the first of those who submit.

39:13. Say: I fear, if I disobey my Lord, the chastisement of a grievous day.

39:14. Say: Allah I serve, being sincere to Him in my obedience.

39:15. Serve then what you will beside Him. Say: The losers surely are those who lose themselves and their people on the day of Resurrection. Now surely that is the manifest loss

39:16. They shall have coverings of fire above them and coverings beneath them. With that Allah makes His servants to fear; so keen your duty to Me, O My servants.

39:17. And those who eschew the worship of the idols and turn to Allah, for them is good news. So give good news to My servants,

39:18. Who listen to the Word, then follow the best of it. Such are they whom Allah has guided, and such are the men of understanding.

39:19. He against whom the sentence of chastisement is due -- canst thou save him who is in the Fire?

39:20. But those who keep their duty to their Lord, for them are high places, above them higher places, built (for them), wherein rivers flow. (It is) the promise of Allah. Allah fails not in (His) promise.

39:21. Seest thou not that Allah sends down water from the clouds, then makes it go down into the earth in springs, then brings forth therewith herbage of various hues; then it withers so that thou seest it turn yellow, then He makes it chaff? Surely there is a reminder in this for men of understanding.

***

39:22. Is he whose breast Allah has opened to Islam so that he follows a light from his Lord --? So woe to those whose hearts are hardened against the remembrance of Allah! Such are in clear error.

39:23. Allah has revealed the best announcement, a Book consistent, repeating (its injunctions), whereat do shudder the skins of those who fear their Lord, then their skins and their hearts soften to Allah's remembrance. This is Allah's guidance -- He guides with it whom He pleases. And he whom Allah leaves in error, there is no guide for him.

39:24. Is then he who has to guard himself with his own person against the evil chastisement on the Resurrection day --? And it will be said to the iniquitous: Taste what you earned.

39:25. Those before them denied, so the chastisement came to them from whence they perceived not.

39:26. So Allah made them taste disgrace in this world's life, and certainly the chastisement of the Hereafter is greater. Did they but know!

39:27. And certainly We have set forth for men in this Qur'an similitudes of every sort that they may mind.

39:28. An Arabic Qur'an without any crookedness, that they may guard against evil.

39:29. Allah sets forth a parable: A man belonging to partners differing with one another, and a man (devoted) wholly to one man. Are the two alike in condition? Praise be to Allah! Nay, most of them know not.

39:30. Surely thou wilt die and they (too) will die;

39:31. Then surely on the day of Resurrection you will contend one with another before your Lord.

***

39:32. Who is then more unjust than he who utters a lie against Allah and denies the truth, when it comes to him? Is there not in hell an abode for the disbelievers?

39:33. And he who brings the truth and accepts the truth -- such are the dutiful.

39:34. They shall have with their Lord what they please. Such is the reward of the doers of good --

39:35. That Allah may ward off from them the worst of what they did, and give them their reward for the best of what they did.

39:36. Is not Allah sufficient for His servant? And they seek to frighten thee with those besides Him. And whomsoever Allah leaves in error, there is no guide for him.

39:37. And whom Allah guides, there is none that can lead him astray. Is not Allah Mighty, the Lord of retribution?

39:38. And if thou ask them, Who created the heavens and the earth? They will say: Allah. Say: See you then that those you call upon besides Allah, would they, if Allah desire to afflict me with harm, remove His harm? Or if He desire to show me mercy, could they withhold His mercy? Say: Allah is sufficient for me. On Him do the reliant rely.

39:39. Say: O my people, work in your place. Surely I am a worker, so you will come to know,

39:40. Who it is to whom there comes a chastisement abasing him, and on whom falls a lasting chastisement.

39:41. Surely We have revealed to thee the Book with truth for (the good of) men. So whoever follows the right way, it is for his own soul, and whoever errs, he errs only to its detriment. And thou art not a custodian over them.

***

39:42. Allah takes (men's) souls at the

39. The Companies

time of their death, and those that die not, during their sleep. Then He withholds those on whom He has passed the decree of death and sends the others back till an appointed term. Surely there are signs in this for a people who reflect.

39:43. Or, take they intercessors besides Allah? Say: What! Even though they control naught, nor do they understand.

39:44. Say: Allah's is the intercession altogether. His is the kingdom of the heavens and the earth. Then to Him you will be returned.

39:45. And when Allah alone is mentioned, the hearts of those who believe not in the Hereafter shrink, and when those besides Him are mentioned, lo! they are joyful.

39:46. Say: O Allah, Originator of the heavens and the earth, Knower of the unseen and the seen, Thou judgest between Thy servants as to that wherein they differ.

39:47. And had those who do wrong all that is in the earth and the like of it with it, they would certainly offer it as ransom from the evil of the chastisement on the day of Resurrection. And what they never thought of shall become plain to them from Allah.

39:48. And the evil of what they wrought will become plain to them, and that which they mocked at will beset them.

39:49. So when harm afflicts a man he calls upon Us; then, when We give him a boon from Us, he says: I have been given it only by means of knowledge. Nay, it is a trial, but most of them know not.

39:50. Those before them did say it indeed, but what they earned availed them not.

39:51. So there befell them the evil which they had earned. And those who

الَّذِينَ مِنْ دُونِهِ إِذَا هُمْ يَسْتَبْشِرُونَ (٤٥)

قُلِ اللَّهُمَّ فَاطِرَ السَّمَاوَاتِ وَالْأَرْضِ عَالِمَ الْغَيْبِ وَالشَّهَادَةِ أَنْتَ تَحْكُمُ بَيْنَ عِبَادِكَ فِي مَا كَانُوا فِيهِ يَخْتَلِفُونَ (٤٦)

وَلَوْ أَنَّ لِلَّذِينَ ظَلَمُوا مَا فِي الْأَرْضِ جَمِيعًا وَمِثْلَهُ مَعَهُ لَافْتَدَوْا بِهِ مِنْ سُوءِ الْعَذَابِ يَوْمَ الْقِيَامَةِ وَبَدَا لَهُمْ مِنَ اللَّهِ مَا لَمْ يَكُونُوا يَحْتَسِبُونَ (٤٧)

وَبَدَا لَهُمْ سَيِّئَاتُ مَا كَسَبُوا وَحَاقَ بِهِمْ مَا كَانُوا بِهِ يَسْتَهْزِئُونَ (٤٨)

فَإِذَا مَسَّ الْإِنْسَانَ ضُرٌّ دَعَانَا ثُمَّ إِذَا خَوَّلْنَاهُ نِعْمَةً مِنَّا قَالَ إِنَّمَا أُوتِيتُهُ عَلَى عِلْمٍ بَلْ هِيَ فِتْنَةٌ وَلَكِنَّ أَكْثَرَهُمْ لَا يَعْلَمُونَ (٤٩)

قَدْ قَالَهَا الَّذِينَ مِنْ قَبْلِهِمْ فَمَا أَغْنَى عَنْهُمْ مَا كَانُوا يَكْسِبُونَ (٥٠)

فَأَصَابَهُمْ سَيِّئَاتُ مَا كَسَبُوا وَالَّذِينَ ظَلَمُوا مِنْ هَؤُلَاءِ سَيُصِيبُهُمْ سَيِّئَاتُ مَا كَسَبُوا وَمَا هُمْ بِمُعْجِزِينَ (٥١)

أَوَلَمْ يَعْلَمُوا أَنَّ اللَّهَ يَبْسُطُ الرِّزْقَ لِمَنْ يَشَاءُ وَيَقْدِرُ إِنَّ فِي ذَلِكَ لَآيَاتٍ لِقَوْمٍ يُؤْمِنُونَ (٥٢)

قُلْ يَا عِبَادِيَ الَّذِينَ أَسْرَفُوا عَلَى أَنْفُسِهِمْ لَا تَقْنَطُوا مِنْ رَحْمَةِ اللَّهِ إِنَّ اللَّهَ يَغْفِرُ الذُّنُوبَ جَمِيعًا إِنَّهُ هُوَ الْغَفُورُ الرَّحِيمُ (٥٣)

وَأَنِيبُوا إِلَى رَبِّكُمْ وَأَسْلِمُوا لَهُ مِنْ قَبْلِ أَنْ يَأْتِيَكُمُ الْعَذَابُ ثُمَّ لَا تُنْصَرُونَ (٥٤)

وَاتَّبِعُوا أَحْسَنَ مَا أُنْزِلَ إِلَيْكُمْ مِنْ رَبِّكُمْ مِنْ قَبْلِ أَنْ يَأْتِيَكُمُ الْعَذَابُ بَغْتَةً وَأَنْتُمْ لَا تَشْعُرُونَ (٥٥)

are unjust from among these, there shall befall them the evil which they earn, and they shall not escape.

39:52. Know they not that Allah gives ample subsistence to whom He pleases, and He straitens; surely there are signs in this for a people who believe.

* * *

39:53. Say: O My servants who have been prodigal regarding their souls, despair not of the mercy of Allah; surely Allah forgives sins altogether. He is indeed the Forgiving, the Merciful.

39:54. And turn to your Lord and submit to Him before chastisement comes to you, then you will not be helped.

39:55. And follow the best that has been revealed to you from your Lord before chastisement comes to you all of a sudden, while you perceive not --

39:56. Lest a soul should say: O woe is me, that I fell short of my duty to Allah! and surely I was of those who laughed to scorn;

39:57. Or it should say: Had Allah guided me, I should have been dutiful;

39:58. Or it should say, when it sees the chastisement: Had I another chance I should be a doer of good.

39:59. Aye! My communications came to thee, but thou didst reject them, and wast proud and wast of the disbelievers.

39:60. And on the day of resurrection thou wilt see those who lied against Allah, their faces will be blackened. Is there not in hell an abode for the proud?

39:61. And Allah delivers those who keep their duty with their achievement -- evil touches them not, nor do they grieve.

39:62. Allah is the Creator of all things and He has charge over everything.

39:63. His are the treasures of the heavens and the earth. And those who

39. The Companies

disbelieve in the messages of Allah, such are the losers.

***

39:64. Say: Do you bid me serve others than Allah, O ye ignorant ones?

39:65. And certainly, it has been revealed to thee and to those before thee: If thou associate (with Allah), thy work would certainly come to naught and thou wouldst be a loser.

39:66. Nay, but serve Allah alone and be of the thankful.

39:67. And they honour not Allah with the honour due to Him; and the whole earth will be in His grip on the day of Resurrection and the heavens rolled up in His right hand. Glory be to Him! and highly exalted is He above what they associate (with Him).

39:68. And the trumpet is blown, so all those in the heavens and all those in the earth will swoon, except such as Allah please. Then it will be blown again, when lo! they stand up, awaiting.

39:69. And the earth beams with the light of its Lord, and the Book is laid down, and the prophets and the witnesses are brought up, and judgment is given between them with justice, and they are not wronged.

39:70. And every soul is paid back fully for what it did, and He knows best what they do.

***

39:71. And those who disbelieve are driven to hell in companies; until, when they come to it, its doors are opened, and the keepers of it say to them: Did not there come to you messengers from among you reciting to you the messages of your Lord and warning you of the meeting of this day of yours? They say: Yea. But the word of punishment proved true against the disbelievers.

39:72. It is said: Enter the gates of hell to abide therein; so evil is the abode of the proud.

39:73. And those who keep their duty to their Lord are conveyed to the Garden in companies until when they come to it, and its doors are opened and the keepers of it say to them Peace be to you! you led pure lives so enter it to abide.

39:74. And they say: Praise be to Allah Who has made good to us His promise, and He has made us inherit the land; we abide in the Garden where we please. So goodly is the reward of the workers.

39:75. And thou seest the angels going round about the Throne of Power, glorifying their Lord with praise. And they are judged with justice, and it is said: Praise be to Allah, the Lord of the worlds!

40. The Believer

In the name of Allah, Beneficent, the Merciful.

40:1. Beneficent God!

40:2. The revelation of the Book is from Allah, the Mighty, the Knowing,

40:3. Forgiver of sin and Acceptor of repentance, Severe to punish, Lord of bounty. There is no God but He; to Him is the eventual coming.

40:4. None dispute concerning the messages of Allah but those who disbelieve, so let not their control in the land deceive thee.

40:5. Before them the people of Noah and the parties after them rejected (prophets), and every nation purposed against its messenger to destroy him, and disputed by means of falsehood to render null thereby the truth, so I seized them; how (terrible) was then My retribution!

40:6. And thus did the word of thy Lord prove true against those who disbelieve that they are the

٤٠ـ سورة غافر

بِسْمِ اللَّهِ الرَّحْمَنِ الرَّحِيمِ

حم (١)

تَنزِيلُ الْكِتَابِ مِنَ اللَّهِ الْعَزِيزِ الْعَلِيمِ (٢)

غَافِرِ الذَّنبِ وَقَابِلِ التَّوْبِ شَدِيدِ الْعِقَابِ ذِي الطَّوْلِ لَا إِلَهَ إِلَّا هُوَ إِلَيْهِ الْمَصِيرُ (٣)

مَا يُجَادِلُ فِي آيَاتِ اللَّهِ إِلَّا الَّذِينَ كَفَرُوا فَلَا يَغْرُرْكَ تَقَلُّبُهُمْ فِي الْبِلَادِ (٤)

كَذَّبَتْ قَبْلَهُمْ قَوْمُ نُوحٍ وَالْأَحْزَابُ مِن بَعْدِهِمْ وَهَمَّتْ كُلُّ أُمَّةٍ بِرَسُولِهِمْ لِيَأْخُذُوهُ وَجَادَلُوا بِالْبَاطِلِ لِيُدْحِضُوا بِهِ الْحَقَّ فَأَخَذْتُهُمْ فَكَيْفَ كَانَ عِقَابِ (٥)

وَكَذَلِكَ حَقَّتْ كَلِمَةُ رَبِّكَ عَلَى الَّذِينَ كَفَرُوا أَنَّهُمْ أَصْحَابُ النَّارِ (٦)

40. The Believer

companions of the Fire.

40:7. Those who bear the Throne of Power and those around it celebrate the praise of their Lord and believe in Him and ask protection for those who believe: Our Lord, Thou embracest all things in mercy and knowledge, so protect those who turn (to Thee) and follow Thy way, and save them from the chastisement of hell.

40:8. Our Lord, make them enter the Gardens of perpetuity, which Thou hast promised them and such of their fathers and their wives and their offspring as are good. Surely Thou art the Mighty, the Wise:

40:9. And guard them from evil, and whom Thou guardest from evil this day, Thou hast indeed mercy on him. And that is the mighty achievement.

* * *

40:10. Those who disbelieve are told: Certainly Allah's hatred (of you), when you were called upon to the faith and you rejected, was much greater than your hatred (now) of yourselves.

40:11. They say Our Lord, twice hast Thou made us die, and twice hast Thou given us life; so we confess our sins. Is there then a way of escape?

40:12. That is because when Allah alone was called upon, you disbelieved, and when associates were given to Him, you believed. So judgment belongs to Allah, the High, the Great.

40:13. He it is Who shows you His signs and sends down for you sustenance from heaven, and none minds but he who turns (to Him).

40:14. So call upon Allah, being sincere to Him in obedience, though the disbelievers are averse --

40:15. Exalter of degrees, Lord of the Throne of Power, He makes the spirit to light by His command upon whom Re pleases of His servants, that he may warn (men) of the day of Meeting --

40:16. The day when they come forth.

40. The Believer

Nothing concerning them remains hidden from Allah. To whom belongs the kingdom this day? To Allah, the One, the Subduer (of all).

40:17. This day every soul is rewarded what it has earned. No injustice this day! Surely Allah is Swift in Reckoning.

40:18. And warn them of the day that draws near, when hearts, grieving inwardly, rise up to the throats. The iniquitous will have no friend, nor any intercessor who should be obeyed.

40:19. He knows the dishonesty of eyes and that which the breasts conceal.

40:20. And Allah judges with truth. And those whom they call upon besides Him judge naught! Surely Allah is the Hearing, the Seeing.

* * *

40:21. Have they not travelled in the land and seen what was the end of those who were before them? Mightier than these were they in strength and in fortifications in the land, but Allah destroyed them for their sins. And they had none to protect them from Allah.

40:22. That was because there came to them their messengers with clear arguments, but they disbelieved, so Allah destroyed them. Surely He is Strong, Severe in Retribution.

40:23. And certainly We sent Moses with Our messages and clear authority,

40:24. To Pharaoh and Haman and Korah, but they said: A lying enchanter!

40:25. So when he brought to them the Truth from Us, they said: Slay the sons of those who believe with him and keep their women alive. And the plot of the disbelievers is bound to fail.

40:26. And Pharaoh said: Leave me to slay Moses and let him call upon his Lord. Surely I fear that he will change your religion or that he will make mischief to appear in the land.

40:27. And Moses said: Truly I seek

40. The Believer

refuge in my Lord and your Lord from every proud one who believes not in the day of Reckoning.

* * *

40:28. And a believing man of Pharaoh's people, who hid his faith, said: Will you slay a man because he says, My Lord is Allah, and indeed he has brought you clear arguments from your Lord? And if he be a liar, on him will be his lie, and if he be truthful, there will befall you some of that which he threatens you with. Surely Allah guides not one who is a prodigal, a liar.

40:29. O my people, yours is the kingdom this day, being masters in the land, but who will help us against the punishment of Allah, if it comes to us? Pharaoh said: I only show you that which I see and I guide you only to the right way.

40:30. And he who believed said: O my people, surely I fear for you the like of what befell the parties,

40:31. The like of what befell the people of Noah and 'Ad and Thamud and those after them. And Allah wishes no injustice for (His) servants.

40:32. And, O my people, I fear for you the day of Calling out --

40:33. The day on which you will turn back retreating, having none to save you from Allah; and whomsoever Allah leaves in error there is no guide for him.

40:34. And Joseph indeed came to you before with clear arguments, but you ever remained in doubt as to what he brought you; until, when he died, you said: Allah will never raise a messenger after him. Thus does Allah leave him in error who is a prodigal, a doubter --

40:35. Those who dispute concerning the messages of Allah without any authority that has come to them. Greatly hated is it by Allah and by those who believe. Thus does Allah

يَكْتُمُ إِيمَانَهُ أَتَقْتُلُونَ رَجُلًا أَنْ يَقُولَ رَبِّيَ اللَّهُ وَقَدْ جَاءَكُمْ بِالْبَيِّنَاتِ مِنْ رَبِّكُمْ وَإِنْ يَكُ كَاذِبًا فَعَلَيْهِ كَذِبُهُ وَإِنْ يَكُ صَادِقًا يُصِبْكُمْ بَعْضُ الَّذِي يَعِدُكُمْ إِنَّ اللَّهَ لَا يَهْدِي مَنْ هُوَ مُسْرِفٌ كَذَّابٌ (٢٨)

يَا قَوْمِ لَكُمُ الْمُلْكُ الْيَوْمَ ظَاهِرِينَ فِي الْأَرْضِ فَمَنْ يَنْصُرُنَا مِنْ بَأْسِ اللَّهِ إِنْ جَاءَنَا قَالَ فِرْعَوْنُ مَا أُرِيكُمْ إِلَّا مَا أَرَى وَمَا أَهْدِيكُمْ إِلَّا سَبِيلَ الرَّشَادِ (٢٩)

وَقَالَ الَّذِي آمَنَ يَا قَوْمِ إِنِّي أَخَافُ عَلَيْكُمْ مِثْلَ يَوْمِ الْأَحْزَابِ (٣٠) مِثْلَ دَأْبِ قَوْمِ نُوحٍ وَعَادٍ وَثَمُودَ وَالَّذِينَ مِنْ بَعْدِهِمْ وَمَا اللَّهُ يُرِيدُ ظُلْمًا لِلْعِبَادِ (٣١)

وَيَا قَوْمِ إِنِّي أَخَافُ عَلَيْكُمْ يَوْمَ التَّنَادِ (٣٢) يَوْمَ تُوَلُّونَ مُدْبِرِينَ مَا لَكُمْ مِنَ اللَّهِ مِنْ عَاصِمٍ وَمَنْ يُضْلِلِ اللَّهُ فَمَا لَهُ مِنْ هَادٍ (٣٣)

وَلَقَدْ جَاءَكُمْ يُوسُفُ مِنْ قَبْلُ بِالْبَيِّنَاتِ فَمَا زِلْتُمْ فِي شَكٍّ مِمَّا جَاءَكُمْ بِهِ حَتَّى إِذَا هَلَكَ قُلْتُمْ لَنْ يَبْعَثَ اللَّهُ مِنْ بَعْدِهِ رَسُولًا كَذَلِكَ يُضِلُّ اللَّهُ مَنْ هُوَ مُسْرِفٌ مُرْتَابٌ (٣٤)

الَّذِينَ يُجَادِلُونَ فِي آيَاتِ اللَّهِ بِغَيْرِ سُلْطَانٍ أَتَاهُمْ كَبُرَ مَقْتًا عِنْدَ اللَّهِ وَعِنْدَ الَّذِينَ آمَنُوا كَذَلِكَ يَطْبَعُ اللَّهُ عَلَى كُلِّ قَلْبِ مُتَكَبِّرٍ جَبَّارٍ (٣٥)

وَقَالَ فِرْعَوْنُ يَا هَامَانُ ابْنِ لِي صَرْحًا لَعَلِّي أَبْلُغُ الْأَسْبَابَ (٣٦) أَسْبَابَ السَّمَاوَاتِ فَأَطَّلِعَ إِلَى إِلَهِ مُوسَى وَإِنِّي لَأَظُنُّهُ كَاذِبًا وَكَذَلِكَ

40. The Believer

seal every heart, of a proud, haughty one.

40:36. And Pharaoh said: O Haman, build for me a tower that I may attain the means of access --

40:37. The means of access to the heavens, then reach the God of Moses, and I surely think him to be a liar. And thus the evil of his deed was made fair-seeming to Pharaoh, and he was turned aside from the way. And the plot of Pharaoh ended in naught but ruin.

* * *

40:38. And he who believed said: O my people, follow me I will guide you to the right way.

40:39. O my people, this life of the world is but a (passing) enjoyment, and the Hereafter, that is the abode to settle.

40:40. Whoever does evil, he is requited only with the like of it; and whoever does good, whether male or female, and he is a believer, these shall enter the Garden, to be given therein sustenance without measure.

40:41. And, O my people, how is it that I call you to salvation and you call me to the Fire?

40:42. You call me to disbelieve in Allah and to associate with Him that of which I have no knowledge, and I call you to the Mighty, the Forgiving.

40:43. Without doubt that which you call me to has no title to be called to in this world, or in the Hereafter, and our return is to Allah, and the prodigals are companions of the Fire.

40:44. So you will remember what I say to you, and I entrust my affair to Allah. Surely Allah is Seer of the servants.

40:45. So Allah protected him from the evil that they planned; and evil chastisement overtook Pharaoh's people --

40:46. The Fire. They are brought before it (every) morning and evening, and on the day when the Hour comes

40. The Believer

to pass: Make Pharaoh's people enter the severest chastisement.

40:47. And when they contend One with another in the Fire, the weak saying to those who were proud: Surely we were your followers; will you then avert from us a portion of the Fire?

40:48. Those who were proud say: Now we are all in it: Allah has indeed judged between the servants.

40:49. And those in the Fire will say to the guards of hell: Pray to your Lord to lighten our chastisement for a day.

40:50. They will say: Did not your messengers come to you with clear arguments? They will say: Yea. They will say: Then pray. And the prayer of the disbelievers goes only astray.

* * *

40:51. We certainly help Our messengers, and those who believe, in this world's life and on the day when the witnesses arise --

40:52. The day on which their excuse will not benefit the unjust, and for them is a curse and for them is the evil abode.

40:53. And We indeed gave Moses the guidance, and We made the Children of Israel inherit the Book --

40:54. A guidance and a reminder for men of understanding.

40:55. So be patient; surely the promise of Allah is true; and ask protection for thy sin and celebrate the praise of thy Lord in the evening and the morning.

40:56. Those who dispute about the messages of Allah without any authority having come to them, there is naught in their breasts but (a desire) to become great, which they will never attain. So seek refuge in Allah. Surely He is the Hearing, the Seeing.

40:57. Assuredly the creation of the heavens and the earth is greater than the creation of men; but most people know not.

وَقَالَ الَّذِينَ فِي النَّارِ لِخَزَنَةِ جَهَنَّمَ ادْعُوا رَبَّكُمْ يُخَفِّفْ عَنَّا يَوْمًا مِنَ الْعَذَابِ (٤٩)

قَالُوا أَوَلَمْ تَكُ تَأْتِيكُمْ رُسُلُكُمْ بِالْبَيِّنَاتِ قَالُوا بَلَى قَالُوا فَادْعُوا وَمَا دُعَاءُ الْكَافِرِينَ إِلَّا فِي ضَلَالٍ (٥٠)

إِنَّا لَنَنْصُرُ رُسُلَنَا وَالَّذِينَ آمَنُوا فِي الْحَيَاةِ الدُّنْيَا وَيَوْمَ يَقُومُ الْأَشْهَادُ (٥١)

يَوْمَ لَا يَنْفَعُ الظَّالِمِينَ مَعْذِرَتُهُمْ وَلَهُمُ اللَّعْنَةُ وَلَهُمْ سُوءُ الدَّارِ (٥٢)

وَلَقَدْ آتَيْنَا مُوسَى الْهُدَى وَأَوْرَثْنَا بَنِي إِسْرَائِيلَ الْكِتَابَ (٥٣)

هُدًى وَذِكْرَى لِأُولِي الْأَلْبَابِ (٥٤)

فَاصْبِرْ إِنَّ وَعْدَ اللَّهِ حَقٌّ وَاسْتَغْفِرْ لِذَنْبِكَ وَسَبِّحْ بِحَمْدِ رَبِّكَ بِالْعَشِيِّ وَالْإِبْكَارِ (٥٥)

إِنَّ الَّذِينَ يُجَادِلُونَ فِي آيَاتِ اللَّهِ بِغَيْرِ سُلْطَانٍ أَتَاهُمْ إِنْ فِي صُدُورِهِمْ إِلَّا كِبْرٌ مَا هُمْ بِبَالِغِيهِ فَاسْتَعِذْ بِاللَّهِ إِنَّهُ هُوَ السَّمِيعُ الْبَصِيرُ (٥٦)

لَخَلْقُ السَّمَاوَاتِ وَالْأَرْضِ أَكْبَرُ مِنْ خَلْقِ النَّاسِ وَلَكِنَّ أَكْثَرَ النَّاسِ لَا يَعْلَمُونَ (٥٧)

وَمَا يَسْتَوِي الْأَعْمَى وَالْبَصِيرُ وَالَّذِينَ آمَنُوا وَعَمِلُوا الصَّالِحَاتِ وَلَا الْمُسِيءُ قَلِيلًا مَا تَتَذَكَّرُونَ (٥٨)

إِنَّ السَّاعَةَ لَآتِيَةٌ لَا رَيْبَ فِيهَا وَلَكِنَّ أَكْثَرَ النَّاسِ لَا يُؤْمِنُونَ (٥٩)

وَقَالَ رَبُّكُمُ ادْعُونِي أَسْتَجِبْ لَكُمْ إِنَّ الَّذِينَ يَسْتَكْبِرُونَ عَنْ عِبَادَتِي سَيَدْخُلُونَ جَهَنَّمَ دَاخِرِينَ (٦٠)

اللَّهُ الَّذِي جَعَلَ لَكُمُ اللَّيْلَ لِتَسْكُنُوا فِيهِ وَالنَّهَارَ مُبْصِرًا إِنَّ اللَّهَ لَذُو فَضْلٍ

40. The Believer

40:58. And the blind and the seeing are not alike, not those who believe and do good and the evildoers. Little do you mind!

40:59. The Hour is surely coming -- there is no doubt therein -- but most people believe not.

40:60. And your Lord says: Pray to Me, I will answer you. Those who disdain My service will surely enter hell, abased.

* * *

40:61. Allah is He Who made for you the night for resting in and the day for seeing. Surely Allah is Full of Grace to men, but most men give not thanks.

40:62. That is Allah, your Lord, the Creator of all things. There is no God but He. Whence are you then turned away?

40:63. Thus are turned away those who deny the messages of Allah.

40:64. Allah is He Who made the earth a resting-place for you and the heaven a structure, and He formed you, then made goodly your forms, and He provided you with goodly things. That is Allah, your Lord -- so blessed is Allah, the Lord of the worlds.

40:65. He is the Living, there is no God but He; so call on Him, being sincere to Him in obedience. Praise be to Allah, the Lord of the worlds!

40:66. Say: I am forbidden to serve those whom you call upon besides Allah, when clear arguments have come to me from my Lord; and I am commanded to submit to the Lord of the worlds.

40:67. He it is Who created you from dust, then from a small life-germ, then from a clot, then He brings you forth as a child, then that you may attain your maturity, then that you may be old; and of you are some who die before and that you may reach an appointed term, and that you may understand.

40:68. He it is Who gives life and causes

40. The Believer

death, so when He decrees an affair, He only says to it, Be, and it is.

***

40:69. Seest thou not those who dispute concerning the messages of Allah? How are they turned away? --

40:70. Those who reject the Book and that with which We have sent Our messengers. But they shall soon know.

40:71. When the fetters are on their necks and the chains. They are dragged

40:72. Into hot water; then in the Fire they are burned.

40:73. Then it is said to them: Where is that which you used to set up

40:74. Besides Allah? They will say They have failed us; nay, we used not to call upon anything before. Thus does Allah confound the disbelievers.

40:75. That is because you exulted in the land unjustly and because you behaved insolently.

40:76. Enter the gates of hell to abide therein; so evil is the abode of the proud.

40:77. Therefore be patient, surely the promise of Allah is true. But whether We make thee see part of what We threaten them with, or cause thee to die, to Us shall they be returned.

40:78. And certainly We sent messengers before thee -- of them are those We have mentioned to thee and of them are those We have not mentioned to thee. Nor was it possible for a messenger to bring a sign except with Allah's permission so when Allah's command comes, judgment is given with truth, and those who treat (it) as a lie are lost.

***

40:79. Allah is He Who made the cattle for you that you may ride on some of them, and some of them you eat.

40:80. And there are advantages in them for you, and that you may attain through them a need which is in your breasts, and on them and on ships you

(٧٣) مِنْ دُونِ اللَّهِ قَالُوا ضَلُّوا عَنَّا بَلْ لَمْ نَكُنْ نَدْعُو مِنْ قَبْلُ شَيْئًا كَذَلِكَ يُضِلُّ اللَّهُ الْكَافِرِينَ (٧٤) ذَلِكُمْ بِمَا كُنْتُمْ تَفْرَحُونَ فِي الْأَرْضِ بِغَيْرِ الْحَقِّ وَبِمَا كُنْتُمْ تَمْرَحُونَ (٧٥) ادْخُلُوا أَبْوَابَ جَهَنَّمَ خَالِدِينَ فِيهَا فَبِئْسَ مَثْوَى الْمُتَكَبِّرِينَ (٧٦) فَاصْبِرْ إِنَّ وَعْدَ اللَّهِ حَقٌّ فَإِمَّا نُرِيَنَّكَ بَعْضَ الَّذِي نَعِدُهُمْ أَوْ نَتَوَفَّيَنَّكَ فَإِلَيْنَا يُرْجَعُونَ (٧٧) وَلَقَدْ أَرْسَلْنَا رُسُلًا مِنْ قَبْلِكَ مِنْهُمْ مَنْ قَصَصْنَا عَلَيْكَ وَمِنْهُمْ مَنْ لَمْ نَقْصُصْ عَلَيْكَ وَمَا كَانَ لِرَسُولٍ أَنْ يَأْتِيَ بِآيَةٍ إِلَّا بِإِذْنِ اللَّهِ فَإِذَا جَاءَ أَمْرُ اللَّهِ قُضِيَ بِالْحَقِّ وَخَسِرَ هُنَالِكَ الْمُبْطِلُونَ (٧٨) اللَّهُ الَّذِي جَعَلَ لَكُمُ الْأَنْعَامَ لِتَرْكَبُوا مِنْهَا وَمِنْهَا تَأْكُلُونَ (٧٩) وَلَكُمْ فِيهَا مَنَافِعُ وَلِتَبْلُغُوا عَلَيْهَا حَاجَةً فِي صُدُورِكُمْ وَعَلَيْهَا وَعَلَى الْفُلْكِ تُحْمَلُونَ (٨٠) وَيُرِيكُمْ آيَاتِهِ فَأَيَّ آيَاتِ اللَّهِ تُنْكِرُونَ (٨١) أَفَلَمْ يَسِيرُوا فِي الْأَرْضِ فَيَنْظُرُوا كَيْفَ كَانَ عَاقِبَةُ الَّذِينَ مِنْ قَبْلِهِمْ كَانُوا أَكْثَرَ مِنْهُمْ وَأَشَدَّ قُوَّةً وَآثَارًا فِي الْأَرْضِ فَمَا أَغْنَى عَنْهُمْ مَا كَانُوا يَكْسِبُونَ (٨٢) فَلَمَّا جَاءَتْهُمْ رُسُلُهُمْ بِالْبَيِّنَاتِ فَرِحُوا بِمَا عِنْدَهُمْ مِنَ الْعِلْمِ وَحَاقَ بِهِمْ مَا كَانُوا بِهِ يَسْتَهْزِئُونَ (٨٣) فَلَمَّا رَأَوْا بَأْسَنَا قَالُوا آمَنَّا بِاللَّهِ وَحْدَهُ

are borne.

40:81. And He shows you His signs which then of Allah's signs will you deny?

40:82. Do they not travel in the land and see what was the end of those before them? They were more numerous than these and greater in strength and in fortifications in the land, but what they earned availed them not.

40:83. Then when their messengers came to them with clear arguments, they exulted in what they had with them of knowledge and that at which they used to mock befell them.

40:84. So when they saw Our punishment, they said: We believe in Allah alone, and we deny what we used to associate with Him.

40:85. But their faith could not profit them when they saw Our punishment. Such is Allah's law, which ever takes its course in the matter of His servants; and there the disbelievers are lost.

41. Ha Min

In the name of Allah, the Beneficent, the Merciful.

41:1. Beneficent God!

41:2. A revelation from the Beneficent, the Merciful.

41:3. A Book of which the verses are made plain, an Arabic Qur'an for a people who know --

41:4. Good news and a warning. But most of them turn away, so they hear not.

41:5. And they say: Our hearts are under coverings from that to which thou callest us, and there is a deafness in our ears, and there is a veil between us and thee, so act, we too are acting.

41:6. Say: I am only a mortal like you. It is revealed to me that your God is one God, so keep in the straight path to

وَكَفَرْنَا بِمَا كُنَّا بِهِ مُشْرِكِينَ (٨٤)
فَلَمْ يَكُ يَنْفَعُهُمْ إِيمَانُهُمْ لَمَّا رَأَوْا بَأْسَنَا سُنَّةَ اللَّهِ الَّتِي قَدْ خَلَتْ فِي عِبَادِهِ وَخَسِرَ هُنَالِكَ الْكَافِرُونَ (٨٥)

٤١ ـ سورة فصلت

بِسْمِ اللَّهِ الرَّحْمَنِ الرَّحِيمِ
حم (١)
تَنْزِيلٌ مِنَ الرَّحْمَنِ الرَّحِيمِ (٢)
كِتَابٌ فُصِّلَتْ آيَاتُهُ قُرْآنًا عَرَبِيًّا لِقَوْمٍ يَعْلَمُونَ (٣)
بَشِيرًا وَنَذِيرًا فَأَعْرَضَ أَكْثَرُهُمْ فَهُمْ لَا يَسْمَعُونَ (٤)
وَقَالُوا قُلُوبُنَا فِي أَكِنَّةٍ مِمَّا تَدْعُونَا إِلَيْهِ وَفِي آذَانِنَا وَقْرٌ وَمِنْ بَيْنِنَا وَبَيْنِكَ حِجَابٌ فَاعْمَلْ إِنَّنَا عَامِلُونَ (٥)
قُلْ إِنَّمَا أَنَا بَشَرٌ مِثْلُكُمْ يُوحَى إِلَيَّ أَنَّمَا إِلَهُكُمْ إِلَهٌ وَاحِدٌ فَاسْتَقِيمُوا إِلَيْهِ وَاسْتَغْفِرُوهُ وَوَيْلٌ لِلْمُشْرِكِينَ (٦)

41. Ha Min

Him, and ask His protection. And woe to the polytheists!

41:7. Who give not the poor-rate, and who are disbelievers in the Hereafter.

41:8. Those who believe and do good, for them is surely a reward never to be cut off.

***

41:9. Say: Do you indeed disbelieve in Him Who created the earth in two days, and do you set up equals with Him? That is the Lord of the worlds.

41:10. And He made in it mountains above its surface, and He blessed therein and ordained therein its foods, in four days; alike for (all) seekers.

41:11. Then He directed Himself to the heaven and it was a vapour, so He said to it and to the earth: Come both, willingly or unwillingly. They both said: We come willingly.

41:12. So He ordained them seven heavens in two days, and revealed in every heaven its affair. And We adorned the lower heaven with lights, and (made it) to guard. That is the decree of the Mighty, the Knowing.

41:13. But if they turn away, then say I warn you of a scourge like the scourge of 'Ad and Thamud.

41:14. When messengers came to them from before them and behind them, saying, Serve nothing but Allah, they said: If our Lord had pleased, He would have sent down angels. So we are disbelievers in that with which you are sent.

41:15. Then as to 'Ad, they were unjustly proud in the land, and said: Who is mightier than we in power? See they not that Allah Who created them is mightier than they in power? And they denied Our messages.

41:16. So We sent on them a furious wind in unlucky days that We might make them taste the chastisement of abasement in this world's life. And the chastisement of the Hereafter is truly

الَّذِينَ لَا يُؤْتُونَ الزَّكَاةَ وَهُم بِالْآخِرَةِ هُمْ كَافِرُونَ (٧)

إِنَّ الَّذِينَ آمَنُوا وَعَمِلُوا الصَّالِحَاتِ لَهُمْ أَجْرٌ غَيْرُ مَمْنُونٍ (٨)

قُلْ أَئِنَّكُمْ لَتَكْفُرُونَ بِالَّذِي خَلَقَ الْأَرْضَ فِي يَوْمَيْنِ وَتَجْعَلُونَ لَهُ أَندَادًا ذَلِكَ رَبُّ الْعَالَمِينَ (٩)

وَجَعَلَ فِيهَا رَوَاسِيَ مِن فَوْقِهَا وَبَارَكَ فِيهَا وَقَدَّرَ فِيهَا أَقْوَاتَهَا فِي أَرْبَعَةِ أَيَّامٍ سَوَاءً لِّلسَّائِلِينَ (١٠)

ثُمَّ اسْتَوَى إِلَى السَّمَاءِ وَهِيَ دُخَانٌ فَقَالَ لَهَا وَلِلْأَرْضِ ائْتِيَا طَوْعًا أَوْ كَرْهًا قَالَتَا أَتَيْنَا طَائِعِينَ (١١)

فَقَضَاهُنَّ سَبْعَ سَمَاوَاتٍ فِي يَوْمَيْنِ وَأَوْحَى فِي كُلِّ سَمَاءٍ أَمْرَهَا وَزَيَّنَّا السَّمَاءَ الدُّنْيَا بِمَصَابِيحَ وَحِفْظًا ذَلِكَ تَقْدِيرُ الْعَزِيزِ الْعَلِيمِ (١٢)

فَإِنْ أَعْرَضُوا فَقُلْ أَنذَرْتُكُمْ صَاعِقَةً مِثْلَ صَاعِقَةِ عَادٍ وَثَمُودَ (١٣)

إِذْ جَاءَتْهُمُ الرُّسُلُ مِن بَيْنِ أَيْدِيهِمْ وَمِنْ خَلْفِهِمْ أَلَّا تَعْبُدُوا إِلَّا اللَّهَ قَالُوا لَوْ شَاءَ رَبُّنَا لَأَنزَلَ مَلَائِكَةً فَإِنَّا بِمَا أُرْسِلْتُم بِهِ كَافِرُونَ (١٤)

فَأَمَّا عَادٌ فَاسْتَكْبَرُوا فِي الْأَرْضِ بِغَيْرِ الْحَقِّ وَقَالُوا مَنْ أَشَدُّ مِنَّا قُوَّةً أَوَلَمْ يَرَوْا أَنَّ اللَّهَ الَّذِي خَلَقَهُمْ هُوَ أَشَدُّ مِنْهُمْ قُوَّةً وَكَانُوا بِآيَاتِنَا يَجْحَدُونَ (١٥)

فَأَرْسَلْنَا عَلَيْهِمْ رِيحًا صَرْصَرًا فِي أَيَّامٍ نَحِسَاتٍ لِّنُذِيقَهُمْ عَذَابَ الْخِزْيِ فِي الْحَيَاةِ الدُّنْيَا وَلَعَذَابُ الْآخِرَةِ أَخْزَى وَهُمْ لَا يُنصَرُونَ (١٦)

وَأَمَّا ثَمُودُ فَهَدَيْنَاهُمْ فَاسْتَحَبُّوا الْعَمَى عَلَى الْهُدَى فَأَخَذَتْهُمْ صَاعِقَةُ الْعَذَابِ

more abasing, and they will not be helped.

41:17. And as for Thamud, We showed them the right way, but they preferred blindness to guidance, so the scourge of an abasing chastisement overtook them for what they had earned.

41:18. And We delivered those who believed and kept their duty.

***

41:19. And the day when the enemies of Allah are gathered to the Fire, they will be formed into groups.

41:20. Until, when they come to it, their ears and their eyes and their skins will bear witness against them as to what they did.

41:21. And they will say to their skins Why bear ye witness against us They will say: Allah Who makes everything speak has made us speak, and He created you at first, and to Him you are returned.

41:22. And you did not cover yourselves lest your ears and your eyes and your skins should bear witness against you, but you thought that Allah knew not much of what you did.

41:23. And that, your (evil) thought which you entertained about your Lord, ruined you, so have you become of the lost ones.

41:24. Then if they are patient, the Fire is their abode. And if they ask for goodwill, they are not of those who are granted goodwill.

41:25. And We have appointed for them comrades, so they make fair-seeming to them what is before them and what is behind them, and the word proved true against them among the nations of jinn and men that have passed away before them they are surely losers.

***

41:26. And those who disbelieve say: Listen not to this Qur'an but make noise therein, perhaps you may overcome.

41:27. So We shall certainly make those who disbelieve taste a severe chastisement, and We shall certainly requite them for the worst of what they did.

41:28. That is the reward of Allah's enemies -- the Fire. For them therein is the home to abide. A requital for their denying Our messages.

41:29. And those who disbelieve will say: Our Lord, show us those who led us astray from among the jinn and the men that we may trample them under our feet, so that they may be of the lowest.

41:30. Those who say, Our Lord is Allah, then continue in the right way, the angels descend upon them, saying: Fear not, nor be grieved, and receive good news of the Garden which you were promised.

41:31. We are your friends in this world's life and in the Hereafter, and you have therein what your souls desire and you have therein what you ask for.

41:32. A welcome gift from the Forgiving, the Merciful.

***

41:33. And who is better in speech than one who calls to Allah and does good, and says: I am surely of those who submit?

41:34. And not alike are the good and the evil. Repel (evil) with what is best, when lo! he between whom and thee is enmity would be as if he were a warm friend.

41:35. And none is granted it but those who are patient, and none is granted it but the owner of a mighty good fortune.

41:36. And if a false imputation from the devil afflict thee, seek refuge in Allah. Surely He is the Hearing, the Knowing.

41:37. And of His signs are the night

and the day and the sun and the moon. Adore not the sun nor the moon, but adore Allah Who created them, if He it is that you serve.

41:38. But if they are proud, yet those with thy Lord glorify Him night and day, and they tire not.

41:39. And of His signs is this, that thou seest the earth still, but when We send down water thereon, it stirs and swells. He Who gives it life is surely the Giver of life to the dead. Surely He is Possessor of Power over all things.

41:40. Those who distort Our messages are not hidden from Us. Is he then who is cast into the Fire better or he who comes safe on the day of Resurrection? Do what you like, surely He is Seer of what you do.

41:41. Those who disbelieve in the Reminder when it comes to them, and surely it is an Invincible Book:

41:42. Falsehood cannot come at it from before or behind it: a revelation from the Wise, the Praised One.

41:43. Naught is said to thee but what was said to messengers before thee. Surely thy Lord is the Lord of Forgiveness and the Lord of painful Retribution.

41:44. And if We had made it a Qur'an in a foreign tongue, they would have said: Why have not its messages been made clear? What a foreign (tongue) and an Arab! Say: It is to those who believe a guidance and a healing, and those who believe not, there is a deafness in their ears and it is obscure to them. These are called to from a place afar.

***

41:45. And indeed We gave Moses the Book, but differences arose therein. And had not a word already gone forth from thy Lord, judgment would have been given between them. And surely they are in a disquieting doubt about it.

41:46. Whoever does good, it is for his

(٣٩)
إِنَّ الَّذِينَ يُلْحِدُونَ فِي آيَاتِنَا لَا يَخْفَوْنَ عَلَيْنَا أَفَمَنْ يُلْقَى فِي النَّارِ خَيْرٌ أَمْ مَنْ يَأْتِي آمِنًا يَوْمَ الْقِيَامَةِ اعْمَلُوا مَا شِئْتُمْ إِنَّهُ بِمَا تَعْمَلُونَ بَصِيرٌ (٤٠) إِنَّ الَّذِينَ كَفَرُوا بِالذِّكْرِ لَمَّا جَاءَهُمْ وَإِنَّهُ لَكِتَابٌ عَزِيزٌ (٤١) لَا يَأْتِيهِ الْبَاطِلُ مِنْ بَيْنِ يَدَيْهِ وَلَا مِنْ خَلْفِهِ تَنْزِيلٌ مِنْ حَكِيمٍ حَمِيدٍ (٤٢) مَا يُقَالُ لَكَ إِلَّا مَا قَدْ قِيلَ لِلرُّسُلِ مِنْ قَبْلِكَ إِنَّ رَبَّكَ لَذُو مَغْفِرَةٍ وَذُو عِقَابٍ أَلِيمٍ (٤٣) وَلَوْ جَعَلْنَاهُ قُرْآنًا أَعْجَمِيًّا لَقَالُوا لَوْلَا فُصِّلَتْ آيَاتُهُ أَأَعْجَمِيٌّ وَعَرَبِيٌّ قُلْ هُوَ لِلَّذِينَ آمَنُوا هُدًى وَشِفَاءٌ وَالَّذِينَ لَا يُؤْمِنُونَ فِي آذَانِهِمْ وَقْرٌ وَهُوَ عَلَيْهِمْ عَمًى أُولَئِكَ يُنَادَوْنَ مِنْ مَكَانٍ بَعِيدٍ (٤٤) وَلَقَدْ آتَيْنَا مُوسَى الْكِتَابَ فَاخْتُلِفَ فِيهِ وَلَوْلَا كَلِمَةٌ سَبَقَتْ مِنْ رَبِّكَ لَقُضِيَ بَيْنَهُمْ وَإِنَّهُمْ لَفِي شَكٍّ مِنْهُ مُرِيبٍ (٤٥) مَنْ عَمِلَ صَالِحًا فَلِنَفْسِهِ وَمَنْ أَسَاءَ فَعَلَيْهَا وَمَا رَبُّكَ بِظَلَّامٍ لِلْعَبِيدِ (٤٦) إِلَيْهِ يُرَدُّ عِلْمُ السَّاعَةِ وَمَا تَخْرُجُ مِنْ ثَمَرَاتٍ مِنْ أَكْمَامِهَا وَمَا تَحْمِلُ مِنْ أُنْثَى وَلَا تَضَعُ إِلَّا بِعِلْمِهِ وَيَوْمَ يُنَادِيهِمْ أَيْنَ شُرَكَائِي قَالُوا آذَنَّاكَ مَا مِنَّا مِنْ شَهِيدٍ (٤٧) وَضَلَّ عَنْهُمْ مَا كَانُوا يَدْعُونَ مِنْ قَبْلُ وَظَنُّوا مَا لَهُمْ مِنْ مَحِيصٍ (٤٨) لَا يَسْأَمُ الْإِنْسَانُ مِنْ دُعَاءِ الْخَيْرِ وَإِنْ مَسَّهُ الشَّرُّ فَيَئُوسٌ قَنُوطٌ (٤٩) وَلَئِنْ أَذَقْنَاهُ رَحْمَةً مِنَّا مِنْ بَعْدِ

own soul; and whoever does evil, it is against it. And thy Lord is not in the least unjust to the servants.

***

41:47. To Him is referred the knowledge of the Hour And no fruit comes forth from its coverings, nor does a female bear or bring forth but with His knowledge. And on the day when He calls out to them: Where are My associates? they will say: We declare to Thee, not one of us can bear witness.

41:48. And those whom they called upon before will fail them, and they will know that they cannot escape.

41:49. Man tires not of praying for good, but, if evil touch him, he is despairing, hopeless.

41:50. And if We make him taste mercy from ifs after distress has touched him, he says: This is due to me, and I think not that the Hour will come to pass; and if I am sent back to my Lord, I shall have sure good with Him. So We shall certainly inform those who disbelieve of what they do, and We shall make them taste of hard chastisement.

41:51. And when We show favour to man, he turns away and withdraws himself; but when evil touches him, he is full of lengthy supplications.

41:52. Say: See you, if it is from Allah, then you disbelieve in it, who is in greater error than he who is in opposition far away?

41:53. We will soon show them Our signs in farthest regions and among their own people, until it is quite dear to them that it is the Truth. Is it not enough that thy Lord is a Witness over all things?

41:54. Now surely they are in doubt as to the meeting with their Lord. Lo! He surely encompasses all things.

ضَرَّاءَ مَسَّتْهُ لَيَقُولَنَّ هَذَا لِي وَمَا أَظُنُّ السَّاعَةَ قَائِمَةً وَلَئِنْ رُجِعْتُ إِلَى رَبِّي إِنَّ لِي عِنْدَهُ لَلْحُسْنَى فَلَنُنَبِّئَنَّ الَّذِينَ كَفَرُوا بِمَا عَمِلُوا وَلَنُذِيقَنَّهُمْ مِنْ عَذَابٍ غَلِيظٍ (٥٠)
وَإِذَا أَنْعَمْنَا عَلَى الْإِنْسَانِ أَعْرَضَ وَنَأَى بِجَانِبِهِ وَإِذَا مَسَّهُ الشَّرُّ فَذُو دُعَاءٍ عَرِيضٍ (٥١)
قُلْ أَرَأَيْتُمْ إِنْ كَانَ مِنْ عِنْدِ اللَّهِ ثُمَّ كَفَرْتُمْ بِهِ مَنْ أَضَلُّ مِمَّنْ هُوَ فِي شِقَاقٍ بَعِيدٍ (٥٢)
سَنُرِيهِمْ آيَاتِنَا فِي الْآفَاقِ وَفِي أَنْفُسِهِمْ حَتَّى يَتَبَيَّنَ لَهُمْ أَنَّهُ الْحَقُّ أَوَلَمْ يَكْفِ بِرَبِّكَ أَنَّهُ عَلَى كُلِّ شَيْءٍ شَهِيدٌ (٥٣)
أَلَا إِنَّهُمْ فِي مِرْيَةٍ مِنْ لِقَاءِ رَبِّهِمْ أَلَا إِنَّهُ بِكُلِّ شَيْءٍ مُحِيطٌ (٥٤)

42. The Counsel

In the name of Allah, the Beneficent, the Merciful.

42:1. Beneficent God!
42:2. Knowing, Heating, Powerful God
42:3. Thus does Allah, the Mighty, the Wise, reveal to thee, and (He revealed) to those before thee.
42:4. To Him belongs whatever is in the heavens and whatever is in the earth; and He is the High, the Great.
42:5. The heavens may almost be rent asunder above them, while the angels celebrate the praise of their Lord and ask forgiveness for those on earth. Now surely Allah is the Forgiving, the Merciful.
42:6. And those who take protectors besides Him -- Allah watches over them; and thou hast not charge over them.
42:7. And thus have We revealed to thee an Arabic Qur'an, that thou mayest warn the mother-town and those around it, and give warning of the day of Gathering, wherein is no doubt. A party will be in the Garden and (another) party in the burning Fire.
42:8. And if Allah had pleased, He would surely have made them a single nation, but He admits whom He pleases to His mercy. And the wrong doers have no protector not helper.
42:9. Or have they taken protectors besides Him? But Allah is the Protector, and He gives life to the dead, and He is Possessor of power over all things.

* * *

42:10. And in whatever you differ, the judgment thereof is with Allah. That is Allah, my Lord; on Him I rely, and to Him I turn.
42:11. The Originator of the heavens and the earth. He has made for you pairs from among yourselves, and pairs of the cattle, too, multiplying you

42. The Counsel

thereby. Nothing is like Him; and He is the Hearing, the Seeing.

42:12. His are the treasures of the heavens and the earth -- He amplifies and straitens subsistence for whom He pleases. Surely He is Knower of all things.

42:13. He has made plain to you the religion which He enjoined upon Noah and which We have revealed to thee, and which We enjoined on Abraham and Moses and Jesus to establish religion and not to be divided therein. Hard for the polytheists is that to which thou callest them. Allah chooses for Himself whom He pleases, and guides to Himself him who turns (to Him).

42:14. And they were not divided until knowledge had come to them, out of envy among themselves. And had not a word gone forth from thy Lord for an appointed term, the matter would surely have been judged between them. And those who were made to inherit the Book after them are surely in disquieting doubt about it.

42:15. To this then go on inviting, and be steadfast as thou art commanded, and follow not their low desires, and say: I believe in what Allah has revealed of the Book, and I am commanded to do justice between you. Allah is our Lord and your Lord. For us are our deeds; and for you your deeds. There is no contention between us and you. Allah will gather us together, and to Him is the eventual coming.

42:16. And those who dispute about Allah after obedience has been rendered to Him, their plea is null with their Lord, and upon them is wrath, and for them is severe chastisement.

42:17. Allah is He Who revealed the Book with truth, and the Balance; and what will make thee know that perhaps the Hour is nigh.

لَهُ مَقَالِيدُ السَّمَاوَاتِ وَالْأَرْضِ يَبْسُطُ الرِّزْقَ لِمَنْ يَشَاءُ وَيَقْدِرُ إِنَّهُ بِكُلِّ شَيْءٍ عَلِيمٌ (١٢) شَرَعَ لَكُمْ مِنَ الدِّينِ مَا وَصَّى بِهِ نُوحًا وَالَّذِي أَوْحَيْنَا إِلَيْكَ وَمَا وَصَّيْنَا بِهِ إِبْرَاهِيمَ وَمُوسَى وَعِيسَى أَنْ أَقِيمُوا الدِّينَ وَلَا تَتَفَرَّقُوا فِيهِ كَبُرَ عَلَى الْمُشْرِكِينَ مَا تَدْعُوهُمْ إِلَيْهِ اللَّهُ يَجْتَبِي إِلَيْهِ مَنْ يَشَاءُ وَيَهْدِي إِلَيْهِ مَنْ يُنِيبُ (١٣) وَمَا تَفَرَّقُوا إِلَّا مِنْ بَعْدِ مَا جَاءَهُمُ الْعِلْمُ بَغْيًا بَيْنَهُمْ وَلَوْلَا كَلِمَةٌ سَبَقَتْ مِنْ رَبِّكَ إِلَى أَجَلٍ مُسَمًّى لَقُضِيَ بَيْنَهُمْ وَإِنَّ الَّذِينَ أُورِثُوا الْكِتَابَ مِنْ بَعْدِهِمْ لَفِي شَكٍّ مِنْهُ مُرِيبٍ (١٤) فَلِذَلِكَ فَادْعُ وَاسْتَقِمْ كَمَا أُمِرْتَ وَلَا تَتَّبِعْ أَهْوَاءَهُمْ وَقُلْ آمَنْتُ بِمَا أَنْزَلَ اللَّهُ مِنْ كِتَابٍ وَأُمِرْتُ لِأَعْدِلَ بَيْنَكُمُ اللَّهُ رَبُّنَا وَرَبُّكُمْ لَنَا أَعْمَالُنَا وَلَكُمْ أَعْمَالُكُمْ لَا حُجَّةَ بَيْنَنَا وَبَيْنَكُمُ اللَّهُ يَجْمَعُ بَيْنَنَا وَإِلَيْهِ الْمَصِيرُ (١٥) وَالَّذِينَ يُحَاجُّونَ فِي اللَّهِ مِنْ بَعْدِ مَا اسْتُجِيبَ لَهُ حُجَّتُهُمْ دَاحِضَةٌ عِنْدَ رَبِّهِمْ وَعَلَيْهِمْ غَضَبٌ وَلَهُمْ عَذَابٌ شَدِيدٌ (١٦) اللَّهُ الَّذِي أَنْزَلَ الْكِتَابَ بِالْحَقِّ وَالْمِيزَانَ وَمَا يُدْرِيكَ لَعَلَّ السَّاعَةَ قَرِيبٌ (١٧) يَسْتَعْجِلُ بِهَا الَّذِينَ لَا يُؤْمِنُونَ بِهَا وَالَّذِينَ آمَنُوا مُشْفِقُونَ مِنْهَا وَيَعْلَمُونَ أَنَّهَا الْحَقُّ أَلَا إِنَّ الَّذِينَ يُمَارُونَ فِي السَّاعَةِ لَفِي ضَلَالٍ بَعِيدٍ (١٨) اللَّهُ لَطِيفٌ بِعِبَادِهِ يَرْزُقُ مَنْ يَشَاءُ وَهُوَ الْقَوِيُّ الْعَزِيزُ (١٩)

42. The Counsel

42:18. Those who believe not in it would hasten it on, and those who believe are in fear from it, and they know that it is the Truth. Now surely those who dispute concerning the Hour are far astray.

42:19. Allah is Benignant to His servants; He gives sustenance to whom He pleases; and He is the Strong, the Mighty.

***

42:20. Whoso desires the tilth (fields) of the Hereafter, We give him increase in his tilth and whoso desires the tilth of this world, We give him thereof and he has no portion in the Hereafter.

42:21. Or have they associates who have prescribed for them any religion that Allah does not sanction? And were it not for the word of judgment, it would have been decided between them. And surely for the wrongdoers is a painful chastisement.

42:22. Thou seest the unjust fearing on account of what they have earned, and it must befall them. And those who believe and do good are in the meadows of the Gardens -- they have what they please with their Lord. That is the great grace.

42:23. This it is of which Allah gives the good news to His servants, who believe and do good. Say: I ask of you naught in return for it but love for relatives. And whoever earns good, We give him more of good therein. Surely Allah is Forgiving, Grateful.

42:24. Or say they: He has forged a lie against Allah? So, if Allah please, He would seal thy heart (against them). And Allah blots out the falsehood and confirms the Truth with His words. Surely He is Knower of what is in the breasts.

42:25. And He it is Who accepts repentance from His servants and pardons evil deeds, and He knows what you do;

مَنْ كَانَ يُرِيدُ حَرْثَ الْآخِرَةِ نَزِدْ لَهُ فِي حَرْثِهِ وَمَنْ كَانَ يُرِيدُ حَرْثَ الدُّنْيَا نُؤْتِهِ مِنْهَا وَمَا لَهُ فِي الْآخِرَةِ مِنْ نَصِيبٍ (٢٠)

أَمْ لَهُمْ شُرَكَاءُ شَرَعُوا لَهُمْ مِنَ الدِّينِ مَا لَمْ يَأْذَنْ بِهِ اللَّهُ وَلَوْلَا كَلِمَةُ الْفَصْلِ لَقُضِيَ بَيْنَهُمْ وَإِنَّ الظَّالِمِينَ لَهُمْ عَذَابٌ أَلِيمٌ (٢١)

تَرَى الظَّالِمِينَ مُشْفِقِينَ مِمَّا كَسَبُوا وَهُوَ وَاقِعٌ بِهِمْ وَالَّذِينَ آمَنُوا وَعَمِلُوا الصَّالِحَاتِ فِي رَوْضَاتِ الْجَنَّاتِ لَهُمْ مَا يَشَاءُونَ عِنْدَ رَبِّهِمْ ذَلِكَ هُوَ الْفَضْلُ الْكَبِيرُ (٢٢)

ذَلِكَ الَّذِي يُبَشِّرُ اللَّهُ عِبَادَهُ الَّذِينَ آمَنُوا وَعَمِلُوا الصَّالِحَاتِ قُلْ لَا أَسْأَلُكُمْ عَلَيْهِ أَجْرًا إِلَّا الْمَوَدَّةَ فِي الْقُرْبَى وَمَنْ يَقْتَرِفْ حَسَنَةً نَزِدْ لَهُ فِيهَا حُسْنًا إِنَّ اللَّهَ غَفُورٌ شَكُورٌ (٢٣)

أَمْ يَقُولُونَ افْتَرَى عَلَى اللَّهِ كَذِبًا فَإِنْ يَشَأِ اللَّهُ يَخْتِمْ عَلَى قَلْبِكَ وَيَمْحُ اللَّهُ الْبَاطِلَ وَيُحِقُّ الْحَقَّ بِكَلِمَاتِهِ إِنَّهُ عَلِيمٌ بِذَاتِ الصُّدُورِ (٢٤)

وَهُوَ الَّذِي يَقْبَلُ التَّوْبَةَ عَنْ عِبَادِهِ وَيَعْفُو عَنِ السَّيِّئَاتِ وَيَعْلَمُ مَا تَفْعَلُونَ (٢٥)

وَيَسْتَجِيبُ الَّذِينَ آمَنُوا وَعَمِلُوا الصَّالِحَاتِ وَيَزِيدُهُمْ مِنْ فَضْلِهِ وَالْكَافِرُونَ لَهُمْ عَذَابٌ شَدِيدٌ (٢٦)

وَلَوْ بَسَطَ اللَّهُ الرِّزْقَ لِعِبَادِهِ لَبَغَوْا فِي الْأَرْضِ وَلَكِنْ يُنَزِّلُ بِقَدَرٍ مَا يَشَاءُ إِنَّهُ بِعِبَادِهِ خَبِيرٌ بَصِيرٌ (٢٧)

وَهُوَ الَّذِي يُنَزِّلُ الْغَيْثَ مِنْ بَعْدِ مَا قَنَطُوا وَيَنْشُرُ رَحْمَتَهُ وَهُوَ الْوَلِيُّ

42. The Counsel

42:26. And He answers those who believe and do good deeds, and gives them more out of His grace. And for the disbelievers is a severe chastisement.

42:27. And if Allah were to amplify the provision for His servants, they would rebel in the earth; but He sends (it) down by measure, as He pleases. Surely He is Aware, Seer of His servants.

42:28. And He it is Who sends down the rain after they have despaired, and He unfolds His mercy. And He is the Friend, the Praised One.

42:29. And of His signs is the creation of the heavens and the earth and what He has spread forth in both of them of living beings. And He is All-powerful to gather them together, when He will.

* * *

42:30. And whatever misfortune befalls you, it is on account of what your hands have wrought and He pardons much.

42:31. And you cannot escape in the earth, and besides Allah you have no protector nor helper.

42:32. And of His signs are the ships, like mountains on the sea.

42:33. If He will, He stills the wind so that they lie motionless on its back. Surely there are signs in this for every patient, grateful one,

42:34. Or He causes them to perish for what they have earned, and He pardons much;

42:35. And (that) those who dispute about Our messages may know. There is no refuge for them.

42:36. So whatever you are given is but a provision of this word's life, and that which Allah has is better and more lasting for those who believe and rely on their Lord;

42:37. And those who shun the great sins and indecencies, and whenever they are angry they forgive;

الْحَمِيدُ (٢٨)
وَمِنْ آيَاتِهِ خَلْقُ السَّمَاوَاتِ وَالْأَرْضِ وَمَا بَثَّ فِيهِمَا مِنْ دَابَّةٍ وَهُوَ عَلَى جَمْعِهِمْ إِذَا يَشَاءُ قَدِيرٌ (٢٩)
وَمَا أَصَابَكُمْ مِنْ مُصِيبَةٍ فَبِمَا كَسَبَتْ أَيْدِيكُمْ وَيَعْفُو عَنْ كَثِيرٍ (٣٠)
وَمَا أَنْتُمْ بِمُعْجِزِينَ فِي الْأَرْضِ وَمَا لَكُمْ مِنْ دُونِ اللَّهِ مِنْ وَلِيٍّ وَلَا نَصِيرٍ (٣١)
وَمِنْ آيَاتِهِ الْجَوَارِ فِي الْبَحْرِ كَالْأَعْلَامِ (٣٢)
إِنْ يَشَأْ يُسْكِنِ الرِّيحَ فَيَظْلَلْنَ رَوَاكِدَ عَلَى ظَهْرِهِ إِنَّ فِي ذَلِكَ لَآيَاتٍ لِكُلِّ صَبَّارٍ شَكُورٍ (٣٣)
أَوْ يُوبِقْهُنَّ بِمَا كَسَبُوا وَيَعْفُ عَنْ كَثِيرٍ (٣٤)
وَيَعْلَمَ الَّذِينَ يُجَادِلُونَ فِي آيَاتِنَا مَا لَهُمْ مِنْ مَحِيصٍ (٣٥)
فَمَا أُوتِيتُمْ مِنْ شَيْءٍ فَمَتَاعُ الْحَيَاةِ الدُّنْيَا وَمَا عِنْدَ اللَّهِ خَيْرٌ وَأَبْقَى لِلَّذِينَ آمَنُوا وَعَلَى رَبِّهِمْ يَتَوَكَّلُونَ (٣٦)
وَالَّذِينَ يَجْتَنِبُونَ كَبَائِرَ الْإِثْمِ وَالْفَوَاحِشَ وَإِذَا مَا غَضِبُوا هُمْ يَغْفِرُونَ (٣٧)
وَالَّذِينَ اسْتَجَابُوا لِرَبِّهِمْ وَأَقَامُوا الصَّلَاةَ وَأَمْرُهُمْ شُورَى بَيْنَهُمْ وَمِمَّا رَزَقْنَاهُمْ يُنْفِقُونَ (٣٨)
وَالَّذِينَ إِذَا أَصَابَهُمُ الْبَغْيُ هُمْ يَنْتَصِرُونَ (٣٩)
وَجَزَاءُ سَيِّئَةٍ سَيِّئَةٌ مِثْلُهَا فَمَنْ عَفَا وَأَصْلَحَ فَأَجْرُهُ عَلَى اللَّهِ إِنَّهُ لَا يُحِبُّ الظَّالِمِينَ (٤٠)
وَلَمَنِ انْتَصَرَ بَعْدَ ظُلْمِهِ فَأُولَئِكَ مَا

42. The Counsel

42:38. And those who respond to their Lord and keep up prayer, and whose affairs are (decided) by counsel among themselves, and who spend out of what We have given them;

42:39. And those who, when great wrong afflicts them, defend themselves.

42:40. And the recompense of evil is punishment like it; but whoever forgives and amends, his reward is with Allah. Surely He loves not the wrongdoers.

42:41. And whoever defends himself after his being oppressed, these it is against whom there is no way (of blame).

42:42. The way (of blame) is only against those who oppress men and revolt in the earth unjustly. For such there is a painful chastisement.

42:43. And whoever is patient and forgives -- that surely is an affair of great resolution.

* * *

42:44. And he whom Allah leaves in error, has no friend after Him. And thou wilt see the iniquitous, when they see the chastisement, saying Is there any way of return?

42:45. And thou wilt see them brought before it, humbling themselves because of abasement, looking with a faint glance. And those who believe will say: Surely the losers are they who lose themselves and their followers on the Resurrection day. Now surely the iniquitous are in lasting chastisement.

42:46. And they will have no friends to help them besides Allah. And he whom Allah leaves in error cannot find a way.

42:47. Hearken to your Lord before there comes from Allah the day which there is no averting. You will have no refuge on that day, nor will it be yours to make a denial.

42:48. But if they turn away, We have

not sent thee as a watcher over them. Thy duty is only to deliver (the message). And surely when We make man taste mercy from Us, he rejoices thereat; and if an evil afflicts them on account of what their hands have sent before, then surely man is ungrateful.

42:49. Allah's is the kingdom of the heavens and the earth. He creates what He pleases. He grants females to whom He pleases and grants males to whom He pleases,

42:50. Or He grants them both males and females, and He makes whom He pleases, barren. Surely He is Knower, Powerful.

42:51. And it is nor vouchsafed to a mortal that Allah should speak to him, except by revelation or from behind a veil, or by sending a messenger and revealing by His permission what He pleases. Surely He is High, Wise.

42:52. And thus did We reveal to thee an inspired Book by Our command. Thou knewest nor what the Book was, nor (what) Faith (was), but We made it a light, guiding thereby whom We please of Our servants. And surely thou guidest to the right path --

42:53. The path of Allah, to Whom belongs whatsoever is in the heavens and whatsoever is in the earth. Now surely to Allah do all affairs eventually come.

43. Gold

In the name of Allah, the Beneficent, the Merciful.

43:1. Beneficent God!
43:2. By the Book that makes manifest!
43:3. Surely We have made it an Arabic Qur'an that you may understand.
43:4. And it is in the Original of the Book with Us, truly elevated, full of wisdom.
43:5. Shall We then turn away the Reminder from you altogether because

| 43. Gold | | 43-سورة الزخرف |

you are a prodigal people?
43:6. And how many a prophet did We send among the ancients!
43:7. And no prophet came to them but they mocked him.
43:8. Then We destroyed those stronger than these in prowess, and the example of the ancients has gone before.
43:9. And if thou ask them, Who created the heavens and the earth? they would say: The Mighty, the Knowing One, has created them,
43:10. Who made the earth a resting-place for you, and made in it ways for you that you might go aright.
43:11. And Who sends down water from the cloud according to a measure, then We raise to life thereby a dead land; even so will you be brought forth.
43:12. And Who created pairs of all things, and made for you ships and cattle oh which you ride,
43:13. That you may sit firm on their backs, then remember the favour of your Lord, when you are firmly seated thereon, and say: Glory be to Him Who made this subservient to us and we were not able to do it,
43:14. And surely to our Lord we must return.
43:15. And they assign to Him a part of His servants. Man, to be sure, is clearly ungrateful.

***

43:16. Or has He taken daughters to Himself of what He creates and chosen you to have sons?
43:17. And when one of them is given news of that of which he sets up a likeness for the Beneficent, his face becomes black and he is full of rage.
43:18. Is one decked with ornaments and unable to make plain speech in disputes (a partner with God)?
43:19. And they make the angels, who are the servants of the Beneficent, females. Did they witness their creation? Their evidence will be

أَفَنَضْرِبُ عَنْكُمُ الذِّكْرَ صَفْحًا أَنْ كُنْتُمْ قَوْمًا مُسْرِفِينَ (٥)
وَكَمْ أَرْسَلْنَا مِنْ نَبِيٍّ فِي الْأَوَّلِينَ (٦)
وَمَا يَأْتِيهِمْ مِنْ نَبِيٍّ إِلَّا كَانُوا بِهِ يَسْتَهْزِئُونَ (٧)
فَأَهْلَكْنَا أَشَدَّ مِنْهُمْ بَطْشًا وَمَضَى مَثَلُ الْأَوَّلِينَ (٨)
وَلَئِنْ سَأَلْتَهُمْ مَنْ خَلَقَ السَّمَاوَاتِ وَالْأَرْضَ لَيَقُولُنَّ خَلَقَهُنَّ الْعَزِيزُ الْعَلِيمُ (٩)
الَّذِي جَعَلَ لَكُمُ الْأَرْضَ مَهْدًا وَجَعَلَ لَكُمْ فِيهَا سُبُلًا لَعَلَّكُمْ تَهْتَدُونَ (١٠)
وَالَّذِي نَزَّلَ مِنَ السَّمَاءِ مَاءً بِقَدَرٍ فَأَنْشَرْنَا بِهِ بَلْدَةً مَيْتًا كَذَلِكَ تُخْرَجُونَ (١١)
وَالَّذِي خَلَقَ الْأَزْوَاجَ كُلَّهَا وَجَعَلَ لَكُمْ مِنَ الْفُلْكِ وَالْأَنْعَامِ مَا تَرْكَبُونَ (١٢)
لِتَسْتَوُوا عَلَى ظُهُورِهِ ثُمَّ تَذْكُرُوا نِعْمَةَ رَبِّكُمْ إِذَا اسْتَوَيْتُمْ عَلَيْهِ وَتَقُولُوا سُبْحَانَ الَّذِي سَخَّرَ لَنَا هَذَا وَمَا كُنَّا لَهُ مُقْرِنِينَ (١٣)
وَإِنَّا إِلَى رَبِّنَا لَمُنْقَلِبُونَ (١٤)
وَجَعَلُوا لَهُ مِنْ عِبَادِهِ جُزْءًا إِنَّ الْإِنْسَانَ لَكَفُورٌ مُبِينٌ (١٥)
أَمِ اتَّخَذَ مِمَّا يَخْلُقُ بَنَاتٍ وَأَصْفَاكُمْ بِالْبَنِينَ (١٦)
وَإِذَا بُشِّرَ أَحَدُهُمْ بِمَا ضَرَبَ لِلرَّحْمَنِ مَثَلًا ظَلَّ وَجْهُهُ مُسْوَدًّا وَهُوَ كَظِيمٌ (١٧)
أَوَمَنْ يُنَشَّأُ فِي الْحِلْيَةِ وَهُوَ فِي الْخِصَامِ غَيْرُ مُبِينٍ (١٨)
وَجَعَلُوا الْمَلَائِكَةَ الَّذِينَ هُمْ عِبَادُ الرَّحْمَنِ إِنَاثًا أَشَهِدُوا خَلْقَهُمْ سَتُكْتَبُ

recorded and they will be questioned.

43:20. And they say if the Beneficent had pleased, we should not have worshipped them. They have no knowledge of this; they only lie.

43:21. Or have We given them a Book before it so that they hold fast to it?

43:22. Nay, they say We found our fathers on a course, and surely we are guided by their footsteps.

43:23. And thus, We sent not before thee a warner in a town, but its wealthy ones said: Surely we found our fathers following a religion, and we follow their footsteps.

43:24. (The warner) said And even if I bring tn you a better guide than that which you found your fathers following? They said: We surely disbelieve in that with which you are sent.

43:25. So We exacted retribution from them, then see what was the end of the rejectors!

***

43:26. And when Abraham said to his sire and his people: I am clear of what you worship,

43:27. Save Him Who created me, for surely He will guide me.

43:28. And he made it a word to continue in his posterity that they might return.

43:29. Nay! I let these and their fathers enjoy till there came to them the Truth and a Messenger making manifest.

43:30. And when the Truth came to them they said: This is enchantment, and surely we are disbelievers in it.

43:31. And they say: Why was not this Qur'an revealed to a man of importance in the two towns?

43:32. Do they apportion the mercy of thy Lord? We portion out among them their livelihood in the life of this world, and We exalt some of them above others in rank, that some of them may take others in service. And the mercy of thy Lord is better than that which they amass.

43:33. And were it not that all people would become one (disbelieving) community, We would provide for those who disbelieve in the Beneficent, roofs of silver for their houses and stairs (of silver) by which they ascend,

43:34. And (of silver) the doors of their houses and the couches on which they recline,

43:35. And of gold. And all this is naught but a provision of this world's life; and the Hereafter is with thy Lord only for the dutiful.

* * *

43:36. And whoever turns himself away from the remembrance of the Beneficent, We appoint for him a devil, so he is his associate.

43:37. And surety they hinder them from the (right) path, and they think that they are guided aright.

43:38. Until when he comes to Us, he says: O would that between me and thee there were the distance of the East and the West! so evil is the associate

43:39. And as you did wrong, it will profit you naught this day that you are sharers in the chastisement.

43:40. Canst thou then make the deaf to hear or guide the blind and him who is in clear error?

43:41. So if We take thee away, still We shall exact retribution from them,

43:42. Or We shall show thee that which We promise them surely We are Possessors of power over them.

43:43. So hold fast to that which has been revealed to thee; surely thou art on the right path.

43:44. And surely it is a reminder for thee and thy people, and you will be questioned.

43:45. And ask those of Our messengers whom We sent before thee: Did We ever appoint gods to be worshipped besides the Beneficent?

وَلَوْلَا أَنْ يَكُونَ النَّاسُ أُمَّةً وَاحِدَةً لَجَعَلْنَا لِمَنْ يَكْفُرُ بِالرَّحْمَنِ لِبُيُوتِهِمْ سُقُفًا مِنْ فِضَّةٍ وَمَعَارِجَ عَلَيْهَا يَظْهَرُونَ (٣٣)
وَلِبُيُوتِهِمْ أَبْوَابًا وَسُرُرًا عَلَيْهَا يَتَّكِئُونَ (٣٤)
وَزُخْرُفًا وَإِنْ كُلُّ ذَلِكَ لَمَّا مَتَاعُ الْحَيَاةِ الدُّنْيَا وَالْآخِرَةُ عِنْدَ رَبِّكَ لِلْمُتَّقِينَ (٣٥)
وَمَنْ يَعْشُ عَنْ ذِكْرِ الرَّحْمَنِ نُقَيِّضْ لَهُ شَيْطَانًا فَهُوَ لَهُ قَرِينٌ (٣٦)
وَإِنَّهُمْ لَيَصُدُّونَهُمْ عَنِ السَّبِيلِ وَيَحْسَبُونَ أَنَّهُمْ مُهْتَدُونَ (٣٧)
حَتَّى إِذَا جَاءَنَا قَالَ يَا لَيْتَ بَيْنِي وَبَيْنَكَ بُعْدَ الْمَشْرِقَيْنِ فَبِئْسَ الْقَرِينُ (٣٨)
وَلَنْ يَنْفَعَكُمُ الْيَوْمَ إِذْ ظَلَمْتُمْ أَنَّكُمْ فِي الْعَذَابِ مُشْتَرِكُونَ (٣٩)
أَفَأَنْتَ تُسْمِعُ الصُّمَّ أَوْ تَهْدِي الْعُمْيَ وَمَنْ كَانَ فِي ضَلَالٍ مُبِينٍ (٤٠)
فَإِمَّا نَذْهَبَنَّ بِكَ فَإِنَّا مِنْهُمْ مُنْتَقِمُونَ (٤١)
أَوْ نُرِيَنَّكَ الَّذِي وَعَدْنَاهُمْ فَإِنَّا عَلَيْهِمْ مُقْتَدِرُونَ (٤٢)
فَاسْتَمْسِكْ بِالَّذِي أُوحِيَ إِلَيْكَ إِنَّكَ عَلَى صِرَاطٍ مُسْتَقِيمٍ (٤٣)
وَإِنَّهُ لَذِكْرٌ لَكَ وَلِقَوْمِكَ وَسَوْفَ تُسْأَلُونَ (٤٤)
وَاسْأَلْ مَنْ أَرْسَلْنَا مِنْ قَبْلِكَ مِنْ رُسُلِنَا أَجَعَلْنَا مِنْ دُونِ الرَّحْمَنِ آلِهَةً يُعْبَدُونَ (٤٥)
وَلَقَدْ أَرْسَلْنَا مُوسَى بِآيَاتِنَا إِلَى فِرْعَوْنَ وَمَلَئِهِ فَقَالَ إِنِّي رَسُولُ رَبِّ

***

43:46. And truly We sent Moses with Our messages to Pharaoh and his chiefs, so he said: I am the messenger of the Lord of the worlds;
43:47. But when he brought them Our signs, lo! they laughed at them.
43:48. And We showed them not a sign but it was greater than its fellow, and We seized them with chastisement that they might turn.
43:49. And they said: O enchanter, call on thy Lord for us, as He has made the covenant with thee; we shall surely follow guidance.
43:50. But when We removed from them the chastisement, lo! they broke the pledge.
43:51. And Pharaoh proclaimed amongst his people, saying: O my people, is not the kingdom of Egypt mine and these rivers flowing beneath me? Do you not see?
43:52. Rather I am better than this (fellow) who is contemptible, and can hardly express himself clearly.
43:53. Why, then, have bracelets of gold not been bestowed on him or angels come along with him in procession?
43:54. So he incited his people to levity and they obeyed him. Surely they were a transgressing people
43:55. Then when they displeased Us, We exacted retribution from them, so We drowned them all together.
43:56. And We made them a thing past and an example for later generations.

***

43:57. And when the son of Mary is mentioned as an example, lo! thy people raise a clamour thereat.
43:58. And they say: Are our gods better, or is he? They set it forth to thee only by way of disputation. Nay, they are a contentious people.
43:59. He was naught but a servant on whom We bestowed favour and We made him an example for the Children

of Israel.

43:60. And if We pleased, We could make among you angels to be (Our) vicegerents in the land.

43:61. And this (revelation) is surely knowledge of the Hour, so have no doubt about it and follow me. This is the right path.

43:62. And let not the devil hinder you; surely he is your open enemy.

43:63. And when Jesus came with clear arguments, he said: I have come to you indeed with wisdom, and to make clear to you some of that about which you differ. So keep your duty to Allah and obey me.

43:64. Surely Allah is my Lord and your Lord, so serve Him. This is the right path.

43:65. But parties among them differed, so woe to those who did wrong for the chastisement of a painful day!

43:66. Wait they for aught but the Hour, that it should come on them all of a sudden, while they perceive not?

43:67. Friends on that day will be foes one to another, except those who keep their duty.

***

43:68. O My servants, there is no fear for you this day, nor will you grieve

43:69. Those who believed in Our messages and submitted (to Us),

43:70. Enter the Garden, you and your wives, being made happy.

43:71. Sent round to them are golden bowls and drinking-cups, and therein Is that which (their) souls yearn for and the eyes delight in, and therein you will abide.

72 And this is the Garden, which you are made to inherit on account of what you did.

73 For you therein is abundant fruit to eat thereof.

43:74. Surely the guilty will abide in the chastisement of hell.

43:75. It is not abated for them and they

وَاتَّبِعُونِ هَذَا صِرَاطٌ مُسْتَقِيمٌ (٦١) وَلَا يَصُدَّنَّكُمُ الشَّيْطَانُ إِنَّهُ لَكُمْ عَدُوٌّ مُبِينٌ (٦٢) وَلَمَّا جَاءَ عِيسَى بِالْبَيِّنَاتِ قَالَ قَدْ جِئْتُكُمْ بِالْحِكْمَةِ وَلِأُبَيِّنَ لَكُمْ بَعْضَ الَّذِي تَخْتَلِفُونَ فِيهِ فَاتَّقُوا اللَّهَ وَأَطِيعُونِ (٦٣) إِنَّ اللَّهَ هُوَ رَبِّي وَرَبُّكُمْ فَاعْبُدُوهُ هَذَا صِرَاطٌ مُسْتَقِيمٌ (٦٤) فَاخْتَلَفَ الْأَحْزَابُ مِنْ بَيْنِهِمْ فَوَيْلٌ لِلَّذِينَ ظَلَمُوا مِنْ عَذَابِ يَوْمٍ أَلِيمٍ (٦٥) هَلْ يَنْظُرُونَ إِلَّا السَّاعَةَ أَنْ تَأْتِيَهُمْ بَغْتَةً وَهُمْ لَا يَشْعُرُونَ (٦٦) الْأَخِلَّاءُ يَوْمَئِذٍ بَعْضُهُمْ لِبَعْضٍ عَدُوٌّ إِلَّا الْمُتَّقِينَ (٦٧) يَا عِبَادِ لَا خَوْفٌ عَلَيْكُمُ الْيَوْمَ وَلَا أَنْتُمْ تَحْزَنُونَ (٦٨) الَّذِينَ آمَنُوا بِآيَاتِنَا وَكَانُوا مُسْلِمِينَ (٦٩) ادْخُلُوا الْجَنَّةَ أَنْتُمْ وَأَزْوَاجُكُمْ تُحْبَرُونَ (٧٠) يُطَافُ عَلَيْهِمْ بِصِحَافٍ مِنْ ذَهَبٍ وَأَكْوَابٍ وَفِيهَا مَا تَشْتَهِيهِ الْأَنْفُسُ وَتَلَذُّ الْأَعْيُنُ وَأَنْتُمْ فِيهَا خَالِدُونَ (٧١) وَتِلْكَ الْجَنَّةُ الَّتِي أُورِثْتُمُوهَا بِمَا كُنْتُمْ تَعْمَلُونَ (٧٢) لَكُمْ فِيهَا فَاكِهَةٌ كَثِيرَةٌ مِنْهَا تَأْكُلُونَ (٧٣) إِنَّ الْمُجْرِمِينَ فِي عَذَابِ جَهَنَّمَ خَالِدُونَ (٧٤) لَا يُفَتَّرُ عَنْهُمْ وَهُمْ فِيهِ مُبْلِسُونَ

will therein despair.

43:76. And We wronged them not but they were themselves the wrongdoers.

43:77. And they cry: O Malik, let thy Lord make an end of us. He will say: You shall stay (here).

43:78. Certainly We bring the Truth to you, but most of you are averse to the Truth.

43:79. Or have they settled an affair? But it is We Who settle (affairs).

43:80. Or do they think that We hear not their secrets and their private counsels? Aye, and Our messengers with them write down.

43:81. Say: The Beneficent has no son; so I am the foremost of those who serve (God).

43:82. Glory to the Lord of the heavens and the earth, the Lord of the Throne of Power, from what they describe

43:83. So let them talk and sport until they meet their day which they are promised.

43:84. And He it is Who is God in the heavens and God in the earth. And He is the Wise, the Knowing.

43:85. And blessed is He Whose is the kingdom of the heavens and the earth and all between them; and with Him is the knowledge of the Hour, and to Him you will be returned.

43:86. And those whom they call upon besides Him control not intercession, but he who bears witness to the Truth and they know (him).

43:87. And if thou wert to ask them who created them, they would say: Allah. How are they then turned back?

43:88. And his cry -- O my Lord, these are a people who believe not!

43:89. So turn away from them and say, Peace! They will soon come to know.

(٧٥)

وَمَا ظَلَمْنَاهُمْ وَلَكِنْ كَانُوا هُمُ الظَّالِمِينَ (٧٦)

وَنَادَوْا يَا مَالِكُ لِيَقْضِ عَلَيْنَا رَبُّكَ قَالَ إِنَّكُمْ مَاكِثُونَ (٧٧)

لَقَدْ جِئْنَاكُمْ بِالْحَقِّ وَلَكِنَّ أَكْثَرَكُمْ لِلْحَقِّ كَارِهُونَ (٧٨)

أَمْ أَبْرَمُوا أَمْرًا فَإِنَّا مُبْرِمُونَ (٧٩)

أَمْ يَحْسَبُونَ أَنَّا لَا نَسْمَعُ سِرَّهُمْ وَنَجْوَاهُمْ بَلَى وَرُسُلُنَا لَدَيْهِمْ يَكْتُبُونَ (٨٠)

قُلْ إِنْ كَانَ لِلرَّحْمَنِ وَلَدٌ فَأَنَا أَوَّلُ الْعَابِدِينَ (٨١)

سُبْحَانَ رَبِّ السَّمَاوَاتِ وَالْأَرْضِ رَبِّ الْعَرْشِ عَمَّا يَصِفُونَ (٨٢)

فَذَرْهُمْ يَخُوضُوا وَيَلْعَبُوا حَتَّى يُلَاقُوا يَوْمَهُمُ الَّذِي يُوعَدُونَ (٨٣)

وَهُوَ الَّذِي فِي السَّمَاءِ إِلَهٌ وَفِي الْأَرْضِ إِلَهٌ وَهُوَ الْحَكِيمُ الْعَلِيمُ (٨٤)

وَتَبَارَكَ الَّذِي لَهُ مُلْكُ السَّمَاوَاتِ وَالْأَرْضِ وَمَا بَيْنَهُمَا وَعِنْدَهُ عِلْمُ السَّاعَةِ وَإِلَيْهِ تُرْجَعُونَ (٨٥)

وَلَا يَمْلِكُ الَّذِينَ يَدْعُونَ مِنْ دُونِهِ الشَّفَاعَةَ إِلَّا مَنْ شَهِدَ بِالْحَقِّ وَهُمْ يَعْلَمُونَ (٨٦)

وَلَئِنْ سَأَلْتَهُمْ مَنْ خَلَقَهُمْ لَيَقُولُنَّ اللَّهُ فَأَنَّى يُؤْفَكُونَ (٨٧)

وَقِيلِهِ يَا رَبِّ إِنَّ هَؤُلَاءِ قَوْمٌ لَا يُؤْمِنُونَ (٨٨)

فَاصْفَحْ عَنْهُمْ وَقُلْ سَلَامٌ فَسَوْفَ يَعْلَمُونَ (٨٩)

44. The Drought

In the name of Allah, the Beneficent, the Merciful.

44:1. Beneficent God!
44:2. By the Book that makes manifest!
44:3. We revealed it On a blessed night truly We are ever warning.
44:4. Therein is made clear every affair full of wisdom --
44:5. A command from Us -- truly We are ever sending messengers --
44:6. A mercy from thy Lord -- truly He is the Hearing, the Knowing,
44:7. The Lord of the heavens and the earth and what is between them, if you would be sure.
44:8. There is no God but He; He gives life and causes death -- your Lord and the Lord of your fathers of yore.
44:9. Nay, in doubt they sport.
44:10. So wait for the day when the heaven brings a clear drought,
44:11. Enveloping men. This is a painful chastisement.
44:12. Our Lord, remove from us the chastisement -- surely we are believers.
44:13. When will they be reminded? And a Messenger has indeed come, making clear;
44:14. Yet they turned away from him and said: One taught (by others), a madman!
44:15. We shall remove the chastisement a little, (but) you will surely return (to evil).
44:16. On the day when We seize (them) with the most violent seizing surely We shall exact retribution.
44:17. And certainly We tried before them Pharaoh's people and a noble messenger came to them,
44:18. Saying: Deliver to me the servants of Allah. Surely I am a faithful messenger to you.
44:19. And exalt not yourselves against Allah. Surely I bring to you a clear authority.

44. The Drought

44:20. And I take refuge with my Lord and your Lord, lest you stone me to death.
44:21. And if you believe not in me, leave me alone.
44:22. Then he called upon his Lord: These are a guilty people.
44:23. So go forth with My servants by night; surely you will be pursued,
44:24. And leave the sea behind calm. Surely they are a host to be drowned.
44:25. How many the gardens and springs they left behind!
44:26. And cornfields and noble places!
44:27. And goodly things wherein they rejoiced!
44:28. Thus (it was). And We made other people inherit them.
44:29. So the heaven and the earth wept not for them, nor were they respited.

* * *

44:30. And We indeed delivered the Children of Israel from the abasing chastisement,
44:31. From Pharaoh. Surely he was haughty, prodigal.
44:32. And certainly We chose them above the nations, having knowledge.
44:33. And We gave them signs wherein was clear blessing.
44:34. These do indeed say:
44:35. There is naught but our first death and we shall not be raised again.
44:36. So bring our fathers (back), if you are truthful.
44:37. Are they better or the people of Tubba', and those before them? We destroyed them, for surely they were guilty.
44:38. And We did not create the heavens and the earth and that which is between them in sport.
44:39. We created them not but with truth, but most of them know not.
44:40. Surely the day of Decision is the term for them all,
44:41. The day when friend will avail friend in naught, nor will they be

وَأَنْ لَا تَعْلُوا عَلَى اللَّهِ إِنِّي آتِيكُمْ بِسُلْطَانٍ مُبِينٍ (١٩)
وَإِنِّي عُذْتُ بِرَبِّي وَرَبِّكُمْ أَنْ تَرْجُمُونِ (٢٠)
وَإِنْ لَمْ تُؤْمِنُوا لِي فَاعْتَزِلُونِ (٢١)
فَدَعَا رَبَّهُ أَنَّ هَؤُلَاءِ قَوْمٌ مُجْرِمُونَ (٢٢)
فَأَسْرِ بِعِبَادِي لَيْلًا إِنَّكُمْ مُتَّبَعُونَ (٢٣)
وَاتْرُكِ الْبَحْرَ رَهْوًا إِنَّهُمْ جُنْدٌ مُغْرَقُونَ (٢٤)
كَمْ تَرَكُوا مِنْ جَنَّاتٍ وَعُيُونٍ (٢٥)
وَزُرُوعٍ وَمَقَامٍ كَرِيمٍ (٢٦)
وَنَعْمَةٍ كَانُوا فِيهَا فَاكِهِينَ (٢٧)
كَذَلِكَ وَأَوْرَثْنَاهَا قَوْمًا آخَرِينَ (٢٨)
فَمَا بَكَتْ عَلَيْهِمُ السَّمَاءُ وَالْأَرْضُ وَمَا كَانُوا مُنْظَرِينَ (٢٩)
وَلَقَدْ نَجَّيْنَا بَنِي إِسْرَائِيلَ مِنَ الْعَذَابِ الْمُهِينِ (٣٠)
مِنْ فِرْعَوْنَ إِنَّهُ كَانَ عَالِيًا مِنَ الْمُسْرِفِينَ (٣١)
وَلَقَدِ اخْتَرْنَاهُمْ عَلَى عِلْمٍ عَلَى الْعَالَمِينَ (٣٢)
وَآتَيْنَاهُمْ مِنَ الْآيَاتِ مَا فِيهِ بَلَاءٌ مُبِينٌ (٣٣)
إِنَّ هَؤُلَاءِ لَيَقُولُونَ (٣٤)
إِنْ هِيَ إِلَّا مَوْتَتُنَا الْأُولَى وَمَا نَحْنُ بِمُنْشَرِينَ (٣٥)
فَأْتُوا بِآبَائِنَا إِنْ كُنْتُمْ صَادِقِينَ (٣٦)
أَهُمْ خَيْرٌ أَمْ قَوْمُ تُبَّعٍ وَالَّذِينَ مِنْ قَبْلِهِمْ أَهْلَكْنَاهُمْ إِنَّهُمْ كَانُوا مُجْرِمِينَ (٣٧)
وَمَا خَلَقْنَا السَّمَاوَاتِ وَالْأَرْضَ وَمَا بَيْنَهُمَا لَاعِبِينَ (٣٨)

44. The Drought

helped --
44:42. Save those on whom Allah has mercy. Surely He is the Mighty, the Merciful.

* * *

44:43. Surely the tree of Zaqqum
44:44. Is the food of the sinful,
44:45. Like molten brass; it seethes in (their) bellies
44:46. Like boiling water.
44:47. Seize him, then drag him into the midst of hell;
44:48. Then pour on his head of the torment of boiling water --
44:49. Taste -- thou art forsooth the mighty, the honourable!
44:50. Surely this is what you doubted.
44:51. Those who keep their duty are indeed in a secure place --
44:52. In gardens and springs,
44:53. Wearing fine and thick silk, facing one another --
44:54. Thus (shall it be). And We shall join them to pure, beautiful ones.
44:55. They call therein for every fruit in security --
44:56. They taste not therein death, except the first death; and He will save them from the chastisement of hell --
44:57. A grace from thy Lord. This is the great achievement.
44:58. So We have made it easy in thy tongue that they may mind.
44:59. Wait then; surely they (too) are waiting.

مَا خَلَقْنَاهُمَا إِلَّا بِالْحَقِّ وَلَكِنَّ أَكْثَرَهُمْ لَا يَعْلَمُونَ (٣٩)
إِنَّ يَوْمَ الْفَصْلِ مِيقَاتُهُمْ أَجْمَعِينَ (٤٠)
يَوْمَ لَا يُغْنِي مَوْلًى عَنْ مَوْلًى شَيْئًا وَلَا هُمْ يُنْصَرُونَ (٤١)
إِلَّا مَنْ رَحِمَ اللَّهُ إِنَّهُ هُوَ الْعَزِيزُ الرَّحِيمُ (٤٢)
إِنَّ شَجَرَةَ الزَّقُّومِ (٤٣)
طَعَامُ الْأَثِيمِ (٤٤)
كَالْمُهْلِ يَغْلِي فِي الْبُطُونِ (٤٥)
كَغَلْيِ الْحَمِيمِ (٤٦)
خُذُوهُ فَاعْتِلُوهُ إِلَى سَوَاءِ الْجَحِيمِ (٤٧)
ثُمَّ صُبُّوا فَوْقَ رَأْسِهِ مِنْ عَذَابِ الْحَمِيمِ (٤٨)
ذُقْ إِنَّكَ أَنْتَ الْعَزِيزُ الْكَرِيمُ (٤٩)
إِنَّ هَذَا مَا كُنْتُمْ بِهِ تَمْتَرُونَ (٥٠)
إِنَّ الْمُتَّقِينَ فِي مَقَامٍ أَمِينٍ (٥١)
فِي جَنَّاتٍ وَعُيُونٍ (٥٢)
يَلْبَسُونَ مِنْ سُنْدُسٍ وَإِسْتَبْرَقٍ مُتَقَابِلِينَ (٥٣)
كَذَلِكَ وَزَوَّجْنَاهُمْ بِحُورٍ عِينٍ (٥٤)
يَدْعُونَ فِيهَا بِكُلِّ فَاكِهَةٍ آمِنِينَ (٥٥)
لَا يَذُوقُونَ فِيهَا الْمَوْتَ إِلَّا الْمَوْتَةَ الْأُولَى وَوَقَاهُمْ عَذَابَ الْجَحِيمِ (٥٦)
فَضْلًا مِنْ رَبِّكَ ذَلِكَ هُوَ الْفَوْزُ الْعَظِيمُ (٥٧)
فَإِنَّمَا يَسَّرْنَاهُ بِلِسَانِكَ لَعَلَّهُمْ يَتَذَكَّرُونَ (٥٨)
فَارْتَقِبْ إِنَّهُمْ مُرْتَقِبُونَ (٥٩)

45. The Kneeling

In the name of Allah, the Beneficent, the Merciful.

45:1. Beneficent God!

45:2. The revelation of the Book is from Allah, the Mighty, the Wise.

45:3. Surely in the heavens and the earth are signs for believers.

45:4. And in your creation and in the animals He spreads abroad are signs for a people who are sure

5 And (in) the variation of the night and the day and (in) the sustenance which Allah sends down from the heaven, then gives life thereby to the earth after its death, and (in) the changing of the winds, are signs for a people who understand. 6 These are the messages of Allah, which We recite to thee with truth. In what announcement will they then believe after Allah and His signs?

45:7. Woe to every sinful liar!

45:8. Who hears the messages of Allah recited to him then persists in haughtiness, as though he had not heard them. So announce to him a painful chastisement.

45:9. And when he comes to know of any of Our messages, he takes them for a jest. For such is an abasing chastisement.

45:10. In front of them is hell, and that which they have earned will avail them naught, nor those whom they take for protectors besides Allah, and for them is a grievous chastisement.

45:11. This is guidance; and those who disbelieve in the~ messages of their Lord, for them is a painful chastisement of an evil (kind).

***

45:12. Allah is He Who made subservient to you the sea that the ships may glide therein by His command, and that you may seek of His grace, and that you may give

٤٥ ـ سورة الجاثية

بِسْمِ اللهِ الرَّحْمَنِ الرَّحِيمِ

حم (١)

تَنْزِيلُ الْكِتَابِ مِنَ اللهِ الْعَزِيزِ الْحَكِيمِ (٢)

إِنَّ فِي السَّمَاوَاتِ وَالْأَرْضِ لَآيَاتٍ لِلْمُؤْمِنِينَ (٣)

وَفِي خَلْقِكُمْ وَمَا يَبُثُّ مِنْ دَابَّةٍ آيَاتٌ لِقَوْمٍ يُوقِنُونَ (٤)

وَاخْتِلَافِ اللَّيْلِ وَالنَّهَارِ وَمَا أَنْزَلَ اللهُ مِنَ السَّمَاءِ مِنْ رِزْقٍ فَأَحْيَا بِهِ الْأَرْضَ بَعْدَ مَوْتِهَا وَتَصْرِيفِ الرِّيَاحِ آيَاتٌ لِقَوْمٍ يَعْقِلُونَ (٥)

تِلْكَ آيَاتُ اللهِ نَتْلُوهَا عَلَيْكَ بِالْحَقِّ فَبِأَيِّ حَدِيثٍ بَعْدَ اللهِ وَآيَاتِهِ يُؤْمِنُونَ (٦)

وَيْلٌ لِكُلِّ أَفَّاكٍ أَثِيمٍ (٧)

يَسْمَعُ آيَاتِ اللهِ تُتْلَى عَلَيْهِ ثُمَّ يُصِرُّ مُسْتَكْبِرًا كَأَنْ لَمْ يَسْمَعْهَا فَبَشِّرْهُ بِعَذَابٍ أَلِيمٍ (٨)

وَإِذَا عَلِمَ مِنْ آيَاتِنَا شَيْئًا اتَّخَذَهَا هُزُوًا أُولَئِكَ لَهُمْ عَذَابٌ مُهِينٌ (٩)

مِنْ وَرَائِهِمْ جَهَنَّمُ وَلَا يُغْنِي عَنْهُمْ مَا كَسَبُوا شَيْئًا وَلَا مَا اتَّخَذُوا مِنْ دُونِ اللهِ أَوْلِيَاءَ وَلَهُمْ عَذَابٌ عَظِيمٌ (١٠)

هَذَا هُدًى وَالَّذِينَ كَفَرُوا بِآيَاتِ رَبِّهِمْ لَهُمْ عَذَابٌ مِنْ رِجْزٍ أَلِيمٌ (١١)

اللهُ الَّذِي سَخَّرَ لَكُمُ الْبَحْرَ لِتَجْرِيَ الْفُلْكُ فِيهِ بِأَمْرِهِ وَلِتَبْتَغُوا مِنْ فَضْلِهِ وَلَعَلَّكُمْ تَشْكُرُونَ (١٢)

وَسَخَّرَ لَكُمْ مَا فِي السَّمَاوَاتِ وَمَا فِي الْأَرْضِ جَمِيعًا مِنْهُ إِنَّ فِي ذَلِكَ لَآيَاتٍ لِقَوْمٍ يَتَفَكَّرُونَ (١٣)

45. The Kneeling

thanks.

45:13. And He has made subservient to you whatsoever is in the heavens and whatsoever is in the earth, all, from Himself. Surely there are signs in this for a people who reflect.

45:14. Tell those who believe to forgive those who fear not the days of Allah that He may reward a people for what they earn.

45:15. Whoever does good it is for himself, and whoever does evil, it is against himself; then to your Lord you will be brought back.

45:16. And certainly We gave the Children of Israel the Book and judgment and prophethood and provided them with good things, and made them excel the nations.

45:17. And we gave them clear arguments in the Affair. So they differed not until after knowledge had come to them, out of envy among themselves. Surely thy Lord will judge between them on the day of Resurrection concerning that wherein they differed.

1$ Then We made thee follow a course in the Affair, so follow it, and follow not the low desires of those who know not. 19 Surely they can avail thee naught against Allah. And surely the wrongdoers are friends of each Other, and Allah is the Friend of the dutiful.

45:20. These are clear proofs for men, and a guidance and a merry for a people who are sure.

45:21. Or do those who do evil deeds think that We shall make them as those who believe and do good -- their life and their death being equal? Evil is what they judge!

***

45:22. And Allah created the heavens and the earth with truth, and that every soul may be rewarded for what it has earned, and they will not be wronged.

45:23. Seest thou him who takes his

قُلْ لِلَّذِينَ آمَنُوا يَغْفِرُوا لِلَّذِينَ لَا يَرْجُونَ أَيَّامَ اللَّهِ لِيَجْزِيَ قَوْمًا بِمَا كَانُوا يَكْسِبُونَ (١٤)

مَنْ عَمِلَ صَالِحًا فَلِنَفْسِهِ وَمَنْ أَسَاءَ فَعَلَيْهَا ثُمَّ إِلَى رَبِّكُمْ تُرْجَعُونَ (١٥)

وَلَقَدْ آتَيْنَا بَنِي إِسْرَائِيلَ الْكِتَابَ وَالْحُكْمَ وَالنُّبُوَّةَ وَرَزَقْنَاهُمْ مِنَ الطَّيِّبَاتِ وَفَضَّلْنَاهُمْ عَلَى الْعَالَمِينَ (١٦)

وَآتَيْنَاهُمْ بَيِّنَاتٍ مِنَ الْأَمْرِ فَمَا اخْتَلَفُوا إِلَّا مِنْ بَعْدِ مَا جَاءَهُمُ الْعِلْمُ بَغْيًا بَيْنَهُمْ إِنَّ رَبَّكَ يَقْضِي بَيْنَهُمْ يَوْمَ الْقِيَامَةِ فِيمَا كَانُوا فِيهِ يَخْتَلِفُونَ (١٧)

ثُمَّ جَعَلْنَاكَ عَلَى شَرِيعَةٍ مِنَ الْأَمْرِ فَاتَّبِعْهَا وَلَا تَتَّبِعْ أَهْوَاءَ الَّذِينَ لَا يَعْلَمُونَ (١٨)

إِنَّهُمْ لَنْ يُغْنُوا عَنْكَ مِنَ اللَّهِ شَيْئًا وَإِنَّ الظَّالِمِينَ بَعْضُهُمْ أَوْلِيَاءُ بَعْضٍ وَاللَّهُ وَلِيُّ الْمُتَّقِينَ (١٩)

هَذَا بَصَائِرُ لِلنَّاسِ وَهُدًى وَرَحْمَةٌ لِقَوْمٍ يُوقِنُونَ (٢٠)

أَمْ حَسِبَ الَّذِينَ اجْتَرَحُوا السَّيِّئَاتِ أَنْ نَجْعَلَهُمْ كَالَّذِينَ آمَنُوا وَعَمِلُوا الصَّالِحَاتِ سَوَاءً مَحْيَاهُمْ وَمَمَاتُهُمْ سَاءَ مَا يَحْكُمُونَ (٢١)

وَخَلَقَ اللَّهُ السَّمَاوَاتِ وَالْأَرْضَ بِالْحَقِّ وَلِتُجْزَى كُلُّ نَفْسٍ بِمَا كَسَبَتْ وَهُمْ لَا يُظْلَمُونَ (٢٢)

أَفَرَأَيْتَ مَنِ اتَّخَذَ إِلَهَهُ هَوَاهُ وَأَضَلَّهُ اللَّهُ عَلَى عِلْمٍ وَخَتَمَ عَلَى سَمْعِهِ وَقَلْبِهِ وَجَعَلَ عَلَى بَصَرِهِ غِشَاوَةً فَمَنْ يَهْدِيهِ مِنْ بَعْدِ اللَّهِ أَفَلَا تَذَكَّرُونَ (٢٣)

وَقَالُوا مَا هِيَ إِلَّا حَيَاتُنَا الدُّنْيَا نَمُوتُ

45. The Kneeling

desire for his god, and Allah leaves him in error knowingly, and seals his hearing and his heart and puts a covering on his sight? Who can then guide him after Allah? Will you not mind?

45:24. And they say: There is naught but our life of the world; we die and we live and nothing destroys us bur time, and they have no knowledge of that; they only conjecture.

45:25. And when Our clear messages are recited to them, their only argument is that they say: Bring (back) our fathers, if you are truthful.

45:26. Say: Allah gives you life, then makes you die, then will He gather you to the day' of Resurrection, wherein is no doubt, but most people know not.

***

45:27. And Allah's is the kingdom of the heavens and the earth. And on the day when the Hour comes to pass, on that day will the followers of falsehood perish.

45:28. And thou wilt see every nation kneeling down. Every nation will be called to its record. This day you are requited for what you did.

45:29. This is Our record that speaks against you with truth. Surely We wrote what you did.

45:30. Then as to those who believed and did good, their Lord will admit them to His mercy. That is the manifest achievement.

45:31. And as to those who disbelieved -- were not My messages recited to you? But you were proud and you were a guilty people.

45:32. And when it was said, Surely the promise of Allah is true and the Hour -- there is no doubt about it, you said: We know not what the Hour is. We think (it) only a conjecture and we are not at all sure.

45:33. And the evil of what they did will become manifest to them, and that at which they mocked will encompass them.

45:34. And it will be said: This day We forsake you as you neglected the meeting of this day of yours, and your abode is the Fire, and you have no helpers.

45:35. That is because you made the messages of Allah a jest and the life of this world deceived you. So on that day they shall not be taken out of it, nor shall they be granted goodwill.

45:36. So praise be to Allah, the Lord of the heavens and the Lord of the earth, the Lord of the worlds!

45:37. And to Him belongs greatness in the heavens and the earth; and He is the Mighty, the Wise.

46. The Sandhills

In the name of Allah, the Beneficent, the Merciful.

46:1. Beneficent God!

46:2. The revelation of the Book is from Allah, the Mighty, the Wise.

46:3. We created not the heavens and the earth and all between them save with truth and for an appointed term. And those who disbelieve turn away from that whereof they are warned.

46:4. Say Have you considered that which you invoke besides Allah? Show me what they have created of the earth, or have they a share in the heavens? Bring me a Book before this or any relics of knowledge, if you are truthful.

46:5. And who is in greater error than he who invokes besides Allah such as answer him not till the day of Resurrection, and they are heedless of their call?

46:6. And when men are gathered together, they will be their enemies, and will deny their worshipping (them).

46:7. And when Our clear messages are

46. The Sandhills

recited to them, those who disbelieve say of the Truth when it comes to them: This is clear enchantment.

46:8. Nay, they say: He has forged it. Say: If I have forged it, you control naught for me from Allah. He knows best what you utter concerning it. He is enough as a witness between me and you. And He is the Forgiving, the Merciful.

46:9. Say: I am nor the first of the messengers, and I know not what will be done with me or with you. I follow naught but that which is revealed to me, and I am but a plain warner.

46:10. Say: See you if it is from Allah, and you disbelieve in it, and a witness from among the Children of Israel has borne witness of one like him, so he believed, while you are big with pride. Surely Allah guides not the iniquitous people.

* * *

46:11. And those who disbelieve say of those who believe: If it had been a good, they would not have attained it before us. And as they are not guided thereby, they say: It is an old lie.

46:12. And before it was the Book of Moses, a guide and a mercy. And this is a Book verifying (it) in the Arabic language, that it may warn those who do wrong, and as good news for the doers of good.

46:13. Surely those who say, Our Lord is Allah, then continue on the right way, on them is no fear, nor shall they grieve.

46:14. These are the owners of the Garden, abiding therein -- a reward for what they did.

46:15. And We have enjoined on man the doing of good to his parents. His mother bears him with trouble and she brings him forth in pain. And the bearing of him and the weaning of him is thirty months. Till, when he attains his maturity and reaches forty years, he

46. The Sandhills

says: My Lord, grant me that I may give thanks for Thy favour, which Thou hast bestowed on me and on my patents, and that I may do good which pleases Thee; and be good to me in respect of my offspring. Truly I turn to Thee, and truly I am of those who submit.

46:16. These are they from whom We accept the best of what they do and pass by their evil deeds -- among the owners of the Garden. A promise of truth, which they were promised.

46:17. And he who says to his parents: Fie on you! Do you threaten me that I shall be brought forth, when generations have passed away before me? And they both call for Allah's aid Woe to thee! Believe; surely the promise of Allah is true. But he says This is nothing but stories of the ancients.

46:18. These are they against whom the word proves true, among nations of the jinn and the men that have passed away before them. Surely they are losers.

46:19. And for all are degrees according to what they do, and that He may pay them for their deeds and they will not be wronged.

46:20. And on the day when those who disbelieve are brought before the Fire: You did away with your good things in your life of the world and you enjoyed them; so this day you are rewarded with the chastisement of abasement because you were unjustly proud in the land and because you transgressed.

* * *

46:21. And mention the brother of 'Ad; when he warned his people in the sandy plains -- and warners indeed came before him and after him -- saying: Serve none but Allah. Surely I fear for you the chastisement of a grievous day.

46:22. They said: Hast thou come to us

to turn us away from our gods? Then bring us that with which thou threatenest us, if thou art truthful.

46:23. He said: The knowledge is only with Allah, and I deliver to you that wherewith I am sent, but I see you are an ignorant people.

46:24. So when they saw it -- a cloud advancing towards their valleys, they said: This is a cloud bringing us rain. Nay, it is that which you sought to hasten, a wind wherein is painful chastisement,

46:25. Destroying every thing by the command of its Lord. So at dawn naught could be seen except their dwellings. Thus do We reward the guilty people.

46:26. And certainly We had given them power in matters in which We have not empowered you, and We had given them ears and eyes and hearts, but neither their ears, nor their eyes, nor their hearts availed them aught, since they 'denied the messages of Allah, and that which they mocked at encompassed them.

* * *

46:27. And certainly We destroyed the towns round about you, and We repeat the messages that they may turn.

46:28. Then why did those whom they took for gods besides Allah to draw (them) nigh (to Rim) not help them? Nay, they failed them. And this was their lie and what they forged.

46:29. And when We turned towards thee a party of the jinn, who listened to the Qur'an; so when they were in its presence, they said: Be silent. Then when it was finished, they turned back to their people warning (them).

46:30. They said: O our people, we have heard a Book revealed after Moses, verifying that which is before it, guiding to the truth and to a right path.

46:31. O our people, accept the Inviter to Allah and believe in Him. He will

تَجْهَلُونَ (٢٣) فَلَمَّا رَأَوْهُ عَارِضًا مُسْتَقْبِلَ أَوْدِيَتِهِمْ قَالُوا هَذَا عَارِضٌ مُمْطِرُنَا بَلْ هُوَ مَا اسْتَعْجَلْتُمْ بِهِ رِيحٌ فِيهَا عَذَابٌ أَلِيمٌ (٢٤) تُدَمِّرُ كُلَّ شَيْءٍ بِأَمْرِ رَبِّهَا فَأَصْبَحُوا لَا يُرَى إِلَّا مَسَاكِنُهُمْ كَذَلِكَ نَجْزِي الْقَوْمَ الْمُجْرِمِينَ (٢٥) وَلَقَدْ مَكَّنَّاهُمْ فِيمَا إِنْ مَكَّنَّاكُمْ فِيهِ وَجَعَلْنَا لَهُمْ سَمْعًا وَأَبْصَارًا وَأَفْئِدَةً فَمَا أَغْنَى عَنْهُمْ سَمْعُهُمْ وَلَا أَبْصَارُهُمْ وَلَا أَفْئِدَتُهُمْ مِنْ شَيْءٍ إِذْ كَانُوا يَجْحَدُونَ بِآيَاتِ اللَّهِ وَحَاقَ بِهِمْ مَا كَانُوا بِهِ يَسْتَهْزِئُونَ (٢٦) وَلَقَدْ أَهْلَكْنَا مَا حَوْلَكُمْ مِنَ الْقُرَى وَصَرَّفْنَا الْآيَاتِ لَعَلَّهُمْ يَرْجِعُونَ (٢٧) فَلَوْلَا نَصَرَهُمُ الَّذِينَ اتَّخَذُوا مِنْ دُونِ اللَّهِ قُرْبَانًا آلِهَةً بَلْ ضَلُّوا عَنْهُمْ وَذَلِكَ إِفْكُهُمْ وَمَا كَانُوا يَفْتَرُونَ (٢٨) وَإِذْ صَرَفْنَا إِلَيْكَ نَفَرًا مِنَ الْجِنِّ يَسْتَمِعُونَ الْقُرْآنَ فَلَمَّا حَضَرُوهُ قَالُوا أَنْصِتُوا فَلَمَّا قُضِيَ وَلَّوْا إِلَى قَوْمِهِمْ مُنْذِرِينَ (٢٩) قَالُوا يَا قَوْمَنَا إِنَّا سَمِعْنَا كِتَابًا أُنْزِلَ مِنْ بَعْدِ مُوسَى مُصَدِّقًا لِمَا بَيْنَ يَدَيْهِ يَهْدِي إِلَى الْحَقِّ وَإِلَى طَرِيقٍ مُسْتَقِيمٍ (٣٠) يَا قَوْمَنَا أَجِيبُوا دَاعِيَ اللَّهِ وَآمِنُوا بِهِ يَغْفِرْ لَكُمْ مِنْ ذُنُوبِكُمْ وَيُجِرْكُمْ مِنْ عَذَابٍ أَلِيمٍ (٣١) وَمَنْ لَا يُجِبْ دَاعِيَ اللَّهِ فَلَيْسَ بِمُعْجِزٍ فِي الْأَرْضِ وَلَيْسَ لَهُ مِنْ دُونِهِ أَوْلِيَاءُ أُولَئِكَ فِي ضَلَالٍ مُبِينٍ

forgive you some of your sins and protect you from a painful chastisement.

46:32. And whoever accepts not the Inviter to Allah, he cannot escape in the earth, nor has he protectors besides Him. These are in manifest error.

46:33. See they not that Allah, Who created the heavens and the earth and was not tired by their creation, is able to give life to the dead? Aye, He is surely Possessor of power over all things.

46:34. And on the day when those who disbelieve are brought before the Fire: Is it not true? They will say Yea, by our Lord He will say: Then taste the chastisement, because you disbelieved.

46:35. So have patience, as men of resolution, the messengers, had patience, and seek not to hasten on for them (their doom). On the day when they see that which they are promised, (it will be) as if they had not tarried save an hour of the, day. (Thine is) to deliver. Shall then any be destroyed save the transgressing people?

47. Muhammad

In the name of Allah, the Beneficent, the Merciful.

47:1. Those who disbelieve and turn (men) from Allah's way, He will destroy their works.

47:2. And those who believe and do good, and believe in that which has been revealed to Muhammad -- and it is the Truth from their Lord -- He will remove their evil from them and improve their condition.

47:3. That is because those who disbelieve follow falsehood, and those who believe follow the Truth from their Lord. Thus does Allah set forth their descriptions for men.

47:4. So when you meet in battle those who disbelieve, smite the necks; then,

when you have overcome them, make (them) prisoners, and afterwards (set them free) as a favour or for ransom till the war lay down its burdens. That (shall be so). And if Allah please, He would certainly exact retribution from them, but that He may try some of you by means of others. And those who are slain in the way of Allah, He will never allow their deeds to perish.
47:5. He will guide them and improve their condition.
47:6. And make them enter the Garden, which He has made known to them.
47:7. O you who believe, if you help Allah, He will help you and make firm your feet.
47:8. And those who disbelieve, for them is destruction, and He will destroy their works.
47:9. That is because they hate that which Allah reveals, so He has rendered their deeds fruitless.
47:10. Have they not travelled in the land and seen what was the end of those before them? Allah destroyed them. And for the disbelievers is the like thereof.
47:11. That is because Allah is the patron of those who believe, and because the disbelievers have no patron.

***

47:12. Surely Allah will make those who believe and do good enter Gardens wherein flow rivers. And those who disbelieve enjoy themselves and eat as the cattle eat, and the Fire is their abode.
47:13. And how many a town, more powerful than thy town which has driven thee out -- We destroyed them, so there was no helper for them.
47:14. Is then he who has a clear argument from his Lord like him to whom his evil conduct is made fair-seeming; and they follow their low desires.

الرِّقَابِ حَتَّىٰ إِذَا أَثْخَنْتُمُوهُمْ فَشُدُّوا الْوَثَاقَ فَإِمَّا مَنًّا بَعْدُ وَإِمَّا فِدَاءً حَتَّىٰ تَضَعَ الْحَرْبُ أَوْزَارَهَا ذَٰلِكَ وَلَوْ يَشَاءُ اللَّهُ لَانْتَصَرَ مِنْهُمْ وَلَٰكِنْ لِيَبْلُوَ بَعْضَكُمْ بِبَعْضٍ وَالَّذِينَ قُتِلُوا فِي سَبِيلِ اللَّهِ فَلَنْ يُضِلَّ أَعْمَالَهُمْ (٤)
سَيَهْدِيهِمْ وَيُصْلِحُ بَالَهُمْ (٥)
وَيُدْخِلُهُمُ الْجَنَّةَ عَرَّفَهَا لَهُمْ (٦)
يَا أَيُّهَا الَّذِينَ آمَنُوا إِنْ تَنْصُرُوا اللَّهَ يَنْصُرْكُمْ وَيُثَبِّتْ أَقْدَامَكُمْ (٧)
وَالَّذِينَ كَفَرُوا فَتَعْسًا لَهُمْ وَأَضَلَّ أَعْمَالَهُمْ (٨)
ذَٰلِكَ بِأَنَّهُمْ كَرِهُوا مَا أَنْزَلَ اللَّهُ فَأَحْبَطَ أَعْمَالَهُمْ (٩)
أَفَلَمْ يَسِيرُوا فِي الْأَرْضِ فَيَنْظُرُوا كَيْفَ كَانَ عَاقِبَةُ الَّذِينَ مِنْ قَبْلِهِمْ دَمَّرَ اللَّهُ عَلَيْهِمْ وَلِلْكَافِرِينَ أَمْثَالُهَا (١٠)
ذَٰلِكَ بِأَنَّ اللَّهَ مَوْلَى الَّذِينَ آمَنُوا وَأَنَّ الْكَافِرِينَ لَا مَوْلَىٰ لَهُمْ (١١)
إِنَّ اللَّهَ يُدْخِلُ الَّذِينَ آمَنُوا وَعَمِلُوا الصَّالِحَاتِ جَنَّاتٍ تَجْرِي مِنْ تَحْتِهَا الْأَنْهَارُ وَالَّذِينَ كَفَرُوا يَتَمَتَّعُونَ وَيَأْكُلُونَ كَمَا تَأْكُلُ الْأَنْعَامُ وَالنَّارُ مَثْوًى لَهُمْ (١٢)
وَكَأَيِّنْ مِنْ قَرْيَةٍ هِيَ أَشَدُّ قُوَّةً مِنْ قَرْيَتِكَ الَّتِي أَخْرَجَتْكَ أَهْلَكْنَاهُمْ فَلَا نَاصِرَ لَهُمْ (١٣)
أَفَمَنْ كَانَ عَلَىٰ بَيِّنَةٍ مِنْ رَبِّهِ كَمَنْ زُيِّنَ لَهُ سُوءُ عَمَلِهِ وَاتَّبَعُوا أَهْوَاءَهُمْ (١٤)
مَثَلُ الْجَنَّةِ الَّتِي وُعِدَ الْمُتَّقُونَ فِيهَا أَنْهَارٌ مِنْ مَاءٍ غَيْرِ آسِنٍ وَأَنْهَارٌ مِنْ لَبَنٍ لَمْ يَتَغَيَّرْ طَعْمُهُ وَأَنْهَارٌ مِنْ خَمْرٍ لَذَّةٍ لِلشَّارِبِينَ وَأَنْهَارٌ مِنْ عَسَلٍ

47:15. A parable of the Garden which the dutiful are promised: Therein are rivers of water not altering for the worse, and rivers of milk whereof the taste changes not, and rivers of wine delicious to the drinkers, and rivers of honey clarified; and for them therein are all fruits and protection from their Lord. (Are these) like those who abide in the Fire and who are made to drink boiling water, so it tends their bowels asunder?

47:16. And there are those of them who seek to listen to thee, till, when they go forth from thee, they say to those who have been given knowledge: What was it that he said just now? These are they whose hearts Allah has sealed and they follow their low desires.

47:17. And those who follow guidance, He increases them in guidance and grants them their observance of duty.

47:18. Wait they for aught but the Hour that it should come upon them of a sudden? Now tokens thereof have already come. Fur how will they have their reminder, when it comes on them?

47:19. So know that there is no God but Allah and ask protection for thy sin and for the believing men and the believing women. And Allah knows your moving about and your staying (in a place).

***

47:20. And those who believe say: Why is not a chapter revealed? But when a decisive chapter is revealed, and fighting is mentioned therein, thou seest those in whose hearts is a disease look to thee with the look of one fainting at death So woe to them!

47:21. Obedience and a gentle word (was proper). Then when the affair is settled, it is better for them if they remain true to Allah.

47:22. But if you turn away, you are sure to make mischief in the land and

مُصَفًّى وَلَهُمْ فِيهَا مِنْ كُلِّ الثَّمَرَاتِ وَمَغْفِرَةٌ مِنْ رَبِّهِمْ كَمَنْ هُوَ خَالِدٌ فِي النَّارِ وَسُقُوا مَاءً حَمِيمًا فَقَطَّعَ أَمْعَاءَهُمْ (١٥)

وَمِنْهُمْ مَنْ يَسْتَمِعُ إِلَيْكَ حَتَّى إِذَا خَرَجُوا مِنْ عِنْدِكَ قَالُوا لِلَّذِينَ أُوتُوا الْعِلْمَ مَاذَا قَالَ آنِفًا أُولَئِكَ الَّذِينَ طَبَعَ اللَّهُ عَلَى قُلُوبِهِمْ وَاتَّبَعُوا أَهْوَاءَهُمْ (١٦)

وَالَّذِينَ اهْتَدَوْا زَادَهُمْ هُدًى وَآتَاهُمْ تَقْوَاهُمْ (١٧)

فَهَلْ يَنْظُرُونَ إِلَّا السَّاعَةَ أَنْ تَأْتِيَهُمْ بَغْتَةً فَقَدْ جَاءَ أَشْرَاطُهَا فَأَنَّى لَهُمْ إِذَا جَاءَتْهُمْ ذِكْرَاهُمْ (١٨)

فَاعْلَمْ أَنَّهُ لَا إِلَهَ إِلَّا اللَّهُ وَاسْتَغْفِرْ لِذَنْبِكَ وَلِلْمُؤْمِنِينَ وَالْمُؤْمِنَاتِ وَاللَّهُ يَعْلَمُ مُتَقَلَّبَكُمْ وَمَثْوَاكُمْ (١٩)

وَيَقُولُ الَّذِينَ آمَنُوا لَوْلَا نُزِّلَتْ سُورَةٌ فَإِذَا أُنْزِلَتْ سُورَةٌ مُحْكَمَةٌ وَذُكِرَ فِيهَا الْقِتَالُ رَأَيْتَ الَّذِينَ فِي قُلُوبِهِمْ مَرَضٌ يَنْظُرُونَ إِلَيْكَ نَظَرَ الْمَغْشِيِّ عَلَيْهِ مِنَ الْمَوْتِ فَأَوْلَى لَهُمْ (٢٠)

طَاعَةٌ وَقَوْلٌ مَعْرُوفٌ فَإِذَا عَزَمَ الْأَمْرُ فَلَوْ صَدَقُوا اللَّهَ لَكَانَ خَيْرًا لَهُمْ (٢١)

فَهَلْ عَسَيْتُمْ إِنْ تَوَلَّيْتُمْ أَنْ تُفْسِدُوا فِي الْأَرْضِ وَتُقَطِّعُوا أَرْحَامَكُمْ (٢٢) أُولَئِكَ الَّذِينَ لَعَنَهُمُ اللَّهُ فَأَصَمَّهُمْ وَأَعْمَى أَبْصَارَهُمْ (٢٣)

أَفَلَا يَتَدَبَّرُونَ الْقُرْآنَ أَمْ عَلَى قُلُوبٍ أَقْفَالُهَا (٢٤)

إِنَّ الَّذِينَ ارْتَدُّوا عَلَى أَدْبَارِهِمْ مِنْ بَعْدِ مَا تَبَيَّنَ لَهُمُ الْهُدَى الشَّيْطَانُ سَوَّلَ لَهُمْ وَأَمْلَى لَهُمْ (٢٥)

cut off the ties of kinship!

47:23. Those it is whom Allah has cursed, so He has made them deaf and blinded their eyes.

47:24. Do they not reflect on the Qur'an? Or, are there locks on the hearts?

47:25. Surely those who turn back after guidance is manifest to them, the devil embellishes it for them and lengthens false hopes for them.

47:26. That is because they say to those who hate what Allah has revealed We will obey you in some matters. And Allah knows their secrets.

47:27. But how will it be when the angels cause them to die, smiting their faces and their hacks?

47:28. That is because they follow that which displeases Allah and are averse to His pleasure, so He makes their deeds fruitless.

* * *

47:29. Or do those in whose hearts is a disease think that Allah will nor bring forth their spite?

47:30. And if We please, We could show them to thee so that thou shouldst know them by their marks. And certainly thou canst recognize them by the tone of (their) speech. And Allah knows your deeds.

47:31. And certainly We shall try you, till We know those among you who strive hard, and the steadfast, and manifest your news.

47:32. Surely those who disbelieve and hinder (men) from Allah's way and oppose the Messenger after guidance is quite clear to them, cannot harm Allah in any way, and He will make their deeds fruitless.

47:33. O you who believe, obey Allah and obey the Messenger and make not your deeds vain.

47:34. Surely those who disbelieve and hinder (men) from Allah's way, then die disbelievers, Allah will not forgive

ذَٰلِكَ بِأَنَّهُمْ قَالُوا لِلَّذِينَ كَرِهُوا مَا نَزَّلَ اللَّهُ سَنُطِيعُكُمْ فِي بَعْضِ الْأَمْرِ وَاللَّهُ يَعْلَمُ إِسْرَارَهُمْ (٢٦)

فَكَيْفَ إِذَا تَوَفَّتْهُمُ الْمَلَائِكَةُ يَضْرِبُونَ وُجُوهَهُمْ وَأَدْبَارَهُمْ (٢٧)

ذَٰلِكَ بِأَنَّهُمُ اتَّبَعُوا مَا أَسْخَطَ اللَّهَ وَكَرِهُوا رِضْوَانَهُ فَأَحْبَطَ أَعْمَالَهُمْ (٢٨)

أَمْ حَسِبَ الَّذِينَ فِي قُلُوبِهِمْ مَرَضٌ أَنْ لَنْ يُخْرِجَ اللَّهُ أَضْغَانَهُمْ (٢٩)

وَلَوْ نَشَاءُ لَأَرَيْنَاكَهُمْ فَلَعَرَفْتَهُمْ بِسِيمَاهُمْ وَلَتَعْرِفَنَّهُمْ فِي لَحْنِ الْقَوْلِ وَاللَّهُ يَعْلَمُ أَعْمَالَكُمْ (٣٠)

وَلَنَبْلُوَنَّكُمْ حَتَّىٰ نَعْلَمَ الْمُجَاهِدِينَ مِنْكُمْ وَالصَّابِرِينَ وَنَبْلُوَ أَخْبَارَكُمْ (٣١)

إِنَّ الَّذِينَ كَفَرُوا وَصَدُّوا عَنْ سَبِيلِ اللَّهِ وَشَاقُّوا الرَّسُولَ مِنْ بَعْدِ مَا تَبَيَّنَ لَهُمُ الْهُدَىٰ لَنْ يَضُرُّوا اللَّهَ شَيْئًا وَسَيُحْبِطُ أَعْمَالَهُمْ (٣٢)

يَا أَيُّهَا الَّذِينَ آمَنُوا أَطِيعُوا اللَّهَ وَأَطِيعُوا الرَّسُولَ وَلَا تُبْطِلُوا أَعْمَالَكُمْ (٣٣)

إِنَّ الَّذِينَ كَفَرُوا وَصَدُّوا عَنْ سَبِيلِ اللَّهِ ثُمَّ مَاتُوا وَهُمْ كُفَّارٌ فَلَنْ يَغْفِرَ اللَّهُ لَهُمْ (٣٤)

فَلَا تَهِنُوا وَتَدْعُوا إِلَى السَّلْمِ وَأَنْتُمُ الْأَعْلَوْنَ وَاللَّهُ مَعَكُمْ وَلَنْ يَتِرَكُمْ أَعْمَالَكُمْ (٣٥)

إِنَّمَا الْحَيَاةُ الدُّنْيَا لَعِبٌ وَلَهْوٌ وَإِنْ تُؤْمِنُوا وَتَتَّقُوا يُؤْتِكُمْ أُجُورَكُمْ وَلَا يَسْأَلْكُمْ أَمْوَالَكُمْ (٣٦)

إِنْ يَسْأَلْكُمُوهَا فَيُحْفِكُمْ تَبْخَلُوا وَيُخْرِجْ أَضْغَانَكُمْ (٣٧)

هَاأَنْتُمْ هَٰؤُلَاءِ تُدْعَوْنَ لِتُنْفِقُوا فِي

them.

47:35. And be nor slack so as to cry for peace -- and you are the uppermost -- and Allah is with you, and He will not bring your deeds to naught.

47:36. The life of this world is but idle sport and play, and, if you believe and keep your duty, He will give you your reward, and He does not ask of you your wealth.

47:37. If He should ask you for it and press you, you will be niggardly, and He will bring forth your malice.

47:38. Behold! you are those who are called to spend in Allah's way, but among you are those who are niggardly; and whoever is niggardly, is niggardly against his own soul. And Allah is Self-Sufficient and you are needy. And if you turn back He will bring in your place another people, then they will not be like you.

48. The Victory

In the name of Allah, the Beneficent, the Merciful.

48:1. Surely We have granted thee a clear victory,

48:2. That Allah may cover for thee thy (alleged) shortcomings in the past and those to come, and complete His favour to thee and guide thee on a right path,

48:3. And that Allah might help thee with a mighty help.

48:4. He it is who sent down tranquillity into the hearts of the believers that they might add faith to their faith. And Allah's are the hosts of the heavens and the earth, and Allah is ever Knowing, Wise --

48:5. That He may cause the believing men and the believing women to enter Gardens wherein flow rivers to abide therein and remove from them their evil. And that is a grand achievement

48. The Victory

with Allah,

48:6. And (that) He may chastise the hypocritical men and the hypocritical women, and the polytheistic men and the polytheistic women, the entertainers of evil thoughts about Allah. On them is the evil turn, and Allah is wroth with them and has cursed them and prepared hell for them and evil is the resort.

48:7. And Allah's are the hosts of the heavens and the earth; and Allah is ever Mighty, Wise.

48:8. Surely We have sent thee as a witness and as a bearer of good news and as a warner,

48:9. That you may believe in Allah and His Messenger and may aid him and revere him. And (that) you may declare His glory, morning and evening.

48:10. Those who swear allegiance to thee do but swear allegiance to Allah. The hand of Allah is above their hands. So whoever breaks (his faith), he breaks it only to his soul's injury. And whoever fulfils his covenant with Allah, He will grant him a mighty reward.

* * *

48:11. Those of the dwellers of the desert who lagged behind will say to thee: Our property and our families kept us busy, so ask forgiveness for us. They say with their tongues what is not in their hearts. Say: Then who can control aught for you from Allah, if He intends to do you harm or if He intends to do you good. Nay, Allah is ever Aware of what you do.

48:12. Nay, you thought that the Messenger and the believers would never return to their families, and that was made fair-seeming in your hearts, and you thought an evil thought, and you are a people doomed to perish.

48:13. And whoever believes not in Allah and His Messenger -- then surely

وَالْمُشْرِكِينَ وَالْمُشْرِكَاتِ الظَّانِّينَ بِاللَّهِ ظَنَّ السَّوْءِ عَلَيْهِمْ دَائِرَةُ السَّوْءِ وَغَضِبَ اللَّهُ عَلَيْهِمْ وَلَعَنَهُمْ وَأَعَدَّ لَهُمْ جَهَنَّمَ وَسَاءَتْ مَصِيرًا (٦)
وَلِلَّهِ جُنُودُ السَّمَاوَاتِ وَالْأَرْضِ وَكَانَ اللَّهُ عَزِيزًا حَكِيمًا (٧)
إِنَّا أَرْسَلْنَاكَ شَاهِدًا وَمُبَشِّرًا وَنَذِيرًا (٨)
لِتُؤْمِنُوا بِاللَّهِ وَرَسُولِهِ وَتُعَزِّرُوهُ وَتُوَقِّرُوهُ وَتُسَبِّحُوهُ بُكْرَةً وَأَصِيلًا (٩)
إِنَّ الَّذِينَ يُبَايِعُونَكَ إِنَّمَا يُبَايِعُونَ اللَّهَ يَدُ اللَّهِ فَوْقَ أَيْدِيهِمْ فَمَنْ نَكَثَ فَإِنَّمَا يَنْكُثُ عَلَى نَفْسِهِ وَمَنْ أَوْفَى بِمَا عَاهَدَ عَلَيْهُ اللَّهَ فَسَيُؤْتِيهِ أَجْرًا عَظِيمًا (١٠)
سَيَقُولُ لَكَ الْمُخَلَّفُونَ مِنَ الْأَعْرَابِ شَغَلَتْنَا أَمْوَالُنَا وَأَهْلُونَا فَاسْتَغْفِرْ لَنَا يَقُولُونَ بِأَلْسِنَتِهِمْ مَا لَيْسَ فِي قُلُوبِهِمْ قُلْ فَمَنْ يَمْلِكُ لَكُمْ مِنَ اللَّهِ شَيْئًا إِنْ أَرَادَ بِكُمْ ضَرًّا أَوْ أَرَادَ بِكُمْ نَفْعًا بَلْ كَانَ اللَّهُ بِمَا تَعْمَلُونَ خَبِيرًا (١١)
بَلْ ظَنَنْتُمْ أَنْ لَنْ يَنْقَلِبَ الرَّسُولُ وَالْمُؤْمِنُونَ إِلَى أَهْلِيهِمْ أَبَدًا وَزُيِّنَ ذَلِكَ فِي قُلُوبِكُمْ وَظَنَنْتُمْ ظَنَّ السَّوْءِ وَكُنْتُمْ قَوْمًا بُورًا (١٢)
وَمَنْ لَمْ يُؤْمِنْ بِاللَّهِ وَرَسُولِهِ فَإِنَّا أَعْتَدْنَا لِلْكَافِرِينَ سَعِيرًا (١٣)
وَلِلَّهِ مُلْكُ السَّمَاوَاتِ وَالْأَرْضِ يَغْفِرُ لِمَنْ يَشَاءُ وَيُعَذِّبُ مَنْ يَشَاءُ وَكَانَ اللَّهُ غَفُورًا رَحِيمًا (١٤)
سَيَقُولُ الْمُخَلَّفُونَ إِذَا انْطَلَقْتُمْ إِلَى مَغَانِمَ لِتَأْخُذُوهَا ذَرُونَا نَتَّبِعْكُمْ يُرِيدُونَ أَنْ يُبَدِّلُوا كَلَامَ اللَّهِ قُلْ لَنْ

48. The Victory

We have prepared burning Fire for the disbelievers.

48:14. And Allah's is the kingdom of the heavens and the earth. He forgives whom He pleases and chastises whom He pleases. And Allah is ever Forgiving, Merciful.

48:15. Those who lagged behind will say, when you set forth to acquire gains: Allow us to follow you They desire to change the word of Allah. Say; You shall not follow us. Thus did Allah say before. But they will say: Nay, you are jealous of us. Nay, they understand not but a little.

48:16. Say to those of the dwellers of the desert who lagged behind: You will soon be called against a people of mighty prowess to fight against them until they submit. Then if you obey, Allah will grant you a good reward; but, if you turn back as you turned back before, He will chastise you with a painful chastisement.

48:17. There is no blame on the blind, nor is there blame on the lame, nor is there blame on the sick. And whoever obeys Allah and His Messenger, He will cause him to enter Gardens wherein flow rivers. And whoever turns back, He will chastise him with a painful chastisement.

* * *

48:18. Allah indeed was well pleased with the believers, when they swore allegiance to thee under the tree, and He knew what was in their hearts, so He sent down tranquillity on them and rewarded them with a near victory,

48:19. And many gains which they will acquire. And Allah is ever Mighty, Wise.

48:20. Allah promised you many gains which you will acquire, then He hastened this on for you, and held back the hands of men from you; and that it may be a sign for the believers and that He may guide you on a right path,

تَتَّبِعُونَا كَذَلِكُمْ قَالَ اللَّهُ مِنْ قَبْلُ فَسَيَقُولُونَ بَلْ تَحْسُدُونَنَا بَلْ كَانُوا لَا يَفْقَهُونَ إِلَّا قَلِيلًا (١٥)

قُلْ لِلْمُخَلَّفِينَ مِنَ الْأَعْرَابِ سَتُدْعَوْنَ إِلَى قَوْمٍ أُولِي بَأْسٍ شَدِيدٍ تُقَاتِلُونَهُمْ أَوْ يُسْلِمُونَ فَإِنْ تُطِيعُوا يُؤْتِكُمُ اللَّهُ أَجْرًا حَسَنًا وَإِنْ تَتَوَلَّوْا كَمَا تَوَلَّيْتُمْ مِنْ قَبْلُ يُعَذِّبْكُمْ عَذَابًا أَلِيمًا (١٦)

لَيْسَ عَلَى الْأَعْمَى حَرَجٌ وَلَا عَلَى الْأَعْرَجِ حَرَجٌ وَلَا عَلَى الْمَرِيضِ حَرَجٌ وَمَنْ يُطِعِ اللَّهَ وَرَسُولَهُ يُدْخِلْهُ جَنَّاتٍ تَجْرِي مِنْ تَحْتِهَا الْأَنْهَارُ وَمَنْ يَتَوَلَّ يُعَذِّبْهُ عَذَابًا أَلِيمًا (١٧)

لَقَدْ رَضِيَ اللَّهُ عَنِ الْمُؤْمِنِينَ إِذْ يُبَايِعُونَكَ تَحْتَ الشَّجَرَةِ فَعَلِمَ مَا فِي قُلُوبِهِمْ فَأَنْزَلَ السَّكِينَةَ عَلَيْهِمْ وَأَثَابَهُمْ فَتْحًا قَرِيبًا (١٨)

وَمَغَانِمَ كَثِيرَةً يَأْخُذُونَهَا وَكَانَ اللَّهُ عَزِيزًا حَكِيمًا (١٩)

وَعَدَكُمُ اللَّهُ مَغَانِمَ كَثِيرَةً تَأْخُذُونَهَا فَعَجَّلَ لَكُمْ هَذِهِ وَكَفَّ أَيْدِيَ النَّاسِ عَنْكُمْ وَلِتَكُونَ آيَةً لِلْمُؤْمِنِينَ وَيَهْدِيَكُمْ صِرَاطًا مُسْتَقِيمًا (٢٠)

وَأُخْرَى لَمْ تَقْدِرُوا عَلَيْهَا قَدْ أَحَاطَ اللَّهُ بِهَا وَكَانَ اللَّهُ عَلَى كُلِّ شَيْءٍ قَدِيرًا (٢١)

وَلَوْ قَاتَلَكُمُ الَّذِينَ كَفَرُوا لَوَلَّوُا الْأَدْبَارَ ثُمَّ لَا يَجِدُونَ وَلِيًّا وَلَا نَصِيرًا (٢٢)

سُنَّةَ اللَّهِ الَّتِي قَدْ خَلَتْ مِنْ قَبْلُ وَلَنْ تَجِدَ لِسُنَّةِ اللَّهِ تَبْدِيلًا (٢٣)

وَهُوَ الَّذِي كَفَّ أَيْدِيَهُمْ عَنْكُمْ وَأَيْدِيَكُمْ عَنْهُمْ بِبَطْنِ مَكَّةَ مِنْ بَعْدِ أَنْ أَظْفَرَكُمْ عَلَيْهِمْ وَكَانَ اللَّهُ بِمَا تَعْمَلُونَ بَصِيرًا (٢٤)

48. The Victory

48:21. And others which you have not yet been able to achieve Allah has surely encompassed them. And Allah is ever Powerful over all things.

48:22. And if those who disbelieve fight with you, they will certainly turn (their) backs, then they will find no protector nor helper.

48:23. (Such has been) the course of Allah that has run before, and thou wilt not find a change in Allah's course.

48:24. And He it is Who held back their hands from you and your hands from them in the valley of Makkah after He had given you victory over them. And Allah is ever Seer of what you do.

48:25. It is they who disbelieved and debarred you from the Sacred Mosque -- and the offering withheld from reaching its goal. And were it not for the believing men and the believing women, whom, not having known, you might have trodden down, and thus something hateful might have afflicted you on their account without knowledge -- so that Allah may admit to His mercy whom He pleases. Had they been apart, We would surely have chastised those who disbelieved from among them with a painful chastisement.

48:26. When those who disbelieved harboured disdain in their hearts, the disdain of Ignorance, but Allah sent down His tranquillity on His Messenger and on the believers and made them keep the word of observance of duty, and they were entitled to it and worthy of it. And Allah is ever Knower of all things.

***

48:27. Allah indeed fulfilled the vision for His Messenger with truth. You shall certainly enter the Sacred Mosque, if Allah please, in security, your heads shaved and hair cut short, not fearing. But He knows what you know not, so He has ordained a near victory before that.

48:28. He it is Who has sent His Messenger with the guidance and the religion of Truth that He may make it prevail over all religions. And Allah is enough for a witness.

48:29. Muhammad is the Messenger of Allah, and those with him are firm of heart against the disbelievers, compassionate among themselves. Thou seest them bowing down, prostrating themselves, seeking Allah's grace and pleasure. Their marks are on their faces in consequence of prostration. That is their description in the Torah -- and their description in the Gospel -- like seed-produce that puts forth its sprout, then strengthens it, so it becomes stout and stands firmly on its stem, delighting the sowers that He may enrage the disbelievers on account of them. Allah has promised such of them as believe and do good, forgiveness and a great reward.

49. The Apartments

In the name of Allah, the Beneficent, the Merciful.

49:1. O you who believe, be not forward in the presence of Allah and His Messenger, and keep your duty to Allah. Surely Allah is Hearing, Knowing.

49:2. O you who believe, raise not your voices above the Prophet's voice, nor speak loudly to him as you speak loudly one to another, lest your deeds become null, while you perceive not.

49:3. Surely those who lower their voices before Allah's Messenger are they whose hearts Allah has proved for dutifulness. For them is forgiveness and a great reward.

49:4. Those who call out to thee from behind the private apartments, most of them have no sense:

٤٩ - سورة الحجرات

بِسْمِ اللهِ الرَّحْمَنِ الرَّحِيمِ
يَا أَيُّهَا الَّذِينَ آمَنُوا لَا تُقَدِّمُوا بَيْنَ يَدَيِ اللهِ وَرَسُولِهِ وَاتَّقُوا اللهَ إِنَّ اللهَ سَمِيعٌ عَلِيمٌ (١)
يَا أَيُّهَا الَّذِينَ آمَنُوا لَا تَرْفَعُوا أَصْوَاتَكُمْ فَوْقَ صَوْتِ النَّبِيِّ وَلَا تَجْهَرُوا لَهُ بِالْقَوْلِ كَجَهْرِ بَعْضِكُمْ لِبَعْضٍ أَنْ تَحْبَطَ أَعْمَالُكُمْ وَأَنْتُمْ لَا تَشْعُرُونَ (٢)
إِنَّ الَّذِينَ يَغُضُّونَ أَصْوَاتَهُمْ عِنْدَ رَسُولِ اللهِ أُولَئِكَ الَّذِينَ امْتَحَنَ اللهُ قُلُوبَهُمْ لِلتَّقْوَى لَهُمْ مَغْفِرَةٌ وَأَجْرٌ عَظِيمٌ (٣)
إِنَّ الَّذِينَ يُنَادُونَكَ مِنْ وَرَاءِ

49. The Apartments

49:5. And if they had patience till thou come out to them, it would be better for them. And Allah is Forgiving, Merciful.

49:6. O you who believe, if an unrighteous man brings you news, look carefully into it, lest you harm a people in ignorance, then be sorry for what you did.

49:7. And know that among you is Allah's Messenger. Were he to obey you in many a matter, you would surely fall into distress but Allah has endeared the faith to you and has made it seemly in your hearts, and He has made hateful to you disbelief and transgression and disobedience. Such are those who are rightly guided --

49:8. A grace from Allah and a favour. And Allah is Knowing, Wise.

49:9. And if two parties of the believers quarrel, make peace between them. Then if one of them does wrong to the other, fight that which does wrong, till it return to Allah's command. Then, if it returns, make peace between them with justice and act equitably. Surely Allah loves the equitable.

49:10. The believers are brethren so make peace between your brethren, and keep your duty to Allah that mercy may be had on you.

* * *

49:11. O you who believe, let not people laugh at people, perchance they may be better than they; nor let women (laugh) at women, perchance they may be better than they. Neither find fault with your own people, nor call one another by nick-names. Evil is a bad name after faith; and whoso turns not, these it is that are the iniquitous.

49:12. O you who believe, avoid most of suspicion, for surely suspicion in some cases is sin and spy not nor let some of you backbite others. Does one of you like to eat the flesh of his dead brother? You abhor it! And keep your duty to Allah, surely Allah is Oft-returning (to mercy), Merciful.

49:13. O mankind, surely We have created you from a male and a female, and made you tribes and families that you may know each other. Surely the noblest of you with Allah is the most dutiful of you. Surely Allah is Knowing, Aware.

49:14. The dwellers of the desert say We believe. Say: You believe not, but say, We submit; and faith has not yet entered into your hearts. 'And if you obey Allah and His Messenger, He will not diminish aught of your deeds. Surely Allah is Forgiving, Merciful.

49:15. The believers are those only who believe in Allah and His Messenger, then they doubt not, and struggle hard with their wealth and their lives in the way of Allah. Such are the truthful ones.

49:16. Say: Would you apprise Allah of your religion? and Allah knows what is in the heavens and what is in the earth And Allah is Knower of all things.

49:17. They presume to lay thee under an obligation by becoming Muslims. Say: Lay me not under an obligation by your Islam; rather Allah lays you under an obligation by guiding you to the faith, if you are truthful.

49:18. Surely Allah knows the unseen of the heavens and the earth. And Allah is Seer of what you do.

50. Qaf

In the name of Allah, the Beneficent, the Merciful.

50:1. Almighty (God)! By the glorious Qur'an!

50:2. Nay, they wonder that a warner has come to them from among themselves; so the disbelievers say: This is a wonderful thing

50:3. When we die and become dust that is a far return.

50:4. We know indeed what the earth diminishes of them and with Us is a book that preserves.

50:5. Nay, they reject the Truth when it comes to them, so they are in a state of confusion.

50:6. Do they not look at the sky above them? -- how We have made it and adorned it and it has no gaps.

50:7. And the earth, We have spread it out, and cast therein mountains, and We have made to grow therein of every beautiful kind --

50:8. To give sight and as a reminder to every servant who turns (to Allah).

50:9. And We send down from the clouds water abounding in good, then We cause to grow thereby gardens and the grain that is reaped,

50:10. And the tall palm-trees having flower spikes piled one above another --

50:11. A sustenance for the servants, and We give life thereby to a dead land. Thus is the rising.

50:12. Before them the people of Noah rejected (the Truth) and (so did) the dwellers of al-Rass and Thamud

50:13. And 'Ad and Pharaoh and Lot's brethren,

50:14. And the dwellers of the grove and the people of Tubba'. They all rejected the messengers, so My threat came to pass.

50:15. Were We then fatigued with the first creation? Yet they are in doubt about a new creation.

***

50:16. And certainly We created man, and We know what his mind suggests to him -- and We are nearer to him than his life-vein.

50:17. When the two receivers receive, sitting on the right and on the left,

50:18. He utters not a word but there is by him a watcher at hand.

أَئِذَا مِتْنَا وَكُنَّا تُرَابًا ذَلِكَ رَجْعٌ بَعِيدٌ (٣)

قَدْ عَلِمْنَا مَا تَنْقُصُ الْأَرْضُ مِنْهُمْ وَعِنْدَنَا كِتَابٌ حَفِيظٌ (٤)

بَلْ كَذَّبُوا بِالْحَقِّ لَمَّا جَاءَهُمْ فَهُمْ فِي أَمْرٍ مَرِيجٍ (٥)

أَفَلَمْ يَنْظُرُوا إِلَى السَّمَاءِ فَوْقَهُمْ كَيْفَ بَنَيْنَاهَا وَزَيَّنَّاهَا وَمَا لَهَا مِنْ فُرُوجٍ (٦)

وَالْأَرْضَ مَدَدْنَاهَا وَأَلْقَيْنَا فِيهَا رَوَاسِيَ وَأَنْبَتْنَا فِيهَا مِنْ كُلِّ زَوْجٍ بَهِيجٍ (٧)

تَبْصِرَةً وَذِكْرَى لِكُلِّ عَبْدٍ مُنِيبٍ (٨)

وَنَزَّلْنَا مِنَ السَّمَاءِ مَاءً مُبَارَكًا فَأَنْبَتْنَا بِهِ جَنَّاتٍ وَحَبَّ الْحَصِيدِ (٩)

وَالنَّخْلَ بَاسِقَاتٍ لَهَا طَلْعٌ نَضِيدٌ (١٠)

رِزْقًا لِلْعِبَادِ وَأَحْيَيْنَا بِهِ بَلْدَةً مَيْتًا كَذَلِكَ الْخُرُوجُ (١١)

كَذَّبَتْ قَبْلَهُمْ قَوْمُ نُوحٍ وَأَصْحَابُ الرَّسِّ وَثَمُودُ (١٢)

وَعَادٌ وَفِرْعَوْنُ وَإِخْوَانُ لُوطٍ (١٣)

وَأَصْحَابُ الْأَيْكَةِ وَقَوْمُ تُبَّعٍ كُلٌّ كَذَّبَ الرُّسُلَ فَحَقَّ وَعِيدِ (١٤)

أَفَعَيِينَا بِالْخَلْقِ الْأَوَّلِ بَلْ هُمْ فِي لَبْسٍ مِنْ خَلْقٍ جَدِيدٍ (١٥)

وَلَقَدْ خَلَقْنَا الْإِنْسَانَ وَنَعْلَمُ مَا تُوَسْوِسُ بِهِ نَفْسُهُ وَنَحْنُ أَقْرَبُ إِلَيْهِ مِنْ حَبْلِ الْوَرِيدِ (١٦)

إِذْ يَتَلَقَّى الْمُتَلَقِّيَانِ عَنِ الْيَمِينِ وَعَنِ الشِّمَالِ قَعِيدٌ (١٧)

مَا يَلْفِظُ مِنْ قَوْلٍ إِلَّا لَدَيْهِ رَقِيبٌ عَتِيدٌ (١٨)

50:19. And the stupor of death comes in truth; that is what thou wouldst shun.
50:20. And the trumpet is blown. That is the day of threatening.
50:21. And every soul comes, with it a driver and a witness.
50:22. Thou wast indeed heedless of this, but now We have removed from thee thy veil, so thy sight is sharp this day.
50:23. And his companion will say: This is what is ready with me.
50:24. Cast into hell every ungrateful, rebellious one,
50:25. Forbidder of good, exceeder of limits, doubter,
50:26. Who sets up another god with Allah, so cast him into severe chastisement.
50:27. His companion will say: Our Lord, I did not cause him to rebel but he himself went far in error.
50:28. He will say: Dispute not in My presence, and indeed I gave you warning beforehand.
50:29. My sentence cannot be changed, nor am I in the least unjust to the servants.

* * *

50:30. On the day when We say to hell: Art thou filled up? And it will say: Are there any more?
50:31. And the Garden is brought near for those who guard against evil -- (it is) not disrant.
50:32. This is what you are promised -- for every one turning (to Allah), keeping (the limits) --
50:33. Who fears the Beneficent in secret, and comes with a penitent heart:
50:34. Enter it in peace. That is the day of abiding.
50:35. For them therein is all they wish, and with Us is yet more.
50:36. And how many a generation We destroyed before them who were mightier in prowess than they! so they went about in the lands. Is there a place

وَجَاءَتْ سَكْرَةُ الْمَوْتِ بِالْحَقِّ ذَلِكَ مَا كُنْتَ مِنْهُ تَحِيدُ (١٩)
وَنُفِخَ فِي الصُّورِ ذَلِكَ يَوْمُ الْوَعِيدِ (٢٠)
وَجَاءَتْ كُلُّ نَفْسٍ مَعَهَا سَائِقٌ وَشَهِيدٌ (٢١)
لَقَدْ كُنْتَ فِي غَفْلَةٍ مِنْ هَذَا فَكَشَفْنَا عَنْكَ غِطَاءَكَ فَبَصَرُكَ الْيَوْمَ حَدِيدٌ (٢٢)
وَقَالَ قَرِينُهُ هَذَا مَا لَدَيَّ عَتِيدٌ (٢٣)
أَلْقِيَا فِي جَهَنَّمَ كُلَّ كَفَّارٍ عَنِيدٍ (٢٤)
مَنَّاعٍ لِلْخَيْرِ مُعْتَدٍ مُرِيبٍ (٢٥)
الَّذِي جَعَلَ مَعَ اللَّهِ إِلَهًا آخَرَ فَأَلْقِيَاهُ فِي الْعَذَابِ الشَّدِيدِ (٢٦)
قَالَ قَرِينُهُ رَبَّنَا مَا أَطْغَيْتُهُ وَلَكِنْ كَانَ فِي ضَلَالٍ بَعِيدٍ (٢٧)
قَالَ لَا تَخْتَصِمُوا لَدَيَّ وَقَدْ قَدَّمْتُ إِلَيْكُمْ بِالْوَعِيدِ (٢٨)
مَا يُبَدَّلُ الْقَوْلُ لَدَيَّ وَمَا أَنَا بِظَلَّامٍ لِلْعَبِيدِ (٢٩)
يَوْمَ نَقُولُ لِجَهَنَّمَ هَلِ امْتَلَأْتِ وَتَقُولُ هَلْ مِنْ مَزِيدٍ (٣٠)
وَأُزْلِفَتِ الْجَنَّةُ لِلْمُتَّقِينَ غَيْرَ بَعِيدٍ (٣١)
هَذَا مَا تُوعَدُونَ لِكُلِّ أَوَّابٍ حَفِيظٍ (٣٢)
مَنْ خَشِيَ الرَّحْمَنَ بِالْغَيْبِ وَجَاءَ بِقَلْبٍ مُنِيبٍ (٣٣)
ادْخُلُوهَا بِسَلَامٍ ذَلِكَ يَوْمُ الْخُلُودِ (٣٤)
لَهُمْ مَا يَشَاءُونَ فِيهَا وَلَدَيْنَا مَزِيدٌ (٣٥)
وَكَمْ أَهْلَكْنَا قَبْلَهُمْ مِنْ قَرْنٍ هُمْ أَشَدُّ

of refuge?

50:37. Surely there is a reminder in this for him who has a heart or he gives ear and is a witness.

50:38. And certainly We created the heavens and the earth and what is between them in six periods, and no fatigue touched Us.

50:39. So bear with what they say, and celebrate the praise of thy Lord before the rising of the sun and before the setting.

50:40. And glorify Him in the night and after prostration.

50:41. And listen on the day when the crier cries from a near place --

50:42. The day when they hear the cry in truth. That is the day of coming forth.

50:43. Surely We give life and cause to die, and to Us is the eventual coming --

50:44. The day when the earth cleaves asunder from them, hastening forth. That is a gathering easy to Us.

50:45. We know best what they say, and thou art not one to compel them. So remind by means of the Qur'an him who fears My threat.

51. The Scatterers

In the name of Allah, the Beneficent, the Merciful.

51:1. By those scattering broadcast
51:2. And those bearing the load!
51:3. And those running easily!
51:4. And those distributing the Affair! --
51:5. What you are promised is surely true,
51:6. And the Judgment will surely come to pass.

51. The Scatterers

51:7. By the heaven full of paths!
51:8. Surely you are of varying opinion --
51:9. He is turned away from it who would be turned away.
51:10. Cursed be the liars!
51:11. Who are in an abyss, neglectful;
51:12. They ask: When is the day of Judgment?
51:13. (It is) the day when they are tried at the Fire.
51:14. Taste your persecution! This is what you would hasten on.
51:15. Surely the dutiful are amidst Gardens and fountains,
51:16. Taking that which their Lord gives them. Surely they were before that the doers of good.
51:17. They used to sleep but little at night.
51:18. And in the morning they asked (Divine) protection.
51:19. And in their wealth there was a due share for the beggar and for one who is denied (good).
51:20. And in the earth are signs for those who are sure,
51:21. And in yourselves do you not see?
51:22. And in the heavens is your sustenance and that which you are promised.
51:23. So by the Lord of the heavens and the earth! it is surely the truth, just as you speak.

* * *

51:24. Has the story of Abraham's honoured guests reached thee?
51:25. When they came to him, they said Peace! Peace! said he. Strangers!
51:26. Then he turned aside to his family and brought a fat calf.
51:27. So he placed it before them. He said: Will you not eat?
51:28. So he conceived a fear of them. They said: Fear not. And they gave him the good news of a boy possessing knowledge.

51. The Scatterers

51:29. Then his wife came up in grief, and she smote her face and said: A barren old woman!

51:30. They said: Thus says thy Lord. Surely He is the Wise, the Knowing.

* * *

51:31. He said: What is your errand, O messengers!

51:32. They said: We have been sent to a guilty people

51:33. That we may send upon them stones of clay,

51:34. Marked from thy Lord for the prodigal.

51:35. Then We brought forth such believers as were there.

51:36. And We found there but a (single) house of Muslims.

51:37. And We left therein a sign for those who fear the painful chastisement.

51:38. And in Moses, when We sent him to Pharaoh with clear authority.

51:39. But he turned away on account of his might and said: An enchanter or a madman!

51:40. So We seized him and his hosts and hurled them into the sea, and he was blameable.

51:41. And in 'Ad, when We sent upon them the destructive wind.

51:42. It spared naught that it came against, but it made it like ashes.

51:43. And in Thamad, when it was said to them: Enjoy yourselves for a while.

51:44. But they revolted against the commandment of their Lord, so the punishment overtook them, while they saw.

51:45. So they were unable to rise up, nor could they defend themselves;

51:46. And the people of Noah before. Surely they were a transgressing people.

* * *

51:47. And the heaven, We raised it high with power, and We are Makers

فَأَقْبَلَتِ امْرَأَتُهُ فِي صَرَّةٍ فَصَكَّتْ وَجْهَهَا وَقَالَتْ عَجُوزٌ عَقِيمٌ (٢٩)

قَالُوا كَذَلِكِ قَالَ رَبُّكِ إِنَّهُ هُوَ الْحَكِيمُ الْعَلِيمُ (٣٠)

قَالَ فَمَا خَطْبُكُمْ أَيُّهَا الْمُرْسَلُونَ (٣١)

قَالُوا إِنَّا أُرْسِلْنَا إِلَى قَوْمٍ مُجْرِمِينَ (٣٢)

لِنُرْسِلَ عَلَيْهِمْ حِجَارَةً مِنْ طِينٍ (٣٣)

مُسَوَّمَةً عِنْدَ رَبِّكَ لِلْمُسْرِفِينَ (٣٤)

فَأَخْرَجْنَا مَنْ كَانَ فِيهَا مِنَ الْمُؤْمِنِينَ (٣٥)

فَمَا وَجَدْنَا فِيهَا غَيْرَ بَيْتٍ مِنَ الْمُسْلِمِينَ (٣٦)

وَتَرَكْنَا فِيهَا آيَةً لِلَّذِينَ يَخَافُونَ الْعَذَابَ الْأَلِيمَ (٣٧)

وَفِي مُوسَى إِذْ أَرْسَلْنَاهُ إِلَى فِرْعَوْنَ بِسُلْطَانٍ مُبِينٍ (٣٨)

فَتَوَلَّى بِرُكْنِهِ وَقَالَ سَاحِرٌ أَوْ مَجْنُونٌ (٣٩)

فَأَخَذْنَاهُ وَجُنُودَهُ فَنَبَذْنَاهُمْ فِي الْيَمِّ وَهُوَ مُلِيمٌ (٤٠)

وَفِي عَادٍ إِذْ أَرْسَلْنَا عَلَيْهِمُ الرِّيحَ الْعَقِيمَ (٤١)

مَا تَذَرُ مِنْ شَيْءٍ أَتَتْ عَلَيْهِ إِلَّا جَعَلَتْهُ كَالرَّمِيمِ (٤٢)

وَفِي ثَمُودَ إِذْ قِيلَ لَهُمْ تَمَتَّعُوا حَتَّى حِينٍ (٤٣)

فَعَتَوْا عَنْ أَمْرِ رَبِّهِمْ فَأَخَذَتْهُمُ الصَّاعِقَةُ وَهُمْ يَنْظُرُونَ (٤٤)

فَمَا اسْتَطَاعُوا مِنْ قِيَامٍ وَمَا كَانُوا مُنْتَصِرِينَ (٤٥)

of the vast extent.

51:48. And the earth, We have spread it out. How well We prepared it!

51:49. And of everything We have created pairs that you may be mindful.

51:50. So flee to Allah. Surely I am a plain warner to you from Him.

51:51. And do not set up with Allah another god. Surely I am a plain warner to you from Him.

51:52. Thus there came not a messenger to those before them but they said: An enchanter or a madman!

51:53. Have they charged each other with this? Nay, they are an inordinate people.

51:54. So turn away from them, for thou art not to blame;

51:55. And remind, for reminding profits the believers.

51:56. And I have not created the jinn and the men except that they should serve Me.

51:57. I desire no sustenance from them, nor do I desire that they should feed Me.

51:58. Surely Allah is the Bestower of sustenance, the Lord of Power, the Strong.

51:59. Surely the lot of the wrongdoers is as was the lot of their companions, so let them not ask Me to hasten on.

51:60. Woe, then, to those who disbelieve because of that day of theirs which they are promised!

وَقَوْمَ نُوحٍ مِنْ قَبْلُ إِنَّهُمْ كَانُوا قَوْمًا فَاسِقِينَ (٤٦)

وَالسَّمَاءَ بَنَيْنَاهَا بِأَيْدٍ وَإِنَّا لَمُوسِعُونَ (٤٧)

وَالْأَرْضَ فَرَشْنَاهَا فَنِعْمَ الْمَاهِدُونَ (٤٨)

وَمِنْ كُلِّ شَيْءٍ خَلَقْنَا زَوْجَيْنِ لَعَلَّكُمْ تَذَكَّرُونَ (٤٩)

فَفِرُّوا إِلَى اللَّهِ إِنِّي لَكُمْ مِنْهُ نَذِيرٌ مُبِينٌ (٥٠)

وَلَا تَجْعَلُوا مَعَ اللَّهِ إِلَهًا آخَرَ إِنِّي لَكُمْ مِنْهُ نَذِيرٌ مُبِينٌ (٥١)

كَذَلِكَ مَا أَتَى الَّذِينَ مِنْ قَبْلِهِمْ مِنْ رَسُولٍ إِلَّا قَالُوا سَاحِرٌ أَوْ مَجْنُونٌ (٥٢)

أَتَوَاصَوْا بِهِ بَلْ هُمْ قَوْمٌ طَاغُونَ (٥٣)

فَتَوَلَّ عَنْهُمْ فَمَا أَنْتَ بِمَلُومٍ (٥٤)

وَذَكِّرْ فَإِنَّ الذِّكْرَى تَنْفَعُ الْمُؤْمِنِينَ (٥٥)

وَمَا خَلَقْتُ الْجِنَّ وَالْإِنْسَ إِلَّا لِيَعْبُدُونِ (٥٦)

مَا أُرِيدُ مِنْهُمْ مِنْ رِزْقٍ وَمَا أُرِيدُ أَنْ يُطْعِمُونِ (٥٧)

إِنَّ اللَّهَ هُوَ الرَّزَّاقُ ذُو الْقُوَّةِ الْمَتِينُ (٥٨)

فَإِنَّ لِلَّذِينَ ظَلَمُوا ذَنُوبًا مِثْلَ ذَنُوبِ أَصْحَابِهِمْ فَلَا يَسْتَعْجِلُونِ (٥٩)

فَوَيْلٌ لِلَّذِينَ كَفَرُوا مِنْ يَوْمِهِمُ الَّذِي يُوعَدُونَ (٦٠)

52. The Mountain

In the name of Allah, the Beneficent, the Merciful.
52:1. By the Mountain!
52:2. And a Book written
52:3. On unfolded vellum!
52:4. And the frequented House,
52:5. And the elevated canopy,
52:6. And the swollen sea!
52:7. The chastisement of thy Lord will surely come to pass --
52:8. There is none to avert it;
52:9. On the day when the heaven will be in a state of commotion,
52:10. And the mountains will pass away, fleeing.
52:11. Woe on that day to the deniers,
52:12. Who amuse themselves by vain talk.
52:13. The day when they are driven to hell-fire with violence.
52:14. This is the Fire, which you gave the lie to.
52:15. Is it magic or do you not see?
52:16. Burn in it, then bear (it) patiently, or bear (it) not, it is the same to you. You are requited only for what you did.
52:17. The dutiful will be surely in Gardens and bliss,
52:18. Rejoicing because of what their Lord has given them; and their Lord saved them from the chastisement of the burning Fire.
52:19. Eat and drink with pleasure for what you did,
52:20. Reclining on thrones set in lines, and We shall join them to pure beautiful ones.
52:21. And those who believe and whose offspring follow them in faith -- We unite with them their offspring and We shall deprive them of naught of their work. Every man is pledged for what he does.
52:22. And We shall aid them with fruit and flesh, as they desire.

52. The Mountain

52:23. They pass therein from one to another a cup, wherein is neither vanity, nor sin.
52:24. And round them go boys of theirs as if they were hidden pearls.
52:25. And they will advance to each other, questioning
52:26. Saying: Surely we feared before on account of our families.
52:27. But Allah has been gracious to us and He has saved us from the chastisement of the hot wind.
52:28. Surely We called upon Him before. Surely, He is the Benign, the Merciful.

* * *

52:29. So remind for, by the grace of thy Lord thou art no soothsayer, nor madman.
52:30. Or say they: A poet -- we wait for him the evil accidents of time.
52:31. Say: Wait, I too wait along with you.
52:32. Or do their understandings bid them this? Or are they an inordinate people?
52:33. Or say they: He has forged it. Nay, they have no faith.
52:34. Then let them bring a saying like it, if they are truthful.
52:35. Or were they created without a (creative) agency? Or are they the creators?
52:36. Or did they create the heavens and the earth? Nay, they are sure of nothing.
52:37. Or have they the treasures of thy Lord with them? Or have they absolute authority?
52:38. Or have they the means by which they listen? Then let their listener bring a clear authority.
52:39. Or has He daughters and you have sons?
52:40. Or askest thou a reward from them so that they are over-burdened by a debt?
52:41. Or possess they the unseen, so

كَسَبَ رَهِينٌ (٢١)
وَأَمْدَدْنَاهُم بِفَاكِهَةٍ وَلَحْمٍ مِّمَّا يَشْتَهُونَ (٢٢)
يَتَنَازَعُونَ فِيهَا كَأْسًا لَّا لَغْوٌ فِيهَا وَلَا تَأْثِيمٌ (٢٣)
وَيَطُوفُ عَلَيْهِمْ غِلْمَانٌ لَّهُمْ كَأَنَّهُمْ لُؤْلُؤٌ مَّكْنُونٌ (٢٤)
وَأَقْبَلَ بَعْضُهُمْ عَلَىٰ بَعْضٍ يَتَسَاءَلُونَ (٢٥)
قَالُوا إِنَّا كُنَّا قَبْلُ فِي أَهْلِنَا مُشْفِقِينَ (٢٦)
فَمَنَّ اللَّهُ عَلَيْنَا وَوَقَانَا عَذَابَ السَّمُومِ (٢٧)
إِنَّا كُنَّا مِن قَبْلُ نَدْعُوهُ إِنَّهُ هُوَ الْبَرُّ الرَّحِيمُ (٢٨)
فَذَكِّرْ فَمَا أَنتَ بِنِعْمَتِ رَبِّكَ بِكَاهِنٍ وَلَا مَجْنُونٍ (٢٩)
أَمْ يَقُولُونَ شَاعِرٌ نَّتَرَبَّصُ بِهِ رَيْبَ الْمَنُونِ (٣٠)
قُلْ تَرَبَّصُوا فَإِنِّي مَعَكُم مِّنَ الْمُتَرَبِّصِينَ (٣١)
أَمْ تَأْمُرُهُمْ أَحْلَامُهُم بِهَٰذَا أَمْ هُمْ قَوْمٌ طَاغُونَ (٣٢)
أَمْ يَقُولُونَ تَقَوَّلَهُ بَل لَّا يُؤْمِنُونَ (٣٣)
فَلْيَأْتُوا بِحَدِيثٍ مِّثْلِهِ إِن كَانُوا صَادِقِينَ (٣٤)
أَمْ خُلِقُوا مِنْ غَيْرِ شَيْءٍ أَمْ هُمُ الْخَالِقُونَ (٣٥)
أَمْ خَلَقُوا السَّمَاوَاتِ وَالْأَرْضَ بَل لَّا يُوقِنُونَ (٣٦)
أَمْ عِندَهُمْ خَزَائِنُ رَبِّكَ أَمْ هُمُ الْمُسَيْطِرُونَ (٣٧)

they write (it) down?
52:42. Or do they intend a plot? But those who disbelieve will be the ensnared ones in the plot.
52:43. Or have they a god other than Allah? Glory be to Allah from what they set up (with Him)
52:44. And if they were to see a portion of the heaven coming down, they would say: Piled-up clouds!
52:45. Leave them then till they meet that day of theirs wherein they are smitten with punishment:
52:46. The day when their struggle will avail them naught, nor will they be helped.
52:47. And surely for those who do wrong there is a chastisement besides that; but most of them knnw not.
52:48. And wait patiently for the judgment of thy Lord, for surely thou art before Our eyes, and celebrate the praise of thy Lord, when thou risest,
52:49. And in the night, give Him glory, too, and at the setting of the stars.

53. The Star

In the name of Allah, the Beneficent, the Merciful.
53:1. By the star when it sets!
53:2. Your companion errs not, nor does he deviate.
53:3. Nor does he speak out of desire.
53:4. It is naught but revelation that is revealed --
53:5. One Mighty in Power has taught him,
53:6. The Lord of Strength. So he attained to perfection,

53. The Star

53:7. And he is in the highest part of the horizon.
53:8. Then he drew near, drew nearer yet,
53:9. So he was the measure of two bows or closer still.
53:10. So He revealed to His servant what He revealed.
53:11. The heart was not untrue in seeing what he saw.
53:12. Do you then dispute with him as to what he saw?
53:13. And certainly he saw Him in another descent,
53:14. At the farthest lote-tree.
53:15. Near it is the Garden of Abode.
53:16. When that which covers covered the lote-tree
53:17. The eye turned not aside, nor did it exceed the limit.
53:18. Certainly he saw of the greatest signs of his Lord.
53:19. Have you then considered Lat and 'Uzzi,
53:20. And another, the third, Manit?
53:21. Are the males for you and for Him the females?
53:22. This indeed is an unjust division!
53:23. They are naught but names which you have named, you and your fathers -- Allah has sent no authority for them. They follow but conjecture and what (their) souls desire. And certainly the guidance has come to them from their Lord.
53:24. Or shall man have what he wishes?
53:25. But for Allah is the Hereafter and the former (life).

***

53:26. And how many angels are in the heavens, whose intercession avails naught except after Allah gives permission to whom He pleases and chooses.
53:27. Surely those who believe not in the Hereafter name the angels with female names.

ثُمَّ دَنَا فَتَدَلَّى (٨)
فَكَانَ قَابَ قَوْسَيْنِ أَوْ أَدْنَى (٩)
فَأَوْحَى إِلَى عَبْدِهِ مَا أَوْحَى (١٠)
مَا كَذَبَ الْفُؤَادُ مَا رَأَى (١١)
أَفَتُمَارُونَهُ عَلَى مَا يَرَى (١٢)
وَلَقَدْ رَآهُ نَزْلَةً أُخْرَى (١٣)
عِنْدَ سِدْرَةِ الْمُنْتَهَى (١٤)
عِنْدَهَا جَنَّةُ الْمَأْوَى (١٥)
إِذْ يَغْشَى السِّدْرَةَ مَا يَغْشَى (١٦)
مَا زَاغَ الْبَصَرُ وَمَا طَغَى (١٧)
لَقَدْ رَأَى مِنْ آيَاتِ رَبِّهِ الْكُبْرَى (١٨)
أَفَرَأَيْتُمُ اللَّاتَ وَالْعُزَّى (١٩)
وَمَنَاةَ الثَّالِثَةَ الْأُخْرَى (٢٠)
أَلَكُمُ الذَّكَرُ وَلَهُ الْأُنْثَى (٢١)
تِلْكَ إِذًا قِسْمَةٌ ضِيزَى (٢٢)
إِنْ هِيَ إِلَّا أَسْمَاءٌ سَمَّيْتُمُوهَا أَنْتُمْ وَآبَاؤُكُمْ مَا أَنْزَلَ اللَّهُ بِهَا مِنْ سُلْطَانٍ إِنْ يَتَّبِعُونَ إِلَّا الظَّنَّ وَمَا تَهْوَى الْأَنْفُسُ وَلَقَدْ جَاءَهُمْ مِنْ رَبِّهِمُ الْهُدَى (٢٣)
أَمْ لِلْإِنْسَانِ مَا تَمَنَّى (٢٤)
فَلِلَّهِ الْآخِرَةُ وَالْأُولَى (٢٥)
وَكَمْ مِنْ مَلَكٍ فِي السَّمَاوَاتِ لَا تُغْنِي شَفَاعَتُهُمْ شَيْئًا إِلَّا مِنْ بَعْدِ أَنْ يَأْذَنَ اللَّهُ لِمَنْ يَشَاءُ وَيَرْضَى (٢٦)
إِنَّ الَّذِينَ لَا يُؤْمِنُونَ بِالْآخِرَةِ لَيُسَمُّونَ الْمَلَائِكَةَ تَسْمِيَةَ الْأُنْثَى (٢٧)
وَمَا لَهُمْ بِهِ مِنْ عِلْمٍ إِنْ يَتَّبِعُونَ إِلَّا الظَّنَّ وَإِنَّ الظَّنَّ لَا يُغْنِي مِنَ الْحَقِّ شَيْئًا (٢٨)

53. The Star

53:28. And they have no knowledge of it. They follow but conjecture, and surely conjecture avails naught against Truth.
53:29. So shun him who turns his back upon Our Reminder, and desires nothing but this world's life.
53:30. That is their goal of knowledge. Surely thy Lord knows best him who strays from His path and He knows best him who goes aright.
53:31. And Allah's is whatever is in the heavens and whatever is in the earth, that He may reward those who do evil for that which they do, and reward those who do good with goodness.
53:32. Those who avoid the great sins and the indecencies, but the passing idea surely thy Lord is Liberal in Forgiving. He knows best when He brings you forth from the earth and when you are embryos in the wombs of your mothers; so ascribe not purity to yourselves. He knows him best who guards against evil.

* * *

53:33. Seest thou him who turns back,
53:34. And gives a little, then withholds?
53:35. Has he the knowledge of the unseen so that he can see?
53:36. Or has he not been informed of what is in the scriptures of Moses,
53:37. And (of) Abraham who fulfilled (commandments)?
53:38. That no bearer of a burden bears another's burden:
53:39. And that man can have nothing but what he strives for:
53:40. And that his striving will soon be seen.
53:41. Then he will be rewarded for it with the fullest reward:
53:42. And that to thy Lord is the goal:
53:43. And that He it is Who makes (men) laugh and makes (them) weep:
53:44. And that He it is Who causes death and gives life:

فَأَعْرِضْ عَنْ مَنْ تَوَلَّى عَنْ ذِكْرِنَا وَلَمْ يُرِدْ إِلَّا الْحَيَاةَ الدُّنْيَا (٢٩) ذَلِكَ مَبْلَغُهُمْ مِنَ الْعِلْمِ إِنَّ رَبَّكَ هُوَ أَعْلَمُ بِمَنْ ضَلَّ عَنْ سَبِيلِهِ وَهُوَ أَعْلَمُ بِمَنِ اهْتَدَى (٣٠) وَلِلَّهِ مَا فِي السَّمَاوَاتِ وَمَا فِي الْأَرْضِ لِيَجْزِيَ الَّذِينَ أَسَاءُوا بِمَا عَمِلُوا وَيَجْزِيَ الَّذِينَ أَحْسَنُوا بِالْحُسْنَى (٣١) الَّذِينَ يَجْتَنِبُونَ كَبَائِرَ الْإِثْمِ وَالْفَوَاحِشَ إِلَّا اللَّمَمَ إِنَّ رَبَّكَ وَاسِعُ الْمَغْفِرَةِ هُوَ أَعْلَمُ بِكُمْ إِذْ أَنْشَأَكُمْ مِنَ الْأَرْضِ وَإِذْ أَنْتُمْ أَجِنَّةٌ فِي بُطُونِ أُمَّهَاتِكُمْ فَلَا تُزَكُّوا أَنْفُسَكُمْ هُوَ أَعْلَمُ بِمَنِ اتَّقَى (٣٢) أَفَرَأَيْتَ الَّذِي تَوَلَّى (٣٣) وَأَعْطَى قَلِيلًا وَأَكْدَى (٣٤) أَعِنْدَهُ عِلْمُ الْغَيْبِ فَهُوَ يَرَى (٣٥) أَمْ لَمْ يُنَبَّأْ بِمَا فِي صُحُفِ مُوسَى (٣٦) وَإِبْرَاهِيمَ الَّذِي وَفَّى (٣٧) أَلَّا تَزِرُ وَازِرَةٌ وِزْرَ أُخْرَى (٣٨) وَأَنْ لَيْسَ لِلْإِنْسَانِ إِلَّا مَا سَعَى (٣٩) وَأَنَّ سَعْيَهُ سَوْفَ يُرَى (٤٠) ثُمَّ يُجْزَاهُ الْجَزَاءَ الْأَوْفَى (٤١) وَأَنَّ إِلَى رَبِّكَ الْمُنْتَهَى (٤٢) وَأَنَّهُ هُوَ أَضْحَكَ وَأَبْكَى (٤٣) وَأَنَّهُ هُوَ أَمَاتَ وَأَحْيَا (٤٤) وَأَنَّهُ خَلَقَ الزَّوْجَيْنِ الذَّكَرَ وَالْأُنْثَى (٤٥) مِنْ نُطْفَةٍ إِذَا تُمْنَى (٤٦) وَأَنَّ عَلَيْهِ النَّشْأَةَ الْأُخْرَى (٤٧) وَأَنَّهُ هُوَ أَغْنَى وَأَقْنَى (٤٨)

53:45. And that He creates pairs, the male and the female:
53:46. From the small life-germ when it is adapted:
53:47. And that He has ordained the second bringing forth:
53:48. And that He it is Who gives wealth and contentment:
53:49. And that He is the Lord of Sirius:
53:50. And that He destroyed the first 'Ad:
53:51. And Thamud, so He spared not:
53:52. And the people of Noah before. Surely they were most iniquitous and inordinate.
53:53. And the overthrown cities, He hurled down:
53:54. So there covered them that which coveted.
53:55. Which, then, of thy Lord's benefits wilt thou dispute?
53:56. This is a warner of the warners of old.
53:57. The near Event draws nigh.
53:58. There is none besides Allah to remove it.
53:59. Wonder you then at this announcement?
53:60. And do you laugh and not weep,
53:61. While you sport?
53:62. So bow down in prostration before Allah and serve (Him).

54. The Moon

In the name of Allah, the Beneficent, the Merciful.
54:1. The hour drew nigh and the moon was rent asunder.
54:2. And if they see a sign, they turn away and say: Strong enchantment!
54:3. And they deny and follow their low desires; and every affair is settled.
54:4. And certainly narratives have come to them, which should deter --
54:5. Consummate wisdom but warnings avail not;

54. The Moon

54:6. So turn away from them. On the day when the Inviter invites them to a hard task --
54:7. Their eyes cast down, they will go forth from their graves as if they were scattered locusts,
54:8. Hastening to the Inviter. The disbelievers will say: This is a hard day!
54:9. Before them the people of Noah rejected -- they rejected Our servant and called (him) mad, and he was driven away.
54:10. So he called upon his Lord: I am overcome, so do Thou help.
54:11. Then We opened the gates of heaven with water pouring down,
54:12. And made water to flow forth in the land in springs, so the water gathered together according to a measure already ordained.
54:13. And We bore him on that which was made of planks and nails,
54:14. Floating on, before Our eyes -- a reward for him who was denied.
54:15. And certainly We left it as a sign, but is there any that will mind?
54:16. How terrible was then My chastisement and My warning!
54:17. And certainly We have made the Qur'an easy to remember, but is there any one who will mind?
54:18. 'Ad denied, so how terrible was My chastisement and My warning!
54:19. Surely We sent on them a furious wind in a day of bitter ill-luck,
54:20. Tearing men away as if they were the trunks of palm-trees torn up.
54:21. How terrible was then My chastisement and My warning!
54:22. And certainly We have made the Qur'an easy to remember, but is there any one who will mind?

* * *

54:23. Thamud rejected the warning.
54:24. So they said: What! A single mortal from among us! Shall we follow him? We shall then be in sure error and

54. The Moon

distress.

54:25. Has the reminder been sent to him from among us? Nay, he is an insolent liar!

54:26. To-morrow they will know who is the liar, the insolent one.

54:27. Surely We are going to send the she-camel as a trial for them; so watch them and have patience.

54:28. And inform them that the water is shared between them; every share of the water shall be attended.

54:29. But they called their companion, so he took (a sword) and hamstrung (her).

54:30. How (terrible) was then My chastisement and My warning!

54:31. Surely We sent upon them a single cry, so they were like the dry fragments of trees, which the maker of an enclosure collects.

54:32. And certainly We have made the Qur'an easy to remember, but is there any one who will mind?

54:33. The people of Lot treated the warning as a lie.

54:34. Surely We sent upon them a stone-storm, except Lot's followers; We saved them a little before daybreak --

54:35. A favour from Us. Thus do We reward him who gives thanks.

54:36. And certainly he warned them of Our violent seizure, but they disputed the warning.

54:37. And certainly they endeavoured to turn him from his guests, but We blinded their eyes so taste My chastisement and My warning.

54:38. And certainly a lasting chastisement overtook them in the morning.

54:39. So taste My chastisement and My warning.

54:40. And certainly We have made the Qur'an easy to remember, but is there any one who will mind?

* * *

54:41. And certainly the warning came

كَذَّبَتْ ثَمُودُ بِالنُّذُرِ (٢٣)

فَقَالُوا أَبَشَرًا مِنَّا وَاحِدًا نَتَّبِعُهُ إِنَّا إِذًا لَفِي ضَلَالٍ وَسُعُرٍ (٢٤)

أَؤُلْقِيَ الذِّكْرُ عَلَيْهِ مِنْ بَيْنِنَا بَلْ هُوَ كَذَّابٌ أَشِرٌ (٢٥)

سَيَعْلَمُونَ غَدًا مَنِ الْكَذَّابُ الْأَشِرُ (٢٦)

إِنَّا مُرْسِلُو النَّاقَةِ فِتْنَةً لَهُمْ فَارْتَقِبْهُمْ وَاصْطَبِرْ (٢٧)

وَنَبِّئْهُمْ أَنَّ الْمَاءَ قِسْمَةٌ بَيْنَهُمْ كُلُّ شِرْبٍ مُحْتَضَرٌ (٢٨)

فَنَادَوْا صَاحِبَهُمْ فَتَعَاطَى فَعَقَرَ (٢٩)

فَكَيْفَ كَانَ عَذَابِي وَنُذُرِ (٣٠)

إِنَّا أَرْسَلْنَا عَلَيْهِمْ صَيْحَةً وَاحِدَةً فَكَانُوا كَهَشِيمِ الْمُحْتَظِرِ (٣١)

وَلَقَدْ يَسَّرْنَا الْقُرْآنَ لِلذِّكْرِ فَهَلْ مِنْ مُدَّكِرٍ (٣٢)

كَذَّبَتْ قَوْمُ لُوطٍ بِالنُّذُرِ (٣٣)

إِنَّا أَرْسَلْنَا عَلَيْهِمْ حَاصِبًا إِلَّا آلَ لُوطٍ نَجَّيْنَاهُمْ بِسَحَرٍ (٣٤)

نِعْمَةً مِنْ عِنْدِنَا كَذَلِكَ نَجْزِي مَنْ شَكَرَ (٣٥)

وَلَقَدْ أَنْذَرَهُمْ بَطْشَتَنَا فَتَمَارَوْا بِالنُّذُرِ (٣٦)

وَلَقَدْ رَاوَدُوهُ عَنْ ضَيْفِهِ فَطَمَسْنَا أَعْيُنَهُمْ فَذُوقُوا عَذَابِي وَنُذُرِ (٣٧)

وَلَقَدْ صَبَّحَهُمْ بُكْرَةً عَذَابٌ مُسْتَقِرٌّ (٣٨)

فَذُوقُوا عَذَابِي وَنُذُرِ (٣٩)

وَلَقَدْ يَسَّرْنَا الْقُرْآنَ لِلذِّكْرِ فَهَلْ مِنْ مُدَّكِرٍ (٤٠)

وَلَقَدْ جَاءَ آلَ فِرْعَوْنَ النُّذُرُ (٤١)

كَذَّبُوا بِآيَاتِنَا كُلِّهَا فَأَخَذْنَاهُمْ أَخْذَ

to Pharaoh's people.

54:42. They rejected all Our signs, so We overtook them with the seizing of the Mighty, the Powerful.

54:43. Are your disbelievers better than these, or have you an immunity in the scriptures?

54:44. Or say they We are a host allied together to help each other?

54:45. Soon shall the hosts be routed, and they will show (their) backs.

54:46. Nay, the Hour is their promised time, and the Hour is most grievous and bitter,

54:47. Surely the guilty are in error and distress,

54:48. On the day when they are dragged into the Fire upon their faces: Taste the touch of hell.

54:49. Surely We have created everything according to a measure.

54:50. And Our command is but once, as the twinkling of an eye.

54:51. And certainly We destroyed your fellows, but is there any one who will mind?

54:52. And everything they do is in the writings.

54:53. And everything small and great is written down.

54:54. Surely the dutiful will be among Gardens and rivers,

54:55. In the seat of truth, with a most Powerful King.

55. The Beneficent

In the name of Allah, The Beneficent, the Merciful.

55:1. The Beneficent
55:2. Taught the Qur'an.
55:3. He created man,
55:4. Taught him expression.
55:5. The sun and the moon follow a reckoning,
55:6. And the herbs and the trees adore (Him).

55. The Beneficent

وَالسَّمَاءَ رَفَعَهَا وَوَضَعَ الْمِيزَانَ (٧) أَلَّا تَطْغَوْا فِي الْمِيزَانِ (٨) وَأَقِيمُوا الْوَزْنَ بِالْقِسْطِ وَلَا تُخْسِرُوا الْمِيزَانَ (٩) وَالْأَرْضَ وَضَعَهَا لِلْأَنَامِ (١٠) فِيهَا فَاكِهَةٌ وَالنَّخْلُ ذَاتُ الْأَكْمَامِ (١١) وَالْحَبُّ ذُو الْعَصْفِ وَالرَّيْحَانُ (١٢) فَبِأَيِّ آلَاءِ رَبِّكُمَا تُكَذِّبَانِ (١٣) خَلَقَ الْإِنْسَانَ مِنْ صَلْصَالٍ كَالْفَخَّارِ (١٤) وَخَلَقَ الْجَانَّ مِنْ مَارِجٍ مِنْ نَارٍ (١٥) فَبِأَيِّ آلَاءِ رَبِّكُمَا تُكَذِّبَانِ (١٦) رَبُّ الْمَشْرِقَيْنِ وَرَبُّ الْمَغْرِبَيْنِ (١٧) فَبِأَيِّ آلَاءِ رَبِّكُمَا تُكَذِّبَانِ (١٨) مَرَجَ الْبَحْرَيْنِ يَلْتَقِيَانِ (١٩) بَيْنَهُمَا بَرْزَخٌ لَا يَبْغِيَانِ (٢٠) فَبِأَيِّ آلَاءِ رَبِّكُمَا تُكَذِّبَانِ (٢١) يَخْرُجُ مِنْهُمَا اللُّؤْلُؤُ وَالْمَرْجَانُ (٢٢) فَبِأَيِّ آلَاءِ رَبِّكُمَا تُكَذِّبَانِ (٢٣) وَلَهُ الْجَوَارِ الْمُنْشَآتُ فِي الْبَحْرِ كَالْأَعْلَامِ (٢٤) فَبِأَيِّ آلَاءِ رَبِّكُمَا تُكَذِّبَانِ (٢٥) كُلُّ مَنْ عَلَيْهَا فَانٍ (٢٦) وَيَبْقَىٰ وَجْهُ رَبِّكَ ذُو الْجَلَالِ وَالْإِكْرَامِ (٢٧) فَبِأَيِّ آلَاءِ رَبِّكُمَا تُكَذِّبَانِ (٢٨) يَسْأَلُهُ مَنْ فِي السَّمَاوَاتِ وَالْأَرْضِ كُلَّ يَوْمٍ هُوَ فِي شَأْنٍ (٢٩)

55:7. And the heaven, He raised it high, and He set up the measure,
55:8. That you may not exceed the measure,
55:9. And keep up the balance with equity, nor fall short in the measure.
55:10. And the earth, He has set it for (His) creatures;
55:11. Therein is fruit and palms having sheathed clusters,
55:12. And the grain with (its) husk and fragrance.
55:13. Which then of the bounties of your Lord will you deny?
55:14. He created man from dry clay like earthen vessels,
55:15. And He created the jinn of a flame of fire.
55:16. Which then of the bounties of your Lord will you deny?
55:17. Lord of the two Easts, and Lord of the two Wests.
55:18. Which then of the bounties of your Lord will you deny?
55:19. He has made the two seas to flow freely they meet:
55:20. Between them is a barrier which they cannot pass.
55:21. Which then of the bounties of your Lord will you deny?
55:22. There come forth from them both, pearls large and small.
55:23. Which then of the bounties of your Lord will you deny?
55:24. And His are the ships reared aloft in the sea like mountains.
55:25. Which then of the bounties of your Lord will you deny?

***

55:26. Every one on it passes away --
55:27. And there endures for ever the person of thy Lord, the Lord of glory and honour.
55:28. Which then of the bounties of your Lord will you deny?
55:29. All those in the heavens and the earth ask of Him. Every moment He is in a state (of glory).

55. The Beneficent

55:30. Which then of the bounties of your Lord will you deny?
55:31. Soon shall We apply Ourselves to you, O you two armies.
55:32. Which then of the bounties of your Lord will you deny?
55:33. O assembly of jinn and men, if you are able to pass through the regions of the heavens and the earth, then pass through. You cannot pass through but with authority.
55:34. Which then of the bounties of your Lord will you deny?
55:35. The flames of fire and sparks of brass will be sent upon you, then you will not be able to defend yourselves.
55:36. Which then of the bounties of your Lord will you deny?
55:37. So when the heaven is rent asunder, so it becomes red like red hide.
55:38. Which then of the bounties of your Lord will you deny?
55:39. So on that day neither man nor jinni will be asked about his sin.
55:40. Which then of the bounties of your Lord will you deny?
55:41. The guilty will be known by their marks, so they shall be seized by the forelocks and the feet.
55:42. Which then of the bounties of your Lord will you deny?
55:43. This is the hell which the guilty deny.
55:44. Round about shall they go between it and hot, boiling water.
55:45. Which then of the bounties of your Lord will you deny?

* * *

55:46. And for him who fears to stand before his Lord are two Gardens.
55:47. Which then of the bounties of your Lord will you deny?
55:48. Full of varieties,
55:49. Which then of the bounties of your Lord will you deny?
55:50. Therein are two fountains flowing.

فَبِأَيِّ آلَاءِ رَبِّكُمَا تُكَذِّبَانِ (٣٠)
سَنَفْرُغُ لَكُمْ أَيُّهَ الثَّقَلَانِ (٣١)
فَبِأَيِّ آلَاءِ رَبِّكُمَا تُكَذِّبَانِ (٣٢)
يَا مَعْشَرَ الْجِنِّ وَالْإِنْسِ إِنِ اسْتَطَعْتُمْ أَنْ تَنْفُذُوا مِنْ أَقْطَارِ السَّمَاوَاتِ وَالْأَرْضِ فَانْفُذُوا لَا تَنْفُذُونَ إِلَّا بِسُلْطَانٍ (٣٣)
فَبِأَيِّ آلَاءِ رَبِّكُمَا تُكَذِّبَانِ (٣٤)
يُرْسَلُ عَلَيْكُمَا شُوَاظٌ مِنْ نَارٍ وَنُحَاسٌ فَلَا تَنْتَصِرَانِ (٣٥)
فَبِأَيِّ آلَاءِ رَبِّكُمَا تُكَذِّبَانِ (٣٦)
فَإِذَا انْشَقَّتِ السَّمَاءُ فَكَانَتْ وَرْدَةً كَالدِّهَانِ (٣٧)
فَبِأَيِّ آلَاءِ رَبِّكُمَا تُكَذِّبَانِ (٣٨)
فَيَوْمَئِذٍ لَا يُسْأَلُ عَنْ ذَنْبِهِ إِنْسٌ وَلَا جَانٌّ (٣٩)
فَبِأَيِّ آلَاءِ رَبِّكُمَا تُكَذِّبَانِ (٤٠)
يُعْرَفُ الْمُجْرِمُونَ بِسِيمَاهُمْ فَيُؤْخَذُ بِالنَّوَاصِي وَالْأَقْدَامِ (٤١)
فَبِأَيِّ آلَاءِ رَبِّكُمَا تُكَذِّبَانِ (٤٢)
هَذِهِ جَهَنَّمُ الَّتِي يُكَذِّبُ بِهَا الْمُجْرِمُونَ (٤٣)
يَطُوفُونَ بَيْنَهَا وَبَيْنَ حَمِيمٍ آنٍ (٤٤)
فَبِأَيِّ آلَاءِ رَبِّكُمَا تُكَذِّبَانِ (٤٥)
وَلِمَنْ خَافَ مَقَامَ رَبِّهِ جَنَّتَانِ (٤٦)
فَبِأَيِّ آلَاءِ رَبِّكُمَا تُكَذِّبَانِ (٤٧)
ذَوَاتَا أَفْنَانٍ (٤٨)
فَبِأَيِّ آلَاءِ رَبِّكُمَا تُكَذِّبَانِ (٤٩)
فِيهِمَا عَيْنَانِ تَجْرِيَانِ (٥٠)
فَبِأَيِّ آلَاءِ رَبِّكُمَا تُكَذِّبَانِ (٥١)
فِيهِمَا مِنْ كُلِّ فَاكِهَةٍ زَوْجَانِ (٥٢)
فَبِأَيِّ آلَاءِ رَبِّكُمَا تُكَذِّبَانِ (٥٣)

55. The Beneficent

55:51. Which then of the bounties of your Lord will you deny?
55:52. Therein are pairs of every fruit.
55:53. Which then of the bounties of your Lord will you deny?
55:54. Reclining on beds, whose inner coverings are of silk brocade. And the fruits of the two Gardens are within reach.
55:55. Which then of the bounties of your Lord will you deny?
55:56. Therein are those restraining their glances, whom no man nor jinni has touched before them.
55:57. Which then of the bounties of your Lord will you deny?
55:58. As though they were rubies and pearls.
55:59. Which then of the bounties of your Lord will you deny?
55:60. Is the reward of goodness aught but goodness?
55:61. Which then of the bounties of your Lord will you deny?
55:62. And besides those are two (other) Gardens.
55:63. Which then of the bounties of your Lord will you deny?
55:64. Inclining to blackness.
55:65. Which then of the bounties of your Lord will you deny?
55:66. Therein are two springs gushing forth.
55:67. Which then of the bounties of your Lord will you deny?
55:68. Therein are fruits and palms and pomegranates.
55:69. Which then of the bounties of your Lord will you deny?
55:70. Therein are goodly beautiful ones.
55:71. Which then of the bounties of your Lord will you deny?
55:72. Pure ones confined to pavilions.
55:73. Which then of the bounties of your Lord will you deny?
55:74. Before them man has not touched them, nor jinni.

مُتَّكِئِينَ عَلَىٰ فُرُشٍ بَطَائِنُهَا مِنْ إِسْتَبْرَقٍ وَجَنَى الْجَنَّتَيْنِ دَانٍ (٥٤)
فَبِأَيِّ آلَاءِ رَبِّكُمَا تُكَذِّبَانِ (٥٥)
فِيهِنَّ قَاصِرَاتُ الطَّرْفِ لَمْ يَطْمِثْهُنَّ إِنْسٌ قَبْلَهُمْ وَلَا جَانٌّ (٥٦)
فَبِأَيِّ آلَاءِ رَبِّكُمَا تُكَذِّبَانِ (٥٧)
كَأَنَّهُنَّ الْيَاقُوتُ وَالْمَرْجَانُ (٥٨)
فَبِأَيِّ آلَاءِ رَبِّكُمَا تُكَذِّبَانِ (٥٩)
هَلْ جَزَاءُ الْإِحْسَانِ إِلَّا الْإِحْسَانُ (٦٠)
فَبِأَيِّ آلَاءِ رَبِّكُمَا تُكَذِّبَانِ (٦١)
وَمِنْ دُونِهِمَا جَنَّتَانِ (٦٢)
فَبِأَيِّ آلَاءِ رَبِّكُمَا تُكَذِّبَانِ (٦٣)
مُدْهَامَّتَانِ (٦٤)
فَبِأَيِّ آلَاءِ رَبِّكُمَا تُكَذِّبَانِ (٦٥)
فِيهِمَا عَيْنَانِ نَضَّاخَتَانِ (٦٦)
فَبِأَيِّ آلَاءِ رَبِّكُمَا تُكَذِّبَانِ (٦٧)
فِيهِمَا فَاكِهَةٌ وَنَخْلٌ وَرُمَّانٌ (٦٨)
فَبِأَيِّ آلَاءِ رَبِّكُمَا تُكَذِّبَانِ (٦٩)
فِيهِنَّ خَيْرَاتٌ حِسَانٌ (٧٠)
فَبِأَيِّ آلَاءِ رَبِّكُمَا تُكَذِّبَانِ (٧١)
حُورٌ مَقْصُورَاتٌ فِي الْخِيَامِ (٧٢)
فَبِأَيِّ آلَاءِ رَبِّكُمَا تُكَذِّبَانِ (٧٣)
لَمْ يَطْمِثْهُنَّ إِنْسٌ قَبْلَهُمْ وَلَا جَانٌّ (٧٤)
فَبِأَيِّ آلَاءِ رَبِّكُمَا تُكَذِّبَانِ (٧٥)
مُتَّكِئِينَ عَلَىٰ رَفْرَفٍ خُضْرٍ وَعَبْقَرِيٍّ حِسَانٍ (٧٦)
فَبِأَيِّ آلَاءِ رَبِّكُمَا تُكَذِّبَانِ (٧٧)
تَبَارَكَ اسْمُ رَبِّكَ ذِي الْجَلَالِ وَالْإِكْرَامِ (٧٨)

55:75. Which then of the bounties of your Lord will you deny?
55:76. Reclining on green cushions and beautiful carpets.
55:77. Which then of the bounties of your Lord will you deny?
55:78. Blessed be the name of thy Lord, the Lord of Glory and Honour!

56. The Event

In the name of Allah, the Beneficient, the Merciful.
56:1. When the Event comes to pass --
56:2. There is no belying its coming to pass-3 Abasing (some), exalting (others) --
56:4. When the earth is shaken with a (severe) shaking,
56:5. And the mountains are crumbled to pieces,
56:6. So they are as scattered dust,
56:7. And you are three sorts.
56:8. So those on the right-hand how (happy) are those on the right-hand!
56:9. And those on the left; how (wretched) are those on the left!
56:10. And the foremost are the foremost --
56:11. These are drawn nigh (to Allah).
56:12. In Gardens of bliss
56:13. A multitude from among the first,
56:14. And a few from among those of later times,
56:15. On thrones inwrought,
56:16. Reclining on them, facing each other.
56:17. Round about them will go youths never altering in age,
56:18. With goblets and ewers, and a cup of pure drink --
56:19. They are not affected with headache thereby, nor are they intoxicated,
56:20. And fruits that they choose,
56:21. And flesh of fowl that they

٥٦- سورة الواقعة

بِسْمِ اللَّهِ الرَّحْمَنِ الرَّحِيمِ
إِذَا وَقَعَتِ الْوَاقِعَةُ (١)
لَيْسَ لِوَقْعَتِهَا كَاذِبَةٌ (٢)
خَافِضَةٌ رَافِعَةٌ (٣)
إِذَا رُجَّتِ الْأَرْضُ رَجًّا (٤)
وَبُسَّتِ الْجِبَالُ بَسًّا (٥)
فَكَانَتْ هَبَاءً مُنْبَثًّا (٦)
وَكُنْتُمْ أَزْوَاجًا ثَلَاثَةً (٧)
فَأَصْحَابُ الْمَيْمَنَةِ مَا أَصْحَابُ الْمَيْمَنَةِ (٨)
وَأَصْحَابُ الْمَشْأَمَةِ مَا أَصْحَابُ الْمَشْأَمَةِ (٩)
وَالسَّابِقُونَ السَّابِقُونَ (١٠)
أُولَئِكَ الْمُقَرَّبُونَ (١١)
فِي جَنَّاتِ النَّعِيمِ (١٢)
ثُلَّةٌ مِنَ الْأَوَّلِينَ (١٣)
وَقَلِيلٌ مِنَ الْآخِرِينَ (١٤)
عَلَى سُرُرٍ مَوْضُونَةٍ (١٥)
مُتَّكِئِينَ عَلَيْهَا مُتَقَابِلِينَ (١٦)
يَطُوفُ عَلَيْهِمْ وِلْدَانٌ مُخَلَّدُونَ (١٧)
بِأَكْوَابٍ وَأَبَارِيقَ وَكَأْسٍ مِنْ مَعِينٍ (١٨)
لَا يُصَدَّعُونَ عَنْهَا وَلَا يُنْزِفُونَ (١٩)

desire,
56:22. And pure, beautiful ones,
56:23. Like to hidden pearls.
56:24. A reward for what they did.
56:25. They hear therein no vain or sinful talk --
56:26. But only the saying, Peace! Peace!
56:27. And those on the right hand; how (happy) are those on the right hand!
56:28. Amid thornless lote-trees,
56:29. And clustered banana-trees,
56:30. And extensive shade,
56:31. And water gushing,
56:32. And abundant fruit.
56:33. Neither intercepted, nor forbidden,
56:34. And exalted couches.
56:35. Surely We have created them a (new) creation,
56:36. So We have made them virgins,
56:37. Loving, equals in age,
56:38. For those on the right hand.
56:39. A multitude from among the first,
56:40. And a multitude from among those of later times.

* * *

56:41. And those on the left hand; how (wretched) are those on the left hand!
56:42. In hot wind and boiling water,
56:43. And shadow of black smoke,
56:44. Neither cool nor refreshing.
56:45. Surely they lived before that in ease.
56:46. And they persisted in the great violation.
56:47. And they used to say: When we die and become dust and bones, shall we then indeed be raised?
56:48. Or our fathers of yore?
56:49. Say: The ancients and those of later times
56:50. Will surely be gathered together for the appointed hour of a known day.
56:51. Then shall you, O you who err and deny,

56. The Event

56:52. Eat of the tree of Zaqqum,
56:53. And fill (your) bellies with it
56:54. Then drink after it of boiling water;
56:55. And drink as drinks the thirsty camel.
56:56. This is their entertainment on the day of Requital.
56:57. We have created you, why do you not then accept?
56:58. See you that which you emit?
56:59. Is it you that create it or are We the Creators?
56:60. We have ordained death among you and We are not to be overcome,
56:61. That We may change your state and make you grow into what you know not.
56:62. And certainly you know the first growth, why do you not then mind?
56:63. See you what you sow?
56:64. Is it you that cause it to grow, or arc We the Causer of growth.
56:65. If We pleased, We would make it chaff, then would you lament:
56:66. Surely we are burdened with debt:
56:67. Nay, we are deprived.
56:68. See you the water which you drink?
56:69. Do you bring it down from the clouds, or are We the Bringer?
56:70. If We pleased, We could make it saltish; why give you not thanks?
56:71. See you the fire which you kindle?
56:72. Is it you that produce the trees for it, or are We the Producer?
56:73. We have made it a reminder and an advantage for the wayfarers of the desert.
56:74. So glorify the name of thy Lord, the Incomparably Great.

***

56:75. But nay, I swear by revelation of portions (of the Qur'an)
56:76. And it is a great oath indeed, if you knew --

56. The Event

56:77. Surely it is a bounteous Qur'an,
56:78. In a book that is protected,
56:79. Which none touches save the purified ones.
56:80. A revelation from the Lord of the worlds.
56:81. Is it this announcement that you disdain?
56:82. And make your denial your means of subsistence. --
56:83. Why is it nor then that when it comes up to the throat,
56:84. And you at that time look on --
56:85. And We are nearer to it than you, but you see not --
56:86. Why then, if you are not held under authority,
56:87. Do you not send it back, if you are truthful?
56:88. Then if he is one of those drawn nigh (to Allah),
56:89. Then happiness and bounty and a Garden of bliss.
56:90. And if he is one of those on the right hand,
56:91. Then peace to thee from those on the right hand.
56:92. And if he is one of the rejectors, the erring ones,
56:93. He has an entertainment of boiling water,
56:94. And burning in hell.
56:95. Surely this is a certain truth.
56:96. So glorify the name of thy Lord. the Incomparably Great.

لَوْ نَشَاءُ جَعَلْنَاهُ أُجَاجًا فَلَوْلَا تَشْكُرُونَ (٧٠)
أَفَرَأَيْتُمُ النَّارَ الَّتِي تُورُونَ (٧١)
أَأَنْتُمْ أَنْشَأْتُمْ شَجَرَتَهَا أَمْ نَحْنُ الْمُنْشِئُونَ (٧٢)
نَحْنُ جَعَلْنَاهَا تَذْكِرَةً وَمَتَاعًا لِلْمُقْوِينَ (٧٣)
فَسَبِّحْ بِاسْمِ رَبِّكَ الْعَظِيمِ (٧٤)
فَلَا أُقْسِمُ بِمَوَاقِعِ النُّجُومِ (٧٥)
وَإِنَّهُ لَقَسَمٌ لَوْ تَعْلَمُونَ عَظِيمٌ (٧٦)
إِنَّهُ لَقُرْآنٌ كَرِيمٌ (٧٧)
فِي كِتَابٍ مَكْنُونٍ (٧٨)
لَا يَمَسُّهُ إِلَّا الْمُطَهَّرُونَ (٧٩)
تَنْزِيلٌ مِنْ رَبِّ الْعَالَمِينَ (٨٠)
أَفَبِهَذَا الْحَدِيثِ أَنْتُمْ مُدْهِنُونَ (٨١)
وَتَجْعَلُونَ رِزْقَكُمْ أَنَّكُمْ تُكَذِّبُونَ (٨٢)
فَلَوْلَا إِذَا بَلَغَتِ الْحُلْقُومَ (٨٣)
وَأَنْتُمْ حِينَئِذٍ تَنْظُرُونَ (٨٤)
وَنَحْنُ أَقْرَبُ إِلَيْهِ مِنْكُمْ وَلَكِنْ لَا تُبْصِرُونَ (٨٥)
فَلَوْلَا إِنْ كُنْتُمْ غَيْرَ مَدِينِينَ (٨٦)
تَرْجِعُونَهَا إِنْ كُنْتُمْ صَادِقِينَ (٨٧)
فَأَمَّا إِنْ كَانَ مِنَ الْمُقَرَّبِينَ (٨٨)
فَرَوْحٌ وَرَيْحَانٌ وَجَنَّةُ نَعِيمٍ (٨٩)
وَأَمَّا إِنْ كَانَ مِنْ أَصْحَابِ الْيَمِينِ (٩٠)
فَسَلَامٌ لَكَ مِنْ أَصْحَابِ الْيَمِينِ (٩١)
وَأَمَّا إِنْ كَانَ مِنَ الْمُكَذِّبِينَ الضَّالِّينَ (٩٢)
فَنُزُلٌ مِنْ حَمِيمٍ (٩٣)
وَتَصْلِيَةُ جَحِيمٍ (٩٤)
إِنَّ هَذَا لَهُوَ حَقُّ الْيَقِينِ (٩٥)

57. Iron

In the name of Allah, the Beneficent, the Merciful.

57:1. Whatever is in the heavens and the earth declares the glory of Allah, and He is the Mighty, the Wise.

57:2. His is the kingdom of the heavens and the earth. He gives life and causes death; and He is Possessor of power over all things.

57:3. He is the First and the Last and the Manifest and the Hidden, and He is Knower of all things.

57:4. He it is Who created the heavens and the earth in six periods, and He is established on the Throne of Power. He knows that which goes down into the earth and that which comes forth out of it, and that which comes down from heaven and that which goes up to it. And He is with you wherever you are. And Allah is Seer of what you do.

57:5. His is the kingdom of the heavens and the earth; and to Allah are (all) affairs returned.

57:6. He causes the night to pass into the day, and causes the day to pass into the night. And He is Knower of what is in the hearts.

57:7. Believe in Allah and His Messenger, and spend of that whereof He has made you heirs. So those of you who believe and spend for them is a great reward.

57:8. And what reason have you that you believe not in Allah? And the Messenger invites you to believe in your Lord, and He has indeed accepted your covenant, if you are believers.

57:9. He it is Who sends down clear messages to His servant, that he may bring you forth from darkness into light. And surely Allah is Kind, Merciful to you.

57. Iron

57:10. And what reason have you that you spend not in Allah's way? And Allah's is the inheritance of the heavens and the earth. Those of you who spent before the Victory and fought are not on a level (with others). They are greater in rank than those who spent and fought afterwards. And Allah has promised good to all. And Allah is Aware of what you do.

***

57:11. Who is he that will offer to Allah a good gift, so He will double it for him, and he will have a generous reward.

57:12. On that day thou wilt see the faithful men and the faithful women, their light gleaming before them and on their right hand. Good news for you this day -- Gardens wherein rivers flow, to abide therein! That is the grand achievement.

57:13. On the day when the hypocrites? men and women, will say to those who believe: Wait for us, that we may borrow from your light. It will be said: Turn back and seek a light. Then a wall, with a door in it, will be raised between them. Within it shall be mercy, and outside of it chastisement.

57:14. They will cry out to them: Were we not with you? They will say: Yea, but you caused yourselves to fall into temptation, and you waited and doubted, and vain desire deceived you, till the threatened punishment of Allah came, and the arch-deceiver deceived you about Allah.

57:15. So this day no ransom will be accepted from you, nor from those who disbelieved. Your abode is the Fire it is your patron and evil is the resort.

57:16. Has not the time yet come for the believers that their hearts should be humble for the remembrance of Allah and the Truth that is revealed, and (that) they should not be like those who were given the Book before, but

مِيرَاثُ السَّمَاوَاتِ وَالْأَرْضِ لَا يَسْتَوِي مِنْكُمْ مَنْ أَنْفَقَ مِنْ قَبْلِ الْفَتْحِ وَقَاتَلَ أُولَئِكَ أَعْظَمُ دَرَجَةً مِنَ الَّذِينَ أَنْفَقُوا مِنْ بَعْدُ وَقَاتَلُوا وَكُلًّا وَعَدَ اللَّهُ الْحُسْنَى وَاللَّهُ بِمَا تَعْمَلُونَ خَبِيرٌ (١٠) مَنْ ذَا الَّذِي يُقْرِضُ اللَّهَ قَرْضًا حَسَنًا فَيُضَاعِفَهُ لَهُ وَلَهُ أَجْرٌ كَرِيمٌ (١١) يَوْمَ تَرَى الْمُؤْمِنِينَ وَالْمُؤْمِنَاتِ يَسْعَى نُورُهُمْ بَيْنَ أَيْدِيهِمْ وَبِأَيْمَانِهِمْ بُشْرَاكُمُ الْيَوْمَ جَنَّاتٌ تَجْرِي مِنْ تَحْتِهَا الْأَنْهَارُ خَالِدِينَ فِيهَا ذَلِكَ هُوَ الْفَوْزُ الْعَظِيمُ (١٢) يَوْمَ يَقُولُ الْمُنَافِقُونَ وَالْمُنَافِقَاتُ لِلَّذِينَ آمَنُوا انْظُرُونَا نَقْتَبِسْ مِنْ نُورِكُمْ قِيلَ ارْجِعُوا وَرَاءَكُمْ فَالْتَمِسُوا نُورًا فَضُرِبَ بَيْنَهُمْ بِسُورٍ لَهُ بَابٌ بَاطِنُهُ فِيهِ الرَّحْمَةُ وَظَاهِرُهُ مِنْ قِبَلِهِ الْعَذَابُ (١٣) يُنَادُونَهُمْ أَلَمْ نَكُنْ مَعَكُمْ قَالُوا بَلَى وَلَكِنَّكُمْ فَتَنْتُمْ أَنْفُسَكُمْ وَتَرَبَّصْتُمْ وَارْتَبْتُمْ وَغَرَّتْكُمُ الْأَمَانِيُّ حَتَّى جَاءَ أَمْرُ اللَّهِ وَغَرَّكُمْ بِاللَّهِ الْغَرُورُ (١٤) فَالْيَوْمَ لَا يُؤْخَذُ مِنْكُمْ فِدْيَةٌ وَلَا مِنَ الَّذِينَ كَفَرُوا مَأْوَاكُمُ النَّارُ هِيَ مَوْلَاكُمْ وَبِئْسَ الْمَصِيرُ (١٥) أَلَمْ يَأْنِ لِلَّذِينَ آمَنُوا أَنْ تَخْشَعَ قُلُوبُهُمْ لِذِكْرِ اللَّهِ وَمَا نَزَلَ مِنَ الْحَقِّ وَلَا يَكُونُوا كَالَّذِينَ أُوتُوا الْكِتَابَ مِنْ قَبْلُ فَطَالَ عَلَيْهِمُ الْأَمَدُ فَقَسَتْ قُلُوبُهُمْ وَكَثِيرٌ مِنْهُمْ فَاسِقُونَ (١٦) اعْلَمُوا أَنَّ اللَّهَ يُحْيِي الْأَرْضَ بَعْدَ مَوْتِهَا قَدْ بَيَّنَّا لَكُمُ الْآيَاتِ لَعَلَّكُمْ تَعْقِلُونَ (١٧)

time was prolonged for them, so their hearts hardened. And most of them are transgressors.

57:17. Know that Allah gives life to the earth after its death. Indeed, We have made the signs clear for you that you may understand.

57:18. The men who give in charity and the women who give in charity and set apart for Allah a goodly portion, it will be doubled for them, and theirs is a generous reward.

57:19. And those who believe in Allah and His messengers, they are the truthful and the faithful ones with their Lord. They have their reward and their light. And those who disbelieve and reject Our messages, they are the inmates of hell.

***

57:20. Know that this world's life is only sport and play and gaiety and boasting among yourselves and a vying in the multiplication of wealth and children. It is as rain, whose causing the vegetation to grow pleases the husbandmen, then it withers away so that thou seest it turning yellow, then it becomes chaff. And in the Hereafter is a severe chastisement, and (also) forgiveness from Allah and (His) pleasure. And this world's life is naught but a source of vanity.

57:21. Vie one with another for forgiveness from your Lord and a Garden the extensiveness of which is as the extensiveness of the heaven and the earth -- it is prepared for those who believe in Allah and His messengers. That is the grace of Allah; He gives it to whom He pleases. And Allah is the Lord of mighty grace.

57:22. No disaster befalls in the earth, or in yourselves, but it is in a book before We bring it into existence -- surely that is easy to Allah --

57:23. So that you grieve not for what has escaped you, nor exult in that which He has given you. And Allah loves not any arrogant boaster:

57:24. Such as are niggardly and enjoin niggardliness on men. And whoever turns back, then surely Allah is the Self-Sufficient, the Praised.

57:25. Certainly We sent Our messengers with clear arguments, and sent down with them the Book and the measure, that men may conduct themselves with equity. And We sent down iron, wherein is great violence and advantages to men, and that Allah may know who helps Him and His messengers, unseen. Surely Allah is Strong, Mighty.

* * *

57:26. And certainly We sent Noah and Abraham, and We gave prophethood and the Book to their offspring; so among them is he who goes aright, but most of them are transgressors.

57:27. Then We made Out messengers to follow in their footsteps, and We made Jesus son of Mary to follow, and We gave him the Gospel. And We put. compassion and mercy in the hearts of those who followed him. And (as for) monkery, they innovated it -- We did not prescribe it to them -- only to seek Allah's pleasure, but they did not observe it with its due observance. So We gave those of them who believed their reward, but most of them are transgressors.

57:28. O you who believe, keep your duty. to Allah and believe in His Messenger -- He will give you two portions of His mercy, and give you a light in which you shall walk, and forgive you. And Allah is Forgiving, Merciful --

57:29. That the People of the Book may know that they control naught of the grace of Allah, and that grace is in Allah's hand. He gives it to whom He pleases. And Allah is the Lord of mighty grace.

وَرُسُلِهِ بِالْغَيْبِ إِنَّ اللَّهَ قَوِيٌّ عَزِيزٌ (٢٥) وَلَقَدْ أَرْسَلْنَا نُوحًا وَإِبْرَاهِيمَ وَجَعَلْنَا فِي ذُرِّيَّتِهِمَا النُّبُوَّةَ وَالْكِتَابَ فَمِنْهُمْ مُهْتَدٍ وَكَثِيرٌ مِنْهُمْ فَاسِقُونَ (٢٦) ثُمَّ قَفَّيْنَا عَلَى آثَارِهِمْ بِرُسُلِنَا وَقَفَّيْنَا بِعِيسَى ابْنِ مَرْيَمَ وَآتَيْنَاهُ الْإِنْجِيلَ وَجَعَلْنَا فِي قُلُوبِ الَّذِينَ اتَّبَعُوهُ رَأْفَةً وَرَحْمَةً وَرَهْبَانِيَّةً ابْتَدَعُوهَا مَا كَتَبْنَاهَا عَلَيْهِمْ إِلَّا ابْتِغَاءَ رِضْوَانِ اللَّهِ فَمَا رَعَوْهَا حَقَّ رِعَايَتِهَا فَآتَيْنَا الَّذِينَ آمَنُوا مِنْهُمْ أَجْرَهُمْ وَكَثِيرٌ مِنْهُمْ فَاسِقُونَ (٢٧) يَا أَيُّهَا الَّذِينَ آمَنُوا اتَّقُوا اللَّهَ وَآمِنُوا بِرَسُولِهِ يُؤْتِكُمْ كِفْلَيْنِ مِنْ رَحْمَتِهِ وَيَجْعَلْ لَكُمْ نُورًا تَمْشُونَ بِهِ وَيَغْفِرْ لَكُمْ وَاللَّهُ غَفُورٌ رَحِيمٌ (٢٨) لِئَلَّا يَعْلَمَ أَهْلُ الْكِتَابِ أَلَّا يَقْدِرُونَ عَلَى شَيْءٍ مِنْ فَضْلِ اللَّهِ وَأَنَّ الْفَضْلَ بِيَدِ اللَّهِ يُؤْتِيهِ مَنْ يَشَاءُ وَاللَّهُ ذُو الْفَضْلِ الْعَظِيمِ (٢٩)

58. The Pleading Woman

In the name of Allah, the Beneficent, the Merciful.

58:1. Allah indeed has heard the plea of her who pleads with thee about her husband and complains to Allah and Allah hears the contentions of both of you. Surely Allah is Hearing, Seeing.

58:2. Those of you who put away their wives by calling them their mothers -- they are not their mothers. None are their mothers save those who gave them birth, and they utter indeed a hateful word and a lie. And surely Allah is Pardoning, Forgiving.

58:3. And those who put away their wives by calling them their mothers, then go back on that which they said, must free a captive before they touch one another. To this you are exhorted; and Allah is Aware of what you do.

58:4. But he who has not the means, should fast for two months successively before they touch one another, and he who is unable to do so should feed sixty needy ones. That is in order that you may have faith in Allah and His Messenger. And these are Allah's limits. And for the disbelievers is a painful chastisement.

58:5. Surely those who oppose Allah and His Messenger will be humbled as those before them were humbled; and indeed We have revealed clear messages. And for the disbelievers is an abasing chastisement.

58:6. On the day when Allah will raise them all together, then inform them of what they did. Allah records it, while they forget it. And Allah is Witness over all things.

***

58:7. Seest thou not that Allah knows whatever is in the heavens and whatever is in the earth? There is no secret counsel between, three but He is the fourth of them, nor between five

58. The Pleading Woman

but He is the sixth of them, nor between less than that nor more but He is with them wheresoever they are; then He will inform them of what they did on the day of Resurrection. Surely Allah is Knower of all things.

58:8. Seest thou not those who are forbidden secret counsels, then they return to that which they are forbidden, and hold secret counsels for sin and revolt and disobedience to the Messenger. And when they come to thee they greet thee with a greeting with which Allah greets thee not, and say within themselves: Why does not Allah punish us for what we say? Hell is enough for them; they will burn in it, and evil is the resort!

58:9. O you who believe, when you confer together in private, give not to each other counsel of sin and revolt and disobedience to the Messenger, but give to each other counsel of goodness and observance of duty. And keep your duty to Allah, to Whom you will be gathered together.

58:10. Secret counsels are only of the devil that he may cause to grieve those who believe, and he can hurt them naught except with Allah's permission. And on Allah let the believers rely.

58:11. O you who believe, when it is said to you, Make room in assemblies, make room. Allah will give you ample. And when it is said, Rise up, rise up. Allah will exalt those of you who believe, and those who are given knowledge, to high ranks. And Allah is Aware of what you do.

58:12. O you who believe, when you consult the Messenger, offer something in charity before your consultation. That is better for you and purer. But if you have not (the means), then surely Allah is Forgiving, Merciful.

58:13. Do you fear that you will not (be able to) give in charity before your consultation? So when you do it not,

ثُمَّ يَعُودُونَ لِمَا نُهُوا عَنْهُ وَيَتَنَاجَوْنَ بِالْإِثْمِ وَالْعُدْوَانِ وَمَعْصِيَةِ الرَّسُولِ وَإِذَا جَاءُوكَ حَيَّوْكَ بِمَا لَمْ يُحَيِّكَ بِهِ اللَّهُ وَيَقُولُونَ فِي أَنْفُسِهِمْ لَوْلَا يُعَذِّبُنَا اللَّهُ بِمَا نَقُولُ حَسْبُهُمْ جَهَنَّمُ يَصْلَوْنَهَا فَبِئْسَ الْمَصِيرُ (٨)

يَا أَيُّهَا الَّذِينَ آمَنُوا إِذَا تَنَاجَيْتُمْ فَلَا تَتَنَاجَوْا بِالْإِثْمِ وَالْعُدْوَانِ وَمَعْصِيَةِ الرَّسُولِ وَتَنَاجَوْا بِالْبِرِّ وَالتَّقْوَى وَاتَّقُوا اللَّهَ الَّذِي إِلَيْهِ تُحْشَرُونَ (٩)

إِنَّمَا النَّجْوَى مِنَ الشَّيْطَانِ لِيَحْزُنَ الَّذِينَ آمَنُوا وَلَيْسَ بِضَارِّهِمْ شَيْئًا إِلَّا بِإِذْنِ اللَّهِ وَعَلَى اللَّهِ فَلْيَتَوَكَّلِ الْمُؤْمِنُونَ (١٠)

يَا أَيُّهَا الَّذِينَ آمَنُوا إِذَا قِيلَ لَكُمْ تَفَسَّحُوا فِي الْمَجَالِسِ فَافْسَحُوا يَفْسَحِ اللَّهُ لَكُمْ وَإِذَا قِيلَ انْشُزُوا فَانْشُزُوا يَرْفَعِ اللَّهُ الَّذِينَ آمَنُوا مِنْكُمْ وَالَّذِينَ أُوتُوا الْعِلْمَ دَرَجَاتٍ وَاللَّهُ بِمَا تَعْمَلُونَ خَبِيرٌ (١١)

يَا أَيُّهَا الَّذِينَ آمَنُوا إِذَا نَاجَيْتُمُ الرَّسُولَ فَقَدِّمُوا بَيْنَ يَدَيْ نَجْوَاكُمْ صَدَقَةً ذَلِكَ خَيْرٌ لَكُمْ وَأَطْهَرُ فَإِنْ لَمْ تَجِدُوا فَإِنَّ اللَّهَ غَفُورٌ رَحِيمٌ (١٢)

أَأَشْفَقْتُمْ أَنْ تُقَدِّمُوا بَيْنَ يَدَيْ نَجْوَاكُمْ صَدَقَاتٍ فَإِذْ لَمْ تَفْعَلُوا وَتَابَ اللَّهُ عَلَيْكُمْ فَأَقِيمُوا الصَّلَاةَ وَآتُوا الزَّكَاةَ وَأَطِيعُوا اللَّهَ وَرَسُولَهُ وَاللَّهُ خَبِيرٌ بِمَا تَعْمَلُونَ (١٣)

أَلَمْ تَرَ إِلَى الَّذِينَ تَوَلَّوْا قَوْمًا غَضِبَ اللَّهُ عَلَيْهِمْ مَا هُمْ مِنْكُمْ وَلَا مِنْهُمْ وَيَحْلِفُونَ عَلَى الْكَذِبِ وَهُمْ يَعْلَمُونَ (١٤)

أَعَدَّ اللَّهُ لَهُمْ عَذَابًا شَدِيدًا إِنَّهُمْ سَاءَ مَا

58. The Pleading Woman

and Allah has turned to you (mercifully), keep up prayer and pay the poor-rate and obey Allah and His Messenger. And Allah is Aware of what you do.

* * *

58:14. Hast thou not seen those who take for friends a people with whom Allah is wroth? They are neither of you nor of them, and they swear falsely, while they know.

58:15. Allah has prepared for them a severe chastisement. Evil indeed is that which they do!

58:16. They take shelter under their oaths, so they turn (men) from Allah's way for them is an abasing chastisement.

58:17. Of no avail against Allah, will be to them their wealth or their children. They are the companions of the Fire therein they will abide.

58:18. On the day when Allah will raise them all up, they will swear to Him as they swear to you, and they think that they have some (excuse). Now surely they are the liars.

58:19. The devil has gained the mastery over them, so he has made them forget the remembrance of Allah. They are the devil's party. Now surely the devil's party are the losers.

58:20. Those who oppose Allah and His Messenger, they shall be among the most abased.

58:21. Allah has written down: I shall certainly prevail, I and My messengers. Surely Allah is Strong, Mighty.

58:22. Thou wilt not find a people who believe in Allah and the latter day loving those who oppose Allah and His Messenger, even though they be their fathers, or their sons, or their brothers, or their kinsfolk. These are they into whose hearts He has impressed faith, and strengthened them with a Spirit from Himself, and He will cause them to enter Gardens wherein flow rivers, abiding therein. Allah is well-pleased with them and they are well-pleased with Him. These are Allah's party. Now surely it is Allah's party who are the successful!

59. The Banishment

In the name of Allah, the Beneficent, the Merciful.

59:1. Whatever is in the heavens and whatever is in the earth glorifies Allah; and He is the Mighty, the Wise;

59:2. He it is Who caused those who disbelieved of the People of the Book to go forth from their homes at the first banishment. You deemed not that they would go forth, while they thought that their fortresses would defend them against Allah. But Allah came to them from a place they expected not and cast terror into their hearts they demolished their houses with their own hands and the hands of the believers. So take a lesson, O you who have eyes!

59:3. And had it not been that Allah had decreed for them the exile, He would certainly have chastised them in this world; and for them in the Hereafter is the chastisement of Fire.

59:4. That is because they were opposed to Allah and His Messenger, and whoever is opposed to Allah, surely Allah is Severe in retribution.

59:5. Whatever palm-tree you cut down or leave it standing upon its roots, it is by Allah's permission, and that He may abase the transgressors.

59:6. And whatever Allah restored to His Messenger from them, you did not press forward against it any horse or any riding-camel, but Allah gives authority to His messengers against whom He pleases. And Allah is Possessor of power over all things.

59:7. Whatever Allah restored to His Messenger from the people of the

59. The Banishment

towns, it is for Allah and for the Messenger, and for the near of kin and the orphans and the needy and the wayfarer, so that it be not taken by turns by the rich among you. And whatever the Messenger gives you, accept it, and whatever he forbids you, abstain (therefrom); and keep your duty to Allah. Surely Allah is Severe in retribution.--

59:8. (It is) for the poor who fled, who were driven from their homes and their possessions, seeking grace of Allah and (His) pleasure, and helping Allah and His Messenger. These it is that are the truthful.--

59:9. And those who made their abode in the City and in faith before them love those who have fled to them, and find in their hearts no need of what they are given, and prefer (them) before themselves, though poverty may afflict them. And whoever is saved from the niggardliness of his soul, these it is that are the successful.

59:10. And those who come after them say Our Lord, forgive us and our brethren who had precedence of us in faith, and leave no spite in our hearts towards those who believe. Our Lord, surely Thou art Kind, Merciful.

***

59:11. Hast thou not seen the hypocrites? They say to their brethren who disbelieve from among the People of the Book: If you are expelled, we certainly will go forth with you, and we will never obey any one concerning you; and if you are fought against, we will certainly help you. And Allah bears witness that they surely are liars.

59:12. If they are expelled, they will not go forth with them, and if they are fought against, they will not help them; and even if they help them, they will certainly turn (their) backs then they shall not be helped.

59:13. Your fear in their hearts is

59. The Banishment

indeed greater than Allah's. That is because they are a people who understand not.

59:14. They will not fight against you in a body save in fortified towns or from behind walls. Their fighting between them is severe. Thou wouldst think them united, but their hearts are divided. That is because they are a people who have no sense.

59:15. Like those before them shortly: they taste the evil consequences of their conduct, and for them is a painful chastisement.

59:16. Like the devil when he says to man: Disbelieve. But when he disbelieves, he says: I am free of thee surely I fear Allah, the Lord of the worlds.

59:17. So the end of both of them is that they are both in the Fire to abide therein. And that is the reward of the wrong-doers.

* * *

59:18. O you who believe, keep your duty to Allah, and let every soul consider that which it sends forth for the morrow, and keep your duty to Allah. Surely Allah is Aware of what you do.

59:19. And be not like those who forget Allah, so He makes them forget their own souls. These are the transgressors.

59:20. Not alike are the companions of the Fire and the owners of the Garden. The owners of the Garden are the achievers.

59:21. Had We sent down this Qur'an on a mountain, thou wouldst certainly have seen it falling down, splitting asunder because of the fear of Allah. And We set forth these parables to men that they may reflect.

59:22. He is Allah besides Whom there is no God: The Knower of the unseen and the seen; He is the Beneficent, the Merciful.

59:23. He is Allah, besides Whom there

is no God; the King, the Holy, the Author of Peace, the Granter of Security, Guardian over all, the Mighty, the Supreme, the Possessor of greatness. Glory be to Allah from that which they set up (with Him)!

59:24. He is Allah; the Creator, the Maker, the Fashioner His are the most beautiful names. Whatever is in the heavens and the earth declares His glory; and He is the Mighty, the Wise.

60. The Examined Woman

In the name of Allah, the Beneficent, the Merciful.

60:1. O you who believe, take not My enemy and your enemy for friends. Would you offer them love, while they deny the Truth that has come to you, driving out the Messenger and yourselves because you believe in Allah, your Lord? If you have come forth to strive in My way and to seek My pleasure, would you love them in secret? And I know what you conceal and what you manifest. And whoever of you does this, he indeed strays from the straight path.

60:2. If they overcome you, they will be your enemies, and will stretch forth their hands and their tongues towards you with evil, and they desire that you may disbelieve.

60:3. Your relationships and your children would not profit you, on the day of Resurrection -- He will decide between you. And Allah is Seer of what you do.

60:4. Indeed, there is for you a good example in Abraham and those with him, when they said to their people: We are clear of you and of that which you serve besides Allah. We disbelieve in you and there has arisen enmity and hatred between us and you forever until you believe in Allah alone --

60. The Examined Woman

except Abraham's saying to his sire I would ask forgiveness for thee, and I control naught for thee from Allah. Our Lord, on Thee do we rely, and to Thee do we turn, and to Thee is the eventual coming.

60:5. Our Lord, make us not a trial for those who disbelieve, and forgive us, our Lord. Surely Thou art the Mighty, the Wise.

60:6. Certainly there is for you in them a good example, for him who hopes for Allah and the Last Day. And who-ever turns away, surely Allah is the Self-Sufficient, the Praised.

* * *

60:7. It may be that Allah will bring about friendship between you and those of them whom you hold as enemies. And Allah is Powerful and Allah is Forgiving, Merciful.

60:8. Allah forbids you not respecting those who fight you not for religion, nor drive you forth from your homes, that you show them kindness and deal with them justly. Surely Allah loves the doers of justice.

60:9. Allah forbids you only respecting those who fight you for religion, and drive you forth from your homes and help (others) in your expulsion, that you make friends of them; and whoever makes friends of them, these are the wrongdoers.

60:10. O you who believe, when believing women come to you fleeing, examine them. Allah knows best their faith. Then if you know them to be believers send them not back to the disbelievers. Neither are these (women) lawful for them, nor are those (men) lawful for them. And give them what they have spent; and there is no blame on you in marrying them, when you give them their dowries. And hold not to the ties of marriage of disbelieving women, and ask for what you have spent, and let them ask for

أَنَبْنَا وَإِلَيْكَ الْمَصِيرُ (٤) رَبَّنَا لَا تَجْعَلْنَا فِتْنَةً لِلَّذِينَ كَفَرُوا وَاغْفِرْ لَنَا رَبَّنَا إِنَّكَ أَنْتَ الْعَزِيزُ الْحَكِيمُ (٥) لَقَدْ كَانَ لَكُمْ فِيهِمْ أُسْوَةٌ حَسَنَةٌ لِمَنْ كَانَ يَرْجُو اللَّهَ وَالْيَوْمَ الْآخِرَ وَمَنْ يَتَوَلَّ فَإِنَّ اللَّهَ هُوَ الْغَنِيُّ الْحَمِيدُ (٦) عَسَى اللَّهُ أَنْ يَجْعَلَ بَيْنَكُمْ وَبَيْنَ الَّذِينَ عَادَيْتُمْ مِنْهُمْ مَوَدَّةً وَاللَّهُ قَدِيرٌ وَاللَّهُ غَفُورٌ رَحِيمٌ (٧) لَا يَنْهَاكُمُ اللَّهُ عَنِ الَّذِينَ لَمْ يُقَاتِلُوكُمْ فِي الدِّينِ وَلَمْ يُخْرِجُوكُمْ مِنْ دِيَارِكُمْ أَنْ تَبَرُّوهُمْ وَتُقْسِطُوا إِلَيْهِمْ إِنَّ اللَّهَ يُحِبُّ الْمُقْسِطِينَ (٨) إِنَّمَا يَنْهَاكُمُ اللَّهُ عَنِ الَّذِينَ قَاتَلُوكُمْ فِي الدِّينِ وَأَخْرَجُوكُمْ مِنْ دِيَارِكُمْ وَظَاهَرُوا عَلَى إِخْرَاجِكُمْ أَنْ تَوَلَّوْهُمْ وَمَنْ يَتَوَلَّهُمْ فَأُولَئِكَ هُمُ الظَّالِمُونَ (٩) يَا أَيُّهَا الَّذِينَ آمَنُوا إِذَا جَاءَكُمُ الْمُؤْمِنَاتُ مُهَاجِرَاتٍ فَامْتَحِنُوهُنَّ اللَّهُ أَعْلَمُ بِإِيمَانِهِنَّ فَإِنْ عَلِمْتُمُوهُنَّ مُؤْمِنَاتٍ فَلَا تَرْجِعُوهُنَّ إِلَى الْكُفَّارِ لَا هُنَّ حِلٌّ لَهُمْ وَلَا هُمْ يَحِلُّونَ لَهُنَّ وَآتُوهُمْ مَا أَنْفَقُوا وَلَا جُنَاحَ عَلَيْكُمْ أَنْ تَنْكِحُوهُنَّ إِذَا آتَيْتُمُوهُنَّ أُجُورَهُنَّ وَلَا تُمْسِكُوا بِعِصَمِ الْكَوَافِرِ وَاسْأَلُوا مَا أَنْفَقْتُمْ وَلْيَسْأَلُوا مَا أَنْفَقُوا ذَلِكُمْ حُكْمُ اللَّهِ يَحْكُمُ بَيْنَكُمْ وَاللَّهُ عَلِيمٌ حَكِيمٌ (١٠) وَإِنْ فَاتَكُمْ شَيْءٌ مِنْ أَزْوَاجِكُمْ إِلَى الْكُفَّارِ فَعَاقَبْتُمْ فَآتُوا الَّذِينَ ذَهَبَتْ أَزْوَاجُهُمْ مِثْلَ مَا أَنْفَقُوا وَاتَّقُوا اللَّهَ الَّذِي أَنْتُمْ بِهِ مُؤْمِنُونَ (١١)

what they have spent. That is Allah's judgment; He judges between you. And Allah is Knowing, Wise.

60:11. And if any part (of the dowries) of your wives has passed away from you to the disbelievers, then your turn comes, give to those whose wives have gone away the like of what they have spent, and keep your duty to Allah in Whom you believe.

60:12. O Prophet, when believing women come to thee giving thee a pledge that they will not associate aught with Allah, and will not steal, nor commit adultery; nor kill their children, nor bring a calumny which they have forged of themselves, nor disobey thee in what is good, accept their pledge, and ask forgiveness for them from Allah. Surely Allah is Forgiving, Merciful.

60:13. O you who believe, take not for friends a people with whom Allah is wroth they indeed despair of the Hereafter, as the disbelievers despair of those in the graves.

61. The Ranks

In the name of Allah, the Beneficent, the Merciful.

61:1. Whatever is in the heavens and whatever is in the earth glorifies Allah; and He is the Mighty, the Wise.

61:2. O you who believe, why say you that which you do not?

61:3. It is most hateful in the sight of Allah that you say that which you do

61:4. Surely Allah loves those who fight in His way in ranks, as if they were a solid wall.

61:5. And when Moses said to his people O my people, why do you malign me, when you know that I am Allah's messenger to you? But when they deviated, Allah made their hearts deviate. And Allah guides not the

61. The Ranks

transgressing people.

61:6. And when Jesus, son of Mary, said O Children of Israel, surely I am the messenger of Allah to you, verifying that which is before me of the Torah and giving the good news of a Messenger who will come after me, his name being Ahmad. But when he came to them with clear arguments, they said: This is clear enchantment.

61:7. And who is more unjust than he who forges a lie against Allah and he is invited to Islam. And Allah guides not the unjust people.

61:8. They desire to put out the light of Allah with their mouths, but Allah will perfect His light, though the disbelievers may be averse.

61:9. He it is Who sent His Messenger with the guidance and the true religion, that He may make it overcome the religions, all of them, though the polytheists may be averse.

* * *

61:10. O you who believe, shall I lead you to a merchandise which will deliver you from a painful chastisement?

61:11. You should believe in Allah and His Messenger, and strive hard in Allah's way with your wealth and your lives. That is better for you, did you but know!

61:12. He will forgive you your sins and cause you to enter Gardens wherein rivers flow, and goodly dwellings in Gardens of perpetuity that is the mighty achievement --

61:13. And yet another (blessing) that you love: help from Allah and a victory near at hand; and give good news to the believers.

61:14. O you who believe, be helpers (in the cause) of Allah, as Jesus, son of Mary, said to the disciples: Who are my helpers in the cause of Allah? The disciples said: We are helpers (in the cause) of Allah. So a party of the

وَإِذْ قَالَ عِيسَى ابْنُ مَرْيَمَ يَا بَنِي إِسْرَائِيلَ إِنِّي رَسُولُ اللَّهِ إِلَيْكُمْ مُصَدِّقًا لِمَا بَيْنَ يَدَيَّ مِنَ التَّوْرَاةِ وَمُبَشِّرًا بِرَسُولٍ يَأْتِي مِنْ بَعْدِي اسْمُهُ أَحْمَدُ فَلَمَّا جَاءَهُمْ بِالْبَيِّنَاتِ قَالُوا هَذَا سِحْرٌ مُبِينٌ (٦)

وَمَنْ أَظْلَمُ مِمَّنِ افْتَرَى عَلَى اللَّهِ الْكَذِبَ وَهُوَ يُدْعَى إِلَى الْإِسْلَامِ وَاللَّهُ لَا يَهْدِي الْقَوْمَ الظَّالِمِينَ (٧)

يُرِيدُونَ لِيُطْفِئُوا نُورَ اللَّهِ بِأَفْوَاهِهِمْ وَاللَّهُ مُتِمُّ نُورِهِ وَلَوْ كَرِهَ الْكَافِرُونَ (٨)

هُوَ الَّذِي أَرْسَلَ رَسُولَهُ بِالْهُدَى وَدِينِ الْحَقِّ لِيُظْهِرَهُ عَلَى الدِّينِ كُلِّهِ وَلَوْ كَرِهَ الْمُشْرِكُونَ (٩)

يَا أَيُّهَا الَّذِينَ آمَنُوا هَلْ أَدُلُّكُمْ عَلَى تِجَارَةٍ تُنْجِيكُمْ مِنْ عَذَابٍ أَلِيمٍ (١٠)

تُؤْمِنُونَ بِاللَّهِ وَرَسُولِهِ وَتُجَاهِدُونَ فِي سَبِيلِ اللَّهِ بِأَمْوَالِكُمْ وَأَنْفُسِكُمْ ذَلِكُمْ خَيْرٌ لَكُمْ إِنْ كُنْتُمْ تَعْلَمُونَ (١١)

يَغْفِرْ لَكُمْ ذُنُوبَكُمْ وَيُدْخِلْكُمْ جَنَّاتٍ تَجْرِي مِنْ تَحْتِهَا الْأَنْهَارُ وَمَسَاكِنَ طَيِّبَةً فِي جَنَّاتِ عَدْنٍ ذَلِكَ الْفَوْزُ الْعَظِيمُ (١٢)

وَأُخْرَى تُحِبُّونَهَا نَصْرٌ مِنَ اللَّهِ وَفَتْحٌ قَرِيبٌ وَبَشِّرِ الْمُؤْمِنِينَ (١٣)

يَا أَيُّهَا الَّذِينَ آمَنُوا كُونُوا أَنْصَارَ اللَّهِ كَمَا قَالَ عِيسَى ابْنُ مَرْيَمَ لِلْحَوَارِيِّينَ مَنْ أَنْصَارِي إِلَى اللَّهِ قَالَ الْحَوَارِيُّونَ نَحْنُ أَنْصَارُ اللَّهِ فَآمَنَتْ طَائِفَةٌ مِنْ بَنِي إِسْرَائِيلَ وَكَفَرَتْ طَائِفَةٌ فَأَيَّدْنَا الَّذِينَ آمَنُوا عَلَى عَدُوِّهِمْ فَأَصْبَحُوا ظَاهِرِينَ (١٤)

Children of Israel believed and another party disbelieved; then We aided those who believed against their enemy, and they became predominant.

62. The Congregation

In the name of Allah, the Beneficent, the Merciful.

62:1. Whatever is in the heavens and whatever is in the earth glorifies Allah, the King, the Holy, the Mighty, the Wise.

62:2. He it is, Who raised among the illiterates a Messenger from among themselves, who recites to them His messages and purifies them, and teaches them the Book and the Wisdom -- although they were before certainly in manifest error --

62:3. And others from among them who have not yet joined them. And He is the Mighty, the Wise.

62:4. That is Allah's grace; He grants it to whom He pleases. And Allah is the Lord of mighty grace.

62:5. The likeness of those who were charged with the Torah, then they observed it not, is as the likeness of the ass carrying books. Evil is the likeness of the people who reject the messages of Allah. And Allah guides not the iniquitous people.

62:6. Say: O you who are Jews, if you think that you are the favourites of Allah to the exclusion of other people, then invoke death, if you are truthful.

62:7. But they will never invoke it because of what their hands have sent before. And Allah is Knower of the wrongdoers.

62:8. Say: The death from which you flee, that will surely overtake you; then you will be sent back to the Knower of the unseen and the seen, so He will inform you of that which you did.

***

٦٢- سورة الجمعة

بِسْمِ اللهِ الرَّحْمَٰنِ الرَّحِيمِ

يُسَبِّحُ لِلَّهِ مَا فِي السَّمَاوَاتِ وَمَا فِي الْأَرْضِ الْمَلِكِ الْقُدُّوسِ الْعَزِيزِ الْحَكِيمِ (١)

هُوَ الَّذِي بَعَثَ فِي الْأُمِّيِّينَ رَسُولًا مِنْهُمْ يَتْلُو عَلَيْهِمْ آيَاتِهِ وَيُزَكِّيهِمْ وَيُعَلِّمُهُمُ الْكِتَابَ وَالْحِكْمَةَ وَإِنْ كَانُوا مِنْ قَبْلُ لَفِي ضَلَالٍ مُبِينٍ (٢)

وَآخَرِينَ مِنْهُمْ لَمَّا يَلْحَقُوا بِهِمْ وَهُوَ الْعَزِيزُ الْحَكِيمُ (٣)

ذَٰلِكَ فَضْلُ اللَّهِ يُؤْتِيهِ مَنْ يَشَاءُ وَاللَّهُ ذُو الْفَضْلِ الْعَظِيمِ (٤)

مَثَلُ الَّذِينَ حُمِّلُوا التَّوْرَاةَ ثُمَّ لَمْ يَحْمِلُوهَا كَمَثَلِ الْحِمَارِ يَحْمِلُ أَسْفَارًا بِئْسَ مَثَلُ الْقَوْمِ الَّذِينَ كَذَّبُوا بِآيَاتِ اللَّهِ وَاللَّهُ لَا يَهْدِي الْقَوْمَ الظَّالِمِينَ (٥)

قُلْ يَا أَيُّهَا الَّذِينَ هَادُوا إِنْ زَعَمْتُمْ أَنَّكُمْ أَوْلِيَاءُ لِلَّهِ مِنْ دُونِ النَّاسِ فَتَمَنَّوُا الْمَوْتَ إِنْ كُنْتُمْ صَادِقِينَ (٦)

وَلَا يَتَمَنَّوْنَهُ أَبَدًا بِمَا قَدَّمَتْ أَيْدِيهِمْ وَاللَّهُ عَلِيمٌ بِالظَّالِمِينَ (٧)

قُلْ إِنَّ الْمَوْتَ الَّذِي تَفِرُّونَ مِنْهُ فَإِنَّهُ مُلَاقِيكُمْ ثُمَّ تُرَدُّونَ إِلَىٰ عَالِمِ الْغَيْبِ وَالشَّهَادَةِ فَيُنَبِّئُكُمْ بِمَا كُنْتُمْ تَعْمَلُونَ (٨)

يَا أَيُّهَا الَّذِينَ آمَنُوا إِذَا نُودِيَ لِلصَّلَاةِ مِنْ يَوْمِ الْجُمُعَةِ فَاسْعَوْا إِلَىٰ ذِكْرِ اللَّهِ

62:9. O you who believe, when the call is sounded for prayer on Friday, hasten to the remembrance of Allah and leave off traffic. That is better for you, if you know.

62:10. But when the prayer is ended, disperse abroad in the land and seek of Allah's grace, and remember Allah much, that you may be successful.

62:11. And when they see merchandise or sport, they break away to it, and leave thee sranding. Say: What is with Allah is better than sport and merchandise. And Allah is the Best of Providers.

63. The Hypocrites

In the name of Allah, the Beneficent, the Merciful.

63:1. When the hypocrites come to thee, they say: We bear witness that thou art indeed Allah's Messenger. And Allah knows thou art indeed His Messenger. And Allah bears witness that the hypocrites are surely liars.

63:2. They take shelter under their oaths, thus turning (men) from Allah's way. Surely evil is that which they do.

63:3. That is because they believed, then disbelieved; thus their hearts are sealed, so they understand not.

63:4. And when thou seest them, their persons please thee; and if they speak, thou listenest to their speech. They are like pieces of wood, clad with garments. They think every cry to be against them. They are the enemy, so beware of them, May Allah destroy them How they are turned back!

63:5. And when it is said to them Come, the Messenger of Allah will ask forgiveness for you, they turn away their heads and thou seest them hindering (others), and they are big with pride.

63:6. It is alike to them whether thou

ask forgiveness for them or ask not forgiveness for them -- Allah will never forgive them. Surely Allah guides not the transgressing people.

63:7. They it is who sa~: Spend not on those who are with the Messenger of Allah that they may disperse. And Allah's are the treasures of the heavens and the earth, but the hypocrites understand not.

63:8. They say: If we return to Madinah, the mightier will surely drive out the meaner therefrom. And might belongs to Allah and His Messenger and the believers, but the hypocrites know not.

***

63:9. O you who believe, let not your wealth nor your children divert you from the remembrance of Allah; and whoever does that, these are the losers.

63:10. And spend our of that which We have given you before death comes to one of you, and he says: My Lord, why didst Thou not respire me to a near term, so that I should have given alms and been of the doers of good deeds?

63:11. But Allah respites not a soul, when its term comes. And Allah is Aware of what you do.

64. Manifestation of Losses

In the name of Allah, the Beneficent, the Merciful.

64:1. Whatever is in the heavens and whatever is in the earth glorifies Allah. His is the kingdom, and His the praise; and He is Possessor of power over all things.

64:2. He it is Who created you, but one of you is a disbeliever and one of you is a believer. And Allah is Seer of what you do.

64:3. He created the heavens and the earth with truth, and He shaped you, then made goodly your shapes; and to

64. Manifestation of Losses

Him is the resort.

64:4. He knows what is in the heavens and the earth, and He knows what you hide and what you manifest. And Allah is Knower of what is in the hearts.

64:5. Has there not come to you the story of those who disbelieved before, then tasted the evil consequences of their conduct, and they had a painful chastisement?

64:6. That is because there came to them their messengers with clear arguments, but they said: Shall mortals guide us? So they disbelieved and turned away, and Allah is above all need. And Allah is Self-Sufficient, Praised.

64:7. Those who disbelieve think that they will not be raised. Say: Aye, by my Lord you will certainly be raised; then you will certainly be informed of what you did. And that is easy to Allah.

64:8. So believe in Allah and His Messenger and the Light which We have revealed. And Allah is Aware of what you do.

64:9. The day when He will gather you for the day of Gathering, that is the day of the Manifestation of losses. And whoever believes in Allah and does good, He will remove from him his evil and cause him to enter Gardens wherein rivers flow, to abide therein for ever. That is the great achievement.

64:10. And those who disbelieve and reject Our messages, they are the companions of the Fire, abiding therein and evil is the resort.

***

64:11. No calamity befalls but by Allah's permission. And whoever believes in Allah, He guides his heart. And Allah is Knower of all things.

64:12. And obey Allah and obey the Messenger; but if you turn away, the duty of Our Messenger is only to deliver (the message) clearly.

64:13. Allah, there is no God but He. And on Allah let the believers rely.

64:14. O you who believe, surely of your wives and your children there are enemies to you, so beware of them. And if you pardon and forbear and forgive, surely Allah is Forgiving, Merciful.

64:15. Your wealth and your children are only a trial, and Allah with Him is a great reward.

64:16. So keep your duty to Allah as much as you can, and hear and obey and spend; it is better for your souls. And whoever is saved from the greediness of his soul, these it is that are the successful.

64:17. If you set apart for Allah a goodly portion, He will double it for you and forgive you. And Allah is the Multiplier (of rewards), Forbearing,

64:18. The Knower of the unseen and the seen, the Mighty, the Wise.

65. Divorce

In the name of Allah, the Beneficent, the Merciful.

65:1. O Prophet, when you divorce women, divorce them for their prescribed period, and calculate the period; and keep your duty to Allah, your Lord. Turn them nor out of their houses -- nor should they themselves go forth -- unless they commit an open indecency. And these are the limits of Allah. And whoever goes beyond the limits of Allah, he indeed wrongs his own soul. Thou knowest not that Allah may after that bring about an event.

65:2. So when they have reached their prescribed time, retain them with kindness or dismiss them with kindness, and call to witness two just ones from among you, and give upright testimony for Allah. With that is admonished he who believes in Allah and the Latter Day. And whoever keeps his duty to Allah, He ordains a way out for him,

65:3. And gives him sustenance from whence he imagines not. And whoever trusts in Allah, He is sufficient for him. Surely Allah attains His purpose. Allah indeed has appointed a measure for everything.

65:4. And those of your women who despair of menstruation, if you have a doubt, their prescribed time is three months, and of those, too, who have not had their courses. And the pregnant women, their prescribed time is that they lay down their burden. And whoever keeps his duty to Allah, He makes his affair easy for him.

65:5. That is the command of Allah, which He has revealed to you. And whoever keeps his duty to Allah, He will remove from him his evils and give him a big reward.

65:6. Lodge them where you live according to your means, and injure them not to straiten them. And if they are pregnant, spend on them until they lay down their burden. Then if they suckle for you, give them their recompense, and enjoin one another to do good and if you disagree, another will suckle for him.

65:7. Let him who has abundance spend out of his abundance, and whoever has his means of subsistence straitened to him, let him spend out of that which Allah has given him. Allah lays not on any soul a burden beyond that which He has given it. Allah brings about ease after difficulty.

***

65:8. And how many a town which rebelled against the commandment of its Lord and His messengers, so We called it to severe account and We chastised it with a stern chastisement!

65:9. So it tasted the evil consequences of its conduct, and the end of its affair was perdition.

66. The Prohibition

65:10. Allah has prepared for them severe chastisement, so keep your duty to Allah, O men of understanding, who believe. Allah has indeed sent down to you a Reminder --

65:11. A Messenger who recites to you the clear messages of Allah, so that he may bring forth those who believe and do good deeds from darkness into light. And whoever believes in Allah and does good deeds, He will cause him to enter Gardens wherein rivers flow, to abide therein for ever. Allah has indeed given him a goodly sustenance.

65:12. Allah is He who created seven heavens, and of the earth the like thereof. The command descends among them, that you may know that Allah is Possessor of power over all things, and that Allah encompasses all things in (His) knowledge.

66. The Prohibition

In the name of Allah, the Beneficent, the Merciful.

66:1. O Prophet, why dost thou forbid (thyself) that which Allah has made lawful for thee? Seekest thou to please thy wives? And Allah is Forgiving, Merciful.

66:2. Allah indeed has sanctioned for you the expiation of your oaths; and Allah is your Patron, and He is the Knowing, the Wise.

66:3. And when the Prophet confided an information to one of his wives -- but when she informed (others) of it, and Allah informed him of it, he made known part of it and passed over part. So when he told her of it, she said Who informed thee of this? He said The Knowing, the One Aware, informed me.

66:4. If you both turn to Allah, then indeed your hearts are inclined (to

66. The Prohibition

this); and if you back up one another against him, then surely Allah is his Patron, and Gabriel and the righteous believers, and the angels after that are the aiders.

66:5. Maybe, his Lord, if he divorce you, will give him in your place wives better than you, submissive, faithful, obedient, penitent, adorers, fasters, widows, and virgins.

66:6. O you who believe, save yourselves and your families from a Fire whose fuel is men and stones; over it are angels, stern and strong. They do not disobey Allah in that which He commands them, but do as they are commanded.

66:7. O you who disbelieve, make no excuses this day. You are rewarded only as you did.

***

66:8. O you who believe, turn to Allah with sincere repentance. It may be your Lord will remove from you your evil and cause you to enter Gardens wherein flow rivers, on the day on which Allah will not abase the Prophet and those who believe with him. Their light will gleam before them and on their right hands -- they will say: Our Lord, make perfect for us our light, and grant us protection surely Thou art Possessor of power over all things.

66:9. O Prophet, strive against the disbelievers and the hypocrites, and remain firm against them, and their abode is hell; and evil is the resort.

66:10. Allah sets forth an example for those who disbelieve -- the wife of Noah and the wife of Lot. They were both under two of Our righteous servants, but they acted treacherously towards them, so they availed them naught against Allah, and it was said Enter the Fire with those who enter.

66:11. And Allah sets forth an example for those who believe -- the wife of Pharaoh, when she said: My Lord,

67. The Kingdom

build for me a house with Thee in the Garden and deliver me from Pharaoh and his work, and deliver me from the iniquitous people.

66:12. And Mary, the daughter of Amran, who guarded her chastity, so We breathed into him Our inspiration, and she accepted the truth of the words of her Lord and His Books, and she was of the obedient ones.

67. The Kingdom

In the name of Allah, the Beneficent, the Merciful.

67:1. Blessed is He in Whose hand is the Kingdom, and He is Possessor of power over all thing.

67:2. Who created death and life that He might try you -- which of you is best in deeds. And He is the Mighty, the Forgiving,

67:3. Who created the seven heavens alike. Thou seest no incongruity in the creation of the Beneficent. Then look again: Canst thou see any disorder?

67:4. Then turn the eye again and again -- thy look will return to thee confused, while it is fatigued.

67:5. And certainly We have adorned this lower heaven with lamps and We make them means of conjectures for the devils, and We have prepared for them the chastisement of burning.

67:6. And for those who disbelieve in their Lord is the chastisement of hell, and evil is the resort.

67:7. When they are cast therein, they will hear a loud moaning of it as it heaves,

67:8. Almost bursting for fury. Whenever a group is cast into it, its keepers ask them: Did not a warner come to you?

67:9. They say: Yea, indeed a warner came to us, but we denied and said Allah has revealed nothing you are

67. The Kingdom

only in great error.

67:10. And they say: Had we but listened or pondered, we should not have been among the inmates of the burning Fire.

67:11. Thus they will confess their stns so far (from good) are the inmates of the burning Fire.

67:12. Those who fear their Lord in secret, for them is surely forgiveness and a great reward.

67:13. And conceal your word or manifest it, truly He is Knower of that which is in the hearts.

67:14. Does He not know Who created? And He is the Knower of subtilties, the Aware.

* * *

67:15. He it is Who made the earth subservient to you, so go about in the spacious sides thereof, and eat of His sustenance. And to Him is the rising (after death).

67:16. Do you feel secure that He Who is in the heaven will not make the earth to swallow you up? Then lo! it will shake.

67:17. Or do you feel secure that He Who is in the Heaven will not send on you a violent wind? Then shall you. know how (truthful) was My warning!

67:18. And cettainly those before them denied, then how (terrible) was My disapproval.

67:19. Do they not see the birds above them spreading and contracting (their wings)? Naught upholds them save the Beneficent. Surely He is Seer of all things.

67:20. Or who is it that will be a host for you to help you against the Beneficent? The disbelievers are in naught but delusion.

67:21. Or who is it that will give you sustenance, if He should withhold His sustenance? Nay, they persist in disdain and aversion.

67:22. Is, then, he who goes prone upon

ضَلَالٍ كَبِيرٍ (٩)
وَقَالُوا لَوْ كُنَّا نَسْمَعُ أَوْ نَعْقِلُ مَا كُنَّا فِي أَصْحَابِ السَّعِيرِ (١٠)
فَاعْتَرَفُوا بِذَنْبِهِمْ فَسُحْقًا لِأَصْحَابِ السَّعِيرِ (١١)
إِنَّ الَّذِينَ يَخْشَوْنَ رَبَّهُمْ بِالْغَيْبِ لَهُمْ مَغْفِرَةٌ وَأَجْرٌ كَبِيرٌ (١٢)
وَأَسِرُّوا قَوْلَكُمْ أَوِ اجْهَرُوا بِهِ إِنَّهُ عَلِيمٌ بِذَاتِ الصُّدُورِ (١٣)
أَلَا يَعْلَمُ مَنْ خَلَقَ وَهُوَ اللَّطِيفُ الْخَبِيرُ (١٤)
هُوَ الَّذِي جَعَلَ لَكُمُ الْأَرْضَ ذَلُولًا فَامْشُوا فِي مَنَاكِبِهَا وَكُلُوا مِنْ رِزْقِهِ وَإِلَيْهِ النُّشُورُ (١٥)
أَأَمِنْتُمْ مَنْ فِي السَّمَاءِ أَنْ يَخْسِفَ بِكُمُ الْأَرْضَ فَإِذَا هِيَ تَمُورُ (١٦)
أَمْ أَمِنْتُمْ مَنْ فِي السَّمَاءِ أَنْ يُرْسِلَ عَلَيْكُمْ حَاصِبًا فَسَتَعْلَمُونَ كَيْفَ نَذِيرِ (١٧)
وَلَقَدْ كَذَّبَ الَّذِينَ مِنْ قَبْلِهِمْ فَكَيْفَ كَانَ نَكِيرِ (١٨)
أَوَلَمْ يَرَوْا إِلَى الطَّيْرِ فَوْقَهُمْ صَافَّاتٍ وَيَقْبِضْنَ مَا يُمْسِكُهُنَّ إِلَّا الرَّحْمَنُ إِنَّهُ بِكُلِّ شَيْءٍ بَصِيرٌ (١٩)
أَمَّنْ هَذَا الَّذِي هُوَ جُنْدٌ لَكُمْ يَنْصُرُكُمْ مِنْ دُونِ الرَّحْمَنِ إِنِ الْكَافِرُونَ إِلَّا فِي غُرُورٍ (٢٠)
أَمَّنْ هَذَا الَّذِي يَرْزُقُكُمْ إِنْ أَمْسَكَ رِزْقَهُ بَلْ لَجُّوا فِي عُتُوٍّ وَنُفُورٍ (٢١)
أَفَمَنْ يَمْشِي مُكِبًّا عَلَى وَجْهِهِ أَهْدَى أَمَّنْ يَمْشِي سَوِيًّا عَلَى صِرَاطٍ مُسْتَقِيمٍ (٢٢)
قُلْ هُوَ الَّذِي أَنْشَأَكُمْ وَجَعَلَ لَكُمُ

68. The Pen

his face better guided or he who walks upright on a straight path?

67:23. Say: He it is Who brought you into being and made for you ears and eyes and hearts. Little thanks it is you give!

67:24. Say: He it is Who multiplies you in the earth and to Him you will be gathered.

67:25. And they say: When will this threat be (executed), if you are truthful?

67:26. Say: The knowledge is with Allah only, and I am only a plain warner.

67:27. But when they see it nigh, the faces of those who disbelieve will be grieved, and it will be said: This is that which you used to call for.

67:28. Say: Have you considered if Allah should destroy me and those with me -- rather He will have mercy on us yet who will protect the disbelievers from a painful chastisement?

67:29. Say: He is the Beneficent -- we believe in Him and on Him do we rely. So you will come to know who it is that is in clear error.

67:30. Say: Have you considered if your water should subside, who is it then that will bring you flowing water?

68. The Pen

In the name of Allah, the Beneficent, the Merciful.

68:1. (By) the inkstand and the pen and that which they write!

68:2. By the grace of thy Lord thou art not mad.

68:3. And surely thine is a reward never to be cut off.

68:4. And surely thou hast sublime morals.

68:5. So thou wilt see, and they (too) will see,

68. The Pen

68:6. Which of you is mad.
68:7. Surely thy Lord knows best who is erring from His way, and He knows best those who go aright.
68:8. So obey not the rejectors.
68:9. They wish that thou shouldst be pliant, so they (too) would be pliant.
68:10. And obey not any mean swearer,
68:11. Defamer, going about with slander,
68:12. Hinderer of good, out-stepping the limits, sinful,
68:13. Ignoble, besides all that, notoriously mischievous --
68:14. Because he possesses wealth and sons.
68:15. When Our messages are recited to him, he says: Stories of those of yore!
68:16. We shall brand him on the snout.
68:17. We shall try them as We tried the owners of the garden, when they swore to pluck its fruits in the morning,
68:18. And would not set aside a portion (for the poor).
68:19. But a visitation from thy Lord came on it, While they slept.
68:20. So it became as black, barren land --
68:21. Then they called out one to another in the morning,
68:22. Saying: Go early to your tilth, if you would pluck (the fruit).
68:23. So they went, while they said one to another in low tones:
68:24. No poor man shall enter it to-day to you --
68:25. And in the morning they went, having the power to prevent.
68:26. But when they saw it, they said: Surely we are in error;
68:27. Nay, we are made to suffer privation.
68:28. The best of them said: Said I not to you, Why do you not glorify (Allah)?
68:29. They said: Glory be to our Lord! surely we were unjust.
68:30. Then some of them advanced

سَبِيلِهِ وَهُوَ أَعْلَمُ بِالْمُهْتَدِينَ (٧)
فَلَا تُطِعِ الْمُكَذِّبِينَ (٨)
وَدُّوا لَوْ تُدْهِنُ فَيُدْهِنُونَ (٩)
وَلَا تُطِعْ كُلَّ حَلَّافٍ مَهِينٍ (١٠)
هَمَّازٍ مَشَّاءٍ بِنَمِيمٍ (١١)
مَنَّاعٍ لِلْخَيْرِ مُعْتَدٍ أَثِيمٍ (١٢)
عُتُلٍّ بَعْدَ ذَلِكَ زَنِيمٍ (١٣)
أَنْ كَانَ ذَا مَالٍ وَبَنِينَ (١٤)
إِذَا تُتْلَى عَلَيْهِ آيَاتُنَا قَالَ أَسَاطِيرُ الْأَوَّلِينَ (١٥)
سَنَسِمُهُ عَلَى الْخُرْطُومِ (١٦)
إِنَّا بَلَوْنَاهُمْ كَمَا بَلَوْنَا أَصْحَابَ الْجَنَّةِ إِذْ أَقْسَمُوا لَيَصْرِمُنَّهَا مُصْبِحِينَ (١٧)
وَلَا يَسْتَثْنُونَ (١٨)
فَطَافَ عَلَيْهَا طَائِفٌ مِنْ رَبِّكَ وَهُمْ نَائِمُونَ (١٩)
فَأَصْبَحَتْ كَالصَّرِيمِ (٢٠)
فَتَنَادَوْا مُصْبِحِينَ (٢١)
أَنِ اغْدُوا عَلَى حَرْثِكُمْ إِنْ كُنْتُمْ صَارِمِينَ (٢٢)
فَانْطَلَقُوا وَهُمْ يَتَخَافَتُونَ (٢٣)
أَنْ لَا يَدْخُلَنَّهَا الْيَوْمَ عَلَيْكُمْ مِسْكِينٌ (٢٤)
وَغَدَوْا عَلَى حَرْدٍ قَادِرِينَ (٢٥)
فَلَمَّا رَأَوْهَا قَالُوا إِنَّا لَضَالُّونَ (٢٦)
بَلْ نَحْنُ مَحْرُومُونَ (٢٧)
قَالَ أَوْسَطُهُمْ أَلَمْ أَقُلْ لَكُمْ لَوْلَا تُسَبِّحُونَ (٢٨)
قَالُوا سُبْحَانَ رَبِّنَا إِنَّا كُنَّا ظَالِمِينَ (٢٩)
فَأَقْبَلَ بَعْضُهُمْ عَلَى بَعْضٍ يَتَلَاوَمُونَ

68. The Pen

against others, blaming each other.
68:31. Said they: O woe to us! Surely we were inordinate --
68:32. Maybe, our Lord will give us instead one better than it surely to our Lord we make petition.
68:33. Such is the chastisement. And certainly the chastisement of the Hereafter is greater, did they but know!

***

68:34. Surely the dutiful have with their Lord Gardens of bliss.
68:35. Shall We then make those who submit as the guilty?
68:36. What is the matter with you? How do you judge?
68:37. Or have you a book wherein you read
68:38. That you shall surely have therein what you choose?
68:39. Or have you covenants from Us on oath, extending to the day of Resurrection, that yours is surely what you judge?
68:40. Ask them which of them will vouch for that.
68:41. Or have they associate-gods? Then let them bring their associates, if they are truthful.
68:42. On the day when there is a severe affliction, and they are called upon to prostrate themselves, but they are not able --
68:43. Their looks cast down, abasement will cover them. And they were indeed called upon to prostrate themselves, while yet they were safe.
68:44. So leave Me alone with him who rejects this announcement. We shall overtake them by degrees, from whence they know not.
68:45. And I bear with them, surely My plan is firm.
68:46. Or dost thou ask from them a reward, so that they are burdened with debt?
68:47. Or is the unseen with them so

(٣٠)
قَالُوا يَا وَيْلَنَا إِنَّا كُنَّا طَاغِينَ (٣١)
عَسَىٰ رَبُّنَا أَنْ يُبْدِلَنَا خَيْرًا مِنْهَا إِنَّا إِلَىٰ رَبِّنَا رَاغِبُونَ (٣٢)
كَذَٰلِكَ الْعَذَابُ وَلَعَذَابُ الْآخِرَةِ أَكْبَرُ لَوْ كَانُوا يَعْلَمُونَ (٣٣)
إِنَّ لِلْمُتَّقِينَ عِنْدَ رَبِّهِمْ جَنَّاتِ النَّعِيمِ (٣٤)
أَفَنَجْعَلُ الْمُسْلِمِينَ كَالْمُجْرِمِينَ (٣٥)
مَا لَكُمْ كَيْفَ تَحْكُمُونَ (٣٦)
أَمْ لَكُمْ كِتَابٌ فِيهِ تَدْرُسُونَ (٣٧)
إِنَّ لَكُمْ فِيهِ لَمَا تَخَيَّرُونَ (٣٨)
أَمْ لَكُمْ أَيْمَانٌ عَلَيْنَا بَالِغَةٌ إِلَىٰ يَوْمِ الْقِيَامَةِ إِنَّ لَكُمْ لَمَا تَحْكُمُونَ (٣٩)
سَلْهُمْ أَيُّهُمْ بِذَٰلِكَ زَعِيمٌ (٤٠)
أَمْ لَهُمْ شُرَكَاءُ فَلْيَأْتُوا بِشُرَكَائِهِمْ إِنْ كَانُوا صَادِقِينَ (٤١)
يَوْمَ يُكْشَفُ عَنْ سَاقٍ وَيُدْعَوْنَ إِلَى السُّجُودِ فَلَا يَسْتَطِيعُونَ (٤٢)
خَاشِعَةً أَبْصَارُهُمْ تَرْهَقُهُمْ ذِلَّةٌ وَقَدْ كَانُوا يُدْعَوْنَ إِلَى السُّجُودِ وَهُمْ سَالِمُونَ (٤٣)
فَذَرْنِي وَمَنْ يُكَذِّبُ بِهَٰذَا الْحَدِيثِ سَنَسْتَدْرِجُهُمْ مِنْ حَيْثُ لَا يَعْلَمُونَ (٤٤)
وَأُمْلِي لَهُمْ إِنَّ كَيْدِي مَتِينٌ (٤٥)
أَمْ تَسْأَلُهُمْ أَجْرًا فَهُمْ مِنْ مَغْرَمٍ مُثْقَلُونَ (٤٦)
أَمْ عِنْدَهُمُ الْغَيْبُ فَهُمْ يَكْتُبُونَ (٤٧)
فَاصْبِرْ لِحُكْمِ رَبِّكَ وَلَا تَكُنْ كَصَاحِبِ الْحُوتِ إِذْ نَادَىٰ وَهُوَ مَكْظُومٌ (٤٨)
لَوْلَا أَنْ تَدَارَكَهُ نِعْمَةٌ مِنْ رَبِّهِ لَنُبِذَ

that they write (it) down?

68:48. So wait patiently for the judgment of thy Lord, and be not like the Companion of the fish, when he cried while he was in distress.

68:49. Had not favour from his Lord reached him, he would certainly have been cast down on naked ground, while he was blamed.

68:50. Then his Lord chose him, and He made him of the righteous.

68:51. And those who disbelieve would almost smite thee with their eyes when they hear the Reminder, and they say: Surely he is mad!

68:52. And it is naught but a Reminder for the nations.

69. The Sure Truth

In the name of Allah, the Beneficent, the Merciful.

69:1. The sure Truth!

69:2. What is the sure Truth?

69:3. And what would make thee realize what the sure Truth is?

69:4. Thamud and 'Ad called the calamity a lie.

69:5. Then as for Thamud, they were destroyed by the severe punishment.

69:6. And as for 'Ad, they were destroyed by a roaring, violent wind,

69:7. Which He made to prevail against them for seven nights and eight days continuously, so that thou mightest have seen the people therein prostrate as if they were trunks of hollow palm-trees.

69:8. So canst thou see a remnant of them?

69:9. And Pharaoh and those before him and the overthrown cities wrought evil.

69:10. And they disobeyed the messenger of their Lord, so He punished them with a vehement punishment.

69. The Sure Truth

69:11. Surely We carried you in the ship, when the water rose high,
69:12. That We might make it a reminder for you, and that the retaining ear might retain it.
69:13. So when the trumpet is blown with a single blast,
69:14. And the earth and the mountains are borne away and crushed with one crash --
69:15. On that day will the Event come to pass,
69:16. And the heaven will be cleft asunder; so that day it will be frail,
69:17. And the angels will be on its sides. And above them eight will bear that day thy Lord's Throne of Power.
69:18. On that day you will be exposed to view -- no secret of yours will remain hidden.
69:19. Then as for him who is given his book in his right hand, he will say: Lo! Read my book.
69:20. Surely I knew that I should meet my account.
69:21. So he will be in a life of bliss,
69:22. In a lofty Garden,
69:23. Its fruits are near.
69:24. Eat and drink pleasantly for that which you sent on before in bygone days.
69:25. And as for him who is given his book in his left hand -- he will say: O would that my book had not been given to me!
69:26. And I had not known what my account was!
69:27. O would that (death) had made an end (of me)!
69:28. My wealth has not availed me.
69:29. My authority has gone from me.
69:30. Seize him, then fetter him,
69:31. Then cast him into the burning Fire,
69:32. Then insert him in a chain the length of which is seventy cubits.
69:33. Surely he believed not in Allah, the Great,

لِنَجْعَلَهَا لَكُمْ تَذْكِرَةً وَتَعِيَهَا أُذُنٌ وَاعِيَةٌ (١٢)
فَإِذَا نُفِخَ فِي الصُّورِ نَفْخَةٌ وَاحِدَةٌ (١٣)
وَحُمِلَتِ الْأَرْضُ وَالْجِبَالُ فَدُكَّتَا دَكَّةً وَاحِدَةً (١٤)
فَيَوْمَئِذٍ وَقَعَتِ الْوَاقِعَةُ (١٥)
وَانْشَقَّتِ السَّمَاءُ فَهِيَ يَوْمَئِذٍ وَاهِيَةٌ (١٦)
وَالْمَلَكُ عَلَى أَرْجَائِهَا وَيَحْمِلُ عَرْشَ رَبِّكَ فَوْقَهُمْ يَوْمَئِذٍ ثَمَانِيَةٌ (١٧)
يَوْمَئِذٍ تُعْرَضُونَ لَا تَخْفَى مِنْكُمْ خَافِيَةٌ (١٨)
فَأَمَّا مَنْ أُوتِيَ كِتَابَهُ بِيَمِينِهِ فَيَقُولُ هَاؤُمُ اقْرَءُوا كِتَابِيَهْ (١٩)
إِنِّي ظَنَنْتُ أَنِّي مُلَاقٍ حِسَابِيَهْ (٢٠)
فَهُوَ فِي عِيشَةٍ رَاضِيَةٍ (٢١)
فِي جَنَّةٍ عَالِيَةٍ (٢٢)
قُطُوفُهَا دَانِيَةٌ (٢٣)
كُلُوا وَاشْرَبُوا هَنِيئًا بِمَا أَسْلَفْتُمْ فِي الْأَيَّامِ الْخَالِيَةِ (٢٤)
وَأَمَّا مَنْ أُوتِيَ كِتَابَهُ بِشِمَالِهِ فَيَقُولُ يَا لَيْتَنِي لَمْ أُوتَ كِتَابِيَهْ (٢٥)
وَلَمْ أَدْرِ مَا حِسَابِيَهْ (٢٦)
يَا لَيْتَهَا كَانَتِ الْقَاضِيَةَ (٢٧)
مَا أَغْنَى عَنِّي مَالِيَهْ (٢٨)
هَلَكَ عَنِّي سُلْطَانِيَهْ (٢٩)
خُذُوهُ فَغُلُّوهُ (٣٠)
ثُمَّ الْجَحِيمَ صَلُّوهُ (٣١)
ثُمَّ فِي سِلْسِلَةٍ ذَرْعُهَا سَبْعُونَ ذِرَاعًا فَاسْلُكُوهُ (٣٢)
إِنَّهُ كَانَ لَا يُؤْمِنُ بِاللَّهِ الْعَظِيمِ (٣٣)

69:34. Nor did he urge the feeding of the poor.
69:35. Therefore he has nor here this day a true friend,
69:36. Nor any fond except refuse,
69:37. Which none but the wrongdoers eat.

* * *

69:38. But nay! I sweat by that which you see,
69:39. And that which you see not!
69:40. Surely, it is the word of an honoured Messenger;
69:41. And it is not the word of a poet. Little is it that you believe!
69:42. Nor the word of a soothsayer. Little is it that you mind!
69:43. It is a revelation from the Lord of the worlds.
69:44. And if he had fabricated against Us certain sayings,
69:45. We would certainly have seized him by the right hand,
69:46. Then cut off his heart's vein.
69:47. And not one of you could have withheld Us from him.
69:48. And surely it is a Reminder for the dutiful.
69:49. And We certainly know that some of you are rejectors.
69:50. And it is indeed a (source of) grief to the disbelievers.
69:51. And surely it is the certain Truth.
69:52. So glorify the name of thy Lord, the Incomparably Great.

70. The Ways of Ascent

In the name of Allah, the Beneficent, the Merciful.
70:1. A questioner asks about the chastisement to befall
70:2. The disbelievers - there is none to avert it --
70:3. From Allah, Lord of the ways of Ascent.

70. The Ways of Ascent

70:4. To Him ascend the angels and the Spirit in a day the measure of which is fifty thousand years.
70:5. So be patient with a goodly patience.
70:6. Surely they see it far off,
70:7. And We see it nigh.
70:8. The day when the heaven is as molten brass,
70:9. And the mountains are as wool;
70:10. And no friend will ask of friend,
70:11. (Though) they are made to see them. The guilty one would fain redeem himself from the chastisement of that day by his children,
70:12. And his wife and his brother,
70:13. And his kin that gave him shelter,
70:14. And all that are in the earth -- then deliver him --
70:15. By no means! Surely it is a flaming Fire,
70:16. Plucking out the extremities --
70:17. It shall claim him who retreats and turns his back,
70:18. And hoards then withholds.
70:19. Surely man is created impatient --
70:20. Fretful when evil afflicts him,
70:21. And niggardly when good befalls him --
70:22. Except those who pray,
70:23. Who are constant at their prayer,
70:24. And in whose wealth there is a known right
70:25. For the beggar and the destitute,
70:26. And those who accept the truth of the day of Judgment:
70:27. And those who are fearful of the chastisement of their Lord --
70:28. Surely the chastisement of their Lord is (a thing) not to be felt secure from --
70:29. And those who restrain their sexual passions,
70:30. Except in the presence of their mates or those whom their right hands possess -- for such surely are not to be

كَانَ مِقْدَارُهُ خَمْسِينَ أَلْفَ سَنَةٍ (٤)
فَاصْبِرْ صَبْرًا جَمِيلًا (٥)
إِنَّهُمْ يَرَوْنَهُ بَعِيدًا (٦)
وَنَرَاهُ قَرِيبًا (٧)
يَوْمَ تَكُونُ السَّمَاءُ كَالْمُهْلِ (٨)
وَتَكُونُ الْجِبَالُ كَالْعِهْنِ (٩)
وَلَا يَسْأَلُ حَمِيمٌ حَمِيمًا (١٠)
يُبَصَّرُونَهُمْ يَوَدُّ الْمُجْرِمُ لَوْ يَفْتَدِي مِنْ عَذَابِ يَوْمِئِذٍ بِبَنِيهِ (١١)
وَصَاحِبَتِهِ وَأَخِيهِ (١٢)
وَفَصِيلَتِهِ الَّتِي تُؤْوِيهِ (١٣)
وَمَنْ فِي الْأَرْضِ جَمِيعًا ثُمَّ يُنْجِيهِ (١٤)
كَلَّا إِنَّهَا لَظَى (١٥)
نَزَّاعَةً لِلشَّوَى (١٦)
تَدْعُوا مَنْ أَدْبَرَ وَتَوَلَّى (١٧)
وَجَمَعَ فَأَوْعَى (١٨)
إِنَّ الْإِنْسَانَ خُلِقَ هَلُوعًا (١٩)
إِذَا مَسَّهُ الشَّرُّ جَزُوعًا (٢٠)
وَإِذَا مَسَّهُ الْخَيْرُ مَنُوعًا (٢١)
إِلَّا الْمُصَلِّينَ (٢٢)
الَّذِينَ هُمْ عَلَى صَلَاتِهِمْ دَائِمُونَ (٢٣)
وَالَّذِينَ فِي أَمْوَالِهِمْ حَقٌّ مَعْلُومٌ (٢٤)
لِلسَّائِلِ وَالْمَحْرُومِ (٢٥)
وَالَّذِينَ يُصَدِّقُونَ بِيَوْمِ الدِّينِ (٢٦)
وَالَّذِينَ هُمْ مِنْ عَذَابِ رَبِّهِمْ مُشْفِقُونَ (٢٧)
إِنَّ عَذَابَ رَبِّهِمْ غَيْرُ مَأْمُونٍ (٢٨)
وَالَّذِينَ هُمْ لِفُرُوجِهِمْ حَافِظُونَ (٢٩)
إِلَّا عَلَى أَزْوَاجِهِمْ أَوْ مَا مَلَكَتْ أَيْمَانُهُمْ فَإِنَّهُمْ غَيْرُ مَلُومِينَ (٣٠)

blamed,
70:31. But he who seeks to go beyond this, these are the transgressors.
70:32. And those who are faithful to their trusts and their covenant,
70:33. And those who are upright in their testimonies,
70:34. And those who keep a guard on their prayer.
70:35. These are in Gardens, honoured.

* * *

70:36. But what is the matter with those who disbelieve, that they hasten on to thee,
70:37. On the right hand and on the left, in sundry parties?
70:38. Does every man of them desire to be admitted to the Garden of bliss?
70:39. By no means! Surely We have created them for what they know.
70:40. But nay I swear by the Lord of the Eastern lands and the Western lands that We are certainly Powerful
70:41. To bring in their place (others) better than them, and We shall not be overcome.
70:42. So leave them alone to plunge in vain talk and to sport, until they come face to face with that day of theirs which they are promised --
70:43. The day when they come forth from the graves in haste, as hastening on to a goal,
70:44. Their eyes cast down, disgrace covering them. Such is the day which they are promised.

71. Noah

In the name of Allah, the Beneficent, the Merciful.
71:1. Surely We sent Noah to his people, saying: Warn thy people before there come to them a painful chastisement.
71:2. He said: O my people, surely I am a plain warner to you:

فَمَنِ ابْتَغَىٰ وَرَاءَ ذَٰلِكَ فَأُولَٰئِكَ هُمُ الْعَادُونَ (٣١)
وَالَّذِينَ هُمْ لِأَمَانَاتِهِمْ وَعَهْدِهِمْ رَاعُونَ (٣٢)
وَالَّذِينَ هُم بِشَهَادَاتِهِمْ قَائِمُونَ (٣٣)
وَالَّذِينَ هُمْ عَلَىٰ صَلَاتِهِمْ يُحَافِظُونَ (٣٤)
أُولَٰئِكَ فِي جَنَّاتٍ مُكْرَمُونَ (٣٥)
فَمَالِ الَّذِينَ كَفَرُوا قِبَلَكَ مُهْطِعِينَ (٣٦)
عَنِ الْيَمِينِ وَعَنِ الشِّمَالِ عِزِينَ (٣٧)
أَيَطْمَعُ كُلُّ امْرِئٍ مِنْهُمْ أَن يُدْخَلَ جَنَّةَ نَعِيمٍ (٣٨)
كَلَّا إِنَّا خَلَقْنَاهُم مِّمَّا يَعْلَمُونَ (٣٩)
فَلَا أُقْسِمُ بِرَبِّ الْمَشَارِقِ وَالْمَغَارِبِ إِنَّا لَقَادِرُونَ (٤٠)
عَلَىٰ أَن نُّبَدِّلَ خَيْرًا مِّنْهُمْ وَمَا نَحْنُ بِمَسْبُوقِينَ (٤١)
فَذَرْهُمْ يَخُوضُوا وَيَلْعَبُوا حَتَّىٰ يُلَاقُوا يَوْمَهُمُ الَّذِي يُوعَدُونَ (٤٢)
يَوْمَ يَخْرُجُونَ مِنَ الْأَجْدَاثِ سِرَاعًا كَأَنَّهُمْ إِلَىٰ نُصُبٍ يُوفِضُونَ (٤٣)
خَاشِعَةً أَبْصَارُهُمْ تَرْهَقُهُمْ ذِلَّةٌ ذَٰلِكَ الْيَوْمُ الَّذِي كَانُوا يُوعَدُونَ (٤٤)

٧١- سورة نوح

بِسْمِ اللَّهِ الرَّحْمَٰنِ الرَّحِيمِ
إِنَّا أَرْسَلْنَا نُوحًا إِلَىٰ قَوْمِهِ أَنْ أَنذِرْ قَوْمَكَ مِن قَبْلِ أَن يَأْتِيَهُمْ عَذَابٌ أَلِيمٌ (١)
قَالَ يَا قَوْمِ إِنِّي لَكُمْ نَذِيرٌ مُّبِينٌ (٢)

71:3. That you should serve Allah and keep your duty to Him and obey me --
71:4. He will forgive you some of your sins and grant you respite to an appointed term. Surely the term of Allah, when it comes, is not postponed. Did you but know!
71:5. He said: My Lord, I have called my people night and day:
71:6. But my call has only made them flee the more.
71:7. And whenever I call to them that Thou mayest forgive them, they thrust their fingers in their ears and cover themselves with their garments, and persist and are big with pride.
71:8. Then surely I have called to them aloud,
71:9. Then spoken to them in public and spoken to them in private,
71:10. So I have said: Ask forgiveness of your Lord; surely He is ever Forgiving:
71:11. He will send down upon you rain, pouring in abundance,
71:12. And help you with wealth and sons, and make for you gardens, and make for you rivers.
71:13. What is the matter with you that you hope not for greatness from Allah?
71:14. And indeed He has created you by various stages.
71:15. See you not how Allah has created the seven heavens alike,
71:16. And made the moon therein a light, and made the sun a lamp?
71:17. And Allah has caused you to grow out of the earth as a growth,
71:18. Then He returns you to it, then will He bring you forth a (new) bringing forth.
71:19. And Allah has made the earth a wide expanse for you;
71:20. That you may go along therein in spacious paths.

* * *

71:21. Noah said: My Lord, surely they disobey me and follow him whose

أَنِ اعْبُدُوا اللَّهَ وَاتَّقُوهُ وَأَطِيعُونِ (٣)
يَغْفِرْ لَكُمْ مِنْ ذُنُوبِكُمْ وَيُؤَخِّرْكُمْ إِلَى أَجَلٍ مُسَمًّى إِنَّ أَجَلَ اللَّهِ إِذَا جَاءَ لَا يُؤَخَّرُ لَوْ كُنْتُمْ تَعْلَمُونَ (٤)
قَالَ رَبِّ إِنِّي دَعَوْتُ قَوْمِي لَيْلًا وَنَهَارًا (٥)
فَلَمْ يَزِدْهُمْ دُعَائِي إِلَّا فِرَارًا (٦)
وَإِنِّي كُلَّمَا دَعَوْتُهُمْ لِتَغْفِرَ لَهُمْ جَعَلُوا أَصَابِعَهُمْ فِي آذَانِهِمْ وَاسْتَغْشَوْا ثِيَابَهُمْ وَأَصَرُّوا وَاسْتَكْبَرُوا اسْتِكْبَارًا (٧)
ثُمَّ إِنِّي دَعَوْتُهُمْ جِهَارًا (٨)
ثُمَّ إِنِّي أَعْلَنْتُ لَهُمْ وَأَسْرَرْتُ لَهُمْ إِسْرَارًا (٩)
فَقُلْتُ اسْتَغْفِرُوا رَبَّكُمْ إِنَّهُ كَانَ غَفَّارًا (١٠)
يُرْسِلِ السَّمَاءَ عَلَيْكُمْ مِدْرَارًا (١١)
وَيُمْدِدْكُمْ بِأَمْوَالٍ وَبَنِينَ وَيَجْعَلْ لَكُمْ جَنَّاتٍ وَيَجْعَلْ لَكُمْ أَنْهَارًا (١٢)
مَا لَكُمْ لَا تَرْجُونَ لِلَّهِ وَقَارًا (١٣)
وَقَدْ خَلَقَكُمْ أَطْوَارًا (١٤)
أَلَمْ تَرَوْا كَيْفَ خَلَقَ اللَّهُ سَبْعَ سَمَوَاتٍ طِبَاقًا (١٥)
وَجَعَلَ الْقَمَرَ فِيهِنَّ نُورًا وَجَعَلَ الشَّمْسَ سِرَاجًا (١٦)
وَاللَّهُ أَنْبَتَكُمْ مِنَ الْأَرْضِ نَبَاتًا (١٧)
ثُمَّ يُعِيدُكُمْ فِيهَا وَيُخْرِجُكُمْ إِخْرَاجًا (١٨)
وَاللَّهُ جَعَلَ لَكُمُ الْأَرْضَ بِسَاطًا (١٩)
لِتَسْلُكُوا مِنْهَا سُبُلًا فِجَاجًا (٢٠)
قَالَ نُوحٌ رَبِّ إِنَّهُمْ عَصَوْنِي وَاتَّبَعُوا مَنْ لَمْ يَزِدْهُ مَالُهُ وَوَلَدُهُ إِلَّا خَسَارًا (٢١)

wealth and children have increased him in naught but loss.
71:22. And they have planned a mighty plan.
71:23. And they say: Forsake not your gods; nor forsake Wadd, nor Suwa', nor Yaguth and Ya'uq and Nasr.
71:24. And indeed they have led many astray. And increase Thou the wrongdoers in naught but perdition.
71:25. Because of their wrongs they were drowned, then made to enter Fire, so they found no helpers besides Allah.
71:26. And Noah said My Lord, leave not of the disbelievers any dweller on the land.
71:27. For if Thou leave them, they will lead astray Thy servants, and will not beget any but immoral, ungrateful ones.
71:28. My Lord, forgive me and my parents and him who enters my house believing, and the believing men and the believing women. And increase nor the wrongdoers in aught but destruction!

72. The Jinn

In the name of Allah, the Beneficent, the Merciful.
72:1. Say It has been revealed to me that a party of the jinn listened, so they said: Surely we have heard a wonderful Qur'an,
72:2. Guiding to the right way -- so we believe in it. And we shall nor set up any one with our Lord:
72:3. And He -- exalted be the majesty of our Lord! -- has not taken a consort, nor a son:
72:4. And the foolish among us used to forge extravagant lies against Allah:
72:5. And we thought that men and jinn did not utter a lie against Allah:
72:6. And persons from among men used to seek refuge with persons from

72. The Jinn

among the jinn, so they increased them in evil doing:

72:7. And they thought, as you think, that Allah would not raise anyone:

72:8. And we sought to reach heaven, but we found it filled with strong guards and flames:

72:9. And we used to sit in some of the sitting-places thereof to steal a hearing. But he who tries to listen now finds a flame lying in wait for him:

72:10. And we know not whether evil is meant for those on earth or whether their Lord means to direct them aright:

72:11. And some of us are good and others of us are below that -- we are sects following different ways:

72:12. And we know that we cannot escape Allah in the earth, nor can we escape Him by flight:

72:13. And when we heard the guidance, we believed in it. So whoever believes in his Lord, he fears neither loss nor injustice:

72:14. And some of us are those who submit, and some of us are deviators. So whoever submits, these aim at the right way.

72:15. And as to deviators, they are fuel of hell:

72:16. And if they keep to the (right) way, We would certainly give them to drink of abundant water,

72:17. So that We may try them thereby. And whoever turns away from the reminder of his Lord, He will make him enter into an afflicting chastisement:

72:18. And the mosques are Allah's, so call not upon any one with Allah:

72:19. And when the Servant of Allah stood up praying to Him, they well-nigh crowded him (to death).

***

72:20. Say: I only call upon my Lord, and associate naught with Him.

72:21. Say: I control not evil nor good for you.

بِرِجَالٍ مِنَ الْجِنِّ فَزَادُوهُمْ رَهَقًا (٦) وَأَنَّهُمْ ظَنُّوا كَمَا ظَنَنْتُمْ أَنْ لَنْ يَبْعَثَ اللَّهُ أَحَدًا (٧) وَأَنَّا لَمَسْنَا السَّمَاءَ فَوَجَدْنَاهَا مُلِئَتْ حَرَسًا شَدِيدًا وَشُهُبًا (٨) وَأَنَّا كُنَّا نَقْعُدُ مِنْهَا مَقَاعِدَ لِلسَّمْعِ فَمَنْ يَسْتَمِعِ الْآنَ يَجِدْ لَهُ شِهَابًا رَصَدًا (٩) وَأَنَّا لَا نَدْرِي أَشَرٌّ أُرِيدَ بِمَنْ فِي الْأَرْضِ أَمْ أَرَادَ بِهِمْ رَبُّهُمْ رَشَدًا (١٠) وَأَنَّا مِنَّا الصَّالِحُونَ وَمِنَّا دُونَ ذَلِكَ كُنَّا طَرَائِقَ قِدَدًا (١١) وَأَنَّا ظَنَنَّا أَنْ لَنْ نُعْجِزَ اللَّهَ فِي الْأَرْضِ وَلَنْ نُعْجِزَهُ هَرَبًا (١٢) وَأَنَّا لَمَّا سَمِعْنَا الْهُدَى آمَنَّا بِهِ فَمَنْ يُؤْمِنْ بِرَبِّهِ فَلَا يَخَافُ بَخْسًا وَلَا رَهَقًا (١٣) وَأَنَّا مِنَّا الْمُسْلِمُونَ وَمِنَّا الْقَاسِطُونَ فَمَنْ أَسْلَمَ فَأُولَئِكَ تَحَرَّوْا رَشَدًا (١٤) وَأَمَّا الْقَاسِطُونَ فَكَانُوا لِجَهَنَّمَ حَطَبًا (١٥) وَأَنْ لَوِ اسْتَقَامُوا عَلَى الطَّرِيقَةِ لَأَسْقَيْنَاهُمْ مَاءً غَدَقًا (١٦) لِنَفْتِنَهُمْ فِيهِ وَمَنْ يُعْرِضْ عَنْ ذِكْرِ رَبِّهِ يَسْلُكْهُ عَذَابًا صَعَدًا (١٧) وَأَنَّ الْمَسَاجِدَ لِلَّهِ فَلَا تَدْعُوا مَعَ اللَّهِ أَحَدًا (١٨) وَأَنَّهُ لَمَّا قَامَ عَبْدُ اللَّهِ يَدْعُوهُ كَادُوا يَكُونُونَ عَلَيْهِ لِبَدًا (١٩) قُلْ إِنَّمَا أَدْعُو رَبِّي وَلَا أُشْرِكُ بِهِ أَحَدًا (٢٠) قُلْ إِنِّي لَا أَمْلِكُ لَكُمْ ضَرًّا وَلَا رَشَدًا

72:22. Say: None can protect me against Allah, nor can I find any refuge besides Him:
72:23. (Mine is naught) but to deliver (the command) of Allah and His messages. And whoever disobeys Allah and His Messenger, surely for him is the Fire of hell, to abide therein for ages,
72:24. Till when they see that which they are promised, they will know who is weaker in helpers and less in numbers.
72:25. Say: I know nor whether that which you are promised is nigh or if my Lord will appoint for it a distant term.
72:26. The Knower of the unseen, so He makes His secrets known to none,
72:27. Except a messenger whom He chooses. For surely He makes a guard to go before him and after him,
72:28. That He may know that they have truly delivered the messages of their Lord; and He encompasses what is with them, and He keeps account of all things.

73. Folded in Garments

In the name of Allah, the Beneficent, the Merciful.
73:1. O thou covering thyself up!
73:2. Rise to pray by night except a little,
73:3. Half of it, or lessen it a little,
73:4. Or add to it, and recite the Qur'an in a leisurely manner.
73:5. Surely We shall charge thee with a weighty word.
73:6. The rising by night is surely the firmest way to tread and most effective in speech.
73:7. Truly thou hast by day prolonged occupation.
73:8. And remember the name of thy Lord and devote thyself to Him with

73. Folded in Garments

(complete) devotion.

73:9. The Lord of the East and the West -- there is no God but He -- so take Him for Protector.

73:10. And bear patiently what they say and forsake them with a becoming withdrawal.

73:11. And leave Me and the deniers, possessors of plenty, and respite them a little.

73:12. Surely with Us are heavy fetters and a flaming Fire,

73:13. And food that chokes and a painful chastisement.

73:14. On the day when the earth and the mountains quake and the mountains become (as) heaps of sand let loose.

73:15. Surely We have sent to you a Messenger, a witness against you, as We sent a messenger to Pharaoh.

73:16. But Pharaoh disobeyed the messenger, so We seized him with a violent grip.

73:17. How, then, if you disbelieve, will you guard yourselves on the day which will make children grey-headed?

73:18. The heaven being rent asunder thereby. His promise is ever fulfilled.

73:19. Surely this is a Reminder so let him, who will, take a way to his Lord.

* * *

73:20. Thy Lord knows indeed that thou passest in prayer nearly two-thirds of the night, and (sometimes) half of it, and (sometimes) a third of it, as do a party of those with thee. And Allah measures the night and the day. He knows that (all of) you are not able to do it, so He has turned to you (mercifully); so read of the Qur'an that which is easy for you. He knows that there are sick among you, and others who travel in the land seeking of Allah's bounty, and others who fight in Allah's way. So read as much of it as is easy (for you), and keep up prayer and pay the poor-rate and offer to Allah a goodly gift. And whatever of good you send on before hand for yourselves, you will find it with Allah -- that is best and greatest in reward. And ask forgiveness of Allah. Surely Allah is Forgiving, Merciful.

74. Wrapped Up

In the name of Allah, the Beneficent, the Merciful.
74:1. O thou who wrappest thyself up,
74:2. Arise and warn,
74:3. And thy Lord do magnify,
74:4. And thy garments do purify,
74:5. And uncleanness do shun,
74:6. And do no favour seeking gain,
74:7. And for the sake of thy Lord, be patient.
74:8. For when the trumpet is sounded,
74:9. That will be that day -- a difficult day,
74:10. For the disbelievers, anything but easy.
74:11. Leave Me alone with him whom I created,
74:12. And gave him vast riches,
74:13. And sons dwelling in his presence,
74:14. And made matters easy for him,
74:15. And yet he desires that I should give more!
74:16. By no means! Surely he is inimical to Our messages.
74:17. I will make a distressing punishment overtake him.
74:18. Surely he reflected and determined,
74:19. But may he be destroyed how he determined!
74:20. Again, may he be destroyed how he determined!
74:21. Then he looked,
74:22. Then frowned and scowled,
74:23. Then turned back and was big with pride,

74. Wrapped Up

74:24. Then said: This is naught but magic from of old!
74:25. This is naught but the word of a mortal!
74:26. I will cast him into hell.
74:27. And what will make thee realize what hell is?
74:28. It leaves naught, and spares naught.
74:29. It scorches the mortal.
74:30. Over it are nineteen.
74:31. And We have made none but angels wardens of the Fire, and We have not made their number but as a trial for those who disbelieve, that those who have been given the Book may be certain and those who believe may increase in faith, and those who have been given the Book and the believers may not doubt; and that those in whose hearts is a disease and the disbelievers may say: What does Allah mean by this parable? Thus Allah leaves in error whom He pleases, and guides whom He pleases. And none knows the hosts of thy Lord but He. And this is naught but a Reminder to mortals.

* * *

74:32. Nay, by the moon!
74:33. And the night when it departs!
74:34. And the dawn when it shines!
74:35. Surely it is one of the gravest (misfortunes),
74:36. A warning to mortals,
74:37. To him among you who will go forward or will remain behind.
74:38. Every soul is. held in pledge for what it earns,
74:39. Except the people of the right hand.
74:40. In Gardens, they ask one another,
74:41. About the guilty:
74:42. What has brought you into hell?
74:43. They will say: We were not of those who prayed;
74:44. Nor did we feed the poor;

فَقَالَ إِنْ هَذَا إِلَّا سِحْرٌ يُؤْثَرُ (٢٤)
إِنْ هَذَا إِلَّا قَوْلُ الْبَشَرِ (٢٥)
سَأُصْلِيهِ سَقَرَ (٢٦)
وَمَا أَدْرَاكَ مَا سَقَرُ (٢٧)
لَا تُبْقِي وَلَا تَذَرُ (٢٨)
لَوَّاحَةٌ لِلْبَشَرِ (٢٩)
عَلَيْهَا تِسْعَةَ عَشَرَ (٣٠)
وَمَا جَعَلْنَا أَصْحَابَ النَّارِ إِلَّا مَلَائِكَةً وَمَا جَعَلْنَا عِدَّتَهُمْ إِلَّا فِتْنَةً لِلَّذِينَ كَفَرُوا لِيَسْتَيْقِنَ الَّذِينَ أُوتُوا الْكِتَابَ وَيَزْدَادَ الَّذِينَ آمَنُوا إِيمَانًا وَلَا يَرْتَابَ الَّذِينَ أُوتُوا الْكِتَابَ وَالْمُؤْمِنُونَ وَلِيَقُولَ الَّذِينَ فِي قُلُوبِهِمْ مَرَضٌ وَالْكَافِرُونَ مَاذَا أَرَادَ اللَّهُ بِهَذَا مَثَلًا كَذَلِكَ يُضِلُّ اللَّهُ مَنْ يَشَاءُ وَيَهْدِي مَنْ يَشَاءُ وَمَا يَعْلَمُ جُنُودَ رَبِّكَ إِلَّا هُوَ وَمَا هِيَ إِلَّا ذِكْرَى لِلْبَشَرِ (٣١)
كَلَّا وَالْقَمَرِ (٣٢)
وَاللَّيْلِ إِذْ أَدْبَرَ (٣٣)
وَالصُّبْحِ إِذَا أَسْفَرَ (٣٤)
إِنَّهَا لَإِحْدَى الْكُبَرِ (٣٥)
نَذِيرًا لِلْبَشَرِ (٣٦)
لِمَنْ شَاءَ مِنْكُمْ أَنْ يَتَقَدَّمَ أَوْ يَتَأَخَّرَ (٣٧)
كُلُّ نَفْسٍ بِمَا كَسَبَتْ رَهِينَةٌ (٣٨)
إِلَّا أَصْحَابَ الْيَمِينِ (٣٩)
فِي جَنَّاتٍ يَتَسَاءَلُونَ (٤٠)
عَنِ الْمُجْرِمِينَ (٤١)
مَا سَلَكَكُمْ فِي سَقَرَ (٤٢)
قَالُوا لَمْ نَكُ مِنَ الْمُصَلِّينَ (٤٣)
وَلَمْ نَكُ نُطْعِمُ الْمِسْكِينَ (٤٤)
وَكُنَّا نَخُوضُ مَعَ الْخَائِضِينَ (٤٥)

74:45. And we indulged in vain talk with vain talkers;
74:46. And we called the day of Judgment a lie;
74:47. Till the inevitable overtook us.
74:48. So the intercession or intercessors will not avail them.
74:49. What is then the matter with them, that they turn away from the Reminder.
74:50. As if they were frightened asses,
74:51. Fleeing from a lion?
74:52. Nay, every one of them desires that he should be given pages spread out --
74:53. By no means! But they fear not the Hereafter.
74:54. Nay, it is surely a Reminder.
74:55. So whoever pleases may mind it.
74:56. And they will not mind unless Allah please. He is Worthy that duty should be kept to Him and Worthy to forgive.

75. The Resurrection

In the name of Allah, the Beneficent, the Merciful.
75:1. Nay, I swear by the day of resurrection!
75:2. Nay, I swear by the self-accusing spirit!
75:3. Does man think that We shall not gather his bones?
75:4. Yea, We are Powerful to make complete his whole make.
75:5. Nay, man desires to go on doing evil in front of him.
75:6. He asks: When is the day of Resurrection?
75:7. So when the sight is confused,
75:8. And the moon becomes dark,
75:9. And the sun and the moon are brought together --
75:10. Man will say on that day Whither to flee?
75:11. No! There is no refuge!

وَكُنَّا نُكَذِّبُ بِيَوْمِ الدِّينِ (٤٦)
حَتَّى أَتَانَا الْيَقِينُ (٤٧)
فَمَا تَنْفَعُهُمْ شَفَاعَةُ الشَّافِعِينَ (٤٨)
فَمَا لَهُمْ عَنِ التَّذْكِرَةِ مُعْرِضِينَ (٤٩)
كَأَنَّهُمْ حُمُرٌ مُسْتَنْفِرَةٌ (٥٠)
فَرَّتْ مِنْ قَسْوَرَةٍ (٥١)
بَلْ يُرِيدُ كُلُّ امْرِئٍ مِنْهُمْ أَنْ يُؤْتَى صُحُفًا مُنَشَّرَةً (٥٢)
كَلَّا بَلْ لَا يَخَافُونَ الْآخِرَةَ (٥٣)
كَلَّا إِنَّهُ تَذْكِرَةٌ (٥٤)
فَمَنْ شَاءَ ذَكَرَهُ (٥٥)
وَمَا يَذْكُرُونَ إِلَّا أَنْ يَشَاءَ اللَّهُ هُوَ أَهْلُ التَّقْوَى وَأَهْلُ الْمَغْفِرَةِ (٥٦)

٧٥- سورة القيامة

بِسْمِ اللَّهِ الرَّحْمَنِ الرَّحِيمِ
لَا أُقْسِمُ بِيَوْمِ الْقِيَامَةِ (١)
وَلَا أُقْسِمُ بِالنَّفْسِ اللَّوَّامَةِ (٢)
أَيَحْسَبُ الْإِنْسَانُ أَلَّنْ نَجْمَعَ عِظَامَهُ (٣)
بَلَى قَادِرِينَ عَلَى أَنْ نُسَوِّيَ بَنَانَهُ (٤)
بَلْ يُرِيدُ الْإِنْسَانُ لِيَفْجُرَ أَمَامَهُ (٥)
يَسْأَلُ أَيَّانَ يَوْمُ الْقِيَامَةِ (٦)
فَإِذَا بَرِقَ الْبَصَرُ (٧)
وَخَسَفَ الْقَمَرُ (٨)
وَجُمِعَ الشَّمْسُ وَالْقَمَرُ (٩)
يَقُولُ الْإِنْسَانُ يَوْمَئِذٍ أَيْنَ الْمَفَرُّ (١٠)
كَلَّا لَا وَزَرَ (١١)

75. The Resurrection

75:12. With thy Lord on that day is the place of rest.
75:13. Man will that day be informed of what he sent before and what he put off.
75:14. Nay, man is evidence against himself,
75:15. Though he put up excuses.
75:16. Move not thy tongue therewith to make haste with it.
75:17. Surely on Us rests the collecting of it and the reciting of it.
75:18. So when We recite it, follow its recitation.
75:19. Again on Us rests the explaining of it.
75:20. Nay, but you love the present life,
75:21. And neglect the Hereafter.
75:22. (Some) faces that day will be bright,
75:23. Looking to their Lord.
75:24. And (other) faces that day will be gloomy,
75:25. Knowing that a great disaster will be made to befall them.
75:26. Nay, when it comes up to the throat,
75:27. And it is said: Who will ascend (with it)?
75:28. And he is sure that it is the parting,
75:29. And affliction is combined with affliction --
75:30. To thy Lord on that day is the driving.

* * *

75:31. So he accepted not the truth, nor prayed,
75:32. But denied and turned back,
75:33. Then he went to his people in haughtiness.
75:34. Nearer to thee and nearer,
75:35. Again, neater to thee and nearer (is woe).
75:36. Does man think that he will be left aimless?
75:37. Was he not a small life-germ in

إِلَى رَبِّكَ يَوْمَئِذٍ الْمُسْتَقَرُّ (١٢)
يُنَبَّأُ الْإِنْسَانُ يَوْمَئِذٍ بِمَا قَدَّمَ وَأَخَّرَ (١٣)
بَلِ الْإِنْسَانُ عَلَى نَفْسِهِ بَصِيرَةٌ (١٤)
وَلَوْ أَلْقَى مَعَاذِيرَهُ (١٥)
لَا تُحَرِّكْ بِهِ لِسَانَكَ لِتَعْجَلَ بِهِ (١٦)
إِنَّ عَلَيْنَا جَمْعَهُ وَقُرْآنَهُ (١٧)
فَإِذَا قَرَأْنَاهُ فَاتَّبِعْ قُرْآنَهُ (١٨)
ثُمَّ إِنَّ عَلَيْنَا بَيَانَهُ (١٩)
كَلَّا بَلْ تُحِبُّونَ الْعَاجِلَةَ (٢٠)
وَتَذَرُونَ الْآخِرَةَ (٢١)
وُجُوهٌ يَوْمَئِذٍ نَاضِرَةٌ (٢٢)
إِلَى رَبِّهَا نَاظِرَةٌ (٢٣)
وَوُجُوهٌ يَوْمَئِذٍ بَاسِرَةٌ (٢٤)
تَظُنُّ أَنْ يُفْعَلَ بِهَا فَاقِرَةٌ (٢٥)
كَلَّا إِذَا بَلَغَتِ التَّرَاقِيَ (٢٦)
وَقِيلَ مَنْ رَاقٍ (٢٧)
وَظَنَّ أَنَّهُ الْفِرَاقُ (٢٨)
وَالْتَفَّتِ السَّاقُ بِالسَّاقِ (٢٩)
إِلَى رَبِّكَ يَوْمَئِذٍ الْمَسَاقُ (٣٠)
فَلَا صَدَّقَ وَلَا صَلَّى (٣١)
وَلَكِنْ كَذَّبَ وَتَوَلَّى (٣٢)
ثُمَّ ذَهَبَ إِلَى أَهْلِهِ يَتَمَطَّى (٣٣)
أَوْلَى لَكَ فَأَوْلَى (٣٤)
ثُمَّ أَوْلَى لَكَ فَأَوْلَى (٣٥)
أَيَحْسَبُ الْإِنْسَانُ أَنْ يُتْرَكَ سُدًى (٣٦)
أَلَمْ يَكُ نُطْفَةً مِنْ مَنِيٍّ يُمْنَى (٣٧)
ثُمَّ كَانَ عَلَقَةً فَخَلَقَ فَسَوَّى (٣٨)
فَجَعَلَ مِنْهُ الزَّوْجَيْنِ الذَّكَرَ وَالْأُنْثَى (٣٩)
أَلَيْسَ ذَلِكَ بِقَادِرٍ عَلَى أَنْ يُحْيِيَ

sperm emitted?
75:38. Then he was a clot; so He created (him), then made (him) perfect.
75:39. Then He made of him two kinds, the male and the female.
75:40. Is not He Powerful to give life to the dead?

76. Man

In the name of Allah, the Beneficent, the Merciful.

76:1. Surely there came over man a time when he was nothing that could be mentioned.
76:2. Surely We have created man from sperm mixed (with ovum), to try him, so We have made him hearing, seeing.
76:3. We have truly shown him the way; he may be thankful or unthankful.
76:4. Surely we have prepared for the disbelievers chains and shackles and a burning Fire.
76:5. The righteous truly drink of a cup tempered with camphor --
76:6. A fountain from which the servants of Allah drink, making it flow in abundance.
76:7. They fulfil vows and fear a day, the evil of which is widespread.
76:8. And they give food, out of love for Him, to the poor and the orphan and the captive.
76:9. We feed you, for Allah's pleasure only We desire from you neither reward nor thanks.
76:10. Surely we fear from our Lord a stern, distressful day.
76:11. So Allah will ward off from them the evil of that day, and cause them to meet with splendour and happiness;
76:12. And reward them, for their steadfastness, with a Garden and with silk,
76:13. Reclining therein on raised couches; they will see therein neither (excessive heat of) sun nor intense cold.

الْمَوْتَىٰ (٤٠)

٧٦- سورة الإنسان

بِسْمِ اللَّهِ الرَّحْمَٰنِ الرَّحِيمِ
هَلْ أَتَىٰ عَلَى الْإِنْسَانِ حِينٌ مِنَ الدَّهْرِ لَمْ يَكُنْ شَيْئًا مَذْكُورًا (١)
إِنَّا خَلَقْنَا الْإِنْسَانَ مِنْ نُطْفَةٍ أَمْشَاجٍ نَبْتَلِيهِ فَجَعَلْنَاهُ سَمِيعًا بَصِيرًا (٢)
إِنَّا هَدَيْنَاهُ السَّبِيلَ إِمَّا شَاكِرًا وَإِمَّا كَفُورًا (٣)
إِنَّا أَعْتَدْنَا لِلْكَافِرِينَ سَلَاسِلَ وَأَغْلَالًا وَسَعِيرًا (٤)
إِنَّ الْأَبْرَارَ يَشْرَبُونَ مِنْ كَأْسٍ كَانَ مِزَاجُهَا كَافُورًا (٥)
عَيْنًا يَشْرَبُ بِهَا عِبَادُ اللَّهِ يُفَجِّرُونَهَا تَفْجِيرًا (٦)
يُوفُونَ بِالنَّذْرِ وَيَخَافُونَ يَوْمًا كَانَ شَرُّهُ مُسْتَطِيرًا (٧)
وَيُطْعِمُونَ الطَّعَامَ عَلَىٰ حُبِّهِ مِسْكِينًا وَيَتِيمًا وَأَسِيرًا (٨)
إِنَّمَا نُطْعِمُكُمْ لِوَجْهِ اللَّهِ لَا نُرِيدُ مِنْكُمْ جَزَاءً وَلَا شُكُورًا (٩)
إِنَّا نَخَافُ مِنْ رَبِّنَا يَوْمًا عَبُوسًا قَمْطَرِيرًا (١٠)
فَوَقَاهُمُ اللَّهُ شَرَّ ذَٰلِكَ الْيَوْمِ وَلَقَّاهُمْ نَضْرَةً وَسُرُورًا (١١)
وَجَزَاهُمْ بِمَا صَبَرُوا جَنَّةً وَحَرِيرًا (١٢)
مُتَّكِئِينَ فِيهَا عَلَى الْأَرَائِكِ لَا يَرَوْنَ

76:14. And close down upon them are its shadows, and its fruits are made near (to them), easy to reach.

76:15. And round about them are made to go vessels of silver and goblets of glass,

76:16. Crystal-clear, made of silver -- they have measured them according to a measure.

76:17. And they are made to drink therein a cup tempered with ginger --

76:18. (Of) a fountain therein called Salsabil.

76:19. And round about them will go youths, never altering in age; when thou seest them thou wilt think them to be scattered pearls.

76:20. And when thou lookest thither, thou seest blessings and a great kingdom.

76:21. On them are garments of fine green silk and thick brocade, and they are adorned with bracelets of silver, and their Lord makes them to drink a pure drink.

76:22. Surely this is a reward for you, and your striving is recompensed.

* * *

76:23. Surely We have revealed the Qur'an to thee, in portions.

76:24. So wait patiently for the judgment of thy Lord, and obey not a sinner or an ungrateful one among them.

76:25. And glorify the name of thy Lord morning and evening.

76:26. And during part of the night adore Him, and glorify Him throughout a long night.

76:27. Surely these love the transitory life and neglect a grievous day before them.

76:28. We created them and made firm their make, and, when We will, We can bring in their place the like of them by change.

76:29. Surely this is a Reminder; so whoever will, let him take a way to his

فِيهَا شَمْسًا وَلَا زَمْهَرِيرًا (١٣)
وَدَانِيَةً عَلَيْهِمْ ظِلَالُهَا وَذُلِّلَتْ قُطُوفُهَا تَذْلِيلًا (١٤)
وَيُطَافُ عَلَيْهِمْ بِآنِيَةٍ مِنْ فِضَّةٍ وَأَكْوَابٍ كَانَتْ قَوَارِيرَ (١٥)
قَوَارِيرَ مِنْ فِضَّةٍ قَدَّرُوهَا تَقْدِيرًا (١٦)
وَيُسْقَوْنَ فِيهَا كَأْسًا كَانَ مِزَاجُهَا زَنْجَبِيلًا (١٧)
عَيْنًا فِيهَا تُسَمَّى سَلْسَبِيلًا (١٨)
وَيَطُوفُ عَلَيْهِمْ وِلْدَانٌ مُخَلَّدُونَ إِذَا رَأَيْتَهُمْ حَسِبْتَهُمْ لُؤْلُؤًا مَنْثُورًا (١٩)
وَإِذَا رَأَيْتَ ثَمَّ رَأَيْتَ نَعِيمًا وَمُلْكًا كَبِيرًا (٢٠)
عَالِيَهُمْ ثِيَابُ سُنْدُسٍ خُضْرٌ وَإِسْتَبْرَقٌ وَحُلُّوا أَسَاوِرَ مِنْ فِضَّةٍ وَسَقَاهُمْ رَبُّهُمْ شَرَابًا طَهُورًا (٢١)
إِنَّ هَذَا كَانَ لَكُمْ جَزَاءً وَكَانَ سَعْيُكُمْ مَشْكُورًا (٢٢)
إِنَّا نَحْنُ نَزَّلْنَا عَلَيْكَ الْقُرْآنَ تَنْزِيلًا (٢٣)
فَاصْبِرْ لِحُكْمِ رَبِّكَ وَلَا تُطِعْ مِنْهُمْ آثِمًا أَوْ كَفُورًا (٢٤)
وَاذْكُرِ اسْمَ رَبِّكَ بُكْرَةً وَأَصِيلًا (٢٥)
وَمِنَ اللَّيْلِ فَاسْجُدْ لَهُ وَسَبِّحْهُ لَيْلًا طَوِيلًا (٢٦)
إِنَّ هَؤُلَاءِ يُحِبُّونَ الْعَاجِلَةَ وَيَذَرُونَ وَرَاءَهُمْ يَوْمًا ثَقِيلًا (٢٧)
نَحْنُ خَلَقْنَاهُمْ وَشَدَدْنَا أَسْرَهُمْ وَإِذَا شِئْنَا بَدَّلْنَا أَمْثَالَهُمْ تَبْدِيلًا (٢٨)
إِنَّ هَذِهِ تَذْكِرَةٌ فَمَنْ شَاءَ اتَّخَذَ إِلَى رَبِّهِ سَبِيلًا (٢٩)

Lord.

76:30. And you will not, unless Allah please. Surely Allah is ever Knowing, Wise.

76:31. He admits whom He pleases to His mercy; and the wrongdoers -- He has prepared for them a painful chastisement.

77. Those Sent Forth

In the name of Allah, the Beneficent, the Merciful.

77:1. By those sent forth to spread goodness!

77:2. Then those driving off the chaff!

77:3. And those spreading (goodness), far and wide

77:4. Then those making a distinction!

77:5. Then those offering the Reminder,

77:6. To clear or to warn! --

77:7. Surely that which you are promised will come to pass.

77:8. So when the stars are made to disappear,

77:9. And when the heaven is rent asunder,

77:10. And when the mountains are carried away as dust,

77:11. And when the messengers are made to reach their appointed time,

77:12. To what day is the doom fixed?

77:13. To the day of Decision.

77:14. And what will make thee comprehend what the day of Decision is?

77:15. Woe on that day to the rejectors!

77:16. Did We not destroy the former generations?

77:17. Then We followed them up with later ones.

77:18. Thus do We deal with the guilty.

77:19. Woe on that day to the rejectors!

77:20. Did We not create you from ordinary water?

77:21. Then We placed it in a secure resting-place,

77. Those Sent Forth

77:22. Till an appointed term,
77:23. So We determined -- how well are We at determining!
77:24. Woe on that day to the rejectors!
77:25. Have We not made the earth draw to itself
77:26. The living and the dead,
77:27. And made therein lofty mountains, and given you to drink of sweet water?
77:28. Woe on that day to the rejectors!
77:29. Walk on to that which you called a lie.
77:30. Walk on to the shadow, having three branches,
77:31. Neither cool, nor availing against the flame.
77:32. It sends up sparks like palaces,
77:33. As if they were tawny camels.
77:34. Woe on that day to the rejectors!
77:35. This is the day on which they speak not,
77:36. Nor are they allowed to offer excuses.
77:37. Woe on that day to the rejectors!
77:38. This is the day of Decision We have gathered you and those of yore.
77:39. So if you have a plan, plan against me (now).
77:40. Woe on that day to the rejectors!

***

77:41. Surely the dutiful are amid shades and fountains,
77:42. And fruits such as they desire.
77:43. Eat and drink pleasantly for what you did.
77:44. Thus do We reward the doers of good.
77:45. Woe on that day to the rejectors!
77:46. Eat and enjoy yourselves for a little; surely you are guilty.
77:47. Woe on that day to the rejectors!
77:48. And when it is said to them, Bow down, they bow not down.
77:49. Woe on that day to the rejectors!
77:50. In what narration after it, will they believe?

وَيْلٌ يَوْمَئِذٍ لِلْمُكَذِّبِينَ (٢٤)
أَلَمْ نَجْعَلِ الْأَرْضَ كِفَاتًا (٢٥)
أَحْيَاءً وَأَمْوَاتًا (٢٦)
وَجَعَلْنَا فِيهَا رَوَاسِيَ شَامِخَاتٍ وَأَسْقَيْنَاكُمْ مَاءً فُرَاتًا (٢٧)
وَيْلٌ يَوْمَئِذٍ لِلْمُكَذِّبِينَ (٢٨)
انْطَلِقُوا إِلَى مَا كُنْتُمْ بِهِ تُكَذِّبُونَ (٢٩)
انْطَلِقُوا إِلَى ظِلٍّ ذِي ثَلَاثِ شُعَبٍ (٣٠)
لَا ظَلِيلٍ وَلَا يُغْنِي مِنَ اللَّهَبِ (٣١)
إِنَّهَا تَرْمِي بِشَرَرٍ كَالْقَصْرِ (٣٢)
كَأَنَّهُ جِمَالَةٌ صُفْرٌ (٣٣)
وَيْلٌ يَوْمَئِذٍ لِلْمُكَذِّبِينَ (٣٤)
هَذَا يَوْمُ لَا يَنْطِقُونَ (٣٥)
وَلَا يُؤْذَنُ لَهُمْ فَيَعْتَذِرُونَ (٣٦)
وَيْلٌ يَوْمَئِذٍ لِلْمُكَذِّبِينَ (٣٧)
هَذَا يَوْمُ الْفَصْلِ جَمَعْنَاكُمْ وَالْأَوَّلِينَ (٣٨)
فَإِنْ كَانَ لَكُمْ كَيْدٌ فَكِيدُونِ (٣٩)
وَيْلٌ يَوْمَئِذٍ لِلْمُكَذِّبِينَ (٤٠)
إِنَّ الْمُتَّقِينَ فِي ظِلَالٍ وَعُيُونٍ (٤١)
وَفَوَاكِهَ مِمَّا يَشْتَهُونَ (٤٢)
كُلُوا وَاشْرَبُوا هَنِيئًا بِمَا كُنْتُمْ تَعْمَلُونَ (٤٣)
إِنَّا كَذَلِكَ نَجْزِي الْمُحْسِنِينَ (٤٤)
وَيْلٌ يَوْمَئِذٍ لِلْمُكَذِّبِينَ (٤٥)
كُلُوا وَتَمَتَّعُوا قَلِيلًا إِنَّكُمْ مُجْرِمُونَ (٤٦)
وَيْلٌ يَوْمَئِذٍ لِلْمُكَذِّبِينَ (٤٧)
وَإِذَا قِيلَ لَهُمُ ارْكَعُوا لَا يَرْكَعُونَ (٤٨)

78. The Announcement

In the name of Allah, the Beneficent, the Merciful.

78:1. Of what do they ask one another?
78:2. Of the tremendous announcement
78:3. About which they differ.
78:4. Nay, they will soon know;
78:5. Nay, again, they will soon know.
78:6. Have We not made the earth an expanse
78:7. And the mountains as pegs?
78:8. And We have created you in pairs,
78:9. And made your sleep for rest,
78:10. And made the night a covering,
78:11. And made the day for seeking livelihood.
78:12. And We have made above you seven strong (bodies),
78:13. And made a shining lamp,
78:14. And We send down from the clouds water pouring forth in abundance,
78:15. That We may bring forth thereby grain and herbs,
78:16. And luxuriant gardens.
78:17. Surely the day of Decision is appointed --
78:18. The day when the trumpet is blown, so you come forth in hosts,
78:19. And the heaven is opened so it becomes as doors,
78:20. And the mountains are moved off, so they remain a semblance.
78:21. Surely hell lies in wait,
78:22. A resort for the inordinate,
78:23. Living therein for long years.
78:24. They taste not therein coolness nor drink,
78:25. But boiling and intensely cold water,
78:26. Requital corresponding.

78:27. Surely they feared not the reckoning,
78:28. And rejected Our messages, giving the lie (thereto).
78:29. And We have recorded every thing in a book,
78:30. So taste, for We shall add to you naught but chastisement.

* * *

78:31. Surely for those who keep their duty is achievement,
78:32. Gardens and vineyards,
78:33. And youthful (companions), equals in age,
78:34. And a pure cup.
78:35. They hear not therein vain words, nor lying --
78:36. A reward from thy Lord, a gift sufficient;
78:37. The Lord of the heavens and the earth and what is between them~ the Beneficent, they are not able to address Him.
78:38. The day when the spirit and the angels stand in ranks; none shall speak except he whom the Beneficent permits and he speaks aright.
78:39. That is the True Day, so whoever desires may take refuge with his Lord.
78:40. Truly We warn you of a chastisement near at hand -- the day when man will see what his hands have sent before, and the disbeliever will say O would that I were dust!

79. Those Who Yearn

In the name of Allah, the Beneficent, the Merciful.
79:1. By those yearning vehemently!
79:2. And those going forth cheerfully!
79:3. And those running swiftly!
79:4. And those that are foremost going ahead!
79:5. And those regulating the Affair!
79:6. The day when the quaking one

79. Those Who Yearn

shall quake --
79:7. The consequence will follow it.
79:8. Hearts that day will palpitate,
79:9. Their eyes downcast.
79:10. They say: Shall we indeed be restored to (out) first state?
79:11. What! After we are rotten bones?
79:12. They say; That would then be a return with loss.
79:13. It is only a single cry,
79:14. When lo! they will be awakened.
79:15. Has not there come to thee the story of Moses,
79:16. When his Lord called him in the holy valley, Tuwa?
79:17. Go to Pharaoh, surely he has rebelled.
79:18. And say: Wilt thou purify thyself?
79:19. And I will guide thee to thy Lord so that thou fear (Him).
79:20. So he showed him the mighty sign;
79:21. But he denied and disobeyed.
79:22. Then he went back hastily,
79:23. So he gathered and called out.
79:24. Then he said: I am your Lord, the most High.
79:25. So Allah seized him with the punishment of the Hereafter and of this life.
79:26. Surely there is in this a lesson for him who fears.

* * *

79:27. Are you the stronger in creation or the heaven? He made it.
79:28. He raised high its height, and made it perfect,
79:29. And He made dark its night and brought out its light.
79:30. And the earth, He cast It after that.
79:31. He brought forth from it its water and its pasture.
79:32. And the mountains, He made them firm,
79:33. A provision for you and for your cattle.

يَوْمَ تَرْجُفُ الرَّاجِفَةُ (٦)
تَتْبَعُهَا الرَّادِفَةُ (٧)
قُلُوبٌ يَوْمَئِذٍ وَاجِفَةٌ (٨)
أَبْصَارُهَا خَاشِعَةٌ (٩)
يَقُولُونَ أَئِنَّا لَمَرْدُودُونَ فِي الْحَافِرَةِ (١٠)
أَئِذَا كُنَّا عِظَامًا نَخِرَةً (١١)
قَالُوا تِلْكَ إِذًا كَرَّةٌ خَاسِرَةٌ (١٢)
فَإِنَّمَا هِيَ زَجْرَةٌ وَاحِدَةٌ (١٣)
فَإِذَا هُمْ بِالسَّاهِرَةِ (١٤)
هَلْ أَتَاكَ حَدِيثُ مُوسَى (١٥)
إِذْ نَادَاهُ رَبُّهُ بِالْوَادِ الْمُقَدَّسِ طُوًى (١٦)
اذْهَبْ إِلَى فِرْعَوْنَ إِنَّهُ طَغَى (١٧)
فَقُلْ هَلْ لَكَ إِلَى أَنْ تَزَكَّى (١٨)
وَأَهْدِيَكَ إِلَى رَبِّكَ فَتَخْشَى (١٩)
فَأَرَاهُ الْآيَةَ الْكُبْرَى (٢٠)
فَكَذَّبَ وَعَصَى (٢١)
ثُمَّ أَدْبَرَ يَسْعَى (٢٢)
فَحَشَرَ فَنَادَى (٢٣)
فَقَالَ أَنَا رَبُّكُمُ الْأَعْلَى (٢٤)
فَأَخَذَهُ اللَّهُ نَكَالَ الْآخِرَةِ وَالْأُولَى (٢٥)
إِنَّ فِي ذَلِكَ لَعِبْرَةً لِمَنْ يَخْشَى (٢٦)
أَأَنْتُمْ أَشَدُّ خَلْقًا أَمِ السَّمَاءُ بَنَاهَا (٢٧)
رَفَعَ سَمْكَهَا فَسَوَّاهَا (٢٨)
وَأَغْطَشَ لَيْلَهَا وَأَخْرَجَ ضُحَاهَا (٢٩)
وَالْأَرْضَ بَعْدَ ذَلِكَ دَحَاهَا (٣٠)
أَخْرَجَ مِنْهَا مَاءَهَا وَمَرْعَاهَا (٣١)
وَالْجِبَالَ أَرْسَاهَا (٣٢)
مَتَاعًا لَكُمْ وَلِأَنْعَامِكُمْ (٣٣)

79:34. So when the great Calamity comes;
79:35. The day when man remembers all that he strove for,
79:36. And hell is made manifest to him who sees.
79:37. Then as for him who is inordinate,
79:38. And prefers the life of this world,
79:39. Hell is surely the abode.
79:40. And as for him who fears to stand before his Lord and restrains himself from low desires,
79:41. The Garden is surely the abode.
79:42. They ask thee about the Hour, When will that take place,
79:43. About which thou remindest?
79:44. To thy Lord is the goal of it.
79:45. Thou art only a warner to him who fears it.
79:46. On the day when they see it, it will be as if they had but tarried for an evening or a morning.

80. Frowned

In the name of Allah, the Beneficent, the Merciful.
80:1. He frowned and turned away,
80:2. Because the blind man came to him.
80:3. And what would make thee know that he might purify himself,
80:4. Or be mindful, so the Reminder should profit him?
80:5. As for him who considers himself free from need
80:6. To him thou dost attend.
80:7. And no blame is on thee, if he purify himself not.
80:8. And as to him who comes to thee striving hard,
80:9. And he fears --
80:10. To him thou payest no regard.
80:11. Nay, surely it is a Reminder.
80:12. So let him who will mind it.
80:13. In honoured books,

80:14. Exalted, purified,
80:15. In the hands of scribes,
80:16. Noble, virtuous.
80:17. Woe to man! How ungrateful is he!
80:18. Of what thing did He create him?
80:19. Of a small life-germ. He creates him, then proportions him,
80:20. Then makes the way easy for him,
80:21. Then He causes him to die, then assigns to him a grave,
80:22. Then; when He will, He raises him to life again.
80:23. Nay, but he does not what He commands him.
80:24. Then let man look at his food --
80:25. How We pour down abundant water,
80:26. Then cleave the earth, cleaving (it) asunder,
80:27. Then cause the grain to grow therein,
80:28. And grapes and clover,
80:29. And the olive and the palm,
80:30. And thick gardens,
80:31. And fruits and herbage --
80:32. A provision for you and your cattle.
80:33. But when the deafening cry comes,
80:34. The day when a man flees from his brother,
80:35. And his mother and his father,
80:36. And his spouse and his sons.
80:37. Every man of them, that day, will have concern enough to make him indifferent to others.
80:38. Faces on that day will be bright,
80:39. Laughing, joyous.
80:40. And faces on that day will have dust on them,
80:41. Darkness covering them?
80:42. Those are the disbelievers, the wicked.

فِي صُحُفٍ مُكَرَّمَةٍ (١٣)
مَرْفُوعَةٍ مُطَهَّرَةٍ (١٤)
بِأَيْدِي سَفَرَةٍ (١٥)
كِرَامٍ بَرَرَةٍ (١٦)
قُتِلَ الْإِنْسَانُ مَا أَكْفَرَهُ (١٧)
مِنْ أَيِّ شَيْءٍ خَلَقَهُ (١٨)
مِنْ نُطْفَةٍ خَلَقَهُ فَقَدَّرَهُ (١٩)
ثُمَّ السَّبِيلَ يَسَّرَهُ (٢٠)
ثُمَّ أَمَاتَهُ فَأَقْبَرَهُ (٢١)
ثُمَّ إِذَا شَاءَ أَنْشَرَهُ (٢٢)
كَلَّا لَمَّا يَقْضِ مَا أَمَرَهُ (٢٣)
فَلْيَنْظُرِ الْإِنْسَانُ إِلَى طَعَامِهِ (٢٤)
أَنَّا صَبَبْنَا الْمَاءَ صَبًّا (٢٥)
ثُمَّ شَقَقْنَا الْأَرْضَ شَقًّا (٢٦)
فَأَنْبَتْنَا فِيهَا حَبًّا (٢٧)
وَعِنَبًا وَقَضْبًا (٢٨)
وَزَيْتُونًا وَنَخْلًا (٢٩)
وَحَدَائِقَ غُلْبًا (٣٠)
وَفَاكِهَةً وَأَبًّا (٣١)
مَتَاعًا لَكُمْ وَلِأَنْعَامِكُمْ (٣٢)
فَإِذَا جَاءَتِ الصَّاخَّةُ (٣٣)
يَوْمَ يَفِرُّ الْمَرْءُ مِنْ أَخِيهِ (٣٤)
وَأُمِّهِ وَأَبِيهِ (٣٥)
وَصَاحِبَتِهِ وَبَنِيهِ (٣٦)
لِكُلِّ امْرِئٍ مِنْهُمْ يَوْمَئِذٍ شَأْنٌ يُغْنِيهِ (٣٧)
وُجُوهٌ يَوْمَئِذٍ مُسْفِرَةٌ (٣٨)
ضَاحِكَةٌ مُسْتَبْشِرَةٌ (٣٩)
وَوُجُوهٌ يَوْمَئِذٍ عَلَيْهَا غَبَرَةٌ (٤٠)
تَرْهَقُهَا قَتَرَةٌ (٤١)
أُولَئِكَ هُمُ الْكَفَرَةُ الْفَجَرَةُ (٤٢)

81. The Folding Up

In the name of Allah, the Beneficent, the Merciful.

81:1. When the sun is folded up,
81:2. And when the stars are dust-coloured,
81:3. And when the mountains are made to pass away,
81:4. And when the camels are abandoned,
81:5. And when the wild animals are gathered together,
81:6. And when the cities are made to swell,
81:7. And when men are united,
81:8. And when the one buried alive is asked
81:9. For what sin she was killed,
81:10. And when the books are spread,
81:11. And when the heaven has its covering removed,
81:12. And when hell is kindled,
81:13. And when the Garden is brought nigh --
81:14. Every soul will know what it has prepared.
81:15. Nay, I call to witness the stars,
81:16. Running their course, (and) setting,
81:17. And the night when it departs,
81:18. And the morning when it brightens,
81:19. Surely it is the word of a bountiful Messenger,
81:20. The possessor of strength, established in the presence of the Lord of the Throne,
81:21. One (to be) obeyed, and faithful.
81:22. And your companion is not mad.
81:23. And truly he saw himself on the clear horizon.
81:24. Nor is he niggardly of the unseen.
81:25. Nor is it the word of an accursed devil --
81:26. Whither then are you going?
81:27. It is naught but a Reminder for

٨١ - سورة التكوير

بِسْمِ اللَّهِ الرَّحْمَنِ الرَّحِيمِ
إِذَا الشَّمْسُ كُوِّرَتْ (١)
وَإِذَا النُّجُومُ انكَدَرَتْ (٢)
وَإِذَا الْجِبَالُ سُيِّرَتْ (٣)
وَإِذَا الْعِشَارُ عُطِّلَتْ (٤)
وَإِذَا الْوُحُوشُ حُشِرَتْ (٥)
وَإِذَا الْبِحَارُ سُجِّرَتْ (٦)
وَإِذَا النُّفُوسُ زُوِّجَتْ (٧)
وَإِذَا الْمَوْءُودَةُ سُئِلَتْ (٨)
بِأَيِّ ذَنبٍ قُتِلَتْ (٩)
وَإِذَا الصُّحُفُ نُشِرَتْ (١٠)
وَإِذَا السَّمَاءُ كُشِطَتْ (١١)
وَإِذَا الْجَحِيمُ سُعِّرَتْ (١٢)
وَإِذَا الْجَنَّةُ أُزْلِفَتْ (١٣)
عَلِمَتْ نَفْسٌ مَا أَحْضَرَتْ (١٤)
فَلَا أُقْسِمُ بِالْخُنَّسِ (١٥)
الْجَوَارِ الْكُنَّسِ (١٦)
وَاللَّيْلِ إِذَا عَسْعَسَ (١٧)
وَالصُّبْحِ إِذَا تَنَفَّسَ (١٨)
إِنَّهُ لَقَوْلُ رَسُولٍ كَرِيمٍ (١٩)
ذِي قُوَّةٍ عِنْدَ ذِي الْعَرْشِ مَكِينٍ (٢٠)
مُطَاعٍ ثَمَّ أَمِينٍ (٢١)
وَمَا صَاحِبُكُمْ بِمَجْنُونٍ (٢٢)
وَلَقَدْ رَآهُ بِالْأُفُقِ الْمُبِينِ (٢٣)
وَمَا هُوَ عَلَى الْغَيْبِ بِضَنِينٍ (٢٤)
وَمَا هُوَ بِقَوْلِ شَيْطَانٍ رَجِيمٍ (٢٥)
فَأَيْنَ تَذْهَبُونَ (٢٦)
إِنْ هُوَ إِلَّا ذِكْرٌ لِلْعَالَمِينَ (٢٧)
لِمَنْ شَاءَ مِنْكُمْ أَنْ يَسْتَقِيمَ (٢٨)

the nations,
81:28. For him among you who will go straight.
81:29. And you will not, except Allah please, the Lord of the worlds.

82. The Cleaving

In the name of Allah, the Beneficent, the Merciful.

82:1. When the heaven is cleft asunder,
82:2. And when the stars become dispersed,
82:3. And when the rivers are made to flow forth,
82:4. And when the graves are laid open --
82:5. Every soul will know what it has sent before and what it has held back.
82:6. O man, what beguiles thee from thy Lord, the Gracious?
82:7. Who created thee, then made thee complete, then made thee in a right good state --
82:8. Into whatever form He pleases He casts thee.
82:9. Nay, but you give the lie to the Judgment,
82:10. And surely there are keepers over you,
82:11. Honourable recorders,
82:12. They know what you do.
82:13. Surely the righteous are in bliss,
82:14. And the wicked are truly in burning Fire --
82:15. They will enter it on the day of judgment,
82:16. And will not be absent from it.
82:17. And what will make thee realize what the day of Judgment is?
82:18. Again, what will make thee realize what the day of Judgment is?
82:19. The day when no soul controls aught for another soul. And the command on that day is Allah's.

وَمَا تَشَاءُونَ إِلَّا أَنْ يَشَاءَ اللَّهُ رَبُّ الْعَالَمِينَ (٢٩)

٨٢- سورة الإنفطار

بِسْمِ اللَّهِ الرَّحْمَنِ الرَّحِيمِ
إِذَا السَّمَاءُ انْفَطَرَتْ (١)
وَإِذَا الْكَوَاكِبُ انْتَثَرَتْ (٢)
وَإِذَا الْبِحَارُ فُجِّرَتْ (٣)
وَإِذَا الْقُبُورُ بُعْثِرَتْ (٤)
عَلِمَتْ نَفْسٌ مَا قَدَّمَتْ وَأَخَّرَتْ (٥)
يَا أَيُّهَا الْإِنْسَانُ مَا غَرَّكَ بِرَبِّكَ الْكَرِيمِ (٦)
الَّذِي خَلَقَكَ فَسَوَّاكَ فَعَدَلَكَ (٧)
فِي أَيِّ صُورَةٍ مَا شَاءَ رَكَّبَكَ (٨)
كَلَّا بَلْ تُكَذِّبُونَ بِالدِّينِ (٩)
وَإِنَّ عَلَيْكُمْ لَحَافِظِينَ (١٠)
كِرَامًا كَاتِبِينَ (١١)
يَعْلَمُونَ مَا تَفْعَلُونَ (١٢)
إِنَّ الْأَبْرَارَ لَفِي نَعِيمٍ (١٣)
وَإِنَّ الْفُجَّارَ لَفِي جَحِيمٍ (١٤)
يَصْلَوْنَهَا يَوْمَ الدِّينِ (١٥)
وَمَا هُمْ عَنْهَا بِغَائِبِينَ (١٦)
وَمَا أَدْرَاكَ مَا يَوْمُ الدِّينِ (١٧)
ثُمَّ مَا أَدْرَاكَ مَا يَوْمُ الدِّينِ (١٨)
يَوْمَ لَا تَمْلِكُ نَفْسٌ لِنَفْسٍ شَيْئًا وَالْأَمْرُ يَوْمَئِذٍ لِلَّهِ (١٩)

83. Default in Duty

In the name of Allah the Beneficent, the Merciful.

83:1. Woe to the cheaters!
83:2. Who, when they take the measure (of their dues) from men, take it fully,
83:3. And when they measure out to others or weigh out for them, they give less than is due.
83:4. Do they not think that they will be raised again,
83:5. To a mighty day? --
83:6. The day when men will stand before the Lord of the worlds.
83:7. Nay, surely the record of the wicked is in the prison.
83:8. And what will make thee know what the prison is?
83:9. It is a written book.
83:10. Woe on that day to the rejectors!
83:11. Who give the lie to the day of Judgment.
83:12. And none gives the lie to it but every exceeder of limits, every sinful one;
83:13. When Our messages are recited to him, he says Stories of those of yore!
83:14. Nay, rather, what they earned is rust upon their hearts.
83:15. Nay, surely they are that day debarred from their Lord.
83:16. Then they will surely enter the burning Fire. --
83:17. Then it will be said: This is what you gave the lie to.
83:18. Nay, surely the record of the righteous is in the highest places.
83:19. And what will make thee know what the highest places are?
83:20. It is a written book.
83:21. Those drawn near (to Allah) witness it.
83:22. Surely the righteous are in bliss,
83:23. On raised couches, gazing --
83:24. Thou recognizest in their faces the brightness of bliss.
83:25. They are given to drink of a pure

٨٣- سورة المطففين

بِسْمِ اللهِ الرَّحْمَنِ الرَّحِيمِ
وَيْلٌ لِلْمُطَفِّفِينَ (١)
الَّذِينَ إِذَا اكْتَالُوا عَلَى النَّاسِ يَسْتَوْفُونَ (٢)
وَإِذَا كَالُوهُمْ أَوْ وَزَنُوهُمْ يُخْسِرُونَ (٣)
أَلَا يَظُنُّ أُولَئِكَ أَنَّهُمْ مَبْعُوثُونَ (٤)
لِيَوْمٍ عَظِيمٍ (٥)
يَوْمَ يَقُومُ النَّاسُ لِرَبِّ الْعَالَمِينَ (٦)
كَلَّا إِنَّ كِتَابَ الْفُجَّارِ لَفِي سِجِّينٍ (٧)
وَمَا أَدْرَاكَ مَا سِجِّينٌ (٨)
كِتَابٌ مَرْقُومٌ (٩)
وَيْلٌ يَوْمَئِذٍ لِلْمُكَذِّبِينَ (١٠)
الَّذِينَ يُكَذِّبُونَ بِيَوْمِ الدِّينِ (١١)
وَمَا يُكَذِّبُ بِهِ إِلَّا كُلُّ مُعْتَدٍ أَثِيمٍ (١٢)
إِذَا تُتْلَى عَلَيْهِ آيَاتُنَا قَالَ أَسَاطِيرُ الْأَوَّلِينَ (١٣)
كَلَّا بَلْ رَانَ عَلَى قُلُوبِهِمْ مَا كَانُوا يَكْسِبُونَ (١٤)
كَلَّا إِنَّهُمْ عَنْ رَبِّهِمْ يَوْمَئِذٍ لَمَحْجُوبُونَ (١٥)
ثُمَّ إِنَّهُمْ لَصَالُو الْجَحِيمِ (١٦)
ثُمَّ يُقَالُ هَذَا الَّذِي كُنْتُمْ بِهِ تُكَذِّبُونَ (١٧)
كَلَّا إِنَّ كِتَابَ الْأَبْرَارِ لَفِي عِلِّيِّينَ (١٨)
وَمَا أَدْرَاكَ مَا عِلِّيُّونَ (١٩)
كِتَابٌ مَرْقُومٌ (٢٠)
يَشْهَدُهُ الْمُقَرَّبُونَ (٢١)
إِنَّ الْأَبْرَارَ لَفِي نَعِيمٍ (٢٢)
عَلَى الْأَرَائِكِ يَنْظُرُونَ (٢٣)

drink, sealed.
83:26. The sealing of it is (with) musk. And for that let the aspirers aspire.
83:27. And it is tempered with water coming from above --
83:28. A fountain from which drink those drawn near (to Allah).
83:29. Surely they who are guilty used to laugh at those who believe.
83:30. And when they passed by them, they winked at one another,
83:31. And when they returned to their people, they returned exulting.
83:32. And when they saw them, they said Surely these are in error --
83:33. And they were not sent as keepers over them.
83:34. So this day those who believe laugh at the disbelievers --
83:35. On raised couches, gazing.
83:36. Surely the disbelievers are rewarded as they did.

84. The Bursting Asunder

In the name of Allah, the Beneficent, the Merciful.
84:1. When the heaven bursts asunder,
84:2. And listens to its Lord and is made fit;
84:3. And when the earth is stretched,
84:4. And casts forth what is in it and becomes empty,
84:5. And listens to its Lord and is made fit.
84:6. O man, thou must strive a hard striving (to attain) to thy Lord, until thou meet Him.
84:7. Then as to him who is given his book in his right hand,

84:8. His account will be taken by an easy reckoning,
84:9. And he will go back to his people rejoicing.
84:10. And as to him who is given his book behind his back,
84:11. He will call for perdition,
84:12. And enter into burning Fire.
84:13. Surely he was (erstwhile) joyful among his people.
84:14. Surely he thought that he would never return (to Allah) --
84:15. Yea, surely his Lord is ever Seer of him.
84:16. But nay, I call to witness the sunset redness,
84:17. And the night and that which it drives on,
84:18. And the moon when it grows full,
84:19. That you shall certainly ascend to one state after another.
84:20. But what is the matter with them that they believe not?
84:21. And, when the Qur'an is recited to them, they adore (Him) not?
84:22. Nay, those who disbelieve give the lie --
84:23. And Allah knows best what they hide.
84:24. So announce to them a painful chastisement,
84:25. Except those who believe and do good -- for them is a reward that shall never be cut off.

85. The Stars

In the name of Allah, the Beneficent, the Merciful.
85:1. By the heaven full of stars!
85:2. And the Promised day!
85:3. And the bearer of witness and that to which witness is borne!
85:4. Destruction overtake the companions of the trench!
85:5. The fire fed with fuel --

86. The Comer by Night

85:6. When they sit by it,
85:7. And they are witnesses of what they do with the believers.
85:8. And they punished them for naught but that they believed in Allah, the Mighty, the Praised,
85:9. Whose is the kingdom of the heavens and the earth. And Allah is Witness of all things.
85:10. Those who persecute believing men and believing women, then repent not, theirs is the chastisement of hell, and theirs the chastisement of burning.
85:11. Those who believe and do good, theirs are Gardens wherein flow rivers. That is the great achievement.
85:12. Surely the grip of thy Lord is severe.
85:13. Surely He it is Who creates first and reproduces;
85:14. And He is the Forgiving, the Loving,
85:15. Lord of the Throne of Power, the Glorious,
85:16. Doer of what He intends.
85:17. Has not there come to thee the story of the hosts,
85:18. Of Pharaoh and Thamud?
85:19. Nay, those who disbelieve give the lie --
85:20. And Allah encompasses them on all sides.
85:21. Nay, it is a glorious Qur'an,
85:22. In a guarded tablet.

إِذْ هُمْ عَلَيْهَا قُعُودٌ (٦)
وَهُمْ عَلَى مَا يَفْعَلُونَ بِالْمُؤْمِنِينَ شُهُودٌ (٧)
وَمَا نَقَمُوا مِنْهُمْ إِلَّا أَنْ يُؤْمِنُوا بِاللَّهِ الْعَزِيزِ الْحَمِيدِ (٨)
الَّذِي لَهُ مُلْكُ السَّمَاوَاتِ وَالْأَرْضِ وَاللَّهُ عَلَى كُلِّ شَيْءٍ شَهِيدٌ (٩)
إِنَّ الَّذِينَ فَتَنُوا الْمُؤْمِنِينَ وَالْمُؤْمِنَاتِ ثُمَّ لَمْ يَتُوبُوا فَلَهُمْ عَذَابُ جَهَنَّمَ وَلَهُمْ عَذَابُ الْحَرِيقِ (١٠)
إِنَّ الَّذِينَ آمَنُوا وَعَمِلُوا الصَّالِحَاتِ لَهُمْ جَنَّاتٌ تَجْرِي مِنْ تَحْتِهَا الْأَنْهَارُ ذَلِكَ الْفَوْزُ الْكَبِيرُ (١١)
إِنَّ بَطْشَ رَبِّكَ لَشَدِيدٌ (١٢)
إِنَّهُ هُوَ يُبْدِئُ وَيُعِيدُ (١٣)
وَهُوَ الْغَفُورُ الْوَدُودُ (١٤)
ذُو الْعَرْشِ الْمَجِيدُ (١٥)
فَعَّالٌ لِمَا يُرِيدُ (١٦)
هَلْ أَتَاكَ حَدِيثُ الْجُنُودِ (١٧)
فِرْعَوْنَ وَثَمُودَ (١٨)
بَلِ الَّذِينَ كَفَرُوا فِي تَكْذِيبٍ (١٩)
وَاللَّهُ مِنْ وَرَائِهِمْ مُحِيطٌ (٢٠)
بَلْ هُوَ قُرْآنٌ مَجِيدٌ (٢١)
فِي لَوْحٍ مَحْفُوظٍ (٢٢)

86. The Comer by Night

In the name of Allah, the Beneficent, the Merciful.
86:1. By the heaven and the Comer by night!
86:2. And what will make thee know what the Comer by night is?
86:3. The star of piercing brightness --
86:4. There is nor a soul but over it is a keeper.

٨٦- سورة الطارق

بِسْمِ اللَّهِ الرَّحْمَنِ الرَّحِيمِ
وَالسَّمَاءِ وَالطَّارِقِ (١)
وَمَا أَدْرَاكَ مَا الطَّارِقُ (٢)
النَّجْمُ الثَّاقِبُ (٣)
إِنْ كُلُّ نَفْسٍ لَمَّا عَلَيْهَا حَافِظٌ (٤)
فَلْيَنْظُرِ الْإِنْسَانُ مِمَّ خُلِقَ (٥)

87. The Most High

86:5. So let man consider of what he is ejected.
86:6. He is created of water pouring forth,
86:7. Coming from between the back and the ribs.
86:8. Surely He is able to return him (to life).
86:9. On the day when hidden things are manifested,
86:10. Then he will have no strength nor helper.
86:11. By the cloud giving rain,
86:12. And the earth opening (with herbage)!
86:13. Surely it is a decisive word,
86:14. And it is not a joke.
86:15. Surely they plan a plan,
86:16. And I plan a plan.
86:17. So grant the disbelievers a respite -- let them alone for a while.

87. The Most High

In the name of Allah, the Beneficent, the Merciful.
87:1. Glorify the name of thy Lord, the Most High!
87:2. Who creates, then makes complete,
87:3. And Who measures, then guides,
87:4. And Who brings forth herbage,
87:5. Then makes it dried up, dust-coloured.
87:6. We shall make thee recite so thou shalt not forget --
87:7. Except what Allah please. Surely He knows the manifest, and what is hidden.
87:8. And We shall make thy way smooth to a state of ease.
87:9. So remind, reminding indeed profits.
87:10. He who fears will mind,
87:11. And the most unfortunate one will avoid it,
87:12. Who will burn in the great Fire.

خُلِقَ مِنْ مَاءٍ دَافِقٍ (٦)
يَخْرُجُ مِنْ بَيْنِ الصُّلْبِ وَالتَّرَائِبِ (٧)
إِنَّهُ عَلَىٰ رَجْعِهِ لَقَادِرٌ (٨)
يَوْمَ تُبْلَى السَّرَائِرُ (٩)
فَمَا لَهُ مِنْ قُوَّةٍ وَلَا نَاصِرٍ (١٠)
وَالسَّمَاءِ ذَاتِ الرَّجْعِ (١١)
وَالْأَرْضِ ذَاتِ الصَّدْعِ (١٢)
إِنَّهُ لَقَوْلٌ فَصْلٌ (١٣)
وَمَا هُوَ بِالْهَزْلِ (١٤)
إِنَّهُمْ يَكِيدُونَ كَيْدًا (١٥)
وَأَكِيدُ كَيْدًا (١٦)
فَمَهِّلِ الْكَافِرِينَ أَمْهِلْهُمْ رُوَيْدًا (١٧)

٨٧- سورة الأعلى

بِسْمِ اللَّهِ الرَّحْمَٰنِ الرَّحِيمِ
سَبِّحِ اسْمَ رَبِّكَ الْأَعْلَى (١)
الَّذِي خَلَقَ فَسَوَّىٰ (٢)
وَالَّذِي قَدَّرَ فَهَدَىٰ (٣)
وَالَّذِي أَخْرَجَ الْمَرْعَىٰ (٤)
فَجَعَلَهُ غُثَاءً أَحْوَىٰ (٥)
سَنُقْرِئُكَ فَلَا تَنْسَىٰ (٦)
إِلَّا مَا شَاءَ اللَّهُ إِنَّهُ يَعْلَمُ الْجَهْرَ وَمَا يَخْفَىٰ (٧)
وَنُيَسِّرُكَ لِلْيُسْرَىٰ (٨)
فَذَكِّرْ إِنْ نَفَعَتِ الذِّكْرَىٰ (٩)
سَيَذَّكَّرُ مَنْ يَخْشَىٰ (١٠)
وَيَتَجَنَّبُهَا الْأَشْقَى (١١)
الَّذِي يَصْلَى النَّارَ الْكُبْرَى (١٢)
ثُمَّ لَا يَمُوتُ فِيهَا وَلَا يَحْيَا (١٣)

87:13. Then therein he will neither live nor die.
87:14. He indeed is successful who purifies himself,
87:15. And remembers the name of his Lord, then prays.
87:16. But, you prefer the life of this world,
87:17. While the Hereafter is better and mote lasting.
87:18. Surely this is in the earlier scriptures
87:19. The scriptures of Abraham and Moses.

قَدْ أَفْلَحَ مَنْ تَزَكَّى (١٤)
وَذَكَرَ اسْمَ رَبِّهِ فَصَلَّى (١٥)
بَلْ تُؤْثِرُونَ الْحَيَاةَ الدُّنْيَا (١٦)
وَالْآخِرَةُ خَيْرٌ وَأَبْقَى (١٧)
إِنَّ هَذَا لَفِي الصُّحُفِ الْأُولَى (١٨)
صُحُفِ إِبْرَاهِيمَ وَمُوسَى (١٩)

88. The Overwhelming Event

٨٨- سورة الغاشية

In the name of Allah, the Beneficent, the Merciful.
88:1. Has there come to thee the news of the Overwhelming Event?
88:2. Faces on that day will be downcast,
88:3. Labouring, toiling,
88:4. Entering burning Fire,
88:5. Made to drink from a boiling spring.
88:6. They will have no food but of thorns,
88:7. Neither nourishing nor satisfying hunger.
88:8. Faces on that day will be happy,
88:9. Glad for their striving,
88:10. In a lofty Garden,
88:11. Wherein thou wilt hear no vain talk.
88:12. Therein is a fountain flowing.
88:13. Therein are thrones raised high,
88:14. And drinking-cups ready placed,
88:15. And cushions set in rows,
88:16. And carpets spread out.
88:17. See they not the clouds, how they are created?
88:18. And the heaven, how it is raised high?
88:19. And the mountains, how they are fixed?

بِسْمِ اللَّهِ الرَّحْمَنِ الرَّحِيمِ
هَلْ أَتَاكَ حَدِيثُ الْغَاشِيَةِ (١)
وُجُوهٌ يَوْمَئِذٍ خَاشِعَةٌ (٢)
عَامِلَةٌ نَاصِبَةٌ (٣)
تَصْلَى نَارًا حَامِيَةً (٤)
تُسْقَى مِنْ عَيْنٍ آنِيَةٍ (٥)
لَيْسَ لَهُمْ طَعَامٌ إِلَّا مِنْ ضَرِيعٍ (٦)
لَا يُسْمِنُ وَلَا يُغْنِي مِنْ جُوعٍ (٧)
وُجُوهٌ يَوْمَئِذٍ نَاعِمَةٌ (٨)
لِسَعْيِهَا رَاضِيَةٌ (٩)
فِي جَنَّةٍ عَالِيَةٍ (١٠)
لَا تَسْمَعُ فِيهَا لَاغِيَةً (١١)
فِيهَا عَيْنٌ جَارِيَةٌ (١٢)
فِيهَا سُرُرٌ مَرْفُوعَةٌ (١٣)
وَأَكْوَابٌ مَوْضُوعَةٌ (١٤)
وَنَمَارِقُ مَصْفُوفَةٌ (١٥)
وَزَرَابِيُّ مَبْثُوثَةٌ (١٦)
أَفَلَا يَنْظُرُونَ إِلَى الْإِبِلِ كَيْفَ خُلِقَتْ (١٧)
وَإِلَى السَّمَاءِ كَيْفَ رُفِعَتْ (١٨)

88:20. And the earth, how it is spread out?
88:21. So remind. Thou art only one to remind.
88:22. Thou art not a warder over them -
88:23. But whoever turns back and disbelieves,
88:24. Allah will chastise him with the greatest chastisement.
88:25. Surely to Us is their return,
88:26. Then it is for Us to call them to account.

89. The Daybreak

In the name of Allah, the Beneficent, the Merciful.
89:1. By the daybreak!
89:2. And the ten nights!
89:3. And the even and the odd!
89:4. And the night when it departs!
89:5. Truly in this is an oath for men of understanding.
89:6. Hast thou not considered how thy Lord dealt with 'Ad,
89:7. (Of) Iram, having lofty buildings,
89:8. The like of which were not created in the land;
89:9. And (with) Thamud who hewed out rocks in the valley;
89:10. And (with) Pharaoh, the lord of hosts,
89:11. Who exceeded limits in the cities,
89:12. And made great mischief therein?
89:13. So thy Lord poured on them a portion of chastisement.
89:14. Surely thy Lord is Watchful;
89:15. As for man, when his Lord tries him, then gives him honour and favours him, he says: My Lord honours me.
89:16. But when He tries him, then straitens to him his subsistence, he says: My Lord has disgraced me.
89:17. Nay, but you honour not the orphan,

89:18. Nor do you urge one another to feed the poor,
89:19. And you devour heritage, devouring all,
89:20. And you love wealth with exceeding love.
89:21. Nay, when the earth is made to crumble to pieces,
89:22. And thy Lord comes with the angels, ranks on ranks;
89:23. And hell is made to appear that day. On that day man will be mindful, and of what use will being mindful be then?
89:24. He will say: O would that I had sent before for (this) my life!
89:25. But none can punish as He will punish on that day.
89:26. And none can bind as He will bind on that day.
89:27. O soul that art at rest,
89:28. Return to thy Lord, well-pleased, well-pleasing,
89:29. So enter among My servants,
89:30. And enter My Garden!

90. The City

In the name of Allah, the Beneficent, the Merciful.
90:1. Nay, I call to witness this City!
90:2. And thou wilt be made free from obligation in this City --
90:3. And the begetter and he whom he begot!
90:4. We have certainly created man to face difficulties.
90:5. Does he think that no one has power over him?
90:6. He will say I have wasted much wealth.
90:7. Does he think that no one sees him?
90:8. Have We not given him two eyes,
90:9. And a tongue and two lips,

90:10. And pointed out to him the two conspicuous ways?
90:11. But he attempts not the uphill road;
90:12. And what will make thee comprehend what the uphill road is?
90:13. (It is) to free a slave,
90:14. Or to feed in a day of hunger
90:15. An orphan nearly related,
90:16. Or the poor man lying in the dust.
90:17. Then he is of those who believe and exhort one another to patience, and exhort one another to mercy.
90:18. These are the people of the right hand.
90:19. And those who disbelieve in Our messages, they are the people of the left hand.
90:20. On them is Fire closed over.

91. The Sun

In the name of Allah, the Beneficent, the Merciful.
91:1. By the sun and his brightness!
91:2. And the moon when she borrows light from him!
91:3. And the day when it exposes it to view!
91:4. And the night when it draws a veil over it!
91:5. And the heaven and its make!
91:6. And the earth and its extension!
91:7. And the soul and its perfection!
91:8. So He reveals to it its way of evil and its way of good;
91:9. He is indeed successful who causes it to grow,
91:10. And he indeed fails who buries it.
91:11. Thamud rejected (the truth) in their inordinacy,
91:12. When the basest of them broke forth with mischief --
91:13. So Allah's messenger said to them (Leave alone) Allah's she-camel,

and (give) her (to) drink.
91:14. But they called him a liar and slaughtered her. So their Lord destroyed them for their sin and levelled them (with the ground)
91:15. And He fears not its consequence.

92. The Night

In the name of Allah, the Beneficent, the Merciful.
92:1. By the night when it draws a veil!
92:2. And the day when it shines!
92:3. And the creating of the male and the female! --
92:4. Your striving is surely (for) diverse (ends).
92:5. Then as for him who gives and keeps his duty,
92:6. And accepts what is good --
92:7. We facilitate for him (the way to) ease.
92:8. And as for him who is niggardly and considers himself self-sufficient,
92:9. And rejects what is good --
92:10. We facilitate for him (the way to) distress.
92:11. And his wealth will not avail him when he perishes.
92:12. Surely Ours is it to show the way,
92:13. And surely Ours is the Hereafter and the former.
92:14. So I warn you of the Fire that flames.
92:15. None will enter it but the most unfortunate,
92:16. Who rejects (the truth) and turns (his) back.
92:17. And away from it shall be kept the most faithful to duty,
92:18. Who gives his wealth, purifying himself,
92:19. And none has with him any boon for a reward,
92:20. Except the seeking of the

بِذَنْبِهِمْ فَسَوَّاهَا (١٤)
وَلَا يَخَافُ عُقْبَاهَا (١٥)

٩٢- سورة الليل

بِسْمِ اللَّهِ الرَّحْمَنِ الرَّحِيمِ
وَاللَّيْلِ إِذَا يَغْشَى (١)
وَالنَّهَارِ إِذَا تَجَلَّى (٢)
وَمَا خَلَقَ الذَّكَرَ وَالْأُنْثَى (٣)
إِنَّ سَعْيَكُمْ لَشَتَّى (٤)
فَأَمَّا مَنْ أَعْطَى وَاتَّقَى (٥)
وَصَدَّقَ بِالْحُسْنَى (٦)
فَسَنُيَسِّرُهُ لِلْيُسْرَى (٧)
وَأَمَّا مَنْ بَخِلَ وَاسْتَغْنَى (٨)
وَكَذَّبَ بِالْحُسْنَى (٩)
فَسَنُيَسِّرُهُ لِلْعُسْرَى (١٠)
وَمَا يُغْنِي عَنْهُ مَالُهُ إِذَا تَرَدَّى (١١)
إِنَّ عَلَيْنَا لَلْهُدَى (١٢)
وَإِنَّ لَنَا لَلْآخِرَةَ وَالْأُولَى (١٣)
فَأَنْذَرْتُكُمْ نَارًا تَلَظَّى (١٤)
لَا يَصْلَاهَا إِلَّا الْأَشْقَى (١٥)
الَّذِي كَذَّبَ وَتَوَلَّى (١٦)
وَسَيُجَنَّبُهَا الْأَتْقَى (١٧)
الَّذِي يُؤْتِي مَالَهُ يَتَزَكَّى (١٨)
وَمَا لِأَحَدٍ عِنْدَهُ مِنْ نِعْمَةٍ تُجْزَى (١٩)
إِلَّا ابْتِغَاءَ وَجْهِ رَبِّهِ الْأَعْلَى (٢٠)
وَلَسَوْفَ يَرْضَى (٢١)

pleasure of his Lord, the Most High.
92:21. And he will soon be well-pleased.

93. The Brightness of the Day

In the name of Allah, the Beneficent, the Merciful.
93:1. By the brightness of the day!
93:2. And the night when it is still! --
93:3. Thy Lord has not forsaken thee, not is He displeased.
93:4. And surely the latter state is better for thee than the former.
93:5. And soon will thy Lord give thee so that thou wilt be well pleased.
93:6. Did He not find thee an orphan and give (thee) shelter?
93:7. And find thee groping, so He showed the way?
93:8. And find thee in want, so He enriched thee?
93:9. Therefore the orphan, oppress not.
93:10. And him who asks, chide not.
93:11. And the favour of thy Lord, proclaim.

94. The Expansion

In the name of Allah, the Beneficent, the Merciful.
94:1. Have We not expanded for thee thy breast,
94:2. And removed from thee thy burden,
94:3. Which weighed down thy back,
94:4. And exalted for thee thy mention?
94:5. Surely with difficulty is ease,
94:6. With difficulty is surely ease:
94:7. So when thou art free (from anxiety), work hard,
94:8. And make thy Lord thy exclusive object.

95. The Fig

In the name of Allah, the Beneficent, the Merciful.

95:1. By the fig and the olive!
95:2. And mount Sinai!
95:3. And this City made secure! --
95:4. Certainly We created man in the best make.
95:5. Then We render him the lowest of the low,
95:6. Except those who believe and do good; so theirs is a reward never to be cut off.
95:7. So who can give the lie to thee after (this) about the Judgment?
95:8. Is not Allah the Best of the Judges?

بِسْمِ اللهِ الرَّحْمَنِ الرَّحِيمِ
وَالتِّينِ وَالزَّيْتُونِ (١)
وَطُورِ سِينِينَ (٢)
وَهَذَا الْبَلَدِ الْأَمِينِ (٣)
لَقَدْ خَلَقْنَا الْإِنْسَانَ فِي أَحْسَنِ تَقْوِيمٍ (٤)
ثُمَّ رَدَدْنَاهُ أَسْفَلَ سَافِلِينَ (٥)
إِلَّا الَّذِينَ آمَنُوا وَعَمِلُوا الصَّالِحَاتِ فَلَهُمْ أَجْرٌ غَيْرُ مَمْنُونٍ (٦)
فَمَا يُكَذِّبُكَ بَعْدُ بِالدِّينِ (٧)
أَلَيْسَ اللهُ بِأَحْكَمِ الْحَاكِمِينَ (٨)

96. The Clot

In the name of Allah, the Beneficent, the Merciful.

96:1. Read in the name of thy Lord who creates --
96:2. Creates man from a clot,
96:3. Read and thy Lord is most Generous,
96:4. Who taught by the pen,
96:5. Taught man what he knew not.
96:6. Nay, man is surely inordinate,
96:7. Because he looks upon himself as self-sufficient.
96:8. Surely to thy Lord is the return.
96:9. Hast thou seen him who forbids
96:10. A servant when he prays?
96:11. Seest thou if he is on the right way,
96:12. Or enjoins observance of duty?
96:13. Seest thou if he denies and turns away?
96:14. Knows he not that Allah sees?
96:15. Nay, if he desist not, We will seize him by the forelock --
96:16. A lying, sinful forelock!
96:17. Then let him summon his council,

بِسْمِ اللهِ الرَّحْمَنِ الرَّحِيمِ
اقْرَأْ بِاسْمِ رَبِّكَ الَّذِي خَلَقَ (١)
خَلَقَ الْإِنْسَانَ مِنْ عَلَقٍ (٢)
اقْرَأْ وَرَبُّكَ الْأَكْرَمُ (٣)
الَّذِي عَلَّمَ بِالْقَلَمِ (٤)
عَلَّمَ الْإِنْسَانَ مَا لَمْ يَعْلَمْ (٥)
كَلَّا إِنَّ الْإِنْسَانَ لَيَطْغَى (٦)
أَنْ رَآهُ اسْتَغْنَى (٧)
إِنَّ إِلَى رَبِّكَ الرُّجْعَى (٨)
أَرَأَيْتَ الَّذِي يَنْهَى (٩)
عَبْدًا إِذَا صَلَّى (١٠)
أَرَأَيْتَ إِنْ كَانَ عَلَى الْهُدَى (١١)
أَوْ أَمَرَ بِالتَّقْوَى (١٢)
أَرَأَيْتَ إِنْ كَذَّبَ وَتَوَلَّى (١٣)
أَلَمْ يَعْلَمْ بِأَنَّ اللهَ يَرَى (١٤)
كَلَّا لَئِنْ لَمْ يَنْتَهِ لَنَسْفَعَنْ بِالنَّاصِيَةِ (١٥)

96:18. We will summon the braves of the army.
96:19. Nay! Obey him not, but prostrate thyself, and draw nigh (to Allah).

97. The Majesty

In the name of Allah, the Beneficent, the Merciful.
97:1. Surely We revealed it on the Night of Majesty --
97:2. And what will make thee comprehend what the Night of Majesty is?
97:3. The Night of Majesty is better than a thousand months.
97:4. The angels and the Spirit descend in it by the permission of their Lord -- for every affair --
97:5. Peace it is till the rising of the morning.

98. The Clear Evidence

In the name of Allah, the Beneficent, the Merciful.
98:1. Those who disbelieve from among the People of the Book and the idolaters could not have been freed till clear evidence came to them --
98:2. A Messenger from Allah, reciting pure pages,
98:3. Wherein are (all) right books.
98:4. Nor did those to whom the Book was given become divided till clear evidence came to them.
98:5. And they are enjoined naught but to serve Allah, being sincere to Him in obedience, upright, and to keep up prayer and pay the poor-rate, and that is the right religion.
98:6. Those who disbelieve from among the People of the Book and the idolaters will be in the Fire of hell, abiding therein. They are the worst of

creatures.
98:7. Those who believe and do good, they are the best of creatures.
98:8. Their reward is with their Lord Gardens of perpetuity wherein flow rivers, abiding therein for ever. Allah is well pleased with them and they are well pleased with Him. That is for him who fears his Lord.

99. The Shaking

In the name of Allah, the Beneficent, the Merciful.
99:1. When the earth is shaken with her shaking,
99:2. And the earth brings forth her burdens,
99:3. And man says: What has befallen her?
99:4. On that day she will tell her news,
99:5. As if thy Lord had revealed to her.
99:6. On that day men will come forth in sundry bodies that they may be shown their works.
99:7. So he who does an atom's weight of good will see it
99:8. And he who does an atom's weight of evil will see it.

100. The Assaulters

In the name of Allah, the Beneficent, the Merciful.
100:1. By those running and uttering cries!
100:2. And those producing fire, striking!
100:3. And those suddenly attacking at morn!
100:4. Then thereby they raise dust,
100:5. Then penetrate thereby gatherings --
100:6. Surely man is ungrateful to his Lord.
100:7. And surely he is a witness of

that.
100:8. And truly on account of the love of wealth he is niggardly.
100:9. Knows he not when that which is in the graves is raised,
100:10. And that which is in the breasts is made manifest?
100:11. Surely their Lord this day is Aware of them.

101. The Calamity

In the name of Allah, the Beneficent, the Merciful.
101:1. The calamity!
101:2. What is the calamity?
101:3. And what will make thee know how terrible is the calamity?
101:4. The day wherein men will be as scattered moths,
101:5. And the mountains will be as carded wool.
101:6. Then as for him whose measure (of good deeds) is heavy,
101:7. He will live a pleasant life.
101:8. And as for him whose measure (of good deeds) is light,
101:9. The abyss is a mother to him.
101:10. And what will make thee know what that is?
101:11. A burning Fire.

102. Abundance of Wealth

In the name of Allah, the Beneficent, the Merciful.
102:1. Abundance diverts you,
102:2. Until you come to the graves.
102:3. Nay, you will soon know,
102:4. Nay, again, you will soon know.
102:5. Nay, would that you knew with a certain knowledge!
102:6. You will certainly see hell;
102:7. Then you will see it with certainty of sight;
102:8. Then on that day you shall

certainly be questioned about the boons.

103. The Time

In the name of Allah, the Beneficent, the Merciful.
103:1. By the time!
103:2. Surely man is in loss,
103:3. Except those who believe and do good, and exhort one another to Truth, and exhort one another to patience.

104. The Slanderer

In the name of Allah, the Beneficent, the Merciful.
104:1. Woe to every slanderer, defamer!
104:2. Who amasses wealth and counts it --
104:3. He thinks that his wealth will make him abide.
104:4. Nay, he will certainly be hurled into the crushing disaster;
104:5. And what will make thee realize what the crushing disaster is?
104:6. It is the Fire kindled by Allah,
104:7. Which rises over the hearts.
104:8. Surely it is closed in on them,
104:9. In extended columns.

105. The Elephant

In the name of Allah, the Beneficent, the Merciful.
105:1. Hast thou not seen how thy Lord dealt with the possessors of the elephant?
105:2. Did He not cause their war to end in confusion?
105:3. And send against them birds in flocks?
105:4. Casting at them decreed stones -
105:5. So He rendered them like straw

ثُمَّ لَتُسْأَلُنَّ يَوْمَئِذٍ عَنِ النَّعِيمِ (٨)

١٠٣- سورة العصر

بِسْمِ اللَّهِ الرَّحْمَنِ الرَّحِيمِ
وَالْعَصْرِ (١)
إِنَّ الْإِنْسَانَ لَفِي خُسْرٍ (٢)
إِلَّا الَّذِينَ آمَنُوا وَعَمِلُوا الصَّالِحَاتِ وَتَوَاصَوْا بِالْحَقِّ وَتَوَاصَوْا بِالصَّبْرِ (٣)

١٠٤- سورة الهمزة

بِسْمِ اللَّهِ الرَّحْمَنِ الرَّحِيمِ
وَيْلٌ لِكُلِّ هُمَزَةٍ لُمَزَةٍ (١)
الَّذِي جَمَعَ مَالًا وَعَدَّدَهُ (٢)
يَحْسَبُ أَنَّ مَالَهُ أَخْلَدَهُ (٣)
كَلَّا لَيُنْبَذَنَّ فِي الْحُطَمَةِ (٤)
وَمَا أَدْرَاكَ مَا الْحُطَمَةُ (٥)
نَارُ اللَّهِ الْمُوقَدَةُ (٦)
الَّتِي تَطَّلِعُ عَلَى الْأَفْئِدَةِ (٧)
إِنَّهَا عَلَيْهِمْ مُؤْصَدَةٌ (٨)
فِي عَمَدٍ مُمَدَّدَةٍ (٩)

١٠٥- سورة الفيل

بِسْمِ اللَّهِ الرَّحْمَنِ الرَّحِيمِ
أَلَمْ تَرَ كَيْفَ فَعَلَ رَبُّكَ بِأَصْحَابِ الْفِيلِ (١)
أَلَمْ يَجْعَلْ كَيْدَهُمْ فِي تَضْلِيلٍ (٢)
وَأَرْسَلَ عَلَيْهِمْ طَيْرًا أَبَابِيلَ (٣)
تَرْمِيهِمْ بِحِجَارَةٍ مِنْ سِجِّيلٍ (٤)
فَجَعَلَهُمْ كَعَصْفٍ مَأْكُولٍ (٥)

eaten up.

106. The Quraish

١٠٦ـ سورة قريش

In the name of Allah, the Beneficent, the Merciful.

106:1. For the protection of the Quraish —

106:2. Their protection during their journey in the winter and the summer.

106:3. So let them serve the Lord of this House,

106:4. Who feeds them against hunger and gives them security against fear.

بِسْمِ اللهِ الرَّحْمَنِ الرَّحِيمِ
لِإِيلَافِ قُرَيْشٍ (١)
إِيلَافِهِمْ رِحْلَةَ الشِّتَاءِ وَالصَّيْفِ (٢)
فَلْيَعْبُدُوا رَبَّ هَذَا الْبَيْتِ (٣)
الَّذِي أَطْعَمَهُمْ مِنْ جُوعٍ وَآمَنَهُمْ مِنْ خَوْفٍ (٤)

107. Acts of Kindness

١٠٧ـ سورة الماعون

In the name of Allah, the Beneficent, the Merciful.

107:1. Hast thou seen him who belies religion?

107:2. That is the one who is rough to the orphan,

107:3. And urges not the feeding of the needy.

107:4. So woe to the praying ones,

107:5. Who are unmindful of their prayer!

107:6. Who do (good) to be seen,

107:7. And refrain from acts of kindness!

بِسْمِ اللهِ الرَّحْمَنِ الرَّحِيمِ
أَرَأَيْتَ الَّذِي يُكَذِّبُ بِالدِّينِ (١)
فَذَلِكَ الَّذِي يَدُعُّ الْيَتِيمَ (٢)
وَلَا يَحُضُّ عَلَى طَعَامِ الْمِسْكِينِ (٣)
فَوَيْلٌ لِلْمُصَلِّينَ (٤)
الَّذِينَ هُمْ عَنْ صَلَاتِهِمْ سَاهُونَ (٥)
الَّذِينَ هُمْ يُرَاءُونَ (٦)
وَيَمْنَعُونَ الْمَاعُونَ (٧)

108. The Abundance of Good

١٠٨ـ سورة الكوثر

In the name of Allah, the Beneficent, the Merciful.

1 Surely We have given thee abundance of good.

108:2. So pray to thy Lord and sacrifice.

108:3. Surely thy enemy is cut off (from good).

بِسْمِ اللهِ الرَّحْمَنِ الرَّحِيمِ
إِنَّا أَعْطَيْنَاكَ الْكَوْثَرَ (١)
فَصَلِّ لِرَبِّكَ وَانْحَرْ (٢)
إِنَّ شَانِئَكَ هُوَ الْأَبْتَرُ (٣)

109. The Disbelievers

١٠٩ـ سورة الكافرون

In the name of Allah, the Beneficent, the Merciful.

بِسْمِ اللهِ الرَّحْمَنِ الرَّحِيمِ

109:1. Say: O disbelievers,
109:2. I serve not that which you serve,
109:3. Nor do you serve Him Whom I serve,
109:4. Nor shall I serve that which ye serve,
109:5. Nor do you serve Him Whom I serve.
109:6. For you is your recompense [religion] and for me my recompense [religion].

قُلْ يَا أَيُّهَا الْكَافِرُونَ (١)
لَا أَعْبُدُ مَا تَعْبُدُونَ (٢)
وَلَا أَنْتُمْ عَابِدُونَ مَا أَعْبُدُ (٣)
وَلَا أَنَا عَابِدٌ مَا عَبَدْتُمْ (٤)
وَلَا أَنْتُمْ عَابِدُونَ مَا أَعْبُدُ (٥)
لَكُمْ دِينُكُمْ وَلِيَ دِينِ (٦)

110. The Help

In the name of Allah, the Beneficent, the Merciful.
110:1. When Allah's help and victory comes,
110:2. And thou seest men entering the religion of Allah in companies,
110:3. Celebrate the praise of thy Lord and ask His protection. Surely He is ever Returning (to mercy).

بِسْمِ اللَّهِ الرَّحْمَنِ الرَّحِيمِ
إِذَا جَاءَ نَصْرُ اللَّهِ وَالْفَتْحُ (١)
وَرَأَيْتَ النَّاسَ يَدْخُلُونَ فِي دِينِ اللَّهِ أَفْوَاجًا (٢)
فَسَبِّحْ بِحَمْدِ رَبِّكَ وَاسْتَغْفِرْهُ إِنَّهُ كَانَ تَوَّابًا (٣)

111. The Flame

In the name of Allah, the Beneficent, the Merciful.
111:1. Abu Lahab's hands will perish and he will perish.
111:2. His wealth and that which he earns will not avail him.
111:3. He will burn in fire giving rise to flames --
111:4. And his wife the bearer of slander;
111:5. Upon her neck a halter of twisted rope!

بِسْمِ اللَّهِ الرَّحْمَنِ الرَّحِيمِ
تَبَّتْ يَدَا أَبِي لَهَبٍ وَتَبَّ (١)
مَا أَغْنَى عَنْهُ مَالُهُ وَمَا كَسَبَ (٢)
سَيَصْلَى نَارًا ذَاتَ لَهَبٍ (٣)
وَامْرَأَتُهُ حَمَّالَةَ الْحَطَبِ (٤)
فِي جِيدِهَا حَبْلٌ مِنْ مَسَدٍ (٥)

112. The Unity

In the name of Allah, the Beneficent, the Merciful.
112:1. Say: He, Allah, is One.
112:2. Allah is He on Whom all depend.

بِسْمِ اللَّهِ الرَّحْمَنِ الرَّحِيمِ
قُلْ هُوَ اللَّهُ أَحَدٌ (١)
اللَّهُ الصَّمَدُ (٢)

112:3. He begets not, nor is He begotten;
112:4. And none is like Him.

113. The Dawn

In the name of Allah, the Beneficent, the Merciful.
113:1. Say: I seek refuge in the Lord of the dawn,
113:2. From the evil of that which He has created,
113:3. And from the evil of intense darkness, when it comes,
113:4. And from the evil of those who cast (evil suggestions) in firm resolutions,
113:5. And from the evil of the envier when he envies.

114. The Men

In the name of Allah, the Beneficent, the Merciful.
114:1. Say I seek refuge in the Lord of men,
114:2. The King of men,
114:3. The God of men,
114:4. From the evil of the whisperings of the slinking (devil),
114:5. Who whispers into the hearts of men,
114:6. From among the jinn and the men.

www.ingramcontent.com/pod-product-compliance
Lightning Source LLC
Chambersburg PA
CBHW070327240426
43665CB00045B/1150